The New York Times

Guide to Listening Pleasure

𝔈𝔥𝔢 𝔑𝔢𝔴 𝔜𝔬𝔯𝔨 𝔗𝔦𝔪𝔢𝔰

Guide to Listening Pleasure

Edited and with an Introduction by

HOWARD TAUBMAN

A NEW YORK TIMES BOOK

THE MACMILLAN COMPANY, NEW YORK

COLLIER-MACMILLAN LTD., LONDON

Library of Congress Catalog Card Number: 68-27038

FIRST PRINTING

The Macmillan Company, New York
Collier-Macmillan Canada Ltd., Toronto, Ontario
Printed in the United States of America

1479395

Contents

Preface

WQXR has been called "radio with a soul" and many other complimentary things. Those of us who are associated with this good-music station believe that these pleasant epithets are all well deserved. We must admit, however, that it all started by accident. The idea for WQXR was the unexpected by-product of experiments whose real purpose was the technical development of TV.

It happened back in the early 1930's. John V. L. Hogan, a radio engineer with scores of patents to his credit, had techniques in mind for simultaneous image and sound broadcast, and he obtained an FCC permit for an experimental station, W2XR, to carry his sound signals. The radio frequency granted was well above the normal end of the broadcasting range, so listeners weren't expected to be bothered by whatever Mr. Hogan put on the air to go along with his test pictures.

As a fortunate coincidence, in addition to being an engineer, Hogan was a lover of good music. It was perfectly natural for him to draw on his own record collection to provide the sound for his experiments. When he broadcast pictures of a waterfall, he put on Handel's *Water Music,* for example. This was just a private indulgence, he thought, because no one would hear the music on his unfrequented frequency. Anyway, he was in operation only an hour or so in the evening.

To his astonishment Hogan began to hear from the unknown

listening public "out there." First a trickle, than a torrent of cards and letters: "This is great"; "Keep it up"; "At last." A few dial fiddlers had found the spot and spread the word to their friends. W2XR had an audience, an audience in which each member felt he had his own personal, secret radio station.

Although they had scientific value, the television efforts came to naught, chiefly because there was no one to receive them. But Hogan thought he had made another discovery of importance. There must be a place in the radio spectrum for a station that offered good music and other selected programming for an intelligent, cultured audience. Friendly radio professionals tried to set him straight. They urged him not to be misled by the odd-ball fans who had communicated their thanks. "Who wants to listen to records on the air?" they asked. Anyone who wanted to hear recordings would play his own. He didn't need a radio set for that. Radio was for *Amos and Andy, The Goldbergs* and the *A & P Gypsies.*

But Hogan persisted. Good-music programming did have a future, he felt, even though there already were about twenty-five radio stations in New York. He received enthusiastic support from his friend Elliott M. Sanger, and in 1936 the two men formed the Interstate Broadcasting Company.

The start was inauspicious. Headquarters consisted of a desk for Sanger in Hogan's engineering offices at 41 Park Row. The transmitter was located on the second floor of a garage in Long Island City, near Queensborough Bridge. There, if you looked carefully, you would have seen a wooden pole on the roof which was W2XR's homemade antenna. You would have said that the whole venture looked pretty precarious, and it was, except for one thing: Hogan and Sanger were absolutely right; there *was* a great, unsatisfied thirst for good music on the air. Although W2XR (later in 1936 it became WQXR) had power of only 250 watts, just about enough to reach midtown Manhattan and parts of Queens, the response to its programming brought successive power increases to 1,000, 5,000, 10,000 and 50,000 watts, enabling WQXR to reach an audience of millions throughout the East.

Interstate was a pioneer on the FM scene, and its experimental station, W2XQR, the first FM affiliate of a commercial broadcaster in New York, went on the air in 1939. Today it has one of the largest FM audiences in the city.

The New York Times purchased WQXR in 1944 and has steadfastly maintained the station's basic good-music policies. Elliott Sanger joined *The Times* as executive vice president of WQXR and supervised its operations until retirement in 1967.

In the course of this compressed history, the phrase *good music* has popped up several times. It might be well to define that term, as WQXR sees it. It is not a synonym for high-brow or even classical. To us, any music that has lasting value is good music: symphonies, concertos, chamber works, opera, of course; but also the best of the lighter forms, including operettas, Broadway show tunes, folk music, and the world of jazz. WQXR listeners have wide and varied tastes. They like all kinds of music: they only demand the best of each kind. Serving them through the years has been an education for all of us on the station. Our special audience, difficult and impatient whenever standards sag, has helped us learn a lot about music and recordings. We're glad to pass on some of what they have taught us in this book.

Ivan Veit
President
WQXR

Editor's Introduction

HOWARD TAUBMAN

D RIVING alone to New York from my place in the country one morning, I switched on the car radio—naturally, to WQXR. Not that I am in the habit of casually listening to music, certainly not to great music. I could not, even if I wanted to do so. Music has a way of seizing and holding my attention. Once in a while I am unlucky enough to visit a home where fine music is used as a backdrop to conversation, and I find myself in an uncomfortable quandary. I want to be polite and share in the talk, but the music, like the ancient mariner, fastens me in its grip, and I end by seeming distant and abstracted, like an absentminded professor. However, I can understand how people turn to music while they are occupied with routine tasks. My route to New York is so familiar that the music from WQXR beguiles my journey.

On the particular morning of which I speak, I snapped on the radio to hear what I could hear. I had not looked at the program listings in advance, and I did not know what to expect. It happened to be the hour for *Piano Personalities,* and the music that filled my car was unfamiliar. It was sunny and lilting and capricious in its turns of phrase and mood. What could it be? Obviously there were more than ten fingers at work. Two pianists? Yes. Two pianos? Not likely, probably something for four hands on one piano. Mozart and Schubert, I knew, had written lovely things for this intimate form of music-making, designed for the delectation of their friends in their homes. Hardly anyone plays these pieces in public these days, and one can spend a long lifetime of devoted concert-going without encountering even the best pieces in this form. This piece, I was sure, could not have been on many programs. But how appealing it was! And how it shortened the miles! When it was over, I listened carefully for the announcement of title and author. *Divertissement à la Hongroise* by Franz Schubert, for four hands. The composer was not too great a surprise, but the music? I confess I had never heard it before. WQXR had done me and anyone interested in a different musical experience a good turn.

There is another dividend I get from tuning in WQXR. Actually it is a game I play to challenge myself. I do not look at the programs in advance, and I am pleased when I turn on the radio after a piece has begun. The first requirement of the game is to identify the composer. The next is to name the composition. The third is to say who is playing, and that is often the tough part of the game. It is not too difficult when one hears an orchestra playing with a wonderful momentum, with a tone that never fails to sing, with a Mediterranean clarity, in which attacks and releases have a dazzling crispness, and the inner voices are so cannily articulated that they are both clearly defined and deftly blended into the tonal pattern as a whole. It must be Toscanini at the helm, and I am rarely mistaken. Or the piano has a tone that caresses or bursts with power, without ever sacrificing its songfulness, while every resource—sensitivity to form, regality of rhythm, and freedom of phrase—is directed to a total experience of the music, whether it be an étude or a sonata. Several distinguished pianists have the skill and penetration for such an achievement, but the little touches, as well as the grasp of the grand design, are the hallmark of only one man: Horowitz. Or the violin strides forth with a poise, an elegance, an aristocratic style which are in the command of one man: Heifetz. Or the cello manages as many as four gradations of tone in what can only be one bow, while the music is proclaimed with sovereign power or unimaginable serenity. Who but Casals? But these are the relatively easy ones to recognize. In a lifetime of professional concert-going, I have sat at the feet of these men, have listened again and again to their recordings, and I feel that I am as acquainted with their musical personalities as I am with the traits of my family and best friends. There are others with whom I have had as long a musical intimacy, and I have little difficulty identifying them: Bruno Walter, Artur Rubinstein, Rudolf Serkin, Nathan Milstein, Lotte Lehmann, Enrico Caruso. After all, I was virtually weaned on Caruso records. I heard that magnificent voice on the primitive records of my youth and did not realize how truly magnificent it was until electronic advances made it possible for the engineers to let us hear something approximating what the tenor had sounded like on a stage. But new performers of quality keep coming along, and recordings have grown into a flood. There are musicians I could not possibly identify; I had never heard their names until the WQXR announcer spoke them. There are pieces, not only new, but old—think of the torrents of baroque music that have been poured onto discs—I could not possibly recognize, for the simple reason that I did not know they existed, and I am not unfamiliar with the baroque literature.

Failures and frustrations do not discourage me from testing myself in my WQXR game. Better ears than mine have been fooled by recordings. There is the authenticated story about Toscanini and an unheralded conductor whose work he first heard on a disc. This chap had made several recordings with a pick-up group of exceptionally skilled orchestral players, and the result was truly impressive. Toscanini could not be blamed for getting excited over the quality of the ensemble tone and the perceptive style of the interpretation. There was the record to prove that it had not been accomplished with knobs or mixers. And it hadn't, though we know that musician-engineers can do wonders for performers, from converting pipsqueak voices into thunderers to substituting the right note for a false one. What was exhilarating on these discs was the interpretations, and these had to be the conductor's. But were they? Well, Toscanini invited the conductor to do some guest appearances with the NBC Symphony during the summer series, and it turned out that the man was what Maestro called an *assasino*. It was the crack musicians under the man's temporary command who had contributed the quality to the discs.

If the record was misleading about the conductor's gifts, it was nothing of the sort about the music. And that is what counts. Music is our theme. Indeed, it is a vast congeries of worlds. One may find it in everything from trifling charm to exalting sub-limity. One may dwell always on the heights amid apocalyptic masterpieces, or one may romp happily along the gentle valleys with the humble works that have no ambitions other than to amuse and entertain. Or one can be tolerant and wise and choose to relish the exalted and the modest at different times, depending on one's mood and taste.

For myself I am not doctrinaire about any school, form, or epoch. All I seek is excellence, which, of course, is a great deal to ask, and I am happy to find it in any style or genre. For me, music has been and is an endless source of enjoyment. I get a kick out of a tenor singing a thrice familiar aria, provided it is a tenor like Caruso doing an aria like "Vesti la Giubba" from *Pagliacci,* and I can get a lift out of a Sousa march, a Strauss waltz, or an honest and evocative treatment of an old jazz fixture like "The Saints Go Marching In." More often my preference is for a late Beethoven quartet, with its relentless searching for the elusive, mysterious truth of our common mortality and our un-common reach for immortality, or a Chopin ballade, with its unexpected refractions of the sweetness and heartbreak of the human predicament. But I exclude no area. I welcome new ex-periences in the concert hall and opera house, on the radio and through the phonograph and tape recorder in my home.

It is the aim of this book, as it is of WQXR itself, to encourage you to be as ardent an explorer as you wish or dare to be. The writers of the individual chapters have been guides to the pub-lic on the air, and they now have given their enthusiasms a more permanent form. If you follow them into any section of the musi-cal cosmos, you will find their personal distillations of years of experience. If you take advantage of their discographies, you can become as knowledgeable—well, almost as knowledgeable—as they are. I don't mind confessing that I intend to take some of the hints of my colleagues in fields where I have less experience than they.

I don't pretend that I agree with every judgment in these chap-ters. I have great respect for Robert Lawrence's command of opera, and I join in most of his views. But I do not agree with his estimate of either *Carmen* or *Otello*. I grant that he makes his points cogently, and I feel that when Bizet stops to let Micaela, that innocuous milksop of an ingenue, sing a long, show-stopping aria, he is less than true to the passion and intensity of his subject, and that Verdi retrogresses to his earlier style when he pauses to have Iago sing the surefire *Brindisi*, or drinking song. But even as I agree with the need for rigorous artistic standards, I find myself recalling the pleasure I have derived from a Bori singing Micaela or a Leonard Warren belting out the *Brindisi*. But what about my demands for excellence? Well, the singing is excellent, and I welcome any manifestation of grace.

I am especially pleased with the independence of judgment to be found in these chapters. Does Mr. Lawrence dare to declare his preference for Kappel over Flagstad? Bravo for him! I, too, felt that Flagstad often sounded like some inhumanly glorious machine when she poured out those shining cascades of rich, dark tone, but there were moments when her power to transcend apparently human limits of sound were unbelievably thrilling—and right. In the *Liebestod*, when her voice, with its unearthly coolness, pierced and surmounted the surging orchestra, she seemed to me to achieve the transfiguration—the passage beyond human desire and the merging with a kind of brooding, exulting world spirit—that Wagner intended.

Each of us has his own treasured memories. Like Mr. Lawrence, I have a higher opinion than most connoisseurs of *Fidelio*, and like him, I recall with admiration Flagstad's Lenora and René Maison's Florestan. I have grateful recollections of a more recent *Fidelio* with Nilsson in the title role and John Vickers as Florestan. But the *Fidelio* I remember best is the one I heard in Salzburg in 1935, during one of those brief, magical years when Toscanini, who had turned his back on a Bayreuth dominated by Hitler, joined Bruno Walter and others to make the Austrian festival the most unforgettable of my musical experiences. Lotte Lehmann was the Maestro's Fidelio, and though her voice never had the sheen and amplitude of either Flagstad's or Nilsson's, it had a humanity, a vulnerability that enhanced the character's courage, that was immensely touching. With Toscanini holding everything together with a tight, yet incandescent force, Lehmann sang with a tenderness and intensity remarkable even for her. At that year's Salzburg Festival, if I may permit myself to wallow in rich memories, Toscanini also conducted a *Falstaff* of incomparable lightness and radiance, and Walter presided over a luminous and enchanting *Don Giovanni*. I have always regretted that those performances were not captured on discs. I know that Toscanini did another *Falstaff* years later with the NBC Symphony Orchestra, not long before his retirement, and I feel that in this performance he caught more of the sunset glow and undercurrent of melancholy that are so clearly part of Verdi's operatic swansong than in the Salzburg performance. But it would be wonderful to have records of both performances, as well as, say, a much earlier Toscanini *Falstaff* from his first Scala years at the turn of the century. I am sure that one would discover unexpected subtleties of interpretation in each version, and one would learn something about the growth and change in attitudes of a great performer as well as discover different views of a lovely and abiding masterpiece.

My colleagues have confined themselves for the most part to recommendations of one performance of certain works, though there may be dozens of different recordings. The purpose is to simplify difficult decisions for you. But no one will be offended if you go your own way and select a different recording. I would recommend that occasionally you might try different versions just for the fun of checking how much difference you can discern. Jascha Zayde, in his chapter on the piano, its literature and interpreters, has brought an expert musician's discrimination to an analysis of the individual excellences as well as the differences between the Horowitz and Rubinstein performances of the *Waldstein Sonata*. I would also suggest that you investigate the differences in a great pianist's various interpretations of the same piece. I have spent some time comparing Horowitz's old Victor recording of Chopin's *B flat Minor Sonata* with his more recent Columbia recording. I thought I had a distinct notion of the pianist's way with this sonata; I was astonished to find how much alteration and penetration had developed in the years between the two versions. The Funeral March movement in the later one has arrived at a dignity and nobility that leaves one humble and grateful. If there is any music that has become shopworn from reuse, this is it. One does not need to hark back to meetings of a provincial Kiwanis Club of decades ago where grown men stood up and bleated the words, "Where will all be a hundred years from now? Pushing up the daisies, pushing up the daisies," in an embarrasing caricature of Chopin's music. Heaven alone knows how many times in my thirty years of music criticism I sat through overly sentimental or deliberately unsentimentalized and arid treatments of this movement. I developed, I fear, a kind of instant nausea at the thought of having to endure another traversal, even by a fine pianist. But listening to the later Horowitz version, I was led to rediscover the shattering simplicity and purity of Chopin's emotion.

I hope that you will give yourself a chance to broaden the range of your musical interests by accepting the counsel of my colleagues to try a variety of styles and performances in whatever fields your interest lies. I happen not to be an admirer of the operettas of Romberg and Friml, but I am gratified that Alfred Simon is willing to defend their good qualities at a time when it is unfashionable to do so. I might just go back and listen to his recommendations and find that he speaks with the voice of wisdom.

I would also hope that if your first preferences are for music that is readily accessible, whether a Gilbert and Sullivan song or a Tchaikovsky symphony, you will take chances and try other and more challenging things. You might find yourself on an unexpectedly adventurous course. I recall a friend of years gone by, a man whose principal preoccupation was sports, whom I sent one night to see and hear his first opera. I don't think he was at all interested, but here was a pair of tickets down front on the aisle for *Lucia di Lammermoor* at the Met. The next day my friend was shiny-eyed. Why hadn't anyone told him about her? I wondered for an instant whether he was talking about Lucia. Not at all; he was ecstatic about Lily Pons, and if he remembered that a chap named Donizetti had had something to do with the occasion, he did not mention him. Well, my friend, a meticulous man, not only caught every Pons performance at the Met that season, but also kept a log with the dates and the roles. For several seasons he was a dedicated Pons follower; if he could not get away for the entire performance, he managed to hear at least an act, for he could not bear to have his log remind him that he had missed a Pons evening. Was this the fidelity of a man in love from a distance? Who knows? I do know that my friend was exposing himself to all the operas in which Miss Pons sang. And then, one year, Miss Pons was away from the Met for quite a long time, and my bereaved friend decided that he might as well as try another singer. This time he hit on Verdi's *Traviata,* and another enchanted world opened up for him. Thereafter he became the slave of Verdi, and presently he broadened his experience—and the scope of his log—to embrace nearly all the Italian and French operas. I assumed that his zeal would stop there, but it was not many years before he thought he ought to venture on Wagner. Strauss followed, and then almost anything new or different that the Met did. In time the Met became inadequate to his curiosity, and he began to attend other performances when they were available, in and out of New York. Finally, the thing happened that I would have regarded as most unlikely: He decided to explore something besides opera. Toward the end of his enormously enriched life he went to all sorts of concerts—recitalists as well as ensembles—and he had lovingly accumulated a record collection of amazing diversity and catholicity.

I daresay that many of us have had comparable, if not similar, adventures with music. I remember that as a high-school lad in New York in the twenties, I sat in the cheapest seats at Lewisohn Stadium. They cost twenty-five cents in those days, and there was the nickel fare each way in the subway. But like so many New Yorkers, I had my first experience of the staples of the symphonic repertoire at the Stadium. The inevitable echo was an annoyance, and the performances were often routine, if not downright slipshod. But how could you quibble when you found yourself listening to marvels of eloquence for a total outlay of thirty-five cents? Radio in those days, you must remember, was a primitive affair; you were lucky to get a shadow of a voice or an instrument if you held your earphones snugly to your ears. I remember that my dream of felicity was to have a season pass so that I might attend every Stadium concert every summer. Alas, for the disillusionment of maturity. I reached the point where I did have a season pass, and I used it only when I had to go to the Stadium in the line of reviewing duty. By then I knew that there were better ways to hear symphonic music. By then I was also eager for much greater variety.

I have learned that there are no limits to the ways in which people discover and respond to music, and I am constantly reminded of the rewards for those who come unexpectedly upon something moving or stirring. I remember spending summer vacations in the late thirties in the White Mountain area of northern New Hampshire. My wife and I rented a little wooden shack on a knoll surrounded by sloping fields, with the Presidential range in the distance. We brought with us one summer a portable phonograph, not bad in quality of sound for its time, but thoroughly rudimentary by present-day standards, and a limited number of albums. I need hardly remind the old-timers among my readers how brutally heavy a load of the old shellac 78-rpm discs could be. I have forgotten exactly what was in the collection, though I know it was diversified, including several big pieces, some works for soloists, a Beethoven quartet, a Mozart quintet, some songs. Among the items on my list was an acetate disc of Toscanini's performance of Sibelius's *Second Symphony.* I admit readily that this was a pirated recording, and if my friends among the Toscaninis think they have a cause for action, so be it. It was a full-voiced, dramatic performance of a symphony that may sound corny to impatient and sophisticated ears, and somehow it was perfect for our porch on the knoll, with all of northern New Hampshire to absorb the sound of the phonograph played at top volume and to give back a reflection of Sibelius's affinity for the forests and hills. It happened that our house was on a road over which a group of young actors—members of the newly installed company at the Chase Barn Playhouse—passed each afternoon, on foot I might say, on their way to dinner before the evening's rehearsal or show. It became habitual for them to pause on our knoll and stretch out on the grass while we regaled them with a spot of music from the portable. We went through our tiny repertory several times, but the piece they nearly always demanded was the Sibelius *Second.* Its drama and its orotundity thrilled them and picked them up better than a cocktail could have done. I have run into some of these actors and actresses in later years, and they have told me that no music reached them so readily and that Sibelius's *Second* became, no matter how they fared in their careers, a kind of symbol of how it felt to aspire to a grand utterance.

Music was for me not only a career but a way of life for so many years that I was desolated at the thought of being without it. When *The New York Times* requested in 1960 that I shift from the post of music critic to that of drama critic, I knew I would miss enkindling experiences in the opera house and concert hall, and I did. But I did not miss music, because I sought after it. If my evenings were occupied with theatre openings, I could turn to my record collection and to the radio, especially WQXR, for things I wanted to hear when the mood struck me.

I found that I rarely listened to the familiar repertory. While my blood could still be stirred by a grand performance of Beethoven's *Eroica,* I rarely turned to it of my own accord. If it was Beethoven I wanted to hear again, I went to the less frequently performed pieces. I listened to the piano sonatas, especially the late ones, that are not on every recitalist's program. I lived on intimate terms—and still do—with the late quartets; repetition does not diminish their spiritual strength. I can go back to Mozart's *G Minor Quintet* without fear of being disappointed. In its passion and anguish it tells me as much as any work of art, whether Shakespeare's *King Lear* or a Rembrandt self-portrait of the later years, about the truth of human suffering and courage. And on the same level of greatness is Schubert's *C Major Quintet.* I find inexpressible beauty in all sorts of places—in the slow movement of a Bach concerto, like the one for two violins, in a Corelli concerto grosso, in a long, declamatory, and piercingly emotional passage by Monteverdi, in a spacious, sunny air by Handel, in a moment of shy tenderness of a Schumann piano piece, in the exuberant playfulness of a Mendelssohn scherzo, in the heartbreak of a Schubert song, in the fragmented, eerie pointillism of Webern, in the rarefied atmosphere of the late, still adventurous, Stravinsky, as exemplified in a piece like *Threni.*

The rewards of music are unending, and the directions one can take in seeking them are unlimited. Familiar pieces can yield new discoveries, and unfamiliar ones can provide unexpected delight and illumination. The other day I decided to try Prokofiev's *Quartet No. 1*, Opus 50, which was written in 1930 on commission from the Library of Congress and Elizabeth Sprague Coolidge, that great and good benefactor of music of our century. I must have heard this quartet at one time or another during the years I haunted the concert halls, but it struck me with the force of an utter and agreeable stranger. I was particularly taken by the lovely slow movement.

Another evening I selected Horowitz's record of twelve Scarlatti sonatas. You will notice, when you read Igor Kipnis's chapter and discography, that he recommends Landowska and Kirkpatrick, both harpsichordists, for the Scarlatti sonatas. There is no doubt that this was the instrument for which Scarlatti wrote, and that each interpreter has something worthwhile to reveal of the composer and his music; but I would also suggest listening to a pianist like Horowitz bringing his own resources and those of the modern piano to bear on Scarlatti. The result is entrancing. Listen to Horowitz play the *F Minor Sonata*, Longo 118, and note the poignancy and sweetness of Scarlatti's enamoring inspiration. This music is like the prefiguring of a melting aria by Bellini. Then listen to Joan Sutherland reviving the glories of bel canto in Bellini, and perhaps even as you relish the commanding control of the singer, note how this music bears a slight, incipient kinship to Chopin, who was touched and influenced by its composer.

As you read through the ensuing chapters and consult the accompanying discographies, you will observe that there are some duplications. Thus David Randolph and Igor Kipnis list Handel's *Messiah*, but in different interpretations. I welcome such differences of opinion, and I hope that you will have the opportunity to take advantage of them by testing various performances for yourself. I suppose that you will dissent from some of the choices our experts have made. I know that I do. I could argue with Martin Bookspan, for example, about interpreters of Beethoven's symphonies. I could certainly want people to have some idea of the way Toscanini conducted these works. But there is no doubt in my mind that the recommended discs in all categories are deserving. Our object in limiting ourselves to a minimum of suggestions was to provide immediate guidance to the reader who is not yet sure of his own predilections. In time he will make his own way, ignoring the hints of his advisers. That is as it should be.

Let me make another confession. I am a little unhappy that we have not done more with contemporary music. I happen to think that one of America's distinguished composers is Elliott Carter and that his string quartets, though novel in structure and difficult to apprehend on first acquaintance, are works of stature, which will repay repeated hearings. But in our desire to range over the vast literature in all the forms, we found we had to make choices, lest the discographies themselves form a book as thick as the Schwann catalogue. We were mindful of our purpose—to provide a guide for family listening pleasure. We assumed and hoped we would be reaching into families for whom the vast, overflowing worlds of music remained largely to be explored. We are confident that those individuals and families well on their way in musical exploration will also find these pages useful, and that they will be encouraged to leave us for bypaths we have not mapped. We hope that you will get fresh ideas from these chapters, and that you will keep telling WQXR how it can continue to enhance your family's listening pleasure. In your home, in the opera house and concert hall, in the schools and churches, and on the airwaves, especially WQXR's, AM and FM, happy listening!

1

Opera

ROBERT LAWRENCE

Opera is less an art than a state of being. The allegiance it exacts is total, engulfing, lifelong. Emotion reigns as in a cult; logic is secondary; even the most objective critic, in framing his verdict, will start from only one of several possible viewpoints. The charm of opera—and its strength—lies in the power to disunite, stir aesthetic conflict among all who prize it. Learned men have stated, from time to time, that opera is dying; but no moribund organism could possibly generate such passions.

The word *opera*, really an omnibus term, has been used rather loosely across the years—especially in this country, where "Grand Opera" is still taken to mean any sung and staged work calling for expensive soloists, large orchestra, chorus, and production by a multiple staff. This is an illusion. Style, not size, is the determining factor in opera's identity; yet size alone seems to have written its calling card in the United States. Any art taken up by the rich and highly placed (as opera has been in the past) is assumed to be "grand"; and the inflating process, inspired by the word *opera* and its association with crystal chandeliers, imposing halls, elegant audiences, went down the line during the last century until most small towns in America called their largest theater—housing vaudeville and occasionally a spoken drama—the *Opera House*, not because opera was being given there, but because the place was grander and more sumptuous than any other in town.

The majority of works produced in a season of "Grand Opera" are, technically speaking, not *grand* at all. Most of them may be classified as *lyric drama,* with a libretto (generally the equivalent of a modern play) set to music which not only sounds well in itself but continually heightens the action. There are few, if any, formal arias. Historical pageantry does not exist; ballet, infrequently. The scale of production, despite a few big scenes, is generally intimate. All the scores of Puccini, with the exception of *Turandot,* are *lyric drama;* and so is the preponderance of those by Massenet.

An even more intimate style, closely connected with the French theater, is *opéra-comique,* which features set numbers (as in modern Broadway musicals) linked by spoken dialogue. *Carmen* and *Mignon* are perhaps the best known examples. Their German cousins—*The Magic Flute, Fidelio, Der Freischütz*—are put together in exactly the same way, though designated across the border as *singspiel.* It should be noted that despite the French term *comique,* this type of opera is not so lighthearted (plenty of the plots are tragic) as it is intimate, evoking life at close quarters, and reminiscent of the *genre* paintings of Greuze as opposed to the monumental canvases of a Rubens.

Opera buffa, a style beloved of the Italian theater (this time read *buffa* for real comedy), also uses set numbers; but instead of being linked by spoken dialogue, they are bound together by a freely moving song-speech called *recitativo.* The numbers themselves concentrate on antic, often zany farce. *Folk opera*— a mood rather than a style, often comic, sometimes rich in pathos—draws on national coloring, ranges widely in repertoire from *The Bartered Bride* to *Porgy and Bess.*

There are many avenues of approach to this flexible and diversified art. Richard Wagner spurned old-fashioned opera (*arias* alternating with *recitativo*) in favor of *music drama,* with its uninterrupted chain of melody and symphonic dominance of the orchestra. Musorgski, using much but not all of the same philosophy (voice and orchestra are equally prominent in his scores), created the *chronicle* type of music drama: short historical scenes varying sharply in characterization, wild humor contrasting with bleakest tragedy.

Most of the great Verdi scores (and a majority of those by Rossini, Bellini, and Donizetti) are labeled simply *opera*, no less, no more—a design of formal numbers known as *arias* alternating with *recitativo* in convincingly dramatic sequence. *Lucia di Lammermoor, Luisa Miller, Rigoletto, Il Trovatore,* and *La Traviata* are among the masterpieces that come to mind. As for the redoubtable style labeled *grand opera*, only the giant machines of Spontini, Meyerbeer, late Rossini (*Mosè, William Tell*), early Verdi (*Nabucco, I Lombardi, Macbeth*), quite late Verdi (*Simon Boccanegra, Don Carlo, Aida, Otello*), Ponchielli's *La Gioconda* and a few twentieth-century loners, such as Puccini's *Turandot*, conform technically to the concept of historical background, vast concerted numbers, frequent use of ballet, and elaborate pageantry which make it very special.

This variety of approach strengthens, in the long run, the fascination of opera. The diverse types of work, such as *grand opera, opera buffa, opéra-comique,* complement rather than vie with one another. There is plenty of room in the musical theater for every sort of style. No basis for conflict here. The real battle line, over which many wars in opera have been waged, has to do with the relative importance of words and music. Which comes first? Which rates a priority? For centuries we have had tugs of war between admirers of the vocal melodists—Handel, Scarlatti, Bellini, Donizetti—and champions of the dramatic reformers—Gluck, Wagner, Musorgski, Berg—with fans of some of the greatest composers (Mozart, Verdi, Strauss) standing dead center.

Allied with this conflict—on a performing rather than a compositional level—is the question of how singers should behave when the music comes first. How far can they go in milking a climax and yet stand within the bounds of good taste? These are issues that can still bring opera buffs to blows, or at least to the breaking of long-time friendships.

Since all of opera is a personal experience, and every writer—subconsciously or otherwise—advances his own point of view, I trust the reader will permit me to present my own, imbedded in reminiscences of New York performance. Light—admittedly subjective—may thereby be shed on certain styles and artists.

Personal Memories

My first preparations for listening to opera took place in movie palaces. It is almost impossible today to imagine the quantity of good music performed in New York, thirty-five or forty years ago, in the vast, cathedral-like motion picture theaters. Every one of them had its permanent orchestra of from sixty to seventy-five players, expert musicians all. The Capitol Theater's ensemble provided a base of development for Eugene Ormandy, first as assistant concertmaster, later as associate conductor.

These orchestras at the Strand, Capitol, Roxy, Rivoli and Rialto, under the direction of competent leaders and with musical programs arranged by men of taste and imagination, played a widely ranging repertoire of overtures, tone poems, and excerpted symphonic movements. During a brief stint as usher at the Rialto I came to know Bruckner's *Fourth Symphony* as incidental music for a silent film featuring Emil Jannings, "The Way of All Flesh." This score was performed by the orchestra at two of the five shows daily (the organ took over at the other performances). I was so drawn, night after night, by the symphony's opening horn call that I stood listening in the aisle, forgetting the flow of patrons waiting for seats.

Vocally, too, the movie houses had interesting things to offer. They maintained, in addition to resident orchestra and ballet, a permanent chorus and often very good soloists. We had Verdi— the triumphal scene from *Aida*—on the stage of the Capitol and the beauties of Russian opera, in excerpted form, at the Rivoli.

New York in those days was starting on its career as a cultural beehive. My musical background was formed at popular roots not only in the movie houses but the ball parks (a first encounter with *Aida* took place one night long ago at the Polo Grounds), open-air concerts in Central Park by the Goldman Band, and at the Lewisohn Stadium by the New York Philharmonic. A first memory of the Stadium—and an operatic one—goes back to the night following the death of President Harding, when the Philharmonic played "Siegfried's Funeral March" in memoriam. So heroic a send-off may not have been warranted; but to the youngster drinking in this music as a new experience, the evening lent Warren G. Harding a special aura. I wonder if he ever heard of Wagner.

The most vivid preparation for life as an opera buff came with a musical play imported from Berlin: *Johannes Kreisler*. It was based on short stories by E. T. A. Hoffmann, some of whose tales had already inspired the famous piece by Offenbach. Years have gone by since this production in the early twenties, sumptuously mounted, with Jacob Ben-Ami as the protagonist. I have tried checking with any number of contemporaries, brought up in New York, as to their impressions. No one today recalls *Johannes Kreisler*.

There were over sixty scenes, made possible through a revolving stage and the ingenious use of cutouts. At one point, as the platform swung around, the interior of a rococo opera house came into sight, while on the stage within a stage, Mozart's *Don Giovanni* was being performed. Indeed the central theme of the play was the art of Mozart, and its crowning point the moment when Johannes Kreisler—in love with the soprano who sings the rôle of Donna Anna—returns late at night to the empty opera house. He sits brooding in his box, suddenly perceives the ghost of the soprano on the stage below, hears her sing a spectral "Non mi dir." In a surge of feeling which defies gravity itself, he soars (on wires) from the box, descends to the stage, and holds out his arms to the phantom, who disappears. Exaggerated, ridiculous? Not at all. A way of life eternally operatic, illusory, expressive.

Then at last came an encounter with opera at the Metropolitan. Newspaper pictures of Maria Jeritza as Turandot, wearing a cloth-of-gold train that spread from the top of a majestic staircase to footlights apparently hundreds of feet away, led me to the spectacle by Puccini. I bought a ticket in that part of the old house perpendicular to the stage, from which one could see very little of what was happening on stage. Moreover I was poorly prepared, having read only a brief synopsis, instead of the libretto word for word. Yet certain elements in the performances made their mark: the clatter of the xylophone in the opening bars; the entrance of Turandot, silent and implacable, extending a hand tipped with clawlike nails to signal death for the Prince of Persia. These were among the externals that impressed. The work itself, as I learned later, suffers from variations in quality.

Even before attending *Turandot*, I had succumbed to that love for the music of Wagner, which, once it sets in, holds one captive for years. There were weekly visits to the shelves of the New York Public Library, borrowing piano-vocal scores of the *Ring*, playing them through. I resolved to hear every work of Wagner then being offered by the Metropolitan. To raise funds for standing room, I tutored in Latin; but my mind was not much on the work. What held me fast were *Tristan und Isolde, Götterdämmerung, Parsifal*, and a dramatic soprano, new to the Metropolitan, who sang in all of them: Gertrude Kappel.

The night of January 16, 1928, was a significant one for me. Life, at the age of fifteen, seemed to hold no limits. The thrill of a first *Tristan*—toward which I had built through months of studying the score, playing it, dreaming it—was about to be realized. I stood in back of the house, impatient for the opening notes of the prelude. When the music began, my critical sense told me this was not a good orchestra (Metropolitan instrumental standards have risen immeasurably since then); but once the soprano from Munich, who was making her debut that evening, had embarked on Isolde's first-act narrative, the performance cast its spell. There were other aspects that have stayed with me: the intensity of Artur Bodanzky's conducting, despite the poor ensemble he had to work with; the sumptuous singing of Karin Branzell as Brangaene; the vigor and authority of Friedrich Schorr as Kurvenal; the cast-iron sound of Rudolf Laubenthal as Tristan; but my chief impression was of the Isolde, a performer I was rarely to miss from that night until her departure from the Metropolitan eight years later. Gertrude Kappel, from the other side of the footlights, taught me more about drama through vocal coloring than any artist in recall.

Was this just a puppy love, the indiscriminate worship of a youngster taking his first steps in opera? I do not think so; for on the basis of much that was told me later, there were other articulate, sensitive opera-goers growing up at that time who felt the same way. Some three decades after that memorable first *Tristan*, I was seated at a performance of *La Traviata* with a group that included the conductor Erich Leinsdorf and his wife, Anne, who as a child had been taken to almost all of the Bodanzky performances. That night we were hearing Renata Tebaldi's first New York Violetta—a mellifluous study in surface gloss. Suddenly Mrs. Leinsdorf shot me a glance and muttered, "*We* heard Kappel!" An odd remark, evoking the name of a soprano who had never in her life sung Violetta; but I understood at once what was meant: the chasm between that beloved voice, which had come from the soul, and the well-negotiated singing of the moment.

I often disagree about opera with George Marek, author of *Puccini* and *Richard Strauss*, but never about Kappel. He and his wife were standees in that era; they too were held by the vocal colors Kappel used for revealing psychological states, and they still talk about it. The late Robert Bagar, a perceptive music critic, told me that on a Sunday afternoon in April, 1934, when Kappel sang Brünnhilde's Immolation at Carnegie Hall with the New York Philharmonic under Toscanini's direction, he was so unstrung following the concert that he walked miles before recovering himself. In short, I did not stand alone as an enthusiast.

Why was it, then, that this remarkable artist, for all her gifts, never reaped the public acclaim of a Flagstad? I should say in answer—and this is a question over which I have pondered long—that one had to tune in, provide one's own reception on her very special wave length. Before hearing her sing, one had to know the *word*. It was the extension, the transformation of this word into music that melted one. The voice itself had superb natural beauty, especially in the deeper tones, with a dark opulence I have heard from no other soprano. Then just before the emergence of the extreme top it had a fullness, richness, eloquence, which haunt one in retrospect. If my words, at this point, read like those of a physician recounting a case history, it is because this voice etched itself on my mind and heart, because I knew—just as the lover knows every impulse of the woman he has been courting—the most minute responses of this instrument in performance. There were passing technical lapses; the top tones, basically thrilling, were sometimes strained, for this great interpreter varied perceptively from one evening to the next. Her voice did not possess the Niagara-like plenitude that marked the Flagstad tone, the metallic gleam of Frida Leider or Germaine Lubin, other leading Wagner singers of Kappel's generation.

Yet it had something more to say than any of the voices I have mentioned; it brought—when in best condition—a matchless sense of illumination to the role.

Outwardly Kappel was jovial—blonde, attractive, modest. I have heard it said by those who sang with her that she was among the most considerate of colleagues. The wonderful carriage of her head, the regal bearing of the shoulders were attributes onstage and offstage. One of her most winning qualities as a person was her simplicity, her bubbling and spontaneous warmth.

Yet was she really simple? I cannot believe so; for over the years, my ears attuned to many voices, I have never heard another so mysterious, so elusive. This is perhaps the reason it was never a successful recording voice. The few discs (pallid pre-electrical) that are available can give no idea of its color, its unique overtones. When, in Isolde's first-act narrative, she reflected on the wounded Tristan and sang the words *Er sah mir in die Augen* ("He looked into my eyes"), the voice glided softly, almost opaquely, up those half-steps to the final note, then opened like some fabled flower. Yet this was only one facet of Kappel's art. Loftiness and nobility, as in the *Götterdämmerung* Brünnhilde, were another; and a third lay in the subtle, almost insidious projection of evil. Her Ortrud and Kundry were complex, malevolent creations both, a journey into the extrasensory.

To have summoned this sound out of the depths of her consciousness, projected her inner world to those willing to get in touch, must have demanded a complexity that still has me baffled when I recall the modest, smiling woman offstage. The enigma remains.

If I have dwelled on Gertrude Kappel at length, it is because her singing determined for me the standard by which I still judge opera in performance: expressivity. There are many ways, all entirely personal, of appraising this art. Some listeners prefer vocal brilliance; others, intellectual discipline; a third group, purity of phrasing; and so on down the line. It is possible, of course, for the same buff to prize all these qualities in varying degree; but usually one who lives for opera has his own hard-core approach, his own well-defined aesthetic. And so, with a bow to the intellectual, to the purely musical, to the vocally

pyrotechnical, I shall explore operatic values in the remainder
of this piece with an ear for the expressive.

Singing Style

Before long the seductive air of the opera house, the desire
to be there at all times, no matter what the work to be sung, cut
through my limiting Wagnerian preference. I learned that every
part of the repertoire can have its special appeal. There came as
fresh discoveries the grandeur of *Norma,* pathos of *Manon,* high
spirits of *The Bartered Bride.* Three distinguished sopranos were
appearing in these works: Rosa Ponselle, Lucrezia Bori, Elisabeth Rethberg—all of them strikingly different in sound, yet
almost equally fine. Ponselle, though American by birth, exemplified the tradition of the Italian dramatic soprano: vocal majesty, command of ornamentation. Bori was the singing actress,
relying less on opulence of tone than unfailing charm and insight.
Rethberg had perhaps the most appealing voice of all—a lyrical
instrument, capable of dramatic flight—plus enormous taste and
musicality.

When one is new to opera and to the halls where it is given,
almost every detail on both sides of the footlights lingers through
the years. In those early days as a standee at the old Met, I had
my counterpoint notebook before me, propped against the rail.
There were exercises to be done for next morning's class, and
intermissions were the time in which to get started. As I worked,
those idols of my youth, the New York music critics, would
saunter up the aisle in the midst of the crowd. These were the
mysterious ones, unrecognized by most of the audience, but
known to my fellow standees. They ranged through their empire
incognito, much as Haroun al Raschid must have gone in disguise among his people. Olin Downes, Lawrence Gilman, Oscar
Thompson, journalists all, looked to us, behind the rail, like sages
from some Caliphate in space. These were first impressions, re-
fracted and romanticized.

Other great singers held sway in those days—the last of the
Gatti regime—in addition to the artists already mentioned. Law-

rence Tibbett, at his vibrant best; John Charles Thomas, a model of vocal elegance; Giuseppe De Luca, all suavity and lyricism; Ezio Pinza, one of the noblest bassos in the world. And with the demise of the old Chicago Civic Opera, some of its leading singers came to perform—outstandingly—at the Metropolitan. Frida Leider, Maria Olszewska, Lotte Lehmann, Tito Schipa, and Richard Bonelli established themselves among the elect. There were brief but memorable returns by Claudia Muzio and Edith Mason, both of whom had sung in New York prior to their days in Chicago. This was the firmament of the time, made even brighter by the debut of Kirsten Flagstad in 1935.

It was before the huge success of Flagstad that I had begun to wonder about the aesthetics of opera in performance. Could it be that some of the world's most celebrated artists, the recognized "greats," were not to the taste of all who heard them? Might one concede that stylistic preference, previous education, helped shape one's judgment just as definitely as the sound of the singer's voice?

The lack of an absolute standard for judging operatic artists first made itself known to me during certain performances that featured Beniamino Gigli. Here was a tenor with an indisputably beautiful voice, lionized by the public; yet I found much of his work uncongenial. The compressing of all emotion into the passing sigh, the vulgar sob, put me off then and still does whenever I hear his records—excepting a first-rate *Andrea Chénier*, which, sung straight, shows how great an artist he might have been. In the case of his contemporary, Giacomo Lauri-Volpi, the brilliantly trumpeted top tones, arrogantly held ad infinitum, again could bring offense. There was little real expressivity in either of these men, for all their conventionalized show of it. Their art, though based on quality singing, was contrived; "sold" to a public out front via routine theatrical effects.

One has only to hear a recording by Enrico Caruso with its manly, straightforward account of the music to realize that Italian tenors need not exaggerate in order to make their point. Aureliano Pertile, Giovanni Martinelli, and in our time Carlo Bergonzi have upheld the dignity and emotional directness of the Latin performer, with such distinguished foreigners as the late

Jussi Bjoerling, Jan Peerce, Nicolai Gedda, and Richard Tucker seconding their approach. Franco Corelli, who continues to grow artistically from one season to the next, still has enough of the Lauri-Volpi vocal strut to alienate me in part. The point of view is admittedly subjective. Which school of singing, in short, does one prefer? Best make a choice and judge accordingly.

Now back to Kirsten Flagstad, with that same subjectivity as guide. There can be no doubt that hers was one of the phenomenal voices of the century. The grandeur of sound, ease of emission, and feeling of limitless reserve made her art—from the technical standpoint—unique and unsurpassable. On occasion the size and splendor of the voice created an aura that matched the excitement of the music—as in Brünnhilde's oath on the spear, Leonora's rapture at the freeing of Florestan. In general, however, her acting and much of her singing lacked (for me and for others) that inner expressivity one had cherished so greatly in Kappel and found in the art of a Frida Leider, a Lotte Lehmann.

Recently I have studied several Flagstad recordings with a view to playing them on the air; and in almost every case, though admiring the tone and musicianship, I have been put off by their austerity, the separation of notes within the phrase, so that the climactic ones come out detached and sometimes dry. A more basic source of alienation lies in the small amount of nuance, the limited gradations of color. Yet I am aware, more now than ever before, that it is not so much the individual singer who determines the listener's reaction as the school he or she represents. Substitute, in this year of publication, Christa Ludwig and Régine Crespin for Kappel and Leider; replace Flagstad with Birgit Nilsson, and the lines are clearly drawn. Here are two opposing schools of thought, their patterns running from one generation to the next: the expressive and the overwhelming. Take your pick, and mark X on the ballot.

There comes a time in the life of most opera fans when the focus of energy and admiration shifts from their contemplation of the singer to the work itself. This, in short, is maturity; and, regrettably, some of the more impassioned bobby-soxers never make it. They end as they started—with a permanent crush on performers, endless talk about singers, their fees and foibles. To them, opera is a parlor game, a checkerboard of personalities; or a sport, with high C's bearing the same importance as a home run or a matador thrust.

Turning away from all this, one can concentrate on *opera*—the sum rather than its parts—the most complex and fascinating of theatrical arts. Having reached expressivity as my critical norm, with the understanding that certain great singers fall within this category and others do not, I began to approach the art of the performers with less personal involvement, learned to take their achievements more in stride. It was the music itself that held me more than before.

This is not to imply a lack of major artists during the regime of Edward Johnson, who followed Gatti-Casazza as general manager. The brief but fiery presence of Maria Caniglia, an outstanding dramatic soprano, and of Mafalda Favero, a cherishable lyric, just before World War II, helped maintain international standards. The success of such American singers as Helen Traubel and Eleanor Steber did much for the development of native talents. Zinka Milanov, vocally authoritative in the big Verdi roles, brought a special glow to the 1940's, as did those two admirable lyric sopranos, Licia Albanese and Bidu Sayao.

There followed, after the war, a gifted group of Italian singers who bloomed dramatically and faded too quickly: Giuseppe Di Stefano, Mario Del Monaco, Cloe Elmo, Fedora Barbieri (now enjoying a resurgence as "character" mezzo)—all prime voices lacking in the moderation that preserves. Then, well into the administration of Rudolf Bing, came Maria Callas (expressive school) and Renata Tebaldi (overwhelming) with their famous rivalry.

At the risk of being charged with inconsistency, I must admit to playing few recordings by Callas on the air, for the fine intelligence, the creativity of her singing do not always neutralize what for me is an unpleasant sound. I respect her artistry, but choose not to live with it. Yet Callas holds, and deserves, a stature that will never be lessened by adverse reaction from any critic. She has given significantly of herself in dramatic projection and musical splendor. Her case illustrates again—more strikingly than most—the hotly subjective nature of one's feelings about opera. The recordings of her rival, Madame Tebaldi, though smoother and more luscious, disaffect me from another standpoint. They have little to offer interpretatively. Tebaldi is the surer vocalist, Callas the greater artist.

Still one further credit, a large one, must be chalked on the Callas scoreboard: her versatility in portraying many roles, and more important, her enterprise in reviving single-handedly a whole branch of the repertoire fallen into disuse: the *bel canto* operas, which concentrate on vocal agility as well as expressive song. *Anna Bolena, Il Pirata, I Puritani, La Sonnambula* are among the works that have returned to life through this singer's initiative. Whether or not one relishes their music is another question, part of the eternal subjectivity of opera, but her contribution is undeniable.

It remained for Joan Sutherland to follow the road opened by Miss Callas and to add certain dazzling accomplishments of her own. Starting purely as a vocalist (the overwhelming school), Miss Sutherland has developed the expressive side of her art until she now stands among the best-rounded of today's performers.

These conflicting elements of expressivity and vocal glamor may sometimes overlap in the same artist—as with Miss Sutherland and the excellent basso, Nicolai Ghiaurov—but more often they occur singly. Then it is up to us and our tastes, how much the performer pleases. Along such basic lines, Evelyn Lear—with a good voice and superb theatrical instincts—would be ranked among the leaders of today's expressive school. Leontyne Price, with wonderful vocal equipment and routine acting ability, would be hailed for her eminence in song. Each, according to the reader's lights, will have filled a valid place.

Worship of the prima donna, for many years in eclipse, is being revived for commercial reasons. A group of operatic susceptibles (turbulent fans) has been indoctrinated into nostalgia for a bygone era when princes, archdukes and railroad magnates drank champagne out of a diva's slipper and students unhitched the horses from their favorite soprano's carriage and bore her in triumph on their shoulders. This neogaslight cult—set in motion by a skillfully handled advertising campaign for recording artists—has been under way since the early 1950's. No more unhitched carriages, of course; and we are too hygienic to drink out of slippers. But florid titles, suggestive of old-time Havana cigars, have been invented for modern singers: *La Divina, La Stupenda, La Diva Imperial.* Recording companies, out to surround their artists with the type of fervent mystique that greeted Jenny Lind on a tour of America in the 1850's (whipped up by her New York representative, P. T. Barnum), would seem to have convinced some of our buffs that it is history relived to turn the opera house into a bedlam of shouts and cheers *during* the act. They rip the music as it sounds, smash the mood before its spell has ended, and take over the show in a belief that exhibitionist madness can restore the fabled past. This group has been spoiling opera at its source, driving many devotees to give up live performance for the privacy of stereo in the home, which no bellowing extrovert can mar. (The sale of discs has ironically been increased by all this, but not on the basis of divas.) Certainly the LP recordings of today offer an ideal, uninterrupted listening experience, which most opera houses (with the exception of Bayreuth, where special festival conditions prevail) would find it hard to match.

Another good reason for listening to records at home is one's own choice of repertoire. In this country, where the major opera houses are not—as in Europe—state-supported, an impresario must be guided by the public's taste in the production of new works or the revival of rare old ones. He depends, financially, upon its preference.

New York's operatic audience is in the main conservative. *Bohème* and *Traviata*, both admirable yet frayed, still reign at the ticket window. Rather than face a new musical experience, many patrons prefer rotating stars in the same old works. It *is* true, and fortunately, that unfamiliar scores sometimes do take hold. Strauss's *Die Frau ohne Schatten,* given its first New York stage production during the Metropolitan season of 1966-1967, succeeded with the public; and a superb revival of *Peter Grimes* in the same winter also found favor. But when the Hamburg Opera arrived in June, 1967, on an official visit to Lincoln Center, bringing with it a group of works never before presented here, response at the box-office was initially slow and ultimately disappointing. This, in effect, would constitute a mandate to any local impresario for the exercise of caution. Music-lovers with a taste for modern masterpieces will have to go it alone until the public, through its support, permits these works to enter the repertoire. Meanwhile *Lulu, Mathis der Maler,* and *Les Dialogues des Carmélites* make for good listening at home, complete on stereo, or in excerpted form, via radio.

Opera Companies

With the single exception of repertoire—in which they can afford to be more adventurous—the state-subsidized houses of Europe are run on a similar scale and with the same performing ideals as the great opera theaters of the United States. First-class orchestras and choruses are the rule; there is generally elaborate staging; famous singers divide their time among the various companies. Most celebrated today—and this is a rating that can always change—are La Scala, Italy's leading theater at Milan; the Vienna State Opera; the Hamburg, Munich, and Berlin operas; the Paris Opéra (more, perhaps, as a memory than a current achievement); the Bolshoi in Moscow; the Stockholm Opera; London's Covent Garden; in South America, the Teatro Colón of Buenos Aires; and here at home the Metropolitan.

So much for the crystal chandelier division. There remains another type of house, popularly priced, that fills a definite need. Vienna has its Volksoper, London its Sadler's Wells, New York its City Opera—theaters with good, often inventive repertoire and rising young artists to perform it. These companies are stable; their working conditions range from modest to excellent.

Those of us with memories of New York before the advent of the City Opera can recall more sketchy ensembles, which nevertheless gave pleasure. I remember, for example, a traveling troupe known as the *Art of Musical Russia.* This threadbare company brought to many young opera-goers a first, and startlingly wonderful, taste of *Khovantschina* and *The Golden Cockerel.* It mattered little that the orchestra was small, the singers only so-so, the scenery kept standing by the grace of God. The group, in its warmhearted abandon, radiated true musical theater.

Not all production need be luxurious. Low budget in itself is no crime against opera, and only mediocrity of spirit can do real damage. Memories go back to a shoestring venture which shaped the tastes of many buffs in my time. Following its great days as a home for extravaganza, the old New York Hippodrome had been converted into a vaudeville house, the big stage shorn to half its former size, the orchestra pit foreshortened. The auditorium, still overpowering in a moldy sort of way, was taken over during the early 1930's by a showman with a flair: Alfredo Salmaggi. He wore luxuriant black hair almost shoulder length, topped it with a broad-brimmed Borsalino, carried a gold-headed cane, and called himself Maestro. This flashy exuberance marked one side of the man. He also brought to the Hippodrome a vein of idealism for which few have given him credit. Many operagoers heard their first *Otello, Mefistofele, Ballo in Maschera, Andrea Chénier,* during the long years when these works were out of the Metropolitan repertoire, and some very superior performances of *Norma,* all at a widely publicized "ninety-nine-cent top."

Those who recall the workings of this theater from the inside tell me that its operation was filled with intrigue of a low order; but I, from out front, remember with gratitude a large selection of Italian operas done quite acceptably at prices that made it possible for one to attend night after night. When success came to Salmaggi, he did not stint, but extended himself by attempting—like Don Quixote combating the windmills—such formidable works as *Tannhäuser, Die Walküre,* and *Tristan und Isolde.* His productions of Wagner were weird; nor could they have been otherwise. A good *Ring* orchestra is hard to come by even with adequate rehearsals and a balanced budget. More importantly, Wagner cannot be improvised, while within certain definable limits, Verdi and Puccini can. I have heard, when the flame burned bright, a *Trovatore* or a *Tosca* come off at the Hippodrome with tremendous excitement. It was the unpredictability of those performances that made one eager to be there. Many evenings went unbelievably well, and in retrospect one thanks the Maestro.

Some of the rough-and-ready qualities of the old Hippodrome survive today in a company known as the Brooklyn Opera, under the direction of a second-generation Salmaggi: Felix, one of Alfredo's four sons. I go there, drawn by the lure of Brooklyn's

Academy of Music, its cozily fading splendor, perfect sight lines, and fine acoustics. The audience, too, attracts me. Only at the Academy can one still find the unjaded. The star system, its piddling rival camps and sniveling fan clubs, are unknown to these young people who shout with joy as Tosca—*any* Tosca—stabs the villainous Scarpia, for they are totally involved with the drama. The Brooklyn scenery is often wild. The orchestra can sound as if it were reading the music for the first time. And yet the singers are convincing, the performance weaves its spell, conjures up that sense of the homemade, the authentically popular, which remains an endearing part of the Italian operatic world below top performance level.

The control of that top level has shifted with the years. We read a good deal about the Golden Age of Song, during which star singers were virtually in command. Then, fired by enthusiasm, we rush out to buy whatever discs remain of these great personalities, and are often disappointed.

Their voices come off solidly; their technique sounds more flexible, in many instances, than the singing of today; the dramatic intensity is high. Yet the performances, to put it plainly, can be sloppy, wanting in accuracy. Even so famous an artist as Mattia Battistini took signal liberties with the composer's rhythms, and his less talented contemporaries went further. The carelessness to which I refer is not to be confused with the freedom and improvisation so appropriate in the old *bel canto* operas. I have in mind music composed during the artists' own careers. In addition to being lax, their performances bear a trace of arrogance.

Opera Conductors

Centralized control was needed to check such abuses. It came in the person of Arturo Toscanini, who battled for authority over the performance as a whole and won. The singers gradually fell into line, embraced the concept of responsibility. In the recordings of a Caruso may be heard, to an ideal degree, the wedding of the old brilliance and the new integrity.

Then, in the wake of Toscanini's reform, came the golden

period of opera conducting. Singers and musical directors worked jointly for the glory of the performance, the last word emanating from the maestro. Bruno Walter, Fritz Reiner, Otto Klemperer, Erich Kleiber, Fritz Busch and Sir Thomas Beecham were the distinguished men who presided—no mere accompanists, but masters of the orchestra.

This development was in a sense ordained. Had Toscanini not come forward, some other great conductor with fire and initiative would have created the new order, for it was implicit in the needs of the music. Composers, rather than performers, are the ultimate force for change. When the suave *bel canto* operas of Donizetti and Bellini gave way to the fierce, earthy scores of young Verdi, an adjustment in vocal style had to be made. The newer operas called for savage accents, ringing tones, a violence quite alien to what had gone before. The size of the orchestra, too, was enlarged. Singers had to cope with increased instrumental volume, and so the stentorian style still prevalent in Italian opera was evolved. No one performer dictated this transition. It lay in the nature of the music.

It was the composer too, with his new symphonic needs, who shaped the rise of the all-powerful conductor. No mere time-beater or accompanist could do justice to the orchestral intricacies of mature Wagner, middle and late Verdi, Debussy, and Strauss. *Parsifal, Falstaff, Pelléas et Mélisande, Elektra* all demand consummate skill on the part of the musical director, full control of the complicated forces. For every recording today of an operatic masterpiece, there is a famous conductor at the helm.

Ironically, much of the arrogance marking the attitude of the old-time star has more recently crept into the approach of the conductor. We may substitute for liberties taken by the storybook prima donna a rigidity of tempo imposed by the maestro. Even the great Toscanini (as evidenced in his recordings with the NBC Symphony of *Aida* and *La Traviata*) was known in later years to force his singers, instead of breathing with them. This was the whim of a Titan, who instead of relaxing toward the end, recharged his strength excessively and drove not only his colleagues but himself.

In truth there can be no imposed, *absolute* tempo in opera. The speed, the travel of the music, are determined by the physical condition of the singer. One soprano will have shorter breath than another; one tenor, instead of sustaining a top note, will be compelled to cut it relatively short. This is part of the give-and-take in operatic performance, calling ultimately for a meeting of minds in rehearsal rather than a ruthless dictatorship at performance. Many younger conductors, lacking the special gifts of a Toscanini, have captured his outward manner instead of his inner genius, interfered with singers of talent and good will, interrupted or congealed their flow of song.

Yet the wheel still turns in this evolving art, and the power of the maestro today is being largely eroded by a comparative newcomer to the scene: the *régisseur*. It all started with Richard Wagner, who declared his works to be a complete union of music, drama and décor. He acted as his own stage director, bringing what he considered theatrical truth to the scene. For more than sixty years after Wagner's death in 1883, the quest that he had started, for convincing movement and psychological insight, grew mainly in Central Europe, with offshoots in Italy, Russia, and less notably, France and the United States. I am referring not to the great individual acting performances of a Feodor Chaliapin, Mary Garden, Geraldine Farrar, Germaine Lubin, but to the drawing together by one person—the stage director—of *all* the theatrical elements in opera. The popularity of motion pictures, from the beginning of this century, put an additional demand upon the *régisseur*. Scenic credibility and dramatic motivation were called for by audiences in the great opera houses, as well as beauty of song, splendor of orchestral playing.

Then suddenly, as the end of World War II, there began in Germany and spread around the world what might be called the implosion of operatic stage direction. Sparked by the success of Wieland Wagner at Bayreuth—the grandson of Richard Wagner, modernizing the visual texture of the *Ring* in the very theater built for its first performance, fusing singers, conductors and designers into one performing unit on which to work his concept—the *régisseur* soon became king in many places. It was he who would now have the last word in policy decisions and dominate the music as well as the scene. Using this philosophy, Herbert von Karajan, always a controlling force as conductor, extended his sway to lighting, grouping and décor, thus keeping a grip on the entire production. In the cases of other less versatile (or influential) maestri it has been a losing struggle to exercise the old authority from the orchestra pit in the face of steadily growing power from the stage. Tyrone Guthrie, Walter Felsenstein, and Giorgio Strehler are among the masters of this comparatively new element in opera. Their function, in the highest sense, is not so much to illustrate as illumine the music.

Occasionally, as with conductors who have tended to throw their weight around, certain *régisseurs* can go too far. I recall, for example, a production of Poulenc's *Les Dialogues des Carmélites* not long ago in Rio de Janeiro by a visiting Frenchman who deliberately changed the structure of the work. He declared, in a program note, that Poulenc's division into three acts was dramatically weak. Therefore he, the *régisseur*, had arranged matters differently. There would be only two acts, with the intermission coming at a moment of his choice. The intent was presumptuous; the resulting performance, lopsided.

The editing of a work centuries old, launched under conditions that never approximated our own, is, within discretion, justifiable. Tampering with an opera whose composer, a man of the theater, has been dead less than five years would appear to be a crime. At best the modern stage director is a vitalizing force. On a lower level, he could endanger the artistic climate.

Recorded Opera

Thus far we have been considering what happens inside an opera house. When production is transferred to a medium outside the theater—recording—changes in the power structure inevitably take place.

The earliest recordings, primitive by modern standards of presence and fidelity, were based on the star system, on the desire of the public at the turn of the century to hear its favorite artists in familiar excerpts. The voice was everything. Standards of orchestral performance were generally neglected, personnel kept to a minimum. Not until the early 1920's did the practice of recording complete operas under first-class conditions take hold, as in the pioneering series by La Scala of Milan. So gradually have refinements been added since then as to make us forget that the long-playing record, with what would seem its immemorial advantages, is at this time of writing (1968) less than twenty years old. The complete opera albums of 78's were weighty affairs, containing thirteen or fourteen double-faced discs, and often running into two volumes.

LP changed all that. It also brought, on associated technical fronts, a dramatic improvement in orchestral sound. New clarity of texture, of over-all dimension, has added to one's pleasure in listening. And the emergence of another person in command—the producer, as distinguished from the musical director—has altered the sonic face of opera. The conductor no longer controls the blend of voice and orchestra, the ideal balance as he has imagined it. This is determined by specialists. And in their search for recorded perfection, shortcuts may be brought into play. Small voices have been beefed up, ringing top tones substituted for tired ones, by mechanical means. Expediency may here be pleaded. But what is one to say when inner strands of the orchestra, designed as background, suddenly take over and dominate?

This free-swinging approach, the deliberate reshaping of operatic sound in the image of the producer, has rung the bell of controversy. For those who believe—as do I—that the goal of recording is to document, make accessible, translate artistically, not arbitrarily, from one medium to another, the trend is distasteful.

History of Opera

When I first attended opera at the Metropolitan, the company was divided into three wings: Italian, German, and French. The first two units were a matter of nationality, the third (since there were few singers actually from France), of language.

All that has changed. Today we classify operatic production largely in terms of style and period. With a new awareness of history, we are more conscious of the Baroque (an era which, in theater music, would range roughly from 1600 to 1760). Many works of that age have been unjustly neglected. Few have survived in common knowledge, except on library shelves. And all were performed differently from opera in our time. Gone is the pristine *castrato* (male soprano or alto) whose prowess—a combination of agility, sweetness of tone, and muscular brilliance—once inspired so much theatrical song. His music has been arranged, perforce, for other voices. And many of the instruments that played in the early opera orchestras are obsolete. We have had to make do with near-authentic substitutes. For these retouchings, modern scholarship has been called into service.

Again, even in the distant Baroque, we meet the old struggle between the expressive and the decorative in music. Opera began with dramatic truth, and Claudio Monteverdi was its earliest master. The nobility and psychological strength of his stage works would assure their effectiveness in any age. His *Orfeo* moved the princely court of Mantua. And the superb love duet (first of its kind, they say, in the history of opera) that brings *L'Incoronazione di Poppea* to so glowing a close captivates the heart and mind today.

This is the art of the early Baroque. In its later mazes we come upon a more formalized idiom—the operas of Handel. Unlike the starkly sculptured works of a Monteverdi, these are full of floridity, shaped by vocal rather than dramatic line. Elaborate scenic pageantry marks their revival. And in well-handled productions, care is taken that the musical repeats should be embellished, to charm the ear and avoid monotony, as in the time of Handel himself. What emerges in performance (one recalls the beautiful *Giulio Cesare* by the New York City Opera) is a stately and beguiling masque, a melodious ramble on an antique poetic theme. When one has learned to pry oneself loose from motile theater and surrender to the spell of Handel's music, enjoyment can be strong.

This whole tradition of the *opera seria*—the stiff but impressive medium in which Handel excelled—was to continue into the 1700's past the midcentury mark. Even so progressive a composer as Mozart wrote vestigial works in this style (for special occasions)—notably, *Idomeneo* and *La Clemenza di Tito*, last traces of a disappearing age. But in general Mozart cut to the heart of the drama and created characters rather than types. And in this he was preceded, in a lovable mixture of clumsiness and grandeur, by Christoph Willibald Gluck, the oldest composer still represented, season after season, in our standard repertoire.

It was *Orfeo ed Euridice* that established Gluck as a leading composer of opera and has maintained him ever since. Created for male alto at its Vienna premiere in 1762, the work was revised for tenor by Gluck himself when given twelve years later at the Paris Opéra. The form in which we generally hear it today was devised by Hector Berlioz in 1859 for a revival of which he was in charge. Berlioz, known for his devotion to the music of Gluck, combined the finest pages of both the original and the French versions, avoiding the problem of a *castrato* (extinct even then) by assigning the rôle of Orfeo, *en travesti*, to the great mezzo-soprano, Pauline Viardot-García. Eventually the new design was shifted, for international performance, into Italian. In our own time Margaret Matzenauer, Kerstin Thorborg, Kathleen Ferrier, Risë Stevens, Giulietta Simionato, and Kerstin Meyer have followed the Berlioz tradition.

This was the last change for modern performance in Gluck. Once the master, in full career, had settled in Paris and was writing expressly for the Opéra, he composed scores that are given today as they were in his time. Gossec, it is true, reworked Act III of *Alceste;* Richard Wagner edited *Iphigénie en Aulide;* and Richard Strauss, *Iphigénie en Tauride*, but these revisions have gone out of fashion. The works are now performed as Gluck composed them. And especially in *Armide*, the pearl among his operas, brilliantly in touch with the modern theater, no single note might be changed or revised without weakening the drama. *Armide* was last heard in New York (1912) with Olive Fremstad and Enrico Caruso in the leading roles, Toscanini conducting.

As a reformer, a champion of the expressive, Gluck took excess floridity out of opera and tightened the lines of music and plot. His characters, while godlike rather than human, were able to communicate with the public in terms of direct emotional experience. When Alceste, loyal wife of Admète, vows—in the aria, "Divinités du Styx"—to save her husband from the rulers of Hades and yield herself in his place, the nobility and passion of her song can conquer even now.

The closing scene of *Armide*, a work little known to modern audiences and never recorded, is still more interesting in its play of emotion, its range of theatrical effect. The temptress who has laid bare her heart, renounced hatred, and given herself to the Christian knight whom the Saracens have set her to corrupt, finally loses him. Invoking the demons of air to destroy her pleasure dome—an act suggesting the modern death-wish—she vanishes in a chariot of fire, and the music that Gluck has provided matches every changing facet of the text.

For all the nobility that animates his operas, certain pages come off as melodically stilted, striving for dramatic ease rather than achieving it. Yet in the full flight of *Armide*, the grandeur of *Alceste*, and those parts of *Orfeo* that are tinged with a rare sensibility, Gluck must be accounted the first of our modern masters.

Modern—but he was still not idiomatic. His melodies suggest, at times, the old walls of a city, the outer fortifications that once protected the town and are still a part of the urban plan. Now they stand at the periphery—they contain, rather than animate— whereas the operas of Mozart, chronologically on the heels of Gluck, are well inside the walls.

Mozart was not a reformer or a theorist. He worked with existing styles, improved rather than changed them. What made for the radical difference between his operas and all that had gone before (always excepting Monteverdi) was his theatrical grasp of modern man, his ability to fix upon people like ourselves and set them to music. Since Mozart was a genius, the beauty of his scores is to be taken for granted. What astounds freshly, every time one restudies *Don Giovanni, The Marriage of Figaro, Così fan tutte,* and *The Magic Flute,* is the humanity of these operas, their almost Shakespearean understanding of men and women, their commentary—alternately witty and tragic—on our daily lives.

Part of this achievment, it is true, came about through the skill of Lorenzo da Ponte, Mozart's librettist for *Giovanni, Figaro* and *Così.* Here was a man completely of the theater, a dramatic

poet to be ranked with—or perhaps above—Arrigo Boito and
Hugo von Hofmannsthal for his literary contributions to opera.
But da Ponte only set the stage. Mozart took over psychologically
where his collaborator stopped. The sophistication of a *Così fan
tutte* could never have been achieved by text alone without the
knowing poise and sparkle of the music. That Mozart was equal
to any demands of the theater, in whatever style, is shown by
his triumphant treatment of the libretto given him by Emmanuel
Schickaneder for *The Magic Flute*. Fantasy, pathos, farce, Masonic ritual, all side by side; and the composer evoking every
mood with mastery.

Mozart did not wear his heart on his sleeve. For all the expressivity to be found in his scores, there exists a patrician manner that cannot be denied. His music is not to be barked, its
subtleties made obvious. Neither is it served by performers too
precious in voice and bearing. The hallmark of the great Mozart
operas is their humanity. Affectation has no place in them.
Neither has the vocal poverty that masquerades as refinement.
If a performer cannot sing out, if he takes refuge from technical
requirements in an elegant crooning, then—just as surely as the
singer who belts—he is unsuited to this repertoire.

Still another demanding element enters the picture with
Mozart: the need for an *ensemble* in which all the leading artists
—while maintaining their individual skills—must unite in a singing and acting style that brings gloss to the performance as a
whole. Too often the word *ensemble* has been taken to mean an
amalgamation of vocal mediocrities. The true galaxy in these
operas must be made up of stars who, instead of colliding on
their courses, unite for greater brilliance. The finest festival performances at Glyndebourne and Salzburg have operated on this
principle. And star conductors are always in charge of such
events—from Bruno Walter and Fritz Busch of earlier times to
Carlo Maria Giulini today.

With the passing of the Mozart era, European opera entered
the nineteenth century by splitting into two main streams—
German Romantic and Italian *bel canto*—with further tributaries
—French and Slavic—opening up in the years that followed.

There were a few works, stirring and important, that fitted
into none of these categories: the *Médée*, for example, of Luigi

Cherubini. This powerful opera, first given at Paris in 1797, started as an *opéra-comique*, spoken dialogue alternating with the musical numbers. Then, on the German stage, it underwent plastic surgery, being provided in 1855, at Frankfurt am Main, with musical recitatives composed by Franz Lachmann (these are still in use), to replace all spoken dialogue. By virtue of this new material, the work came to be considered a full-dress opera. Its most famous revival has taken place in our own era (Florence, 1953)—in Italian translation as *Medea*—with Maria Callas a brilliant interpreter of the title rôle.

Another anomaly, from the standpoint of the revisions it has undergone since the Vienna premiere of 1805, is Beethoven's *Fidelio*. Twice revised by the composer, provided by him with no fewer than four different overtures (three of them named *Leonore*, after the heroine, and the fourth, *Fidelio*), the score remains technically a *singspiel*, with spoken dialogue linking the set numbers. After Beethoven's death, still others tried to reshape the work.

More than one prominent musician (Michael Balfe in London, Artur Bodanzky in New York) composed his own recitatives to replace the spoken dialogue—with no lasting result. The original lines are still spoken. And Gustav Mahler, in a celebrated Viennese revival, changed the face of the opera by establishing a custom followed even now: beginning the evening with the *Fidelio* overture, then using the *Leonore No. 3* as a bridge, a kind of Wagnerian interlude, between the two scenes of the second act (prison cell and castle gate). Since the opera is symphonic by nature, the interpolation of *Leonore No. 3* does no violence to the styles; but dramatically it is a point-killer. The offstage trumpet announcing the Minister of Justice has already sounded. Its reintroduction a few minutes later, in the midst of an interlude, weakens the theatrical impact, no matter how overpowering the music.

As for the score itself, how many detractors it has had across the years! Because Beethoven composed nine symphonies and only one opera, historians have taxed him with a lack of dramatic flair, basing their judgment for the most part on the ratio of nine to one rather than any considered examination of the music. This opera, in reality, is shot through with the strongest, most cogent kind of theater, and one special moment ranks among the exalted in any medium: the passage (Scene 1) for divided violins and cellos that precedes the canon quartet, "Mir ist so wunderbar." Outwardly poised and serene, these measures transmit a throbbing inner life.

Fidelio has also been called unvocal. This, I submit, depends upon who is singing it. When the test has been joined, the result can be glorious. Among the renowned Leonores of our time have been Lotte Lehmann, Kirsten Flagstad (her most convincing role), Birgit Nilsson, Leonie Rysanek, and Christa Ludwig. Jon Vickers and René Maison stand as the most ardent Florestans, and Alexander Kipnis as the ideal Rocco, the benevolent jailer. I have never heard a Pizarro quite equal to the demands Beethoven put upon this villainous character, but Michael Bohnen, in the recording of a single aria, "Ha! welch' ein Augenblick!," made in the 1920's, suggests how fearsome his full-length version of the part must have been. Ironically, Bohnen sang Rocco, not Pizarro, during his years at the Metropolitan.

In the short space of time between Beethoven's *Fidelio* and Karl Maria von Weber's *Der Freischütz*, the structure of German opera did not change—it was still based on the *singspiel*—but the style was remarkably transformed. The new Romanticism that was sweeping Europe found in Weber a musical apostle. His stage works, filled with stirring scenes of the superhuman (as, in the Wolf's Glen episode of *Der Freischütz*, the casting of the magic bullet while infernal hounds bay in the darkness and firewheels roll by), the knightly feeling of the Middle Ages, and the evocation of old peasant festivals, were to lead directly— through their fantastic musical coloring—into the youthful operas of Richard Wagner.

Der Freischütz, however, is by no means to be taken as just a historical link. It remains, on its own account, a work of genius, full of marvelous melodies, a superb hunting chorus, and thrilling orchestral effects. With his next, *Euryanthe*, Weber moved into the field of full-dress opera, abandoning the spoken dialogue so characteristic of the *singspiel*. He replaced it not with *recitativo* but with a fluid connecting tissue that anticipates the finest type of music drama. Indeed *Euryanthe* is a splendid work, worthy of modern revival. I heard it in 1937 at Salzburg, under the direction of Bruno Walter; and the beauty of the score rings in the memory. Weber's *Oberon,* set to an English text for Covent Garden and conducted by the master in the last year of his life, was never completed to his satisfaction. It survives as a problem piece, subject to editing of one sort or another (usually a condensation of the numerous scenes and characters), but the great moments, such as the heroine's "Ocean, thou mighty monster," are equal in grandeur to anything in opera.

While Weber and Romanticism were holding the stage in Germany, the type of opera known as *bel canto* began its reign in Italy, spread to the Théâtre-Italien in Paris and from there to Covent Garden. It should be noted at once that the expression *bel canto* has less connection with style or form than with sound. In this kind of opera, entirely vocal in inspiration, the singing— even when dramatic—had to flow purely. Technical hurdles were set up in advance for the singer, so they might be surmounted with bravura. As for structure, it was the traditional full-dress opera: *arias,* concerted numbers (duets, trios, quartets), and choruses, linked by *recitativo.*

The *bel canto* operas developed a formula that became in time a stereotype. At its heart lay the solo number, allocated to most of the leading singers in turn. This consisted of an opening *recitativo* (to display the artist's feeling for dramatic accent), a *cavatina* (proof of his ability to spin out a slowly moving melodic line), and a concluding *cabaletta* filled with fast, dazzling runs and scales. The three-part entity was known, in sum, as a *scene and aria.* It had been used more passionately, and with greater orchestral complexity, by Mozart, Beethoven, and Weber. In *bel canto* the emphasis was frankly on voice.

Masterpieces could spring from this restricted soil. Rossini's *Otello,* Bellini's *Norma,* and Donizetti's *Lucrezia Borgia* are commanding works by virtue of the melodic sweep and dramatic intensity that transcend their conventional design. All are vehicles for singing stars, and *Norma* in particular has maintained a tradition of stellar performance. Within a span of memories dating from the late 1920's, no other diva has approached Rosa Ponselle in the vocal grandeur needed for Bellini's heroine.

Norma, however, was only an isolated opera in the twenties.

The modern *bel canto* revival had yet to come. Set in motion thirty years later by Maria Callas, it became a platform for other singers of outstanding ability: Joan Sutherland, Montserrat Caballé, Leyla Gençer. Audiences roared their approval of works and of artists, both in concert and opera. To meet a demand for fresh vehicles, forgotten operas by Bellini, Rossini, and Donizetti were taken off the shelf, and almost every salient musical idea was stalked by a smothering formula.

These noted composers at their best—Rossini (in his Italian period) with *Otello, The Barber of Seville,* and *Cenerentola,* Bellini with *Norma,* Donizetti with *Lucia, Don Pasquale,* and *L'Elisir d'Amore*—offer treasures of beautiful sound, and occasionally, dramatic glory. But they wrote in bulk. Their lesser, grade B, products, dusted off hastily for recent revival, fizzed not only in our era, but even in their own. Most of the *bel canto* repertoire disappeared quite naturally, its sighing elegance replaced by the new vigor of Giuseppe Verdi.

During the ascendancy of *bel canto* in Italy, the beginnings of *grand opera*—in its technical sense as a style—were stirring in France. I must point out, of course, that theater music in Paris and Versailles had enjoyed an illustrious history for well over a century before the Revolution. Lully and later Rameau had set a dignified, dramatic, and often imaginative tone. Then Gluck had come from Austria, under the patronage of Marie Antoinette.

After the Terror had passed, and years later, Napoleon had gone into exile, Paris became the first city of Europe. A newly enriched bourgeoisie supported the arts. Writers, painters, musicians, and dancers formed an ambiance unique in modern times. Chopin, Liszt, Berlioz, George Sand, Balzac, Delacroix, de Musset, Flaubert, Gautier, Taglioni, Grisi, Heine, Meyerbeer, Auber, and Rossini (in his French period) brought a cosmopolitan outlook, a large-scale interest in the theater that made *grand opera* inevitable. This was the concept of the "big machine": a story with historical background, calling for mammoth pageantry, brilliant ballet, and grandiose vocal and orchestral power.

Gasparo Spontini, the Italian composer who settled in Paris and later moved on to Berlin, was a pioneer in the field with *La Vestale* and *Fernand Cortez;* but the first *grand opera* to make an absolute and overpowering contact with its audience is said to have been Auber's *La Muette de Portici* in 1828. One year later, Rossini—then living in Paris—had *William Tell* produced in the French capital. Like the work of Auber, it became a beacon in the development of epic style. I say "style" rather than form because *grand opera* differed not at all structurally from the traditional Italian opera. There were the same arias, concerted numbers, choruses, but less vocal display, with the melodies more tightly drawn and a heightened sense of dramatic awareness.

These qualities came to stay in French *grand opera*. No matter how elaborate the framework, the music is spare, often severe. And this type of writing found its apogee in the works of Giacomo Meyerbeer, born in Berlin, educated in Venice, triumphant in Paris. The wild fantasy of his *Robert le Diable*, with its ballet of unfrocked nuns, burst upon the public in 1831; *Les Huguenots*, based on the massacre of St. Bartholomew's Day, came five years later; then *Le Prophète*, taking for its story the infamous career of John of Leyden; and finally *L'Africaine*, with Vasco da Gama and a fictional Indian queen as its central figures. This last work was given a posthumous premiere in 1865, a year after the composer's death.

Most of the estimates of Meyerbeer's music still in print today were launched over sixty or seventy years ago. They came from critics indoctrinated by Wagner's well-known (and highly personal) dislike of this composer. There is only one way in which to form a valid estimate of Meyerbeer, and that lies in studying his scores first hand. Unfortunately, none of his operas has been recorded complete, and few of the great scenes, except in German on sonically faded discs. There are indications that some of the big works will presently be revived, at least in concert form.

It is easy, of course, to go along with condemnations of the sensational element in Meyerbeer. His plots, to attract the public, had their bizarre and erotic moments (but is this not also a tendency of well-respected opera in our time—the orgy in Schönberg's *Moses and Aaron* and the voluptuous events in Ginastera's *Bomarzo?*). Some of the music is plodding on occasion. Yet when it soars, as in the grand duo of *Les Huguenots*, the final act of *L'Africaine*, the closing scene of *Le Prophète*, and a miraculous trio (unaccompanied) in the third act of *Robert le Diable*, this is writing of supreme imagination. The framework is definitely grand; and with Meyerbeer the structure of the "big machine" is established in five acts, one of which contains a large-scale ballet.

It will be noted that Spontini, Rossini, and Meyerbeer, all practitioners of Parisian *grand opera*, were foreigners. A great native Frenchman Hector Berlioz tried his hand at the style— in *Les Troyens*—and turned out a work of full-blown genius. The entrance of the Grecian horse into Troy, hailed by an enormous chorus, with three stage bands converging stereophonically upon the scene, and the tragic Cassandra crying out her prophecies in vain, affords the noblest example of how *grand* opera can become, with no literary element distended, no part of the music banal or overblown. In those portions of the work taking place in Carthage, there is a softer, more lyrical quality, culminating in a nocturnal septet by the sea that has remained one of the glories of the French repertoire. The work is too long—not for its content, which is almost continuously beautiful, but for the staying power of the audience. Cuts are usually made; when discreet, they prove successful. *Les Troyens* has yet to be heard in stage form at the Metropolitan Opera House.

Secondary composers of French *grand opera* include Halévy (*La Juive*), Saint-Saëns (*Samson et Dalila*), Reyer (*Salammbo*). Massenet, whose glowing skill lay in lyric opera, attempted the grand in *Hérodiade*, but his most winning achievements stem from the intimacy, poetry, and theatrical flair of *Manon, Werther,* and *Le Jongleur de Notre Dame*. I vibrate personally to this composer, to the economy of his orchestral scoring, his supple writing for voice and refinement of dramatic style. Charles Gounod in *grand opera* (*Faust*) I salute with more respect than affection, Delibes, in *Lakmé*, with neither. It was in the lyrical sphere that Gounod was to win out with a captivating version of *Romeo and Juliet*.

Masterpieces of French lyric opera have been those in which music and the stage are as one—song, action, and orchestra fused with absolute equality: the finer works of Massenet, Charpentier's *Louise*, Debussy's *Pelléas et Mélisande*, Poulenc's *Les Dialogues des Carmélites*. In *opéra-comique* one must mention

Carmen, if only for the sake of the record. I have never enjoyed it, except for that dramatic last act, finding in its music too many diabetic turns of phrase. The lyric operas bring no over-all stress on voice, no stentorian underlining by the orchestra. The fusion of elements is complete, the balance perfect.

Yet Gallic elegance, though gaining in favor today, is still a specialized taste. If one were to point out the heartland of opera, one's finger would inevitably move toward the works of Giuseppe Verdi. This great composer, who with Mozart and Wagner remains among the pillars of musical theater, outstrips his rivals in one important respect: his scores, like the Bible, speak with equal persuasion to men of all intellects. The simple and sophisticated are inspired by them. There is, in this music, a miraculous force that dignifies the crude, refines but never softens.

After the suave and long-lined *bel canto* operas, Verdi's output came upon the scene with violence. His early works had a vein of rugged exaggeration, a gusto that bordered on the uncouth. Yet cheek by jowl with exuberance, as in his first big success, *Nabucco*, lay enormous nobility. We still hear the threadbare advice to bypass early Verdi and start admiring him with *Don Carlo;* one cannot protest too strongly the assumption that this genius, in his younger years, was writing only trash. Grave inequalities do exist in *Rigoletto;* yet consider the strength of *Il Trovatore* (I have reference not to an addled libretto but the unfailing excitement of the music); the warmth of *La Traviata*, marking a new threshold of sensitivity in this master's approach; the splendor and *terribilità* of a *Macbeth*, flawed though it be in certain pages.

Personally I take keenest enjoyment in Verdi's experimental works that followed the "popular" period of *Trovatore* and *Traviata*. Here was a famous man reaching for new devices, sometimes failing, more often succeeding in an attempt to broaden his horizons. It is the flux of this period, the trial and achievement, that makes it so vivid and brings such power to a work like *Don Carlo*, which incorporates not only music and drama but psychology on a scale not attempted in the Italian theater since Monteverdi. *Don Carlo*, to be accurate, has a few substandard pages. These are, however, exceptional and minimal. The ability of Verdi to read the human soul and communicate his findings

has never been more explicit (or polished) than in this masterpiece, written for the Paris Opéra and then translated, revised,
and improved for its place in the Italian repertoire.

La Forza del Destino, of this same period, represents the
master at white heat. No matter the extravagances of the plot!
Into no other score did he pour such molten melody. Skill of
characterization, too, runs high. All of the principals are strongly
painted; the secondary figures—such as the gypsy girl, Preziosilla;
the muleteer, Trabucco; the whining friar, Melitone—have a
sharpness of definition never before encountered in Verdi's supporting roles. There is humor—incisive and mature—in addition
to tragedy. And the orchestra mirrors superbly the darkling
Spanish background of the first two acts and the brio of the
military scenes in Italy.

Simon Boccanegra, also of this era, has top pages—the Prologue, Council Chamber scene, final duo (unforgettably sung, in
our time, by Lawrence Tibbett and Ezio Pinza)—along with
others which might better have been suppressed when Verdi
revised the work. I feel less drawn (a minority of one) to *Un
Ballo in Maschera*, where great places—the scene in the fields,
Renato's "Eri tu!," the quintet that follows—yield to crashing dis-
appointments, notably the masked ball itself.

As for Verdi's final period, this was largely glory. *Aida* is perfection from almost every standpoint. It has become the archetype
of Italian *grand opera* (in four acts, rather than the five of the
Parisian stage), with a carefully worked historical background,
grandiose solo and concerted numbers, rousing choruses, spectacular pageantry, and a glittering ballet. The humanity of *Don
Carlo* is still there, limited only by a somewhat stiff libretto. Aida
herself and Radames stir us musically rather than through
drama; but Amonasro, the father of Aida, comes fiercely to life;
and Amneris, torn by pride and jealousy, yields to few other
operatic characters in total rapport with the listener.

It has for so long been the fashion to consider *Otello* as the
greatest of Verdi's works that I must with apologies name it
an overrated opera. The score contains dramatic music of high
quality: the whole of the first act, much of the last. Yet aside
from the famous Kiss motive, the melodic ideas fall below the
best of *La Forza, Don Carlo, Aida,* even *Trovatore* in appeal and

spontaneity. They are superbly worked, but tired. Characterization is skillful—in the case of the Moor, eloquent; but Iago sounds more orotund than evil (exception: the delicately spun, insidious page known as "Era la notte"). And I should question the finale of Act III, a big old-fashioned number that is out of joint in style and pacing with the rest of the opera.

It is a different story with *Falstaff*. Youth regained, and at the same time made wise, hovers over the music—joyous, spare, modern. Verdi is here in tune with the contemporary world. And in the stunning fugue that ends the opera ("Tutto nel mondo è burla") he has put, as in a time capsule, the best of his musical heritage together with a prospect of things to come.

Wagner is not so much a branch of the repertoire as a way of life, and there remains little to be written that can throw new light on this most engulfing of composers. In youth, one submits almost totally to the power of *Der Ring des Nibelungen, Tristan und Isolde, Die Meistersinger von Nürnberg,* and *Parsifal.* Inevitably the confirmed Wagnerite will revolt against the system; but just as surely he will return, armed with reservations, yet basically loyal. My own residue of disquiet about Wagner has to do with the *Ring,* which I feel—despite page after page of magnificent music—is orchestrally inflated, its counterpoint forced. No such hesitancy stays me in the other great works.

The Wagnerian music dramas stand or fall through their performers. We are told, for example, that Gurnemanz, aging knight of the Grail in *Parsifal,* is a bore, and he usually is, when sung by the average basso. But those who have heard a Kipnis in this role will recall not a measure that might be spared. And as to the long scene of Tristan's death, so often undersung and overacted: for the listener who doubts its power, I recommend an old recording, made in Buenos Aires over a quarter-century ago, by Lauritz Melchior. The splendor of his voice is not matched by the sonics of the disc, but what tremendous intensity comes through!

Above all, we have been losing in most performances of Wagner the lyricism and the introspection that mark his music at its finest. We are settling for volume in place of depth. I am averse, by nature and training, to the chilly, monumental sound. These works can be sung intimately, warmly. Kappel and Leider succeeded in the past. Perhaps Christa Ludwig and Régine Crespin will do it again.   **1479395**

The operas of Richard Strauss—an extension orchestrally, vocally, and dramatically of Wagnerian principles—can still, in our time, stir men to battle. One army of buffs declares that Strauss's inspiration stopped short after *Salome, Elektra, Der Rosenkavalier,* and *Ariadne auf Naxos.* The opposing side claims that his inspiration only began at that point. Their argument is inconclusive, since so much of value may be found in Strauss on either side of the Great Divide. *Die Frau ohne Schatten* and, among his later works, *Arabella* and *Capriccio,* have reservoirs of enormous worth.

My own feeling is that Strauss's operas at their shortest are also at their best. *Salome* and *Elektra,* each in a single act, each a study in dramatic conciseness, go on to magnificent climaxes. Some of the details in *Salome*—especially the music of Jochanaan, with its revivalist overtones—are coarse. But in *Elektra* the Furies are at work, driving music and drama forward, flaying the participants, beating the audience into ultimate, pleasurable insensibility. *Elektra,* when paced by a great conductor (Fritz Reiner!) and sung by an inspired singing-actress, can furnish one of the stirring theatrical experiences of this century.

Brevity also enhances *Ariadne auf Naxos.* Strauss's idea of scoring this opera for an orchestra of only thirty-seven, resulting in a chamber atmosphere throughout, makes for a work that can charm on a number of levels. And its prologue, with the portrait of a young composer tricked into sacrificing art for expediency, brings us Strauss at his most moving. As for *Der Rosenkavalier,* having once loved the work, I must confess to finding it too long, repetitive, and (for a comedy) ponderous. While the superb moments remain—the Marschallin's monologue, the presentation of the silver rose, the final trio—the acres of "situation" music grow less interesting to a listener not bound up with Ringstrasse tradition.

Again too long, though irresistible in its finest pages, is *Die Frau ohne Schatten.* The score has enormous power; most of the action sweeps one forward—but Strauss's great librettist, Hugo von Hofmannsthal, is often grandiosely obscure, bringing to mind those famous words by an Emperor of Japan:

> All prosy dull society sinners
> Who chatter and bleat and bore,
> Are sent to hear sermons by mystical Germans
> Who preach from ten till four.

The least familiar part of the repertoire is the Slavic division. Of these operas unsurpassed for emotional surge, only *Boris Godunov* has become standard. Because the composer, Musorgski, was notoriously lacking in skill as an orchestrator, we have heard it at the Metropolitan—within a span of twenty years—in three different editions: by Rimski-Korsakov, by Karol Rathaus, and by Shostakovich. Rimski, in addition to reorchestrating the opera, softened certain of its harmonies, and deleted an amount of basic material. In spite of these indignities, his version surpasses the other two. It sounds; it conveys the gorgeous, barbaric essence of medieval Russia. As for the work itself, any performance with a prime singing-actor must impress the listener, and when played for ensemble (*every* part is important), the result can be extraordinary.

Musorgski's other great opera, *Khovanshchina*, is also a chronicle play, dealing with that dark part of Russian history in which three factions—the old nobility, a fanatical clergy, a liberally minded prince—wrestled with and destroyed one another, all disappearing in the upheaval that gave rise to the Romanov dynasty. Despite loose ends, caused by its sprawling structure, *Khovanshchina* is magnificent music drama: superb choruses, imaginative solo scenes, and a finale—the mass suicide of the Old Believers—the recollection of which may never be shaken off, once it has been seen in the theater.

There are other fine works in the Russian repertoire, but they reach us only intermittently. Borodin's *Prince Igor*, Rimski-Korsakov's *Sadko* and *The Snow Maiden*, once popular in New York, have vanished from the scene. *The Golden Cockerel* comes and goes. We have had, to be sure, revivals of those Tchaikovsky masterpieces, *Eugene Onegin* and *Pique Dame*, but neither in a performance that touched the springs of their greatness.

As to Czech opera, we live in twilight. Smetana's *The Bartered Bride* has not been given these many years on a professional level. The same composer's epic *Dalibor* does not exist for us, nor does Dvořák's *Rusalka*. The works of Leoš Janáček (save for a very occasional *Jenufa*) stand apart. Ambitious music schools sometimes attempt them, but thoroughly skilled productions of *Katya Kabanova, The Sly Little Vixen,* and *The Makropoulos Affair* are still awaited in New York. From reports in other places, they are said to match one's expectations.

Save for the big pieces of Verdi, there have been few *grand operas* out of Italy in almost a century. Among the few, one would note Ponchielli's *La Gioconda,* Boito's *Mefistofele* and *Nerone,* and Puccini's *Turandot.* These are, generally, relics. The trend has run to works of an intimate nature, some realistic, others sentimental.

Mascagni in *Cavalleria Rusticana* and Leoncavallo in *Pagliacci* produced operas that broke with the romantic past and emphasized the everyday aspects—some of them grim—of small town life in Italy. Their heroes were the poor and illiterate. Refinement was not their aim, but violent impact. And their best works, despite moments of outhouse vulgarity, cannot be dismissed on grounds of taste, for they also have dramatic truth and compassion. When these operas are given straight, free of hamming, with the Sicilian or Calabrian countryside bearing in relentlessly on the actors, they come off with power—and with empathy for an audience of today. There is not much difference, really, between this dispossessed *verismo* world of the nineties and the convulsed, unromantic Italy cast up by World War II (well known to us through the early films of De Sica). Life in both was hard, fundamentally tragic.

Umberto Giordano was a glossier composer than the others, cross-pollinating realism with the last vestiges of *grand opera.* The combination worked. One tends in our time, without justification, to underrate *Andrea Chénier,* that gusty score inspired by the French Revolution, the scintillating *Madame Sans-Gêne,* a comedy set in the same period and in the Napoleonic era that followed, and *Fedora,* based on a lushly old-fashioned stage play of Sardou and worth reviving for a white-gloved, tiara-topped diva.

Since these judgments are personal, I trust the reader will

indulge me in a one-sided approach to the theater of Puccini. I am not a fan. The excitement is there; so are the hit tunes; so is the sentimentality. We know from his letters that Puccini, a gifted composer, took great pains with his operas. He had an expert sense of theater, a unique flair for melody, but he often wasted these assets on the obvious. There are, of course, stunning exceptions: the superb score for *Il Tabarro;* the climax of Act II (the poker game) in *Girl of the Golden West,* where the power of the music transcends the hokey plot; and most of *La Bohème,* with its very special flavor of young love. What has prejudiced me against certain of the Puccini works—notably large parts of *Tosca* and almost all of *Madama Butterfly*—is their literalism, their show biz exploitation of the surefire. Counter in spirit runs the motto inscribed on the proscenium of the Royal Opera House in Copenhagen: MORE THAN ENTERTAINMENT.

I am for contemporary opera. Out of experimentation must come the great new works of which we have need, if music theater is to stay alive. Today's undisputed masterpieces are Berg's *Wozzeck,* Prokofiev's *The Flaming Angel,* Britten's *Peter Grimes,* all represented—not equally well—in New York during the past decade, and, fortunately, all superbly recorded. I cannot admire the elegant conceits of *The Rake's Progress,* despite the prestige of its composer, Igor Stravinsky. I find infinitely more rewarding the modest but penetrating little music drama by Luigi Dallapiccola, *Il Prigioniero.*

American opera? Coming up, hopefully.

2

Orchestral Music

MARTIN BOOKSPAN

I⊤ is only during the past four hundred years that music for a combination of instruments has become prominent in Western civilization. During the first fifteen hundred years of the Christian Era, the literature of music was largely for the human voice—and mostly for the church, at that. Two sixteenth-century Italian composers named Gabrieli—Andrea and his nephew Giovanni—are generally credited with expanding the horizons of music to include instruments within the framework of choral writing; it was not long before the Gabrielis were composing music for instruments alone, and the whole course of music history was changed.

The earliest of Andrea Gabrieli's works for combinations of instruments bore the designation Sonatas, literally, *sounded pieces* (as contrasted with Canzonas, *sung pieces*). Pivotal works produced by the Gabrielis are Andrea's *Sonatas for Five Instruments* and Giovanni's *Sonata pian' e forte* in which contrast between loud and soft is explored for the first time in instrumental music.

Giovanni Gabrieli died in 1612, and for the most part the composers who followed him during the seventeenth century experimented with the concepts and forms first formulated and codified by him and his uncle. Orlando Gibbons and William Byrd, both of whom outlived Giovanni Gabrieli by about a dozen years, were important composers in England who seized upon the newfound emancipation of instrumental music and wrote a considerable body of works for combinations of stringed instruments. One of the most fascinating musical figures of the period was the Frenchman Jean-Baptiste Lully, who was born Giovanni Battista Lulli in Florence, Italy, in 1632, but who was brought to France at the tender age of about twelve to teach Italian to the niece of a French nobleman. Lully spent the rest of his life in France and became her most famous and influential musician, an intimate of Louis XIV, for whose court he composed innumerable ballets, and a friend of Molière, with whom he collaborated in the composition of many ballets. Lully was also an expert dancer and a comic actor of considerable ability.

During the last fifteen years of his life, Lully was the director of the Paris Opéra, and he ruled the musical life of France with an iron hand that was reinforced by royal edict. The King proclaimed that no opera could be performed anywhere within the kingdom without Lully's permission. Along with his administrative and other musical activities at the Opéra, Lully also took it upon himself to conduct many of the performances. This he accomplished by standing in front of his instrumentalists and rapping a long wooden pole on the floor in order to establish the tempo and keep the musicians playing together. Legend has it that he clubbed himself right out of this world: In mid-performance, one day, he missed the floor and came down hard with the pole on one of his feet; the resulting wound abscessed, and Lully died from the infection.

During the century between the death of Andrea Gabrieli in 1586 and the death of Lully in 1687, instrumental music developed rapidly. Certain principles of form were already well established, and the basic foundation of orchestral music as an expressive medium had been well laid. It remained for three composers, all of them born just a few years before Lully died, to bring this particular phase of musical history, the Baroque period, to its finest flowering. In his chapter on Baroque, Igor Kipnis details the facts and the figures of this fascinating epoch, but I must touch briefly on the music of Johann Sebastian Bach, George Frederick Handel, and Antonio Vivaldi. The veteran among them was Vivaldi—his birth date is given variously as

1669, 1675, and 1678; Bach and Handel were both born in 1685.

Not until the post-World War II period was the musical community fully aware of Vivaldi's importance as a composer. Recent scholarship, along with vigorous championing of Vivaldi's music by the recording companies, has revealed the true dimensions of Vivaldi's art. He was a seminal influence in the development of two musical forms—the concerto grosso and the solo concerto—and he even pointed the way for the later development of the symphony itself by Haydn and Mozart.

Vivaldi left behind him an astonishing profusion of compositions—operas, choral works, sonatas—but my concern is with his instrumental music, particularly the concerti grossi and the solo concerti. The concerto grosso form was pioneered by Italian composers toward the end of the seventeenth century, notably Arcangelo Corelli and Giuseppe Torelli. It was Torelli who created the standard form of Baroque concerto grosso with three movements, fast-slow-fast. In textural design, the concerto grosso pits a small group of soloists (called the *concertino*) against a larger group of players, usually strings only (called the *tutti* or *ripieno*). With these as the basic ground rules, Vivaldi produced dozens of masterful orchestral concerti grossi, distinguished by rhythmic vitality and drive and requiring brilliant precision work from the performers. Similarly, Vivaldi's dozens of solo concerti are remarkable examples of a music bursting with energy and vitality. His best-known orchestral score is *The Four Seasons*, a cycle of four violin concerti deliberately calculated to conjure up visions and emotions associated with the four seasons of the year. "Program music"—both descriptive and narrative—existed before Vivaldi composed *The Four Seasons*, but this is the oldest example of the genre still in the active repertoire.

If Vivaldi's greatest accomplishments as we know them today were in the field of instrumental music, then surely the major contributions of Bach and Handel were their large-scale choral works, as discussed by David Randolph in this volume. Yet the contributions of both composers to instrumental and orchestral music are among the glories of the literature. The principal works of Bach's output for orchestra are the six *Brandenburg Concerti*, the four *Suites for Orchestra*, and the various concerti for solo and multiple instruments. Handel's orchestral works include two famous sets of concerti grossi, along with the *Water Music* and the *Royal Fireworks Music*.

Bach composed his set of six orchestral concerti on commission from Christian Ludwig, the Margrave of Brandenburg, who was a deeply committed musical amateur. The composer seized upon the opportunity offered him, and the six scores that he produced represent the ultimate in Baroque concerto grosso expression. Each is scored for a different group of solo instruments—the *Third* and *Sixth* for strings only, the other four for various instrumental combinations. They are endlessly fascinating, and repeated hearings only increase the listener's respect for the fertile inventiveness of Bach's creative genius.

The four *Suites for Orchestra* seem to have been composed by Bach at about the same time he produced the *Brandenburgs*. During the six-year period between 1717 and 1723 Bach was in the service of Prince Leopold of Anhalt-Cöthen, where an orchestra of eighteen musicians was placed at his disposal. It is not hard to imagine with what joy Bach threw himself into the task of providing music for the ensemble; and the players, in turn, must have been first-class virtuosi, for the works are by no means easy to play. The *Second Suite* has a prominent part for solo flute and the *Third* contains the long-breathed song for strings that became famous as the "Air for the G String" by virtue of August Wilhelmj's arrangement for violin solo. Structurally, each of the *Suites* is built along the same lines: an elaborate French Overture (in the slow-fast-slow Lully tradition), followed by a series of dances popular in Bach's time—bourrées, gigues, gavottes, and the like.

No less inventive and stimulating than the *Brandenburgs* and the *Suites* are Bach's numerous concerti for solo and multiple instruments. Chief among these are the *Violin Concerti in A minor* and *E Major* and the *D Minor Concerto for Two Violins*, the *Concerto in C minor for Violin and Oboe*, several of the concerti for solo keyboard instrument, the two for two solo keyboards, and those for three and four solo keyboards. The principal keyboard instrument of Bach's time was the harpsichord, and it was for the harpsichord that the Bach keyboard concerti were composed. Until the Baroque revival of recent years, these scores were more often than not given in performances utilizing the modern piano. Today, however, performances on the harpsichord are the rule rather than the exception.

The most important of the concerti grossi that Handel composed are the eighteen contained in two sets: Opus 3, made up of six works for woodwinds and strings, and Opus 6, twelve concerti for strings alone. Much of the music in both sets was freely adapted and rewritten by Handel from earlier works. It remains astonishing, nevertheless, that the twelve superb Baroque concerti of Opus 6 could all have been completed in a single month during 1739.

The *Water Music* and the *Music for the Royal Fireworks* were both composed for the entertainment of the King and his court. During the early years of the eighteenth century, the Thames River served not only as London's main commercial artery, but also as the city's chief pleasure arcade. King George I frequently organized barge parties on the river and for one, probably in July, 1717, Handel composed a series of brief pieces, later collected under the generic title *Water Music*. According to an account in the London *Daily Courant* at the time of the King's party, his entourage was accompanied by another barge "wherein were fifty instruments of all sorts," which performed "the finest symphonies, compos'd express for this occasion by Mr. Hendel, which His Majesty liked so well that he caused it to be played over three times in going and returning."

More than thirty years later Handel composed his other great piece of "outdoor" music, the *Royal Fireworks* score written for the celebration of the Treaty of Aix-la-Chapelle, which ended the War of the Austrian Succession. Because of the festive nature of the occasion, Handel seized the opportunity to score the work for an enormous body of winds which included twenty-four oboes, twelve bassoons, nine trumpets, and nine horns. A special pavilion was built in London's Green Park to house the "machine" that would set off the imposing fireworks display at the climax of the celebration. Suddenly there was a totally different kind of climax: the hundred-foot high wooden pavilion caught fire, panic ensued, and in the turmoil the architect of the building engaged the director of the fireworks in a duel. No one apparently considered substituting the *Water Music* for the *Fireworks* score to help quench the flames.

During this period composers throughout central Europe were busy creating instrumental works of increasingly elaborate proportions and formal structure. The most important activity along these lines took place in the court of Mannheim, whose elector, Karl Theodor, was a devoted music lover. A first-class orchestra came into being there during the middle of the eighteenth century, and the place was alive with orchestral composition and performance. The most important composers active in the Mannheim group were Richter (1709–1789), Holzbauer (1711–1783), Johann Stamitz (1717–1757), and his son Carl (1746–1801), Filtz (1725–1760), and Cannabich (1731–1798). Their influence extended far beyond Mannheim, and their attitudes and stylistic designs are to be found in the orchestral scores of their contemporaries all over Europe: William Boyce and Johann Christian Bach in England, Giuseppe Sammartini in Italy, Carl Philipp Emanuel Bach and F. A. Rössler (who composed under the name of Rosetti) in Germany, Carl Ditters von Dittersdorf in Austria. Each of them produced instrumental music in abundance, with special emphasis on the newly emerging form, the symphony.

Haydn and Mozart

In defining the symphony, *Grove's Dictionary of Music and Musicians* and the *Harvard Dictionary of Music* agree that it is the most exalted form of instrumental music. The word is derived from the Greek and means merely "a musical ensemble." By the time of the Mannheim composers and their contemporaries, the symphony had come to represent its creator's noblest and most advanced musical thoughts. The first truly great symphonic composer was Franz Josef Haydn, whose *Symphony No. 1* appeared in 1759, nine years after Johann Sebastian Bach died.

Over the next thirty-five years Haydn produced more than one hundred more symphonies, many of which are staples of the concert repertoire today. His last twelve, composed in sets of six each for two different visits to London during the 1790's under the auspices of the impresario Salomon, have always figured in the mainstream of symphonic life. The Haydn revival of the past couple of decades has served to focus attention on many of the composer's earlier symphonies and to enrich our experience and knowledge of his incredible output. My own favorites among the lesser-known symphonies are the trilogy of works titled *Morning, Noon,* and *Night* (the *Symphonies Nos. 6, 7,* and *8*); the *Symphony No. 13* (whose last movement's principal theme is a remarkable anticipation of the main theme in the last movement of Mozart's *Jupiter Symphony*); the *Symphony No. 22,* called the *Philosopher,* because of the weighty and serious aspect of its first movement; the dramatic and impassioned *Symphony No. 39 in G minor;* the intense *Symphony No. 44 in E minor,* which is known as the *Mourning Symphony;* the turbulent and storm-tossed *Symphony No. 49 in F minor;* the *Symphony No. 80 in D minor,* which begins as a serious contemplative work and ends as a lighthearted romp; and the *Symphony No. 86 in D,* alive with spontaneous sparkle and joy, especially in its captivating last movement.

Haydn also left us a large body of instrumental concerti, including several for solo violin, cello, horn, organ, harpsichord, and flute. But perhaps his most widely played concerto today is the irrepressible *Trumpet Concerto in E flat,* a virtuoso player's paradise. Another gem for solo instruments is the *Sinfonia Concertante in B flat,* scored for orchestra with principal solo parts for oboe, bassoon, violin, and cello. As with Vivaldi, our present broader knowledge of the total creativity of Haydn is due in no small measure to the sense of creative repertory adventure shown by the recording industry in recent years. Many of the works by Haydn listed in the discography at the end of the book were not available in recordings until fairly recently.

During the year when Haydn produced his *First Symphony,* there was a three-year old boy named Wolfgang Amadeus Mozart in Salzburg, Austria, who was astonishing his musician-father with an incredibly precocious display of musical gifts. He would sit for hours at the family harpsichord and play by ear the pieces he heard his older sister, Marianne, practicing. The father began to give his son music lessons as a game, but the game quickly became serious business as the full measure of the child's capacities made themselves known. Soon the father began to take young Wolfgang on concert tours all over the continent, exhibiting him as a prodigy pianist and violinist. The nomadic concert life was the only existence young Wolfgang knew for many years, and other circumstances of his personal life were anything but sanguine. And yet in a life-span that barely covered thirty-five years, Mozart composed more than six hundred works in nearly every conceivable musical form. The percentage of masterpieces is astonishingly high; and even the slightest among Mozart's creations radiates a quality of elevated invention and superior craftsmanship. In recent years New York's Lincoln Center for the Performing Arts has undertaken month-long festivals of Mozart's music which have surveyed its wealth and dynamism; I can think of no other composer whose works could sustain such concentrated scrutiny without falling victim to the law of diminishing returns.

I could single out two dozen or more of Mozart's works which are special favorites of mine for discussion in these pages; the problem is that at least an equal number of favorites would go neglected. I propose, therefore, merely to mention some that come to mind immediately. Since I am a frustrated violinist from way back, perhaps a good place to begin would be with the violin concerti. Mozart often produced works in clusters, either because he was commissioned to produce series of scores in the same genre, or because an inner need compelled him. Between April and December of 1775, in his twentieth year, Mozart composed no fewer than five violin concerti; the *Third, Fourth* and *Fifth* have been standard concert fare almost from the moment of their creation. Each has its individual character—the *Third* has as its centerpiece a deeply felt, melancholy Adagio which is one of the most moving of all Mozart's works; the *Fourth* is a sunny outpouring of joy; and the *Fifth* is a frolicsome romp which in the last movement introduces a raucous orchestral episode borrowed by Mozart from music he had earlier composed for a ballet appended to his early opera, *Lucio Silla*. These three violin concerti stand at the apex of Mozart's music for solo instrument and orchestra.

Another absolutely unforgettable Mozart masterpiece is scored for two solo string instruments and orchestra; this is the *Sinfonia Concertante in E flat for Violin, Viola, and Orchestra*. Alfred Einstein, in his authoritative study of Mozart's music, calls the *Sinfonia Concertante* Mozart's "crowning achievement in the field of the violin concerto." Like the *Third Violin Concerto*, the *Sinfonia Concertante* has a profound and elegiac slow movement, which scales the heights of nobility and passion.

There is another *Sinfonia Concertante in E flat* by Mozart, this one scored for four solo woodwind instruments and orchestra: oboe, clarinet, bassoon, and French horn. Some doubt exists concerning the authenticity of this score, but I am prepared to include it unquestioningly in the Mozart canon. If this score is not authentic Mozart, whoever *did* write it deserves a place in music history alongside Mozart. This is music that overflows with a wealth of rich and inspired melody, and its blending of the four solo instruments is the work of a master.

When we come to Mozart's piano concerti, we are faced with works incredibly rich in quantity and quality. It could almost be said, indeed, that Mozart created the piano concerto as a form. When he came upon the scene, it was little more than a sonata for keyboard instrument with a modest string accompaniment. He left it a full orchestral vehicle, more complex even than a symphony, for the two elements of solo instrument and orchestra had to blend or alternate in perfect integration. Any one of Mozart's later piano concerti is fully symphonic in character—often richer in color and variety than a symphony. He "composed" his first four piano concerti when he was ten years old; the quotes are around the word *composed* because these four works are actually nothing more than concertolike arrangements of keyboard sonata movements by several now-forgotten composers popular during Mozart's early youth. But from his first original concerto onward (the *Concerto No. 5 in D*), he produced a body of music that is perhaps unrivaled in the orchestral repertoire by any other group of works by any composer. *Numbers 9, 12,* and *14* are my own favorites among the earlier ones, and from *No. 15* through the last, *No. 27,* there is an unbroken string of masterpieces. If I were pinned against a wall and forced to name my unqualified favorite, my choice would be the *Concerto No. 20 in D minor*. The epic-heroic nature of this particular concerto made it for years not only *a* Mozart piano concerto but *the* Mozart piano concerto. My own reasons for my special love for this work are quite personal, however. I have already alluded to my violin playing days. When I was about twelve, I was a member of the second violin section in the symphony orchestra of the Boston Music School. The climax of each year's activities was the annual recital on the stage of Jordan Hall in Boston— and one of the pieces on the program my first year in the orchestra was this concerto, with my friend Bernie Siff as soloist. Not only did that performance open up for me the whole magical world of the Mozart piano concerto literature, but I am convinced I have never heard a better performance of it than the one Bernie and I played!

Before continuing with the Mozart orchestral music, let me at this point introduce the mysterious letter *K.* It has taken considerable restraint for me thus far to refrain from using *K* numbers in connection with the several Mozart scores we have already discussed. Concert programs, record catalogues, and all other reference material always append a capital letter *K,* followed by some combination of numbers in their listings of Mozart's works. What is this strange mumbo-jumbo? Nothing more than the indication of the catalogue number assigned to every known Mozart composition by the nineteenth-century musicologist and scholar, Ludwig Köchel, who devoted years of research to cataloging, codifying, and chronologically listing Mozart's entire output. Thus Mozart's first original piano concerto, the *No. 5 in D,* carries the number 175 in Köchel's catalogue, and the *Concerto No. 20 in D minor* is numbered 466 by Köchel's reckoning.

Prominent in Mozart's orchestral output is a series of works titled variously Cassation, Divertimento, or Serenade. The titles, really interchangeable, refer to a body of entertainment music. But even here Mozart was incapable of turning out music automatically, and some of his most inspired musical creativity is to be found in these works. My favorites? Four in the key of D Major among the Divertimenti—K 131, K 136, K 251 and K 334— along with the *Divertimento No. 15 in B flat,* K 287, an endlessly melodic and inventive work, scored for strings and two horns. Among the Serenades I particularly treasure the little

Serenata Notturna, K 239, with its antiphonal effects and drum flourishes; the mighty *Serenade in B flat for Thirteen Wind Instruments,* K 361; the two that follow it, also scored for woodwind instruments (K 375 and K 388); and the *Serenade in G Major* for strings only, K 525, titled *Eine kleine Nachtmusik—A Little Night Music.*

And so we come to the Mozart symphonies; again the fertility of the total output is astonishing. The first two symphonies, K 16 and 19 (K 17 and 18 are copies of works by other composers), were written while the eight-year-old lad was recuperating in London from a serious childhood disease, and the last three—the great *Symphonies Nos. 39 in E flat, 40 in G minor,* and *41 in C,* the *Jupiter*—were created in one enormous gush during a six-week period in the summer of 1788. From the *Symphony No. 32* onward, each one exerts some special claim to my affections. Among the earlier ones my favorites are the *Symphony No. 20 in D;* the *No. 25 in G minor,* an absolute miracle of concentrated drama and passion; *No. 28 in C;* and *No. 29 in A.*

Beethoven and the Romantics

When Mozart was creating his last three symphonies during the summer of 1788, a youth of seventeen was playing viola in the opera orchestra in Bonn, the place of his birth. A year earlier he had spent several weeks in Vienna, and may even have taken a few lessons in composition from Mozart—the record is unclear—but he had hurriedly returned to Bonn because of the serious illness of his mother. His name, of course, was Ludwig van Beethoven, and by the turn of the nineteenth century he was to become well established in Vienna as her most famous musical figure. No only did Beethoven usher in the nineteenth century literally, he was also the figure who dominated and pointed the way toward the whole musical philosophy of the century. In all the arts, the nineteenth century was the era of Romanticism. In music this meant that composers gave free expression to their own emotional urgings; it also meant the slow dissolution of many of the principles of form and structure established by composers during the two previous centuries.

By and large Beethoven worked on a broad musical canvas. His ideas could not be contained within the framework of eighteenth-century thought, hence there is a visionary quality about much of his music. He wrote in all forms and left his personal stamp on every one. In this chapter, of course, we are concerned with his orchestral music—which is to say that we shall be dealing with the very backbone of the orchestral repertoire.

Beethoven's nine symphonies may be said to be the cornerstones of Western symphonic culture. It has been traditional to divide the composer's creative life into three definite periods— early, middle, and late. Where the symphonies are concerned, this almost works, but not quite. The symphonies numbered 3 through 8—composed during the decade between 1803 and 1812—can legitimately be called "middle period," and the monumental *Ninth,* a product of the six years between 1817 and 1823, certainly is representative of the impulses of Beethoven's "late period." What of the first two? It has been convenient in the past to pigeonhole them as youthful muscle-flexing: the emerging composer taking a fling at the form so gloriously developed by Haydn and Mozart. The trouble with this theory is that it ignores the impact and daring of Beethoven's first two symphonies; each represents a significant break with the traditions of the past, and both herald the arrival of a great and original creator.

It has been observed that in his even-numbered symphonies Beethoven sought after gentler beauties, reserving his defiances, his true depths of passion, for the odd-numbered ones. Let us take a brief look at the nine Beethoven symphonies with this thought in mind. The *First* immediately breaks with the past by ambiguously hovering in two rather alien keys before it settles down to its fundamental tonality, C Major. It is a virile, extroverted work that has a particularly playful last movement. The *Third Symphony* is the mighty *Eroica,* dedicated at first to Napoleon Bonaparte, but then dedicated simply "to the memory of a great man" after the Little Corporal had proclaimed himself Emperor. The *Eroica* has been called by Paul Henry Lang in his admirable *Music in Western Civilization* "one of the incomprehensible deeds in arts and letters, the greatest single step made by an individual composer in the his-

tory of the symphony and in the history of music in general."
The colossal score stretched all the symphonic ground rules.
Its length, for example, is about twice that of the average
Haydn or Mozart symphony; the first movement alone is as
long as many complete four-movement symphonies written during the eighteenth century. And in its harmony, rhythm, and formal structure, the *Eroica* looks ahead to a new era of music. The
Fifth Symphony is that bold, fist-shaking score that opens with
the four-note motif that has been characterized as Fate knock-
ing at the door. During World War II the opening motif of the
Fifth Symphony was adopted by the Allies as the musical signature of the coming victory, and at the Victory Concert played
by the Israel Philharmonic Orchestra in Jerusalem in June, 1967,
to celebrate the cessation of the six-day war against the Arab
countries, it was again Beethoven's *Fifth Symphony* that marked
the occasion. The *Seventh* is a rhythmic romp from first to last.
Characterized by Richard Wagner as "the apotheosis of the
dance," the *Seventh* is one of the most spontaneous and vigorous works in the entire literature. The *Ninth* is the symphony in
which instruments no longer sufficed; Beethoven had to turn to
the human voice for the expression of his muse. The last movement is a setting for orchestra, chorus, and four vocal soloists of
the *Ode to Joy* by the German playwright and poet, Friedrich
von Schiller.

Performances of the *Ninth Symphony* have taken on special
meaning because of the unique message and significance of
the music. It is not uncommon for conductors to open or close
their annual subscription series of concerts with the *Ninth
Symphony*, or for the score to figure on Pension Fund or other
such special programs. I have heard the *Ninth* under many
different circumstances and in many extraordinary situations,
but the performance that remains indelibly engraved on my
memory is the one given in Symphony Hall, Boston, on the last
Saturday in April, 1945, with chorus, soloists, and the Boston
Symphony Orchestra conducted by Serge Koussevitzky. At that
time the last remnants of the German war machine were being
overwhelmed by the United States and its Allies, and the war in
Europe was rapidly rushing to its triumphal conclusion. Koussevitzky had scheduled the *Ninth* for the final concerts of his

season as an act of rededication to the higher principles of humanity. Promptly at the scheduled starting time, he strode out to the podium, acknowledged the welcoming applause of the audience, and then with a motion of his arms silenced us and indicated that he had something to tell us. "Germany has surrendered!" he proclaimed, "and I now dedicate this performance of Beethoven's *Ninth Symphony* to the victorious Allies and to the cause of universal peace!" Pandemonium broke loose in Symphony Hall as strangers hugged and kissed each other; the members of the orchestra cheered and shouted, and tears streamed down Koussevitzky's face. And then he wheeled around on the podium and led his combined forces in a performance of the *Ninth Symphony* that I can only describe as apocalyptic. It was of little consequence that we learned after the concert that the radio reports on which Koussevitzky had based his announcement were a bit premature; it was not until a week later that the unconditional German surrender was finally effected. But the high emotion of that Saturday evening in Symphony Hall will live with me forever—as will that performance of Beethoven's *Ninth Symphony*.

Beethoven's *Second Symphony* may be termed a transitional work from the *First* to the great *Eroica*. It treats its material in a more relaxed manner; perhaps its most distinctive section is the long and lyrical slow movement. The *Fourth Symphony* was called by Robert Schumann "a slender Greek maiden between two Norse giants"—a reference to its position in the Beethoven chronology between the *Eroica* and the *Fifth*. It, too, is a free-flowing, lyrical outpouring whose mood is always sunny. The *Sixth* is the *Pastoral Symphony*, modeled in its formal and pictorial outlines after a similar symphony by one of Beethoven's contemporaries. But how marvelously Beethoven characterizes the pastoral scenes portrayed in the music! The *Eighth* is altogether a more robust and rambunctious score than any of the other even-numbered ones, but it, too, deals with superficial pleasures rather than profound ones. As the reader may by now have gathered, I consider all nine of the Beethoven symphonies completely indispensable in any representative home library of the great musical masterpieces of our civilization.

Similarly indispensable are Beethoven's concerti for solo instrument and orchestra—five for piano and one for violin. One can almost apply to the piano concerti the same generalization applicable to the symphonies—the odd-numbered ones are the heaven-stormers, the even-numbered ones, the more placid and lyrical expressions. The last is the so-called *Emperor Concerto,* a nickname attached to it by a soldier, who at one of its first performances is reputed to have shouted, at its conclusion, "This is the Emperor among concerti!" The *Violin Concerto* is a more rhapsodic, elegiac work. In Beethoven's output it came into being between the *Fourth* and *Fifth Symphonies;* in spirit and content it relates more closely to the *Fourth.*

Beethoven also composed a sizable body of instrumental music for performance with dramatic works in the theater. For Goethe's drama, *Egmont,* there is incidental music, including an overture that is one of Beethoven's most powerful and concise scores. Similarly, his overture to Collin's drama, *Coriolan,* is a miniature tone poem of the conflicting elements in the makeup and personality of the central figure of the play. And there are no fewer than four different overtures to Beethoven's only opera, *Fidelio*—the *Leonore Overtures Nos. 1, 2,* and *3* and the *Fidelio Overture* itself. They are all staples of the active symphonic repertoire, and each has its individual character.

In the five years between 1812 and 1817, when Beethoven composed no symphonies, a young Viennese musician named Franz Schubert produced his first six symphonies. Schubert was seventeen years younger than Beethoven, and he admired the older composer with a fervor that bordered on adulation. There is much to admire in these first six Schubert symphonies—especially in the rollicking *Second,* the darker-hued *Fourth* and the easy and genial *Fifth.* In 1821 Schubert drafted a *Seventh Symphony* in quite some detail, but dropped it and never returned to it. The following year he turned again to the composition of a symphony, completed two movements, sketched out a third, and orchestrated a few measures, then dropped that symphony too. Did he intend to return to it? Did he indeed return to it and complete two more movements, which were subsequently lost? Neither question has yet been satisfactorily answered; the fact remains, however, that the two-movement torso of a symphony, which was discovered some years after

Schubert died, and which has been known ever since as his *Unfinished Symphony*, is an unquestioned masterpiece. It is utterly different from any symphony that had been composed before it; the music is extremely dramatic and passionate, yet at all times under complete control. It is an "unfinished" symphony only in the sense that it consists of two movements rather than the four that were customary in Schubert's time. In every other respect, however, the work is a fully developed, completely fulfilled gem. Schubert's last symphony, composed during the last year of his tragically brief thirty-one-year life span, is the *Great C Major Symphony*, so called because of its magnitude and content, and to distinguish it from his earlier *C Major Symphony*, his *Sixth*. The *Great C Major* Schubert *Symphony* is one I particularly love; it is a symphony that soars constantly, ever striving to burst its bonds and go careening off into space. Because of its magnitude it has sometimes been called "The Symphony of Heavenly Length." As far as I am concerned, the score could just as easily sustain a one-word mark of identification as the "Heavenly" symphony.

Two years after Schubert completed his *Great C Major Symphony* there appeared another epoch-making symphony of heroic dimensions. This was the *Fantastic Symphony* by the twenty-six-year-old Frenchman, Hector Berlioz. If Beethoven, in the *Pastoral Symphony*, had created pictorial effects, then Berlioz' *Fantastic Symphony* is the first hallucinogenic score in music history. Berlioz is very explicit on this point; outlining the program for the *Fantastic Symphony*, he wrote: "A young musician of morbid sensibility and ardent imagination is in love and has poisoned himself with opium in a fit of desperation. Not having taken a lethal dose, he falls into a long sleep during which he has the strangest dreams, in which his feelings, sentiments and memories are translated by his sick brain into musical ideas and figures." The *Fantastic*, with its vividly descriptive tone painting, was as influential a work in its way as Beethoven's *Eroica*.

One of the most hilarious experiences I have ever had in the concert hall occurred in a performance of the *Fantastic*. Charles Munch is single-handedly responsible for the great revival of this score during our time; his white-hot, impetuous

reading of the symphony has influenced a generation of conductors and audiences and has set the standard for current
performances. During the summer of 1956 Munch toured
Europe and the Soviet Union with the Boston Symphony Orchestra, and one of the most frequently scheduled works was
the *Fantastic*. A highlight for Munch was the concert scheduled in his home town, Strasbourg; understandably, he was
especially anxious to "wow" his fellow Strasbourgians, and the
Fantastic was scheduled as the central focus of the program.
As luck would have it, one crisis after another conspired to
bring orchestra, instruments, and conductor into Strasbourg
almost literally at the last minute. The stage crew hurriedly
arranged the chairs, stands, and instruments on the stage and
finally the concert began—with the *Fantastic*. One of the most
chilling episodes in the music occurs in the last movement—
"Dream of a Witches' Sabbath"—when two large bells, tuned to
C and G, are struck successively just before and during the
playing of the theme of the *Dies Irae*, the Roman Catholic
liturgy for the dead. In their haste to assemble the stage, unfortunately, the stage crew had reversed the positions of the
two bells, so that the C bell was where the G bell was normally
positioned—and vice versa. Came the time for the two bells to be
struck, and the percussion player made a mighty hammer blow
in the direction of the C bell—except that the note that came
out was not C but G! By the time the poor player realized that
the position of the bells on stage was reversed, a sequence of
G-G-C (instead of C-C-G) had been intoned. You can imagine
the range of emotions that gripped everyone on stage! First
there was incredulity, then rage, then uncontrollable shock, and
finally contorting, aching inner laughter. Mr. Munch's face
changed colors several times, from ashen white to tumultuous red
to apoplectic purple. During his thirteen seasons with the Boston
Symphony, Munch led many extraordinary performances of the
Fantastic, but surely this one in Strasbourg was the most unforgettable!

In many respects Berlioz was the archetypal Romantic composer. He was the possessor of a perfervid imagination, he was
brilliantly gifted as a writer and critic, and he was in touch
with all the movements in the artistic ferment of his time. His

Harold in Italy Symphony, scored for solo viola and orchestra, is a depiction in sound of the adventures of Lord Byron's hero, Childe Harold. And Berlioz composed many operas on literary subjects—among them the *Faust* legend, *Romeo and Juliet, Beatrice and Benedict,* and *The Corsair.*

Another musician whose temperament and talents closely resembled those of Berlioz was Robert Schumann, who was born seven years after Berlioz and died thirteen years earlier. Schumann, too, was a man of extraordinary literary accomplishments as writer, editor, and critic. And he, too, was drawn to literary subjects for some of his compositions: Goethe's *Faust* and Byron's *Manfred* were among them. Schumann's most important orchestral scores, however, were his four symphonies and his individual concerti for piano, cello, and violin. Schumann was also a remarkable pianist, and until recent years it was fashionable in certain circles to denigrate his orchestral music as amateurish in scoring. That attitude has undergone considerable change of late, and some conductors—notably Leonard Bernstein—find it possible to conduct the Schumann symphonies without tinkering with the scoring at all. Schumann's *Piano Concerto* is one of the best known and best loved of all works for piano and orchestra. It began its life as a single-movement *Fantasy for Piano and Orchestra,* written for the composer's wife, Clara; Schumann later added two movements and created the *Concerto.* The *Cello Concerto* likewise is a staple of the literature; and the *Violin Concerto,* after nearly a century of neglect, is beginning to find its champions.

An almost exact contemporary of Schumann was Felix Mendelssohn, who was born in 1809 and died in 1847. Into his short life Mendelssohn crammed a wealth of musical activity, including important conducting accomplishments, reviving some of the great works of Bach. As a composer Mendelssohn produced no fewer than seventeen symphonies. The first dozen are juvenilia, however, and are not generally counted in his over-all output. Of the five that are, two are masterpieces: the *A Minor Symphony* titled *Scotch* and the *A Major Symphony* titled *Italian.* Both reveal a fertile imagination and a sure hand for orchestral color. Mendelssohn also composed two concerti each for violin and piano. The early *D Minor Violin Concerto* is something of a curiosity, but his later *Violin Concerto in E minor* has been called "the most perfect" concerto for the violin ever written. It sings all the way and has a quality of innocent purity that sweeps all before it. The *First Piano Concerto* has a similar quality of simplicity, but it has not been able to maintain as consistent a hold on the affections of performers and public as has the *Violin Concerto.* By far the best known of Mendelssohn's works is the *Wedding March* he composed as part of a set of instrumental pieces for Shakespeare's play *A Midsummer Night's Dream.* Interestingly, the music for the play came into being in two installments: the Overture was composed as an independent work when Mendelssohn was all of seventeen; the other pieces were composed seventeen years later, on commission from the King of Prussia, for a scheduled performance of the Shakespeare play.

One of the most fascinating musical figures of the nineteenth century was Franz Liszt. No less important than Liszt's piano music is his output for orchestra. As an innovator, he created the symphonic poem. Taking Berlioz' *Fantastic Symphony* as his model, Liszt achieved a new kind of musical and poetic unity in his thirteen symphonic poems. The best known are *Les Preludes* and *Mazepa,* the former being a musical reflection of Lamartine's philosophy that life is but a series of preludes to death, the latter depicting a wild ride across the Ukrainian steppes by a Cossack hero. Liszt's two piano concerti are brilliant display vehicles for a virtuoso pianist, as is his *Hungarian Fantasy for Piano and Orchestra.* By far his most ambitious score for orchestra is his *Faust Symphony,* a three-panel musical canvas on which are delineated the characters and personalities of the story's principal figures: Faust, Gretchen, and Mephistopheles.

During the second half of the nineteenth century there were five great composers of symphonies: Brahms, Bruckner, Dvořák, Mahler, and Tchaikovsky. At the same time there were many composers all over Europe writing music for orchestra that can generally be categorized within the broad framework of the political climate that was sweeping the continent: nationalism.

Brahms's four great symphonies are in the direct Beethoven

tradition. They are visionary, heroic, noble—and quite outside the mainstream of the music of his time. We tend to take it as a sign of admiration that someone at the time called Brahms's *First Symphony* "Beethoven's Tenth." And yet was it admiration, or was it a comment of condescension, a criticism of Brahms for looking to the giants of the past and away from the musical currents of his own time? A bitter rivalry existed between the supporters of Wagner and the admirers of Brahms; the Wagner champions considered Brahms old hat and reactionary. Yet there is little question that the music of Brahms has stood the test of time.

Along with the four symphonies, Brahms's orchestral output consists principally of two companion concert overtures, the *Academic Festival Overture* and the *Tragic Overture*, and four concerti—two for piano, one for violin, and one for violin and cello. Brahms himself, speaking of the two overtures, said the first laughs while the second weeps. Although this characterization may be simplistic, it conveys the essential nature of the two pieces. Each of the concerti is a score of large and sweeping dimensions, and each engages in an intense musical confrontation, emerging at the end on a note of high triumph and affirmation.

One of my own most exciting adventures as a broadcaster occurred during a performance by Rudolf Serkin of Brahms's *Second Piano Concerto*. Serkin, as is well known, is not a reticent performer. He almost literally throws himself into his playing, and the piano absorbs a good deal of physical punishment. On the day in question I arrived at the hall several hours prior to the start of the concert, and there was Serkin on stage, practicing some of the trickier passages and flailing away at the piano for all he was worth. After a dinner break I returned to the hall and prepared for the broadcast. The first part of the concert consisted of music by Aaron Copland conducted by the composer, with Serkin and the Brahms concerto conducted by Charles Munch following after intermission. I had some matters to discuss with Copland, and after I introduced the concerto, I left my broadcast booth and proceeded to the conductor's room to chat with Copland. Shortly after the third movement of the concerto began, the stage door leading to the conductor's room opened and one of the double bass players of the orchestra ambled slowly offstage, to be followed in an instant by one of the assistant managers of the orchestra, who came bounding backstage through another door. I didn't know what had happened, but quite obviously something had gone wrong. I immediately bounced up from my conversation with Copland, ran to the other side of the stage and then up the two flights of stairs that led to the broadcast booth, picking up en route the information that the lyre mechanism at the bottom of the piano had literally torn away from the main body of the instrument! When I arrived at my microphone, I was as thoroughly out of breath as though I had run the mile in three minutes. Between gasps for air I signaled for the engineer to let me tell the radio audience what had happened, and then after some seconds of "dead air" while I caught my breath, I described to the audience the various stages of piano repair work that were taking place on stage. After a delay of about fifteen minutes a makeshift arrangement was completed that allowed the performance to proceed to its conclusion. To this day I cannot hear Brahms's *Second Piano Concerto* without uttering a silent prayer that the piano and the soloist will hold out until the very end of the music!

Finally, I must mention Brahms's two *Serenades* for small orchestra and his *Variations on a Theme by Haydn.* The *Serenades* are easy-going, genial works that reveal a far more relaxed side of their composer's nature. I defy anyone to listen to the last movement of the *Second Serenade in A Major* and not break into a smile of pure joy. The *Variations on a Theme by Haydn,* Brahms's last purely orchestral work before he produced his *First Symphony,* is actually a misnomer; the so-called Haydn theme on which the music is based is actually an old Austrian peasants' hymn, the *St. Anthony Chorale.* A more accurate title would be *Variations on the St. Anthony Chorale—* and the score is so listed in the WQXR library.

The case of Anton Bruckner is another instance of modern-day revival. During his own time Bruckner was admired by some, reviled by most, and did not experience the joy of public acceptance of his music until fairly late in life. When he died in 1896, much of the interest in his music died with him. Dur-

ing his lifetime Bruckner was so grateful for whatever performances his music received, he allowed conductors and editors
to retouch and reorchestrate his symphonies. The modern-day
interest in Bruckner began with a Munich performance in the
early 1930's of the original version of the *Ninth Symphony.* It
was seen that the variously edited and reorchestrated editions
had wiped away much of the power and originality of Bruckner's music. From that time on, the swing was back to Bruckner's original scoring. Bruckner today enjoys unprecedented
popularity. His nine symphonies are massive splashes of orchestral weight and sound; they are repetitious and long; and there
are patches of dull note-spinning in nearly every one. Yet the
best contain pages of exalted musical inspiration that cannot
fail to impress any fair-minded listener. My own choices among
the Bruckner symphonies are the *Fourth, Seventh, Eighth,* and
Ninth—each a monolith, but each exerting a strong and cumulative impact.

Dvořák, for my money, is the most underrated symphonist
of the nineteenth century. For years his last symphony, the one
called *From the New World,* quite obliterated his other works
in this form. Indeed, for years he was credited with only five
symphonies, because his first four works in the form remained
unpublished. Now the nine symphonies of Dvořák—isn't it amazing how many composers produced nine symphonies?—are seen
as a total symphonic output of heroic proportions. The recent
publication of the four early Dvořák symphonies has brought
about a renumbering of the other five; the *Symphony From the
New World,* for example, formerly bore the number 5—now it is
correctly identified as the *Ninth;* the old *No. 4* is now the
No. 8, and so forth. Dvořák's *Symphonies Nos. 6, 7, 8,* and *9*
(the old *Nos. 1, 2, 4,* and *5*) form a quartet of exuberant and
exhilarating works on the very highest level, and among the four
newly mined Dvořák symphonies, my favorites are the *Third* (in
E flat, Opus 10) and *Fourth* (in D minor, Opus 13).

Dvořák also composed symphonic poems, concerti, concert
overtures, and a series of *Slavonic Dances.* His *Cello Concerto
in B minor,* supposedly suggested to him after he had attended
a performance in New York of Victor Herbert's *Second Cello
Concerto,* is the *locus classicus* of the literature for cello and

orchestra. The *Violin Concerto* is a less successful work but it nonetheless is a full-blooded expression of Dvořák's rich melodic invention and is beginning to find increasing favor with performers and audiences. The *G Minor Piano Concerto* went virtually ignored for years, partly because of the thickness of its orchestral scoring, but now this work, too—thanks largely to the championing of Rudolf Firkusny and Sviatoslav Richter—is beginning to make its way in the repertoire. An interesting trilogy is formed by the three overtures, *In Nature's Realm, Carnival,* and *Othello.* Dvořák created them as a group, and they share some thematic material, but they can be, and often are, played separately. The Dvořák symphonic poems are perhaps his least frequently played orchestral compositions. They carry fanciful titles—*The Golden Spinning Wheel, The Watersprite, The Wood Dove,* and so forth—and are full of inventive orchestral imagery. There are two quite extraordinary *Serenades:* the *First, in E Major,* is scored for strings and is a lyrical outpouring of irresistible charm; the *Second, in D minor,* is scored for woodwinds, cello, and double bass, and is a darker-hued but equally affecting score. The *Slavonic Dances* run the gamut of expression from the boisterous extroversion of the first, in C Major, to the atmospheric calm of the last, in A flat.

Tchaikovsky (1840–1893) produced what is probably the most popular body of orchestral music in the whole of the literature. Symphonies, symphonic poems, concerti, overtures, concert pieces, ballets—Tchaikovsky wrote them all, and he left his mark on every form. There is a quality of melancholia about much of Tchaikovsky's music, and this has tempted some interpreters to go overboard in "emotionalizing" their performances of Tchaikovsky. For me, the most successful performances are those that take full advantage of the sentiment without swooning. The last three Tchaikovsky symphonies, *Nos. 4, 5,* and *6,* are his most popular. The *Fourth* builds to a cumulative excitement which can be quite overwhelming, the *Fifth* is in the victory-through-struggle tradition of Beethoven's *Fifth,* and the *Sixth* is the gloomy, despairing *Pathétique.* Before he composed the *Pathétique,* Tchaikovsky sketched out another symphony and then abandoned it. In 1956 the Soviet musician Semyon Bogatyryev reconstructed this abandoned symphony from

Tchaikovsky's sketches, and it now has some currency as Tchai-kovsky's "*Seventh*" *Symphony.*

Tchaikovsky composed one *Violin Concerto,* one score for cello and orchestra titled *Variations on a Rococo Theme,* and three concerti for piano and orchestra. The first is probably the best-known of all works for piano and orchestra. During the 1940's, when composers of Tin Pan Alley appropriated a good many of Tchaikovsky's works for their own purposes, the majestic opening of Tchaikovsky's *First Piano Concerto* turned up on the Hit Parade as "Tonight We Love." Tchaikovsky's *Second Piano Concerto* is a far more serene score, but it is full of typical Tchaikovsky melodies, and it is beginning to be heard in our concert halls more frequently. The *Violin Concerto* is one of the half-dozen most popular works of its kind and the *Rococo Variations* is a charming and subtle score.

Many other Tchaikovsky compositions are part of the bread-and-butter orchestral repertory: the *Romeo and Juliet* and *Francesca da Rimini* fantasies, both extremely dramatic and melodious; the *Serenade in C Major for Strings,* with its liquid waltz movement; the *Capriccio Italien,* a dazzling display of colorful orchestration; the *March Slav* and *1812 Overture,* two intensely nationalistic scores. But there are those who maintain, and with considerable justification, that the essence of Tchaikovsky is to be found in his three great ballet scores: *Swan Lake, The Nutcracker,* and *The Sleeping Beauty.*

Unlike Tchaikovsky, who composed in many different musical forms, Gustav Mahler was primarily a symphonist. A superb conductor of the operatic and symphonic literature, Mahler was forced for the most part to be an avocational composer during his summer vacations. Despite this restriction, however, he managed to produce nine symphonies—there is that magical number "nine" again—which are truly colossal in mystical and philosophical terms. "A symphony is like the world," Mahler once stated. "It must embrace everything." And the nine Mahler symphonies go into the recesses of wild and secret territory, probing and challenging established truths about the nature of the universe. In an extraordinary letter to Mahler in 1904 Arnold Schönberg wrote: "I must not speak as a musician to a musician if I am to give any idea of the incredible impression your symphony made on me: I can speak only as one human being to another. . . . I felt it as an event of nature, which after scouring us with its terrors puts a rainbow in the sky. . . . I believed in your symphony. I shared in the battling for illusion; I suffered the pangs of disillusionment; I saw the forces of evil and good wrestling with each other; I saw a man in torment struggling toward inward harmony; I divined a personality, a drama, and truthfulness, the most uncompromising truthfulness." What characterizes the specific also serves the general. Mahler's symphonies, all of them, are immense frescoes of life, which we are only now beginning to understand.

Because of his mystical and superstitious nature, Mahler hesitated to put a number *nine* on a symphony—out of fear that it would be his last. He dodged the issue for a while by putting a title with words onto what actually *was* his *Ninth Symphony*— this is the sublime song-symphony *Das Lied von der Erde* (*The Song of the Earth*). But then he did put the number nine onto his next full-blown orchestral score, and he even sketched out a *Tenth*, which was painstakingly reconstructed recently by the British Mahler connoisseur, Deryck Cooke, and performed and recorded. The year 1960 marked the centennial of the birth of Mahler; it also marked the real beginning of a wide public appreciation of Mahler's importance in music history.

The Nationalists among the composers of the latter half of the nineteenth century were responding to the prevailing political climate throughout Europe. The Bohemian Bedřich Smetana rebelled against the repressive measures of the Austrian Empire in his native land and fled for a time to Sweden, where he could more freely function as a creative artist. When he returned to his homeland, he created a series of Czech national scores, including the cycle of six symphonic poems titled collectively *My Country*. The second and fourth—*The Moldau* and *From Bohemia's Meadows and Forests*—are the best known.

In Russia, Mikhail Glinka was the founder of the Russian school of nationalist music, which ultimately brought into being the group of composers who banded together as "The Five": Balakirev, Cui, Rimski-Korsakov, Borodin, and Musorgski. Each of them composed orchestral music chiefly distinguished by exotic and colorful orchestration. The most prolific was Rimski-

Korsakov, whose *Scheherazade, Capriccio Espagnole,* and *Russian Easter Overture* are perennial favorites.

In Norway, Edvard Grieg became the national musical spokesman, and his incidental music for Ibsen's fantasy *Peer Gynt* is one of his nation's richest natural resources. Also reflective of Grieg's national character is his *Piano Concerto in A minor*—solid, tough and richly romantic.

A Spanish national music was beginning to emerge under the impetus provided by the success of the music of Albéniz and Granados, and toward the very end of the century Sibelius appeared in Finland as that country's representative of a national musical expression.

In France, too, there was a musical ferment, though it would be overstating the case to say that the composers active in France were creating a distinctive French musical nationalism. Rather, each was expressing his own musical point of view, and in the aggregate what they came up with are some of the qualities we today characterize as being typically French: wit, urbanity, polish, and meticulous craftsmanship. To this group of composers belong such figures as Franck (though Belgian-born), Chausson, d'Indy, Lalo, Fauré, Bizet, and Saint-Saëns.

In the Austrian Empire the musical nationalism that reigned supreme was the waltz, and its chief apostle, of course, was the man who quickly came to be dubbed The Waltz King, Johann Strauss the Younger.

Although his life span covered the first half of the twentieth century, Richard Strauss (no relation to the waltzing Strausses from Vienna) must be evaluated in the context of his orchestral output as a composer of the nineteenth century. Though he composed a delectable *Oboe Concerto* and a few other instrumental scores late in life, his principal orchestral scores date mostly from the last decade and a half of the previous century. That he was a Romantic to the core is proven by his addiction to literary subjects for many of his works—*Don Juan, Macbeth, Don Quixote, Thus Spake Zarathustra,* and even *Death and Transfiguration* all have literary programs. So does *Till Eulenspiegel's Merry Pranks.* The symphonic poem *Ein Heldenleben* (*A Hero's Life*), which may be said to sum up the first period of Strauss's creativity, is similarly tied to an explicit program, albeit one of Strauss's own devising. All these scores have a plush and luxuriant sound and a truly sensual impact.

The Twentieth Century

In our own century orchestral music has flourished. There have been many different trends along the way, to be sure, and the situation seems constantly to be changing. I label as nonsense the dire predictions of those who forecast the disappearance of the symphony orchestra through atrophy. Before we examine some of the most recent contributions to the orchestral literature, let us briefly look at some of the great composers of the recent past.

During the early years of this century Debussy, Schönberg, and Stravinsky were busily enriching orchestral literature. Debussy's *La Mer, Nocturnes,* orchestral *Images,* and *Jeux* are highly evocative scores, which seem to challenge all the senses at once. Schönberg's first orchestral works are in the style of lush Romanticism—*Pelleas and Melisande,* the *Gurre-Lieder,* and *Transfigured Night.* And the three great ballet scores Stravinsky composed between 1910 and 1913—*The Firebird, Petrouchka,* and *The Rite of Spring*—are all brilliantly scored orchestral tours de force very much in the Rimski-Korsakov tradition—yes, even the savage and barbaric *Rite of Spring.* Similarly, the orchestral works of Ravel are natural outgrowths from the evolving French style of the 1880's and 1890's and the early 1900's.

What makes the music of the twentieth century such a fascinating and complex literature is its many-sidedness. Composers like Nielsen, Bartók, Prokofiev, and Britten have worked within traditional frameworks and formal concepts, and each has enriched the art with the power of his own musical thought. Free spirits like Ives and Varèse have cast aside the motivational principles that have guided other composers, and have struck out in their own new directions. Composers like Copland and Shostakovich have consciously striven to communicate directly to their audiences while others, of whom John Cage is perhaps the principal example, seem to devote their energies toward finding new ways to confound the public. In short, there is something for every taste.

To conclude this chapter, I would merely like to touch upon some of the music of the present and the recent past that I find particularly satisfying.

The emergence of the Danish composer Carl Nielsen as a powerful figure in twentieth-century music is especially gratifying to me. Nielsen was a unique figure, and his six symphonies are among the most engaging in the entire realm of music. My own favorites are the graceful and pastoral *Third* and the sardonic, menacing *Fifth*.

Bartók, who died so tragically unappreciated in New York as recently as 1945, left us a heritage of many superb orchestral creations. Chief among them are the *Concerto for Orchestra;* the *Music for Strings, Percussion and Celesta;* the *Second Violin Concerto;* the *Divertimento for String Orchestra;* the *Dance Suite;* and the *Second* and *Third Piano Concerti.*

Bartók's *Concerto for Orchestra* was composed on commission from Serge Koussevitzky for the Koussevitzky Music Foundation. Its first performances were given in Boston under Koussevitzky's direction by the Boston Symphony Orchestra early in December, 1944, and a few weeks later Koussevitzky took the unprecedented step of repeating the score in the same subscription series. Precarious health had prevented Bartók from attending the first performances, but when the repeats came along a few weeks later, he journeyed to Boston to be present at the rehearsals and performances. Koussevitzky saw to it that Bartók was comfortably seated in Symphony Hall's first balcony, overlooking the stage, for the rehearsals. No sooner did the conductor begin to rehearse the concerto than the composer, seated directly overhead, interrupted with the suggestion that the tempo was a bit too slow for what he had in mind. Koussevitzky began again, this time with a slightly faster tempo. Before long, however, Bartók again interrupted with another comment, and then another and another. After a while Koussevitzky patiently suggested to Bartók that perhaps he could write his comments down on a sheet of paper, and then the two of them could discuss matters during the rehearsal's intermission, rather than using up valuable rehearsal time for their deliberations. To this Bartók readily agreed, and a pad of paper and pencil were brought to him. The rehearsal proceeded without further interruption from Bartók, but he was observed to be writing furiously, filling page after page with notes. When the intermission break arrived, composer and conductor closeted themselves behind the locked door of the conductor's room to go over Bartók's notes and suggestions. Only Koussevitzky and Bartók know the details of the discussion that followed, and neither, unfortunately, is around today to offer testimony. Not a sound was heard by the bystanders who were stationed outside the door, but in a very few minutes the door was unlocked from the inside, and Bartók and Koussevitzky emerged wreathed in smiles. When the rehearsal session was reconvened on the stage, the conductor announced beatifically: "Gentlemen, during the intermission of our rehearsal I was able to go over the score of this masterpiece with its inspired composer, and I am happy to report to you that he agrees in every detail with *my* interpretation. Let us go now to the fourth movement!"

Prokofiev was an extremely important creative figure of this century, and his symphonies, concerti, and incidental scores form one of the richest lodes of the music of our time. His *Classical, Fifth,* and *Sixth Symphonies* are true classics, his two violin concerti and five for piano are endlessly fascinating, and several of his miscellaneous orchestral scores, including the *Scythian Suite,* the *Lieutenant Kije Suite,* and *Peter and the Wolf,* are among the best-known works of our time. Prokofiev was also a superb composer of music for the ballet, and his *Cinderella* and *Romeo and Juliet* are full-scale masterpieces.

Of the output of that other great Soviet composer of the twentieth century, Shostakovich, I particularly recommend five of the symphonies: the *First, Fifth, Sixth, Eighth,* and *Tenth.* Each packs a powerful and long-lasting message.

In addition to the three great ballets, there is much other Stravinsky music worth cultivating: the *Symphony in C* and the *Symphony in Three Movements,* the *Capriccio for Piano and Orchestra,* the *Violin Concerto, The Soldier's Tale,* the *Symphony of Psalms, Card Game,* and *Oedipus Rex.*

Of Aaron Copland's music I particularly like *Appalachian*

Spring, Billy the Kid, El Salon Mexico, the *Dance Symphony,* the *Piano Concerto, Rodeo,* and *Music for the Theater.*

Though Benjamin Britten's major reputation rests on his operas and other theater works, I would additionally commend to your attention his *Sinfonia da Requiem,* his *Variations on a Theme by Frank Bridge,* the *Young Person's Guide to the Orchestra,* and the *Symphony for Cello and Orchestra.*

The symphonies by Sibelius and Ralph Vaughan Williams are distinguished twentieth-century additions to the form that so dominated orchestral music during the nineteenth century. In addition, both Sibelius and Vaughan Williams composed much other orchestral music of outstanding and lasting importance. Chief among Sibelius' output in this area are the symphonic poems *Pohjola's Daughter, Tapiola, En Saga, The Swan of Tuonela,* and *Finlandia;* Vaughan Williams' principal orchestral scores in addition to his symphonies are the *Fantasia on a Theme by Tallis,* the *Fantasia on "Greensleeves,"* the *Romance for Violin and Orchestra* titled *The Lark Ascending,* and the *English Folk Song Suite.*

Finally, I would call to your attention some of the music of the Czechoslovakian-born composer, Bohuslav Martinu, who spent the years of the Second World War in this country. Unfortunately, not much of Martinu's music is performed or recorded. His was a distinctive voice, however, and he had a rich sense of orchestral color and symphonic design. Of the available recordings of his works, perhaps the most representative are his *Fourth Symphony,* the *Third* and *Fourth Piano Concerti,* and the *Violin Concerto.*

This brief panoramic survey of four centuries of orchestral music is of necessity highly condensed. Many important composers have not even been mentioned. I hope, however, that the reader will be encouraged to do some exploring of his own, for only through personal discovery can one fully participate in what Leonard Bernstein has so rightly termed *The Joy of Music.*

3

Music of the Baroque

IGOR KIPNIS

To some listeners Baroque music represents a somewhat vague historical period, somewhere around the time of Bach or earlier. To them this is music of a faintly antiseptic nature, anti-emotional in content, usually involving reduced performing forces, who are utilizing antiquarian instruments. The bulk of compositions stemming from this time is looked on as an early and undeveloped form of expression. It is regarded as music still in a fairly primitive state, music that has not yet attained the full flowering it would achieve with the rise of the symphony in the age of Mozart or Beethoven.

Another company of music lovers has a somewhat less restricted view of that era. But they look upon Baroque music as a passionless antidote for the Romantic excesses of the late nineteenth and early twentieth centuries. They appreciate their Vivaldi or Teleman because they think that these composers have the characteristics of classicism, purity and formalism. Even Mozart has been viewed by this school of listeners as an essentially classical composer, whose emotional penetration is seldom profound.

This attitude, like the first, is a limited one. It applies neither to the early Baroque (the beginnings of the seventeenth century—the time of Giovanni Gabrieli and Monteverdi) or to the late (the Baroque in music is usually said to end with the death of Johann Sebastian Bach in 1750). The one distinguishing characteristic that emerges from any study of this period, whether it deals with music or the visual arts, is an unusually strong element of passion. This quality, of which a great many music lovers are unaware, runs throughout the entire 150-year span of what we call *Baroque music*. What I would like to stress here most of all is that in this period of music history, with its tremendous concentration on the emotions, there was an immense amount of vitality. There was, to be sure, an occasional undercurrent of classicism, but by and large it was an era of overt expression. This passionate communication was not couched, however, in the Romantic style, a rhapsodic revelation of a later century, but rather in the controlled expression of an exceptionally rhetorical and brilliantly varied age, an age whose intensity and desire to explore very much matches our own.

What we think of today as a historical period of music was originally a descriptive term, and not a very complimentary one at that. First used over three centuries ago in reference to irregularly shaped pearls, *Baroque*, by the middle of the eighteenth century, had attained a derogatory meaning that was applied to art, implying something contorted, eccentric, bizarre, and even tasteless. The word did not lose its pejorative connotation until close to the beginning of this century, when *Baroque* began to be used to describe a stylistic period in the visual arts. The attachment to music did not come until around 1918, but several decades had to pass before its general acceptance as a stylistic label for the music of the seventeenth and first half of the eighteenth centuries.

This style of composition was an outgrowth of the Renaissance, the aesthetic ideal of which was the discovery and control of the world and mankind. The Renaissance concept was one of serene formalism and reality; the Baroque involved an exaggeration, a striving beyond formal structure. The Renaissance held its own equilibrium, the Baroque pushed out of it, but without entirely foregoing the formalistic elements.

Music between 1600 and 1750 may be pictured as involving two opposing forces, a formal structure (fugue, aria, concerto) and an equally powerful desire to escape the structure (the free cadenza at the conclusion of the aria, the spontaneously embellished repeats of a formal dance movement in an equally formal setting of the suite, the virtuosic flights of fancy of a toccata). The interaction between these two forces results in tension; tension is also achieved by a new harmonic language, in which the emphasis is rather more strongly on the discord than the concord (the reason why trills begin on the upper note rather than the main note). There is, of course, relaxation as well, but tension, the driving impulse of the Baroque, is always present to some degree. One may hear it in a 1610 *Magnificat* by Monteverdi, a keyboard lament for the death of a lutenist by the mid-seventeenth-century Austrian, Froberger, or a French-styled suite by Bach. In the Monteverdi work, which derives from a musical setting of the Vespers for the Feasts of the Blessed Virgin, the symmetrical spirit of the Renaissance has been magnified, even distorted, with the most grandiose results.

Innovations

Monteverdi, who parallels the beginnings of the Baroque, was also intensely interested in a new development of musical composition—monody; here the concept of melody and accompaniment displaced an earlier polyphonic style, where all voices (or parts) of a composition has equal importance. The manner in which Monteverdi approached this idea, with its supreme emphasis on the importance of the text, sometimes resulted in an affective expression that becomes manneristic, which of course is Baroque exaggeration carried to its furthest extreme (for instance the highly chromatic passage of some of his madrigals, or one hundred years later, the strange harmonic progressions of a Bach chorale prelude).

Monody was to have far-reaching influence, for out of it came the opera aria. Opera developed at the beginnings of the Baroque, as did another important principle from Italy (this country was the musical leader throughout not only the Renaissance but also the Baroque): the idea of contrast (*concertato*). Early examples of such contrast in Baroque music are particularly stimulating for stereo-minded listeners, for such composers as Giovanni Gabrieli wrote both instrumental and choral pieces

involving spectacular antiphonal effects. *Concertato* eventually
developed into the concerto, in which either a single instrument or a group was pitted against a larger, accompanying
body. So far as Baroque composers were concerned, the solo
forces involved in a concerto could not only be variable (ranging from a single violin, oboe, or even, as in the renowned Bolognese school, the trumpet, all the way to a small ensemble,
as in a concerto grosso), but the principle of contrast could be
achieved as well by dynamics and differing tonal characteristics. Perfectly in keeping with the concerto principle are works
of that name by Bach (the *Italian Concerto* for a solo harpsichord with two keyboards), by the early eighteenth-century
French bourgeois favorite Joseph Bodin de Boismortier, who
wrote a delightful *Concerto in E minor,* Opus 37, just for flute,
oboe, violin, bassoon, and continuo, and by Vivaldi, who composed numerous concertos for orchestra without any solo instruments at all.

The Baroque age is sometimes called the period of the continuo, or to use its full name, the basso continuo. This was the
system of the figured bass or thorough bass, and it refers to the
harmonic underpinning for any piece of music. Composers developed a musical shorthand for indicating with each bass note
what harmony was to be required at any given moment, a
method that has its counterpart today in the system of guitar
chords for popular music. "Continuo" really refers to the bass
line of a composition, a part that has considerable aural importance. That line would normally be played by the low
stringed instruments, together with one or more keyboard instruments, such as harpsichord and organ and even lute or harp.
The instruments that were capable of playing more than just
the bottom line would also fill out the indicated harmonies from
the figures. So far as the execution of the harmonies was concerned, this was an entirely improvisational system.

Among other innovations developed during the Baroque age
was the instrumental sonata (solo plus continuo, or more instruments, as in the trio sonata, where two soloists are heard
above the continuo—in other words, involving three separate
parts, although as many as four or five players may be participating). Then there was the suite, which derived from pair-

ings of dance movements. The Renaissance Pavan and Galliard metamorphosed, roughly speaking, into the Baroque Allemande and Courante. To these were added a slow and stately Sarabande and a bouncy Gigue (as in a Froberger suite); eventually additional movements were provided, some free, some not dance movements at all, but descriptive pieces (as in the harpsichord suites of Couperin and Rameau), and some movements that could serve as introductions (Prelude, Fantasia, Toccata, or French Overture).

The French Overture, itself a highly stylized form, consisting of a slow section with dotted rhythms, followed by a fast fugal section with, usually, a return to the slow pompous opening material, was developed by Lully in the latter half of the seventeenth century. It was used both orchestrally and instrumentally by composers both French and non-French, and it is one of the most common musical forms to be found during this era (*viz.*, Handel, *Royal Fireworks Music;* Telemann, *Don Quichotte Suite;* Bach, *Goldberg Variations, No. 16*). The Sinfonia, a more Italianate development, was made up of three movements in a fast-slow-fast sequence, and it eventually became transformed in the later eighteenth century into the classical symphony.

Among the innovations, it might be wise to mention the development of certain instruments, notably the violin. Music for it began to be written at the very outset of the Baroque, although not until the end of the seventeenth century could it be considered a serious rather than a popular instrument whose function had to be restricted mainly to dance music. By the close of the Baroque, Corelli had ennobled the violin through his sonatas, Vivaldi had helped to develop the violin concerto and broadened its technical capabilities, Tartini extended them even further, and Locatelli (whose *L'arte del violino,* Opus 3, appeared in 1733) provided opportunities for violin virtuosity that were not to be equaled until the time of Paganini.

The lute and the viols, however, proceeded rather in the opposite direction. Their heyday was at the close of the Renaissance, when they were beloved by amateurs. By the close of the seventeenth century both had diminished considerably in appeal. The lute had evolved from an instrument any gentleman could play to an incredibly complex device, which might be effective only in the hands of the most skilled virtuoso (for example, Bach's intricate lute pieces).

Among the keyboard instruments, three held sway: the harpsichord, which could be played solo, in ensemble or with orchestra (in its continuo as well as in a concerted function); the organ, whose main use was connected with the church; and the clavichord, an intimate-voiced home instrument.

As a harpsichordist I cannot refrain from adding a few remarks about my own instrument. Contrary to the popular belief, the harpsichord is not an ancestor of the modern piano; it is, however, a kind of great granduncle, for the simple reason that it bears the same approximate shape as the later instrument and because it uses a keyboard. Mechanically, however, the harpsichord has its strings plucked, as against the struck strings of the piano. In that respect, the clavichord, for all its tiny dynamic span, is the true ancestor of the piano, since its strings are struck, by metal tangents, to produce a tone. That instrument, incidentally, is the only keyboard instrument able to produce a vibrato, which the player can accomplish by gently wiggling any key up and down. Both the harpsichord and clavichord possess an enormous repertoire, most of it, of course, Baroque, though modern composers have become attracted to them as well. The new enthusiasm for the harpsichord has been only one of the factors in the Baroque revival that indicate to what extent musical tastes have shifted.

The Baroque Revival

The enormous interest in, and appreciation of, Baroque music, which has reached peak proportions in the last few years, could hardly have been envisaged a mere two decades ago. At that time the standard repertoire for concerts or records lay almost exclusively within nineteenth-century boundaries, with only occasional forays into earlier or later fields. There were eloquent spokesmen for these fringe areas, but so far as an enlightened public response might be concerned, a phonograph representation or concert performance of Schönberg's *Pierrot*

Lunaire had about as much general appeal as Handel's *Semele* or Monteverdi's 1607 opera *Orfeo,* which is to say hardly any at all, certainly not enough curiosity to make such a performance commercially worthwhile.

In the late 1940's the situation changed dramatically. A wealth of unusual repertoire, embracing music of many different periods, became available, and a public that for so long had been content with oft-performed Beethoven, Brahms, and Tchaikovsky suddenly became aware of names and works that, though largely unfamiliar, were no less attractive. This repertoire explosion can be ascribed partly to changing tastes, but it got its principal impetus from a commercial development— the long-playing record.

For many listeners the chance to venture beyond standard fare came as a relief after a surfeit of Beethoven *Fifths* and Tchaikovsky *Pathétiques;* there was a reaction against the excesses of Romanticism—overlush harmonies and an overdose of sentimentality. Perhaps because we live in a scientific age, the clarity of Baroque writing, as exemplified in a Vivaldi concerto, had much to do with its appeal. As much may be said about interest engendered in the pointillistic effects of a twentieth-century Webern composition. The music was different, and this in itself was a source of attraction. However, curiosity in this drastically different repertoire remained largely unexpressed, until record producers in the late forties discovered that a Vivaldi concerto was far less expensive to make than a nineteenth-century piece. Baroque music (as well as a good deal of contemporary material) was akin to chamber music in its demands of manpower. A Bach *Brandenburg Concerto* not only did not need the resources of a full-scale symphony orchestra, it sounded better with the small ensemble for which the composer intended it.

A large number of the Baroque works that were finding their way into the hands of record buyers originated in Europe, where recording costs, primarily musician's fees, were lower. The result was that a number of young, small firms began making excellent reputations and achieving respectable, if not overwhelming, sales based on releases of this repertoire. As more records were sold, the repertoire widened and was duplicated by other companies. The larger companies began to realize that there was money to be made in this area, though the biggest began to make their inroads into the Baroque only a few years ago. Once the momentum began to be felt, the effects on the record market were startling, to say the least. At latest count, according to the Schwann LP-record catalogue, there were twenty-three recordings of the Tchaikovsky *Nutcracker Suite,* as against twenty-one of Vivaldi's *Four Seasons.* Schwann lists thirty-three Beethoven *Fifths* compared with twenty-four sets of the complete Bach *Brandenburg Concerti.*

The Four Seasons and the *Brandenburg Concerti* are the evergreens of their fields. With the more esoteric pieces, the numbers are far less, though in a few curious instances (for example, there have been four recordings of an early Baroque oratorio, Carissimi's *Jepthe*) there exist more duplications than one might reasonably expect.

Because recordings have so dramatically broadened the standard repertoire, there has also been a striking change in live concert programming. To be sure, the Beethoven symphonies have not been displaced, but symphony orchestras do occasionally delve into orchestral repertoire of the early eighteenth century. Instrumentalists no longer are content to begin their recitals with the usual Handel sonata; they even go so far as to program a piece by the seventeenth-century Biber. I might mention here in passing that instruments once considered museum curiosities—the viola da gamba, lute, recorder, viola d'amore, and of course, the harpsichord and clavichord—have successfully been revived and are now appreciated on their own merits and no longer thought of as inferior ancestors of our "improved" modern instruments. A manifestation of the remarkable Baroque advance occurred at the 1967 Berkshire Festival at Tanglewood when an all-Vivaldi orchestral program attracted an audience of over six thousand.

Vivaldi may be considered the key composer responsible for the Baroque revival. It was around 1950 that the first recording of *The Four Seasons* was issued on long-playing discs. People who had never heard a note of Vivaldi suddenly were charmed by that Italian composer's marvelous rhythmic verve. They began investigating other Vivaldi works available in the record stores. They asked for more, and they discovered, especially after the record companies realized that there was a huge potential Vivaldi market, that this early eighteenth-century Venetian wrote hundreds of orchestral pieces, most of them concertos for almost every instrument available at that time (bassoon, cello, flute, lute, horn, mandolin, oboe, piccolo, recorder, trumpet, viola d'amore, violin, as well as combinations of these and other instruments).

A wag once observed that Vivaldi didn't write four hundred concerti, but merely wrote one concerto four hundred times. Though exaggerated, the comment has a slight touch of truth. When one is forced to listen to a great deal of Vivaldi at one time, the harmonic patterns and sewing-machine sequences (those energetic rhythms so typical of nearly all late Baroque Italian music) do begin to pall, but cannot one say the same of nearly all other composers?

If Vivaldi began as one of the principal heroes of the Baroque revival during the fifties, today he seems to have been supplanted at least partially by Telemann, who was even more prolific. Georg Philipp Telemann (1681–1767) not only outlived Johann Sebastian Bach by seventeen years, but was in his time considered a far greater composer; it was he who was offered first choice at the position Bach eventually attained, cantor of the Thomaskirche in Leipzig. When the Bach revival began, toward the middle of the nineteenth century, Telemann also came in for investigation (Bach had transcribed some of Telemann's concertos for keyboard), and in comparison with the astounding Bach, he was found wanting. He was considered facile (how could one not consider the creator of some eight hundred orchestral suites facile?) and unprofound, a poor runner-up to the great composers of the epoch—Bach, Handel, Corelli, Vivaldi, Couperin, and Rameau, to mention only some of the late Baroque names. Even at the start of the LP era, Telemann was vastly underrepresented on records. Today the situation is quite changed; within the last few years there have appeared three separate recordings of Telemann's three *Tafelmusik* productions (music for banquets, consisting of both orchestral pieces and chamber works, each set of which lasts about an hour and a half), not to mention a plethora of discs

involving almost every aspect of the composer's widespread
activity, from Passions and that favorite chamber music form
of the eighteenth century, the trio sonata, to orchestral suites
and concertos. If Telemann still cannot be considered an equal
to Bach (and who can?), there is often far more to his writing
than can be glossed over by the superficial description "eighteenth-century Muzak." Certainly equal in intrinsic musical merit
to some of the best Vivaldi (*The Four Seasons,* the *D Minor
Concerto Grosso,* Opus 3, No. 11, or the *Concerto in C Major for
Ottavino* [usually played on the piccolo], *Strings, and Continuo*)
are Telemann's *A Minor Suite for Recorder, Strings, and Continuo,* the *Don Quichotte Suite,* or his *Concerto in B flat Major
for Three Oboes, Three Violins, and Continuo.*

Johann Sebastian Bach has not been neglected since the early
nineteenth century, though the variety and scope of his compositions did not achieve representation in performance and recordings for many years. The Baroque revival has helped immeasurably. There is now not only a multitude of recordings of such
standard works as the *St. Matthew* and *St. John Passions,* the *B
Minor Mass,* the *Magnificat,* the cantatas, such as *Nc. 140
(Wachet auf!)* or *No. 4 (Christ lag in Todesbanden),* the suites,
concertos, keyboard and instrumental pieces (the *Italian Concerto,* the *D Minor Organ Toccata and Fugue,* the unaccompanied violin *Chaconne),* but there has been added to the recorded and concert repertoire a considerable number of curiosities, from a thirty-three-bar exercise for organ pedals to such
spurious attributions as the *St. Luke Passion.* There was a time
when, to propagate the greatness of Bach, composers, arrangers,
and conductors resorted to transcriptions, and indeed, a great
many music lovers came to know such works as the *D Minor
Organ Toccata* from Leopold Stokowski's orchestration, or some
of the chorale preludes from the piano transcriptions of Busoni.
Today, with a change in tastes and aesthetic attitudes, the arrangements are often looked upon as passé; one can hear the
originals with a better appreciation of the music and the instrument for which it was written.

If the Baroque revival has succeeded in broadening the Bach
repertoire to an amazing extent (I sometimes think that our
era's mania for completeness is a kind of library neurosis), it

is a little surprising to find that not all the two hundred-plus cantatas have yet been committed to discs. With George Frederick Handel, the other giant of the late Baroque, the public's appreciation has been rather more narrowly centered on fewer works. These pieces—*Messiah, Israel in Egypt,* the *Water Music, Royal Fireworks Music,* and some instrumental favorites—have long been held in affection. While Bach in his own day was esteemed by only a small body of connoisseurs (mainly for his organ playing) and was known but regionally, Handel was widely admired on an international level; he was an impresario of opera and oratorio performances, he hobnobbed with royalty, made money and lost it, and not least, was one of the most cosmopolitan of composers. The popularity of his music—primarily certain oratorios—has never diminished, not so much because of the style of his writing but, curiously, because of social and religious reasons. The works the public refused to relinquish were invariably connected with the idea of music being good for the uplift of the soul.

Handel had considerable difficulties with his operatic productions. Audience tastes were changing in the first half of the eighteenth century, and the lavishly staged but incredibly stylized opera of the day was rapidly losing appeal. The Puritans considered the form sinful, while oratorio, which was musically almost identical with opera but basically unstaged, was considered morally acceptable. It must be remembered that from the standpoint of entertainment opera and oratorio stood about equal in Handel's eyes. In the years after his death in 1759, however, the dramatic character of the composer's oratorios became sadly diluted in favor of the concept of the oratorio as a religious experience. This metamorphosis, evidence of which may be heard in most seasonal presentations of *Messiah,* is the principal reason Handel's name did not fade out by the nineteenth century, as did Bach's. On the other hand, what remained, in its pompous and inflated way, was principally, due to the participation of vast performing organizations, choirs and orchestras, a far cry from the dramatic entertainment Handel had originally intended.

Fortunately, the vestiges of the Victorian approach to Handel are dissolving today, and his sacred and secular music is again being performed and admired on its own terms. Even the operas, so different in their relatively static quality from the conventional opera we know, are being revived with success.

So far I have singled out for specific mention four composers—Vivaldi, Telemann, Bach, and Handel—who in the eyes of the casual onlooker might epitomize Baroque music. There are of course many other distinguished names, even though they might not have attained the same level of popularity: Domenico Scarlatti, the composer of over 550 harpsichord sonatas; Jean Philippe Rameau, whose opera-ballet productions are slowly being revived, and whose clavecin (harpsichord) music, along with that of his earlier contemporary, François Couperin, is a mainstay of Baroque keyboard literature; and Giovanni Battista Pergolesi, whose fame after his early death at the age of twenty-six eclipsed that of the majority of his contemporaries. There is also a host of less important Italians, whose liberal outpourings of concerti and orchestral pieces have brought them into the Baroque popularity boom: the Marcello brothers (Alessandro and Benedetto—Alessandro is now believed to have written the popular *Oboe Concerto*), Geminiani, Tartini, Sammartini, Locatelli, and Albinoni.

Not all these composers are equally outstanding, but all have become virtually household names in the fields of Baroque music. It is essential to realize, however, that everyone of them, from Vivaldi through Albinoni, belong to the *late* Baroque. For the neophyte listener approaching the Baroque from other later musical interests, these are the personalities he will find most congenial. From the popular Bach, Handel, and Vivaldi to the more esoteric Geminiani or Rameau is not too big a step, though there are fairly profound stylistic differences among them, especially between the fairly clear-cut Italians and the more sophisticated, rhythmically complex French. It is logical to assume that if one becomes familiar with the late Baroque, the music of the previous one hundred years or so can also be assimilated without too much feeling of strangeness.

The music of the Baroque, viewed as a whole, had incredible variety. Much of it was composed for specific occasions. In this category we may include not only all the sacred literature and many large-scale operatic undertakings designed for royal patronage, but also a large variety of spectacular display pieces composed for wedding, victory, and peace celebrations (my own favorite is Handel's *Royal Fireworks Music*).

Different Styles

It was an age for strong trends in musical fashions and tastes. There were two principal styles of writing, and both had nationalism as their basis. The Italian manner was fairly clear cut rhythmically, songful in slow sections and highly energized in fast ones. Melodiousness was much admired. The typical Italian "sound" may be easily traced through 150 years in such works as a Gabrieli canzona, a Frescobaldi ballo, a Corelli concerto grosso, or a Tartini sinfonia. The opposing style was French, and it was characterized by complex rhythms, an intricate manner of writing which was far more subtle in expression, often convoluted, and quite stylized, with a great profusion of ornaments. Whereas the Italians glorified in the voice, the French preferred the ballet. A representative cross section of the French Baroque "sound" might include a Lully ballet suite, lute pieces by Denis Gaultier, a Charpentier *Te Deum,* one of Couperin's *Leçons de Ténèbres,* and a Rameau suite for harpsichord.

These two principal national schools (there was also the German polyphonic style) had enormous influence over virtually all composers of the period, no matter what their country of origin. There was, in addition, a considerable interchange of influences, so Couperin and Rameau wrote French music with some distinctly Italian elements, while Vivaldi and Geminiani delved into French dotted rhythmic patterns from time to time. As for non-French and non-Italian composers, they took liberally from whatever they liked. In England Henry Purcell wrote vocal and instrumental pieces based on Italian models but with strong French characteristics (including much use of the French overture).

Incidentally, Purcell may, along with Monteverdi, be the next Baroque hero. His writing is quite extraordinary in its appeal and expression. I would strongly recommend that anyone not

familiar with this composer sample his *Dido and Aeneas,* some
of the incidental music to his plays, and several of the fantasias
for string consort.

Toward the close of the Baroque, one can see the nationalist
influences in French and Italian movements coexisting side by
side in, for instance, the concerti grossi of Handel and the cantatas of Bach.

Near the end of the first quarter of the eighteenth century
a new style became manifest, and this shift in taste signaled the
end of the Baroque. This was the *galant,* a supersensitive, elegant, sighing, polite manner of composing, in which sensibility
rather than deep emotions was stressed. It developed through
the latent classical qualities of the Baroque, and as a style it
may be heard in many works of Telemann (who, in contrast
to Bach, was rather an avant-gardist; the two men were close
contemporaries, but Bach was distinctly conservative), in the
post-Baroque works of the Bach sons, and in the music of Haydn
and Mozart. Another offshoot of the Baroque was the Rococo,
in which the intricate ornaments of music and the visual arts
became more convoluted and overembroidered; it was a typically French development, a heightening not of the essential
structure but of the purely decorative. Although François Couperin may be considered an example of a late Baroque composer (he died in 1733), his music features very obvious Rococo
elements.

Of the different styles of writing during the Baroque era,
the Italian is the one easiest for present-day audiences to assim-
ilate; perhaps this is why Vivaldi has made such a conquest
in our own time. On the other hand, the considerable quantity
of Vivaldi-like pieces of the late Baroque—those by Marcello,
Albinoni, Torelli, Corelli, Geminiani, Manfredini, Locatelli, and
the like—can begin to pall after a while. At their best they can
be most enjoyable, but one cannot deny a certain repetitiveness
when they are taken in large quantities.

When these works pall, it is time to explore earlier periods
and men—Monteverdi, Purcell, the great German sacred composer Heinrich Schütz (his *Christmas Story* is one of the gems
of the entire period), and the French school. The French,
whether in their stylized ballets, somewhat overpompous sa-

cred music (I am thinking particularly of Charpentier), often effete but refined harpsichord pieces, or deliberate and quite delightful cultivation of rural or pastoral atmosphere (hence the many musettes and tambourins in basically aristocratic music, such as Boismortier's *Daphnis et Chloë*), are perhaps more difficult to appreciate, but the extra effort may be worthwhile in terms of eventual enjoyment and understanding.

4

Sonatas and Chamber Music

MARTIN BOOKSPAN

IN this chapter we shall be dealing with the vast body of music scored for solo or ensemble players. Ensemble music for small forces, whether for two or ten players, requires the most perceptive and delicately balanced teamwork in performance, hence the medium has frequently served composers as the vessel into which they have poured some of their most deeply felt and intimate musical thoughts.

There was a time, in the not too distant past, when the chamber music literature was regarded by large segments of the music-loving public as a kind of rarified, untouchable commodity, which yielded its innermost secrets only to the most sophisticated of listeners. Nothing could be farther from the truth. Much of the chamber music literature came into being because composers of the past and present created music that could be played by small groups of their own friends and colleagues, often with their own personal participation in the performances. Haydn, Mozart, Schubert, Schumann, and Mendelssohn all composed the great bulk of their chamber music for immediate performance by ensembles comprised of their dearest friends. And though the chamber music literature does contain some of the most profound and sublime music ever written, one must never lose sight of the fact that in chamber music, perhaps more than in any other serious compositional medium, the aim of the composer is to communicate.

For the performer there is no musical satisfaction quite like the one to be derived from playing chamber music with a small ensemble of one's peers. It is for this reason that Jascha Heifetz and Gregor Piatigorsky have in recent years limited their public music-making almost exclusively to chamber music, or that such distinguished individual artists as Isaac Stern, Leonard Rose, and Eugene Istomin devote part of their professional lives to public performance of the great piano trios.

The annals of musical legend and lore are full of amusing anecdotes relating to the performance of chamber music. Before we get to the historical elements, a few of these anecdotes might not be out of place.

Brahms, who was an inveterate chamber music participant as a pianist, was playing one of the Beethoven cello sonatas with a friend when he rather enthusiastically came down hard on the pedal. "Softer," pleaded the other musician, "I can't hear my cello." To this Brahms is supposed to have replied, "You're lucky. I can."

The pianist Moriz Rosenthal used to take along on his tours a dumb piano that produced no sound, but which contained a full eighty-eight-note keyboard, so he could practice fingerings. A maid in a Southern hotel room, seeing him so occupied, asked what he was doing. He replied that he was playing on a magic piano that could be heard only by people who had not sinned within the past twenty-four hours. She hesitated for a moment, and then bolted out of the room!

Fritz Kreisler and Sergei Rachmaninoff often played violin and piano sonatas for their own amusement; occasionally they consented to appear in public together. On one such memorable evening in New York's Carnegie Hall, Kreisler had a memory lapse in the middle of a piece and could not extricate himself from his difficulty. Inching over to his partner at the keyboard he managed to whisper, "Where are we?" To this came Rachmaninoff's instantaneous and dead-pan response: "In Carnegie Hall."

And so to the literature of chamber music and sonatas. It is always hazardous to generalize, but the composers who loom largest in the creation of symphonies, tone poems, and concerti are also those who have enriched the repertoire of smaller concerted ensemble music.

Bach, Haydn, Boccherini, and Mozart

We have seen how the symphony as a form evolved from the rather modest beginnings of the sixteenth and seventeenth centuries. Because of the development of expert violin makers in the little Italian town of Cremona during that time, the evolution of the solo sonata was principally of Italian origin and largely violin-derived. Some of the leading composers of violin sonatas three and four hundred years ago were Corelli, Tartini, Geminiani, Vivaldi, Locatelli, and Veracini. That the art was not wholly an Italian monopoly, however, is proved by the appearance in other countries of composers who toiled in the same vineyards as their Italian colleagues—Heinrich von Biber in Bohemia, or Henry Purcell in England. By the time of Bach and Handel, the violin sonata had become pretty well established as one of the most popular musical forms of the day, and Domenico Scarlatti, also born in 1685 (the year of birth for both Bach and Handel), was composing harpsichord sonatas by the dozens.

Bach's principal works for solo violin are the six *Sonatas and Partitas for Unaccompanied Violin* and the six *Sonatas for Violin and Harpsichord.* Handel, for his part, composed many sonatas for violin and harpsichord, and both composers also contributed a vast body of music for other solo instruments with harpsichord accompaniment and for harpsichord alone. Not until the second half of the eighteenth century did the ultimate form of so-called chamber music come into being with the development by Franz Josef Haydn of the string quartet.

Composers before Haydn employed the combination of two violins, viola, and cello for concerted and intimate musical conversation. Haydn's great leap forward was the assigning of equal weight to all four instruments and in freeing the small ensemble from the control of an extra continuo instrument which filled in the composer's figured bass line. Further, Haydn set the formal pattern for the structure of the string quartet, a structure that proved to be fundamental to the advancement of the medium. Before he was finished, Haydn composed more than eighty string quartets, not to mention other works for different combinations of four instruments. He also produced piano sonatas by the yard. What is incredible is the astonishingly high level of inspiration he was able to maintain throughout his overflowing output. Because of some special characteristic, many of the Haydn string quartets have identifying nicknames: the *D Major Quartet* of Opus 64 is called the *Lark* because of the first violin's singing, soaring solo melody in the first movement; the *C Major Quartet* of Opus 76 is called the *Emperor* because its slow movement is a set of variations on an original Haydn melody, which later became the Austrian national anthem. Haydn also composed more than two dozen trios for piano, violin, and cello—fifteen after 1790, the year of his first visit to England. The best-known is the *G Major* with a Gypsy Rondo as its final movement.

Before we move on to Mozart, there is one other significant composer of chamber music who must be mentioned: Luigi Boccherini, who was born in 1743 and died in 1805. Boccherini, too, was extraordinarily prolific; he composed twenty-one symphonies, eight sinfonias concertante, and assorted concerti for solo instruments. But he was primarily a composer of chamber music! In addition to a large body of duos, trios, quartets, and quintets for combinations that included wind instruments, Boccherini composed ninety-one string quartets and 113 string quintets. The famous "Boccherini Minuet" is the third movement from his *String Quintet in E Major*, Opus 13, No. 5.

Though the list of Mozart's sonata and chamber music output is not so voluminous as that of Haydn or Boccherini—about sixty completed works of chamber music, along with the piano sonatas, the sonatas for violin and piano, and for other instrumental combinations—it contains one masterpiece after another in many different combinations: string trios, piano quartets, string quartets, string quintets, and so forth. The fertility of Mozart's musical imagination was truly beyond belief!

Of the string quartets there are perhaps a dozen that I particularly cherish; among them are the six that Mozart dedicated to Haydn (*Nos. 14* through *19*) and the final four (*Nos. 20* through *23*). The *G Major Quartet, No. 14*, has a particularly frolicsome final movement full of fugal passages; the *D Minor Quartet, No. 15*, is an impassioned work with a concluding movement—a set of variations—which has about it an unsettling feeling of urgency; the next quartet in the series, *No. 16 in E flat*, opens arrestingly with absolutely no harmony at all—the theme is stated at the beginning in octave unison—and then a few bars later the opening is restated, this time fully harmonized and with some dissonances that are like needle pricks; the fourth quartet of the "Haydn" series is the *No. 17 in B flat*, called the *Hunt Quartet* because the opening somewhat resembles a hunting call; *No. 18 in A* has a particularly free theme and variations as a slow movement, which culminates in a coda of sheer magic; the last quartet of the series, *No. 19 in C*, is called the *Dissonant Quartet* because of the harmonies in the slow introduction.

Mozart's two *Quartets for Piano and Strings*, in *G minor* and *E flat*, also deserve special mention. The *G Minor* is the more dramatic and hence the better known. Both, however, reveal Mozart's unending source of inspired melody and his constant ability to thrill us with unexpected surprises—for example, the episode in five-beat meter in the first movement of the *G Minor Quartet*.

Speaking of unexpected surprises in Mozart's chamber music brings me to the *Divertimento in E flat for String Trio* (violin, viola, and cello), K 563. The texture these three instruments afford the composer is not very broad, and the fourth of the six movements of this work is again a theme and variations. Mozart deliberately further restricts the texture of the opening of the movement by casting it principally for violin and viola in octave unison, with a rather pedestrian bass line in the cello. Just when the ear begins to question the wisdom of this restricted tonal framework, the music bursts into three-part writing that now seems all the richer. Further adding to the suddenly expanded sound is the frequent scoring of double stops for the viola, so that in many places the trio sounds like a quartet.

Of Mozart's six string quintets, those in *C Major*, K 515, and *G minor*, K 516, are especially rewarding. The addition of a second viola to the string quartet gives the whole sound a richer, more vibrant quality. The *G Minor Quintet*, indeed, is one of the most tragically beautiful things in all music. Two other quintets I must mention are the *E flat for Piano and Woodwinds* and the *A Major for Clarinet and String Quartet*. Mozart himself, in a letter to his father, wrote that he considered the *E flat Piano Quintet* his finest work to date; it is certainly one of the most perfectly organized and unified works in the literature—a joy for both performers and listeners. The *Clarinet Quintet* is perhaps the perfect introduction to chamber music; its mood is all sunshine and warmth, and its quality of spontaneity and freshness, always self-renewing.

There are so many marvelous sonatas by Mozart for various instruments, we can only scratch the surface. The piano sonatas I leave to Jascha Zayde. Where the violin sonatas are concerned, the one in *A Major*, K 305, used to be my big show-stopper in my violin-playing days; hence, I retain a special affection for it, even though it is admittedly one of the slighter sonatas. The biggest are the two in *B flat*, K 378 and K 454, in which the two instruments operate at equal levels of musical interest.

Beethoven

And so to Beethoven, whose collective chamber music output is among the most varied in the entire literature. At the center, of course, are his sixteen string quartets and the *Great Fugue* for string quartet. Beethoven's string quartets fit very handily into the early, middle, and late categorization. The first six were composed during the years 1798–1800, before Beethoven was thirty; they were published in 1801. The next three, the so-called *Rasumovsky Quartets* of Opus 59, were composed about 1806 on commission from the Russian ambassador to Vienna, Count Rasumovsky. Two more quartets followed in 1809 and 1810. And then in the last years of his life, between 1824 and 1826, Beethoven returned once again to the string quartet to produce his final five visionary quartets and the *Great Fugue*. These were the last works Beethoven wrote, and he composed no other music at this time.

All seventeen works are indispensable to any chamber music lover; I merely wish to point out a few highlights. The first quartet in the Opus 18 group is the biggest and the boldest of the six; the second, in *G Major,* is the gentlest and perhaps the most charming of the group; the fourth, in *C minor,* is the most passionate and the one that makes the most immediate impression. The first of the *Rasumovsky Quartets* is bigger in conception than its two companions, and it is, arguably, the finest of the three. The second, in *E minor,* has a kind of Slavic melancholy—and in the trio section of the third movement Beethoven incorporated the well-known "Slava" ("Glory") theme that later was to form the central musical material in the Coronation Scene in Musorgski's *Boris Godunov.* The last of the *Rasumovsky Quartets* is perhaps the most accessible of the three, especially its muscle-flexing and athletic last movement. The next two quartets, Opus 74 and Opus 95, have won for themselves identifying nicknames because of particular characteristics: the many pizzicato accompaniments in the opening movement of the Opus 74 *Quartet in E flat* have led to its being dubbed the *Harp Quartet,* and the serious nature of the Opus 95 *Quartet in F minor* has brought about its *Serioso* identity.

The last five quartets are the work of a master far removed from temporal affairs. It once was fashionable to regard these five works with a respectful but distant awe—as though their inner being and meaning could not be comprehended by mortal man. I take violent exception to this point of view. True, all require concentrated listening and study, but there are no abstruse secrets in these works; they are merely the ultimate expression of Beethoven's remarkable imagination. Interestingly, three of the five are multimovement affairs: the *B flat Quartet, No. 13,* has six movements; the *C sharp Minor, No. 14,* has seven; and the *A Minor, No. 15,* has five. The *Quartet No. 12 in E flat* is a genial, contented work, with an especially moving slow movement; the *Quartet No. 13* is a headlong plunge into the unknown, whose fifth movement is a tragic Cavatina about which Beethoven is supposed to have remarked, "Never have I written a melody that affected me so much"; the *Quartet No. 14 in C sharp minor* is perhaps the most consistently "other-worldly" and sublime—its seven movements are played without pause, and more than one symphony conductor (Mitropoulos and Bernstein among them) has included the *C sharp Minor Quartet* on symphony concerts by assigning the four voices of the music to the massed orchestral strings; the *Quartet No. 15 in A minor,* among many special features, has two that are outstanding—the slow movement carries with it the heading "Song of thanksgiving to the Deity on recovering from an illness, written in the Lydian mode," and the quartet concludes with a rather gentle movement whose main theme Beethoven at one time had intended for the last movement of the *Ninth Symphony;* the last quartet, in *F Major,* is a relaxation from the tremendous emotional and intellectual challenges of its companions—it is about half their length and poses none of the refined problems presented by the others.

A word about the *Great Fugue.* This was originally the last movement of *Quartet No. 13.* Beethoven's publisher, however, insisted that it made an already long work quite undigestible. Beethoven, in an unexpectedly conciliatory gesture, set about composing a new last movement for the quartet (which became the last music he completed) and the *Great Fugue* assumed an independent life of its own. It is a craggy, granitelike score, which taxes the playing capacities of four instrumentalists almost to the breaking-point. Like the *C sharp Minor Quartet,* it, too, is sometimes played at symphony concerts by the combined strings of an orchestra.

In addition to the string quartets there is a considerable body of chamber music by Beethoven, including piano trios and quartets, five string trios, a septet for strings and winds, a string quintet, a quartet for piano and strings, a quintet for piano and winds, and a sextet for winds. Chief among the piano trios are the two of Opus 70, in *D flat* and *E flat,* and the *B flat Trio,* Opus 97, titled the *Archduke.* The first of the Opus 70 trios also has an identifying name: because of the low rumblings in the piano part it has come to be known as the *Ghost Trio.* The *Archduke Trio* is so called because Beethoven dedicated it to the younger brother of the Austrian Emperor, Archduke Rudolf, who was a devoted amateur musician. It was the Archduke who in 1809 set up an annual annuity to be paid to Beethoven by the government, the only condition of which was that Beethoven could not accept employment outside Vienna. The

Archduke Trio is a constantly inventive and fascinating score and marks the high point of Beethoven's music for piano and strings. Another masterpiece for the combination of violin, cello, and piano is the *G Major Trio*, called the *Kakadu Variations* because the basis for the music is a silly little tune titled "I Am the Tailor Kakadu" from an opera by a Viennese contemporary of Beethoven's, one W. Müller. The variations that Beethoven contrives for the tune are remarkable, and they include one for piano alone, one that shows off the violin, one that spotlights the cello, and one for violin and cello together with no piano at all.

What about the *Septet*, scored for clarinet, bassoon, horn, violin, viola, cello, and bass? From its very creation the work has been extremely popular, which caused Beethoven himself to downgrade it. He did it a disservice, however; it is one of his finest ensemble pieces, blending together in masterful fashion the seven different sonorities. Its Minuet is one of the most familiar of all Beethoven's creations.

In the fashion of his day, Beethoven allowed his violin and piano sonatas to be published as works for piano "with violin," or for piano "with violin accompaniment." The implied secondary role for the violin is not at all justified, however; the two instruments are equal partners even in the early sonatas, and in the later ones it is the piano that gets the shorter end of the stick. The first really arresting sonata among the ten is the *Fourth, in A minor*, Opus 23; rather than flowing along in the accepted classical mould, this piece is full of stops, starts, and surprises. The *Fifth, in F Major*, appeared in the same year as the *Fourth*, 1801. Its easy-flowing lyricism long ago earned for it the nickname *Spring*, and it seems particularly appropriate. The last two are the brilliant *Kreutzer Sonata*, Opus 47, and the much more relaxed *G Major Sonata*, Opus 96. The *Kreutzer* comes by its subtitle from the name of the French violinist, Rudolphe Kreutzer, to whom Beethoven dedicated the work.

The *Third, Fourth,* and *Fifth* of Beethoven's five cello and piano sonatas come from the composer's middle and late periods. The *Third, in A Major*, Opus 69, is a broad, singing work; the *Fourth* and *Fifth*, which together form the composer's Opus 102, are more in the form of free fantasias, rhapsodic and improvisational in nature. As the Beethoven sonatas for violin and piano form the backbone of the violin recitalist's repertory, so the cello and piano sonatas serve the solo cellist.

Schubert, Mendelssohn, and Schumann

Franz Schubert left us about thirty works of ensemble chamber music, some among the most beloved in the entire literature. His last three string quartets—in *A minor, D minor,* and *G Major*—are profoundly melancholy works but with a particular and pervading beauty; that the three were composed by a lad still in his twenties is one of those miracles of the creative process. Each plumbs emotional depths, and each is an ennobling listening experience. The *D Minor Quartet, No. 14,* is known as *Death and the Maiden,* because its second movement borrows the melody of the second half of the song Schubert had written seven years earlier.

On a similarly exalted level of spiritual communication is the great *Quintet in C Major* for strings by Schubert. In range of emotion, quality of material, and perfection of form there is little question that the *Quintet* is Schubert's chamber music masterpiece. Where Mozart employed an extra viola in his string quintets, Schubert went back to the model of Boccherini and employed an extra cello. The added velvety texture contributes in no small measure to the over-all impact of the music. The heart of the *Quintet* is the long and almost unbearably poignant slow movement marked "Adagio," one of the most serenely beautiful creations in all music.

Another Schubert quintet that offers a different kind of pleasure is the *A Major* for piano, violin, viola, cello, and double bass—the *Trout Quintet,* so called because the fourth movement is a set of variations on Schubert's song, "The Trout." If the *C Major Quintet* is an impassioned, stormy work, the *Trout* is all headlong rapture. Because of the odd scoring, the *Trout* is not heard in the concert hall nearly frequently enough; several supremely good recordings of it exist, however.

Another blissfully happy Schubert chamber work is the *Trio in B flat* for violin, cello, and piano, Opus 99. The first move-

ment has a blustering extroversion which sweeps all before it;
the second is a freely developed extension of the simple cello
melody announced at the beginning; the Scherzo is a brusque,
dancelike affair, which becomes an out-and-out waltz in the
middle section; the concluding Rondo is full of bustle and
excitement.

Nor should we forget Schubert's *Octet* for clarinet, horn,
bassoon, string quartet, and double bass. The score was commissioned by Count Ferdinand Troyer, an amateur clarinetist
in the court of Archduke Rudolf. Troyer wanted from Schubert
a score like Beethoven's *Septet*, and he got it. The *Octet* has
six movements and is delightful entertainment.

Schubert also composed a variety of music for violin and
piano. The three sonatas of Opus 137 are particularly outstanding. They were composed when Schubert was nineteen
and are really sonatas in miniature. The first is amiable and
gentle, the second is dramatic and fiery, and the third has elements of both.

Felix Mendelssohn contributed several outstanding works to
the chamber music repertoire, among them the *Octet for Strings,*
the *D Minor Piano Trio,* and several string quartets. The *Octet*
is scored for double string quartet, with each part a vital element in the fabric. The music has a marvelous swing and lift.
The third movement is one of Mendelssohn's winged Scherzos,
all gossamer and shimmer. The English pianist, composer, and
musical scholar Sir Donald Francis Tovey wrote of this movement: "Eight string players might easily practice it for a lifetime without coming to an end of their delight in producing
its marvels of tone color." The *D Minor Piano Trio* has had its
ups and downs in public affection; right now it seems to be in
an "up" period. Much of the effect of this music can be vitiated
by performers insensitive to the fragile beauties it contains.
But I have heard Isaac Stern, Leonard Rose, and Eugene Istomin
play this score to perfection. Fortunately, we now have a recording of the music from them.

Among Robert Schumann's five chamber music works are
three string quartets, the magnificent *Piano Quintet in E flat,*
the *Piano Quartet* in the same key, and three piano trios.
Astonishingly, Schumann's *Quintet* was the first work ever com-

posed for that combination of instruments. The work is one of Schumann's perfect inspirations. After an impetuous first movement comes a slow movement rather like a funeral march; impetuosity returns in a Scherzo which makes much of ascending and descending scales, and the last movement is a tour de force of contrapuntal dexterity: in the coda the main theme of the first movement returns as the subject of a fugal section, with the first theme of the Finale as the countersubject. In spontaneity, daring, and manipulation of musical materials, the *Piano Quintet* is probably Schumann's most successful large-scale work.

Brahms, Smetana, and Dvořák

We move on to Brahms. This most self-critical of composers once stated that he had written twenty string quartets before he produced one that he considered good enough to publish. At least four sonatas for violin and piano were composed and then destroyed before he allowed the appearance of the one we label his *First, in G Major,* Opus 78. His most important works in the field are three string quartets; two string quintets; two string sextets; three piano trios; three piano quartets; a piano quintet; a trio for clarinet, cello, and piano; a trio for horn, violin, and piano; and a quintet for clarinet and strings. In addition there are three sonatas for violin and piano, two for cello and piano, and two for clarinet (or viola, interchangeably) and piano. Considering the lengths to which Brahms went to destroy many of his own compositions, the list of chamber music and sonata scores that survives is quite formidable!

The kinship of Brahms with the musical impulses that motivated Beethoven and Bach is to be found everywhere in his music, but nowhere more pointedly than in the chamber music. The string quartets, though characteristic of Brahms, follow directly in the path trodden by Beethoven. In the string sextets one finds Brahms constantly shifting the texture to lighten it, in the manner of Bach. With but a single exception, the *Horn Trio,* the first movement of every chamber music work by Brahms is in classical sonata form. The *Horn Trio,* a magically rhapsodic and elegiac work, occupies a special place not only in the Brahms catalogue but in all chamber music literature. The quartets for piano and strings are gems for that combination of instruments, with a special nod in the direction of the *First, in G minor,* with its Gypsy Rondo final movement. Despite my abiding love for this score as Brahms cast it for piano and three strings, I consider Arnold Schönberg's orchestral version an overwhelmingly successful realization of the music's character, and I wish more symphony conductors would program it. Finally, I want to direct special attention toward Brahms's *Clarinet Quintet,* a work of his later years that has the sweet autumnal quality of Brahms's final works.

Brahms's two Bohemian contemporaries, Smetana and Dvořák, also composed works of importance in the chamber music medium. Smetana's mature years saw him produce only three chamber music compositions, the *G Minor Piano Trio* and two string quartets, of which the *First, in E minor,* was titled by Smetana himself *From My Life.* Smetana appended a fairly detailed program to the quartet: the first movement is about the composer's youth, his yearnings and aspirations and his love of art; the second movement, a rustic polka, finds Smetana reminiscing about the days of his youth when he composed much dance music (he himself was an expert dancer); the slow movement recalls the esctasy of his love for the girl who became his first wife; and the final movement deals with his ability to be a national spokesman through his music—toward the end of the movement a high, sustained note is introduced, signalizing the whistling in Smetana's ears that preceded his deafness, and the autobiographical quartet ends in a mood of painful regret. This quartet, like the Brahms *G Minor Piano Quartet,* has been transcribed for orchestra most successfully; the arranger in this case is George Szell, and it is time that we had a new recording of the music from Szell and the Cleveland Orchestra. Though infrequently performed, Smetana's *Second Quartet, in D minor,* is also quasiautobiographical. Smetana stated that the quartet was his attempt to put on paper "the whirlwind of music in the head of one who has lost his hearing."

Dvořák's chamber music list is long and largely neglected.

He composed at least fourteen string quartets, several piano quartets, string quintets, a quintet for piano and strings, and several trios for violin, cello, and piano. The popularity of three works—the *Piano Quintet*, the *American Quartet*, and the *Dumky Trio*—tended until recently to overshadow Dvořák's other chamber music works, much as the *Symphony From the New World* all but obliterated Dvořák's eight other symphonies. There are now encouraging signs that some of Dvořák's other chamber music creations are beginning to emerge from the shadows. The *Quartet No. 3 in E flat,* Opus 51, and the *Seventh, in A flat,* Opus 105, to name just two, are fully mature, deeply expressive works which deserve to be far better known. This is not to deny that the *American Quartet (No. 6 in F Major)* is a gorgeous, colorful and exciting score, or that the *Piano Quintet* is a vibrant, melodious, rhythmically vital composition. What I am suggesting is that a healthy curiosity about some of the lesser-known Dvořák chamber music compositions will pay the listener handsome dividends.

Though the second half of the nineteenth century was the period of the bestirring of Russian composers in the field of orchestral music, there was comparatively little activity by these men in the chamber music area. There are only two nineteenth-century Russian string quartets in the international repertoire—Tchaikovsky's *First* and Borodin's *Second,* both in the key of *D Major.* Both have individual movements that have been taken out of context and arranged for every possible (and some impossible!) combination of instruments and voices. In the case of Tchaikovsky's quartet it is the slow movement, marked "Andante Cantabile," which has been butchered. (Does anybody remember a lunatic song on the Hit Parade a quarter of a century ago whose verse ran something like ". . . and it was June, June on the Isle of May"?) In Borodin's quartet it is the third movement, the Nocturne, that has been variously appropriated; in the musical show *Kismet* it turned up as "And This Is My Beloved."

The Late Nineteenth and the Twentieth Centuries

Before we get to some of the important composers of chamber music in the twentieth century—Bloch, Bartók, Schönberg, and Berg—we must briefly touch upon some other nineteenth-century figures. Edvard Grieg in Norway produced a very fine *String Quartet* and four sonatas—three for violin and piano and one for cello and piano. The *Third Violin Sonata* is especially fine; though it seems to hold little interest for the present generation of fiddlers, it was a great favorite of Fritz Kreisler and one of the happiest of all recorded performances is the version played by Kreisler and Rachmaninoff.

César Franck was an important figure in the development of sonata and chamber music composition in France. His *Sonata in A Major for Violin and Piano* is one of the richest products of his entire creative life; it is music of elegance, poetry, and drama, with the two instruments complementing each other to perfection. Franck's two other vitally important works to chamber music literature were the passionate and sensual *F Minor Piano Quintet* and the *String Quartet in D*. The latter, his most ambitious work, was completed just a few months before he died. At the beginning of the last movement Franck borrows Beethoven's technique from the last movement of the *Choral Symphony:* He recalls the themes from the earlier movements before the music settles down contrapuntally on the basic motif of the first movement.

Another important French figure was Gabriel Fauré, whose music includes two violin and piano sonatas, two piano quintets, two piano quartets, a piano trio, a string quartet, and two cello and piano sonatas. The sonatas for violin and piano were composed forty-one years apart; the earlier one, in *A Major*, is one of Fauré's best-known works, sparkling and spontaneous in character. The *First Piano Quartet* has the same qualities of grace and poise; the *Second* is more intense and powerful. In the last year of his life, 1924, the seventy-nine-year-old composer produced his vibrant and impulsive *Piano Trio* and his only *String Quartet*, an enigmatic, fragmentary work that has a beatific, farewell glow.

Claude Debussy composed four principal works of chamber music: his early *String Quartet* and the three late sonatas for different combinations of instruments. The *Quartet* is a marvelously atmospheric piece, full of shifting moods and mosaiclike patterns. The three sonatas, composed impulsively while Debussy was dying of cancer, reveal that he had lost none of his powers of evocation.

The *String Quartet* of Maurice Ravel, composed in 1902—nine years after Debussy's—has many traits in common with the Debussy, yet it is unquestionably the work of a strong and independent new voice. The other concerted piece by Ravel that belongs in the present discussion is the *Introduction and Allegro for Harp, String Quartet, Flute, and Clarinet*—a brilliant display vehicle for a virtuoso harp performer which nevertheless manages to sustain musical interest from first to last. Ravel's *Piano Trio* has a Spanish character, his *Sonata for Violin and Cello* has a sparse severity and the *Sonata for Violin and Piano* finds Ravel composing a "Blues" movement.

Ernest Bloch, with five string quartets, and Béla Bartók, with six, are thus far the twentieth century's principal practitioners in the string quartet medium. True, Dimitri Shostakovich has produced a dozen or so string quartets by the most recent reckoning, but his quartets are wildly uneven, while the four by Bloch that I know and the six by Bartók are all masterpieces. Bloch's *No. 1*, dating from 1916, is a sprawling colossus; an indication of its character is to be found in some of the markings in the score: *frenetico, furioso, feroce,* and *strepitoso*. Some thirty years passed before Bloch turned again to the string quartet. He produced four more quartets between 1945 and 1956. The *Second Quartet* is more controlled, less explosive than the *First;* it makes a devastating impression. The *Third* is closely knit but mellow and profoundly moving; the *Fourth* is lyrical and poetic.

Bloch also left us a superb *Piano Quintet*, several pieces of a descriptive nature for piano trio and string quartet, two violin sonatas, and a suite for viola and piano (which also exists in an alternative version by Bloch himself for viola and orchestra). The *Piano Quintet* was a problematic work when it appeared in the 1920's; its use of harsh dissonance and quarter-tones repelled some listeners. Today it is seen as an uncommonly symbolic work, with an optimistic faith that even the most hopeless and despairing struggle is capable of resolution. At the end of the *Quintet* order and calm have been retrieved out of chaos and trouble, and the work ends on an innocent C Major chord.

The six Bartók string quartets have been likened to the last five of Beethoven in their prophetic vision and their challenge to listeners. They cover very nearly Bartók's entire creative life-span: the *First String Quartet* appeared in 1908, when Bartók was twenty-seven; the *Sixth* is a product of 1939, when Bartók was fifty-eight. In December, 1944, nine months before he died, he sketched out a few ideas for a seventh quartet but was never able to pursue them. The *First Quartet* is an eclectic work—the principal influence would appear to be Beethoven's *C sharp Minor Quartet*—but the wild rhythms of the last movement are indicative of the Bartók to come. The *Second Quartet* is essentially romantic and lyrical. The *Third* is the shortest, the most concentrated, and generally considered the most difficult to listen to of the six. The *Fourth* followed the *Third* by only a year, and it has much the same toughness, though not quite the same austerity. The *Fifth* shows a further relaxation, with an ironic parody in the last movement of second-rate Hungarian cafe music. In the *Sixth Quartet* Bartók finally arrives at the classical sequence of four contrasting movements. The form is relatively simpler, and the themes have a more sustained, broader nature. It is a short step from the Bartók of the *Sixth Quartet* to the Bartók who composed such popular works as the *Sonata for Two Pianos and Percussion*, the *Concerto for Orchestra* and the *Third Piano Concerto*.

Much of the experimentation of Arnold Schönberg, which ultimately led to the strict twelve-tone method, was accomplished in various chamber music pieces. In his *First String Quartet* of 1904–1905 the four movements are played without a pause, and the developments are no longer identifiable sections but are fused into the over-all structure. In his *Second String Quartet* (1907–1908) there is no development at all in the first two movements; instead, the third movement becomes the arena in which material from the first two movements is developed. In the last movement Schönberg dissolves all contact with a recognizable tonal center. Here was the turning point, and this principle was to motivate all of Schönberg's thinking, as well as that of his disciples, for many years. Among those disciples, Alban Berg and Anton von Webern composed a considerable body of music for chamber ensembles.

Now, in the late 1960's, more and more composers are concentrating their attentions and resources upon music for small ensemble and solo performance. There is still plenty of life in the chamber music medium.

5

Piano Music

JASCHA ZAYDE

I WOULD have an easier time counting the stars at night than trying to cover the gamut of keyboard music. It is my sincere hope, however, that I may be able to give the reader a somewhat clearer insight into some of the great literature written for the one true solo instrument that is able to fulfill totally all musical requirements of the immortal composers. Do not misunderstand me. I am fully aware of the significant contributions made by clavier writers prior to the invention of the piano (by Bartolomeo Christofori about 1707), but with the exception of Johann Sebastian Bach and Domenico Scarlatti, whose keyboard compositions are part of every pianist's repertoire, the works of the other composers are still played mainly on the instruments for which they were originally intended: the clavichord, harpsichord, and organ.

I am always irritated when I hear people say that Bach's music is cold and without feeling. Nothing could be further from the truth. From the relatively simple two-part inventions, the not so simple partitas, the forty-eight preludes and fugues, the French and English suites (nobody really knows why they are called French or English—the music certainly shows no nationalistic tendencies) to the profound and complex *Goldberg Variations*, Bach's clavier music is full of lyric passion, emotion, and monumental architectural construction. There is never a dull moment in any of his works. The melodies or counter-melodies (Richard Wagner was a great admirer of Bach's melodic writing) are always on the move, always soaring and searching for something new to say and a new way to say it. The wonderful and at times daring harmonies hold a special degree of importance in all of the master's works. They never sound jaded or old-fashioned; on the contrary, they are fresh, and vital. Bach wrote magnificent fantasias and toccatas and fugues for the organ, and we can never sufficiently thank Ferruccio Busoni, Eugene d'Albert, Franz Liszt, Alexander Siloti, and others for transcribing them for the piano. I'm sure that they did this so that pianists might also share in the joy of playing these extraordinary works with their organist cousins. Bach's fantasias are exactly what the title indicates. They are written in a free style, unhampered by rigid rules and regulations (Bach broke all conventional rules regarding form and harmony, whenever his inventive mind required it) and display an enormous variety of moods and styles. Some passages are brilliant and fast, and the performer must accomplish incredibly spectacular feats of digital proficiency. Other passages are quite somber and create a chorale atmosphere. But at all times there is a feeling of spontaneity. Therein lies part of the genius of Bach. The *Fantasia and Fugue in G minor*, as arranged for the piano by Liszt, is a choice example of that.

Bach was meticulous in many ways, but when it came to leaving musical instructions on paper for the artist to follow, he was negligent. Take the *Goldberg Variations*. There are almost no indications of tempo or dynamics. When a pianist plays this almost superhuman work, he may do as he pleases with the notes. He may play them loudly or softly, quickly or slowly, smoothly or detached, and he will not transgress the composer's requirements. Bach apparently had a very free attitude toward his music (or tremendous faith in the players of his day) as well as to the compositions of others, which he would change and arrange (sometimes signing his own name to the product without so much as a second thought). He left no detailed instructions as to how he wanted his ornamentations (little signs above certain notes that tell you to embroider them in a special way) executed. One of Bach's sons, Johann Christoph, published a manual for the correct playing of these signs,

but there are those who say that young Johann had a minor
falling out with his father and spitefully indicated the wrong
way to finger the ornaments. Two of the most admired Bach
specialists, Rosalyn Tureck (she is "untouchable" in the forty-
eight *Preludes and Fugues*) and the slightly eccentric but
formidable musician and pianist, Glenn Gould, approach the
Goldberg Variations with a different outlook. Miss Tureck adds
very little to what is on paper. She loves each note and pays
fond attention to each, like a mother afraid to show favoritism
to any of her young. She takes no liberties with tempo. Once
she chooses one, it never varies. But within this strict framework she manages subtle nuances of tone color and phrasing to
interpret the mood of each of the thirty variations that make
up this colossal masterpiece. It is an unforgettable performance.
Gould's version on the other hand (the one I prefer) is more
thrilling. He rips into the piece with an enormous amount of
vitality and energy. He breathes fire and brimstone. He takes
many liberties with tempo and voicing and sometimes adds
ornaments of his own. On occasion he even transposes entire
passages up or down an octave. Everything, however, is under
perfect control. All I can say is *bravo* to both. Each sounds
perfectly correct, artistic, and beautiful.

There rises on occasion a rather provocative question: Should
keyboard works of Bach be played on the modern piano? After
all, Bach conceived his works for the harpsichord or clavichord,
and there are those who feel they owe it to history to perform
the music on the instrument for which it was composed. I am
not among them. I am sure Bach would have agreed with me,
had a piano been available to him, that it is much more satisfactory for the expression of a complete musical concept than
is the harpsichord. Although the harpsichord can produce various degrees of dynamics by means of coupling or uncoupling
octaves with the pedals, it cannot be made to bring out enough
different shades of loud and soft. The mechanics of the instrument do not allow notes to be sustained for any length of time
or to be played smoothly. The naturally detached sound cannot
be altered, nor is there a personal approach to tone quality.
One might compare the relationship of the harpsichord and the
piano to that of a black-and-white sketch and a color portrait.

I do not mean to belittle the art of a great harpsichordist like the late Wanda Landowska. She was a beacon for twentieth-century Bach interpretation; her understanding and performance of the repertoire for her instrument were sheer magic. Igor Kipnis, Ralph Kirkpatrick, and Rafael Puyana, among our present-day performers, are artists of the highest level and project everything the harpsichord has to offer. Nor do I deny the charm of the harpsichord as an ensemble supplement, but I prefer the piano, which permits the performer to produce dynamic expression and phrasing. Harpsichord or piano, Tureck or Kipnis, Gould or Landowska, does it really matter? I have my preference, you may disagree, but a mutual bond unites us in our veneration of Bach. Although Handel was a keyboard virtuoso, his contribution towards its literature is, unfortunately, quite limited. (The organ, for some strange reason, is not considered part of the keyboard family.)

Alongside these two giants, Domenico Scarlatti, also born in 1685, was a tiny giant who wrote about six hundred works for the harpsichord, which are now played on the piano. Even though they are called sonatas, they in no way resemble the sonata of later development. They are, however, miniature masterpieces. Only a few pages in length, and taking but a few minutes to play, they require extreme dexterity of fingers and arms. In many you have to crisscross your hands in rapid tempo. These sonatas brim over with limpid melodies, excitement, rhythmic pulsation, and many sudden changes of mood and color. If you want to spend an exhilarating hour, I suggest you listen to the twelve Scarlatti sonatas recorded by Vladimir Horowitz. Pay special attention to the extraordinary sequence of sounds in the *D Major*, L 164, the lyric beauty of the *F Minor*, L 187, and the unbelievably rapid hammering of the *A Major*, L 391.

Mozart and Haydn

To the average listener the obvious thing about the music of Mozart is that it seems to be endlessly bright, gay or serene, cheerful, witty and full of spirit. One thinks of Mozart in white

wig, lace cuffs, and silk pants. Consider the *Sonata in A Major*
(K 331), the one with the "Marcia alla Turca" as its final movement. I remember an unforgettable performance many years
ago by Ossip Gabrilowitsch.

Although I was quite young, I was impressed by his playing
of the opening theme, soft and songlike, as if he were humming
a lullaby. There were occasional slight swells and dips in dynamics, minute waits before stressing certain notes, but an
over-all feeling of quiet and contentment. The six variations
that followed were handled with a delicacy of fine china, yet
each had its own character. The "Marcia alla Turca" (every child
plays it as a separate piece of music and bangs like mad, trying
to imitate the snare and bass drum) was played in miniature
style, but big in scope, so that the whole sonata hung together.

The other side of Mozart is the tragic one, the Mozart of
financial difficulties, illness, and frustration, a musician whose
music is somber, melancholy, and intense. The superlative and
profound *Fantasia in C minor* (K 475) belongs to this category.
It offers sudden and extreme dynamic changes, gentle phrases
that explode into violent ones, and slow passages followed by
rapid ones. It is a true fantasy and a great one. Daniel Barenboim
gives it an exceptional treatment in his recording.

Except for the concertos, Mozart's greatest contribution to
the piano literature is his *Sonata in F* (K 497) for four hands,
one piano. In a letter to his father Mozart wrote that he would
prefer to have this piece played on two pianos. He undoubtedly
realized the stupendous grandeur of this composition. In view
of the limited sound and volume the piano was capable of producing in his time, Mozart probably wished for some striking
way to enhance this sonata. For me it is truly a symphony for
the keyboard. A gentle slow opening leads into a fast movement, with a heavenly, lyrical second movement, and a boisterous and gay rondo, to complete a masterpiece. The work is so
rich in concept, melody, harmony, and rhythmic novelties that
after playing it for more than twenty years, I feel I need another twenty before I can be sure I am doing more than scratch-
ing its surface.

Included in Haydn's vast output are more than fifty piano
sonatas, themes and variations (the one in *F minor* is best

known), and shorter pieces. Haydn was highly resourceful and imaginative in the development of his thematic material, if I may say so, and actually more daring than Mozart in exploring and experimenting with new ideas. It's a pity his piano music is heard so rarely on the concert stage. There certainly is a place for it. My colleagues have recorded quite a few of his pieces, and of these I highly recommend Nadia Reisenberg's delightful and ingratiating version of the *Sonata No. 50 in C Major* and the *Sonata No. 52 in E flat Major,* Opus 78. Artur Balsam plays the *Sonatas Nos. 21* and *48,* both in *C Major, No. 31 in E Major,* and *No. 32 in B minor,* with impeccable musical taste and technique. The *Andante and Variations in F minor* is performed by Artur Rubinstein. Need I say more.

Beethoven

And now we come to Beethoven. His piano sonatas were twice the length of any previous composer's. He would use two themes where only one had been the practice. He changed piano technique to suit his needs. Into almost all his piano works he introduced new kinds of rhythms, harmonic progressions, and an infinite variety of moods, ranging from deepest sadness to the most radiant happiness.

For me one of his finest piano pieces is the *Sonata in C,* known as the *Waldstein* because Beethoven dedicated it to one of his patrons, Count von Waldstein. This sonata requires the ultimate artistry to do it justice. Certainly Artur Rubinstein and Vladimir Horowitz qualify for the job. Each is a great interpreter, and each seeks to be faithful to Beethoven's wishes. Unlike Bach, Beethoven left many notations, but such are the mystery and wonder that, though Rubinstein and Horowitz play loud and soft where Beethoven indicated, though each plays legato and staccato according to the score, though each follows all the other markings, the two end up with renditions that sound completely different and completely persuasive. How does this happen?

The Horowitz version goes with a great deal of drive and power. Every atom of his being is focused on the task at hand.

The result is an intensity in the pianissimos, as well as the fortissimos, which electrifies the listener.

Rubinstein's interpretation, on the other hand, is broad and relaxed, shimmering with a velvety sonority which beguiles the listener. Horowitz's tempos are barely a hair's breadth faster than Rubinstein's, but because of the differences in tone and concept (his nervous drive compared with Rubinstein's relaxed authority), he seems quite a bit faster. In short, a great artist is always convincing.

Beethoven's sonatas are illustrative of the course of Beethoven's development. The first thirteen, with the possible exception of the *No. 8 in C minor,* the *Pathétique,* belong to the first stage, where the influence of Haydn and Mozart is clearly evident. With the *Sonata No. 14 in C sharp minor,* Opus 27, No. 2, or *Moonlight* as it is popularly known, we see Beethoven making a clean break with tradition and settling into his own style. I remember the magnificent conception of Josef Hofmann, who made this sonata a personal message from the pianist to the composer, especially the first movement, which took on an improvisational flavor, as if it were being thought of for the first time. This middle Beethoven period reached its peak with the *Waldstein* and the *Sonata No. 23 in F minor,* Opus 57, the *Appassionata.* These titanic works require vast imagination plus gorgeous tone quality and lots of nervous energy. They sound best when a Horowitz brings his power and infinite varieties of dynamics to them.

The "unpianistic and unplayable" *Hammerklavier,* the *Sonata No. 29 in B flat Major,* Opus 106, marks the third and last Beethoven period, intense and introspective. The *Hammerklavier* abounds in technical nightmares for the performer. It is a sonata that should be played only by the elite. Then it becomes Beethoven's greatest contribution to the piano literature. I am most satisfied by the Rudolph Serkin and Daniel Barenboim performances, but hasten to add that the lesser-known Hans Richter-Hasser's reading is also to be greatly admired. For these artists the *Hammerklavier* is certainly not unpianistic or unplayable.

I have been asked whether I thought Beethoven could adequately handle it. I most certainly think so, for he was renowned as a virtuoso pianist. Like all great creators writing music for their own instruments, he invariably wrote for his own capabilities.

Another aspect of Beethoven's genius as composer and pianist was his remarkable ability to improvise. He would on occasion give public demonstrations of this wonderful gift. I can very well imagine how these extemperaneous works sounded. There must have been glory in his melody and harmony, as well as power, vitality, force, and even the brute strength of a demonic artist seeking to enlarge the instrument's capacities and extract every last ounce of delicacy and sonority from it.

Weber through Brahms

During Beethoven's lifetime, there occurred six wondrous musical events. A seventh came six years after his death. What were they? The birth of seven of the most illustrious pianists and composers of all time.

First came Carl Maria von Weber (1786), then Franz Schubert (1797), Felix Mendelssohn (1809), Frederic Chopin and Robert Schumann, (1810), Franz Liszt (1811), and last, Johannes Brahms (1833). Although all the composers were ardent admirers of Beethoven, they felt the need to create new forms and a new language of musical expression. They exploited new harmonic structures, and this resulted in an extraordinarily varied palette, expressive devices and dynamic exaggerations. The piano itself was improved. Keys were added at both ends of the range, and the action was accelerated, making possible increased sonority. Pedals for the sustaining, blending, and muting of sounds were invented, and made an indispensable contribution to the evolution of new, creative ideas.

Weber, with large hands and slim fingers, must have been a virtuoso pianist. His compositions offer many opportunities for the pianist to display pyrotechnics. Huge, rapid leaps, intricate finger passages, and immense chords are characteristic of his piano works. He wrote brilliant polonaises, excellent themes and variations, attractive sonatas, and other fine music for the instrument. His melodies, full of charm and grace, are unmistakably original. His fame today rests on his operas and over-

tures; unfortunately, his solo piano music has been discarded
as concert fare and relegated to the practice room.

Schubert left imperishable compositions for almost every
form and combination, but none surpassed in quality his works
for the piano. Whether one listens to his delightful short pieces,
the impromptus, *Moments Musicaux,* waltzes, the great *Fantasy
in C minor* known as the *Wanderer* (the Artur Rubinstein
version is the most beautiful I've ever heard), the sonatas, or
the compositions for one piano, four-hands, certain basic traits
are always in evidence. The melodies have unutterable loveliness in their mixture of sensitivity, strength, dignity, emotion,
and dramatic intensity. He succeeded in imparting to all his
music a feeling of youthful romance, poetic tenderness, variety,
and charm.

Some people complain that Schubert's sonatas are too long.
I disagree. I enjoy the soulful melodies and distinctive modula-
tions. They are sublime. Long-windedness in some composers
may be a sin, but with Schubert it is a blessing.

The wolf that seemed to howl at Schubert's door did not
exist for Mendelssohn. His music reflects his taste and culture.
It makes me think of a young gentleman, immaculately dressed,
exuding personal charm, refinement, and suavity, completely
capable of handling any situation. Mendelssohn has never been
given enough credit for his talent; he was a first-rate and individualistic composer. His scherzi, capriccios, and rondos are
in a class by themselves. They are gay and lighthearted in
spirit, elfin in character, and very humorous. His beautiful,
lyrical *Songs Without Words* are a permanent part of the
pianistic repertory. Of his more serious works for solo piano or
piano four-hands, the *Andante and Rondo Capriccioso,* the
Variations Sérieuses, and the *Allegro Brillante* are among his
finest. Two recordings of the *Andante and Rondo Capriccioso*
are absolute standouts: one by the immortal Hofmann and the
other by Serkin. The interpretations are vastly different, but
both are superb. The *Variations* are given a glorious treatment
by Horowitz.

If I had to say whom I regarded as the greatest writer of
music for the piano, I would nominate Chopin. He wrote almost exclusively for the instrument, and in the handful of com-

positions where the piano is not the prime factor, it is effective. He is the perfect poet and lyricist of the keyboard. He experimented with new and subtle harmonies. He investigated and brought into focus the full sonority of the piano. Novel and original forms and a new piano technique were his creations. All of his works have boldness, richness, exuberance, and charm. They remain unalterably attractive, brilliant, and daring; the critics of his day called them barbaric, wild, and dissonant.

To Chopin must go the credit for bringing to the fore a new style of performance called *rubato* playing. According to Chopin, *rubato* means that the right hand plays freely while the left plays in strict time. What happens in practice is that a little is taken away from the time value of one note and added to another, thus giving the latter note unexpected importance. The musical effect is to permit greater freedom of expression and a more rhapsodic style. Without *rubato* the compositions of the Romantic school, from Schubert through Brahms, would be dull and mechanical, and would be false to the mood and contour of the melodic line. It would be wonderful if we had discs or tapes of Chopin playing, for we would then know exactly how he conceived his *rubatos* rather than having to rely on the conflicting and not always dependable authorities.

There is an abundance of recordings of Chopin's piano music. If I were starting a collection, I would certainly include some of the following compositions played by artists who most closely approach what, I imagine, were Chopin's own interpretations: the stately and vigorous polonaises, the ones in *A Major,* Opus 4, No. 1, and *A flat Major,* Opus 53, No. 6, played by Rubinstein; the coquettish *Waltz No. 1 in E flat Major,* better known as the *Grande Valse Brilliante,* and the one in *C sharp minor,* again Rubinstein; the *Etudes in G flat Major,* Opus 10, No. 5 (*Black Key*), *C minor,* Opus 10, No. 12 (*Revolutionary*), the *G flat Major,* Opus 25, No. 9 (*Butterfly*), and the *A Minor,* Opus 25, No. 11 (*Winter Wind*), excitingly performed by Vladimir Ashkenazy; the *Fantaisie in F minor,* Opus 59, Van Cliburn; the *Sonata No. 3 in B minor,* played by the late Dinu Lipatti with ravishing subtlety of nuances. Although the name Moura Lympany may not be too well known to the average music lover, she is nonetheless a first-rate artist, and her performances of the delicious and beautiful *Nocturnes in E flat Major, A flat Major, F sharp Major,* and *C sharp minor* are exquisite. However, if I had to start with just one recording, my choice would be the *Scherzos Nos. 1, 2,* and *3,* dazzlingly played by Josef Hofmann.

Schumann did not write for the virtuoso school of piano playing. His conceptions demand a variety of tone and contrasts of color and pedal effects. His music is brimful of poetic inspirations. His imagination is fanciful rather than profound; he delighted in writing about subjects of fantastic grace. He developed what we call program music, music that expresses a definite, firm, and external idea. In almost all his best-known piano compositions, such as the *Kinderscenen, Papillons, Carnaval, Davidsbündlertänze,* and *Fantasiestücke,* Schumann paints charming vignettes. Each vignette is a complete composition; yet a series may be held together by a single, binding thought. (By the way, don't miss Rubinstein's playing of *Carnaval.* Sheer heaven!)

While Schumann was writing program music, and Chopin was developing and enlarging the sonorities and capabilities of the piano, Liszt, a pianistic cyclone, was sweeping the world. As an interpreter his blazing drive, unbelievable virtuosity, and diabolic strength overwhelmed all who heard him play. As a creator his exotic harmonies and original forms opened new doors not only for composers of his generation but also for those of later periods.

Liszt played for Beethoven and Schubert and was still giving concerts when Bartók and Stravinsky were starting to take piano lessons. He is yet another example of an outstanding creator whose worth has never been fully recognized by the public and who has, save in rare instances, been neglected by concert pianists. The monumental *B Minor Sonata* (a terrific performance by Emil Gilels), a few etudes, a nocturne or two, one of the *Mephisto Waltzes* (the William Kapell recording is superb), a half-dozen rhapsodies, and some of the pieces in *Années de Pèlerinage* are about all we are likely to get during an entire season of piano recitals. Yet the number of original works Liszt wrote for the piano is immense and diversified. Not all of his pieces are bombastic, as you might think from a glancing acquaintance with his music. Many contain some of the most exquisite melodies and delicate improvisations anyone ever conceived for the piano. There are those of his compositions that prefigure the dawn of the twentieth century and its use of dissonant harmonies, and some are the foundation for styles used by Debussy and Ravel. Liszt's transcriptions of operatic themes and arias for solo piano set a trend for the future in their virtuoso demands. These transcriptions call for great surety in leaps, crossing of the hands, brilliant and elaborate runs in single and double notes, and chords in each hand played at breakneck speed. He transcribed the great organ fugues of Bach, the songs of Schubert, and many symphonic works, including all the Beethoven symphonies, four-hands, one piano. His influence was widespread. He started societies to publish the music of Bach, Handel, and Mozart. He gave free piano lessons to gifted students (I was fortunate to call two of his students my friends, Moritz Rosenthal and Alexander Siloti). He was the patron of Schumann, Chopin, Wagner, Tchaikovsky, Dvořák, Grieg, Borodin, and a host of others. He originated the piano recital, doing away with the custom of performing publicly only with orchestral accompaniment. I am sorry he did not record for the old cylinder discs; after all, the phonograph was invented when he was sixty-six and still, I am sure, a giant as a pianist. I would dearly love to hear him, even on a scratchy, primitive recording.

Liszt always enjoyed the music of Brahms, especially the short compositions. It is strange but nonetheless true that Brahms wrote his longer works for solo piano before he was forty, and for the rest of his life was content to compose, at least for the piano, poetic gems like ballades, rhapsodies, intermezzi, and capriccios; and for piano duet, a simple and charming cycle of waltzes and Hungarian dances. I feel particularly close to Brahms, since I studied for many years with the great and benevolent Carl Friedberg, who was a pupil of Brahms and Clara Schumann.

Brahms's place in music has caused a great deal of controversy, perhaps because he did not seek new forms or harmonies. He was no revolutionary; he worked along traditional lines, using the sonata form and that of the variations for big piano compositions. Tchaikovsky pronounced him "ungifted, pretentious, and lacking in creative power." Is it possible that Tchaikovsky was jealous of Brahms? Although Brahms may have been conservative, his works overflow with romantic inspiration, technical interest (he was a virtuoso pianist), and vitality. I find it difficult to sit through an entire program devoted to the works of one composer. Yet I listened gladly to a series of four programs, presented within a few days, encompassing all Brahms's piano music. The recitals were not only enjoyable but exhilarating. The dignity, force, and nobility of the large works, contrasted with the lighthearted merriment and childlike gaiety of the smaller pieces, gave each concert an endless variety of moods. Julius Katchen, who played the series, was superb.

The Late Nineteenth and the Twentieth Centuries

While Brahms in his mature years was writing some of his loveliest romantic-lyrical compositions, a young generation was striving to find new ways of translating their impressions and emotions into music. Claude Debussy, who was to become perhaps the greatest harmonic innovator of the late nineteenth and early twentieth centuries, succeeded by avoiding clear-cut pictures and by resorting to misty sonorities and a revolutionary approach to the pedals, giving them unprecedented importance and using them in heretofore unimagined combinations. (I was told by a pupil of Debussy that the composer spent at least an hour a day improving and advancing pedal technique.) Logically, the most effective way to create a misty, veiled impression is to superimpose sonority upon sonority; thus each detracts from the clarity of the other and leaves details to the imagination of the listener. It is the moon under many thin layers of clouds, or a forest as seen through a frosted pane of glass. Debussy loved to paint pianistic tonal pictures of colorful subjects. *Footprints in the Sand, Gardens in the Rain, Fireworks, Sails, Goldfish, Reflections in the Water:* These are among the pieces in his marvelous set of twenty-four piano preludes. His many piano works under the fingers of masters like Robert Casadesus or Walter Gieseking are priceless.

With modified variations in harmony and form, the piano music of Maurice Ravel is in many ways quite similar to that of Debussy. I find in Ravel a great deal more absolute music (compositions without any extramusical association, written purely for the beauty of their sound) than in Debussy. However, in *Gaspard de la Nuit* there is the same building of veiled sonorities, important and intricate pedal manipulations, and sparkling colors (let me recommend a dazzling performance on a disc by Vladimir Ashkenazy). Ravel sometimes reverts to strict and old musical forms like those of Bach's partitas and suites. A striking example is *Le Tombeau de Couperin*.

The polar opposite of Debussy's innovations was created by Arnold Schönberg. He devised a new system of musical structure, which produced harmonies and tonal colors previously unheard. But where Debussy's are blurred and veiled, Schönberg's intensify sonorous images, defining them to a point of jagged distortion and harsh dissonance. Most of Schönberg's music is without title and specific program. It can best be described as an expression of anger or frustration, sometimes illuminated in a wild outburst, sometimes in subdued brooding and melancholia. It is his musical way of showing his dissatisfaction with the world. The *Piano Pieces*, Opus 33, as recorded by Glenn Gould, reveal the special creativity of Schönberg.

His disciples Alban Berg and Anton Webern branched out in opposite directions. Berg took the Schönberg doctrines and shaped them toward the conservative side, while Webern, with a far more liberal viewpoint, crystallized and intensified them to a point that went beyond Schönberg, as disclosed in his *Piano Variations*, Opus 27.

It is difficult to describe the music of Stravinsky, Bartók, or Prokofiev without going into great detail. Dissonance is flaunted as never before, often with two or more alienated harmonies used at the same time. There are compelling rhythms, deriving from a kind of barbaric and brutal primitivism, with an inexhaustible supply of energy and extraordinary coloristic effects. The melodic line is as romantic and lyrical as any ever written, but because of the harshness and caustic fence built around the melody, the beauty and elegance of the phrase are often difficult to discern. Try Stravinsky's

Concerto for Two Solo Pianos (Gold and Fizdale), the *Out of Doors Suite* by Béla Bartók (Leonid Hambro), and the Prokofiev *Sonata No. 7* (Vladimir Horowitz).

Of the piano works being written today, little can yet be said authoritatively. They must be given a chance to stand the test of time. You and I may or may not like what we hear, and audiences may hiss, boo, and deride some of the new works. But I believe that much thought and originality are being shown by some of today's young composers. I discern imagination and organization in the works of Boulez, Stockhausen, Babbit, and Carter. History will be the judge. I hope that this generation's creators will compare favorably with those of the past.

What impresses me as I go back in history over the long and noble line of creators is how many have been superlative keyboard artists. All these men I have mentioned in this chapter were wonderfully at home at the keyboard. So were such composers as Granados, Albéniz, Nin, Turina, and scores of others. Among contemporaries, Copland, Gould, Shostakovich, Kabalevsky, Britten, Barber, and Bernstein belong to the line of composer-pianists. How many of the great symphonists and opera composers were not pianists? Very few indeed. Wagner, though known primarily for his operas, was an accomplished pianist. Saint-Saëns, De Falla, Fauré, Richard Strauss, who are known for their symphonic, chamber, and choral music and not especially for piano works, were fine pianists, and the list goes on and on. Where, I might ask, would music be without the piano?

6

Choral Music

DAVID RANDOLPH

Strange as it may seem, my enthusiasm for choral music started rather late. I had, I suppose, the average music lover's lack of interest in choral music and much preferred symphonies, concertos, chamber music, and opera. Curiosity impelled me to visit a rehearsal of a glee club. However, that single rehearsal discouraged me, partly because of the low quality of the music, and partly because of the undifferentiated shouting that passed for singing.

A radio broadcast of Beethoven's *Ninth Symphony* served to bolster my slight interest in choral music and, in turn, made me more receptive to a fellow student's suggestion that I join a chorus that was being formed at the New School in New York City. I wasn't much of a singer and was not even particularly interested in singing, so I approached the experience rather warily. The fact that I became as enthusiastic as I later did is a tribute to the taste and musicianship of the conductor, Arthur Lief. The repertoire he chose served to open a whole new world of beauty to me. It included Bach's *Cantata No. 106, God's Time Is Best,* madrigals by the early English composers Dowland, Wilbye, and Morley, Handel's *Acis and Galatea,* Purcell's *The Fairy Queen,* Mozart's *Requiem,* Brahms's *Schicksalslied,* Bartók's *Slovak Folk Songs,* and Howard Hanson's *Lament for Beowulf.*

I can still recall my sense of wonderment as each new work

revealed a new facet of the composer's musical personality. Bach, in his cantata *God's Time Is Best,* emerged with a more "human" quality than I had known in his instrumental music, and the rich romanticism of the symphonic Brahms took on another dimension when applied to voices in his *Schicksalslied.* I found in the sound of concerted voices an additional sensuous satisfaction that was not present in purely instrumental music.

One other factor contributed to my enjoyment of the medium —one that I often refer to in my rehearsals with my own choruses. I have often pointed out to, let's say the baritones, that the cellos are capable of making equally beautiful sounds. But the singer has an advantage over an instrument. He can evoke feelings by the use of words and their attendant emotional connotations. For example, if the text contains the word *bitterly,* the cellos might accent the beginning of the passage. But that would not evoke the same emotional response as the singers could by intensifying the first syllable of the word. In addition, the listener actually has more in common with vocal music than with instrumental music, since it is with the voice that he most readily expresses his own feelings.

Vocal music developed earlier than did instrumental music, for the simple reason that man was able to manipulate his own voice more easily than he could the crude instruments at his disposal in early times. In fact, in the "Golden Age" of vocal music, the Elizabethan period, when the madrigal reigned supreme, instrumental music was largely an imitation of vocal music. True orchestral music developed long after choral music had attained a great degree of polish and sophistication.

Let me return to my first enthusiasms in the choral field. The work that reached me with the greatest impact was Mozart's *Requiem.* The drama and excitement of that music were the equivalent of any I had known in his orchestral output. Moreover, there was the exhilaration of making the music myself! I can very clearly recall that I was able to close the score for about sixty consecutive pages and sing from memory. Participating in that performance was probably my greatest musical experience up to that time, even though the accompaniment was played on an electronic organ. Later there was the thrill of singing Howard Hanson's stirring *Lament for Beowulf* under the composer's direction, and with full orchestra. Not long after, I wrote a work that had the distinction of being the second student's composition ever performed by the Teachers' College Choir of Columbia University. (The first was by William Schuman.) Years later, at a meeting with Howard Hanson, I told him how greatly my composition had been influenced by his work.

Curiously, my first encounter with the best known of all choral works was the result of an unusual circumstance.

The story begins in New York City's Washington Square Park on a beautiful spring night. A gentle rain was falling—the kind of soft, caressing rain in which young people in love enjoy walking. I was a young person in love—aged seventeen, and I was walking with the first girl whom I ever loved. Quietly, yet with an intensity I could not hide, I confessed to her that I had been in love with her for a year and a half, only to be told that while she liked me, her feelings toward me were merely those of a close friend.

We completed the walk around the park in silence, and then, perhaps in order to ease our embarrassment, we stopped in at one of the churches on lower Fifth Avenue, where an oratorio was being presented. I was in no state to notice the name of the work being performed, but the first sound to greet our ears was a tenor voice, singing a slow, expressive melody to the words "Thy rebuke hath broken His heart"! This was my first exposure to Handel's *Messiah*.

I have since conducted that work any number of times in Carnegie and Philharmonic Halls. It is not difficult to imagine the thoughts that go through my mind each time we reach that section.

Handel and Bach

Messiah is the most popular single large choral work ever written. It may be said to hold the position in choral literature that Beethoven's *Fifth Symphony* occupies in the symphonic repertoire. This, in spite of the fact that it has been the victim of more mishandling, by major and minor performers alike, than any other choral work.

It is the British who are largely responsible for the prevalent misconceptions regarding the manner in which *Messiah* should be performed, though they love choral music and have adopted the German-born Handel as their own. It is they who fostered the custom of performing his *Messiah* with ever-increasing forces. This megalomania began with the first Handel Festival in England, which took place in 1784, twenty-five years after the composer's death. Since then the tradition of the ponderous performance has grown, reaching a climax in a performance given in 1859, by a chorus of 2,765 singers (almost the capacity of Carnegie Hall) and an orchestra of nearly four hundred!

The English scholar Sir Richard Terry wrote in 1927 about the British Handelian as follows:

> He has evolved a heavy, lumbering carthorse-like method of singing Handel. He calls this big bow-wow "the Handel tradition". . . . You may tell him 'til you are black in the face that Handel was (musically) an Italian by training, that he has all the Italian grace and elegance of style that will not stand rough handling. All to no purpose; he will return to his "Messiah" and bellow out "And He shall purify" for all the world like a corpulent Dutch galliot wallowing in the trough of a heavy sea.

Fortunately, within the last decade, we have realized that Handel was a composer of the Baroque era, and that his style was closer to Vivaldi's than Verdi's. Thus Thomas Beecham's recording of the work, rescored for a full nineteenth-century symphony orchestra (such as Handel never knew), and the equally stodgy versions by Malcolm Sargent and Adrian Boult have been supplanted recently by no fewer than three recordings, all of which restore the authentic texture of the work. All are listed in the discography.

Messiah is by no means the only oratorio Handel wrote. In fact there is even more dramatic music in such works as *Israel in Egypt*, which contains many exciting double choruses.

An unaccountably neglected work is *Solomon*, which contains some of Handel's most beautiful writing, both for soloists and chorus. Here I must agree with Beecham, who in his recorded version has omitted certain portions of the work and rearranged the order of the remaining numbers. Having investigated the score in preparation for my own performances, and having found it too long and of uneven quality, I discovered that Sir Thomas's omissions largely reflected my own tastes. I do regret, though, the fact that Beecham did not allow Handel's original scoring to speak for itself, but as in the case of *Messiah,* he reorchestrated the work for a symphonic aggregate of romantic proportions.

I would especially commend to your attention the so-called "Masque" in *Solomon.* Under the guise of presenting an entertainment for the Queen of Sheba, Solomon proposes a series of highly contrasting choruses, one more beautiful than the next. Another high spot is the so-called "Nightingale Chorus," which in its delicacy of treatment is nothing short of entrancing.

There are riches to be found in other Handel oratorios. *Judas Maccabaeus* contains a most moving opening chorus, as well as the famous bravura aria for tenor, "Sound an Alarm." And did you, as I did when a pupil in grammar school, sing "See the-huh conq'ring he-he-he-he-hero comes"? Well, that comes from this oratorio, and it turns out to be quite appealing when properly sung.

Another oratorio, *Saul,* contains many felicities that are worthy of investigation. And if you'd like to hear a shorter work, which is an absolute gem, locate a performance or a recording of Handel's so-called *Chandos Anthem No. VI.* This is a setting of the Forty-second Psalm, and it represents Handel in a tender vein, with some meltingly beautiful music.

One cannot mention Handel without thinking of the other giant of the Baroque period: Bach. Needless to say, his four "big" works—the *Mass in B minor,* the *Passion According to St. Matthew,* the *Passion According to St. John,* and the *Christmas Oratorio*—are musts for any lover of choral music. That does not mean I don't find occasional dull spots in some of these works. My devotion to the truth compels me to report that in the *St. John Passion,* I find the tenor aria "Erwäge" too long— and I could point out a few more such examples. My reason for making this declaration is solely to make all the more convincing my expressions of enthusiasm for the remainder of the music. Perhaps one way to convey my admiration is to confess that each time I conduct one of those four works, I feel as if I were approaching it for the first time. They are such endless sources of wonder that each rehearsal and each performance reveals something new.

Of the four, the *Mass in B minor* is to me the greatest source of musical riches. The *St. Matthew Passion* is the warmest and most human, while the *St. John Passion* is more compact and possibly the most dramatic. Let me stress, though, that these opinions are subject to change—and above all, they are not meant to influence your own reactions.

With this brief bow in the direction of the four "big" Bach choral works, let me call your attention to the beauty in the cantatas—that body of about 250 works that Bach was *required* to write for the church holidays, and of which 199 are still in existence. Note that I used the word *required*. The composer of Bach's era was not just "expressing his inmost feelings" when he wrote music. He was responding to a specific need for music— music for a specific time and place. Under those circumstances it is all the more amazing that Bach was able to maintain such a high level. To be sure, he often borrowed from himself; several portions of the *Mass in B minor* were simply taken from previously written cantatas, with the original German words replaced by the Latin text.

Let us investigate some of the cantatas. There is one cantata for which I have a soft spot. It is *No. 106, Gottes Zeit ist die allerbeste Zeit* (*God's Time Is Best*), also known as the *Actus Tragicus*. For a long time I felt this was "my" cantata. It was the first cantata I had ever sung and the first Bach work I had ever conducted. When a recording of it was issued, and it was my duty to write a criticism of the performance, I approached it almost defensively—as if to say: "Who dares perform *my* cantata?" But I was completely captivated by the performance, which I found to be a revelation. It was conducted by Hermann Scherchen. I would strongly recommend this disc for its insight into the stylistic requirements of a Bach performance.

Some years after this record appeared, I was introduced to Scherchen at a gathering after one of his New York concerts. I told him about my proprietary feeling toward Bach's *Cantata No. 106*, and that I was, nevertheless, completely won over by his recording. A smile gradually appeared on his face. His only answer was to sing the melody of one of the choruses: "Es ist der alte Bund: Mensch, du musst sterben" ("It is the old decree: Man, thou must perish"), making the appropriate conductorial gestures, as if he were directing an imaginary ensemble. I nodded in recognition, and our conversation was interrupted there. About a year later, Scherchen died. How curious that he should have chosen that particular phrase to sing that evening!

Here are a few more of the Bach cantatas I have found particularly appealing. *Number 104, Du Hirte Israël, höre (Thou Guide of Israel, Hear Us)*, has a lilting opening chorus. *Number 140, Wachet auf! (Sleepers, Wake)*, explores a single chorale melody in its opening movement, and again in a later movement, where it is combined with a beautiful melody in the violins. I'm quite certain that you will recognize the latter treatment of it. There is also an expressive duet for the bass and soprano soloists in this cantata.

Cantata No. 76, Die Himmel erzählen die Ehre Gottes (The Heavens Declare the Glory of God), is one of the longer cantatas. As the title implies, some of it is rather exuberant in feeling. There is a most delicious opening chorus in the little-known *Cantata No. 8, Liebster Gott, wann werd' ich sterben.* Unfortunately, the only recording of it at this writing uses boy sopranos and altos, who, for me, leave something to be desired. However, the sound of the solo flute weaving its florid melody above the plucked strings of the orchestra is not easily forgotten.

The opening chorus of *No. 12, Weinen, Klagen,* is the original from which the "Crucifixus" of the *B Minor Mass* was taken. *Number 50, Nun ist das Heil,* is a brief, single-movement work that makes up in power what it lacks in length. But there is no end to the possible recommendations of Bach cantatas. Dip in. They are an endless source of pleasure.

Let us go back in time to an era preceding that of Bach and

Handel: the Italian Renaissance, a source of much beautiful music. One of the supreme masters of this period is Claudio Monteverdi, who lived from 1567 to 1643. One of my favorites for many years has been his "Lagrime d'amante al sepolcro dell' amata" ("Tears of a Lover at the Tomb of the Beloved"). In fact, I was so haunted by it that I could not rest until I had published my own edition of the printed score and had recorded it. As the title indicates, the work is a somber one. It was composed upon the death of an actual person, a beautiful and talented young student of Monteverdi, Caterina Martinelli, who died in 1608 at the age of eighteen.

In my rehearsals of the work with The Masterwork Chorus, in preparation for making the recording, I warned the singers that in the beginning, they might not be aware of the beauties of the work. It is scored for five-part unaccompanied chorus, and it seems for a time as if nothing happens. Only gradually do the subtleties and the expressive qualities of the music emerge. Just as I had predicted, though, the members of the chorus came to me to tell me that they were being haunted by the music, even between rehearsals.

I cannot leave the pre-Bach era without mentioning a few other composers who have produced some beautiful music. The French had an individual style, sometimes ceremonial and at other times greatly expressive. For example, the moving "De Profundis" by Lalande, the "Dies Irae" and "Miserere Mei Deus" of Lully and the "Te Deum" and "Grand Magnificat" of Marc-Antoine Charpentier, not to be confused with the nineteenth-century's Gustave Charpentier, composer of *Louise*.

Haydn, Mozart, and Beethoven

It would be pleasant to linger over the early composers, but we must move on to the two great representatives of the classic period, Haydn and Mozart.

Haydn's two best-known choral works are *The Seasons* and *The Creation*, but we are just beginning to be aware of the beautiful music in his various masses. The *Mass in Time of War* is a fine work, as is the *Lord Nelson Mass in D minor*, which sometimes goes under the name *Imperial Mass*. The *St. Cecilia Mass* is a large-scale work, which begins most beautifully, and most originally, with a hushed opening. Any of these works is well worth exploring.

Mozart's best-known single choral work probably is *Ave Verum Corpus*, simple and appealing enough to be done by many amateur choruses. The *Requiem*, I suspect, would come next in popularity. Certain it is one of the greatest works in the choral literature, though Mozart left it unfinished at his death. Parts of it were completed by his student Felix Süssmayer, who did a most excellent job. Süssmayer left a clear indication of those portions that had been completely written by Mozart, those in which he carried out Mozart's intentions, and those he composed completely by himself. One of the sections I find extremely appealing, the "Benedictus," is entirely the work of Süssmayer.

If you'd like a chilling experience, play the recording of the "Lacrymosa" of the *Requiem*, up to the climax at the words "homo reus," and then stop the music suddenly. Those were the last notes ever composed by Mozart! The remainder of the movement was completed by Süssmayer.

Then there is the *Mass in C minor*, again a work left incomplete by Mozart. But what a powerful opening chorus it contains, and what a wealth of other beauties! For Mozart in a truly relaxed mood, there are his canons. Some of the texts are so free, however, that the literal translations are seldom supplied in present-day performances and recordings!

After Haydn and Mozart, the next great figure is Beethoven. It has become the custom to denigrate almost all Beethoven's choral music, with the exception of the *Ninth Symphony* and the *Missa Solemnis*. While I acknowledge the existence of weak spots in the output of the greatest composers, I should like to guard against the too-easy dismissal of certain works *in toto*, merely because writers and commentators repeat the generalizations of their predecessors, without taking the trouble to investigate the music. The mere fact that Beethoven sometimes wrote without consideration for the comfort of the singers is not sufficient reason, in my opinion, for consigning his choral music to the scrap heap. (An analogy comes to my mind: Once, when

a violinist complained to Beethoven about how difficult some
of his music was for the violin, Beethoven replied, "Do you
think that I'm thinking about your puny little fiddle when I
write?" In all likelihood, he took the same attitude toward the
singers, when he composed some of those fiendishly high passages.)

Those who are familiar with Beethoven's *Ninth Symphony*
and its famous choral finale may be interested in his lesser-
known *Fantasia in C minor for Piano, Chorus, and Orchestra,*
Opus 80. In effect, this was a "study" for the choral finale of
the *Ninth Symphony.* Its closing section for chorus and six vocal soloists sounds very much like the later symphony, since it,
like the rest of the *Fantasia,* is the exploration of a theme which
is very similar to the famous "Ode to Joy" melody of the *Ninth.*
In addition to the pleasure obtainable from the music itself, this
work is of great historic interest, since it gives us an insight into
Beethoven's own development. The entire piece, which lasts
about nineteen minutes, is in essence a series of variations on
the melody. Moreover, while this is a rather strange combination, the first three-quarters of the work actually amounts to a
concerto for piano and orchestra.

I have a fond personal recollection in connection with this
work. I had trained The Masterwork Chorus for a performance
of it with The Philadelphia Orchestra under Eugene Ormandy.
At the single rehearsal of the chorus and orchestra together,
late in the afternoon on the day of the performance, Mr. Ormandy read through the work once. He then turned the baton
over to his assistant and walked to the rear of the auditorium to
listen. I recall that both of us were standing in the center aisle,
and after a few minutes of listening, he turned to me slowly
and quietly uttered one word: "Beautiful!" That constituted
the entire rehearsal.

I omit discussion of Beethoven's *Ninth Symphony,* because
it is so familiar. I prefer to call your attention to a lesser-known
work, his *Mass in C Major,* Opus 86, which is not to be
confused with the better-known *Missa Solemnis.* The later work
has overshadowed the *Mass in C Major* to the point where
many music lovers are not even aware of its existence. This is
a pity, since it is a beautiful, melodious work in Beethoven's

middle-period style, and while it does not reach the heights of the *Missa Solemnis,* it does generate its own excitement. Of course, the *Missa Solemnis* is not to be overlooked. I grant that it is not as immediately accessible as some of Beethoven's other music. Yet it more than repays the time spent getting to know it. And did you know that Beethoven composed an oratorio? This is his *Christus am Oelberg (Christ on the Mount of Olives),* Opus 85. Fate seems to be unkind to certain works by even the greatest of composers. This work merits a hearing.

Nineteenth Century

The romanticism of the nineteenth century made itself felt in choral music. Berlioz, one of the prime influences in this movement, is a composer who affords me increasing pleasure. His *Requiem* was described by an early critic as "beautiful and strange, wild, convulsed and dolorous." True, there is a spot where the flutes are bunched up high in their register and are accompanied by eight trombones in the lower part of their register. And what a weird effect they create! But that same imagination served him well in the creation of many arresting passages in the *Requiem* and the exquisite *Romeo and Juliet.*

Of special appeal is *L'Enfance du Christ.* For a man who was capable of some of the greatest excesses, his restraint in this work is nothing short of remarkable. Indeed, Berlioz originally pretended that some of the music of *L'Enfance du Christ* was the work of an unknown, earlier composer!

Should your mood call for drama, I would suggest the *Requiem* by Verdi. Do not expect any of the restraint so often associated with religious music. It is my feeling that Verdi has here written another opera, without scenery and without action. It is one of the most overpowering works in the entire choral repertoire. In judging any recording of it, by the way, I suggest you turn immediately to the second movement, the "Dies Irae," or "Day of Wrath," section. If your room doesn't shake with the power of the music, then reject the recording. There is a part for a bass drum that will be a good test of your equipment.

The *Requiem* of Brahms—to me, surely one of the most beautiful nineteenth-century compositions—has overshadowed another work of his which I regard as equally fine. It is the *Shicksalslied* (*Song of Destiny*), Opus 54. Brahms himself was said to have been especially fond of this work. It begins with a slow, lyrical opening followed by a very turbulent section. Curiously, though, this second portion leaves the chorus "up in the air," so to speak. The music has a feeling of uncertainty, which is resolved only by the orchestra, as it returns to the consoling opening portion.

If there is any composer whose music can be said to lack "heroic" quality, he is Gabriel Fauré. His aesthetic creed apparently had no place for the "monumental." Instead he substituted a refined lyricism. But within his self-prescribed limits, he is a minor master. Listen to his *Requiem*. There are no huge crescendos, no overpowering climaxes. Even the violinists sit there for most of the performance, doing nothing. Fauré prefers the muted sounds of the lower strings and the darker woodwinds. But what a hypnotically beautiful work it is, with its graceful melodies and exquisite harmonies! In 1887, the year in which he composed his *Requiem*, Fauré also wrote his *Pavanne*, Opus 50, for chorus and orchestra. This is a work lasting about five minutes, but its beauty will haunt you. It exists in two versions—with and without chorus. Either version is beautiful, but the chorus adds the distinctive quality that only the human voices can impart.

Twentieth Century

The twentieth century has seen the creation of a number of exciting choral works. In fact, the 1920's and 1930's alone have accounted for at least a half-dozen compositions that are all-time favorites for me as both conductor and listener.

A work I found intriguing from the moment I first heard it is the *Slavonic Mass*, or as it is also known, the *Glagolitic Mass*, by Leoš Janáček. Written in 1926, when its composer was seventy-three years old, it was performed for the first time two years later, shortly after Janáček's death. Two years later, on the occasion of its first New York performance, the conductor,

Artur Bodanzky, remarked: "I can realize that anyone who comes to hear this Mass of Janáček's with the Masses of Mozart or Palestrina or the Passions of Bach in mind will be shocked by the barbaric peasantlike strength of this new music."

I would suggest that in approaching this work you banish from your mind all preconceptions of how religious music should sound. To me the work suggests Stravinsky's *Sacre du Printemps,* as it might sound if it had been filtered through Moravian folk music. As one commentator aptly said: "An old man had here flung before the world a work filled with tempestuous vitality."

Speaking of rough-hewn music inevitably brings to my mind one of the most exciting choral works of the twentieth century: William Walton's *Belshazzar's Feast.* It should be borne in mind that when this work was given its *premiere* in 1931, its composer was only twenty-nine years old. It is an interesting commentary on the taste of the times that Walton's composition was accepted for performance at the Leeds Festival only after considerable controversy, because its idiom was considered so extreme; this, despite its use of a Biblical text. Since then it has caught on in England, though performances in the United States are unfortunately still a rarity. Perhaps the British love of choral music has helped the work to gain a foothold there. The scarcity of performances in the United States may be attributable to the unusually large orchestra required. Besides a full symphonic complement, including an organ and a piano, with extra wind instruments, the score calls for an amplified percussion battery: bass and snare drums, cymbals, triangle, tambourine, gong, glockenspiel, a slapstick, a Chinese block, and an anvil! In addition, Walton calls for no fewer than two extra brass bands, facing each other from opposite sides of the chorus! Sheer economics make it difficult, if not prohibitive, for the average American choral society to engage the requisite number of players. But when the text comes to the words "Make a joyful noise," the effect of these enormous forces is overwhelmingly exciting.

Another outstanding section is the one in which, after a tremendous climax and a moment of silence, the baritone soloist (the only solo voice) intones, entirely without accompaniment:

"And in that same hour, as they feasted, came forth the fingers of a man's hand, and the King saw the part of the hand that wrote." Then, against a quiet but foreboding accompaniment, he continues: "And this was the writing that was written: 'Mene, mene, tekel upharsin.'" A four-part male chorus, singing fortissimo and reinforced by four French horns, translates: "Thou art weighed in the balance and found wanting." The soloist returns with another unaccompanied recitative: "In that night was Belshazzar the King slain," with a momentary pause before the final word—a pause that sends shivers up one's spine. Immediately upon the completion of that phrase, the full chorus of men and women, supplemented by the brass and percussion instruments, shouts the single word "Slain!" For sheer dramatic impact, this is a most thrilling moment.

Also English, but at the opposite end of the emotional scale, is the lovely *Mass in G minor* by Ralph Vaughan Williams. It is well known that Vaughan Williams had great admiration for the music of his compatriots of the sixteenth century, an admiration reflected in his beautiful *Fantasia on a Theme by Thomas Tallis,* which is based on a hymn composed by Tallis in 1567. The *Mass in G minor* might be said to be the vocal counterpart of the *Tallis Fantasia,* which is composed for two string orchestras and a string quartet, while the *Mass* is written for two unaccompanied choruses and a vocal quartet. The similarity in textures is readily apparent. In both works the two choirs (whether of strings or voices) are treated antiphonally—that is, they answer one another from different locations. At times they are used as one massive choir. In addition, the presence of the string quartet and the vocal quartet in the respective works supplies a contrast in weight of sound. It should be obvious that in the cases of both of these works the composer's intentions are best realized in a stereophonic recording, which reproduces the spatial relationships of the two choirs.

While the *Mass* evokes the feeling of early English music, it should not be thought that Vaughan Williams attempts merely to imitate the old composers. The work bears the unmistakable stamp of a twentieth-century musical personality. (And just in passing, lest any choral conductor be led to the conclusion that the work, with its many serene sections, is an easy one to per-

form, let him be forewarned. Behind the *apparent* simplicity
of the music lie many pitfalls for the chorus. It takes quite some
time for a chorus to accustom itself, not only to the notes, but
also to the stylistic requirements of the music.) There is frequent fluctuation between major and minor harmonies, which
together with the "false relations" (the presence of, say, an E
flat in one part, followed immediately by an E natural in another part), lends the work a modern feeling, at the same time
evoking the old modal style. The chorus is sometimes divided
into as many as ten or twelve parts, with a consequent richness
of sound. This, contrasted with the sections given over to only
the four solo voices, makes for some exquisite contrasts. Listen
to Vaughan Williams's setting, in the "Crucifixus," of the words
"passus, et sepultus est," in which both choruses combine, in some
extremely soft and simple chords. It is an absolutely magical
moment.

While we are in the period of the 1920's and 1930's, I must
mention Ernest Bloch's *Sacred Service,* composed in 1933. Aside
from the inherent beauties of the music, the work occupies a
unique place historically. The various Catholic and Protestant
services have been set numerous times by great composers, but
the *Sacred Service* is the first large-scale choral-orchestral composition written for Jewish worship by a composer of stature.

The work has a power and drive which will come as no surprise to anyone familiar with Bloch's earlier composition, *Sche-
lomo,* a rhapsody for cello and orchestra. The scoring has a richness which matches that of the earlier work, combined at times
with a fine lyrical quality. A wonderful excitement pervades
both chorus and orchestra at the words "Yimloch Adonoy leolom,"
with its irresistible rhythmic drive. The only portion of the work
that is given over to the unaccompanied chorus (the hushed
setting of the words "Yihyu L'rotzon" ["May the words of my
mouth"]), coming immediately after, supplies a beautiful contrast
in mood.

Stravinsky has contributed an exciting work in his *Symphony
of Psalms,* which I regard as one of the major choral compositions of this century. It contains a rhythmic propulsiveness and
a fine lyrical quality. I regard myself as fortunate in having
been present to hear the composer himself conduct the work

during Lincoln Center's Stravinsky Festival in the summer of 1966.

Another Stravinsky composition that can afford considerable pleasure is *Les Noces*. The accompaniment of four pianos and percussion gives some idea of the texture of this music, which is characterized, above all, by rhythmic vitality.

Three works by the twentieth-century French composer Francis Poulenc have been most gratifying to me. They are the *Mass in G* of 1937, the *Stabat Mater* of 1951, and the *Gloria*, which dates from 1961, only two years before the composer's death. Poulenc seems to have two different musical personalities. He often appears to aim for nothing more than witty effects, peppering his music with what sound like Paris music-hall tunes. One example that comes to my mind occurs in the closing movement of his *Concerto for Two Pianos and Orchestra*. But these three choral works reveal another side of him. Always the superb craftsman, here he shows a more serious face as well. His is a distinctive voice—no mean accomplishment in an era that boasts so many composers. My own feeling is that he has been somewhat underrated because of the urbanity and playfulness of so many of his compositions. Dip into any of the three works I have listed—the first is for *a cappella* chorus, the other two are with orchestra, each with a soprano soloist. I think you will be gratified by the results.

Speaking of unaccompanied choruses, I must mention a few groups that have given me great pleasure, not only for the charm and appeal of their musical fare, but also for the high caliber of the performances. One is the Agrupación Coral de Pamplona de España, under Luis Morondo. I suspect there is very little music of any school to which this virtuosic group of nine women and seven men could not do complete justice. There seems to be no end to the variety of tone quality they can produce. Listen to their performance of *Five Songs* by Manuel de Falla—music you will probably recognize—and as you do so, you will gradually become aware of the fact that the guitar accompaniment you are hearing is produced by the voices! Their technical polish is truly outstanding. Moreover, the solos are sung by various members of the chorus.

Another remarkably fine group is the National Chorus of

Russian Song, a ninety-five-voice mixed chorus which was founded during World War II. How artistically these performers sing even so popular a war horse as "The Volga Boatmen," and what tonal richness they bring to the soft opening and close! However, their most outstanding contributions are two songs called "On the Mounts of Manchuria" and "The Little Birch Brooms." The first is one of those typical sentimental, lilting Russian folk melodies sung by the tenors to a simulated guitar (or is it balalaika?) accompaniment—with the basses singing the "oomp" and the women supplying the "plink, plink." Words can hardly convey the beauty of the music or the artistry with which it is sung. I have almost worn out my copy of the recording of this number as a result of repeated playings for both myself and my friends. The other number is a humorous song about the tied-up bunches of birch twigs used for sweeping and scrubbing in every peasant household. Listen to the wonderful ensemble achieved by the chorus and its conductor, A. V. Sveshnikov, as the music speeds up and slows down. Here is real musical excitement!

I cannot leave the field of folk music without mentioning another group—the Mazowsze Choral Ensemble and Orchestra, conducted by Tadeusz Sygietynski. There is a naïve but refreshing charm to their arrangements and performances. The tone of the chorus, and especially of the soloists, is hardly what we would consider polished, "professional" quality. Yet it has the ring of authenticity, and it fits the music perfectly.

Here is a quick mention of other choral works I would recommend without hesitation. Zoltán Kodály's *Missa Brevis* and *Te Deum* are first rate, alternating power with appealing melody. Bernstein's *Chichester Psalms* is a surprisingly accessible work, considering the amount of avant-garde music that its creator has espoused. Dvořák's *Requiem* and his *Stabat Mater* are rewarding works, with many felicities. He is another composer who is not sufficiently appreciated. Then there are *Trois Chansons de Charles d'Orléans* for unaccompanied chorus by Debussy, Ravel's *Trois Chansons*, Erik Satie's *Mass for the Poor*, the appealing work called *Psalms* for chorus and two pianos by Lukas Foss, and *The Christmas Story* by Hugo Distler, and . . . and . . .

7

The Art Song

DAVID RANDOLPH

O NE cannot think of the art song without immediately thinking of German Lieder. In fact, I suspect the German word for
songs has almost replaced the English word in the minds of
most devotees of this art. If this is so, the reason is not hard
to find. The art song has been brought to its greatest heights
by four composers: Franz Schubert, Robert Schumann, Johannes Brahms, and Hugo Wolf, all of whom set German poems to
music. Other composers and other nations have made significant contributions, but nothing can approach the extent to
which these four composers devoted themselves to the creation
of songs. Schubert alone wrote over six hundred!

Why is it that we so readily expose ourselves to sadness and
tragedy in art when we go out of our way to avoid them in
real life? Be that as it may (and to answer that question would
lead us into an involved discussion of the nature of the artistic experience), I shall start with one of the last and most
somber of Schubert's song cycles. It is his group of twenty-four
songs known collectively as *Die Winterreise* (*The Winter Journey*). The text has to do with a man who is sick at heart because he has been betrayed in love. He travels through the
snow-covered countryside, assailed at every turn by desolation.
The streams are frozen, nature is lifeless. At night he hears the
prolonged barking of dogs, the creaking of the weather vane.
He pushes on without hope, finally encountering an organ-
grinder, whose one tune becomes his own song.

Out of this pessimistic cycle of poems, Schubert has fashioned some of the most touching music ever written for solo voice and piano. Each of the twenty-four songs has some musical felicity to recommend it. For me the crowning touch is the final song, "Der Leiermann" ("The Organ Grinder"). In its very simplicity, it is the most moving of all. The entire song is accompanied only by a drone bass, intended to suggest the hand organ. The mere snatches of melody allotted to the voice help to intensify the sense of loneliness. As a musico-dramatic entity, this is a masterpiece of writing.

Another of my favorites, and one of the best known, is "Der Doppelgänger" ("The Double"). What subtle musical wonders Schubert creates in this work! The introduction consists of four somber chords, which are repeated almost identically for fully two-thirds of the song. But notice the magical effect produced near the end of the song, when Schubert changes just the fourth chord! This song is one of fourteen which comprise the cycle known as the *Schwanengesang* (*Swan Song*)—a title given to the set not by Schubert but by his publisher. The cycle also contains the now famous "Serenade."

Let us leave the rather somber feelings expressed in these Schubert song cycles for the emotional relief afforded by a slightly less pessimistic cycle composed by Schumann, the *Dichterliebe* (*Poet's Love*), to poems by Heine. While it does seem characteristic of the German romanticists always to be lamenting a lost love, there are some lighter works in this collection of sixteen songs. Listen to the third song in this collection, "Die Rose, die Lilie, die Taube, die Sonne," a brief but ecstatic outpouring of love. And there is certainly an infectious excitement in "Das ist ein Flöten und Geigen" and "Aus alten Märchen winkt es," with their powerful piano accompaniments. And what a felicitous touch Schumann imparts to the entire cycle by ending it with a thoughtful postlude in the piano, after the poet has gradually become disillusioned by his faithless sweetheart.

Another beautiful cycle by Schumann is *Frauenliebe und Leben* (*Woman's Love and Life*). As the title suggests, this group of eight songs runs the gamut from the ecstasy of a woman in love, to her sadness upon the death of her beloved. It is one of the pinnacles of the romantic song literature.

There were, of course, songs before those by the four I have mentioned. Let me touch briefly on two of their predecessors. Although he is acknowledged as one of the most universal of composers, because he wrote so superbly in nearly all the forms, Mozart is not regarded as preeminent in the field of the song; nor is Beethoven. The art song did not become an important aspect of music until the later, romantic period. Nevertheless, both giants wrote songs that, while they may not possess the intimate, personal quality of the songs by the later composers, are worthy of attention on their own terms. One of Mozart's songs, "Die Alte," represents a woman who is lamenting the fact that "everything was better in the old days." Mozart directs that the song is to be sung "a little bit through the nose"!

Beethoven composed a group of six songs titled *An die ferne Geliebte* (*To the Distant Beloved*). Because the subject matter of the texts is related, and because Beethoven linked several of the songs by reusing some of the musical material, these are considered to be the first "song cycle" and are of importance in the development of the art song.

Mozart's songs reveal the approach of the classic period—an almost folklike simplicity in which the piano accompaniment supplies mostly harmonic background.

Later in the nineteenth century it fell to the lot of Brahms to carry on the Lieder tradition. For years I have been in love with his *Vier Ernste Gesänge* (*Four Serious Songs*). As the title indicates, their subject matter is rather somber. But there is a richness about the music that makes these songs irresistible to me, regardless of the texts. I invite you to listen especially to the culmination of the fourth song. For beauty of melody I know of few things that match it.

Of perhaps even more immediate appeal is his "Immer leiser wird mein Schlummer." The melody of this song will be familiar to those who know the composer's *Piano Concerto No. 2*, since it appears in the second movement as a cello solo. His "Ständchen" is a light-hearted serenade, while the dramatic "Auf dem Kirchhofe" finds Brahms in a somber mood. Perhaps his best-known work in this genre is the familiar "Wiegenlied," the cradle song. Although it is not readily apparent to us, the piano accompaniment of this work incorporates a traditional Viennese love song. While Brahms was the conductor of the Hamburg Ladies' Choir, one of its members brought the song to his attention. Some time later, on the birth of her second son, Brahms dedicated this cradle song to her and her husband. Accompanying the music was a note saying that "since the song is suitable for boys or girls, you need not order a new one each time."

The fourth of the great pinnacles in the field of German Lieder is Hugo Wolf. Curiously, despite the fact that both Brahms and Wolf occupy comparable positions as song composers, Wolf was nothing short of vitriolic in his opinions of the music of Brahms. These opinions were expressed in print, since Wolf was a music critic for one of the Viennese newspapers. His hatred of Brahms's music extended into a detestation of Brahms the man, with the result that his reviews reached the heights (or should we say the depths?) of critical invective. Incidentally, the last few years of his relatively brief life were spent in an insane asylum.

Be that as it may, Wolf did compose many magnificent songs. In one period of a little more than two years, he wrote more than one hundred and sixty songs. I would call your attention to just two. They are the very lyrical "Benedeit die sel'ge Mutter," and the vigorous and outgoing "Fussreise."

Another composer who has contributed some of the most beautiful songs to the literature is Gustav Mahler. Many of his songs, however, are written with orchestral accompaniment. Where to begin? Let us start chronologically, with the *Lieder eines fahrenden Gesellen* (*Songs of a Wayfarer*), composed when Mahler was in his twenty-third year. These four songs are tremendously appealing. In addition, a melody in the second song served as the principal theme of the opening movement of his *First Symphony,* and a refrain in the fourth song appears in the slow movement.

There is a later cycle for contralto, baritone, and orchestra, called *Des Knaben Wunderhorn* (*The Youth's Magic Horn*). Here, too, we find beautiful music as well as the source material for another symphony. You'll find the origin of the scherzo of the *Second Symphony* in the song "St. Anthony and the Fishes," and the song "Urlicht" ("Primeval Light") serves as the basis of part of the fourth movement.

Early in the twentieth century Mahler composed his *Kindertotenlieder* (*Songs on the Death of Children*), and again we find some of the most magnificently expressive songs ever conceived. Here indeed, in Mahler, is a fitting successor to Schubert and Brahms as a creator of the romantic song.

If you would like to follow the German song into more recent manifestations, I would recommend the three *Geistliche Motetten*, composed in 1941 and 1944 by Paul Hindemith. There is a simplicity to these three works that makes them immediately accessible, and at times they are downright haunting.

Italian, Spanish, and French

So much for songs in the Germanic tradition. There are many beauties to be found in the songs of Spanish, Italian, and French composers. Some of the very earliest examples, even those going back as far as the fourteenth century, contain music that should not be overlooked.

It sometimes happens that one particular song will appeal to us above all others of its kind. This has been my experience in the case of a two-and-a-half-minute song by the early eighteenth-century Italian composer Alessandro Scarlatti, called "Cara e dolce." I have played it on radio broadcasts numberless times and have always had requests that it be repeated, thanks to its haunting quality. For those who are interested in the vocal music of sixteenth-century Spain, I would recommend two composers: Luis Milan and Alonzo de Mudarra. The latter's "Triste estaba" is a dignified yet moving setting of David's Lament for Absalom.

French composers seem to have been attracted to the song almost as much as the Germans. There is a cycle of six by Berlioz called *Les Nuits d'Été* for soprano and orchestra, which is one of my all-time favorites. Here is Berlioz at his best. Not only is the vocal line at all times expressive, but the orchestra is used so imaginatively that the ear is constantly being ravished. There is none of the bombastic Berlioz here—no attempt to bowl you over with tremendous orchestral forces. This is intimate music—music that envelops you with a bittersweet sadness, as it conveys the essence of Theophile Gautier's romantic poems.

One cannot discuss the songs of French composers without mentioning Gabriel Fauré and Claude Debussy. Fauré, who was treated with mere respect during his lifetime, mainly because of his position as a pedagogue, has still not fully come into his own. Yet for those listeners who are sensitive to his subtleties, his music can afford considerable pleasure. I would particularly recommend his cycle of nine love songs called *La Bonne Chanson.*

Debussy, too, brought all his individual genius to his songs. His "Beau Soir," "Green," and "Mandoline" have justly become favorites among devotees of this type of music. There is one song in particular whose text I have found especially moving, since it deals not with some imagined poetic situation but with real life. It is "Noel des Enfants Qui n'Ont Plus de Maisons"—"Christmas of the Children Who Have No Home." The song was composed during the First World War as Debussy's protest against the inhumanities of war. It was the last song he ever wrote, and one of the few for which he wrote his own text. By showing the effects of war upon homeless children, he brings the horror down to a personal and intimate level. The text reads, in part: "We have no house any more, the enemies have taken all, taken all, down to our little bed!" The words "taken all"—in French, "tout pris"—are repeated at each appearance, to a brief descending musical figure that becomes quite heartbreaking in its effect.

The words continue: "To be sure, papa is at war and poor mama is dead. Before she could see all this. What are we going to do?" What a far cry this is from the typical romantic descriptions of the beauties of nature which form the texts of so many songs! The music has a restless quality that matches the plaintiveness of the children's outcry, and the piano accompaniment, with its constant motion, adds to the emotional impact.

The songs by another French composer, Francis Poulenc, reveal both his originality and lyricism in full measure. His set-

tings of four brief poems by Guillaume Apollinaire are delightful. I recommend especially "Avant le Cinéma." The heights of
soaring lyricism are attained in his "Tu Vois le Feu du Soir,"
with its fiendishly difficult range. "Main Dominée par le Coeur"
has a wonderful sense of urgency, and each of his seven brief
Calligrammes by Guillaume Apollinaire is more expressive than
the last.

I cherish the memory of my only contact with Poulenc, which
took the form of a brief telephone conversation with him in the
1950's, during one of his visits to New York. My purpose was
to ask him whether at one place in the opening movement of
his *Concerto for Two Pianos and Orchestra* he did not consciously
attempt to imitate the Balinese gamelan, despite the fact that
the jacket notes on the recording made no mention of it.
His answer was an impetuous "But, of course!"

Should you wish to venture even farther into the byways of
French song, I would call to your attention the songs of Emanuel Chabrier, and Erik Satie's *Trois Melodies.*

Middle European and Slavic

The songs I have discussed so far make relatively little use of
folk melodies. Generally speaking, it was the middle European
and Slavic composers who seemed to draw to a greater degree
upon their folk heritage in their art songs.

A truly unconventional song cycle is Leoš Janáček's *Diary of
One Who Vanished,* composed in 1916. The text deals with the
mysterious disappearance of a young Moravian peasant. A group
of short poems were found in his room. They were at first
thought to be folk songs, but a legal investigation revealed that
they were an account of his love affair and his subsequent suicide. These poems form the basis of the text of this song cycle.
The greater part of the twenty-two songs are sung by a tenor,
but the girl is represented by a mezzo-soprano voice. A few
magical moments are supplied by two brief appearances of
three women's voices.

A precursor of Janáček is Modest Musorgski, whose *Songs
and Dances of Death* are a must for any lover of the art song.

I can still recall the chills I experienced upon first hearing an old 78-rpm recording by the baritone Igor Gorin of "The Field Marshall," the final song in this cycle of four. Both Musorgski and Janáček made use of the folk music of their respective countries without attempting to prettify it. They preserved the simpler aspects of their native music, which other composers might have rejected as too crude. This authenticity of feeling, coupled with the observance of the inherent rhythms of their respective languages, imparts a tremendous sense of conviction to the works of both men. When Musorgski deals with death in four different guises in his song cycle, the effect is dramatic in the extreme. The first, "Trepak," is about a toil-worn peasant. The second, "Lullaby," is concerned with a mother nursing a sick child. "Serenade" finds death in the form of a lover courting a maiden, and in the final song, death appears on a battlefield as a field marshall, crying out: "Struggle no more, the fight is over. I am the conqueror of all . . . In life you were bitter enemies, but in death you are joined together . . . I will rule over you, all powerful." The emotional tension is in marked contrast to the relatively restrained feelings found in the typical German Lied or the French Song.

Another aspect of Musorgski's art is represented by his *The Nursery*, a cycle of seven songs of great charm and originality. It would be difficult to imagine a greater contrast in emotional tone than that supplied by this cycle. There are also two other delightful songs by the same composer—"The He-Goat" and "Hopak."

Are you willing to seek out the unfamiliar in song literature? You will find a delightful surprise in a cycle of eleven songs called *From Jewish Folk Poetry*, the Opus 79 of Shostakovich. The Soviet composer has set eight old Jewish folk texts and has added three more from recent times. The result is most appealing. Shostakovich employs a soprano, a mezzo-soprano, and a tenor, using them in solo capacity and in various combinations.

Another prominent Soviet composer, Dmitri Kabalevsky, has made a setting for bass voice and piano of three of Shakespeare's sonnets. How strange to have Shakespeare emerge as Russian music! In its own terms, however, the music is gratifying to hear.

English and American

Let us not overlook the considerable contribution of English and American composers to the song literature. The undisputed master of the art of setting the English language to music is the seventeenth-century English composer Henry Purcell. Four of his works display several facets of his genius. Dramatic declamation is the basis of "Not All My Torment," while in contrast "If Music Be the Food of Love" contains some appealing lyricism. (The words of the latter song, by the way, come not from Shakespeare, but from a poem by a Colonel Heveningham.) A variety of moods is to be found in "From Rosy Bowers." It was composed for D'Urfey's *Don Quixote* and is a fairly lengthy *scena* in which Altisidora attempts to seduce the knight from his allegiance to Dulcinea. In its five parts, it is alternately dramatic and lyrical, and it ends with a section intended to illustrate the lady's frenzy when she discovers that her attempts are in vain. "Man Is for the Woman Made" is a jocose work whose original text is so free that some modern record versions are discreetly bowdlerized.

In our time some of the most gratifying music for the human voice has been composed by Benjamin Britten. Indeed, Britten has been spoken of as the first English composer to match Purcell in his ability to set the English language to music.

One of his most rewarding works is *Les Illuminations*, for high voice and string orchestra, written in 1939 when the composer was only twenty-six. What color Britten draws from the strings, right from the start of the opening movement, called "Fanfare"! And what excitement is created as the voice intones over the strings, as if in defiance, the opening line of Arthur Rimbaud's poem "I alone hold the key to this savage parade"! At the opposite end of the scale is the exquisite setting of the poem "Being Beauteous," in which the voice floats above a quietly sustained accompaniment in the strings. This is one of the truly outstanding examples of twentieth-century lyricism. Immediately following, and in the sharpest contrast possible, is the movement called "Parade," in which both voice and strings seem to pile color upon color, as they match the feelings of the wildly exotic text.

Two other song cycles dating from this period in Britten's life have been sources of pleasure to me, though they both take more time to yield their riches. They are his settings of *Seven Sonnets of Michelangelo*, and *The Holy Sonnets of John Donne*. In the latter set Britten gives us some intensely passionate writing for the voice, in the sonnet beginning "Since she whom I lov'd hath payed her last debt to Nature." And there is a dramatic and powerful setting of the sonnet beginning with the words: "Thou hast made me, and shall thy work decay?"

For some years I have been intrigued by a novel work of the American composer Henry Cowell, who died in December, 1966. It was composed in 1938 for the unusual combination of soprano voice, flute, cello, and piano. But more noteworthy than the instrumentation is the fact that the voice sings a wordless vocalise and is treated simply as one of the instruments in a chamber group. I am in favor of this approach to vocal music, since it frees the composer from the strictures of a text. At the same time it enables him to take advantage of the warmth inherent in the human voice, and thereby to imbue his music with human expressiveness.

Cowell's work is titled *Toccanta*. This is a rather clever combination of the word *toccata,* which since Bach's time has meant a rhapsodic show piece for an instrument, and *cantata,* meaning a work for voices. Its five short movements employ the voice in a variety of manners which are unusual and quite appealing.

Henry Cowell subsequently returned to his idea of writing wordless music for voices. Some years ago he agreed to compose a work for The Randolph Singers, a madrigal group of five voices that I conducted. The result was his "Hymn and Fuguing Tune No. 5," which contained no text and not even any indication of the sounds to which the notes were to be sung. We experimented with various sounds, and finally decided to hum the opening "Hymn" and sing the faster and more complex "Fuguing Tune" to the syllables "la-la-la-." This made possible the clearer articulation of the faster notes. For contrast we also hummed a few of the interludes in the "Fuguing Tune," thus achieving changes of color. The results are preserved in the recording we made of *English Madrigals and American Part Songs,* a disc which has since become a collector's item.

Twentieth-century America also boasts the songs of Samuel Barber. His *Hermit Songs* were first performed in 1953 by the soprano Leontyne Price at the Library of Congress, with the composer accompanying at the piano. The text consists of ten short poems by Irish monks and scholars of the eighth to thirteenth centuries. They are actually observations written on the margins of manuscripts they were copying. I quote here the complete text of one of the songs, called "Promiscuity":

I do not know with whom Edan will sleep
But I do know that fair Edan will not sleep alone.

The songs display Barber's lyrical talents and contain enough dissonance to enable them to be considered "modern."

I have also enjoyed two more modern song cycles. They are *Pomes Penyeach,* to words by James Joyce, and *Thirteen Ways of Looking at a Blackbird,* to words by Wallace Stevens. Both are by the American composer John Gruen, and both reveal a genuine feeling for vocal writing.

In the interest of accuracy, let me amend somewhat the statement I made earlier about the relative lack of folk melodies in the songs by the German composers. There are some, notably in Brahms. If you would like to share the pleasure I have received from Brahms in a folk mood, try his *Zigeunerlieder* (*Gypsy Songs*), Opus 103. He set these songs in two forms—for solo voice and piano and for four-part chorus and piano. I have conducted the works in their choral setting, but I must admit that the solo version is equally satisfying. If you can resist the infectious quality of these songs, perhaps you don't like music after all.

The Art of Singing Lieder

A final word about the art of Lieder singing. It is not to be assumed that every singer—even among famous opera stars—is necessarily a good Lieder singer. This is a specialized art, requiring not only a flexible voice but also great understanding of the emotional implications of the text. In place of the sheer volume so often required for opera, the art song demands a variety of tone colors and great control of the voice, often in *pianissimo* passages. This is a more severe test of musicianship than is the more brilliant kind of singing called for in opera. To me, the outstanding Lieder singers of our era are Dietrich Fischer-Dieskau, Gerard Souzay, Ernst Haefliger, Hermann Prey and Pierre Bernac. Among the women, I find Elisabeth Schwarzkopf, Maria Stader, Evelyn Lear, Régine Crespin and Judith Raskin pre-eminent.

8

The Musical Theater

ALFRED SIMON

WHEN I was eight or nine, a cousin presented me with a phonograph record—the first I could call my own. It was Jerome Kern's "Babes in the Wood" from *Very Good Eddie*, as pounded out relentlessly by the Emerson Military Band. Hardly the most sensitive performance for this tender, caressing melody, but at that point in my life it did not matter. There was a folklike simplicity about "Babes in the Wood" which I loved, and the record would be played over and over until the hissing surface noise made the music almost unrecognizable. The name Jerome Kern, or indeed, any other name in the musical comedy world, had no significance for me. But from that record on, I was hooked for life on show tunes. On succeeding birthdays and Christmases I'd acquire more records of theater music for my small, but growing collection. These were set forth in quite traditional style, as solos and duets, by Miss Lucy Isabelle Marsh, Mr. Lambert Murphy, and other genteel sopranos and tenors with beautiful voices.

Even better were the *Gems from* . . . records, a series of vocal medleys, sung by the Victor Light Opera Company, which in a fat four minutes would race through four or five songs (plus a reprise of the hit number) from each of the better Broadway musicals of that era. What a marvelous way to learn the highlights from the new shows, through the earliest ancestor of today's original-cast albums. Happily, almost every new

Victor list would include a new *Gems* record, for in those days there was no scarcity of fine songs. Not only were there the current musicals, but sometimes new versions of earlier operetta scores. In that way I discovered the lilting melodies of Lehár, Kálmán, Oscar Straus, Herbert, Friml, and Romberg. Though born and musically trained in Europe, the last three of these masters achieved their great and lasting fame in the Broadway theater.

During the last generation or so it has become fashionable to be contemptuous of anything as sentimental as operettas. Indeed, there was a period during my adolescent days when I would not dare admit liking such frankly romantic melodies as "Will You Remember?" from Romberg's *Maytime,* or "Only a Rose" from Friml's *The Vagabond King,* or "When You're Away" from Herbert's *The Only Girl.* Pure hypocrisy, of course, but I had to pretend to go along with the snobbishness of my contemporaries, or risk their ridicule.

There is no doubt that indifference or disdain for operetta music is completely genuine in many instances; with that I do not quarrel. But far too many people find it necessary to apologize for really liking the songs from *The Student Prince, Rose Marie,* or *The Red Mill.*

One basic and unfortunately valid reason for the prevailing disdain of operetta music could well be the inept and uninspired performances by some of our light-music maestros. Because the music is old-fashioned, must it always be orchestrally gimmicked-up with echo chambers and other studio tricks? Such treatment is justified when the songs are dull and cheap, but the operetta boys were gifted composers, and they deserve to be properly preserved. Let us at least have room for *both* approaches.

Victor Herbert himself, to judge by some Victor recordings he made in the early years of the century, was a top-notch conductor and had a joyful, yet sensitive way of conducting his music, as well as that of other composers. What a boon it would be to have some of these vintage performances restored on LP's.

Among today's conductors the only one who seems to have the knack for performing Herbert is Eugene Ormandy. His now-deleted record with the Philadelphia Orchestra of selec-

tions from *Naughty Marietta* and *The Fortune Teller* has all
the zest and understanding the music should have.

While on the subject of authentic operetta records, it is interesting to listen to music by Rudolf Friml as performed by
the composer. There is still one disc available, which consists
of individual songs played by a large orchestra, with Friml
ostensibly conducting from the keyboard. His piano playing is
rather charming in an overflorid style, with many pianistic
flourishes and ornamentations. Were it not for the presence of
the orchestra, one would have the impression of listening to
him play in an old-fashioned parlor, surrounded by overstuffed
furniture, autographed photos of operetta stars, heavy drap-
eries, and the inevitable scarf on the piano.

That traditional stage performances of period pieces can be
commercially successful was delightfully demonstrated as recently as the mid-1940's, when Herbert's *The Red Mill* was produced at New York's Ziegfeld Theater without any tongue-in-
cheek staging, and still managed to run for fifteen months. *The
Merry Widow* and *Die Fledermaus* also enjoyed long runs about
that time. Unfortunately, though, most revivals of famous
operettas, other than Gilbert and Sullivan, have not fared too
well in New York.

The summer theater is another matter. Since audiences in a
vacation mood go to the theater with less rigid standards, it is
much easier to please them with simple sets, a small orchestra,
and good voices singing familiar melodies. And so the theaters-
in-the-round, the converted barns and larger auditoriums, like
those in St. Louis, Kansas City, Fort Worth, San Francisco, and
Los Angeles, are filled with audiences returning year after year
to wallow in the nostalgic pleasure of the music they know and
love. They can almost be forgiven for humming along and tap-
ping their feet against the back of your chair, completely out of
rhythm!

The great vogue for operettas during the early years of the
century diminished as the pace of life quickened. Nevertheless,
there has always been a substantial audience not only for the old
standards, but for such newer favorites as Noel Coward's *Bitter
Sweet, Up in Central Park* by Sigmund Romberg and the Grieg-

oriented *Song of Norway* and Borodin-oriented *Kismet*, both by Wright and Forrest. Thanks to Jerome Kern, Richard Rodgers, and particularly to Oscar Hammerstein II, the operetta form has grown into a newer, more mature, and infinitely more satisfying theater experience through masterpieces like *Show Boat, Carousel,* and *The King and I.*

Years ago the need for swifter-paced musicals was satisfied to some extent by the brash, breezy works of George M. Cohan, the source of the first truly American show tunes. "Give My Regards to Broadway," "You're a Grand Old Flag," "Mary's a Grand Old Name," and "The Yankee Doodle Boy" are still being sung, but are often thought of as folk songs rather than show tunes. The shows were hardly distinguished in themselves; they were just cheerful showcases for the talents of the song-and-dance man and his engaging parents and sister.

Jerome Kern

Unlike most of his colleagues on Broadway, Kern was brought up in a household where there was much music. His mother, a proficient pianist, was his earliest teacher. Being of Bohemian descent, she taught him gay and charming folk tunes, and these served him well much later. He used one for the march played by the stage band that accompanies Cap'n Andy's first entrance in *Show Boat.* Another is a little polka Kern adapted for "Pick Yourself Up," in the Astaire-Rogers film *Swing Time.* This polka, by the way, served not only Bedřich Smetana in "The Merry Chicken Yard," but also Jaromir Weinberger in "Schwanda."

Kern's earliest professional experience was at the music publishing firm T. B. Harms, which later became his publisher. Once his flair for composing was discovered by the head of the firm, Max Dreyfus, Kern got the job of adding new songs with an American flavor to the scores of foreign musicals. The songs he added were not outstanding, especially compared with what was to come, but they had a distinctive quality. Alan Dale, a leading dramatic critic of the day, wrote about one show: "Its music by Jerome D. Kern towers in such an Eiffel way above the hurdy-gurdy, penny-in-slot primitive accompaniment to the musical show that criticism is disarmed."

A British importation to which Kern added music was called *The Girl from Utah*. For it he wrote his first great hit, "They Didn't Believe Me," the song that opened the door to a flood of offers. Kern responded with a succession of intimate musical comedies, full of endearing ballads, comedy numbers, and danceable tunes. Kern was represented on Broadway in the year 1917 by no fewer than five shows. Two of these, *Have a Heart* and *Love o' Mike,* opened five nights apart, and *Oh, Boy!* came along just five weeks later!

Kern was well aware of the importance of intelligent lyrics to go with his new musical style. Guy Bolton and P. G. Wodehouse—both British—collaborated effectively with him in breaking away from the stilted operetta pattern. Their lyrics were models of charm and wit. As far back as 1917 Kern said, "It is my opinion that the musical numbers should carry the action of the play and should be representative of the personalities of the characters who sing them. Songs must be suited to the action and mood of the play."

Although not as productive in the 1920's, each year Kern brought forth new scores, most of them head and shoulders above anything else being produced at the time. While still retaining his lyrical, flowing style, he was able to keep up with changing styles and fads in rhythms. Songs like "Look for the Silver Lining," "Ka-Lu-A," and "Who?" became great favorites, even perennial standards. To no one's surprise, it was Kern who, with Oscar Hammerstein II, created from an Edna Ferber novel the finest musical play of the 1920's, *Show Boat*. Here at last was the perfect blend of libretto, lyrics, and music. Six of the songs have become a part of our heritage; in addition the incidental music is full of wonderfully tender and joyful themes. On records there are excerpts from the score, but *Show Boat* deserves a complete version.

Great as *Show Boat* was, Kern later wrote two musicals that are in some ways even superior. *The Cat and the Fiddle* does not contain as many well-known songs, nor does *Music in the Air,* but each show is more fully developed musically. No matter how often I play through these two piano scores, I marvel at the beauty and variety of the melodies. *The Cat and the Fiddle* and *Music in the Air* have been even more shabbily treated on records, with not even one set of excerpts available today.

It is often difficult to pick one's own favorite among the songs of any composer. But oddly enough, in all that wealth of Kern music, I do have one favorite—"All the Things You Are," with a lyric by Hammerstein to match the endearing melody. It was gratifying for me to learn from Hammerstein himself that this happened to be both his and Kern's favorite among all they had written.

This composer's place in American music is well demonstrated by the fact that no matter how strongly fanciers of show music may differ about other men, they almost invariably agree in their estimate of and affection for Kern.

Richard Rodgers spoke for all of us when he wrote in *The New York Times* some years ago:

> Kern was typical of what was and still is good in our general maturity in this country in that he had his musical roots in the fertile European and English school of operetta writing, and amalgamated it with everything that was fresh in the American scene, to give us something wonderfully new and clear in music writing in the world. Actually, he was a giant with one foot in Europe and the other in America. Before he died, he picked up the European foot and planted it squarely alongside the American one. . . . If we were to look for one example of each extreme of his geographical range, we might find *Look for the Silver Lining* with its almost beer hall simplicity at one end, and discover *Ol' Man River* with its deep turmoil and strong native inflection at the other. Both are fine music and both are Kern.

Irving Berlin

Because Irving Berlin wrote many hit songs not intended for musical comedies, he is often overlooked in discussions of theater composers. The truth is that his contribution to musical theater is more impressive and spans a longer period than any contemporary. The 1911 edition of the *Ziegfeld Follies* contained the first Berlin show music. Fifty-five years later, well into his seventies, Berlin added the hilarious show-stopper "An Old-Fashioned Wedding" to an already bountiful score for *Annie Get Your Gun*, when the show was revived at Lincoln Center in 1966. Captious critics have complained that Berlin keeps reverting to the same old formula, that he never breaks new ground. Perhaps so, but the breaking of new ground is not necessarily a criterion for evaluating a song writer. Even though Berlin has played it safe, he has managed to keep up with the times, writing topical songs for such satiric shows as *Face the Music, As Thousands Cheer,* and *Call Me Madam.* But it is for his disarmingly simple ballads that Berlin will always be remembered. Composers in the current theater are able to write simply, sometimes, but the results are just not the same as "A Pretty Girl Is Like a Melody," "Say It with Music," "Easter Parade," or "They Say It's Wonderful." There is something basic and wonderfully down-to-earth in Berlin's music and lyrics when he expresses the soldier's plight in "Oh, How I Hate to Get Up in the Morning." Despite the fact that much of his fame springs from Tin Pan Alley and Hollywood, the man who wrote "There's No Business Like Show Business" is very much of the theater.

George Gershwin

The particular magic George Gershwin has always held for me is quite indescribable. It probably began when I discovered something unusual about his song "Somebody Loves Me." If you are familiar with the melody, you will note that after the rising, affirmative melody of the first line, there is a sudden doubting effect in the second line, as a beat comes before "I wonder who," and another beat before "I wonder who he can be." This imaginative blending of music and lyric intrigued me, though it seems to be lost on many pop singers, who insist on beginning the song with the beat. As time went on, I became

increasingly bowled over by the combination of humor, wist-
fulness, vitality, and invention in song after song, from show
after show. What a joy it is to discover songs like "Fascinating
Rhythm," "The Man I Love," "Do Do Do," "Someone to Watch
over Me," "My One and Only"—each with its own innovations.

Yet it is interesting to note that it was Kern whom Gershwin
called his greatest influence. Gershwin's biographer, Isaac Goldberg, quotes the composer as follows:

> Kern was the first composer who made me conscious that
> most popular music was of inferior quality and that musical
> comedy music was made of better material. I followed Kern's
> work and studied each song that he composed. I paid him
> the tribute of frank imitation, and many things I wrote at this
> period sounded as though Kern had written them himself.

Indeed, Gershwin was imitative of Kern, as I discovered in the
obscure "Some Far-Away Someone," from the 1924 musical *Primrose,* a song Kern could well have written.

Playing the piano versions of Gershwin songs, with their
often intricate arrangements, made me an avid student of all
show music, and improved my facility at the piano as well. In
the fall of 1931 I had the incredible audacity to ask Gershwin,
whom I had met through my oldest brother, whether I could
be of any use to him playing piano for rehearsals of his new
show, *Of Thee I Sing.* He told me that rehearsal pianists had
already been engaged, but kindly and generously recommended
that I drop in at the theater any time to watch rehearsals, that it
would be an interesting and instructive experience, if I wanted
to get into the musical comedy field, which I did, desperately.
As things turned out, I was soon put to work, playing mostly
for the chorus numbers, headed by George Murphy, a young
dancer who later made good in Hollywood, and still later in
Washington.

Listening to Gershwin himself take over the piano was a
memorable feature of rehearsals. There was a special kind of
electric excitement in everything he played. Fortunately for
everyone who listened, he loved playing his own music. George
S. Kaufman once remarked, "George's music gets around so

much before an opening that the first-night audience thinks it's at a revival."

Gershwin recorded several piano solos of his songs for English Columbia; hopefully these will some day be reissued, for they capture marvelously his own joy in playing. His recorded up-tempo performance of "Someone to Watch over Me" is unusually interesting historically. Ira Gershwin's fascinating book, *Lyrics on Several Occasions*, has this to say about the song:

> As originally conceived by the composer, this tune would probably not be around much today. At the piano in its early existence, it was fast and jazzy, and undoubtedly I would have written it up as another dance-and-ensemble number. One day, for no particular reason and hardly aware of what he was at, George started and continued it in a comparatively slow tempo; and half of it hadn't been sounded when both of us had the same reaction; this was really no rhythm tune, but rather a wistful and warm one—to be held out until the proper stage occasion arose for it.

That "proper stage occasion" turned out to be Gertrude Lawrence's unforgettable performance of "Someone to Watch over Me" in *Oh, Kay!*

In view of Gershwin's ability to compose in such a wide variety of moods for the theater, and his gratifying success in the concert field, it was not surprising that he combined these talents for the creation of an opera. *Porgy and Bess* was rather cautiously received by the critics and public when it first opened on Broadway. Theatergoers seemed wary of the term *opera;* the opera world reacted condescendingly to a modern work which dared to include so many accessible tunes, and was hardly opera in the traditional sense. It is not in my province to argue whether or not the term *opera* applies to *Porgy and Bess.* The fact remains that it is an exceptional theater achievement. It is hard to think of any musical play that so effectively portrays varied emotions as does *Porgy and Bess* in the tragic song "My Man's Gone Now," the carefree "I Got Plenty o' Nuttin'," the soothing "Summertime," the soaring "Bess, You Is My Woman Now," or the menacing "There's a Boat Dat's Leavin' Soon for New York."

Generosity toward his colleagues was a trait of Gershwin's which is rare in the theater. He was especially enthusiastic about the music of Vincent Youmans (exactly one day younger than Gershwin, incidentally), and he was directly responsible for Youmans' receiving his first Broadway assignment, *Two Little Girls in Blue*. That show had lyrics by one Arthur Francis, who later forsook the pseudonym in favor of his actual name, Ira Gershwin.

Vincent Youmans

Of all the major theater composers, Youmans had the shortest career—eleven years, during which he managed to turn out twelve shows. *Wildflower, No, No, Nanette,* and *Hit the Deck* were outstanding hits, which is not a bad percentage, and out of them came such classics as "Tea for Two," "I Want to Be Happy," "Hallelujah!" "Sometimes I'm Happy," and "Bambalina." Even when Youmans had little commercial luck on Broadway, his songs survived. Most of us are familiar with "Time on My Hands," "More Than You Know," "Without a Song," "Great Day," and "Through the Years," but how many of us realize that these songs were introduced in disastrous shows?

Even during his short career, Youmans developed a style peculiarly his own, and oddly enough, it has never been imitated. There is a quiet, inner strength and great inventiveness in his songs. Even when the melody is not particularly original, his insinuating harmonic and rhythmic effects are often quite striking. While the main opening theme of "Tea for Two" is not outstanding in itself, the sly variations are arrestingly ingenious, and they have had much to do with the song's enduring popularity.

Youmans' own favorite was "Through the Years," the title melody from one of his last shows. This ambitious and beautiful score represented a marked advance over what he had done before, and it points up the great loss that was Broadway's and ours when the composer's frail health forced him to retire at the age of thirty-five.

Richard Rodgers

The *Garrick Gaieties* of 1925 and 1926 made theatergoers aware of music by Richard Rodgers and lyrics by Lorenz Hart. However, I am somewhat proud of having discovered their talents for myself as early as 1920 in the Columbia Varsity show *Fly with Me;* their gay, lilting songs danced in my head for months and months. Two of the Rodgers melodies in that college show had lyrics by Oscar Hammerstein II. *Oklahoma!,* their first professional collaboration, was twenty-three years in the future.

Despite the early Kern influence on him, Rodgers, even at seventeen, was definitely developing a style of his own—an easy, graceful melodic line. One of the songs in *Fly with Me,* called "Peek in Pekin," is completely Rodgers, not at all like Kern. (Larry Hart, never averse to puns, later wrote new lyrics for "Peek in Pekin," and the song, now called "Love's Intense in Tents," appeared in the show *Poor Little Ritz Girl.*)

Between the first and second editions of the *Garrick Gaieties* Rodgers and Hart were represented on Broadway by an exceptionally charming period piece called *Dearest Enemy.* Set in New York City during the American Revolution, it was perfectly, if surprisingly, suited to the partners' light, airy style. The only song that may still be familiar to you is "Here in My Arms," but the score is full of characteristically lilting ballads and infectious production tunes, with wonderfully literate and sly lyrics, the likes of which are almost unheard of in a costume piece. Very possibly this was the progenitor of the Rodgers and Hammerstein era; it would be gratifying to have *Dearest Enemy* revived both on the stage and on records.

It is hard to pick one favorite in the Rodgers and Hart show catalog. I particularly like *On Your Toes,* with its devastating satire on ballet; *Babes in Arms,* full of such marvelous songs as "Where or When," "My Funny Valentine," "The Lady Is a Tramp," and "Johnny One Note"; *Pal Joey,* with one of the most adult books any musical ever had; *The Boys from Syracuse,* which contained "Falling in Love with Love," "This Can't Be

Love," "Sing for Your Supper," and the beautiful and less familiar "You Have Cast Your Shadow on the Sea."

The last Rodgers and Hart collaboration, *By Jupiter*, enjoyed the longest run, but was less inspired than those listed previously. The songs seemed to be oversophisticated and labored, with the notable exception of "Wait Till You See Her," which was cut from the show soon after it came to Broadway. How good it was to hear that lovely waltz, now restored, stop the show when *By Jupiter* was revived Off-Broadway in 1967.

When Rodgers began collaborating with Hammerstein on *Oklahoma!*, the sprightly quality of his music remained, but there also appeared a new open-air freshness, an added warmth and maturity. Hammerstein's previous experience with warm, believable characters in *Show Boat* and *Music in the Air* gave Rodgers a new dimension on his musical life. The sunniness of *Oklahoma!*'s opening song, "Oh, What a Beautiful Mornin'," established the show's mood brilliantly; it also set the appropriate tone for the start of the collaboration itself.

Instead of following with another musical in the breezy vein of *Oklahoma!*, Rodgers and Hammerstein turned to the poignant, bittersweet *Carousel*—as wise a move as it was triumphant in accomplishment. The score for *Carousel* represented Rodgers' greatest advance, with its abundance of wonderful melodies and its complementing of the tender glow of Hammerstein's lyrics. The music for *South Pacific* is not in the richly romantic vein of *Carousel*, nor should it be, but it is exactly right for the predominantly exuberant mood of the show.

The most beautifully conceived of all their shows, for me, is *The King and I*. The touching story of *Anna and the King of Siam* seems to have been made to order for their particular talents. Each of them had pertinent things to say about the adaptation. Hammerstein said, "What was required was the Eastern sense of dignity and pageantry—none of this business of girls dressed in Oriental costumes and dancing onto the stage and singing 'ching-a-ling' with their fingers in the air." Rodgers maintained that "a too-accurate reproduction of the sound of 1860 Siam would give less than small pleasure to an Occidental ear, and an evening of it would drive an American

audience howling into the streets. The score makes an occasional pass at the five-tone scale, but only in the interest of
color. I finally decided to write a score that would be analagous
in sound to the look of a series of Siamese paintings by Grant
Wood. I myself remained a Broadway character, not somebody
disguised in Oriental get-up."

If *The Sound of Music* is not up to the mark set by *Carousel,
South Pacific,* or *The King and I,* it does have much of the
warmth and simplicity so typical of Rodgers and Hammerstein.
One of its songs, the folklike "Edelweiss," has a lyric that re-
minds me of "I've Told Every Little Star," which Hammerstein
wrote with Jerome Kern for *Music in the Air.* There is even a
feeling of Kern in Rodgers' gentle melody. This was their
last song; a tenderly appropriate one to mark the end of a
memorable collaboration.

Admirers of Rodgers sometimes feel they must take sides on
the subject of Hart versus Hammerstein. This is nonsensical,
for both were wonderful in their completely disparate styles.
Hart would scarcely have done right by *Carousel* or *The King
and I,* and Hammerstein would hardly have been the ideal
lyricist for *Pal Joey* or *On Your Toes.*

Never content to repeat a formula, Rodgers followed *The
Sound of Music* with *No Strings,* a breezy affair which reverted
in some ways to the sophisticated quality of the Rodgers and
Hart shows, but with some inventive effects in staging and
orchestration. Another recent score, the one for *Do I Hear a
Waltz?,* is once again in a relaxed, melodic vein. Altogether,
Rodgers has been a refreshingly adventurous man in the musical
theater.

Cole Porter

Cole Porter's first song hit gave no hint of the sophistication
for which he was to gain his greatest fame. That first song was
"An Old-Fashioned Garden," introduced by Lillian Kemble
Cooper in a revue called *Hitchy-Koo, 1919.* This was a frankly
sentimental ballad, undoubtedly setting the scene for a lavish production number. Though Cole Porter was the most sophisticated

and worldly of all songwriters, there was more simplicity in him than his devotees would have us believe. There was also enormous variety. Most typical are the sparklers, like "You're the Top," "I Get a Kick Out of You," "Let's Do It," "My Heart Belongs to Daddy," and "Just One of Those Things." But when the occasion called for it, he could turn out a clog-waltz like "Me and Marie," a quasihillbilly tune called "The Ozarks Are Calling Me Home," or an outrageously corny duet like "Friendship." As something of a sentimentalist, I melt at such haunting ballads as "So in Love," "Night and Day," and the neglected "Ev'ry Time We Say Goodbye."

As for the shows themselves, there is little, if any, argument about what is Porter's masterpiece. *Kiss Me, Kate* has a succession of marvelous songs of infinite variety and imagination. Until *Kiss Me, Kate* came along, most lovers of show music considered *Anything Goes* his best score. Not I. My vote goes to *Jubilee*, which contains not only one of the greatest show songs by any composer, "Begin the Beguine," but also "Just One of Those Things," "Why Shouldn't I?" and a host of other winning numbers which may be a bit too special outside of the show itself to get much recognition. Notable among these is "When Love Comes Your Way," an affectionate takeoff on a typical Noel Coward waltz ballad. As for *Anything Goes*, it contains four fine standards: "You're the Top," "I Get a Kick Out of You," "All Through the Night," and "Blow, Gabriel, Blow." The other songs for the most part are second-rate Porter. When the show was revived Off-Broadway some seasons ago, the producers wisely substituted several other obscure songs by Porter for the ones in the original score. Ordinarily, I do not approve of indiscriminate substitutions; but in this case it was warranted.

There was another team that contributed a great deal to the gaiety of Broadway during the 1920's and 1930's. This was the trio of Buddy De Sylva, Lew Brown, and Ray Henderson. Like Irving Berlin, they played it safe, but also like Berlin, they wrote many attractive and breezy songs. George White's *Scandals* contained "The Birth of the Blues," "Black Bottom," and "Life Is Just a Bowl of Cherries." Then there were such high-spirited shows as *Good News, Follow Thru* and *Hold Every-*

thing. For these they wrote "The Best Things in Life Are Free," "The Varsity Drag," "Button Up Your Overcoat," and "You're the Cream in My Coffee."

Schwartz and Dietz

If Rodgers and Hart proved in the *Garrick Gaieties* that revue scores need not be just a hodgepodge of sentimental ballads and rhythm numbers to accompany production numbers and dance routines, Arthur Schwartz and Howard Dietz continued and developed the intimate revue tradition. Their first success, the litlting "I Guess I'll Have to Change My Plan," was introduced by Clifton Webb in *The Little Show* in 1929. The next year came the first Schwartz and Dietz song to become a lasting hit: "Something to Remember You By," which Libby Holman sang in *Three's a Crowd*. Like Gershwin's "Someone to Watch over Me," this lovely ballad started life as a fast dance tune under a different title by another lyricist. But Dietz suggested to Schwartz that he slow down the rhythm to accommodate the romantic mood of the new lyric he had in mind.

Their greatest triumph was *The Band Wagon*, which starred Fred and Adele Astaire, and which even today is remembered as something perfect in the way of revues. While the show was running, RCA-Victor issued a 33⅓-rpm record (the term *long-playing* had not yet entered the vocabularly), which featured Leo Reisman's Orchestra and the Astaires performing "I Love Louisa," "New Sun in the Sky," and the unforgettable "Dancing in the Dark." Arthur Schwartz supplied a piano solo for "White Heat." This, then, was the first original-cast LP. *The Band Wagon* was never produced in England, but as recently as 1966 the enterprising English branch of RCA-Victor issued this treasurable disc as a modern LP. A note to record collectors: the English number is RD-7756.

Adept as he was in the revue form, Schwartz was even more effective in writing romantic songs. In 1934 came *Revenge with Music*, a lavish version of *The Three-Cornered Hat*. The Spanish locale afforded him and Dietz the opportunity for richly melodic and colorfully exciting numbers. Two exceptionally fine ballads came from this show; one, "If There Is Someone Lovelier Than You," is Schwartz's own favorite among his songs. The other, "You and the Night and the Music," was initially banned from radio broadcasting because of its suggestive opening lines: "You and the night and the music/Fill me with flaming desire/Setting my being completely on fire." The fire has long since died down, and the song is one of our most respected and respectable standards. Twenty-five years after *Revenge with Music*, Schwartz and Dietz were still in top form, writing bubbling numbers for *The Gay Life*, with slightly but appropriately Viennese touches.

Aside from the score for *The Band Wagon*, the most appealing songs Schwartz has written are those for *A Tree Grows in Brooklyn*. The gay, tender quality of the lyrics by Dorothy Fields were beautifully caught by her collaborator. Each song seems exactly right—lyrically and musically.

Harold Rome

Like Schwartz, Harold Rome made his first impact on the musical theater with bright topical revues. *Pins and Needles,* produced by the International Ladies Garment Workers Union, contained, not unexpectedly, songs of social significance, as one song put it plainly in its title, but the big hit turned out to be a pleasant little item, which had little bearing on social consciousness—"Sunday in the Park." Quite different, and most rousing, was "Franklin D. Roosevelt Jones," a choral number from Rome's next show, *Sing Out the News*. The joys and problems of GI's returning to civilian life after World War II were dealt with penetratingly in *Call Me Mister*. The best-remembered of Rome's songs in that show is the riotously funny "South America, Take It Away."

By the end of the 1940's, when the revue form seemed to have been absorbed by television specials, Rome turned his attention and talents to book musicals. His first try was also one of his most resounding hits—*Wish You Were Here*, a good-natured musical about life in a summer camp for adults. The wistful title number summed up the mood of the show well, in addition to becoming the most popular song in the Rome catalogue. The composer's diversified talents were heard next in *Fanny*, far more ambitious than anything he had tried before. The result was a charmingly colorful and melodious set of songs, which beautifully underscored the many varied emotions and characters created by Marcel Pagnol in the film trilogy on which *Fanny* was based. Ironically, not a note of Rome's score was sung in the film version adapted from the musical; however, its themes served most handsomely in the background score.

Destry Rides Again, another stage adaptation of a famous film, was far more conventional, and had a most disappointing set of songs. The most recent score by Harold Rome, for *The Zulu and the Zayda,* found him in an unusual setting—the tense atmosphere of South Africa. Unlikely as this might seem for a musical play, the songs were properly atmospheric. And not surprisingly, the most effective were those he wrote for Menasha Skulnik, the Zayda.

Harold Arlen

Certain show composers, despite their considerable accomplishments, are not nearly as well known by name as they should be. Vincent Youmans, mentioned earlier, was one in that category. Another is Harold Arlen. Many of Arlen's greatest songs, like "Stormy Weather," "Over the Rainbow," "Blues in the Night," and "That Old Black Magic," did not originate on the Broadway stage. Perhaps that is why he is not immediately thought of with Gershwin, Rodgers, Kern, and Porter, when the illustrious musical names of the theater are mentioned. But Arlen has written memorable songs for Broadway. The most famous, "Come Rain or Come Shine," is from *St. Louis Woman,* which had indifferent success. *House of Flowers* did not fare much better on Broadway, but it had a hauntingly lovely score, including "A Sleepin' Bee" and "I Never Has Seen Snow," as well as the more exotic and exciting "Bamboo Cage."

Little of the wistful, deeply felt blues quality that is usually associated with Arlen's music is to be found in *Bloomer Girl,* a period piece about the Civil War. But the score has charm and grace, and it is a pity the songs are not heard more often these days.

Arlen, fortunately, is a persuasive singer of his own songs, whether something as plaintive as "Stormy Weather" or as jubilant as "Ac-cent-tchuate the Positive." The many records he has made of his own songs should help toward making him as well known as he should be.

Weill, Styne, Sondheim, Loesser

The notable career Kurt Weill achieved in Germany during the pre-Hitler years was matched by the remarkable way in which he was able to adapt to the American theater. The bitter, sardonic feeling of his German music was still evident in *Johnny Johnson,* his first Broadway show, produced in 1936. Indeed, it was appropriate to the antiwar theme of the plot. But by 1938 and *Knickerbocker Holiday,* his composing style, to some, seemed to have softened; to me it seemed to have acquired some degree of beauty and warmth, especially in the memorable "September Song." Two seasons later came a landmark in his career, as well as in the history of musical shows: *Lady in the Dark.* Weill's experience writing music for the theater and his incredibly rapid grasp of Broadway styles had resulted in a rich, broadly varied score (including such masterpieces as "My Ship" and "The Saga of Jenny"), which matched the incomparable lyrics by Ira Gershwin and book by Moss Hart. *One Touch of Venus* was a pleasant score in a rather more conventional style, notable mostly for another all-time favorite, "Speak Low." Weill resumed collaboration with Ira Gershwin in *The Firebrand of Florence.* Colorful as it was, the show itself was hardly a masterpiece, but the seldom-heard score had much interesting material and deserves more recognition.

Weill's two most impressive scores are the highly dramatic *Street Scene* and *Lost in the Stars,* a singularly moving work. It was during the run of the latter that Weill died. What irony that he could not have lived to enjoy the tremendous American success of his greatest European hit, *The Three-Penny Opera,*

when it was revived Off-Broadway. Its "Mack the Knife" also
proved to be the great hit of Weill's American career. Thus,
in a sense, his entire professional life came full cycle.

Among the most prolific contributors to the Broadway scene
is Jule Styne, responsible for the scores of such hits as *High
Button Shoes, Gentlemen Prefer Blondes,* and *Bells Are Ringing.* There is a professional, craftsmanlike, and occasionally
dynamic quality about his songs, but they are seldom distinguished. The exception is *Gypsy,* in which he captured so
vividly the brashest, gaudiest, and seamiest aspects of show
biz, and provided Ethel Merman with some rousing material.
Of tremendous value in making the songs so effective were
the sharp, funny, and knowing lyrics of Stephen Sondheim.
Although Sondheim is recognized for his lyric writing (*West
Side Story* and *Do I Hear a Waltz?* particularly), his musical
gifts are not so well known. The songs he wrote for *A Funny
Thing Happened on the Way to the Forum* were rightfully
subordinate to the comedy, but the music had some quietly sly
twists. Some day when he is given the opportunity to write a
show in which music plays a prominent part, Sondheim may
turn out to be one of the theater's most important composers.

Few composers have had as much interesting and original
versatility as Frank Loesser. After beginning with *Where's
Charley?* in 1948, he switched from its conventional formula to
Guys and Dolls, which portrayed superbly the raffish characters
and atmosphere of the Damon Runyon stories. Next he turned
almost operatic with *The Most Happy Fella.* Perhaps there was
too much variety in this ambitious score, as if he could not
make up his mind about the prevailing mood. But there is no
denying that the score contains an immense amount of colorful
musical material.

How to Succeed in Business Without Really Trying is far
from a memorable score, apart from the production itself, and
it has been judged unfavorably on that basis. I suspect, though,
that rather than write a series of lively, attractive songs, Loesser
decided to write music that underscored the fast-paced and

hilarious action in the show, as if he were doing a film background score. In that sense, he succeeded admirably. Unless one has seen and enjoyed the show itself, though, the record album is disappointing.

Leonard Bernstein

Leonard Bernstein has written only four major scores for the Broadway stage, but all four are such exciting experiences that he ranks as one of the musical theater's most impressive figures. Three are set in New York, but each has its own individuality. *On the Town*, an off-shoot of Bernstein's ballet *Fancy Free*, is full of dance music, with a humorous, quasi-Gershwin flavor, but still a good quota of romantic moods. *Wonderful Town* reveals Bernstein in a more satirical mood, with the foibles of the 1930's as his target. *West Side Story*, without question a great masterpiece of the American theater, is a marvelous mixture of highly dramatic songs, ballads, comedy numbers, and ballet music. *Candide* gets away from New York, but not from satire. Although the adaptation of the Voltaire classic left a lot to be desired, the Bernstein score is full of delights. With other serious composers, it could have come perilously close to conventional operetta, but that's just what Bernstein satirized so impishly. The result: a collection of such European rhythms as the waltz, tango, gavotte, and mazurka, all dressed up in totally irreverent style. He does not overlook opera, either, for the highlight is a devastating lampoon of coloratura singing in "Glitter and Be Gay."

Of the composers who have performed their own music on records, Bernstein is incomparably the most brilliant. His conducting of *On the Town* makes the score sound better than it did originally. And to add to the authenticity, four original cast members—Betty Comden and Adolph Green (who collaborated on the book and lyrics), Nancy Walker, and Cris Alexander—participate on this superb disc. Conductor Bernstein should give us more of composer Bernstein on records.

Lerner and Loewe, Burton Lane

The team of Alan Jay Lerner and Frederick Loewe has given great distinction and beauty to the American musical theater. Their first collaborations were amiable shows with a contemporary setting. However, when they broke away from the present and wrote about the past, their brilliance as writers came into prominence. In *Brigadoon,* Loewe, a Viennese, caught the Scottish flavor magnificently in his ballads, and especially in his themes for the ballet sequences and ensemble numbers. Next was *Paint Your Wagon.* Again, hardly the ideal locale for a composer with a Viennese background, but the score was rousing Americana, with a folklike quality in many songs.

My Fair Lady deserves more space in this chapter, and needs less than any show of which I can think. It comes quite close to being the perfect musical in every respect. There are purists who consider it a desecration of Shaw's *Pygmalion.* To me it is a highly respectful and beautiful extension of a brilliant comedy.

Camelot, which followed, was expected to be an anticlimax, and possibly it was to a certain extent; anything would have been. But *Camelot,* on its own terms, was a lovely show to listen to and to watch. Loewe's score is full of delectable melodies, some lilting and gay, and others in the haunting, almost rueful mood of *Brigadoon.*

Loewe's decision to retire from the musical theater is sad, indeed, even if it is hard to blame him for wanting to forgo the rigors it entails. If we are to look for the silver lining, we can find it in the fact that Alan Jay Lerner found a collaborator in the person of a composer who had been absent from Broadway for much too long—Burton Lane, whose delightful *Finian's Rainbow* enchanted us back in 1946. The songs which Lane wrote with Lerner for *On a Clear Day You Can See Forever* were among the most captivating in many seasons. There is nothing ambitious about the score; it just happens to have what the American musical theater so often lacks today—a series of wonderfully tuneful, bouncy, affectionate, and well-constructed songs. E. Y. Harburg, who wrote the lyrics for *Finian's*

Rainbow, once remarked that of all the modern composers, Lane has come the closest to capturing the effervescence so characteristic of George Gershwin. The music for *On a Clear Day* must, if anything, confirm Harburg's observation. It definitely does so for me.

A great many of the best show tunes of the 1930's, 1940's, and 1950's are not actually show tunes at all. They are the songs written by the theater's top composers and lyricists when they migrated to Hollywood during the heyday of screen musicals. De Sylva, Brown, and Henderson were the first to head westward, and they turned out a typically fresh set of songs for the Janet Gaynor-Charles Farrell film, *Sunny Side Up.* Soon they were followed by the Gershwins, Berlin, Kern, Hammerstein, Dorothy Fields, Rodgers and Hart, Porter, Schwartz, and more recently, Lerner and Loewe. These writers did not lower their standards in Hollywood; they turned out some of their most enchanting songs out there, especially in such films as *Shall We Dance, Swing Time, Top Hat, State Fair,* and *Gigi.*

In time, most of these writers returned to New York, but still contributed to the film song literature by long-distance. As this is being written, a number of Broadway musicals are being prepared for lavish screen production. Many will include additional songs by the original writers. And so these may very justifiably be called show tunes, even if they began life on the screen.

Time was when the principal requirement of a Broadway show was a good set of catchy songs and some unrelated comedy scenes, to punctuate as well as disguise the deficiencies of the wobbly book. The average musical would stand a reasonable chance of success, and could even play to half-empty houses for weeks and months without losing a fortune for the producer and his backers. However, today, with the musical theater facing so much competition from television and musical films, and with sky-rocketing admission costs resulting from economic pressures, audiences have become much more selective. Producers therefore have had to be more selective about the quality of the librettos for the musicals they bring to Broadway. The result has been far greater cohesion in book, lyrics, and music. The exception is the musical tailored for a big box-office name. There is a comparatively small group of writers gifted and knowledgeable enough to cope with the exacting requirements of tying together the components of a musical show. Most active are Jerry Herman (*Milk and Honey, Hello, Dolly!, Mame*), Jerry Bock and Sheldon Harnick (*Fiddler on the Roof, Fiorello, She Loves Me*), Harvey Schmidt and Tom Jones (*The Fantasticks, 110 in the Shade, I Do! I Do!*), Charles Strouse and Lee Adams (*Bye, Bye, Birdie, Golden Boy*), and John Kander and Fred Ebb (*Cabaret, The Happy Time*). Admirable as their work is, what I miss about it is an individual style. I miss the pleasure of being able to recognize a character-istic tune by this or that composer. The younger writers are too preoccupied with the integration of the ingredients, and not sufficiently concerned with the importance and permanence of a fine melody with distinctive turns of phrases and har-monies. Consequently, there is a certain sameness about the scores.

I believe that the music should serve as more than a con-venient crutch for engaging lyrics. It should have a separate life of its own, away from the theater. That may seem impos-sible, but it can be done—look at *My Fair Lady*.

9

Light Music

ROBERT SHERMAN

I HAVE always been unhappy with the phrase *light music*. It suggests bits of fluff, unworthy of serious discussion or attention. It calls to mind the sort of faceless tonal wallpaper we find with distressing frequency in department stores, supermarkets, and other places of commercial worship. Its connotation is that of music with little substance and less inspiration, not music to listen to, just music to be heard. Besides, it implies that Mozart and company are "heavy," and I am not ready to concede that either.

How then can we define light music? Simple. We cannot. The term is too vague, and the field encompasses far too diverse a range of material to permit any convenient pigeonholing. Generally speaking, though, I think it's fair to say that marches, dances, orchestral novelties, and all the other categories we tend to call "light," have one important attribute in common: They make their musical points directly, with a minimum of artistic subterfuge. By that I mean that a beautiful melody counts more than intricate thematic interplay, infectious rhythm, more than complex counterpoint. In terms of Sonata Form (to borrow a phrase from those "heavy" composers), light music frequently involves exposition without development, and consequently it flourishes in short forms rather than extended ones. Even the more expansive works in the genre (operettas, for example) are usually made up of comparatively concise, uncomplicated segments. A piece of light music, however, is not inherently any less imaginative or creative than a full-scale symphony. Brevity, as Shakespeare remarked in one of his heavier plays, is the soul of wit, and a miniature like "The Beautiful Blue Danube" is, in its own way, as perfect a work of art as the *Eroica*. This is not, of course, to credit Johann Strauss with the profound inspiration of Beethoven, but merely to point out that it would be pretty tricky to waltz to the *Third Symphony*.

The idea of music for casual entertainment is not exactly brand new. Cleopatra had her household musicians, Nero loved to play the lute (he once won first musical prize at the Olympics, possibly because he thoughtfully stationed the judges right next to his soldiers, where they could hear better), and Elizabeth I could not really enjoy her supper unless an ensemble of fifes, trumpets, and kettledrums came by to serenade her.

In bygone eras, like today, many of the most skilled and famous composers were engaged in producing this type of "light" music. We tend to think of Handel in rather staid, reverent terms, but old George Frederick wrote pieces to shoot off fireworks by. Telemann churned out dozens of suites of dinner music, Boyce concocted nearly two dozen birthday songs, and Bach devised a set of harpsichord variations to help out a fellow who could not get to sleep at night.

Long before the Strauss family got the idea, Mozart, Beethoven, and Schubert were keeping the Viennese well supplied with dance music. The stage comedies of Europe, from Shakespeare's day on, came equipped with songs and dances by all the big names: Lully, Purcell, Mendelssohn, Sibelius, *et al.* Saint-Saëns and Satie wrote music for the movies; so, more recently, have Copland, Walton, and Shostakovich.

Light music, then, cannot and should not be equated with inconsequential music. A waltz may be easier to understand than a symphonic poem, it may require less concentration, it may serve a subsidiary purpose aside from pure listening enjoyment; but it is not necessarily a less valid or important part of the musical scene. It is for this reason that we at WQXR program Coates or Offenbach or Gilbert and Sullivan with pride and conviction, and why we feel that a light-music wing is a logical adjunct to any well-rounded library of classical recordings.

Having established the fact that light music is a Good Thing, we are now faced with the far trickier task of coming down to specifics. As previously noted, the term embraces such a diversity of styles and musical types that completeness, or even comprehensiveness, is virtually out of the question. As it happens, four prime divisions of light music (folk, theatrical, Latin American, and jazz) are taken up in separate chapters; what I would like to do, therefore, is merely to go poking about the rest of the field, name-dropping composers, arrangers, and performers who have contributed to it in some special fashion, and talking about a few of the pieces I have found especially appealing.

Pop Concerts

Let us begin with the Pops Concert, a colorful institution, which surprisingly enough was not invented by Arthur Fiedler. In England they had Promenade Concerts as far back as 1838, the name apparently deriving from the informality of the occasion, which allowed the audience to walk about during the program. The musical menu was not terribly exciting—according to one contemporary report, the fare almost invariably consisted of four overtures, four quadrilles, four waltzes, and one solo number—but the concerts themselves were quite successful. About twenty years later the famous Monday Evening Pops were organized "to collect a permanent audience from the lovers of music resident in London and the suburbs." They did precisely that, flourishing for the rest of the nineteenth century, and eventually attracting such topflight guest artists as Clara Schumann, Anton Rubinstein, Grieg, and Paderewski.

One of the conductors of the English proms, Louis Antoine Jullien, came to America in the late 1840's, and it was probably this master showman who introduced the pops concert idea over here. I would give anything to have seen this fellow in action. They say he conducted with a jeweled baton, from a

crimson podium edged with gold, and if the piece were by
Beethoven, he insisted on wearing white kid gloves, which were
ceremoniously presented to him on a silver platter. His music
stand was formed by a fantastic giltcarved figure, and an
ornately decorated velvet throne stood ready to receive his ex-
hausted, collapsing form at the end of a performance. Despite
all the gimmickry, however, Jullien apparently was a fine musician, and since he made a point of including symphonic music
on all his programs, he did much to popularize the music of
the European masters in America.

The earliest American concerts with a definite tie to our own
day were organized in 1885, when the Boston Symphony Orchestra, barely four years old itself, began a series of daily
"Music Hall Promenades" (the Boston Music Hall being the
orchestra's home at that time). When Symphony Hall was
built in 1900, these summer concerts were renamed Symphony
Hall Pops, and later they became known more simply as the
Boston Pops. And now we *do* come to Arthur Fiedler, who took
over as conductor of the Pops in 1930 (after fifteen years playing violin, viola, celesta, organ, and piano for the Boston Symphony), and quietly ushered in a new era in American light
music.

From the start Fiedler had an uncanny knack for devising
programs that appealed to everybody. He made the Pops Concert an eagerly awaited event, not only in Boston but everywhere in the country that his extensive tours took him. He also
evolved the pattern that almost all other orchestral pops would
follow. I first heard the Boston Pops about twenty years ago (it
was at one of the outdoor concerts on the banks of the Charles
River, and Fiedler conducted the *Water Music*, which seemed
terribly appropriate), and as I recall, the general makeup of the
program was about the same as it is today. The first section
contains popular overtures, short symphonic suites, and a few
novelty encores; the second part ventures into more ambitious
literature, perhaps including one of the familiar concertos; and
the last segment blends show and film music, popular standards,
and humorous medleys into a razzle-dazzle finale. How can
anybody have the theme from *Batman* and the Grieg *Piano
Concerto* on the same program? I don't know, but Fiedler does

it, and it works, and I guess that is all we really have to know about it.

Although Fiedler's thirty-five-year-plus tenure as King of the Pops is altogether unique, a number of other conductors have successfully followed his lead, combining the more entertaining elements of light music and the classics. Louis Lane has done a fine job with the Cleveland Orchestra Pops; so have Howard Mitchell with the Washington National Pops, Frederick Fennell with the Eastman-Rochester Pops, and Carmen Dragon with the summer festival concerts at the Hollywood Bowl.

André Kostelanetz, despite his lack of a permanent orchestral affiliation, has been even more influential. He plays fugues, foxtrots, and everything in between; he has transcribed opera arias, children's pieces, and ballads by The Beatles, and his concert tours have built up a large and loyal following over the years. I find that Kostelanetz is particularly effective as an arranger of popular, show, and movie music, but his interests and energies have taken him far afield. For more than a dozen years, he has been a regular guest conductor of the New York Philharmonic, and he has commissioned and premiered an impressive list of contemporary scores (including the stirring *Lincoln Portrait* by Aaron Copland).

Over in England things have been bubbling too, thanks to such gifted composer-arranger-conductors as Stanley Black, Frank Chacksfield, and Robert Farnon. Their work is known here primarily through recordings, but it is consistently tasteful and appealing. Another famous English light-music man, and certainly the most imitated, has parlayed lush harmonies and cascading strings into a million-dollar empire. It was in 1951 that Annunzio Paulo Mantovani developed his "new music"—arrangements of popular airs and symphonic favorites, which emphasized overlapping violins and a warm, honeyed orchestral tone. Since then his record sales have been phenomenal (more than sixteen million albums in America alone) and his concert tours are invariably sold out. I must confess I used to look down a highly dubious nose at Mantovani's wall-to-wall background music, but I came to respect it more after attending one of his Philharmonic Hall programs a couple of years ago.

Watching him at work, I realized that he is a sensitive musician as well as a clever showman. And if he does go off the deep end sometimes, with soupy arrangements of *Carmen* and other classical items that should have been left alone, many of his lighter selections do have warmth and an engaging lyric sweep.

Composers

Of all the composers who have made light music their exclusive metier (not counting, for the moment, writers for stage and screen), I find Leroy Anderson the most refreshing. Not only does he have a marvelous flair for melody, but his pieces are laced through with sophisticated wit and all sorts of deftly amusing scoring techniques. "Concert music with a pop quality" is how Anderson himself described his work, and probably that is as close as we are going to get to a proper definition of his indefinable style. All I know is that an Anderson miniature is as immediately recognizable as a Strauss waltz, and most often just as captivating. We have used "Forgotten Dreams," "The Typewriter," "Sleigh Ride," "Serenata," and several others as theme music for various WQXR programs, and it is amazing how well they hold up after repeated hearings. In Anderson's case, at least, familiarity breeds added delight.

An English composer whose music has much the same sort of appeal for me is Eric Coates. He too is a superb orchestral colorist, and he shares Anderson's ability to come up time and again with seemingly inconsequential tunes, which quickly give the listener a severe case of can't-get-it-out-of-my-headitis. Not too much of Coates's music has been available on records in America, and I do not know nearly as much of it as I would like, but such gracious little suites as *London, London Again, The Three Elizabeths,* and *Four Centuries* all have their highly attractive moments, as does his charming concert overture "The Merrymakers."

In America we have the three G's of light music: Ferde Grofé, George Gershwin, and Morton Gould. Gould and Gershwin have several points in common: both were, and Gould still *is,* wonderful pianists; both wrote music for films, shows, and the concert hall; both have distinctly American styles, full of buoyancy and exuberance.

Much of Gershwin's most important work was done for the stage, and accordingly is described in the chapter on Musical Theater. The few concert works that come within our purview, however, are scintillating pieces of Americana: *Rhapsody in Blue, An American in Paris, Variations on "I Got Rhythm."* Gershwin once said all music, in fact all art, should be a product of the period in which it is produced, and he wanted his own scores to reflect the spirit of his age, even as those of the old masters had done in earlier times. He was, of course, totally successful. In the pieces just named, the roaring twenties are alive again, ebullient, impudent, and irresistible.

Morton Gould has split his allegiances even more thoroughly than Gershwin. He is a major symphonic conductor, he has made hundreds of transcriptions from both the classical and popular repertoires, he gives lecture-recitals, composes all manner of pieces for films, TV, ballet, and the concert stage, and he generally keeps himself among the busiest musicians in the country today. Gould's style as a symphonist can be severe and quite dissonant, but his music in the lighter vein bubbles along with a wonderfully jaunty spirit, abetted by bright tunes and highly inventive orchestrations. I have always had a particular fondness for *Interplay,* a zesty piano concerto of sorts which borrows the blues and other pseudofolk rhythms, and the *Latin American Symphonette,* with its heady, south-of-the-border lilt.

A fairly high proportion of light orchestral pieces are descriptive in nature, but one man has set up shop as our chief portraitist in sound. Ferde Grofé has sketched profiles of famous Americans (*Knute Rockne, Henry Ford*), captured the vibrant pulsations of the country at work (*Tabloid Suite, Symphony in Steel*), and painted the natural wonders of the land in rich, soaring strokes of instrumental color (*Mississippi Suite, Hudson River Suite*).

The inspiration for his best, and best-known, work dates back about half a century, when Grofé was a young, itinerant pianist, roaming the desert and mountain country of Arizona, playing in hotel bands, vaudeville houses, nickel-a-turn dance halls, and sundry other gathering places of the Western elite. In due course, he fell under the spell of the Grand Canyon. "It became an obsession," he wrote later; "the richness of the land and the rugged optimism of its people had fired my imagination. I was determined to put it all to music someday." That someday was more than a decade coming, but Grofé accomplished what he set out to do—he portrayed the incredibly vast panorama of the Canyon, with its drifting shadows and ever-changing moods. I love the *Grand Canyon Suite*. I know it is corny, and I know it is derivative, and I know it is played to death, and I love it anyway.

Whenever we think of music that is distinctly and uniquely American, we are bound to come around to the March King. John Philip Sousa was an international monarch, of course. At Queen Victoria's sixty-year jubilee celebrations in London, the Regimental Bands struck up a Sousa march, and in Germany, a Sousa tune was played at the dedication of a Wagner monument (some thirty years earlier, Wagner had conned the Philadelphia Exposition out of $5,000 for a perfectly dreadful "American Centennial March," so the turnabout was only poetic justice). Here in the States, no self-respecting parade for the last seventy years or more would have dreamt of stepping off without at least one Sousa march on tap, and for a while Congress debated making "The Stars and Stripes Forever" our national anthem. Sousa's music even sparked a dance fad which pushed the waltz out of favor in America. It turned out you could do a perfect two-step to "Washington Post," and before long, folks were not dancing anything else.

Ironically, Sousa always wanted to write bigger and better things than marches, and though he produced bigger, they were never better. He wrote ten operas, and all sorts of songs, choral pieces, orchestral suites, even a cantata. All are now forgotten, revived as curios once in a while, perhaps, and then allowed to slip gratefully back into oblivion. The march is what Sousa did magnificently, more magnificently than anybody else before him or since. As someone who spent three years struggling through third clarinet parts in an Army band, I can vouch for the fact that really good marches are in shamefully short supply. There are several fine ones by Edwin Franko Goldman, a couple by

Alford (the "Colonel Bogey" man), and some nifty circus marches too, but by and large, the great ones belong to Sousa.

The Waltz and Operetta Tradition

If Sousa ruled undisputedly as the King of the March, there was a bit of a scuffle before the crown settled on the true Waltz King of Vienna. The waltz, as you may know, came to favor over the collective dead bodies of defenders of the public morality, who found it indecent, immodest, scandalous, and otherwise much too enjoyable for comfort. It was, after all, the first dance where the partners actually embraced each other, and as late as 1896 a reformed dancing master, one T. A. Faulkner, published a graphic exposé of the ballroom, that "hotbed of vice, within whose treacherous embrace so many sweet young things have been whirled to perdition." With recommendations like that it was only a matter of time before the waltz became the rage of Europe, and nowhere did it catch on with greater fervor than in the glittering city of Vienna.

Johann Strauss, the elder, was the first Waltz King, and as properly befitting a royal title, it was passed down from father to son (albeit not without quite a struggle on the part of the father). For a while the men were bitter competitors, but by the time the senior Strauss died, in 1849, there was no longer any doubt that Johann Strauss Jr. was the monarch-in-chief. He soon merged his own orchestra with his father's old ensemble, and within a few years had built up a fantastic organization, numbering some two hundred copyists, singers, musicians, assistant conductors, and even press agents. On a busy night Strauss would have three orchestras playing simultaneously at different ballrooms in Vienna, with the Maestro himself merely stopping in for brief personal appearances at each. Waltz King or no Waltz King, Strauss also wrote hundreds of polkas, galops, quadrilles, and polonaises (not to mention sixteen operettas, about which I shall have more to say presently). And behind the ingratiating melodies lie inspiration and craftsmanship of the very first rank. Strauss may have operated within a comparatively limited sphere, but there he reigned supreme.

Although he was one of its most eloquent practitioners, Strauss himself didn't pioneer the operetta form in Vienna. That task fell to Francesco Ezechiele Ermenegildo Cavaliere Suppé Demelli, who quite understandably condensed his name to Franz von Suppé. In 1860 he produced the first of his successful operettas, and many more followed before Strauss began to corner the market effectively about a dozen years later. Little of Suppé's vocal music is heard these days, but you can hardly escape the overtures (nor would you particularly want to do so). "Poet and Peasant," for instance, is a marvelous curtain-raiser and still fun to hear, despite its ritual murder by first-year piano students, and so is "Light Cavalry," without which half the Westerns in Hollywood could never have been made.

As for Strauss himself, he sometimes was a bit ill at ease with the longer, more involved format of the operetta, but at his best he was, as usual, unbeatable. *Die Fledermaus* is a frothy farce, a fast and funny show with more whistleable tunes than anything you will find on Broadway today. Not far behind (musically speaking at least—I have never seen it produced on stage) is another brilliant Strauss creation, *The Gypsy Baron.*

The waltz and operetta tradition that the Strauss family brought to such elegant heights was continued into the twentieth century by several other composers, all operating at a worthy, if necessarily reduced, level of genius. In Paris there was Emil Waldteufel, whose charming "Skaters Waltz" helped earn him the nickname The French Johann Strauss, while in Denmark, Hans Christian Lumbye enticed dancers to famed Tivoli Gardens with a whole raft of tasty tonal bon-bons. He was duly dubbed The Waltz King of the North.

In Vienna itself, the torch was taken by such men as Franz Lehár, Emmerich Kálmán, Oscar Straus, Edmund Eysler, and Robert Stolz, who at the age of eighty-five or so is still going strong. My own favorite among them is Lehár, whose big hit romped into town three days after Christmas in 1905. *The Merry Widow*, of course, has hardly had a day's rest since, and deservedly so. The operetta is not so much fun to see on stage as *Fledermaus* (book trouble, I think the ailment is called), but musically it is every bit as good, with "Vilia" standing among the loveliest songs of all. Lehár also inherited Strauss's mantle in the waltz department, writing such twinkling pieces as the popular "Gold and Silver."

If nineteenth-century Vienna whirled to the graceful rhythms of the waltz, Paris was cavorting to the frenetic beat of the can-can, an escapade Mark Twain once described as "a mixture of shouts, laughter, furious music, gay dresses, bobbing heads, flying arms, and then a grand final riot, with a terrific hubbub and a wild stampede." And what Strauss did for the waltz, Jacques Offenbach did for the can-can: he brought it stage center, gave it cheery tunes to thrive on, and made it the throbbing heartbeat of a fun-loving city. I suppose the best way to enjoy the full flavor of the Offenbach operettas is to hear them in their original form, but I must admit to a personal preference for their enshrinement as songs without words, either in the various overtures, or as the buoyant melodies for Manuel Rosenthal's ballet *Gâité Parisienne*. Rosenthal picked themes from seven Offenbach stage works, and the impudent, saucy tunes, spiced further by the brilliant new orchestrations, seem to evoke perfectly the giddy spirit of La Belle France just about a century ago.

Meanwhile, over in London town, the reluctant team of William S. Gilbert and Arthur Seymour Sullivan was producing the cream of the operetta crop, the pieces that are to the lyric theater what Beethoven's symphonies are to the concert hall. You could write a book on this subject alone (several people have, in fact) without exhausting the fascinating details of this incompatible couple, who tolerated their collaborations as trifles that helped pay the rent, but hoped and expected to be remembered for more important works (in Gilbert's case, some of his seventy plays; in Sullivan's, his cantatas, songs, and his grand opera *Ivanhoe*).

I am not at all a true Savoyard, in the sense of knowing every song or even every opera. Still, a good production of *Mikado*, *Ruddigore*, *Patience*, or any of a half-dozen others never loses its luster for me. The satire of Gilbert's lyrics is remarkably fresh and pungent today (tell members of the Senate that their seats are henceforth subject to competitive examination, and their reactions would undoubtedly be a fair reenactment of the

Act I finale from *Iolanthe*), while Sullivan's music remains as fresh and warmly appealing as ever it was.

Just as Strauss had his disciples in Vienna, the Gilbert and Sullivan syndrome continued for a while after their partnership had collapsed. Sullivan himself teamed up with Basil Hood in 1899 for something called *The Rose of Persia*, and his protégé, Edward German, also wrote some fine pieces for the Savoy Theatre, including the delightful *Merrie England*.

In the 1920's and 1930's Ivor Novello achieved a pleasing, romantic fusion of operetta and show music, and Noel Coward brought the drawing-room comedy to superb musical life with such bitter-sweet concoctions as *Conversation Piece* and (come to think of it) *Bitter Sweet*. I also am enormously partial to Coward singing Coward, and have been since I stumbled, as a teen-ager, upon his recordings of "Mad Dogs and Englishmen" and the slashingly satiric "Don't Let's Be Beastly to the Germans."

In America the operetta influence came to Broadway for a long run, and later to Hollywood, with the vastly popular shows of Victor Herbert, Rudolf Friml and Sigmund Romberg. All three men were European-born (respectively in Ireland, Czechoslovakia and Hungary), concert-trained (Friml toured America as a classical pianist, while Herbert was the conductor of the Pittsburgh Symphony Orchestra for more than five years), and blessed with a gift for melody which really allowed the lyric theater to live up to its billing.

I came to know their works almost exclusively through the movies. *Naughty Marietta* was my first Jeanette MacDonald-Nelson Eddy film, and perhaps for that reason it remains my favorite Herbert score. From Friml I would choose *Rose Marie*, since I saw it in two different versions. Romberg immediately brings to mind such classics as *The Desert Song*, *The Student Prince*, and *The New Moon*.

I must confess that various stage revivals of these and other American operettas have not tempted me into attendance. I find something terribly dated about the plots, the lines, the whole heart-on-sleeve romantic atmosphere, and I much prefer to hear the lovely scores on disc, unencumbered by all the extramusical trappings. It is either that, or stay up and wait for MacDonald and Eddy to come around on the *Late Show*.

Films

The entire subject of movies is another of those vast categories, which necessarily will have to be short-shrifted here. On the other hand, a significant amount of first-rate light music has been cinematically inspired, and I do want to touch briefly on a little of it.

On October 5, 1927, movies cracked the sound barrier. It was at the old Warner's Theater in New York, and the picture was a creaky bit of soap opera, which cast Al Jolson as *The Jazz Singer*. It started out quietly enough—the first several reels were silent—but then Jolson spoke a soundtrack line heard round the world. "You ain't heard nothin' yet, folks," he roared, launching into "Mammy," one of the songs that heralded the beginning of the end of the silent era. Within months the studios were at work on the first all-talkies, and in 1929 MGM came out with the first "100% All Talking! All Singing! All Dancing!" original film musical. This was *Broadway Melody,* a typical backstage romance, with a score by Nacio Herb Brown and Arthur Freed, and it set a pattern for screen extravaganzas that held for more than a quarter of a century.

The vogue for musicals continued in the 1930's, heightened by the spectacular success of the aforementioned MacDonald-Eddy pictures and the equally famous series with Fred Astaire and Ginger Rogers. The latter films were especially rich in original music, since the roster of composers included such masters of the Broadway musical as Kern, Berlin, and the brothers Gershwin. Richard Rodgers is another stalwart of the Great White Way who has contributed songs to Hollywood films throughout the sound era, from "Lover," "Mimi," and "Isn't It Romantic," which dotted the 1932 hit *Love Me Tonight,* on through the two new ballads he wrote (both words and music) for the Hollywood adaptation of *The Sound of Music.*

By the late 1930's and early 1940's Hollywood was turning out musicals as fast as MGM could feed its lion, but gradually the well then began to run dry. Costs were rising, TV competition became a problem, and talent got scarce. Studios just were not willing to chance an original venture; they preferred to shell out huge sums for what they knew were sure things—the screen rights to such Broadway hits as *My Fair Lady* and *Oklahoma*. Outside of Elvis Presley musicals and similar films, there have not been more than a handful of originals in the past decade or so. *Dr. Dolittle* was the only one of consequence in 1967; then we'd have to go back to *Mary Poppins* in 1964; and I can't think of another really good one before that unless we return to *Gigi* in 1958.

A parallel development in the cinematic world has involved what Aaron Copland once called "a small lamp placed beneath the screen to warm it": the background score. Long before the advent of sound composers wrote incidental music—or at the very least, songs—which were played "live" by the local theater pianists. In more affluent houses, of course, this task might be taken over by a virtuoso at the "mighty Wurlitzer organ," or sometimes even by an orchestra of up to thirty players. When the talkies arrived, background music suffered a temporary setback. For one thing the recording techniques were fairly crude, so a ninety-piece orchestra on the soundtrack might not sound any more imposing than our friend at the Wurlitzer; for another, directors were so engrossed with their new task of putting dialogue on film, they seemed to dump in music as an afterthought, with little consideration for quality, or even awareness of the very real potential of music as an adjunct to the screen drama. Max Steiner was one of the first studio composers to change this concept, with his pioneering scores for *King Kong* and *The Informer* (the latter using *leitmotivs* to help with the flashbacks). Others who joined him in converting film music from a craft to a genuine art form were Alfred Newman, Dimitri Tiomkin, Victor Young, Miklós Rózsa, Erich Korngold, and dozens more as well. Most of them were classically trained musicians, and they brought to the movie score a whole new sense of form and proportion.

More recently a new breed of film composer has taken over; men often associated with the jazz idiom, musicians who can combine the melodic suavity of the old school with the modern sounds and tempos of our atomic age. Alex North, Henry Mancini, Ernest Gold—the list is long, and growing every day. Add to it some of the greatly talented composers of Europe—England's John Barry, France's Maurice Jarre, Italy's Riz Ortolani, etc.—and it becomes clear why movie scores (if not the movies themselves) are better than ever.

I have one final set of recommendations. Our discussion has centered almost entirely about the light music of America and England, with sporadic side trips to France and Austria. Obviously, there is much to explore from other lands as well.

From Spain, listen to some of the zarzuelas. These light-hearted stageworks are the Iberian equivalent of Viennese operetta, and they have much the same blend of frothy tunes and eminently danceable rhythms. Even if you do not like singing, there are plenty of nonvocal samplers about, containing fresh and not frequently encountered overtures, intermezzi, and other instrumental extracts.

Tap the wonderfully wide gamut of popular styles in countries around the world: English music hall ditties, French chansons, Neapolitan ballads, Mexican mariachi bands, the moody fados of Portugal, the pseudoswingy pop tunes of Russia.

Seek out concert music in the lighter vein from faraway places, and delve into some of the fascinating specialty items (several such discs are listed in the discography).

The world of light music, in short, knows no boundaries, and the world of enjoyment it can provide is similarly limited only by your own energy and enthusiasm in seeking it.

10

Jazz

JOHN S. WILSON

I KNOW exactly when I became aware of the joy of jazz. It was the day I stole my first record.

The record was "Wolverine Blues" by the Jelly Roll Morton Trio. I had never heard of Jelly Roll Morton, and I was not aware that what his trio played might be considered jazz. All I knew was what I heard when I cranked up our next-door neighbor's phonograph and lowered the needle on that shiny black shellac disc. A pianist played with a romping, stomping gaiety I found irresistible, followed by a low-register clarinet solo which sang with merriment. The piece was full of little asides and breaks, climaxed by a sudden, brief, high piano note, rapidly repeated, which for some reason sent me into ecstacies (it still does, I am still not sure why, and I have no intention of destroying this cobweb of pleasure by examining it too closely).

No one who lived in our neighbor's house ever played this record—at least, not when I was there. It seemed to me that it would be more convenient for everybody if I took the record home where I could play it at will and the neighbors would not have to listen to it over and over again.

I treasured this record because there was something about it that was different from the other records we had around the house—records that ranged from Wagner and Beethoven through Gilbert and Sullivan and Harry Lauder to "Cohen on the Telephone" and "The Two Black Crows" along with such dance bands as those of Joseph C. Smith, Edwin McEnelly, Joe Raymond, and of course, Paul Whiteman. One Paul Whiteman record stood out from the rest and impressed me almost as much as Jelly Roll Morton's "Wolverine Blues." It was "Mississippi Mud." All through it a trumpet kept appearing, played with a crisp, ringing tone and a punching way of phrasing which had an exciting quality I didn't hear in other dance bands, or for that matter, in Wagner or in Gilbert and Sullivan.

It was not until years later that I learned the trumpeter who had caught my ear was Bix Beiderbecke. By that time I had found out I was a jazz fan, and unwittingly, had been one for some time. On records and radio I had been listening to a wide range of what I thought of simply as "pop" music. But of the "pop" music I encountered in this fashion, the things I responded to most strongly were played by Duke Ellington and McKinney's Cotton Pickers and Red Nichols and Bennie Moten (his "Moten Stomp," played on a portable phonograph through a grating coat of sand on a beach all one summer, was another landmark "new sound" to me, like "Wolverine Blues" and "Mississippi Mud").

Discovering, in retrospect, that these were all jazz bands gave me the first indication that my musical interests were moving in a specific direction. Even the technically nonjazz bands that appealed to me then had some underlying jazz colorations —Coon-Sanders Original Kansas City Nighthawks, Ray Noble's inimitable English recording band (its inimitability proven when Noble came to the United States and recorded with an American band), even Guy Lombardo, whose essentially Dixieland orientation was quite apparent in his early records, are examples.

Because I arrived at jazz in this fashion, totally undirected, responding simply to sounds that provided a kind of stimulation unlike my responses to other music, I tend to look on jazz as an emotional vehicle rather than an intellectual one.

Some Background

In its early days, up until World War II, jazz was functional music, an accompaniment for dancing, and on its own, music that was basically entertaining. When jazz was removed from this functional role after World War II and became concert or listening music, an intellectual view of jazz began to take precedence over the emotional reaction. Along with this came a term that puzzles me, and possibly because it puzzles me, disturbs me.

This term, a descriptive phrase which has turned up frequently in writings about jazz during the past decade, is "the serious jazz listener." I'm not sure what it means. It has such a distant, austere sound I have difficulty relating it to the spontaneous, joyous, thoroughly emotional response I have to a really good jazz performance. And I resent the condescension toward us emotional respondents that the term implies.

I am not suggesting that jazz is not to be taken seriously, that it should be dismissed as something trivial. But I do feel that the best jazz performances are those that stir the blood first, the brain cells later. Lift me out of my seat, out of myself, and if I am so inclined, I will go back afterward and find out how you did it.

In any event, there are usually elements in the best jazz performances that simply cannot be dissected and labeled. The unique texture and intonation produced by Duke Ellington's magnificent growl-trumpet specialist, Cootie Williams, is partially a result of the personal chemistry of this man, Cootie Williams. You can isolate and identify certain aspects of his performance—notes, dynamics, manner of attack—but there is always an unidentifiable, unreproduceable X representing the quality that gives a Cootie Williams performance its individuality.

Jazz is the music of individuals, whether they are playing as improvising soloists or as part of an ensemble. Cootie Williams has his own X quality, and when he is sitting in Duke Ellington's orchestra, he is one of several outstanding and inimitable X's—Johnny Hodges on alto saxophone, Harry Carney on baritone saxophone, Lawrence Brown on trombone, the Duke himself at the piano, each of whom thinks, phrases, and sounds like no other musician. Together they produce an orchestral result that defies analysis or reproduction because there are too many X's involved.

As a result of all these X's the phonograph record has played an important role in the development of jazz—a more essential role, I would judge, than in any other type of music.

It is not possible to convey the vital qualities of a jazz performance in written notes, because the essence of jazz lies both in its improvisational nature and in the individual manner of expression within the improvisation. A jazz performance exists in its finished form only in the moment of its creation, when the musicians play it—and they never play it precisely the same way twice.

If the phonograph record had not come along, jazz would have had no permanence. It originated as a form of urban folk-pop music, played by and for a submerged minority: the Negro. The phonograph record provided both a vehicle for reporting a jazz performance and a means of lifting it beyond its ghetto origins to an audience which otherwise might never have become aware of it.

A Thumbnail History

Until jazz was first recorded in 1917 (by the Original Dixieland Jazz Band, a group of white musicians from New Orleans who were inspired by New Orleans Negro bands), it had apparently gone through relatively little change since it had taken shape as an identifiable musical form about twenty years earlier. But once jazz was recorded, interest in it spread far beyond the Negro neighborhoods of New Orleans, Chicago, New York, St. Louis, Memphis, and Kansas City, where it had its roots.

It reached out to such a distant spot as Ogden, Utah, where young Red Nichols, cornetist son of a traditional bandmaster, tried to emulate Nick LaRocca, the cornetist on the ODJB records. In Davenport, Iowa, Bix Beiderbecke heard the same records and fell under the same influence. And when Beiderbecke, having evolved his own musical personality, began making records, Nichols's playing began to reflect what he heard in Beiderbecke on top of the basic LaRocca inspiration from which both musicians worked.

Through records this chain effect has continued ever since, providing a constant stream of readily available examples for fledgling jazzmen, and whenever a strong and provocative musical personality appears—a Charlie Parker, a Charlie Christian, an Ornette Coleman—the whole body of jazz moves quickly in new directions indicated by these seminal personalities. As a result, the character of jazz has changed quite drastically and frequently since jazz became available on records.

In the twenties, the first recorded decade of jazz, it moved out of the small-group (six to seven pieces) ensemble improvisation which had characterized it until then, splitting in two directions: small groups featuring virtuoso solo improvisation; and orchestrated big-band (thirteen to fourteen pieces) performances, which allowed for short improvised solos. Louis Armstrong was the catalytic figure in the first category, while Fletcher Henderson's orchestra was the groundbreaker in the second.

The thirties were the decade of the big bands, the swing bands, epitomized by Benny Goodman's orchestra. In the forties came the be-bop revolution, led by Charlie Parker and Dizzy Gillespie. New harmonic and rhythmic approaches to jazz were introduced, and small groups returned to a dominant position.

The fifties were characterized by various forms of regression —"cool" jazz, a subdued, withdrawn, return-to-the-womb type of expression, as well as a search for roots. This search led some musicians (Dave Brubeck, John Lewis of the Modern Jazz Quartet) to an exploration of the jazz uses of traditional European musical forms, while others (Horace Silver, Art Blakey, Cannonball Adderley) emphasized the basic blues aspects of jazz, playing what came to be known as "soul jazz."

Freedom has been the focal point of jazz in the sixties— freedom in one degree or another from the traditional disciplines both of jazz and of Western music in general. Ornette

Coleman, John Coltrane, and Cecil Taylor have been in the fore-front of these innovations.

Despite these constant changes in the immediate directions of jazz, the music has developed lines of continuity. A musi-cian who reached maturity in one decade usually continued to reflect the jazz mannerisms of that decade for the rest of his career. In the 1960's Louis Armstrong was still a representative of the jazz of the twenties, Benny Goodman continued to play in the style of the thirties, and Dizzy Gillespie reflected the be-bop mannerisms of the forties. In all of these cases, however, as in the cases of most other jazzmen, the passage of time has tempered the playing to some extent. The real thing—Arm-strong in the twenties, Goodman in the thirties, Gillespie in the forties—can still be heard on records along with the work of other musicians, who have not survived so long. Records, in fact, carry in their grooves almost the entire history and de-velopment of jazz.

Learning to Listen to Jazz

Faced with this opportunity to hear the whole historical panorama of jazz, where should one start? At the beginning—that is, the recorded beginning with the first jazz records by the Original Dixieland Jazz Band?

It might seem logical but I would not recommend it. The contemporary ear must first become adjusted both to the musi-cal style of the Original Dixieland Jazz Band and to the limita-tions of its acoustical discs.

The best beginning, I think, is the unintentional one—the one in which you hear something that appeals to you, which turns out to be jazz. The next best thing is a reasonable ap-proximation of that situation: Start with whatever jazz you have heard that rouses a responsive interest on your part. This gives you a focal point from which to expand.

Let us say you have heard something by Miles Davis that caught your fancy. You like the pungent tone of his trumpet, and you respond to the attack of his group. This could provide you with an introduction to the avant-garde jazz of the sixties, since Davis's group, as of 1968, was touching the edges of that jazz style. It might lead you to the Third Stream music of the midfifties, through Davis's recordings of big band arrangements by Gil Evans. Or it could take you to the "cool" jazz of the early fifties, which was given identification by an octet Davis led.

If you start here, or anywhere, it is the opening door to adventure. Once you have made some form of personal contact, once you have had a positive reaction of your own, then you are on your way.

You are on your way provided you do not allow yourself to become stuck in the rut of your first discovery. You miss the point completely if you settle for the first jazz sounds you hear, and say, "This is it. I like it. I'm a jazz fan."

You are not a jazz fan yet. There is still a lot more to be discovered. Jazz is a music of constant stimulations. It can provide excitement on a variety of levels, from simple, direct, elementary rhythmic pulsation to highly sophisticated responses.

From whatever your starting point, you can, with the help of recordings, fill in the full panorama. The reason I do not suggest that you start at the recorded beginning, with the Original Dixieland Jazz Band, is the ear adjustments that must be made first. Once you have heard Dixieland recorded by a good band, under more advanced recording circumstances than those primitive beginnings in 1917, you can, quite literally, *hear* much more in the Original Dixieland Jazz Band's 1917 recordings than if you try to listen to them with no preparation.

An ideal introduction is *The Great 16* by Muggsy Spanier and His Ragtime Band (RCA Victor LPM 1295), even though this collection of recordings, made in 1939, was "enhanced" when it was transferred to LP—"enhanced" being an RCA Victor promotional term that means "distorted by the addition of echo." Spanier's band plays many of the very same tunes that were created and recorded by the Original Dixieland Jazz Band, which have become standards of the Dixieland repertory—"At the Jazz Band Ball," "Eccentric," "Bluin' the Blues," and others. In the Spanier versions the basic tune can be heard clearly, and the relationships of the lines of cornet, clarinet, and trombone are quite apparent.

Going from this to the ODJB recordings of the same tunes, you are much more likely to be able to follow what is happening than if you approach the Original Dixieland Jazz Band with nothing to guide you. Superficially, the Original Dixieland Jazz Band recordings might seem to be shrill and repetitious (but undeniably energetic). But if your ear can penetrate beyond the limitations of the recording, if it is aware of the lines the various instruments are taking (all of which is made explicit in the Spanier recordings), then you are much better prepared to absorb early jazz in its original reproductions.

And it is worth doing. The Spanier recordings are good representations of this type of music twenty years after the Original Dixieland Jazz Band made its mark. In fact they have a quality that has been caught by no other group before or since (largely due to Muggsy Spanier's individual X as a jazz musician). Even so, they do not have the same special spark given off by the Original Dixieland Jazz Band. They do not have Larry Shields's singing clarinet (another X quality) or Nick LaRocca's soaring cornet (more X). This differentiation is repeated time and time again in the course of jazz history. The same tunes are played repeatedly by various groups. Entire arrangements may be copied, but the final result is always different. It may be equal. It may even be better. But it is never the same.

Once your ear can supply some of the things that were left out by the acoustical recording system (which prevailed until the late 1920's), you can appreciate the distinctive spirit that enlivened the Original Dixieland Jazz Band. You can sense the drive and depth of King Oliver's Creole Jazz Band, which in recordings made during 1922 and 1923, provided the recorded epitome of the basic New Orleans ensemble jazz style.

Oliver's band, which played and recorded in Chicago, was made up of the cream of New Orleans musicians, including twenty-two-year-old Louis Armstrong on second cornet (Oliver also played cornet). In this context Armstrong can be heard as one of several sparkling elements—as an occasional lead cornetist, in slashing duets with Oliver, and with the additional stimulus of Johnny Dodds's wry and plaintive clarinet.

But the full stature of Armstrong as a creative jazzman was revealed in a series of records by his Hot Five and Hot Seven (recording groups with somewhat varying personnel), made between 1925 and 1929. If you listen to these recordings in chronological sequence—or even just highlights of the series in sequence—you can hear the sound of jazz changing.

The early recordings in this series reflect the traditional ensemble style that had been characteristic of Oliver's band. But as the series moves along, Armstrong's brilliance as a virtuoso soloist steadily takes command. The early ensemble performances change to a series of solos in which Dodds on clarinet, Kid Ory on trombone, and Armstrong, each have equal opportunities. And soon the whole object is to give Armstrong as much of the three-minute time limit of a 78-rpm disc as possible. Thus we hear him in a dazzling display of runs and breaks on "Cornet Chop Suey," his slow, insistent build-up during "Hear Me Talkin' to You," and the incredible excursions he takes on "Potato Head Blues." Tallulah Bankhead is reputed to have survived a long run on Broadway in a revival of *Private Lives* (Miss Bankhead, despite her flamboyant reputation, was not used to long runs), only because she kept Armstrong's record of "Potato Head Blues" spinning on a phonograph in her dressing room.

Armstrong's performances on these records changed the direction of jazz. This music, which had been identified until then with ensemble improvisation, was redirected toward solo improvisation as a result of his virtuosity, a direction that jazz was to follow with increasing concentration for the next forty years.

As a rule the early virtuosos were, like Armstrong, cornetists or trumpeters—Bix Beiderbecke, Red Nichols, and Joe Smith of Fletcher Henderson's band, who was blues singer Bessie Smith's favorite accompanist.

But the only jazz musician whose work in the twenties left as lasting an impression as Armstrong's was Jelly Roll Morton, a pianist, composer, and idea man whose musical conception was so personal, it began and ended with him. Morton's Red Hot Peppers, a group that recorded between 1926 and 1930, paralleled Armstrong's Hot Five and Hot Seven chronologically, and was almost as influential. Morton, a pianist, did not inspire followers, stylistically, as Armstrong did on cornet. Morton's main impact was in bringing an orchestral style to jazz.

His Red Hot Peppers was in the tradition of the small jazz ensemble, seven or eight pieces at most. But instead of turning every man loose on his own, Morton played his musicians as though they were the keyboard of his piano. The Red Hot Peppers were an extension of his own distinctively personal approach to the piano—an orchestration of his use of breaks, fills, runs, and phrasing. He knew precisely what he wanted, and dealing with musicians who were more accustomed to ad libbing than reading, he often had difficulty bending them to his will ("I just want you to play those little black dots," he insisted to a reluctant Sidney Bechet, whose natural inclination was to close his eyes and let his fingers find their own way on his soprano saxophone).

Depending on whom he had at his disposal at his recording sessions, Morton's directions sometimes worked and sometimes did not. When they did, the result was some of the most delightfully inventive jazz recordings ever made by a small group.

By the time Morton made these recordings, he was reaching the peak of a career as a wandering pianist whose mixture of arrogance and talent had lost him at least as many opportunities as it had won. In the Red Hot Peppers recordings he was able to bring together all his capabilities as performer and organizer. At exactly the same time a younger, less experienced pianist, Duke Ellington, was also beginning to create in orchestral terms in much the same way Morton did with his Red Hot Peppers.

Ellington's orchestral approach differed from Morton's in that he worked with larger groups—twelve or thirteen pieces in the early stages and on up to twenty or so in later periods. It also differed from Morton's in that it was less self-centered, and as a result, became threaded with a variety of dazzling colors. Morton's orchestrations were simply an extension of himself. A Morton sideman, given a solo spot, could inject some of his own musical personality into his solo, but he did it within limitations dictated by Morton.

Ellington, on the other hand, built an orchestral style that was based on the distinctive personal sounds of the musicians in his band (the fact that he was able to keep an unusually stable

personnel in his band between 1927 and 1942 had a great deal
to do with the establishment of an Ellington "sound"). The
growl-trumpet style originally brought to the band by Bubber
Miley and later carried on by Cootie Williams and Ray Nance;
the adaptation of this style to the trombone by Joe Nanton, who
was justifiably known as Tricky Sam, since none of his successors in the band since his death in 1944 have had his creative
touch with this strange musical tool; the peculiar talent of
Johnny Hodges for bending and stretching notes on his alto
saxophone; the imaginative use of half-valve positions on cornet
by Rex Stewart; the soaring lyricism achieved by Lawrence
Brown on trombone; the superb, visceral power in Harry
Carney's baritone saxophone; the dark, flowing warmth in
Barney Bigard's clarinet—all these and other very individual
sounds are the elements out of which Ellington has woven an
orchestral style that has taken on an inimitable identity. Ellington is the pianist in the band, and as pianist he contributes his
own distinctive sound. But his main instrument, as it was
pointed out early in his career, is not the piano—it is his orchestra.

Yet it was not Ellington who made the transition in jazz from
the small group to the big band. That was accomplished by
Fletcher Henderson's orchestra. Henderson was a pianist with
good connections in the New York recording world of the early
twenties. He had a band which was primarily a dance band,
but because it worked regularly both in dance halls (primarily
Roseland Ballroom) and on a variety of recording jobs (his
musicians frequently backed Bessie Smith and other blues
singers on records), he could get and hold very good musicians.
In 1924 Henderson lured Louis Armstrong away from Chicago,
where he had been playing with King Oliver.

In the course of a year spent in Henderson's trumpet section,
Armstrong helped to transform a dance band into a jazz band.
He did it mostly by example and inspiration (Henderson's men
were largely Easterners who had not had close contact with the
New Orleans-based mainstream of jazz until they met Armstrong) and through the presence of some musicians who were
on the verge of blossoming. Coleman Hawkins, for example, can
be heard on Henderson's 1923 and 1924 records playing a tenor

saxophone that runs a gamut from ordinary to utterly corny, while on the 1926 and 1927 records he has become the first vital and influential tenor saxophonist in jazz.

The enlargement of jazz from its early small-group limitations to big bands involving sections of saxophones and brass was made possible by Henderson's alto saxophonist and arranger, Don Redman, a conservatory-trained musician at a time when this kind of background was rare in jazz. Redman was able to write arrangements that permitted the jazz feeling of a small group to be transformed into a big-band context, though it took a little while for this to become apparent. Henderson's musicians, good as they were, did not begin to translate Redman's arrangements into really viable jazz terms until Armstrong's arrival gave the band a strong jazz voice and an equally strong jazz direction.

The Henderson band, which hit its stride in 1925, set the pattern for big jazz bands, a pattern that dominated jazz in the 1930's and carried on until the end of World War II. Benny Goodman's success in the midthirties—his acclamation as King of Swing and the subsequent arrival of the Swing Era—came very directly from Fletcher Henderson's band because Goodman's initial successes were made with arrangements that had been recorded years earlier by Henderson (this happened because Henderson, in 1935, was a staff arranger for Goodman). You can still rouse some strong arguments about the relative merits of the Henderson and Goodman recordings of such Henderson arrangements as "King Porter Stomp" and "Down South Camp Meeting." Henderson's performances are relatively rough and casual, built on striking solos. Goodman's have occasional solo moments, but their outstanding qualities are polish and smoothness. As a rule the newcomer to jazz prefers the clean impact of the Goodman versions, but as you get deeper into the music, the freewheeling Henderson records may take precedence. And there comes a time, I find, when one can appreciate the special merits of both approaches.

Even though Goodman won public acclaim as the King of Swing, the exemplification of swing in the Swing Era was provided by Count Basie's band, a loose, hungry, and tremendously exciting group when it first came out of Kansas City in 1936.

This was a band that played largely by instinct. There was no money to pay for arrangements, and the band relied on "head" arrangements (extemporized arrangements) based on the blues and built on riffs created on the bandstand. The core of this band was a remarkable rhythm section (Basie, piano; Freddie Green, guitar; Walter Page, bass; Jo Jones, drums), which provided a flowing sense of pulsation as opposed to the heavy, solid, 4/4 beat of other bands of that day.

The Basie rhythm section (and such Basie sidemen as saxophonist Lester Young) formed an important part of the transition from Swing Era jazz to the be-bop style of the 1940's. The easy flow of Basie's rhythm—one step removed from the strict, relatively static beat that preceded it—led in turn to a looser, more varied type of drumming, which came in with be-bop and has continued to be characteristic of jazz ever since.

This change in rhythm, which took place during and just after World War II, is an important dividing line in gauging responses to jazz. The whole aspect of jazz changed at this time. It changed from dance music to listening music. Solo improvisations, which had previously been based on melody, now used chord patterns as a basis. Harmonic structures became more complex. All these aspects of the new jazz of the forties set up barriers for the old jazz listeners—barriers that were intensified by the fact that most of these old listeners were cut off from jazz for three or four years while they served in World War II and came back to civilian life unaware that jazz had changed while they were gone.

At first it seemed to be the lack of traditional "melody" in be-bop that bothered the old listeners (there was melody but it was a new, nervous kind of melody). But the real source of the old listeners' problem with be-bop was, I think, the new approach to rhythm. For the same reason, listeners who have picked up jazz since World War II are apt to find the older jazz, of the Swing Era and before, difficult to appreciate. They are disturbed by rhythm to which they do not respond naturally.

This difference was brought home to me during a series of uninhibited jazz seminars I conducted at the University of Hawaii for several weeks in 1966. The participants—undergraduates and graduate students, some of them in their early thirties—were interested in exploring the various periods of jazz. Their curiosity took them into every decade, but their interest usually flagged when examples from the pre-World War II period were played. Our discussions of why this should be so invariably pointed to the rhythm. To them the rhythm of Benny Goodman's band, which had stirred a generation of youngsters to mad exhilaration, was utterly leaden. They heard it with different ears.

This is one of the challenges that keeps cropping up in jazz. It constantly demands that its listeners have new ears—a willingness to listen to "different" sounds. It is a challenge not all those who have considered themselves jazz fans are willing to meet. The change from ensemble improvisation to an emphasis on soloists, in the twenties, lost some early jazz followers, who would not go along with the new move ("It's not jazz," they said). The appearance of big bands playing jazz disturbed others ("A big band can't play jazz," they said). A really violent upheaval was caused by the arrival of be-bop ("That's got nothing to do with jazz," said the objectors). Every step along the way loses somebody who thought of himself as a jazz fan—the European influences introduced in the 1950's by the Modern Jazz Quartet and Gunther Schuller's Third Stream of music ("That's not jazz"), or the "new thing" of Ornette Coleman in the early sixties ("That's not jazz"), or the free expression, later in the sixties, of Archie Shepp and Albert Ayler ("That's not jazz").

Maybe it is not jazz. Or maybe it is. Or maybe it does not matter, particularly since *jazz,* as a term, has never been pinned down to anyone's satisfaction. (Duke Ellington, for example, does not consider what he plays to be "jazz"—he calls it music.)

But all this is part of the fun of listening to what is, for one reason or another, categorized as jazz. This is a maverick's area. This is the territory for people who don't go by the rules. It was created by musicians who did not know the rules. Even though, down through the years, it has developed traditions of its own, which tend to solidify into rules, the excitement continues to be created by those who are ignoring the rules.

So Charlie Parker and Dizzy Gillespie found their own ways into what became known as be-bop in the forties. To the Jazz

Establishment they were pretty shocking. But they anticipated
the musical temper of their times, and the tight, jabbing lines
they played are now part of the jazz mainstream. The cycle
turned, and in 1960 we find Dizzy Gillespie, the radical of the
be-bop era, frowning on the newly arrived, radical Ornette
Coleman, who was playing his own set of shocking sounds, and
asking, "Is he kidding?" Within five years Ornette Coleman's
ideas had joined Gillespie's in the jazz mainstream.

The process of action and reaction goes on constantly in jazz,
contributing to its mobility and to its quicksilver elusiveness.
Be-bop was a reaction to the apparent (to the be-boppers)
dead end at which the swing bands had arrived. The reaction
to the nervous agitation of the boppers was "cool" jazz, a dis-
passionate, vibratoless, withdrawn type of music exemplified by
a Miles Davis "Nonet" of 1948 and 1949, which in its style and
personnel forecast the influences of jazz in the fifties. The group
included Gerry Mulligan, John Lewis (who was to become
musical director and pianist of the Modern Jazz Quartet), and
Gunther Schuller (the propagator of the idea that there could
be a Third Stream of music flowing between European "classical" music and jazz). Gil Evans was the primary arranger for
the group. After a lapse of more than six years Evans wrote
and conducted some big-band arrangements for Davis (*Miles
Ahead*, Columbia CL 1041; CS 8633) which placed the trumpeter in a setting that brought out his lyrical brilliance and
helped to establish his present stature in jazz.

During the fifties, jazz—cool, subdued, fumbling back toward
its roots—tended to reflect the cautious blandness that affected
American life in general in those McCarthy-influenced years.
There were a few adventurers—notably Charlie Mingus, the
bassist, an individualist who got some attention, and Cecil
Taylor, the pianist, a groundbreaker who got none. But it was
largely a period of marking time between the explosions of the
be-boppers in the forties and the even louder explosions of the
free-formites in the sixties.

The major figure who rose in these later years was John
Coltrane, a saxophonist who had been around all through the
fifties. At first he appeared on the fringes as a capable member
of such groups as Johnny Hodges's band, Miles Davis's, and

Thelonious Monk's. Then, starting in 1960, he became the prickly and exploratory leader of his own group, moving rapidly from postbop explorations to an examination of Indian-oriented ideas (played on the soprano saxophone), and just before his death in 1967, moving into the free-form company of Archie Shepp and Pharoah Sanders.

In Coltrane's playing, particularly his last work, I find the feeling of wonder and surprise I first encountered on Jelly Roll Morton's "Wolverine Blues." It is still, to me, the most exciting thing about jazz. When you have listened to jazz over a long period, there are inevitably old, familiar sounds for which you have a very warm feeling. Those sounds are heard now invariably on records, because they are old sounds. Jazz—live jazz—is music of immediacy. You will never hear live jazz today the way it was played yesterday—even by the musicians who played it yesterday. The sense of immediacy will not allow it. When a jazz muscian delves into his past, you will either hear a tired version of something that once had life, or if you and the musician are both lucky, a new, immediate version which offers new wonders and new surprises—something that Duke Ellington, above all others, seems consistently able to do when he reexamines his past successes.

Jazz survives because it continues to be full of these wonders and surprises, whether they are provided by the remarkably varied virtuosity shown by John Coltrane on one of his last LP's, *Kulu Se Mama* (Impulse S 9106), by Erroll Garner remembering tunes he composed twenty years earlier in his 1967 recording, *That's My Kick* (MGM S 4463), or by Wild Bill Davison, showing that the vital juices of a basic but exciting cornet style need never dry up, on *Blowin' Wild* (Jazzology 18).

11

Folk Music

ROBERT SHERMAN

Girls and Folk Music began to interest me at just about the same time, and for some strange reason I have been partial to both ever since. It all began in 1946 or so, when I took my very first full-fledged evening date to my very first hootenanny. I did not know exactly what a hootenanny was then (I'm not sure I do yet), but according to the ad in the paper, it had something to do with singing and it cost only fifty cents. That was an unbeatable combination.

It turned out, musically speaking at least, to be an unbeatable evening too. A number of people I had never heard of got up and sang a number of songs I had never heard, and by the time they sat down again, I was hooked. At intermission I signed up as a member of a new folk-song organization called Peoples Songs, and when the show was over, I spent the wildly extravagant sum of seventy-five cents for a recording by one of the performers who had particularly thrilled me. My poor date had to go without an ice-cream soda that night, but I returned home in an advanced state of euphoria, clutching my membership receipt, my record, and the knowledge that I had stumbled upon a whole new world of music. I still have that 10-inch, 78-rpm disc, by the way. It is a triple header, with Pete Seeger singing "T for Texas," "Keep My Skillet Good and Greasy," and the story-song-with-banjo that was only the most sensational thing I had ever heard in my life, "The Cumberland Mountain Bear Chase."

At this distance in time I cannot say for sure just what excited me so much about folk music. I like to think I was perceptive enough to recognize the more substantial nature of the tunes and the more genuine emotion of the lyrics, as compared with much of the claptrap being spewed out by Tin Pan Alley. I doubt it, though. I suspect it was the vitality of the performers that swept me along. They sang with an infectious sense of joy, a high-spirited exuberance which gave the music a special impact quite apart from its intrinsic merit. There was also something vastly intoxicating about the way in which the audience was part of that music. I was much too shy to sing along myself, but even so, I couldn't help sharing in the electricity flowing so generously back and forth between the folks on stage and those in the hall.

At any rate I started going to hootenannies as often as I could, I became a charter member of the Pete Seeger Fan Club, and I practiced yelling for the "Cumberland Mountain Bear Chase" until I could usually outshout any other encore-seeker in the house.

It was another struggling young balladeer who administered the two-punch to Seeger's one, and completed my wholehearted conversion to folk music—Oscar Brand. One day he came down to my history class at Stuyvesant High School in New York City to sing American folk songs and explain how they had grown out of various episodes in the country's development. It was a great topic (I should know—I used it, in various disguises, for three different term papers in college), and it fired my enthusiasm to new heights. The very idea that something I liked so much could be both Worthwhile and Educational at the same time was folk music to my ears. I do not know about warm puppies, but happiness for me that day was walking my new hero back to the Lexington Avenue Subway, and listening entranced to him talk about his experiences as a minstrel. Needless to say I became a charter member of the Oscar Brand Fan Club forthwith (Pete, forgive me!), and from that date forward, woe betide the villain who came between me and Oscar's regular Sunday night radio show on WNYC.

There was an amusing sidelight to that radio business. Usually Oscar did his show from a small studio, but once a year he would move it to an auditorium and have an audience. Naturally I wrote for tickets, but then, suspecting they would be scarce, I cajoled my mother into sending away for an extra set, just in case. She is a concert pianist, and she used her professional name. Well, I got a form letter back: sorry, no room, try again next year. And Mother? She received a warm, personal note from Oscar, saying how pleased he was that so distinguished a musician appreciated his work, and that of course she could have the tickets and wouldn't she please come backstage afterward and say hello. So, prepared for the worst, Mother reluctantly went with me to a folk concert for the first time in her life. What is more, she enjoyed herself thoroughly (except for complaining that one of the guest singers was off-key), and was able to meet and congratulate Oscar with a clear conscience.

I started drifting away from the hootenannies in the late 1940's, mainly because many of them were becoming political rallies more than songfests, but my interest in folk music continued unabated. I sought out the occasional concerts given in New York by such (then) little-known performers as Josh White, Richard Dyer-Bennet, and Burl Ives, and I bought their recordings on such long-extinct labels as Asch, Charter, and Musicraft. Looking back on it now, I feel we owe a tremendous debt of gratitude to these crusading minstrels who spread the gospel of folk music long before it was either fashionable or profitable to do so. The late Carl Sandburg was another of those valued pioneers; so was John Jacob Niles, who still has a remarkable penchant for writing songs that turn into public-domain folk material almost before the first ASCAP check arrives (he has quietly composed many of our most beautiful "traditional" ballads, including "Black Is the Color," "I Wonder as I Wander," and dozens more). On the distaff side there were Susan Reed, Hally Wood, and Betty Sanders, all of whom have more or less retired now, and Jean Ritchie, who is still a vital personality on the folk scene.

I came to other, more international loves in various ways: Russian music, because our family had a friend in the Don Cossack Choir, and we kept getting free tickets; Welsh music because the New York University Glee Club had a language coach who had been to Wales, and we consequently sang a whole group of Welsh songs; South African music because I developed a violent crush on Miranda and kept going to Marais and Miranda concerts.

I must confess that the music part of folk music always interested me more than the folk. I sat in on one of Henry Cowell's courses on ethnic folk music at the New School, but somehow I could not work up any real enthusiasm for analytical comparisons of different versions of "Barbara Allen." I felt vaguely guilty about not being more fascinated by the field recordings from the Library of Congress and a host of other authentic performances, but unquestionably I preferred the more professional approach. Perhaps because I came to love folk music from the outside, as it were, rather than growing up with it as part of my own background and environment, I wanted a little showmanship with my songs, a certain basic level of refinement.

Now I certainly do not mean to imply that I could not—and do not—appreciate the earthy wit of someone like Woody Guthrie or the gravelly nonvoice of someone like Leadbelly. These men, though, were more than just authentic singers— they were born entertainers! Music was as natural to them as breathing; it reflected their whole life and gave it meaning, and their songs came to an audience imbued with the spark of their very special genius.

Nor do I want to suggest even remotely that ethnic recordings are oddball items, of concern only to the folk scholar. Nothing could be farther from the truth. It is often intriguing to compare an original version of a song with its transfiguration by a professional balladeer, and sometimes you will run across a farmer or a coal miner who sings with more spirit and musicality than half the recitalists at Carnegie Hall. By and large, though, these unpolished, roughhewn, sometimes primitively recorded discs are an acquired taste, and the beginning folk *aficionado* will do better to cast his listening lot with the professionals.

Again, and at the risk of belaboring the point, let me emphasize that there is nothing shameful about being a "professional" folk singer. Purists will argue the issue (and do, incessantly), but a balladeer, as Theodore Bikel once pointed out, is a storyteller, and it is hardly necessary for him to live the story he tells. You do not have to be a cowboy to sing a Western song, or a sailing man to shout a shanty. You do not need to be in love to whisper a love song (although, come to think of it, it might help at that), or be miserable to sing the blues. I grant that the performance of a blues singer with a hefty recording contract in his pocket will be quite different from the mournful wail of a starved-out sharecropper, but that is not to say that it must necessarily be worse.

The medieval troubador—the journeyman minstrel who literally sang for his suppers—was just this kind of storyteller. He did not fight the battles himself, or rescue the damsels or topple the kings, but he made up ballads about those who did, and he sang them just as entertainingly and as beautifully as he could.

So it is, I feel, with the Pete Seegers and the Oscar Brands and the Richard Dyer-Bennets. They are singers of folk songs rather than authentic folksingers, and in this lies their greatest strength. They can sing of many lands, in many styles, even in many languages, and since they are masters of their trade, be convincing in all of them. By combining sincerity and showmanship, they not only capture the essence of the music they sing but convey it glowingly to an audience.

So far as I am concerned, it is to these professionals that we owe the present high level of interest in folk music all over America. By showing that folk songs can be fun, they kindled a new awareness of our treasury of traditional music. By showing that folk songs can be popular, they removed the ballad from its rather suspect position as the darling of small, arty cliques in a few big cities. By showing that folk songs can earn their purveyors a fair number of coins of the realm, they paved the way for the incredible revival that swept the country in the 1950's and 1960's. Thanks largely to their efforts and accomplishments, folk music—which very nearly was a casualty of our ultramodern, ultrasophisticated society—made a dramatic comeback, and now gives every evidence of being here to stay.

The Revival

It is not easy to pinpoint any one person or event as having sparked this great revival, but certainly it would not be far wrong to suggest that the die was cast on the day four modern minstrels decided to form a singing group. They were my old idol Pete Seeger, Ronnie Gilbert, Fred Hellerman, and a rumbling-voiced ex-preacher named Lee Hays, and they called themselves the Weavers. Somehow the Weavers crystallized for me all the things I like best about folk music—the freshness, vitality, humor, depth of feeling and the spontaneous give-and-take among the performers and between performers and audience. I had heard each Weaver sing many times before at various hootenannies, but their work as a team was a revelation.

I remember cheering myself hoarse at their first Town Hall concert. "Wimoweh," a pulsing South African chant, promptly pushed out "The Bear Chase" as my all-time favorite number, and a meltingly beautiful Indonesian lullaby called "Suliram" moved into second place. I liked "Goodnight Irene" so much I even broke down and sang along.

This was in 1949, I believe, and by the following year, something astounding had happened. The Weavers' recordings of "Goodnight Irene" and an Israeli hora called "Tzena Tzena" were back-to-back best sellers, edging out such immortal pop items as "The Thing" and "Music, Music, Music." Folk songs on the Hit Parade! This was an incredible development, quite as inconceivable as jazz at the Philharmonic (this was Before Bernstein, of course), and yet, there it was. From that point the American folk renaissance was on in earnest.

Significantly, if not surprisingly, those early recordings were not really representative of the Weavers' art in actual performance. The big recording companies were scared out of their collective wits by the term *folk music,* and decreed that it must be made as unfolksy as possible in order to get folks to listen to it. The Weavers thus were saddled with flashy arrangements, added choirs, sometimes even jazz-band accompaniments. ("Yours truly has made a lot of records I cannot bear listening to," wrote Pete Seeger a few years ago, "but some of the worst were those which were made under pressure to turn out pop hits.") And yet, despite (or, who knows? because of) those atrocious trimmings, the records sold, and millions of people suddenly were introduced to this strange new music form called folk.

What the Weavers started, other groups and solo singers helped continue. A fellow named Harry Belafonte came along with his sensuous voice and galvanic stage presence, and there were millions of new converts. It was by choice that Belafonte used rich, cleverly sophisticated choral and orchestral back-drops. He never played an instrument because he wanted his hands free to act out his songs and help make his performance a unified theatrical experience. You may like his style or find it oppressively fussy (different Belafonte recordings have led me to each of those conclusions), but there is no denying its impact. Belafonte brought the Calypso craze to America almost singlehandedly, and he went on to place spirituals, blues, even lullabies on the top of the pop charts.

Then, in 1959, the Kingston Trio, a collegiate group that used ballads as a jumping-off point for semipop song stylings, recorded a song called "Tom Dooley," and the simmering folk revival exploded full force. It was just one band out of the dozen on a long-playing disc, but after a few months it caught on, zoomed to overnight popularity, and quickly became a public nuisance. Its syncopated rhythms came blaring out of every jukebox, every record shop, every top-ten radio station. "Tom Dooley Fan Clubs" sprang up in every state (even though the real-life Tom was long since dead and buried) and pilgrimages were undertaken to visit his tomb. The whole affair was the subject of long spreads in the major magazines, and by the end of the year the Kingstons—totally unknown a few months earlier—found themselves the most sought after entertainers in the land.

Far more meaningful than the personal success of the Trio, of course, was the fact that into the spotlight with the group went their folk songs. Dozens of other young performers, smelling gold in them thar ballads, hastened to work the same rich vein. There came the Travelers Three and the Brothers Four, the

Journeymen and the Highwaymen, the Raftsmen and the Shan-
tymen, until the art of folk singing was all but submerged in
the swoosh of an arriving fad.

The Nineteen Sixties

To speak of a folk fad is to project a basic contradiction in
terms. Traditional music, after all, suggests longevity, while a
fad, by definition, is a passing fancy. What happened in the
1960's, though, was far more than the pressing of traditional
music into one particular mold; it was its use as a catalyst, a
generating force for a long succession of musical vogues. When
the craze for folk groups subsided, there was an upsurge of interest in gospel singing. Then came blue-grass music (which
Alan Lomax once described as a sort of Southern mountain
Dixieland), and the even more jazz-influenced Jug Band music.
Joan Baez started what amounted to a cult with her pure
soprano, and her stark, intensely concentrated singing. Bob
Dylan came along and spawned a budding new crop of protest
and topical ballad writers. Lately the pop trends have sped off
in still other folk-oriented directions: folk-rock, soul-folk, folk-
jazz.

One glorious truth has emerged from all this: Folk music
has had, does have, and presumably always will have the re-
silience to survive both fad and faction. It may be a farfetched
analogy, but I cannot help thinking of all the feverish pop-folk
activity over the past few years in terms of the fabled Nile
River floods. It came on in a rush, with a huge wave that in-
undated what we might call the heartland of true folk expression. As the swirling currents receded, the trash and trivia
washed away with them, but some of the more worthy elements
remained, enriching and revitalizing the old traditions. There
also was left behind a more fertile soil of receptivity to folk
music. People who had been attracted by the surface glitter of
the pop trimmings stayed on to enjoy the deeper satisfactions
of the folk music at its core. Sure, there were a lot of horrors
perpetrated in the name of folk music, but on balance it
certainly would seem that the pop interplay has been a good

thing. The veteran minstrels have won a host of new admirers, and the crusading newcomers—both singers and songwriters— have given the decade one of the most prolific folksong harvests in history.

The "New" Folk Music

It might not be amiss to dispense a few thoughts on this pesky subject of "new" folk songs. Are we not again dealing in mutually exclusive terms? How can any song bearing a 1967 copyright be called a folk song? That is a good question. In fact, it is a good two questions, and they cannot be answered categorically.

My feeling is that the word "authentic" has many gradations in folk music, and that anonymity and extreme old age are not necessarily attributes of a genuine folk song. If they were, any minstrel who sang "Waterboy" (which is *not* a traditional spiritual, but a composed song by Avery Robinson) would immediately be drummed out of the fraternity. Was it not Mark Twain who said "a folk song is a song nobody ever wrote"? The point of his whimsy is that somebody wrote the song, all right, but nobody can remember who. In the old days that was quite understandable. They did not have publishing societies and publishing offices in the fourteenth century, and ballads served quite a different purpose. They were the newspapers, magazines, and back-fence gossip sessions rolled into one. They told of murders, hangings, wars, political intrigues, and all the other niceties of civilization. They were no more intended for posterity than the news page of today's Late City Edition.

When equivalent songs were penned in the twentieth century, our improved communications systems often meant that they were anonymous no longer, but it did not at all mean that the new songs were inferior to the old. We know that Woody Guthrie wrote "This Land Is Your Land," and John Jacob Niles wrote "Venezuela," and an itinerant entertainer named "Banjo" Patterson wrote "Waltzing Matilda," but the knowledge in no way lessens their status as genuine folk songs. They have entered the oral tradition, and are firmly part of the folk heritage.

What about the protest songs? They too have a parallel in years gone by—the broadside ballads, which not only told a story, but commented on it. They were the editorials, to continue our newspaper analogy, and whether angry, compassionate, or satiric, they bespeak the era that gave them birth. These songs have frequently served as the conscience of a nation and sometimes (as with the union ballads of the 1930's, for instance) they have played a vital role in its history. Old Man Plato knew whereof he spoke when he said (in the *Republic*): "Musical innovation is full of danger to the State, for when modes of music change, the laws of the State always change with them."

The singers of today's topical songs are doing precisely what their counterparts in past centuries have done. They are commenting on their life and times, and more often than not, trying to change them. And so Bob Dylan sings of the generation gap, Tom Paxton of war and peace, Buffy Saint-Marie of the plight of the American Indian. Which of their songs have value primarily as polemics, and which will actually go on to enter the folk mainstream? With a few exceptions (such as Lee Hays and Pete Seeger's "If I Had a Hammer," which has already entered the oral folk tradition in the South as a civil-rights anthem), it is too early to tell. I prefer to think of these contemporary ballads as folk songs in the making—songs, the worth of which will be judged, and the fate of which will be decided, by you and me and people everywhere, through immersion in that mysterious musical melting pot known as the folk process.

12

Music from Latin America

PRU DEVON

PEOPLE came to the Americas from all over the world, often bringing with them not much but their ambitions, beliefs, and creative abilities. From Mexico and the Caribbean islands down to the Straits of Magellan the dominant influence was Spanish, with the gigantic exception of Portuguese Brazil. Realizing that basic fact, people are inclined to imagine that Latin American music will sound like the fiery flamenco they heard in Spain or the dolorous fado of Portugal. It does not. Rich broth is a blend of good tastes, and Latin American music is like that.

I think one appreciates an unfamiliar art form in direct ratio to one's understanding of it. Rather than a little knowledge being a dangerous thing, I believe it to be the road to deep enjoyment. Thus even a casual grasp of the background of Latin American music increases one's listening pleasure.

Latin America may be the last area, and these might be the last decades in that last area, where genuinely exciting, viable music of the people is a way of life. Up to the present these people have sung their own songs and danced their own dances with a great deal of flair and spontaneity, since relatively few could afford the luxury of commercial entertainment. True, the ubiquitous juke-box made inroads, and movies were available in towns. But these were only drops compared to the avalanche of constantly available sound provided by the inexpensive transistor radio. I brought my transistor with me on my last visit to South America, and I was delighted that most of the radio stations had up to that time escaped serious commercialization and were broadcasting authentic music of the region many hours daily. My dread is that some day the fine sharp differences will become blurred, so that there will be a homogenized genre, a sort of basic Latin American music.

Latin American popular dance rhythms have spread virtually around the globe. (I have a weird little subcollection of tangos from such unexpected countries as Iceland, Australia, Japan, and Saudi Arabia.) Many people get their first taste of Latin American music on the dance floor, finding the tricky rhythm patterns and varied percussion instruments intriguing. Apparently my inner rhythm went counterclockwise and for an ironic reason. When I first heard such innovations as rumba, conga, and son (not a law-firm, the son is a dance), I definitely disliked them! I came from England to the United States in my teens, and I now realize that I was a musical prig. I had had a fine piano and singing teacher who not only got me through the annual Royal Academy exams but also gave me a great enthusiasm for European folk music. I sneered at popular dance music generally, but for some absurd reason I sneered even more haughtily at the vigorous Caribbean dances just coming in at that time.

Later I went to Mexico, where I fell in love with the melodic and richly varied songs. A series of voyages of musical discovery to central South America turned this love affair into an enduring marriage, and I have had the delight and fulfillment of presenting *Nights in Latin America* for more than twenty years.

Folk music traditionally is born "from the soil." I know of no other area in the world so dominated by the dramatic structure of the land as is Latin America. From the Sierra Madres in Mexico, the Central American volcanic chain and the majestic ramparts of the Andes, to enormous, barely passable rain forests and the incredible Amazon, the land itself creates massive barriers. Jungle, pampa, the vast sierras, deep valleys, and canyons all compel much of the population to live in comparative isolation. This is why archaic, curious instruments and strands of melody survive despite the rapid advances of the machine age in and about cities.

The term *folk music* is so elastic, particularly in Latin America, that I prefer to say *regional* unless I am certain there is no known composer or arranger. In South America several composers have specialized in writing in a style that has the qualities of folk music. In other words, they create songs and dances which express the flavor of a specific region in an "enriched" tonality. Two such recordings of unsurpassed beauty listed in my discography are *The South American Suite* based on typical music of Peru, Uruguay, Paraguay, and Argentina, and the magnificent *Misa Criolla* in which the Mass is brilliantly set to authentic Argentine folk forms. On a slighter scale, the opening and closing theme of *Nights in Latin America*, "Los Carnavales," is an example of authentic Indian melody, a Peruvian circle dance known as a Huayño, which was collected by Rosendo Huirse and arranged and orchestrated by his son Jorge.

"Los Carnavales"

The story about "Los Carnavales" that I like best is so fantastic you will find it hard to accept. I swear, however, that every word is true:

Cuzco was the capital city of the Incas (an accepted misnomer, since only the emperor was "the Inca"). The town lies far from Lima, up in the easternmost fold of the Peruvian Andes. Quite far from Cuzco is a village called Pisac, which visitors remember because the men blow conch-shell trumpets there every Sunday. Quite far from Pisac, over a precarious switchback road called *muy sinuouso*, is a tiny hamlet called Paucartambo, which looks as if no white man had ever been there. Its music, played only on pipes and drums, is unadulterated Indian.

The Director of Indian Affairs in Lima had advised me that a unique fiesta took place in July in Paucartambo. So there, after a series of almost-accidents and ludicrous problems, was

"your commentator and guide to *Nights in Latin America*," alone
and unable to speak the Quechuan Indian tongue of highland
Peru. I could write a hundred pages of this enchanted episode,
from the moment the burly handsome mayor in pantomime
basic Spanish invited me to "sleep with him" (it was a great
family dormitory set up for the occasion) to my affectionate
leavetaking five days later (at fiesta time jeeps come in one day
and out the other because the road is so narrow).

One after another, little groups of costumed Indians arrived,
mostly in wonderful, vividly colored costumes, some with huge
feathered headdresses, some with weird masks. They came from
enormous distances to pay homage to the Virgin of Paucartambo. For three days and the two intervening nights there was
rarely a moment of silence, though the people were not vocally
noisy at all. It was a trancelike experience, a timeless ballet of
oddly simple dances and haunting pentatonic melodies breathed
through a variety of flutes and pipes to the occasional thudding
of a drum. I was astonished at the acumen of the mayor's tiny
grandson, who sat on my lap and identified each dancing group
by its special little tune. "Eso es Los Chunchos," he would explain, or "Eso es Los Llameros." After all, he had attended this
fiesta each of his six years.

When a small Andean village has a special fiesta it enjoys
splurging a bit in the evening and having mestizo entertainment
rather than unmixed Indian fare. Lack of electricity rules out
loud radios or juke boxes, so the villagers arrange for a truck
to come from Cuzco with a generator, a record player, and a
selection of locally popular records. The mayor had most gra-
ciously invited me to come with him to the opening of the
temporary outdoor cantina. We pushed our way through a herd
of llamas that had been "parked" while their owners celebrated.
And then, just as we entered the enclosure all decorated with
paper flowers, fringed tissue paper and rush lanterns, *what* do
you suppose came blasting out from the sound truck? With
literally hundreds of Huayños to choose from, it was the theme
of my program, the Peruvian Huayño "Los Carnavales!" You
could say it was sheer coincidence, and I would agree rationally.
But I assure you that as the mayor and I solemnly drank each

other's health in the fiery chicha, I listened with almost agonized delight to "Los Carnavales" in its native setting, something I will never forget.

Before the white men came, nomadic Indians wandered the land with primitive culture and minimal music. Their instruments were made of cane, earth, bones, and shells. In Mexico and the central Andes, however, there were two advanced and splendid civilizations boasting a highly developed music, which was considered an essential part of a nobleman's life.

The Aztecs and the Incas had the gold that drew the conquistadores and subsequent adventurers and treasure hunters. These men came from Spain without wives or families. They intermarried with the Indian women, thereby starting a new race. African slaves were brought in to cultivate the lucrative tropical crops, and here again new mutations resulted.

To me the rainbow beautifully symbolizes the emotional and musical life of Latin America. While it has pure red, yellow, and blue, the rainbow's loveliness is enhanced by its graduated shadings. Similarly, the blends of the primary Indian, Iberian, and African musical colors rival their basic ingredients in appeal and variety.

Because these three elements and all their prismatic blendings dazzle and at times confuse, for clarity I would like to discuss them separately: Aztec and Inca foundations, Spain the conqueror and catalyst, Africa as a tropical modifier, and Brazil, where Portuguese and African elements combine.

Aztec and Inca

Latin American music owes to the Aztecs and Incas whatever pre-Columbian flavor it has. From the musical point of view it is remarkable how similar these two widely separated civilizations were in their five-toned scale, use of flutes and percussion instruments, and even their attitudes toward singing, dancing, and playing, which they considered virtually inseparable. Neither the Aztecs nor the Incas had any word for *music* as an abstract concept, but both highly valued its performance. The Aztecs, in fact, were known to have put performers to death for a missed dance step, a crude voice, or a false rhythm, because this might well offend the gods!

Both the Aztecs and the Indians used their music ceremonially. It was tied in with their respective sun gods and the pantheon of deities controlled by the powerful priest-aristocracy. It was used for military encouragement and victory celebrations also. For both of these reasons, the pagan music was almost doomed once the Spanish missionaries got to work. What saved it was that many of the priests cleverly adapted the agricultural cycle of festivals to the Catholic cycle of fiestas, exactly as they had superimposed churches on the foundations of temples which they had destroyed. "Operation Superimpose," if I may so call it, affected Mexican music more than Peruvian, Ecuadorian, and Bolivian. I think part of the reason for this is the actual structure of the land.

Mexico, while mostly a high mountainous plateau gouged by occasional canyons, is far more accessible than the Andean altiplano. It was relatively easy for zealous missionaries to infiltrate most of the country and in so doing to affect the music deeply. They did this by introducing guitars and harps to accompany the religious songs and by outlawing instruments directly associated with ritual or the military. They converted the complex dances in elaborate costume, headdress, or mask into something of an Hispanic cast, such as battles between the Moors and the Christians or little Bible stories in pantomime. Thus the dances and costumes fared better than the music. Other elements of pre-Columbian "sound" were quickly absorbed and enriched by the addition of stringed instruments. Today Mexican music is a fusion from which it is impossible to pluck out one melody or one rhythm and say with authority: "This is pure Indian" or "This is pure Spanish."

The Central Andean phases of "Operation Superimpose" developed quite differently from the Mexican. The overpowering ramparts of the Andes tended to discourage missionary work. Exceptions were the great capitals at Cuzco and Quito, where priests flocked to stamp out paganism at its chief centers. As for the highlands generally, they were so vast, and the pastoral valleys where Indians lived were so separated, that relatively few priests penetrated them. Those who did settle in villages had to cover so much territory they simply could not know about the many rituals of sun worship, llama-shearing, plowing, and harvesting. In this manner many of the archaic songs and dances endured.

Even the instruments themselves conspired. The large unique drums, so essential to the Aztecs' complicated dances, were quickly destroyed on the grounds they were flagrantly pagan. The Incas, who stressed melody more strongly than rhythm, used smaller tools: conch shells, flutes of great variety, and above all, superb pipes of pan. These were much easier to conceal, and also much easier to replace if confiscated.

There are recordings that give an idea of how these virtually extinct pre-Columbian instruments sounded, as well as the pan pipes still in use, like those of Carlos Chavez, Ballet Folklorico, GNP, Mexican Fiesta (Monitor), Laura Boulton (Folkways), and Gods and Demons of Bolivia (Vanguard).

A postscript to the Indian chapter of the story: In the mammoth Amazonian jungles and other rain-forest areas there still are nomadic Indians whose lives and music are almost untouched by five centuries of white men's presence. They were untouched also by the high cultural levels of the Aztec and Inca. Theirs is a pragmatic, special-purpose music, used to accompany the grinding of manioc, the roasting of fish, the coming-of-age of children, the propitiation of forest spirits, and the intricate machinations of witchcraft. I know of one tune used exclusively while trimming a chief's headdress with macaw feathers! Another useful and specialized form is animal sounds employed as a hunting lure. This was elegantly utilized by the fabulous but real Yma Sumac, whose superb "Chuncho" jungle song is on the regrettably out-of-print *Voice of the Xtabay* (Capitol W-684). Generally speaking, however, this ethnic music has limited appeal and rarely merges with any other.

European Influence

The second rainbow color or ethnic influence came from the Iberian Peninsula. Spain influenced indigenous music from the moment the first wave of priests followed the conquistadores.

Because the invaders' first step was to obliterate everything associated with the pre-Columbian religions, they destroyed hundreds of instruments and prohibited ritual dancing. Then they contrived to teach the Indians versions of Christianity, which they hoped would appeal to a naïve audience. They used songs and playlets dealing with Bible stories. "Civilized" dancing was introduced, to the accompaniment of the first stringed instruments to be heard in this hemisphere—small portable harps and guitars.

These instruments were a tremendous success almost immediately. Previously, the priests had got nowhere in Paraguay, where the nomadic Guarani tribes slipped through the Chaco like elusive deer. Jesuit missionaries found it was as difficult to pick up quicksilver as to win these people by conversion. But when the priests took to sailing down the rivers on rafts, playing and singing, the lovely sound of their harps completely seduced the Indians, who eagerly crept closer and closer to accept baptism. To this day, the harp is by far the most popular instrument in Paraguay.

By the time colonists were starting to make up a sizable slice of the population, religious music had become well established in Mexico and was making itself heard throughout the conquered areas. The colonists also brought their secular songs and their marvelous, vibrant dances. Spain has always been marked by a dazzling musical diversity, as you will realize if you try to hear in your imagination, say, flamenco seguidillas from Andalucia, a Basque choral group, a fandango from Castile, bagpipes from Galicia, and a vivacious jota from La Mancha. (Incidentally, if you want to make this imagined sampling actual, try to track down a copy of the volume on Spain in Columbia's *World Library of Folk and Primitive Music* [SL 216].)

We skip lightly over several centuries, during which the church gradually relaxed its tight control and various tidal waves of musical impulses swept in from abroad. Soon Viceregal Lima (and to a lesser degree such other emerging cities as Bogota, Caracas, and Santiago) delightedly welcomed various dances that came direct from the courts of Europe. The gavotte, minuet, sarabande, pavana, pasacalle, and chacona, in transmuted form, became the backbone of at least half of

southern Latin America's important regional dances. Argentina
absorbed these stately forms and sent them radiating from her
cities throughout the rural provinces and pampas. Rough gauchos and paysanos, intrigued by these dances' curiously dignified qualities, refurbished them to suit the new environment of
pampa or Andean foothill, where they would crash head-on
with traditional Inca music.

I have seen gauchos and their Chilean counterparts, called
Huasos, dancing the zamba and cueca, gracefully twirling a
kerchief overhead, bowing with dignity as their partners curtsy
in the correct court manner. Then a few seconds later I have
watched them revert to type, and stamp and twirl in their own
gusty style more in keeping with their trade. (*Argentine
Dances,* Folkways ST 6 7148, and *Gaucho,* Columbia WL 120,
give the general flavor.)

The next, much later, important musical impulse was,
strangely enough, Italian opera. How often you hear tunes,
particularly in Mexico, which are pure Verdi or Rossini. Then
there were operetta and musical comedy, known as *Zarzuela,*
the latest light music of Spain. On top of these came a deluge
of such ballroom dances as the waltz, mazurka, polka, and paso-
doble. It was remarkable how distinctively the new musical
forms adapted themselves to the new ambience, and how differently they combined with the already intermixed music. A
Paraguayan polka, for instance, is not in the least like a Mexican
one, which in turn does not sound like one from Bolivia.

Such a Bolivian polka, by the way, might be played on a
curious little mandolin made from an armadillo shell, one of
the most ingenious instruments produced by Indians anywhere.
When I had at last tracked one down in La Paz, its ruddy-
cheeked owner did not want to sell it to a gringo. When he
relented, he gave me the Cassandra-like warning that my amaz-
ingly hairy armadillo was "con pelo buena suerte, pero sin pelo
mala suerte" (Should it shed its hair, it would bring me ter-
rible luck). I asked how I could escape such a misfortune, and
he explained that to keep the little creature from going bald
I should rub it every night with chicha. *Faute de mieux,* I try
beer whenever I remember, and so far all is well!

That year the big popular hit in Bolivia was the nicely swinging "O Linda La Paz," extolling the joys of that city two and one quarter miles above the sea. Everybody sang it; it was very catchy. I brought a record home and played it on the program. To my surprise I was swamped with mail and phone calls which made me thoroughly aware of my stupidity in failing to recognize this famous tune, which had apparently encircled the earth. It was known variously as "Sing Everyone Sing" (USA), "O Viene sul Mar" (Italian), "Zwei Augen so Blau" (German), "Zing Faigele Zing" (Yiddish), "Two Lovely Black Eyes" and "My Nellie's Mince Pies" (English), "Poi Lastachka Poi" (Russian), and "Namide No Umibe" (Japanese).

While stringed instruments and religious songs brought new dimensions to pre-Columbian music, perhaps even more important was the Hispanic attitude. This reveling in spirited melodies and this intricate dancing to springy, fiery rhythms formed a new concept. The long story-telling romances—which would translate into corridos in Mexico, decima in Puerto Rico, and estilo in Argentina, songs for children to sing, lullabies, serenades, and all the songs about fishing, plowing, galloping, and even living and dying—were unheard of previously. In the past, one sang and danced because one was told to do so. It was part of one's religious duty. Now one sang and danced because it was a joy!

From the first Catholic fiesta, held at Lake Titicaca, and the moment in 1526 when a companion of Cortéz established a music school in Mexico with professional instructors, the imprint of Spain was stamped on Latin American music in unforgettable fashion.

African Influence

Africans, the third race, the third color in the rainbow, were brought over in a crescendo from the sixteenth to eighteenth centuries. Thanks to the universal popularity of jazz, everybody is thoroughly aware of the superlative rhythmic sophistication of Negro musicians. In the southern new world, the fascinating variety of innumerable percussion instruments fared much better than in the more puritan north. This alone would help to keep the rhythms vital. In addition there was an easier racial assimilation, leading to a stronger musical synthesis.

Once again the structure of the land decided a people's distribution. Slaves were needed in the hot tropical lowlands to produce sugar, coffee, cotton, and fruits. (Africans teemed into the lands bordering on the Caribbean Sea, into coastal Ecuador and Colombia, and overwhelmingly into Brazil, leaving a strong mark on regional music.) On enormous plantations, under varying degrees of tolerance, the slaves managed to keep alive a large proportion of their African heritage of folklore, dance, drumming, and song. Their cults assumed the outer cloak of Catholicism in much the same manner as had the earlier Indian religions. These secret cults (Ñanigo in Cuba, Vodoun in Haiti, and Candomblé in Brazil) preserved, along with their strong African musical elements, intricate drum rhythms, and they affected every dance along the way.

The best-known examples of African-influenced dances are urban, as are the many popular ones that came to us from Cuba and Puerto Rico. They need neither introduction nor champion. They provide a showcase for the strange and ingenious African percussion instruments that form a rhythmic counterpoint to all the many sizes and shapes of drums. There is the slightly macabre-looking quijada, a horse's jawbone complete with rattling teeth, and the marimbola, made from a large wooden box with several metal tongues nailed onto it. Occasionally a large earthenware jug is employed exactly as it was by old-time North American "jug bands." Most widely used and familiar are maracas, which are rattles and claves, two sticks which make a crisp "tic-toc" and are poetically known as "the heartbeat of the Caribbean," and a serrated gourd that is scratched with a fork (guiro).

African-influenced music has a strong dance tradition and is highly syncopated and polyrhythmic. Song is secondary, often a simple chant alternately sung by solo and answering chorus.

Brazil

While there is not space here to discuss the always shifting cultural relationships of each republic individually, it is quite apparent that Brazil must be considered as distinct from the Spanish-speaking lands. Brazil's acculturation story is similar to Spanish America's, but with one striking difference: There were no highly developed pre-Columbian cultures on which to perform "Operation Superimpose." The Indians of that vast land were either Amazon rain-forest tribes or the more advanced Tupi-Burani, who had sweet lyrical songs which occasionally filter into the musical mainstream. (Two of these rarities are on the old Aravel AB 2001, by now a collector's item. They were sung by Los Indios Taba-Jaras.) For practical purposes there are simply two colors of the cultural rainbow in Brazil—Portugal and Africa.

Bandeirantes, bands who pioneered the limitless interior, were followed by agricultural settlers who kept their Portuguese musical traditions alive. Others remained fishermen as they had been at home, with their elegiac songs of lovers parted and husbands drowned at sea. (Dorival Caymmi was to make this genre completely his own in such beautiful recordings as *Cancoes Praieiras*, Odeon LDS 3.004.)

Portuguese aristocrats brought their melancholy fado accompanied by vialao (guitar). These fados, marked by sad yearning, sparked the Brazilian moda, modinha, and toada. This cherished sorrow and homesickness they call *saudades* can be felt in many forms besides fado. There are hundreds of lyrical songs in this mood, nostalgically recalling the immensity of the Amazon, the mysterious beauty of the lush jungle, or the hardships of the sertao. (In listing, note singers Olga Coelho, Clara Petraglia, and Alice Ribeiro.)

Some of the wealthier Portuguese chose to live in towns such as Bahia. Others, if rich enough, became owners of large coastal plantations called *fazendas,* worked by slaves. As early as 1538 the first full shipment of slaves had made the short crossing from the bulge of Africa to the bulge of Brazil. They came from Nigeria, Dahomey, Angola, and Guinea. In the following three centuries over three million slaves were brought to this area. There was an easy-going relationship between owners and field hands. In many cases they were allowed weekends off and could then keep their Candomblé and Macumba rituals intact. There were nonreligious festivities, too, preserving other African musical forms: coco, originally a witchcraft song; batuque, a circle dance accompanied by hand-clapping; and lundu, a rapid song-dance with comic words. All of these were part of the samba family tree. Besides the familiar drums and maracas of Latin dance-bands, Brazil has a whole "bateria" of such curious African instruments as the friction-drum, known as a *cuica* or *pig-squeek*, and chocalho, a very large gourd rattle strung around with conch shells.

Brazil was unique in South America in the 1800's with its transplanted Emperor. (Pedro the First was highly musical, an amateur composer in fact. In 1822 he wrote a hymn of independence and sang it himself in a public performance, accompanied by a chorus!) Cultivated music flourished in this environment. The royal decree abolishing slavery in 1888 immediately impoverished the fazendas but increased the exuberance and musical expression of the masses. The former slaves now migrated in large numbers to towns, where they were introduced to feshta. Like the Spanish fiestas for innumerable saints' days, Portuguese feshta gave many opportunities for musical exchange between the races. Greatest of all feshtas, of course, is carnaval—an unbelievable impetus to the creation of the marchas and sambas that form the backbone of Brazilian popular music.

Brazilian samba and the fragile bossa nova, Argentine tango and an encyclopedia of Caribbean dances, the ubiquitous and romantic bolero and the cheerfully brassy Mexican mariachi band are probably recognized by most aficionados. But there are many stories which must be left untold: how the Mexican Revolution was musically interpreted; how General San Martin (incidentally, an enthusiastic musician and singer) changed the course of Argentina's folk music; the gold rush, which forged an unexpected musical liaison between Chile and Mexico; North American jazz as half-brother to the current bossa nova; a dejected Spanish priest with an Andean llama-bone flute; and even mambo with its peculiar grunts originally attributed to a local piano mover!

There are innumerable other indirect elements that embellish the background, but there is not space here to discuss them. I do want to leave you with an aroused interest in the music of Latin America, and some understanding of how it came to be. Sometimes when you hear it, you might like to try asking yourself such questions as: Which of the three primary racial groups are most represented in this selection? Was there a geographic or historic reason for this? Was it then modified or fertilized by a second or a third ethnic group? How did this come about? Do I enjoy the hybrid more than the components? Why? Indian music can be hauntingly evocative; Spanish, electric and exuberant; African, melodically simple and rhythmically amazing; but it is their myriad combinations that make up the unique, dazzling, and ever-changing spectrum which is Latin American music.

As your interest and perception grow, perhaps you will come to share my hope that electronics will not homogenize this phenomenal variety of songs, dances, chants, and all the diverse sounds of fiesta and carnival. You will, I feel sure, join with me in crying: "Viva las diferencias!"

Discography[*]

OPERA

In every choice of recordings I have made for this list, the performance has been the payoff. I am not concerned here with sophistication of sound, with the subtleties of stereo versus mono. It is the music *per se* that counts.

Bartók, Béla
 Bluebeard's Castle (in Hungarian), Christa Ludwig, Walter Berry, London Symphony Orchestra, conducted by Istvan Kertesz   (LONDON OSA 1158)
 ▶ *Brief, distinguished score, well recorded.*
Beethoven, Ludwig van
 Fidelio, Christa Ludwig, Jon Vickers, Walter Berry, Gottlob Frick, Philharmonia Orchestra and Chorus, conducted by Otto Klemperer   (ANGEL S 3625)
 ▶ *First-rate Beethoven from all concerned, with Ludwig a great Leonore.*
Bellini, Vincenzo
 Norma, Gina Cigna, Ebe Stignani, Giovanni Breviario, Tancredi Pasero, Orchestra and Chorus of Torino Radiotelevisione Italiana, conducted by Vittorio Gui   (EVEREST/CETRA S 423/3)
 ▶ *A rough, rather inelegant prewar performance (reissued in LP), but so very exciting. I find Callas's recorded* NORMA *unpleasant vocally, and Sutherland's not sufficiently dramatic.*
 Norma, "Casta Diva" (aria), Rosa Ponselle; "Mira Norma" (duet), Rosa Ponselle and Marion Telva
                         (RCA VICTOR ALBUM: TEN GREAT SINGERS)
 ▶ *Classic and distinguished.*

* Compiled by the individual contributors to this volume.

I Puritani, Maria Callas, Giuseppe Di Stefano, Orchestra and Chorus of La Scala, conducted by Tullio Serafin   (ANGEL 3502)
▶ *Callas and Di Stefano at their pristine best. An excellent performance.*

La Sonnambula, Joan Sutherland, Nicola Monti, Fernando Corena, Orchestra and Chorus of the Maggio Musicale Fiorentino, conducted by Richard Bonynge   (LONDON OSA 1365)
▶ *Fading score, expertly done.*

Berg, Alban

Wozzeck, Evelyn Lear, Dietrich Fischer-Dieskau, Orchestra of the German Opera, Berlin, conducted by Karl Böhm
(DEUTSCHE GRAMMOPHON GESELLSCHAFT S 138991/2)
▶ *Wonderfully human, accessible performance of a masterpiece.*

Lulu, Evelyn Lear, Patricia Johnson, Dietrich Fischer-Dieskau, Donald Grobe, Orchestra of the German Opera, Berlin, conducted by Karl Böhm
(DEUTSCHE GRAMMOPHON GESELLSCHAFT S 139273/5)
▶ *A problematical opera, gripping yet remote, superbly presented.*

Berlioz, Hector

Béatrice et Bénédict, Josephine Veasey, April Cantelo, John Mitchinson, London Symphony Orchestra and St. Anthony Singers, conducted by Colin Davies   (OISEAU-LYRE S 256/7)
▶ *A charming comedy with sentimental overtones, deftly performed.*

Les Troyens (scenes), Régine Crespin, Guy Chauvet, Paris Opéra Orchestra, conducted by Georges Prêtre   (ANGEL S 3670)
▶ *Badly cut, but gives some idea of the superb score by Berlioz. Crespin is effective as Didon.*

Bizet, Georges

Carmen, Victoria de los Angeles, Janine Micheau, Nicolai Gedda, Ernest Blanc, French National Radio Orchestra, conducted by Sir Thomas Beecham   (ANGEL S 3613)
▶ *If CARMEN is your preference, this is the best of its many recordings.*

Boito, Arrigo

Mefistofele. There has been no really adequate recording of this grand old work since the Scala issue of the 1920's with Mafalda Favero, Gianna Arangi-Lombardi, Antonio Melandri, and Nazzareno De Angelis, with Cav. Lorenzo Molajoli conducting (Columbia Operatic Set No. 17, unfortunately not reissued).
▶ *Toscanini directs a splendid performance of the Prologue on RCA Victor LM-1849.*

Borodin, Aleksandr
Prince Igor, Boris Christoff (doubling as Prince Galitsky and Khan Kontchak), Soloists, Chorus, and Orchestra of the National Theatre of Sofia, conducted by Jerzy Semkow
(USSR MELODIYA-ANGEL S 3714)
▶ *A striking performance, with benefit of Western recording techniques.*

Britten, Benjamin
Peter Grimes, Claire Watson, Peter Pears, James Pease, Royal Opera Orchestra, Covent Garden, conducted by Benjamin Britten
(LONDON OSA 1305)
▶ *One could wish for a newer recording, perhaps a different cast, but the current artists are all communicative, and the orchestra under the direction of the composer is first-rate.*

Charpentier, Gustave
Louise, Berthe Monmart, Solange Michel, André Laroze, Louis Musy, Orchestra and Chorus of the Paris Opéra-Comique, conducted by Jean Fournet
(EPIC SC 6018)
▶ *Singers excellent, but the heart of the performance is Jean Fournet's superb conducting.*

Cherubini, Luigi
Medea, Maria Callas, Orchestra and Chorus of La Scala, conducted by Tullio Serafin
(MERCURY SR 3-9000)
▶ *The Callas sound is here acceptable, the interpretation overwhelming.*

Debussy, Claude
Pelléas et Mélisande, Janine Micheau, Rita Gorr, Camille Maurane, Michel Roux, Xavier Depraz, Orchestre des Concerts Lamoureux, conducted by Jean Fournet
(EPIC SC 6003)
▶ *Fournet and the singers score again. Surpasses every other recorded* PELLÉAS.

Donizetti, Gaetano
Don Pasquale, Graziella Sciutti, Juan Oncina, Tom Krause, Fernando Corena, Vienna Opera Orchestra and Chorus, conducted by Istvan Kertesz
(LONDON OSA 1260)
▶ *This recording has its ups and downs, but unfortunately, there is no better available.*

L'elisir d'amore, Mirella Freni, Nicolai Gedda, Mario Sereni, Rome Opera Orchestra and Chorus, conducted by Francesco Molinari-Pradelli
(ANGEL S 3701)
▶ *Sheer joy, as music and performance, from beginning to end.*

Lucia di Lammermoor, Joan Sutherland, Renato Cioni, Robert Merrill, Cesare Siepi, Orchestra and Chorus of L'Accademia di Santa Cecilia, conducted by John Pritchard
(LONDON OSA 1327)
▶ *The definitive modern performance of* LUCIA.

Lucrezia Borgia, Montserrat Caballé, Shirley Verrett, Alfredo
Kraus, Ezio Flagello, RCA Italiana Opera Orchestra and
Chorus, conducted by Jonel Perlea   (RCA LSC-6176)
▶ *Caballé in one of her more congenial assignments.*

Dvořák, Anton
Rusalka, Soloists, Chorus, and Orchestra of the National Theater, Prague, conducted by Zdeněk Chalabala   (ARTIA s 89D)
▶ *The last act compensates for all longueurs in the earlier
scenes. It is wonderful music, strongly performed.*

Giordano, Umberto
Andrea Chénier, Renata Tebaldi, Mario Del Monaco, Ettore
Bastianini, Orchestra and Chorus of L'Accademia di Santa
Cecilia, Rome, conducted by Gianandrea Gavazzeni
(LONDON OSA 1303)
▶ *Powerful score in a reputable recording.*
Fedora, Maria Caniglia, Giacinto Prandelli, Orchestra and Chorus
of Radiotelevisione Italiana, conducted by Mario Rossi
(CETRA 1222)
▶ *Both opera and performance slightly moldy, but eloquent.*

Gluck, Christoph Willibald
Orfeo ed Euridice, Maureen Forrester, Teresa Stich-Randall,
Hanny Steffek, Akademie Choir and Vienna State Opera Or-
chestra, conducted by Charles Mackerras
(THE BACH GUILD BGS 70686/7)
▶ *Dignified reading, expressively sung.*

Gounod, Charles
Faust, Victoria de los Angeles, Nicolai Gedda, Michel Dens, Boris
Christoff, Orchestra and Chorus of the Paris Opéra, conducted
by André Cluytens   (ANGEL s 3622)
▶ *If it is* FAUST *you want, this is the best, even with Christoff's
heavily accented Méphistophélès.*
Roméo et Juliette (scenes), Rosanna Carteri, Nicolai Gedda,
Paris Opéra Orchestra, conducted by Alain Lombard
(ANGEL s 36287)
▶ *Carteri sounds a bit mature as Juliette, with Gedda the per-
fect Roméo.*

Handel, George Frederick
Alcina, Joan Sutherland, Teresa Berganza, Monica Sinclair,
Graziella Sciutti, Mirella Freni, Ezio Flagello, London Sym-
phony Orchestra and Chorus, conducted by Richard Bonynge
(LONDON s 1361)
▶ *A feast of virtuoso singing. Baroque style and ornamenta-
tion are imaginatively recreated.*

Hindemith, Paul
Mathis der Maler (scenes), Pilar Lorengar, Dietrich Fischer-

Dieskau, Berlin Radio Orchestra, conducted by Leopold Ludwig   (DEUTSCHE GRAMMOPHON GESELLSCHAFT S 138769)
▶ *This noble work sounds better in excerpts than as an integrated whole, for many of the parts are greater than the sum.*

Janáček, Leoš
Jenufa, Soloists, Chorus, and Orchestra of the National Theater, Prague, conducted by Jaroslav Vogel   (ARTIA ALPO 80 C/L)
▶ *A strong, but currently overrated opera, adequately performed.*
The Sly Little Vixen, Soloists, Chorus, and Orchestra of the National Theater, Prague, conducted by Václav Neumann
(ARTIA ALPO 88 B/L)
▶ *What an affecting mixture of wisdom, satire, and pathos! So human, and well played.*

Leoncavallo, Ruggiero
Pagliacci, Lucine Amara, Franco Corelli, Tito Gobbi, Mario Zanasi, Orchestra and Chorus of La Scala, conducted by Lovro von Matacic   (ANGEL S 3618 B/L)
▶ *Brilliant, consuming performance.*

Mascagni, Pietro
L'Amico Fritz, Ferruccio Tagliavini and Pia Tassinari, Orchestra and Chorus of Torino Radiotelevisione Italiana, conducted by Pietro Mascagni   (EVEREST/CETRA S 429/2)
▶ *A charming miniature, well sung. This recording (a reissue) has the additional interest of the composer on the podium.*
Cavalleria Rusticana, Giulietta Simionato, Mario Del Monaco, Cornell MacNeil, Orchestra and Chorus of L'Accademia di Santa Cecilia, Rome, conducted by Tullio Serafin
(LONDON S 1213)
▶ *Good, routine performance, but without much of the ferocity implicit in the score.*

Massenet, Jules
Hérodiade (scenes), Régine Crespin, Rita Gorr, Albert Lance, Michel Dens, Orchestra of the Paris Opéra, conducted by Georges Prêtre   (ANGEL S 36145)
▶ *The best pages of a debatable opera, well performed.*
Manon, Victoria de los Angeles, Henri Legay, Michel Dens, Jean Borthayre, Orchestra and Chorus of the Paris Opéra-Comique, conducted by Pierre Monteux   (CAPITOL GDR-7171)
▶ *The standard* MANON *on discs. First-rate.*
Thaïs (scenes), Jacqueline Brumaire, Christiane Gayraud, Michel Dens, Orchestra of the Paris Opéra, conducted by Pierre Dervaux   (ANGEL S 36286)
▶ *The opera's important moments, surprisingly well done by a modest cast.*

Werther, Ninon Vallin, Germaine Feraldy, Georges Thill, Marcel Roque, Orchestra of the Paris Opéra-Comique, conducted by Elie Cohen   (PATHÉ FHX 5009/5011)
▸ *The poetry of this prewar recording of* WERTHER *(in an LP reissue) has not yet been surpassed.*

Meyerbeer, Giacomo
Les Huguenots. Marcel's aria "Piff, paff, pouff" from *Les Huguenots* is performed by Nicolai Ghiaurov on his album of French and Russian arias, with the London Symphony Orchestra, conducted by Edward Downes   (LONDON OS 25911)
▸ *Bravo!*

Les Huguenots. The Queen's aria "O beau pays de Touraine" is sung by Joan Sutherland on her album *Art of Prima Donna*, with the Orchestra of the Royal Opera House, Covent Garden, conducted by Francesco Molinari-Pradelli   (LONDON OS 1214)
▸ *And brava!*

Montemezzi, Italo
L'Amore dei Tre Re, Clara Petrella, Amedeo Berdini, Renato Capecchi, Sesto Bruscantini, Orchestra and Chorus of Radio-televisione Italiana, conducted by Arturo Basile   (CETRA 1212)
▸ *The score, though eclectic, is still worth hearing. A good recording.*

Monteverdi, Claudio
L'Incoronazione de Poppea (selections), edited by Raymond Leppard; Magda Laszlo, Frances Bible, Oralia Dominguez, Richard Lewis, Carlo Cava, Glyndebourne Festival Chorus and Royal Philharmonic Orchestra, conducted by John Pritchard
(ANGEL SBL 3644)
▸ *Sensitively, magnificently recorded. The closing duet is one of the landmarks in opera.*

Mozart, Wolfgang Amadeus
Così fan tutte, Elisabeth Schwarzkopf, Christa Ludwig, Hanny Steffek, Alfredo Kraus, Giuseppe Taddei, Walter Berry, Philharmonia Orchestra and Chorus, conducted by Karl Böhm
(ANGEL S 3631 D/L)
▸ *Polished, persuasive Mozart in today's best performing tradition.*

Don Giovanni, Joan Sutherland, Elisabeth Schwarzkopf, Graziella Sciutti, Eberhard Wächter, Luigi Alva, Giuseppe Taddei, Philharmonia Orchestra and Chorus, conducted by Carlo Maria Giulini   (ANGEL S 3605 D/L)
▸ *Same critical comment as on* COSÌ FAN TUTTE.

Idomeneo, Sena Jurinac, Lucille Udovick, Richard Lewis, Leopold Simoneau, Glyndebourne Festival Orchestra and Chorus, conducted by John Pritchard   (ANGEL 3574 C/L)

▶ *A dedicated performance of an opera that deserves to be better known.*

The Magic Flute, Tiana Lemnitz, Erna Berger, Helge Roswänge, Gerhard Hüsch, Wilhelm Strienz, Berlin Philharmonic Chorus and Orchestra, conducted by Sir Thomas Beecham
(TURNABOUT [MOZART SOCIETY EDITION] 4111/3)

▶ *A reissue (in LP) of the famous prewar Beecham recording. Still the best* FLUTE *on discs.*

The Marriage of Figaro, Anna Moffo, Elisabeth Schwarzkopf, Fiorenza Cossotto, Eberhard Wächter, Giuseppe Taddei, Philharmonia Orchestra and Chorus, conducted by Carlo Maria Giulini
(ANGEL S 3608)

▶ *Same critical comment as on* COSÌ FAN TUTTE.

Musorgski, Modest

Boris Godunov (Rimski-Korsakov version), George London, Irina Arkhipova, Vladimir Ivanovsky, Orchestra and Chorus of the Bolshoi Theater, Moscow, conducted by Alexander Melik-Pashaev
(COLUMBIA M4S 696)

▶ *Great performance, sumptuous sound.*

Offenbach, Jacques

The Tales of Hoffmann, Gianna D'Angelo, Elisabeth Schwarzkopf, Victoria de los Angeles, Nicolai Gedda, George London, Ernest Blanc, Jean-Christophe Benoit, Orchestre de la Société des Concerts du Conservatoire, conducted by André Cluytens
(ANGEL SCLX 3667)

▶ *Adequate but frequently uneven recording of a fascinating work. Gedda consistently stylish.*

Ponchielli, Amilcare

La Gioconda, Renata Tebaldi, Marilyn Horne, Carlo Bergonzi, Robert Merrill, Orchestra and Chorus of L'Accademia di Santa Cecilia, Rome, conducted by Lambert Gardelli
(LONDON OSA 1388)

▶ *Vigorous, red-blooded, extrovert performance.*

Poulenc, Francis

Les Dialogues des Carmélites, Denise Duval, Régine Crespin, Rita Gorr, Xavier Depraz, Paul Finel, Orchestra of the Paris Opéra, conducted by Pierre Dervaux
(ANGEL 3585)

▶ *Sumptuous recording of an outstanding modern score.*

Prokofiev, Sergei

The Flaming Angel, Jane Rhodes, Irma Kolassi, Xavier Depraz, Orchestra of the Paris Opéra and Chorus of Radiodiffusion-Télévision Française, conducted by Charles Bruck
(WESTMINSTER 1304)

▶ *The Gothic mood is expertly sustained; and the opera itself comes off as one of the major works of our time.*

Puccini, Giacomo

La Bohème, Mirella Freni, Mariella Adani, Nicolai Gedda, Mario Sereni, Rome Opera Orchestra and Chorus, conducted by Thomas Schippers (ANGEL S 3643)
▶ *Tastefully and often movingly sung. Good conducting.*

Gianni Schicchi, Fernando Corena, Renata Tebaldi, Agostino Lazzari, Orchestra of the Maggio Musicale Fiorentino, conducted by Lamberto Gardelli (LONDON OSA 1153)
▶ *Singing only fair, orchestra very good.*

Girl of the Golden West, Birgit Nilsson, Joaõ Gibin, Andrea Mongelli, Orchestra and Chorus of La Scala, conducted by Lovro von Matacic (ANGEL S 3593 C/L)
▶ *Puccini's most important score, with von Matacic firmly in command.*

Madama Butterfly, Renata Tebaldi, Nell Rankin, Giuseppe Campora, Giovanni Inghilleri, Orchestra and Chorus of L'Accademia di Santa Cecilia, Rome, conducted by Alberto Erede
(RICHMOND 63001)
▶ *A reissue of Tebaldi's first recorded BUTTERFLY. It was this album, with its bloom of vocal youth, that originally, and justifiably, helped build her reputation.*

Manon Lescaut, Licia Albanese, Jussi Bjoerling, Robert Merrill, Orchestra and Chorus of Rome Opera, conducted by Jonel Perlea (RCA LM-6116)
▶ *Puccini COME SI DEVE. An impassioned performance.*

La Rondine, Anna Moffo, Graziella Sciutti, Daniele Barioni, Piero Di Palma, RCA Italiana Opera Orchestra and Chorus, conducted by Francesco Molinari-Pradelli (RCA LSC-7048)
▶ *A fragile and frequently appealing little opera, generally well performed.*

Suor Angelica, Victoria de los Angeles, Fedora Barbieri, Rome Opera Chorus and Orchestra, conducted by Tullio Serafin
(ANGEL 35748)
▶ *Sensitive projection of a work alternately inert and moving.*

Il Tabarro, Clara Petrella, Antenore Reali, Glauco Scarlino, Orchestra Lirica di Torino della Radiotelevisione Italiana, conducted by Giuseppe Barone (CETRA LPC 50029)
▶ *The oldest, and finest, TABARRO on records. No other Giorgietta comes within miles of Clara Petrella for dramatic and vocal penetration. The entire cast and conductor are excellent.*

Tosca, Maria Callas, Giuseppe Di Stefano, Tito Gobbi, Orchestra and Chorus of La Scala, conducted by Vittorio De Sabata
(ANGEL 3508)
▶ *Not to be confused with a later stereo release (also by Angel)*

featuring Callas and Gobbi. Here, every one of the artists is at his and her respective best. De Sabata magnificent. Easily the finest recording of TOSCA.

Turandot, Birgit Nilsson, Renata Scotto, Franco Corelli, Rome Opera Orchestra and Chorus, conducted by Francesco Molinari-Pradelli   (ANGEL S 3671)
▶ *Nilsson's big voice meets Puccini's big opera in a perfect union. Stunning performance of an extroverted score.*

Rameau, Jean Philippe

Hippolyte et Aricie, Janet Baker, John Shirley-Quirk, English Chamber Orchestra and St. Anthony Singers, conducted by Anthony Lewis   (OISEAU-LYRE S 286/8)
▶ *Much of the opera is dull, yet some of its scenes have great lyrical beauty.*

Ravel, Maurice

L'Enfant et les Sortilèges, Françoise Ogéas, Michel Sénéchal, Sylvaine Gelma, French National Radio Orchestra, conducted by Lorin Maazel
(DEUTSCHE GRAMMOPHON GESELLSCHAFT S 138675)
▶ *Brilliant, glittering, virtuosic performance.*

L'Heure Espagnole, Jeanne Berbié, Michel Sénéchal, Gabriel Bacquier, French National Radio Orchestra, conducted by Lorin Maazel (DEUTSCHE GRAMMOPHON GESELLSCHAFT S 138970)
▶ *Brilliant, glittering, virtuosic performance.*

Rimski-Korsakov, Nikolai

The Golden Cockerel (*Le Coq d'Or*), Soloists, Moscow Radio Chorus and Radio-Symphony Orchestra, conducted by Alexei Kovalyov   (ULTRAPHONE ULP 108/110)
▶ *Engagingly performed, poorly recorded.*

Sadko, Soloists, Chorus, and Orchestra of the Bolshoi Theater, conducted by Nicolai Golovanov   (ULTRAPHONE ULP 127/130)
▶ *Same critical comment as on* THE GOLDEN COCKEREL.

Rossini, Gioacchino

The Barber of Seville, Victoria de los Angeles, Sesto Bruscantini, Luigi Alva, Carlo Cava, Glyndebourne Festival Orchestra and Chorus, conducted by Vittorio Gui   (ANGEL S 3638)
▶ *This performance is so aristocratic in design as to erase for us every miserable travesty of* THE BARBER *in the past.*

La Cenerentola, Giulietta Simionato, Ugo Benelli, Sesto Bruscantini, Orchestra and Chorus of the Maggio Musicale Fiorentino, conducted by Oliviero de Febritiis   (LONDON OSA 1376)
▶ *Able and sparkling Rossini.*

Le Comte Ory, Jeanette Sinclair, Cora Canne-Meijer, Juan Oncina, Michel Roux, Glyndebourne Festival Orchestra and Chorus, conducted by Vittorio Gui   (ANGEL 3565 B/L)

▶ *A scintillating, jewel-like score. The performance is adequate.*

L'Italiana in Algeri, Teresa Berganza, Luigi Alva, Fernando Corena, Orchestra of the Maggio Musicale Fiorentino, conducted by Silvio Varviso   (LONDON OAS 1376)
▶ *Same critical comment as on* CENERENTOLA.

Semiramide, Joan Sutherland, Marilyn Horne, Joseph Rouleau, London Symphony Orchestra and Ambrosian Opera Chorus, conducted by Richard Bonynge   (LONDON OAS 1383)
▶ *The apex of modern* BEL CANTO *singing is reached by Sutherland and Horne in their great duet.*

Saint-Saëns, Camille

Samson et Dalila, Rita Gorr, Jon Vickers, Ernest Blanc, Paris Opéra Orchestra and Choeur René Duclos, conducted by Georges Prêtre   (ANGEL S 3639)
▶ *Hardly a voluptuous performance, but a good one.*

Shostakovich, Dimitri

Katerina Ismailova, Artists, Chorus, and Orchestra of the Stanislavsky/Nemirov-Danchenko Musical Drama Theatre of Moscow, conducted by Gennay Provatorov
                    (USSR MELODIYA-ANGEL S 4100)
▶ *A striking performance, with benefit of Western recording techniques.*

Smetana, Bedřich

The Bartered Bride, Soloists, Chorus, and Orchestra of the National Theater, Prague, conducted by Zdeněk Chalabala
                    (ARTIA S 82 C/L)
▶ *Said by ethnic specialists to be an authentic performance.*

Strauss, Richard

Arabella, Lisa Della Casa, Hilde Gueden, George London, Vienna Philharmonic Orchestra, conducted by Georg Solti
                    (LONDON OSA 1404)
▶ *Spirited reading of a charming minor work.*

Ariadne auf Naxos, Elisabeth Schwarzkopf, Irmgard Seefried, Rita Streich, Rudolf Schock, Vienna Philharmonic Orchestra, conducted by Herbert von Karajan   (ANGEL 3532)
▶ *Seefried and Streich excel. The orchestral performance is sterling, the over-all mood poetically conveyed.*

Capriccio, Elisabeth Schwarzkopf, Christa Ludwig, Nicolai Gedda, Dietrich Fischer-Dieskau, Hans Hotter, Philharmonia Orchestra, conducted by Wolfgang Sawallisch   (ANGEL 3580)
▶ *An all-star cast lives up to expectations. Brilliantly performed in every way. The opera itself is a tough nut to crack (for the listener) and takes many hearings.*

Elektra, Birgit Nilsson, Marie Collier, Regina Resnik, Tom Krause, Gerhard Stolze, Vienna Philharmonic Orchestra, conducted by Georg Solti   (LONDON OSA 1269)
▶ *Much impressive singing, manipulated orchestral sound.*

Die Frau ohne Schatten, Inge Borkh, Ingrid Bjoner, Marta Mödl, Jess Thomas, Dietrich Fischer-Dieskau, Bavarian State Opera Orchestra, conducted by Joseph Keilberth
(DEUTSCHE GRAMMOPHON GESELLSCHAFT S 138911/4)
▶ *A performance recorded "live" at the National Theater, Munich. Much of it is good. Better, as a memento of* DIE FRAU *in microcosm, is the recording of the duet for the Dyer and his wife (Act III, Scene 1), beautifully sung by Christa Ludwig and Walter Berry, with the orchestra of the German Opera, Berlin, conducted by Heinrich Hollreiser (RCA VICS-1269).*

Der Rosenkavalier (scenes), Lotte Lehmann, Maria Olszewska, Elisabeth Schumann, Richard Mayr, Vienna Philharmonic Orchestra, conducted by Robert Heger   (ANGEL GRB-4001)
▶ *The classic prewar performance (reissued in LP), with memorable artists, bearing a mark of authenticity and enchantment not approached by any other recording of* ROSENKAVALIER. *An added attraction: all the duller scenes in the opera are eliminated, and only its shining pages retained.*

Salome (final scene), Ljuba Welitsch and Metropolitan Opera Orchestra, conducted by Fritz Reiner   (ODYSSEY 32160077)
▶ *The model performance in every way (reissued). The complete recording by London (OSA 1218), starring Birgit Nilsson, is for my taste overengineered.*

Tchaikovsky, Pëtr Ilich

Eugene Onegin (scenes), Galina Vishnevskaya and artists of the Bolshoi Theater, conducted by Boris Khaikin   (MONITOR S 2072)
▶ *Said by ethnic specialists to be an authentic performance.*

Pique Dame, Soloists, Chorus, and Orchestra of Bolshoi Theater, conducted by Alexander Melik-Pashaev   (BRUNO 32004/6L)
▶ *Engagingly performed, poorly recorded.*

Thomas, Ambroise

Mignon (scenes), Jeanne Berbié, Mady Mesplé, Gérard Dunan, Xavier Depraz, Orchestra Lamoureux and Choeur St. Paul, conducted by Jean Fournet
(DEUTSCHE GRAMMOPHON GESELLSCHAFT S 136279)
▶ *So excellently performed is this series of excerpts that one could have wished for the opera complete.*

Verdi, Giuseppe

Aida, Leontyne Price, Rita Gorr, Jon Vickers, Robert Merrill, Giorgio Tozzi, Rome Opera Orchestra and Chorus, conducted by Georg Solti   (RCA LSC-6158)
▶ *Conventional, satisfying performance.*

Un Ballo in Maschera, Birgit Nilsson, Giulietta Simionato, Sylvia Stahlman, Carlo Bergonzi, Cornell MacNeil, Orchestra and Chorus of L'Accademia di Santa Cecilia, Rome, conducted by Georg Solti   (LONDON OSA 1328)
▶ *Strongly sung and effectively played.*

Don Carlos, Renata Tebaldi, Grace Bumbry, Carlo Bergonzi, Dietrich Fischer-Dieskau, Nicolai Ghiaurov, Royal Opera Orchestra, Covent Garden, conducted by Georg Solti
(LONDON OSA 1432)
▶ *Distinguished cast, well fused.*

Falstaff, Ilva Ligabue, Mirella Freni, Giulietta Simionato, Rosalind Elias, Alfredo Kraus, Geraint Evans, Robert Merrill, RCA Italiana Orchestra, conducted by Georg Solti   (RCA LSC-6163)
▶ *Vocally the best* FALSTAFF *on records. In the orchestra, I prefer Leonard Bernstein's reading (Columbia M3S-750) to Solti's.*

La Forza del Destino, Renata Tebaldi, Giulietta Simionato, Mario Del Monaco, Ettore Bastianini, Cesare Siepi, Orchestra and Chorus of L'Accademia di Santa Cecilia, Rome, conducted by Francesco Molinari-Pradelli   (LONDON OSA 1405)
▶ *Same critical comment as on* UN BALLO IN MASCHERA.

Luisa Miller, Anna Moffo, Shirley Verrett, Carlo Bergonzi, Cornell MacNeil, Giorgio Tozzi, Ezio Flagello, RCA Italiana Opera Orchestra and Chorus, conducted by Fausto Cleva
(RCA LSC-6168)
▶ *All-around good performance, with Bergonzi excelling as Rodolfo. The final act, musically, is top-rank Verdi.*

Macbeth, Birgit Nilsson, Giuseppe Taddei, Bruno Prevedi, Orchestra and Chorus of L'Accademia di Santa Cecilia, Rome, conducted by Thomas Schippers   (LONDON OSA 1380)
▶ *Nilsson's Lady Macbeth is controversial in regard to Italian vocal style, but as characterization, I like its steely quality.*

Nabucco, Elena Suliotis, Tito Gobbi, Bruno Prevedi, Carlo Cava, Vienna State Opera Orchestra and Chorus, conducted by Lamberto Gardelli   (LONDON OSA 1382)
▶ *Rough vocalism, but dramatically convincing.*

Otello, Leonie Rysanek, Jon Vickers, Tito Gobbi, Rome Opera Orchestra and Chorus, conducted by Tullio Serafin
(RCA LDS-6155)
▶ *Impressively sung and conducted.*

Rigoletto, Anna Moffo, Rosalind Elias, Alfredo Kraus, Robert
Merrill, Ezio Flagello, RCA Italiana Opera Orchestra and
Chorus, conducted by Georg Solti   (RCA LSC-7027)
▶ *Solid, meat-and-potatoes performance.*

Simon Boccanegra, Tito Gobbi, Boris Christoff, Victoria de los
Angeles, Giuseppe Campora, Rome Opera Orchestra and
Chorus, conducted by Gabriele Santini   (ANGEL 3617)
▶ *A towering opera, for the most part well recorded.*

La Traviata, Anna Moffo, Richard Tucker, Robert Merrill, Rome
Opera Orchestra and Chorus, conducted by Fernando Previ-
tali   (RCA LSC-6154)
▶ *Same critical comment as on* RIGOLETTO.

Il Trovatore, Antonietta Stella, Fiorenza Cossotto, Carlo Bergonzi,
Ettore Bastianini, Orchestra and Chorus of La Scala, con-
ducted by Tullio Serafin
              (DEUTSCHE GRAMMOPHON GESELLSCHAFT 138835/7)
▶ *Fluctuating job, but at best quite acceptable.*

Wagner, Richard

Der Fliegende Holländer, Leonie Rysanek, George London,
Giorgio Tozzi, Royal Opera Orchestra, Covent Garden, con-
ducted by Antal Dorati   (RCA LSC-6156)
▶ *Good, durable, and often eloquent Wagner.*

Lohengrin, Elisabeth Grümmer, Christa Ludwig, Jess Thomas,
Dietrich Fischer-Dieskau, Gottlob Frick, Vienna Philharmonic
and State Opera Chorus, conducted by Rudolf Kempe
                                            (ANGEL S 3641)
▶ *A poetic, sensitive performance.*

Die Meistersinger, Elisabeth Grümmer, Rudolf Schock, Ferdinand Frantz, Berlin Philharmonic Orchestra, conducted by
Rudolf Kempe   (ANGEL 3572)
▶ *I cannot recommend unreservedly any complete* MEISTER-
SINGER *on records, although the Frantz-Kempe performance
will do in a pinch. Better, for savoring the essence of this
work, is the reissue of scenes (Angel COLH-137) featuring
that incomparable Hans Sachs, Friedrich Schorr.*

Parsifal, Irene Dalis, Jess Thomas, George London, Hans Hotter,
Bayreuth Festival Orchestra and Chorus, conducted by Hans
Knappertsbusch   (PHILLIPS PHS 5-950)
▶ *Wonderfully conducted and played, a good deal of uneven
singing. I recommend, as an example of how this music* HAS
*been sung, the reissue (Angel COLH-132) of Frida Leider
in Kundry's monologue, "Ich sah das Kind."*

Der Ring des Nibelungen

Das Rheingold, Kirsten Flagstad, George London, Gustav
Neidlinger, Set Svanholm, Vienna Philharmonic, conducted
by Georg Solti   (LONDON OSA 1309)

Die Walküre, Birgit Nilsson, Régine Crespin, Christa Ludwig, James King, Hans Hotter, Gottlob Frick, Vienna Philharmonic, conducted by Georg Solti   (LONDON OSA 1509)

Siegfried, Birgit Nilsson, Marga Höffgen, Joan Sutherland (Forest Bird), Wolfgang Windgassen, Gerhard Stolze, Hans Hotter, Vienna Philharmonic, conducted by Georg Solti
(LONDON OSA 1508)

Götterdämmerung, Birgit Nilsson, Claire Watson, Christa Ludwig, Wolfgang Windgassen, Dietrich Fischer-Dieskau, Gottlob Frick, Vienna Philharmonic, conducted by Georg Solti
(LONDON OSA 1604)

▶ *The London* RING *is a monumental project, unmatched on records, with a high standard of performance, but I find much of the sound (via engineering) intrusive and pretentious.*

Tristan und Isolde, Birgit Nilsson, Christa Ludwig, Wolfgang Windgassen, Eberhard Wächter, Marti Talvela, Bayreuth Festival Orchestra, conducted by Karl Böhm
(DEUTSCHE GRAMMOPHON GESELLSCHAFT S 139221/5)

▶ *For my taste, the finest orchestral performance on records of* ANY *opera. The singers are good.*

Weber, Karl Maria von

Der Freischütz, Irmgard Seefried, Rita Streich, Richard Holm, Kurt Böhme, Eberhard Wächter, Bavarian Broadcasting Orchestra and Chorus, conducted by Eugen Jochum
(DEUTSCHE GRAMMOPHON GESELLSCHAFT S 138639/40)

▶ *Kurt Böhme especially fine as the diabolical Kaspar. Rita Streich an adorable Aennchen.*

ORCHESTRAL MUSIC

Bach, Johann Sebastian

Violin Concerto No. 1 in A minor, Szeryng, Wintherthur Collegium Musicum   (MERCURY 90466, 50466)

Violin Concerto No. 2 in E, Menuhin, with Masters Chamber Orchestra   (CAPITOL SG 7210, G 7210)

Clavier Concerto No. 1 in D minor, Ashkenazy, London Symphony Orchestra, Zinman   (LONDON CS 6440, CM 9440)

Six Brandenburg Concertos, Lucerne Festival Strings, Baumgartner   (ARCHIVE 73156/7, 3156/7)

Suites for Orchestra, Bath Festival Chamber Orchestra, Menuhin
(CAPITOL SGBR 7252, GBR 7252)

Bartók, Béla
  Concerto for Orchestra, New York Philharmonic, Bernstein
                          (COLUMBIA MS 6140, ML 5471)
  Piano Concerto No. 3, Peter Serkin, Chicago Symphony Orches-
    tra, Ozawa   (RCA LSC/LM 2929)
  Violin Concerto No. 2, Stern, New York Philharmonic, Bernstein
                          (COLUMBIA MS 6002, ML 5283)
  Music for Strings, Percussion and Celesta, Chicago Symphony
    Orchestra, Reiner   (RCA LSC/LM 2374)
Beethoven, Ludwig van
  Incidental Music for Egmont, Philharmonia Orchestra, Klem-
    perer   (ANGEL S 3577, 3577)
  The Five Piano Concertos, Fleisher, Cleveland Orchestra, Szell
                       (EPIC BSC 151, SC 6051)
  Piano Concerto No. 1, Richter, Boston Symphony Orchestra,
    Munch   (RCA LSC/LM 2544)
  Piano Concerto No. 3, Rubinstein, Boston Symphony Orchestra,
    Leinsdorf   (RCA LSC/LM 2947)
  Piano Concerto No. 5, Serkin, New York Philharmonic, Bern-
    stein   (COLUMBIA MS 6366, ML 5766)
  Violin Concerto, Francescatti, Columbia Symphony Orchestra,
    Walter   (COLUMBIA MS 6263, ML 5663)
  Fidelio and *Leonore Overtures,* Cleveland Orchestra, Szell
                 (COLUMBIA MS 7068) stereo only
  Symphony No. 1, Cleveland Orchestra, Szell
                   (EPIC BC 1292, LC 3892)
  Symphony No. 2, Royal Philharmonic Orchestra, Beecham,
                 (ANGEL S 35509, 35509)
  Symphony No. 3, Philharmonia Orchestra, Klemperer
                 (ANGEL 35328) mono only
  ▶ *This earlier performance is far preferable to Klemperer's*
    later rerecording with the same orchestra (Angel S 35853,
    35853). If this earlier Klemperer recording is unobtainable,
    I would recommend the Barbirolli performance (Angel
    S 36461, stereo only).
  Symphony No. 4, Columbia Symphony Orchestra, Walter
                 (COLUMBIA MS 6055, ML 5365)
  Symphony No. 5, Amsterdam Concertgebouw Orchestra, Kleiber
                 (RICHMOND 19105) mono only
  ▶ *The best performance of Beethoven's Fifth ever committed*
    to the permanency of recording!
  Symphony No. 6, Columbia Symphony Orchestra, Walter
                 (COLUMBIA MS 6012, ML 5284)
  Symphony No. 7, Columbia Symphony Orchestra, Walter
                 (COLUMBIA MS 6082, ML 5404)

Symphony No. 8, Marlboro Festival Orchestra, Casals
(COLUMBIA MS 6931, ML 6331)
Symphony No. 9, Vienna Philharmonic Orchestra, Schmidt-
Isserstedt   (LONDON CS 1159, CM 4159)
Berlioz, Hector
Harold in Italy, Primrose, Boston Symphony Orchestra, Munch
(RCA LSC/LM 2228)
Symphonie Fantastique, Boston Symphony Orchestra, Munch
(RCA LSC/LM 2608); or London Symphony Orchestra, Davis
(PHILIPS SR 900101, MG 500101)
Brahms, Johannes
Academic Festival Overture and *Tragic Overture,* Cleveland Or-
chestra, Szell   (COLUMBIA MS 6965, ML 6365)
Double Concerto for Violin and Cello, Francescatti and Fournier,
Columbia Symphony Orchestra, Walter
(COLUMBIA MS 6158, ML 5493)
Piano Concerto No. 1, Curzon, London Symphony Orchestra,
Szell   (LONDON CS 6329, CM 9329)
Piano Concerto No. 2, Serkin, Cleveland Orchestra, Szell
(COLUMBIA MS 6967, ML 6367)
Violin Concerto, Oistrakh, French National Orchestra, Klem-
perer   (ANGEL S 35836, 35836)
Serenade No. 1, London Symphony Orchestra, Kertesz
(LONDON CS 6567) stereo only
Serenade No. 2, New York Philharmonic, Bernstein
(COLUMBIA MS 7132) stereo only
Symphony No. 1, Cleveland Orchestra, Szell
(COLUMBIA D3S 758, D3L 358)
▶ *A three-disc set that has all four Brahms Symphonies in
Szell, Cleveland performances.*
Symphony No. 2, Vienna Philharmonic Orchestra, Monteux
(RCA VICS/VIC 1055)
Symphony No. 3, Cleveland Orchestra, Szell, (COLUMBIA MS
6685, ML 6085); or included in   (COLUMBIA D3S 758, D3L 358)
Symphony No. 4, Cleveland Orchestra, Szell
(COLUMBIA D3S 758, D3L 358)
Variations on the St. Anthony Chorale, Cleveland Orchestra,
Szell   (COLUMBIA MS 6965, ML 6365)
Britten, Benjamin
Sinfonia da Requiem, New Philharmonia Orchestra, Britten
(LONDON OS 25937, CM 5937)
Young Person's Guide to the Orchestra, London Symphony Or-
chestra, Britten   (LONDON CS 6398, CM 9398)
Variations on a Theme by Frank Bridge, Bath Festival Chamber
Orchestra, Menuhin   (ANGEL S 36303, 36303)

Bruch, Max
Violin Concerto No. 1, Heifetz, New Symphony Orchestra, Sargent   (RCA LSC/LM 2652)
Bruckner, Anton
Symphony No. 4, Columbia Symphony Orchestra, Walter, included in   (COLUMBIA M2S 622, M2L 273)
Symphony No. 7, Philharmonia Orchestra, Klemperer
(ANGEL S 3626, 3626)
Symphony No. 8, Berlin Philharmonic Orchestra, Jochum
(DEUTSCHE GRAMMOPHON GESELLSCHAFT 138918/9, 18918/9)
Symphony No. 9, Vienna Philharmonic Orchestra, Mehta
(LONDON CS 6462, CM 9462)
Chopin, Frederic
Piano Concerto No. 1, Rubinstein, New Symphony Orchestra,
Skrowaczewski   (RCA LSC/LM 2575)
Piano Concerto No. 2, Ashkenazy, London Symphony Orchestra,
Zinman   (LONDON CS 6440, CM 9440)
Copland, Aaron
Appalachian Spring, New York Philharmonic, Bernstein
(COLUMBIA MS 6355, ML 5755)
Billy the Kid and *Rodeo*, New York Philharmonic, Bernstein
(COLUMBIA MS 6175, ML 5575)
Music for the Theater, New York Philharmonic, Bernstein
(COLUMBIA MS 6698, ML 6098)
Debussy, Claude
Iberia, NBC Symphony Orchestra, Toscanini
(RCA VIC 1246), mono only
La Mer, NBC Symphony Orchestra, Toscanini
(RCA VIC 1246), mono only
Nocturnes, Boston Symphony Orchestra, Monteux
(RCA VICS/VIC 1027)
Dvořák, Anton
Cello Concerto, Casals, Czech Philharmonic Orchestra, Szell
(ANGEL COLH 30), mono only
▶ *One of the truly Great Recordings of the Century.*
Overture Trilogy, Vienna State Opera Orchestra, Somogyi
(WESTMINSTER WST 17072, XWN 19072)
Serenade No. 1, Israel Philharmonic, Kubelik
(LONDON STS 15037) stereo only
Serenade No. 2, Musica Aeterna Chamber Orchestra, Waldman
(DECCA 710137, 10137)
Symphony No. 3, London Symphony Orchestra, Kertesz
(LONDON CS 6525, CM 9525)
Symphony No. 4, London Symphony Orchestra, Kertesz
(LONDON CS 6526, CM 9526)

Symphony No. 6, London Symphony Orchestra, Kertesz
(LONDON CS 6495, CM 9495)
Symphony No. 7, London Symphony Orchestra, Monteux
(RCA VICS/VIC 1310)
Symphony No. 8, Hallé Orchestra, Barbirolli
(VANGUARD 133SD, 133)
Symphony No. 9, NBC Symphony Orchestra, Toscanini
(RCA VIC 1249), mono only
▶ *One of the best of all the Toscanini recordings.*
Dukas, Paul
The Sorcerer's Apprentice, Boston Symphony Orchestra, Munch
(RCA VICS/VIC 1060)
Enesco, Georges
Roumanian Rhapsodies Nos. 1 and 2, Philadelphia Orchestra,
Ormandy   (COLUMBIA MS 6018, ML 5299)
Falla, Manuel de
Nights in the Gardens of Spain, Soriano, Paris Conservatory Or-
chestra, Burgos   (ANGEL S 36131, 36131)
The Three-Cornered Hat, De los Angeles, Philharmonia Orches-
tra, Burgos   (ANGEL S 36235, 36235)
Franck, César
Symphonic Variations, Casadesus, Philadelphia Orchestra, Or-
mandy   (COLUMBIA MS 6070, ML 5388)
Symphony in D minor, Chicago Symphony Orchestra, Monteux
(RCA LSC/LM 2514)
Gabrieli, Giovanni
Sonata pian' e forte, London Gabrieli Brass Ensemble
(NONESUCH 71118, 1118)
Gershwin, George
An American in Paris, New York Philharmonic, Bernstein
(COLUMBIA MS 6091, ML 5413)
Piano Concerto, Wild, Boston Pops Orchestra, Fiedler
(RCA LSC/LM 2586)
Rhapsody in Blue, Bernstein, Columbia Symphony Orchestra,
Bernstein   (COLUMBIA MS 6091, ML 5413)
Grieg, Edvard
Piano Concerto, Rubinstein with Orchestra, Wallenstein
(RCA LSC/LM 2566)
Peer Gynt Suite No. 1, Cleveland Orchestra, Szell
(COLUMBIA MS 6877, ML 6277)
Handel, George Frederick
Concerti Grossi, Opus 6, Bath Festival Orchestra, Menuhin
(ANGEL S 3647, 3647)
Royal Fireworks Music, Chamber Orchestra, Mackerras
(VANGUARD BACH GUILD 5046, 630)

Water Music, Bath Festival Orchestra, Menuhin
(ANGEL S 36173, 36173)

Haydn, Franz Josef
Trumpet Concerto, Wobitsch, Zagreb Soloists, Janigro
(VANGUARD BACH GUILD 5053, 641)
Cello Concerto in C, Rostropovitch, English Chamber Orchestra,
Britten   (LONDON CS 6419, CM 9419)
Cello Concerto in D, Starker, Philharmonia Orchestra, Giulini
(ANGEL S 35725, 35725)
Symphonies Nos. 6, 7, and 8, Saar Chamber Orchestra, Risten-
part   (NONESUCH 71015, 1015)
Symphony No. 13, London Little Orchestra, Jones
(NONESUCH 71121, 1121)
Symphony No. 22, Suisse Romande Orchestra, Ansermet
(LONDON CS 6481, CM 9481)
Symphony No. 39, Esterhazy Orchestra, Blum
(VANGUARD 71123, 1123)
Symphony No. 44, Zagreb Symphony, Janigro
(VANGUARD 2145, 1106)
Symphony No. 49, Zagreb Symphony, Janigro
(VANGUARD 2147, 1108)
Symphony No. 80, London Little Orchestra, Jones
(NONESUCH 71131, 1131)
Symphony No. 86, Cincinnati Symphony Orchestra, Rudolf
(DECCA 710107, 10107)
Last six *London Symphonies Nos. 99 to 104,* Royal Philharmonic
Orchestra, Beecham   (ANGEL S 36254/6, 36254/6)

Hindemith, Paul
Mathis der Maler, Philadelphia Orchestra, Ormandy
(COLUMBIA MS 6562, ML 5962)
Symphonic Metamorphosis on Themes of Weber, Philadelphia
Orchestra, Ormandy   (COLUMBIA MS 6562, ML 5962)

Ives, Charles
Symphony No. 2, New York Philharmonic, Bernstein
(COLUMBIA MS 6889, ML 6289)
Symphony No. 4, American Symphony Orchestra, Stokowski
(COLUMBIA MS 6775, ML 6175)

Khatchaturian, Aram
Piano Concerto, Hollander, Royal Philharmonic Orchestra, Previn
(RCA LSC/LM 2801)
Violin Concerto, Kogan, Boston Symphony Orchestra, Monteux
(RCA VICS/VIC 1153)
Gayne Ballet, London Symphony Orchestra, Fistoulari
(EVEREST 3052, 6052)

Masquerade Suite, RCA Victor Orchestra, Kondrashin
                                    (RCA LSC/LM 2398)
Liszt, Franz
  Piano Concerto No. 1, Richter, London Symphony Orchestra,
    Kondrashin   (PHILIPS 900000, 500000)
  Piano Concerto No. 2, Richter, London Symphony Orchestra,
    Kondrashin   (PHILIPS 900000, 500000)
  Faust Symphony, New York Philharmonic, Bernstein
                                    (COLUMBIA M2S 699, M2L 299)
  Hungarian Fantasy, Cherkassky, Berlin Philharmonic Orchestra,
    Karajan
          (DEUTSCHE GRAMMOPHON GESELLSCHAFT 138692, 18692)
  Mazeppa, Boston Pops Orchestra, Fiedler   (RCA LSC/LM 2442)
  Les Préludes, London Symphony Orchestra, Dorati
                                    (MERCURY SR 90214, MG 50214)
Lully, Jean Baptiste
  Le Bourgeois Gentilhomme, Mainz Chamber Orchestra, Kehr
                                    (VOX 501070, 1070)
Mahler, Gustav
  Das Lied von der Erde, Vienna Philharmonic Orchestra, Bern-
    stein   (LONDON OS 26005, CM 36005)
  Symphony No. 1, London Symphony Orchestra, Solti
                                    (LONDON CS 6401, CM 9401)
  Symphony No. 2, London Symphony Orchestra, Solti
                                    (LONDON CSA 2217, CMA 7217)
  Symphony No. 4, New York Philharmonic, Bernstein, (COLUMBIA
    MS 6152, ML 5485); or Cleveland Orchestra, Szell
                                    (COLUMBIA MS 6833, ML 6233)
  Symphony No. 5, New York Philharmonic, Bernstein
                                    (COLUMBIA M2S 698, M2L 298)
  Symphony No. 8, London Symphony Orchestra, Bernstein
                                    (COLUMBIA M2S 751, M2L 351)
  Symphony No. 9, Vienna Symphony Orchestra, Horenstein (VOX
    VBX 116), mono only, a 3-disc set also containing Horenstein-
    conducted performances of *Symphony No. 1* and *Kindertoten-
    lieder.*
    ▸ *An album absolutely indispensable to any Mahler addict,
    especially since Horenstein is revealed as one of the great-
    est of all Mahler interpreters ever to record any of the
    master's music.*
Martinu, Bohuslav
  Piano Concerto No. 3, Palenicek, Czech Philharmonic Orchestra,
    Ancerl   (ARTIA 7205, 205)
  Piano Concerto No. 4, Palenicek, Brno State Philharmonic, Pinkas
                                    (ARTIA S 712, 712)

Violin Concerto, Belcik, Prague Symphony Orchestra, Neumann
(ARTIA 7205, 205)
Symphony No. 4, Czech Philharmonic Orchestra, Turnovsky
(PARLIAMENT S 621, 621)

Mendelssohn, Felix
A Midsummer Night's Dream, London Symphony Orchestra,
Chorus and Soloists, Maag   (LONDON CS 6001, CM 9201)
  ▶ *Of the several recordings of a Suite from the complete score,
  my first recommendation would be Cleveland Orchestra,
  Szell, (Columbia MS 7002, ML 6402).*
Piano Concerto No. 1, Serkin, Philadelphia Orchestra, Ormandy
(COLUMBIA MS 6128, ML 5456)
Violin Concerto in E minor, Szeryng, London Symphony Orches-
tra, Dorati   (MERCURY SR 90406, MG 50406)
Symphony No. 3, London Symphony Orchestra, Maag
(LONDON CS 6191, CM 9252)
Symphony No. 4, Marlboro Festival Orchestra, Casals
(COLUMBIA MS 6931, ML 6331)

Mozart, Wolfgang A.
Piano Concerto No. 9, Ashkenazy, London Symphony Orchestra,
Kertesz   (LONDON CS 6501, CM 9501)
Piano Concerto No. 15, Bernstein, Vienna Philharmonic Orches-
tra, Bernstein   (LONDON CS 6499, CM 9499)
Piano Concerto No. 19, Serkin, Columbia Symphony Orchestra,
Szell   (COLUMBIA MS 6534, ML 5934)
Piano Concerto No. 20
  ▶ *Unfortunately, Bernie Siff has never recorded the score. My
  second choice, therefore, is Rubinstein with Orchestra, Wal-
  lenstein, (RCA LSC/LM 2635).*
Piano Concerto No. 21, Rubinstein with Orchestra, Wallenstein
(RCA LSC/LM 2634)
Piano Concerto No. 23, Casadesus, Columbia Symphony, Szell
(COLUMBIA MS 6194, ML 5594)
Piano Concerto No. 24, Haskil, Lamoureux Orchestra, Marke-
vitch   (EPIC BC 1143, LC 3798)
Piano Concerto No. 27, Casadesus, Columbia Symphony Orches-
tra, Szell   (COLUMBIA MS 6403, ML 5803)
Violin Concerto No. 3, Francescatti, Columbia Symphony Or-
chestra, Walter   (COLUMBIA MS 6063, ML 5381)
Violin Concerto No. 4, Heifetz, New Symphony Orchestra, Sar-
gent   (RCA LSC/LM 2652)
Violin Concerto No. 5, Stern, Columbia Symphony Orchestra,
Szell   (COLUMBIA MS 6557, ML 5957)
Divertimento, K 131, Cleveland Orchestra, Szell
(COLUMBIA MS 6968, ML 6368)

Divertimento, K 136, Bath Festival Orchestra, Menuhin
(ANGEL S 36429, 36429)
Divertimento, K 251, English Chamber Orchestra, Davis
(OISEAU LYRE 60029, 50198)
Divertimento, K 287, Vienna Octet　(LONDON CS 6352, CM 9352)
Divertimento, K 334, Berlin Philharmonic Orchestra, Karajan
(DEUTSCHE GRAMMOPHON GESELLSCHAFT 139008, 39008)
Eine kleine Nachtmusik, Columbia Symphony Orchestra, Walter
(COLUMBIA MS 6356, ML 5756)
Serenade, K 239, Lucerne Festival Strings, Baumgartner
(DEUTSCHE GRAMMOPHON GESELLSCHAFT 136480) stereo only
Serenade, K 361, London Wind Soloists
(LONDON CS 6346, CM 9346)
Symphony No. 20, Mainz Chamber Orchestra, Kehr
(TURNABOUT 34002, 4002)
Symphony No. 25, London Symphony Orchestra, Davis
(PHILIPS 900133, 500133)
Symphony No. 28, Cleveland Orchestra, Szell
(COLUMBIA MS 6858, ML 6258)
Symphony No. 29, New Philharmonia Orchestra, Klemperer
(ANGEL S 36329, 36329)
Symphony No. 35, Columbia Symphony Orchestra, Walter
(COLUMBIA MS 6255, ML 5655)
Symphony No. 36, Vienna Philharmonic Orchestra, Bernstein
(LONDON CS 6499, CM 9499)
Symphony No. 38, London Symphony Orchestra, Maag
(LONDON CS 6107), stereo only
Symphony No. 39, Cleveland Orchestra, Szell
(EPIC BC 1106, LC 3740)
Symphony No. 40, Philharmonia Orchestra, Klemperer, (ANGEL
S 36183, 36183); or Columbia Symphony Orchestra, Walter
(COLUMBIA MS 6494, ML 5894)
Symphony No. 41, Columbia Symphony Orchestra, Walter, (CO-
LUMBIA MS 6255, ML 5655); or NBC Symphony Orchestra,
Toscanini　(RCA LM 1030), mono only
Sinfonia Concertante, K 364, Druian and Skernick, Cleveland Or-
chestra, Szell　(COLUMBIA MS 6625, ML 6025)
Musorgski, Modest
Pictures at an Exhibition (orchestrated by Ravel), Suisse Ro-
mande Orchestra, Ansermet　(LONDON CS 6177, CM 9246)
Nielsen, Carl
Symphony No. 3, Royal Danish Orchestra, Bernstein
(COLUMBIA MS 6769, ML 6169)
Symphony No. 5, New York Philharmonic, Bernstein
(COLUMBIA MS 6414, ML 5814)

Offenbach, Jacques
Gaîté Parisienne, Ballet score arranged by Rosenthal, New Philharmonia Orchestra, Munch (LONDON 21011, 55009)

Paganini, Nicolo
Violin Concerto No. 1, Friedman, Chicago Symphony Orchestra, Hendl (RCA LSC/LM 2610)

Prokofiev, Serge
Piano Concerto No. 3, Graffman, Cleveland Orchestra, Szell
(COLUMBIA MS 6925, ML 6325)
Violin Concerto No. 1, Stern, Philadelphia Orchestra, Ormandy
(COLUMBIA MS 6635, ML 6035)
Violin Concerto No. 2, Perlman, Boston Symphony Orchestra, Leinsdorf (RCA LSC/LM 2962)
Lieutenant Kije Suite, Philadelphia Orchestra, Ormandy
(COLUMBIA MS 6545, ML 5945)
Peter and the Wolf, Flanders, Philharmonia Orchestra, Kurtz
(CAPITOL SG/G 7211)
Romeo and Juliet (Suites), Minneapolis Symphony Orchestra, Skrowaczewski (MERCURY SR 90315, MG 50315)
Scythian Suite, Boston Symphony Orchestra, Leinsdorf
(RCA LSC/LM 2934)
Symphony No. 1, Classical, Philadelphia Orchestra, Ormandy
(COLUMBIA MS 6545, ML 5945)
Symphony No. 5, New York Philharmonic, Bernstein
(COLUMBIA MS 7005, ML 6405)
Symphony No. 6, Philadelphia Orchestra, Ormandy
(COLUMBIA MS 6489, ML 5889)

Rachmaninoff, Sergei
Piano Concerto No. 2, Ashkenazy, Moscow Philharmonic Orchestra, Kondrashin (LONDON CS 6390, CM 9390)
Piano Concerto No. 3, Cliburn, Symphony of the Air, Kondrashin
(RCA LSC/LM 2355)
Rhapsody on a Theme by Paganini, Graffman, New York Philharmonic, Bernstein (COLUMBIA MS 6634, ML 6034)

Ravel, Maurice
Bolero, New York Philharmonic, Bernstein
(COLUMBIA MS 6011, ML 5293)
Piano Concerto, Katchen, London Symphony Orchestra, Kertesz
(LONDON CS 6487, CM 9487)
Daphnis et Chloé, Boston Symphony Orchestra, Munch
(RCA LSC/LM 2568)
Rapsodie Espagnole, London Symphony Orchestra, Monteux
(LONDON CS 6248, CM 9317)
La Valse, New York Philharmonic, Bernstein
(COLUMBIA MS 6011, ML 5293)

Respighi, Ottorino
Fountains of Rome and *Pines of Rome*, NBC Symphony Orchestra, Toscanini (RCA VIC 1244, mono only); New Philharmonia Orchestra, Munch   (LONDON 21024) stereo only
Rimski-Korsakov, Nikolai
Capriccio Espagnole, London Symphony Orchestra, Argenta
                              (LONDON CS 6006, CM 9192)
Scheherazade, Royal Philharmonic Orchestra, Beecham
                              (ANGEL S 35505, 35505)
Rossini, Gioacchino
La Boutique Fantasque, Ballet score arranged by Respighi, Israel Philharmonic Orchestra, Solti   (LONDON CSTS 15005)
Saint-Saëns, Camille
Cello Concerto No. 1, Fournier, Lamoureux Orchestra, Martinon
              (DEUTSCHE GRAMMOPHON GESELLSCHAFT 138669, 18669)
Piano Concerto No. 2, Entremont, Philadelphia Orchestra, Ormandy   (COLUMBIA MS 6778, ML 6178)
Piano Concerto No. 4, Casadesus, New York Philharmonic, Bernstein   (COLUMBIA MS 6377, ML 5777)
Symphony No. 3, Boston Symphony Orchestra, Munch
                              (RCA LSC/LM 2341)
Schönberg, Arnold
Transfigured Night, Southwest German Radio Symphony Orchestra, Horenstein   (VOX 510460, 10460)
Schubert, Franz
Rosamunde, Incidental Music, Cleveland Orchestra, Szell
                              (COLUMBIA MS 7002, ML 6402)
Symphony No. 5, Royal Philharmonic Orchestra, Beecham
                              (CAPITOL SG/G 7212)
Symphony No. 8, Columbia Symphony Orchestra, Walter
                              (COLUMBIA MS 6218, ML 5618)
Symphony No. 9, London Symphony Orchestra, Krips
                              (LONDON CS 6061, CM 9007)
Schumann, Robert
Piano Concerto, Serkin, Philadelphia Orchestra, Ormandy
                              (COLUMBIA MS 6688, ML 6088)
Cello Concerto, Rostropovitch, Leningrad Philharmonic Orchestra, Rozhdestvensky
              (DEUTSCHE GRAMMOPHON GESELLSCHAFT 138674, 18674)
Symphony No. 1, Berlin Philharmonic Orchestra, Kubelik
              (DEUTSCHE GRAMMOPHON GESELLSCHAFT 138860, 18860)
Symphony No. 4, New York Philharmonic, Bernstein
                              (COLUMBIA MS 6256, ML 5656)
Shostakovitch, Dmitri
Piano Concerto No. 1, Previn, New York Philharmonic, Bernstein
                              (COLUMBIA MS 6392, ML 5792)

Symphony No. 1, Symphony of the Air, Stokowski
(UNITED ARTISTS 8004, 7004)
Symphony No. 5, New York Philharmonic, Bernstein
(COLUMBIA MS 6115, ML 5445)
Symphony No. 10, USSR Symphony Orchestra, Svetlanov
(ANGEL/MELODIYA S 40025, 40025)
Sibelius, Jean
Finlandia and *Swan of Tuonela,* Symphony Orchestra, Stokowski
(CAPITOL SP/P 8399)
Violin Concerto, Heifetz, Chicago Symphony Orchestra, Hendl
(RCA LSC/LM 2435)
Symphony No. 1, Vienna Philharmonic Orchestra, Maazel
(LONDON CS 6375, CM 9375)
Symphony No. 2, Amsterdam Concertgebouw Orchestra, Szell
(PHILIPS PHS 900092, PHM 500092)
Symphony No. 5, New York Philharmonic, Bernstein
(COLUMBIA MS 6749, ML 6149)
Symphony No. 7, Vienna Philharmonic Orchestra, Maazel
(LONDON CS 6488, CM 9488)
Smetana, Bedřich
The Moldau, Symphony Orchestra, Stokowski (RCA LSC/LM 2471)
Strauss, Richard
Death and Transfiguration, Philharmonia Orchestra, Klemperer
(ANGEL S 35976, 35976)
Don Juan, Stadium Concerts Orchestra, Stokowski
(EVEREST SDBR 3023, LPBR 6023)
Ein Heldenleben, Royal Philharmonic Orchestra, Beecham
(SERAPHIM S 60041, 60041)
Till Eulenspiegel's Merry Pranks, Cleveland Orchestra, Szell
(EPIC BC 1011, LC 3439)
Stravinsky, Igor
The Firebird Suite, Symphony Orchestra, Stravinsky
(COLUMBIA MS 7011, ML 6411)
Petrouchka, Suisse Romande Orchestra, Ansermet, (LONDON CS
6009, CM 9229); or Boston Symphony Orchestra, Monteux
(RCA LSC/LM 2376)
The Rite of Spring, New York Philharmonic, Bernstein
(COLUMBIA MS 6319, ML 5719)
Symphony of Psalms, CBC Symphony, Stravinsky
(COLUMBIA MS 6548, ML 5948)
Symphony in Three Movements, Columbia Symphony Orchestra,
Stravinsky (COLUMBIA MS 6331, ML 5731)
Tchaikovsky, Pëtr Ilich
Piano Concerto No. 1, Cliburn, Symphony Orchestra, Kondrashin
(RCA LSC/LM 2252)

Violin Concerto, Heifetz, Chicago Symphony Orchestra, Reiner
(RCA LSC/LM 2129)
Capriccio Italien, Symphony Orchestra, Kondrashin
(RCA LSC/LM 2323)
Francesca da Rimini, New York Philharmonic, Bernstein
(COLUMBIA MS 6258), stereo only
Nutcracker Suite, New York Philharmonic, Bernstein
(COLUMBIA MS 6193, ML 5593)
Romeo and Juliet, Boston Symphony Orchestra, Munch
(RCA LSC/LM 2565)
Serenade for Strings, London Symphony Orchestra, Barbirolli
(ANGEL S 36269, 36269)
Sleeping Beauty Suite, New Philharmonia Orchestra, Stokowski
(LONDON 21008, 55006)
Swan Lake Suite, New Philharmonia Orchestra, Stokowski
(LONDON 21008, 55006)
Symphony No. 4, Vienna Philharmonic Orchestra, Maazel
(LONDON CS 6429, CM 9429)
Symphony No. 5, Boston Symphony Orchestra, Koussevitzky,
(RCA LM 2901), mono only; or Philadelphia Orchestra, Or-
mandy, Columbia   (MS 6109, ML 5435)
Symphony No. 6, Philharmonia Orchestra, Giulini
(SERAPHIM S 60031, 60031)
Variations on a Rococo Theme, Starker, London Symphony Or-
chestra, Dorati   (MERCURY SR 90409, MG 50409)
Vaughan Williams, Ralph
Fantasia on a Theme by Thomas Tallis, London Sinfonia, Bar-
birolli   (ANGEL S 36101, 36101)
Symphony No. 2, London, Hallé Orchestra, Barbirolli
(VANGUARD S 134, 134)
Vivaldi, Antonio
Concerti for Diverse Instruments, New York Philharmonic, Bern-
stein   (COLUMBIA MS 6131, ML 5459)
The Four Seasons, New York Sinfonietta, Goberman
(ODYSSEY 32160132, 32160131)
Wagner, Richard
Miscellaneous Orchestral Works, NBC Symphony Orchestra,
Toscanini   (RCA VIC 1247), mono only
Miscellaneous Orchestral Works, London Symphony Orchestra,
Stokowski   (LONDON 21016), stereo only

MUSIC OF THE BAROQUE

This list of recordings has been chosen with two points in mind: providing a representative sample of Baroque composers, styles, and forms; and including primarily those recordings whose style of performance matches most closely the spirit of the Baroque era.

As we have learned more about the age itself, so have we discovered that the musicians of the seventeenth and eighteenth centuries did not interpret in the style we inherited from our nineteenth-century ancestors. The most obvious differences have to do with ornamentation, phrasing, articulation, dynamics, tempo, instrumental forces, and embellishment. There are quite a few performers today, as distinct from only a few years ago, who have applied themselves to learning about the performance practices of the Baroque age, who understand the necessity for tightening the dotted rhythms of a French Overture, for playing correct ornaments, for phrasing in considerable detail, and for providing embellishments for repeats of a movement. These are the recordings I enjoy the most and which I prefer to recommend.

Albinoni, Tomaso
Concerto a Cinque, Opus 5, No. 5; also includes Handel, *Concerto Grosso, Opus 6, No. 1;* Avison, *Concerto, Opus 9, No. 11;* Manfredini, *Concerto, Opus 3, No. 10;* Telemann, *Concerto in F, (Tafelmusik II),* Marriner, St. Martin-in-the-Fields Academy   (L'OISEAU-LYRE S 264)
▶ *Marriner and his splendid British ensemble bring enormous* ESPRIT *and sensitivity to all their discs.*

Bach, C. P. E.
Concerto in E flat for Harpsichord, Fortepiano, and Orchestra; also includes Fasch, *Sonata for Flute, 2 Recorders, and Continuo;* Quantz, *Trio Sonata in C,* Stadelman, Neumeyer, Wenzinger, Schola Cantorum Basiliensis
      (DEUTSCHE GRAMMOPHON GESELLSCHAFT ARC-73173)
▶ *Interesting blend of old and new instruments, illustrating the* GALANT *perfectly.*

Bach, J. S.
Six Brandenburg Concerti, Dart, London Philomusica (2-OISEAU-
LYRE S 60005/6); mono version includes *Double Violin Con-
certo* and *Suites Nos. 3 and 4* (3-OISEAU-LYRE 50167, 50160,
50159); or Harnoncourt, Vienna Concentus Musicus (original
instruments)   (2-TELEFUNKEN S 9459/60)
▸ *Both stylish, with Harnoncourt using original instruments.*
*Cantatas Nos. 4, Christ lag in Todesbanden, and 111, Was mein
Got will,* Giebel, Höffgen, Rotzsch, Adam, Thomas, Leipzig
Gewandhaus Orchestra and Thomanerchor (TURNABOUT 3 4048)
Cantatas Nos. 57, Selig ist der Mann, and 140, Wachet auf!
Buckel, Stämpfli, Ristenpart, Saar Choir and Orchestra
                              (NONESUCH 7 1029)
*Cantatas Nos. 159, Sehet, wir geh'n hinauf, and 170, Vergnügte
Ruh', beliebte Seelenlust,* Baker, Tear, Shirley-Quick, Marriner,
St. Martin-in-the-Fields Academy   (L'OISEAU-LYRE S 295)
Harpsichord Concerti Nos. 1 in D minor and 2 in E Major,
Malcolm, Münchinger, Stuttgart Chamber Orchestra
                              (LONDON 9392/6392)
*Concerto in D minor for Two Violins; Violin Concerti Nos. 1 in
A minor and 2 in E Major,* Menuhin, Ferras, Masters Chamber
Orchestra   (CAPITOL S G-7210)
Six French Suites, Dart on clavichord
                              (L'OISEAU-LYRE 50208/60039)
Goldberg Variations, Kirkpatrick on harpsichord (DEUTSCHE
GRAMMOPHON GESELLSCHAFT ARC 7 3138); or Landowska on
harpsichord   (RCA VICTOR LM-1080)
▸ *Equally valid, with Landowska the more flamboyant but
older recording.*
Italian Concerto; also includes *English Suite No. 2, Twelve Lit-
tle Preludes, Fantasia in A minor, Adagio in G, Prelude and
Fughetta in C,* Kipnis on harpsichord (It. Conc. & Suite) and
clavichord (remainder)   (EPIC LC 3932/BC 1332)
▸ *Good contrast between harpsichord and clavichord, with
one brief Prelude played on each instrument.*
Lute Music, Gerwig   (NONESUCH 7 1137)
Magnificat; also includes *Cantata No. 78,* Stader, Töpper, Hae-
fliger, Fischer-Dieskau, Richter, Munich Bach Chorus and
Orchestra   (DEUTSCHE GRAMMOPHON GESELLSCHAFT ARC-73197)
Mass in B minor, Stader, Töpper, Haefliger, Engen, Fischer-
Dieskau, Richter, Munich Bach Chorus and Orchestra
        (3-DEUTSCHE GRAMMOPHON GESELLSCHAFT ARC-73177/9)
Motets Nos. 2, 3, and 5, Wolters, N. German Singkreis
                              (NONESUCH 7 1060)
Musical Offering, Menuhin, Bath Festival Orchestra
                              (ANGEL S 35731)

Organ Music, including *Toccata in D minor, Passacaglia, Preludes and Fugues, Chorales,* etc., Walcha
(5-DEUTSCHE GRAMMOPHON GESELLSCHAFT ARC S KL 1 306/10)
▶ *Excellent selection, played by one of the most distinguished organists of our time.*

Orgelbüchlein (with settings of original chorales), Rilling, Gedaechtniskirche Chorus   (4-NONESUCH 73015)

Partita in B minor; also includes *Concerto after Vivaldi No. 15, Fantasia in C minor, Toccata in F sharp minor,* Puyana on harpsichord   (MERCURY 50369/90369)

St. John Passion, Equiluz, Van t'Hoff, Van Egmond, Villisech, Schneeweis, Gillesberger, Vienna Concentus Musicus (original instruments) (3-TELEFUNKEN S KH-19); or Harwood, Pears, Watts, Willcocks, London Philomusica (in English)
(3-LONDON 4348/1320)
▶ *German versus English performance—former particularly interesting attempt at authenticity.*

Eight Sonatas for Flute, Harpsichord, Larrieu, Puyana (2-MERCURY SR 2 9125); or Shaffer, Malcolm (seven sonatas)
(2-ANGEL S 36337, 36350)

Six Sonatas for Violin and Harpsichord, Menuhin, Malcolm, Gauntlett   (2-ANGEL S 3629)

Four Suites for Orchestra, Harnoncourt, Vienna Concentus Musicus (original instruments)   (2-TELEFUNKEN S 9509/10)
▶ *Like the Concentus Musicus* BRANDENBURGS, *very stylish and controversial, with original instruments in greatly reduced forces.*

The Well-Tempered Clavier, Books I and II, Landowska on harpsichord   (6-RCA VICTOR LM 6801)
▶ *A landmark in the extensive Landowska discography.*

Biber, Heinrich Johann

Battalia, Sonata No. 8, Pavern Kirchfahrt, etc.; also includes Muffat, *Concerto Grosso, Suite No. 8,* Harnoncourt, Vienna Concentus Musicus
(DEUTSCHE GRAMMOPHON GESELLSCHAFT ARC-73262)

Mystery Sonatas for Violin and Continuo, Monosoff, Smith, Scholz, Miller   (3-CAMBRIDGE 1 811)

Böhm, Georg

Organ Music; also includes Buxtehude and Walther Organ Music, Gilbert   (PIROUETTE S 19034)

Boismortier, Joseph Bodin de

Concerto à 5 in E minor, Opus 37; included in *French 18th-Century Concert of Chamber Music,* Paris Baroque Ensemble
(MUSIC GUILD S 111)

Daphnis et Chloë ballet suite; also includes La Barre, *Flute*

Suite; Leclair, *Violin Sonata (Tombeau);* Mouton, *Lute Suite,*
Seiler, Chamber Orchestra   (HELIODOR S 25018)
▶ *The* DAPHNIS ET CHLOË *suite is an unparalleled charmer.*
Boyce, William
Eight Symphonies, Janigro, Solisti di Zagreb   (BACH GUILD 70 668)
▶ *Brief, delightful, in Handelian style.*
Buxtehude, Dietrich
Five Cantatas, Krebs, Fischer-Dieskau, Gorvin, Bach Orchestra,
Berlin   (DEUTSCHE GRAMMOPHON GESELLSCHAFT ARC-3096)
Carissimi, Giacomo
Jepthe, Judicium Salomonis, Rilling, Spandauer Kantorei
                                              (TURNABOUT 3 4089)
Charpentier, Marc-Antoine
Magnificat, Te Deum, Martinia, Paillard Orchestra, Chorus
                                              (BACH GUILD 70 663)
Corelli, Arcangelo
Twelve Concerti Grossi, Opus 6, Goberman, Vienna Sinfonietta
                          (3-ODYSSEY 32360001/32360002)
Corrette, Michel
Concertos comique Nos. 3, 4, and 6, Opus 8, for flutes, Rampal,
Baron, Bennett, Schaeffer, Robison, Veyron-Lacroix, Soyer;
also includes Boismortier, *Concertos for Flutes*
                                     (CONNOISSEUR SOCIETY S 362)
Couperin, Louis
Works of, Blanchard Chorus, Chapuis on organ, Mueller on harp-
sichord, Wind ensemble
               (DEUTSCHE GRAMMOPHON GESELLSCHAFT ARC-73261)
Daquin, Louis-Claude
Noëls for Organ, Biggs   (COLUMBIA ML 5567, MS 6167)
Frescobaldi, Girolamo
Toccate canzoni, Arie Musicali; also includes Monteverdi,
Madrigals, Curtis, Berkeley Collegium Musicum
                                              (CAMBRIDGE 1 708)
Froberger, Johann
Le Tombeau de M. Blancrocher, Suites, Dart on clavichord
                                     (L'OISEAU-LYRE 50207/60038)
▶ *The sensitivity of the clavichord is wonderfully revealed.*
Fux, Johann
Ouverture, Sonata; also includes instrumental works by Biber,
Legrenzi, and Schmelzer, Harnoncourt, Vienna Concentus
Musicus   (BACH GUILD 70 690)
Gabrieli, Giovanni
Canzonas and other instrumental works; also includes works by
Gabrieli contemporaries, Wenzinger, Schola Cantorum Basil-
iensis (original instruments)
               (DEUTSCHE GRAMMOPHON GESELLSCHAFT ARC-73154)

Motets, Negri, Biggs, Smith Singers, Texas Boys Choir
(COLUMBIA MS 7071)
Motets and Canzonas by Giovanni and Andrea Gabrieli, Stevens,
Ambrosian Singers   (ANGEL S 36443)
▶ *Relatively little duplication in these well-recorded collections.*
Geminiani, Francesco
Concerto Grosso, Opus 3, No. 3; also includes Bellini, *Oboe Concerto;* Corelli, *Concerto Grosso, Opus 6, No. 1;* Vivaldi,
Cello Concerto in C minor, Marriner, St. Martin-in-the-Fields
Academy   (L'OISEAU-LYRE S 277)
Handel, George Frederick
Arias, Oberlin, Dunn, Baroque Orchestra   (DECCA 7 9407)
Berenice Overture, "Arrival of the Queen of Sheba" from Solomon, Oboe Concertos, Marriner, St. Martin-in-the-Fields Academy   (LONDON ARGO 5 442)
Six Concerti Grossi, Opus 3, Marriner, St. Martin-in-the-Fields
Academy   (LONDON ARGO 5 400)
▶ *One of the most outstanding Baroque discs.*
Twelve Concerti Grossi, Opus 6, Wenzinger, Schola Cantorum
Basiliensis (original instruments) (3-DEUTSCHE GRAMMOPHON
GESELLSCHAFT ARC-73246/8); or Menuhin, Bath Festival Orchestra   (4-ANGEL S 3647)
▶ *Each version commendable; Wenzinger's attempts to be
particularly authentic. A new version by Marriner and the
Academy of St. Martin-in-the-Fields, unissued as of this
writing, promises to be the preferred interpretation.*
*Concerto in C, Alexanderfest; Concerto for Harp, Opus 4, No. 5;
Concerto for Harp and Lute, Opus 4, No. 6,* Jones, London
Philomusica   (L'OISEAU-LYRE 50181/60013)
Dixit Dominus, Willcocks, King's College, Cambridge
(ANGEL S 36331)
Julius Caesar (excerpts), Sutherland, Elkins, Sinclair, Horne,
Conrad, Bonynge, New Symphony
(LONDON 5876/25876)
Messiah, Harper, Watts, Wakefield, Shirley-Quirk, David, London Symphony Orchestra and Chorus, (3-PHILIPS PHM 3 592/
PHS 3 992); or Harwood, Baker, Esswood, Tear, Herincx,
Mackerras, English Chamber Orchestra, Ambrosian Singers
(3-ANGEL S 3705)
▶ *Each is stripped of Victorian overtones; Mackerras more
daring and imaginative in embellishments.*
*Royal Fireworks Music, Concerto for Two Wind Choirs and
Strings,* Mackerras, Wind Band, Pro Arte Orchestra
(BACH GUILD 630/5046)
*Sonatas for Recorder and Continuo, Opus 1, Nos. 1, 2, 4, 7, and
11,* Brüggen, Leonhardt   (TELEFUNKEN S 9421)

Suite in B flat for Harpsichord (Book II); included in collection
of English Harpsichord Music, Kipnis   (EPIC LC 3898/BC 1298)
Water Music (complete), Dart, London Philomusica (L'OISEAU-
LYRE 50178/60010); or Menuhin, Bath Festival Orchestra
(ANGEL S 36173)
▶ *Dart has perhaps the best flavor and lightness.*

Keiser, Reinhard
Croesus (excerpts); also includes operatic excerpts from Handel,
Almira; Mattheson, *Boris Gudenov;* Telemann, *Pimpinone,*
Prey, Otto, Brückner-Rüggeberg, Berlin Philharmonic
(ANGEL S 36273)
▶ *Unusual collection of early 18th-century Hamburg operatic
excerpts.*

Lalande, Michel-Richard de
Symphonies pour les soupers du roi, No. 1; also includes Mouret,
Suites de Simphonies, Scherbaum, Kuentz Chamber Orchestra
(DEUTSCHE GRAMMOPHON GESELLSCHAFT ARC-73233)

Leclair, Jean Marie
Concerto in C, Opus 7, No. 4; also includes *Flute Concerti* by
Grétry, Jacques Loeillet, and Quantz; C. Monteux, Marriner,
St. Martin-in-the-Fields Academy   (L'OISEAU-LYRE S 279)

Locatelli, Pietro
L'Arte del Violino, Opus 3, Concerti Nos. 1 to 4, Lautenbacher,
Kehr, Mainz Chamber Orchestra   (2-VOX 500 500)
Concerto Grosso, Opus 1, No. 9; also includes Corelli, *Concerto
Grosso, Opus 6, No. 7;* Torelli, *Concerto, Opus 6, No. 10;*
Albicastro, *Concerto No. 6 in B flat;* Handel, *Concerto Grosso,
Opus 6, No. 6,* Marriner, St. Martin-in-the-Fields Academy
(L'OISEAU-LYRE 50214/60045)

Louis XIII
Ballet de Merlaison; also includes Charpentier, *Messe pour
Plusieurs Instruments,* Chailley, Instrumental and Vocal En-
semble   (NONESUCH 7 1130)
▶ *Even kings could be composers, though not so distinguished
as the professionals.*

Lully, Jean Baptiste
Le Temple de la paix (ballet); also includes Fischer, *Journal de
printemps, Opus 1 (Suites);* Muffat, *Nobles Jeunesse Suite,* Fro-
ment, L'Oiseau-Lyre Ensemble   (L'OISEAU-LYRE 50136)
▶ *There is relatively little well-performed Lully on discs. This
is one of the better ones.*

Marcello, Alessandro
Oboe Concerto; Concerti Nos. 2, 3, 4, and 6, La Cetra, Cantore
(oboe), I Musici   (PHILIPS WS 9085)
▶ *Competently played, but not the last word in stylistic
acumen.*

Monteverdi, Claudio
  Combattimento di Tancredi e Clorinda, Ballo delle Ingrate,
    Stevens, Accademia Monteverdiana (EXPÉRIENCES ANONYMES 72)
  Lamento d'Arianna and other madrigals; also includes madrigals
    by Marenzio, Gesualdo, etc., Deller Consort
                                          (BACH GUILD 70 671)
  Madrigals, Deller Consort, Baroque Ensemble, (BACH GUILD
    579/5007); or Jürgens, Hamburg Monteverdi Chorus
                                          (TELEFUNKEN S 9438)
  Madrigals; also includes Banchieri, *La Pazzia senile,* Sestetto
    Italiano Luca Marenzio   (HELIODOR S 25060)
    ▶ *Relatively little duplication in these madrigal collections;
    the Sestetto Luca Marenzio has unusual charm.*
  Magnificat for Six Voices, Mass for Four Voices, Malcolm,
    Carmelite Priory (London) Chorus   (L'OISEAU-LYRE S 263)
    ▶ *Particular emphasis on emotional impact.*
  Orfeo, Krebs, Guilleaume, Wenzinger
              (DEUTSCHE GRAMMOPHON GESELLSCHAFT ARC-3035/6)
    ▶ *An old though serviceable recording; at least two new re-
    cordings are in preparation.*
  Vespro della Beata Vergine (1610), Hansmann, Jacobeit, Rogers,
    Van t'Hoff, Van Egmond, Villisech, Harnoncourt, Jürgens,
    Concentus Musicus, Vienna Boys Choir, Hamburg Monteverdi
    Chorus, (Original instruments)   (2-TELEFUNKEN S 9501/2)
Pergolesi, Giovanni Battista
  Six Concertinos (attrib.), *Two Flute Concerti* (attrib.), Rampal,
    Münchinger, Stuttgart Chamber Orchestra
                          (LONDON 9393 & 9395/6393 & 6395)
Praetorius, Michael
  Terpsichore (Dances); also includes Schein, *Banchetto musicale
    Suites;* Widmann, *Dances,* Terpsichore Collegium
              (DEUTSCHE GRAMMOPHON GESELLSCHAFT ARC-73153)
    ▶ *Beautifully performed collection of early Baroque German
    dances.*
Purcell, Henry
  Come Ye Sons of Art; also includes *Anthems,* Deller, Oriana
    Chorus and Orchestra   (BACH GUILD 635/5047)
    ▶ *The piece with spectacular duet for countertenors is* SOUND
    THE TRUMPET.
  Dido and Aeneas, Baker, Clark, Sinclair, Herincx, Lewis, Cham-
    ber Orchestra, St. Anthony Singers (L'OISEAU-LYRE 50216/
    60047); or Troyanos, McDaniel, Esswood, Mackerras, NW
    German Radio Chamber Orchestra, Monteverdi Chorus
              (DEUTSCHE GRAMMOPHON GESELLSCHAFT ARC-198424)
    ▶ *Distinguished performances of Purcell's short but great
    opera.*

Fantasias and Sonatas (selection), Menuhin, Bath Festival Ensemble   (ANGEL S 36270)
Suites from The Gordian Knot Untied and *The Virtuous Wife, Trumpet Sonata, Keyboard pieces,* Kehr, Cologne Rhenish Orchestra, Gerlin (harpsichord)   (NONESUCH 7 1027)
▶ *The orchestral work is quite stylish but heavy-handed keyboard work disappoints.*
Indian Queen, Cantelo, Tear, Brown Patridge, Keyte, Mackerras, English Chamber Orchestra, St. Anthony Singers
                                          (L'OISEAU-LYRE S 294)
▶ *Purcell at both his most humorous and affecting.*
Dioclesian: Incidental Music, Deller, Vienna Concentus Musicus
                                          (BACH GUILD 70 682)
Songs, Oberlin (countertenor) (COUNTERPOINT/ESOTERIC 5 535);
Songs (also includes instrumental music), Deller, Cantelo, Bevan   (2-BACH GUILD 70 570/1)

Rameau, Jean Philippe
Hippolyte et Aricie, Lewis, English Chamber Orchestra, St. Anthony Singers   (3-L'OISEAU-LYRE S 286/8)
Suite in E minor for Harpsichord; also includes F. Couperin and L. Couperin, *Harpsichord Pieces;* Boismortier, *Suite No. 3 in E,* Kipnis (harpsichord)   (EPIC LC 3889/BC 1289)
Gavotte varié; also includes harpsichord works of C.P.E. Bach, Scarlatti, Fischer, F. and L. Couperin, Chambonnières, Dieupart, and Telemann, Puyana (harpsichord)
                                          (MERCURY 50411/90411)
▶ *The last two discs provide a partial anthology of French Baroque harpsichord music.*
Pygmalion (ballet), Couraud, Lamoureux Chamber Orchestra
                    (DEUTSCHE GRAMMOPHON GESELLSCHAFT ARC-73202)
Le Temple de la Gloire, Suite; also includes Grétry, *Suite,* Leppard, English Chamber Orchestra   (L'OISEAU-LYRE S 297)

Scarlatti, Alessandro
Concertato in D; also includes concertos by Albinoni, Pergolesi, Tartini, and Vivaldi. Haas, London Baroque Ensemble
                                          (VANGUARD EVERYMAN S 192)
▶ *Excellent Italian repertoire, played fairly well, but also with great conviction.*
Cantata, Su le Sponde del Tebro; also includes Mozart, *Exsultate Jubilate,* etc., Stader, Richter, Munich Bach Orchestra
             (DEUTSCHE GRAMMOPHON GESELLSCHAFT 19291/136291)
Toccata No. 7 in D minor for Harpsichord; also includes harpsichord works by Pasquini, Cimarosa, Frescobaldi, Rossi, and Galuppi, Kipnis   (EPIC LC 3911/BC 1311)

Scarlatti, Domenico
Sonatas for Harpsichord, Kirkpatrick *(60 Sonatas)* (4-ODYSSEY
32260007, 32260012); or Landowska *(40 Sonatas)*
(2-ANGEL COLH 73/304)
▶ *The Landowska 1930's recordings have great atmosphere.
Kirkpatrick is the renowned Scarlatti authority.*
Schein, Johann Hermann
Banchetto musicale, Suites Nos. 1 and 2; also includes Prae-
torius, *Dances,* Conrad Ensemble   (NONESUCH 7 1128)
Schütz, Heinrich
The Christmas Story, Ehmann, Westphalian Kantorei
(VANGUARD EVERYMAN S 232)
▶ *The most accessible Schütz I know.*
Klein Geistliche Konzerte, Book I, Ehmann, Westphalian Kan-
torei   (2-NONESUCH 7 3012)
Cantiones Sacrae, Eighteen Motets, Träder, Hannover Nieder-
sächsischer Singkreis   (NONESUCH 1062/71062)
Soler, Padre Antonio
Fandango, Two Sonatas; also includes sonatas by Scarlatti and
Blasco de Nebra; Kipnis on harpsichord   (EPIC BC 1374)
Stölzel, Gottfried Heinrich
*Concerto Grosso in D for Six Trumpets, Timpani, Double String
Orchestra, and Continuo;* also includes Graupner, *Concerto for
Two Flutes;* Pisendel, *Violin Concerto No. 1,* Redel, Chamber
Orchestra   (DEUTSCHE GRAMMOPHON GESELLSCHAFT ARC-73266)
▶ *The late-Baroque Stölzel has enormous brilliance; the rest
is somewhat dull.*
Tartini, Giuseppe
Violin Concertos in D and G; also includes Nardini, *Violin Con-
certo in E flat,* Melkus, Wenzinger, Vienna Capella Academy
(DEUTSCHE GRAMMOPHON GESELLSCHAFT ARC-73270)
Symphony in A; also includes orchestral works of Albinoni,
Geminiani, and Locatelli; De Stoutz, Zurich Chamber Orchestra
(VANGUARD EVERYMAN S 212)
Telemann, Georg Philipp
Concerto in D for Horn and Orchestra; also includes Albinoni,
Oboe Concerto, Opus 9, No. 4; Fasch, *Concerto in D for
Trumpet;* K. Stamitz, *Clarinet Concerto;* Vivaldi, *Flute Con-
certo (P. 77),* Penzel, Winschermann, Deutsche Bachsolisten
(NONESUCH 7 1148)
▶ *Performance of* HORN CONCERTO *particularly virtuosic.*
Concerto in C for Recorder, Strings, and Continuo; also includes
Recorder Concerti by Handel and Vivaldi, Krainis, Marriner,
London Strings   (MERCURY 50443/90443)
Concerto in E minor for Recorder, Flute, and Strings; also in-

cludes *Concerto for Four Violins, Concerto for Flute and Oboe d'Amore, Concerto for Three Oboes and Three Violins,* Sparr, Schaeffer, Meyer
(DEUTSCHE GRAMMOPHON GESELLSCHAFT ARC-3109)
▶ *Telemann both old-fashioned and* AVANT-GARDE.
Don Quichotte Suite; also includes Purcell: Suite from *The Fairy Queen;* Haydn: *Echo Divertimento,* Böttcher, Vienna Solisten
(BACH GUILD 70 662)
Musique de Table (Tafelmusik) (Productions 1-3), Brüggen, Concerto Amsterdam   (6-TELEFUNKEN S TDL-1 S 9449/54)
▶ *Mostly first-rate Telemann, brilliantly and stylishly recorded.*
Paris Quartets Nos. 1, 4, and 6, Quadro Amsterdam
(TELEFUNKEN S 9448)
Overture No. 1 in G minor for Harpsichord; also includes Pachelbel, *Chorale Partita;* Buxtehude, *Variations;* Kuhnau, *Biblical Sonata No. 1, David and Goliath;* Works by J. S. and C. P. E. Bach, and Kirmaier, Kipnis (harpsichord and clavichord)   (EPIC LC 3963/BC 1363)
Suite in A minor for Recorder and Strings; also includes *Concerto for Flute and Recorder in E minor, Overture in G (Nations: Ancient and Modern),* Brüggen, Tilegant, Southwest German Chamber Orchestra   (TELEFUNKEN S 9413)
Water Music; also includes *Concerto in A for Flute, Harpsichord, and Continuo; Suite No. 6 for Oboe, Violin, and Continuo; Trio Sonata in E flat for Oboe, Harpsichord, and Continuo;* Wenzinger, Schola Cantorum Basiliensis
(DEUTSCHE GRAMMOPHON GESELLSCHAFT ARC-73198)

Torelli, Giuseppe
Trumpet Concerto in D; also includes trumpet pieces by Alberti, Biber, Manfredini, Haydn, and L. Mozart; Wobisch, Janigro, Solisti di Zagreb   (BACH GUILD 641/5053)

Vivaldi, Antonio
Concerto in C for Ottavino (P. 79); also includes *Cello Concerto (P. 434), Concerto for Guitar and Viola d'Amore (P. 266),* and *Concerto for Two Violins (P. 222),* Linde (sopranino recorder), Hofmann, Seiler Chamber Orchestra (DEUTSCHE GRAMMOPHON GESELLSCHAFT ARC-73218); or Brüggen (soprano recorder), Rieu, Amsterdam Chamber Orchestra, which also includes *Concerto alla Rustica (P. 143), Concerti Grossi in A (P. 235), C minor (P. 427),* and *D minor, Opus 3, No. 11*
(TELEFUNKEN S 9426)
▶ *Either version of P. 79 is worth obtaining. The concerto is usually played on piccolo, which was unknown to Vivaldi.*
The Four Seasons, Opus 8, Nos. 1 to 4, Bronne, Monosoff, Kwalwasser, Koutzen, Goberman, New York Sinfonietta, (ODYSSEY

32160131/32160132); or Tomasow, Janigro, I Solisti di
Zagreb, (BACH 564/5001); or Corigliano, Bernstein, New York
Philharmonic, (COLUMBIA ML 6144/MS 6744); or Buechner,
Redel, Munich Pro Arte Chamber Orchestra
                              (MUSICAL HERITAGE SOCIETY MHS S 579)
▶ *There is as yet no stylistically satisfactory* FOUR SEASONS,
though Redel, in mediocre-sounding monophonic recording,
adds more embellishments than most. The rest may be well
played but are conservative.
Concerto in C for Two Trumpets (P. 75); Flute Concertos in G
minor, Opus 10, No. 2, La Notte, and D, Opus 10, No. 3, Il
Gardellino; Concerto in B minor for Four Violins, Opus 3, No.
10; Violin Concerto in E minor, Opus 4, No. 2, Redel, Munich
Pro Arte Chamber Orchestra
                              (MUSICAL HERITAGE SOCIETY MHS S 593)
Concerto in B minor for Four Violins, Opus 3, No. 10; also in-
cludes Handel, *Concerto Grosso, Opus 6, No. 4;* Gabrieli,
Canzona noni toni; Telemann, *Viola Concerto in G,* Marriner,
St. Martin-in-the-Fields Academy   (L'OISEAU-LYRE S 276)
▶ *One of great Vivaldi performances for sheer* ESPRIT.
Gloria in D; also includes Pergolesi, *Magnificat,* Baker, Vaughan,
Willcocks, King's College Choir   (LONDON ARGO Z 505)

SONATAS AND CHAMBER MUSIC

Bach, Johann Sebastian
Sonatas and Partitas for Unaccompanied Violin, Szigeti
                    (VANGUARD BACH GUILD 926/9), MONO ONLY
Sonatas for Violin and Harpsichord, Grumiaux and Sartori
                    (PHILIPS PHS 2-997, PHM 2-597)
Suites for Unaccompanied Cello, Starker
                    (MERCURY SR 3-9016, OL 3-116)
Bartók, Béla
Six String Quartets, Juilliard Quartet
                    (COLUMBIA D3S 717, D3L 317)
Sonata for Two Pianos and Percussion, Votapek, Vosgerchian,
etc.   (CAMBRIDGE 1803, 803)
Beethoven, Ludwig van
Great Fugue, Fine Arts Quartet   (CONCERT DISC 249, 1249)
String Quartets, Opus 18, Amadeus Quartet
        (DEUTSCHE GRAMMOPHON GESELLSCHAFT 138531/3, 18531/3)

String Quartets, Opera 59, 74, 95, Budapest String Quartet
(COLUMBIA M4S 616, M4L 254)
String Quartets, Opera 127, 130/1/2/5, Budapest String Quartet
(COLUMBIA M5S 677, M5L 277)
Septet, Vienna Octet Members (LONDON CS 6132, CM 9129)
Sonatas for Cello and Piano, Fournier and Kempff
(DEUTSCHE GRAMMOPHON GESELLSCHAFT 138993/5), STEREO ONLY
Sonatas for Violin and Piano, Szigeti and Arrau (VANGUARD
1109/12, MONO ONLY); *Kreutzer,* Szeryng and Rubinstein
(RCA LSC/LM 2377)
Trios for Piano and Strings: Kakadu, Senofsky, Trepel, Graffman
(RCA LSC/LM 2715); *Opus 70, Nos. 1 and 2,* Alma Trio
(DECCA 710064, 10064); *Archduke,* Stern, Rose, Istomin
(COLUMBIA MS 6819, ML 6219)
Bloch, Ernest
Piano Quintet, Glazer with Fine Arts Quartet
(CONCERT DISC 252, 1252)
String Quartet No. 3, Edinburgh String Quartet
(MONITOR S 2123, 2123)
String Quartet No. 5, Fine Arts Quartet (CONCERT DISC 225, 1225)
Sonata for Violin and Piano No. 1, Stern and Zakin
(COLUMBIA MS 6717, ML 6117)
Boccherini, Luigi
Quintet in C for Guitar and Strings, Diaz, Schneider, etc.
(VANGUARD 71147, 1147)
Quintet in E for Strings, Schneider, Galimir, etc.
(VANGUARD 71147, 1147)
Borodin, Alexander
Quartet No. 2 in D, Hollywood String Quartet
(CAPITOL P 8187), MONO ONLY
Brahms, Johannes
Three String Quartets, Budapest String Quartet
(COLUMBIA M2S 734, M2L 334)
Piano Quartet No. 1, Quartetto di Roma
(DEUTSCHE GRAMMOPHON GESELLSCHAFT 138104), STEREO ONLY
Clarinet Quintet, Boskovsky and Vienna Octet Members
(LONDON CS 6234, CM 9301)
Piano Quintet, Rubinstein and Guarneri String Quartet
(RCA LSC/LM 2971)
Sextet No. 1 for Strings, Opus 18, Menuhin, Masters, etc.
(ANGEL S 36234, 36234)
Sextet No. 2 for Strings, Opus 36, Heifetz, Baker, etc.
(RCA LSC/LM 2739)
Violin and Piano Sonatas Nos. 1 and 3, Stern and Zakin
(COLUMBIA MS 6522, ML 5922)

Trios for Piano and Strings, Stern, Rose, Istomin
(COLUMBIA M2S 760, M2L 360)
Trio for Horn, Piano, and Violin, Bloom, Serkin and Tree
(COLUMBIA MS 6243, ML 5643)

Chopin, Frederic
Piano Sonatas Nos. 2 and 3, Rubinstein   (RCA LSC/LM 2554)

Corelli, Arcangelo
La Follia, Bress   (FOLKWAYS 3351), MONO ONLY

Debussy, Claude
String Quartet, Juilliard String Quartet   (RCA LSC/LM 2413)
Sonata No. 1 for Cello and Piano, Starker and Sebok
(MERCURY SR 90405, MG 50405)
Sonata No. 2 for Flute, Viola, and Harp, Melos Ensemble Members   (OISEAU LYRE 60048, 50217)
Sonata No. 3 for Violin and Piano, Stern and Zakin
(COLUMBIA MS 6139, ML 5470)

Dvořák, Anton
String Quartet No. 3, Vlach Quartet   (ARTIA S 706, 706)
String Quartet No. 6, Janacek Quartet (LONDON CS 6394, CM 9394)
String Quartet No. 7, Guarneri Quartet   (RCA LSC/LM 2887)
Piano Quintet, Peter Serkin, Schneider, etc.
(VANGUARD 71148, 1148)
Dumka Trio, Dumka Trio   (TURNABOUT 34075, 4075)

Fauré, Gabriel
Piano Quartet No. 1, Pennario, Shapiro, etc. (CAPITOL SP/P 8558)
Piano Quartet No. 2, Babin, Goldberg, etc.   (RCA LSC/LM 2735)
String Quartet, Loewenguth Quartet   (TURNABOUT 34014, 4014)

Franck, César
Piano Quintet, Curzon with Vienna Philharmonic Quartet
(LONDON CS 6226, CM 9294)
Violin and Piano Sonata, Morini and Firkusny
(DECCA 710038, 10038)

Geminiani, Francesco
Sonata for Solo Violin, Staryk   (BAROQUE 2851, 1851)

Handel, George Frederick
Sonatas for Violin and Harpsichord, Opus 1, Olevsky and Valenti   (WESTMINSTER 9064/6), MONO ONLY

Haydn, Franz Josef
String Quartets: Opus 3, No. 5, Janacek String Quartet (LONDON CS 6385, CM 9385); *Opus 33, No. 2, Joke,* Janacek Quartet (LONDON CS 6385, CM 9385); *Opus 33, No. 3, Bird,* Hungarian Quartet (TURNABOUT 34062, 4062); *Opus 64, No. 5, Lark,* Hungarian Quartet (TURNABOUT 34062, 4062); *Opus 76, No. 3, Emperor,* Amadeus Quartet
(DEUTSCHE GRAMMOPHON GESELLSCHAFT 138886, 18886)

Piano Trio No. 1, Cortot, Thibaud, Casals
(ANGEL COLH 12), MONO ONLY

Mendelssohn, Felix
String Quartets Nos. 2 and 3, Juilliard String Quartet
(EPIC BC 1287, LC 3887)
Piano Trio No. 1, Stern, Rose, Istomin
(COLUMBIA MS 7083), STEREO ONLY
Octet, Laredo, Schneider, etc.   (COLUMBIA MS 6848, ML 6248)

Mozart, Wolfgang A.
Quartets Nos. 14-19, "Haydn" Quartets, Juilliard String Quartet
(EPIC BSC 143, SC 6043)
Quartets Nos. 20-23, Budapest String Quartet
(COLUMBIA ML 5007/8), MONO ONLY
Quartets Nos. 22 and 23, Guarneri String Quartet
(RCA LSC/LM 2888)
Piano Quartets No. 1 and 2, Peter Serkin, Schneider, etc.
(VANGUARD 71140, 1140)
Clarinet Quintet, Boskovsky and Vienna Octet Members
(LONDON CS 6379, CM 9379)
String Quintets Nos. 3-6, Griller Quartet and Primrose
(VANGUARD S 158, 194; 158, 194)
String Divertimento, K 563, Italian String Trio
(DEUTSCHE GRAMMOPHON GESELLSCHAFT 139150, 39150)
Quintet for Piano and Winds, Ashkenazy and London Wind
Soloists   (LONDON CS 6494, CM 9494)
Violin and Piano Sonatas, (6 of them), Kroll and Balsam
(OISEAU LYRE 60043/4, 50212/3)
Violin and Piano Sonatas, K 378 and 454, Heifetz and Smith
(RCA LM 1958)

Ravel, Maurice
Introduction and Allegro, Challan, etc.   (ANGEL S 36290, 36290)
String Quartet, Quartetto Italiano   (PHILIPS 900154) STEREO ONLY
Violin Sonata, Oistrakh, Bauer   (PHILIPS 900112, 500112)

Schönberg, Arnold
Four String Quartets, Juilliard String Quartet
(COLUMBIA ML 4735/7), MONO ONLY

Schubert, Franz
Octet, Vienna Octet   (LONDON CS 6051, CM 9110)
String Quartet No. 13, Juilliard String Quartet
(EPIC BC 1313, LC 3913)
String Quartet No. 14, Death and the Maiden, Vienna Philhar-
monic Quartet   (LONDON CS 6384, CM 9384)
String Quartet No. 15, Juilliard String Quartet
(EPIC BC 12360, LC 3860)

Piano Quintet in A, Trout, Peter Serkin, Schneider, etc.
(VANGUARD 71145, 1145)
String Quintet in C, Vienna Philharmonic Members
(LONDON CS 6441, CM 9441)
Sonatinas for Violin and Piano, Schneider and Peter Serkin
(VANGUARD 71128, 1128)
Trio No. 1, Stern, Rose, Istomin   (COLUMBIA MS 6716, ML 6116)
Schumann, Robert
Piano Quartet, Pennario, Shapiro, etc.   (CAPITOL SP/P 8558)
Piano Quintet, Bernstein, Juilliard String Quartet
(COLUMBIA MS 6929, ML 6329)
Smetana, Bedřich
String Quartet No. 1, Guarneri String Quartet   (RCA LSC/LM 2887)
String Quartet No. 2, Smetana Quartet
(CROSSROADS 22160112, 22160111)
Tartini, Giuseppe
Violin Sonata No. 10, Didone Abbandonnata, Morini and Pom-
mers   (DECCA 710014, 10014)
Violin Sonata in G Minor, Devil's Trill, Szeryng
(RCA VICS/VIC 1037)
Tchaikovsky, Pëtr Ilich
String Quartet No. 1, Hollywood String Quartet
(CAPITOL P 8187), MONO ONLY

PIANO MUSIC

Albeniz, Isaac
Iberia, (Complete), Alicia de Larrocha   (EPIC SC 6058/BSC 158)
Alkan, Charles-Henri
Symphony for Piano, Raymond Lewenthal   (RCA LM/LSC 2815)
Bach, Johann Sebastian
Chromatic Fantasy and Fugue in D minor, Rudolf Serkin
(COLUMBIA ML 4350)
French Suite No. 5 in G, Emil Gilels   (RCA LM/LSC 2868)
Goldberg Variations, Glenn Gould   (COLUMBIA ML 5060)
Italian Concerto in F, Glenn Gould
(COLUMBIA ML 5472/MS 6141)
Partitas, (Complete), Glenn Gould
(COLUMBIA M2L 293/M2S 693)
Toccata, Adagio and Fugue in C (arranged by Busoni), Vladi-
mir Horowitz   (COLUMBIA M2L 382/M2S 728)
Well-Tempered Clavier, (Complete), Rosalyn Tureck
(DECCA DX 127/8)

Balakirev, Mili
  Islamey, Julius Katchen   (LONDON CS 6064)
Barber, Samuel
  Piano Sonata, Vladimir Horowitz   (RCA LD 7021)
Bartók, Béla
  Out of Doors, Suite, Leonid Hambro   (BARTOK 902)
  Sonata for Two Pianos and Percussion, Gyorgy Sandor and Rolf
    Reinhardt, pianists; Otto Schad and Richard Sohm, percussion-
    ists   (TURNABOUT 4036/34036)
  Suite for Piano, Opus 14, Béla Bartók   (BARTOK 903)

Beethoven, Ludwig van
  Bagatelles, (Complete), Alfred Brendel (TURNABOUT 4077/34077)
  Piano Sonata No. 3 in C, Opus 2, No. 3, *Piano Sonata No. 14
    in C sharp minor,* Opus 27, No. 2 *(Moonlight),* Josef Hofmann
                        (ARCHIVE OF PIANO MUSIC X 903)
  Piano Sonata No. 8 in C minor, Opus 13, *(Pathétique),* Arthur
    Rubinstein   (RCA LM/LSC 2654)
  Piano Sonata No. 21 in C, Opus 53, *(Waldstein),* Vladimir Horo-
    witz   (RCA LM 2009)
  Piano Sonata No. 23 in F minor, Opus 57, *(Appassionata),*
    Vladimir Horowitz   (RCA LM/LSC 2366)
  Piano Sonata No. 26 in E flat, Opus 81, *(Les Adieux),* Van
    Cliburn   (RCA LM/LSC 2931)
  Piano Sonata No. 29 in B flat, Opus 106, *(Hammerklavier),*
    Daniel Barenboim   (COMMAND 11026)
  Piano Sonata No. 31 in A flat, Opus 110, *Piano Sonata No. 32
    in C,* Opus 111, Hans Richter-Haaser   (ANGEL S 35749)
  Variations in C minor, Alfred Brendel   (VOX SVBX 5416)
  Variations on a Theme by Diabelli, Rudolf Serkin
                                       (COLUMBIA ML 5246)

Brahms, Johannes
  Piano Sonatas Nos. 1 and 2, Julius Katchen
                        (LONDON CM 9410/CS 6410)
  Piano Sonata No. 3 in F minor, Julius Katchen
                        (LONDON CM 9482/CS 6482)
  *Variations on a Theme by Handel, Variations on a Theme by
    Paganini,* Julius Katchen   (LONDON CM 9474/CS 6474)
  Six Intermezzi, Three Rhapsodies, One Capriccio, Artur Rubin-
    stein   (RCA LM 1787)

Chabrier, Emmanuel
  Complete Piano Works, Rena Kyrakou   (VOX SVBX 5400)

Chopin, Frederic
  Andante Spianato and Grande Polonaise, Vladimir Horowitz
                                       (RCA LD 7021)
  The Four Ballades, Artur Rubinstein   (RCA LM/LSC 2370)

The Etudes, (Complete) Vladimir Ashkenazy   (ARTIA MK 203)
Fantaisie in F minor, Van Cliburn   (RCA LM/LSC 2576)
The Four Impromptus, Artur Rubinstein   (RCA LM/LSC 7037)
The Mazurkas, (Complete), Artur Rubinstein   (RCA LM/LSC 6177)
Nocturnes, Moura Lympany   (ANGEL S 3602)
Polonaises, Artur Rubinstein   (RCA LM/LSC 7037)
Scherzos Nos. 1, 2 and 3, Josef Hofmann
                          (ARCHIVE OF PIANO MUSIC X 904)
Scherzo No. 4, Vladimir Horowitz   (ANGEL COLH 300)
Piano Sonata No. 2 in B flat minor, Vladimir Horowitz
                          (COLUMBIA KL 5771/KS 6371)
Piano Sonata No. 3 in B minor, Dinu Lipatti (COLUMBIA ML 4721)
Waltzes, Artur Rubinstein   (RCA LM/LSC 2726)

Clementi, Muzio
Sonatas, Vladimir Horowitz   (RCA LM 1902)

Debussy, Claude
Two Arabesques, Leonard Pennario   (CAPITOL S P 8648)
Children's Corner Suite, Walter Gieseking   (ANGEL 35067)
En Blanc et Noir, Leonid Hambro and Jascha Zayde
                          (COMMAND 11013)
Estampes, Walter Gieseking   (ANGEL 35065)
Preludes, (Complete), Robert Casadesus
                          (COLUMBIA ML 4977/78)

Dello Joio, Norman
Piano Sonata No. 3, Frank Glazer   (CONCERT-DISC 1217, 217)

Dvořák, Anton
The Slavonic Dances, (Complete), Alfred Brendel and Walter
    Klien   (TURNABOUT 4064, 34064)

Fauré, Gabriel
Piano Music, (Complete), Grant Johannessen
                          (GOLDEN CREST 4030, 4046, 4048)

Ginastera, Alberto
Piano Sonata, Hilde Somer   (DESTO 6402)

Gottschalk, Louis Moreau
Piano Music, Eugene List   (VANGUARD 485)

Granados, Enrique
Spanish Dances, Alicia de Larrocha   (EPIC LC 3943/BC 1343)

Grieg, Edvard
Lyric Pieces, Walter Gieseking   (ANGEL 35450/1)

Griffes, Charles Tomlinson
Roman Sketches, Leonid Hambro   (LYRICHORD 105)

Haydn, Franz Josef
Piano Sonatas, (Nos. 6, 18, 20, 23, 28, 30, 31, 38, 40, 46, and
    48), Artur Balsam   (L'OISEAU-LYRE S 273/5)
Piano Sonatas Nos. 50 and 52, Nadia Reisenberg
                          (MONITOR S 2097)

Hindemith, Paul
  Piano Sonata No. 3, Paul Badura-Skoda   (WESTMINSTER 9309)
Ives, Charles
  Piano Sonata No. 1, William Masselos   (RCA LM/LSC 2941)
Kodály, Zoltán
  Dances of Marosszek, Andor Foldes   (DECCA 9913)
Liszt, Franz
  Dante Sonata, David Bar-Illan   (RCA LM/LSC 2943)
  Hungarian Rhapsodies Nos. 2 and 6, Vladimir Horowitz
                                          (RCA LM 2584)
    Hungarian Rhapsody No. 11, William Kapell   (RCA LM 2585)
    Hungarian Rhapsody No. 12, Ruth Slenczynska   (DECCA 79991)
    Mephisto Waltz, William Kapell   (RCA LM 2588)
    Mazeppa, Erwin Nyireghazy   (ARGO DA 43)
    Piano Sonata in B minor, Emil Gilels   (RCA LM/LSC 2811)
    Transcendental Etudes, Gyorgy Cziffra   (ANGEL 3591)
Mendelssohn, Felix
  Allegro Brillant, Leonid Hambro and Jascha Zayde
                                          (COMMAND 11010)
    Songs Without Words, Guiomar Novaes   (VOX 12000/512000)
    Variations sérieuses, Vladimir Horowitz   (RCA LVT 1043)
Mozart, Wolfgang Amadeus
  Fantasia in C minor, (K 396), Lili Kraus   (HAYDN SOCIETY 9044)
  Fantasia in D minor, (K 397), Wilhelm Kempff
          (DEUTSCHE GRAMMOPHON GESELLSCHAFT 18707/138707)
  Fantasia in C minor, (K 475), Daniel Barenboim
                                          (WESTMINSTER 19120/17120)
  Piano Sonata No. 8 in A minor, (K 310), Dinu Lipatti
                                          (COLUMBIA ML 4633)
  Piano Sonata No. 11 in A (K 331), Guiomar Novaes   (VOX 9080)
  Piano Sonata in D for Two Pianos, (K 448), Josef and Rosina
    Lhevinne   (RCA LM 2824)
  Variations on "Ah, Vous Dirai-Je, Maman," (K 265), Andre
    Previn   (COLUMBIA ML 5986/MS 6586)
Musorgski, Modest
  Pictures at an Exhibition, Vladimir Horowitz   (RCA LM 2357)
Prokofiev, Sergei
  Piano Sonata No. 2 in D minor, Emil Gilels   (ARTIA 163)
  Piano Sonata No. 7, Vladimir Horowitz   (RCA LD 7021)
  Piano Sonata No. 9 in C, Sviatoslav Richter   (MONITOR 2034)
Rachmaninoff, Sergei
  Humoresque, Barcarolle, Polichinelle, Etude Tableau, Opus 39,
    No. 6, Sergei Rachmaninoff   (ARGO DA 42)
  Prelude in C sharp minor, Prelude in F minor, Etude in E flat,

Opus 33, No. 7, and *Polka de W.R.*, Sergei Rachmaninoff
(RCA LM 2587)
Preludes, Constance Keene   (PHILIPS WS 2 006)
Ravel, Maurice
Gaspard de la Nuit, Vladimir Ashkenazy
(LONDON CM 9472, CS 6472)
Complete Piano Music, Robert Casadesus   (ODYSSEY 323 60003)
Roussel, Albert
Suite pour Piano, Francoise Petit   (L'OISEAU-LYRE 50221/60052)
Scarlatti, Domenico
Sonatas, Vladimir Horowitz   (COLUMBIA ML 6058/MS 6658)
Schubert, Franz
German Dances, Walter Hautzig   (TURNABOUT 4006/34006)
Impromptus, Sviatoslav Richter   (MONITOR 2027)
Piano Sonata in A, Opus 120, Sviatoslav Richter   (ANGEL S 36150)
Piano Sonata in A, Opus Posthumous, Rudolf Serkin
(COLUMBIA ML 6249/MS 6849)
Piano Sonata in A minor, Opus 42, Wilhelm Kempff
(DEUTSCHE GRAMMOPHON GESELLSCHAFT 39104/139104)
Piano Sonata in C minor, Opus Posthumous, Alfred Brendel
(VANGUARD 7 1157)
Wanderer Fantasy, Artur Rubinstein   (RCA LM/LSC 2871)
Schumann, Robert
Andante and Variations in B flat, Vladimir Ashkenazy and Mal-
colm Frager   (LONDON CM 9411/CS 6411)
Carnaval, Artur Rubinstein   (RCA LM/LSC 2669)
Kinderscenen, Benno Moiseiwitsch   (DECCA 10048/710048)
Papillons, Sviatoslav Richter   (ANGEL S 36104)
Symphonic Etudes, Vladimir Ashkenazy
(LONDON CM 9471/CS 6471)
Toccata, Vladimir Horowitz   (ANGEL COLH 72)
Scriabin, Alexander
Piano Sonata No. 9, Vladimir Horowitz
(COLUMBIA M2L 328/M2S 728)
Piano Sonata No. 10, Vladimir Horowitz
(COLUMBIA M2L 357/M2S 757)
Shostakovich, Dimitri
Preludes and Fugues, Dimitri Shostakovich   (SERAPHIM 60024)
Stravinsky, Igor
Concerto for Two Solo Pianos, Arthur Gold and Robert Fizdale
(COLUMBIA ML 5733/MS 6333)
Tchaikovsky, Pëtr Ilich
Piano Music, Philippe Entremont   (COLUMBIA ML 5846/MS 6446)
Wagner, Richard
Piano Music, (Complete), Martin Galling   (VOX SVUX 52022)

CHORAL MUSIC

Bach, Carl Philipp Emanuel
  Magnificat, Prohaska, Vienna State Opera Orchestra
                                              (BACH GUILD 552)
Bach, Johann Sebastian
  Cantata No. 4, Christ lag in Todesbanden, Wagner, Wagner
    Chorale, Concert Arts Orchestra   (ANGEL S 36014)
  Cantata No. 12, Weinen, Klagen, Sorgen, Zagen, Wöldike,
    Vienna State Opera Orchestra   (BACH GUILD 610, 5036)
  Cantata No. 21, Ich hatte viel Bekümmernis, Lehmann, Berlin
    Motet Choir and Philharmonic
                (DEUTSCHE GRAMMOPHON GESELLSCHAFT ARC-3064)
  Cantata No. 76, Die Himmel erzählen die Ehre Gottes, Scherchen
                                      (3-WESTMINSTER S 1019)
  Cantata No. 78, Jesu, der du meine Seele, Prohaska, Bach Guild
    Chorus   (BACH GUILD 537)
  Cantata No. 80, Ein feste Burg ist unser Gott, Prohaska, Aka-
    demiechor   (BACH GUILD 508)
  Cantata No. 104, Du Hirte Israël, höre, Vandernoot, Amsterdam
    Philharmonic Society Orchestra, Bach Chorus
                                              (VANGUARD S 219)
  Cantata No. 106, Gottes Zeit ist die allerbeste Zeit, Scherchen,
    Vienna Akademie Kammerchor   (WESTMINSTER 18394)
  Cantata No. 140, Wachet auf!, Prohaska, Vienna Chamber
    Chorus and State Opera Orchestra   (BACH GUILD 598, 5026)
  Cantata No. 198, Trauer-Ode, Scherchen
                                      (3-WESTMINSTER S 1019)
  Christmas Oratorio, S.248, Thomas, Detmold Orchestra and
    Chorus   (3-OISEAU-LYRE 50001/3)
  Mass in b minor, S.232, Richter, Munich Bach Orchestra and
    Chorus   (DEUTSCHE GRAMMOPHON GESELLSCHAFT ARC-73177/9)
  St. John Passion, S.245, Richter, Munich Bach Orchestra and
    Chorus
          (3-DEUTSCHE GRAMMOPHON GESELLSCHAFT ARC-73228/30)
  St. Matthew Passion, S.244, Scherchen   (4-WESTMINSTER 4402)
Barber, Samuel
  Stopwatch & Ordnance Map, Opus 15, Golschmann, De Cormier
    Chorus, Symphony of the Air   (VANGUARD 1065)
Bartók, Béla
  Cantata Profana, Süsskind, New Symphony   (BARTOK 312)

Beethoven, Ludwig van
Christus am Oelberg, Opus 85, Scherchen, Vienna State Opera
  Orchestra and Academy Chorus   (WESTMINSTER 19033, 17033)
Fantasia in C minor for Piano, Chorus, Orch., Op. 80, Somogyi,
  Vienna State Opera Orchestra and Chorus
                                    (WESTMINSTER 19078, 17078)
Mass in C, Opus 86, Beecham Chorus, Royal Philharmonic
                                    (CAPITOL S G 7168)
Missa Solemnis in D, Opus 123, Bernstein, NY Philharmonic
                                    (2-COLUMBIA M2L 270, M2S 619)
Symphony No. 9 in D minor, Opus 125, Monteux, London Sym-
  phony and Chorus (with rehearsal) (2-WESTMINSTER 2234, 234)

Berlioz, Hector
L'Enfance du Christ, Davis, Goldsbrough Orchestra, St. Anthony
  Singers   (2-OISEAU-LYRE 50201/2, 60032/3)
Requiem, Opus 5 (Grande Messe des Morts), Scherchen, Orches-
  tre Théâtre National Opéra   (2-WESTMINSTER 2227, 201)
Roméo et Juliette, Opus 17, Monteux, Boston Symphony, NE
  Conservatory Chorus   (2-RCA LD/LDS 6098)

Bernstein, Leonard
Chichester Psalms, for Chorus and Orchestra, Bernstein, NY Philharmonic, Camerata Singers   (COLUMBIA ML 6192, MS 6792)

Bloch, Ernest
Sacred Service, Avodath Hakodesh, Bernstein, NY Philharmonic
                                    (COLUMBIA ML 5621, MS 6221)

Brahms, Johannes
German Requiem, Opus 45, Bamburger, Hamburg No. German
  Radio Symphony and Chorus   (2-NONESUCH 7 3003)
Liebeslieder Waltzes, Opera 52, 65, Shaw Chorale
                                    (RCA LM/LSC 2864)
Song of Destiny, Opus 54, Beecham, Beecham Choral Society,
  Royal Philharmonic   (ANGEL S 35400)

Britten, Benjamin
Spring Symphony, Britten, Royal Opera House Orchestra and
  Chorus   (LONDON 5612, 25242)
War Requiem, Britten, London Symphony and Chorus
                                    (2-LONDON 4225, 1255)

Bruckner, Anton
Mass No. 3 in F minor, Great, Forster, Berlin Symphony
                        •   (ANGEL S 35982)
Te Deum, Walter, Westminster Choir, NY Philharmonic
                                    (COLUMBIA ML 4980)

Buxtehude, Dietrich
Missa Brevis, Magnificat in D, Cantata Singers
                                    (URANIA 8018, 58018)

Byrd, William
  Ave Verum Corpus, Magnificat, Nunc Dimittis, Willcocks, King's
     College Chorus   (LONDON ARGO 5 226; LONDON 5725, 25725)
  Mass in Three Parts; Mass in Four Parts; Mass in Five Parts,
     Little, Montreal Bach Choir   (VOX 500 880)
Campra, André
  Requiem (Messe des Morts), Frémaux, Paillard Orchestra, Cail-
     lard and Caillat Chorales   (WESTMINSTER 19007, 17007)
Carissimi, Giacomo
  Jepthe, Rilling, Spandauer Kantorei   (TURNABOUT 3 4089)
Charpentier, Marc-Antoine
  Magnificat, Te Deum, Martini, Paillard Orchestra, Chorus
                                                  (BACH GUILD 70 663)
Cherubini, Luigi
  Mass in C, Portsmouth Philharmonic   (LYRICHORD 28)
Copland, Aaron
  In the Beginning, Copland, N.E. Conservatory Chorus
                                      (CBS 32110017, 32110018)
Debussy, Claude
  Le Martyre de St. Sébastien, Ormandy, Philadelphia Orchestra
                                      (2-COLUMBIA M2L 353, M2S 753)
  Nocturnes (Nuages, Fêtes, Sirènes), Ormandy, Philadelphia Or-
     chestra, Temple University Women's Chorus
                                      (COLUMBIA ML 6097, MS 6697)
  Trois Chansons de Charles d'Orléans, Concordia Chorus
                                      (CONCORDIA 8, S-2)
Des Prez, Josquin
  Mass: L'homme Armé, Venhoda, Prague Madrigal Singers
                                 (CROSSROADS 22160093, 22160094)
Duruflé, Maurice
  Requiem, Opus 9, Duruflé, Orchestre Concerts Lamoureux
                                      (EPIC LC 3856, BC 1256)
Dvořák, Anton
  Requiem, Opus 89, Ancerl, Czech Philharmonic
     (2-DEUTSCHE GRAMMOPHON GESELLSCHAFT 18547/8, 138026/7)
  Stabat Mater, Opus 58, Reichert, Recklinghausen Chorus, West-
     phalian Symphony   (2-VOX S VUX 5 2026)
Elgar, Edward
  Dream of Gerontius, Barbirolli, Hallé Orchestra and Chorus,
     Sheffield Philharmonic Chorus, Ambrosian Singers
                                      (2-ANGEL S 3660)
Falla, Manuel de
  Five Songs (and other Spanish music), Luis Morondo, Agrupación
     Coral de Pamplona de España   (COLUMBIA ML 5278)

Fauré, Gabriel
Requiem, Opus 48, Frémaux, Monte Carlo Opera National Orchestra, Caillard Chorus (EPIC LC 3885, BC 1285)
Foss, Lukas
Psalms; Behold! I Build an House, Wagner Chorale
(COMPOSERS RECORDINGS, INC. S 123)
Gabrieli, Giovanni
Processional and Ceremonial Music, Appia, Gabrieli Fest.
(BACH GUILD 581, 5004)
Gounod, Charles
Messe Solennelle (St. Cecilia), Markevitch, Czech Philharmonic Orchestra and Chorus
(DEUTSCHE GRAMMOPHON GESELLSCHAFT 39111, 139111)
Handel, George Frederick
Acis and Galatea, Boult (2-OISEAU-LYRE 50179/80, 60011/2)
Chandos Anthems, Mann, Rutgers University Collegium Musicum
(3-VANGUARD S 227/9)
Israel in Egypt, Waldman, Musica Aeterna (2-DECCA DX S 7 178)
Judas Maccabaeus, Abravanel, Utah Symphony
(3-WESTMINSTER 3310/301)
Messiah, Davis, London Symphony Orchestra and Chorus, (3-PHILIPS PHM 3 592, PHS 3 992); or Mackerras, English Chamber Orchestra, Ambrosian Singers, (3-ANGEL S 3705); or Shaw Orchestra and Chorus, (3-RCA VICTOR LM/LSC 6175); or Scherchen, London Symphony and Philharmonic Chorus
(3-BACH GUILD 631/3)
Saul, Wöldike, Copenhagen Boys Choir, Vienna Symphony Orchestra (VANGUARD 3-BGS 5054/6)
Hanson, Howard
Lament for Beowulf, Opus 25, Hanson, Eastman-Rochester Orchestra (MERCURY 50192, 90192)
Harris, Roy
Symphony No. 4, Folksong, Golschmann (VANGUARD 1064, 2082)
Haydn, Franz Joseph
Creation, Waldman, Musica Aeterna (2-DECCA DX S 7 191)
Mass No. 3 in C, Missa Sanctae Caeciliae, Jochum
(2-DEUTSCHE GRAMMOPHON GESELLSCHAFT 138028/9)
Mass No. 7, Missa in Tempore Belli (Paukenmesse), Wöldike, Vienna State Opera Orchestra (VANGUARD S 153)
Mass No. 9 in D minor, Missa Solemnis (Nelson Mass), Rossi, Vienna State Opera Orchestra (VANGUARD 470)
Seasons, Goehr, North German Radio Symphony Chorus
(3-NONESUCH 7 3009)
Seven Last Words of Christ, Scherchen, Vienna State Opera Orchestra and Academy Chorus (WESTMINSTER 19006, 17006)

Hindemith, Paul
Requiem "For Those We Love," Hindemith, NY Philharmonic,
   Schola Cantorum   (COLUMBIA ML 5973, MS 6573)
Holst, Gustav
Choral Hymns from the Rig-Veda, Opus 26, Holst, English Cham-
   ber Orchestra, Purcell Singers   (LONDON ARGO Z NF 6)
Honegger, Arthur
Christmas Cantata, Ansermet, L'Orchestre de la Suisse Romande,
   Choruses   (LONDON 5686, 25320)
Judith, Abravanel, Utah Symphony, Chorus   (VANGUARD 7 1139)
Roi David, Abravanel, Utah Symphony
                              (2-VANGUARD 1090/1, 2117/8)
Janáček, Leoš
Slavonic Mass (M'ša Glagolskaja), Bernstein, NY Philharmonic,
   Westminster Chorus   (COLUMBIA ML 6137, MS 6737)
Kodály, Zoltán
Missa Brevis, Hokans, Peloquin Chorale
                              (GREGORIAN INSTITUTE S 205)
Te Deum, Swoboda, Vienna Chorus and Symphony
                              (WESTMINSTER 18455)
Lalande, Michel-Richard de
De Profundis, Couraud, Stuttgart Pro Musica and Chorus
                              (VOX 9040)
Te Deum; Confitemini, Boyd Neel Orchestra, St. Anthony Chorus
                              (OISEAU-LYRE 50153)
Liszt, Franz
Missa Choralis in A minor, Gillesberger, Vienna Chamber Choir
                              (VOX 50 1040)
Mahler, Gustav
Symphony No. 2 in C minor (Resurrection), Bernstein, NY Phil-
   harmonic, Collegiate Chorale   (2-COLUMBIA M2L 295, M2S 695)
Symphony No. 8 in E flat (Symphony of a Thousand), Bernstein,
   London Symphony   (2-COLUMBIA M2L 351, M2S 751)
Mendelssohn, Felix
Elijah, Opus 70, Krips, London Philharmonic, Choir
                              (3-LONDON 4315)
Midsummer Night's Dream, Incidental Music, Opera 21 and 61,
   Maag, London Symphony, Royal Opera House Female Chorus
                              (LONDON 9201, 6001)
Milhaud, Darius
Choëphores, Bernstein, NY Philharmonic, NY Schola Cantorum
                              (COLUMBIA ML 5796, MS 6396)
Sabbath Morning Service, Milhaud, Orchestre du Théâtre Na-
   tional de L'Opéra, Choeurs de la Radiodiffusion-Télévision
   Française   (WESTMINSTER 19052, 17052)

Symphony No. 3, Hymnus Ambrosianus, Milhaud, Conservatory
Society Orchestra, Brasseur Chorus
(WESTMINSTER 19101, 17101)

Monteverdi, Claudio
Lagrime d'Amante (from Madrigals, Book VI), Randolph, Mas-
terwork Chorus   (WESTMINSTER 9622)
Magnificat a 6 Voci, Wallenstein, Los Angeles Philharmonic,
Wagner Chorale   (CAPITOL S P 8572)
Vespro della Beata Vergine, Craft, Columbia Baroque Ensemble,
Smith Singers, Ft. Worth Tex. Boys Chorus
(2-COLUMBIA M2L 363, M2S 763)

Mozart, Wolfgang Amadeus
Cantata: Eine kleine Freimaurer, K.623, Meyer, Vienna Pro
Musica Orchestra, Mulhouse Oratorio Chorus
(3-TURNABOUT 4111/3)
Mass in C, K.317, *(Coronation),* Moralt, Vienna Symphony and
Choir Boys   (EPIC LC 3415)
Mass in C minor, K.427, *(The Great),* Fricsay, Berlin Radio
Symphony
(DEUTSCHE GRAMMOPHON GESELLSCHAFT 18624, 138124)
Requiem, K.626, Walter, NY Philharmonic, Westminster Choir
(COLUMBIA ML 5012)
Sacred Music, Leibowitz, Vienna Academy Chorus and State
Opera Orchestra   (2-WESTMINSTER 2230, 205)
Vesperae Solennes de Confessore in C, K.339, Ristenpart
(NONESUCH 7 1041)

Orff, Carl
Carmina Burana, Frühbeck de Burgos, New Philharmonic
(ANGEL S 36333)
Catulli Carmina, Smetáček, Prague Symphony, Czech Philhar-
monic Chorus   (CROSSROADS 22160003, 22160004)

Palestrina, Giovanni
Choral Works, De Nobel, Netherlands Chamber Choir
(ANGEL 35667)
Missa Papae Marcelli, Schrems, Regensburg Cathedral Chorus
(DEUTSCHE GRAMMOPHON GESELLSCHAFT ARC-73182)

Pergolesi, Giovanni Battista
Stabat Mater, Rossi   (VANGUARD S 195)

Poland
Folk Songs of, Mazowsze Choral Ensemble and Orchestra,
Tadeusz Sygietynski   (VANGUARD VRS 9061)

Poulenc, Francis
Gloria in G, Prêtre, French National Radio-Television Orchestra
and Chorus   (ANGEL S 35953)
Mass in G, Whikehart Chorus   (LYRICHORD 7 127)
Stabat Mater, Frémaux, Colonne Orchestra   (WESTMINSTER 9618)

Prokofiev, Serge
  Alexander Nevsky, Opus 78, Schippers, NY Philharmonic, West-
    minster Chorus   (COLUMBIA ML 5706, MS 6306)
Purcell, Henry
  Hail! Bright Cecilia (Ode for St. Cecilia), Tippett, Ambrosian
    Singers   (BACH GUILD 559)
  Music for the Funeral of Queen Mary, Somary, Amor Artis
    Chorus   (DECCA 7 10114)
Rachmaninoff, Sergei
  The Bells, Opus 35, Ormandy, Temple University Choir, Phila-
    delphia Orchestra   (COLUMBIA ML 5043)
Ravel, Maurice
  Daphnis et Chloé: Suite No. 2, Bernstein, NY Philharmonic,
    Schola Cantorum   (COLUMBIA ML 6154, MS 6754)
  Trois Chansons, Shaw Chorale   (RCA LM/LSC 2676)
Respighi, Ottorino
  Laud to the Nativity, Wallenstein, Los Angeles Philharmonic
                            (CAPITOL S P 8572)
Rossini, Gioacchino
  Messe Solennelle, Vitalini, Societa del Quartetto Orchestra and
    Chorus   (PERIOD 588)
  Stabat Mater, Schippers, NY Philharmonic, Camerata
                  (COLUMBIA ML 6142, MS 6742)
Russia
  National Chorus of Russian Song, A. V. Sveshnikov
                          (DECCA DL 9985)
Satie, Erik
  Mass for the Poor, Randolph, Chorus   (COUNTERPOINT 90435)
Scarlatti, Alessandro
  St. John Passion, Boatwright, Yale Orchestra   (OVERTONE 1)
Schönberg, Arnold
  Friede auf Erden, Opus 13, Berlin Radio Chorus (MONITOR 2047)
  Gurre-Lieder, Kubelik, Bavarian Radio Orchestra and Chorus
    (2-DEUTSCHE GRAMMOPHON GESELLSCHAFT 18984/5, 138984/5)
Schubert, Franz
  Mass No. 2 in G, D.167, Froitzheim, Freiburg Orchestra and
    Chorus   (DECCA 7 10091)
  Mass No. 6 in E flat, D.950, Waldman, Musica Aeterna
                          (DECCA 7 9422)
  Rosamunde: Incidental music, Opus 26, Abravanel, Utah Sym-
    phony and University Chorus   (VANGUARD 1087, 2114)
Schuman, William
  Carols of Death, Smith Singers   (EVEREST 6129, 3129)
Schütz, Heinrich
  Musicalische Exequien, Gillesberger, Vienna Chamber Chorus
                         (VOX ST DL 50 1160)

Stravinsky, Igor
  Mass, Davis, English Chamber Orchestra, St. Anthony Singers
                                          (OISEAU-LYRE S 265)
  Les Noces, Stravinsky   (COLUMBIA ML 5772, MS 6372)
  Oedipus Rex, Stravinsky, Washington Opera Society
                                   (COLUMBIA ML 5872, MS 6646)
  Symphony of Psalms, Stravinsky, CBS Symphony, Toronto Fes-
      tival Chorus   (COLUMBIA ML 5948, MS 6548)
Telemann, Georg Philipp
  St. Matthew Passion, Redel, Swiss Festival Orchestra, Lucerne
      Festival Chorus   (2-PHILIPS PHM 2 594, PHS 2 994)
Thompson, Randall
  Peaceable Kingdom, San José Chorus   (MUSIC LIBRARY 7065)
Vaughan Williams, Ralph
  Flos Campi (Suite for Viola, Small Orchestra and Chorus), Abra-
      vanel, Utah Symphony and University Chamber Chorus
                                          (VANGUARD 7 1159)
  Mass in G minor, Wagner Chorale   (CAPITOL S 8535)
Verdi, Giuseppe
  Pezzi Sacri, Giulini, Philharmonic Orchestra and Chorus
                                          (ANGEL S 36125)
  Requiem Mass, in memory of Manzoni, Reiner, Vienna Phil-
      harmonic   (2-RCA LD/LDS 6091)
Vivaldi, Antonio
  Gloria in D, Scherchen, Vienna State Opera Orchestra
                                   (WESTMINSTER 18958, 14139)
  Juditha Triumphans, Ephrikian, Scuola Veneziana
                                          (3-PERIOD 1043)

Wagner, Richard
  Choruses, Pitz, Bayreuth Festival
                  (DEUTSCHE GRAMMOPHON GESELLSCHAFT 136006)
Walton, William
  Belshazzar's Feast, Walton, Philharmonia Orchestra and Chorus
                                          (ANGEL S 35681)

THE ART SONG

Arne, Thomas
  Songs to Shakespeare's Plays, Forrester, Young, Priestman,
      Vienna Radio Orchestra and Chorus
                             (WESTMINSTER 19075, 17075)

Bach, Johann Sebastian
  Songs, Cuénod   (CAMBRIDGE 1 702)

Barber, Samuel
  Hermit Songs, Leontyne Price, Barber   (COLUMBIA ML 4988)
  Knoxville: Summer of 1915, Steber, Strickland, Dumbarton Oaks
    Chamber Orchestra   (COLUMBIA ML 5843)
Bartók, Béla
  Songs, Opus 15, Laszlo, Hambro   (BARTOK 927)
Beethoven, Ludwig van
  An die ferne Geliebte, Opus 98, Haefliger   (HELIODOR S 25048)
  Songs, (fifteen), Fischer-Dieskau
    (DEUTSCHE GRAMMOPHON GESELLSCHAFT 139197)
Berg, Alban
  Songs (Seven Early Songs), Beardslee
    (2-COLUMBIA M2L 271, M2S 620)
Brahms, Johannes
  Songs, Fischer-Dieskau (Opus 32, Nos. 1 through 6, and 9)
    (ANGEL 35522)
  Songs for Alto, Viola, Piano, Opus 91, and Opus 47, No. 1;
    Opus 94, No. 4; Ferrier   (LONDON 5098)
Britten, Benjamin
  Les Illuminations for Solo Voice and Orchestra, Opus 18, J.
    Harsanyi, N. Harsanyi, Princeton Chamber Orchestra
    (DECCA 7 10138)
  *Seven Sonnets of Michelangelo, The Holy Sonnets of John
    Donne,* Alexander Young, Watson, Westminster   (ARGO RG 25)
  Serenade for Tenor, Horn, Strings, Opus 31, Pears, Tuckwell,
    Britten, London Symphony   (LONDON 9398, 6398)
  Songs (Six) from the Chinese, Opus 58, Pears (RCA LM/LSC 2718)
Canteloube, Joseph
  Songs of the Auvergne, Grey, Cohen, Orchestra (ANGEL COLC 152)
Chanler, Theodore
  Epitaphs, (nine), Curtin   (COLUMBIA ML 5598, MS 6198)
Chausson, Ernest
  Poème de l'Amour et de la Mer, Opus 19, Verna
    (MUSIC LIBRARY 7009)
Copland, Aaron
  Twelve Poems of Emily Dickinson, Addison
    (CBS 32110017, 32110018)
Couperin, Francois
  Leçons de Ténèbres (Lamentations of Jeremiah), Cuénod, Sinim-
    berghi, Holetschek, Harand   (WESTMINSTER 9601)
Cowell, Henry
  Toccanta for Soprano, Flute, Cello, and Piano, Boatwright,
    Ensemble   (COLUMBIA ML 4986)
  Hymn and Fuguing Tune No. 5, Randolph Singers (included in
    English Madrigals and American Part Songs)
    (CONCERT HALL SOCIETY CHC-52)

Debussy, Claude
Songs, Fischer-Dieskau
(DEUTSCHE GRAMMOPHON GESELLSCHAFT 18615, 138115)
Songs, Teyte   (ANGEL COLH 134)
Dowland, John
Lute Songs, Oberlin, Iadone   (EXPÉRIENCES ANONYMES 34)
Duke, John
Songs, (four), Tassie   (MUSIC LIBRARY 7117)
Duparc, Henri
Songs, (twelve), Souzay   (PHILIPS 500027, 900027)
Falla, Manuel de
Seven Popular Spanish Songs, De Los Angeles   (ANGEL S 35775)
Fauré, Gabriel
Songs, (six), Curtin   (CAMBRIDGE 1 706)
Flagello, Nicholas
Songs, (three), Reardon   (SERENUS 1019, 12019)
Grieg, Edvard
Songs, Nilsson, Bokstedt, Vienna Opera Orchestra
(LONDON 5942, 25942)
Hindemith, Paul
Marienleben (Song Cycle), Opus 27, Lammers
(2-NONESUCH 7 3007)
Italian and Spanish Songs of the 16th and 17th Centuries, Cuénod,
Leeb   (WESTMINSTER WL 5059/9611)
Janáček, Leoš
Diary of One Who Vanished, Haefliger, Griffel, Women's Chorus,
Kubelik (DEUTSCHE GRAMMOPHON GESELLSCHAFT 18904, 138904)
Loewe, Karl
Ballades, Prey   (VOX 5 510)
Mahler, Gustav
Kindertotenlieder, Fischer-Dieskau
(DEUTSCHE GRAMMOPHON GESELLSCHAFT 18879, 138879)
Das Lied von der Erde, Lewis, Forrester, Reiner, Chicago Sym-
phony   (2-RCA LM/LSC 6087)
Songs of a Wayfarer, Fischer-Dieskau, Furtwängler, Philhar-
monia Orchestra   (ANGEL 35522)
Monteverdi, Claudio
Songs (Duets), Schwarzkopf, Seefried   (ANGEL 35290)
Musorgski, Modest
Nursery (song cycle), Dorlyak   (MONITOR 2020)
Songs and Dances of Death, Davrath   (VANGUARD 1068)
Songs and Dances of Death, London
(COLUMBIA ML 6134, MS 6734)
Poulenc, Francis
Songs; also includes Chabrier, Debussy, and Satie, Bernac,
Poulenc   (COLUMBIA ML 4484)

Ravel, Maurice
  Chansons Madécasses, Fischer-Dieskau
         (DEUTSCHE GRAMMOPHON GESELLSCHAFT 18615, 138115)
  Shéhérazade, Tourel, Bernstein, NY Philharmonic
         (COLUMBIA ML 5838, MS 6438)
Schubert, Franz
  Die Schöne Müllerin, Opus 25, D.795, Fischer-Dieskau
         (2-ANGEL S 36283s)
  Schwanengesang, D.957, Fischer-Dieskau   (ANGEL S 36127)
  Winterreise, Opus 89, D.911, Fischer-Dieskau
     (2-DEUTSCHE GRAMMOPHON GESELLSCHAFT 139201/2)
Schumann, Robert
  Dichterliebe, Opus 48, Fischer-Dieskau
       (DEUTSCHE GRAMMOPHON GESELLSCHAFT 139109)
  Frauenliebe und Leben, Opus 42, Stader
         (WESTMINSTER 19029, 17029)
Shostakovich, Dmitri
  From Jewish Folk Poetry, Dolukhanova, Dorlyak, Maslenikov
         (MONITOR 2020)
Spain
  Five Centuries of Spanish Song, Victoria de Los Angeles
         (RCA LM 2144)
Strauss, Richard
  Songs, (seventeen), Souzay   (PHILIPS 500060, 900060)
Wagner, Richard
  Wesendonck Songs, Farrell, Bernstein, NY Philharmonic
         (COLUMBIA MS 6353)
Warlock, Peter
  Curlew (song cycle), Young, Solomon, Graeme, Sebastian
         (LONDON ARGO 26)
Wolf, Hugo
  Italienisches Liederbuch, Berger, Prey   (2-VOX 5 532)
  Songs, (seventeen, miscellaneous), Lear
     (DEUTSCHE GRAMMOPHON GESELLSCHAFT 18979, 138979)

MUSICAL THEATER

Annie Get Your Gun (Irving Berlin), Ethel Merman, Bruce Yar-
  nell   (RCA LOC/LSO 1124)
Babes in Arms (Richard Rodgers, Lorenz Hart), Mary Martin, Jack
  Cassidy, Mardi Bayne   (COLUMBIA OL 7070/OS 2570)

Bells Are Ringing (Jule Styne, Betty Comden, Adolph Green),
  Judy Holliday, Sydney Chaplin   (COLUMBIA OL 5170/OS 2006)
The Boy Friend (Sandy Wilson), Julie Andrews in her Broadway
  debut   (RCA LOC 1018)
The Boys from Syracuse (Richard Rodgers, Lorenz Hart), Portia
  Nelson, Jack Cassidy   (COLUMBIA OL 7080/OS 2580)
  ▶ *My preference is for the 1963 Off-Broadway cast recording
  on Capitol, but this has been discontinued.*
Brigadoon (Frederick Loewe, Alan Jay Lerner), Shirley Jones, Jack
  Cassidy, Frank Poretta, Susan Johnson
                                    (COLUMBIA OL 7040/OS 2580)
Bye Bye Birdie (Charles Strouse, Lee Adams), Chita Rivera, Dick
  Van Dyke, Paul Lynde, Dick Gautier
                                    (COLUMBIA OL 5510/OS 2025)
Cabaret (John Kander, Fred Ebb), Joel Grey, Lotte Lenya, Jack
  Gilford, Jill Haworth   (COLUMBIA KOL 6640/KOS 3040)
Camelot (Frederick Loewe, Alan Jay Lerner), Julie Andrews,
  Richard Burton, Robert Goulet
                                  (COLUMBIA KOL 5620/KOS 2031)
Candide (Leonard Bernstein, Richard Wilbur, John Latouche),
  Barbara Cook, Robert Rounseville, Irra Pettina, Max Adrian
                                    (COLUMBIA OS 5180/OS 2350)
Carousel (Richard Rodgers, Oscar Hammerstein II), John Raitt,
  Eileen Christy, Reid Shelton, Susan Watson
                                          (RCA LOC/LSO 1114)
Cinderella (Richard Rodgers, Oscar Hammerstein II), Julie An-
  drews, Jon Cypher, Edie Adams   (COLUMBIA OL 5190/OS 2005)
  ▶ *While not written as a stage musical, this rates inclusion
  because its songs are in the best theater tradition.*
The Desert Song (Sigmund Romberg, Otto Harbach, Oscar Ham-
  merstein II), Edmund Hockridge, June Bronhill
                                           (ANGEL 35905) (M&S)
Do I Hear a Waltz? (Richard Rodgers, Stephen Sondheim), Sergio
  Franchi, Elizabeth Allen, Carol Bruce
                                  (COLUMBIA KOL 6370/KOS 2770)
Fanny (Harold Rome), Ezio Pinza, Walter Slezak, William Tab-
  bert, Florence Henderson   (RCA LOC/LSO 1015)
The Fantasticks (Harvey Schmidt, Tom Jones), Jerry Orbach, Rita
  Gardner, Kenneth Nelson   (MGM 3872) (M&S)
Fiddler on the Roof (Jerry Bock, Sheldon Harnick), Zero Mostel,
  Maria Karnilova, Julia Migenes, Bert Convy
                                          (RCA LOC/LSO 1093)
Finian's Rainbow (Burton Lane, E. Y. Harburg), Ella Logan, Don-
  ald Richards, David Wayne   (COLUMBIA OL 4062/OS 2080)
Gigi (Frederick Loewe, Alan Jay Lerner), Maurice Chevalier, Leslie
  Caron, Louis Jourdan, Hermione Gingold   (MGM 3641) (M&S)

Girl Crazy (George Gershwin, Ira Gershwin), Mary Martin, Louise
    Carlyle, Eddie Chappell   (COLUMBIA OL 7060/OS 2560)
Guys and Dolls (Frank Loesser), Robert Alda, Isabel Bigley,
    Vivian Blaine, Sam Levene   (DECCA 9023) (M&S)
Gypsy (Jule Styne, Stephen Sondheim), Ethel Merman, Jack Klug-
    man, Sandra Church, Paul Wallace
                         (COLUMBIA OL 5420/OS 2017)
Hello, Dolly! (Jerry Herman), Carol Channing, David Burns,
    Charles Nelson Reilly, Eileen Brennan   (RCA LOCD/LSOD 1087)
High Society (Cole Porter), Bing Crosby, Frank Sinatra, Grace
    Kelly, Louis Armstrong, Celeste Holm   (CAPITOL W 750) (M&S)
Hit the Deck (Vincent Youmans, Clifford Grey, Leo Robin), Tony
    Martin, Jane Powell, Debbie Reynolds, Vic Damone   (MGM 3163)
House of Flowers (Harold Arlen, Truman Capote), Diahann Car-
    roll, Pearl Bailey, Rawn Spearman, Juanita Hall
                         (COLUMBIA OL 4969/OS 2320)
The King and I (Richard Rodgers, Oscar Hammerstein II), Ger-
    trude Lawrence, Yul Brynner, Dorothy Sarnoff, Larry Doug-
    las, Doretta Morrow   (DECCA 9008) (M&S)
Kismet (Robert Wright, George Forrest—based on Borodin), Al-
    fred Drake, Lee Venora, Richard Banke   (RCA LOC/LSO 1112)
Kiss Me, Kate (Cole Porter), Alfred Drake, Patricia Morison,
    Harold Lang, Lisa Kirk
      (COLUMBIA OL 4140/OS 2300, or CAPITOL TAO 1267) (M&S)
   ▶ *Same principals in both versions.*
Lady in the Dark (Kurt Weill, Ira Gershwin), Gertrude Lawrence
    in very condensed version   (RCA LPV 503)
Little Mary Sunshine (Rick Besoyan), Eileen Brennan, William
    Graham, John McMartin   (CAPITOL WAO 1240) (M&S)
Lost in the Stars (Kurt Weill, Maxwell Anderson), Todd Duncan,
    Inez Matthews, Frank Roane   (DECCA 9120) (M&S)
Mame (Jerry Herman), Angela Lansbury, Beatrice Arthur, Jerry
    Lanning, Frankie Michaels,   (COLUMBIA KOL 6600/OS 3000)
Man of La Mancha (Mitch Leigh, Joe Darion), Richard Kiley,
    Joan Diener, Robert Rounseville, Irving Jacobson
                           (KAPP 4505) (M&S)
The Merry Widow (Franz Lehar), Lisa Della Casa, John Reardon,
    Laurel Hurley, Charles K. L. Davis
                       (COLUMBIA OL 5880/OS 2280)
The Most Happy Fella (Frank Loesser), Robert Weede, Jo Sul-
    livan, Art Lund, Susan Johnson
      (COLUMBIA OL 5118/OS 2330, or 03L-240 COMPLETE VERSION)
The Music Man (Meredith Willson), Robert Preston, Barbara
    Cook   (CAPITOL W 990) (M&S)
My Fair Lady (Frederick Loewe, Alan Jay Lerner), Rex Harrison,
    Julie Andrews, Stanley Holloway (COLUMBIA OL 5090/OS 2015)

The New Moon (Sigmund Romberg, Oscar Hammerstein II), Dorothy Kirsten, Gordon MacRae (CAPITOL W 1966) (M&S)
No Strings (Richard Rodgers), Richard Kiley, Diahann Carroll (CAPITOL O 1695) (M&S)
Oh, Kay! (George Gershwin, Ira Gershwin), Barbara Ruick, Jack Cassidy, Allen Case (COLUMBIA OL 7050/OS 2550)
Oklahoma! (Richard Rodgers, Oscar Hammerstein II), Alfred Drake, Joan Roberts, Celeste Holm (DECCA 9017) (M&S)
On a Clear Day You Can See Forever (Burton Lane, Alan Jay Lerner), Barbara Harris, John Cullum, Clifford David (RCA LOCD/LSOD 2006)
On the Town (Leonard Bernstein, Betty Comden, Adolph Green), Nancy Walker, Betty Comden, Adolph Green, Cris Alexander, John Reardon (COLUMBIA OL 5540/OS 2828)
On Your Toes (Richard Rodgers, Lorenz Hart), Jack Cassidy, Portia Nelson (COLUMBIA OL 7090/OS 2590)
110 in the Shade (Harvey Schmidt, Tom Jones), Inga Swenson, Robert Horton, Stephen Douglass (RCA LOC/LSO 1085)
One Touch of Venus (Kurt Weill, Ogden Nash), Mary Martin, Kenny Baker (DECCA 9122) (M&S)
Paint Your Wagon (Frederick Loewe, Alan Jay Lerner), James Barton, Olga San Juan, Tony Bavaar (RCA LOC/LSO 1006)
The Pajama Game (Richard Adler, Jerry Ross), John Raitt, Janis Paige, Eddie Foy, Jr., Carol Haney (COLUMBIA OL 4840)
Pal Joey (Richard Rodgers, Lorenz Hart), Vivienne Segal, Harold Lang (COLUMBIA OL 4364)
Peter Pan (Mark Charlap, Jule Styne, Carolyn Leigh, Betty Comden, Adolph Green), Mary Martin, Cyril Ritchard (RCA LOC/LSO 1019)
Porgy and Bess (George Gershwin, Ira Gershwin, DuBose Heyward), Lawrence Winters, Camilla Williams, Avon Long (complete version) (COLUMBIA OSL 162)
The Red Mill (Victor Herbert, Henry Blossom), Eileen Farrell, Felix Knight (DECCA 8016)
Roberta (Jerome Kern, Otto Harbach, Dorothy Fields, Jimmy McHugh), Joan Roberts, Jack Cassidy, Stephen Douglass, Kaye Ballard (COLUMBIA OL 7030/OS 2530)
She Loves Me (Jerry Bock, Sheldon Harnick), Barbara Cook, Daniel Massey, Barbara Baxley, Ludwig Donath (MGM 4118) (M&S)
Show Boat (Jerome Kern, Oscar Hammerstein II), Barbara Cook, John Raitt, Anita Darian (COLUMBIA OL 5820/OS 2220)
The Sound of Music (Richard Rodgers, Oscar Hammerstein II), Film version, starring Julie Andrews (RCA LOC/LSO 1032)

South Pacific (Richard Rodgers, Oscar Hammerstein II), Mary
    Martin, Ezio Pinza, Juanita Hall, William Tabbert
                                    (COLUMBIA OL 4180/OS 2040)
Street Scene (Kurt Weill, Langston Hughes), Anne Jeffreys, Brian
    Sullivan, Polyna Stoska   (COLUMBIA OL 4139)
The Student Prince (Sigmund Romberg, Dorothy Donnelly), Jan
    Peerce, Roberta Peters, Giorgio Tozzi
                                    (COLUMBIA OL 5980/OS 2380)
Sweet Charity (Cy Coleman, Dorothy Fields), Gwen Verdon,
    John McMartin, Helen Gallagher, Thelma Oliver
                                    (COLUMBIA KOL 6500/KOS 2900)
A Tree Grows in Brooklyn (Arthur Schwartz, Dorothy Fields),
    Shirley Booth, Johnny Johnston, Marcia Van Dyke
                                    (COLUMBIA OL 4405)
Up in Central Park (Sigmund Romberg, Dorothy Fields), Eileen
    Farrell, Wilbur Evans   (DECCA 8016)
West Side Story (Leonard Bernstein, Stephen Sondheim), Carol
    Lawrence, Larry Kert, Chita Rivera
                                    (COLUMBIA OL 5230/OS 2001)
Wish You Were Here (Harold Rome), Jack Cassidy, Patricia
    Marand, Sheila Bond   (RCA LOC/LSO 1108)
Wonderful Town (Leonard Bernstein, Betty Comden, Adolph
    Green), Rosalind Russell, Edie Adams, George Gaynes
                                    (DECCA 9010) (M&S)

Miscellaneous Songs by One Composer

Noel Coward, Joan Sutherland, Noel Coward, John Wakefield
                                    (LONDON 5992/25992)
Rudolf Friml, featuring composer as pianist and conductor
                                    (WESTMINSTER 6069/15008)
George Gershwin, Barbara Cook, Bobby Short, Elaine Stritch,
    Anthony Perkins   (MGM 4375) (M&S)
Victor Herbert, Robert Shaw Chorale and Orchestra
                                    (RCA LM/LSC 2515)
Jerome Kern, Barbara Cook, Bobby Short, Harold Lang, Nancy
    Andrews   (COLUMBIA OL 6440/OS 2840)
Jerome Kern, Reid Shelton, Susan Watson, Danny Carroll
                                    (MONMOUTH-EVERGREEN MES 6808)
Cole Porter, Mabel Mercer   (ATLANTIC 1213)
Cole Porter, Cesare Siepi   (LONDON 5705/25705)
Arthur Schwartz, Nancy Dussault, Karen Morrow, Clifford David,
    Neal Kenyon   (MONMOUTH-EVERGREEN 6604/5) (M&S)
Kurt Weill (American shows), Lotte Lenya   (COLUMBIA KL 5229)
Vincent Youmans, Nolan Van Way, Ellie Quint, Bob Quint
                                    (MONMOUTH-EVERGREEN 6401/2) (M&S)

In addition to the Victor Herbert album listed above, the Robert Shaw Chorale and Orchestra have recorded two miscellaneous collections of operetta and musical comedy songs, beautifully performed in fine arrangements by Robert Russell Bennett. Several of the songs are not available in any other version. There are on Victor LM/LSC 2231, and Victor VCM/VCS 7023. Also recommended is a *Treasury of Great Operettas*, a set containing condensed versions of eighteen operettas, performed by Anna Moffo, William Lewis, Jeannette Scovotti, Rosalind Elias, Stanley Grover, etc., with musical direction by Lehman Engel. Available only directly from *The Reader's Digest* in Album # RD 40.

LIGHT MUSIC

This list of recommended recordings will follow the general outlines already established in Chapter 9: Part I will consider some of the important arranger-conductors, Part II is a composer's corner, Part III deals with music from the movies, and Part IV is a rapid roundup of light music on the international scene.

Naturally there will be some duplication of artists (Arthur Fiedler, for instance, shows up in Parts I, II, and III), but otherwise I have limited the selections to one, or occasionally two discs per man. This will, I hope, emphasize what must already be clear: The list is only a suggested sampling intended as a guide and not an index. If you like one recording by somebody, the chances are excellent that you will enjoy others, and you are hereby urged to take a Schwann-dive into the many more currently available.

Part I: The Conductors

Black, Stanley
 Music of France   (LONDON 44090) STEREO ONLY
Chacksfield, Frank
 New Limelight   (LONDON 3421, STEREO 44066)
Dragon, Carmen
 Fiesta!   (CAPITOL 8335) MONO AND STEREO

Farnon, Robert
Music from the Emerald Isle   (LONDON 3050) MONO ONLY
Fennell, Frederick
Popovers   (MERCURY 50222, STEREO 90222)
Fiedler, Arthur
Evening at the Pops   (RCA 2827) MONO AND STEREO
Goldman, Richard Franko
Greatest Band in the Land   (CAPITOL 8631) MONO AND STEREO
    ▶ *A fascinating assortment of original and rarely heard music for band, including a march by Stephen Foster and a non-march—"The Presidential Polonaise"—by John Philip Sousa.*
Gould, Morton
Beyond the Blue Horizon   (RCA 2552) MONO AND STEREO
Kostelanetz, Andre
Promenade Favorites   (COLUMBIA ML 6206, STEREO MS 6806)
Lane, Louis
Pop Concert, U.S.A.   (EPIC 3539, STEREO 1013)
Mitchell, Howard
Music to Have Fun By   (RCA 2813) MONO AND STEREO
Mantovani
Folk Songs Around the World   (LONDON 3360, STEREO 360)

Part II: The Composers

Anderson, Leroy
Anderson Conducts Anderson   (DECCA 8865, STEREO 78865)
Anderson Conducts His Music   (DECCA 8954, STEREO 78954)
    ▶ *Between them, these two albums contain the most popular Anderson miniatures, some two dozen in all.*
Coates, Eric
London and *London Again Suites,* Eric Johnson, conductor
     (WESTMINSTER 18951, STEREO 14132)
3 Elizabeths and *4 Centuries Suites,* Eric Coates, conductor
     (LONDON 9065) MONO ONLY
Coward, Noel
Noel and Gertie, with Gertrude Lawrence
     (ODEON 1050) MONO ONLY
Joan Sutherland Sings Noel Coward
     (LONDON 5992, STEREO 25992)
    ▶ *The Odeon disc is vintage Coward, recorded in 1936, with songs and dialogue from PRIVATE LIVES, RED PEPPERS and other shows. Also included are two of his great specialty numbers: "Mrs. Worthington" and "Mad Dogs and Englishmen." The London album is, of course, something of an anachronism, but it is lots of fun anyway.*

Friml, Rudolf
  Indian Love Call   (WESTMINSTER 6069, STEREO 15008)
  ▶ *A bouquet of memorable tunes, with composer Friml dou-*
  bling as pianist and conductor.
German, Edward
  Merrie England (excerpts), *Dances from Henry VIII,* and *Nell*
  Gwynn, Victor Olof, conductor   (LONDON 772) MONO ONLY
  ▶ *This disc was discontinued a few years ago, but it is a fine*
  one, and worth a hunt. The complete MERRIE ENGLAND *was*
  recorded in England, and with a little bit of luck, can be
  located in import specialty shops; its label is Odeon, 1311/2.
Gershwin, George
  An American in Paris and *Rhapsody in Blue,* Leonard Bernstein,
  pianist and conductor   (COLUMBIA 5413, STEREO 6091)
  Variations on "I Got Rhythm," Cuban Overture, and *Second*
  Rhapsody, Leonard Pennario, pianist; Alfred Newman, con-
  ductor   (CAPITOL 8581) MONO AND STEREO
  ▶ *Also see under Morton Gould, below.*
Gilbert and Sullivan
  Overtures, Sir Malcolm Sargent, conductor
          (ANGEL 35929) MONO AND STEREO
  Pineapple Poll, Charles Mackerras, conductor
          (CAPITOL 8663) MONO AND STEREO
  ▶ *Sullivan's music is gloriously served in both albums, the*
  second being a ballet derived by Mackerras from sundry
  themes in the operas. The full operas are, of course, heartily
  recommended, and only space limitations preclude their
  listing here. If stylistic perfection is what you want, go with
  the d'Oyly Carte productions on the London label; if vocal
  beauty is of greater concern, the Angel series with soloists
  and chorus of the Glyndebourne Festival is preferable.
Goldman, Edwin Franko
  March Time, Frederick Fennell, conductor
          (MERCURY 50170, STEREO 90170)
Gould, Morton
  Interplay and *Fall River Legend,* Morton Gould, conductor
          (RCA 2532) MONO AND STEREO
  Latin American Symphonette, and *Porgy and Bess Suite* by
  Gershwin, Howard Hanson, conductor
          (MERCURY 50394, STEREO 90394)
Grofé, Ferde
  Grand Canyon Suite, Eugene Ormandy, conductor
          (COLUMBIA 5286, STEREO 6003)
Herbert, Victor
  The Immortal Victor Herbert, Robert Shaw Chorale
          (RCA 2515) MONO AND STEREO

Kálmán, Emmerich
  Countess Maritza and *Czardas Princess* (Excerpts), Soloists,
    Vienna Symphony Chorus and Orchestra
                    (WESTMINSTER 18966, STEREO 14147)
Lehár, Franz
  The Merry Widow (complete), Schwarzkopf, Gedda, *et al.*
                    (ANGEL 3630) MONO AND STEREO
  Waltzes, Robert Sharples, conductor
                    (RCA 1106) MONO AND STEREO
Lumbye, Hans Christian
  Copenhagen Pops, Lavard Friisholm, conductor
                    (CAPITOL 7253) MONO AND STEREO
Novello, Ivor
  Ivor Novello's Music Hall, Eric Johnson, conductor
                    (WESTMINSTER 18953, STEREO 14134)
Offenbach, Jacques
  Operetta Overtures, Hermann Scherchen, conductor
                    (WESTMINSTER 19035, STEREO 17035)
  Gaîté Parisienne, Charles Munch, conductor
                    (LONDON 55009, STEREO 21011)
Romberg, Sigmund
  A Night with Romberg, Lois Hunt and Earl Wrightson
                    (COLUMBIA 1302, STEREO 8102)
Sousa, John Philip
  Sousa Forever, Morton Gould, conductor
                    (RCA 2569) MONO AND STEREO
  Sound Off, Frederic Fennell, conductor
                    (MERCURY 50264, STEREO 90264)
Stolz, Robert
  The Vienna of Robert Stolz, Robert Stolz, conductor
                    (EPIC LN 3374) MONO ONLY
Strauss, Johann, Jr.
  Gypsy Baron and *Die Fledermaus Suites*, Arthur Fiedler, con-
    ductor   (RCA 2130) MONO AND STEREO
  Die Fledermaus (complete), Gueden, Resnik, *et al.*
                    (LONDON 4249, STEREO 1249)
  Tales of Old Vienna, Willi Boskovsky, conductor
                    (LONDON 9340, STEREO 6340)
  ▶ *This sparkling set also contains music by Papa Strauss, and
    Johann Jr.'s two younger brothers, Josef and Eduard.*
  The Blue Danube, Josef Krips, conductor
                    (LONDON 9232, STEREO 6007)
Suppé, Franz von
  Overtures, Henry Krips, conductor
                    (ANGEL 35427) MONO AND STEREO

Waldteufel, Emil
Waldteufel Waltzes, Henry Krips, conductor
(ANGEL 53426) MONO AND STEREO

Part III: Music from the Movies

FEATURE PRESENTATIONS
(original soundtrack scores)

The Alamo, Dimitri Tiomkin   (COLUMBIA 1558, STEREO 8358)
Cleopatra, Alex North
(20TH CENTURY FOX 5008) MONO AND STEREO
Gigi, Lerner and Loewe   (MGM 3641) MONO AND STEREO
Gone with the Wind, Max Steiner   (MGM 1E10) MONO AND STEREO
Hans Christian Andersen, Frank Loesser
(DECCA 8479, STEREO 78479)
How the West Was Won, Alfred Newman
(MGM 1E5) MONO AND STEREO
Lawrence of Arabia, Maurice Jarre
(COLGEMS 5004) MONO AND STEREO
Mary Poppins, Sherman and Sherman
(BUENA VISTA 4026) MONO AND STEREO
Those Magnificent Men in Their Flying Machines, Ron Goodwin
(20TH CENTURY FOX 3174, STEREO 4174)
Windjammer, Morton Gould   (COLUMBIA 1158, STEREO 8651)
Wizard of Oz, Arlen and Harburg   (MGM 3996) MONO ONLY
Zorba the Greek, Mikis Theodorakis
(20TH CENTURY FOX 3167, STEREO 4167)

STAR ATTRACTIONS
(Nostalgia, Incorporated)

Astaire, Fred
Nothing Thrilled Us Half as Much   (EPIC 13103, STEREO 15103)
Cantor, Eddie
Cantor Sings   (CAMDEN 870) MONO AND STEREO
Chevalier, Maurice
The Best of Chevalier   (MGM 4205) MONO AND STEREO
Garland, Judy
Hollywood Years   (MGM 4005) MONO ONLY
Jolson, Al
Rock-a-bye Your Baby   (DECCA 9035, STEREO 79035)
Kaye, Danny
The Best of Kaye   (DECCA 175, STEREO 7175)
MacDonald, Jeanette, and Nelson Eddy
Original Recordings   (RCA 526) MONO ONLY

Temple, Shirley
Animal Crackers in My Soup
(20TH CENTURY FOX 3006) MONO ONLY
Tucker, Sophie, Gloria Swanson, Fanny Brice, Dennis King, et al.
Stars of the Silver Screen, 1929-1930   (RCA 538) MONO ONLY

SELECTED SHORT SUBJECTS
(miscellaneous collections)

Black, Stanley
Film Spectacular   (LONDON 3313, STEREO 44025)
Farnon, Robert
Great Movie Themes   (PHILIPS 200,098, STEREO 600,098)
Fiedler, Arthur
Music from Million Dollar Movies   (RCA 2380) MONO AND STEREO
Gold, Ernest
Film Themes   (LONDON 3320, STEREO 320)
Kleiner, Arthur
Musical Moods from the Silent Films
(GOLDEN CREST 4019) MONO ONLY
▶ *Until his recent retirement, Kleiner presided at the piano for
all the silent film showings at the Museum of Modern Art,
in New York. This intriguing collection includes music from*
THE KID, BIRTH OF A NATION, COVERED WAGON, *etc.*
Korngold, Erich
Film Themes   (WARNER BROS. 1438) MONO AND STEREO
Mancini, Henry
The Academy Award Songs, 1934-1964
(RCA 6013) MONO AND STEREO
Muller, Werner
International Film Festival
(WARNER BROS. 1548) MONO AND STEREO
Ortolani, Riz
Made in Rome   (UNITED ARTISTS 3360, STEREO 6360)
Rozsa, Miklos
Great Movie Themes   (MGM 4112) MONO AND STEREO
Shaindlin, Jack
Fifty Years of Movie Music   (DECCA 9079, STEREO 79079)
▶ *A most intriguing excursion, including Chase and Newsreel
Music, "Charmaine" on the Mighty Wurlitzer, and the Max
Steiner scores for* KING KONG *and* THE INFORMER.
Young, Victor
Love Themes from Hollywood   (DECCA 8364) MONO ONLY

Part IV: International and Specialty Items

Africa
Drum Fever, Saka Acquaye ensemble
(CRESTVIEW 805, STEREO 7805)

England
Cheers, Tessie O'Shea   (COMMAND 872) MONO AND STEREO
Trooping the Colour, Band of the Grenadier Guards
(LONDON SP 44044) STEREO ONLY

France
The Best of Edith Piaf   (CAPITOL 2616) MONO ONLY
Sixty French Girls Sing Encore, Les Djinns Singers
(ABC PARAMOUNT 368) MONO AND STEREO

Indonesia
Bali Island and *Ceylon Island Suites,* composed by Saburo Iida
(LONDON 91379, STEREO 99379)

Italy
San Remo's Greatest Hits   (EPIC 18047, STEREO 19047)
Songs of Venice, I Gondolieri Chorus
(LONDON 91391, STEREO 99391)

Lebanon
Evening in Beirut   (CAPITOL 10189) MONO ONLY

Malaya
Popular Music of the Far East   (CAPITOL 10256) MONO ONLY

Mexico
Hottest Mariachi in Mexico   (REQUEST 8041) MONO AND STEREO

Portugal
Lisbon by Night   (MONITOR 393) MONO AND STEREO

Russia
Pops à la Russe   (MONITOR 591) MONO ONLY

South America
South American Suite, composed and conducted by Waldo de los
Rios   (COLUMBIA 5162, STEREO 1862)
▶ *One of the most inventive scores of its type, and a work
that has proved to be a great favorite with WQXR audiences.
The recording was out-of-print for several years, and I sus-
pect that it was the clamor by disappointed listeners that
prompted Columbia to reissue the Suite.*

Spain
Zarzuela Arias, Montserrat Caballé   (RCA 2894) MONO AND STEREO
Zarzuela Preludes and Intermezzi, conducted by Rafael Frühbeck
de Burgos   (LONDON 9424, STEREO 6424)
Bullfight! sounds and music   (LONDON 44082) STEREO ONLY

Tahiti
Dream Island   (CAPITOL 10281) MONO ONLY

Sweden
  Swinging Swedish Schottisches and Waltzes
                                      (CAPITOL 10172) MONO ONLY
Yugoslavia
  Hit Parade   (MONITOR 601) MONO ONLY

JAZZ

The 1920's

Armstrong, Louis
  The Louis Armstrong Story   (4-COLUMBIA CL 851/4)
  ▸ *Classic small group jazz played by Armstrong's Hot Five and*
    Hot Seven between 1925 and 1929, showing emergence of
    Armstrong as a virtuoso soloist.
  In the '30's and '40's   (RCA LPM/LSP 2971)
  ▸ *Mostly with big bands.*
Beiderbecke, Bix
  The Bix Beiderbecke Story   (3-COLUMBIA CL 844/6)
  ▸ *A style-setting trumpeter shining through groups that are*
    less interesting than he is.
Henderson, Fletcher
  A Study in Frustration   (4-COLUMBIA C4L 19)
  ▸ *A ten-year survey of the first of the big jazz bands, a star-*
    studded group, tracing the development of the jazz potential
    of a large ensemble.
Jazz, Vols. 1-11   (FOLKWAYS 2801/11)
  ▸ *A unique series of discs presenting aspects of jazz from*
    African origins to World War II.
Johnson, James P.
  Father of the Stride Piano   (COLUMBIA CL 1780)
  ▸ *A magnificent "stride" pianist, teacher of Fats Waller, in*
    solo and small-group performances.
Jugs, Washboards and Kazoos   (RCA LPV 540)
  ▸ *Groups using simple or homemade instruments that reflect*
    the early jazz era before recordings.
Morton, Jelly Roll
  King of New Orleans Jazz   (RCA LPM 1649)
  Stomps & Joys   (RCA LPV 508)
  Hot Jazz, Pop Jazz, Hokum and Hilarity   (RCA LPV 524)
  Mr. Jelly Lord   (RCA LPV 546)

Jelly Roll Morton   (MAINSTREAM 56020, 6020)
▸ *The RCA's contain almost all the work of Morton's Red Hot Peppers (1926-1930), fascinating expressions of his pioneering orchestral style, plus solos, trios, and oddities of "hokum." The Mainstream disc is a definitive collection of Morton as piano soloist, composer, and singer.*

Moten, Bennie
Count Basie in Kansas City   (RCA LPV 514)
▸ *Greatest of the Midwestern bands at its peak with young Count Basie at the piano.*

Nichols, Red
The Red Nichols Story   (BRUNSWICK 54047)
▸ *Small groups loaded with stars on the rise (Teagarden, Goodman, Krupa, Jimmy Dorsey) playing a crisp, bright extension of Dixieland.*

Oliver, King   (EPIC 16003)
▸ *Acoustical recordings, made in 1923, of a superb band playing New Orleans ensemble style with Louis Armstrong on second cornet.*

Original Dixieland Jazz Band   (RCA LPV 547)
▸ *A landmark—first jazz records ever made (1917), played by a group that established a style and repertory which is still being heard half a century later.*

The 1930's

Basie, Count
The Best of Count Basie   (2-DECCA DX S 7 170)
Basie   (ROULETTE S 52003)
▸ *The loose, swinging excitement of the original Basie band of the thirties is on the Decca discs; the Roulette is a peak effort of a second, more polished, but less provocative, Basie band of the fifties and sixties.*

Berigan, Bunny
Great Dance Bands of the '30's   (RCA LPM 2078)
▸ *Berigan's classic recording of* I CAN'T GET STARTED *and other examples of his lusty trumpet-playing with his big band.*

Crosby, Bob
Greatest Hits   (DECCA 7 4856)
▸ *Big band Dixieland crossed with swing.*

Ellington, Duke
The Beginning (1926-28), Vol. 1   (DECCA 7 9224)
The Ellington Era, Vol. 1   (3-COLUMBIA C3L 27)
The Ellington Era, Vol. 2   (3-COLUMBIA C3L 39)

Music of Ellington   (COLUMBIA CL 558)
▶ *The two* ELLINGTON ERA *albums trace the development of Ellington's band and his work as a composer from 1926 to 1939. Columbia CL 558 collects high spots of the same period.*

Goodman, Benny
King of Swing   (2-COLUMBIA OSL 180)
Carnegie Hall Jazz Concert   (2-COLUMBIA OSL 160)
Small Groups   (RCA LPV 521)
▶ *The Swing Era is recaptured at its height and with audience excitement in the 1937-1938 radio broadcasts on* KING OF SWING. *The Concert, first of its kind in Carnegie Hall, was a significant musical event of the thirties. The small groups are the original Goodman trio and quartet (Teddy Wilson, Gene Krupa, Lionel Hampton).*

Hampton, Lionel
Swing Classics   (RCA LPM 3318)
▶ *All-star recording groups in superb jam sessions.*

Hawkins, Coleman
Body and Soul   (RCA LPV 501)
▶ *Highlights covering thirty-six years in the career of the first major jazz saxophonist.*

Holiday, Billie
Golden Years   (3-COLUMBIA C3L 21)
Golden Years, Vol. 2   (3-COLUMBIA C3L 40)
Billie Holiday   (MAINSTREAM 56000, 6000)
▶ *One of the greatest jazz vocalists (the first who was not basically a blues singer) in the performances that established her. On the* GOLDEN YEARS *sets, she is accompanied by many of the major jazzmen of the thirties; the Mainstream includes her famous* STRANGE FRUIT.

Lunceford, Jimmie
Lunceford Special   (COLUMBIA CL 2715, CS 9515)
▶ *A big band with a distinctive style that joined subtlety and wit to a strongly rhythmic attack.*

Reinhardt, Django
Best of Django Reinhardt   (2-CAPITOL T 10457/8)
▶ *A gypsy guitarist, the first European to win international recognition in jazz, playing with the Quintet of the Hot Club of France as well as some visiting Americans.*

Russell, Pee Wee
A Legend   (MAINSTREAM 56026, 6026)
▶ *A highly individualistic clarinetist in definitive performances in a Dixieland-swing style.*

Spanier, Muggsy
The Great 16   (RCA LPM 1295)
▶ *A magnificent set of small group recordings that epitomize the latter-day Dixieland style.*

Teagarden, Jack
King of the Blues Trombone   (3-EPIC SN 6044)
Jack Teagarden   (RCA LPV 528)
▶ *Surveys of the work of a masterful trombonist and singer from the late twenties through the thirties (Epic) and into the forties and fifties (Victor).*

Waller, Fats
'34/'35   (RCA LPV 516)
Valentine Stomp   (RCA LPV 525)
Fractious Fingering   (RCA LPV 537)
Smashing Thirds   (RCA LPV 550)
▶ *Fun, swing, and a jazz piano style that has had an effect on almost every jazz pianist since the midtwenties.*

Webb, Chick
Vol. 1, Legend (1929-36)   (DECCA 7 9222)
Vol. 2 (1937-39)   (DECCA 7 9223)

The 1940's

Bechet, Sidney
Jazz Classics   (BLUE NOTE 1201)
Blue Bechet   (RCA LPV 535)
▶ *One of the great jazz originals, a clarinetist and soprano saxophonist who played with a fierce overpowering lyricism, in the performance that established him (SUMMERTIME on Blue Note 1201) and with various small groups.*

Christian, Charlie
With the Benny Goodman Sextet   (COLUMBIA CL 652)
▶ *Performances that established the electric guitar in jazz and set a guitar style that dominated jazz for twenty years.*

Ellington, Duke
At His Very Best   (RCA LPM 1715)
The Indispensable Duke Ellington   (2-RCA LPM 6009)
▶ *The Ellington band at one of its highest points (possibly the highest) coincides with an unusually fertile period for the Duke as a composer.*

Gillespie, Dizzy
Groovin' High   (SAVOY 12020)
Jazz at Massey Hall   (FANTASY 8 6003)
▶ *These two and the Parker recording, listed later in this sec-*

*tion, are three definitive be-bop recordings by its two most
vital proponents. The Savoy discs, made in the midforties,
are the basic be-bop statements. The Fantasy reports a concert in 1953 at which Gillespie, Parker, Bud Powell, Max
Roach, and Charlie Mingus play the best recorded versions
of their be-bop successes of the forties.*

Herman, Woody
  The Thundering Herds (3-COLUMBIA C3L 25)
Hines, Earl
  Grand Terrace Band (RCA LPV 512)
Kenton, Stan
  Artistry in Rhythm (CAPITOL T-167)
  Milestones (CAPITOL T-190) OUT OF PRINT
Krupa, Gene
  Drummin' Man (2-COLUMBIA C2L-29)
  ▶ *Big bands that carried the Swing Era into the forties. Hines'
band, 1940-1941, is a crisply swinging group, just on the
verge of taking on some early signs of be-bop. Krupa's and
Herman's midforties bands show the vitality of the new
blood then entering jazz, while Kenton was exploring dis-
tinctive sounds—rich sonorities and blazing walls of brass.*
Parker, Charlie
  The Genius of Charlie Parker (SAVOY 12009, 12014)
Powell, Bud
  The Amazing Bud Powell, Vol. 1, Vol. 2 (BLUE NOTE 1503, 1504)
  ▶ THE *pianist of the be-bop movement in the performances
that gave him his stature.*
Watters, Lu
  San Francisco Style (3-GOOD TIME JAZZ 12001/3)
  ▶ *The primary source of the traditional jazz revival of the late
forties and the prototype of almost all revivalist bands since
then.*
Young, Lester
  Memorial Album (2-EPIC SN 6031)
  ▶ *Recordings by the original Count Basie band featuring
Young's tenor saxophone playing, which formed a bridge
between the swing period and the post-bop cool jazz era of
the fifties.*

The 1950's

Brown, Clifford
  The Immortal Clifford Brown (LIMELIGHT 28201, 28601)
  ▶ *A varied collection by a trumpeter who influenced trum-
peters of the fifties and sixties as Armstrong and Beider-*

becke influenced those of the twenties and thirties and as Gillespie influenced those of the forties.

Brubeck, Dave
Jazz Goes to College   (COLUMBIA CL 566)
▶ *The most consistently successful jazz group of the fifties and sixties in live performances which project the group's relationship and response to its audience.*

Davis, Miles
Birth of the Cool   (CAPITOL TT 1974)
Miles Ahead   (COLUMBIA CL 1041, CS 9633)
Kind of Blue   (COLUMBIA CS 1355, CS 8763)
▶ *Three aspects of one of the dominant trumpeters of post-World War II jazz: leading a nonet (BIRTH OF THE COOL), which established the "cool" jazz idiom of the early fifties; in big band settings by Gil Evans which brought out Davis' lyrical resources; leading a hard-driving small group which has been his usual vehicle since the late fifties.*

Garner, Erroll
Concert by the Sea   (COLUMBIA CL 883)
▶ *The first disc to capture the full flavor of Garner's highly personal piano style. Along with THAT'S MY KICK, (MGM S 4463), recorded a decade later (1966), the definitive Garner.*

Lewis, George
Concert!   (BLUE NOTE 1208)
▶ *A group of veteran New Orleans musicians, the sturdiest remnants of the traditional jazz revival of the forties. They had a widespread influence on European jazz musicians and were the prime source of the "trad" bands that were THE popular fare in England until the Beatles came along.*

Modern Jazz Quartet
European Concert   (2-ATLANTIC S 1385/6)
▶ *High points in the repertory of a group that often draws on European forms (particularly the fugue) as much as it does on jazz but manages to give its precise, subtle performances a compellingly swinging character.*

Mulligan, Gerry
The Genius of Gerry Mulligan   (PACIFIC JAZZ 8)
▶ *The original records by Mulligan's pianoless quartet in 1952 and examples of subsequent Mulligan groups through 1957.*

Outstanding Jazz Compositions of the 20th Century
                                   (2-COLUMBIA C2L 31, C2S 831)
▶ *Never mind the title. The set is largely devoted to efforts at Third Stream music (drawing on both jazz and European music) by Gunther Schuller, the chief proponent of Third Stream music, Jimmy Giuffre, Milton Babbitt, George Rus-*

sell and others. As a bonus there's a long, thoroughly mainstream work by Duke Ellington, IDIOM '59.

Silver, Horace
Blowin' the Blues Away (BLUE NOTE 8 4017)
▶ The driving, blues-rooted "hard bop" that came as a reaction
to the withdrawn qualities of "cool" jazz in the midfifties.

Tatum, Art
This Is Art Tatum (2-20TH CENTURY FOX 3162/3)
▶ A pianist with extraordinary facility and a fertile imagination
in informal performances which show him at his best.

The 1960's

Allen, Red
Feelin' Good (COLUMBIA CL 2447, CS 9247)
Davison, Wild Bill
Blowin' Wild (JAZZOLOGY 18)
▶ A trumpeter (Allen) and a cornetist (Davison) whose basic
styles were formed in the twenties, playing with tremendous
vitality, freshness and enthusiasm in the sixties. Excellent
examples of the long-lasting potential of what might have
become dated playing.

Coleman, Ornette
At the Golden Circle (2-BLUE NOTE 8 4224/5)
▶ The pioneer of the modern jazz idiom of the sixties in the
performances that lifted him from the status of a curiosity
to the ranks of the unquestioned jazz greats.

Coltrane, John
My Favorite Things (ATLANTIC S 1361)
Kulu Se Mama (IMPULSE S 9106)
▶ The final, climactic phases of Coltrane's consistent develop-
ment during his thirty-year career: his amalgamation of
Indian influences and jazz in his use of the soprano saxo-
phone (MY FAVORITE THINGS) and his polar position in the
AVANT-GARDE of the sixties (KULU).

Dolphy, Eric
Last Date (LIMELIGHT 82013, 86013)
▶ A summation of an exceptionally versatile and exploratory
saxophonist, flutist, and clarinetist who had had a strong influence on the direction of the jazz in the sixties when he
died in 1964 at the age of thirty-six.

Ellis, Don
Electric Bath (COLUMBIA CL 2785, CS 9585)
▶ A big band that colors a strong, basic, swinging attack with
odd time signatures, electronic devices, and unusual instrumentation.

Evans, Bill, and Hall, Jim
Undercurrent   (UNITED ARTISTS 14003, 15003)
▶ *Piano and guitar duets by a pair of unusually well-grounded, subtle, and technically adroit jazzmen.*

Fitzgerald, Ella
At Juan Les Pins   (VERVE 6 4065)
▶ *The jazz-derived phrasing that colors Miss Fitzgerald's ballad-singing and the warm lyricism in her rhythm numbers are caught at their best in this relaxed, "in-person" recording.*

Getz, Stan
Jazz Samba   (VERVE 6 8432)
▶ *This disc was a major factor in popularizing* BOSSA NOVA *and in turning Getz toward a more deeply lyrical use of his saxophone. Good on both counts and for a third—the presence of Charlie Byrd, playing guitar in the classical, finger-plucking manner.*

Hines, Earl
The Real Earl Hines   (FOCUS S 335)
▶ *Recording of a concert in 1964, the first Hines had ever given, which showcased his talents so brilliantly that it brought him back into the jazz limelight after a decade of obscurity.*

Lloyd, Charles
At Monterey   (ATLANTIC S 1473)
▶ *A tenor saxophonist who is one of the more readily communicative members of the* AVANT-GARDE *of the sixties with a quartet that features an extremely provocative pianist, Keith Jarrett.*

Mingus, Charles
The Black Saint and the Sinner Lady   (IMPULSE S 1385/6)
▶ *A fascinating jazz iconoclast who has built a highly personal form of ensemble expression on a foundation of church music, the blues, and Duke Ellington. The Ellington influence is particularly strong in this well-developed set.*

Monk, Thelonious
Two Hours with Thelonious   (2-RIVERSIDE 9 460/1)
▶ *A collection of solo and quartet performances by a pianist and composer who has a wry and individualistic approach.*

Shepp, Archie
Mama Too Tight   (IMPULSE S 9134)

Taylor, Cecil
Unit Structures   (BLUE NOTE 8 4237)
▶ *Two of the foremost jazzmen in the* AVANT-GARDE *of the sixties in sets that exemplify their work.*

Blues Singers

Charles, Ray
Live Concert   (ABC S 500)
▸ *This and the King recording, listed later in this section, are
representative of the Blues.*

Johnson, Robert
Delta Blues   (COLUMBIA CL 1654)
▸ *The country Blues of the thirties.*

King, B. B.
Blues Is King   (BLUESWAY S 6001)

Rushing, Jimmy
Listen to the Blues   (VANGUARD 3007, 73007)
▸ *This and the Turner recording, listed later in this section,
are representative of the Urban Blues of the thirties and
forties.*

Smith, Bessie
The Bessie Smith Story   (4-COLUMBIA CL 855/8)
▸ *The Classic Blues of the twenties.*

Turner, Joe
Boss of the Blues   (ATLANTIC S 1234)

Vinson, Eddie "Cleanhead"
Cherry Red   (BLUESWAY S 6007)

FOLK

As we get down to the specific business of suggesting the
wherewithal of a basic folk library, things start getting complicated. There are, literally, thousands of albums to choose
from, in an endless variety of styles, categories, languages, and
repertoires. What I plan to do, then, is simply set down an
assortment of recordings that have been a source of pleasure to
me over the years. Most of them, incidentally, seem to have
struck a similarly responsive chord in the hearts of listeners to
WQXR's *Folk Music of the World* program. We have an all-
request show once a month and we keep pretty good tabs on
the songs and singers our audience likes best.

Enjoyment, or if you will, listenability is the keynote. I have
specifically refrained from listing albums merely because they

are historically important or educationally valid or anything except sources of highly agreeable music. Admittedly, it is a highly subjective list, too. You won't find Bob Dylan on it, for instance, even though he has exerted a vast influence on the younger generation of ballad composers. This is because, as much as I admire many of Dylan's songs, I personally find his singing whiny, mumbly, and bleaty, and would much rather recommend other performances of his music.

I have tried to choose albums that will be fun for the casual folknik as well as the connoisseur. For this reason, and others already mentioned, I have generally steered away from ethnic field recordings and other esoteric material (*i.e.*, Indian ragas) likely to appeal to specialized tastes. I have also eliminated the host of albums by such singers as Trini Lopez and such groups as The Byrds, since they are really geared more to the pop trade than to the folk.

Essentially, this leaves us with the traditional-style performances of professional folk singers (whether individually, in small groups, or as a chorus), and the rather more sophisticated concert interpretations of trained musicians. I do not really want to get into a discussion of the relative merits of the two, *per se*, except to suggest that both have their place. I feel the test of a valid performance is the degree to which it succeeds in conveying the basic emotional content of a given song. This is true whether the singer happens to be a farmer in Kentucky or a star of the Metropolitan Opera, and this is why you will find on the list both a Kentucky farmer and a contralto who sang at the Met.

For reasons of clarity, convenience and—considering the huge discography at hand—self-preservation, I have divided my recommendations into four major compartments.

Part I lists ten of my very favorite albums—recordings I have found particularly meaningful and appealing, and the ones to which I seem to keep returning time and again. There is no attempt at a preferential order within this category.

Part II contains fifty American soloists and groups (a few are Canadian), representing among them virtually every shade of musical opinion in the folk field. The solo singers are listed first in alphabetical order, then the groups and choirs.

Part III maintains the setup of Part II, except that it taps the wonderfully rich heritage of Great Britain and Ireland.

Part IV is at once the most extensive and restricted compilation of all; extensive because it ranges over music from a couple of dozen countries, restricted because no list of fifty albums can even begin to suggest the full international array currently available for the record-buyer here in the U.S.A.

I think I need hardly stress again that these are personal choices, which I feel will provide the nucleus of a well-rounded and (most importantly) an easily expandable library of folk recordings. There are many deserving artists and recordings which, for reasons of space or (I apologize in advance) oversight, have not been included. Please do not look on this selection as definitive or all-inclusive. Use it, rather, as a tentative guide. If it helps you to a wider appreciation of folk music in even one of its myriad guises, it will have served its purpose well.

Part I: Favorites

Belafonte, Harry
  Love Is a Gentle Thing   (RCA 1927) MONO AND STEREO
  ▶ *Belafonte's soothing, meltingly tender songside manner works wonders with eleven wistful tunes of love lost and found.*

Bibb, Leon
  Cherries and Plums   (LIBERTY 3358, STEREO 7358)
  ▶ *More love songs, including an exquisite modern romance called "The Honey Wind." Bibb's singing is gentle, his musicianship impeccable.*

Bikel, Theodore
  Jewish Folk Songs   (ELEKTRA 141, STEREO 7141)
  ▶ *These are the songs his mother taught him, and Bikel recalls them with affection and uncommon warmth.*

Damari, Shoshana
  Shoshana!   (VANGUARD 9126, STEREO 2144)
  ▶ *The vibrant Israeli CHANTEUSE has long been an incomparable interpreter of Jewish and Israeli music. Here she widens her tonal horizons to include songs from Turkey, Romania, and South America as well.*

Gibson, Bob
  There's a Meeting Here Tonight   (RIVERSIDE 830) MONO ONLY

▶ *A light, fluid voice, boundless energy, and a knack for picking good songs are among Gibson's attributes. Add a generous supply of personal charm, and you have the story of this buoyant album. It may be hard to find, incidentally, but it IS still listed in the Schwann Catalogue, and it is worth the hunt.*

Hinton, Sam
Whoever Shall Have Some Good Peanuts

(FOLKWAYS FC 7530) MONO ONLY

▶ *One of those children's albums guaranteed to captivate us erstwhile kiddies too. Hinton is among the most underrated balladeers in America today, and his witty assemblage of songs, stories, and sundry musical oddments is sheer delight.*

Kennedy, Calum
Islands of Scotland   (LONDON 91322) MONO ONLY

▶ *I think this must be my favorite of all favorite albums—a totally enchanting garland of songs from the Hebrides. The arrangements are tasteful, the performances by Kennedy (himself a native of the Isle of Lewis) serene, sensitive, and radiant.*

The Soviet Army Chorus and Band

(ANGEL 35411) MONO AND STEREO

▶ *Rip-roaring songs à la Russe by the best chorus in the world, along with two delicious extras: "O No John" and "It's a Long Long Way to Tipperary," both sung in English (of sorts).*

Tracey, Andrew, et al.
Wait a Minim!   (LONDON 58002, STEREO 88002)

▶ *What is a nice show album doing in a folk discography like this? Simple. The original cast recording of the South African revue is made up entirely of international ballads. The arrangements by Andrew Tracey are fresh and inventive; the performances have enormous flair.*

The Weavers
At Home   (VANGUARD 9024, STEREO 2030)

▶ *My favorite among the many fine Weavers albums, this one also boasts first-rate solo turns by Pete Seeger ("Empty Pockets Blues") and Ronnie Gilbert ("Every Night").*

Part II: America

Anderson, Marian
He's Got the Whole World in His Hands

(RCA 2592) MONO AND STEREO

Baez, Joan (VANGUARD 9078, STEREO 2077)
▶ *Baez's solo album debut contains all traditional songs, and is still a winner. For a more representative sampling of her later style, with its switch in emphasis to newly composed material, try* FAREWELL ANGELINA *(Vanguard 9200, stereo 79200). Included are four Bob Dylan ballads, and one each by Pete Seeger, Lee Hays, and Woody Guthrie.*

Belafonte, Harry
Swing Dat Hammer (RCA 2194) MONO AND STEREO

Bikel, Theodore
From Bondage to Freedom (ELEKTRA 200, STEREO 7200)

Bok, Gordon
Johnny Todd and Other Songs
(VERVE-FOLKWAYS 3016) MONO AND STEREO
▶ *A new talent, and a fine one.*

Brand, Oscar
Laughing America (TRADITION 1014) MONO ONLY
▶ *Oscar's predilection for making history come alive is also revealed in the equally entertaining* ELECTION SONGS OF THE U.S.A., *(Folkways 5280), mono only.*

Collins, Judy
The Fifth Album (ELEKTRA 300, STEREO 7300)
▶ *A top-notch collection of contemporary ballads, beautifully sung.*

Dobson, Bonnie
For the Love of Him (MERCURY 20987, STEREO 60987)

Dyer-Bennet, Richard
Of Ships and Seafaring Men
(DYER-BENNET RECORDS #12) MONO ONLY

Felix, Julie
Debut Album (LONDON 3395, STEREO 395)

Guthrie, Woody
Dust Bowl Ballads (FOLKWAYS 5212) MONO ONLY
▶ *A classic recording by America's greatest ballad composer.*

Hinton, Sam
Songs for Men (FOLKWAYS 2400) MONO ONLY

Houston, Cisco
I Ain't Got No Home (VANGUARD 3006, STEREO 73006)
▶ *The last testament of a superb balladeer, recorded less than two months before he died of cancer, at the age of forty-two. Another fine Houston album is* WOODY GUTHRIE SONGS *(Vanguard 9089, stereo 2131).*

Ives, Burl
The Wayfaring Stranger (COLUMBIA 628, STEREO 9041)
▶ *The old master, in the halcyon days before he turned pop singer.*

Jackson, Mahalia
The World's Greatest Gospel Singer
(COLUMBIA 644, STEREO 8759)
▸ *The title says it.*

Langstaff, John
Songs for Singing Children   (HMV 1604) MONO ONLY
▸ *An imported disc, probably available only at specialty shops, this rollicking songfest stands among the best children's recordings ever made.*

Leadbelly
Take This Hammer   (VERVE-FOLKWAYS 9001) MONO AND STEREO

McCurdy, Ed
Treasure Chest of American Song   (ELEKTRA 205) MONO ONLY

Mitchell, Howie
Folk Songs   (FOLK-LEGACY 2) MONO ONLY
▸ *Pleasing, unaffected singing in traditional style. Mitchell can also be heard, with seven friends, in a refreshingly spontaneous round of group music-making, called "Golden Ring" (Folk-Legacy 16, mono only).*

Niles, John Jacob
I Wonder as I Wander   (TRADITION 1023) MONO ONLY
▸ *Niles, with his eccentric manner and eerily high-pitched voice, is the very model of an unauthentic folksinger, but his compelling personality holds your attention unflaggingly. The album is named for one of the many famous tunes Niles has "collected" from his own fertile imagination; others here include "Black Is the Color," "Go Way from My Window," and "Venezuela."*

Odetta
At Carnegie Hall   (VANGUARD 3003, STEREO 73003)

Paxton, Tom
Ain't That News!   (ELEKTRA 298, STEREO 7298)
▸ *Our most talented young folk composer, Paxton has a gift both for incisive lyrics and affecting melodies.*

Reed, Susan
Folk Songs   (ELEKTRA 116) MONO ONLY

Ritchie, Jean
A Time for Singing   (WARNER BROS. 1592) MONO AND STEREO

Robeson, Paul
Favorite Songs   (MONITOR 580) MONO ONLY
▸ *The resonant Robeson voice imparts a rare grandeur to these spirituals and other folk songs.*

Sainte-Marie, Buffy
Little Wheel Spin and Spin   (VANGUARD 9211, STEREO 79211)
▸ *Another gifted young singer-composer.*

Sandburg, Carl
Folk Songs   (LYRICHORD 66) MONO ONLY
▶ *Rumbling, rambling versions of seventeen ballads, love
  songs, and what Sandburg called "darn fool ditties."*

Seeger, Pete
Birds, Beasts, Bugs and Bigger Fishes
                                             (FOLKWAYS 711) MONO ONLY
▶ *Choosing one "best" Pete Seeger record is akin to selecting
  one best book to be marooned with on a desert island—it
  just cannot be done. This disc has the ineffable advantage
  of containing "The Cumberland Mountain Bear Chase," but
  I will not be at all insulted if you prefer Pete's later and
  more socially significant collections. Especially recommended
  among these are* STRANGERS AND COUSINS *(Columbia 2334,
  stereo 9134),* DANGEROUS SONGS!? *(Columbia 2503, stereo
  9303), and* GOD BLESS THE GRASS *(Columbia 2432, stereo
  9232).*

Terri, Salli
I Know My Love   (CAPITOL 8556) MONO AND STEREO

Washington, Jackie
Folk Songs   (VANGUARD 9110) MONO ONLY

Watson, Doc
Southbound   (VANGUARD 9170, STEREO 79170)

Wheeler, Billy Edd
Billy Edd, U.S.A.   (MONITOR 354) MONO ONLY
▶ *A protégé of John Jacob Niles, Wheeler writes lovely songs,
  and sings them most effectively. He shares billing here with
  sultry-voiced Joan Sommer (who subsequently changed her
  style to pop-blues and her name to Joan Tolliver).*

White, Josh
Spirituals and Blues   (ELEKTRA 193, STEREO 7193)

Addiss, Steve, and Crofut, Bill
Folk Songs   (COLUMBIA 2611, STEREO 9411)
▶ *Ballads from many lands by two personable young singers
  who have been touring the world on State Department-
  sponsored trips for a good many years now.*

The Baby Sitters
Folk Songs for Babies, Small Children and Parents
                               (VANGUARD 3002, STEREO 73002)
▶ *Charming songs for the younger set.*

The Beers Family
An American Folk Tradition   (COLUMBIA 6105, STEREO 6705)

DeCormier Singers
Folk Album   (COMMAND 897) MONO AND STEREO
▶ *A little overblown, but exciting performances nonetheless.*

Gene and Francesca
Love and War Between the Sexes   (ELEKTRA 164) MONO ONLY

Ian and Sylvia
Northern Journey   (VANGUARD 9154, STEREO 79154)
▶ *One of the best albums by the duo before their recent (and lamented) conversion to pop, country-and-western, and folk-rock stylings.*

Kathy and Carol
Folk Songs   (ELEKTRA 289, STEREO 7289)

Kingston Trio
Folk Era   (CAPITOL 2180) MONO AND STEREO
▶ *A three-disc set chronicling the work of this popular group, from "Tom Dooley" on down. If that's too big a dose, one of the Trio's best single albums is their early in-concert performance* FROM THE HUNGRY I *(Capitol 1107), mono only.*

The Limeliters
14 Karat Folk Songs   (RCA 2671) MONO AND STEREO

Luboff Choir, Norman
Songs of the World   (COLUMBIA C2L-13) MONO ONLY
▶ *Lush, but lovely choral settings of folk favorites from twenty-four countries.*

Marais, Josef, and Miranda
In Person   (DECCA 9026) MONO ONLY
▶ *Songs of the South African veld, and many other lands too. A companion album, also recorded in actual performance, is also excellent (Decca 9027, mono only).*

Mitchell Trio
Slightly Irreverent   (MERCURY 20944) STEREO 60944
▶ *I liked the Trio much better when it was named for (and led by) Chad Mitchell, so my choice is the group's last album before Chad left it, in 1965.*

Paton, Sandy and Caroline
Folk Songs   (FOLK-LEGACY 30) MONO ONLY
▶ *Charming duets, family style.*

Peter, Paul and Mary
See What Tomorrow Brings
                    (WARNER BROS. 1615) MONO AND STEREO

de Paur Chorus
Dansé Calinda!   (MERCURY 50418, STEREO 90418)
▶ *Exciting choral versions of Creole songs and Negro Spirituals.*

The Weavers
   Reunion at Carnegie Hall   (VANGUARD 2150, STEREO 9130)
    ▶ *I just could not let the list go without a final wave to The
    Weavers. This marvelous set contains "Wimoweh," "Guan-
    tanamera," "Goodnight Irene," and "If I Had a Hammer."*
The Womenfolk
   Never Underestimate the Power   (RCA 2919) MONO AND STEREO

Part III: Britain and Ireland

Clancy, Liam
   Folk Songs   (VANGUARD 9169, STEREO 79169)
    ▶ *One of the Clancy boys (see below) takes off on his own
    with a beguiling bouquet of Irish song.*
Deller, Alfred
   Wraggle Taggle Gipsies   (VANGUARD 1001) MONO ONLY
    ▶ *The strangely pure, semifalsetto timbre of a counter-tenor's
    voice is not to everyone's taste, but Deller's performances
    are impeccable.*
Ferrier, Kathleen
   English Folk Songs   (LONDON 5411) MONO ONLY
    ▶ *Glowing concert performances by the beloved contralto.*
MacColl, Ewan
   Songs of Robert Burns   (FOLKWAYS 8758) MONO ONLY
McCormack, John
   Irish Songs and Ballads   (ANGEL 124) MONO ONLY
    ▶ *The greatest Irish tenor of them all.*
McKellar, Kenneth
   Songs from Scotland   (LONDON 91331, STEREO 99331)
O'Dowda, Brendan
   Immortal Irish Ballads   (CAPITOL 10213) MONO AND STEREO
O'Duffy, Michael
   Songs of Ireland   (AVOCA 122) MONO AND STEREO
O'Hara, Mary
   Songs of Ireland   (TRADITION 1024) MONO ONLY
    ▶ *Winsome and winning.*
O'Shea, Tessie
   Cheers   (COMMAND 872) MONO AND STEREO
    ▶ *Bright, brassy memories of the British music hall.*
Redpath, Jean
   Laddie Lie Near Me   (ELEKTRA 274, STEREO 7274)
Stewart, Andy
   A Scottish Soldier   (EPIC 18027, STEREO 19027)
    ▶ *Highland songs with a swagger, by modern Scotland's
    answer to Sir Harry Lauder.*

Thomas, Thomas L.
  Welsh Traditional Songs   (LONDON 5172) MONO ONLY

Cameron, Isla, and Britton, Tony
  Songs of Love, Lust and Loose Living (LONDON 5808) MONO ONLY
  ▶ *Not for the kiddies.*
Ian Campbell Folk Group
  The Rights of Man   (ELEKTRA 309, STEREO 7309)
Clancy Brothers and Tommy Makem
  The First Hurrah   (COLUMBIA 2165, STEREO 8965)
  ▶ *One of many first-rate albums by these four exuberant,
  exultant, irrepressible sons of the auld sod.*
Corrie Folk Trio and Paddie Bell
  The Promise of the Day   (ELEKTRA 304, STEREO 7304)
Galliards
  England's Great Folk Group   (MONITOR 407) MONO AND STEREO
Hall, Robin, and MacGregor, Jimmie
  Two Heads Are Better Than One   (MONITOR 365) MONO ONLY
  ▶ *Fine songs and singing by the talented pair who later
  founded the Galliards.*
Morriston Orpheus Choir
  The Glory of Wales   (EPIC 18039, STEREO 19039)
  ▶ *One of the most marvelous male choirs in a land of marvel-
  ous male choirs, the Morriston Orpheus offers thrilling ver-
  sions of such favorites as "Ar Hyd Y Nos" and "Rhyfelgyrch
  Gwyr Harlech" (or, if you insist, "All Through the Night"
  and "Men of Harlech").*

Part IV: Other Lands

AFRICA
(see also Marais and Miranda, Part II)

Fodeba, Keita, et al.
  Voices and Drums of Africa   (MONITOR 373) MONO ONLY
Makeba, Miriam
  Folk Songs   (RCA 2267) MONO AND STEREO
  ▶ *This delectable album, which also contains international as
  well as South African songs, just missed my list of top-ten
  favorites in Part I by the proverbial whisker. Makeba's
  "Suliram" is not to be missed.*
de Paur Chorus
  Songs of New Nations   (MERCURY 50382, STEREO 90382)

Troubadors of King Baudouin
Misa Luba and *Native Songs of the Congo*
(PHILIPS 206, STEREO 606)
▶ *The* MISA LUBA *is absolutely fascinating. The form and Latin words of the traditional Catholic Mass are fused with the pulsing drums, intricate cross-rhythms, and improvised themes of tribal Africa.*

ARMENIA

Various Soloists
Armenian Folk Songs   (MONITOR 303) MONO ONLY

AUSTRALIA

Clauson, William
Songs of Australia   (MONITOR 424) MONO ONLY
Harris, Rolf
The Court of King Caractacus   (EPIC 24110, STEREO 26110)

AUSTRIA

The Engel Children (Die Engelkinder)
Music from the Tyrol   (VOX 15050, STEREO 515050)
Tauber, Richard
21 Favorite Volkslieder   (CAPITOL 10369) MONO ONLY
▶ *German and Austrian songs by the pride of old Vienna.*

CANADA

Les Feux Follets
Canadian Mosaic   (RCA 1088) MONO AND STEREO
▶ *It will probably take some hunting in imported record shops to locate a copy of this release, but it contains an entertaining panorama of music from various areas of the country. Les Feux Follets is Canada's national folklore ensemble.*
Mills, Alan
Folk Songs of Newfoundland   (FOLKWAYS 8771) MONO ONLY

CHINA

Chang, Grace
Nightingale of the Orient   (CAPITOL 10272) MONO ONLY

CZECHOSLOVAKIA

Melnik Folk Ensemble
Czechoslovakia in Song and Dance   (MONITOR 329) MONO ONLY

FRANCE

Davrath, Netania
Songs of the Auvergne   (VANGUARD 9085, STEREO 2090)
▶ *The wonderful settings by Joseph Canteloube and Davrath's luxurious singing make this set, and its companion Volume II (Vanguard 9120, stereo 2132), a treat from beginning to end.*
Malkine, Sonia
French Songs from the Provinces   (FOLKWAYS 8743) MONO ONLY

GERMANY

Kunz, Erich
German University Songs, Vol. II   (VANGUARD 1010, STEREO 2009)
▶ *There are five volumes of these robust songs of wine and women, all of them delightful.*
Prey, Hermann
Famous German Folk Songs   (ANGEL 36414) MONO AND STEREO

GREECE

Fleury
Isles of Greece   (VANGUARD 9168, STEREO 79168)
Yapapa, Stella
Love Ballads and Folk Songs of Greece
                    (MONITOR 369) MONO ONLY

HUNGARY

Horvath, Toki
King of the Gypsies   (ANGEL 65040) MONO ONLY
▶ *Fabulous fiddling, and some good songs by Mihaly Szekely.*
Sandor Lakatos Ensemble
The Gypsies Are Singing   (WESTMINSTER 19022, STEREO 17022)

ISRAEL

Ahroni, Hanna
Songs of Israel   (DECCA 8937, STEREO 78937)
Schlamme, Martha
Israeli Folk Songs   (VANGUARD 9072, STEREO 2070)

ITALY

Bastianini, Ettore
Songs of Italy   (LONDON 91412, STEREO 99412)
Corelli, Franco
Memories of Naples   (ANGEL 36126) MONO AND STEREO

JEWISH-YIDDISH

Bernardi, Herschel
  Chocolate Covered Matzohs   (VANGUARD 9074) MONO ONLY
  ▸ Songs and hilarious comedy routines by the noted actor
    whose most recent Broadway triumph was in the role of
    Tevye, in FIDDLER ON THE ROOF.

Davrath, Netania
  Yiddish Folk Songs   (VANGUARD 9117, STEREO 2127)

LATIN AMERICA
(with apologies to Pru Devon)

Buchino, Maria Luisa
  Music of Chile   (MONITOR 342) MONO AND STEREO

Curtin, Phyllis
  Cantigas y Canciones   (VANGUARD 1125, STEREO 71125)
  ▸ Concert arrangements and composed songs in folk style by
    Villa Lobos, Ginastera, and other Latin American masters.
    Beautiful performances.

Jimenez, Alfonso Cruz
  Folk Songs of Mexico   (FOLKWAYS 8727) MONO ONLY
  ▸ Gentle, almost intimate singing by a blind street minstrel
    from the state of Oaxaca.

Petraglia, Clara
  Songs from Brazil   (WESTMINSTER 9807) MONO ONLY

Various Artists
  Latin American Festival   (MONITOR 390) MONO ONLY

PHILIPPINE ISLANDS

Bayanihan Ensemble
  Songs and Dances from the Philippines
                            (MONITOR 322) MONO AND STEREO

POLAND

Slask Ensemble
  Songs and Dances of Poland   (MONITOR 325) MONO ONLY

PORTUGAL

Marques, Maria, and Fernandes, Manuel
  Fados and Folk Songs   (MONITOR 340) MONO AND STEREO

Rodrigues, Amalia
  World's Greatest Fado Singer   (KAPP 1310, STEREO 3310)

ROMANIA

Ciocarlia Ensemble
  Rumanian Folk Songs and Dances   (MONITOR 304) MONO ONLY

▶ *Enesco's "Rumanian Rhapsody"* AU NATUREL, *and other musical enticements.*

RUSSIA

Piatnitsky Chorus
Ballads and Balalaikas (ARTIA 192) MONO AND STEREO
Various Artists
Moscow Nights (MONITOR 590) MONO ONLY
▶ *The pop scene, Russian style.*

SCANDINAVIA

Clauson, William
Swedish Songs (MGM 4198) MONO AND STEREO
Saga Sjöberg and Arne Dørumsgaard
Scandinavian Folk Songs (MONITOR 333) MONO ONLY
▶ *Gracious settings (by Dørumsgaard) and warmly appealing singing, too.*

SPAIN

Berganza, Teresa
Airs of Aragon and the Basque Country
(LONDON 5543, STEREO 25116)

Herrero, Miguel
Creaciones (MONTILLA 104) MONO ONLY
Montero, Germaine
Canciones de Espana (VANGUARD 9050) MONO ONLY
Plata, Manitas de
Flamenco Guitar (CONNOISSEUR SOCIETY 263) MONO AND STEREO

SWITZERLAND

Various Artists
Alpine Festival (COLUMBIA 159) MONO ONLY
Various Artists
Swiss Mountain Music (CAPITOL 10161) MONO ONLY
Various Artists
A Visit to Switzerland (CAPITOL 10264) MONO AND STEREO

YUGOSLAVIA

Radio Zagreb Children's Choir
Yugoslav Melodies and Folk Songs
(VANGUARD 9138, STEREO 79138)

Various Artists
Folk Songs and Dances of Yugoslavia (MONITOR 312) MONO ONLY

MUSIC FROM LATIN AMERICA

Twenty years ago you could buy very little authentic Latin
American music in the United States. Now, however, there is an
incredible number of popular dance and sentimental songs very
readily available. Because such popularity flickers, and supply
and demand has its own mysterious dynamics, I have left this
classification virtually untouched. Similarly, the various popular
solo or trio performers, whose output is prodigious and somewhat
standardized, have been given short shrift just because their discs
are so numerous. (Note that the words "and others," appearing in
parentheses, signify that the artist or artists have many similar
releases.) With these things in mind, and twenty years of answering listener's inquiries, I have listed material that is characteristic and generally less commercially exploited.

Some of these will be currently stocked by the large record
shops, and they will order the others for you. Two labels that
may be unfamiliar to you are SMC, Spanish Music Center, 319
West 48th Street, New York, New York, 10036, and Folkways,
701 Seventh Avenue, New York, New York 10036. The latter
company has a listing of some sixty-five albums from the entire
inclusive area of Latin America, in many cases not represented
at all elsewhere. They generally include excellent pamphlets of
explanation. However, their musical appeal varies; often they are
of more value to the ethnomusician than to the typical WQXR
listener. If concerned, I suggest you obtain their catalogue.

I confess to a certain inconsistency in my alphabetizing. This
is due not to indifference to order, but the knotty problem concerning which word should be the key to the reader, *i.e.,* "Guitar"
under G, or the name of the record, its composer, or its performer, all frequently unknown here.

This list as an introductory guideline should add to your appreciation and enjoyment of a music of tremendous vitality, excitement, and variety.

Assorted Countries

Alma del Bandoneon (el)   (SMC 1104)
▶ *Instrumental featuring distinctively Argentine type of accordion.*
Boleros y Folklore (and others), Los Hermanos Silva
                                                             (RCA MKL 1203)
Bravo Hi-Fi, Morton Gould, George Gershwin, Robert McBride
                                                             (MERCURY MG 50166)
▶ *Striking non-Latin Latin Americana.*
Cantigas y Canciones, Phyllis Curtin
                              (VANGUARD VRS 1125, STEREO VSD 71125)
▶ *Beautifully sung Villa-Lobos, Barrios, etc.*
Caramba (and others), Los Machucambos (LONDON INT, SP 44084)
Exitos de Sudamerica   (DECCA DL 4722)
▶ *There are several Paraguayan groups who present recordings of great variety. This is one of the best.*
Greatest Hits (and others), Los Paraguayos
                              (PHILIPS PHM 200-235, STEREO PHM 200-235)
Guitar Classics, Elias Marreiro   (SMC 1111, 1112, 1113)
▶ *Classic composers of Europe, Spain, Latin America.*
Guitar Moods, Jorge Morel   (SMC 1110)
Himnos Nacionales   (MONTILLA FM 95)
▶ *All of the National Anthems.*
Latin American Best Sellers (and others), Trio Los Panchos
                              (COLUMBIA EX 5183, STEREO ES 1883)
Latin American Festival   (MONITOR MF 390)
▶ *Wide, characteristic sampler.*
Latin American Fiesta, Villa-Lobos, Guernieri
                              (COLUMBIA ML 5914, STEREO MS 6514)
▶ *Fernandez, Chavez, Revueltas.*
Maravilloso, Los Indios   (EPIC LN 3530)
Pan American Folk Dances   (SMC 1030)
▶ *Includes songs, words, and dance instructions.*
Panorama Folklorico, Los de Ramón   (RCA MKL 6001)
▶ *Astonishingly varied assemblage from everywhere.*
Xango, Olga Coelho   (DECCA DL 10018)
▶ *Predominantly from the renowned singer's Brazil repertoire.*

Andean Republics (Ecuador, Peru, Bolivia)

Cancionero Incaico, Vols. 1 and 2   (SMC 518, 557)
Canciones Peruanas   (SMC 1105)
Ecos de los Andes   (SMC 1043)

> **Gods and Demons of Bolivia**   (VANGUARD VRS 9054)
>   ▶ *Extremely interesting and well documented.*
> **Incaica,** Vols. 1 and 2   (SMC 1089, 1090)
> **Musique Indienne des Andes**   (BAM LD 349-M)
> **Realm of the Incas,** Elisabeth Waldo (GNP 603) MONO AND STEREO
>   ▶ *Good "re-creation" using authentic themes and instruments.*
> **Songs and Dances of Bolivia**   (FOLKWAYS FW 6871)
> **Traditional Music of Peru**   (FOLKWAYS FE 4456)

Argentina

> **Argentina,** Maria Luisa Buchino   (MONITOR MF 343)
> **Argentine Folkdances**   (FOLKWAYS FW 8841)
> **Aromas de Pampa**   (SMC 1103)
>   ▶ *Instrumental, featuring harp.*
> **Cantata para America Magica,** Alberto Ginastera
>   (COLUMBIA MS 6447, STEREO ML 5847)
>   ▶ *Striking. Contemporary yet pre-Columbian in concept. So-*
>   *prano and wild instruments. (*TOCCATA FOR PERCUSSION, *by*
>   *Carlos Chavez, on reverse.)*
> **Color en Folklore,** Los Fronterizos
>   (PHILIPS PHS 600-246, STEREO PHM 200-246)
> **Danzas Folkloricas Argentina**
>   (RCA INTERNATIONAL FPM 165, STEREO FSP 165)
>   ▶ *Superb instrumental.*
> **Folklore Argentino,** Maria Luisa Buchino   (SMC 1096)
> **Folklore Argentino (el)**   (SMC 558)
> **Guitarra (una),** Eduardo Falú
>   (PHILIPS PHM 200-244, STEREO PHS 600-244)
> **Misa Criolla,** Ariel Ramírez   (PHILIPS PCC 219)
>   ▶ *Magnificent creation, the traditional Mass magically set in*
>   *folklore lyrics and rhythms.*
> **Nuestro Folklore en Hollywood,** Los Chalchaleros   (RCA AVL 3554)
>   ▶ *Do not be put off by the title. This is entirely authentic.*
> **South American Suite,** Waldo de los Rios
>   (COLUMBIA EX 5162, STEREO ES 1862)
>   ▶ *A symphonic tone-poem, with some folk-themes used. Para-*
>   *guay, Uraguay, and Peru are included.*
> **Trovadores (los)**   (COLUMBIA EX 5169)
>   ▶ *Irresistible quintet. South American prizewinners.*
> **Tangos,** Lo Mejor de Carlos Gardel   (RCA MKLA 34)
> **Tangos (and others),** Amor en la Sombra, Libertad Lamarque
>   (RCA MKL 1245)
> **Tangos (and others),** Sarita Montiel   (COLUMBIA EX 5071)
> **Tangos,** Julio Sosa   (COLUMBIA EX 5164)
> **Tangos,** Instrumental   (MONTILLA FMS 2100)

Tangos, Besos Brujos, Blanca Mooney   (COLUMBIA EX 5041)
Tangos, (more Argentine), Instrumental   (CAPITOL T 10303)
Tangos (and others), Los Cinco Latinos   (COLUMBIA EX 5086)
▶ *Young, nontraditional, swingers.*

Brazil

Bonfá, Luiz, Guitar   (EPIC LN 24124)
Bonfá, O Vialaõ de   (COOK 1134)
Bossa Nova, Miltinho   (AUDIO FIDELITY AFLP 1984)
Brasil e Samba, Instrumental   (RCA BBL 1173)
Debut, "Poly," Guitar and Winds   (EPIC LN 24193)
Esto es Carnaval   (COLUMBIA EX 5083)
Jequibau   (EPIC LN 24192)
▶ *Instrumental in current off-beat 5/8 and other odd time.*
Songs of Brasil, Clara Petraglia   (WESTMINSTER 9807)
▶ *Delicate songs, guitar accompaniment.*
Tren do Caipira (el), Villa-Lobos
          (EVEREST LPBR 6041, STEREO SDBR 3041)
▶ *Beguiling descriptive nostalgia from Bachianas Brasileiras.*
  Argentine Ginastera on reverse with two Ballets.
Uirapuru, Villa-Lobos   (EVEREST LPBR 6016)
▶ *Symphonic synthesis for ballet drawn from strange Bra-*
  zilian folk legend.
Xango and Eight Brasilian Folk Songs   (WESTMINSTER 9807)
▶ *Jose Siqueira's richly textured contemporary Negro cantata.*
  On reverse, soprano Alice Ribeira sings.

Caribbean

Bomba   (MONITOR MF 355)
▶ *Mostly interesting Puerto Rican and Haitian.*
Caribbean Calypsos   (CAPITOL T-10071)
Caribbean Folkmusic   (FOLKWAYS FE 4533)
▶ *Two-disc broad sampling of rustic material.*
Cuba, Rapsodia de, Esther Borja   (MONTILLA LD 21)
Cuban Ballet, Tambó   (MONTILLA FM 92)
Cuban Nights, Miguelito Valdes   (DECCA DL 8716)
▶ *This and* MACHITO Y SUS AFRO-CUBANS, *listed below, include*
  old-style Afro-Cuban dance hits of the past.
Haiti (Fiesta en), Jean León Destiné   (ELEKTRA EKL 130)
Haitian Folksongs, Lolita Cuevas   (FOLKWAYS FP 811)
Homenaje a Los Santos   (SEECO SCLP 4269)
▶ *This, and* NAÑIGO *and* ORIZA, *listed below, are reasonably*
  authentic Afro-Cuban examples. They are semiritual and
  semisocial.

Jamaican Children's Songs (FOLKWAYS FC 7250)
Jamaican Folk Songs, Louise Bennett (FOLKWAYS FP 6846)
Machito y sus Afro-Cubans (DECCA DL 4505)
Nañigo, Ruth Fernandez (MONTILLA FM 54)
▶ *Famous ultra contralto of Cecilia Valdez.*
Oriza (SEECO CELP 4260)
Panama (Sylvia de Grasse en) (MONTILLA FM 161)
Petite Musicale (la), Olive Walkes (RCA LPS 3001)
▶ *Trinidad and Tobago in well-modulated chorus.*
Puerto Rico (Sons and Dances of) (FOLKWAYS FP 80-2)
Steel Band (the Original Trinidad) (ELEKTRA 139)
Trinidad (Limbo from)
(RCA LPB 3013, STEREO LPS 3013)
Trio Vegabajeño (RCA LPR 1009)
▶ *So very typical of Puerto Rican Bolero.*

Chile

Chile, Maria Luisa Buchino and group (MONITOR MF 342)
▶ *Sterling, vital, and regional.*
Folklore Chileno (el), Los Quincheros (SMC 562)
Folk Songs of Chile (FOLKWAYS FW 8817)
Peña de los Parra (MUSIC HALL 12 586)
Traditional Songs of Chile (FOLKWAYS FW 8748)

Colombia

Canta un Tiple, Pacho Benavides (MONTILLA FM 89)
▶ *Instrument resembling guitar but with twelve strings, di-
vided in groups of four.*
Cumbia (a bailar la) (COLUMBIA EX 5136)
Cumbia (Señorita) (COLUMBIA EX 5148)
Flores Negras, Carolos Ramirez sings (SMC 541)
Pajaros (los) (PHILIPS PHM 200-240, STEREO PHS 600-240)

Mexico

Bailes Regionales, Instrumental (RCA MKL 1448)
Ballet Folklorico de Mexico (RCA MKL 1530, STEREO MKS 1530)
Cancionero Mexicana, Vols. 1 and 2, includes words
(SMC 559, 560)
Cantos de las Posadas, includes words (FOLKWAYS FC 7745)
Corridos de la Revolución (RCA MKL 1309)
Fantasia Mexicana, Mariachi (MONTILLA DM 1115)
Fiesta Mexicana, Mariachi (MONITOR MF 472, STEREO MFS 472)

Folklore de Mexico (lo Mejor del)   (RCA MKLA 46)
▶ *Three-disc cross-section of all regions.*
Lourdes, Maria de Mariachi   (COLUMBIA EX 5067)
Mejia, Miguel Aceves   (RCA MKL 1140)
Mexican Folk Songs, Trio, words included   (SMC 1059)
Mexican Panorama   (VANGUARD VRS 9014)
Mexican Rancheras, Dora Maria   (CAPITOL T-10102)
Mexico, Carlos Chavez   (COLUMBIA LL 1015)
▶ *Famed concert of 1940 in superbly illustrated book. Includes re-created Aztec music and Paloma Azul.*
Mexico, Alta Fidelidad   (VANGUARD VRS 9009)
▶ *Like* MEXICAN PANORAMA, *listed above, an authentic group of songs.*
Mexico, Music of   (DECCA DL 9527)
▶ *Sinfonia India, El Sol, Oberatura Republicana, Carlos Chavez, Huapango, José Pablo Moncayo.*
Misa en Mexico (la)   (COLUMBIA EX 5155)
▶ *Exciting rendition of traditional Mass set in folklore forms.*
Negrete, Jorge (and others)   (RCA MKL 1157)
▶ *Marvelously vigorous and typical singer.*
Salon Mexico, Aaron Copland   (RCA LM 1928)
Sones de Mexico   (FOLKWAYS FP 15)
Viva Mexico   (CAPITOL T-10083)
▶ *Four fine contemporary composers: Galindo, Moncayo, Revueltas, Ayala.*

Paraguay

Azucena con los Comuneros del Paraguay   (DECCA DL 4722)
Chiriguanos (los)   (ELEKTRA EKL 202)
Guantanamera, Los Tres Paraguayos   (MONITOR MFS 490)
Guaranies (los)   (VENEVOX BL 411)
Maravilloso, Los Indios   (EPIC LN 3530)
Trio del Paraguay with Digno Garcia (and others)
          (MONTILLA FM 131)

Venezuela

Dances of Venezuela   (FOLKWAYS FW 8844)
▶ *One of my favorites in the Folkways Catalogue.*
Por los Caminos de Venezuela, Adilia Castillo
          (COLUMBIA EX 5063)
Venezuela, Vols. 1 and 2   (SMC 1044, 1045)
▶ *Very typical orshera and male singer.*
Venezuelan Fiesta, Salon Orchestra   (RCA LPM 1203)

Index

ANTIQUES
PRICE GUIDE 2008

ANTIQUES
PRICE GUIDE 2008

Judith Miller

A DORLING KINDERSLEY BOOK

LONDON, NEW YORK,
MELBOURNE, MUNICH, DELHI

A joint production from DORLING KINDERSLEY
and THE PRICE GUIDE COMPANY

THE PRICE GUIDE COMPANY LIMITED

Publisher Judith Miller

Publishing Manager Julie Brooke

Senior Managing Editor Carolyn Madden

Editor Jessica Bishop

Editorial Assistants Carolyn Malarkey, Louisa Wheeler

Design & DTP Tim & Ali Scrivens, TJ Graphics

Photographers Graham Rae, John McKenzie, Elizabeth Fields, Andy Johnson, Byron Slater, Heike Löwenstein, Adam Gault, Bruce Boyajian, Ellen McDermott

Indexer Hilary Bird

Workflow Consultant Bob Bousfield

Publishing Advisor Nick Croydon

DORLING KINDERSLEY LIMITED

Publisher Jonathan Metcalf

Managing Art Editor Christine Keilty

Managing Editor Angela Wilkes

Production Editor Clare McLean

Production Controller Linda Dare

Production Manager Joanna Bull

While every care has been taken in the compilation of this guide, neither the authors nor the publishers accept any liability for any financial or other loss incurred by reliance placed on the information contained in *Antiques Price Guide 2008*

First American edition, 2007

Published in the United States by
DK Publishing
375 Hudson Street
New York, NY 10014

07 08 09 10 11 10 9 8 7 6 5 4 3 2 1

AD344 – August 2007

The Price Guide Company Ltd
info@thepriceguidecompany.com

Published in Great Britain by Dorling Kindersley Limited.

A catalog record for this book is available from the Library of Congress.

ISBN: 978-0-7566-2843-7

Printed and bound in China by Hung Hing Offset Printing Company Limited

DK books are available at special discounts for bulk purchases for sales promotions, premiums, fund-raising, or educational use. For details, contact: DK Publishing Special Markets, 375 Hudson Street, New York, NY 10014 or SpecialSales@dk.com

Discover more at **www.dk.com**

CONTENTS

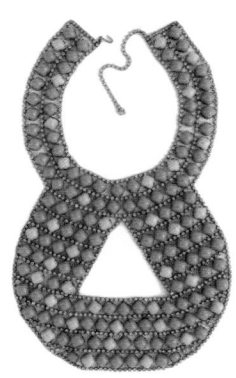

LIST OF CONSULTANTS

JUDITH MILLER – General editor
Judith has been collecting antiques since the 1960s. Since then she has extended and reinforced her knowledge of antiques. Since 1979 she has written more than 100 books on antiques and historic interiors which are held in high regard by collectors and dealers alike.

DUDLEY BROWNE – Glass
Dudley's parents were antique dealers in Sheridan, Wyoming. After working as a stock broker, he realized his true passion was the antique business and he opened an antique shop in Spokane, Washington. He is Head of the Lamp & Glass Division at James D. Julia Auctioneers, Fairfield, ME.

SEBASTIAN CLARKE – Furniture
Sebastian has been active in the antiques field for nearly 20 years, having started at the age of 16. He has worked primarily at Sotheby's and Doyle's in New York and now heads the English and Continental Furniture and Decorative Arts department at Freeman's in Philadelphia.

NICHOLAS D. LOWRY – Posters
Nicholas is President and Principal Auctioneer of Swann Auction Galleries in New York City. He is also the Director of Swann's Vintage Poster Department. He is the third generation in this family-owned business and the youngest auction house president in the world.

DUNCAN McLEAN – Inuit
Duncan is President of Waddington's auction house in Toronto. He is recognized as one of the leading international experts in Inuit Art. Duncan is credited with bringing Inuit art to an international audience. He is also a respected expert on Canadian art.

ALASDAIR NICHOL – Paintings
Born in Scotland, Alasdair worked for Phillips Auction House in Glasgow as Head of Fine Art. He moved to London to specialize in Modern and Contemporary Art and was made Director of Paintings for Phillips New York. In 1999 he joined Freeman's in Philadelphia as Vice President.

RONALD POOK – Folk Art
Ronald began his career in antiques as a dealer, and in 1984 he and his wife Debra created Pook & Pook, Inc. Auctioneers and Appraisers in Donwingtown, PA. They have been committed to the field of antique furniture, accessories and fine art for more than thirty years.

DAVID RAGO – Decorative Arts
David has been a specialist in American and European 20th Century decorative arts and furnishings for 35 years. A leading dealer in the field of American Arts and Crafts, he is the founder of the Rago Arts and Auction Center, one of the country's principal specialty auction houses.

JOHN SOLLO – Modern Design
John is a premier authority in 20th Century Modern decorative art and furnishings and the author of several books on Modern design. He is the principal auctioneer at the Rago Arts and Auction Center in Lambertville, NJ where he holds Modern auctions with David Rago and Meredith Hilferty.

WHAT'S HOT?

The antiques market has seen a return to some old favourites this year, as long as the pieces are of excellent quality. The top end of the market has remained very strong with ever more record prices paid for 'the best', whether it be a painting, a ceramic or a piece of furniture. The middle market has also seen a slow strengthening, albeit patchy. 'Brown furniture' is still slow and my collection of 18thC blue and white porcelain has still to see a resurgence of interest – although any rarity will confound predictions, even if damaged.

A set of four Georgian mahogany window benches c1762 **$1,000,000+** PAR

A George Ohr vase, with red and green mottled glaze, **$90,000-110,000** DRA

FINEST FURNITURE

Good quality English, French and American furniture has seen the market strengthen substantially with collectors old and new excited when anything of high quality comes on to the scene, particularly if the piece is fresh. This area of the market did not suffer the fate of the infamous 'brown furniture' in recent years. Instead, it soared ahead, buoyed up by its very rarity, desirability, intrinsic quality and often rock solid provenance.

"MARY HAD A LITTLE LAMB AND BILOXI HAD A POTTER"

Arts and Crafts ceramics is a strong global collecting market. In the UK Ruskin Pottery has a strong and growing collecting base. While in the US old standbys such as Grueby and Roseville languish in the place between the market that was and the market yet to come, George Ohr, the Biloxi genius, would be either very happy, or very sad about how much money his best work continues to bring. Why the attention? Instead of depending on only one set of collectors, the Ohr market is bulwarked by modern art collectors, folk art collectors, museum interest, and even those modernists who are intrigued by the architect Frank Gehry, who is building the George Ohr museum in Biloxi, Miss, Ohr's home.

RISING IN THE EAST

The Chinese porcelain market is again strong and growing, with many collectors from mainland China buying

*A Chinese Kangxi period yen yen vase, painted with figures, **$18,000-20,000** WW*

into pieces of Chinese taste. Early celadons and fine blue and white examples are at a premium. Export wares, although performing well, have not had the same level of growth. They may well be set for a little surge.

CLEAR AS DAY
18thC English glassware has always had its devotees but prices have been steady rather than stellar. However there are new collectors coming into the marketplace who are buying into 18thC wineglasses, this development could well see prices escalate. And my heartfelt plea – check out antique English decanters, they are so under-priced.

ARCTIC ART
And lastly an area emerging from the 'quaint craft' Tribal Art category to be taken seriously as modern sculpture of the 20th and 21st centuries – Inuit Art. Works from the early 'Classic' period (1950-1970) are generally highly valued for their powerful simplicity. Art

created over the last thirty years has a more contemporary look, and has developed a following of its own. Karoo Ashevak, is one of the most respected artists based in Talurqjuaq, which is one of the last areas to be touched by the outside world.

To look for a general rule about 'What's Hot' it is pieces that are rare and desirable. Also those with a crossover interest that appeal to a wide range of collectors and are perceived as a part of a continuum, and not compart-mentalized into a specific genre or era.

Judith Miller.

*A Karoo Ashevak 'Whimsical Figure' **$35,000-45,000** WAD*

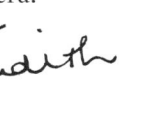

*An English heavy baluster goblet, c1700-1710 **$5,000-6,000** JH*

HOW TO USE THIS BOOK

Running head – Indicates the sub-category of the main heading.

Page tab – This device appears on every spread and identifies the main category heading as indicated in the Contents List on pp.5–6.

The introduction – The key facts about a factory, maker or style are given, along with stylistic identification points, value tips and advice on fakes.

A closer look at – Does exactly that. This is where we show identifying aspects of a factory or maker, point out rare colors or shapes and explain why a particular piece is so desirable.

The source code – Every item in *The Antiques Price Guide* has been specially photographed at an auction house, a dealer, an antiques market or a private collection. These are credited by the code at the end of the caption, and can be checked against the Key to Illustrations on pages 724–6.

The price guide – The price ranges in the Guide are there to give a ball-park figure of what you should pay for a similar item. The great joy of antiques is that there is not a recommended retail price. The prices guides in this book are based on actual prices – either what a dealer will take or the full auction price – and are then checked by consultants. If you wish to sell an item you may be offered much less; if you want to insure your items the insurance valuation may be considerably more.

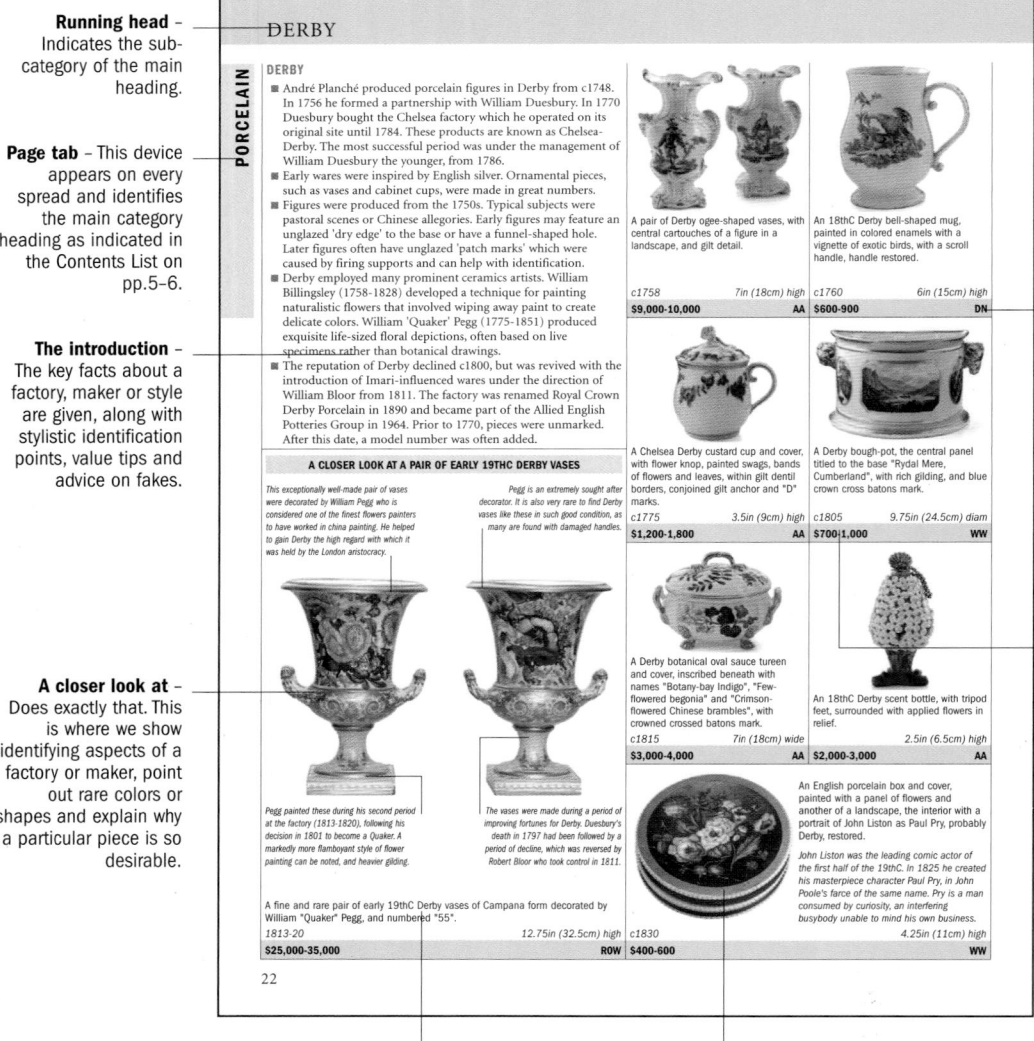

DERBY

PORCELAIN

DERBY

- André Planché produced porcelain figures in Derby from c1748. In 1756 he formed a partnership with William Duesbury. In 1770 Duesbury bought the Chelsea factory which he operated on its original site until 1784. These products are known as Chelsea-Derby. The most successful period was under the management of William Duesbury the younger, from 1786.
- Early wares were inspired by English silver. Ornamental pieces, such as vases and cabinet cups, were made in great numbers.
- Figures were produced from the 1750s. Typical subjects were pastoral scenes or Chinese allegories. Early figures may feature an unglazed 'dry edge' to the base or have a funnel-shaped hole. Later figures often have unglazed 'patch marks' which were caused by firing supports and can help with identification.
- Derby employed many prominent ceramics artists. William Billingsley (1758-1828) developed a technique for painting naturalistic flowers that involved wiping away paint to create delicate colors. William 'Quaker' Pegg (1775-1851) produced exquisite life-sized floral depictions, often based on live specimens rather than botanical drawings.
- The reputation of Derby declined c1800, but was revived with the introduction of Imari-influenced wares under the direction of William Bloor from 1811. The factory was renamed Royal Crown Derby Porcelain in 1890 and became part of the Allied English Potteries Group in 1964. Prior to 1770, pieces were unmarked. After this date, a model number was often added.

A pair of Derby ogee-shaped vases, with central cartouches of a figure in a landscape, and gilt detail.

c1758   7in (18cm) high
$9,000-10,000   AA

An 18thC Derby bell-shaped mug, painted in colored enamels with a vignette of exotic birds, with a scroll handle, handle restored.

c1760   6in (15cm) high
$600-900   DN

A CLOSER LOOK AT A PAIR OF EARLY 19THC DERBY VASES

This exceptionally well-made pair of vases were decorated by William Pegg who is considered one of the finest flowers painters to have worked in china painting. He helped to gain Derby the high regard with which it was held by the London aristocracy.

Pegg is an extremely sought after decorator. It is also very rare to find Derby vases like these in such good condition, as many are found with damaged handles.

A Chelsea Derby custard cup and cover, with flower knop, painted swags, bands of flowers and leaves, within gilt dentil borders, conjoined gilt anchor and "D" marks.

c1775   3.5in (9cm) high
$1,200-1,800   AA

A Derby bough-pot, the central panel titled to the base "Rydal Mere, Cumberland", with rich gilding, and blue crown cross batons mark.

c1805   9.75in (24.5cm) diam
$700-1,000   WW

A Derby botanical oval sauce tureen and cover, inscribed beneath with names "Botany-bay Indigo", "Few-flowered begonia" and "Crimson-flowered Chinese brambles", with crowned crossed batons mark.

c1815   7in (18cm) wide
$3,000-4,000   AA

An 18thC Derby scent bottle, with tripod feet, surrounded with applied flowers in relief.

2.5in (6.5cm) high
$2,000-3,000   AA

Pegg painted these during his second period at the factory (1813-1820), following his decision in 1801 to become a Quaker. A markedly more flamboyant style of flower painting can be noted, and heavier gilding.

The vases were made during a period of improving fortunes for Derby. Duesbury's death in 1797 had been followed by a period of decline, which was reversed by Robert Bloor who took control in 1811.

An English porcelain box and cover, painted with a panel of flowers and another of a landscape, the interior with a portrait of John Liston as Paul Pry, probably Derby, restored.

John Liston was the leading comic actor of the first half of the 19thC. In 1825 he created his masterpiece character Paul Pry, in John Poole's farce of the same name. Pry is a man consumed by curiosity, an interfering busybody unable to mind his own business.

c1830   4.25in (11cm) high
$400-600   WW

A fine and rare pair of early 19thC Derby vases of Campana form decorated by William "Quaker" Pegg, and numbered "55".

1813-20   12.75in (32.5cm) high
$25,000-35,000   ROW

22

Caption – The description of the item illustrated, including, when relevant, the period, the maker or factory, medium, the year it was made, dimensions and condition. Many captions have **footnotes** which explain terminology or give identification or valuation information.

The object – The antiques are shown in full color. This is a vital aid to identification and valuation. With many objects, a slight color variation can signify a large price differential.

CURRENCY CONVERSION					
US Dollar to Canadian Dollar					
USD	**CAD**	**US**	**CAD**	**US**	**CAD**
$1	$1.15	$300	$345.00	$5,000	$5,750
$50	$57.50	$500	$575.00	$7,500	$8,625
$100	$115.00	$750	$862.50	$10,000	$11,500
$150	$172.50	$1,000	$1,150	$20,000	$23,000
$200	$230.00	$2,000	$2,300	$30,000	$34,500

THE CERAMICS MARKET

Pre-1850 ceramics have had an interesting year, with some strong prices and some areas remaining flat. High prices have been achieved for early English porcelain: Chelsea pre-1755, Lund's Bristol and hand-painted Worcester of the 1750s. People are also prepared to pay for early Derby figures. Collectors will pay well for Philadelphia's Tucker porcelain, especially in good condition.

In pottery, again, the earlier the better, especially delft and slipware of the 17thC and 18thC American redware. If the piece is dated or inscribed, the sky is the limit and in such cases a bit of damage does not seem to be much of a drawback.

For other ceramics the year has been a bit tricky, a reasonable increase in price for most of the better middle ranking wares, but problems for a lot of ordinary things such as Staffordshire chimney ornaments. The demand for late 18th and 19thC pieces has diminished and this can be seen in the values pieces fetch.

However, the market for European factories such as Meissen and Sèvres, is performing better than that for British pieces, probably because it is more mature. But again, exceptional pieces are doing better than average ones. The market in late 19thC Berlin porcelain plaques is very strong as long as they are marked KPM, in excellent condition and with an attractive subject. As ever, beautiful young ladies, with flowing tresses and diaphanous gowns, preferably off one shoulder, are the order of the day.

I am often asked for suggestions as to what a person should buy and I always give the answer: "buy what you like" and "buy the best you can afford". If you would like a few tips as to what might do well (but don't blame me if they don't), put a few dollars on English Worcester scale blue and Chelsea gold anchor. Fingers crossed.

Judith Miller

BERLIN

A late 19thC Berlin porcelain plaque, 'Love's Awakening', after G.P Jacomb-Hood, inscribed verso, signed lower left "G.P. Jacomb-Hood and lower right "H. Meisel", impressed KPM and scepter mark.

15.75in (39cm) wide

A 19thC Berlin porcelain plaque, signed "Wagner", depicting a young female with blue flowers in her hair and clutching a birds nest, impressed KPM and scepter mark.

9in (22.75cm) high

A late 19thC Berlin porcelain plaque, finely painted with a young female wearing a pink dress and with a daisy in her hair, framed and signed "Wagner".

5.75in (14.5cm) high

$12,000-18,000	FRE	$7,000-9,000	FRE	$1,500-2,500	FRE

A late 19thC Berlin porcelain plaque of 'Echo', painted with a young maiden wearing a red gown, in an ornate giltwood and gesso frame, signed "Wagner".

7in (18cm) high

A late 19thC Berlin porcelain plaque, after Chatillon, painted with a full length portrait of a chained slave girl in a white gown, impressed "KPM" and scepter mark.

9.25in (23cm) high

A 19thC Berlin porcelain plaque, 'Medea', after Sichel, painted with a classically draped Medea standing before a classical column, impressed "KPM" and scepter mark.

9.25in (23cm) high

A late 19thC Berlin oval porcelain plaque, depicting a young Neapolitan, framed, impressed "KPM" and scepter.

12in (30cm) high

$2,000-3,000	FRE	$4,000-5,000	FRE	$3,000-4,000	FRE	$4,000-6,000	FRE

A fine late 19thC Berlin porcelain plaque, signed "Wagner", painted with two nude young ladies, on a river bank with bulrushes, impressed "KPM" and scepter mark.

11in (27.5cm) wide

$10,000-15,000   **FRE**

A late 19thC Berlin porcelain plaque, painted with an interior scene depicting an elderly Dutch couple in traditional costume, framed and impressed "KPM" scepter mark.

7.25in (18cm) wide

$1,500-2,000   **FRE**

A CLOSER LOOK AT A BERLIN GROUP

This figure is one of a set of 20 from a series depicting a wedding procession, produced to celebrate the marriage of the Prussian Crown Prince William to Cecilie, Duchess of Mecklenburg-Schwerin in 1905.

The figure is reminiscent of depictions of the story of Europa and the Bull. It also exhibits elements of the European Classical tradition while being contemporary in style. The updating of porcelain figures in line with contemporary design trends, by modelers such as Adolph Amberg, helped to revive the waning porcelain figure market.

The Royal family rejected the series because some of the figures were modeled semi-nude. They were, however, very popular with the public and individual pieces were produced for sale.

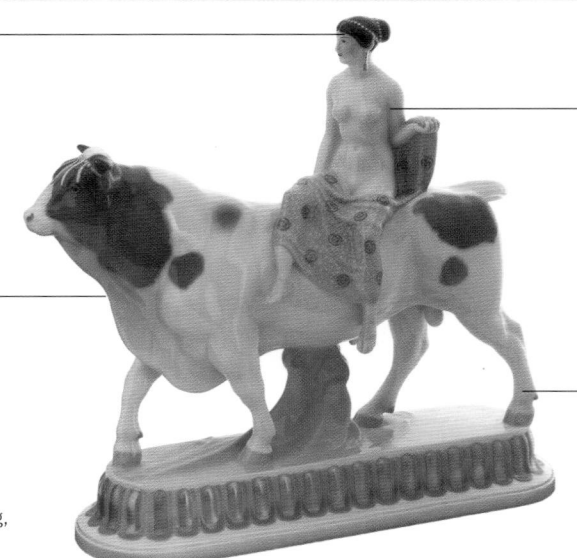

The reputation of the Berlin factory, the relatively high profile of the series and the known modeler make this piece desirable.

A Berlin group, modeled by Adolph Amberg, depicting a woman riding a bull.

c1915

15.5in (39.5cm) long

$5,000-6,000   **DA**

A KPM Berlin porcelain cup and saucer, printed and gilded, depicting a view over a bridge with the castle Osterstein at sunset, printed factory mark.

c1845   *saucer 6.5in (16cm) diam*

$500-600   **KAU**

A Berlin porcelain part breakfast service, printed with a crest, within gilt line borders, comprising: five teacups, four saucers, four plates and three eggcups, printed and stenciled marks in blue and red and impressed numerals.

This service was removed by a custom's officer from The Kaiser's Yacht Germania whilst it was a 'trophy of war' at Southampton Docks following Cowes Week 1914.

$400-600 set   **LFA**

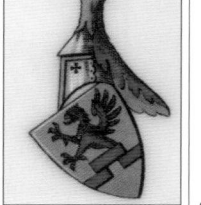

An early 20thC Berlin porcelain figure of Europa on a bull, on an oval natural base, the bull carrying a female, signed "Europa", underglaze blue scepter mark and model number "h 962".

7.5in (19cm) high

$600-900   **KAU**

A pair of Bow figures of a shepherd and shepherdess, each decorated in enamels, the mound bases applied with flowers and leaves, unmarked.

c1755   *6in (15cm) high*

$7,000-10,000   **AA**

A pair of Bow figures of Liberty and Matrimony, each decorated in enamels, the mound base applied with flowers and leaves, unmarked.

c1755   *6in (15cm) high*

$5,000-7,000   **AA**

A CLOSER LOOK AT A PAIR OF BOW FIGURES

These figures, representing Liberty and Matrimony, were produced in the light, flowery Rococo style so typical of Bow.

These figures were press-molded and are therefore rather heavy in comparison to similar examples by Chelsea.

This pair have been decorated in polychrome enamels. Earlier Bow figures were left in the white.

Pieces made before c1765 are usually unmarked.

A pair of Bow figures, of a young man and woman, she holds a bird cage while he carries a nest with three fledglings, restored.

c1760   *7in (18cm) high*

$4,000-6,000   **WW**

Two Bow models of musicians, each sitting on a stump, the young man with a drum and his companion with a zither, restored.

c1760   *6.5in (16.5cm) high*

$4,000-5,000   **WW**

A Bow porcelain figure of a girl playing a tambourine.

c1760   *8.75in (22cm) high*

$2,000-3,000   **AA**

A small Bow model of a flautist, wearing a mauve jacket and flowery breeches.

c1760   *3.75in (9.5cm) high*

$2,000-3,000   **WW**

A pair of Bow models of Harlequin and Columbine, each in a theatrical pose and raised on a pad base, unmarked, restored.

c1760   *5in (13cm) high*

$1,200-1,800   **WW**

A pair of Bow figures of a monk and a nun, decorated with colored enamels, the flower-applied mound base with a puce scroll band, restored.

c1760   *4.5in (11.5cm) high*

$800-1,200   **LFA**

A pair of Bow figures of a shepherd and shepherdess, he with a hound and she with a lamb, raised on pierced scroll bases, anchor and dagger marks.

c1765   *7in (18cm) high*

$3,000-4,000   **WW**

THE BOW FACTORY

- In 1744, Irish painter Thomas Frye (1710-62) established the Bow factory in the east of London with his partner Edward Heylyn. Along with Chelsea, it became the first manufacturer of commercial porcelain in England, and was the first to use bone ash in the body.

- During the 1750s, Frye had developed a new recipe for soft-paste porcelain that involved the addition of bone ash. The resulting formula made Bow porcelain durable with a creamy, chalky appearance.

- Bow specialized in producing everyday tablewares for a wide market, as well as decorative figures. Output was less exclusive than pieces by firms such as Chelsea.

- Wares were decorated in underglaze blue in the Chinese style, or were adorned with Rococo embellishments and polychrome enamels.

- Frye designed many lines and drove the business forward. After his death in 1762, quality declined. The factory finally closed in 1776.

- The glaze is blue-tinged and glassy and is liable to crackle and pool around the base. Pieces are thickly potted, largely as a result of press-molding, and show little translucence when held to the light. The porcelain has a tendency to stain and so pieces in good condition are desirable.

- Early pieces are often unmarked. Anchor and dagger marks were used between 1762-76, possibly by outside decorators.

A pair of Bow sweetmeat figures, in the form of monkeys, finely decorated in enamels, the interior of each bowl particularly well painted with flowers and leaves, unmarked.

c1758   5.5in (14cm) high

$18,000-20,000   **AA**

A Bow octagonal dish, painted with enamels, with numeral "5" to the base.

c1760   7.75in (19.5cm) diam

$1,500-2,000   **AA**

A rare English porcelain white glazed model of a prowling lion, probably Bow or Longton Hall, snarling, and with his head lowered, standing upon a rocky base.

7.25in (18.5cm) wide

$6,000-9,000   **WW**

An 18thC Bow figure of a woman with a sickle, holding a sheaf of wheat and flowers.

The blue palette is typical of Bow.

6.75in (17cm) high

$1,000-1,200   **AA**

An early Bow blue and white coffee can, painted with two Chinese figures, one fishing from a boat, the other sitting beneath a tree, faint glaze crack.

c1750   2.25in (5.5cm) high

$700-1,000   **WW**

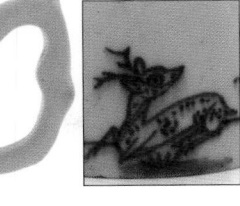

An early Bow coffee can, painted in underglaze blue with two deer beneath a pine tree, damaged.

c1755   2.25in (5.5cm) high

$1,000-1,500   **WW**

A Bow miniature tea bowl, coffee cup and saucer, painted in underglaze blue with vines, within blue line borders.

c1755   bowl 3.5in (9cm) diam

$700-1,000   **LFA**

An early Bow blue and white silver-shaped sauceboat, with a mask head terminal, on three lion's head and paw feet, painted with peony, bamboo and a fence pattern, marked "G", body cracks.

c1750   9in (23cm) high

$1,500-2,000   **WW**

A Bow baluster-shaped sparrow beak milk jug, with loop handle, painted in underglaze blue with flowering branches, rockwork and a fence, decorator's numeral "20" in blue, some damage.

c1750   3.25in (8cm) high

$2,000-3,000   **LFA**

A rare and early Bow blue and white baluster vase, painted with a pavilion, a figure fishing from a boat, flower and scroll border, incised "R" mark, reglazed, hairline crack.

c1750   6.25in (16cm) high

$3,000-4,000   **WW**

A Bow model of a lion, in the white, one front paw raised on a tree stump, on a rocky mound base, unmarked.

c1750   3.25in (8.5cm) high

$5,000-7,000   **AA**

A Bow model of a recumbent lion, in the white, its front paws resting on a ball, on a mound base, unmarked.

c1750   3in (7.5cm) high

$5,000-6,000   **AA**

A very rare and early white glazed Bow model of a cherub, holding up a fruiting vine and raised upon a spiral-molded shaped octagonal base, some old restoration.

This piece is unusually crisp for an early Bow figure.

c1750   7in (17.5cm) high

$2,000-3,000   **WW**

A rare Bow miniature model of a seated fox, in the white, its front left paw resting on a tree stump, on a mound base.

c1760   1.5in (4cm) high

$3,000-4,000   **LFA**

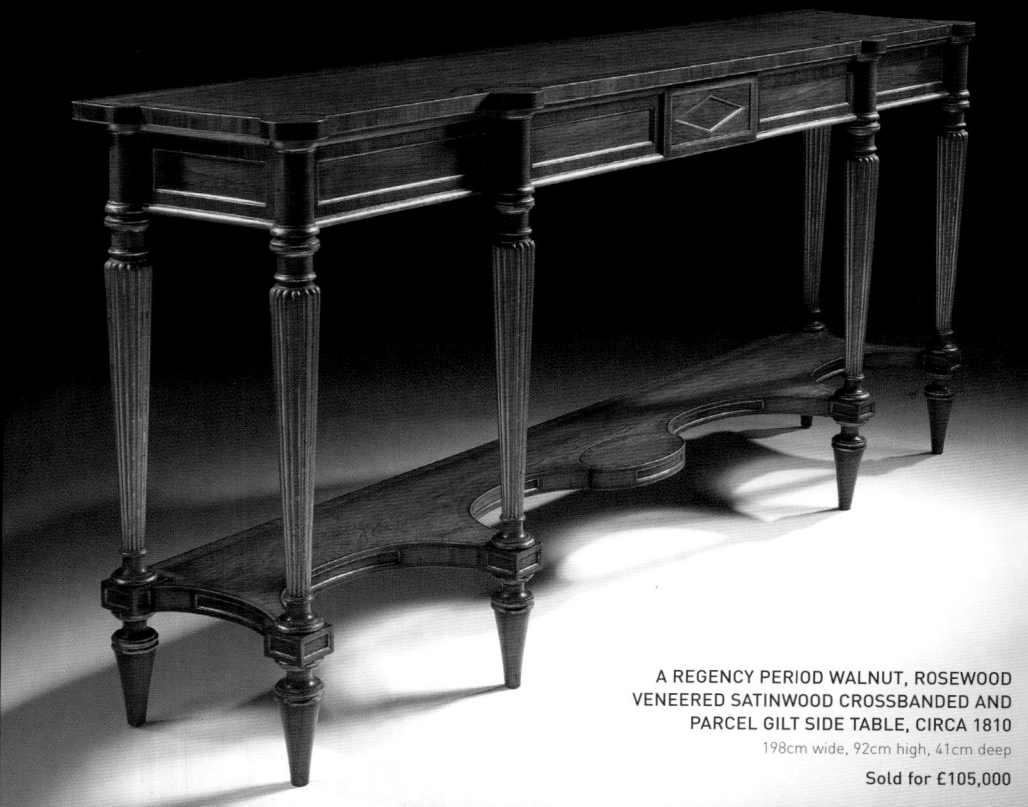
16

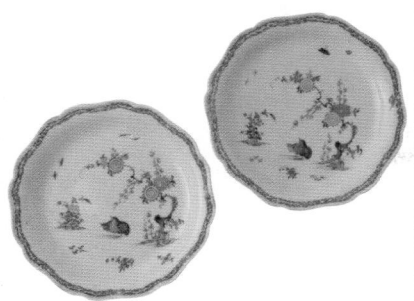

A pair of Bow plates, with shaped edges, painted in the Kakiemon style with the 'Quail' pattern.

c1755	9in (23cm) diam
$2,000-3,000	**WW**

A pair of Bow plates, with shaped edges, painted with birds amidst foliage, the borders with insects, red anchor and dagger marks, one with a flat rim chip.

c1770	7.75in (19.5cm) diam
$2,000-3,000	**WW**

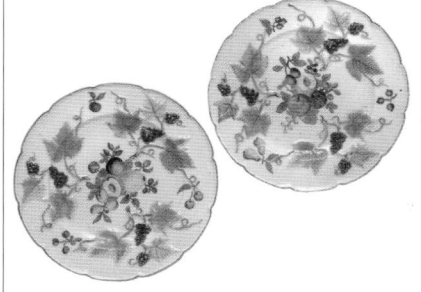

A rare pair of Bow plates, molded in relief with fruiting vines, painted with fruit and foliage, the rims gilded, iron red anchor and dagger marks.

c1770	7.75in (19.5cm) diam
$3,000-4,000	**WW**

A rare Bow canted dish, painted in the famille rose palette, with flowers, leaves and insects, the rim applied with sprays of prunus, two rim chips.

c1755	10.75in (27cm) wide
$700-1,000	**LFA**

A Bow pierced chestnut basket, painted with flowers and floral motifs, applied flowers and leaves around the rim, the handles in the form of stalks.

	11.25in (28.5cm) wide
$4,000-5,000	**AA**

A rare Bow lobed chamber candlestick, with leaf-molded sconce and twig loop handle, with flowerhead thumb piece, with brown line borders, cracked and chipped.

c1765	3in (7.5cm) high
$1,000-1,500	**LFA**

An unusual pair of Bow Rococo vases, applied with flowers around the rims, decorated with flower sprays and colored enamels.

c1765	
$700-1,000	**WW**

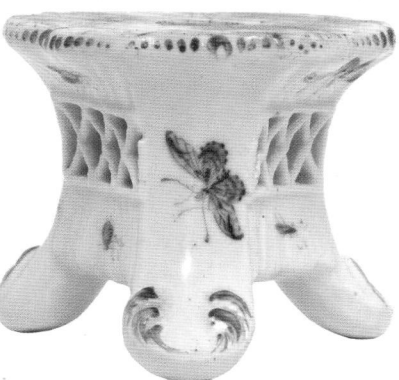

A rare Bow stand, the sides with pierced trelliswork panels and painted with insects, the feet molded with scrolls, the top painted to imitate veined marble.

c1765	2.25in (6cm) high
$1,000-1,500	**WW**

PORCELAIN

A large pair of Chelsea melon-shaped tureens and covers, the stalk loop handles with yellow flower and bud terminals, red anchor marks.

c1755   6.75in (17cm) wide

$100,000-120,000   **AA**

A pair of Chelsea oval sauce tureens and covers, with scroll handles and loop knops, painted in enamels with cut fruit, flowers and leaves, within scrolling claret ground borders, edged in gilt with vines, gold anchor marks.

This style of 'cut fruit' painting closely relates to the output of James Giles' studio at the time. It is possible that these tureens were outside decorated by Giles.

c1765   5.25in (13.5cm) high

$5,000-7,000   **AA**

A pair of Chelsea pierced oval baskets, the wells painted with floral sprays, the pierced work with flowerhead bosses, the entwined handles with flower-encrusted terminals, red-line rims, red anchor marks, one with repaired handle, small chips.

c1755   11.75in (30cm) wide

$4,000-6,000   **DN**

A rare Chelsea wine cooler, with Rococo scroll side handles, the body molded with fruiting vines and painted with flower sprigs, red anchor mark, peppering to glaze, base with drill hole.

c1755   7.75in (20cm) wide

$1,500-2,000   **WW**

A Chelsea fluted bowl, with a scalloped rim, painted in the Kakiemon style with a tiger and dragon amidst prunus and bamboo, raised anchor period but unmarked.

c1750   4in (10cm) wide

$2,000-3,000   **WW**

A Chelsea tea bowl, with everted rim, decorated in gilt with butterflies and leaves, molded 'peacock feather' band, gilt flower spray to interior, gold anchor mark.

c1765   3.25in (8cm) diam

$500-600   **LFA**

A Chelsea teabowl and saucer, decorated in the Kakiemon style with alternate panels of karakusa scrolls, flowers and tied scrolls, raised anchor period but unmarked.

Karakusa is a traditional Japanese winding vine motif, symbolic of luck and long life.

c1750

$2,000-3,000   **WW**

A Chelsea bell-shaped coffee cup and trembleuse saucer, the twig loop handle with molded flowerhead and leaf terminals, painted in enamels with birds, butterflies and an insect, within brown line rims. red anchor marks.

c1755

$2,000-3,000   **AA**

A Chelsea cup and saucer, painted with flowers within gilt rocaille waves and turquoise oeil de perdrix, gold anchor marks.

$2,000-3,000   **CHEF**

A rare Chelsea blanc-de-Chine cup and saucer, with prunus sprigs molded in bold relief, trembleuse-type saucer with molded raised anchor.

4.75in (12cm) diam

$2,000-3,000   **GORL**

Two Derby figures of a gentleman and a lady, seated, holding oval baskets.

c1755   *6.75in (17cm) high*

$8,000-12,000   **RGA**

A Derby figure of Britannia, wearing claret-lined green drapery, with patch marks and a small incised mark, extensive damage.

c1765   *10.75in (27cm) high*

$400-600   **SWO**

A Derby figure of Sir John Falstaff, typically modeled holding a shield and a sword, restored.

c1770   *12.5in (32cm) high*

$500-600   **DN**

A pair of late 18thC Derby musical bocage figures, set on a scroll base, with damage.

7.5in (19.5cm) high

$700-1,000   **ROS**

A late 18thC large pair of Derby figures of Shakespeare and Milton, each poet well modeled and standing beside a plinth, painted in colored enamels and gilt.

12.5in (31cm) high

$2,000-3,000   **WW**

Two late 18thC Derby allegorical figures, 'Water' and 'Earth', modeled as a fisherwoman holding a net, the male as a gardener holding a pot, with incised numerals to bases, damaged.

7.5in (19cm) high

$600-900   **ROS**

An early 19thC Derby model of a red squirrel, modeled seated on its haunches eating a nut, incised numeral "2", ears chipped.

3.25in (8.5cm) high

$1,000-1,500   **DN**

An 18thC Derby squirrel, modeled eating a nut, on a base with applied foliage.

2.75in (7cm) high

$2,000-3,000   **AA**

PORCELAIN

A Derby plate, painted by George Complin with a still life within a gilt scroll border, the turquoise ground with three oval panels of flowers, crowned crossed batons mark in puce and pattern number "115".

c1790

$800-1,200 **LFA**

Two of a set of five late 18thC Derby botanical plates, and a matching lobed dish, with gilt laurel and line borders, titled in blue, pattern number 141, wear and rim chips.

8.75in (22cm) diam

$3,000-4,000 set **WW**

A CLOSER LOOK AT A DERBY BILLINGSLEY PLATE

William Billingsley is hailed by many as the greatest of all English flower painters. He worked for Derby, Coalport and other factories and went on to run the Nantgarw and Swansea potteries.

Derby porcelain from this period is also noted for its fine gilding. Thomas Soar, identifiable by marks on this plate, was the factory's pre-eminent gilder in the late 18thC.

Billingsley's naturalistic style of painting was achieved by switching between a heavily loaded paintbrush for the lowlights and a dry brush for the highlights.

This plate dates from Derby's finest period, when the firm had a team comprising many of the best ceramicists and decorators in Europe.

An extremely rare Derby plate, painted by William Billingsley and gilded by Thomas Soar, with border painted in gilt, yellow ground and central roundel with spray of flowers, marked "D107".

c1790 *9in (23cm) diam*

$12,000-18,000 **AA**

A pair of 18thC Derby plates painted with views named "On Loch Lomond, Scotland" and "Near Coupar in Angus, Scotland", marks in blue, pattern number 270.

8.75in (22cm) diam.

$2,000-3,000 **CHEF**

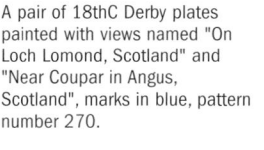

A Derby dish with scalloped gilt border, painted with flowers and inscribed "Lathyrus Odoratus Sweet Pea or Vetchling" and "D115".

8.75in (22cm) diam

$7,000-10,000 **AA**

A Derby dish with scalloped gilt border, painted with flowers, impressed "N" mark, inscribed "Passion Flower" and "D115".

8.75in (22cm) diam

$7,000-10,000 **AA**

A pair of Derby dishes with gilt borders painted with flowers, inscribed "Nasturtiums" to rear, crown mark.

10in (25.5cm) wide

$3,000-4,000 **AA**

A late 18thC Derby can and saucer, painted with pattern number 317 depicting Cupid flying through clouds holding a torch, marks in puce.

$1,000-1,200 **CHEF**

A late 18thC Derby can and saucer, painted with Cupid being disarmed by a lady, marks in gilt and puce.

Barrett and Thorpe in 'Derby Porcelain' attribute the painting of this pattern number to James Banford.

$3,000-4,000 **CHEF**

A Derby cabaret set, painted by George Robertson with nautical scenes, comprising a teapot, sucrier, milk jug, a pair of teabowls and saucers and a lobed oval tray with two loop handles, crowned crossed batons marks in puce, some pieces with pattern number "464".

$100,000-120,000 **AA**

A 19thC Derby cup and saucer, painted with lake views, with gilt swag frieze.

$450-550 **BRI**

A Derby two-handled loving cup, painted with pink roses and gilt, cross-over handles, painted mark.

5in (12cm) high

$500-700 **BRI**

A Derby porcelain ice cup, decorated with floral swags and trails of vines, with gilt detail, crown and crossed swords mark with "D".

2.25in (5.5cm) high

$2,000-3,000 **AA**

A rare Derby fluted creamboat, one side painted with a dwelling, the reverse with a simple flower spray, unmarked.

c1755   *4.5in (11.5cm) wide*

$1,500-2,000 **WW**

A Derby barrel-shaped jug, with flattened 'S' scroll handle, painted in Kakiemon palette with a bird in a branch, the reverse with scattered flowers, restored crack to lip.

c1760   *7.5in (19cm) high*

$1,200-1,800 **LFA**

A miniature Derby jug and bowl of octagonal form, with Imari-style design, red painted mark.

$200-300 **BRI**

A 19thC Derby style two-handled vase, painted with the 'Inverary' pattern, with gilt and blue swags.

8in (20.5cm) high

$450-550 **BRI**

A garniture of three early 19thC campana vases, possibly Derby, painted with a floral panel against a royal blue ground gilded with leaf scrolls and husks, on square gilt bases, unmarked, restored.

tallest 6.75in (17cm) high

$3,000-4,000 **GORL**

A rare Derby documentary miniature biscuit oval basket of flowers, incised beneath "Cocker Derby".

c1800   *1in (2.5cm) wide*

$600-900 **LFA**

PORCELAIN

DERBY

- André Planché produced porcelain figures in Derby from c1748. In 1756 he formed a partnership with William Duesbury. In 1770 Duesbury bought the Chelsea factory which he operated on its original site until 1784. These products are known as Chelsea-Derby. The most successful period was under the management of William Duesbury the younger, from 1786.
- Early wares were inspired by English silver. Ornamental pieces, such as vases and cabinet cups, were made in great numbers.
- Figures were produced from the 1750s. Typical subjects were pastoral scenes or Chinese allegories. Early figures may feature an unglazed 'dry edge' to the base or have a funnel-shaped hole. Later figures often have unglazed 'patch marks' which were caused by firing supports and can help with identification.
- Derby employed many prominent ceramics artists. William Billingsley (1758-1828) developed a technique for painting naturalistic flowers that involved wiping away paint to create delicate colors. William 'Quaker' Pegg (1775-1851) produced exquisite life-sized floral depictions, often based on live specimens rather than botanical drawings.
- The reputation of Derby declined c1800, but was revived with the introduction of Imari-influenced wares under the direction of William Bloor from 1811. The factory was renamed Royal Crown Derby Porcelain in 1890 and became part of the Allied English Potteries Group in 1964. Prior to 1770, pieces were unmarked. After this date, a model number was often added.

A CLOSER LOOK AT A PAIR OF EARLY 19THC DERBY VASES

This exceptionally well-made pair of vases were decorated by William Pegg who is considered one of the finest flowers painters to have worked in china painting. He helped to gain Derby the high regard with which it was held by the London aristocracy.

Pegg is an extremely sought after decorator. It is also very rare to find Derby vases like these in such good condition, as many are found with damaged handles.

Pegg painted these during his second period at the factory (1813-1820), following his decision in 1801 to become a Quaker. A markedly more flamboyant style of flower painting can be noted, and heavier gilding.

The vases were made during a period of improving fortunes for Derby. Duesbury's death in 1797 had been followed by a period of decline, which was reversed by Robert Bloor who took control in 1811.

A fine and rare pair of early 19thC Derby vases of Campana form decorated by William "Quaker" Pegg, and numbered "55".

1813-20   *12.75in (32.5cm) high*

$25,000-35,000   **ROW**

A pair of Derby ogee-shaped vases, with central cartouches of a figure in a landscape, and gilt detail.

c1758   *7in (18cm) high*

$9,000-10,000   **AA**

An 18thC Derby bell-shaped mug, painted in colored enamels with a vignette of exotic birds, with a scroll handle, handle restored.

c1760   *6in (15cm) high*

$600-900   **DN**

A Chelsea Derby custard cup and cover, with flower knop, painted swags, bands of flowers and leaves, within gilt dentil borders, conjoined gilt anchor and "D" marks.

c1775   *3.5in (9cm) high*

$1,200-1,800   **AA**

A Derby bough-pot, the central panel titled to the base "Rydal Mere, Cumberland", with rich gilding, and blue crown cross batons mark.

c1805   *9.75in (24.5cm) diam*

$700-1,000   **WW**

A Derby botanical oval sauce tureen and cover, inscribed beneath with names "Botany-bay Indigo", "Few-flowered begonia" and "Crimson-flowered Chinese brambles", with crowned crossed batons mark.

c1815   *7in (18cm) wide*

$3,000-4,000   **AA**

An 18thC Derby scent bottle, with tripod feet, surrounded with applied flowers in relief.

2.5in (6.5cm) high

$2,000-3,000   **AA**

An English porcelain box and cover, painted with a panel of flowers and another of a landscape, the interior with a portrait of John Liston as Paul Pry, probably Derby, restored.

John Liston was the leading comic actor of the first half of the 19thC. In 1825 he created his masterpiece character Paul Pry, in John Poole's farce of the same name. Pry is a man consumed by curiosity, an interfering busybody unable to mind his own business.

c1830   *4.25in (11cm) high*

$400-600   **WW**

Two views of a late19thC Dresden porcelain figure of The Blown Kiss, after Meissen.

5.75in (14.5cm) high

$900-1,000 **TBK**

A pair of Dresden figures, each decorated in colored enamels, with scroll molded bases picked out in gilt, and marks in blue.

c1900   9.25in (23.5cm) high

$200-300 **LFA**

A 19thC/20thC Dresden porcelain figure group, of a classical maiden with amorini.

6.75in (17cm) high

$200-300 **CLV**

A pair of 19thC/20thC Dresden salt cellars, each in the form of a putto, the interior painted with a harbor scene, with marks in blue.

5.5in (14cm) wide

$400-600 **LFA**

An early 20thC Dresden porcelain seven piece monkey band, including a drummer, a cymbalist, a violinist and two horn players.

5.5in (14cm) high

$600-900 **FRE**

A Dresden/Potschappel porcelain figure bowl, with polychrome flower paintings, gilded, with blue mark, and painters' marks.

c1903   8.5in (21cm) diam

$200-300 **BMN**

A 19thC Dresden porcelain figural centerpiece, with underglaze blue interwoven "S" and "V" above "Dresden", impressed "M11046", inscribed "76 C5".

13in (33.5cm) diam

$700-1,000 **PC**

A Dresden table centerpiece, in the form of three putti, around a flower applied column supporting a pierced painted basket, with a mark in blue.

c1900   16.75in (42.5cm) high

$1,000-1,200 **LFA**

A Carl Thieme, Dresden, porcelain ink stand, polychrome painted, gilded, with molded peacocks, and blue lilies mark with "CT", restored.

c1900   11.5in (29cm) wide

$1,200-1,800 **BMN**

A late 19thC to early 20thC Meissen-style pair of inkwells and stand, enameled by A. Lamm of Dresden, decorated with flowers and a Watteau-style scene.

11in (28cm) wide

$700-1,000 **BMN**

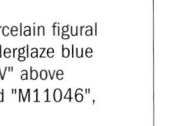

DRESDEN

PORCELAIN

DRESDEN

- Many porcelain factories operated in and around Dresden in the 19thC, copying and imitating the successful styles of Meissen.
- Output was generally of lower quality than Meissen in terms of both body and design. Painted decoration often lacked refinement and colors tended to be stronger. However, there were many exceptions and good quality, appealing pieces were also produced.
- Forms were elaborate and Rococo in style with applied decoration of flowers, shells and scrollwork.
- Carl Thieme is considered to be one of the best Dresden imitators of Meissen. His factory, established at Potschappel in 1872, produced high quality decorative wares. Pieces by the Voigt factory in Sitzendorf are also among the most collectable today.
- Many decorating workshop also opened in the area, such as Donath & Co., Richard Klemm, Oswald Lorenz, and Adolph Hammann. One of the most successful decorators was Helena Wolfsohn.
- Many Dresden pieces are unmarked, although some factories marked their wares with the Meissen crossed swords mark. Today, some pieces have an unglazed patch to the base where marks were removed to disguise their origination.

A late 19thC Dresden porcelain punch bowl and cover, painted with Watteauesque scenes, the cover surmounted with a bacchic putto, and a Berlin-type scepter mark.

10.5in (26.5cm) diam

$1,000-1,500 | **DN**

A pair of Dresden flared round jardinières, each with two scroll handles and brightly painted in colored enamels with birds, flowers and insects.

c1880 *4in (10cm) high*

$300-400 | **LFA**

A late 19thC Dresden porcelain tureen and présentoir, decorated by Helena Wolfsohn with Watteau-style scenes, the tureen with a molded lemon knob, and a blue "AR" mark.

9.5in (24cm) wide

$500-700 | **BMN**

Five Dresden pierced gilded dessert plates painted with flowers, two with damaged borders.

9in (22.5cm) diam

$400-450 | **GORL**

A late 19thC Dresden flower-encrusted wall mirror, mounted with putti and musical motifs, with a blue cross mark, and some small chips and repairs.

17.75in (45cm) high

$1,000-1,500 | **DN**

A 19thC/20thC Dresden porcelain chandelier, in the Meissen style, with six detachable scroll branches, each with applied flowers and leaves and hung with floral bouquets.

23.5in (59.5cm) high

$1,500-2,000 | **PC**

A 19thC/20thC Dresden style salon suite, decorated with painted floral sprays in relief, the table with an impressed crossed swords mark and initials "DKE".

Arm chair 5in (12.5cm) high

$550-650 | **H&L**

A Dresden porcelain oval portrait plaque of a semi-clad woman, the back stamped in blue "Franz Till DRESDEN Pragerstrasse 46".

10.5in (26.5cm) high

$3,000-4,000 | **JN**

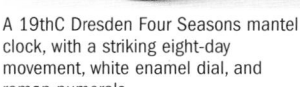

A 19thC Dresden Four Seasons mantel clock, with a striking eight-day movement, white enamel dial, and roman numerals.

19in (48cm) high

$1,500-2,000 | **FRE**

MEISSEN AFTER 1800

- Established c1709, Meissen was Europe's first hard-paste porcelain factory (from c1710). It had a reputation for quality and was hugely successful.
- Despite this, by 1800 the factory was in decline as a result of increasing competition. To counteract these problems, the factory began to rely on more efficient methods of production.
- Output became more diverse to cater for the expanding bourgeoisie and a variety of popular styles such as Neoclassical, Biedermeier and Rococo and Renaissance Revival were incorporated and combined into designs during the 19thC.
- Rococo Revival figures were produced in large numbers. They can be distinguished from original 18thC designs by their elaborate forms, shiny gilding and stronger colors.
- Pieces are often marked with the crossed swords mark and a model number. Painter's marks are also found.

A 19thC Meissen porcelain figure group, with a blue crossed swords mark.

13in (32.5cm) high

$3,000-4,000   **FRE**

A 19thC Meissen porcelain group of the Capture of Tritons, after a model by J. J. Kändler, modeled as two nymphs and a putto, with blue crossed swords mark.

12.75in (32cm) high

$3,000-4,000   **FRE**

A 19thC Meissen porcelain figure representing 'Hearing' from the 'Five Senses' series, crossed swords mark.

4.5in (11.5cm) high

$2,000-3,000   **SWO**

A 19thC near pair of Meissen porcelain groups of 'Amor Fesselung' and 'Cupid Punished', with blue crossed swords marks.

13in (32.5cm) high

$9,000-12,000   **FRE**

A Meissen group of 'The Good Mother', after the original model by Michel Victor Acier, with crossed swords mark, incised "E69 71 40", some damage.

c1880   *8.5in (21cm) high*

$2,000-3,000   **SWO**

A late 19thC Meissen porcelain figure emblematic of Music, modeled as a standing draped classical maiden holding a harp, with a blue crossed swords mark.

20.25in (50.5cm) high

$3,000-4,000   **FRE**

A late 19thC pair of Meissen porcelain figural candlesticks, modeled as a gallant and his companion, with blue crossed swords mark.

13.75in (34cm) high

$3,000-5,000   **FRE**

A late 19thC Meissen porcelain figure of the tailor's wife, modeled as a mother with her child on a goat, with blue crossed swords mark.

7in (17.5cm) high

$2,000-3,000   **FRE**

A pair of late 19thC Meissen porcelain figures of jays, each perched on a tree stump, with a blue crossed swords mark.

11in (27.5cm) high

$3,000-4,000   **FRE**

A late 19thC pair of Meissen porcelain figural candelabra, of tree form, with blue crossed swords marks.

9in (22.5cm) high

$4,000-6,000   **FRE**

A late 19thC large Meissen porcelain figure of Count Brühl's tailor, after a model by J. J. Kändler, blue underglaze crossed swords mark.

Count Brühl was famed for his clothes. When his tailor asked to dine at court he commissioned a satirical model of the tailor.

17in (42.5cm) high

$15,000-20,000   **FRE**

A Meissen porcelain figure representing 'Touch' from the 'Five Senses' series, a woman and a caged parrot, underglaze blue swords mark, model number "E.4".

c1880   6in (15cm) high

$1,000-1,500   **KAU**

A late 19thC Meissen group, with a lady and gentleman standing on a high scroll base with a drummer seated at their feet, crossed swords mark and "1484" incised.

9.75in (25cm) high

$4,000-5,000   **WW**

A CLOSER LOOK AT A MEISSEN GROUP

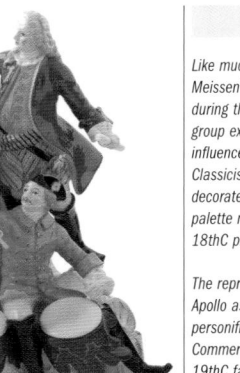

Like much of Meissen's output during the period, the group exhibits the influence of Neo-Classicism and is decorated in a strong palette not seen on 18thC pieces.

The representation of Apollo as a personification of Commerce reflects the 19thC fascination with trade and the virtue of industry.

The lively composition and large size make for a significant, and thus desirable, display piece.

The crossed swords mark is found on many Meissen pieces and was widely used from c1724.

A large 19thC Meissen group, with Apollo as a personification of Commerce, seated on a sack inscribed "E.B. 1794", behind him a cherub holds a sack of gold, crossed swords mark, minor repairs.

7in (28cm) high

$5,500-6,500   **WW**

A late 19thC Meissen figure of a woman, modeled standing at a tripod table playing cards, blue crossed swords mark, Pressnummern, incised F64, repaired and restored.

6.75in (17cm) high

$1,200-1,800   **DN**

A late 19thC Meissen group of Minerva, the goddess seated before a tree, Caesar's War Commentaries in her lap, a putto and a suit of armour at her side, blue crossed swords marks, incised "E16", some chips.

9in (23cm) high

$600-900   **DN**

A late 19thC Meissen porcelain figure of a gentleman wearing 18thC dress, blue crossed swords mark, Pressnummern, top of staff missing, other small chips.

5.5in (14cm) high

$700-1,000   **DN**

A late 19thC Meissen model of Cupid, modeled standing holding a broken love-heart, a quiver slung over his shoulder, blue crossed swords mark, Pressnummer, incised "M.102".

5.75in (14.5cm) high

$1,000-1,500   **DN**

A late 19thC Meissen figure of Harlequin, modeled seated playing bagpipes on a rock work base, arm replaced.

5.25in (13.5cm) high

$1,500-2,000   **ROS**

Two late 19thC Meissen monkey band figures, modeled after originals by J.J. Kändler, comprising a drummer and an oboeist, each with a blue crossed swords mark, restored.

taller 5.75in (14.5cm) high

$1,000-1,500   **DN**

One of a German porcelain part monkey band, modeled after the original Meissen examples by J.J. Kändler, comprising a conductor, cellist, violinist, bag-piper, two horn players, bassoonist, recorder player and drummer, blue crossed sword marks, some damage and repair.

c1900   tallest 6.75in (17cm) high

$1,500-2,000 SET   **DN**

A late 19thC Meissen porcelain figure of a woman with a festoon, glazed, painted and gilded, holding a festoon in her hands, underglaze blue swords mark, stamped "122" and "F.67".

6.75in (17cm) high

$1,000-1,500   **KAU**

A 19thC Meissen model of a Bolognese terrier, raised on a scroll-mounded oval base, crossed swords mark and "26" incised.

6.5in (16.5cm) high

$4,000-6,000 **WW**

A 19thC Meissen model of a Bolognese terrier, crossed swords mark and incised "C77".

5.75in (14.5cm) high

$3,000-4,000 **WW**

A 19thC Meissen group of three pug dog puppies, wearing blue collars with bells and playing upon a grassy mound, crossed swords mark and incised "F186", restored.

$4,500-5,500 **WW**

A pair of 19thC Meissen pugs, the bitch with her puppy between her feet, crossed swords marks, restored.

7in (17.5cm) high

$5,000-7,000 **WW**

A Meissen porcelain model of an ostrich, with red cross motifs to its neck.

6.5in (16.5cm) high

$3,000-4,000 **AA**

A 19thC Meissen model of a swan, standing amidst green reeds and detailed with colored enamels, crossed swords mark.

10.5in (26.5cm) high

$4,000-6,000 **WW**

27

A small Meissen milk jug and cover, with a cone knop and scroll handle, painted in Kakiemon palette with the 'Quail' pattern, crossed swords mark, finial restored.

The quail pattern is a popular motif of Japanese Kakiemon ceramics, symbolizing peace and longevity. It was taken up by European porcelain decorators in the 18thC, who imitated the Kakiemon style.

c1730   6.5in (16.5cm) high

$4,500-5,500   **WW**

A Meissen milk jug and cover, with a flower knop and gilt metal hinge, painted with a panel of flowers on a purple ground, crossed swords mark.

c1745   5.5in (14cm) high

$1,500-2,000   **WW**

A Meissen coffee pot, domed lid with ball knop, with ribbed surface and flowering tree, partially gilded, blue underglaze swords mark with star.

c1800   90.6in (24cm) high

$1,000-1,200   **KAU**

A Meissen tea canister, domed lid with cone knop, the ribbed surface with flowering tree, partially gilded, blue underglaze swords mark with line.

c1800   5.25in (13cm) high

$1,000-1,500   **KAU**

A Meissen porcelain cup and saucer, the cup with square handle, with floral decoration, underglaze blue swords mark with a star.

c1800   Saucer 5.5in (14cm) diam

$100-150   **KAU**

Part of a late 19thC Meissen porcelain dinner service, 'Neuer Ausschnitt' shape, floral decoration with insects, gilded rims, in 47 parts, comprising: 12 soup plates, 13 dinner plates, three oval dishes, one circular plate, one saucière, one rectangular plate, 17 bread plates, underglaze blue swords mark.

$6,000-9,000 SET   **KAU**

A Meissen porcelain cup and saucer, with gilt rims, blue decoration of flowers and insects, crossed swords mark.

4.75in (12cm) high

$1,000-1,500   **AA**

A pair of late 19thC Meissen baskets, the gilt-lined wavy oval rims above diamond lattice-pierced sides encrusted with flowers, canceled cross swords marks.

14.5in (37cm) wide

$500-700 PAIR   CHEF

A 19thC Meissen porcelain mantel clock, with applied decoration of exotic birds and floral encrustations with a brass dial, crossed swords mark, incised "G81".

11.5in (29cm) high

$700-1,000   SWO

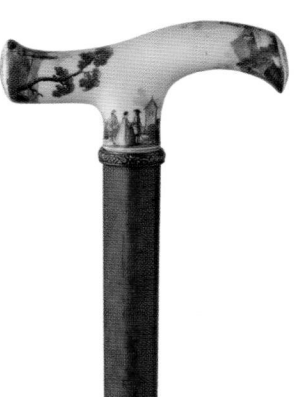

A Meissen clock case, modeled en rocaille and mounted with figures of putti emblematic of the Seasons, set with a two-train movement striking on a bell and with a bob pendulum, blue crossed swords and cancellation marks, damage.

18.5in (47cm) high

$3,000-4,000   DN

A Meissen three-branch candelabra, the flower-applied branches supported by a shepherdess with a pipe, a sheep at her feet, mark in blue and incised "F.156", damaged.

c1870

$450-550   LFA

A late 19thC Meissen flower-encrusted chamberstick, with floriform sconce and twig handle, blue crossed swords mark, restored.

5in (12cm) diam

$600-900   DN

An 18thC Meissen 'Opera' cane, the handle with a bust of woman wearing a tiara, painted with flowers, malacca shaft, gilded collar.

$4,500-5,500   SEG

An 18thC Meissen cane, the handle gilt-copper mounted, painted with merchant scene and flowering branches, malacca shaft.

$4,500-5,500   SEG

A late 19thC Meissen model of a flower-encrusted hand bell, painted with scattered insects, blue crossed swords mark.

4.75in (12cm) high

$300-400   DN

An early 20thC Meissen round dish, with central bar, painted in underglaze blue with the 'Onion' pattern, mark in blue.

4.25in (11cm) diam

$100-150   LFA

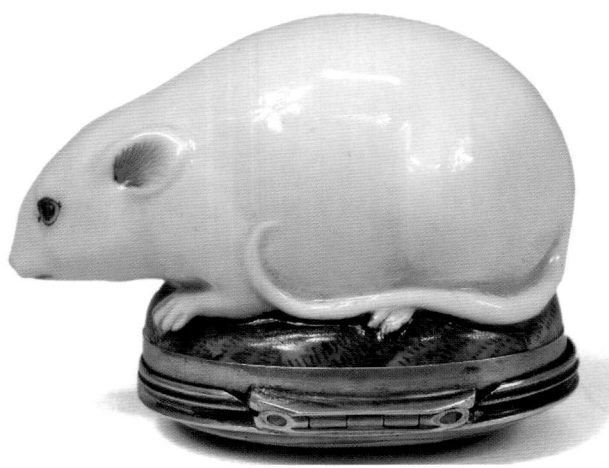

A rare 18thC Paris porcelain pill box in the form of a white mouse, with painted silver mounted lid and marks for London 1797, crack.

2.5in (6cm) wide

$4,500-5,500   **SWO**

A Paris porcelain vase, decorated in relief with masks and Cupids, painted with reserves depicting a figural tavern scene, the reverse with a floral basket.

c1830   *22.5in (56cm) high*

$8,000-10,000   **FRE**

A pair of 19thC Paris porcelain vases, applied with figures and birds, on a white ground enriched with gilt.

15.5in (39cm) high

$800-1,000   **FRE**

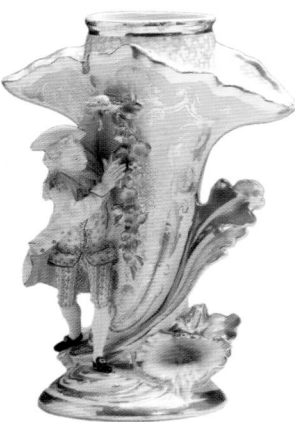

A 19thC pair of Paris porcelain vases, molded with bisque figures, depicting a dandy and his companion, on white gilt enhanced ground.

16in (40cm) high

$1,500-2,000   **FRE**

A 19thC Paris porcelain vase, with ornate Rococo scroll pierced rim, and a reserve depicting two Asian ladies taking tea.

19.5in (49cm) high

$500-700   **FRE**

A 19thC Paris circular porcelain plaque, the central panel inscribed "Bataille De Rocroy 16 Mai 1643", signed "Leber Von Schnetz".

18.25in (45.5cm) diam

$1,000-1,200   **SWO**

A pair of late 19thC Paris gold anchor figures, modeled as an 18thC gentleman and his beau.

15.75in (40cm) high

$1,000-1,200   **L&T**

A 19thC Russian porcelain military plate, by N. Kholshevnikov after Piratsky, the reverse inscribed in Cyrillic "5th Alexandrovsky Hussars of His Highness Prince Ludwig Gessensky and 6th Klyatitsky Hussars of Duke Nikolai Nikolaievich Senior", with blue and green cypher marks, and dated "72".

9.75in (24.5cm) diam

$25,000-35,000   **LAW**

A Royal Copenhagen 'Flora Danica' porcelain covered tureen and underplate, with green underglaze mark, number "203559" decorator's marks and wavy underglaze mark.

16in (40.5cm) wide

$8,000-10,000   **FRE**

A set of three Royal Copenhagen 'Flora Danica' porcelain serving bowls, finely painted with botanical specimens, with green underglaze marks and two of the dishes with numbers "3545".

9.5in (24cm) diam

$3,000-4,000   **FRE**

A Tucker and Hemphill China Factory enamel and gilt decorated porcelain pitcher, of Grecian urn form, with "B" on underside for decorator Charles J. Boulter.

Tucker Porcelain was made from 1826-38 in a factory in Philadelphia PA, US founded by William Ellis Tucker.

1826-32

12in (30.5cm) high

$7,000-10,000   **FRE**

A Tucker and Hemphill China Factory enamel and gilt decorated porcelain pitcher, decorated with the Philadelphia Waterworks and the Upper Ferry Bridge, restored.

1826-32

8in (20.5cm) high

$2,000-3,000   **FRE**

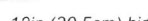

A large pair of 19thC Sèvres-style 'vases des âges', applied with female busts and painted with flowers and figures, with enamel blue interlaced "L" marks.

16.25in (41cm) high

$7,000-10,000   **WW**

A late 19thC pair of Sèvres-style porcelain and gilt-bronze-mounted covered vases, with painted figural reserves, on a blue ground enriched with gilding.

16.5in (41cm) high

$5,000-6,000   **FRE**

A late 19thC pair of Sèvres-style 'jeweled' covered vases, with pineapple finials and a gilt enhanced cobalt blue ground.

11.25in (28cm) high

$4,500-5,500   **FRE**

A late 19thC pair of Sèvres-style porcelain and gilt-bronze-mounted vases, signed "M Demonceaux", with pseudo Sèvres marks.

26.5in (66cm) high

$6,000-9,000   **FRE**

A pair of Sèvres-style vases, with gilt bronze mounts and handles, printed and painted with female figures, signed.

c1890   *17.25in (43cm) high*

$700-1,000   **SWO**

A late 19th to early 20thC pair of Sèvres-style porcelain gilt-bronze mounted covered vases, painted with scenes of lovers, with pseudo Sèvres mark.

23.5in (59cm) high

$6,000-8,000   **FRE**

A late 19thC Sèvres-style 'jeweled' porcelain and gilt-bronze-mounted covered vase, with a continuous figural landscape after Watteau, signed "Schmit de Manufacture de Sevres".

24.5in (61cm) high

$7,000-10,000   **FRE**

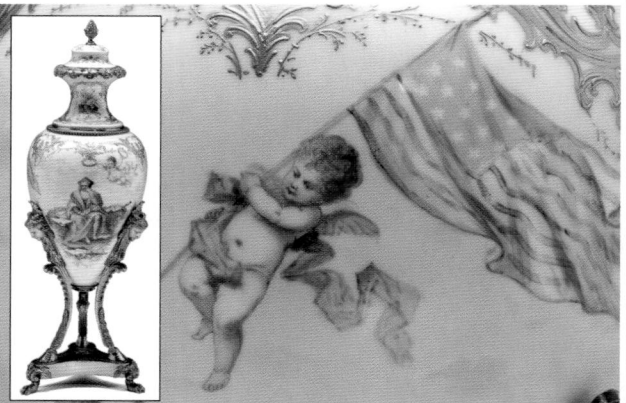

A rare late 19thC Sèvres-style porcelain and gilt metal covered vase, the ovoid sides painted with Columbus discovering the New World.

22.5in (56cm) high

$4,000-5,000   **FRE**

A late 19th to early 20thC Sèvres-style porcelain and gilt bronze mounted vase on a stand, painted with figures in 18thC costume, signed "J Morin".

66in (165cm) high

$10,000-15,000   **FRE**

An early 20thC Sèvres-style porcelain and onyx pedestal, of Doric form, painted with cherubs and female figures.

39.5in (99cm) high

$4,000-6,000   **FRE**

An early 20thC Sèvres-style porcelain, onyx and gilt bronze pedestal, on a Doric-form pilaster painted with cherubs and maidens.

44.5in (111cm) high

$5,000-7,000   **FRE**

A rare pair of Sèvres porcelain busts, of the Comte D'Artois and his daughter-in-law the Duchesse de Berri, he with an impressed Sèvres mark and incised "29 - Nov - SZ", she inscribed "Mas 14 x bu.SZ" (Mas for Mascret).

Jean Mascret was a sculpteur répareur at Sèvres from 1810-1848. The Comte D'Artois, later Charles X, King of France and Navarre, was crowned King of France in 1824 and reigned until the French revolution of 1830. Marie-Caroline Bourbon married the second son of Charles X and was the mother of the Comte de Chambourd (Henri V), the last descendant of the ancient branch of the House of Bourbon.

c1816   *15.25in (38cm) high*

$7,000-10,000   **WW**

A 19thC Sèvres-style plate, painted with figures and a castle within a rural landscape.

11.5in (29cm) diam

$400-600   **ROS**

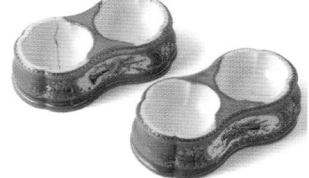

A pair of Sevres-style bleu celeste ground double salts, with late 19thC decoration, one with firing cracks, the other repaired.

5in (13cm) wide

$200-300   **DN**

A set of four 19thC Sèvres porcelain plates, painted with central portraits and inscribed verso, enriched in gilt with insects and palmettes, with painted red marks.

9.5in (24cm) diam

$3,000-4,000   **FRE**

A pair of late 19thC Sèvres-style cabinet plates, decorated with rose and gilt garlands, on a blue ground.

9.5in (24cm) diam

$700-1,000 PAIR   **SWO**

A 19thC Sèvres tête-à-tête, with late 19thC probably Limoges decoration, the cypher of Louis-Philippe, various Sèvres marks, and minor chips, one cup a Limoges replacement.

The piece is decorated in the manner of a service originally ordered by King Louis-Philippe of France (1830-48).

$1,000-1,200   **DN**

A late 19th to early 20thC Sèvres-style porcelain and gilt-metal-mounted bijouterie box, with romantic and Bacchic scenes, signed "Schuler".

14in (35cm) wide

$11,000-15,000   **FRE**

A Louis XV-style gilt-bronze-mounted center table, inset with Sèvres-style porcelain plaques depicting court ladies, the later central plate with a portrait of Louis XV.

32.5in (81cm) high

$10,000-15,000   **FRE**

PORCELAIN

A late 19thC Vienna covered vase, painted with a portrait bust of a young woman, on an iridescent ground, signed "Wagner", with a red shield mark.

25in (62.5cm) high

$7,000-10,000   FRE

A Vienna milk jug and cover, painted in enamels with a "Vue de la Ville de Gerace dans la Calabre ulterieure près de l'ancienne ville de Locres", mark in blue and incised numerals.

c1800 5in (12.5cm) high

$4,500-5,500   AA

A late 19thC Vienna covered vase and stand, depicting Cleopatra holding an asp, with underglaze blue shield mark, signed "Wagner".

24in (60cm) high

$7,000-10,000   FRE

A large late 19thC Vienna porcelain urn on a stand, decorated with cherubs and classical figures, against a blue ground enriched with gilt, lacks cover.

22.5in (57cm) high

$2,000-3,000   FRE

A late 19thC large Vienna porcelain vase, painted with a female, with gilt foliage and Greek key bands, and a blue scepter mark, signed "Wagner".

25.5in (65cm) high

$7,000-10,000   FRE

A late 19thC Vienna porcelain vase, entitled "Summerlust", with a red luster ground and gilt, blue shield mark, signed "Schlesinger".

15.5in (39.5cm) high

$3,000-4,000   FRE

A late 19thC Vienna covered urn, signed "Richter", inscribed "Unschuldig", painted with a portrait bust of a woman on an iridescent olive green ground.

20in (50cm) high

$7,000-10,000   FRE

A 19thC Vienna porcelain plate of a young Neapolitan, painted with a young woman, with a blue shield mark, signed indistinctly.

9.5in (24cm) diam

$1,000-1,200   FRE

A 19thC Vienna porcelain plate depicting Napoleon, signed "Wagner", with a blue shield mark.

9.75in (25cm) diam

$1,500-2,000   FRE

A Vienna painted porcelain plaque, by Josef Zasche, the reverse inscribed "Das Quartett, nach F A Kaulbach", within an ornate carved giltwood frame, signed.

Josef Zasche (1821-1881) was born in Gablonz, Austria, which is now part of the Czech Republic. He worked for the Vienna Porcelain Manufactory from 1844, before setting up his own workshop in 1847.

19.75in (49cm) wide

$7,000-10,000   FRE

WORCESTER

- Since the founding of the company in 1751, Worcester has been famous for the variety and quality of its blue-and-white and polychrome designs, in particular the chinoiserie designs introduced in the early 1750s.
- Early blue-and-white Worcester shows the influence of the Bristol factory, with shapes derived from British silver. Teawares, sauceboats and pickle-dishes were decorated with blue and white copies of Chinese wares and polychrome chinoiseries.
- Worcester invented the process of printing on porcelain. It used this technique extensively to produce overglaze black enamel and underglaze blue printed decoration. By 1770 Worcester even exported blue-and-white ware to the Netherlands.
- The factory perfected a deep, underglaze blue ground, developed its famous 'scale blue' and other colored grounds. Many early blue-and-white wares bear a workman's mark, usually a simple sign of uncertain meaning, prior to the adoption of the crescent mark.
- It lost its position as Britain's premier pottery in the 1780s as wares from Derby, French and cheap Chinese imports took over but late regained its position during the Flight, Chamberlain and Grainger periods.

An 18thC Worcester blue and white bowl, decorated with a coastal scene, with fishermen and figures in boats, and a blue crescent mark.

11in (28cm) diam

$4,500-6,500   **AA**

A Worcester blue and white deep dish, with a wicker pattern in relief and reserve cartouches with floral sprays, and crescent mark.

9.25in (23.5cm) diam

$3,000-4,000   **AA**

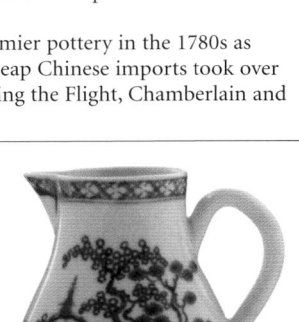

A Worcester blue and white sparrow beak jug and cover, printed with sprays of flowers and a moth, with a hatched crescent mark, and some small chips.

c1770   *5.5in (14cm) high*

$300-400   **DN**

A Worcester blue and white sparrow-beak jug, painted with the so called 'Cannonball' pattern, and open crescent mark.

c1770   *4.25in (11cm) high*

$350-450   **DN**

A Worcester mug, printed in black with a head and shoulders portrait of William Pitt, Earl of Chatham, flanked by Fame and Minerva, unmarked.

This is a rare subject.

c1770   *5.75in (14.5cm) high*

$3,500-4,500   **AA**

A Worcester blue and white cornucopia wall pocket, painted with the so-called 'Cornucopia Prunus' pattern, workmans' mark.

c1760   *10in (25cm) high*

$2,000-3,000   **DN**

A Worcester blue and white guglet, painted with the willow bridge fisherman pattern, open crescent mark to base, rim restored.

c1760   *9.75in (24.5cm) high*

$600-900   **SWO**

A pierced blue and white Worcester bowl, with pierced cover, decorated inside with a boat, trees and pagodas, and with foliage in relief outside.

c1755   *7.75in (19.5cm) diam*

$5,000-7,000   **AA**

A rare Worcester blue and white silver shaped sauceboat, painted with the 'Fisherman on a Towering Rock' pattern, workman's mark.

c1755   *9.25in (23.5cm) wide*

$1,000-1,500   **WW**

A Worcester low oval sauceboat, painted in underglaze blue with a version of the 'Sinking Boat Fisherman' pattern, within molded cartouches, interior painted with flowers, leaves and Chinese emblems, workman's mark, rim chip.

c1755   *5.5in (14cm) wide*

$2,000-3,000   **LFA**

A Worcester silver-shape sauceboat, painted in blue with the 'Sinking Boat Fisherman' pattern, workman's mark.

c1755   *6.25in (16cm) wide*

$1,200-1,800   **WW**

A rare Worcester blue and white cream boat, printed with the 'Obelisk Fisherman' pattern, disguised numeral mark.

c1780   *4.25in (11cm) wide*

$1,500-2,000   **WW**

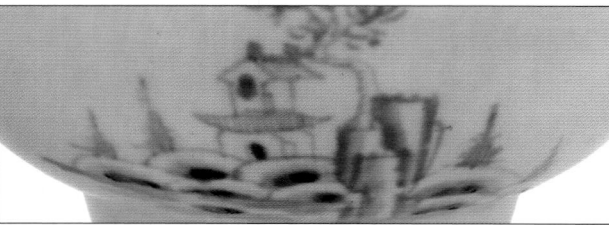

A Worcester bowl, painted in pale blue with a version of 'The Plantation' pattern, workman's mark.

c1755   *4.5in (11cm) diam*

$2,000-3,000   **LFA**

A Worcester blue and white bowl, with floral printed decoration on scallop-molded reserves, shaped rim, crescent mark.

c1780   *10.5in (26.5cm) diam*

$600-900   **BRI**

A Worcester pierced flared basket, the interior painted in underglaze blue with the 'Honeysuckle, Narcissus and Anemone Spray' pattern, the exterior applied with flowerheads, blue crescent mark.

c1770   *7.5in (19cm) diam*

$2,000-3,000   **AA**

A Worcester two-handled pierced basket, printed in blue with the 'Pine Cone' pattern, hatched crescent mark, crack.

c1780   *8.75in (22cm) wide*

$600-900   **DN**

A Worcester flared jardinière and stand, printed in underglaze blue with the 'Pine Cone' pattern, within cell diaper borders, the stand painted with sprays of flowers, blue crescent marks.

c1770   *4in (10cm) high*

$2,200-2,800   **AA**

An early Worcester blue and white baluster vase, with floral printed decoration, Rococo scroll molded handles and crescent mark, damaged. *This would have been part of a garniture.*

12in (30.5cm) high

$700-1,000   **BRI**

A rare Worcester mustard spoon, of Rococo silver form, with round bowl and scroll-molded handle, printed in underglaze blue with a flower spray, tip of handle restored.

c1770   *3.75in (9.5cm) long*

$1,000-1,500   **LFA**

WORCESTER TRANSFER PRINTING

- Several names can be linked to the development of the transfer printing process at Worcester c1756-8. Foremost among them are engraver Robert Hancock, who first applied the method to porcelain, and the Holdship brothers.
- The process involved applying ink to a copper sheet and then transferring this to unglazed porcelain using a sheet of tissue. The cross-hatching made by the engraving tools can often be seen in transfer-printed decoration. The pattern could be reproduced identically on every piece, much more cheaply than hand-painting.
- Worcester used transfer printing extensively for overglaze black enamel and underglaze blue printed pieces.
- Demand for blue and white wares was enormous from the mid-18thC and most English factories began mass-producing transfer-printed wares in the 1770s. Worcester and Caughley were the most successful.
- Some firms later applied transfer printing methods to earthenware, which was cheaper than porcelain. By the end of the 18thC, transfer-printed ceramics were common across Europe.

A Worcester feather-molded coffee cup, with everted barbed rim and C-scroll handle, transfer-printed in black with a finch on a branch and birds in flight, the interior border with a flower-paneled trellis band.

c1760   2.5in (6.5cm) high

$2,000-3,000   AA

A Worcester coffee cup and saucer, with notched loop handle, printed after Robert Hancock with 'The Tea Party' in black, within black line borders.

c1770

$600-900   LFA

A Worcester mug, with notched loop handle, transfer-printed in black with the 'Whitton Anglers' pattern, faint base crack.

c1770   6in (15cm) high

$1,200-1,800   LFA

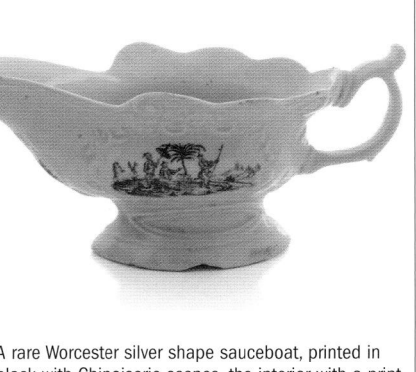

A rare Worcester silver shape sauceboat, printed in black with Chinoiserie scenes, the interior with a print of 'Bubbles', scratched line mark, rim crack and footrim chip.

c1755   7.75in (19.5cm) wide

$1,500-2,000   WW

A large and rare Worcester leaf-molded mask jug, inscribed "Success to the Crosby Hunt", transfer-printed in black with a continuous fox hunting scene, the neck with two vignettes, unmarked, repaired cracks.

c1770   9in (23cm) high

$1,500-2,000   WW

PORCELAIN

A Worcester mug, unusually painted in colored enamels with a cluster of strawberries, and scattered flowers and leaves, unmarked.

c1760   *4.75in (12cm) high*

$3,000-4,000   **AA**

An 18thC Worcester porcelain cup, decorated with Oriental figures in a landscape, with black and gilt patterned border and leaves.

2.5in (6.5cm) high

$700-1,000   **AA**

An 18thC Worcester porcelain cup, decorated with Chinese figures with fans, and a butterfly.

2.25in (5.5cm) high

$1,200-1,500   **AA**

An 18thC Worcester coffee cup, with notched loop handle, decorated in gilt with monograms, within a cartouche flanked by putti.

c1775   *2.5in (6.5cm) high*

$1,200-1,500   **AA**

A fluted Worcester teacup and saucer, with ear-shaped handle, painted in the Kakiemon palette with the 'Two Quail' pattern, unmarked.

c1770   *5.5in (14cm) diam*

$1,800-2,200   **AA**

An 18thC Worcester lobed porcelain cup and saucer, painted in Kakiemon palette with the Sir Joshua Reynolds pattern, marked with cypher.

5in (12.5cm) diam

$2,500-3,000   **AA**

A Worcester cup and saucer with gilt rim, decorated with fruit and flower sprays in magenta on a white ground, and impressed circle to underside.

c1780   *5in (12.5cm) diam*

$500-700   **AA**

An 18thC Worcester lobed porcelain bowl and saucer, painted in Kakiemon palette with the 'Sir Joshua Reynolds' pattern, marked with cypher.

4.75in (12cm) diam

$2,200-2,800   **AA**

A Worcester lobed oval sauce tureen, cover and stand, from the 'Reagan' service, painted in Sèvres style with swags of husks, unmarked.

c1775   *9.5in (24cm) wide*

$9,000-10,000   **AA**

An 18thC Worcester pot pourri holder, with pierced lid and flower knop, decorated with sprays of flowers, and a blue and gilt border.

$12,000-15,000   **AA**

A CLOSER LOOK AT A WORCESTER SCALLOPED BOWL

This bowl dates from the first five years of production at Dr Wall's celebrated Worcester porcelain factory. Such early pieces are rare and generally of immense interest to collectors.

The scalloped rim of this bowl is exaggerated. At the time, Worcester was the only English porcelain manufacturer capable of achieving complex shapes like this.

The quality of the painting on this bowl is very high, and the colors retain their vibrancy.

Much early Worcester is decorated in underglaze blue. This early use of the famille verte palette is rare.

An early Worcester scalloped rim bowl, molded with flowers and leaves and a shell band, painted in the *famille verte* palette with flowers, insects and trailing branches, within an iron red line rim, unmarked.

c1755   4.75in (12cm) diam

$33,000-36,000   **AA**

A Worcester bowl, painted in the *famille rose* palette with flowering branches, a fence and rockwork, the interior with a flower spray, within an iron red and yellow flowerhead and looped band, unmarked.

c1760   4.75in (12cm) diam

$1,500-2,000   **AA**

A Worcester bowl, painted in the 'Jabberwocky' pattern, with a turquoise interior border and red, blue, green and gilt decoration.

c1765   6.5in (16cm) diam

$700-1,000   **SWO**

An early Worcester beaker vase, of waisted form, painted in the Kakiemon palette with a Ho-Ho bird perched on pierced rockwork, flanked by flowering branches, unmarked.

c1755   5.5in (14cm) high

$15,000-18,000   **AA**

A Worcester bowl, painted in the *famille verte* palette with a bird on a flowering branch, the leaves picked out in brown enamel and gilt.

c1760   6in (15cm) diam

$1,000-1,500   **LFA**

A pair of Worcester ovoid vases and covers, painted in the Kakiemon style with reserves of flowering shrubs, blue square seal marks, flower finials missing.

6in (15cm) high

$1,000-1,500   **BRI**

PORCELAIN

A Chamberlain's Worcester plate, painted with naturalistic feathers, within a gilt roundel, gilt band to rim, berry and leaf scroll border, script mark in puce.

c1805   *8.25in (21cm) diam*

$3,000-4,000   **AA**

A Chamberlain's Worcester cabinet cup and saucer, painted with flowers and leaves, within raised paste gilded cartouches, gilt gadrooned rims, printed London address marks in brown.

c1845

$1,200-1,800   **LFA**

A CLOSER LOOK AT A CHAMBERLAIN'S WORCESTER TEA & COFFEE SET

The shape and decoration of the set are typical of the Neo-classical style fashionable at the beginning of the 19thC.

These pieces would originally have been part of a larger service. A complete service would be a very rare find and therefore extremely valuable.

This rich gilding was fashionable at the time and particularly appealed to the nobility. This set would have been made to order for a wealthy family.

A Chamberlain's Worcester porcelain tea and coffee set, comprising a teapot, stand, milk jug, saucers, tea cups and coffee cups, decorated in gilt on a peach ground, each piece painted with a landscape scene.

Each piece carries a different landscape scene. Although the painter is unidentified, the work is very accomplished, enhancing the value of this service.

teapot 10.5in (26.5cm) wide

$7,000-10,000 set   **AA**

A Chamberlain's Worcester two-handled cup, cover and stand, painted with sprays of flowers within gilt C-scroll, diaper and cell pattern borders, the cover with script mark, the saucer with slight glaze crazing.

c1820

$600-900   **DN**

A Chamberlain's Worcester pot pourri vase and cover, painted with a view titled "Eastnor Castle, Herefordshire", on a blue and gilt ground, unmarked, restored cover.

c1820   *7in (17.5cm) high*

$1,000-1,200   **WW**

A Chamberlain's Worcester inkstand, with a central jar, two wells, a cover and a candle snuffer, painted with flowers and leaves, on gilt scroll feet, one cover lacking.

c1840   *11in (28cm) wide*

$600-800   **LFA**

A Chamberlain's Worcester flared inkwell and cover, painted with landscapes and flowers, within scroll-molded borders, on shell and scroll feet, script mark in puce, some restoration.

c1840   *4.25in (11cm) high*

$600-900   **LFA**

A George Grainger miniature milk jug and slop bowl, painted with titled views of Fonthill, Wiltshire, and a thatched cottage, on a gilt scroll ground.

c1830   *2in (5cm) high*

$300-400   **LFA**

A George Grainger miniature ovoid sucrier and cover, with gilt lion mask handles, painted with titled views of the Royal Crescent in Bath and Fonthill in Wiltshire, on a gilt leaf scroll ground.

c1830   *2.25in (5.5cm) high*

$700-1,000   **LFA**

A Grainger's Worcester reticulated pedestal vase, painted with landscape panels, probably by John Stinton, reserved on a turquoise reticulated ground, printed marks and date letter for 1902.

11.75in (30cm) high

$1,500-2,000   **DN**

A George Grainger ovoid ewer, with scroll handle and reticulated rim and neck, painted with pheasants in a landscape, with gilt borders, printed mark and shape number "G965".

6.25in (16cm) high

$1,000-1,500   **LFA**

A Grainger's Worcester plate, depicting pheasants painted by James Stinton, within gilt-enriched foliate scroll borders, printed marks, date letter for 1902.

9in (23cm) diam

$300-400   **DN**

A George Grainger miniature coffee can and saucer, painted with birds in flight, on a blush ivory ground, printed marks in green for 1902.

$200-300   **LFA**

OTHER PORCELAIN FACTORIES

A Belleek basket, the handle modeled as flower stems, the sides applied with flowers, with impressed factory mark to strap.

11in (28cm) wide

$1,500-2,000   **WW**

A mid-19thC glazed parian basket, with entwined branch handle, encrusted with flowers on an ozier-molded ground, possibly early Belleek, unmarked.

11.75 (30cm) wide

$300-400   **DNT**

A Bristol teacup and saucer, from the Lord Nelson service, the cup with harebell-molded ear-shaped handle, blue cross mark and numeral "3".

This service was made for Lord Nelson.

$3,000-4,000   **AA**

A Bristol porcelain figure, by Richard Champion, depicting a zephyr, emblematic of Air from the Four Elements series, colored and gilt in pale enamels, impressed repairer's mark "To" for Tebo, restored.

c1775   *10.75in (27cm) high*

$3,000-4,000   **DN**

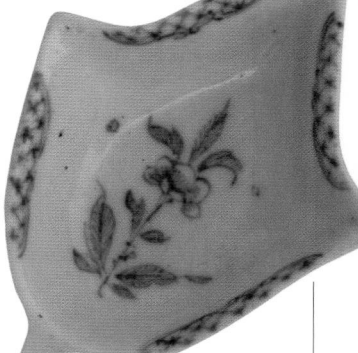

A rare Lund's Bristol leaf-shaped pickle dish, painted with a flower stem and leaves, the reverse molded with veining, minute flake to tip.

This piece is very similar to early Worcester.

c1750   *4in (10cm) wide*

$6,000-9,000   **WW**

PORCELAIN

A Caughley blue and white tankard, decorated with flowers and foliage with "JK" motif beneath a griffon.

The mark makes this a rare piece.

5.25in (13.5cm) high

$3,500-4,500   **AA**

A pair of Chantilly ormolu mounted porcelain perfume burners, in the Kakiemon style and decorated with a bird atop a flowering tree, with pierced foliated cast covers and tripartite bases.

c1780

$5,000-7,000   **FRE**

An 18thC Chelsea porcelain dish, painted with chestnuts on a branch.

c1755   9.5in (24cm) wide

$7,000-8,000   **AA**

A good Chelsea dish, the border molded with diaper panels and scrolls and painted with loose flower sprays, and a brown line rim, with red anchor mark.

c1755   12.75in (32cm) diam

$1,500-2,000   **WW**

A pair of Chelsea dishes, each in the form of two overlapping cabbage leaves, the veining of the leaves picked out in puce, one with red anchor mark and numeral "8".

c1755   10in (25.5cm) long

$10,000-15,000   **AA**

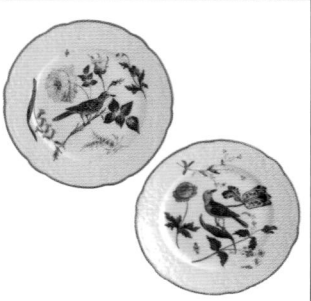

A pair of Coalport plates, with gilt borders and painted with birds and flowers.

c1820

$1,500-2,000   **AA**

A pair of Coalport porcelain tureens, each with four feet and a flower knop, painted with flowers and with gilt decoration.

c1820   8in (20.5cm) wide

$3,500-4,500   **AA**

A 19thC Copeland centerpiece, with a molded frieze of fruiting vines enriched with gilt, supported by three children emblematic of 'Summer', 'Spring' and 'Autumn', impressed "Copeland", copyright reserved.

17.5in (44cm) high

$1,000-1,500   **FRE**

A Copeland Parian model of Marguerite, standing wearing flowing robes, with impressed marks.

c1870   20.75in (52cm) high

$500-700   **WW**

A Copeland Parian miniature model of a rabbit, with a carrot at its side, and impressed mark.

2.75in (7cm) wide

$120-180   **LFA**

A rare Gilbody figure of a Levantine lady, upon a pad base applied with flowers and leaves, with minor faults.

These figures were probably copied from Meissen originals. Versions by Staffordshire and Longton Hall are also known.

c1754-60   7in (17.5cm) high

$7,000-9,000   **WW**

A late 19thC Hutschenreuther porcelain plaque, after Asti, framed, impressed mark and " 311", painted in Germany, signed "Wagner".

7in (18cm) high

$4,000-5,000   **FRE**

A pair of English George Jones pâte-sur-pâte porcelain vases, with white relief decoration, gilt highlights and ring handles, signed "F. Schenck" in one of the reserves, gilt mark "5639" to underside.

The George Jones & Sons factory was in operation in Stoke on Trent from 1861 to 1951. Porcelain was made from 1872.

c1880   6.25in (15.5cm) high

$3,000-4,000   **FRE**

A Liverpool coffee cup, by the Richard Chaffers factory, painted in underglaze blue with a pagoda, in a mountainous Chinese river landscape.

c1760   2.25in (6cm) high

$500-700   **LFA**

A Longton Hall mug, with a loop handle, painted in colored enamels with a figure beside a fence, in Chinese style.

c1755   6.5in (16.5cm) high

$10,000-12,000   **AA**

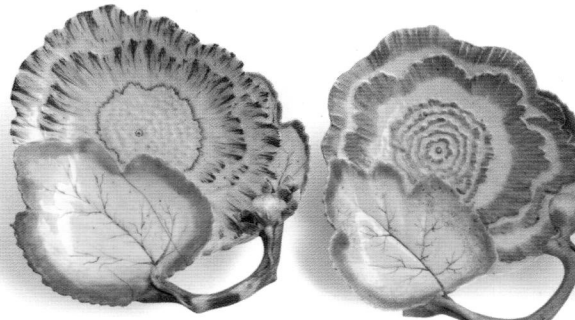

Two Longton Hall dishes, modeled as flowerheads, with green-glazed twig handles with bud terminals.

c1755   8.5in (21.5cm) long

$5,000-7,000   **AA**

A Minton porcelain Rococo Revival two-handled 'Dresden vase' and pierced cover, painted with two panels titled "Winter" and "Summer".

c1835   17in (43cm) high

$2,000-3,000   **DN**

A rare Minton teapot and cover, designed by Sir Henry Cole, with impressed "F" and registration date letter for 1847.

Sir Henry Cole (1802-1882) was the first director of the Victoria & Albert Museum. So few examples of this teapot exist that it was obviously made in limited numbers.

6.75in (17cm) high

$1,500-2,000   **WW**

A mid-19thC Minton vase and cover, with two conjoined cylinders with a griffin standing on Chinese-style mythical beasts, and impressed mark with number "1624".

11.5in (29cm) high

$10,000-12,000   **L&T**

A Minton celadon ewer, decorated with putti and ivy, with a modeled mermaid handle and satyr mask, impressed mark.

1868   7.5in (18.5cm) high

$1,000-1,500   **SWO**

PORCELAIN

A CLOSER LOOK AT A MINTON PEMBROKE GARNITURE

The garniture was produced in the 1820s, a period during which Minton produced some outstanding wares. The presence of high quality gilding indicates the caliber of this garniture and its original position at the higher end of the market.

The presence of three vases increases the visual impact of this display piece and distinguishes it from the many single vases on the market.

The garniture is complete and the gilding is in excellent condition.

The work of Thomas Steele (1792-84) typically depicts tightly grouped fruit or flowers in vivid colors, often framed within a gilt border. Attributing a piece to a known artist increases value. A signature can increase value by 50%.

A garniture of three Minton Pembroke vases, painted with floral panels in the manner of Thomas Steele, with gold handles, necks and bases.

c1820   tallest 10.75in (27cm) high

$7,000-10,000   **WW**

A pair of Naples monteiths, the rims modeled with doves, finely painted in colored enamels with sprays of flowers and leaves, on scroll and paw feet, incised marks.

c1795   11in (28cm) wide

$1,200-1,500 pair   **AA**

A large Nautilus porcelain figure, modeled as Othello the Moor, on naturalistic plinth, red printed factory mark.

A rare Nautilus porcelain centerpiece, the circular bowl with scalloped pierced edge and molded stylized floral and foliate design, the column supported by mermaids, horses emerging from the base, with black printed factory mark.

The Nautilus Porcelain Co. produced highly decorative wares in Glasgow, Scotland from 1896-1913.

A New Hall cream jug, painted with a Chinoiserie figure in landscape, pattern 20, and matching slop bowl.

20in (51cm) high

$1,000-1,500 L&T

19in (48cm) high

$4,500-6,500   **L&T**

4in (10cm) high

$450-550   **BRI**

A New Hall helmet-shaped milk jug, with loop handle, painted in the *famille rose* palette with a woman and a boy in a garden, the interior with loop and pendant flowerhead band, on a round foot.

c1785   3.75in (9.5cm) high

$500-700   **LFA**

Two New Hall polychrome cups, with Chinoiserie floral designs in the *famille rose* palette.

$150-200   **BRI**

A Plymouth baluster-shaped coffee pot and domed cover, painted in underglaze blue with the 'Mansfield' pattern, within diaper paneled scroll borders, unmarked.

c1770   9in (23cm) high

$4,500-6,500   **AA**

A Rockingham porcelain model of a recumbent hare, model no. 106, impressed marks, both ears lacking.

c1830   2.5in (6cm) wide

$1,000-1,200   **DN**

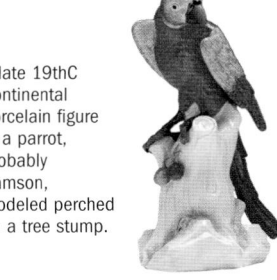

A late 19thC Continental porcelain figure of a parrot, probably Samson, modeled perched on a tree stump.

12.5in (31cm) high

$800-1,100   **FRE**

A Samson & Hancock swan bowl, with gilt rim, crown and crossed swords mark and "SH" in magenta.

5.5in (14cm) long

$1,500-2,000   **AA**

A garniture of three Spode porcelain vases, painted in puce and gilt with convolvulus, painted marks and pattern number "3994", chips.

c1825   tallest 6in (15cm) high

$1,000-1,200   **DN**

A Lloyd Shelton bone china 'The Lion Shall Lie Down with the Lamb' model.

c1815   5in (12cm) high

$1,000-1,200   **SWO**

WELSH PORCELAIN

- Welsh porcelain enjoys a reputation for fine body and beautiful decoration and examples are much coveted. Credit for the success lies largely with porcelain painter William Billingsley who in 1813 brought a soft-paste to Nantgarw. In 1814 he moved to works in Swansea before returning to Nantgarw in 1817 and then leaving for Coalport in 1820.
- Swansea forms were influenced by French styles. The delicate translucent paste was an ideal ground for flower-painting, and realistic botanical designs are typical. Rich decoration was sometimes added in London.
- Firing problems in Swansea led to a return to Nantgarw, where Billingsley built new kilns. Although a relatively substantial number of plates were produced, the firing difficulties persisted, most notably in tewares, making them scarce today. The French-inspired decoration included rich grounds and ornate painting. Many wares were decorated in London. The venture failed to make a profit and closed in 1820.

A Nantgarw plate, London decorated, painted with a flower bouquet within a border of pendant flowers, within a wave scroll border, faint crack.

c1820   10.25in (26cm) diam

$2,000-3,000   **WW**

A pair of Nantgarw ecuelles, covers and stands, painted with bouquets of flowers within gilt borders, the saucers impressed "Nantgarw CW", one saucer cracked and glued.

c1815   7.5in (19cm) diam

$10,000-15,000   **DN**

A 19thC Swansea plate with gilt border and floral decoration, probably painted by William Pollard.

c1815   9.5in (24cm) wide

$3,000-4,000   **AA**

A Swansea cup and saucer, with painted bird's nest and flowers in bright enamels, and pink and gilt border.

$1,000-1,200   **BRI**

A mid-19thC pair of Wedgwood porcelain vases, decorated in relief with profile cameos, laurel wreath swags, palmettes and Greek key bands, impressed "Wedgwood".

8in (20cm) high

$1,500-2,000   **FRE**

A late 18thC Doccia coffee can, painted in puce with an Italianate vignette.

$150-200   DN

A Doccia coffee pot and cover, painted with flower sprays, the handle and spout detailed in puce and blue, flakes.

c1775   8.75in (22.5cm) high

$1,000-1,500   WW

One of a set of 12 Heinrich & Co. 'Selby' service plates with gold borders, each with a floral center and gold border with molded details.

10.75in (27cm) diam

$1,000-1,500 SET   FRE

A Continental porcelain plaque, probably Berlin, painted with a portrait of Princess Louise, signed 'Jager', the reverse inscribed 'Luise' and with impressed numerals, mounted in a giltwood frame.

c1880   22.5in (57cm) high

$6,000-9,000   WW

A 19thC Russian porcelain Easter egg, painted with a crucifixion and the Host, both within oval gilt borders on a dark blue ground.

2.5in (6.5cm) high

$500-700   ROS

A late 19thC continental porcelain fairing, titled to base "A long pull and a Strong Pull", hairline cracks and a small chip.

5in (13cm) wide

$450-550   WW

A late 19thC continental porcelain fairing, titled in gilt to base "Out by Jingo!!", rubbing to the gilt.

5in (13cm) wide

$500-600   WW

CREAMWARE

- Creamware is a light-colored earthenware with a smooth, thin transparent lead glaze, and was developed in the mid 18thC by potteries in Leeds, Liverpool, Bristol and Staffordshire, which was the center of the British pottery industry in the 18thC.
- The most successful creamware maker was Josiah Wedgwood (1730-95), who developed it to such a high standard that by the 1760s it virtually replaced the traditional tin-glazed pottery that had dominated the European market for centuries. The financial success of creamware provided the grounding for Wedgwood's future business ventures.
- Creamware was used for everything from ornaments to everyday tea and coffee wares.
- Importantly, it was accepted by the upper classes, which ensured it became fashionable. It even became known as 'Queensware' after Queen Charlotte ordered a tea service in 1765.
- Creamware is identifiable by its ivory glaze and thin and light body. Pieces by Wedgwood are often marked "WEDGWOOD". It is rarer to find creamware figures than the massively popular tablewares.

A Leeds creamware documentary teapot and cover, one side inscribed and dated "Elizath. Webster Winstrope, 1774", the reverse in polychrome with a Chinaman in a garden, chips to lid and spout.

1774   *5.75in (14.5cm) high*

$3,000-4,000   **SWO**

A late 18thC Wedgwood creamware cylindrical mug, printed in black with shield panel and mottos for the Ancient Order of the Bucks, "Wedgwood" impressed.

6.25in (15.5cm) high

$600-900   **WW**

A Newcastle creamware cylindrical mug, printed with the Shipwright's Arms and marked "Jameson, Newcastle".

c1800   *5.75in (14.5cm) high*

$1,000-1,200   **WW**

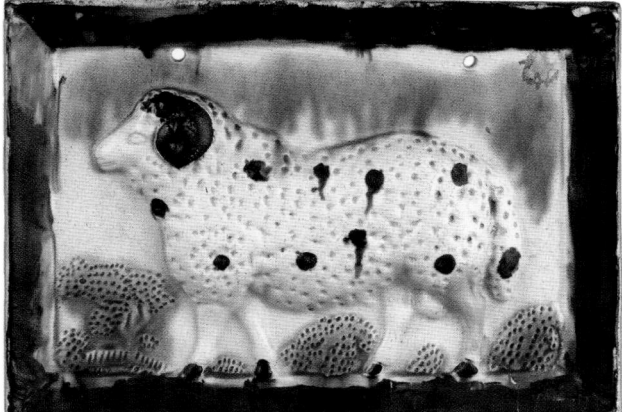

A 19thC Scottish creamware plaque, depicting a ram in a pastoral setting.

11.5in (29cm) wide

$1,500-2,000   **POOK**

A Scottish creamware plaque with relief figure of a ram within a grapevine border.

12.5in (31cm) high

$4,000-5,000   **POOK**

POTTERY

A Dutch Delft polychrome plate, possibly by Adriaen Pynacker, depicting a portrait of William of Orange and his wife Mary II, with an orange tree surmounted by an inscribed "D", inscribed "P V O R".

A near identical plate is in the collection of the Fine Arts Museums of San Francisco.

c1690   9.25in (23.5cm) diam

$500-700   **FRE**

An 18thC Dutch Delft blue and white posset pot, of circular bellied form with scrolled handles, painted with birds perched amongst foliage, various chips and cracks.

5.5in (14cm) high

$700-1,000   **SWO**

A late 18thC pair of Dutch Delft tobacco jars, converted to lamps, each decorated in underglaze blue with native figures smoking pipes, inscribed "MARTENIEK" and "HAVANA".

10in (25cm) high

$1,500-2,000   **FRE**

A Dutch Delft blue and white heart-shaped tulip vase, decorated with a beau proposing to his beloved and a basket of flowers, painted mark "BN132".

c1920   9.25in (23.5cm) high

$400-600   **SWO**

A CLOSER LOOK AT A DUTCH DELFT PLATE

Delft, is tin-glazed earthenware and was made in the town of Delft, and numerous other centers, in the Netherlands. This piece is finely potted with a thick glaze and high quality, detailed brushwork.

The decoration on this piece was probably inspired by a contemporary print. A scene featuring artisans at work is a rare subject matter, making this plate more valuable than a similar example with chinoiserie decoration.

This plate is dated and early, adding to its desirability. It is also in very good condition, another plus point for collectors. However, given the date and subject matter this plate would be valuable even if damaged.

This well-known plate came from James Sorber's large collection of antiques and fine art in Pennsylvania.

An 18thC blue and white Delft plate, depicting cabinetmakers at work, dated.

Pictured on the front cover of The Magazine Antiques, May 1981.

1769   12.5in (31.5cm) diam

$20,000-30,000   **POOK**

48

DELFTWARE

- The Netherlands became a center of production for tin-glazed earthenware from c1500, when immigrant Italian craftsmen settled in Antwerp. This new method of making pottery involved making extremely fine, soft and usually thinly potted wares with a thick, white glaze. These techniques spread north during the 16thC and potteries were established at Haarlem, Amsterdam and Rotterdam, although it was the town of Delft that was really at the forefront of production, hence the term 'Delft ware'.
- Early wares were influenced by Italian pottery and were usually decorated with pine cone motifs, geometric patterns, strapwork and half-shaded petal borders. Decoration was usually in blue but also in polychrome, with designs in copper-green, yellow and ochre.
- From the beginning of the 17thC, Delft ware was heavily influenced by the blue and white porcelain brought to Europe from the Orient by the Dutch East India Company. Within a few years the Italian maiolica colors were replaced by a palette of blue and white. In c1645, imports from China were stopped because the kilns in Jingdezhen had been destroyed by the invading Manchus. This meant that there was a huge increase in production of Dutch Delft ware. Wares included drug jars, tiles, dishes, flower holders and ewers.
- In c1683, Chinese porcelain started being imported again. This led Delft potters to experiment with a polychrome palette, with wares in famille verte and famille rose styles. By the 19thC, the popularity of English creamware led to a decline in the production of Delft, although it is still produced today.

A Bristol delftware tile, with a blue and white chinoiserie scene, with bianco-sopra-bianco border.

c1770

$300-350   **STE**

A Bristol delftware tile, with manganese and blue decoration of a windmill.

c1770

$100-150   **STE**

A Bristol delftware tile, with a yellow flower basket.

c1770

$600-700   **STE**

A Bristol delftware tile, with a polychrome chinoiserie scene and a bianco-sopra-bianco border.

The technique bianco-sopra-bianco originated through 16thC Italian maiolica ware. Opaque white was painted over a white or off-white ground. The Bristol potteries adopted it around 1750.

c1770

$600-700   **STE**

An English delftware chinoiserie plate, possibly Liverpool or Bristol, painted in blue with a Chinese figure in a landscape, minor wear to rim.

c1760   *8.75in (22cm) diam*

$300-400   **DN**

A Bristol delftware plate, painted chinoiserie panels of houses in a landscape, reserved on a manganese pebble ground, rim chip and wear.

c1770   *9in (23cm) diam*

$300-400   **DN**

A Liverpool delftware tile, with blue decoration depicting kilns.

c1750   5in (12.5cm) wide

$180-200   STE

A Liverpool delftware tile, with a blue and white chinoiserie landscape, flower stud border and daisy corners.

c1760   5in (12.5cm) wide

$100-150   STE

A rare Liverpool delftware tile, with blue decoration depicting a goat.

c1760   5in (12.5cm) wide

$550-650   STE

A Liverpool delftware tile, with manganese decoration of cattle, with a stud border and Michaelmas daisy corners.

c1760   5in (12.5cm) wide

$300-400   STE

A Liverpool delftware tile, with blue decoration of a rural scene and cherubs to the corners.

c1760   5in (12.5cm) wide

$500-600   STE

A Liverpool delftware tile, with polychrome decoration of a flower.

c1765   5in (12.5cm) wide

$550-650   STE

A Liverpool delftware tile, with polychrome decoration of a bird.

c1765   5in (12.5cm) wide

$550-650   STE

A pair of Liverpool delftware tiles, with polychrome birds.

c1770   5in (12.5cm) wide

$1,500-2,000   STE

A Liverpool delftware tile, with decoration of a Chinese man with Michaelmas daisy corners.

c1770   5in (12.5cm) wide

$600-700   STE

A Liverpool delftware tile, with blue decoration of two Chinese figures.

c1770   5in (12.5cm) wide

$300-400   STE

A London delftware tile, with blue-and-white figures and a ruin.

c1735

$90-100   STE

A London delftware tile, with blue and white decoration of Ceres on a manganese ground with flower corners.

c1735

$160-180   STE

A London delftware tile, with a polychrome flower bowl on a blue ground with stylized flower corners.

c1740

$300-400   STE

A London delftware tile, with unusual decoration of skaters.

c1740

$150-180   STE

A London delftware tile, with a shepherd on a blue ground with stylized corners.

c1740

$150-180   STE

A London delftware tile, with a hunting scene.

c1750   5in (12.5cm) wide

$200-300   STE

A London delftware tile, with a ship.

c1750   5in (12.5cm) wide

$120-160   STE

A London delftware tile, with a blue-and-white stylized flower basket and cherub corners on a blue ground.

c1750

$100-150   STE

A London delftware tile, with a woman carrying a basket.

c1750

$90-100   STE

A London delftware tile, with a polychrome flower bowl, restored.

c1755

$300-350   STE

A London delftware tile, with blue-and-white entwined trellis decoration, one edge restored.

c1760

$100-150   STE

A London delftware tile, with a couple in a landscape.

c1750

$100-150   STE

51

A mid-18thC English delftware wet drug jar, probably London, painted in blue and named for "S: PAPAV:ERRAT." within a cartouche of foliage, putti and shells, damage.

7in (18cm) high

$700-1,000 **DN**

A London delftware campana vase, with lion mask lifts and a flared foot, each side painted with a church and trees.

c1750 *6in (15cm) high*

$2,000-3,000 **WW**

A CLOSER LOOK AT A DELFTWARE POSSET POT

Early English delftware followed the Dutch polychrome palette but from 1620s onwards, it also began to emulate the imported Chinese blue and white porcelain palette and designs.

The bird on a rock motif was introduced c1618.

The introduction of blue and white coincides with the founding of a pottery in Southwark c1620 by Christian Wilhelm, who also manufactured blue smalt, the cobalt blue color used on delftwares.

The fact that this piece has its original cover and that the handles are intact, adds to its value.

A large late 17thC London delftware posset pot and cover, painted with Chinese figures, birds in flight and perched on rockwork with flowers, leaves and insects, some repairs.

c1680 *12in (30.5cm) wide*

$5,000-7,000 **WW**

OTHER BRITISH DELFTWARE

A delftware lobed shallow bowl, painted with five Chinoiserie figures amongst grassy boulders, restored.

c1680 *12.5in (31.5cm) diam*

$200-400 **WW**

An early 18thC molded delftware dish, the center painted with a bird beside a tree within a stylized border design, probably English.

10in (25.5cm) wide

$700-1,000 **WW**

A large mid-18thC English delftware dish, polychrome painted with a large flower spray, chips.

13in (33cm) diam

$700-1,000 **WW**

A large mid-18thC English delftware dish, painted with stylized flowers and panels, the reverse with circle and dash designs.

13in (33cm) diam

$1,500-2,000 **WW**

A large mid-18thC English delftware dish, painted with flowers and hedge, chipped.

13.25in (33.5cm) diam

$1,000-1,500 **WW**

A large 18thC delftware plate, decorated with flowers issuing from stylized rockwork, restored.

14in (35.5cm) diam

$300-600 **WW**

A delftware plate, silver-shaped and painted with floral sprigs, painted marks, restored.

c1800   *10in (25cm) diam*

$60-90   **DN**

An 18thC delftware plate with pagoda and landscape designs to center, floral border.

9in (23cm) diam

$200-300   **BRI**

An English delftware saucer dish, painted with a pagoda in a river landscape.

$200-300   **DN**

An English delftware plate, painted with oriental flowering shrubs.

c1780

$200-300   **DN**

An early 18thC delftware drug jar, inscribed "C:Anthos", within a Baroque panel edged with cherubs, flowers and shells.

7.5in (19cm) high

$1,000-1,500   **WW**

An early 18thC delftware drug jar, inscribed "E:Diascordi", within an elaborated Baroque panel edged with birds, leaves and flowers.

7.5in (19cm) high

$1,200-1,800   **WW**

An 18thC delftware bowl, painted with a perched bird and flying insects amidst flowers and leaves, restored.

11.75in (30cm) diam

$450-650   **WW**

A delftware wet drug jar, with an applied loop handle, inscribed "S:Croci" within a Baroque panel edged with cherubs, flowers and scrolls on an attenuated flared foot.

c1710   *7in (17.5cm) high*

$2,000-3,000   **WW**

An English delftware flower brick, painted in underglaze blue with scrolling flowers and leaves, within blue line borders, minor rim chips.

c1760   *6in (15cm) wide*

$700-1,000   **LFA**

POTTERY

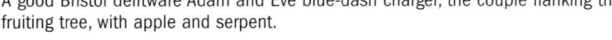

A good Bristol delftware Adam and Eve blue-dash charger, the couple flanking the fruiting tree, with apple and serpent.

c1740   12.5in (31.5cm) diam

$7,000-10,000   **WW**

A mid-18thC Bristol delftware polychrome charger, painted with a Chinese boy with skipping rope in a landscape, some minor chips.

13.5in (34cm) diam

$7,000-10,000   **DN**

An 18thC Delftware small drug or pill pot, the side inscribed "O:Macis", with a panel edged with flowers, birds and a winged cherub's head, restored.

3.5in (9cm) high

$2,000-4,000   **WW**

A rare London delft jar, with a C-scroll handle, painted in shades of blue with a Chinese figure seated in a rocky landscape, slight restoration to the rim.

c1685   4.25in (10.5cm) high

$4,500-6,500   **WW**

A faience plate, by C.F. Hannong of Strasbourg, glazed in white and painted with flowers and insects, marked with a blue "A".

c1735   *9.75in (24.5cm) diam*

$150-200   **KAU**

A Strasbourg faience plate, decorated with flowers, with lilac rim and brown "S" mark.

c1800   *9.75in (24.5cm) diam*

$100-150   **KAU**

A Marseille faience pastry dish, glazed and painted, decorated with a house between trees, the rim with insects.

c1770   *9.5in (23.5cm) wide*

$300-400   **KAU**

An 18thC Rouen faience lozenge-shaped bowl, with two handles, light brown body, glazed and painted with floral decoration.

7.25in (18.5cm) wide

$70-100   **KAU**

A 18thC French faience fluted sauceboat and stand, probably St. Armand, painted in blue and bianco sopra bianco with flowers and leaves.

7.5in (19cm) high

$600-800   **WW**

A French faience water cistern, decorated with garlands of flowers, with a brass tap issuing from a putto face, restored.

17in (43cm) high

$350-450   **DN**

A French faience tobacco jar, inscribed "Tabac Fin" within laurel leaves.

5in (13cm) high

$400-600   **DN**

A Bayeux Langlois faience figure of an Oriental spice seller amongst jars, small repair.

6.5in (16.5cm) wide

$600-800   **BRI**

A Magdeburg faience reticulated oval dish, with floral sprays within a trellis border with flower-head bosses, script "M" mark, glued section to rim.

c1760   *10in (25.5cm) wide*

$200-300   **DN**

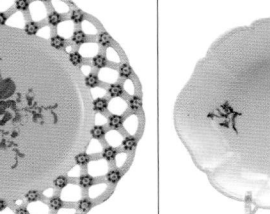

A 18thC Höchst faience serving plate, glazed and painted with floral decoration.

8.25in (20.5cm) wide

$100-150   **KAU**

A 19thC Bruchsal faience oval plate, glazed and painted with floral and leaf decoration.

16.25in (40.5cm) wide

$100-150   **KAU**

A Ludwigsburg faience plate, with brick red body, glazed and painted with a bunch of flowers, the rim with scattered flowers, maker's mark.

c1770   *9.5in (24cm) diam*

$100-150   **KAU**

An 18thC pewter-mounted jug, the hinged lid with a thumb rest, glazed and painted with floral framed cartouches containing floral decoration.

9.5in (24cm) high

$550-650   **KAU**

A Potsdam pewter-mounted jug, with polychrome 'Scharffeuer' painting, with rare manufacturer's mark "PR" corresponding to Rewend period.

c1770   *9.5in (24cm) high*

$6,000-9,000   **VA**

A CLOSER LOOK AT A FAIENCE JUG

Faience production was established in Berlin in 1678. Much of the early output was in the style of Dutch Delft, with which it is often confused.

The maker's mark can often be found under the lid. However, lids are often replaced, so this is an unreliable indicator of date.

Earlier pieces are usually decorated in Chinoiserie style but from the mid-18thC more native designs became popular, such as foliate cartouches, songbirds and naively painted buildings.

Scharffeuer are underglaze colors, applied before firing to create a strong, bright glaze.

A Schrezheim pewter-mounted jug, with polychrome 'Scharffeuer' painting depicting a deer to the front.

c1790   *10in (25.5cm) high*

$2,000-3,000   **VA**

A Crailsheim narrow neck pewter-mounted jug, depicting a man harvesting vines flanked by two castles, the top with geometric decoration, signed and dated.

1748   *13.5in (35cm) high*

$500-700   **KAU**

A Berlin pilaster jug, with polychrome *Scharffeuer* painting, from the Menicus period, with Berlin pewter mounting.

c1750   *10in (25.5cm) high*

$6,000-9,000   **VA**

A late 19thC pewter-mounted jug, of egg-shaped form with ear handle, hinged lid with shell-shaped thumb rest, depicting a bouquet of flowers.

10in (25.5cm) high

$200-300   **KAU**

A late 19thC pewter-mounted jug, the egg-shaped body with ear handle, hinged lid and shell-shaped thumb rest, depicting a cornucopia and floral design, maker's mark.

10in (25.5cm) high

$200-300   **KAU**

A Brunswick stick vase, painted with blue *Scharffeuer* palette, blue painter's mark.

c1740   *10.4in (26cm) high*

$1,500-2,000   **VA**

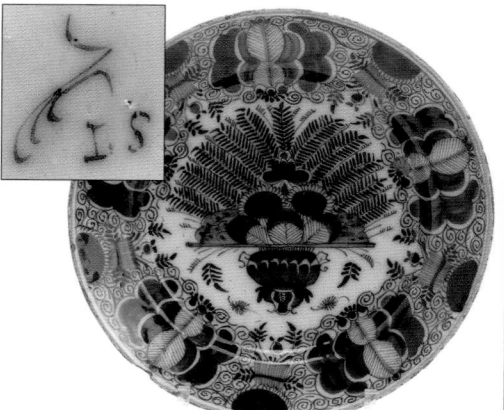

An 18thC plate, painted with a fan and floral decoration, maker's mark, yellow rim.

9.25in (23cm) diam

$1,000-1,500   **KAU**

MAIOLICA

- Maiolica is tin-glazed earthenware that was introduced to Italy around the 13thC. Its name probably derives from the Italian word for the island of Majorca near Spain, through which Hispano-Moresque wares were shipped in the 14thC.

- The clay was twice-fired for durability, then enamels were applied to the glossy surface. Production and decoration before 1400 was limited and naive, but became increasingly sophisticated from the 15thC.

- Production mainly took place in Florence, Faenze, Deruta, Orvieto and Naples. The number of potteries increased in the 16th-17th centuries when manufacturing peaked.

- During this period, maiolica was decorated with colorful and elaborate depictions of biblical and mythical themes. The images on these *istoriato* (narrative) wares were inspired by the works of artists such as Raphael.

- By the late 17thC Chinese porcelain and French faience designs had become more influential and Italian maiolica no longer lead the field.

- In the 19thC, potteries reproduced maiolica wares in earlier styles. Ulysse Cantagalli was famous for his high quality reproductions which can be identified by a rooster mark.

- If a mark on the underside of a piece of maiolica has been scratched off be cautious – a 19thC or later mark may have been removed in an attempt to make the piece appear older.

A pair of late 16thC Venetian globular jars, decorated with a band of boldly painted fruit between bands of crosses.

9in (23cm) high

$15,000-20,000　　　　　　　　**L&T**

A mid- to late 16thC Venetian globular jar, possibly workshop of maestro Domengo da Venezia, decorated with opposed portraits interspersed with flowers and foliage.

9.5in (24cm) high

$3,000-4,000　　**L&T**

A late 19thC large Italian maiolica charger, decorated with figures, beasts and a chariot and a border of mythological figures on a blue ground.

24in (60cm) diam

$600-900　　**FRE**

A 20thC Italian Cantagalli maiolica flattened bottle-form vessel, with a ring-form stopper, the mustard ground with a coat of arms, musical instruments and a pair of winged cherub masks, blue underglaze rooster mark.

14in (35cm) high

$1,000-1,200　　**FRE**

A 20thC Italian maiolica ewer, with a serpent-form handle and a plinth base, decorated with figures and scrolls against a cobalt blue ground.

Ewer 14in (35cm) high

$1,200-1,500　　　　　　　　**FRE**

An early 17thC Sicilian maiolica vase, of bombola form, painted with a saint amongst bold scrolling foliage, restoration.

14in (35cm) high

$1,200-1,800   **SWO**

A late 19thC Renaissance Revival faience vase 'Aux Mascarons', probably Cantagalli of Florence, with floral decoration and antique scenes in oval medallions, with grotesque mask handles.

44in (110cm) high

$6,000-9,000   **GK**

A pair of late 19thC Renaissance Revival faience vases 'Aux Satyrs', probably by Cantagalli, in the style of Urbino, Florence, with painted floral decoration and oval medallions with figures in a landscape, the handles of satyrs sitting on rams' heads, restoration to socle.

38.5in (96cm) high

$7,000-10,000   **GK**

A pair of 19thC blue and white albarello jars, one titled "Plantagine", the other "Marei P Jerba".

8.75in (22cm) high

$500-700   **ROS**

A mid-17thC Italian tin glazed earthenware tazza, depicting Judith beheading Holofernes.

13.5in (34cm) diam

$1,000-1,500   **POOK**

A Nove vase modeled as a boot, painted with flowers, chipped.

The Nove factory was founded by Giovanni Antonibon in 1728, near Bassano, Italy. It produced tin-glazed earthenwares in the Rococo style.

c1900   *8in (20cm) high*

$400-600   **DN**

STONEWARE

A Mettlach beer jug, glazed and painted, the hinged molded lid with a thumb rest in the shape of a female bust, with motto, the lid with a coat-of-arms cartouche with vine, maker's mark and model number "2531".

9.5in (24cm) high

$400-500   **KAU**

A Mettlach beer jug, glazed and painted, with leaf-decorated thumb rest, depicting a couple in a rocaille cartouche, the lid with a pair of birds in a rocaille cartouche, maker's mark and model number "1946".

c1900   *8.75in (22cm) high*

$200-300   **KAU**

A pair of Mettlach vases, glazed, painted, enameled and gilded with geometrical and floral decoration, elephant-shaped handles, maker's mark and model number "1870".

9.5in (24cm) high

$600-800   **KAU**

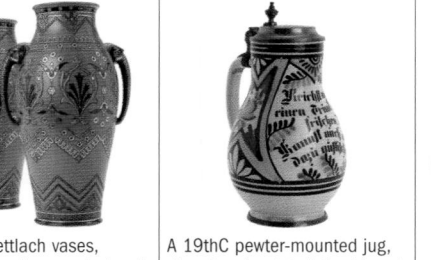

A 19thC pewter-mounted jug, glazed and painted, the hinged lid with molded thumb rest, painted with floral motifs and a German motto.

10in (25.5cm) high

$200-300   **KAU**

A Creussen pewter-mounted planet jug, of brown salt-glazed stoneware with relief decoration painted in enamel colors with an allegorical representation of the planets, dated, restored.

Between the late 16thC and c1730, Creussen produced stoneware with a chocolate-brown salt-glaze.

1690   *5in (13cm) high*

$10,000-12,000   **VA**

An Annaberg pewter-mounted jug, of dark brown stoneware with relief decoration painted with enamel colors, applied Madonna with child and palm frieze, restored.

c1700   *8.5in (21cm) high*

$3,500-4,500   **VA**

A small early 19thC pearlware Montieth, decorated with the tobacco leaf pattern.

5.25in (13.5cm) wide

$300-400   **WW**

An early-19thC small pearlware sauce tureen, in the form of a pigeon on a nest, painted in colored enamels, unmarked.

6.75in (17cm) wide

$700-1,000   **DN**

An early 19thC pearlware sauceboat, in the shape of a duck, probably Staffordshire, the molding with highlights in Pratt-type underglaze colors, unmarked, restored.

7.75in (19.5cm) wide

$1,000-1,500   **DN**

An unusual pearlware quintal flowerhorn, molded initials "IW".

Pearlware was a development of creamware but with a cobalt tinted glaze to make the body look whiter.

c1785   *7.25in (18.5cm) high*

$600-900   **LFA**

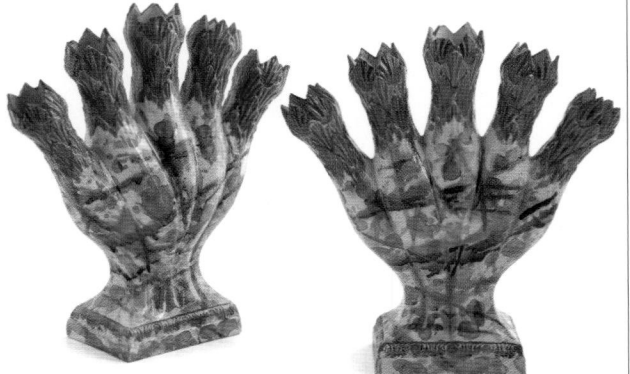

A pair of Sewell & Donkin pearlware quintals, or finger vases, decorated with splashed pink lustre with orange and gray marbling, impressed marks, chips.

c1835   *8.5in (21.5cm) high*

$2,000-3,000   **WW**

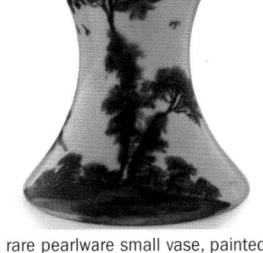

A rare pearlware small vase, painted in underglaze blue with a cottage in a wooded landscape with sponged trees, tiny rim nick.

c1780   *3.5in (9cm) high*

$1,000-1,200   **LFA**

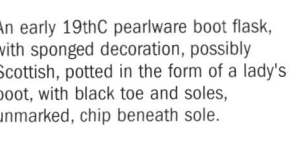

A pair of Staffordshire pearlware demi-lune boughpots, painted with shaped panels of leaves and fruiting vine, reserved on an iron red ground, minor damage.

c1800   *4.75in (12cm) wide*

$1,500-2,000   **DN**

A rare pair of pearlware wall brackets, with pierced tops above stiff leaf-molded bands, on simulated porphyry ground, some glaze flaking.

c1800   *6.75in (17cm) high*

$700-1,000   **LFA**

A pearlware pipe, the large ovoid bowl incised with a hatched design, on a dimpled ground, splashed in blue.

c1790   *7in (18cm) long*

$450-650   **LFA**

An early 19thC pearlware pipe, with bowl molded in the form of a turbanned Turk's head, the long twisted and coiled stem decorated with bands of colored enamels, unmarked.

12in (30.5cm) long

$1,000-1,500   **DN**

An early 19thC pearlware boot flask, with sponged decoration, possibly Scottish, potted in the form of a lady's boot, with black toe and soles, unmarked, chip beneath sole.

7.25in (18.5cm) wide

$300-400   **DN**

A small Staffordshire pearlware egg, printed and painted with two steamers, inscribed "Mary Macklam" and dated 1850.

Similar shapes were made in Whitehaven and used as sock darners.

2.25in (5.5cm) wide

$1,000-1,500   **LFA**

POTTERY

REDWARE

- The term Redware is used to describe the everyday porous red-brown pottery produced largely in America during the 17th and 18thC.
- Early redware was fairly crude in shape and was typically covered with lead glaze to make it watertight. Exteriors were incised with sticks or fingertips, or glazed and applied with splashes of color.
- From the late 17thC, slip-decorated redware became popular. Potters used a brush or slip-cup, a small pot with a hole, to trail simple patterns onto the surface of wares. Potters in different areas developed their own styles of decoration.
- Redware fell out of fashion from the early 19thC when mass-production functional ware became readily available.

A sgraffito-decorated green-glazed redware jar, Pennsylvania, incised with tulips, birds, and leafy reserves enclosing 'May (or Mary) T. Lee' and the date 'A.D. 1819', the underside inscribed 'Mary May'.

7.5in (19cm) high

$20,000-30,000   **FRE**

A covered glazed redware sugar bowl, attributed to John Nase, Upper Salford Township, Montgomery County, with beaded spool-form knop and applied and stamped stylized flower and vine decoration, applied shaped handles with stamped terminals.

c1830   *6.5in (16.5cm) high*

$20,000-30,000   **FRE**

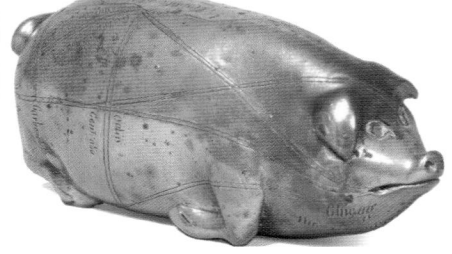

A molded redware pig flask, with incised "Railroad & River Guide with a little Good Old Rye in", attributed to Wallace and Cornwall Kirkpatrick, Anna Pottery, Anna, Illinois, chip to one ear.

8in (20cm) wide

$8,000-10,000   **SK**

A 19thC slip-decorated glazed redware deep dish, decorated with bird-like devices and arched line on rim.

13in (33cm) diam

$7,000-9,000   **FRE**

A small mid-18thC Staffordshire solid agateware teapot and cover, with a compressed circular body and loop handle, chipped.

5.5in (14cm) wide

$1,000-1,500   **WW**

An early George III Staffordshire redware coffee pot and cover, the baluster shape engine turned and with basket molded handle, pseudo Chinese mark.

A rare Staffordshire ashware teapot and cover, the handle and spout in paler clay, the body applied with floral spriging.

c1765   *7in (18cm) long*

$1,000-1,500   **WW**

9.5in (24.5cm) high

$400-600   **CHEF**

An unusual Staffordshire glazed redware mug, the body applied in a cream-colored clay with a lion, unicorn, birds, flowers and leaves, restored.

c1760   *4.75in (12cm) high*

$1,000-1,200   **WW**

A 19thC gray stoneware bear flagon and cover, possibly Denby, the lift-off head with grated clay details, a handle behind.

3.25in (8.5cm) high

$700-1,000   **CHEF**

Two Whieldon-type dishes, each with a sponged manganese brown glaze.

c1760   *12.5in (31.5cm) wide*

$1,200-1,800   **WW**

A Victorian Staffordshire earthenware footbath, of cushion-form with twin cast foliate handles, all over gray glaze with green highlighted diagonals.

$300-400   **BIG**

A mid-19thC Staffordshire model of 'Stanfield Hall', gilded detailing, on an elongated oval base with gilt title, unmarked, slight forward lean.

8in (19.9cm) high

$300-350   **DN**

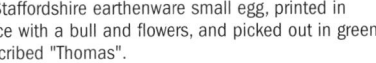

A Staffordshire earthenware small egg, printed in puce with a bull and flowers, and picked out in green, inscribed "Thomas".

c1850   *2.25in (5.5cm) wide*

$1,000-1,500   **LFA**

POTTERY

A pair of early 19thC Staffordshire pottery figures, of Elijah with the ravens and his wife.

$600-900   SWO

An early 19thC Staffordshire pearlware bust of Wesley, inscribed to the inside of the base, restored.

9.75in (25cm) high

$500-700   SWO

A Staffordshire figure of the Reverend Huntington, seated on an armchair in a black coat, brown waistcoat and purple breeches.

c1835   *8.25in (21cm) high*

$500-700   SWO

A pair of Staffordshire lionesses and cubs spill vases, the animals reclining at the base of a tree with entwined a snake.

11.25in (28.5cm) high

$7,000-10,000   JHD

A Victorian Staffordshire figure of a Scotsman with bagpies.

15in (38.5cm) high

$450-650   SWO

A Victorian Staffordshire pottery figure of a huntsman with a bow.

16.5in (42cm) high

$400-600   SWO

A pair of Victorian Staffordshire pottery figures of dancers.

10.25in (26cm) high

$600-900   SWO

A Victorian Staffordshire pottery group, Garrick in his role of King John.

c1880   *13.5in (34.5cm) high*

$500-700   SWO

A Staffordshire figure of the soldier's dream, some restoration.

c1870   *10.75in (27cm) high*

$400-500   SWO

A Staffordshire pottery group, depicting the murder of Thomas Smith by William Collier.

c1865   *13.5in (34cm) high*

$1,000-1,200   SWO

A pair of Staffordshire lions, with glass eyes and on gilded plinths.

c1900   11in (28cm) wide

$1,000-1,800   **RDER**

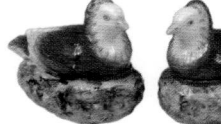

A late 19thC pair of Staffordshire pigeon tureens and covers, chips to beaks, one cracked.

8.75in (22cm) diam

$1,200-1,800   **SWO**

A Royal Staffordshire model, 'The Laughing Cat', by Louis Wain, printed mark.

7.5in (19cm) high

$1,000-1,500   **WW**

A rare Staffordshire pottery model of a thatched house, with a spaniel seated under an arch.

c1860   9.5in (23.5cm) high

$400-500   **SWO**

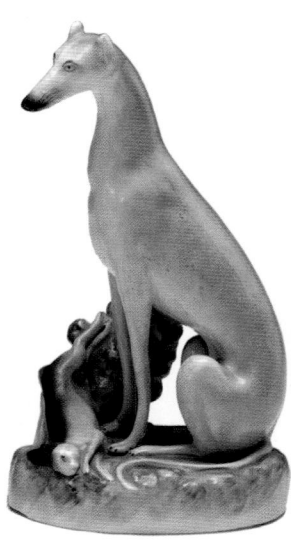

A pair of 19thC Staffordshire Pottery hunting dogs, each modeled as a seated hound on a naturalistic base with a dead hare, unmarked.

11.5in (29cm) high

$1,200-1,800   **FRE**

A Spode pearlware blue and white two-handled pedestal dish, printed with the 'Italian' pattern, gilt line border, impressed mark.

c1820   15in (38cm) long

$500-700   **DN**

A Spode 'Tiber' or 'Rome' pattern sauce tureen, with original ladle and undertray, small amount of restoration to ladle.

c1815   Undertray 6.5in (16.5cm) wide

$800-1,000   **PC**

A Spode pearlware 'Italian' pattern octagonal section garden seat, of typical Chinese form, rare impressed crown and "SPODE" mark.

c1820   19in (47cm) high

$2,000-3,000   **DN**

POTTERY

A Spode 'Turk' pattern bowl, printed in blue, with the Caramanian scene identified as the 'Ancient Granary at Caccamo', with a detail inside the base and rare floral border, broken and restored, unmarked.

c1815   6in (15cm) diam

$500-600   **DN**

A Spode 'Caramanian' series potted meat dish, printed in blue with enlarged scenes from the 'Indian Sporting' animals and inside the rim with a narrow version of the border itself, printed lower-case maker's mark, damage.

c1815   6.25in (16cm) diam

$200-300   **DN**

A Spode 'Forest Landscape' pattern supper set, with four segment dishes and a lidded centerpiece with button knop to the cover, printed with the chinoiserie design and border, impressed upper-case marks on segment dishes, damaged.

c1800   18.5in (47cm) diam

$100-150   **DN**

A 'Flying Pennant' pattern strainer, attributed to Spode, printed in blue with the chinoiserie design and border, unmarked, short firing crack.

c1810   3.25in (8.5cm) diam

$100-150   **DN**

A 19thC Spode blue and white basket and stand printed with floral swags and pierced with guilloche, printed mark.

9in (23cm) wide

$450-550   **CHEF**

An early 19thC Spode blue and white gravy Argyle and cover printed with baskets of flowers, printed marks.

An Argyle is a covered gravy boat with a detachable internal hot water vessel designed to keep the sauce warm.

6.75in (17.5cm) high

$600-800   **CHEF**

A rare Spode medicine spoon, with a short scallop-shell molded handle, printed in blue with a detail from a chinoiserie design, border from the 'Two Figures' pattern, handle replaced, unmarked.

c1800   4in (10cm) wide

$700-1,000   **DN**

A rare Spode medicine spoon, the bowl mounted on a pedestal foot, molded with a scallop-shell design, printed in blue with a detail from a chinoiserie design within the border from the 'Two Figures' pattern, unmarked.

c1800   2.75in (7cm) high

$2,000-3,000   **DN**

A Spode 'Rock' pattern beehive or honey pot, with fixed stand, printed in blue with the chinoiserie pattern and 'Forest Landscape' border, unmarked.

c1810   5in (13cm) diam

$150-200   **DN**

A pair of Spode stone china dessert dishes, printed, colored and gilt in pattern number 4052, impressed "SPODES / NEW STONE" with red-painted pattern numbers.

c1825   10in (26cm) wide

$300-400   **DN**

One of two Spode Greek series dinner plates, printed in blue but heavily clobbered overglaze in red enamel, with 'Zeus in His Chariot' design, border of vases and figure panels, unmarked, wear to enameling.

c1815   9.75in (24.5cm) diam

$300-400 PAIR   **DN**

TRANSFER-PRINTED WARE

- Transfer printing was used by factories including Spode and Wedgwood in the UK and Rorstrand and Marieberg, in Sweden. By the early 19thC potteries in Staffordshire and Leeds, as well as many across Europe, were using the technique to mass produce ceramics.
- The Staffordshire factories exported thousands of pieces to the US every year. exports included pieces decorated with American scenes and events.
- Blue and white chinoiserie designs such as the hugely popular 'Willow' pattern were prevalent. They were mostly applied to tablewares as an inexpensive alternative to hand-painting.
- Production vastly increased around c1815, and by c1835 print methods had advanced hugely and it was possible to produce smoother designs in several colors.
- The popularity of blue and white transfer printed ware began to decrease by the late 19thC.
- Transfer-printed ware may be identified by cross-hatching, created by the engravings on the copper plate. Another identifying mark is where edges of a printed design are not a perfect match.
- Earlier pieces tend to exhibit huge variances of shade, from very strong blue to extremely soft blue. A few rare early examples of outline-printed pieces were filled in by hand in colored enamel.

A mid-19thC Copeland and Garrett Late Spode 'Tower' pattern blue-printed dog bowl, on bracket feet, printed circle mark.

7.25in (18cm) wide

$700-1,000   L&T

An early 19thC John Rogers & Son 'Fallow Deer' pattern blue printed oval dish ring.

5in (12.5cm) wide

$450-650   L&T

A Herculaneum 'Chinese Raft' pattern blue printed chestnut basket and stand, with open trellis work to the sides.

The Herculaneum pottery was based in Toxteth, Liverpool. It produced earthenware and porcelain between 1796 and c1840.

$1,000-1,200   L&T

Two Oriental Birds pattern coffee cans, attributed to Spode, printed in blue with two exotic birds, chinoiserie and bird panels inside the rims, unmarked.

c1805   Taller 2.5in (6.5cm) high

$400-600   DN

A Staffordshire historical blue transfer-decorated platter, by John Rogers & Son, Longport, decorated with the naval battle between "Chesapeake and Shannon".

c1815   19in (48.25cm) long

$3,500-4,500   FRE

A Staffordshire historical blue transfer-decorated sauceboat, by Ralph Stevenson, Cobridge, with molded handle and feet heightened with gilt.

c1820   8in (20.5cm) wide

$1,200-1,500   FRE

A Turner blue and white-printed segmented dish, impressed mark.

c1810   10.5in (26cm) wide

$200-300   SWO

A Staffordshire historical blue transfer-decorated creamer and covered sugar bowl, by E. Wood & Sons, Burslem, with "Washington Standing at Tomb, Scroll in Hand" scene.

c1825   Sugar 6.25in (16cm) high

$1,000-1,500   FRE

A blue and white earthenware feeding bottle, printed with ladies admiring flowers in a landscape.

c1830   6.75in (17cm) wide

$600-900   SWO

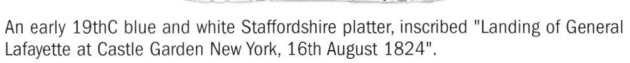

An early 19thC blue and white Staffordshire platter, inscribed "Landing of General Lafayette at Castle Garden New York, 16th August 1824".

17in (43cm) wide

$1,800-2,200   POOK

A 19thC 'Ponte Molle' pattern blue-printed tureen, cover and stand, the cover with flowerhead finial, the twin handles of scrolling foliate form. stand

21.25in (53cm) wide

$1,000-1,500   L&T

A Staffordshire dish, printed with a view of the Crystal Palace, printed mark for Pinder, Bourne & Hope, staining and crack.

c1855   13.5in (34cm) wide

$300-400   **WW**

A Pountney & Goldney 'Bristol Views' series meat dish, printed in blue with a titled view of "Bristol Hot Wells" within the usual floral border, printed title mark and impressed maker's name around a cross.

c1840   18in (46cm) wide

$2,000-3,000   **DN**

A John & William Ridgway 'Christ Church, Oxford' pattern dinner plate from the 'Oxford and Cambridge College' series, printed in blue with the titled view, border with cherub vignettes, printed mark, chip on footrim.

c1820   9.75in (25cm) diam

$100-150   **DN**

Two 'Blind Boy' pattern dinner plates, attributed to Ridgway, printed in blue with the genre scene and floral border, unmarked, small rim chips.

c1820   9.5in (24.5cm) diam

$200-300   **DN**

A 'British Scenery' series dinner plate, attributed to Ridgway, printed in blue with the scene known as 'Cottages and Castle' within the usual flower and leaf border, printed series title mark.

c1825   9.75in (25cm) diam

$120-180   **DN**

A Riley 'Europa' pattern meat dish, printed in blue with the classical scene and floral border, printed maker's "Semi-China" belt mark.

c1820   21in (53cm) wide

$600-900   **DN**

A Riley 'Europa' pattern covered vegetable dish, printed in blue with the classical scene and floral border, printed maker's "Semi-China" belt mark on base, star glaze crack inside cover, chip to foot.

c1820   12in (30.5cm) wide

$200-300   **DN**

A Rogers 'Elephant' pattern meat dish, printed in blue with elephant scene in a Chinese landscape within wide floral border, impressed mark.

c1815   21in (53.5cm) wide

$300-400   **DN**

A Rogers 'Fallow Deer' pattern well-and-tree meat dish, printed in blue with the country scene and usual floral border, impressed maker's mark, wear and chips.

c1820   20.75in (52.5cm) wide

$200-300   **DN**

A pair of William Smith & Co. 'Infant Sports' pattern teabowls and saucers, printed in purple with a scene of children playing, saucers with printed title mark including maker's initials and impressed mark "W.S. & Co's / WEDGWOOD", one bowl cracked.

c1835   Saucers 5in (12.5cm) diam

$100-150   **DN**

A Staffordshire pottery blue-and-white printed meat plate.

c1830   20in (51cm) wide

$550-650   **SWO**

A Wood & Challinor 'Pheasant' pattern meat dish, printed in blue with a landscape featuring pheasants and an urn, within a border featuring scroll-framed vignettes on a geometric ground, printed title mark with maker's initials.

c1835   *22in (55.5cm) wide*

$600-900   **DN**

An Enoch Wood & Sons saucer printed with 'Washington Standing at His Tomb', impressed "WOOD", footrim nick, and a saucer printed with a titled view of "Baltimore Hospital", unmarked, slight damage.

c1825   *larger 6in (15cm) diam*

$400-600   **DN**

An Enoch Wood & Sons 'Grapevine Border' series wash jug, printed in blue with a country house scene beneath the usual grapevine border, cracked, unmarked.

c1825   *9.5in (24cm) high*

$300-400   **DN**

A late 18thC 'Conversation' pattern meat dish, printed in blue with the chinoiserie scene and border, small impressed horn-like symbol.

c1790   *17in (43cm) wide*

$300-400   **DN**

An Enoch Wood & Sons 'Grapevine Border' series cheese cradle, printed in blue with a scene identified as Powderham Castle in Devon, repeated under either end, incorrect printed title mark for "Hollywell Cottage, Cavan", some restoration.

c1825   *20in (51cm) wide*

$3,000-4,000   **DN**

A blue-and-white printed pottery meat plate, decorated with a leopard crouching behind a tree, the border with large flower-heads.

c1820   *20in (51cm) wide*

$1,000-1,500   **WW**

A 'Cathedral Church of Glasgow' pattern well-and-tree meat dish from the 'Antique Scenery' series, printed in blue with the titled scene and usual series border of flowers and foliate scrolls, printed titles mark.

c1820   *18.5in (47cm) wide*

$600-900   **DN**

A 'Ruined Castle and Bridge' pattern well-and-tree meat dish, printed in blue within a narrow border incorporating shell-like motifs, unmarked, minor chipping to foot.

c1820   *19in (48cm) wide*

$200-300   **DN**

A 'Fruit Basket' pattern meat dish, printed in blue with a pattern of a basket and fruit within an open border with fruit and leaves, printed title mark.

c1840   *19.5in (49.5cm) wide*

$400-600   **DN**

POTTERY

A 'Winemakers' pattern dinner plate, printed in blue with the classical scene of winemakers within a grapevine border and with a blue lined rim, rim restored, unmarked.

c1820 *10in (25.5cm) diam*

$70-100 **DN**

A 'Beemaster' pattern soup plate, printed in blue with the central genre scene after George Robertson, within the usual border of flowers and animal vignettes, unmarked.

c1825 *9.5in (24.5cm) diam*

$300-400 **DN**

One of two 'Philosopher' pattern soup plates, printed in blue with the classical scene and floral border, unmarked, one with star crack in side of well.

c1825 *9.75in (24.5cm) diam*

$100-150 pair **DN**

A blue-printed Calais dessert dish, with open crabstock handle, decorated with a copy of the Chinese scene attributed to Robert Hamilton, identified as 'Hotun on the Canton River'.

9in (23cm) wide

$100-150 **DN**

A 'One-Man' Chinoiserie pattern jug, of Dutch shape with an angular handle and ochre lining to both handle and rim, printed in blue with typical border, with a different border featuring stiff leaves around inside the rim, unmarked.

c1800 *7in (18cm) high*

$200-300 **DN**

A small 'Fountain and Statue House' pattern jug, of Dutch shape, the neck and lower body with bands of engine-turning, printed in blue with the chinoiserie scene, unmarked, hole to base.

c1805 *6.25in (11cm) high*

$120-180 **DN**

A large blue-printed jug, of Dutch shape with angular handle, decorated with a basket of flowers and a bird amongst branches of fruit, a floral scroll border, small chips, unmarked.

c1825 *9.25in (23.5cm) high*

$600-900 **DN**

A 'Wanstead House and Gleaner' pattern jug, of Dutch shape, printed with an identified view of Wanstead House in Essex and on reverse with a rural scene, with two floral borders around and inside the neck, unmarked.

c1825 *5.5in (14cm) high*

$450-550 **DN**

A 'Sylvia Flow' blue pitcher, transfer printed in deep blue with birds with birds perched among stylized flowers and scrolls.

13in (33cm) high

$1,000-1,500 **WAD**

A 'Ruined Castle' and 'Milkmaid' patterns coffee pot, printed in dark blue with the 'Ruined Castle' pattern on either side and a version of the Milkmaid pattern on the neck, floral borders, unmarked, chips and repair.

c1820 *11in (28cm) high*

$70-100 **DN**

A Wedgwood smearglazed box and cover modeled as an Antique lamp, sprigged with blue signs of the Zodiac, impressed mark, restored section to cover.

c1810   5.5in (14cm) wide

$200-300   **DN**

A CLOSER LOOK AT A PAIR OF WEDGWOOD AND BENTLEY EWERS

These early ewers were produced by Josiah Wedgwood and his partner Thomas Bentley, a man of sophisticated taste and important social contacts in the arts world.

Bentley was a key influence in Wedgwood's decision to embrace the Neo-classical trend. These fashionable ewers would have met the demands of the market with their distinctly Etruscan style.

Wedgwood was important for innovative processes, such as this painted simulated gilt bronze, which is very unusual and make these ewers particularly desirable.

The simulated porphyry body is an example of Wedgwood's experimentation with simulated stoneware. Porphyry was very desirable amongst the aristocracy and is associated with Imperial Roman times.

A 19thC Wedgwood basalt Portland vase, applied in white relief with Classical draped figures, the underside decorated with a man in a Phrygian hat, impressed "Wedgwood".

11in (28cm) high

$2,000-3,000   **FRE**

An early 20thC Wedgwood deep blue Jasper clock case, sprigged with female figures and peri below Father Time and 'Tempus Fugit', impressed "Wedgwood England".

In Persian mythology, peri are fairy-like descendants of fallen angels.

8.5in (21cm) high

$300-400   **SWO**

A 19thC Wedgwood three color Jasper dip plaque, with white Classical draped figures against a blue ground, within a pale green border, impressed "Wedgwood".

18in (45cm) wide

$3,000-4,000   **FRE**

A pair of Wedgwood and Bentley simulated porphyry ewers, with high scroll handles and lips gilded to simulate ormolu, on mound feet and gilded bases, impressed marks.

c1785   12in (30.5cm) high

$15,000-20,000   **AA**

MISCELLANEOUS

A mid-19thC Masons vase and cover, on an orange ground surmounted with dolphins and decorated with flowers, large chip to neck.

25.25in (64cm) high

$600-900   **SWO**

A large 19thC plaster mastiff, with glass eyes, damage.

21.5in (54cm) high

$400-600   **SWO**

An early 19thC English pottery Rockingham glaze cistern, modeled as a house.

16.5in (41cm) high

$450-550   **FRE**

Four of a collection of 17 Scottish pottery carpet bowls, six sponge-printed with an allover floral motif, nine painted with a checked design and two plain.

$1,500-2,000 SET   **L&T**

A Palissy-style circular charger by Mafra of Caldas De Rainha, with applied lizards, a snake and a beetle, on a bed of extruded clay, impressed mark.

c1880   12.75in (32cm) diam

$700-1,000   **SWO**

POTTERY

A rare pottery bin label, by Spode, with scroll wine name "Bronte" in Sunderland pink lustre, impressed mark.

c1825   5in (13cm) wide

$400-600   **CSA**

A large English pottery wine bin label, impressed "Wedgwood ORV" which denotes the year 1867.

1867   6in (15cm) wide

$100-120   **CSA**

An English sherry pottery label, by Wedgwood, transfer-printed under glaze impressed with "MZW".

c1880   5.5in (14cm) wide

$60-90   **CSA**

A rare "Port 1847" pottery label, transfer-printed under glaze, unmarked.

1847   5in (13cm) wide

$300-400   **CSA**

A rare George Grainger stoneware baluster-shaped flagon, in 16thC style, molded in relief with a seated hound crest, panels and scrolls, plated hinged cover, incised "G. Grainger, Worcester".

This piece has a letter of provenance from Royal Worcester, dated 1971, attesting to its rarity.

c1850   8in (20.5cm) high

$600-900   **LFA**

A large two tone stoneware jug, relief molded with a Crimean war battle scene.

c1880   10.25in (26cm) high

$200-300   **SWO**

An early 19thC Davenport cane ware or 'Terra-cotta' wine cooler, with two dolphin handles, painted in enamel with a Greek Key border and a flute effect lower section.

9.75in (25cm) high

$700-1,000   **DN**

A blue and white pottery '1753 Marriage Act Group' within a simulated brick archway, probably 19thC from an 18thC mold.

6.5in (16.5cm) high

$300-400   **BRI**

An Australian pottery gnome, stamped "JM".

c1900   31.5in (80cm) high

$1,200-1,800   **SWO**

A Ewenny slipware model of a seated cat, the bright yellow glaze incised with eyes, whiskers and a collar, incised mark and dated.

Ewenny Pottery near Bridgend in South Wales is thought to have been established in 1610 and is still operating today.

1907   15in (38cm) high

$2,000-3,000   **LFA**

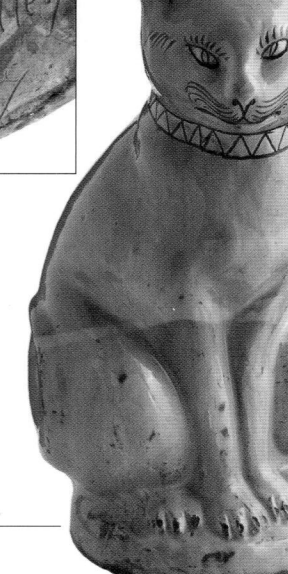

A painted and glazed Nelson memorial tankard, in Delft style, with a portrait of Nelson flanked by floral sprays, inscribed below "in memory of Lord Nelson", with "AG" monogram to the base.

5.5in (14cm) high

$2,000-3,000   **W&W**

A Nelson memorial pearlware jug, printed in blue with a named portrait oval, with Victory and details of Nelson's honor to the reverse, the handle and rim lined in ocher.

6.75in (17cm) high

$1,500-2,000   **W&W**

A Nelson memorial pearlware jug, of baluster form, printed in black with a named oval portrait and Victory to the reverse.

7.25in (18.5cm) high

$1,200-1,800   **W&W**

A late 17thC good Westerwald stoneware krug, molded with a relief portrait of William III of Orange, pewter mount and lid.

Given the iconography of the panel, it is likely that the piece commemorates William's defeat of James II at the Battle of the Boyne in 1690 or success against the French in 1697.

9.5in (24cm) high

$3,000-4,000   **SWO**

A Staffordshire transfer-decorated and enameled creamware pitcher, one side with the 'Philadelphia', the other with a woman resting on an anchor.

The frigate Philadelphia was seized by the enemy during the 1801-05 Barbary Wars. Rather than fight their own ship the US Navy boarded the vessel and burned it.

11in (28cm) high

$5,000-7,000   **FRE**

A creamware Masonic jug, with "The World is in pain, Our secrets to gain, But still them wonder and gaze on, For they ne'er can dine, The word nor the sign of a free and an accepted Mason".

c1800   *8in (20cm) high*

$700-1,000   **SWO**

A Royal Worcester Queen Victoria blush ivory porcelain scent bottle, inscribed "India, Canada and Australia" with a silver-plated coronet screw cap, printed marks.

1897   *3.5in (9cm) high*

$500-700   **SWO**

A Wedgwood King Edward VIII 1937 Coronation mug, designed by Eric Ravilious, printed mark.

1937   *4in (10cm) high*

$2,000-3,000   **SWO**

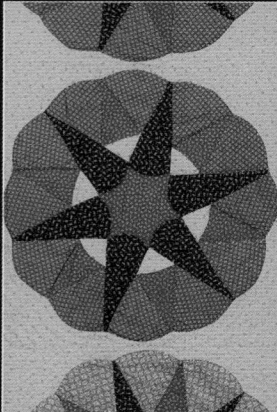

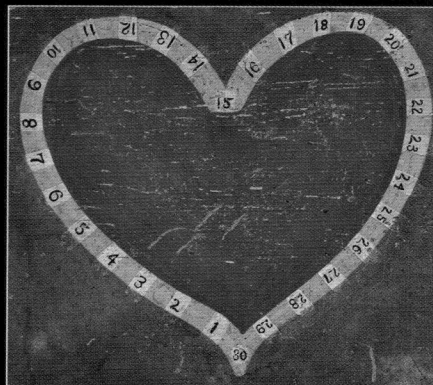

72

THE ORIENTAL MARKET

The market for Chinese art continues to be very strong thanks to the on-going growth of the market in China. However, this does not mean that all areas are performing equally well. Chinese collectors are buying items made to suit the Chinese taste rather than the export wares made for the West. Export and armorial wares, which were bought by American and European collectors, are less popular than they were, and this can be seen in lower prices these pieces are fetching overall.

Items made for scholars' desks, such as brushes, brush pots, brush rests, water droppers and table screens are selling to Chinese, American and European buyers and prices have risen substantially. Chinese collectors are also buying 19th century and early 20th century Republican ceramics, as long as they are of good quality and in good condition.

Also strong at the moment, thanks to Chinese interest, are 17th century blue and white wares such as Transitional and Kangxi porcelain. Jades, if they have good provenance, are also performing well, with Chinese buyers favoring white jade over bright green jadeite.

If you are looking for value for money, then funereal wares and early pottery from the Tang and Hang Dynasties are an area to consider. At present a Tang horse can be bought for $400-1,000, much less than a few years ago, although the best examples continue to sell for $20,000 or more.

An area to watch is Chinese paintings where examples by 20th century artists are starting to fetch large sums of money. In November 2006 Christie's Hong Kong sold Xu Beihong's 1924 painting Slave and Lion for $6.92 million – a record price for a Chinese oil painting.

John Axford

EARLY CHINESE CERAMICS

A Chinese pottery figure of a recumbent dog, Han Dynasty.

14in (36cm) long

$1,000-1,500   **DN**

An Eastern Jin Dynasty Yueyao ewer, with flattened rim and slender neck, the shoulders with a dragon head spout and facetted lugs, rim restored.

AD 217-420   *9in (22cm) high*

$600-900   **DN**

An Eastern Jin Dynasty Yueyao plate mouthed vase with short neck and globular body, the shoulders with four taotie heads, the whole covered in an olive green glaze.

AD 217-420   *6.5in (16.5cm) high*

$500-600   **DN**

One of a group of five pottery horses ridden by warrior archers, in unusual costumes, some have bows and quivers, unusually, some are female.

Substantial numbers of pottery horses and riders began to be placed in tombs during the Qin dynasty (221-206BC). The practice became more widespread during the Han dynasty, due to the struggle against the Xiongmu, a tribe of horsemen from the Ordos region of Inner Mongolia. People of high status would have large numbers of pottery horses and riders placed in their tombs ready to defend them in the next life.

AD c234-581   *15in (38cm) high*

$10,000-15,000 set   **RGA**

A Jin-carved Yaozhou bowl, the outer edges of the bowl are decorated with a comb technique.

Yaozhou refers to the kiln group this piece comes from. It is made with a type of celadon – a glaze color of green tones. Before glazing the middle was carved at an angle to create different depths of glaze giving the pattern a 3D quality.

1115-1234   *5in (13cm) diam*

$1,000-1,500   **R&GM**

A Tang iron splashed ewer, the design is based on metalwork, made of dense stoneware.

This piece is in surprisingly good condition for such an early piece.

AD 618-907   *7.5in (19cm) high*

$800-1,200   **R&GM**

A Tang Dynasty ovoid vase and cover, with an amber brown glaze falling short of the foot and one blue splash, minor chips to rim.

AD 618-906   *9in (22cm) high*

$1,500-2,000   **DN**

A pair of Tang dynasty mottled glaze tea bowls, the green and ochre glazes over a white slip ground, the feet unglazed.

2.5in (6.5cm) diam

$200-300   **CHEF**

A Song dynasty yingching vase, the cylindrical neck incised with fluting below the flared rim, the ovoid body molded with bands of flowers below the pale ice blue glaze.

10.25in (28cm) high

$400-500   CHEF

A large Southern Song Dynasty Henan bottle vase, the ribbed body with short neck, flared rim covered in a black glaze falling evenly short of the foot, minor restoration to rim.

1127-1279   12in (30.5cm) high

$500-600   DN

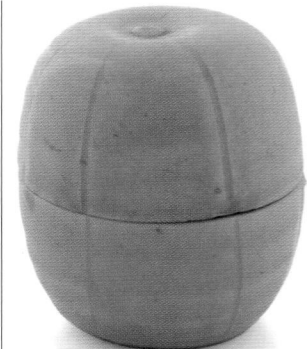

A Song 11th-12thC fruit form box and cover, restored chips, the decorative lines on the outside are marked on with bamboo, the halves are a perfect set.

Without chips the piece would be worth $450.

2.25in (6cm) high

$150-200   R&GM

A Song 12thC Qingbai jar and cover, firing grit to cover.

Used as storage containers, these types of pieces were made in large numbers.

8in (21cm) high

$400-500   R&GM

A Song 12thC Qingbai bowl with incised fish, small chips.

Qingbai is a type of glaze with blue/green color.

7in (18cm) wide

$800-1,200   R&GM

A Chinese celadon charger, centrally incised with basket panel within a scrolling lotus band, Yuan Dynasty.

19in (48cm) diam

$1,000-1,200   DN

A Chinese celadon glazed charger, Ming Dynasty, rim with incised loose scroll motif, well with incised lotus blossom within incised concentric lines, deep foot rim, the underside with unglazed circle.

16.5in (41cm) diam

$1,500-2,000   L&T

A 15thC Ming dynasty Longquan celadon dish.

10.5in (26.5cm) diam

$700-800   R&GM

A Chinese early Ming dynasty Longquan celadon yen yen vase, carved overall with scrolling peony.

20.75in (53cm) high

$3,000-4,000   WW

A rare and early blanc-de-Chine figure of Guanyin, from Dehua in Fujian province.

c1630   9.5in (24cm) high

$3,000-4,000   **R&GM**

A 17thC Dehua blanc-de-Chine figure of Guandi, seated on a rocky outcrop from which emerges a tortoise and serpents.

9.25in (23.5cm) high

$4,000-6,000   **PC**

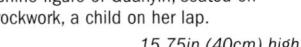

A large Chinese Kangxi period blanc-de-Chine figure of Guanyin, seated on rockwork, a child on her lap.

15.75in (40cm) high

$700-1,000   **WW**

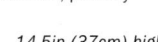

A Dehua blanc-de-Chine figure of The Bodhisattva Avalokitesvara, possibly 18thC.

14.5in (37cm) high

$800-1,200   **PC**

An 18thC Chinese blanc-de-Chine equestrian figure, modeled as a European, one hand holding a sword, the other clenched as if holding a bridle, sword lacking.

11.5in (29cm) high

$7,000-10,000   **L&T**

A massive 19thC Chinese blanc-de-Chine model of Guanyin, raised on a wood stand, impressed "p'u-chi yü-jên" to reverse, restored.

The inscription means "reaching all, even fishermen".

22.5in (57cm) high

$5,000-7,000   **WW**

An early 20thC blanc-de-Chine figure of Guanyin, holding a child and seated on a lotus.

9in (22cm) high

$200-300   **DN**

A pair of 19thC Chinese blanc-de-Chine Buddhist lions, each with a raised paw, on pierced ball and plinth bases.

9in (23cm) high

$300-400   **ROS**

An 18thC au hua decorated stem cup, complete with leather, cotton and wicker carrying case.

5.5in (14cm) diam

$2,000-3,000   **R&GM**

A Jaijing blue and white bowl, decorated with portraits of Shou Xing and other Immortals, stylized pine, deer and ling zhi, with stylized four character mark.

Ling zhi is a type of spore mushroom used in Chinese medicine.

4.75in (12cm) diam

$1,000-1,500   SWO

A 17thC blue and white censer, decorated with a scruffy bird and insects amidst peony and other flowers and foliage, on three feet.

6.75in (17cm) diam

$2,000-3,000   WW

A Wanli period blue and white bowl, decorated with fish, aquatic plants, stylized waves and large peony blooms.

1573-1619   8.5in (21.5cm) diam

$2,000-3,000   WW

An early 19thC square section porcelain bowl, decorated in underglaze blue with buildings, flowers and butterflies in a garden.

10in (25.5cm) wide

$1,000-1,500   DNT

A large 19thC porcelain bowl, glazed and painted in blue, depicting a bush with large blossoms, birds and a butterfly, the rim with floral decoration and four cartouches containing blossoms and insects.

15in (37.5cm) diam

$500-700   KAU

A late 16thC saucer dish, decorated in underglaze blue with a pagoda in a river landscape, the rim with a band of chrysanthemum and lotus, the exterior with cranes amid cloud scrolls.

17in (43cm) diam

$3,000-4,000   DN

An unusual Kraak blue and white dish, decorated with a portrait of Shou Xing and a crane within a border of stylized flowers and fish traps.

Shou Lau is the Chinese god of longevity.

c1600   6.75in (17cm) diam

$500-600   SWO

A rare Tianqi period blue and white leaf-shaped dish, made for the Japanese market, painted with butterflies, a dragonfly and flower sprays, the underside modeled with veining, on three stump feet.

1621-27   6.5in (16.5cm) diam

$800-1,000   WW

A Kraak porcelain blue and white plate, possibly late Ming, painted centrally with a water crustacean within alternating rim panels of boats and flowers, damaged.

8in (20.5cm) diam

$500-600   CHEF

A massive blue and white saucer dish, painted with a stylized calligraphy roundel, within a broad band painted with cranes, peaches and lingzhi, the exterior with a rectangular panel with six character mark for Jiajing and of the period.

23.25in (59cm) diam

$35,000-45,000   **LAW**

A Wanli kraak porcelain plate.
c1600   *8.75in (22cm) diam*

$600-900   **R&GM**

A Chinese blue and white dragon and phoenix dish, the reverse decorated with a continuous lotus scroll, Wanli, six character mark.

11.25in (28.5cm) diam

$5,000-6,000   **WW**

A late Ming blue and white Phoenix design plate.

c1560   *7.5in (19.5cm) diam*

$300-400   **R&GM**

A Chinese blue and white dish, painted with a bird and insect within a floral paneled border, together with another similar, Wanli period.

11.25in (29cm) diam

$600-900   **HAMG**

A Wanli kraak porcelain dish, decorated in a deep underglaze blue with a panel of birds and flowers within a radiating band paneled with flowers and precious emblems.

c1600   *11in (28cm) diam*

$600-900   **DN**

Late Ming small kraak porcelain dish, rim chips, with typical kraak panels, decorated with a cricket, made in a mold.

Kraak porcelain is prone to chips at the edges.

c1600-30   *5.5in (14cm) diam*

$200-300   **R&GM**

A Late Ming dish, for the Japanese market, rim frits, grit from kiln, imprinted mark.

c1620-1640   *8.5in (21.5cm) diam*

$600-900   **R&GM**

A Kangxi dish, chips to rim.

c1700   *8.75in (22cm) diam*

$600-1,000   **R&GM**

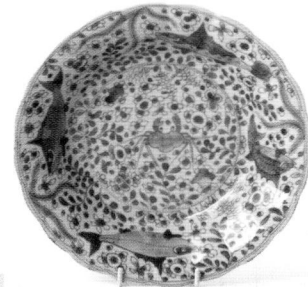

ORIENTAL CERAMICS

CLOSER LOOK AT A KANGXI SAUCER AND A LATER COPY

This finely-potted piece is an original because the painting is of very high quality, each scale has been individually painted and shaded and waterweeds are individually picked out.

The design has been thoughtfully laid-out, with plenty of space between elements.

Molded details are sharply picked out and pleasingly shaped.

Orange iron oxide is evident to the foot rim, suggesting significant age. The sacred fungus mark suggests the Kangxi period (1662-1722).

The branch to the back has been carefully realized using a variety of brush strokes.

A Kangxi hand-painted saucer with decoration of fish, stapled.

c1700   5.25in (13.5cm) diam

$150-200   **R&GM**

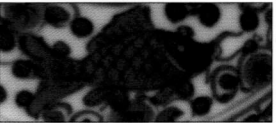

How to tell this is a 19thC copy:

The spacing is far more cluttered.

Glaze is thickly applied so that the molded detail is less pronounced.

There is far less detail in the painting - scales have been summed up and a flat wash applied behind the body of the fish.

A late 19thC hand-painted saucer with decoration of fish, a near copy of the early original design, probably made as a replacement for a broken piece.

5.25in (13.5cm) diam

$20-40   **R&GM**

A Yongzheng mark and period pair of blue and white double phoenix dishes.

1723-35   7.75in (19.5cm) diam

$10,000-12,000   **R&GM**

A Qianlong 'Pompadour' plate, rim chips.

The fish vignettes refer to Madame de Pompadour's original surname, 'Poisson', and the crowned eagle refers to the King Louis XV, to whom she was mistress.

c1750   9in (23cm) diam

$600-800   **R&GM**

A pair of Qianlong blue and white plates, decorated with birds, rocks and flowers.

14.5in (37cm) wide

$800-1,200 pair   **GORL**

A Qianlong blue and white export ware dish, made in imitation of Dutch Delft herring dishes, some rim fritting.

c1775   9.5in (24cm) wide

$4,000-5,000   **R&GM**

A large Chinese Wanli period blue painted bowl, the exterior decorated with cartouche panels of birds in landscapes, flowers and foliage, the interior with birds amongst flowers, the well with a mountain landscape, damage.

13.75in (35cm) diam

$5,000-6,000   **L&T**

A Kangxi bowl, with Chenghua marks.

1662-1722   5.5in (14cm) wide

$2,000-3,000   **R&GM**

A blue and white bowl, with everted flared rim, the exterior painted with maidens and boys in a landscape, the rim with emblems, six character mark for Jiajing, but Kangxi.

6.25in (16cm) diam

$2,000-3,000   **PC**

A blue and white jardinière, of compressed globular form, painted with panels of flowering plants and utensils, reserved on a prunus and cracked ice ground, Kangxi.

10.5in (27cm) diam

$1,500-2,000   **LAW**

A Chinese Kangxi period blue and white molded chrysanthemum bowl, painted with panels of birds amid flowers, unmarked, restored.

9in (22.5cm) diam

$1,500-2,000 WW

A Kangxi bowl, of klapmuts form, Chenghua mark.

c1700 8in (20.25cm) diam

$3,000-4,000 R&GM

A Yongzheng period Chinese blue and white bowl, exterior decorated with children playing beneath a willow tree, interior with a boy kicking a ball, six-character Yongzheng mark, tiny rim chips.

7.75in (19.5cm) diam

$5,000-6,000 WW

A Chinese Qianlong period blue and white bowl, decorated with four roundels of auspicious characters on a lotus scroll ground, the interior decorated with the bajixiang, six-character Qianling mark, tiny rim chips.

7.25in (18.5cm) diam

$4,000-6,000 WW

A Chinese punch bowl with exterior carved with band of peony within underglaze blue borders, interior decorated with carp swimming amongst weed.

16in (41cm) diam

$1,000-1,500 DN

A 19thC mahogany bidet with Canton blue and white porcelain liner, on turned legs and feet, the liner is stained around the upper border.

$1,800-2,000 FRE

A 19thC Canton reticulated basket and undertray.

basket 4.5in (11.5cm) high

$700-1,000 FRE

A 19thC Chinese crackle glaze blue and white wash stand, with a floral rim, painted with floral panels, reserved in a blue ground.

15in (38cm) diam

$400-600 ROS

CLOSER LOOK AT A TRANSITIONAL VASE

A good Chinese blue and white cylindrical vase, the shoulder and foot decorated with anhua bands, the body with figures and a horse beside a waterfall.

c1640 18.75in (47cm) high

$15,000-20,000 WW

The painting of this vase is typical of the 'High Transitional' style and includes banana plants, scholars and rocks.

The shape, with its slight Islamic influence, is typical of the period.

The color, made from expensive cobalt, is intense suggesting a good piece. A similar piece with a poor blue could be worth far less - around $10,000.

The blue decoration is painted onto the pot and so seeps into the body. When the glaze is applied, it also absorbs some of the color, giving the overall a great depth of color.

Has pre-19thC blue and white kiln marks.

A well-painted Transitional bottle-shaped vase, painted in rich blue with figures in a landscape, the neck decorated with stylized tulips in the Islamic style, almost perfect, frit to the glaze of rim.

c1640 14.5in (37cm) high

$30,000-35,000 R&GM

A Chinese Kangxi period blue and white yen yen vase, painted with two pairs of figures standing on rocks in a mountainous landscape.

17.75in (45cm) high

$18,000-20,000   **WW**

A Chinese Kangxi period blue and white yen yen vase, decorated with an all-over prunus pattern.

18.25in (46.5cm) high

$10,000-15,000   **WW**

A Chinese Kangxi blue painted gu shaped vase, painted with frieze of male figures, a carriage and a bull in a rocky landscape, frieze of stylized flowers and scrolling foliage, a band of stiff leaf decoration.

18.5in (47cm) high

$2,000-3,000   **L&T**

A Chinese Kangxi period blue and white bottle vase, painted with antiques and precious objects.

7.75in (20cm) high

$3,000-4,000   **WW**

A Kangxi pot with 19thC mounts.

c1700   *6.75in (17cm) high*

$1,000-1,500   **R&GM**

A Kangxi blue and white oviform vase, painted with an overall design of flowering prunus blossom, within palmette, scroll and flowerhead borders.

13.5in (34cm) high

$2,000-3,000   **ROS**

A Late Kangxi/Yongzheng blue and white bottle vase with extensive watery landscape.

c1720   *8in (20.5cm) high*

$3,000-4,000   **R&GM**

A Yongzheng period blue and white baluster vase, trumpet neck, swelling globular body, painted on the exterior with a broad band enclosing a garden scene with go players, repairs.

c1730   *14.5in (37cm) high*

$3,000-4,000   **BEA**

A Chinese Qianlong period blue and white vase, molded with 12 panels painted with pagoda landscapes on a floral and simulated shagreen ground, six-character Qianlong mark.

14.25in (36cm) high

$3,000-6,000   **WW**

A large 18thC Chinese blue and white vase of archaic form, with molded animal mask and ring handles and decorated with stylized bands of taotie masks, stiff leaves and key fret.

18in (46cm) high

$10,000-15,000   **WW**

A Chinese 19thC blue and white vase, with an ogee-shaped body, decorated with a scene of farmers, women and children, with six-character Kangxi mark.

8.75in (22.5cm) high

$3,000-4,000   **WW**

A pair of early 19thC Chinese blue painted baluster storage jars, with metal fixings to the neck and cover, and foliate and floral decorated panels, damages.

26.75in (68cm) high

$10,000-15,000   **L&T**

A Chinese blue and white vase painted with rocks and bamboo on the downswept shoulders and with four pendant lappets below, each with peony bloom and foliage.

7.25in (18.5cm) high

$300-400   **CHEF**

A Chinese Guangxu vase.

c1890   *14in (36cm) high*

$2,000-3,000   **DB**

A late 19thC Chinese slender bottle vase decorated in underglaze blue with panels of beasts beneath band of stiff leaves to the neck, six character Kangxi mark, fitted case.

18in (46cm) high

$3,000-4,000   **DN**

A late 19thC Chinese Gu shaped vase decorated in underglaze blue with bands of scrolling lotus.

18in (46cm) high

$3,000-4,000   **DN**

ORIENTAL CERAMICS

A Chinese blue and white beaker vase, painted with figures in a garden setting, Qing dynasty, four character mark to the base.

14.25in (36cm) high

$1,000-1,500   **H&L**

A Chinese blue and white cylindrical stick stand, decorated with a dragon amidst flowers.

c1900   *24in (60cm) high*

$500-600   **WW**

A 19thC Chinese blue painted baluster vase, the deep cylindrical neck with stiff leaf frieze, with serrated leaf and blossom decoration.

19.25in (48cm) high

$400-600   **L&T**

A late 19thC pair of Chinese blue and white moon flasks painted with mountainous landscapes.

8.5in (21.5cm) high

$2,000-3,000   **BEA**

A large Transitional mid-17thC Chinese wucai brush pot, body incised with a band of five lines and painted with a pheasant standing on rockwork issuing foliage and flowers, the reverse with two yellow and green birds in flight.

8.5in (21cm) diam

$10,000-15,000   **WW**

A 19thC Chinese underglaze blue and red vase, the meiping shape painted with five clawed dragons chasing flaming pearls through clouds above waves, six character mark of Kangxi, damage.

5.75in (14.5cm) high

$150-200   **CHEF**

A good Chinese Kangxi blue and white cylindrical brush pot, well painted with a dignitary and nine further figures on a veranda, no mark.

c1680   *6.75in (17cm) wide*

$30,000-35,000   **WW**

A large Chinese Kangxi period blue and white brush pot, decorated with a figure carrying a child to the shore, and with figures in boats, and pagodas amidst rockwork, chipping to the inner rim and foot rim, no mark.

c1700   *7.5in (18.5cm) wide*

$6,000-9,000   **WW**

A rare Late Ming miniature kendi of very slender form.

c1625   5.25in (13.25cm) high

$2,000-3,000   **R&GM**

A Transitional blue and white ewer, small chip to rim.

c1645   7.25in (18.5cm) high

$3,000-4,000   **R&GM**

One of a pair of Yongzheng blue and white ewers.

c1730   4.75in (12cm) high

$2,000-3,000 PAIR   **R&GM**

A Yongzheng teapot, tiny chip to spout.

This piece is unusual as it is on three feet, it is of good color with varied tones of strong, rich blue.

c1730   21.5in (8.5cm) high

$2,000-3,000   **R&GM**

A Chinese Qianlong period blue and white pear-shaped ewer, with a later metal cover and broad strap handle, painted with two panels of fruit amidst the flowers of the Four Seasons, seal mark and of the period, damage.

c1760   11in (28cm) high

$5,000-6,000   **WW**

A rare Chinese Wanli or Tanqi period blue and white incense burner, modeled as a Buddhist lion dog, with an open mouth baring its teeth, his front paw raised and resting on a reticulated ball.

c1630   8.25in (21cm) high

$10,000-15,000   **WW**

ORIENTAL CERAMICS

SHIPWRECK CARGOES

- 17thC trade ships, carrying tea, porcelain, spices and silk on the journey from China sometimes sank. Where the fragile cargo has been recovered, the hoard attracts great attention from blue and white porcelain collectors.
- The porcelain on board was occasionally made for the European market and European themes can be seen in the decoration.
- Famous cargoes include: 1752 the Dutch ship Geldermalsen, carrying 25,000 pieces of porcelain for the Amsterdam market. It was salvaged in 1986. It is known as the Nanking cargo.
- In 1817 the Diana sank in the Straits of Malacca. It was salvaged in 1994 with 24,000 intact pieces of blue and white ware.

A Hatcher cargo Chinese Dragon Stem cup.

c1643   2in (5cm) high

$400-500   **R&GM**

Two Hatcher Cargo wine cups, the straight side with sharply waisted base with a small thin foot rim, one with flower heads and leaves and a line border the other similar with a diaper border.

c1643   2.75in (7cm) wide

$400-500 each   **R&GM**

A Hatcher cargo Chinese 'red cliff' bowl, decorated with scenery and calligraphy, chips.

c1643   6in (15cm) diam

$400-500   **R&GM**

A Hatcher cargo Chinese large vase with octagonal neck and cover.

c1643   14.25in (36cm) high

$3,000-4,000   **R&GM**

A handpainted blue and white Chinese miniature vase.

From the Hatcher Junk collection sold at Christie's Amsterdam June 1984 with original label.

1643-1645   4.75in (12cm) high

$300-400   **PC**

A Chinese hand-painted blue and white porcelain teapot (lacking lid).

1643-45   4.5in (11cm) high

$600-900   **PC**

A small Chinese hand-painted blue and white porcelain mustard pot and cover, slight chip to lid.

1643-45   1.5in (4cm) high

$400-500   **PC**

A Vung Tau cargo baluster vase and domed cover, with amusing figures in a rocky landscape, with pines and the sea below.

c1690   *4.5in (11.5cm) high*

$600-900   **RB**

A Vung Tau Cargo beaker, decorated with "penciled" decoration in the style of European engraving with lots of cross-hatching.

c1690   *2.75in (7cm) high*

$400-500   **R&GM**

A small Vung Tau cargo tea bowl and saucer, with floral panels.

c1690   *3.75in (9.5cm) diam*

$500-700   **RB**

One of a set of four late 18thC Nanking cargo blue and white plates, each painted with a crane flying over a pavillion on an island, a boat heading towards it from another island with distant pagoda.

8.75in (22.5cm) diam

$600-900 SET   **CHEF**

A Nanking cargo 'Lattice Fence' pattern soup dish, the borders with three clusters of flowering branches.

c1750   *9in (23cm) diam*

$600-900   **RB**

A large Nanking cargo floral bowl, with enamels, virtually all the pattern in ghost form, leaving gray glaze.

c1750   *7.5in (19cm) diam*

$400-600   **RB**

A Nanking cargo 'Boatman' plate, in blue, white and enamels.

c1750   *9in (23cm) diam*

$600-900   **RB**

A Nanking cargo blue and white 'Scholar on the Bridge' pattern bowl, with scholar crossing bridge, pavillion and trees.

c1750   *7.5in (19cm) diam*

$600-900   **RB**

A large rare Nanking cargo Batavian tea bowl and saucer, with decoration of a pavilion and trees on an island.

c1750   5.25in (13.5cm) diam

$600-700   **RB**

A Nanking cargo 'Blue Pine Tree' pattern tea bowl and saucer.

c1750   4in (10cm) diam

$400-500   **RB**

A Nanking cargo Batavian bowl with landscape decoration.

c1750   10in (25cm) diam

$500-600   **RB**

A large Tek Sing cargo 'Spiral Lotus' dish, decorated with lingzhi fungus, fruiting peach and flowering lotus spray.

c1822   7in (18cm) diam

$300-400   **RB**

A Tek Sing cargo small dish, decorated with basket of chrysanthemums, underside with three stylized flower sprays.

c1822   4.25in (11cm) diam

$120-180   **RB**

A Tek Sing cargo 'Scholar' bowl, standing beside a fence with prunus blossoms.

c1822   6.75in (17cm) diam

$400-500   **RB**

A Tek Sing cargo encrusted storage jar, originally in brown pottery.

c1822   8.25in (21cm) high

$700-1,000   **RB**

A Ca Mau shipwreck plate, after a design by Fivan Fryton from the Yongzheng period.

c1723-1735   9in (22.75cm) diam

$500-700   **R&GM**

A Diana cargo dish.

c1817   11in (28cm) diam

$120-180   **R&GM**

A Diana Cargo 'Chess Player' pattern bowl and saucer.

c1817   6in (15cm) diam

$500-600   **RB**

A Chinese Kangxi period famille verte dish, decorated with peony, rockwork and a large butterfly, Ding mark.

10.75in (27.5cm) diam

$1,000-1,500　　　　WW

A pair of Kangxi famille verte plates.

c1700　　　8.5in (21.5cm) diam

$1,000-1,500　　　　R&GM

A Chinese Kangxi famille-verte charger, with shaped rim and centrally decorated with a basket of flowers within radiating panels of flowers and cell borders.

14.5in (36cm) diam

$1,000-1,500　　　　DN

A Chinese Kangxi famille verte fluted saucer dish, decorated centrally with two kylin within alternate radiating panels of birds and Imari iron red mons, minor chips.

8in (20.5cm) diam

$700-1,000　　　　DN

A large Chinese Kangxi famille verte jar and cover, the baluster body decorated with a narrative frieze, with three figures in a pavilion and six equestrians amongst clouds in a landscape, on a wood stand, damage.

23.5in (60cm) high

$28,000-32,000　　　　L&T

An 18thC Chinese Kangxi period Louis XV gilt bronze mounted famille verte vase, with painted decoration and Rococo scroll cover, stamped "Joubert", fitted as a lamp.

base 19.75in (50cm) high

$10,000-15,000　　　　FRE

An 18thC Kangxi period Chinese famille verte gilt ormolu mounted cooler, decorated with figural scene.

8in (20cm) high

$7,000-10,000　　　　BLA

A Chinese 19thC famille verte vase, of baluster form painted with dignitaries and a rocky outcrop with a tree, painted marks.

8.5in (22cm) high

$600-900　　　　HAMG

A pair of late 19th/early 20thC Chinese porcelain famille verte covered vases, worked to show an immortal, applied white flowers and bamboo to body, restoration and repainting.

35in (89cm) high

$2,000-3,000　　　　FRE

A pair of 20thC famille verte Rouleau vases, painted with a female and a scholar on horseback with attendants, base with Kangxi mark in underglazed blue.

18.5in (47cm) high

$400-600　　　　FRE

A matched pair of Chinese Kangxi famille verte boy figures, each holding a pot with a lotus, one with hexagon painted waist band, the other with flower painted waist band, on decorated plinths.

11.5in (28.5cm) high

$4,000-6,000　　　　L&T

A late 18thC pair of famille verte hawks, each with green backs and yellow breasts, perched on a rocky outcrop.

7.75in (19.5cm) high

$600-900　　　　LAW

ORIENTAL CERAMICS

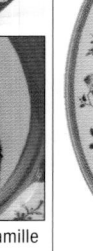

A pair of Yongzheng pink ground famille rose plates.

c1730   8in (20.5cm) wide

$800-1,200   **R&GM**

A Chinese famille rose basin, the center painted with a table and vases containing flowers and fruit, the border with four sprays with flowers, pomegranate and peaches.

c1740   16.5in (42cm) diam

WW   **$8,000-12,000**

An early Qianlong pair of famille rose plates.

c1745   9in (23cm) diam

$600-900   **R&GM**

A Qianlong famille rose oval dish, painted with figures and a traveler outside a pavilion, blue and white border.

11.5in (29cm) wide

$500-600   **PC**

A pair of Qianlong famille rose plates.

c1755   9in (23cm) diam

$150-200   **R&GM**

A Qianlong famille rose blue and white saucer.

c1785   9.5in (24cm) diam

$200-300   **R&GM**

A Cantonese famille rose dish, of shaped square form, painted with figures before a river within a gilt leaf border reserved with iron red scenic panels.

c1800   7.75in (20cm) diam

$400-500   **ROS**

A pair of Chinese Export famille rose Mandarin plates, each decorated with a coronet and inscribed "Exmo Sor Marques de Almendares".

From a service made for the Cuban Marquis de Almendares Ignacio Herrera, ennobled in 1842. Owner of coffee and sugar plantations, railroads and textile mills, Herrera hailed from a prominent Spanish family.

c1845   9.75in (25cm) diam

$2,000-3,000   **FRE**

A pair of Chinese famille rose chargers, painted with a dragon and a rooster fighting against a floral and gilt ground.

c1880   15in (38cm) diam

$1,500-2,000 pair   **HAMG**

A famille rose bowl, painted with panels of figures, birds and landscapes on a foliate gilt ground, restored.

c1760   12.25in (31cm) diam

$700-1,000   **SWO**

A famille rose bowl, painted with two panels of figures on a terrace, within gilt and diaper borders, restored.

c1760   12.25in (31cm) diam

$400-600   **SWO**

A large Qianlong period famille rose bowl, with two large panels containing figures in a landscape and two smaller landscape panels, on a richly enameled and gilded ground, the interior with a cartouche containing a family scene.

1736-95   15in (38cm) diam

$5,000-6,000   **WW**

A famille rose bowl, painted with trailing flowering foliage and rocks, restored.

c1770   15.75in (40cm) diam

$1,200-1,800   **SWO**

A "Mandarin" palette famille rose bowl, with figures and animals in a rural landscape, fine hairline.

c1770   9.75in (25cm) diam

$400-600   **SWO**

A late 18thC Chinese famille rose bowl, painted with flowers and a pink fish-scale diaper band.

10.25in (26cm) diam

$500-700   **CHEF**

A large famille rose bowl, the interior painted with a figural panel and a floral and gilt border, the exterior with figural and landscape panels on a gilt ground, restored.

c1790   16in (41cm) diam

$3,000-4,000   **SWO**

A Daoguang period famille rose medallion bowl, the interior painted in blue with flower sprays and a panel of rockwork and waves, the exterior with four floral panels on a carved yellow enamel ground, with six-character Daoguang seal mark, restored.

1821-50   5.75in (14.5cm) diam

$700-1,000   **WW**

A Chinese Qianlong period famille rose hunting bowl, decorated with two scenes after English hunting engravings showing huntsmen and hounds, the footrim and inner border with gilt spearhead designs, faint cracks.

The painting from which these scenes were engraved is by James Seymour and is entitled 'Beating For A Hare'. Bowls like this were very popular for hunt meetings and would have been ordered in Canton by private traders taking sets of engravings to copy.

c1760   13.25in (33.5cm) diam
$10,000-15,000   **WW**

A large and rare Chinese famille rose hunting bowl, the interior painted with a frieze with huntsmen and hounds encircling a fox, the exterior with panels of Chinese figures hunting a tiger, on a cell-diaper ground.

c1765   15.75in (40cm) diam
$10,000-15,000   **WW**

A Chinese Qianlong period famille rose hunting punch bowl, in the Mandarin palette and gilt, with two shaped panels depicting huntsmen and a pack of hounds, on a 'Y' patterned ground, with further hunting scenes, elaborate rim border, some damage.

c1770   11.75in (30cm) diam
$3,000-4,000   **H&L**

A 19thC Chinese famille rose stick stand, painted in the typical palette with exotic birds, butterflies and foliage, the side molded in high relief with a gilt chilong dragon.

25in (62.5cm) high
$4,000-5,000   **FRE**

A Qianlong period "Mandarin" palette vase, of baluster section, painted with panels of figures.

11.75in. (29.5cm) high
$1,500-2,000   **LAW**

A famille rose vase, of baluster shape, painted with a bird on a flowering branch, signed "Bi Botao" (1885-1961).

Bi Botao was one of the Eight Friends of Zhushan, a group of ceramic artists that painted during the Republic period.

4.25in (11cm) high
$200-300   **LAW**

A Chinese famille rose snuff bottle and stopper, one side painted with figures in a boat and on a bridge in a mountainous landscape, the reverse with calligraphy, the base with a later four character Qianlong mark in iron red.

2.25in (6cm) high
$1,200-1,800   **WW**

A Chinese famille rose enameled glass snuff bottle and stopper, with an octagonal body, one side painted with flowers and pheasants, the other with a bird, rockwork and chrysanthemum, the base with a blue four-character Qianlong mark but later, with gilt metal stopper.

2.25in (5.5cm) high
$500-700   **WW**

A late 19thC Cantonese hexagonal baluster vase decorated in famille rose enamels with continuous band of figures, the neck applied with confronting Dogs of Fo.

23in (59cm) high
$400-600   **DN**

A 19thC pair of pierced Chinese famille rose garden seats, painted in the typical palette with figures, exotic birds, butterflies and foliage.

Provenance: From a private Chester County collection.

18.75in (47cm) high
$5,000-7,000   **FRE**

Two views of a 19thC famille rose figure of a peacock, perched on a rocky outcrop.

12.75in (32.5cm) high
$700-1,000   **LAW**

A Chinese Yongzheng period small saucer, with six-character Yongxheng mark.

5in (13cm) diam

$5,000-6,000 WW

A thinly potted celadon dish, with fluted rim.

11.5in (29.5cm) diam

$300-400 LAW

A 17thC provincial Chinese crackle glazed celadon bulb bowl, with flared rim and standing on three legs.

11.5in (29cm) diam

$1,000-1,500 L&T

A large Chinese Yongzheng period celadon ground bowl, the interior white glazed, six-character Yongzheng mark.

10.25in (26cm) diam

$4,000-6,000 WW

One of a pair of Sang de Boeuf bowls, each with a flared rim, blue square seal mark for Qianlong and of the period.

7.75in (19.5cm) diam

$1,000-1,500 pair LAW

A Chinese Qianlong period coral ground bowl, painted in gilt with a flower spray issuing from the rim, six-character Qianlong seal.

8.25in (21cm) diam

$1,200-1,800 WW

A Sang de Boeuf vase, the squat globular body with an elongated flared neck, probably 18thC.

5.75in (14.5cm) high

$400-600 LAW

An 18thC Chinese celadon kendi form hookah base, designed for the Middle Eastern market, with a metal mounted spout.

9.25in (23.5cm) high

$1,000-1,500 L&T

A Chinese celadon moonflask, Yongzheng mark and period, with scrolled handles to the sides, decorated allover with molded stylized chrysanthemum heads and foliage, blue painted character mark.

11.75in (30cm) high

$500,000-550,000 L&T

A 19thC Chinese bottle vase covered in a thick flambé glaze falling over the foot, the flared neck with dragon handles.

13in (33cm) high

$400-600 DN

A pair of 20thC Chinese green glazed covered vases, worked on the exterior with birds among pine trees, and the base with spurious seal marks.

21in (53.5cm) high

$700-1,000 FRE

One of a large pair of Chinese bottle vases, with fine crackle beneath lustrous green glaze, six-character Kangxi marks but later.

15in (38cm) high

$4,000-6,000 pair WW

A pair of armorial Qianlong plates, inscribed "RS".

c1750	9in (23cm) diam
$1,500-2,000	**R&GM**

A Chinese export enameled porcelain armorial charger with coat of arms over banner in iron red and gilt scroll border.

c1755	14in (36cm) diam
$6,000-9,000	**SK**

A pair of Qianlong armorial meat dishes.

c1785	11.75in (30cm) wide
$4,000-5,000	**R&GM**

A pair of late Kangxi Imari plates.

c1710	8.5in (21.5cm) diam
$600-700	**R&GM**

A Chinese polychrome dragon dish, decorated with five dragons on a breaking wave ground, the reverse with four iron red dragons, with six-character Qianlong mark and probably of the period.

	16in (40.5cm) diam
$4,000-6,000	**WW**

A Qianlong Meissen-style dish, rim chips.

c1750	14in (35.5cm) diam
$2,000-3,000	**R&GM**

A Chinese Qianlong period green dragon dish, painted with a five-clawed dragon in pursuit of a flaming pearl, the reverse with two further dragons and pearls, with six-character Qianlong seal mark, faint hairline.

	7in (18cm) diam
$2,000-4,000	**WW**

An early 19thC Chinese export porcelain gilt bronze mounted dish, with painted scene and underglaze blue border.

	16in (40.5cm) wide
$3,000-4,000	**FRE**

A Qianlong period leaf-shaped dish, decorated with the pseudo tobacco-leaf pattern.

1736-95   8in (20.5cm) wide

$3,000-4,000   **WW**

A rare Wanli period wucai compartmented dish, with six-character Wanli mark within a double circle, some fritting to the edges of the divides, the cover missing.

With the cover this dish could be worth up to ten times more.

1573-1619   8.75in (22cm) diam

$6,000-7,000   **WW**

A rare pair of Kangxi period molded plates, each brightly gilded with pagodas and trees amidst hills and mountains, on a powder blue ground with calligraphy, the borders with cell and flower diaper bands and floral cartouches.

1662-1722   8.25in (21cm) diam

$4,000-6,000   **WW**

An 18thC circular charger, painted with an old man being served saki by a young boy, the border painted in rouge de fer and gilt with precious objects.

13.75in (35cm) diam

$800-1,200   **L&T**

A Canton Persian market dish, decorated with panels of figures, flowers and butterflies on a gold ground, centered with a dated inscription.

1878   15.5in (39cm) diam

$1,500-2,000   **SWO**

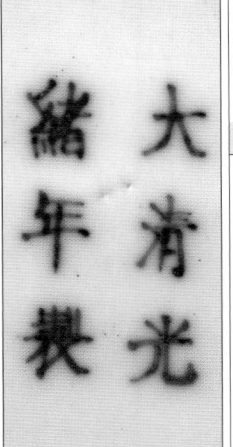

One of a pair of Guangxu period saucer dishes, decorated with aubergine and green dragons on a yellow ground, with six-character Guangxu marks.

4.25in (11cm) diam

$1,500-2,000 PAIR   **WW**

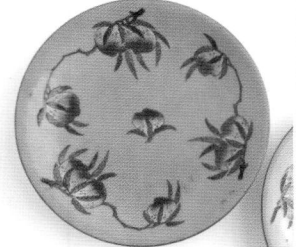

One of a pair of 18thC celadon glazed plates, each of circular form, decorated in enamel with peaches and foliage.

10.25in (26cm) diam

$600-900 PAIR   **ROS**

One of a pair of early 19thC dishes, painted with flowers around the rims, chipped.

10.25in (26cm) diam

$300-400 PAIR   **R&GM**

A Chinese Transitional period Wucai baluster vase, painted with panels of lotus reserved on an iron red ground.

c1650   11in (28cm) high

$2,000-3,000   WW

A large Chinese Kangxi period famille noir vase, decorated with birds perched on rockwork amid peony, the black enamel possibly later, with six-character Chenghua mark.

18in (46cm) high

$2,000-3,000   WW

A small Chinese Kangxi period spinach and egg glazed vase, the sides applied with figures.

6in (15cm) high

$1,500-2,000   WW

A Kangxi double gourd vase, gilt with vases and emblems, on a powder blue ground.

7in (18cm) high

$1,000-1,500   LAW

A Sang de Boeuf and purple flambé double gourd vase, four character mark for Qianlong, but probably later.

10in (25.5cm) high

$700-1,000   LAW

A pair of Chinese export mounted ewers, with 19thC bronze mounts, with sides painted in polychrome and reserves depicting courtiers against a black/white geometric ground.

c1760   6.75in (17cm) high

$5,000-6,000   FRE

A 19thC miniature Chinese export porcelain five piece garniture, comprising two flared cylindrical vases, and three baluster covered vases, decorated with iron red foliage enriched with gilt.

Covered vase 4.5in (11.5cm) high

$1,000-1,500   FRE

A 19thC Chinese slender baluster Wucai vase decorated with figures in a terraced garden, decorative bands to waisted neck.

The 'wucai' (five color) palette was developed during the reign of Jiajing (1522-66). Decoration is in underglaze blue and overglaze iron-red, green, brown, yellow and black.

20in (50cm) high

$3,000-4,000   DN

A 20thC Chinese ruby red ground enameled porcelain vase, with tubular gilt handles, bird and flower cartouches, and scrolling lotus ground, base with Qianlong seal mark.

15.5in (39.5cm) high

$400-600   FRE

Two early 20thC Chinese celadon porcelain jardinières, with molded floral decoration, two shaped reserves with underglaze blue flowers and insects, and printed blue marks, with hardwood stands.

15.5in (39.5cm) wide

$6,000-9,000   FRE

A rare pair of late 18thC Chinese export Pomegranate 'Tobacco leaf' soup tureens, covers and stands, over an oval stand, restored.

7.5in (19cm) wide

$55,000-65,000 PAIR   FRE

A Chinese Qianlong period armorial fluted bowl, decorated with the arms of MacDonald accollée with Forbes, the borders with fruiting vines, a crest and motto "Nec tempore nec fato".

c1795   9.75in (24.5cm) diam

$2,000-3,000   WW

A 19thC export bowl, the interior painted with fish below fruiting vines, the exterior with water birds en grisaille below iron red and gilt flowers on a scrolling foliage rim band.

15.25in (39cm) diam

$500-600   **CHEF**

A Samson copy of a Chinese export bowl, with figures painted in enamels on terraces, on a bronze stand.

c1880   *15.75in (40cm) diam*

$1,500-2,000   **SWO**

GODS IN CHINESE ART

- Religion in China can be broadly summed up as consisting of the 'Three Ways' – Taoism, Buddhism and Confucianism. Chinese popular religion has assimilated aspects from each of these paths.
- Religious art in China depicts many gods. One of the most frequently seen is Hotei, the 'fat Buddha'. Rubbing his belly is said to bring luck and prosperity.
- The Taoist pantheon includes the Eight Immortals, who are most commonly represented by reference to their individual attributes. Li Tieguai, for example, is venerated as the dispenser of medicine and he carries a double gourd.
- True Buddhism has no gods but instead venerates enlightened beings called Bodhisattvas. The most popular Chinese Bodhisattva is Guanyin, associated with mercy and comparable to Mary in the Christian tradition.
- Some historical figures, such as the poet Li Po, have attained the status of minor deities and are often represented in Chinese art.

A Guangxu period bowl, decorated with two green dragons above aubergine waves on a yellow ground, with six-character Guangxu mark, cracked and chipped.

1875-1908   *5.5in (14cm) diam*

$700-1,000   **WW**

A Kangxi period biscuit porcelain figure of Guanyin, seated in meditation on a detachable lotus throne and high stand, with splashes of green, aubergine and yellow glaze, chip and hairline crack.

Guanyin is the Chinese Bodhisattva of mercy.

1662-1722   *10in (25.5cm) high*

$1,000-1,500   **SWO**

An unusual 18thC Kangxi period biscuit figure of Guanyin, seated in lilitasana on a throne and holding a child on her lap, her robes glazed in white, deep blue, turquoise and ochre, hairline fracture.

12.5in (31cm) high

$700-1,000   **SWO**

A rare Kangxi period biscuit porcelain figure of Li Po, modeled asleep in a green robe beside a yellow glazed wine jar, restored.

Li Po was a poet who became the Taoist wine immortal and patron saint of wine merchants.

1662-1722   *6.75in (17cm) high*

$1,000-1,500   **SWO**

A 17thC Kangxi biscuit figure of an Immortal, crisply modeled with robes glazed in deep blue, turquoise and ochre.

8.75in (22cm) high

$700-1,000   **SWO**

A Chinese pale green glazed porcelain pot, with label for "John Sparks Ltd".

2.75in (7cm) diam

$150-200 **GORL**

A mid-18thC cylindrical quart mug, painted in the Imari style with flowers.

5.5in (14cm) high

$500-600 **CHEF**

A porcelain mug, made for the American market, painted with a three-master flying the American flag between blue and red borders.

c1780 *4.25in (11cm) high*

$1,000-1,500 **SWO**

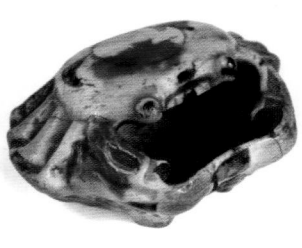

A Kangxi period biscuit porcelain brush washer, in the form of a crab, with a splashed green, yellow and aubergine glaze, hairline crack.

1662-1722 *3in (7.5cm) high*

$700-1,000 **SWO**

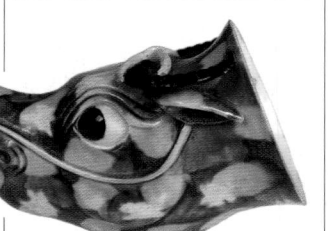

A rare Kangxi period biscuit porcelain rhyton, in the form of a buffalo's head with a rope through the nose, glazed in patches of yellow, aubergine and green.

The rhyton, or libation cup, was used for drinking and pouring liquid on the ground as an offering to the gods.

1662-1722 *4.5in (11cm) long*

$3,000-4,000 **SWO**

A pair of Guangxu period wine cups, each decorated in overglaze iron red with two dragons chasing a flaming pearl above breaking waves, with six-character Guangxu marks.

1875-1908 *2in (5cm) high*

$4,000-5,000 **WW**

A large 19thC tureen and cover, modeled as a carp, molded with scales and painted with brown, pink and black enamels, the interior painted turquoise with Chinese inscription, chipped.

17in (43cm) wide

$3,000-4,000 **WW**

A pair of Canton porcelain Buddhist lion incense holders, damaged.

c1840 *4.25in (11cm) wide*

$500-600 **SWO**

A 20thC circular box and cover, of erotic interest, the cover painted with a horse between trees, the interior with coupling figures, with four-character Qianlong mark.

3.25in (8.5cm) wide

$3,000-5,000 **WW**

A Satsuma earthenware dish with karako at play on a riverbank in a lobed square central cartouche, on a ground of sparrows in flight, above buildings in a river landscape, signed "Nakumura Barkeizo".

8.25in (21cm) diam

$12,000-20,000   BD

A Satsuma earthenware plate with a shaped and pierced rim, raised and flared, of lobed section, decorated with a procession of an elephant and dancing karako, two cartouches to base stating: "This Satsuma ware was first made by lords of Satsuma 300 years ago and received a high accolade. It was first made as a presentation piece in secrecy. After the Emperor's discovery, he granted permission for the ware to be sold publicly throughout the country and made this piece special."

8.25in (21cm) diam

$20,000-30,000   BD

A Satsuma pottery bowl, decorated with a procession of figures, a view of Fuji beyond, the exterior elaborately gilt on a blue ground, signed, some rubbing and staining.

9.75in (25cm) diam

$1,000-1,500   DN

A Satsuma bowl, with a shaped rim, the interior and exterior painted with immortals, signed on a rectangular tablet.

8.5in (22cm) wide

$200-300   LAW

A Japanese Kozan Satsuma bowl and cover, cover painted with seated ceremonial figures, the bowl interior painted with women in a garden setting, the base with signature.

c1900   *5in (12.5cm) diam*

$1,000-1,500   HAMG

A pair of Japanese satsuma vases, Kinkozan.

5.75in (14.5cm) high

$1,000-1,500   **DB**

CLOSER LOOK AT A PAIR OF SATSUMA VASES

Satsuma ware was developed in 16thC Japan but not known in the West until 1872, the Japanese market opened to the West and Satsuma ware became a very desirable and expensive export.

Exceptional pieces from the Meiji period (1868-1912) took months to make, as the miniature paintings took great skill and experience.

This piece shows exceptional detail in the typical scenes of leisure and domestic activities. Foliage and flowers, also painted freehand, typically form backgrounds or borders.

The base is signed and a cartouche, asserting the authenticity of the piece, indicate its quality.

Nakamura Barkei's work is highly collectable and demonstrates quality painting at such a small scale.

Details were added with a single rat-hair to give exceptional detailing on faces and robes.

Enamel and gilding are applied on top of the creamy colored, crazed glaze, in slight relief.

A pair of late 19thC Satsuma vases, necks with mythical animal handles, morning glory in colored enamels and gilt, decorated with four overlapping panels depicting figures at leisure, the borders of scrolling foliage, painted in colored enamels and gilt, signed "Nakamura Barkei".

$20,000-25,000   **BD**

A fine Japanese satsuma vase, signed "Kinkozan", Meiji period (1868-1912), painted in gilt and colored enamels with two reserves depicting Japanese courtiers and Samurai, on a gilt enhanced cobalt blue ground, gilt signature.

10in (25.5cm) high.

$3,000-4,000   **FRE**

A Japanese Satsuma baluster vase, each side decorated with figures beneath bamboo and wisteria on a gilt floral blue ground, no mark, Meiji 1868-1912.

9.5in (24.5cm) high

$700-1,000   **WW**

A large Japanese Satsuma vase, decorated with five storks beneath flowers and foliage, the inner rim with four Satsuma mon, gilt signature, Meiji 1868-1912.

12in (31cm) high

$700-1,000   **WW**

A pair of Japanese Satsuma vases, with elephant head mask handles, and painted with chrysanthemums and prunus trees, Meiji period, chip and hairline to rim.

7.25in (18.5cm) high

$300-400   **HAMG**

A Japanese Satsuma small baluster vase decorated with a panel of Bijin and a landscape panel on floral ground, signed "Senzan".

5in (13cm) high

$1,000-1,500   **DN**

A pair of Japanese Satsuma baluster vases with square necks, the sides finely decorated with panels of Bijin, Fuji and flowers, signed, one broken.

8in (20cm) high

$1,200-1,800   **DN**

A late 19thC Satsuma vase, of square form with re-entrant corners, painted with panels of figures in a landscape, birds, foliage and various devices, the shoulder decorated with flowerheads.

6in (15cm) high

$300-400   **ROS**

A Japanese Meiji period Satsuma hexagonal section vase, decorated with panels of figures in gardens on a blue ground, unsigned, slight wear to gilt.

1868-1912   *10in (25cm) high*

$700-1,000   **WW**

A late 19thC Japanese Satsuma vase.

6in (15cm) high

$1,500-2,000   **DB**

A Japanese Satsuma koro and cover, of square form, with gilt elephant's trunk handles, painted with Japanese ladies seated on a terrace and landscape scenes, painted marks, signed Kiyozan, knop re-stuck.

c1900   *6in (15cm) high*

$300-400   **HAMG**

A late 19th/early 20thC Japanese Satsuma koro, surmounted with a gilded Fu lion, decorated with butterflies and geometric bands in a typical satsuma palette, cracks and restoration.

30in (76cm) high

$1,200-1,500   **FRE**

An early 20thC Japanese Satsuma baluster vase, converted to a lamp, with gilded and painted neck with diaper border, the body decorated with songbirds and flowers.

Vase 23in (58.5cm) high

$2,000-3,000   **FRE**

A Japanese Satsuma cylindrical box and cover decorated with panels of Bijin on an elaborate ground, chrysanthemum finial, signed.

3in (9cm) high

$120-180   **DN**

A Japanese Satsuma wine pot and cover finely decorated with panels of figures, flowers and landscapes on a net ground, chrysanthemum knop, signed "Meizan sei" inside cover, impressed "Taisan" to body.

5in (13cm) high

$7,000-10,000   **DN**

A Satsuma circular box, decorated with a warrior deflecting arrows, signed.

4.25in (10.75cm) diam

$300-400   **GORL**

A Japanese Satsuma figure of Daikoku, by Maruji, in gilt floral and geometrically patterned hat and robes, leaning against a foliate and floral decorated sack.

Daikoku is one of the seven gods of fortune, in Taoist beliefs. He is variously considered to the the god of wealth (or harvest) or of the home, specifically the kitchen. His image featured on the first Japanese bank note.

7.75in (20cm) high

$1,000-1,500   **L&T**

JAPANESE ARITA WARE

A 17thC Arita saucer dish, of lobed shape, well painted with flowering plants, brown rim, the exterior with scrolls, square seal mark.

7.5in (18cm) diam

$150-200   **LAW**

Two large 17thC Japanese Arita kraak style blue and white porcelain chargers.

17.75in (44.5cm) diam

$6,000-9,000   **NAG**

An early 18thC Arita blue and white dish, with an ogee rim, the center painted with waterside cranes, the well with alternate panels of crossed leaves and flowering plants, blue square seal mark.

11in (28cm) diam

$300-500   **LAW**

One of a pair of early 18thC Japanese Arita blue and white dishes, painted in the kraak style, each with a panel containing a large insect, rockwork, flowers and foliage, the reverse with flower scrolls.

16.5in (42cm) diam

$4,000-5,000 PAIR   **WW**

A Japanese Arita blue and white saucer dish, decorated with iris, Kin mark, probably 18thC.

9in (22.5cm)

$600-900   **WW**

An important Japanese Aritaware deep dish of large size, the border with two free-form vignettes of birds, the center with landscape vignette of hawk and waterfall, the reverse with red and underglaze blue floral designs.

From late 17thC, Arita became an important area for the production of blue and white, Imari and Kakiemon porcelain for export to Europe. These were transported to the port of Imari, shipped to the Dutch trading center at Nagasaki and then to Europe.

c1710   *21in (52.5cm) diam*

$5,000-6,000   **NA**

An early 18thC Arita saucer dish, of fluted chrysanthemum form, the interior painted with banded hedges, prunus and chrysanthemum mons, the exterior similarly painted.

7.25in (18.5cm) diam

$200-300   **LAW**

A late 17th to early 18thC set of five Arita Imari saucer dishes, the centers painted with a jetty amongst water plants, the well with paulonia scrolls and chrysanthemums.

9.5in (24.5cm) diam

$2,000-3,000 SET   **LAW**

A late 17thC Arita oviform vase and cover decorated in underglaze blue with panels of floral sprays, decorative borders.

$3,000-4,000   **DN**

An 18thC Japanese Arita tokuri, of square form, painted in underglaze blue with riverscape and swastika.

7.25in (18.5cm) high

$2,000-3,000   **BEA**

A Japanese Arita bottle.

c1800   *10.75in (27.5cm) high*

$600-900   **DB**

A late 17thC/early 18thC Japanese Imari plate painted with central sprig of prunus within pendant floral lappets and pearls alternating with yin and yan shaped pomegranates on the rim.

8.5in (21.5cm) diam

$300-400   **CHEF**

An unusual Japanese Imari blue and white dish, with a crab design.

c1715   *16.25in (41.5cm) diam*

$2,000-3,000   **R&GM**

An early 18thC Imari saucer dish, with molded shaped rim, molded and painted with chrysanthemum sprays.

7.25in (18cm) diam

$200-300   **LAW**

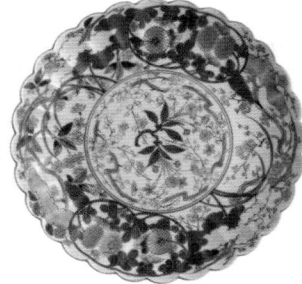

An 18thC Imari saucer dish with fluted body, the center painted with flowering prunus, the rim with panels of chrysanthemum amongst clouds and prunus.

11in (28cm) diam

$300-500   **LAW**

One of a pair of late 19th or early 20thC Japanese Imari chargers, each painted with a vase of peonies, the wide fluted border with panels of flowers and foliate designs.

18.5in (46.5cm) diam

$1,200-1,800 PAIR   **HAMG**

One of a set of six early 20thC Japanese Imari plates, stencilled with central blue flower within alternating panels, on fluted sides within the wavy rims.

8.25in (21cm) diam

$200-300 SET   **CHEF**

An early 20thC Japanese Imari deep dish, painted with a phoenix over a pawlonia tree, the cavetto with scholar and fish vignettes on a blue wave scroll band, barbed rim pawlonia on brocade panels with chrysanthemum heads.

12in (30cm) diam

$300-400   **CHEF**

A pair of early 20thC Imari chargers, the central bowls of flowers within fluted rims painted with shishi panels alternating with peonies.

18.5in (47cm) diam

$1,000-1,500 PAIR   **CHEF**

A late 17th/early 18thC pair of Japanese Imari vases with ribbed sides molded with flowerheads and decorated overall in underglaze blue, iron red and gilt with flowers beneath a collar of flowers.

14in (35cm) diam

$600-900 PAIR   **DN**

A late 17thC/early 18thC Japanese Imari vase, the baluster shape painted with two exotic birds flying above red flowers growing on spindly blue stems.

10in (25cm) high

$400-600   **CHEF**

An Imari pattern chamber pot, the exterior painted with cartouches of flowers, reserved on a peony scrolled ground.

c1750   *9.25in (23.5cm) diam*

$300-400   **LAW**

A rare Japanese Imari tokuri, modeled as Hotie seated on a gourd holding an uchiwa, decorated in iron red and green enamels with flowers, crack to reverse.

Tokuri are sake containers.

c1680   *8.25in (21cm) high*

$5,000-7,000   **WW**

A CLOSER LOOK AT A KAKIEMON ELEPHANT

Kakiemon porcelain has a milky white body, with over-glaze enamels in iron red, blue, turquoise, yellow, black and occasionally purple.

A raised elephant trunk is a sign of good fortune.

From the mid-17thC, animals painted in the Kakiemon style were highly prized by European collectors.

Decorative elements are sparsely applied to emphasize the quality of the milky-white porcelain.

A 17thC Kakiemon porcelain elephant.

It is thought that the first real elephants were seen in Japan in 1408. There are brief mentions of a 'black elephant' brought over from the southern barbarian countries to the court of the Emperor Go-Komatsu. The first known documented models of Kakiemon porcelain elephants to arrive in Europe were those at the magnificent Elizabethan mansion Burghley House in Lincolnshire. These were 'the two large elephants' standing with raised trunks on the bedchamber chimney-piece of John Cecil, fifth Earl of Exeter, inventoried in 1688.

$220,000-280,000   **BD**

A 17thC Japanese Kakiemon porcelain dish.

7.5in (19cm) diam

$1,000-1,500   **NAG**

A small Japanese kakiemon porcelain dish, the center decorated with a plant pot with rocks and flowering plants, the border with flowering prunus branches.

c1700   5in (12.5cm) diam

$1,200-1,800   **R&GM**

A Japanese Kakiemon plate.

c1700   8.5in (21.5cm) diam

$4,000-5,000   **R&GM**

A Japanese Kakiemon style plate, painted with central phoenix, a pomegranate and prunus spray, the reverse with three cloud scrolls.

c1900   9.5in (24cm) diam

$400-600   **WW**

A 19thC Japanese foliate molded bowl, decorated in the Kakiemon style with prunus and pomegranate, the interior with tied sheaves and a flowering prunus tree.

If this were 18thC it would be worth $15,000-20,000.

7.5in (19cm) diam

$3,000-4,000   **WW**

A 19thC Japanese Kutani figure.

11.75in (30cm) high

$1,000-1,500　DB

A Japanese Kutani cat.

14in (36cm) long

$1,000-1,500　DB

A Japanese Kutani dish, probably 19thC, the center painted with a figure surrounded by flowers, foliage and stylized panels, the reverse with a green geometric design and seal mark.

14.25in (36.5cm) diam

$500-700　WW

A Japanese blue and white Nabeshima type dish, painted in blue with flowers and leaves issuing from rockwork, raised on a high comb foot, probably 19thC.

8.25in (21cm) diam

$100-150　WW

A large Japanese molded blue and white dish, depicting figures in a coastal landscape.

c1900　15in (38cm) diam

$120-180　R&GM

A large Japanese blue and white dish, decorated with peony and prunus.

c1900　21.5in (54.5cm) high

$400-600　WW

A Fukagawa small vase painted with flags, signed.

4.25in (11cm) high

$500-700　LAW

A large Japanese earthenware vase finely decorated with panels of warriors on an iron red ground.

14in (35cm) high

$1,000-1,500　DN

A Japanese earthenware figure of Kwannon seated on a rockwork base with flowing stream, robes finely decorated with scattered flowers, signed.

23in (59cm) high

$5,000-7,000　DN

An Osmanic Iznik white tile, painted in underglaze blue, turquoise, green and red with black lines.

c1570　7.75in (19.5cm) wide

$15,000-20,000　NAG

CLOISONNÉ

ORIENTAL

An 18thC Chinese cloisonné censer cast with panels of Arabic inscriptions on red ground scattered with lotus and precious objects, gilt rim pierced with two strap handles, blue interior, seal mark.

6in (14cm) diam

$800-1,000 DN

A Chinese cloisonné globular incense burner and pierced cover on slender stem and round foot, decorated with scrolling lotus on blue ground, bat handles.

9in (23cm) high

$1,000-1,500 DN

A pair of Chinese cloisonné baluster vases decorated with flowers issuing from pierced rockwork on blue ground beneath stiff leaf bands, probably early 19thC.

10in (25cm) high

$700-1,000 DN

A good pair of early 19thC Chinese cloisonne dishes, decorated with butterflies, birds and foliage on a key fret ground, the rims and bases gilt.

1,000-1,500

$1,000-1,500 WW

An impressive matched pair of 19thC Japanese Palace Cloisonne Vases, depicting the cycle of mourning doves, with heavy sprinkling of pyrites to ground brown body, some damage.

Made by J. Ando & Co. Believed to have been exhibited at the 1893 St. Louis Exposition.

60in (152.5cm) high

$60,000-80,000 FRE

A large pair of Japanese cloisonne baluster shaped vases, each decorated with a dragon and a tiger on a dark green ground.

12in (30.5cm) high

$2,000-3,000 L&T

A 20thC Japanese Cloisonne vase, with bamboo and song birds under a red ground, and wire worked to show broad leaf chrysanthemum.

12in (30.5cm) high

$700-900 FRE

A Japanese cloisonné vase, by Ando & Co.

8.25in (21cm) high

$2,000-3,000 DB

A rare Japanese cloisonné vase, by Ando & Co.

7.75in (20cm) high

$5,000-7,000 DB

A fine Japanese cloisonné tripod censer, Meiji Period (1868-1912), the compressed body with pierced cover, twin handles and raised on three splayed feet, decorated in colored enamels.

$4,000-6,000 FRE

A cloisonné box and cover, of rounded rectangular form, the deep blue ground with a sparrow in a flowering branch.

c1900 *4.25in (10.5cm) wide*

$700-1,000 SWO

104

A pair of Chinese gold splash bronze baluster shaped vases with dragon mask and ring handles, dark brown ground, six character Xuande marks but probably 18thC.

11in (29cm) high

$2,000-3,000	DN

A large Chinese bronze incense burner and cover, probably 18thC, in the form of a double finger citron, with seal mark and traces of old gilding.

19.25in (49cm) long

$3,000-4,000	WW

An unusual late 18thC Chinese silver-gilt and enameled jardinière, with a phoenix, an elephant, rockwork, a pagoda and insects beneath a pomegranate tree, the sides applied with filigree, scrollwork cartouches and enameled sprays.

15.75in (40cm) high

$12,000-18,000	WW

A 19thC Chinese sheet bronze figure of a seated Arhat, with red and gold foliate and diaper face gilded with black painted beard and eyebrows.

21in (53.5cm) high

$1,000-1,500	FRE

A 20thC Chinese white metal model of a gun boat, mounted on a wave carved wooden stand.

11in (28cm) long

$1,000-1,500	ROS

Two Chinese iron figures of Dogs of Fo, each seated with left paw on a puppy, re-gilded.

13in (32cm) high

$400-600	DN

A Japanese Meiji period bronze figure of striding elephant with raised trunk, signed "...chika sei".

7in (18cm) long

$400-600	DN

A Japanese Meiji period bronze group of elephant being attacked by tigers, signed "jozan saku", missing tusks.

8in (20cm) high

$500-700	DN

A Japanese bronze figure of prowling tiger, signed.

16in (40cm) long

$600-800	DN

A 19thC Japanese bronze incense burner in the form of a rooster, modeled naturalistically.

10in (25.5cm) high

$1,500-2,000	L&T

A pair of Persian 19thC Qajar damascened steel rams, each in two halves, decorated in gold damascening with stylized hair, with red glass eyes, a band of floral and foliate decoration, the back with a floral cartouche.

7.5in (19cm) wide

$7,000-10,000	L&T

A large Japanese bronze group, Meiji Period (1868-1912), in the form of two fighting samurai, on a naturalistic base.

27in (67.5cm) high

$6,000-9,000　　　　　　　**FRE**

A Japanese Meiji period inlaid bronze koro, formed as a kneeling figure holding an urn surmounted by a fu-lion, raised on a naturalistic base.

13in (33cm) high

$3,000-4,000　　　　　　　**FRE**

A Japanese Meiji period bronze figure, modeled as a young boy holding a bird's nest, signed.

16in (40.5cm) high

$3,000-4,000　　　　　　　**FRE**

A Japanese Meiji period bronze figure, of a grotesque male holding a bowl and cover decorated with cast dragon on a hardwood base.

32.5in (83cm) high

$10,000-15,000　　　　　　　**L&T**

A possibly 17th or 18thC Thai gilt bronze figure of Buddha, probably Sakyamuni, with several skeletal figures, over a painted gilded bronze paneled base, with losses.

12in (30.5cm) high

$1,500-2,000　　　　　　　**FRE**

A Japanese bronze slender ovoid vase finely decorated with Kanzan and Jittoku reading scroll in a mountainous landscape, signed "Shunmin", the base signed "Mitsuyiki".

9in (22cm) high

$5,000-7,000　　　　　　　**DN**

A late Meiji period Japanese reticulated bronze vase, with flower head form neck, elephant mask handles, the side applied with a tea kettle with scrolls, an ovoid vase to reverse, raised on fu-lion mask scroll feet.

27in (68.5cm) high

$5,000-7,000　　　　　　　**FRE**

A small Japanese shibayama vase and cover, with inlaid flowers, dragon form handles, and a white metal flaring foot, signed.

4in (10cm) high

$1,000-1,500　　　　　　　**L&T**

A pair of Japanese white metal vases, decorated with cast flowers and fruit, with fixed pierced hardwood stands.

5.5in (14cm) high

$500-700　　　　　　　**L&T**

A Japanese koro, finely incised ground covered in deep red enamel with pierced wood cover with ivory figure of Hotei on wood stand.

8in (20cm) diam

$600-900　　　　　　　**DN**

A 20thC Japanese bronze urn decorated in high relief dragon decoration.

75in (191cm) high

$6,000-8,000　　　　　　　**POOK**

A Japanese bronze tsuba, very high relief design of fishermen pulling boat and nets from sea among rocks, Tokugawa period.

c1800   2.75in (7cm) diam

$200-300   **BLO**

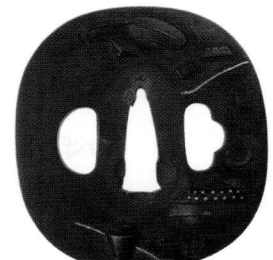

A Japanese bronze tsuba, very high relief design of tea ceremony kettle with inlaid silver studs on ishime, with jar silver and gold spoons and feather, Tokugawa period.

c1820   2.75in (7cm) long

$150-200   **BLO**

A Japanese iron tsuba, openwork and relief design of a carp climbing a waterfall, with blossoms above, gilt inlaid eyes, signed "Tomo-hisa", Tokugawa period.

c1860   3in (7.5cm) diam

$150-200   **BLO**

A Japanese iron tsuba, with inlay and relief design of a dragon entwined in caves, flames flaring, signed faintly, Tokugawa period.

c1860   2.75in (7cm) wide

$120-180   **BLO**

A Japanese iron tsuba, relief carving and openwork design of leaping carp and waves, gilt fins and silvered eyes, with two inset shakudo panels (copper with 5% gold content), Tokugawa period.

c1860   3.25in (8cm) diam

$120-180   **BLO**

A Japanese iron tsuba, with relief design of eagle harassing monkey in cave above a waterfall in mountains, both with gilt inlaid eyes, signed in soshu, a fine Chosu piece, late Tokugawa period.

c1860   3.25in (8cm) wide

$400-600   **BLO**

A Japanese iron tsuba, relief design of a coastal landscape, man punting passenger under gilt awning, signed "Nara Haru-chika", an early Itosukashi piece, Tokugawa period.

c1860   3in (7.5cm) diam

$200-300   **BLO**

A Japanese iron tsuba, openwork design of two Marubori dragons, signed E-gawa Yoshi-hisa of Mito, Tokugawa period.

c1860   3.25in (8cm) diam

$100-150   **BLO**

A Japanese iron tsuba, with relief and inlay design of temples and blossom trees in mountain landscape, two people crossing a bridge, faintly signed, late Tokugawa period.

c1860   2.75in (7cm) wide

$120-180   **BLO**

A Japanese gilt copper (Shibuichi) tsuba, with detailed katakiri engraving of a Shishi (Chinese guardian lion) by a waterfall, signed in sosho Ki-rei, with matching Fuchi (the ring which the hilt base fits into), hardwood case with cords.

Katakiri is a method of incised chiseling using the burin to achieve lines of varying width and depth: capable of producing work of great beauty. Ki-rei's work is rare. He was a samurai of Ki-i.

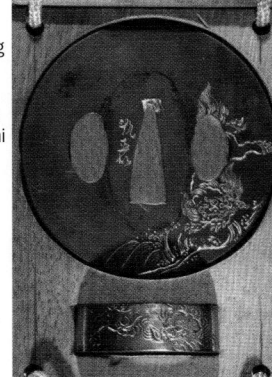

2.75in (7cm) wide

$250-300   **BLO**

A Japanese ivory okimono of an archer, standing holding a staff, quiver of arrows on his back, a further arrow at his feet, his costume with engraved, stained detail, on wooden stand, signed, sword detached.

21in (53.5cm) high

$4,000-6,000   **HAMG**

A late 19thC Japanese carved ivory okimono, modeled as an old farmer with a young child by his side, with a signed red tablet to the base.

8.25in (21cm) high

$600-700   **ROS**

A Japanese ivory okimono of a Geisha, standing holding a song bird and cage, her kimono engraved, signed "Gyoku" with seal, some damage.

c1900   10.75in (27cm) high

$1,000-1,500   **HAMG**

A Japanese ivory okimono of a musician, a basket of masks hung from his shoulder, on wooden stand, signed, sword detached.

21in (53.5cm) high

$3,000-4,000   **HAMG**

A Chinese ivory figure of a goddess, standing with one hand raised and a scrolled brush on lotus leaf base.

10in (25.5cm) high

$200-300   **GORL**

A small fruitwood and ivory figure of an old man, signed.

3.75in (9.5cm) high

$150-200   **CA**

An early 20thC Japanese ivory and shark's tooth figure caught in the moment of raising a knife to ward off an attacking snake.

c1910   7.5in (19cm) high

$300-400   **CHEF**

An early 20thC Japanese ivory and shark's tooth group of two men, one standing holding a basket of lotus on his back and the other seated on his bundle, smoking a pipe.

4.5in (11.5cm) high

$300-400   **CHEF**

An early 20thC Japanese ivory group of a mother with her children, a kettle on a drum shaped table to the other side, lacquer seal mark.

3.5in (9cm) high

$500-700   **CHEF**

A 20thC Japanese carved ivory figure group, depicting an old fisherman and a young boy, with two character mark to the base.

10.25in (26cm) high

$400-600   **ROS**

A 19thC Japanese ivory and hardwood figure, with ivory face, fan, hands, and feet, the body and head dress of carved and colored hardwood, on a timber base.

12in (30.5cm) high

$3,000-5,000   **FRE**

A 19thC Japanese bronze and ivory okimono, in bronze with ivory face, feet and rice basket, on a timber base.

11In (28cm) high

$2,000-3,000   **FRE**

A large Japanese Meiji period sectional ivory carving of a man, carrying a basket of flowers, raised on a large covered wood stand, damaged.

20.5in (52cm) high

$2,000-3,000   **WW**

A Japanese ivory okimono of a musician, standing whilst playing a stringed instrument, a basket of masks hung from his shoulder, his costume with engraved stained detail, wooden stand, signed, sword detached.

21in (53.5cm) high

$3,000-4,000   **HAMG**

A Japanese ivory okimono of a fisherman, standing holding a basket of fish and a club, his coat with engraved, stained decoration, incised signature.

14in (35cm) high

$4,000-6,000   **HAMG**

A late 18th/early 19thC Oriental carved ivory bust of a young lady.

5.5in (14cm) high

$3,000-4,000   **SWO**

CLOSER LOOK AT AN IVORY NETSUKE

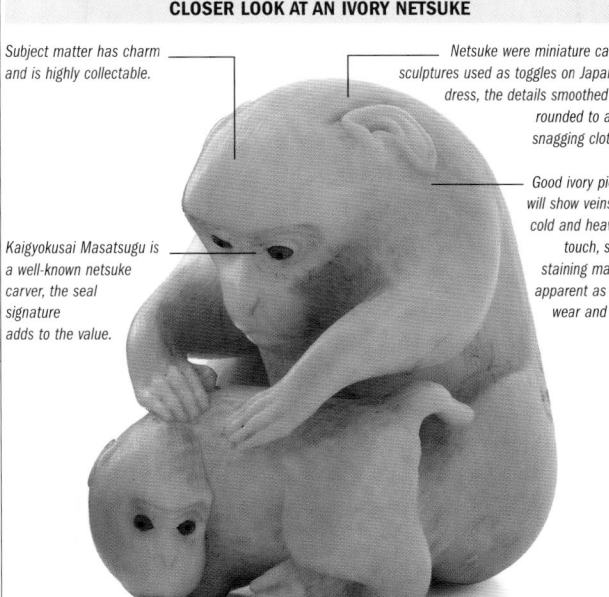

Subject matter has charm and is highly collectable.

Netsuke were miniature carved sculptures used as toggles on Japanese dress, the details smoothed and rounded to avoid snagging clothes.

Good ivory pieces will show veins, be cold and heavy to touch, sepia staining may be apparent as may wear and dirt.

Kaigyokusai Masatsugu is a well-known netsuke carver, the seal signature adds to the value.

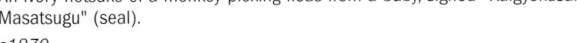

An ivory netsuke of a monkey picking fleas from a baby, signed "Kaigyokusai Masatsugu" (seal).

c1870

$30,000-40,000   **BD**

An 18thC Japanese ivory netsuke, depicting a shishi dog.

2in (5cm) long

$2,000-3,000   **DB**

A stag antler netsuke of Kwangu on horseback.

$6,000-9,000   **BD**

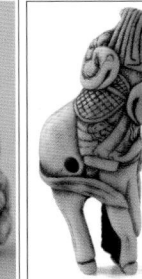

An ivory netsuke of a man seated, partially clothed, holding a gourd and a fan, signed "Rio" (Kawara).

c1850

$8,000-12,000   **BD**

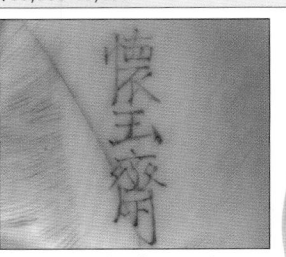

An ivory netsuke of a seated puppy playing with a section of bamboo, signed "Kaigyokusai" (Masatsugu).

$20,000-25,000   **BD**

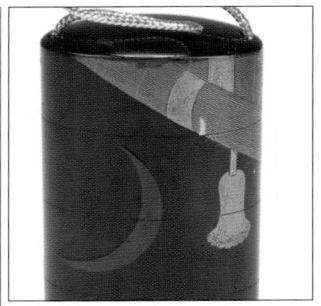

A 19thC Japanese lacquered four case inro decorated with crescent moon scene behind raised bamboo blind, in shades of gold takamakie with gold foil details, gyobu-nashiji interior.

4in (10cm) high

$800-1,000   **DN**

A 19thC Japanese five case inro decorated on a roiro ground in gold hiramakie with a summer retreat by a river flowing through a mountainous landscape, nashiji interior, unsigned, with a lacquered wood netsuke of seated Sarumawashi.

4in (10cm) high

$800-1,000   **DN**

A late 19thC Japanese [maki-e] lacquered 'tortoiseshell' cigar case decorated in tones of gold, black and red with exotic birds in trees above rock pools.

4.5in (12cm) high

$100-150   **CHEF**

A good Japanese gold lacquer five case inro, decorated with tsuba on a complex diaper ground, one end decorated with mother of pearl, three character signature for Kajikawa, Meiji 1868-1912, and a pink hard stone ojime.

$2,000-3,000   **WW**

A Japanese four case gold ground inro decorated with dragons inlaid in ebony, horn and carved in relief to both sides, nashiji interior, signed "Kajkawa".

3in (8cm) high

$800-1,000   **DN**

A Japanese gold lacquer five-case inro, decorated in hiramakie with leafy plants, with nashiji interior, the base with signature.

4in (10cm) long

$600-900   **HAMG**

A 19thC Japanese lacquer box and cover decorated in hiramakie, takamakie and kirigane with flowers on a nashiji ground.

5.5in (14cm) wide

$300-400   **DN**

A late 19thC Chinese cinnabar lacquer covered urn on stand, with geometric design to rim and daoist figures in relief to body, some minor losses, two feet broken off stand.

24in (61cm) high

$3,000-4,000   **FRE**

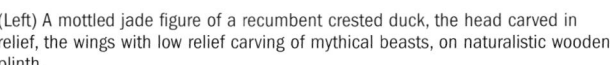

An 18thC Chinese jade deer and young.

3in (7.5cm) long

$4,000-6,000 DB

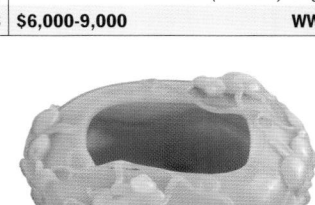

An 18thC Chinese jade carving of two bamboo shoots, partially eaten by bugs.

5in (12.5cm) long

$6,000-9,000 WW

(Left) A mottled jade figure of a recumbent crested duck, the head carved in relief, the wings with low relief carving of mythical beasts, on naturalistic wooden plinth.

8.25in (21cm) wide

$32,000-38,000 L&T

(Right) A Chinese Moghul style twin-handled jade bowl and carved hardwood stand, the bowl of chrysanthemum form.

8.5in (21.5cm) diam

$7,000-10,000 L&T

A Chinese jade oval brush washer, carved with two monkeys and fruiting peach branches.

4in (10cm) wide

$800-1,200 WW

A Chinese Ming dynasty jade toad.

2.75in (7cm) long

$3,000-4,000 DB

A Chinese jade Ming dynasty vase.

4.75in (12cm) high

$1,200-1,800 DB

A large 19thC Chinese Spinach jade archaic covered vase, the cover worked to show Buddhistic lions, Qianlong seal mark to shoulder.

13in (33cm) high

$8,000-10,000 FRE

A 19th/20thC Chinese green hardstone vase and cover, of square section, carved on each face with flowers and foliage.

9.75in (25cm) wide

$1,000-1,500 WW

A pair of probably 20thC Chinese archaic form jade covered censors, surmounted by a fu lion, carved in relief with archaic style motifs, with chips and restoration.

19.75in (50cm) high

$7,000-10,000 FRE

A gray banded agate incense burner and cover, the squat globular body with pierced qilin handles and knop.

2.75in (7cm) diam

$500-700 LAW

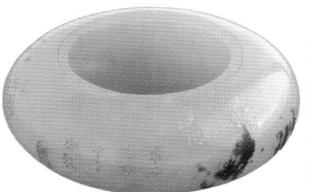

A small Chinese pale green jade compressed circular brush washer, carved with a flowering spray and calligraphy, detailed in gold.

2.5in (6.5cm) wide

$700-1,000 WW

A 20thC Chinese Jade table screen, well carved on the front in relief with a riverscape, the reverse inscribed, glued restoration.

20in (51cm) high

$2,500-3,000 FRE

ORIENTAL

An 18thC Japanese giltwood Buddha, with a bud shaped cintamani, removable central lotus medallion nimbus/halo, and moderate damage to figure.

24in (61cm) high

$6,000-9,000   **FRE**

A 19thC Chinese root carving of an Immortal, his hands held aloft holding a fly whisk.

24.75in (62cm) high

$600-900   **WW**

A fine 19thC Chinese boxwood carved figure of Guanyin seated on a rocky throne.

14in (35.5cm) high

$9,000-11,000   **FRE**

A late Meiji period group carving, portraying a devil crushing an emaciated man with another emaciated figure looking on, upon a scrolled base.

15.25in (38cm) high

$600-900   **BIG**

A pair of Japanese carved wood and ivory figures, Meiji period, in the form of a man and a woman, each with ivory head, hands and feet, the wood inset with mother of pearl motifs, both with inscribed character mark on mother of pearl panel.

11.75in (30cm) high

$25,000-30,000   **L&T**

An early 20thC Chinese carved wood figure of Buddha, seated in dhyanasana on a lotus base and raised plinth, with cracks and major losses of gilt.

24in (61cm) high

$700-1,000   **FRE**

Three Japanese wood toads, carved in all detail.

largest 6in (15cm) high

$1,000-1,500   **GORL**

A Chinese bamboo brush washer carved as a bamboo root.

7in (18cm) long

$600-700   **DN**

A Chinese hardwood brush pot inlaid in lacquer and mother-of-pearl with Zhoulao and other figures, inscribed.

7in (19cm) high

$600-900   **DN**

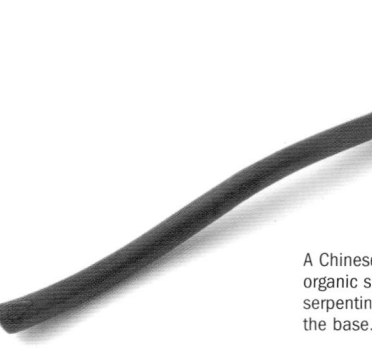

A Chinese boxwood ruyi scepter, the organic shield shaped head on a serpentine stem carved with a leaf at the base.

11.5in (30cm) high

$1,000-1,500   **CHEF**

A Chinese Beijing overlaid glass bottle vase, in green, pink and white, carved with figures on boats and pagodas on islands, the neck with a fruiting gourd vine, four character Qianlong mark and of the period.

7.75in (20cm) high

$10,000-15,000   **WW**

A Chinese blue Beijing glass vase, with a globular body and a tall cylindrical neck, a Daoguang four character mark and of the period.

10.5in (26.5cm) high

$1,000-2,000   **WW**

A 20thC Chinese Beijing glass vase, with red glass overlay to rim and body, depicting an immortal on a crane, showing red applied artist's seal.

11in (28cm) high

$300-400   **FRE**

A 20thC Chinese Beijing glass vase, with red overlay motif, depicting flowering trees above a scholar, applied artist's seal.

11in (28cm) high

$300-400   **FRE**

An 18thC Chinese imperial yellow snuff bottle.

2.25in (6cm) high

$6,000-9,000   **DB**

An 18th or 19thC Chinese seven color overlay snuff bottle and stopper, carved with flowers, bats and auspicious symbols on a white ground.

2.5in (6.5cm) high

$700-1,000   **WW**

An 18th or 19thC Chinese four color overlay glass snuff bottle, carved with flowers and insects.

2.5in (6.5cm) high

$700-1,000   **WW**

A 19thC Chinese amber snuff bottle.

2in (5.5cm) high

$4,000-5,000   **DB**

A 19thC Chinese agate snuff bottle.

2.5in (6.5cm) high

$1,000-1,500   **DB**

A Chinese red overlay glass snuff bottle.

2.25in (5.5cm) high

$1,200-1,800   **DB**

A Chinese inside-painted smokey crystal snuff bottle, by Ye Zhongsa.

2.25in (5.5cm) high

$1,200-1,800   **DB**

A Chinese hair crystal snuff bottle.

2in (5cm) high

$1,000-1,500   **DB**

A Chinese pale jade snuff bottle, of fluted ovular form, with coral stopper.

2.25in (5.5cm) high

$2,000-3,000   **GORL**

A 18thC Fifu or Dragon dress, embroidery with polychrome silk and metal thread on blue silk taffeta, China, Qing Dynasty.

$2,000-3,000   RSS

A 19thC Fifu or Dragon dress, embroidery with polychrome silk and metal thread on blue silk taffeta, China, Qing Dynasty.

$600-900   RSS

A 19thC Long Pao, Chinese woman's court robe, silk and polychrome embroidery on twill weave silk.

Official costume in imperial China was highly regulated, and the decorative motifs of court costumes were specific to rank.

$120-180   RSS

A 19thC Chinese robe, decorated with intricately stitched five-toed dragons.

The decoration suggests that this robe was worn by a high ranking official. It was probably acquired by someone working or traveling in the Far East at the time of the Boxer Rebellion when many artefacts were finding their way into Western hands. It is possible that the sleeves have been shortened, although it is more likely that the robe was produced for summer use.

c1865

$6,000-9,000   TAM

A 19thC Chinese Mandarin dress, embroidered blue silk Pao with couched gold threads depicting nine dragons and mixed religious symbols.

$3,000-4,000   BEA

A 19thC Tibetan Thanka, painted with a Buddha on an orange ground, in a silk brocade mount.

c1800   *17.5in (44.5cm) high*

$50-70   CA

A late 19th/possibly early 20thC Chinese embroidered jacket, ermine lined.

$400-600   WO

An antique Tibetan Thanka, painted with a Buddha surrounded by deities, in a silk brocade mount.

c1800   *23in (58.5cm) high*

$70-100   CA

A Japanese 18thC anonymous fragment of a paravent with a scene from the Genji Monogatari.

17.25in (43cm) high

$1,500-2,000　　　　**NAG**

A Japanese 18thC six-panel folding screen.

per sheet 34in (85cm) high

$7,000-10,000　　　　**NAG**

Ando Hiroshige (Japanese 1797-1858), Konodai Tonegawa from Fuji Sanjurokkei, signed Hiroshige ga, publisher Tsuta-ya Kichizo, color woodcut, Oban, unframed.

$900-1,100　　　　**FRE**

Ando Hiroshige (Japanese 1797-1858), Toto Ichikokubashi from Fuji Sanjrokkei, signed Hiroshige ga, publisher Tsuta-ya Kichizo, color woodcut, Oban, unframed.

$700-900　　　　**FRE**

Ando Hiroshige (Japanese 1797-1858), Kazusa Rokusozan From Fuji Sanjurokkei, signed Hiroshige ga, publisher Tsuta-ya Kichizo, color woodcut, Oban, unframed.

$700-900　　　　**FRE**

A 19thC Japanese anonymous six-panel screen.

per sheet 62.5in (156cm) high

$9,000-10,000　　　　**NAG**

A pair of late 19thC Chinese paintings on silk, each depicting maidens, one within and without a house, the other sailing in a dragon-headed boat, signed.

30.25in (77cm) long

$500-700　　　　**SWO**

Toshi Yoshida (Japanese 1911-1995), Matsu (Pine Tree) from The Friendly Garden Series, 1980, pencil signed Yoshida Toshi in Japanese in the margin, with Yoshida Toshi seal, Toshi signature, and title in the image, color woodcut, Tanzaku, framed.

$900-1,100　　　　**FRE**

Adachi Ginko (Japanese fl. 1874-1897) Intense Battle and Victory in Pyongyang, 1894, signed Ginko and with Ginko seal in the image, publisher Ayabe Hanjiro, color woodcut, Senso-e, Oban triptych, unframed.

$300-500　　　　**FRE**

A Japanese six-panel screen.

per panel 31.25in (78cm) high

$4,000-6,000　　　　**NAG**

ORIENTAL

A fine pair of Japanese red-lacquered folding chairs with brass fittings, Edo period.

39.25in (98cm) high

$6,000-8,000   **NAG**

A pair of 18thC Chinese armchairs, rectangular seats, open-work back and ornamental armrests, hard wood.

44.75in (112cm) high

$10,000-12,000   **NAG**

An 18thC Chinese hardwood open armchair, the curved splat with a carved panel to a sectional curving frame, the panel seat on conforming legs and peripheral stretchers, front missing.

27.5in (70cm) wide

$2,000-3,000   **WW**

A 19thC huang hali open armchair, South China, the yoke toprail above solid splat and open outscrolled arms, the inset rattan board seat above rounded square section legs joined by low stretchers and pierced apron.

$10,000-15,000   **L&T**

A Chinese hardwood ceremonial open armchair, the paneled back decorated with open scrollwork above similarly carved open arms and caned seat with shaped and carved apron on square legs linked by stretchers.

$1,200-1,800   **L&T**

A Chinese hardwood low stand.

c1780   *12in (30.5cm) high*

$500-700   **DL**

A Chinese export brass inlaid solid padouk and inset marble center table, raised on a collapsible turned and reeded six legged stand with a central ropetwist finial on a shaped and reeded base fitted with original brass wheels.

The collapsible base, although evident in Chinese furniture, would have assisted in the table's transport back to Europe.

c1800   *29.5in (75cm) high*

$45,000-55,000   **RGA**

A pair of Chinese hardwood and marble inset occasional tables, each with rectangular marble inset top, above open fruit carved and reeded frieze, on reeded square legs.

20.5in (52cm) high

$3,000-5,000   **L&T**

A pair of Chinese hardwood planter tables, each with marble inset rectangular tops above pierced aprons and undershelf and with shaped legs with claw feet.

31.5in (80cm) high

$2,000-3,000   **L&T**

An early 19thC Chinese presentation shelf on legs, divided into compartments of different size and shape, on square legs, hoof-shaped feet, lacquered soft wood.

58.5in (146cm) high

$2,000-3,000   **NAG**

An early 19thC Chinese hardwood display cabinet, open shelves, each surrounded by fretwork tracing depicting bamboo branches and stylized foliage, above single drawers and paneled doors.

56in (144cm) wide

$3,000-4,000   **L&T**

A 19thC Japanese lacquer display cabinet, the ebonized faux bamboo frame, with inlay of mother-of-pearl and bone, depicting scenes with musicians, panels with faux split bamboo openwork birdcages, on an ebonized faux bamboo stand.

59.25in (148cm) high

$2,000-3,000   **FRE**

A fine late 19thC Japanese lacquer cabinet, in combined lacquer and inlay techniques, three parts, the four-legged stand added later.

58.75in (147cm) high

$10,000-12,000   **NAG**

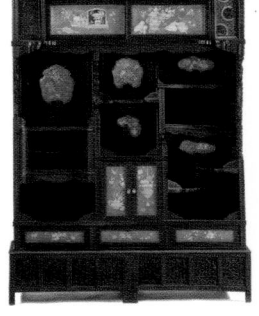

A Japanese Meiji period lacquer cabinet, with cupboards, shelves and drawers, fine takamakie lacquer panels, and bombe form base raised on splayed legs.

1868-1912   47.75in (121.5cm) wide

$5,000-6,000   **FRE**

A Japanese carved wood and lacquer cabinet, Meiji Period (1868-1912), with open shelves and cupboard doors, the lacquer panels decorated with ivory and mother of pearl design elements in relief, raised on a fret pierced paneled base.

49.5in (125.5cm) wide

$3,000-4,000   **FRE**

A Chinese lacquered cabinet on stand, cupboard doors decorated with figures, pagodas and birds with foliage, with ornate brass mounts enclosing decorated drawers, later base fitted with five drawers, the chamfered legs joined by a shaoed galleried undertier.

19.5in (50cm) wide

$3,000-4,000   **L&T**

A Chinese lacquer cabinet on stand, the relief carved lacquer with red ground, green and black highlights, the top with dragon carved cresting, reverse breakfront cupboards, open shelves, cupboards and drawers, three base drawers, shaped plinth, stand with bulbous apron and scrolling legs.

52in (132cm) wide

$4,000-6,000   **L&T**

An 18thC Japanese Byobu gilt six panel screen, with six gilt and painted panels, depicting a Kyoto procession, and bordered by a brocaded silk ribbon, moderate losses.

144in (366cm) long

$7,000-10,000   **FRE**

A Japanese Meiji period carved hardwood and ornamental lacquer bi-fold screen, signed with a seal mark, within diaper framed borders and carved lower apron.

71.25in (181cm) high

$4,000-6,000   **L&T**

A fine Japanese two-panel lacquered wood screen with inlaid silk paintings, gilt mounts, Meiji period.

82.75in (207cm) high

$5,000-7,000   **NAG**

A Chinese eight-fold draught screen, each rectangular fold painted with courtly figural scenes.

each fold 19.75in (50cm) wide

$1,000-1,500   **L&T**

FREEMAN'S
AMERICA'S OLDEST AUCTION HOUSE

The Pennsylvania Sale
11/17/2007

Auction:
Saturday, November 17th, 2007
11am

Inquiries:
LYNDA CAIN ext.3038
lcain@freemansauction.com
NOELLE BURGOYNE ext. 3048
nburgoyne@freemansauction.com

Now accepting consignments

**Green-painted diminutive comb back
Windsor armchair**
PHILADELPHIA, CIRCA 1770
Sold 11/19/06 for $65,725

Freeman's 1808 Chestnut Street Philadelphia, PA 19103 Tel: 215.563.9275 Fax: 215.563.8236 **www.freemansauction.com**

THE FURNITURE MARKET

The continued polarisation of the furniture market means many antique pieces represent excellent value for money. At the top end, buyers will pay a premium for exceptional examples by the best makers, but elsewhere very good furniture can be bought for much less than at the height of the market a few years ago.

The best prices are paid for 18th and early 19th century furniture from the major American centers: Rhode Island, Boston, Philadelphia, New York and Baltimore. However, furniture such as farmhouse and Pembroke tables dating from the same era, but made in provincial areas such as Virginia and Pennsylvania, currently represent excellent value for money. Also undervalued are early American oak and pieces made in the Classical style and dating from the 1820s and 30s. However, good, painted folk art furniture continues to command a premium.

French furniture from the late 19th century and made in the Louis XV style is highly sought after – especially if it is stamped by a good maker such as Linke or Durand. Good quality Louis XIV and XVI revival furniture from the same era is also performing well and unstamped French 18th century furniture is performing better than it has for many years.

The market for brown English furniture is still fairly flat: a good George III bureau currently sells for around $1,000 – much less than half the price you might have excepted a few years ago.

The other trend is that while people do want to furnish their homes with antiques, they are often concerned with the "look" as much as, or even more than, the age or history of a piece. So, decorative pieces are selling exceptionally well while less decorative but more worthy pieces falter.

Sebastian Clarke

WINDSOR CHAIRS

A comb-back Philadelphia windsor armchair, with serpentine crest over a nine-spindle back, retaining an early Spanish brown surface over the original green.

c1765

$10,000-15,000   **POOK**

A pair of early 19thC yew and elm Windsor style armchairs, with tall curved backs, spindle filled with scrolled cut-out splat above molded seat.

$1,500-2,000 PAIR   **L&T**

A late 18thC Pennsylvania Windsor continuous back armchair, the flat crest rail with raised back continuing into flat arms with round ends, ball feet.

$6,000-8,000   **FRE**

A early 19thC English rustic Windsor reclining chair, from East Anglia, the back tipping with adjustable iron brackets.

$600-900   **SWO**

A 19thC Windsor sack back chair, by W. McBride of New York, with rod turned spindles, baluster and tapering legs.

$1,000-1,500   **FRE**

WINDSOR CHAIRS

- Windsor chairs, produced in Britain and the US since the mid-18thC, are identifiable by their shaped seats, into which the spindles, arms and legs are socketed. Most feature little or no decoration, but some British pieces have pierced splats.
- They generally consist of a mix of woods, typically elm for the seats, ash or yew for the bow, and beech for the legs and spindles on British examples, while maple, ash, oak and hickory were commonly used for American pieces.
- The earlier, more sought after chairs tended to be owned by the affluent. These were often painted, with straight top rails (known as comb-backs) and slender legs. Later pieces usually have bowed backs and chunkier legs.
- Because they were designed for use, most surviving pieces will have replacement legs and arms. Chairs made with yew and mahogany are particularly rare and highly desirable, as are 'Gothic' style Windsor chairs from the late 18thC.

Three early 19thC hoop back Windsor armchairs, with baluster turned elements, the other two with bamboo turnings, refinished.

36in (91.5cm) high

$1,000-1,500   **FRE**

A 19thC fruitwood and elm seated Gothic-style Windsor open armchair, on turned legs.

20.5in (52cm) high

$600-900   **WW**

A 20thC child's black-painted sack back Windsor armchair, on vase and ring-turned legs joined by bulbous stretcher.

23in (58.5cm) high

$150-200   **FRE**

A near pair of yew and elm Windsor elbow chairs, each on turned legs with crinoline stretcher.

21.25in (54cm) wide

$3,000-4,000 PAIR   **DN**

FURNITURE

An 18thC pair of Chester County, Pennsylvania, ladderback dining chairs, with rush seats, retaining a 19thC black surface with yellow pinstriping.

$7,000-10,000 POOK

A late 18thC ash corner chair, with a ladder back and a rush seat on turned legs with stretchers.

$500-700   **DN**

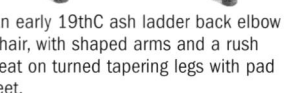

An early 19thC ash ladder back elbow chair, with shaped arms and a rush seat on turned tapering legs with pad feet.

23.5in (60cm) wide

$300-400   **DN**

Two of set of six early 19thC oak country dining chairs, including one open armchair, with arched ladderbacks, on pad and ball feet.

$2,000-3,000 set   **L&T**

A set of six 19thC stained elm ladderback chairs, each with six shaped rails above wicker seats, on turned legs with pad feet.

$1,200-1,800 SET   **L&T**

A set of six 19thC English oak dining chairs, from Lancashire, including one carver, each with spindle-filled backs above rushed seats.

$1,200-1,800 SET   **L&T**

Two of a set of eight 19thC English ash spindle back dining chairs, from Lancashire, the shaped top rails with ears, with rush seats and turned club legs.

$3,000-4,000 SET   **WW**

A large 19thC oak Welsh country chair, with curved top rail and arms, above a spindle-filled back on bowed solid seat with facetted pegged legs.

$3,000-4,000   **L&T**

A 19thC elm open armchair, the curved spindle back incorporating the arms, the solid seat on octagonal turned splayed legs.

$700-1,000   **SWO**

One of a harlequin set of six ash chairs, in the manner of the Clissets, each with a spindle turned back and a rush seat.

18.5in (47cm) wide

$1,000-1,500 SET   **DN**

An early 18thC turned and painted Pennsylvania daybed, the adjustable back with double curved crest rail and spindles, tall turned head posts and rectangular rush seat.

80.5in (204.5cm) long

$15,000-20,000   FRE

A late 18thC pair of low back Pennsylvania Windsor settees, flattened arms, incised plank seat raised on ten baluster turned tapering legs.

83in (211cm) long

$7,000-10,000   FRE

A painted rodback Pennsylvania settee, with red and yellow fruit decoration, above a plank seat supported by bamboo turned legs.

c1830   *78in (198cm) wide*

$6,000-9,000   POOK

An English oak cupboard settle with molded cornice, four cupboard doors enclosing a compartmentalized interior, and open arms with solid seat over two apron drawers.

c1800   *55in (139.5cm) wide*

$1,500-2,000   FRE

A rare child's birdcage Philadelphia Windsor settee, surrounding a salmon seat, parts retaining an old red surface.

c1820   *36.5in (92cm) wide*

$20,000-30,000   POOK

A matched set of four 17thC Derbyshire oak side chairs with pierced and carved backs over solid seats, on baluster turned legs.

Tallest 39in (99cm) high

$2,000-3,000   FRE

An assembled set of four late 18thC New England banisterback side chairs, with typical turnings and rush seats.

$1,200-1,800   POOK

An early 19thC fruitwood and elm elbow chair, the back with reeded rails, with scrolled arms and a solid seat on square tapering legs with 'H' stretcher.

23.5in (60cm) wide

$700-1,000   DN

A 19thC Swiss rural beechwood chair, from Brienz, the seat with beveled corners, carved back.

29.25in (73cm) high

$300-400   KAU

A pair of Victorian oak hall chairs, in the high Victorian style, with pierced quatrefoil splats and spiral twist sides and legs.

$400-500   SWO

An oak-framed child's Orkney chair, with curved woven straw back above open arms and drop in seat raised on square tapering legs linked by stretchers.

$1,000-1,500   L&T

121

A Chippendale style mahogany hall settee, with shaped top rail above four pierced vase-shaped splats, curved open arms and solid seat, raised on cabriole legs.

90.25in (229cm) wide

$2,000-3,000   L&T

A George III oak settle, with five-panel back, scrolled open arms and baluster turned legs.

70.75in (180cm) wide

$1,000-1,200   SWO

A fancy Pennsylvania decorated settee, the rectangular cresting with scrolled ends decorated with metallic stencil fruit and foliate designs, within apple green and gray freehand borders, above lyre-form splats and ring-turned stiles on scrolled arms, with vase- and ring-turned frontal legs joined by rectangular frontal stretchers.

c1830   *79.25in (198cm) wide*

$3,000-4,000   SK

A Pennsylvania painted and decorated settee, with three splats on the plank seat, rolled front rail flanked by scrolled painted arms and turned tapering legs linked with stretchers, with original painted decoration of flowers and leaves.

c1835   *77.5in (197cm) wide*

$3,500-4,500   SK

A 19thC green and gilt painted sofa, with ribbon tie crest, caned back with central rectangular panel painted with two young girls, padded arms with turned supports, caned seat and turned and fluted legs.

43in (109cm) wide

$1,000-1,500   LFA

A 19thC oak five-panel back settle.

73.25in (183cm) wide

$1,000-1,500   SWO

A Victorian oak pew, with carved ends in the Gothic style, pierced with quatrefoils.

45.25in (113cm) wide

$1,500-2,000   SWO

A rare Canadian pine pail bench, from Waterloo County, Ontario.

1865 34.25in (87cm) long

$1,000-1,200   RAON

A Rose Valley oak bench, the rectangular mortized top over a scalloped frame with carved and pierced ends and trestle base.

c1905   *48in (120cm) wide*

$4,500-5,500   POOK

An early 17thC oak chest of drawers, the planked rectangular top above four paneled drawers on turned bun feet.

37.5in (95cm) wide

$1,500-2,000   **L&T**

A 17thC and later oak court cupboard, with a carved frieze with pendants and two paneled doors, carved and with inscription "EH1674", on stile supports.

63.25in (158cm) wide

$4,000-6,000   **L&T**

A late 17thC oak cupboard on stand, with two cupboard doors with octagonal molded panels and turned demi columns, on ball turned and block legs.

41in (104cm) wide

$1,500-2,000   **L&T**

A Welsh oak tridarn, the cavetto cornice above a frieze carved with inscription "MR21 ; 1729".

1729   *76in (190cm) high*

$7,000-10,000   **L&T**

A 17thC oak court cupboard, the top with scrolling foliate frieze above three doors, the base with strapwork carved frieze drawers above a pair of three panel cupboard doors, on stile feet.

74.5in (186cm) high

$8,000-12,000   **L&T**

An 18thC and later oak side cabinet, with a single paneled door and three drawers.

43.75in (111cm) wide

$700-1,000   **SWO**

A George III oak hanging corner cabinet, with a swan neck pediment and paneled door, flanked by fluted pilasters.

31in (79cm) high

$500-700   **SWO**

An early 19thC Welsh oak press cupboard, with two panel doors, the base on bracket feet.

$4,500-5,500   **L&T**

DRESSERS

■ The term "dresser" is derived from the French *dressoir*, a sideboard used for preparing and serving food or storing dishes. Early dressers were simply side tables, later with drawers. Low dressers, made from the late 17th century, featured a 'potboard' or shelf in place of stretchers.

■ As decorative delftware became fashionable during the mid-17th century, householders acquired shelves to display their ceramics. Eventually shelves were added to dressers, particularly in middle class homes in Wales, and the north and south west of England.

■ Dressers from each region had different characteristics. South Wales dressers often feature open backs and bases, while examples from North Wales are often closed with boards behind the upper shelves. Caernarvon dressers, and some northern and south-western English examples, feature spice cupboards set into the rack. Shropshire dressers may feature cabriole legs.

■ Devon examples were typically made of oak or elm and were plain in appearance, while 19th century Cornish examples are known for their elegance.

■ The dresser was essentially a traditional country piece and was less common in metropolitan homes.

■ Be aware of modifications to dressers. Backboards have sometimes been added and feet replaced. Carving may have been added at a later date.

A mid-18thC George II Welsh dresser, in oak with open top and three shelves on a three drawer base.

$6,000-8,000   POOK

A Georgian oak Welsh dresser, with open plate rack and reverse breakfront base with doors with fielded ogee panel, plinth base.

84in (210cm) high

$1,200-1,800   L&T

A Louis XV style provincial oak dresser, with molded cornice over pierced galleried shelves, shaped top and two frieze drawers over three cupboard doors enclosing shelves.

c1780   *95.5in (242.5cm)*

$3,000-4,000   FRE

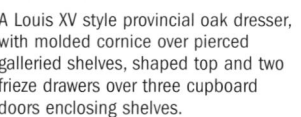

A George III oak, mahogany banded and inlaid dresser, with shelved superstructure, two cupboard doors with conch shell motifs, three drawers and a carved apron, on cabriole legs with pad feet.

c1760   *69in (175cm) wide*

$5,000-8,000   FRE

A 19thC oak dresser, the open plate rack with breakfront cupboard, the base with three drawers and shaped apron on club legs.

64.5in (161cm) wide

$1,500-2,000   L&T

A 19thC North Wales oak dresser, with mahogany banding, the breakfront base on a plinth with shaped bracket feet.

85.25in (213cm) high

$4,000-5,000   L&T

An 18thC oak dresser, with two open plate racks, the base with three drawers, on turned and blocked legs linked by stretchers.

77.5in (194cm) high

$4,000-5,000   L&T

A 17thC walnut refectory table, with rectangular top raised on baluster turned columnar end supports and downswept legs.

89.5in (227.5cm) wide

$5,000-7,000   **FRE**

A mid-18thC oak side table, with two frieze drawers, a shaped apron and square tapering legs.

39.25in (98cm) wide

$300-400   **SWO**

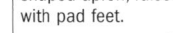

A George III oak lowboy, with plank top and single drawer with a cut and shaped apron, raised on turned legs with pad feet.

30.75in (78cm) wide

$700-1,000   **BIG**

A late 18thC Pennsylvania walnut tavern table, the apron with molded edge and two drawers, on block and baluster turned legs.

27in (68.5cm) high

$900-1,200   **FRE**

An early 19thC large Pennsylvania pine hutch table, with top tilts on a base with slab ends with demilune cutouts enclosing seat with drawer.

30.25in (77cm) high

$800-1,200   **FRE**

A yellow pine table, with cut nails to top, on turned legs with mortise-and-tenon construction, old refinishing, wear.

123in (312.5cm) wide

$2,000-3,000   **BRU**

A Federal inlaid tiger maple sugar box, with a single scratch-beaded drawer, original brass, old refinish, imperfections.

c1825   *42.75in (108.5cm) wide*

$7,000-10,000   **SK**

A 19thC Pennsylvania pine dough box, with rectangular top raised on bulbous-turned splayed legs.

$400-600   **FRE**

A Canadian pine shelf, from Quebec.

c1870   *47.5in (121cm) long*

$400-600   **RAON**

A Canadian carved pine shelf, with traces of original paint, from Quebec.

c1870.   *47.5in (121cm) long*

$300-400   **RAON**

A good Canadian pine shelf, with shaped base, from Quebec.

c1870-1880   *52.5in (133cm) long*

$400-600   **RAON**

A Pennsylvania Windsor cradle, with oval finials, tapering spindles and bamboo turned legs joined by swelled stretchers.

c1795   *24in (61cm) high*

$2,000-3,000   **FRE**

A Massachusetts Federal mahogany canopy bed, the reeded posts with central foliate carving.

c1815

$1,500-2,000   **POOK**

A Pennsylvania late Federal tiger maple canopy bed, with scalloped headboard and turned posts.

c1820   *79.5in (199cm) long*

$2,000-3,000   **POOK**

A 19thC French mahogany lit en bateau, with gilt brass rosette terminals, with a downswept side on a plinth base, castors.

72in (183cm) long

$2,000-3,000   **L&T**

A Classical mahogany bedstead with tester, probably Philadelphia, with spiral-turned and acanthus-leaf carved posts, paneled headboard and engine-turned brass ornament posts.

c1825   *97in (246.5cm) high*

$7,000-10,000   **FRE**

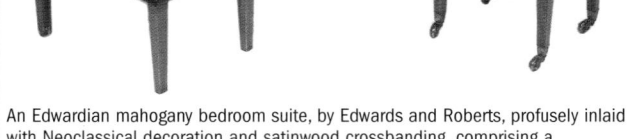

An Edwardian mahogany bedroom suite, by Edwards and Roberts, profusely inlaid with Neoclassical decoration and satinwood crossbanding, comprising a wardrobe, dressing table, night cupboard and chest of drawers.

Dressing table 64cm (162cm) high

$7,000-10,000 SET   **L&T**

A George III octagonal mahogany wine cooler, with brass bound body and ring carrying handles, brass caps and castors.

27in (69cm) high

$3,000-4,000   **L&T**

A Scottish Regency mahogany cellaret, of sarcophagus form, with reeded finial and tapering paneled sides, on castors.

31.5in (79cm) wide

$4,500-5,500   **L&T**

A large Regency mahogany cellaret, of sacophagus form, with panel front and molded plinth, hinged pagoda lid, castors.

31.5in (80cm) wide

$2,000-3,000   **L&T**

A Regency mahogany cellaret, of sarcophagus form with canted angles, vine boss to lid, tin liner, gilt brass lion mask and ring handles.

26in (66cm) wide

$4,500-5,500   **L&T**

A fine Regency mahogany wine cellaret, of sarcophagus form, with central carved leaf motif, carved lion mask and bronze lion mask ring handles, on muscular paw feet, zinc lined interior, lid interior with label for "George Simson, Upholder, of 19 South Side of St Paul's Church Yard, London".

25in (63cm) high deep

$7,000-10,000   **L&T**

A large George IV carved mahogany open wine cooler, the gadrooned top with acanthus carved corners above a roundel frieze and further gadroon carving, the base with anthemion brackets and roundel decoration raised above a shaped plinth with concealed castors, tin lined interior.

20in (51cm) high

$20,000-30,000   **L&T**

A 19thC William IV mahogany wine cooler, with a hinged, gadrooned top, sectioned lined interior, and molded panels, stamped "Miles & Edwards, 134 Oxford St., London, 2425".

32in (81.5cm) wide

$2,000-3,000   **FRE**

FURNITURE

ARMCHAIRS

- Before the late 15th century, only the master of the house, or a visitor, would sit in a chair with arms. Other members of the household sat on stools made of solid, local woods.
- By the early 17th century lighter chairs with upholstered seats and caned or upholstered backs had become fashionable on the Continent. The style gradually spread throughout Europe.
- As home entertaining became popular the comfortable armchair, or fauteuil, became fashionable. Upholstery became more generous and styles more suited to intimate conversation.
- At the end of the 17th century, wings or 'cheeks' appeared and flowing lines and cabriole legs heightened the comfort as well as the visual appeal. Over time an armchair with upholstered sides, known as the bergère in France and the 'easy' chair in England, became popular.
- In the 1820s the development of coiled upholstery springs resulted in more comfortable armchairs, including the archetypal button-back chair.
- 19th century shapes were inspired by the passion for style revivals - from Renaissance to Rococo.
- Look for damage in the most vulnerable areas. Spandrels may have been replaced, arms may have weakened through lifting and fine cabriole legs may have been repaired. On earlier chairs upholstery is rarely original, through original needlework upholstery can be found.

A William and Mary-style wing armchair, on circular section legs with turned knop.

$500-700 — **L&T**

A George II mahogany two seater wing chair, with upholstered double hump back, separate squab, acanthus lion mask carved cabriole front legs, paw feet.

51in (130cm) wide

$6,000-9,000 — **L&T**

A George II wing armchair, the tall upholstered back continuing to shaped wings above upholstered out-scrolled arms, the front cabriole legs carved with lions' masks with stylized plumes above continuing to scrolled brackets, and claw-and-ball feet.

This chair may have formed part of the furnishings of Chesterfield House, London, built for the Earl of Chesterfield in the mid-18th century and demolished in 1937. Much of its contents, including furniture, paintings and the magnificent wrought iron entrance screen were then transferred to Harewood.

1750 — *44in (112cm) high*

$90,000-100,000 — **PAR**

An important late 17thC carved giltwood and upholstered high back chair, the wool fabric covered in restored panels of the original silver thread needlework, on acanthus carved S-scroll legs with corner rosettes, the front apron with a central emblem of the Knights of the Garter, inscribed: "Honi Soit Qui Mal Y Pense", with scroll motifs and foliate garlands to either side.

47.5in (121cm) high

$120,000-180,000 — **L&T**

A Regency mahogany and upholstered bergère armchair, with close nailed back, squab cushion, on reeded square tapering legs with brass caps and castors.

28in (71cm) wide

$4,000-5,000 — **L&T**

A Regency mahogany and caned bergère armchair, with cane filled back, leather button upholstered squab cushion, turned legs terminating in brass caps and castors.

21.5in (55cm) wide

$4,000-6,000 — **L&T**

A William IV simulated rosewood and upholstered armchair, the arm facings with acanthus carving, on lobed and reeded legs with anthemion brass cappings and castors.

$4,000-6,000 — **L&T**

A Victorian upholstered low armchair, with inswept buttoned back, on short turned mahogany front legs with ceramic castors.

$1,500-2,000 — **L&T**

A pair of beech-framed upholstered armchairs, with molded frames, loose squab cushions, on molded cabriole legs with scroll toes.

$2,000-3,000 — **L&T**

A late 17thC carved ebonised and upholstered high back chair, in pink silk with applied 17thC needlework sections, on carved front legs.

51in (130cm) high

$50,000-70,000   **L&T**

A pair of Louis XV carved beechwood fauteuils, the side and top rails of the shaped backs carved with stylized palm fronds, the outward turned arms carved at the elbow with scrolls and at the junction with the seat with foliage, the seat rails centered by a shell with rocaille on a diaper pattern ground, the cabriole front and back legs headed by shells, with interlacing running down the legs and scroll feet, the seats and backs caned, with squab seats.

c1745   *37.5in (95cm) high*

$32,000-38,000   **PAR**

A CLOSER LOOK AT A PAIR OF REGENCY MAHOGANY BERGERES

The chairs are a remarkably fine pair with generous proportions and made from finely toned timber. They are a robust and distinctly English interpretation of the 'Grecian' taste introduced in French design during the late 18th century.

The overall shape and the detailing of the uprights of the backs of these chairs relate to a set of four chairs made for the drawing room of Southill, Bedfordshire, the house designed by Henry Holland for Samuel Whitbread.

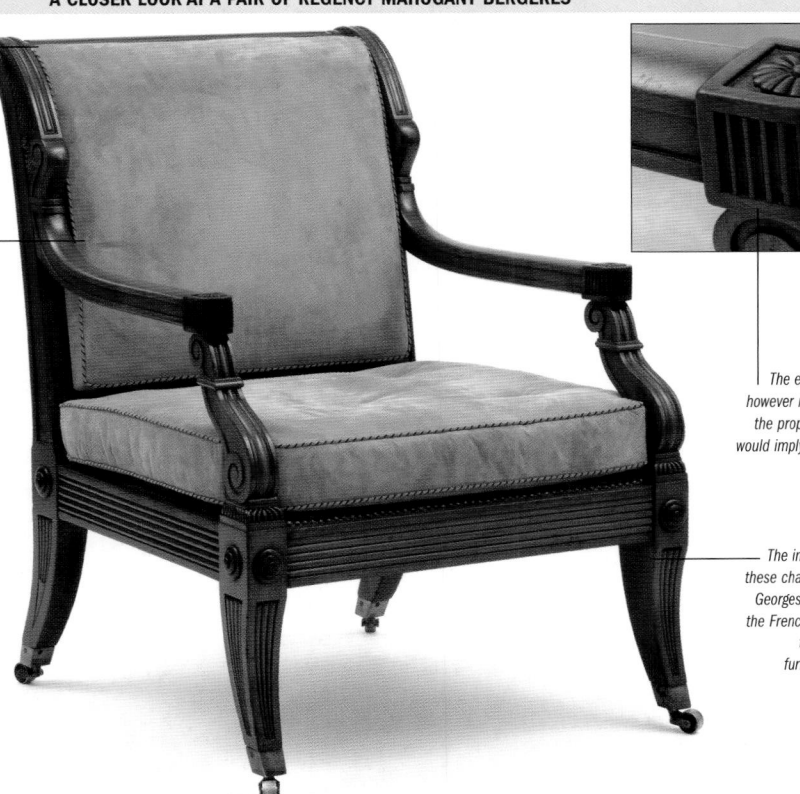

The execution of the chairs is however rather more austere and the proportions are larger which would imply a somewhat later date than the Southill chairs.

The inspiration for the form of these chairs lies in the designs of Georges Jacob who, just prior to the French Revolution, had begun to make chairs and seat furniture in mahogany – an innovation in France.

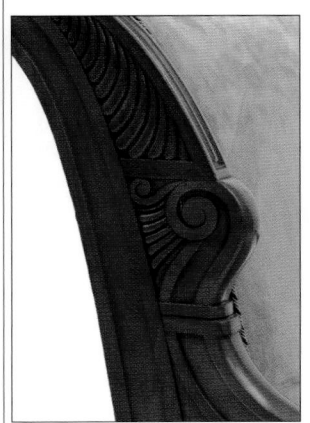

A pair of Regency mahogany bergeres, *c1820*

$180,000-220,000 PAIR   **PAR**

OPEN ARMCHAIRS

A pair of 17thC Italian walnut and tapestry open armchairs, covered in 18thC tapestry fabric depicting lovers and exotic birds in wooded landscapes, with open scroll arms and baluster turned legs.

$11,000-15,000　　　**FRE**

A pair of 17thC and later Italian walnut and tapestry open armchairs, depicting putti with floral swags, on cabriole legs united by stretchers with urn finials.

51in (127.5cm) high

$10,000-15,000　　　**FRE**

18TH CENTURY CHAIRS

- In the early 18th century, the Baroque style continued to be influential. Cabinetmakers favored gilded, carved wood frames.
- Gradually the European upper classes embraced the new French style of informal entertaining and began to copy the new French Rococo styles of the fauteuil and bergère.
- A blight on its walnut trees forced the French to prohibit the export of walnut from 1720. As a result, British cabinetmakers, increased the use of mahogany and walnut from America. The hardness of the wood allowed craftsmen to carve delicate, pierced designs which led to a different style to the carved French designs.
- At first the style known as Queen Anne was popular, but the publication of Thomas Chippendale's The Gentleman and Cabinet-Maker's Director (1754) introduced a new style that remained popular until the 1780s.
- Cabinetmakers in the American colonies interpreted Queen Anne and Chippendale styles with a skill equal to that of British craftsmen.
- In the mid to late 18th century chairs began to be made in the Neoclassical style: squarer and straighter with turned, tapered legs rather than the cabriole legs dictated by Rococo design. Important names include George Hepplewhite, Thomas Sheraton and Robert Adam.

A Massachusetts Queen Anne mahogany open armchair, with arched back and scrolled arm, on cabriole legs and pad feet.

$4,000-5,000　　　**POOK**

A Scottish George II elm corner armchair, the curved back with shaped yoke, cabriole legs with shells and ball and claw feet.

$4,000-5,000　　　**L&T**

A pair of Regence giltwood fauteuils, with caned backs and seats, carved top rails, acanthus carved arms, and upholstered cushion seats over a molded apron.

c1720　　　*36.25in (92cm) high*

$15,000-20,000　　　**FRE**

A French walnut fauteuil, in the Louis XV style, with a channelled frame, on carved cabriole legs.

27.5in (70cm) wide

$1,000-1,500　　　**DN**

A pair of 18thC Louis XVI fauteuils, carved with rosettes and ribbon, suede upholstery and carved molded tapering turned legs.

38.5in (98cm) high

$2,000-3,000　　　**SHA**

A late 18thC set of four Louis XV walnut fauteuils, each with floral carved crest and seat rail supported by cabriole legs.

$3,000-4,000　　　**POOK**

A set of four Louis XVI giltwood fauteuils by Georges Jacob, with molded backs, and loose cushion seats, each stamped "G. IACOB".

Georges Jacob (1739-1814, maitre in 1765) worked extensively in the neoclassical style, his reputation soon spreading outside of France garnering commissions from the future King George IV of England, Gustavus III of Sweden, and Thomas Jefferson.

c1780　　　*36in (91.5cm) high*

$35,000-45,000　　　**FRE**

A part 18thC Scottish mahogany and upholstered armchair, with close nailed back and acanthus carved scroll arm terminals, on imitation bamboo splayed legs.

25in (63cm) wide

$1,000-1,500   **L&T**

A Philadelphia inlaid elbow chair.

This design was probably taken from the drawings in the folios printed by Hepplewhite's widow. The drawings would have been two dimensional giving the appearance that the inlay projected over the edge of the chair back, when Hepplewhite intended it to wrap round the chair. The projecting edges are known as Hepplewhite 'horns'.

The late 18thC was a time of great prosperity for Philadelphia craftsmen. The proximity to Washington increased demand.

c1795   *34.5in (88cm) high*

$1,000-1,500   **AC**

A pair of George III mahogany and hide upholstered Gainsborough armchairs, with close nailed square back and seat, on square legs and brass casters.

28in (71cm) wide

$15,000-20,000   **L&T**

A Scottish George III mahogany cockpen armchair, with stuffover hollow seat on molded curved supports and splayed front legs.

$3,000-4,000   **L&T**

A George III mahogany and upholstered armchair, with shaped back and cockpen type front legs.

$1,000-1,500   **L&T**

A George III mahogany and upholstered library armchair, with serpentine seat and molded scrolling open arms, on square molded legs and brass casters.

$3,000-4,000   **L&T**

A George III mahogany armchair, in the French Hepplewhite taste, with acanthus carved scroll padded open arms, overstuffed seat, on cabriole legs ending in foliate scroll ties.

$6,000-9,000   **L&T**

A George III mahogany and upholstered library armchair, with padded open downswept arms, the square chamfered legs ending in brass casters.

$5,000-6,000   **L&T**

A Federal mahogany adjustable lolling chair, with square tapering legs and reeded leg rest, possibly from New England, imperfections.

c1790   *50in (127cm) high*

$7,000-10,000   **SK**

A George III mahogany and upholstered library armchair, covered in gold patterned fabric, with open downswept arms, restorations.

$5,000-6,000   **L&T**

A pair of 1920s walnut carvers, by Whytock and Reid, Edinburgh, with drop-in serpentine seat and cabriole legs with pad feet.

$1,000-1,500   **L&T**

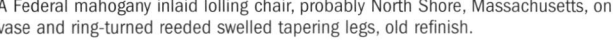

A Federal mahogany inlaid lolling chair, probably North Shore, Massachusetts, on vase and ring-turned reeded swelled tapering legs, old refinish.

c1805   *44in (110cm) high*

$15,000-20,000   **SK**

A painted bentwood armchair, by Samuel Gragg (1772-1855) Boston, MA, with sweep scrolled crestrail, contoured stiles and hoof feet, traces of original paint and landscape scene.

Provenance: Included in exhibit organized by the Winterthur Museum, "The Incredible Elastic Chairs of Samuel Gragg".

c1808   *35.25in (89.5cm) high*

$2,000-3,000   **FRE**

One of a harlequin set of ten mahogany cockpen open armchairs.

c1765

$80,000-100,000 SET   **PAR**

A pair of early 19thC mahogany cockpen armchairs, with lattice backs enclosing open arms above overstuffed concave seats, on outswept legs.

$2,000-3,000   **L&T**

A Scottish Regency mahogany carver, with paneled yoke back above mid rail and reeded uprights, stuffover seat and turned and reeded front legs.

$1,500-2,000   **L&T**

A pair of Regency green, cream and gilt decorated armchairs, in the Grecian Revival taste, re-decorated, with Greek key motifs, on saber legs.

$6,000-9,000   **L&T**

A pair of early Victorian mahogany and leather library armchairs, with button upholstered close nailed backs, on turned tapering legs with brass caps and casters.

24.5in (62cm) wide

$7,000-10,000   **L&T**

A pair of French 19thC beech fauteuils and a settee en suite, in the provincial Louis XV manner, each with molded and carved scrolling frame, on cabriole legs.

$3,000-4,000   **L&T**

Two 19thC French beech fauteuils, each with a flower carved crest, a channelled frame, on cabriole legs.

23.25in (59cm) wide

$700-1,000 PAIR   **DN**

A 19thC German oak wedding chair, from Worpswede, the back with a bust of a local woman, on four fluted legs.

50.75in (127cm) high

$400-600　　　　　　　　**KAU**

A Renaissance Revival carved oak congressional armchair, designed by Thomas U. Walter, manufactured by Bembe and Kimmel, New York, the crest rail carved with American shield, stars and oak leaves, loss of height.

Provenance: Philadelphia born and educated architect Thomas Ustick Walter (1804-87) designed new armchairs for the House of Representatives as part of the commission to renovate and expand the United States Capitol.

1857

$6,000-9,000　　　　　　　　**FRE**

A Victorian mahogany spoon-back fireside chair, with show wood molded frame, on cabriole forelegs with casters.

$1,000-1,500　　**BIG**

One of a pair of Victorian mahogany open armchairs, the showframe carved with patera, foliate scrolls and flutes, on turned tapering legs, ceramic casters.

$500-700 PAIR　　**DN**

A Victorian cast iron and brass campaign type armchair, with upholstered loose cushions, on ceramic casters, incomplete.

27.25in (69cm) wide

$400-500　　**DN**

A Victorian walnut and leather upholstered library armchair, with stiff leaf carved upright and serpentine seat on bulbous reeded legs with brass cappings and casters.

$2,000-3,000　　**L&T**

A late 19thC Louis XV-style patinated, parcel gilt and tapestry armchair, depicting a wooded landscape, raised on foliated carved cabriole legs.

$2,000-3,000　　**FRE**

A pair of Hepplewhite style giltwood open arm chairs, with shield shaped back, bow fronted stuff over seat, on tapering front legs with rosette terminals.

$1,000-1,500 PAIR　　**L&T**

A child's carved mahogany corner chair, in the Chippendale style, with a pierced vase shaped splat, damage.

26in (66cm) high

$600-900　　**SWO**

A painted Regency-style spoonback chair, the hoop back with scrolls and a palmette in red on an ebonized ground, with upholstered seat and saber legs with brass terminals and casters.

36.25in (92cm) high

$700-1,000 **DN**

A Victorian walnut desk chair, with open curved back, three pieced baluster splats, scroll arms and turned tapering legs.

22.5in (57cm) wide

$400-500 **WW**

A pair of 19thC Russian Empire mahogany and parcel gilt armchairs, with rope-twist turned top rails and pierced scroll-carved bar backs centred by palmettes, raised on semi-lobed turned tapered legs.

35.5in (89cm) high

$5,000-6,000 SET **FRE**

A Dutch beech and elm elbow chair, with curved crest rail, lyre-shaped splat and upholstered seat on saber legs.

34.25in (87cm) high

$400-500 **DN**

A pair of Russian Empire painted and parcel gilt armchairs, with shaped backs and carved top rails, padded arms and overstuffed upholstered seats on paterae capped legs and paw feet.

c1830 *46.5in (118cm) high*

$4,000-6,000 **FRE**

A pair of Sheraton style satinwood armchairs, with caned backs centred by painted panels, and caned seats with orange upholstered cushions, on paterae capped legs and spade feet.

c1910 *33.5in (85cm) high*

$1,500-2,000 **FRE**

A Carolean-style carved walnut open armchair, with padded back and stuff-over seat on 'X' frame base.

$700-1,000 **SWO**

One of a pair of 19thC Charles II-style walnut and upholstered armchairs, covered in red velvet, with bobbin-turned open arms, raised on conforming legs joined by stretchers.

$2,000-3,000 pair **FRE**

Two from a set of 12 gilded dining chairs in the George I manner, each with strapwork splat, caned panels and seats on shell carved cabriole legs with paw feet.

$5,000-7,000 SET **L&T**

A CLOSER LOOK AT A PAIR OF GEORGE I SIDE CHAIRS

The provenance is strong. American financier George D. Widener Jr was a member of one of Philadelphia's wealthiest families. His father and brother were killed on the Titanic. The family shared a passion for collecting all kinds of objects.

The restrained carving of these chairs dates them to about 1720.

Details such as the shells, husks and scrolls to the knees can be seen on other chairs of the period but the quality and colour of the veneers and the highly refined carving make them exceptional examples of their period.

One of a set of 12 Italian black-japanned side chairs.
c1720

$270,000-320,000 SET **PAR**

One of a pair of George I side chairs.
Provenance: George D. Widener Jr. (1889-1971), Erdenheim Farm, Pennsylvania
c1720 *39in (99cm) high*

$100,000-120,000 pair **PAR**

A George I walnut side chair, with red silk upholstery, arched padded back and conforming seat over a shaped apron, on cabriole legs with wavy x-form stretcher.

c1715 *48in (122cm) high*

$1,200-1,800 **FRE**

A pair of Queen Anne Pennsylvania walnut dining chairs, the cupid's bow crest over a solid splat and trapezoidal slip seat, on cabriole legs with drake feet.
c1750

$10,000-15,000 **POOK**

A Queen Anne Delaware Valley walnut armchair, with yoke crest, serpentine arms and carved skirt supported by cabriole legs and stocking drake feet.
c1745

$10,000-12,000 **POOK**

A mid-18thC Boston Queen Anne mahogany dining chair, with vasiform splat and compass slip seat on cabriole legs and pad feet, retaining old surface.

$30,000-35,000 **POOK**

THOMAS CHIPPENDALE

■ Outside of documented national collections, little extant furniture can be attributed directly to Thomas Chippendale (1718-1779), yet his style has endured, thanks largely to 'The Gentleman and Cabinet-Maker's Director', produced 1754.

■ The designs in 'The Director' were copied by furniture makers across the globe. Pieces were interpretations of Rococo and Neoclassical styles, but some also feature Chinoiserie - such as fretwork galleries and pagoda motifs - and Gothic revival elements.

■ The 'Chippendale' chair is the best-known example of Chippendale's furniture: more than 60 variations appear in the 'Director'.

■ Despite the different styles, the basic shape of the chair remains the same. With an emphasis on the horizontal, chairs are wide and low.

■ Backs are carved and pierced, often with interlaced splats and scrollwork. A serpentine crest rail - sometimes with ears - rests on inward-curving stiles that continue to form raked back legs. Most chairs have square or trapezoid drop-in seats.

■ Front legs reflect the fashion of the time, most typically Rococo cabriole legs with carved knees and claw-and-ball feet.

■ Mahogany tends to be the wood of choice, allowing for detailed carving, although it is not unusual to see walnut pieces from urban centres and fruitwood pieces from the provinces.

A pair of George II mahogany armchairs, the serpentine and reeded crest over a pierced and carved vasiform splat, over-upholstered seat, on cabriole legs with acanthus carved knees and ball-and-claw feet.

c1740

$12,000-15,000   **POOK**

A pair of Philadelphia walnut side chairs, the serpentine crest rail with a centred shell, gothic pierced vasiform splats, on shell carved cabriole legs and claw-and-ball feet, old finish, wear.

c1765

$10,000-15,000   **FRE**

A pair of late 18thC New England Chippendale cherry side chairs, with a serpentine crestrail with fan above pierced splat, squared legs.

$2,000-3,000   **FRE**

Six late 18thC Chippendale side chairs, probably Delaware Valley, each with pierced splat, on molded squared legs, old horsehair upholstery.

$6,000-9,000   **FRE**

A Philadelphia Chippendale walnut side chair, the crest carved with shell and scrolled ears, pierced splat, on cabriole legs ending in ball and claw feet.

c1760   *39in (99cm) high*

$4,500-6,500   **FRE**

A Philadelphia Chippendale mahogany side chair, with straight crestrail, shaped pierced splat and cabriole legs ending in ball and claw feet.

c1780

$3,000-4,000   **FRE**

A late 18thC Philadelphia mahogany dining chair, with pierced gothic splat with carved seat rail, on cabriole front legs terminating in ball and claw feet, retaining its original surface.

$7,000-9,000   **POOK**

An American Chippendale walnut dining chair, with a pierced and carved splat, on marlborough legs, paper label and provenance information.

The old paper label states that this chair belonged to General George Washington and was taken from Arlington House by Quartermaster's Department during the Civil War.

c1790

$10,000-15,000   **POOK**

Two of a set of ten mahogany dining chairs, six George III and four early 20thC, with pierced vase splat above tan leather stuffover seat.

$8,000-10,000 SET   **L&T**

Two of a set of six Scottish George III laburnum dining chairs, including two carvers, with vase splats and drop-in seats raised on square legs.

***Provenance:** Sir Robert Craigie of Glendoick, Perthshire, thence by descent. Craigie was Lord Advocate of Scotland from 1742-6.*

$10,000-12,000 SET   **L&T**

A set of six George III mahogany dining chairs, with shield shaped backs with foliate and acorn carved rails, drop-in seats on square tapering legs.

20.75in (53cm) wide

$1,500-2,000 set   **DN**

A set of three George III mahogany dining chairs, each with a shield shaped back, carved with wheat ears and with a pierced splat, with a padded seat on square tapering legs and later 'H' stretcher.

20.75in (53cm) wide

$500-700 SET   **DN**

A pair of George III mahogany dining chairs, each with an 'S' scroll carved back, a pierced splat with a central wheel motif, with a padded leather upholstered seat on turned tapering and reeded legs with 'H' stretcher, lacking part of one stretcher.

21.5in (55cm) wide

$500-700 PAIR   **DN**

A set of eight mahogany dining chairs in George III style, one with arms, each with a rounded rail and a pierced splat carved with garrya swags, with a padded seat on channelled square tapering legs with splayed feet. elbow chair

24in (62cm) wide

$3,000-4,000 SET   **DN**

A pair of George III mahogany dining chairs, each with a leaf carved crest and pierced splat, with a padded seat on chamfered legs with 'H' stretcher.

21.25in (54cm) wide

$1,000-1,200 PAIR   **DN**

A pair of Federal mahogany side chairs, probably Baltimore, with a racquet splat with leafage and bellflowers, on square tapering molded legs, repairs, old refinish.

c1790   *35.5in (90cm) high*

$3,000-6,000 PAIR   **FRE**

A set of six George IV mahogany and brass inlaid dining chairs, each with an 'X' shaped back applied with a central lion mask, on turned and pendant carved tapering legs, possibly Irish.

19.25in (49cm) wide

$3,000-4,000 SET   **DN**

A set of eight English Sheraton painted dining chairs, retaining their original rosewood surface with yellow decoration.

$2,000-3,000 SET   **POOK**

A set of ten Hepplewhite style mahogany dining chairs, including two carvers, with pierced splat centred by an anthemion, hollow stuffover gros point seat and fluted legs with spade feet.

$6,000-9,000 SET   **L&T**

FURNITURE

DINING CHAIRS

- By the early 17th century, cabinetmakers had started to lengthen the back legs of traditional stools to create chair backs, and so the earliest side- or dining-chairs were made. These were called 'back-stools'.
- The side chair grew in importance at the end of the 17th century as suites of chairs began to be placed around the edge of a room to emphasize its architectural features.
- During the mid- to late 18th century the Neo-Classical style began to emerge and chairs became light and elegant. Typical features include painted decoration, oval and shield-shaped backs and straight-sided backs.
- In early 19th century France, Neoclassical elements were embellished with decorative motifs from Ancient Rome and Egypt which celebrated Napoleon's successes. This Empire style was exported to much of Europe and America.
- In the UK it was called the Regency style. Common to both these movements was the fashion for sets of dining chairs which included a pair of open armchairs.
- The way a chair was constructed can help identify its age. The earliest chairs had pegged joints. Glue and screws came later.
- The amount of carving, especially where it required extra, detailed work from the craftsman, is a sign of quality.

Two of a set of twelve early 19thC mahogany dining chairs, including two carvers, each with broad curved top rails and curved supports above stuffover seats.

$20,000-30,000 SET   **L&T**

Two of a set of six early 19thC walnut dining chairs, in mid-18thC style, with scrolled top rails and vase-shaped pierced splats above drop-in seat.
c1810

$4,000-6,000 SET   **L&T**

Two of a set of eight early 19thC mahogany 'brander back' dining chairs, with molded triple splat back, above stuff over seats, on tapered legs, includes two carvers.

$2,000-3,000 SET   **L&T**

Two of a set of four Regency simulated rosewood and brass inlaid dining chairs, each with entablature top rails, caned seat on saber legs, later cushions.

$1,000-1,500 SET   **L&T**

One of a set of eight Regency Gothic mahogany chairs, the arched backs with lancet, pierced frieze, with stuff-over seats, on turned and reeded legs.

c1810

$30,000-40,000 SET   **PAR**

Two of a set of eight Regency mahogany dining chairs, in the manner of Gillows, with acanthus carved and pierced lyre horizontal splat, on reeded tapering legs.

$4,000-5,000 SET   **L&T**

A Scottish Regency mahogany carver and side chair, with gadrooned horizontal splat, on channelled saber legs.

22.5in (57cm) wide

$1,000-1,500   **L&T**

Two of a set of nine Scottish Regency and later mahogany dining chairs, each with waved horizontal splats centred by stylized flower heads, two of early 19thC date, inscribed "RAMSAY" in ink to the seat rail.

The scroll on this type of yoke back is referred to as a 'turret end' in the Edinburgh Chair and Cabinet Maker's Books of Prices published in the early 19thC.

$3,000-4,000 SET   **L&T**

Two of a set of eight Regency mahogany dining chairs, each with turned top rail above an entablature and Greek key pierced mid-rail, on turned front legs.

$5,000-7,000 SET   **L&T**

Two of a set of eight Regency mahogany dining chairs, each with bound laurel mid-rails raised above needlework upholstered seats on square tapering legs.

$2,000-3,000 SET   **L&T**

Two of a set of six Scottish Regency mahogany dining chairs, each with scroll-carved top rails above curved and leaf-carved mid-rails, on saber legs, restorations.

$1,200-1,800 SET   **L&T**

Two of a set of 22 Regency mahogany dining chairs, including two carvers, each with plain top rail above molded paneled lower rail, stuffover seat, plain frieze and tapering reeded legs.

$25,000-35,000 SET   **L&T**

Two of a set of ten Regency mahogany chairs. The chairs have a curved tablet top rail above a shaped horizontal splat centred by a pierced and gilded roundel and with gilded anthemion at the ends, with molded uprights. The plain front rail is centred by a patera and laurel with paterae at the angles, on tapering, square section saber legs. With padded drop-in seats. The armchairs have padded arms with scroll supports. Eight chairs and two armchairs.

c1820

$120,000-150,000 SET   **PAR**

Two of a set of six George IV mahogany dining chairs, each with a bar back and reeded supports, with a padded seat on turned and tapering legs

$3,000-4,000 SET   **DN**

Two of a set of eight George IV mahogany side chairs, with curved crestrails, horizontal splats and fluted uprights over olive green upholstered drop-in seats, on turned and tapered legs.

c1825   *34in (86.5cm) high*

$4,000-5,000   **FRE**

A set of 14 chairs Philadelphia Classical mahogany dining chairs, and three associated chairs, each with tablet crest centering figured mahogany panel flanked by backscrolling stiles, above two molded splats joined by three spherules, slip seats, molded legs and seat rails.

PROVENANCE: From the estate of Dr. Benton Hines Marshall of Philadelphia, Pennsylvania

c1820

$25,000-35,000 SET   **FRE**

A William IV rosewood side chair, in the manner of Gillows, waisted back, serpentine stuffover seat and shell cabochon carved cabriole legs.

$600-900   **L&T**

A set of 11 19thC mahogany dining chairs, of Hepplewhite style, the backs carved with acanthus leaves and husk pendants, distressed leather-upholstered seats, fluted legs with block feet.

$7,000-10,000 SET   **L&T**

Three of a 19thC French Second Empire set of 12 mahogany carvers, in pale blue silk damask, with gilt embellishments, on curved square tapering legs.

$10,000-12,000 SET   **SHA**

Two of a set of six Victorian rosewood parlor chairs, each with pierced top rail and c-scrolled mid rail, on molded cabriole legs.

$3,000-4,000 SET   **L&T**

A pair of mid-Victorian rosewood side chairs, each with elaborate pierced and carved backs, on cabriole legs with leaf-scroll feet, painted inventory mark "3908".

$3,000-4,000   **L&T**

A set of eight late 19thC Federal-style mahogany dining chairs, with arched crestrail, carved openwork splat, on reeded legs with spade feet.

$6,000-8,000   **FRE**

Two of a set of 12 Edwardian mahogany dining chairs, inlaid with boxwood stringing, satinwood veneered top rails, trellis arched splat backs, on strung circular tapered legs, one with indistinct maker's name "A. Bowler"?

$1,500-2,000 SET   **L&T**

Two of a set of 14 Edwardian mahogany dining chairs, in the George III style, with molded frames, pierced splats, horsehair fabric drop-in seats, on square tapering legs.

$10,000-12,000 SET   **L&T**

A set of eight early 20thC Queen Anne style walnut dining chairs, with shaped padded backs and drop-in seats, on cabriole legs with pad feet.

$3,000-4,000 SET   **FRE**

A set of five Scottish oak dining chairs, each with reeded yoke back raised on uprights with lotus leaf capitals, stuffover seats and turned and reeded tapering front legs.

$3,000-4,000 SET   **L&T**

A matched 1920s walnut dining room suite, by Whytock and Reid, Edinburgh, comprising a set of six chairs, each with vase splat, drop-in seat and cabriole legs with pad feet, and a rectangular draw leaf table.

98.5in (246cm) long

$1,500-2,000 SET   **L&T**

Two of a set of 12 mahogany and leather upholstered dining chairs, each with trefoil arched close nailed back and seat, on channeled square tapering legs and spade feet.

$5,000-7,000 SET   **L&T**

Two of a harlequin set of eight mahogany dining chairs, including two carvers, with serpentine top rails above pierced waisted splats, and drop in seats on square tapering legs.

$2,000-3,000 SET   **L&T**

A George III mahogany hall chair, with armorial inlaid back depicting an elephant standing on a shield-shaped coat of arms.

$1,000-1,200   **SWO**

A pair of Scottish William IV stained oak hall chairs, after William Playfair's designs for the Royal College of Surgeons, Edinburgh.

$1,200-1,500   **L&T**

A pair of mahogany hall chairs, each with molded ovoid back on hinged seat and ring and baluster-turned tapering legs.
c1840

$1,000-1,200   **FRE**

A pair of Victorian mahogany hall chairs, the ornate pierced backs with painted and applied crests on scrolled front legs.

$700-1,000   **SWO**

A pair of 19thC Italian walnut and ivory sgabello chairs with mother-of-pearl inlay, tapered backs with scroll carved top rails centered by figural reserves, on scroll carved supports.
43in (109cm) high

$3,000-5,000   **FRE**

A pair of Victorian oak hall chairs, with pierced scroll carved oval backs over solid shell carved seats and conforming apron, raised on angular spiral turned legs.
c1880   *35in (89cm) high*

$1,500-2,000   **FRE**

A pair of late Victorian oak hall chairs, with arched cut out back, solid seat enclosed by pierced armrests, and pierced side panels with stud decoration linked by a turned stretcher.

$1,200-1,800   **L&T**

A late 19thC satinwood and parcel gilt low chair, with a padded top rail and seat, the back carved with garrya and wreaths, on turned reeded legs with brass casters.

$450-550   **DN**

A George III leather upholstered porter's chair, with close nailed paneling, the arched hood enclosing a button upholstered interior, with squab cushion above a deep wooden drawer.
67in (170cm) high

$7,000-10,000   **L&T**

A Queen Anne walnut upholstered mahogany side chair, possibly Newport, Rhode Island, on cabriole legs, restoration.

c1730 43in (109cm) high

$35,000-45,000   **SK**

An early 19thC mahogany tub-shaped child's high chair, with crewelwork back and seat, with a removable tray and spindle turned foot guard.
17.75in (45cm) wide

$700-1,000   **DN**

FURNITURE

SOFAS

- The sofa emerged during the early 18th century. It developed at a rapid pace during the Neoclassical era (c.1760-c.1830) in an effort to meet the demand for greater comfort in the home.
- Early forms were based on the designs of contemporary side chairs and had carved backs and upholstered seats.
- By the end of the century the majority of them also had upholstered backs and sides and were covered in luxurious fabrics such as silks, damasks, velvets and chintzes.
- Late 18th century sofas were predominantly rectilinear in shape, having exposed mahogany frames with little ornament and elegant, tapered, reeded or fluted legs. Typical motifs included carved acanthus leaves, guilloche bands and rosettes.
- The more excessive 'Empire' style emerged around the turn of the century in France and quickly spread throughout Europe and the US.
- Empire Forms were generally heavier and reflected an attempt to copy typical Classical forms more closely. Sofa frames were more ornately shaped and stood on sabre legs or lion's paw feet. Carving was more prominent, with common motifs including those from ancient Egypt and ancient Rome.
- Revival style was fashionable throughout the 19th century.

An 18thC French fruitwood window bench with scrolled sides and shell carved apron.

79in (200.5cm) wide

$5,000-7,000   **POOK**

A George III mahogany sofa, the arched back flanked by scrolled arms, on square tapering legs terminating in brass casters.

c1790

$3,000-4,000   **POOK**

A New York Sheraton mahogany sofa, with a straight seat frame supported by turned legs.

c1810   *81in (205.5cm) long*

$7,000-10,000   **POOK**

A Regency mahogany and upholstered settee, the scrolling back centered by a brass inset tablet surmounted by gadrooned scroll, the back, outscrolled arms, seat and cushions upholstered in cream damask fabric, the seat rail with acanthus carved tablet flanked by brass inset tablets, on ring turned tapering legs terminating in brass caps and casters.

77in (196cm) wide

$7,000-10,000   **L&T**

An early 19thC Dutch mahogany and marquetry inlaid sofa, with inlaid and checker strung top rails and stuffover seat.

89.25in (223cm) wide

$2,000-3,000   **L&T**

An early 19thC Dutch mahogany settee, partially gilt, with stuffover seat and squab, the arms with tapering fluted terminals, on turned and lobed front legs.

83in (210cm) wide

$2,000-3,000   **L&T**

A Sheraton mahogany sofa, with molded arms extending to reeded vasiform posts with reeded backing, panel inlaid corners, on reeded legs with tall turned feet.

c1820   *72.5in (184cm) long*

$8,000-10,000   **FRE**

A Southern German Biedermeier cherrywood veneered bench, the back with ebonized wood, on cambered legs.

c1825   *76in (193cm) wide*

$600-900   **KAU**

A small German mahogany framed couch, in the Biedermeier taste, with arched top rail and carved lyre-end arms, on outscrolling legs.

57in (144cm) wide

$1,000-1,500   **L&T**

A Classical mahogany sofa, Boston, rolled crestrail with acanthus carved brackets, scrolled arms with leaf-carved ends, feather carved legs, lion's paw feet. c1825

$3,000-4,000   **FRE**

A mid-19thC Rococo-revival chaise lounge, probably New York, the asymmetrical back carved with floral spray and scrolls, on cabriole legs ending in scrolled feet and casters.

$4,500-6,500   **FRE**

A mid-19thC Rococo Revival walnut sofa, carved with flowers, fruit and leaves, on short curved legs with scroll feet, on casters.

90in (228.5cm) long

$1,500-2,000   **FRE**

A 19thC camel back settee, with a pierced and molded frame.

86.5in (220cm) wide

$1,000-1,500   **SWO**

A five piece American Rococo Revival carved rosewood suite, each carved with flowers and foliage, scrolls and medallion, on cabriole legs carved with bellflowers, scrolled feet, casters, old repairs. c1850

$5,000-7,000   **FRE**

A 19thC New York Classical mahogany love seat, with a gadrooned crest flanked by scrolled foliate carved arms supported by serpent carved legs terminating in animal paw feet.

58in (147.5cm) wide

$1,500-2,000   **POOK**

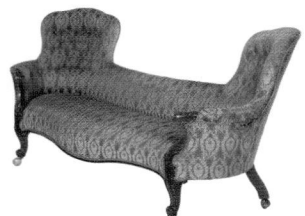

A mid-19thC mahogany framed gallery bench, with brown leather button upholstered seat, central removable back rest, lappet-carved seat rail and scroll supports.

41.25in (105cm) wide

$7,000-10,000   **L&T**

A Victorian walnut framed settee, on turned supports.

188cm (74in) long

$450-550   **SWO**

A pair of Victorian button-upholstered kidney shaped settees, covered in dark green velvet, the curved backs above loose seat cushions, on later casters.

69in (175cm) wide

$10,000-12,000   **L&T**

A 19thC walnut framed triple chair back settee, in the William and Mary taste, with projecting wings and scrollover arms, and upholstered with Jacobean-style floral tapestry.

80in (203cm) wide

$7,000-10,000   **L&T**

A Victorian rosewood framed sofa, the serpentine seat raised on cabriole legs with scroll toes.

84.25in (214cm) wide

$1,500-2,000   **L&T**

A late Victorian three seat Chesterfield settee with out scrolled padded armrests.

35in (90cm) wide

$1,200-1,800   **L&T**

A pair of late 19thC gilt wood and overpainted settees, of bergère form, with laurel moldings, floral cresting, upholstered panel, and seat with loose squab cushion.

43in (108cm) wide

$4,000-6,000   **L&T**

A 20thC mahogany and marquetry sofa, in the Biedemeier style, the back with a central tablet, the lower frieze with marquetry hippocampi, on gilt lion paw feet.

100.75in (256cm) wide

$4,000-6,000   **DN**

FURNITURE

A CLOSER LOOK AT FOUR RARE GEORGE III MAHOGANY BENCHES

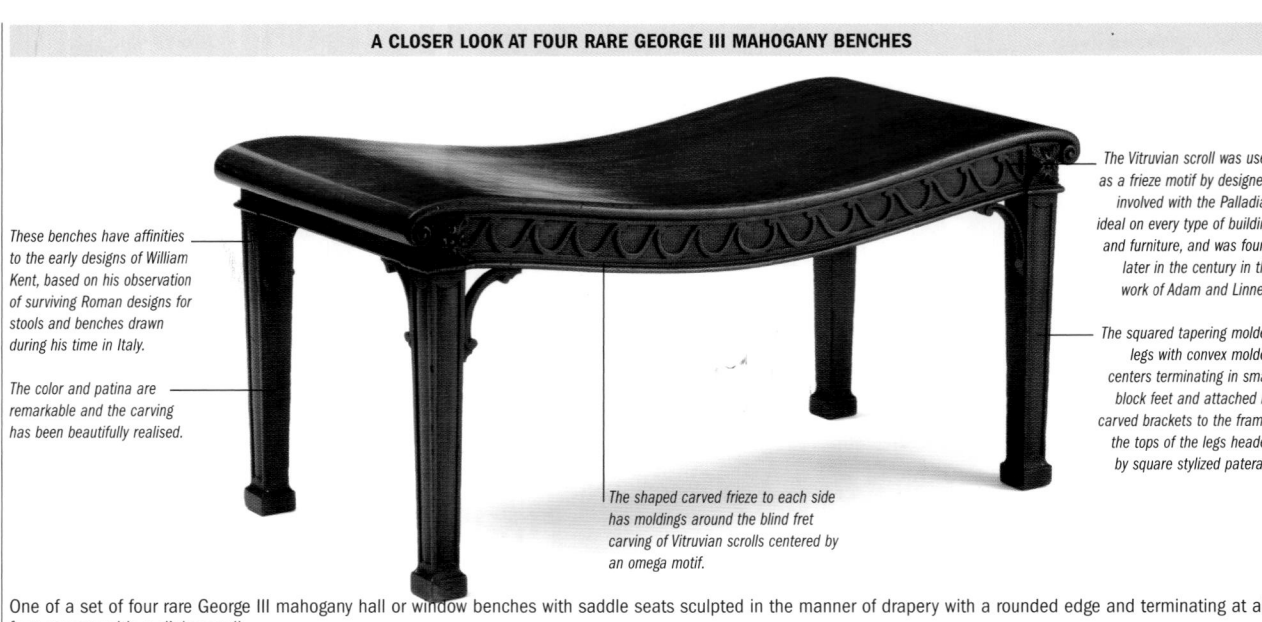

The Vitruvian scroll was used as a frieze motif by designers involved with the Palladian ideal on every type of building and furniture, and was found later in the century in the work of Adam and Linnell.

These benches have affinities to the early designs of William Kent, based on his observation of surviving Roman designs for stools and benches drawn during his time in Italy.

The color and patina are remarkable and the carving has been beautifully realised.

The squared tapering molded legs with convex molded centers terminating in small block feet and attached by carved brackets to the frame, the tops of the legs headed by square stylized paterae.

The shaped carved frieze to each side has moldings around the blind fret carving of Vitruvian scrolls centered by an omega motif.

One of a set of four rare George III mahogany hall or window benches with saddle seats sculpted in the manner of drapery with a rounded edge and terminating at all four corners with a slight scroll.

c1762

$1,000,000+ SET   **PAR**

A pair of George III mahogany window seats, with outscrolled upholstered sides and seat raised on legs with inlaid panels, brass caps and casters.

33.5in (85cm) wide

$6,000-9,000   **L&T**

A pair of George IV mahogany and caned window seats, each with brass mounts and buttoned loose cushions, the reeded and bobbin-turned side arms on scrolled apron supports, the saber legs with brass ball feet.

39in (99cm) wide

$20,000-30,000   **L&T**

A CLOSER LOOK AT A REPLICA GEORGE II SEAT

The lavish carving and use of gilding are typical of furniture dating from the early 18thC and show great craftsmanship – adding to the value of the piece.

This seat probably comes from a Regency copy of a suite of furniture used at Northumberland House in London. The building was demolished in 1874 in the wake of construction work surrounding Charing Cross station. However, it was one of the first interiors to have been photographed, the images reveal the complex history of successive re-decoration throughout the preceding three centuries and show the furniture as arranged by the 1870s. Following a fire in 1780 the building was rebuilt and new furniture made. This bench was designed for one of the re-modeled rooms.

The combination of carved motifs: 'C' scrolls, acanthus leaves and diaperwork (chequered patterns) are typical of the period .

A Regency rectangular bench replicating a George II original, the stuff-over upholstered seat now covered in cerise silk damask above a deeply carved frieze embellished with 'C' scrolls, acanthus leaves and a diaperwork ground merging into the four short cabriole legs carved with husks and further 'C' scrolls on massively carved paw-feet.

c1820   *40in (101.5cm) wide*

$45,000-50,000   **PAR**

A mid-18thC Swedish carved gilt wood bench, in rococo style, with open cartouche, and upholstered walnut seat on carved hairy paw feet.

c1750   *60in (153cm) wide*

$10,000-15,000   **L&T**

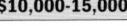

A mid-19thC mahogany bench, the solid seat with turned ends, on turned tapering legs.

37in (94cm) wide

$1,000-1,200   **DN**

A Georgian style walnut stool, the shaped apron raised on carved cabriole legs with ball-and-claw.

23.25in (59cm) high

$600-900   **SWO**

A late Georgian mahogany piano stool, the adjustable padded seat on ring turned legs

$300-400   **SWO**

A pair of Regency mahogany X-framed stools, with incised decoration and scrolling mid-rails, with loose tasseled squab cushions.

27.25in (69cm) high

$10,000-12,000   **L&T**

A Regency style giltwood bench, with green foliate upholstery, twin scroll ends, and Greek Key molded apron, raised on reeded and scroll carved legs with bun feet.

66in (167.5cm) wide

$1,200-1,800   **FRE**

A 19thC Continental oak stool, carved with foliate scrolls and shell motifs on cabriole legs.

23.25in (59cm) wide

$450-650   **DN**

A pair of 19thC Swedish satin birch stools, with 'X' frame bases and upholstered seats.

$400-500   **SWO**

A pair of 19thC Continental wrought iron x-frame stools of typical form.

23in (58.5cm) wide

$2,000-3,000   **FRE**

A Victorian upholstered window seat, on shaped mahogany scrolled legs and a similar small stool.

Seat 40.5in (103cm) wide

$600-900   **SWO**

A Victorian rosewood piano stool, with patent rise and fall action by Brooke Ltd.

$450-650   **BRI**

A late Victorian walnut framed stool, with a modern leather upholstered seat.

$450-650   **SWO**

FURNITURE

A 17thC Italian carved and paint-decorated cassone, with hinged molded top and void interior with candle box, an anthemion decorated frieze and shaped front raised on hairy paw feet.

61in (155cm) wide

$4,000-6,000   **FRE**

A 17thC Italian walnut cassone, the later hinged top over a foliate carved triple panel frieze, raised on carved claw feet joined by a gadrooned apron.

55.5in (141cm) wide

$1,000-1,500   **FRE**

A Charles II oak and marquetry coffer, with hinged paneled top, sectioned interior, anthemion molded frieze front, four arched foliate inlaid panels, and molded panels, anthemion molded apron, raised on later bracket feet.

c1680   *80.5in (204.5cm) wide*

$4,000-6,000   **FRE**

A late 17thC oak coffer, with a molded frame and a three panel front.

43.25in (108cm) wide

$1,000-1,200   **SWO**

A 17thC elm six plank coffer.

32in (80cm) wide

$500-700   **SWO**

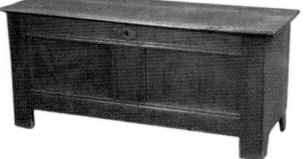

A 17thC made-up Italian walnut cassone with hinged molded top and anthemion carved edge, a later cedar lined interior, stop-fluted sides, and a gadrooned apron, raised on paw feet.

72.5in (184cm) wide

$2,000-3,000   **FRE**

A 17thC Italian walnut cassone, with hinged molded top and void interior, a carved paneled front with masks, and the sides with iron handles, raised on paw feet.

68in (172.5cm) wide

$2,000-3,000   **FRE**

A small 17thC oak coffer, with molded frame, paneled top and sides, and lunette-carved frieze above lozenge-carved inset front panels.

c1650   *38in (97cm) wide*

$1,000-1,500   **L&T**

A late 17thC oak coffer.

$700-1,000   **SWO**

An early 17thC oak six-plank coffer, with routed front plank.

39.75in (101cm) wide

$600-900   **SWO**

A late 17th/early 18thC Italian carved walnut cassone, with a hinged lid and gadrooned edge, over a foliate and figural carved paneled front, raised on stylized claw feet.

67.5in (171.5cm) wide

$2,000-3,000   **FRE**

A late 17thC Charles II oak coffer with twin paneled hinged top, a void interior, palmette carved frieze, and fluted stile feet.

32in (81.5cm) wide

$3,000-5,000   **FRE**

A mid-18thC Bermuda Queen Anne cedar blanket chest, with a dovetailed case resting on a scalloped frame, on cabriole legs and pad feet.

46in (117cm) wide

$18,000-20,000   **POOK**

A rare Southern Pennsylvania or Delaware Chippendale walnut blanket chest, with three drawers and rare three foot front configuration.

c1780   *48.75in (124cm) wide*

$7,000-9,000   **POOK**

A Chippendale walnut miniature blanket chest, Pennsylvania, till inside, two small drawers below with brass knob pulls, on vigorous ogival bracket feet, old finish, repaired.

c1780   *14.75in (37.5cm) wide*

$10,000-12,000   **FRE**

A Pennsylvania walnut blanket chest, with a dovetailed case with inlaid cartouche initialed "C.S.", above two short drawers supported by straight bracket feet, dated.

1781   *45in (114.5cm) wide*

$8,000-10,000   **POOK**

A George III period oak and parquetry-inlaid mule chest, enclosing a candle box and drawer, with chequer banding and molded edge raised above two drawers.

56.75in (144cm) wide

$2,000-3,000   **L&T**

A Pennsylvania inlaid walnut blanket chest, opening to well with till, inlaid with date and initials "17 G M 96" above two drawers and bracket feet.

1796   *29in (73.5cm) high*

$6,000-8,000   **FRE**

A Pennsylvania Chippendale walnut blanket chest, from Lancaster County, inlaid "Magdalena Haglein 1799" centering a star, two drawers and ogee bracket feet.

1799   *50.5in (128.5cm) wide*

$4,500-6,500   **POOK**

A 19thC American folk art pine and oak diminutive blanket chest, with applied carvings of hearts and arrows.

27.75in (69cm) wide

$1,000-1,200   **POOK**

A 19th century Italian walnut cassone, with shaped gadrooned top and plinth base, mask motif interior, lion supports and bearing an "American Express Co., World's Columbian Exposition, from Chicago, Ills, USA" label verso.

68.5in (174cm) wide

$4,000-6,000   **FRE**

PAINTED DOWER CHESTS

- Chests were made for young girls to store household items for use in her future married life. When the girl married, the bride's name and the date of her wedding were often added.

- Painted chests where common in Europe and Scandinavia until the late 18th century. They were an inexpensive way for householders to introduce color to their homes. Paint also disguised inexpensive wood and helped to protect it.

- Immigrants took the tradition to rural areas of North America. New fashions were slower to be adopted and painted chests remained popular during the 19th century.

- Itinerant decorators used European motifs such as hearts, tulips and birds and symbols of the new democracy such as the eagle and American creatures such as the wild turkey.

- Blue was an expensive pigment and hard to use so pieces painted this color command a premium.

- Pieces were sometimes passed on to other couples at a later date. New paint which has been added to take in this change of ownership will not affect value as restoration might.

- An original worn surface with flaking and faded paint is acceptable.

A painted dower chest, probably Northampton County, Pennsylvania, inscribed "Margreta Diefenderfer", over two clover panels and two short drawers supported by bracket feet, dated.

1780   *48in (122cm) wide*

$2,000-3,000   **POOK**

A late 18thC Pennsylvania paint-decorated pine dower chest, with lidded till and pinwheel and tulip design, on bracket feet, old surface, imperfections.

48in (122cm) wide

$7,000-9,000   **SK**

A painted and decorated blanket chest, Pennsylvania, dated and inscribed "Rosina Beutelmann 1788" above birds and flower-filled urn, wear.

A Rosina Beutelmann was born in 1756 in Springfield, Bucks County. This chest was purchased from the Center Bridge, Bucks County home of the painter Edward Willis Redfield (1869-1965) a leading figure of the Pennsylvania Impressionist School.

1788

$4,500-6,500   **FRE**

An 18thC Pennsylvania painted pine dower chest, attributed to Christian Selzer, with three potted tulip panels, on bracket feet.

48in (122cm) wide

$7,000-10,000   **POOK**

A late 18thC Central Pennsylvania painted pine and poplar dower chest, inscribed,"Barbara", with tree and scrolling floral motifs.

48in (122cm) wide

$6,000-8,000   **POOK**

A late 18thC Pennsylvania painted blanket chest, with a dovetailed case with three arched panels depicting urns with tulips, each inscribed "Johanns Rank", dated, on a molded base and cut-out bracket feet.

1798   *51.5in (131cm) wide*

$20,000-30,000   **POOK**

A painted pine dower chest, Dauphin County, Pennsylvania, adorned with three tombstone panels with pinwheels and tulips, inscribed "Sara Farne" and dated.

1808   *50.5in (128.5cm) wide*

$5,000-6,000   **POOK**

A Pennsylvania painted and grained blanket chest, with till and three drawers, decorated with vinegar-grained tulip design, on turned feet.

c1825   *52in (132cm) wide*

$3,500-5,500   **FRE**

A Central Pennsylvania paint-decorated and stenciled poplar blanket chest, the lid with oval wells with till, inscribed 'Lesley Anne Cer 1827', on bracket feet.

1827   *25in (63.5cm) high*

$35,000-40,000   **FRE**

A Schwenkfelder painted blanket chest, Montgomery County, Pennsylvania, dated, with white panel for "Anna Wigner 1847", wear.

1847   *45in (114.5cm) wide*

$8,000-10,000   **FRE**

A Pennsylvania painted and decorated blanket chest, painted and incised with double arches enclosing flowers, and with hearts and vines, molded bracket base.

50in (127cm) wide

$3,000-5,000   **FRE**

CHESTS OF DRAWERS

- In the Middle Ages, chests were simple in construction, a hinged, lidded box or a frame and with a number of panels, and usually made from oak. Many were elaborately carved in high relief.
- All manner of household objects were kept in the chest and, owing to the difficulty in retrieving an item, designs from the middle of the 17th century began to incorporate a single drawer at the bottom of the chest.
- The chest of drawers as we know it today appeared toward the end of the 17th century, making the lidded chest redundant.
- Early versions were rectilinear, often with an arrangement of two short drawers over three long, within a joined frame carcase. The feet were a continuation of the styles of the frame.
- As time progressed, the carcase became made by a cabinetmaker in urban areas and was decorated with veneers. The feet were formed as square or ogee brackets until the 1780s when a curved splay pattern was introduced.
- Variations on the chest of drawers emerged throughout the 18th century and included the cupboard-on-chest, the chest-on-chest or tallboy, known in America as the 'highboy'.

An early 18thC oak chest, of four long drawers with paneled sides.

40.75in (102cm) wide

$700-1,000   **SWO**

An early 18thC George I mahogany and marquetry chest of drawers, with four drawers with foliate and bird decoration, on turned bun feet.

37in (94cm) wide

$5,000-6,000   **POOK**

An early 18thC George I burlwood chest of drawers, with three short drawers and three graduated drawers on bracket feet.

39in (99cm) wide

$3,000-4,000   **POOK**

A George II mahogany bachelor's chest, with a later baize-lined interior, two short and three long graduated drawers, on shaped bracket feet.

30.25in (77cm) high

$6,000-9,000   **L&T**

A Queen Anne Pennsylvania walnut spice chest, from Chester County, with a panel door opening to a 13 drawer interior, on straight bracket feet, inscribed "Made by Richd Riley Goshen".

c1750   *21.25in (54cm) high*

$7,000-10,000   **POOK**

An 18thC French oak chest, with three long drawers with floral carved detail.

53.5in (134cm) wide

$2,000-3,000   **L&T**

An 18thC Pennsylvania Chippendale walnut chest of drawers, with two thumb-molded short drawers and three thumb-molded and graduated long drawers, with ogee bracket feet.

33in (84cm) high

$4,500-6,500   **FRE**

An 18thC and later Chippendale cherry chest of drawers, gadroon-carved base with original bracket feet.

Originally this was the top section of a chest on chest.

34.5in (87.5cm) high

$2,000-3,000   **FRE**

A small early George III mahogany serpentine chest of drawers, with four long graduated drawers, on splayed bracket feet, carry handles to sides.

32.5in (83cm) high

$7,000-10,000   **L&T**

A Philadelphia Chippendale mahogany chest, with four graduated wide lip-molded drawers and quarter-round reeded columns, on ogival bracket feet, brass bails, possibly replaced.

c1770   37.5in (95cm) wide

$7,000-10,000   FRE

A Philadelphia Chippendale mahogany chest of drawers, with four graduated drawers flanked by fluted quarter columns supported by ogee bracket feet.

c1775   38in (96.5cm) wide

$7,000-9,000   POOK

A George III mahogany bachelor's chest, with molded edge top above brushing slide, four graduated drawers and bracket feet.

33in (84cm) wide

$5,000-7,000   L&T

A George III mahogany serpentine chest of drawers, with molded edge top over two short and three long graduated drawers, on bracket feet.

40in (102cm) wide

$6,000-9,000   L&T

A George III mahogany chest, of two short and three long drawers, on bracket feet.

45.75in (116cm) wide

$1,000-1,500   SWO

A George III mahogany serpentine fronted chest of drawers, the top with a molded edge above four long graduated drawers, on later bracket feet.

c1790   39.25in (100cm) wide

$700-1,000   DN

A George III mahogany serpentine chest of drawers, with a long drawer and brushing slide over three further long drawers flanked by canted angles with blind fretwork panels, on ogee bracket feet.

38in (96.5cm) high

$12,000-15,000   L&T

A late 18thC mid-Atlantic States mahogany chest of drawers, possibly Charleston, with four drawers flanked by chamfered satinwood inlaid stiles, on straight bracket feet with line inlays, brasses probably original, the reverse stamped "R. Bringhurst".

46in (116cm) wide

$15,000-20,000   POOK

A George III mahogany and inlaid serpentine commode, with baize lined slide and interior fitted with various items including lidded boxes, glass bottles.

39.25in (98cm) wide

$5,000-7,000   L&T

A late 18thC Connecticut cherry chest of drawers, with serpentine top and four graduated drawers, on a gadrooned skirt and ogee bracket feet.

38in (96.5cm) wide

$13,000-15,000   POOK

An 18thC oak chest of four long drawers, with molded edges, on block feet.

40.75in (102cm) wide

$1,000-1,500   **SWO**

An 18thC walnut chest of five drawers, with an oak top.

41.5in (104cm) wide

$2,000-3,000   **SWO**

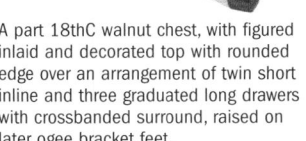

A part 18thC walnut chest, with figured inlaid and decorated top with rounded edge over an arrangement of twin short inline and three graduated long drawers with crossbanded surround, raised on later ogee bracket feet.

44in (110cm) wide

$3,000-4,000   **BIG**

A George III mahogany bachelor's chest, of three long and two short graduating drawers, with later brass drop handles on pierced back plates, having quarter turned and reeded side columns and bracket feet.

35.5in (90cm) wide

$1,000-1,500   **MAX**

A small George II walnut chest of drawers, with later alterations, with a crossbanded caddy top, over a brushing slide, two short and three long drawers and bracket feet.

31.25in (78cm) wide

$4,500-5,500   **SWO**

A George III mahogany bachelor's chest, of three long and two short drawers, with brass swan neck handles and bracket feet.

35.5in (90cm) high

$700-1,000   **MAX**

A George III mahogany chest of drawers, with three drawers below a brushing slide.

$1,800-2,200   **SWO**

A George III mahogany chest of four graduated drawers, with a brushing slide, on bracket feet.

30in (76.5cm) high

$1,000-1,500   **SWO**

A George III mahogany chest of drawers, the molded top over a brushing slide and four long graduated drawers, raised shaped bracket feet.

c1760   *32.5in (81cm) high*

$1,500-2,000   **FRE**

A George III mahogany chest of drawers, with two short and three long drawers, with original brass handles, on bracket feet.

44in (110cm) wide

$1,500-2,000   **SWO**

A late Georgian mahogany bow front chest of two long and two short drawers, with brass ring handles, shaped apron and splay bracket feet.

36in (91.5cm) wide

$700-1,000   **MAX**

A mid-George III burr elm bachelor's chest with brushing slide and 4 graduating cross-banded drawers with oval vase embossed ring handles, on bracket feet, replacement top.

29.5in (75cm) wide

$1,000-1,500   **MAX**

A George III fruitwood small chest, with a slide above four long drawers, brass handles, on bracket feet.

35.75in (91cm) wide

$3,500-5,500   **LFA**

A Regency mahogany three drawer chest, with bun handles and swept legs.

36.5in (91cm) wide

$700-1,000   **SWO**

A Regency mahogany and satinwood strung D-shaped chest, containing four long graduated drawers, between fluted pilasters, on turned feet.

44in (112cm) high

$2,000-3,000   **SWO**

A Regency mahogany bow-front chest of four graduated drawers.

41.25in (104.5cm) high

$1,500-2,000   **SWO**

An early 19thC mahogany and crossbanded bow front chest, containing three short over three long graduated drawers, on bracket feet.

41.25in (105cm) high

$1,000-1,500   **SWO**

An early 19th Century mahogany bowfront chest, with wooden knob handles, on splayed feet.

42in (107cm) wide

$1,500-2,000   **SWO**

A William IV mahogany three drawer chest.

37in (94cm) wide

$700-1,000   **SWO**

A Federal inlaid mahogany bow front chest of drawers, with four graduated drawers with barber pole inlay and inlaid escutcheons, shaped skirt with fan inlay, raised on French feet.

c1800   39.25in (100cm) high

$7,000-9,000   FRE

A Federal cherry inlaid bureau, possibly Connecticut, with four graduated string-inlaid drawers, all on bracket feet, replaced brasses, refinished.

c1800   40.5in (101cm) high

$2,500-3,500   SK

An early 19thC mahogany and brass bound campaign chest, with five graduated drawers with recessed brass handles, made in two sections with brass carrying handles.

41.75in (106cm) wide

$3,000-4,000   L&T

A pair of Federal Philadelphia mahogany swell front chests, each with four graduated and beaded drawers on turned feet.

PROVENANCE: These chests probably belonged to Deborah Bache Duane (1781-1863), granddaughter of Benjamin Franklin. The chests descended through the family to Ellen Duane Davis.

c1800   38.5in (98cm) high

$5,000-7,000   FRE

A Federal Western Pennsylvania walnut chest of drawers, with four long drawers with line and fan inlaid corners, stiles with line and bellflower inlays, skirt with diamond inlays supported by French feet.

c1805   39in (99cm) wide

$8,000-10,000   POOK

Left: A Federal mahogany inlaid bowfront chest of drawers, probably New Hampshire, the cockbeaded drawers with bone-inlaid escutcheons and stringing, front French feet as well as arched, replaced brasses, old refinish.

A brass plaque on the reverse reads, "Property of William and Mary Chandler Sever married Oct 29 1785".

c1810   43.25in (110cm) wide

$4,000-5,000   SK

Right: A Federal cherry and cherry veneer bowfront chest of drawers, probably southeastern New England, with four cockbeaded graduated drawers, on flaring French feet.

c1805   38.75in (98.5cm) wide

$3,000-4,000   SK

A Federal cherry and mahogany veneer inlaid chest of drawers, probably Massachusetts, with four cockbeaded graduated drawers, quarter-engaged vase and ring-turned reeded posts continuing to turned legs, original brasses, old surface, imperfections.

c1815   42.5 (108cm) wide

$3,000-4,000   SK

Left: A Massachusetts Federal mahogany bowfront chest of drawers, probably Salem, with four long drawers, on turned feet.

40in (100cm) wide

$4,000-5,000   POOK

Right: A New England Federal mahogany bowfront chest of drawers, with four long drawers, rope-turned three-quarter columns, on turned feet.

c1815   38.5in (96cm) high

$1,500-1,800   POOK

A Federal stained maple, bird's-eye maple and mahogany veneer bowfront bureau, probably Massachusetts, with quarter-engaged vase and ring-turned reeded columns, old brasses, old refinish.

c1820   43in (107.5cm) high

$7,000-9,000   **SK**

An early 19thC English mahogany veneered chest of drawers, with five drawers with fluted corners, bone inlays, original locks.

51.5in (131cm) wide

$700-1,000   **KAU**

A Federal Pennsylvania inlaid walnut chest of drawers, Mifflin County, with graduated drawers flanked by inlaid chamfered edge, French feet.

c1820   38in (96.5cm) high

$4,000-6,000   **FRE**

A Sheraton bird's eye maple and cherrywood chest, inscribed on bottom of second drawer in pencil "Samuel Slather (?) Shurstown, Lancaster County, State of Pennsylvania, June 7th 1825", refinished.

c1825   42in (106.5cm) high

$2,500-3,000   **FRE**

A Pennsylvania Sheraton tiger maple bureau, with arched backsplash flanked by two short drawers, case with four long drawers, on turned feet.

c1835   55.25in (138cm) high

$3,500-4,500   **POOK**

A 19thC oak table chest of drawers, the top inlaid with a parquetry design of specimen woods, the sides with inlaid panels, brass ringed handles, on a plinth.

19.25in (48cm) high

$1,500-2,000   **L&T**

A 19thC mahogany chest, of two short and two long drawers on splayed front legs, split side.

42.5in (108cm) wide

$500-600   **SWO**

A 19thC mahogany serpentine chest with four long graduated drawers, oval brass handles and tapered bracket feet.

42in (107cm) wide

$2,000-3,000   **L&T**

A pair of walnut veneered chests of drawers, of small proportions, each with ebony lines, five graduated drawers and outswept bracket feet.

27.5in (70cm) high

$1,500-2,000   **L&T**

A mid-Victorian satinwood and bleached wood dressing chest, with two short and three long graduated drawers, period knop handles, on plinth.

47.75in (121cm) wide

$350-550   **BIG**

A 19thC rosewood compact dressing chest the hinged cover enclosing marble top above four long drawers on plinth base.

32in (81.5cm) wide

$500-700   **BRI**

A 19thC continental satin birch chest, the top with inlaid musical instruments within inlaid stringing and crossbanding, over four drawers between a pair of scrolled pilasters.

37.75in (96cm) high

$900-1,100   **SWO**

A Beidermeier satin walnut chest of drawers, the rectangular top over one projecting long drawers, flanked by half doric columns with gilt-metal mounts, on squared block feet.

c1835   *45in (114.5cm) wide*

$2,000-3,000   **FRE**

A 19thC Continental mahogany chest of drawers, with a raised back, over two frieze drawers and four long drawers with ornate molding.

45.5in (114cm) wide

$1,200-1,800   **SWO**

A 19thC continental marquetry chest of drawers.

26in (66cm) wide

$1,200-1,800   **BRI**

FURNITURE

A late 17thC Charles II oak chest on stand, with molded drawer fronts, and a further long drawer, the stand later associated.

41in (104cm) wide

| $7,000-10,000 | DN |

An early 18thC oak chest on stand, with paneled drawers and dummy drawer, shaped apron and square section cabriole legs with pad feet.

56.75in (142cm) high

| $12,000-18,000 | L&T |

An early 18thC walnut chest, with quarter-veneered crossbanded top and six drawers, on barley twist supports with turned feet linked by stretchers, the stand later.

46in (117cm) wide

| $3,000-4,000 | L&T |

An early 18thC English William and Mary burl veneer highboy, with a six drawer upper section resting on a base with six turned legs.

41in (104cm) wide

| $3,000-4,000 | POOK |

An 18thC featherbanded walnut chest on stand, herringbone crossbanded, the molded cornice above six drawers, the later base with two drawers.

63in (160cm) high

| $5,000-7,000 | L&T |

An 18thC American mahogany highboy, with molded cornice, eight drawers with brass handles, central carved fan patera, and shaped apron, on cabriole legs.

40in (102cm) high

| $10,000-15,000 | L&T |

A CLOSER LOOK AT A QUEEN ANNE WALNUT HIGH CHEST OF DRAWERS

The molded cornice over the two short drawers is typical of early American Queen Anne chests. Later examples often have a lavishly carved high bonnet top.

Walnut was favored at this time, often with burl walnut veneers. Maple and cherry were also used by American craftsmen.

The top half should fit snugly onto the bottom. Always check that the drawers in both pieces were made in the same way and that the woods match.

The graceful cabriole legs were carefully designed to support the weight of the chest and contents of the drawers.

An 18thC chest on stand, with chequer stringing, nine drawers, shaped apron, on molded square section chamfered legs.

41.75in (106cm) wide

| $2,000-3,000 | L&T |

An 18thC Queen Anne Rhode Island mahogany band inlaid high chest, with five lip molded drawers, old bat wing brasses, and an arched apron with cock beaded edge.

| $6,000-9,000 | FRE |

A Queen Anne Massachusetts walnut and walnut veneer inlaid high chest of drawers, the engraved brass escutcheons and pulls may be original, refinished, imperfections.

c1730

72in (183cm) high

| $30,000-40,000 | SK |

An 18thC Pennsylvania walnut chest on frame, with eight drawers resting on a base with scalloped skirt, cabriole legs and ball and claw feet.

71in (180.5cm) high

$12,000-15,000 **POOK**

A mid-18thC Delaware Queen Anne walnut high chest, with bonnet top, the middle drawer with shell carving, on cabriole legs.

87in (221cm) high

$8,000-12,000 **POOK**

An 18thC and later Queen Anne-style walnut highboy, with molded waist, the center drawer carved with a fan, shaped skirt and cabriole legs ending in pad feet.

68in (172.5cm) high

$3,000-4,000 **FRE**

A Queen Anne Pennsylvania walnut chest on frame, from Chester County, with molded cornice, nine drawers, scalloped skirt and shell-carved cabriole legs.

c1760   70.5in (179cm) high

$20,000-30,000 **POOK**

A Queen Anne Pennsylvania walnut high chest, in two parts, with molded cornice, twelve drawers, shaped skirt, and cabriole legs ending in pad feet.

c1760   78in (198cm) high

$12,000-18,000 **FRE**

A Queen Anne cherry carved high chest, with scrolled molded top, concave fan, four drawers with valance skirt and original salmon red washed surface, imperfections.

c1760   89in (226cm) high

$250,000-350,000 **SK**

A Queen Anne Pennsylvania walnut highboy, in two parts, with molded cornice, shaped skirt, cabriole legs carved with shell, and trifid 'socked' feet.

PROVENANCE: *From the collection of D. Virginia Armentrout (nee Roosevelt) of Ambler, Pennsylvania*

c1760   69in (175cm) high

$20,000-30,000 **FRE**

A mid-to late 18thC Pennsylvania walnut high chest, with flat molded cornice, carved apron on plain cabriole legs on trifid feet, refinished.

69in (175.5cm) high

$10,000-15,000 **FRE**

A Queen Anne tiger maple brown-painted high chest of drawers, attributed to John Kimball, Deryfield or Concord, New Hampshire, with a deeply valanced apron.

c1765   64in (163cm) high

$80,000-100,000 **SK**

A Massachusetts Queen Anne maple highboy, the molded cornice over four drawers on a base with fan carved long drawer, scalloped skirt and pad feet.

c1765   38in (96.5cm) wide

$6,000-8,000 **POOK**

A Queen Anne New England maple high chest of drawers, with old bat wing brasses, scalloped apron with central shell, refinished, knee blocks are missing.

c1770

$40,000-55,000 **FRE**

A New Hampshire maple chest-on-chest, attributed to Samuel Dunlap, with original brass pulls, escutcheons, and red washed surface, and minor imperfections.

c1780   80in (203cm) high

$110,000-130,000 **SK**

FURNITURE

A George II mahogany chest on chest, the molded cavetto cornice above three short and three long graduated drawers, flanked by canted angles with fluted panels, the base with three long graduated drawers raised on bracket feet.

74.75in (187cm) high

$2,000-3,000   **L&T**

A Chippendale walnut tall chest on chest, Pennsylvania, with three small and four graduated wide lip molded drawers, over three graduated wide lip molded drawers, on ogival bracket feet.

c1770   76in (193cm) high

$10,000-15,000   **FRE**

A George III mahogany chest on chest, cornered by fluted quarter columns, on bracket feet.

c1780   44.5in (113cm) wide

$2,000-3,000   **DN**

A George III mahogany chest-on-chest, with eight drawers and brass handles, canted angles, and bracket feet.

72in (182cm) high

$2,000-3,000   **L&T**

A late 18thC Chippendale carved walnut chest-on-chest Pennsylvania, with three short drawers, the middle drawer carved with a fan, and four long drawers, over three deep drawers, molded base, and ogee bracket feet.

77in (195.5cm) high

$6,000-9,000   **FRE**

A George III mahogany chest on chest, the projecting cornice with dentil frieze above boxwood lined frieze with shell patera and drawers each with fan patera to the angles, the base raised on ogee bracket feet.

78.25in (199cm) high

$6,000-7,000   **L&T**

A late 18thC American mahogany chest-on-chest, with molded dentil cornice, ten drawers, swan neck handles, and ogee bracket feet.

c1775   77in (196cm) high

$6,000-9,000   **L&T**

An 18th to 19thC Chippendale walnut chest on chest, Pennsylvania, with three small and five long drawers and quarter round fluted corners on ogival bracket feet.

73in (185.5cm) high

$10,000-12,000   **FRE**

A mid-18thC Pennsylvania Queen Anne walnut "Octorara" tall chest with molded cornice over five short drawers and four long drawers on screw on Spanish feet.

60in (152cm) high

$10,000-15,000   **POOK**

An 18thC Pennsylvania walnut tall chest with molded cornice over five short drawers above four graduated drawers on bracket feet.

65in (165cm) high

$11,000-14,000   **POOK**

An 18thC Pennsylvania walnut tall chest with five short drawers over three graduated drawers on bracket feet.

63in (160cm) high

$5,500-6,500   **POOK**

A Chippendale Octorara walnut tall chest, Pennsylvania, inlaid "MC", with eight drawers flanked by fluted quarter columns supported by ogee bracket feet.

c1770   *64.5in (162cm) high*

$7,000-10,000   **POOK**

A Federal walnut tall chest, Pennsylvania, with five graduated wide cockbeaded drawers, chamfered corners, on French bracket feet.

c1780   *68.25in (173.5cm) high*

$4,500-6,500   **FRE**

A late 18thC tiger maple tall chest, Pennsylvania, with an arrangement of nine molded drawers, shaped skirt and bracket feet.

57.5in (146cm) high

$4,500-6,500   **FRE**

A late 18thC Pennsylvania Queen Anne walnut tall chest with molded cornice above three small drawers over two short drawers and four graduated drawers on straight bracket feet.

59in (150cm) high

$5,000-6,000   **POOK**

A Federal cherry tall chest, raised on tall bracket feet, the seven drawers lined with pages of 'The Temperance Journal Total Abstinence Gazette', Providence, Rhode Island, 1837.

c1800   *61.25in (155.5cm) high*

$4,500-6,500   **FRE**

A Federal cherry tall chest, Pennsylvania, with three short and five long drawers flanked by fluted chamfered columns, on flaring French feet.

c1810   *65.25in (165.5cm) high*

$4,000-5,500   **POOK**

An early 19thC Pennsylvania cherry tall chest with molded cornice with inlay over three short drawers and five long graduated drawers retaining original crackle varnish.

66in (168cm) high

$6,000-9,000   **POOK**

A late 19thC burr walnut Wellington chest, of small proportions, with quarter-veneered top, ten drawers, and pilasters with carved brackets, one hinged and lockable.

21.25in (54cm) wide

$1,500-2,000   **L&T**

A Pennsylvania Chippendale walnut tall chest, the molded cornice over ten drawers, fluted quarter columns and ogee bracket feet.

68.75in (174.5cm) high

$10,000-15,000   **POOK**

FURNITURE

An early 18thC French Baroque commode, walnut and walnut root, veneered, with three drawers, cambered front, original lock, keys and mountings.

52.5in (131cm) wide

$3,000-4,000   **KAU**

An early 20thC large George I-style japanned and parcel gilt commode, with chinoiserie decoration, arrangement of seven drawers, raised on acanthus carved cabriole legs, ending in claw and ball feet, joined by a shaped carved apron.

64.5in (161cm) wide

$2,000-3,000   **FRE**

A Regence-style rosewood and kingwood crossbanded commode, the shaped top with a brass molded edge over three long drawers, flanked by fluted rounded corners raised on bracket feet with sabots.

36in (91.5cm) wide

$4,000-6,000   **FRE**

A French Regence kingwood-veneered serpentine commode, with gilt metal mounts, the crossbanded drawers with elaborate cast handles, the bombé sides inlaid with parquetry paneling, on bracket feet with cast sabots.

50in (127cm) wide

$15,000-20,000   **L&T**

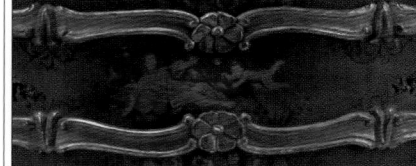

A Venetian 18thC style painted and parcel gilt serpentine commode, the molded rouge marble top of two drawers painted with figures and foliage flanked by two cartouche panels painted with riverside landscapes raised on cabriole legs.

58in (147.5cm) wide

$3,000-4,000   **FRE**

A small French Rococo commode, rosewood, mahogany, plum and kingwood, veneered on oak and pinewood, red-gray marble top, three drawers, gilded bronze mountings, original locks, shellac polish.

c1750   *36.75in (92cm) wide*

$7,000-9,000   **KAU**

An 18thC North Italian walnut and marquetry inlaid commode, in the manner of Maggiolini, with inlaid oval figural panel with scrolling foliate border above three drawers, similarly inlaid, on square tapering supports.

24.5in (62cm) wide

$5,000-6,000   **L&T**

An 18thC and later Italian Neo-classical walnut and marquetry commode, the rectangular marble top over drawers inlaid with flower baskets, swags and central figural reserve, on square tapered legs, restored.

49in (122.5cm) wide

$7,000-9,000   **FRE**

An early 18thC oak and walnut German Baroque commode, veneered, on two ball and two square feet, with three drawers, and original mountings.

51.25in (128cm) wide

$1,500-2,000   KAU

An 18th century Danish walnut and giltwood commode, in the manner of Matthias Ortmann, with molded and crossbanded serpentine top, gilt frieze, ribbon carved gilt apron, on acanthus and lattice carved feet.

32in (81.5cm) high

$10,000-15,000   L&T

A George III Chippendale serpentine commode with rare shaped ends, veneered canted corners and original firegilt brasses with phoenix head bails.

c1770   *32.5in (82.5cm) high*

$35,000-55,000   RGA

A George III mahogany and inlaid serpentine commode, with shaped top, crossbanded drawer containing a baize lined slide and interior fitted with lidded boxes, glass bottles, drawers, mirrors, etc., over three drawers.

39.25in (98cm) wide

$5,000-7,000   L&T

A French walnut and marquetry inlaid commode, in the Louis XVI transitional style, with marble top, semi-bowed front, two drawers, and gilt metal mounts.

44.75in (112cm) wide

$2,000-3,000   L&T

A pair of 18thC Italian walnut serpentine commodes, with shaped tops, one later, over two drawers centred by cartouche escutcheons.

27in (68.5cm) wide

$6,000-9,000   FRE

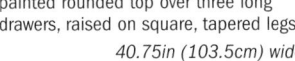

An 18thC Venetian commode, paint decorated with floral swags, and gray painted rounded top over three long drawers, raised on square, tapered legs.

40.75in (103.5cm) wide

$3,000-4,000   FRE

A mid-18thC Italian painted serpentine commode, with shaped simulated marble top, two drawers and foliate decoration, raised on cabriole legs and hoof feet.

27.75in (70.5cm) wide

$3,500-5,500   FRE

A German Baroque walnut commode with rounded rectangular top over three conforming long drawers, raised on bun feet.

c1760   *37.75in (96cm) wide*

$2,500-3,000   FRE

FURNITURE

A Louis XV provincial walnut commode, with shaped top over three long drawers raised on cabriole legs united by a shaped, shell-carved apron.

c1780   47in (119.5cm) wide

$1,800-2,200   **FRE**

A Louis XV provincial walnut commode, with a serpentine top, carved drawers, and acanthus headed canted corners, on cabriole legs with a molded, shaped apron.

c1780   49.75in (126.5cm) wide

$8,000-10,000   **FRE**

A French transitional walnut and kingwood parquetry commode by Leonard Boudin, with gilt bronze mounts, marble top, and stamped "L. Boudin", and "JME" twice.

c1780   50.25in (127.5cm) wide

$15,000-20,000   **FRE**

A late 18thC Venetian paint decorated commode, with Neo-classical decorative motifs, and two short and two long drawers, raised on splayed feet.

39.5in (100.5cm) wide

$7,000-10,000   **FRE**

A Russian Empire burl maple commode, with marble top, single frieze drawer and three long drawers flanked by turned pilasters, on turned column feet.

c1830   51in (129.5cm) wide

$6,000-9,000   **FRE**

A 19thC Louis XV style provincial serpentine oak commode, with three drawers and shaped apron, raised on bracket feet.

49.25in (125cm) wide

$3,000-5,000   **FRE**

A 19thC Louis XV style provincial walnut Santeuse commode, with a shaped top over three serpentine shaped drawers, raised on cabriole legs.

43in (109cm) wide

$3,500-4,500   **FRE**

A 19thC Louis XV style black lacquer bombe commode, with figural chinoiserie decoration, shaped rouge marble top over two drawers, on cabriole legs.

49.5in (125.5cm) wide

$2,000-3,000   **FRE**

A late 19thC Victorian simulated bamboo chest of drawers, in the manner of Holland and Sons, with three long drawers, on a plinth base.

41.75in (106cm) wide

$3,000-4,000   **FRE**

A Louis XV-style kingwood and marquetry bombé-shaped commode, with serpentine-shaped marble top, a pair of inlaid doors, and a shelved interior.

Bears M. Bodet paper label.

c1900   54in (137cm) wide

$1,000-1,300   **FRE**

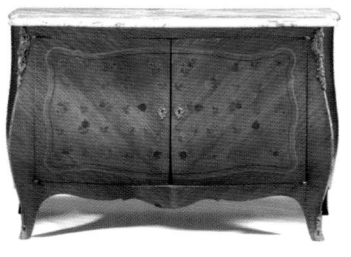

A mahogany and gilt metal mounted serpentine commode, in Louis XV style, of recent manufacture, with marble top, on tapering legs with sabots.

54.75in (139cm) wide

$6,000-9,000   **DN**

LINEN PRESSES

- The princely courts of Europe set the trend for upright storage cupboards from the second half of the 17th century. Early forms were inspired by Renaissance pieces and were typically made of fruitwood or walnut. From the second quarter of the 18th century shapes were often Rococo.
- Many households had an armoire or linen press from the mid-18th to the early 19th century. Used for storing linen, these were large case pieces, often made from walnut.
- Common linen press examples were two piece combinations. They usually had an upper section with two doors and a shelved interior fitted with sliding trays, and a lower section with a drawer.
- Larger examples were based on architectural forms with carved panels and bracket feet.
- Good quality examples sometimes have a pull-out slide for brushing and folding clothes.
- Provincial examples were made in oak or pine and usually lacked the slide and carved decoration.

A George III mahogany three-part linen press, with broken arch bonnet over two recessed panel cupboard doors, and four drawers on bracket feet.

91in (227.5cm) high

$3,000-5,000 **POOK**

A George III mahogany linen press, with paneled and satinwood cross banded doors, four drawers, bracket feet, and replacement brass handles and back plates.

46.5in (118cm) high

$3,500-5,500 **L&T**

A late 18thC George III mahogany two piece linen press, with a molded cornice over two cupboard doors, and three drawers on bracket feet.

74in (188cm) high

$3,000-4,000 **POOK**

A Federal inlaid cherrywood linen press, with diamond-carved frieze, two recessed panel doors inlaid with flower-filled urns, and four graduated drawers.

c1800 79in (200.5cm) high

$6,000-8,000 **FRE**

A late 18th/early 19thC Federal Pennsylvania walnut linen press, with two recessed panel doors opening to four trays, three long drawers and bracket base.

79.5in (202cm) high

$2,000-3,000 **FRE**

A New York Federal cherry linen press, with two line-inlaid doors with parquetry panels, over four long drawers supported by French feet.

c1800 44in (111.5cm) wide

$6,000-7,000 **POOK**

An early 19thC mahogany press cupboard, in the manner of Gillows, with paneled doors and beaded moldings, and two drawers, the interior formerly with sliding shelves.

50.75in (129cm) wide

$4,000-6,000 **L&T**

An early 19thC mahogany linen press, with pair of paneled doors, four sliding trays raised on four graduated crossbanded drawers and scroll front feet.

89in (226cm) high

$2,000-3,000 **L&T**

A late 19thC mahogany and marquetry linen press, with swan neck pediment, satinwood banded frieze, two paneled doors, sliding shelves, and four drawers.

85in (217cm) high

$8,000-10,000 **L&T**

FURNITURE

A Virginia Chippendale walnut two-part linen press, two panel doors on a base with two drawers supported by ogee bracket feet.

c1780   *81.5in (207cm) high*

$25,000-35,000   **POOK**

A George III mahogany linen press, the molded cornice above plain frieze and two doors, each inset with oval panels and enclosing hanging space, the base with two short over two long drawers, raised on bracket feet.

56.25in (143cm) wide

$3,000-4,000   **L&T**

A late 18thC Pennsylvania Queen Anne walnut two-part linen press, with two cupboard doors and five drawers supported by bracket feet.

77in (192.5cm) high

$7,000-10,000   **POOK**

A Scottish George III mahogany bow front linen press, with satinwood crossbanding and boxwood stringing, the dentilled cornice with scalloped cresting and urn finials above oval paneled doors enclosing sliding trays, above two short and two long drawers, on splayed bracket feet.

49.25in (125cm) wide

$15,000-20,000 L&T

A George III strung mahogany linen press, with dentil cornice over paneled doors enclosing slides, the base with two short and three long drawers, raised on splayed bracket feet.

$3,000-4,000   **SWO**

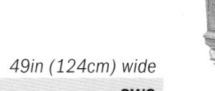

A late Georgian mahogany linen press, with two paneled doors enclosing five slides, over two short and two long drawers, raised on bracket feet.

49in (124cm) wide

$2,000-3,000   **SWO**

A late 18thC George III mahogany two-part corner cupboard, with two cupboard doors and painted interior, scalloped shelves and two doors.

96.5in (241cm) high

$5,000-7,000   **POOK**

A George III painted pine corner cupboard, with a dentil frieze and cornice, a domed back and arched glazed doors, two shelves, and a paneled door.

83.5in (212cm) high

$1,200-1,800   **SWO**

A Georgian-style corner cupboard, with two paneled doors enclosing a series of shaped shelves, supported upon three cabriole legs.

$700-1,000   **SWO**

A late 18thC painted corner cupboard, possibly Virginian, with an interior of shaped shelves and a single shelf, and early painted surface and interior.

84in (213cm) high

$7,000-9,000   **SK**

A Pennsylvania cherry wood two-part corner cabinet, with an arched molding, glazed doors, and two recessed panel doors.

c1800   *87in (221cm) high*

$4,000-6,000   **FRE**

A Pennsylvania pine architectural corner cupboard, with two arched, raised panel doors, reeded pilasters, two smaller cupboard doors, and a molded base.

113in (282.5cm) high

$5,000-7,000   **POOK**

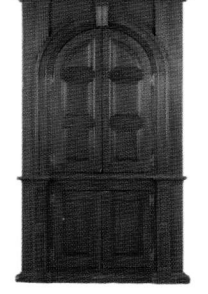

A Pennsylvania pine architectural corner cupboard, with two arched, raised panel doors, two smaller cupboard doors, a molded base, and old red stained surface.

c1810   *104in (260cm) high*

$5,000-7,000   **POOK**

A Western Pennsylvania Federal walnut corner cupboard, with two arched cupboard doors surrounded by floral and line inlays and supported by straight bracket feet.

c1810   *69in (172.5cm) high*

$2,000-3,000   **POOK**

An early 19thC Pennsylvania walnut two-part corner cupboard, with a molded cornice over two arched glazed doors, on a molded base.

92.5in (231cm) high

$5,000-7,000   **POOK**

An early 19thC Pennsylvania cherry corner cupboard, with two glazed doors and two recessed panel doors, above a scalloped skirt supported by bracket feet.

90.5in (230cm) high

$4,000-6,000   **POOK**

An early 19thC New England pine one-piece corner cupboard, with two arched glazed doors and two raised panel cupboard doors.

91.5in (232.5cm) high

$4,000-6,000   **POOK**

A Maryland cherry corner cupboard, with two glazed doors, three paneled drawers, and two recess-paneled doors.

c1820   *85in (216cm) high*

$3,000-4,000   **FRE**

An early 19thC Pennsylvania painted two-part corner cupboard, with glazed doors, two drawers and two cupboard doors, and an old ocher grain decoration.

47in (119.5cm) wide

$2,000-3,000   **POOK**

An early 19thC Pennsylvania two-piece painted pine corner cupboard, from Lancaster County, with old yellow paint.

95in (241cm) high

$2,500-4,000 **POOK**

A Pennsylvania pine corner cupboard, with molded cornice over a glazed door and recessed panel cupboard door supported by straight bracket feet.

c1830 82.75in (207cm) high

$3,000-4,000 **POOK**

An early 19thC two-part cherry corner cupboard, with molded pediment, reeded plinth, glazed door containing three shelves, two drawers and two recessed paneled doors.

98in (249cm) high

$25,000-30,000 **FRE**

A 19thC Pennsylvania late Federal mahogany two-part corner cupboard, with broken arch bonnet over two glazed doors, two short drawers and cupboard doors.

92.5in (231cm) high

$4,000-5,000 **POOK**

A 19thC Pennsylvania walnut glazed corner cupboard, with single glazed door, two recessed panel doors below, bracket feet, and loss of height.

$3,000-4,000 **FRE**

A 19thC cherry corner cupboard, with molded cornice over two glazed doors on two paneled doors supported on bracket feet.

92in (234cm) high

$3,500-4,500 **POOK**

A 19thC Dutch mahogany corner cabinet, with molded dentil cornice, paneled doors with rosette angles, fitted shelves, and fluted apron.

96in (245cm) high

$4,000-6,000 **L&T**

An early 19thC fine carved walnut corner cabinet, probably from Shenandoah County, Virginia, with older refinish, and small splices to one door.

85.25in (216.5cm) high

$30,000-35,000 **FRE**

A Scottish William IV mahogany secretaire cabinet, with two panel doors, a shelved interior and wrythen half columns, and central paneled secretaire drawer.

85.4in (217cm) high

$4,000-6,000 **L&T**

A Victorian mahogany wardrobe, with three paneled doors and double columns with lotus clasping and plinth base with full width drawer.

97in (246cm) high

$3,000-4,000 **L&T**

A William IV mahogany reverse breakfront wardrobe, with six graduated drawers, foliate carved handles, foliate paneled cupboards and a plinth base.

94.4in (240cm) high

$5,000-7,000 **L&T**

A New England pine two-part wall cupboard, with four raised panel doors, on cut-out bracket feet, and a red painted surface.

c1800 *83in (211cm) high*

$1,500-2,000 **POOK**

A late 18thC Pennsylvania painted kas, from Lancaster County, with panel cupboard doors and rattail hinges, three short drawers, inscription, and original ocher grain decoration.

87in (221cm) high

$8,000-12,000 **POOK**

A late 18thC three-part gumwood kas, New Jersey, with two panel cupboard doors, a single drawer and turned bun feet.

70.75in (179.5cm) high

$16,000-20,000 **POOK**

A late 18thC New Jersey gumwood kas, with a boldly molded cornice over two raised panel doors, recessed walnut stiles, and two short drawers.

71in (180.5cm) high

$7,000-9,000 **POOK**

A pine cupboard, probably New England, with two pairs of hinged doors, cockbeading and molding, diagonally cut-out base, and several generations of paint.

c1800 *72in (180cm) high*

$7,000-10,000 **SK**

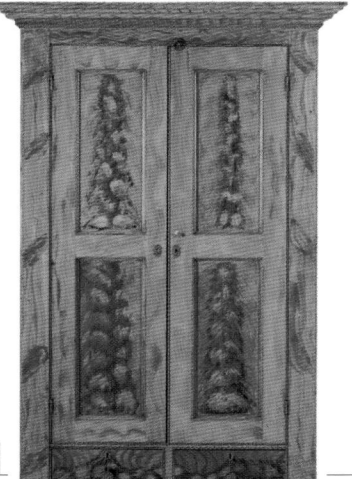

A Pennsylvania painted and grain-painted kas, from Berks county, with two double recessed panel doors, a wide drawer with brass pulls, on turned finished feet.

c1830 *75.25in (191cm) high*

$20,000-30,000 **FRE**

A late 18thC mahogany buffet cabinet, with a Greek key frieze, arched and paneled twin-doors enclosing shelves, and fluted pilasters.

63in (228cm) high

$2,000-3,000 **L&T**

167

A mid-19thC North German mahogany cabinet, with mirrored doors, two drawers and twin doors below with foliate fretwork panels.

74.5in (189cm) high

$3,000-4,000   **L&T**

A mid-17thC large two-part Dutch oak cupboard, of paneled construction, with carved walnut portrait terminals, on large ebonized bun feet.

75in (190cm) high

$1,000-1,500   **L&T**

A pair of figured Pennsylvania maple wardrobes, each with bold ogee molded cornice, mirrored door and drawer below, on flattened ball feet.

c1830   *36.25in (92cm) wide*

$3,000-4,000   **FRE**

A French Louis-Philippe cabinet, with ormolu mounted carotid columns flanking paneled doors on a plinth base.

76in (193cm) wide

$2,000-3,000   **POOK**

An early 19thC Continental painted pine cupboard, the upper section with a pair of arched doors, on a base with canted corners and two narrow doors.

$1,000-1,500   **SWO**

A 19thC French Baroque style buffet a deux corps with a molded pediment of cherubs and mythical beasts, four panel doors enclosing shelves and four drawers between the upper and lower sections, with the cornice and drawers stamped "Jeanneau".

57.25in (145.5cm) wide

$5,000-7,000   **FRE**

An early 19thC Continental painted pine cupboard, the upper section with a pair of arched doors, on a base with canted corners and two narrow doors.

$1,000-1,500   **SWO**

A 17thC French Baroque armoire deux corps, with four carved panel doors of figural reserves and bead and dart molded frieze, on an anthemion carved plinth and block feet.

50.75in (129cm) wide

$8,000-10,000   **FRE**

A Louis XV oak and satinwood inlaid armoire a deux corps, with chevron banding, four paneled doors, four cupboard doors enclosing shelves, and four drawers.

c1780   *106.25in (270cm) wide*

$10,000-15,000   **FRE**

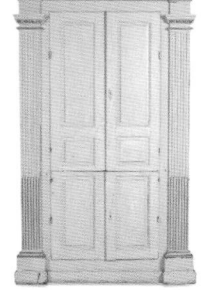

A Scottish George III period over painted buffet niche cabinet, with breakfront cornice, two paneled doors enclosing an interior with shaped shelves, and two paneled doors.

56in (142cm) wide

$4,000-5,000   **L&T**

A CLOSER LOOK AT A GEORGE III BREAKFRONT BOOKCASE

During the latter half of the 18th century library bookcases often had a hidden retractable surface for writing or placing books and maps.

This bookcase is the most sophisticated design incorporating a completely separate fitted pedestal desk and relates to the design of a few famous examples.

Gentlemen's libraries were usually completed furnished with book cabinets, tables, desks and chairs commissioned as a group from a single cabinetmaker, often to a design from the architect responsible for the overall scheme.

The very high quality of this bookcase is reflected overall in the finely figured mahogany, color and patina. The remarkable carving indicating a cabinetmaker of great ability, especially in the apron above the kneehole and the urns surmounting the cornice.

The inclusion of a domestic apothecary's cabinet within the upper section is rare.

The finely chiseled gilt-lacquered metal drawer furniture is original.

An important George III mahogany library breakfront bookcase, centred below by a pedestal library writing table.

c1770

103in (261.5cm) wide

$1,000,000+   **PAR**

A George III mahogany breakfront bookcase, with four glazed doors, each enclosing adjustable shelves, four paneled doors, and a later plinth base.

96.5in (245cm) wide

$10,000-15,000   **L&T**

A George III mahogany breakfront bookcase, with four astragal doors enclosing adjustable shelves, four long drawers, and paneled doors enclosing shelves.

96.5in (245cm) high

$15,000-20,000   **L&T**

A mid-Victorian mahogany breakfront library bookcase, with four trellis astragal glazed doors enclosing shelves, and the base with four paneled cupboard doors.

99in (252cm) wide

$10,000-15,000   **L&T**

An 18thC George III mahogany breakfront library bookcase, with astragal glazed doors enclosing shelves, two central frieze drawers and four fielded panel doors, with restorations.

94in (239cm) wide

$8,000-10,000   **FRE**

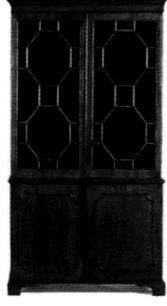

A late 18thC George III mahogany three-part bookcase, with two glazed doors on a base with two cupboard doors supported by straight bracket feet.

87.5in (222.5cm) high

$7,000-9,000   **POOK**

A pair of mahogany breakfront bookcases, each of late 18thC design, with three astragal-glazed doors, frieze drawers and paneled doors.

95in (241cm) high

$3,000-4,000   **L&T**

A Regency mahogany waterfall bookcase cabinet, with graduated shelves flanked by carrying handles on turned legs terminating in brass cappings and casters.

27in (69cm) wide

$3,000-4,000   **SWO**

A large Regency burr oak breakfront open bookcase, with five bays of adjustable shelves divided by pilasters, on a plinth base.

41.5in (105cm) high

$5,000-7,000   **L&T**

An early 19thC walnut "Harvard" bookcase, possibly from Massachusetts, with two hinged doors, recessed panels opening to shelves, and minor imperfections.

64in (163cm) wide

$9,000-11,000   **SK**

A George IV mahogany secretaire breakfront library bookcase, in the manner of Gillow, with a central secretaire drawer containing a fitted interior, and a central cupboard.

c1825   *90in (229cm) wide*

$5,000-7,000   **DN**

An early 19thC stripped pine bookcase, with four sliding upper and lower doors, ogee arched moldings, and lower breakfront moldings.

122in (305cm) wide

$2,000-3,000   **L&T**

A late classical Philadelphia mahogany breakfront, with molded cornice, four glazed doors enclosing shelves, four paneled doors and lion paw feet.

c1825

$30,000-40,000   **FRE**

A William IV mahogany library bookcase, with astragal glazed doors and flat pillars, two double paneled doors, and turned tapering columns.

76.25in (194cm) wide

$4,000-6,000   **SWO**

A fine early Victorian Gothic oak and pollard oak library bookcase, with two astragal glazed doors enclosing adjustable shelves, two frieze drawers and paneled doors.

c1840   *27.5in (70cm) wide*

$15,000-20,000   **FRE**

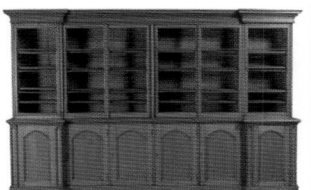

An early Victorian oak reverse breakfront bookcase, with six astragal glazed doors, enclosing adjustable shelves, the base with six doors with lancet arch panels.

135.5in (344cm) wide

$4,000-6,000 **L&T**

A Victorian style mahogany breakfront open bookcase, with a molded top and adjustable shelves on a plinth base.

$1,500-2,000 **SWO**

A late 19th/early 20thC George III style mahogany breakfront bookcase, with blind fret carved frieze, astragal glazed doors, and paneled cupboard doors, on a plinth base.

92in (233.5cm) wide

$4,000-6,000 **FRE**

A mid-Victorian and burr walnut veneered bookcase cabinet, with two glazed doors enclosing adjustable shelves, and blind fretwork paneled doors raised on a plinth.

87.25in (218cm) high

$2,000-3,000 **L&T**

A Lamb of Manchester burl walnut and ebonized library bookcase, with glazed panel doors with mirrors, drawers set with carved cameos and the center cupboard drawer stamped "Lamb, Manchester 35207".

James Lamb was the founder of one of the most successful late 19thC cabinet makers.

c1880   *105in (266.5cm) wide*

$8,000-10,000 **FRE**

A Louis XV style rosewood and kingwood japanned cabinet, with gilt bronze mounts, marble top, central decorated panel, and serpentine cupboard doors enclosing shelves.

c1900   *62.5in (159cm) wide*

$4,000-6,000 **FRE**

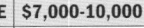

An Edwardian mahogany breakfront bookcase, with boxwood, chequer and feather stringing, dentilled cornice, astragal glazed doors and adjustable shelves.

90in (228cm) high

$7,000-10,000 **L&T**

A large Edwardian four bay walnut bookcase, with glazed doors enclosing adjustable shelves, on a deeper base with paneled doors.

98.5in (250cm) high

$5,000-7,000 **L&T**

An Edwardian mahogany breakfront bookcase, of small proportions, with lancet-arched astragal doors probably of an earlier date, adjustable shelves and four paneled cupboard doors.

63.75in (162cm) wide

$3,000-4,000 **L&T**

A figured walnut breakfront library bookcase, with adjustable interchangeable glass and wooden shelves, central crossbanded doors and ogee outline end sections.

Provenance: *Property of The Drambuie Liqueur Company.*

95in (241cm) high

$7,000-10,000 **L&T**

A pair of mahogany dwarf open bookcases, in Regency style, with three bays, two shelves, and center bay with adjustable shelves, on bracket feet.

51in (130cm) wide

$2,000-3,000 **L&T**

A large Regency mahogany library bookcase, the upper section with a molded cornice, fitted with shelves, the base enclosed by four paneled doors, on a plinth base.

127.25in (318cm) wide

$6,000-9,000 SWO

A Victorian walnut inverted breakfront bookcase, inlaid with floral marquetry and satinwood stringing, the central open section fitted with shelves, flanked by glazed cupboard doors, on a plinth base.

78in (198cm) wide

$4,000-5,000 BRI

A Victorian oak open bookcase, with two adjustable shelves, on a plinth base.

49.5in (124cm) wide

$1,200-1,800 SWO

A Victorian mahogany open bookcase, the shelves flanked by turned columns.

57in (145cm) wide

$1,500-2,000 SWO

An Edwardian inlaid mahogany open bookcase, with three adjustable shelves.

$3,000-4,000 SWO

An early 19thC mahogany wall shelf, with scrolled back and sides, supporting three pine shelves.

39in (99cm) wide

$350-450 SWO

A Victorian hanging wall shelf, the three shelves joined at the front by turned columns.

30in (76cm) wide

$350-550 SWO

A Victorian rosewood three-tier open wall shelf.

53.5in (136cm) wide

$600-700 SWO

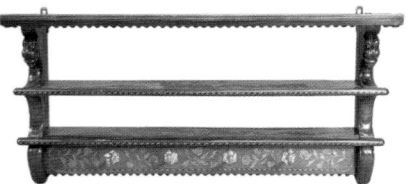

A set of late Victorian walnut wall shelves, with marquetry decoration, carved lion's head and foliate supports and four brass hooks.

48in (120cm) wide

$1,000-1,500 SWO

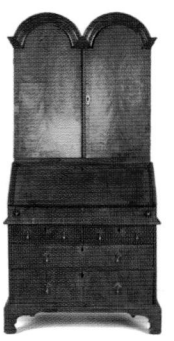

An English Queen Anne burl walnut veneer secretary desk, with a double dome top upper section above a five drawer base with bracket feet.

36in (91.5cm) wide

$6,000-9,000	POOK

An early 18thC George I two-piece secretaire, with mirrored doors, fitted interior, slant front and four drawers, with later Japanned paint.

90in (228.6cm) high

$30,000-35,000	POOK

A CLOSER LOOK AT A BUREAU BOOKCASE

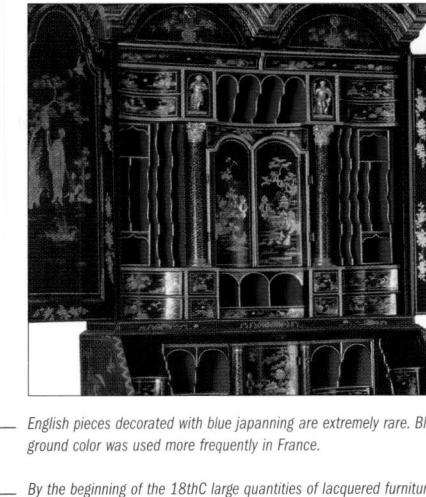

English pieces decorated with blue japanning are extremely rare. Blue as a ground color was used more frequently in France.

By the beginning of the 18thC large quantities of lacquered furniture were being made in the UK. Although craftsmen never rivalled eastern techniques and quality of finish they did reach a high level of accomplishment.

In contemporary records the distinction between European and Oriental work is seldom made; the goods were purchased for their brilliant and exotic appearance and were generally referred to on inventories, bills etc. as 'Japan work' with no indication of their real origin.

The japanners used a large number of sources, both European and Oriental, for their decorative schemes, including imported porcelain and textiles and European architectural designs and prints. This latter category was in turn drawn from fantasy, loose ideas of the East or from travelers' books on China and the Orient.

John Belchier (d.1753) was one of the most important cabinet-makers of the 18th century and had a workshop at The Sun, on the south side of St. Paul's Church Yard in London.

A George I blue and gold japanned bureau bookcase, attributed to John Belchier.

c1715

44in (111.5cm) wide

$1,500,000+	PAR

A Federal cherry inlaid desk bookcase, possibly from Kentucky, with hinged arched doors, inlaid stringing and decoration, and adjustable shelved interior, refinished, replaced pulls, restoration.

c1790 *96in (244cm) high*

$130,000-160,000	SK

A George III mahogany and inlaid secretaire bookcase, with marquetry reserves, astragal glazed doors with kingwood crossbanding, a secretaire drawer with fitted interior.

It is probable that the glazed upper section is associated to the base section.

c1780 *50in (127cm) wide*

$6,000-9,000	DN

A George III mahogany bureau bookcase, with pierced swan neck pediment over a drop front enclosing a fitted interior of drawers and pigeon holes.

89in (225cm) high

$4,000-6,000	L&T

A George III mahogany secretaire bookcase, with pendant frieze, astragal glazed doors, adjustable shelves, a fitted drawer and three graduated drawers.

93.3in (237cm) high

$4,000-6,000	L&T

A late 18thC Pennsylvania mahogany secretary, with two panel cupboard doors above a slant front opening to a fitted interior.

88in (223.5cm) high

$5,000-7,000   POOK

A Federal mahogany and mahogany veneer glazed desk bookcase, probably from Boston, with two glazed doors, cockbeaded desk drawer with fold-out writing surface and multi-drawer compartment interior above three drawers, old pulls.

c1812   81in (202.5cm) high

$5,000-7,000   SK

A CLOSER LOOK AT A CHIPPENDALE MAHOGANY CHEST WITH CABINET

American Chippendale was an adaptation of the ornate designs produced by Thomas Chippendale in London between about 1750 and 1765. This simple style is typical of the more restrained American furniture from the late 18thC.

America, fighting a Revolutionary War between 1775-83, struggled to follow British designs that gravitated towards Robert Adam's Neoclassical style of furniture. This piece shows America's continued development of the Chippendale style.

Mahogany was popular amongst urban cabinet-makers and was one of the most predominant materials.

This chest was made after European craftsmen immigrated to Pennsylvania, and combines Chippendale with newly emerging Federal styles and regional peculiarities.

A late 18thC Pennsylvania Chippendale mahogany chest with cabinet, with three reeded urn finials, floral rosettes and centered inverted fan above twin arched glazed doors, the base with six drawers, on ogival bracket feet.

90in (228.5cm) high

$45,000-50,000   FRE

A New York Federal cherry two part secretary, with two glazed doors and fall front enclosing a fitted bird's eye maple interior.

c1815   86.5in (219.5cm) high

$10,000-15,000   POOK

A classical carved mahogany and mahogany veneer desk bookcase, possibly from New York, with two glazed doors, adjustable shelves, case of inlaid drawers, interior of central prospect door, four drawers and valanced compartments, above two doors containing drawers, refinished, with minor imperfections.

c1820   96.5in (245cm) high

$4,000-6,000   SK

A Classical mahogany desk and bookcase, possibly Anthony Quervelle, Philadelphia, with mirrored cabinet doors, adjustable writing surface and small compartments, with high gloss finish.

c1830   78in (198cm) high

$7,000-10,000   FRE

A 19thC mahogany bureau bookcase, in the George III style, with astragal glazed doors, the fall front enclosing a fitted interior, and a four drawer base.

47in (119cm) high

$2,000-3,000   L&T

A 19thC Vermont painted two-part secretary desk, with birdseye maple drawers, a writing surface, and original red and yellow stippled decoration.

76in (193cm) high

$2,000-3,000   POOK

A 19thC German mahogany fall-front secretaire, with frieze drawer, fitted interior, eight drawers with amboyna veneers, the lower section with two long drawers.

56in (143cm) high

$2,000-3,000   L&T

A Virginia Chippendale walnut secretary, with fluted matchstick frieze, two raised panel doors, a fall front and four drawers.

39in (99cm) wide

$30,000-40,000   POOK

A black lacquer chinoiserie bureau bookcase, with two mirrored doors, candle slides, the fall front enclosing a fitted interior with leather skiver and sliding well, and four drawers with brass handles.

80in (204cm) high

$3,000-4,000   L&T

A Victorian rosewood serpentine vitrine, with ogee sides and foliate gilt brass mounts and moldings, glazed door, velvet lined interior with glass shelves.

55.25in (138cm) high

$7,000-10,000   **L&T**

A late Victorian rosewood Louis XV/XVI-style vitrine, with gilt brass moldings and mounts, marble top, glazed door and velvet lined shelved interior, bears label of Cranston and Elliot, Princes Street, Edinburgh.

60.75in (152cm) high

$6,000-9,000   **L&T**

A late 19thC French Louis XV style kingwood corner vitrine, with gilt brass mounts, glazed door, and quarter veneered lower panel with floral spray.

74in (188cm) high

$4,000-6,000   **L&T**

A fine near pair of early 20thC kingwood and gilt brass mounted vitrines, with crossbanded cavetto frieze set with applied foliate cartouche, glazed doors enclosing a mirrored back with adjustable shelves, and glazed side panels.

65.75in (167cm) high

$15,000-20,000   **L&T**

An Edwardian rosewood and gilt metal mounted display cabinet, with a serpentine glazed door with Vernis Martin style painted panel below.

88in (220cm) high

$6,000-9,000   **L&T**

One of a pair of Edwardian mahogany display cabinets, with an arched molded and dentilled cornice above blind fretwork frieze, carved drapery swags, and glass shelves.

77in (195.5cm) high

$7,000-10,000 PAIR   **L&T**

A fine Edwardian kingwood and gilt brass mounted vitrine, with serpentine glazed door and shelves, and elaborate mounts, on shaped cabriole legs with cast paw sabots.

76.5in (194cm) high

$15,000-20,000   **L&T**

An early 20thC French vitrine, with gilt metal mounts, serpentine front and sides, and decorated panels.

64.5in (161cm) high

$1,200-1,800   **SWO**

A Louis XV style kingwood and gilt metal mounted serpentine vitrine, with glazed door, a velvet lined interior with glass shelves, and pastoral Vernis Martin panels.

80.5in (205cm) high

$6,000-9,000   **L&T**

A French mahogany and gilt brass mounted vitrine, with serpentine glass panels and shelves, and a shaped 'Vernis Martin' panel.

27.25in (69cm) wide

$2,000-3,000   **WW**

A Louis XVI style breakfront kingwood vitrine, London, with gilt mounts, velvet lined interior with glass shelves, above Vernis Martin panels, bearing label of S & H Jewell.

62.5in (158cm) high

$7,000-10,000   **L&T**

FURNITURE

An early 18thC oyster-veneered cabinet, probably olive wood, with a frieze drawer, two doors enclosing a central door and ten drawers.

32in (81cm) wide

$2,000-3,000 SWO

A pair of French Empire mahogany gentleman's presses, with a breakfront top, panel doors enclosing sliding trays and drawers and central drawers.

74in (188cm) wide

$6,000-9,000 PAIR L&T

A Dutch 18thC satinwood and specimen wood bureau abatant, the fall front with lacquer panels and similar drawers below, and a interior fitted with drawers and pigeonholes.

60.5in (154cm) high

$4,000-6,000 L&T

A Federal mahogany inlaid cabinet, with three cockbeaded cabinet doors and drawers, fan inlays to corners, and French bracket feet.

c1800 *46in (117cm) high*

$3,000-4,000 FRE

A Regency mahogany side cabinet, with a cushion frieze, a pair of glazed doors and a pair of paneled doors flanked by leaf carved pilasters.

48.75in (124cm) high

$3,000-4,000 L&T

A Regency mahogany breakfront side cabinet, with later marble top, flame veneer frieze, two central brass lattice and fabric paneled doors.

60.5in (154cm) wide

$4,000-6,000 L&T

A Regency rosewood side cabinet, with marble top, pierced gilt brass gallery, twin doors with pierced brass panels and pleated silk trimmings.

36.25in (92cm) high

$5,000-7,000 L&T

A 19thC Italian ebonized and ivory cabinet, inlaid with ivory, and decorated within hunting scenes.

40in (100cm) wide

$2,000-3,000 FRE

A Victorian burr walnut credenza, with boxwood stringing and marquetry decoration, gilt brass mounts, central paneled door and glazed outer doors.

66in (168cm) wide

$7,000-10,000 L&T

A pair of Victorian burr walnut side cabinets, possibly by Gillows of Lancaster, each with arched doors fretted with arabesques and lined with pleated silk.

c1850

$10,000-15,000 L&T

A Louis XVI style figured mahogany, lacquer and gilt bronze mounted cabinet by Gervais-Maximilien-Eugene Durand, back stamped "G. Durand" twice.

Gervais-Maximilien-Eugene Durand was born in Paris on 30th July 1839. He was the first of three generations of highly successful cabinet makers, exhibiting widely at the series of International Exhibitions.

c1890 *40.5in (103cm) wide*

$17,000-20,000 FRE

A 1920s walnut and burr walnut breakfront side cabinet, by Whytock and Reid, Edinburgh, with glazed central doors and quarter veneered doors.

74in (185cm) wide

$2,000-3,000 L&T

A George III-style painted satinwood side cabinet, with crossbanded top over a frieze drawer, painted with floral sprays and scrolls, with two paneled cupboard doors centered by flowering baskets, raised on shaped bracket feet.

c1910   *37in (92.5cm) high*

$2,000-3,000   **FRE**

A Regency period mahogany dwarf side cabinet, with beaded decoration, molded scroll mounts and reeded bun feet.

34in (86.5cm) wide

$2,000-3,000   **MAX**

One of a pair of Regency mahogany side cabinets, in the manner of Gillows, inlaid with boxwood stringing, the reeded edge tops with protruding corners above a pair of frieze drawers, with a pair of panel doors flanked by three-quarter ribbed tapering pilasters with inlaid line and dot capitols, on ribbed turned feet.

48in (122cm) wide

$18,000-20,000 PAIR   **WW**

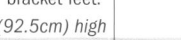

A Regency rosewood breakfront side cabinet, with green marble top over three brass and silk paneled cupboards, the center cupboard flanked by tapering columns, on a plinth base.

82.75in (207cm) wide

$3,500-4,500   **SWO**

A Victorian Regency-style rosewood reverse breakfront side cabinet, the shaped rectangular marble top above three drawers with brass grilles and pleated side panels enclosing shelves, divided by tapering caryatid pilasters with brass bust terminals and feet, on a plinth base.

71.75in (182cm) wide

$3,500-4,500   **L&T**

A Regency-style rosewood breakfront side cabinet, with beveled glass panels, on a plinth base.

$3,000-4,000   **SWO**

A 19thC mahogany side cabinet, parcel gilt with gilt metal mounts, fitted with two drawers over open shelves, on turned feet.

46in (117cm) high

$4,500-5,500   **SWO**

A Victorian mahogany side cabinet, with roll front drawer above a pair of doors with papier-mâché panels painted with church interiors, with a pair of carved corbel brackets on a plinth base, stamped "Jennens & Bettridge".

47.25in (120cm) wide

$2,000-3,000   **SWO**

A Victorian mahogany two-door side cupboard, with a cushion frieze drawer, raised on bun feet.

42.25in (107cm) high

$600-700   **SWO**

A 17thC Flemish tortoiseshell and ebonized cabinet, with gilt bronze mounts, fitted interior and four drawers, on a later lower stand.

51.75in (131.5cm) wide

$10,000-15,000	FRE

A mid-17thC Flemish ebonized and inlaid cabinet on stand, with concave top, hinged lid, paneled doors, and interior fitted with small drawers, on a later base.

$2,000-3,000	L&T

A late 17thC Flemish ebony, ebonized and marquetry inlaid small cabinet on stand, with trailing flowerhead and foliate motifs, the lid revealing a painted 17thC pastoral landscape, tortoiseshell veneered drawers, and 17thC Dutch landscape scenes.

45.25in (115cm) high

$10,000-15,000	L&T

A mid-18thC Louis XV French provincial walnut panetiere, with a compartment enclosed with closely set turned spindles, on a slatted base and scrolled feet.

35.5in (89cm) high

$5,000-7,000	FRE

A Queen Anne Pennsylvania walnut and tulip poplar spice chest, from Chester County, with a secret drawer with Quaker lock, and fitted interior with 12 drawers.

c1760   *24.5in (62cm) high*

$12,000-15,000	POOK

A George III small secretaire writing cabinet on stand, veneered with harewood, with small inlays of satinwood, and three pigeon holes and five drawers to the interior.

c1775

$28,000-32,000	PAR

A George III mahogany bedside commode, with a tray top, three quarter gallery, tambour door and adapted drawer, on square section legs.

29.5in (74cm) high

$2,000-3,000	L&T

A 19thC French walnut and marquetry inlaid meuble d'appui, with applied gilt brass mounts, maple lined interior, and cast caryatid terminals.

44.5in (113.5cm) high

$7,000-10,000	L&T

A mid-19thC walnut and inlaid meuble d'appui, with gilt metal mounts, marble top and single panel door, profusely inlaid with an urn, on turned feet.

44in (112cm) high

$3,000-4,000	L&T

A pair of mahogany pedestal cupboards, centered by an anthemion, with a drawer, cupboard door, circular molded base and shaped plinth.

Provenance: Property of The Drambuie Liqueur Company

32.25in (82cm) high

$10,000-15,000	L&T

BUREAUX

- The bureau emerged in France during the 17th century. These flat-fronted cabinets had a hinged upper section, which opened to reveal a leather-lined writing surface and a lower section with either cupboards or drawers.
- Various new forms of bureau were developed during the 18th and 19th century including the cylinder bureau and the bureau cabinet with its superstructure of shelves.
- Designs became more feminine and delicate and were displayed in the drawing room.
- Combined ladies' writing and toilette desks became popular from the Rococo period. By the 1780s the bonheur du jour, designed for leisure time letter writing, was an established form.
- At the same time plain writing tables were developed for private masculine study areas and for the running of business.
- Kneehole desks appeared from the late 17th century and were conceived as both dressing tables and bureaux. The partners' pedestal desk, with drawers to two sides, enabled two people to work at the same desk.

A late 17th/early 18thC Italian walnut bureau, with hinged slanted front containing a fitted interior with three drawers, and lower cupboard doors with shelved interiors, on stile feet.

39.5in (100.5cm) wide

$1,500-2,000 — **FRE**

An 18thC walnut bureau, with cross and chevron banding, the sloping fall with a fitted interior of drawers and pigeonholes, above five drawers on bracket feet.

36.25in (92cm) wide

$1,500-2,000 — **L&T**

A Pennsylvania Chippendale walnut slant front desk, with fall front enclosing a fitted interior, serpentine front drawers and shell carved prospect door, and four drawers.

c1770   *44in (111.5cm) high*

$7,000-10,000 — **POOK**

A Pennsylvania Chippendale walnut slant front desk, with flat and serpentine drawers, cubbyhole and fan-carved door interior and ogival bracket feet.

c1770   *43in (109cm) high*

$3,000-4,000 — **FRE**

A Massachusetts Chippendale mahogany slant front desk, with fitted interior with fan carved drawers over a four drawer oxbow case with shell drop supported by ogee bracket feet.

c1780   *42.5in (108cm) wide*

$5,000-6,000 — **POOK**

A George III mahogany bureau, the sloping fall enclosing an interior fitted with drawers and pigeonholes, above five drawers raised on bracket feet.

37.75in (96cm) wide

$1,000-1,500 — **L&T**

A Georgian mahogany bureau, with fall front, five graduated drawers later inlaid with marquetry decorated satinwood banding, lopers, and fitted interior.

43.25in (110cm) high

$3,000-4,000 — **L&T**

A New England Chippendale tiger maple slant front desk, the fall front enclosing a fitted interior, above a case with four drawers supported by ogee bracket feet.

c1790   *39.75in (101cm) high*

$5,500-6,500 — **POOK**

A small George III elm bureau, the fall enclosing pigeonholes and small drawers, with engraved brass handles and escutcheons, on bracket feet.

32.25in (82cm) wide

$2,000-3,000 — **LFA**

FURNITURE

A George III mahogany bureau, the interior fitted with a door, two secret drawers, pigeon holes and drawers.

39.5in (99cm) wide

$1,000-1,500   **SWO**

A late 18thC Italian crossbanded walnut bureau, with fall front enclosing a fitted interior of drawers and shelves, and a wavy frieze with a single long drawer.

43.5in (110.5cm) wide

$4,500-6,500   **FRE**

A late 18thC Federal carved walnut slant front desk, with fitted interior, four beaded graduated drawers on a molded base and shaped bracket feet.

42.25in (107.5cm) high

$2,000-3,000   **FRE**

A late 18thC Pennsylvania inlaid walnut slant front desk, with fan and line inlay, a fitted interior, four drawers, and ogee bracket feet.

41in (104cm) high

$2,000-3,000   **FRE**

A late 18thC Pennsylvania Chippendale mahogany slant front desk, with a fitted interior above four beaded drawers, fluted quarter columns, and ogee molded bracket feet.

41.5in (105.5cm) high

$2,000-3,000   **FRE**

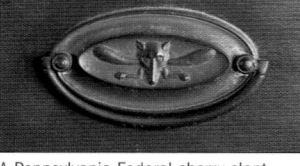

A Pennsylvania Federal cherry slant front desk, with a fitted interior and ash banding, over four drawers with unusual 'Fox' brasses.

c1800   *47in (119.5cm) high*

$5,000-7,000   **POOK**

A Hepplewhite mahogany slant lid desk, bearing the label of William Sinclair, from Flowertown, Pennsylvania, with a fitted interior, four line inlaid drawers, on French feet.

While no furniture can be directly attributed to George Hepplewhite, writer of 'Cabinet Maker and Upholsterer's Guide' in 1788, his designs and methods were hugely influential to Federal design in the late 18thC.

c1810   *44in (111.5cm) high*

$5,000-7,000   **POOK**

An early 19thC Dutch mahogany and floral marquetry bureau, profusely inlaid, the fall front enclosing an interior fitted with a well above three shaped drawers.

47.25in (120cm) high

$5,000-7,000   **L&T**

A late 19thC Sheraton Revival bureau bookcase, in satinwood with mahogany banding, the tambour cylinder front enclosing a two-door fitted cupboard with marquetry inlay.

42in (106.5cm) wide

$6,000-8,000   **BRI**

A Chippendale style cherry oxbow serpentine slant front desk, possibly from eastern Massachusetts, with an interior of drawers and compartments, replaced brass handles, restored.

43in (109cm) wide

$4,000-6,000   **SK**

A Louis XV rosewood and parquetry bureau de dame, with slant front containing an inset leather writing surface and fitted interior of drawers and pigeon holes.

c1760   *22in (56cm) wide*

$4,000-6,000   **FRE**

An Edwardian satinwood bonheur-du-jour, by Maples, with mahogany, boxwood and ebony banding and stringing, astragal glazed doors and pair of frieze drawers.

48.5in (121cm) high

$2,000-3,000   **L&T**

A George III satinwood and marquetry bonheur du jour, attributed to Ince and Mayhew, in two parts, with a leather-lined writing surface, and a central cupboard door inlaid with paterae and flowerheads.

c1790   *48.5in (53.5cm) wide*

$100,000-150,000   **PAR**

An Edwardian mahogany and marquetry kidney-shaped inlaid bonheur du jour, with Neoclassical decoration and snakewood crossbanding, and leather lined writing slope.

51.5in (131cm) high

$3,000-4,000   **L&T**

An Edwardian mahogany and marquetry bonheur du jour, profusely inlaid with Neoclassical decoration and rosewood crossbanding, glazed doors and two drawers, on square tapering legs terminating in brass ball feet.

52in (132cm) high

$4,000-5,000   **L&T**

An Edwardian painted satinwood bonheur du jour, with pierced brass three quarter gallery, secretaire fall front enclosing an interior fitted with drawers, includes two associated brass candelabra.

36.25in (92cm) wide

$2,000-3,000   **L&T**

An Edwardian satinwood and marquetry bonheur du jour, with urn and foliage inlay, a hinged top enclosing a leather writing surface, and single frieze drawer.

c1910   *24in (61cm) wide*

$3,000-4,000   **FRE**

A Louis XV style rosewood and parquetry porcelain mounted bonheur du jour, with pierced galleried, quarter-veneered top, on cabriole legs with sabots.

c1890   *27.5in (70cm) wide*

$5,000-7,000   **FRE**

FURNITURE

A Victorian oak partners' desk, the top with canted angles and inset leatherette surface above six opposing frieze drawers and pedestals with three drawers and opposing cupboards, on plinth base.

57.5in (146cm) wide

$5,000-7,000   **L&T**

A Victorian mahogany pedestal partners desk, with a Greek key tooled leather top, three frieze drawers either side, raised on three graduated drawer pedestals.

55.25in (138cm) wide

$3,000-4,000   **SWO**

A Victorian mahogany writing desk, the superstructure fitted with four short drawers, and a hinged sloping writing surface flanked by four short drawers to either side on a plinth base and casters.

$1,000-1,500   **SWO**

A late Victorian mahogany partners desk, with a green leather writing surface above a series of drawers with Hobbs & Co. locks, paneled sides, supported upon ogee bracket feet with carved knees.

$2,000-3,000   **SWO**

An Edwardian mahogany partners desk, with a red leather writing surface above a series of drawers and paneled sides upon plinth base.

$1,200-1,800   **SWO**

A mahogany partners desk, the shaped top with a leather inset over bowed pedestals, each with drawers and doors.

78in (198cm) wide

$2,000-3,000   **SWO**

A George II mahogany kneehole desk, with a molded top and single frieze drawer, three further short drawers and recessed cupboard door, on carved bracket feet.

c1755   *30in (76cm) wide*

$3,000-4,500   **FRE**

A Victorian inlaid walnut desk, with an inverted central opening, a leather top with three drawers either side of a converted dressing table.

54.75in (137cm) wide

$1,000-1,200   **SWO**

An early 18thC Continental walnut and marquetry kneehole desk, with foliate inlay and chevron banding, two frieze drawers, an adjustable kneehole with marquetry paneled cupboard door enclosing a shelf, with later iron casters.

45.5in (116cm) wide

$6,000-9,000   **L&T**

A 20thC mahogany twin pedestal partners desk, in George II and Thomas Chippendale style, inset with three gilt tooled leather writing surfaces.

Provenance: Property of The Drambuie Liqueur Company

80in (203cm) wide

$7,000-10,000   **L&T**

An 18thC-style Spanish walnut bargueno and table, with steel strapping and hinges and applied gilt mask bosses, fitted interior, the table with turned and blocked trestle supports.

The bargueno, a portable fall front desk, was first produced in Spain during the 15thC.

55in (140cm) high

$3,000-4,000   **L&T**

A walnut and marquetry cabinet-on-stand/'Vargueno', with decorated fall front bearing date "1565", interior of eleven drawers around four cupboard doors, and metal carrying handles.

52in (132cm) high

$5,000-7,000   **L&T**

A George III Hepplewhite mahogany cylinder roll desk, with satinwood inlaid drawers, pigeonholes and inlaid writing surface, on tapering legs with banded cuffs.

c1790   *44.75in (113.5cm) wide*

$7,000-10,000   **POOK**

A late 17thC Italian fruitwood, ivory and ebonized vargueno, with 19thC stand, five drawers inlaid with figural scenes, on claw and ball feet, the stand with three dummy frieze drawers and turned legs.

45.25in (115cm) wide

$4,500-6,500   **FRE**

A 19thC continental walnut and harewood cylinder desk, with raised leather slide, and a fitted interior of drawers, on a square base with tapering legs and brass cappings.

43in (110cm) wide

$700-1,000   **L&T**

A 19thC Louis XV-style mahogany and parquetry bureau cylinder, with gilt bronze mounts, marble top, simulated book end cupboards, and leather inset brushing slide.

43.5in (109cm) wide

$5,000-7,000   **FRE**

A late 19thC walnut veneered bureau a cylindre, with gilt brass mounts, galleried top, curved fall with applied ribbed veneers, and slide-out leather writing surface.

46in (117cm) wide

$4,000-6,000   **L&T**

A late 18thC Philadelphia federal inlaid mahogany secretary and desk, attributed to John Aitken (active 1795-1810), with a fitted interior of maple-faced drawers, pigeonholes and a pull-out lined writing surface.

PROVENANCE: A related secretary cylinder tambour desk, in the collection of Mount Vernon, was purchased from John Aitken by President George Washington in March of 1797. The construction consistency of the two pieces suggest the work of Aitken. It is thought that the secretary section of this piece was made a few years after the desk.

73in (185.5cm) high

| **$20,000-30,000** | **FRE** |

A Federal cherry tambour desk, with tambour that opens to a fitted interior above a hinged writing surface and three drawers on French bracket feet.

c1800   *46.25in (115.5cm) high*

| **$3,000-4,000** | **FRE** |

A New Hampshire maple, cherry, tiger maple, and bird's eye maple inlaid desk, with cockbeaded hinged doors with inlaid panels opening to shelves and drawers.

c1810   *53in (135cm) wide*

| **$14,000-18,000** | **SK** |

An early 19thC mahogany Davenport, with three quarter brass gallery above a sloping hinged fall with swiveling action, interior fitted with drawers, stamped to drawer "* LES & EDWARD, 34 OXFORD STREET, LONDON 3569".

36in (90cm) high

| **$5,000-7,000** | **L&T** |

A 19thC made-up Regency rosewood and brass inlaid desk, with galleried back and nine drawers, and an inset writing surface, on saber legs.

44.5in (113cm) wide

| **$4,000-6,000** | **FRE** |

A late 19thC French rosewood and kingwood escritoire, with a bronzed metal plaque cast and figures, and a top sliding action containing a leather inset writing surface.

c1880   *55.5in (91cm) wide*

| **$6,000-9,000** | **DN** |

A late 19thC Louis XV style kingwood parquetry rococo writing desk, with a pair of gilt bronze candelabra, a central clock, an inset tooled leather writing top and elaborate rococo gilt bronze mounts.

55in (140cm) wide

| **$20,000-30,000** | **SHA** |

A Sheraton Revival style satinwood Carlton House desk, with four short central drawers, cupboards flanked by sloping stationery compartments, and a pull out leather writing surface.

48in (122cm) wide

| **$3,000-4,000** | **L&T** |

GIRANDOLES

- Girandoles are looking glasses or convex mirrors that have candle sconces or candelabra at the base of the frame so that the mirror reflects light into the room.

- Mirrors made of glass backed with metal date back to the age of the Roman Empire, but it was not until the development of plate glass in Paris in the 17thC that mirrors were available in a variety of styles.

- They were particularly popular in the 18thC during the Rococo period, fitting in with the general trend for grand interiors in fine residences with curving, scrolling carved frames.

- Girandole frames of this period were often made from softwoods such as pine or fruitwood, which were then gessoed and applied with gold or silver leaf.

- It is difficult to distinguish American mirrors from European ones. Many European mirrors were exported to the US during this period, but the woods that made up the frames were very similar. Eagles often surmount American examples, particularly on convex mirrors.

- The term 'girandole' originates from the mid-17thC, denoting a revolving cluster of fireworks, and the Latin word 'gyrare' meaning 'gyrate, turn'.

A George III-style oval gilt wood girandole, with a putti, beadwork border with three branch candle holders and scrolling pierced decoration.

40.5in (103cm) high

$700-1,000   SWO

A Federal giltwood mirror, the foliate head with three griffin heads, over a circular mirror and serpent-form girande arms.

c1790   *52in (132cm) high*

$12,000-18,000   POOK

A Regency-style carved and gilt convex wall mirror, surmounted with an eagle.

33.5in (84cm) high

$700-1,000   SWO

An American carved giltwood girandole mirror, with an eagle on a plinth flanked by scrolling foliage, above a molded frame mounted with spherules, and a foliate pendant below.

c1815   *49in (124.5cm) high*

$5,000-7,000   FRE

An English or American Federal giltwood girandole mirror, with an eagle on plinth, double gilt candle arms to the sides, and a foliate pendant below.

c1810   *58in (147.5cm) high*

$15,000-20,000   FRE

An early 19thC George III carved and gilded convex mirror, with an eagle crest, girandole arms, bearing partial Thomas Fentham paper label.

30in (76cm) high

$4,000-6,000   POOK

A pair of 19thC overpainted convex wall mirrors, with leaf-carved crestings with carved eagle surmounts, later overpainting.

36.25in (92cm) high

$3,000-4,000   L&T

A 19thC Federal giltwood girandole mirror, an eagle and leafage surmount the molded and rope-turned frame, two double scrolling candlearms, shaped pendant.

46in (117cm) long

$4,500-6,500   FRE

A 19thC carved and gilded girandole looking glass, probably American, with an eagle and chain on a plinth above a molded frame.

30in (76cm) high

$5,000-7,000   FRE

A carved and gilded convex mirror with lion crest and dolphin girandole arms bearing paper label of "J. Edwards, carver and gilder, Exeter".

54in (137cm) high

$15,000-20,000   POOK

A late 19thC gilt brass dressing mirror, with beveled plate and inlaid molded frame, the scrolled base with two cherubs raised on circular plinths with paw feet.

24in (61cm) high

$4,000-6,000   L&T

FURNITURE

A mid-18thC George II burl and giltwood looking glass, the broken arch crest centering a shell cartouche, flanked by oak leaf appliques.

48.5in (123cm) high

$12,000-15,000	POOK

A Queen Anne mahogany looking glass, with scalloped crest over two stepped mirror plates within an ogee molded frame.

c1760   49in (124.5cm) high

$4,000-6,000	POOK

A George III giltwood mirror, in the Chinese Chippendale manner, with rectangular plate and an ornate scroll and leaf carved frame.

c1770   43.5in (110.5cm) high

$14,000-18,000	FRE

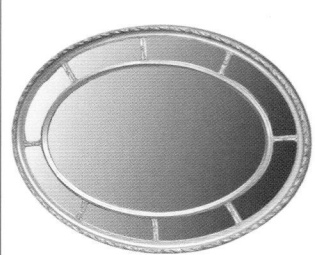

A George III style oval wall mirror, with a central beveled plate surrounded by glass plate panels.

45in (114cm) high

$600-900	SWO

A large Chippendale mahogany looking glass, with scalloped crest and base.

c1790   53.5in (136cm) high

$2,000-3,000	POOK

A late 18thC mahogany mirror with scalloped crest with parcel gilt plume over a rectangular mirror and scalloped base.

40in (101.5cm) high

$1,500-2,000	POOK

A late 18thC George III gilt mirror, with walnut veneer with a phoenix finial and carved floral pilasters.

63in (160cm) high

$4,000-7,000	POOK

A Regency gilt framed upright wall mirror, with verre eglomize landscape frieze, flanked by fluted pilasters with corinthian capitals.

33in (84cm) high

$700-1,000	BRI

An Empire style mahogany wall mirror, with gilt mounts.

50.75in (127cm) high

$400-600	SWO

An early 19thC giltwood pier glass, in the Rococo manner, the frame carved with C scrolls, rocaille work and foliage and enclosing a border of multiple plates.

99.5in (253cm) high

$7,000-10,000	L&T

An early 19thC Northern European painted and parcel gilt wall mirror, with later beveled plate, figural medallion, lion's mask spandrels, and a relief panel.

21.25in (54cm) wide

$1,000-1,500 FRE

An early 19thC New England Federal mahogany and eglomize mirror, with a tablet showing the sea battle 'Frolic and Wasp', with mirror below, imperfections.

The Wasp and the Frolic engaged in battle on 15 Oct 1812.

27in (69cm) high

$1,000-1,500 SK

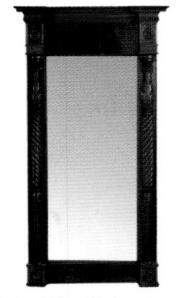

A late Federal New York mahogany mirror, bearing the label of John Williams.

c1825 *51.5in (131cm) high*

$1,000-1,300 POOK

A Classical ebonized, gilded and eglomize panel mirror, with rosettes and eglomize panel depicting two young women, losses and repairs to eglomize panel.

c1825 *31.75in (80.5cm) high*

$700-1,000 FRE

A classical mahogany mirror, from New York or Philadelphia, with stepped and molded cornice above entablature ornamented with classical gilt metal mounts.

c1825 *41.75in (106cm) high*

$500-800 FRE

A Classical giltwood and eglomize mirror, decorated with basket of fruit and drapery swags, some reguilding, craze to guilding.

c1830 *31.75in (80.5cm) high*

$500-800 FRE

A pair of 19thC oval convex wall mirrors, with gilt slip and molded ebonized frames.

15.75in (40cm) high

$1,000-1,500 L&T

A William IV mahogany wall mirror, with split columns around a rectangular plate.

26.75in (68cm) high

$300-400 SWO

A 19thC German hallway mirror, with relief vine and grape decoration, and old mirror glass.

Provenance: Russian Court, Weimar.

74.5in (186cm) high

$2,000-3,000 KAU

A 19thC gilt wall mirror, the heavily cast mirror with egg and dart molding and applied Baccanal mask corner decorations.

33.5in (85cm) wide

$300-400 FRE

A 19thC German mirror, the corners with cartouches, the top with a Baroque coat-of-arms with bay leaves, original mirror glass.

52in (130cm) high

$2,000-3,000 KAU

187

FURNITURE

A 19thC Louis XVI style giltwood trumeau, with rectangular plate and molded foliate carved frame, the upper panel containing a village scene after Brueghel.

61in (155cm) high

$2,000-3,000   **FRE**

A 19thC French carved mirror, the top with cartouches, the center with a putto head framed by a coat-of-arms, original mirror glass.

49.5in (124cm) high

$1,000-1,500   **KAU**

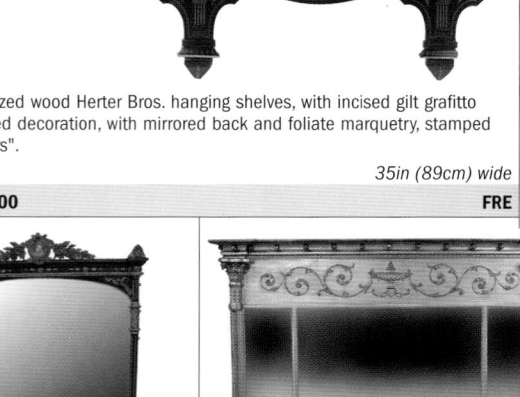

A late 19thC Italian Venician mirror, wood and glass, the cut mirror glass within a floral cut frame.

46in (115cm) high

$700-1,000   **KAU**

A pair of ebonized wood Herter Bros. hanging shelves, with incised gilt grafitto work and carved decoration, with mirrored back and foliate marquetry, stamped "Herter Brothers".

c1880   *35in (89cm) wide*

$20,000-30,000   **FRE**

An ebony framed and marquetry inlaid Dutch wall mirror, of rectangular outline with chequer stringing and floral and foliate inlay, enclosing a beveled plate.

29in (72.5cm) high

$1,500-2,000   **L&T**

A Burmese engraved wall mirror, mounted on velvet ground with three Webb vases.

25in (64cm) high

$3,000-4,000   **JDJ**

A mid-Victorian arched glass over-mantel mirror, with ebonized and gilded frame, floral cresting and bust portrait centerpiece.

72in (183cm) high

$700-1,000   **MAX**

A Regency giltwood over mantel, with a molded and ball decorated cornice over a triple plate, flanked by column pilasters with leaf carved capitals.

57.75in (143cm) wide

$1,000-1,500   **SWO**

A William IV gilt wood over mantel mirror, with a half column frame.

62.5in (156cm) wide

$1,000-1,500   **SWO**

A Victorian carved and gilt overmantel, surmounted with a putti within an oval garland cartouche.

63.25in (158cm) high

$1,000-1,200   **SWO**

A 19thC Continental overpainted pier glass and console table, the mirror with shaped plate enclosed by elaborate carved frame, the matching table with serpentine top and scrolling cabriole legs.

Table 52in (132cm) wide

$12,000-15,000   **L&T**

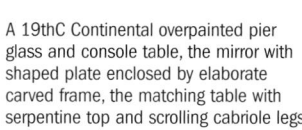

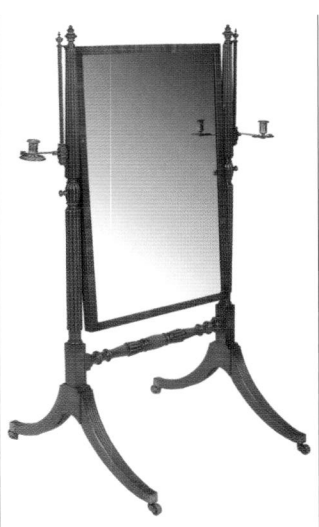

An early 19thC mahogany cheval mirror, with hinged glass with and crossbanded frame, paneled uprights with urn finials, and gilt brass candle sconce.

A Regency mahogany framed cheval dressing glass, with reeded uprights, swivel candle holders and drip trays, on brass caps and casters.

61.5in (156cm) high

$4,000-6,000   **L&T**

A Regency period mahogany cheval mirror, the rectangular glass in a crossbanded frame, on a stand with inlaid stringing and shaped legs.

$1,000-1,500   **SWO**

62.5in (159cm) high

$5,000-7,000   **L&T**

A 19thC mahogany framed cheval mirror, with reeded supports, on a platform base and carved feet.

A Victorian carved mahogany cheval mirror, the arched rectangular plate, between scrolled supports, on a platform base, terminating in scrolled feet and casters.

63.5in (161cm) high

$1,000-1,500   **SWO**

33in (84cm) wide

$1,000-1,500   **SWO**

A Victorian mahogany cheval mirror, with crossbanded plain plate, twin tapered figured horns, on mushroom swept feet with casters.

65.75in (167cm) high

$1,000-1,200   **BIG**

An Edwardian mahogany cheval mirror, on a reeded frame, raised on swept legs.

$500-700   **SWO**

An Edwardian inlaid mahogany cheval mirror, with a beveled plate.

74.75in (187cm) high

$2,000-3,000   **SWO**

An Edwardian mahogany cheval mirror, with an oval shaped plate and rope twist inlay.

69.25in (176cm) high

$700-1,000   **SWO**

FURNITURE

A mid-18thC walnut and feather banded dressing table mirror, with a parcel gilt slip, concave front and three drawers on bracket feet.

18.5in (47cm) wide

$2,000-3,000   **DN**

An 18thC mahogany and hardwood 'China Trade' toilet mirror, with a pigeon-holed interior, and a drawer below with divisions and lidded boxes.

18.5in (46cm) high

$600-900   **SWO**

A Regency mahogany swing frame toilet mirror, the rectangular plate within a simulated bamboo surround, fitted with three short drawers.

23.25in (59cm) high

$450-650   **SWO**

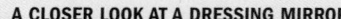

A CLOSER LOOK AT A DRESSING MIRROR

The form of this dressing-mirror is closely related to English examples of the period, but utilizes native Indian timbers and bone inlays.

The style of decoration came to be accepted both in India and England especially in fabrics with the trailing foliate forms exemplified in Paisley shawls.

Vizagapatam is on the Bay of Bengal, between Bombay and Calcutta and was a site of the East India Company's activities from 1668 onwards.

This form of inlay was derived from Mogul traditional work adapted to western taste. The inlays were usually embellished with pen-work etching to the inlays, adding to the overall illusion of depth to the decorative effects achieved.

An Anglo-Indian George III Vizagapatam swing-frame dressing mirror, the ground was usually padouk and the drawers internally of scented sandalwood.

1775

19.25in (49cm) wide

$50,000-60,000   **PAR**

A George III mahogany toilet mirror, with three frieze drawers and a rectangular plate.

20in (51cm) wide

$400-600   **SWO**

A 19thC Dutch marquetry toilet mirror.

15.5in (39.5cm) wide

$200-300   **SWO**

A late 18thC Chippendale mahogany revolving shaving mirror, above three drawers supported by ogee bracket feet and bearing the label of "Wayne and Biddle, Philadelphia".

$5,000-7,000   **POOK**

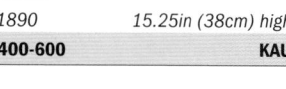

A German Historism table mirror, with silver-plated metal and glass, on two feet, in an open-work frame with floral decoration, and the mirror glass faceted.

c1890   *15.25in (38cm) high*

$400-600   **KAU**

SIDEBOARDS

- From the middle ages, householders demonstrated their social status with abundant food and fine serving dishes displayed on cupboards and dressers.
- Serving tables became popular during the 18th century. They were usually flanked by a pair of cupboard pedestals, each with appropriate fitments to keep food warm in one and cold in the other.
- By the 1760s these three pieces had become combined into the sideboard. Designed specifically for the dining room, early examples tended to be low, rectangular pieces with cupboards at either end separated by one or more drawers.
- In the first half on the 19th century pedestal sideboards, often in figured mahogany, became popular. Bacchic decorative motifs and either backboards or brass galleries were typical.
- The side cabinet and chiffonier were variations of the sideboard, and often had doors with brass grilles backed with silk.
- An additional piece to the dining room, Buffets comprised an open, shelved upper section above drawers and a lower section with cupboards. Such pieces were popular well into the 20th century, where the upper section might also be glazed.
- Alterations are fairly common. Look for later legs, replaced veneers and difference in timber coloring.

An early George III mahogany serving table, with a pair of frieze drawers with engraved silvered handles flanked and divided by oval rosettes.

60.75in (152cm) wide

$10,000-12,000 **L&T**

A George III mahogany bowfront sideboard, with shaped top, central frieze drawer, and cellarette drawers, on square tapered legs with spade feet.

c1760 *65.5in (166.5cm) wide*

$3,000-4,000 **FRE**

A George III mahogany demilune serving table with shaped top and three frieze drawers, on square legs.

c1760 *53.25in (135cm) wide*

$2,000-3,000 **FRE**

A Pennsylvania walnut side table, with three-plank top, two varisized lip molded apron drawers, and plain cabriole legs with claw and ball feet.

c1770 *66.5in (169cm) long*

$4,000-6,000 **FRE**

A George III mahogany serpentine sideboard, with satinwood crossbanding, shaped apron and recessed cupboard with tambour door, the sides dummy fronted with false drawers and cupboards.

67.25in (168cm) wide

$10,000-12,000 **L&T**

A George III mahogany breakfront sideboard, with satinwood banding and ebony stringing, central drawer and arched apron below, with fitted interior.

67.5in (169cm) wide

$3,000-4,000 **L&T**

A George III bow fronted mahogany serving table, with a brass curtain rail, inlaid stringing and a long drawer, on square tapering legs and spade feet.

45.5in (116cm) wide

$1,200-1,800 **SWO**

A George III strung mahogany bow-fronted sideboard, with two deep drawers flanking a central drawer, on square tapering legs and spade feet.

41in (104cm) high

$1,200-1,800 **SWO**

A George III mahogany and satinwood crossbanded sideboard, of semi-bowed form, with boxwood and ebony stringing above a central drawer, an apron with inlaid patera, twin false drawer front with fitted cellar interior, and two corresponding short drawers.

35.5in (90cm) high

$10,000-15,000 **L&T**

A George III mahogany and boxwood strung sideboard, of semi bowed form, with crossbanded top above three central drawers with a single inlaid drawer below.

37.75in (96cm) high

$7,000-10,000 **L&T**

A George III mahogany sideboard, with a rectangular top over a three drawer frieze and two deep drawers.

c1790   56in (142cm) wide

$3,000-4,000   FRE

A Federal mahogany inlaid sideboard, with bow front top, double pencil line to drawers and door, oval 'eagle' brasses and ivory 'diamond' escutcheons.

c1795   43in (109.25cm) high

$7,000-9,000   FRE

A Sheraton side table.

c1800   57in (145cm) high

$35,000-55,000   RGA

A Directoire mahogany table dessert, with inset marble top and pierced gallery, single frieze drawer and cupboard doors flanked by brass mounted pilasters.

c1800   37.5in (95cm) wide

$2,000-3,000   FRE

An early 19thC mahogany serpentine fronted sideboard, inlaid with stringing and geometric motifs, on square tapering legs.

            38.5in (98cm) wide

$3,500-5,500   DN

A late 18th/early 19thC Philadelphia Federal inlaid mahogany sideboard, with central concave long drawer, and square section tapering legs.

PROVENANCE: From the collection of D. Virginia Armentrout (nee Roosevelt) of Ambler, Pennsylvania.

            37in (94cm) high

$7,000-9,000   FRE

An early 19thC Federal New England mahogany veneer and bird's-eye maple sideboard, the swell front top with outset corners, on reeded and ring turned tapering legs, losses, refinished.

$10,000-15,000   FRE

A Federal mahogany and inlaid sideboard, with five drawers and two concave doors, raised on square tapered legs.

c1810   67in (167.5cm) wide

$5,000-7,000   FRE

A Classical Philadelphia mahogany sideboard, attributed to Henry Connelly, with case of kidney-shape, three drawers and two doors on turned and reeded legs.

c1810   40in (101.5cm) high

$10,000-15,000   FRE

A Federal inlaid sideboard, possibly from Boston, with three drawers above central hinged doors, crossbanded and string-inlaid borders, and replaced brass pulls, refinished, imperfections.

c1810   42in (107cm) wide

$12,000-15,000   SK

A Massachusetts Federal mahogany sideboard, with a single frieze drawer and four cupboard doors, conch shell inlay and reeded legs.

c1815   65.5in (164cm) wide

$4,000-6,000   POOK

A late Federal inlaid mahogany sideboard, with seven drawers, reeded uprights, acanthus-carved and tapering reeded legs, and brass casters.

c1815   42in (106.5cm) high

$4,000-6,000   FRE

A Pennsylvania late Federal tiger maple and cherry sideboard, with arched pediment, three drawers and cupboard doors flanked by turned columns.

c1830   59.75in (152cm) wide

$2,000-2,500   POOK

A George II mahogany bowfront sideboard, with a central drawer flanked by two graduated drawers and one deep cellar drawer with two false drawers raised on square tapering legs.

58.25in (148cm) wide

$4,000-6,000	L&T

A George III mahogany serpentine sideboard, with boxwood stringing, with three frieze drawers and square section tapering legs with block feet.

79.5in (202cm) wide

$4,000-6,000	L&T

A George III mahogany serpentine sideboard, the strung and crossbanded top over two cellaret drawers and two central drawers on six square tapering legs and spade feet, the front with ornate crossbanding and stringing, the shaped legs strung.

73.25in (183cm) wide

$6,000-7,000	SWO

A George III mahogany serpentine serving table, the top with a chequer strung edge over a plain frieze and four square tapering legs, the front legs with inlaid oval paterae.

59.25in (148cm) wide

$3,500-4,500	SWO

A Regency mahogany bow-front sideboard, ebony strung with a central drawer over an arched drawer, flanked by cupboards and raised on turned tapering legs.

$2,800-3,200	SWO

A Regency strung mahogany D-shaped sideboard, with three frieze drawers, over two pedestal doors.

56in (140cm) wide

$2,000-3,000	SWO

A Regency strung mahogany sideboard, with satinwood crossbanding and a brass gallery, the superstructure fitted with drawers on cupboards flanking a central drawer on square tapered legs and spade feet.

87.25in (218cm) wide

$4,500-5,500	SWO

A Regency period mahogany breakfront sideboard, the top with a three-quarter gallery over a rope-molded edge, the front with a central indented drawer and cupboard, between a pair of drawers and cupboards on turned tapering paw feet.

61in (155cm) wide

$3,500-4,500	SWO

A Scottish Regency mahogany serving table, with brass baluster columns and table top with three drawers, on tapering fluted legs and muscular paw feet, alterations.

44in (112cm) high

$4,500-6,500   **L&T**

A small Regency style mahogany reverse breakfront sideboard, with a brass rail above frieze drawers and applied anthemia to panels.

61in (154cm) wide

$4,000-6,000   **L&T**

A Regency mahogany breakfront serving table, with central circular molding, curved panels, stiff leaf carved, reeded tapering legs and toupie feet.

36.25in (92cm) high

$20,000-30,000   **L&T**

A Regency mahogany serpentine sideboard with brass gallery back above three frieze drawers, pair of cellarette drawers, on tapering legs with spade feet.

60in (153cm) wide

$2,000-3,000   **L&T**

A Scottish Regency mahogany breakfront sideboard, with reverse breakfront stage, carved ledge back centred by a shell, sliding doors and drawers, on a plinth base.

90.5in (230cm) wide

$3,000-4,000   **L&T**

A Classical Pennsylvania inlaid mahogany and mahogany veneer sideboard, with double pencil line inlays, on square tapering legs, new brasses.

c1825   *73in (185.5cm) wide*

$1,000-1,500   **FRE**

A Classical Philadelphia mahogany sideboard, with low rope-carved splashback, three curved drawers and three cabinet doors, on round carved and ball feet.

c1835   *69.25in (176cm) wide*

$3,000-4,000   **FRE**

A Victorian amboyna and ebonized side cabinet, in Louis XVI style, with gilt-metal mounts, porcelain plaque inlay, central drawer enclosing writing slide, and mirrored back.

$5,000-7,000   **L&T**

A large Edwardian mahogany breakfront sideboard, in the Neo-Classical taste, with central carved drawer above a pair of sliding tambour doors, bears label 'Whytock and Reid, Edinburgh'.

86.25in (219cm) wide

$10,000-15,000   **L&T**

An early 20thC Louis XVI style fiddle mahogany sideboard, with inset marble top and gallery, frieze drawers and cupboard doors, and stop fluted pilasters.

80.75in (205cm) wide

$2,500-3,500   **FRE**

A Rose Valley quarter sawn oak sideboard, with serpentine front top, five drawers, over bottle drawers on cabriole legs, impressed "Rose Valley" on back.

c1915   *60.25in (150.5cm) wide*

$1,200-1,800   **POOK**

TEA & GAMES TABLES

- Tables specifically designed for serving tea started to appear from the late 17th century, though very few of these early tables survive.
- Tripod tables were also made for serving tea. Many had bird-cage mechanisms, and later, tilt tops for easy storage.
- The 18th century witnessed a greater demand for comfort and entertaining in the home. This shift gave rise to all manner of additional tables designed for a wide range of purposes such as playing cards and needlework.
- Many of these tables had drop leaves or tilt tops and drawers, making them more versatile and, therefore, suited to a number of uses.
- Kept to the side of a room when redundant, many tables were mounted on casters to make them easier to move when required.
- Beware of 19th century copies. There was a succession of revival styles in Europe during the 19th century, and early pieces were reproduced, sometimes with great accuracy, using contemporary techniques.

A mid-18thC New England painted tea table, with overhanging top on tapering legs ending in bulbous feet, with original red and brown grain painted surface.

37in (92.5cm) wide

$7,000-10,000   **SK**

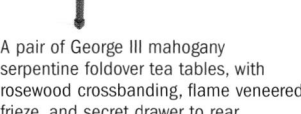

A pair of George III mahogany serpentine foldover tea tables, with rosewood crossbanding, flame veneered frieze, and secret drawer to rear.

29in (74cm) high

$10,000-15,000   **L&T**

A Scottish George III mahogany demi lune foldover tea table, with boxwood stringing, crossbanded top and central tablet on square section tapered legs.

29in (74cm) high

$7,000-10,000   **L&T**

A Scottish George III mahogany demi lune foldover tea table, with boxwood string, crossbanded top and paneled frieze, on square section tapered legs.

29in (74cm) high

$4,000-6,000   **L&T**

An early 19thC mahogany silver table, of Chinese Chippendale style, with three-quarter pierced fretwork gallery, on triple column and chamfered block legs.

29.75in (75.5cm) high

$3,000-4,000   **L&T**

A Scottish Regency mahogany foldover tea table, with shallow bead and reel paneled frieze, and concave quadriform base with reeded sabre legs, with brass caps and casters.

36.25in (92cm) wide

$2,000-3,000   **L&T**

A mid-to late 18thC Pennsylvania Chippendale walnut tea table, with circular dish molded edge and tilting top on a birdcage support, refinished.

38.25in (97cm) diam

$10,000-15,000   **FRE**

A Regency rosewood fold-over tea table, with brass inlaid stringing, paneled frieze on paired octagonal supports and concave rectangular base.

36.25in (92cm) wide

$2,000-3,000   **L&T**

A Scottish Regency mahogany foldover tea table, in the manner of William Trotter, Edinburgh, with a beaded paneled frieze, on four scrolling supports with rosette terminals.

28.5in (72cm) high

$6,000-9,000   **L&T**

A Victorian gonzalo alves and brass-inlaid tea table, with a rosewood and foliate brass-inlaid band, and a satinwood banded interior with ebony-inlaid cross motifs.

30in (76cm) high

$4,000-6,000   **L&T**

A mid-18thC Queen Anne tiger maple and maple Porringer-top table, with shaped overhanging top on four block-turned tapering legs continuing to pad feet and joined by a cut-out apron.

21.5in (54.5cm) wide

$20,000-30,000   **SK**

A George II walnut concertina card table, the hinged top with later lining to counter wells and burr walnut corners, on shell capped and husk cabriole legs to claw and ball feet.

35.25in (89.5cm) wide

$10,000-12,000   **WW**

A George III mahogany and crossbanded card table, with a plain frieze, with ring turned legs.

36.5in (91cm) high

$700-1,000   **SWO**

A George III inlaid mahogany and cross-banded fold-over card table, raised on square tapering legs, with brass caps and casters.

35.75in (91cm) high

$1,000-1,500   **SWO**

A George III mahogany and inlaid serpentine games table, in the manner of Sheraton, the shaped fold-over top centered by a fan medallion, opening to reveal a baize lined interior, over a plain frieze and raised on square tapered legs, surmounted by patera and ending in later ogee block feet.

c1790   *36in (90cm) wide*

$1,500-2,000   **FRE**

A George II demi-lune tea table, the hinged top, over a shaped frieze, on cabriole legs and hoot feet.

32.75in (83.5cm) high

$2,000-3,000   **SWO**

A George III mahogany half-round tea table, on square tapering legs and spade feet.

37.75in (96cm) high

$1,500-2,000   **SWO**

A Regency cross banded mahogany fold over tea table, inlaid with ebony, raised on a turned and carved column and a quadripartite base.

36.5in (91cm) wide

$1,200-1,800   **SWO**

An Edwardian satinwood demi-lune table, in the George III style, the shaped top painted with husk swags and floral border above a mahogany inlaid frieze, on turned legs painted with leaf clasps and husk pendants.

42in (107cm) wide

$2,000-3,000   **L&T**

A Regency rosewood games/writing table, the hinged top with brass sockets for book rest (lacking), sliding to reveal well inlaid for backgammon, above false drawers, the saber legs with block terminals and brass caps and casters.

31in (79cm) high

$6,000-9,000   **L&T**

An early 19thC figured maple games table, the rectangular top with floral decorated edge sliding to reveal a backgammon board interior, over a line inlaid frame supported by reeded legs terminating in brass casters.

c1805   *24in (61cm) wide*

$5,000-7,000   **POOK**

A William IV rosewood fold over card table, raised on a tapering column, a quadripartite base, with claw feet.

36.5in (91cm) wide

$1,500-1,800   **SWO**

A Victorian walnut and marquetry inlaid card table, the serpentine hinged swivel top inlaid foliage and scrolls to a molded edge and baize lining, the frieze carved shells and foliage on a ribbed baluster stem to foliage carved scroll legs with brass casters.

36in (91.5cm) wide

$2,000-3,000   **WW**

A Victorian inlaid walnut fold-over card table, on turned and fluted columns and scrolled legs, united by a stretcher.

34.75in (88.5cm) high

$3,000-4,000   **SWO**

A Victorian rosewood serpentine fronted card table, with lined folding swivel top, on leaf carved cabriole legs, with leaf scroll carved feet.

37.75in (96cm) wide

$1,000-1,500   **LFA**

A Victorian canted rectangular quarter veneered walnut fold-over card table with ebony banded inlay, baize lined interior, twin turned end supports, carved splay feet and casters.

36in (91.5cm) wide

$1,000-1,200   **MAX**

A pair of Edwardian satinwood and rosewood crossbanded card tables, on square tapered legs.

36.25in (92cm) high

$2,000-3,000   **SWO**

An Anglo Indian rosewood games table, inlaid with a cheque board, within banding, and ivory inlay, on a turned and carved support, on three reeded feet.

c1870   *20.5in (52cm) high*

$15,000-20,000   **PAR**

FURNITURE

A George II mahogany foldover card table, with baize lined interior and counter holders, frieze drawer and shell carved apron, later applied bases.

27.5in (70cm) high

$4,000-6,000   **L&T**

A George III mahogany card table, with enclosed baize lined playing surface, tooled leather border, 'gothic' paneled apron, and carved block feet.

Provenance: The leg pilasters, with ribbon frets in the 'modern' Gothic fashion correspond to those of seat furniture, formerly in the possession of J Mallett and Sons of Bath before being exhibited at the Burlington Fine Arts Club, 1920, and on an en-suite armchair bequeathed to the Victoria and Albert Museum in 1938 by Lady W.S.Theobald.

1760   *36in (91.5cm) wide*

$70,000-90,000   **PAR**

A George III Harewood, Satinwood, Tulipwood and Floral Marquetry Card Table, inlaid with floral marquetry and in the center with an oval panel, on square section tapering legs with herring-bone banding and block feet, gateleg, top covered in green baize.

1775   *36in (91.5cm) wide*

$190,000-220,000   **PAR**

A late 18thC Chippendale mahogany card table, rectangular top with molded edge, on molded frieze and square chamfered legs, and old finish.

29.75in (75.5cm) wide

$2,000-3,000   **FRE**

A George III mahogany foldover card table, with boxwood and ebony stringing, and D-shaped top with satinwood banding above plain frieze.

29.5in (75cm) high

$7,000-10,000   **L&T**

A late 18thC George III mahogany card table with serpentine top and skirt with egg and dart border, on cabriole legs with ball and claw feet.

35in (90cm) wide

$5,500-6,500   **POOK**

A New York Hepplewhite mahogany card table, with inlaid demi-lune top, conforming case with paterae capitals and with line, inverted cup and heart inlays.

Provenance: Descended in the duPont family.

c1800   *36in (91.5cm) wide*

$8,000-10,000   **POOK**

A federal inlaid Mahogany card table, the demi-lune top with molded edge above conforming line-inlaid apron, on molded tapering legs.

c1800   *29.5in (75cm) high*

$1,500-2,000   **FRE**

An early 19thC New England Federal folding top card table, with bow-shaped top, front apron panel, mahogany oval inlay and oval leaf inlays.

36in (91.5cm) wide

$7,000-9,000   **FRE**

An early 19thC New England Federal mahogany inlaid card table, with bow shaped folding top, elongated diamond panel, inlaid frieze and diamond inlaid sides.

35.75in (91cm) wide

$6,000-7,000   **FRE**

A Boston Sheraton mahogany folding top game table, with pencil line inlay, maple frieze on ring turned capitals and tapering reeded legs on tall turned feet, old refinish.

With a typed card reading "from Grandmother Lucas Powell Thompson's house, Phila. Staunton".

c1810

$6,000-8,000   **FRE**

A Regency rosewood foldover card table, with satinwood crossbanding above boxwood strung frieze, on tow lyre supports and square section tapered legs.

38in (97cm) wide

$2,000-3,000 **L&T**

A pair of Regency calamander-veneered turnover card tables, with gilt brass mounts, enclosing baize-lined interiors above an entableture frieze with applied anthemion motifs.

30in (76cm) high

$10,000-15,000 **L&T**

A Philadelphia Federal mahogany card table, with reeded edge on conforming frieze, on round ring turned and reeded peg feet.

c1815 *35.75in (91cm) wide*

$2,000-3,000 **FRE**

A late 19thC Louis XVI style satinwood bouillotte table, with gilt brass mounts, marble top above scrolling frieze, and four turned and fluted legs.

30.5in (78cm) high

$700-1,000 **L&T**

A Philadelphia Federal mahogany inlaid folding top card table, with reeded edge, bow-shaped top, pencil line inlays to frieze, on round ring turned and reeded legs.

c1815 *31in (78.5cm) wide*

$1,500-2,000 **FRE**

A late 19thC boulle foldover card table, with gilt metal mounts and brass inlaid tortoiseshell panel, baize lined interior and apron frieze with applied mask cartouche.

37.25in (93cm) wide

$2,000-3,000 **L&T**

A Classical Philadelphia carved mahogany card table, the paneled frieze carved with acanthus leaves, on ring and spiral turned legs ending in peg feet.

c1825 *48in (122cm) wide*

$1,000-1,500 **FRE**

A late 19th to early 20thC inlaid birch games table, probably English, folding and rotating top, inlay and frieze with swags and tassels, old Nieman-Marcus label, damage and separations.

35in (89cm) wide

$1,500-2,000 **BRU**

An early 20thC walnut card table, of Georgian style, with a baise-lined interior, on cabriole legs with claw and ball feet.

32in (81cm) wide

$1,000-1,200 **L&T**

An Edwardian satinwood and inlaid demi-lune foldover card table, in the Sheraton Revival style, with radial veneered top on tapering legs and square feet.

30in (76cm) high

$1,000-1,200 **L&T**

A walnut fold over card table, with marquetry inlay, demi lune hinged top enclosing baize lined interior, frieze with three drawers, baluster turned legs, and bun feet.

36in (91cm) wide

$2,000-3,000 **L&T**

FURNITURE

A late 18thC New Jersey walnut work stand, with single drawer and scalloped skirt supported by delicate turned legs joined by 'H' stretcher.

28.5in (72.5cm) high

| $7,000-9,000 | POOK |

A Victorian inlaid walnut fold over combined games and work table, opening to reveal chess, cribbage and backgammon boards, with a drawer and slide below, on a carved base.

| $3,000-4,000 | SWO |

A Federal mahogany and bird's-eye maple two-drawer work table, North Shore, Massachusetts, with two drawers, refinished, surface scratches.

A Regency rosewood writing/work table, with boxwood stringing, baize liner and secret pen and ink compartments, above frieze drawer and sliding silk wool bin.

30in (75cm) high

| $3,000-4,000 | L&T |

A Massachusetts Federal mahogany sewing stand, with rectangular top over two drawers supported by rope turned legs.

c1815   *29.25in (73cm) high*

| $800-1,200 | POOK |

| $10,000-15,000 | FRE |

A Regency mahogany sewing table, with hinged D-ends, paneled drawer and opposing dummy, solid drum wool bin below, on hoop support and turned pedestal.

24.5in (62cm) wide

| $2,000-3,000 | L&T |

A Regency mahogany work table, in the manner of Gillows, with rosewood crossbanded top above a partially fitted frieze drawer between reeded corners.

29.25in (74.5cm) high

| $4,000-6,000 | L&T |

An early 19thC mahogany sewing table, with hinged top enclosing compartments and tapering solid wool bin, on scroll feet with casters.

19in (48cm) wide

| $1,000-1,500 | L&T |

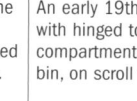

An early 19thC mahogany drop flap sewing table, with a single drawer raised on a turned tapering column.

18.75in (47cm) wide

| $600-900 | SWO |

An early 19thC adjustable rosewood work table, with inset leather writing surface and book rest, the lower drawer fitted with silk-lined compartments and with sewing implements, on turned and reeded legs, with brass caps and casters.

30.25in (77cm) high

$3,000-4,000   **L&T**

A Classical Philadelphia mahogany double pedestal sewing stand, with veneered center section, felt covered work panel, pedestals with fabric containers, on scroll feet on casters.

c1830   30in (76cm) high

$3,000-4,000   **FRE**

An early Victorian rosewood sewing table, with a single drawer and velvet slide.

24in (61cm) wide

$1,000-1,500   **SWO**

A mid-19thC Chinese export lacquered work table, painted with figures and landscapes in gilt, lidded divisions and ivory fittings, lacking the sliding wool bag, some damage to lacquer.

24.5in (62.5cm) wide

$1,000-1,500   **DN**

A 19thC mahogany work table, the chamfered sides enclosing a drawer, fitted together with a secret drawer below, on square tapering legs.

23in (58.5cm) wide

$700-1,000   **SWO**

A Victorian mahogany games table, the fold-over top revealing chess, cribbage and backgammon boards, a well, slide and drawer, on carved legs and a turned stretcher.

*1,000-1,200   **SWO**

A German veneered walnut sewing table, on scroll feet, with fitted interior and one drawer.

c1870   30.5in (76cm) high

$300-400   **KAU**

A Pennsylvania Soap Hollow painted and decorated work stand, from Somerset County, the single drawer with yellow edge, turned legs, brown overall finish, dated, finish crazed.

1875   22in (56cm) wide

$6,000-8,000   **FRE**

A late 19thC gonzalo alves, with rosewood and boxwood strung work table, double hinged top, two burr yew ovals, and square tapering legs with 'X' stretcher.

16.5in (42cm) wide

$1,500-2,000   **DN**

A late 19thC satinwood and painted work table, with a tulipwood crossbanded border and bead decorated edge, hinged to enclose a lined interior.

17.25in (44cm) wide

$1,500-2,000   **DN**

A 17thC made-up Italian walnut centerd table, with octagonal molded top, raised on an acanthus carved columnar support and a scroll carved plinth and paw feet.

27.5in (70cm) high

$1,200-1,800   **FRE**

A late 17th/early 18thC Dutch walnut, ebony, fruitwood, bone and marquetry center table, depicting flowers, birds and acanthus, with some repair, and later feet.

44in (112cm) wide

$10,000-15,000   **DN**

A Regency rosewood and parcel gilt center table, with molded edge above a frieze with applied roundels, raised on a ring turned column with gilded baluster sleeve.

28in (71cm) high

$10,000-12,000   **L&T**

A Classical Philadelphia mahogany and mahogany veneer center loo table, with sectioned flame veneer on a ring-turned and urn form support.

c1830   *28.75in (73cm) high*

$30,000-40,000   **FRE**

A Philadelphia classical carved mahogany center table, with turned and acanthus leaf-carved support, shaped platform and hairy paw feet, on casters.

c1830   *29.5in (75cm) high*

$4,000-6,000   **FRE**

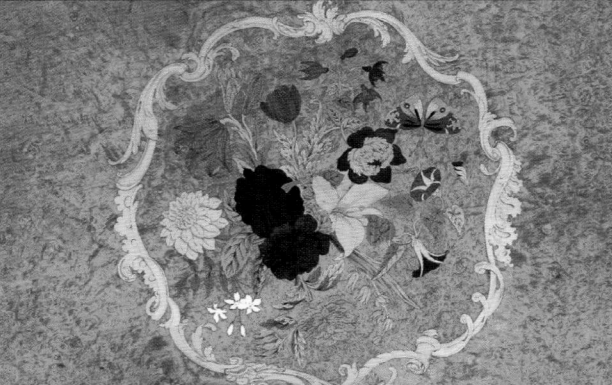

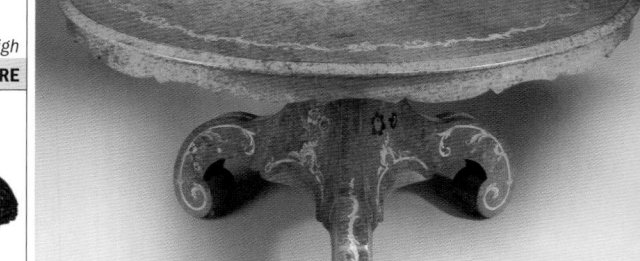

A 19thC burr walnut and marquetry decorated tilt-top center table attributed to Edward Holmes Baldock after a design by Richard Bridgens. The top is veneered with a tightly burred timber, the center inlaid with marquetry flowers, birds and a butterfly in various stained and engraved woods, all encircled with finely inlaid scrolling foliage, the outer edge of the top with a conforming foliate border, raised on a tripartite incurved faceted column continuing to similarly formed down swept legs with scrolled toes fitted with recessed brass casters, all inlaid with flowers and foliage.

c1840   *51in (129.5cm) wide*

$25,000-45,000   **RGA**

A 19thC Continental mahogany and marquetry center table, inlaid throughout with scrolling foliage, on gilt metal mounted turned legs.

29.5in (74cm) high

$800-1,200   **FRE**

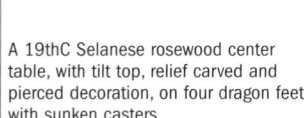

A 19thC Selanese rosewood center table, with tilt top, relief carved and pierced decoration, on four dragon feet with sunken casters.

50.75in (127cm) diam

$5,000-7,000   **L&T**

A 19thC walnut and satinwood inlaid gilt-brass mounted center table, the frieze cast with festoons and Bacchanalian cherubs, and a central drawer, on cabriole legs.

31in (80cm) diam

$10,000-15,000   **L&T**

A specimen marble table, top with games board.

c1860　　　　　　　　　　*29in (74cm) high*

$25,000-45,000　　　　　　　　　　**RGA**

A Victorian rectangular walnut center table, with inlay of flowers and butterflies, on pierced and carved end supports with carved dome finials, on knurled splay feet and later casters.

52in (132cm) long

$6,000-9,000　　　　　　　　　　**MAX**

A Victorian mahogany circular center table, raised on an uptapering octagonal column base, on claw feet.

50in (125cm) diam

$450-650　　　　　　　　　　**SWO**

A mid-Victorian mahogany and specimen-inlaid center table, profusely inlaid with radiating bands of parquetry inlay, the base with maple-inlaid tapering column.

50.75in (129cm) diam

$5,000-7,000　　　　　　**L&T**

A mid-Victorian carved walnut center table, attributed to Henry Eyles, Bath, with burr quarter veneered top centered by a cartouche shaped marquetry panel, boxwood frieze carved in relief with oval panels depicting the 'Ages of Man' and 'Adam and Eve expelled from Paradise', and four concealed compartments.

A similar table by Henry Eyles was exhibited at The Great Exhibition of 1851and is now at the Victoria & Albert Museum in London. It may be that the edge carving was carried out by his relation George Eyles, woodcarver of Claverton Street in Bath. The elaborate carving and decoration to the table may indicate that it also was specifically produced as an exhibition piece. Literature; 'The Pictorial History of British 19th Century Furniture Design', Woodbridge, 1977, p.xxvii

29in (74cm) high

$70,000-100,000　　　　　　**L&T**

A Renaissance Revival Philadelphia center table, inset with leather above an apron with drawer and molded and turned trestle ends on baluster-turned legs.

c1865

$600-800　　　　　　**FRE**

A French 'Japonism' rosewood and gilt bronze mounted center table, attributed to Edouard Lievre, with inset marble top, and ornate fret pierced frieze.

c1880　　　　　　　　　　*47.5in (119cm) wide*

$65,000-85,000　　　　　　**FRE**

A Louis XV style rosewood and parquetry center table, with shaped quarter-folds, on cabriole legs with foliate cast bronze mounts and sabots.

c1900　　　　　　　　　　*35in (89cm) wide*

$800-1,200　　　　　　**FRE**

FURNITURE

A late 18thC Italian decorated console table, with gilt scroll and rosette decoration to frieze on leaf clasped tapered circular stop-fluted legs.

c1780   43.5in (110.5cm) wide

$20,000-30,000	BLO

A rare Regency rosewood, ebonized and parcel gilt console table, in the manner of George Smith, with marble top and twin animal leg supports.

49.5in (126cm) wide

$15,000-20,000	CATO

A CLOSER LOOK AT A PAIR OF GEORGE II CARVED GILTWOOD CONSOLE TABLES

Gilded furniture was a prominent feature of the early 18th century. Pieces were gilded for maximum effect, their sinuous shapes gleaming brilliantly in candlelit salons.

Soft indigenous woods such as pine, lime or beech were used to allow easier and more elaborate carving, then covered in gesso and gilt to give this more extravagant, decorative style.

The form of these tables is similar to that of a pair of console tables in the Queen's Bedchamber at Ham House which have been dated to circa 1740 and thought to have been supplied by George Nix.

The tables may also be related to two designs for 'pier' tables from William Jones's 'The Gentleman or Builder's Companion' of 1739.

The initial influence on the overall concept of these tables partially came from Italian Gaetano Brunetti's 1736 publication 'Sixty Different Sorts of Ornament' which included light, serpentine forms employing only two legs to support the slab top.

One of a pair of George II carved giltwood console tables, with veneered alabaster tops, and a pierced stretcher carved with acanthus on a shaped plinth base carved in low relief.

40.5in (103cm) wide

$400,000-500,000 PAIR	PAR

A highly important English George I gilt gesso side table, with carved giltwood strap-work top embellished with trailing foliate patterns on the usual punched ground within the molded edge, concave frieze centered by a deeply carved cartouche carved around a shell and with a running border of leaves, on cabriole legs carved with masks to the knees decorated with stylized feather head-dresses and the acanthus leaves carved below lead to a fish-scale pattern terminating in remarkable open feet with carved stylized dolphin feet.

A table comparable in quality and outline is similar to the famous example at Erthig Park, Denbighshire supplied by Moore in 1726.

c1725   36.5in (92.5cm) wide

$550,000-700,000	PAR

A Louis XV carved giltwood console table, with a marble top, the frieze carved, the central cartouche of leaves and husks, and carved legs with scrolls and birds.

The vigorous carving of this table gives full expression to the energy of the early rococo in France. The abundance of the flowing decoration and the extravagant asymmetrical curves here reflect the style of the important rococo designer Juste-Aurele Meissonnier (1695-1750), who decorated Louis XV's bedchamber.

c1730   64in (162.5cm) wide

$150,000-200,000   **PAR**

A William and Mary period walnut side table, with cross and feather banding, sunburst burr veneer center with frieze drawer, replacement handle and bun feet.

c1690   34.25in (87cm) wide

$1,000-1,500   **L&T**

A mid-18thC Irish George II walnut side table, with a single frieze drawer and shaped apron, raised on c-scroll and acanthus carved cabriole legs and pad feet.

31in (78.5cm) wide

$3,000-4,000   **FRE**

A George III mahogany side table with marble top on square chamfered legs.

48in (122cm) wide

$10,000-15,000   **L&T**

A pair of late 18thC Continental walnut demilune console tables, probably Italian, with shaped tops, and a frieze drawer, with restorations.

20in (75cm) high

$1,000-1,500   **FRE**

A Classical Philadelphia marble and mahogany pier table, with ogee molded frieze on marble columns with gilt brass collar and base joined by scrolled stretcher.

c1820   35.5in (90cm) high

$12,000-15,000   **FRE**

A Philadelphia Classical mahogany and marble-top pier table, with marble top on conforming apron raised on columns of exotic wood veneer.

c1825   37in (94cm) high

$12,000-16,000   **FRE**

A Philadelphia carved mahogany pier table, with gadrooned edge on ogee molded apron, serpentine shaped platform, mirrored back, and lion paw feet.

c1830   34.5in (87.5cm) high

$3,000-4,000   **FRE**

A William IV rosewood and giltwood console table, with Verde Antico marble top, plain frieze with leaf moldings, and mirrored back supported by scrolling consoles.

34.5in (88cm) high

$4,000-6,000   **L&T**

A William IV mahogany side table, with rosette and leaf scroll terminals, two scrolled consoles with anthemion carvings, raised on a shaped plinth base.

42in (107cm) high

$7,000-10,000   **L&T**

A pair of 19thC carved giltwood palmette console tables, with shaped marble tops on carved scrolling supports, and carved plinth bases.

28in (71cm) wide

$5,000-7,000   **FRE**

A 19thC giltwood and marble-topped side table, with anthemion frieze centered with an entablature, raised to the front on scrolling consoles with acanthus carving.

57in (145cm) wide

$7,000-10,000   **L&T**

DINING TABLES

- Until the early 17thC oak refectory tables were the only form of dining table. Originally the top was formed by one or two planks of wood set on ornately carved legs.
- Gateleg and dropleaf tables were popular well into the 18thC. Gateleg tables had a round or oval tabletop, often with hinged flaps, supported on a gateleg base. The table could be made smaller or larger to suit the occasion and was easily portable.
- Drop leaf tables supersede gateleg tables. They were more comfortable to sit at because they had fewer legs, no stretchers and greater overhang.
- By c1780 the first dining tables with a central pedestal were being made. These tables are often called breakfast tables and are usually rectangular.
- In the 18th and 19thC large tables with D-shaped ends were common. The tops of these were usually supported by two or more pedestals with sections of tabletop which clipped in between them. Tables with original square legs are more sought after than later turned legs.
- In the mid 19thC a cranking mechanism was devized which allowed dining tables to be extended via a series of interlocking supports which removed the need for too many legs.

A good George III mahogany extending dining table, with a fold over top, extending to take five leaves, with brass mounts and fittings.

48in (122cm) wide

$3,000-4,000   **SWO**

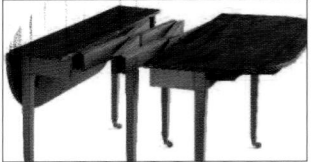

A George III mahogany telescopic dining table, with reeded edge, two loose leaves and drop ends, on square tapering legs with brass casters.

46.5in (118cm) wide

$2,000-3,000   **LFA**

A George III mahogany D-end dining table, in three sections on molded square legs.

120in (305cm) wide

$1,200-1,800   **SWO**

A George III and later mahogany D-end dining table, comprising two D-ends and a drop leaf section on square tapered legs, to include three extra leaves.

115.25in (288cm) wide

$1,500-2,000   **SWO**

A Federal mahogany inlaid three-part banquet table, with deep drop leaves, two demi-lune top end sections, and square tapering legs.

c1800   *151.75in (385.5cm) long*

$7,000-9,000   **FRE**

A Classical two-part cherry and mahogany dining table, from Philadelphia or New York, with a rotating top, and foliate carved decoration supported by scalloped ends.

c1830   *85in (216cm) diam*

$7,000-10,000   **POOK**

An early 19thC mahogany dining table, with boxwood stringing, reeded edge and boxwood paneled frieze on turned and reeded tapering legs with toupie feet.

52.5in (131cm) wide

$10,000-12,000   **L&T**

A two-part Classical cherry dining table, probably from Maryland, with "D" shaped apron and ring-turned tapering legs ending in peg feet, one bears the chalk inscription "Eli[ ]a Ridgely.".

PROVENANCE: The tables may have once belonged to Eliza Eichelberger Ridgely who lived at 'Hampton', a sophisticated country home outside of Baltimore. Ridgely attended Miss Lyman's Institution in Philadelphia. Thomas Sully's full length portrait of Ridgely with her harp, completed in 1818, is in the National Gallery of Arts, Washington D.C.

c1820   *28.5in (72.5cm) high*

$1,500-2,000   **FRE**

A William IV mahogany extending dining table, with rounded angles, above a plain frieze on turned and reeded tapering legs, includes three additional leaves.

28.75in (73cm) high

$20,000-30,000   **L&T**

An early Victorian mahogany extending dining table, with four additional leaves, on baluster turned legs with leaf carved capitals.

134in (340cm) long extended

$15,000-20,000   **L&T**

An Empire mahogany accordian-action extension table, bears pressed brass plate with patent information, a T.P. Sherborne patent 1849, no.127 Walnut St. Philadelphia, with one leaf.

29in (73.5cm) high

$3,000-5,000   **FRE**

A 19thC mahogany extending dining table, with a drop leaf top on turned and reeded legs, now with one leaf.

$1,200-1,800   **SWO**

An early 19thC Delaware Valley mahogany three piece dining table with two matching demilune ends and nearly identical center dropleaf section.

112in (284cm) length open

$3,000-4,000   **POOK**

A Victorian mahogany extending dining table, the molded rectangular top with rounded angles, includes three additional leaves.

131in (333cm) long

$10,000-15,000   **L&T**

DROP LEAF DINING TABLES

An 18thC Queen Anne walnut drop leaf table, with slightly curved ends, deep half-round drop leaves, shaped apron, and round turned legs with pad feet.

52.5in (133.5cm) long

$1,000-1,500   **FRE**

An 18thC Philadelphia walnut drop leaf dining table, supported on cabriole legs with ball and claw feet.

18in (46cm) wide closed

$7,000-9,000   **POOK**

A Pennsylvania Chippendale walnut drop leaf dining table, with rectangular top and leaves, arched carved apron, and cabriole legs with claw and ball feet.

c1770   *28in (71cm) high*

$12,000-15,000   **FRE**

A last third 18thC Chippendale mahogany drop leaf dining table, with slightly curved ends, carved apron, and cabriole legs with claw and ball feet.

60.75in (154cm) long

$2,000-4,000   **FRE**

An 18th/19thC Pennsylvania walnut drop leaf table, with arched carved apron, on square grooved legs with block feet.

43in (109cm) long

$1,000-1,500   **FRE**

An early 19thC Dutch mahogany and floral marquetry drop-leaf table, inlaid with flower sprays and acanthus scrolls, the frieze fitted with opposing frieze drawers.

41in (104cm) wide

$3,000-4,500   **L&T**

A Regency style mahogany triple pedestal metamorphic dining table, with two extra leaves and fillets converting two pedestals to breakfast tables.

154.5in (386cm) long

$7,000-10,000 L&T

A Regency mahogany dining table, with two leaf insertions, on ring turned supports, four legs with brass hairy paw caps and casters.

c1815 *extended 90in (228.5cm) wide*

$4,000-6,000 FRE

A George IV mahogany extending pedestal dining table, with three leaf insertions, two of recent manufacture, above a column and a pair of half columns.

c1825 *60in (152cm) wide*

$10,000-15,000 DN

A Classical Philadelphia two-part mahogany dining table, with D-shape end and deep rectangular leaf with tapering cylindrical support.

c1830 *94in (239cm) long*

$8,000-10,000 FRE

A 19thC triple pedestal mahogany dining table, with crossbanded top raised on quadruped base with four sabre legs, later inlaid and with brass cast paw caps and casters.

120in (300cm) long

$6,000-9,000 L&T

A 20thC mahogany triple pedestal dining table, of Georgian style, on three turned columns, the end two with three legs with pad feet, the central column with four.

143in (363cm) long

$7,000-10,000 L&T

BREAKFAST TABLES

A George III mahogany breakfast table, after the model in Thomas Chippendale's Director, with a pair of concave fretwork doors, similar sides and back.

39.75in (101cm) wide

$4,000-6,000 L&T

An early George III mahogany drop flap breakfast table, in the manner of Thomas Chippendale, with a single drawer above wirework sides and twin concave doors.

29in (73.5cm) high

$6,000-9,000 L&T

A George IV Irish rosewood breakfast table by Williams & Gibson (1830-44), with a beaded border, cylindrical tapering and lappet carved column.

29.5in (75cm) high

$3,000-4,000 DN

A William IV rosewood breakfast table, with turned and gadrooned stem and three lappet carved outswept legs on casters.

48.5in (123cm) diam

$3,000-4,000 DN

A Regency period mahogany period breakfast table, with gadrooned edge, reeded bulbous support and quadruped base, with reeded and leaf-carved sabre legs.

48.75in (124cm) diam

$2,000-3,000 L&T

A mid-18thC Louis XV kingwood and rosewood bureau plat, with an inset leather writing surface, over three real and two dummy frieze drawers, and lateral slides.

65.25in (165.5cm) wide

$5,000-7,000   **FRE**

A late 19thC French mahogany bureau plat with gilt brass mounts, with molded brass edge above fluted paneled breakfront frieze and fluted tapering turned legs.

50.75in (129cm) wide

$5,000-7,000   **L&T**

A Louis XV style kingwood bureau plat, with gilt bronze mounts, shaped top and cabriole legs with a shaped apron, foliate mounts, and sabots.

c1900   40.5in (103cm) wide

$10,000-15,000   **FRE**

A Louis XV style kingwood gilt bronze and porcelain mounted bureau plat, with painted porcelain plaques, serpentine top, shaped frieze and two frieze drawers.

c1900   55in (139.5cm) wide

$20,000-30,000   **FRE**

A Louis XV style kingwood and parquetry bureau plat, with gilt bronze mounts, and inset leather writing surface, over three real and three dummy frieze drawers.

c1900   57.5in (146cm) wide

$1,000-1,300   **FRE**

A French Louis XV style walnut bureau plat, with bronze mounts, inset leather writing surface, and frieze with three real and three dummy drawers.

c1900   52.5in (133.5cm) wide

$1,500-2,500   **FRE**

A 20thC Louis XV-style kingwood bureau plat, with gilt brass cast mounts, inset leather writing surface, with caryatid mounts and cast sabots.

70.5in (176cm) wide

$1,500-2,000   **L&T**

A 20thC Louis XV style kingwood and parquetry bureau plat, with gilt bronze mounts, shaped top and inset leather writing surface, over three real and three dummy drawers.

62in (157.5cm) wide

$800-1,200   **FRE**

WRITING TABLES

A George III mahogany 'universal' table, with twin opposing brushing slides, adjustable felt-lined writing surface and fitted interior of hinged wells, on tapered legs with brass caps and casters.

c1770   41.75in (106cm) wide

$7,000-10,000   **FRE**

A Regency mahogany writing table, attributed to Gillows, with a reeded top, an interior fitted for pens and inkwells, and a frieze drawer.

28.5in (72.5cm) high

$7,000-10,000   **L&T**

A large Regency mahogany partner's writing table, with six opposing drawers, on tapered ring turned legs ending in brass cappings and ceramic casters.

65.25in (166cm) wide

$5,000-7,000   **L&T**

An early 19thC rosewood writing table, by J. Kendell & Co., of Leeds, with tooled tan leather skiver and plain frieze.

c1830   34in (86cm) wide

$10,000-12,000   **L&T**

FURNITURE

A late Regency rosewood library table, with gilt tooled red leather writing surface, two frieze drawers and two false drawers, on turned and gadrooned ball supports.

29.5in (75cm) high

$5,000-7,000   **L&T**

An early 19thC mahogany library table, inset with gilt tooled leather skiver, three frieze drawers and opposing dummies, raised on reeded and turned tapering legs.

60in (150cm) wide

$7,000-10,000   **L&T**

An early 19thC Scottish mahogany lady's writing table, with cupboard enclosing birds eye maple drawers, cupboards enclosing pigeonholes and similar drawers, and foldover top enclosing a gilt tooled skiver, bears the label of "Cunningham & McWilliam, Cabinet Makers, Kilmarnock".

This table conforms closely to the specification of a Lady's Writing Table in the Edinburgh Cabinet and Chair Makers Books of Prices published in 1805 and 1811. It is however finished to an extremely high quality and is of particular note for the label applied to the underside by Cunningham and McWilliam Cabinet Makers.

46in (117cm) high

$10,000-15,000   **L&T**

A Regency mahogany drum library table, inlaid with ebony stringing, the later tooled leather-inset top above alternate real and dummy drawers.

30in (76cm) high

$12,000-18,000   **L&T**

An early 19thC mahogany pedestal reading and writing table, the top on adjustable rack, with frieze with drawer, on baluster column and terminating in three downswept legs.

31in (79cm) high

$3,000-4,000   **L&T**

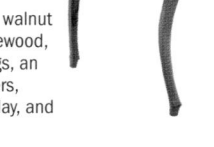

An early 19thC French walnut desk, veneered on pinewood, with four cambered legs, an apron with three drawers, green gilded leather inlay, and bronze decoration.

55.5in (139cm) wide

$2,000-3,000   **KAU**

A 19thC Victorian amboyna writing table, with green leather writing surface, on molded square tapering legs terminating with porcelain casters, and a wavy X-form stretcher.

32in (80cm) wide

$700-1,000   **FRE**

An early 20thC mahogany writing table, with triple inset leather top and carved edge, and three drawers, raised on fluted square tapering legs.

48in (122cm) wide

$1,000-1,500   **L&T**

A mahogany library writing table in the George III style, by Waring & Gillow, with an inset leather top and three drawers, on square tapering legs.

c1920

60.75in (152cm) wide

$1,500-2,000   **SWO**

An early 19thC mahogany writing table, with inset writing surface above fluted edge and three opposed panel drawers with bead and reel moldings, raised on ring-turned baluster legs, brass caps and casters.

50in (127cm) wide

$5,000-7,000 **L&T**

An early Victorian rosewood writing table, with a tooled leather top, inset within a stiff leaf carved edge, over two frieze drawers, stamped "Edwards & Roberts", on carved turned supports, united with a shaped undertier.

53.5in (136cm) wide

$4,000-6,000 **SWO**

A Victorian pitch pine writing table, by Howard & Sons, with a tooled leather top, pair of drawers, on four bamboo effect legs, stamped on both drawers and with the remains of a paper trade label.

41.75in (106cm) wide

$1,500-2,000 **SWO**

A Victorian mahogany library table, with two short drawers, on pierced vase shaped trestle end supports, on rectangular bases with scrolled feet fitted with casters.

55in (140cm) wide

$2,000-3,000 **L&T**

A Victorian mahogany partners writing table, with a tooled leather writing surface and three drawers either side, on turned legs.

60.75in (152cm) wide

$1,500-2,000 **SWO**

A mahogany library table, with gilt tooled leather skiver, above paneled frieze with four drawers, on square section tapering molded legs and block feet with brass caps and casters.

60in (152cm) wide

$3,000-4,000 **L&T**

An early 20thC Louis XV-style kingwood and gilt metal mounted bureau plat, with inset leather writing surface, over one frieze drawer, cabriole legs surmounted by female terms, ending in sabots.

56in (140cm) wide

$3,000-4,000 **FRE**

A 19thC French walnut bureau plat, with gilt brass mounts, inset leather writing surface, single drawer opposing a dummy, cabriole legs with cast mounts to the knees, on cast sabots.

50.75in (129cm) wide

$2,000-3,000 **L&T**

A George I walnut lowboy, the featherbanded and crossbanded molded rectangular top above four similarly banded drawers, molded arch, on cabriole legs with pad feet.

31.5in (80cm) wide

$4,000-6,000   **L&T**

An 18thC Queen Anne New England cherry wood dressing table, with three lip molded drawers, on cabriole legs and pad feet, restorations, replacements.

34.5in (87.5cm) wide

$2,000-3,000   **FRE**

A mid-18thC Delaware Valley Queen Anne walnut dressing table, with five drawers and older etched batwing brasses, and a carved apron with a center pierced 'heart', refinished, top appears to be very close to the top wide drawer.

This dressing table shares stylistic similarities to a high chest and lowboy in the Philadelphia Museum of Art collection

36in (91.5cm) wide

$20,000-30,000   **FRE**

A mid-18thC Philadelphia Chippendale walnut dressing table, with four drawers, 'fishtail' and scalloped apron on plain cabriole legs with claw-and-ball feet.

33.25in (81.5cm) wide

$20,000-30,000   **FRE**

A mid 18thC Philadelphia Queen Anne tiger maple dressing table, possibly the cabinet shop of William Savery with four drawers above a "fish tail" apron on carved cabriole legs on trifid feet.

30in (76cm) wide

$35,000-40,000   **POOK**

A New England Queen Anne maple dressing table, with four drawers, the central fan carved, supported by cabriole legs terminating in pad feet.

c1760   *32.5in (82.5cm) wide*

$15,000-20,000   **POOK**

A Delaware Valley Queen Anne walnut dressing table, with five drawers, above an elaborately scalloped skirt, heart cutout, cabriole legs and trifid feet.

c1765   *32.5in (81cm) wide*

$10,000-15,000   **POOK**

A Georgian mahogany lowboy, with three drawers and shaped apron, on slender cabriole legs with lappet capitals terminating in pad feet.

33in (84cm) wide

$1,500-2,000   **L&T**

An 18th/19thC Chippendale walnut dressing table, enclosing four drawers, with carved central drawer, a shaped skirt, and cabriole legs with shell knees.

35in (89cm) wide

$5,000-7,000   **FRE**

A 19thC Queen Anne-style walnut dressing table, with three short drawers, the central drawer carved with a fan, and cabriole legs ending in pad feet.

32.5in (82.5cm) high

$4,000-6,000   **FRE**

A George III mahogany gentleman's' dressing table or 'Beau Brummel', with roll top and fitted interior, four drawers and three cupboard doors.

c1810   58.75in (149cm) wide

$4,500-6,500   **FRE**

A Regency mahogany campaign dressing chest, the interior fitted with compartments, strut mirror, writing slope, blue and white washing bowls and pan, fittings mostly associated, carry handles to sides.

An early 19thC mahogany kneehole dressing table, with boxwood stringing, three quarter gallery and central drawer flanked by deeper drawers.

36.75in (92cm) high

$4,500-6,500   **L&T**

32.25in (82cm) high

$7,000-10,000   **L&T**

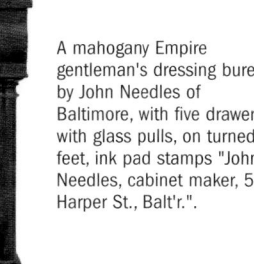

A Classical carved mahogany gentleman's dressing stand, probably Baltimore, with five drawers, twin leaf-carved round pedestals on animal legs with paw feet, old finish.

c1835   64.75in (164.5cm) high

$2,500-3,500   **FRE**

A mahogany Empire gentleman's dressing bureau, by John Needles of Baltimore, with five drawers with glass pulls, on turned feet, ink pad stamps "John Needles, cabinet maker, 54 Harper St., Balt'r.".

.A Victorian dressing chest, with cheval mirror flanked by drawers with turned ebony and ivory handles, and a burr walnut chest of drawers.

c1830   92in (233.5cm) high

$15,000-20,000   **FRE**

35in (89cm) high

$2,000-3,000   **L&T**

A Victorian painted and lacquered nest of three tables.

19.5in (49.5cm) wide

$600-900 | **SWO**

An Edwardian strung mahogany nest of Quartetto tables, the largest with satinwood crossbanding.

$1,200-1,800 | **SWO**

A 1920s quartetto of satinwood tables with moldings to the top on slender turned tapering supports.

$2,000-3,000 | **BRI**

A quartetto of walnut, mahogany and beech occasional tables, each with a figured top with crossbanded surround and molded edge, raised upon bamboo style bobbin turned legs with turned decorative stretchers.

largest 30in (75cm) high

$10,000-12,000 | **BIG**

A Georgian mahogany side table of small proportions, with a single drawer on square tapering legs.

23.25in (59cm) wide

$1,000-1,200 | **SWO**

A George III oak side table with a single frieze drawer, on tapering legs and pad feet.

32.75in (83.5cm) high

$500-700 | **SWO**

A George III mahogany silver table, the rectangular tray top with rounded angles above a single drawer with beaded moldings raised above slender cabriole legs terminating in pad feet.

31.5in (80cm) wide

$3,000-4,000 | **L&T**

A George III mahogany side table, with a single frieze drawer, on square tapering legs.

30in (76cm) high

$1,000-1,200 | **SWO**

A late George III mahogany and boxwood strung reading table, containing a single frieze drawer and fitted with a candle slide to either side, on turned legs.

24in (61cm) wide

$2,000-3,000 | **SWO**

A George III mahogany occasional table, the rectangular top with cock needed molding over two frieze drawers and square tapering legs.

21.5in (55cm) wide

$3,000-4,000 SWO

A 19thC burr elm side table, fitted with two dummy drawers on turned legs.

43in (109cm) high

$600-900 SWO

A late Victorian octagonal inlaid rosewood occasional table, with four turned legs, a shelf, 'X' stretcher and reeded feet.

25.5in (65cm) diam

$1,000-1,200 SWO

A George III laburnum drop flap occasional table, the diamond-shaped top above turned and blocked tapering legs terminating in pad feet.

$1,200-1,800 L&T

A mahogany square occasional table, in Gillows style, with two flaps and a drawer on reeded turned legs.

c1840 *22.5in (56cm) wide*

$1,500-2,000 SWO

A 19thC mahogany and rosewood crossbanded side table, with two frieze drawers, on square tapering legs.

30in (76cm) high

$1,000-1,200 SWO

A 19thC mahogany side table, with two drawers on standard ends joined by a pole stretcher.

42.5in (108cm) high

$1,000-1,200 SWO

A late Victorian inlaid mahogany bijouterie table, of clover leaf shape, with shaped glazed sides, supported upon slender strung legs.

29.5in (75cm) high

$3,000-4,000 SWO

An Edwardian mahogany and satinwood strung kidney shaped bijouterie table, with a hinged lid, on slightly splayed square tapered legs, united by stretchers.

24in (61cm) wide

$1,500-2,000 SWO

FURNITURE

An Edwardian inlaid rosewood drop-leaf table, with a single frieze drawer, on pad feet.

33.75in (86cm) wide

$1,200-1,800   **SWO**

An Edwardian mahogany and satinwood strung occasional table, the radially veneered shaped circular top on turned and fluted legs, united by scrolled stretchers.

29.5in (75cm) high

$1,000-1,500   **SWO**

An Edwardian inlaid satinwood urn table, with canted corners, on square tapering legs, united with a stretcher.

$700-1,000   **SWO**

An Edwardian satinwood inlaid circular occasional table, with tapering legs united by an X-stretcher.

24in (61cm) high

$400-600   **SWO**

A 19thC French transitional kingwood and marquetry gueridon, in the manner of Charles Topino, the oval marble top with a pierced brass gallery, above a frieze with a brushing slide and one drawer, the cabriole legs terminating in sabots.

29.5in (75cm) high

$1,200-1,800   **FRE**

An early 20thC Louis XVI-style onyx, gilt bronze and enamel table, the square top over an ornate enamel frieze, raised on four turned tapered legs united by an undertier and ending in toupie feet.

31in (77.5cm) high

$5,000-7,000   **FRE**

A 17thC Spanish walnut side table, the rectangular top, raised on baluster turned legs united by steel stretchers, with restorations.

41in (104cm) wide

$3,000-4,000   **FRE**

An 18thC Dutch walnut serpentine side table, with gilt metal mounts, the shaped molded top over one frieze drawer, raised on square cabriole legs, ending in sabots.

30.5in (76cm) wide

$2,000-3,000   **FRE**

A fine Regency period sofa table, attributed to Gillows, the top veneered with rosewood, the edge with boxwood inlay, above a frieze containing two real and two dummy drawers, each with original gilded lions mask handles, the 'Hockey Stick' end supports united by twin stretchers and with unusual ivory balls at the base, having superb original color and patina.

The quality of construction and the choice of timbers is indicative of the Gillows workshop of this period. Gillows estimate sketch book shows several examples of sofa tables with this combination of turnings and downswept 'Hockey Stick' legs. The use of decorative ivory balls is unusual but not unprecedented.

c1810   28.25in (72cm) high

$55,000-65,000   **RGA**

A Scottish Regency mahogany dropleaf sofa table, in the manner of William Trotter of Edinburgh, the top and two frieze drawers with quarter beaded border, on four reeded downswept legs, brass caps and casters.

29in (73cm) high

$4,000-5,000   **L&T**

A Regency mahogany sofa table, boxwood and ebony lined, with satinwood crossbanding, twin-flap top above a frieze with two drawers, on trestle, splayed saber legs with brass caps and casters.

28in (71cm) high

$5,000-6,000   **L&T**

A Regency mahogany and satinwood crossbanded sofa table, with ebony and boxwood stringing, rounded drop-flaps above two inlaid drawers opposing two dummy drawers.

27.75in (70.5cm) high

$10,000-15,000   **L&T**

A Scottish Regency mahogany sofa table, in the manner of William Trotter, Edinburgh, with bead and reel molding, opposing drawers, on four scrolling supports.

28.5in (72cm) high

$10,000-15,000   **L&T**

A Regency mahogany simulated rosewood sofa table, by Gillows of Lancaster, with reeded twin flap top, two frieze drawers and two false, and one drawer stamped "Gillows, Lancaster".

29in (73.5cm) high

$6,000-9,000   **L&T**

A Regency rosewood and kingwood banded Pembroke table, inlaid throughout with stringing, the faded top with rounded corners on unusual square tapered cabriole legs.

28.75in (73cm) high

$1,500-2,000   **L&T**

A George IV mahogany sofa table, with hinged leaves, on lappet carved hipped legs with brass caps and casters.

c1825   36in (93cm) long

$3,000-4,000   **DN**

A Victorian gonzalo alves and brass inlaid sofa table, with a rosewood and foliate brass inlaid band, with bulbous parcel gilt lobed column support.

28.75in (73cm) high

$9,000-10,000   **L&T**

A New York Hepplewhite mahogany Pembroke table, with demi-lune leaves, single drawer, paterae inlays, arrow inlaid apron and bellflower chain and banded cuffs.

c1800   31.5in (80cm) diam

$20,000-30,000   **POOK**

FURNITURE

TRIPOD TABLES

- Tripod tables, in the form illustrated here, date from as early as the 17thC and were made in a variety of sizes.
- Small, circular topped tables had been made before this to hold items such as candles and lanterns.
- Only the very smallest tops were fixed to the base. Usually the tops tilt to a vertical position so the table could be stored in the corner of the room. They are often referred to as 'snap' tables because of the sound made by the mechanism as it closed.
- Examples from the mid- to late-18thC are generally made of mahogany and with carved decoration.
- They were designed to be used as tea tables or as stands for silver tea kettles and heaters. However, they tended to be used for many more purposes than that.
- Hollowed out, or "dished", tops with decorative pie crust edges are popular with collectors. Beware plain tops which have been dished later, thinning the wood.
- The 'birdcage' fitment at the junction of the base and top allows the top to revolve as well as tip, and shows added expenditure when new, increasing desirability today.

A CLOSER LOOK AT A MANX TRIPOD TABLE

The Isle of Man is a dependency of the United Kingdom with its own parliament and laws, the Queen being Lord of Man. In the past it has been a Norwegian, and then a Scottish possession.

The color, patina and figuring are good contributing to the desirability.

The three-legged symbol of the Isle, which is 60 miles off the coast of Lancashire, is further distinguished by its motto 'Quocumque Jeceris Stabit' - whichever way you throw me I stand, which is particularly apt for this form of table.

These tables were not always made on the island. Instead, they mark its acquisition by Great Britain in 1765.

A circular mahogany George III Manx tripod table, the solid mahogany top having a good color, patina and figure echoed in the tapering gun-barrel supporting shaft on three distinctively carved legs with shod feet, all typically Manx in form and relating to other known furniture with Isle of Manx connotations.

c1770

$25,000-35,000   **PAR**

A Pennsylvania Queen Anne walnut candlestand, from Downingtown, with circular dish top, over a birdcage support, supported by three cabriole legs and pad feet.

c1760   *27in (68.5cm) high*

$8,000-10,000   **POOK**

A Philadelphia Chippendale carved mahogany tea table, with dished top, tapering support and suppressed ball, with repairs to top, old break to ball and support, and replaced cleat.

c1760   *28.5in (72.5cm) high*

$7,000-10,000   **FRE**

An early George III mahogany tripod table, with circular top and thumbnail rim raised on turned pedestal and cabriole legs.

25in (64cm) high

$3,000-4,000   **L&T**

A George III mahogany tripod table, with molded piecrust edge above the birdcage action and turned stem.

c1780   *27.75in (70.5cm) high*

$6,000-9,000   **DN**

A mid-to late 18thC Pennsylvania Chippendale walnut tea table, with circular dish molded edge and tilting top on a birdcage support, refinished.

38.25in (97cm) diam

$10,000-15,000   **FRE**

A George III mahogany occasional table, with figured plain top, candy twist baluster column raised on tripod base with talon-and-ball feet.

$1,500-2,000   **BIG**

A George III mahogany tip-top occasional table, with Chippendale pie-crust top, foliate-carved column, on tripod cabriole legs with foliate-carved knees and plain pad feet.

30.75in (78cm) diam

$700-1,000   **BIG**

A mahogany tilt top table in George III style, with canted square top and pierced gallery above a bird cage and a turned and reeded column carved with leaves.

24in (61cm) wide

$1,500-2,000   **DN**

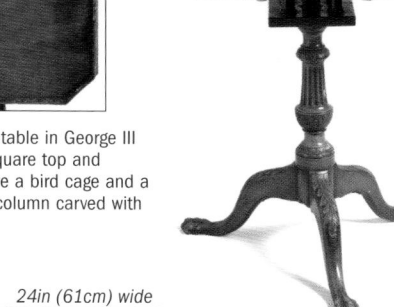

A George III circular mahogany lamp table, with a dished top, raised on a ring turned column, swept legs and ball terminals.

18in (46cm) diam

$450-650   **SWO**

A George III mahogany tripod table, with reeded edge raised on turned column and cabriole legs.

27.5in (70cm) high

$2,000-3,000   **L&T**

A George III mahogany tilt-top tripod table, with pie crust molding, fluted and stiff leaf cast baluster column, harebell carved legs with ball and claw feet.

28in (71cm) high

$4,000-6,000   **L&T**

A George III mahogany wine table, the dished circular top with molded edge, raised on turned column with tripod base of cabriole legs with pad feet.

28in (71.5cm) high

$3,000-4,000   **L&T**

A Regency mahogany tilt-top occasional table, with canted rectangular section column with gadrooned base, on concave tripod base and scrolled feet.

28in (71cm) high

$3,000-4,000   **L&T**

A 19thC carved and turned ivory and rosewood candlestand, the dished top over an elaborately turned standard on three cabriole legs with shell carved knees and animal paw feet.

27in (67.5cm) high

$7,000-10,000   **POOK**

An unusual early 19thC mahogany pedestal table, the dished top raised on plain cylindrical column, terminating in tripod legs emitting from lions masks mounts, and terminating with large claw feet.

24.5in (62cm) high

$4,500-6,500   **L&T**

A 19thC walnut tripod table, with turned baluster column, the tilt top inlaid with a chessboard.

48.5cm (19in) diam

$500-700   **MAX**

A late 19thC mahogany snap top silver table, with 18thC elements, with pierced fretwork gallery, on claw and ball feet.

31.5in (80cm) high

$4,000-6,000   **L&T**

A Chinese ebonized and shell inlaid tripod table, with tilt top inset with a bird, peonies and bamboo, on a turned base with three cabriole legs.

Provenance: Ex Sibyl Colefax and John Fowler

24in (60.5cm) wide

$700-1,000   **DN**

219

FURNITURE

A George III mahogany architect's table, in Chinese Chippendale style, with hinged height adjustable top, and pierced fret carved frieze.

From the collection of the University of Virginia Art Museum

c1770   25.25in (64cm) wide

$2,000-3,000   **FRE**

A late 18thC Louis XVI walnut tric trac table, with removable top and a later felt-lined playing surface on the reverse.

37.25in (94.5cm) wide

$2,500-3,500   **FRE**

An early 19thC mahogany cased Bagatelle table, with a baize lined interior fitted with inset interior holes, numbered cups for balls, and a movable target, stamped "Thurston, 14 Catherine St, London", includes cue, balls, markers, etc.

48.75in (122cm) long

$4,000-6,000   **L&T**

A Victorian mahogany bed table, with twin lift-up sections each with racked supports, mounted on a shaped base with four bun feet.

$500-700   **BIG**

An early 20thC mahogany snooker/dining table, with four leaves over an adjustable slat bed and square tapering fluted legs, stamped "1353" and "2264212".

92.5in (231cm) long

$1,200-1,800   **SWO**

A Victorian maple table, with a burr yew oval within a rosewood marquetry panel, birds eye maple border on pierced lyre shaped supports with splayed feet.

22.5in (57cm) wide

$2,000-3,000   **DN**

A gilt brass gueridon, with inset top above a smaller undershelf with three scrolling supports, with paw feet joined by a further stretcher with cast finial.

29.25in (73cm) high

$6,000-9,000   **L&T**

A pair of Regency period rosewood Canterburies, with five slatted dividers and carrying handle above a single drawer raised on turned legs.

c1810   *24.5in (62cm) wide*

$7,000-10,000   **L&T**

A Regency mahogany Canterbury, the three open X-framed compartments with laurel wreath facings, raised on rectangular base with drawer, turned feet and ball finials.

20in (51cm) wide

$3,000-4,000   **L&T**

A Regency rosewood Canterbury, with three open X-framed compartments, laurel wreath facings, on rectangular base with drawer, and turned feet with brass caps and casters.

20in (51cm) high

$3,000-4,000   **L&T**

A Regency period mahogany canterbury, with four slat-filled dividers, concave top rails, and a single drawer on ring turned legs, with brass caps and casters.

18in (45.5cm) wide

$600-800   **L&T**

A mid-Victorian rosewood etagere/Canterbury, with scroll carved gallery, further tier with scroll supports and base with four pierced dividers over a base drawer.

26.5in (67cm) wide

$1,500-2,000   **L&T**

WHATNOTS

A Scottish early Victorian oak five tier whatnot, the columns with bold vase finials, the tiers with serpentine sides, with drawer to lowest section, on bold lotus clasped scroll feet.

69.5in (176cm) high

$6,000-9,000   **L&T**

A Regency mahogany four-tier whatnot, with four galleried tiers supported by ring turned and block uprights, surmounted by turned finials, above a single drawer.

55in (140cm) high

$4,000-6,000   **L&T**

A George IV mahogany whatnot, with a removable book rest, fitted replaced brass clips, and a frieze drawer fitted with wood handles.

20in (51cm) wide

$1,500-2,000   **WW**

A George IV mahogany four tier whatnot, with rope twist and collar turned columns, four shelves, and baluster turned legs with brass caps and casters.

c1825   *60in (153cm) high*

$2,000-3,000   **DN**

A Victorian mahogany whatnot, with turned finials and barley twist uprights, raised on turned bulb legs with casters.

39.25in (100cm) high

$600-900   **BIG**

A pair of early 20thC mahogany and giltmetal mounted etageres, with cast faux bamboo moldings and uprights, terminating in outswept feet.

38in (95cm) high

$1,500-2,000   **L&T**

A George III mahogany dumb waiter, with three graduated tiers on reeded baluster column, cabriole tripod base, and pad feet.

41in (103cm) high

$1,200-1,800   **L&T**

A CLOSER LOOK AT A PAIR OF GEORGE III PEDESTALS AND VASES

The shapes of the urns and motifs such as festoons and Classical figures of Peace and Plenty are typical of the Neoclassical style which grew in popularity from the mid to late 18thC and was inspired by ancient Greece and Rome and the excavations at Pompeii and Herculaneum.

The vases were made by the renowned manufacturers Matthew Boulton and John Fothergill, adding to their desirability. Boulton was notable for the high quality of the silver and Sheffield plate produced at his Birmingham factory, which he ran with John Fothergill from 1762.

Painted satinwood furniture had become extremely fashionable by the mid 1770s.

Pedestals and vases of this type were frequently found in the grandest dining rooms of the period. One pedestal often served as a plate warmer and might be fitted with racks and a stand for a heater; the other used as a pot cupboard. The vases were often used to hold water for the butler to use, or iced water for drinking.

A magnificent pair of George III pedestals and vases, with satinwood crossbanded in kingwood and ebony on a square plinth of mahogany, the doors painted with an oval reserve hung from ribbons and draped husk festoons, both in the manner of Swiss Neoclassical painter Angelica Kauffmann (1741-1807), with Old Sheffield Plate vases engraved with a coat of arms, crest and motto, with mahogany lined interior, deep lead lined drawer with silvered swag handle, and one having a rack for plates above an iron grid with the interior lined with tin.

c1780

$500,000-600,000   **PAR**

A late Regency mahogany dumb waiter, with two molded tiers between turned brass columns, on baluster turned column and three hipped sabre legs.

41.75in (106cm) high

$3,000-4,000   **L&T**

A Regency mahogany teapoy, with a gadrooned molded top, fitted interior comprising two tea-caddies, on a beaded and leaf carved pedestal.

30in (77cm) high

$2,000-4,000   **SHA**

A Regency period rosewood teapoy, with cavetto molded lid enclosing a fitted interior of removable tea caddies and glass mixing bowls, on concave quadruped base.

18in (46cm) wide

$1,000-1,500   **L&T**

A Regency mahogany reading stand, with ebony strung adjustable slope and protruding book rest, frieze drawer and swivelling circular candle stand.

32.5in (83cm) high

$6,000-9,000   **L&T**

An early 19thC Federal figured maple corner washstand, with bowed front, shaped splash board, medial shelf and shaped stretchers.

37in (94cm) high

$1,400-1,800   **FRE**

A George IV mahogany adjustable folio stand, with slatted sides with turned stretchers and tapering end supports, the platform base with brass terminals and casters.

30.75in (78cm) wide

$3,000-4,000   **DN**

A mid-19thC stained beech hall stand, with latticed back, turned bosses and applied gilt brass coat hooks, above a fluted support for sticks.

50.5in (128cm) wide

$2,000-3,000   **L&T**

A mid-18thC style mahogany plant stand, with round boxwood strung top on turned column and tripod base, lacking flower inlay to top.

37in (94cm) high

$500-700   **DN**

A mahogany polescreen in early 19thC style, the oval banner with a silk embroidered panel of flowers, on a turned and tapering reeded column.

Provenance: Estate of the late The Lady Adam Gordon

17.25in (44cm) wide

$300-400 — **DN**

An early Victorian and later mahogany firescreen, with period needlework panel, rod column raised on a triform base with herringbone inlay on turned feet.

52in (130cm) high

$400-600 — **BIG**

A Victorian cased firescreen, with faux bamboo frame, later gilt painted and enclosing a glazed case filled with exotic birds including humming birds.

$1,200-1,800 — **L&T**

A Victorian walnut firescreen with carved surmount, above a needlework map of England and Wales, on shaped supports and casters.

$700-1,000 — **BRI**

A Victorian rosewood firescreen, the screen with a watercolor still life of a basket of flowers.

$700-1,000 — **SWO**

MINIATURE FURNITURE

MINIATURE FURNITURE

- Miniature furniture has always had great appeal amongst collectors. It has been produced in one form or another since toys were first made, although examples dating before the 17th century are extremely rare.
- The range of quality is wide indeed, from the naive piece made by a loving parent or fiancé to the sophisticated version made to the standard of a working scale model for an interior designer.
- While doll's house furniture, usually made on a scale of 1/12th, and furniture such as chairs designed for children on one half scale, have obvious purposes, the reason for the production of 1/8th scale furniture is still unclear and widely debated.
- Many believe that apprentices made miniature furniture as 'exam' pieces to prove their skill to their employers. Others argue that it was produced as samples for travelling salesmen. Alternatively, there is a popular belief that it was made as window-display pieces by cabinetmakers.
- A large number of small chests of drawers were made, which could hold gloves or trinkets, and so are easy to come by. However, chairs, cupboards and bookcases are rarer.
- Up until around 1840, toy-makers and cabinetmakers were the main producers. From then on miniature furniture was a more commercialized business, particularly in Germany, where the majority of pieces were mass-produced.

A rare 18thC miniature four-slat ladderback armchair, from Pennsylvania, retaining an old green surface.

11in (28cm) high

$10,000-12,000 — **POOK**

A mid-19thC Pennsylvania painted doll's Windsor side chair, with floral decoration on a mustard ground with green pinstriping.

16in (40.5cm) high

$3,000-4,000 — **POOK**

A French Louis XVI miniature walnut commode, on four bracket feet, with four drawers, flanked by half columns.

c1790 *13.25in (33cm) wide*

$700-1,000 — **KAU**

A miniature George III mahogany and ash chest of drawers, of serpentine form, inlaid with stringing and chequer banding.

20in (51cm) wide

$7,000-10,000 — **L&T**

A Victorian mahogany miniature chest, with two short and three long graduated drawers with ebonized knob handles, on a plinth base.

10.75in (27cm) wide

$500-700 — **DN**

An early 19thC mahogany, boxwood and ebony strung miniature bowfront chest, with five short and two long drawers, a carved apron and bracket feet.

11.75in (30cm) wide

$1,000-1,500 — **DN**

An 18thC miniature feather-banded walnut bureau, the hinged top opening to reveal a pigeon holed interior.

15.5in (39.5cm) high

$1,000-1,500   **SWO**

An early Victorian mahogany miniature pedestal sideboard, each pedestal enclosing five internal drawers.

27in (69cm) wide

$3,000-4,000   **SWO**

A late Victorian miniature mahogany chest of drawers, the two short and three long drawers with walnut fronts.

15in (38cm) high

$500-600   **SWO**

A 19thC walnut veneered bachelor's chest, with hinged top enclosing baize lined interior, above four long graduated drawers, on bracket feet.

$4,000-6,000   **L&T**

A miniature oyster veneered walnut chest of drawers, the boxwood strung top with crossbanded edge above three long drawers on bun feet.

12.75in (32cm) wide

$700-1,000   **L&T**

A Victorian mahogany miniature tilt top table, inlaid with a parquetry top and base.

10in (25cm) diam

$400-600   **SWO**

A Victorian mahogany miniature tilt top circular table, with an inlaid chequer board parquetry top.

10.5in (26cm) diam

$300-400   **SWO**

A Victorian mahogany miniature tripod table, the tilt top with a parquetry star motif inlay.

6.75in (17cm) diam

$500-600   **SWO**

A late 19th to early 20thC miniature Anglo-Indian parquetry, ivory and horn games table, complete with a boxed miniature stained and natural ivory chess set.

10.25in (25.5cm) wide

$500-700   **FRE**

A George III mahogany ovoid tray, with a pie crust border.

22in (56cm) wide

$500-700   **DN**

An early Victorian green and gilt japanned papier mâché tray-on-stand, decorated with an urn, with everted lip, the underside stamped "Jennens & Bettridge's / London", on a conforming later stand.

1850   31in (78.5cm) wide

$60,000-70,000   **PAR**

A Victorian papier mâché and mother of pearl inlaid oval tray, by Jennens and Bettridge, with a molded border painted with a central flower spray, stamped to rear, possibly later painted.

31in (79cm) wide

$400-600   **DN**

A 19th to 20thC painted papier-mâché tray, with a scene of an Afro-American banjo player and boy by a fireplace, small chip.

15.25in (38.5cm) wide

$600-900   **FRE**

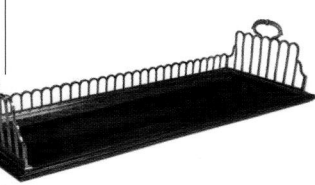

A Regency rosewood and brass book tray, with molded edge, pierced and arcaded gallery and leaf-cast carrying handle.

24in (61cm) wide

$1,200-1,800   **L&T**

An early Victorian rosewood book tray, with baluster turned galleries on S-scroll end supports, and an ogee molded plinth base, one handle later.

17.25in (44cm) wide

$3,000-4,000   **L&T**

A 19thC painted bentwood and wire bird cage, with a turned finial to a waisted frame, with sprung doors.

35in (89cm) high

$600-900   **WW**

A 19thC Dutch bucket, with colored and ebonized wood and a brass liner and handle.

$700-1,000   **SWO**

A Victorian gilt brass hall stand, with three turned uprights with guilloche cast decoration, supporting three adjustable hoops with scrolling bracket supports.

43.25in (110cm) wide

$5,000-7,000   **L&T**

A mahogany step commode, now with leather inset steps and turned feet.

$1,500-2,000   **SWO**

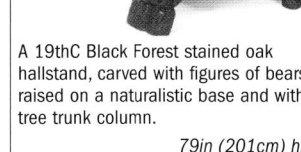

A 19thC Black Forest stained oak hallstand, carved with figures of bears, raised on a naturalistic base and with tree trunk column.

79in (201cm) high

$10,000-15,000   **L&T**

TEA CADDIES

- Tea was extremely expensive in the 18thC and was kept in locked boxes or caddies. The high cost meant that objects connected to tea tended to be well-made.
- The term caddy comes from the Malaysian word Kati, which was used in China as a measure of weight.
- 18thC caddies usually had two compartments, to hold two types of tea, often flanking a mixing or sugar bowl. Typically made from mahogany, chinoiserie, walnut and tortoiseshell versions are fairly rare.
- From the mid 18thC a variety of new shapes and designs were introduced. These were often decorated with wood veneers and marquetry. Fruit-shaped caddies, which were carved from fruitwoods, are particularly popular with collectors.
- Paper was also used in the decoration of tea caddies but fewer examples have survived in good condition. One favorite method involved gluing strips of rolled paper to the surface of the caddy. Papier mâché caddies from the period are also rare.
- 19thC caddies were made of exotic hardwoods, mahogany or walnut. The sarcophagus shape became popular at this time, as did decorative techniques such as penwork.

A George III mahogany and rosewood tea chest, with checkered parquetry top and brass swing handle, enclosing three caddies, on ogee bracket feet.

$400-600   **DN**

A George III mahogany, rosewood banded and inlaid tea chest, with a gilt metal swing handle, enclosing three caddies.

9.75in (25cm) wide

$400-600   **DN**

A George III satinwood, rosewood, ebony and boxwood strung tea chest, with a copper ring handle, enclosing two caddies and an associated cut glass bowl.

12in (30.5cm) wide

$700-1,000   **DN**

A George III mahogany rectangular tea chest, with a brass handle, the base with a shaped escutcheon enclosing three caddies, on ball feet.

$400-600   **DN**

A George III satinwood, tulipwood, ebony and boxwood strung tea caddy, with a central marquetry fan, lacking interior fittings.

7.5in (19cm) wide

$600-700   **DN**

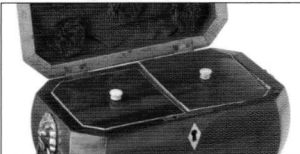

A George III rosewood and boxwood strung bombé shaped tea chest, with turned ivory knops, flanked by brass lion mask ring handles, on stiff leaf capped lion paw feet.

9in (23cm) wide

$600-900   **DN**

A George III partridge wood and parquetry tea caddy, the hinged lid with perspective cube specimen timbers and a herringbone border, ebonized turned knob handle.

4.5in (11.5cm) wide

$300-500   **DN**

A late George III satinwood tea caddy, of plain rectangular shape, fitted with twin canisters and a cut glass mixing bowl, on bun feet.

12in (30.5cm) wide

$3,000-4,000   **SWO**

A Regency rosewood sarcophagus-shaped tea chest, inlaid with mother-of-pearl, enclosing two caddies, the base with a gadrooned border, on bun feet.

9.25in (23.5cm) wide

$300-500   **DN**

(left) A Regency rosewood sarcophagus caddy, with boxwood stringing and fitted interior, embossed brass ring handles and paw bracket feet.

12in (30cm) wide

$200-300   **L&T**

A George III fruitwood tea caddy, in the form of an apple with a scalloped steel escutcheon and hinged lid.

(Right) An early 19thC Vizagapatam sarcophagus work box, inlaid with panels of porcupine quills within bone borders decorated with penwork, interior fitted with compartments.

5in (13cm) high

12.25in (31cm) wide

$2,000-3,000   **SWO**

$3,000-4,000   **L&T**

A George IV octagonal mahogany and boxwood strung tea caddy, inset with a beadwork panel, the base with a foil lining and gilt brass side handles on bun feet.

A William IV mahogany sarcophagus-shaped tea chest, enclosing two caddies with hinged lids, flanked by brass shell ring handles.

12.5in (32cm) wide

$400-600   **DN**

$400-600   **DN**

A George III tortoiseshell tea caddy, inlaid with flowers in mother of pearl, twin-covered canisters enclosed, on ball feet.

7.5in (19cm) wide

$2,000-3,000 **GORL**

An early 19thC tortoiseshell and ivory tea caddy, with pewter stringing enclosing two lidded compartments, the base with a molded border.

7in (18cm) wide

$1,000-1,500 **DN**

A Regency tortoiseshell and ivory strung tea caddy, with silver plate leaf cast ring handles, pewter stringing and bun feet, with pair of associated Sheffield plate lidded caddies and brass spoons bearing initials "JB".

7.25in (18cm) wide

$5,000-6,000 **L&T**

A Regency blonde tortoiseshell and ivory tea caddy, with ogee molded hinged lid and lidded lined interior.

4.75in (25cm) high

$5,000-6,000 **FRE**

A Regency tortoiseshell and ivory tea caddy, with ball finial and lidded lined interior.

5in (12.5cm) high

$5,000-6,000 **FRE**

LEFT: A Regency tortoiseshell tea caddy, with silvered blank plaque, enclosing two lidded compartments for tea, on flattened brass feet.

8.25in (21cm) wide

$2,000-3,000 **L&T**

RIGHT: A Regency tortoiseshell tea caddy, with interior fitted with two lidded compartments for tea, on turned ivory feet.

5.75in (14.5cm) wide

$1,500-2,000 **L&T**

An octagonal pressed tortoiseshell tea caddy, with embossed Gothic panels.

c1820 · *7in (18cm) high*

$30,000-35,000 **RGA**

An early Victorian tortoiseshell tea caddy, the top with silver tableau and interior with ivory knopped finials, profusely decorated with mother of pearl floral inlay, raised on later brass feet.

7.25in (18cm) wide

$2,000-3,000 **BIG**

An early Victorian tortoiseshell tea caddy, of bombé form, with mother-of-pearl floral inlay, two lidded compartments, raised on carved ivory, part lobed ball feet.

c1840 · *14in (35.5cm) wide*

$6,000-7,000 **FRE**

An early 19thC Dutch mahogany decanter box, modeled as a bureau, with six fitted decanters and stoppers.

11in (28cm) wide

$300-400   **GOR**

A CLOSER LOOK AT A DECANTER BOX

The extensive selection of glass elements, comprising 16 stemmed glasses and four decanters, contributes to the value.

The fine stems of the glasses have remained intact and the stoppers on the decanters are present.

A 19thC boulle and gilt metal mounted liqueur set, with tortoiseshell veneer and elaborately inlaid with engraved brass, fitted with 16 stemmed glasses and four decanters and stoppers, each with all-over gilded decoration.

11in (27.5cm) high

The box has a locking mechanism designed to keep servants away from the alcohol stored within.

The set is decorated to a high standard with gilding and boullework, a type of marquetry involving tortoiseshell and brass developed by Andre Charles Boulle in 18th century France. The box would have been on display and used for entertaining visitors at home.

$3,000-4,000   **L&T**

A Regency mahogany tantalus, with marquetry inlaid decoration, the hinged opening revealing a period four bottle lined interior.

$400-600   **BIG**

A burr walnut decanter traveling box, with brass recessed handles, engraved plaque "Be Merry & Wise", fitted with four cut glass decanters and stoppers.

c1850   *10.75in (27cm) high*

$600-900   **ROS**

A Victorian burr oak decanter box with gothic brass mounts and lock.

8.5in (21.5cm) wide

$120-180   **BRI**

A Victorian ebonized liqueur box, with brass and mother of pearl inlay within brass strung and crossbanded borders, the interior with four etched decanters and stoppers and twelve glasses.

12.5in (32cm) wide

$1,200-1,500   **SWO**

An Edwardian electroplate-mounted oak tantalus and games box, with three square cut glass decanters and stoppers, four glasses and cribbage board.

$600-700   **BRI**

A mid-19thC tortoiseshell, mother-of-pearl and ivory inlaid inkstand, with a gilt metal handle cast with cornucopia and flowers, later cut glass inkwells and later ebonized feet.

11in (28cm) wide

$1,000-1,500 DN

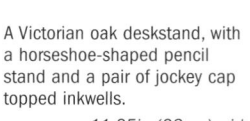

An early 19thC George III mahogany portable inkstand, with three associated glass inkwells.

15in (37.5cm) wide

$200-300 FRE

A Victorian oak deskstand, with a horseshoe-shaped pencil stand and a pair of jockey cap topped inkwells.

11.25in (28cm) wide

$400-500 SWO

A papier-mâché and mother-of-pearl inkstand, by Jennens & Bettridge, with two cut glass inkwells and stamp box, on squat bun feet.

c1860 *16in (40cm) wide*

$300-400 FRE

A late 19thC French rouge marble and gilt-bronze inkstand, with figure of Shakespeare, on toupie feet.

14in (35cm) wide

$300-400 FRE

A late 19thC French Neoclassical-style bronze and rouge marble inkwell and blotter, signed "Burgstaller".

12in (30cm) wide

$800-1,200 FRE

A Victorian tortoiseshell and silver-mounted three piece desk set, by William Comyns, London, comprising an inkstand, stationery casket and a rectangular blotter.

1892

$2,000-3,000 DNT

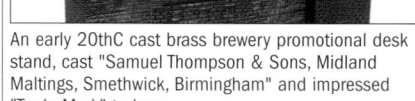

An early 20thC cast brass brewery promotional desk stand, cast "Samuel Thompson & Sons, Midland Maltings, Smethwick, Birmingham" and impressed "Trade Mark" to base.

11.25in (28cm) wide

$300-400 BIG

A Continental walnut deskstand, possibly German, in the form of a dog's kennel, with a slide and pen stand, the dog's head opening to an inkwell.

$1,000-1,500 SWO

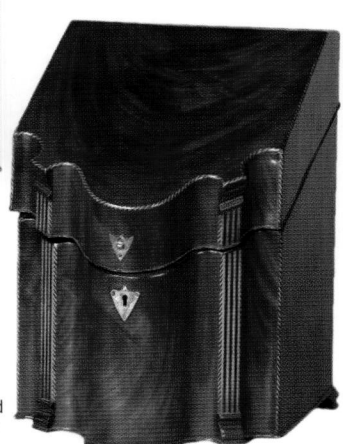

A George III mahogany, rosewood, ebony and box lined inlaid serpentine shaped knife box, later fitted interior.

15in (38cm) high

$1,000-1,500   **DN**

A George III figured mahogany and box lined inlaid knife box of serpentine form, the hinged top with a shaped brass ring handle.

7.5in (19cm) high

$700-1,000   **DN**

A pair of George III mahogany knife boxes, with boxwood stringing, inlaid in boxwood with urns, fitted interior, front with silvered escutcheon, on later feet.

13.5in (34cm) high

$4,000-6,000   **L&T**

A pair of English mahogany knife boxes, of serpentine form, in light and dark wood with bookend inlays, silver mounts, and fitted interior.

c1790

14.25in (35.5cm) high

$6,000-9,000   **POOK**

WORK BOXES

An early 19thC East Indian hardwood, ivory and bone inlaid dressing box, fitted with a central beveled mirror, compartments, and lined tray revealing two small drawers, with key.

18in (46cm) wide

$4,000-6,000   **L&T**

A George IV rosewood and ivory sarcophagus-shaped work box, inlaid with flowers within a beaded border, flanked by patera, on later brass feet.

11.75in (30cm) wide

$300-400   **DN**

A Vizagapatam ivory, horn, pen work and sandalwood sewing box, with lidded lift-out tray, on ivory bun feet.

8in (20cm) wide

$700-1,000   **SWO**

A 19thC Anglo Indian coromandel work box, with lift out tray with nine inlaid lidded compartments.

16.25in (41cm) high

$600-900   **SWO**

A Victorian rosewood workbox, of sarcophagus shape with the mother of pearl inlay to the top and front.

30cm (11.75in) wide

$200-300   **SWO**

A George III satinwood, harewood and boxwood strung writing box, with stationer's label, tooled green leather writing surface, compartments and an inkwell with plated cover.

12.25in (31cm) wide

$600-900   **DN**

A 19thC kingwood and brass bound table top writing desk, with fitted compartment with two glass inkwells with gilt-metal lids.

12.75in (32cm) wide

$600-900   **DN**

A Victorian burr walnut and rosewood writing box, with silvered scrolling panels and engraved initials, fitted compartments, two clear glass inkwells and a tooled leather writing slope.

15.75in (40cm) wide

$500-600   **DN**

A lady's Victorian rosewood, brass-bound and mother-of-pearl inlaid table top writing desk, with compartments, two clear glass inkwells with brass lids and tooled leather writing surface.

15.75in (40cm) wide

$700-1,000   **DN**

A lady's Victorian rosewood and mother-of-pearl table top writing desk, inlaid with shell scrolls and inscribed "Gertrude", fitted compartment with glass inkwell and a tooled leather writing slope.

10.5in (26.5cm) wide

$400-600   **DN**

A Victorian burr walnut and rosewood writing box, with silvered scrolling panels and engraved initials, fitted compartments, two clear glass inkwells and a tooled leather writing slope.

15.75in (40cm) wide

$500-600   **DN**

A mahogany table top letter box, with brass letter slot and glazed post times aperture, above glazed front on molded base.

14.5in (37cm) wide

$2,000-3,000   **L&T**

A Victorian coromandel Gothic brass bound letter box, inset with a jasperware medallion, opening to reveal a compartmented interior.

c1880   *9.25in (24cm) wide*

$300-400   **FRE**

A late 18thC painted candle box, with carved fans painted olive green on cream ground with salmon-painted scrollwork.

16in (41cm) high

$4,000-5,000   **SK**

A mid-19thC Pennsylvania painted poplar slide lid candlebox, with chamfered lid and dovetailed construction, with original decoration.

17.5in (44cm) wide

$5,000-6,000   **POOK**

A Pennsylvania painted poplar candlebox, dated "1854" and initialed "E + RW" painted red with black stylized tulips and birds.

9in (23cm) long

$4,000-6,000   **POOK**

A 19thC rosewood and mother-of-pearl rectangular box, the hinged lid inlaid with playing cards and floral sprays.

9.5in (24cm) wide

$200-300   **DN**

A 19thC Paris games box, by Tahan, with removable compartments and over 100 mother-of-pearl counters, signed, missing key.

13.25in (33cm) wide

$600-700   **KAU**

A walnut and bandwork cribbage box, inlaid with marquetry, enclosing a purple velvet-lined interior.

11.75in (30cm) wide

$200-300   **DNT**

A Victorian oak and brass bound tobacco chest, with brass shield shaped plaque engraved "C. H. Saunders, 9th September 1885", lead lined lid interior.

6.25in (16cm) wide

$300-400   **DN**

A Victorian silver mounted oak cigarette box "Made from wood of Nelson's 'Victory'".

7.5in (19cm) wide

$300-400   **BRI**

A mahogany cigar vending machine, by John Miller Jacobs, Norristown, Pennsylvania, with glass enclosed top, coin slot and crank.

c1903   *18.5in (47cm) high*

$10,000-15,000   **FRE**

A Victorian burr walnut and brass bound watch stand, of casket form, the domed hinged cover enclosing a folding watch stand.

4.5in (11.5cm) wide

$120-180   **DNT**

A Victorian carved mahogany watch stand.

9.5in (23.5cm) high

$300-400   **SWO**

BOXES

BOXES & TREEN

 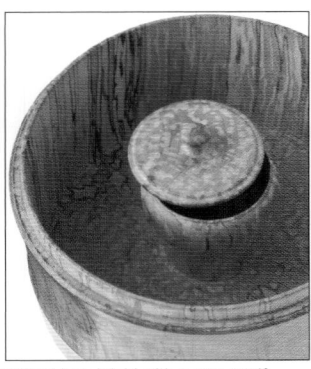

An early 19thC lignum stud and collar cylindrical box, inlaid with a star motif, enclosing a turned lidded urn.

6.25in (16cm) wide

$400-600   **DN**

A late 19thC Killarney marquetry inlaid jewelry box, inlaid with a view of 'Muckross Abbey' above a clasp compartment, four hinged trays and a base compartment, the back inlaid with a stag.

11in (28cm) wide

$1,200-1,800   **DNT**

A Victorian crossbanded figured walnut rectangular box, with brass plaque engraved "Gloves and Handkerchiefs".

10.25in (26cm) wide

$300-400   **CLV**

A CLOSER LOOK AT SHAKER BOXES

The Shakers were a religious group who emigrated to America from England in 1774. Within 50 years there were 19 communities made up of over 5,000 men and women. They were celibate, relying on adoption and conversion to expand.

The Shakers took the simple forms of the 18th century design – the gambrel roofed building, the ladderback chair, the trestle table, the cupboard, and the chest of drawers – and created pieces that facilitated their own mode of living in the 19th century.

They were self sufficient and so all their furnishings were made from woods such as pine, maple, cherry, walnut, butternut, poplar and birch which they found on their own property.

The Shakers produced oval boxes with uniformly slender sides, symmetrical joints, and neat, tight-fitting lids. They were made in eleven sizes and categorized using a numbering system (number 11 is the smallest and number one the biggest).

The Shakers used oval boxes for sewing and quilting items and kitchen storage.

A set of late 19thC Shaker boxes, probably from New England, with pine top and bottom and maple sides secured with copper tacks, stained.

3.75in (9.5cm) diam

$20,000-25,000   **SK**

A mid-19thC painted pine apothecary cabinet, from New Hampshire, with 11 drawers supported by straight bracket feet, old brown-red surface.

24.5in (62cm) wide

$6,000-9,000   **POOK**

An early 19thC rosewood paint box, the hinged lid with a manufacturer's label for "G. Blackman, London", enclosing lift-out paint trays.

$300-400   **DN**

A 19thC marquetry money box in the form of a house, with a sliding cover and back, on a plinth base, damage.

4.75in (12cm) wide

$120-180   **SWO**

A Regency brass inlaid rosewood bonbon box, of gondola form, with twin tambour doors opening to reveal a satinwood interior.

c1820   *11in (30cm) wide*

$2,000-3,000   **FRE**

A George III satinwood, rosewood, fruitwood, harewood, and tulipwood featherbanded box, with shell, flowerheads and oval panels, flanked by side handles.

$700-1,000   **DN**

A Kashmiri lacquer and ivory box, finely incised with feathery scrolls through black and red lacquer and set with pierced ivory discs and finials, some losses.

A large 16thC South German iron-bound casket, with wrought iron side carrying handles and faint later overpainted decoration, the central lock with eagle escutcheon, keys and padlocks.

37.75in (96cm) wide

$6,000-9,000   **L&T**

c1840   *10in (25.5cm) wide*

$400-500   **SWO**

A 19thC German walnut steel mounted box.

28cm (11in) wide

$600-900   **SWO**

A 19thC painted and decorated box, with sliding cover, painted yellow and decorated with buildings and trees in green, pumpkin and cream.

3in (7.5cm) high

$3,000-4,000   **FRE**

A Victorian walnut box in Gothic style, with applied brass strapwork mounts and escutcheon, with a swing handle.

8.25in (21cm) wide

$400-600   **DN**

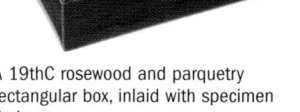

A 19thC rosewood and parquetry rectangular box, inlaid with specimen timbers.

11in (28cm) wide

$400-600   **DN**

A Victorian walnut and brass-mounted rectangular box in Gothic style, with foliate engraved brass mounts.

10.5in (26.5cm) wide

$200-300   **DN**

A Victorian walnut chest, with shaped brass and silvered panels, above a small slide and two drawers with brass handles.

6.75in (17cm) wide

$400-600   **DN**

A Victorian Gothic novelty table cabinet, the white wood ground with ebony mounts modeled as a medieval doorway and medieval knights, some losses.

15.75in (40cm) high

$800-1,200   **DNT**

A carved walnut rectangular box, the lid mounted with a base metal model of a recumbent German Shepherd pup, within an egg and dart border.

8in (20.5cm) wide

$60-90   **GORL**

TUNBRIDGEWARE

- Craftsmen from the spa town Tunbridge Wells began producing a vast array of decorative wooden objects to sell to the growing number of 19th century visitors.
- Early items were initially painted, printed or decorated with parquetry. Designs became increasingly complicated and, in the early 1830s, James Burrows invented the famous tessellated mosaic technique now associated with Tunbridgeware.
- Sticks of wood called tesserae were glued together to create detailed representations of flowers, animals and landscapes as well as abstract designs. The assembled tesserae were cut into thin slices which were applied to boxes and other items. These souvenirs appealed to 19thC tastes and the industry became highly profitable.
- Princess Victoria was so fond of Tunbridgeware that in 1826 the town presented her with a specially made worktable worth twenty-five guineas.
- Thomas Barton (1819-1903) is one of the best-known manufacturers of Tunbridgeware. He started his career working for another well-known manufacturer, the Nye family. Other makers to look out for are Hollamby, Fenner and Wise.
- When buying Tunbridgeware, it is important to check for damage, as warping, discoloration and losses greatly decrease value.
- Pieces with intricate decoration in bold colors, which can be attributed to a known maker, command a premium.

A Tunbridgeware marquetry and parquetry desk stand, by T. Barton, with two lift-up inlaid square panels and a lift-up parquetry panel, supported on bun feet.

10.5in (27cm) wide

$1,000-1,500   JN

A Tunbridgeware games box, with fitted interior, the lid inlaid with a border of flowers and a ruined castle, the concave sides with a band of roses.

10.5in (27cm) wide

$1,000-1,500   JN

A large Tunbridgeware two division tea caddy, the lid inlaid with a castle and border of flowers, with flowers to the concave sides, on ball feet.

11.75in (30cm) wide

$1,500-2,000   JN

A Tunbridgeware rectangular inlaid tray, by Burroughs.

c1810   *11in (28cm) wide*

$1,500-2,000   JN

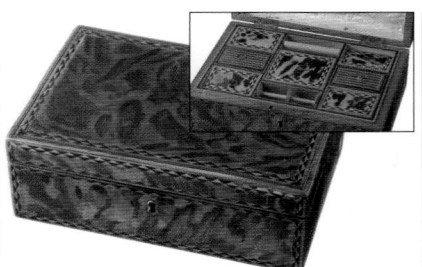

A rare Tunbridgeware inlaid fitted workbox.

9.5in (24cm) wide

$400-600   **JN**

An 18thC Tunbridgeware japanned ware work box, probably from Wise's manufacturer, with swing handle, the lid decorated with an Oriental scene and the sides with penwork decoration.

8.25in (21cm) wide

$200-300   **DNT**

A Tunbridgeware rectangular two division tea caddy, the top inlaid with a ruined castle, the sides inlaid with a band of roses.

8.5in (21.5cm) wide

$400-600   **JN**

A Tunbridgeware rectangular tea caddy, with flared inlaid top and band of roses to the base.

5.75in (14.5cm) wide

$400-600   **JN**

A Tunbridgeware perfume box with two cut glass bottles, the dome top inlaid with a butterfly.

4.5in (11.5cm) wide

$400-600   **JN**

A Tunbridgeware rectangular glove box and cover, the top inlaid with a butterfly and diamonds, scrolls to the sides.

9.5in (24cm) wide

$900-1,100   **JN**

A good Tunbridgeware parquetry rectangular box and cover, inlaid with specimen woods, bears label "Edmund Nye, Tunbridge Wells".

9.5in (24cm) wide

$800-1,200   **JN**

A Tunbridgeware rosewood playing card box, the lid with tesserae mosaic rose spray on a dark ground within narrow tesserae banding.

4.5in (11.5cm) wide

$150-200   **DNT**

A Tunbridgeware rosewood stamp box, with tesserae flower spray panel within chequered stringing, the sides with stylized flower head bands.

1.5in (4cm) wide

$200-300   **DNT**

A Tunbridgeware rosewood netting box, with rectangular red velvet pin cushion over a single end drawer with stickware handle.

7.75in (20cm) wide

$600-900   **DNT**

TUNBRIDGEWARE

BOXES & TREEN

An early 19thC Tunbridgeware yew wood box, the lid with elongated octagonal white wood lozenge within ripple parquetry cross banding.

9.75in (25cm) wide

$200-300   DNT

A Tunbridgeware rosewood box, the cushion shaped lid with perspective cube panel within running tesserae flower banding, the concave sides with similar flower banding, some lifting to perspective cubes.

7.75in (20cm) wide

$400-500   DNT

A Tunbridgeware rosewood box, the pin hinged lid with perspective cube panel within geometric tesserae banding.

5.5in (14cm) wide

$200-300   DNT

An early 19th century Tunbridgeware rosewood box, the lid with half square mosaic panel with palm wood centers and similar banding, the hinged lid with bright interior with half square mosaic lozenge and central removable tray.

8.25in (21cm) wide

$300-400   DNT

A Tunbridgeware rosewood box, the pin hinged lid with tesserae flower spray within a geometric banding, the sides with similar banding.

6.25in (16cm) wide

$150-200   DNT

A Tunbridgeware rosewood box, the oblong lid with geometric half square mosaic panel with chequer stringing.

4.25in (10.5cm) wide

$200-300   DNT

A Tunbridgeware ebony box, the cushion shaped lid with tesserae mosaic view of Hever Castle within tesserae rose banding, the concave sides with similar light ground banding, cracked veneers and filling to tesserae mosaic.

9.75in (25cm) wide

$300-400   DNT

A Tunbridgeware rosewood stamp box, depicting young head of Queen Victoria, said to contain some 1,000 pieces of inlay.

5.75in (14.5cm) wide

$300-400   DNT

A Tunbridgeware rosewood stamp box, depicting young head of Queen Victoria, said to contain some 1,000 pieces of inlay.

5.75in (14.5cm) wide

$300-400   DNT

A Tunbridgeware rosewood stamp box, depicting the young head of Queen Victoria, said to contain some 1,000 pieces of inlay.

$300-400   DNT

An unusual Tunbridgeware stamp box, the lid depicting the young head of Queen Victoria, with the addition of tesserae lettering spelling "postage one penny".

1.5in (4cm) wide

$600-700   DNT

A Tunbridgeware combination tape measure, pin cushion and emery, with stickware collars.

2.25in (5.5cm) high

$200-300   DNT

A Tunbridgeware inlaid inkstand, with cut glass bottle.

5in (13cm) wide

$200-300   JN

A Tunbridgeware combination tape measure, pin cushion and thread waxer, with stickware collars, the base with paper label "of Brighton Trifle".

Stickware were composed from clustered blocks of differently colored wooden sticks of triangular and diamond cross-section.

2.25in (6cm) high

$300-400   DNT

A Tunbridgeware rosewood watch stand, the arched hanger on twin baluster columns with stickware collars.

6.75in (17cm) high

$300-400   DNT

A Tunbridgeware crossover frame, with running flower tesserae bands housing colored engraving of Southborough Church and School, some damage.

9in (23cm) wide

$300-400   DN

A Tunbridgeware rosewood book slide, the folding ends with tesserae mosaic flower sprays on whitewood ground, some damage.

closed 11in (28cm) wide

$150-200   DNT

A Tartanware cigar case, the interior with four divisions, bruising and surface damage.

5in (12.5cm) high

$200-300   DNT

A Tartanware McDuff pattern vinaigrette case, of cylindrical form, inscribed to the lift-off top.

2in (5cm) high

$200-300   DNT

A Mauchlineware egg timer, decorated with a view of The Needles, Isle of Wight.

7.5in (19cm) high

$200-300   GORL

A Mauchlineware wall bracket, made from wood from Abbotsford, decorated with two views of Edinburgh.

$150-200   GORL

A 19thC carved snuff box, in the form of a bearded man, wearing a waistcoat and overcoat, with a hinged lid, slight damage.

7.75in (27cm) wide

$400-500 | **SWO**

A wrought iron rush-nip and candleholder, on a tapering conical elm base.

12in (30.5cm) high

$400-500 | **WW**

A wrought iron rush-nip and candleholder, on a faceted elm base.

10.75in (27.5cm) high

$400-500 | **WW**

An Italian Sorrento Ware folding basket, the octagonal base and fretwork cut sides with tesserae mosaic panels.

11.75in (30cm) diam

$150-200 | **DNT**

A pair of 20thC treen carved and turned lignum vitae and ivory candlesticks, each with ringed and tapered baluster stems carved with spiral decoration on circular base.

Turned by the late S.G. Abell, founder member of the Society of Ornamental Turners.

c1938-68 *13in (33cm) high*

$2,000-3,000 | **BIG**

A 19thC lignum vitae string box, of cylindrical form with a metal blade incorporated into the lid finial.

7.25in (18cm) high

$200-300 | **SWO**

A George V lignum vitae police truncheon, with royal cypher and crown printed transfers.

15in (38cm) long

$150-200 | **GORL**

A 19thC South German carved wooden baking mold, with a tulip bouquet heart.

13.5in (33.5cm) high

$300-400 KAU

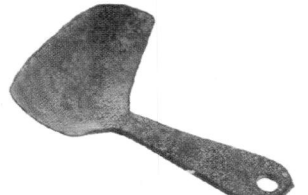

An early 18thC wooden ladle, in good condition.

$40-60 MUR

A 19thC South German carved wooden baking mold, with five designs including a fish, baby and dancing bear, the reverse with eleven further motifs including a dog and sleigh.

13.75in (34.5cm) wide

$200-300 KAU

LEFT: A 19thC Black Forest oak wall mounted brush set, carved as a dancing bear with chained nose, supporting two clothes brushes.

9.5in (24cm) high

$600-900 L&T

CENTER: A 19thC Black Forest carved oak and steel desk bell, supported by the carved figure of a seated bear.

5.25in (13cm) high

$400-600 L&T

RIGHT: A 19thC Black Forest carved oak inkstand, with cut glass inkwell and crouching beaver, raised on a naturalistic rocky base with pen stand.

9.5in (24cm) wide

$300-400 L&T

A 19thC Scottish burr birch snuff mull, stamped "Geo. Sinclair, Bonnington", of shaped oval form, with hinged split lid.

4in (10.5cm) wide

$600-700 L&T

A 19thC Scottish burr elm snuff mull, stamped "Geo. Sinclair, Bonnington", of shaped oval form, with hinged split lid.

4in (10cm) wide

$700-1,000 L&T

A treen snuff box modeled as a chiseled toe boot with brass studded decoration.

4in (10cm) long

$150-200 CA

A pair of carved mahogany wall brackets.

$600-700

8.75in (22cm) high

SWO

A 14thC English alabaster relief carving of the flagellation of Christ.

9.5in (24cm) high

$5,000-6,000   **POOK**

A 14thC carved and painted wooden Holy Wolfgang, wearing bishop's regalia, holding a model of St Wolfgang's church at Aberlake, worm damage.

26in (65cm) high

$7,000-10,000   **KAU**

A 15thC Italian polychrome deep walnut relief plaque of the pieta, with attendants in a landscape.

10.25in (26cm) wide

$2,000-3,000   **POOK**

A 15thC German carved oak figure of the Virgin Mary.

40in (101.5cm) high

$6,000-9,000   **POOK**

A 16thC Franco Flemish oak carved figure of Ecclesia.

28.75in (73cm) high

$4,000-5,000   **POOK**

A 16thC German carved limewood figure of the Madonna and child, losses.

29.5in (75cm) high

$3,000-4,000   **POOK**

A late 16th to early 17thC Italian carved fruitwood figure of a bishop, with outstretched arm and staff, on a plinth with the Medici coat of arms.

27in (67.5cm) high

$2,000-3,000   **POOK**

A mid-18thC German relief carved walnut panel of a bishop, holding a staff with outstretched hand.

52.25in (130.5cm) high

$1,000-2,000   **POOK**

A mid-18thC Franco Flemish carved pine figure of the assumption of the Virgin, hands of later date.

44.5in (111.25cm) high

$5,000-6,000   **POOK**

A mid-18thC Franco Flemish carved soft stone figure of Madonna and child.

30.5in (76cm) high

$5,000-6,000   **POOK**

A pair of late 19thC Franco-Flemish carved giltwood angel figure torcheres, each holding foliate branches, with iron pricket cups.

tallest 24in (60cm) high

$6,000-9,000   **POOK**

A pair of 19thC South German carved pearwood figural pawns, raised on circular pedestal bases.

3.75in (9.5cm) high

$500-600   **BLO**

A pair of 19thC carved and painted wooden putti, each with single wing.

10.75in (27cm) high

$700-1,000   **KAU**

A 19thC carved, painted and partially gilded wooden Holy Zeno, wearing bishop regalia, holding a book and a fish, chipped.

46.75in (117cm) high

$1,500-2,000   **KAU**

A 19thC carved, painted and partially gilded wooden figure, wearing priest's regalia, missing cross.

30.5in (76.5cm) high

$1,500-2,000   **KAU**

A pair of 19thC English School carved oak busts of John Milton and Robert Byron, unsigned.

21in (53cm) high

$6,000-9,000   **L&T**

A late 19thC carved figure, mounted on a wooden plinth, with painted ceremonial costume, found in eastern Pennsylvania.

27in (69cm) high

$6,000-9,000   **SK**

A 19th to 20thC carved wooden Corpus Christi, one nail missing, fingers chipped.

35.25in (88cm) high

$600-900   **KAU**

A late 18thC American carved pine spread-winged eagle, with acanthus-carved shield, perched on a rocky plinth.

30.75in (78cm) high

$6,000-7,000   **POOK**

A late 19thC Black Forest carved stag's head.

50in (125cm) high

$3,000-4,000   **FRE**

A Continental carved and ebonized inkwell, in the form of an owl.

6.75in (17cm) high

$300-400   **SWO**

A 20thC American School carved pine panel, of a cabin in the woods with figures, signed "R. Kreider".

28.5in (72.5cm) wide

$800-1,000   **FRE**

A Brugier continental music box, inset with enameled panels, pierced gilt grille and singing bird automaton, with opening beak and flapping wings, fusée movement, key, slight damage.

3.5in (9cm) high

$7,000-10,000   **SHA**

A CLOSER LOOK AT A STREET ORGAN

During the 18thC and early 19thC the street organ player or monkey grinder was a common sight whose music both entertained and annoyed passers by.

This particular monkey organ is the rarest and most desirable version with four stops. It was nicknamed the Clarabella (The Baby) and has additional features including piccolos and violins.

The inlay of eagles, human faces and instruments is unusually detailed and adds interest.

Bacigalupo was a prominent manufacturer and examples are highly collectable.

It plays eight tunes and contains its original play card which includes a Strauss waltz and Irish medley.

A 30-key Bacigalupo Clariton street organ hurdy gurdy, with four stops, 78 pipes, piccolos, violins, flutes, and clarinets, inlaid with 'Cocchi Bacigalupo & Graffigna-Berlin, Schonhauser Allee 78" and with a lithographed image of children, later cart, replaced pipes.

$15,000-20,000   **JDJ**

A Victorian walnut polyphon, made in Germany with English labels, no. 4283, with twin comb movement and 21 19.5in (49cm) discs, locking penny drawer with 18 old pennies.

51.5in (129cm) high

$6,000-9,000   **L&T**

A Victorian quarter-veneered walnut-cased table polyphon, with single comb gilt brass movement, no. 68082, and ten 16in (40cm) discs.

21.5in (54cm) wide

$3,000-4,000   **L&T**

A Regina console music box, style 40, with 30 15.5in (39.5cm) discs, decorated with various Victorian courtship and landscape scenes, wear.

The Regina Music Box Company was incorporated in 1894 in Jersey City and continued to sell musical boxes from stock until about 1921. Between 1892 and 1921, Regina produced over 100,000 musical boxes.

40in (101.50cm) high

$15,000-20,000   **JDJ**

A Regina 15 1/2 inch mahogany music box, the hinged serpentine top with Regina decal and "C.J. Heppe & Son, Philadelphia" label.

$3,000-4,000   **FRE**

An A. Guiot of London cased guitar, signed to the interior and dated "1839", the ebonized pine case with red plush-lined interior.

36.5in (93cm) long

$1,000-1,500   **L&T**

An important Classical stencilled mahogany and rosewood piano, by Loud & Brothers of Philadelphia, with original silk panel and candle arm brackets.

c1830   *79.5in (202cm) high*

$7,000-10,000   **FRE**

A pair of plated ceremonial trumpets.

These were used at the Anglesey Assizes in 1902.

$700-1,000   **BRI**

A Heckel stained beech and silvered contra bassoon, stamped marks, no. 229.

51in (130cm) high

$8,000-12,000   **L&T**

THE GLASS MARKET

As always prices for high quality, rare items in good condition remain extremely high and seem set to continue to climb.

Wine glasses from the 18th century have remained popular, particularly heavy baluster glasses. Another perennial favorite is glasses with color-twist stems. Increase in value in this sector of the market has a lot to do with rarity. When you have many collectors chasing the same scarce objects prices inevitably rise. Interestingly, and against common perception, there are new collectors coming into this market, which is keeping it buoyant.

Rummers, flutes and tumblers are still desirable and can be inexpensive especially when compared to modern examples.

Early 19th century colored wine glasses are under-priced, particularly green examples, where a good glass can still be found for $40-90. Blue and amethyst colored glasses from this period

are more popular, but still a good buy. These have good decorative appeal, particularly with light behind them. Another area to look out for is late Victorian and Edwardian colored wine glasses, many of which are acid etched.

Stevens and Williams glass has a strong following, particularly the designs of Keith Murray.

High quality Bohemian glass continues to have international appeal and prices are strong.

Glass decanters remain relatively overlooked unless they have crossover appeal, such as ship's decanters, which remain popular. This may be an area to watch for the future as the market can be fickle and, as stocks of wine glasses dry up, eyes may turn to this hitherto neglected sibling.

BALUSTER & BALUSTROID STEMS

A bell bowl heavy baluster wine glass, with folded foot.

The weight of this wine glass adds to its value.

c1715   6in (15cm) high

$1,500-2,000   JH

A baluster wine glass, with teared base of bowl over inverted baluster.

c1720

$1,500-2,000   JH

A bell bowl baluster wine glass, with tiered stem and folded foot.

c1725   6in (15cm) high

$800-1,000   JH

A CLOSER LOOK AT AN ENGLISH GOBLET

The majority of antique stemware on the market today dates from the mid-18thC. This glass pre-dates that era and is appealingly heavy.

Early glasses such as this invariably had baluster stems. The baluster was frequently inverted so that the bulbous part is at the top.

Many stems incorporate bulges, called 'knops', in a variety of shapes. Many glasses had air bubble, or 'tear', inclusions before the middle of the 18thC.

Before 1745 the majority of glasses had folded feet, providing a base that was twice as thick as the body, for strength and stability. In the mid-18thC the British Government began to tax glass by weight and the folded foot became a casualty of economy.

A balustroid wine glass, the ribbed bowl with engraved border and central swelling knop, folded foot.

c1730   5.75in (14.5cm) high

$400-500   JH

A Dutch engraved light baluster armorial and ship goblet, the engraved funnel bowl on an angular knop above bearded and inverted baluster knops on a circular domed foot.

c1750   9.75in (25cm) high

$10,000-15,000   L&T

A Dutch engraved Royal armorial light baluster goblet, the funnel bowl engraved with the crowned Royal arms of England, the reverse with seven arrows tied with ribbon, on a slender multi knopped stem above a circular conical foot.

c1760   7in (18cm) diam

$4,000-5,000   L&T

An English heavy baluster goblet, with conical bowl, the inverted baluster stem with a large tear inclusion, on a folded conical foot.

The production of fine drinking glasses in Britain dates back to the late seventeenth century, when George Ravenscroft perfected his formula for making lead glass. Known as 'flint glass' at the time, lead crystal had more clarity and weight than either potash or soda glass and was easier to work.

c1705

$5,000-6,000   JH

JEANETTE HAYHURST
FINE GLASS
32A Kensington Church St. London W8 4HA. 0207 938 1539

A group of rare 18th Century drinking glasses.

We specialise in glass of all ages including Roman
vessels, 17th, 18th, 19th century drinking glasses,
cut, coloured and engraved glass for the table.

Open:Monday-Friday   10AM-5PM
Saturday   12PM-5PM

MEMBER OF THE BRITISH ANTIQUE DEALERS ASSOCIATION

AIR-TWIST GLASSES

■ One of the most striking features of early stemware is the elaborate air-twist that features prominently from around 1750.

■ Many glasses had air bubble, or 'tear', inclusions in the stem before this date, and the air-twist was an extension of this motif, whereby air was drawn through the stem to form a spiral.

■ When two such spirals interlace, this is known as a 'double-series' twist.

■ The next stage in this development was the opaque twist, which substituted strands of white enamel for the beads of air.

■ Eventually, manufacturers were able to include colored strands within their stems – the most common colors being ruby, blue and green.

■ Many of the most sought-after color-twist glasses use just a single strand of color – among these, black and canary yellow are the most scarce.

■ The highest prices are reserved for glasses of particularly fine craftsmanship or those with historically significant engraving.

A mid-18thC wine glass, on fine incised twist stem, the bowl engraved possibly later c1780 with 'Tulip' pattern.

This glass would be worth around $1,000-1,200 with contemporary decoration.

5in (12.5cm) high

$800-1,000   JH

A wine glass, with tulip border and coarse incised twist stem.

c1760   6.5in (16.5cm) high

$1,000-1,200   JH

A large drawn trumpet wine glass, with double series opaque twist stem, with central large gauge, surrounded by multi-ply band, small chip to foot.

c1760

$800-900   JH

A wine glass, the bowl petal-molded with double series opaque twist, pair of tapes surrounded by multi-ply band.

c1765   5.75in (14.5cm) high

$600-700   JH

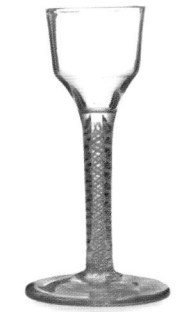

A wine glass, with fluted bowl and single series opaque twist stem.

c1765   6.5in (16.5cm) high

$600-700   JH

A wine glass, with honeycomb molded bowl and double series opaque twist stem.

c1765   5.75in (14.5cm) high

$600-700   JH

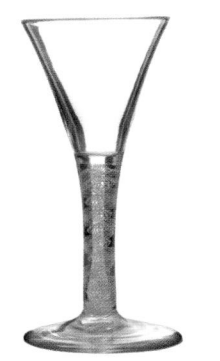

A wine glass, with fluted ogee bowl and double series opaque twist stem.

c1765   6.75in (17cm) high

$600-700   JH

A wine glass, with drawn trumpet bowl and double series opaque twist stem.

c1765   *7in (17.75cm) high*

$600-800   **JH**

A wine glass, with ribbed round funnel bowl and double series opaque twist stem.

c1765   *5.75in (14.5cm) high*

$500-600   **JH**

A wine glass, with ogee bowl and double series opaque twist stem.

c1765   *5.5in (14cm) high*

$500-600   **JH**

A wine glass, with bell bowl and double series opaque twist stem.

c1765   *6.75in (17cm) high*

$500-600   **JH**

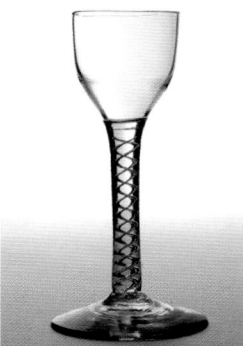

A mercury air twist wine glass.

c1745   *5.5in (14cm) high*

$600-700   **JH**

A wine glass, with round funnel bowl, multi-spiral air twist, shoulder and center knops.

c1745

$700-1,000   **JH**

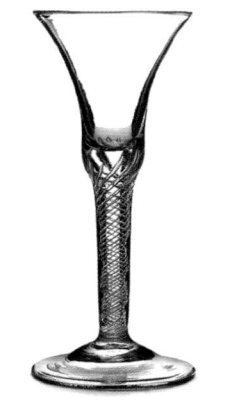

A wine glass, with bell bowl, domed folded foot and multi-spiral air twist stem.

c1745   *6.5in (16.5cm) high*

$600-700   **JH**

A wine glass, with bell bowl and double knopped multi-spiral air twist stem.

c1745   *7.5in (19cm) high*

$800-1,000   **JH**

A rare English color-twist wine glass, with a bell bowl raised on a red, green and white twist stem.

c1760   *6.5in (16.5cm) high*

$6,000-7,000   **WW**

A wine glass, with bell bowl and double knopped multi-spiral air twist stem.

c1750   *6.5in (16.5cm) high*

$800-1,000   **JH**

A wine glass, with fluted bowl, mixed air and enamel twist stem, and plain foot.

c1765   *7.5in (19cm) high*

$1,400-1,600   **JH**

A wine glass, with ogee bowl and series enamel twist stem.

c1765   *6.25in (16cm) high*

$500-600   **JH**

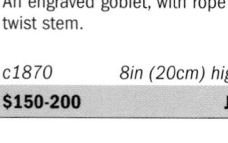
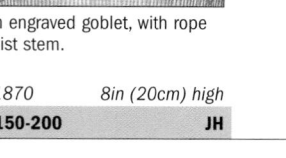

An engraved goblet, with rope twist stem.

c1870   *8in (20cm) high*

$150-200   **JH**

A wine glass, shoulder knopped, with diamond facet-cut stem.

c1760

$400-500   JH

A wine glass, with ovoid bowl, engraved and cut with polished stars and circles on hexagonal facet-cut stem, with rare domed foot.

c1765   5.5in (14cm) high

$400-500   JH

A wine glass, with facet stem and rare cut foot.

c1765   5.5in (14cm) high

$500-600   JH

A small wine glass, the bowl cut and engraved with polished circles and stars, with facet-cut hexagonal stem.

c1770

$150-200   JH

A wine glass, with facet stem.

c1790   6in (15cm) high

$300-400   JH

A wine glass, engraved in James Giles' workshop, with facet stem and stag's head engraving.

c1770   4.5in (11.5cm) high

$450-550   JH

A rummer, with a lemon squeezer base.

c1790   5in (12.5cm) high

$200-300   JH

A petal-molded rummer, with capstan stem.

c1800   5in (12.5cm) high

$120-150   JH

A petal molded capstan stem rummer.

c1800   5.5in (14cm) high

$150-200   JH

A rummer, engraved with fruiting vine and wine lemon squeezer base.

c1800   6.5in (16.5cm) high

$300-400   JH

A sliced cut bucket bowl rummer, with blade knop stem.

c1810   5in (12.5cm) high

$80-100   JH

A rummer, with slice and flute cut bucket bowl.

c1820   5in (12.5cm) high

$80-100   JH

A bucket bowl rummer, with two panels, with Masonic symbols and initials.

c1830-40   5.25in (13cm) high

$400-500   JH

A dimple-molded rummer.

c1850   6in (15cm) high

$50-70   JH

249

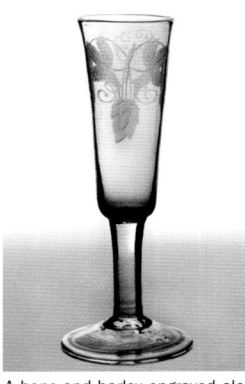

A hops and barley engraved ale glass, with plain stem and folded foot.

c1740   6.5in (16.5cm) high

$400-450   JH

A champagne or ale glass, with drawn trumpet and mixed twist stem, central opaque gauze surrounded by a pair of mercury air tapes.

c1765

$1,000-1,200   JH

An ale glass, with center knopped facet stem.

c1770   7in (17.75cm) high

$400-600   JH

A drawn trumpet hops and barley ale glass.

c1780   6in (15cm) high

$120-150   JH

A dwarf ale glass, the panel-molded bowl on unusual 6-sided molded pedestal foot with star in base.

c1790   4.75in (12cm) high

$120-150   JH

A petal-molded dwarf ale glass. These usually have stems, but this has no effect on value.

c1800   5.25in (13.5cm) high

$80-100   JH

A petal-molded dwarf ale glass, with stem.

c1800   5.25in (13.5cm) high

$80-100   JH

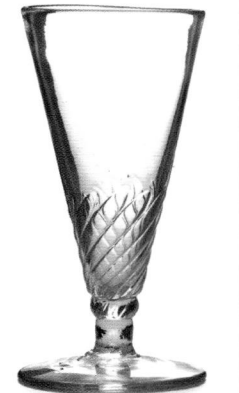

A hops and barley ale glass with knopped stem.

c1800   5in (12.5cm) high

$80-100   JH

A petal molded ale glass.

c1800   4.75in (12cm) high

$80-100   JH

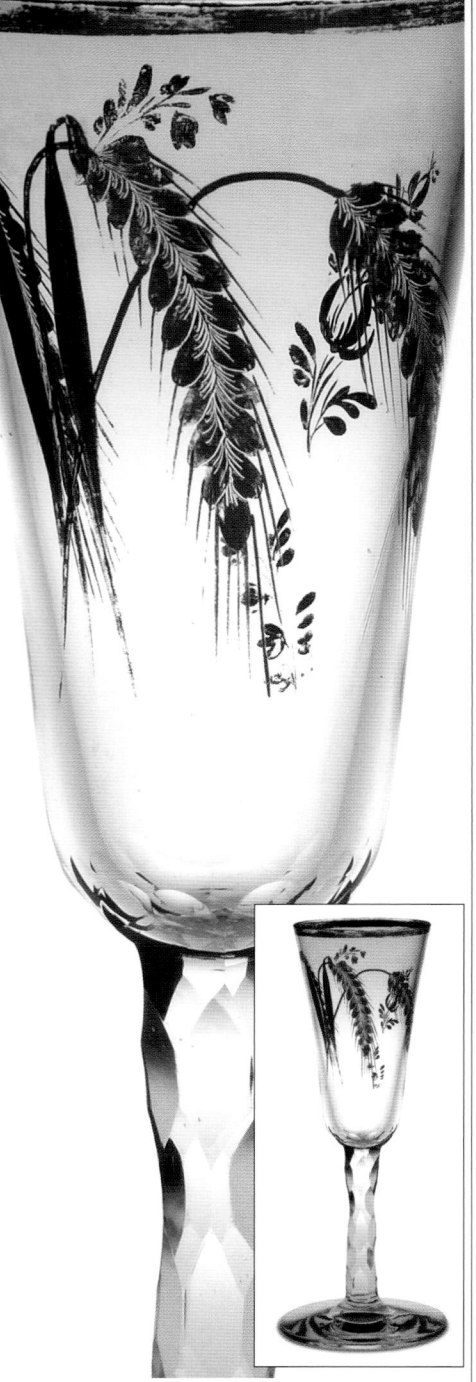

A late 18thC ale glass, the elongated bell shaped bowl painted in gilt with bearded barley and hops above tall diamond faceted stem on circular foot.

7.75in (19.5cm) high

$1,200-1,800   L&T

A jelly glass, with panel molded bowl and domed foot.

c1750   3.75in (9.5cm) high

$150-200   **JH**

A mid-18thC jelly glass, the panel molded bell bowl over air-beaded knop.

The air-beaded knop is rare and on a wine glass adds significantly to the value.

3.5in (9cm) high

$300-400   **JH**

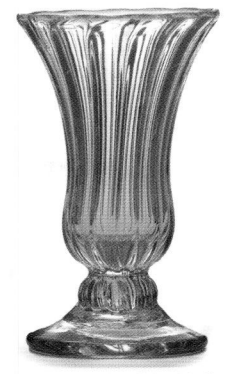

A jelly glass, with ribbed bell bowl.

c1760   3.5in (9cm) high

$80-120   **JH**

A hexagonal jelly glass.

c1770   3.5in (9cm) high

$150-200   **JH**

A jelly glass with flange top rim.

c1770   4in (10cm) high

$50-70   **JH**

A firing glass, the round funnel bowl over double series opaque twist, with central lace gauze, terrace firing foot.

c1765   3.5in (9cm) high

$700-1,000   **JH**

A firing glass, ogee bowl with hammered flutes, stem with double opaque twist around a gauze core, domed foot.

c1770   4in (10cm) high

$700-1,000   **L&T**

A plain stemmed firing glass, the ogee bowl with hammered flutes, on a circular terraced foot.

c1770   3.75in (9.5cm) high

$700-1,000   **L&T**

A plain stem firing glass, the ovoid bowl with hammered flutes on a circular over sewn foot.

c1770   3.75in (9.5cm) high

$700-1,000   **L&T**

An opaque twist stem firing glass, the ogee bowl with hammered flutes, with a thick outer opaque twist surrounding an opaque gauze core stem above a circular terraced foot.

c1770   3.5in (9cm) high

$700-1,000   **L&T**

An opaque twist stem firing glass, the ogee bowl with hammered flutes with a double opaque twist outside an opaque gauze core stem above a molded radially ribbed foot.

c1770   4in (10cm) high

$1,200-1,500   **L&T**

An opaque twist stem firing glass, the plain ogee bowl on a double series multi-thread stem above terraced circular foot.

c1770   3.75in (9.5cm) high

$700-1,000   **L&T**

251

A cordial glass, probably Irish, with plain stem and folded foot.

c1755   6.75in (17cm) high

$1,000-1,200   **JH**

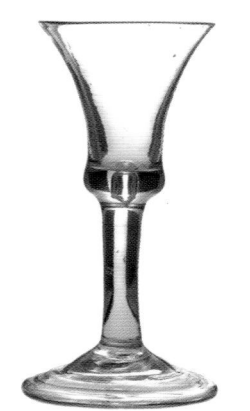

A wine glass, with bell bowl with tear in base, plain stem and folded foot.

c1725   6in (15cm) high

$300-400   **JH**

A CLOSER LOOK AT A DUTCH STIPPLE ENGRAVED 'NEWCASTLE' GLASS

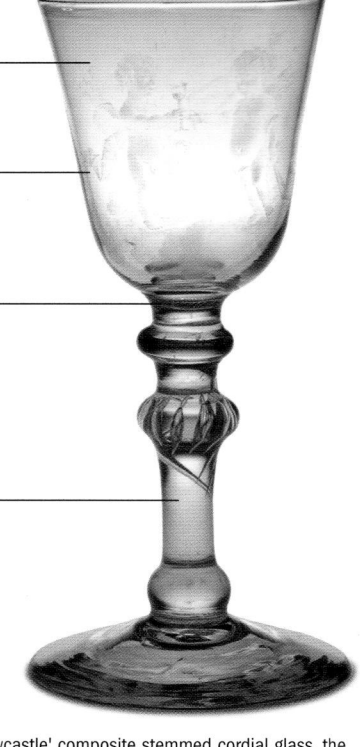

The glass is from a series depicting 'Liberty', 'Peace', 'Friendship', 'Harmony' and 'Fatherland'.

Whilst there are a number of glasses depicting two cherubs on clouds, it is extremely rare to have three.

The technique of stipple engraving, particularly popular in the Netherlands during the 18th century, involved building up a design of dots and lines using a fine diamond needle.

Newcastle was an important center of glass production from the 17th century due to the availability of coal for use in the furnaces. Pieces were sometimes shipped to the Netherlands for decoration and it can be difficult to distinguish from English decorated examples.

A tulip bowl hollow stem champagne glass, with diamond cut stem.

c1875

$70-100   **JH**

A late 19thC hollow stem champagne glass, with slice cutting.

$50-60   **JH**

A fine Dutch stipple engraved 'Newcastle' composite stemmed cordial glass, the rounded funnel bowl with one putti handing a wine glass to the other symbolizing 'friendship', a third putto lying on a cloud and holding a wreath, the bowl supported on a stem with a clear knop, a beaded knop and a plain section with a basal knop, on a circular domed conical foot.

c1760   7in (17.5cm) high

$15,000-20,000   **L&T**

A slice-cut, hollow stem champagne glass.

c1890   5in (12.75cm) high

$55-65   **JH**

A dram glass, the ribbed ovoid bowl over oversewn foot.

Oversewn feet are a feature of dram glasses.

c1770   3in (7.5cm) high

$200-250   **JH**

A dram glass, with facet stem and tavern foot.

c1770   4.25in (10.75cm) high

$150-200   **JH**

A dram glass, with oversewn foot.

c1770   3.75in (9.5cm) high

$300-400   **JH**

An early 19thC Masonic tumbler, with engraved pillars, set square and compass, with star on reverse.

3.5in (9cm) high

$200-300 **JH**

A ceremonial goblet or punch bowl, the incurved cup bowl engraved within a polished frame inscribed "O Willie brew'd a peck o' maut" with scene of three men drinking, initials "J.A. to J.F." and the date "1824", on a stem with flattened knop and a cut square foot with double dome above.

A further inscription reads "Ace o' Hearts/ To say aught less was wrang the cart es/ and flatt'ry I detest". The lines are taken from a song by Robert Burns.

10in (24.5cm) high

$8,000-12,000 **L&T**

One of a pair of goblets, acid etched with Classical scenes after Flaxman.

c1875 *8in (20cm) high*

$1,000-1,200 PAIR **JH**

A Hale Thomas Varnish glass master salt, signed.

c1850 *4.5in (11.5cm) high*

$1,000-1,500 **AL**

A Gilded amethyst wine glass.

c1850 *5.75in (14.5cm) high*

$500-700 **AL**

A Victorian marriage goblet, by John Ford of Edinburgh.

1867 *9.5in (24cm) high*

$1,500-2,000 **AL**

One of a set of six enameled naturalistic drinking glasses.

c1890 *6.75in (17cm) high*

$1,000-1,500 SET **AL**

A Stevens & Williams double case hock glass.

c1900 *8in (20cm) high*

$500-700 **AL**

A Tiffany & Co. opalescent drinking glass.

c1900 *8in (20cm) high*

$600-900 **AL**

A predominantly purple Stevens & Williams two color hock glass.

c1905 *8in (20cm) high*

$600-900 **AL**

A predominantly orange Stevens & Williams two color hock glass.

c1905 *8in (20cm) high*

$600-900 **AL**

An Indiana Glass Company of Dunkirk, Indiana red footed wine or water goblet in the 'Sandwich Daisy' pattern.

1926-31 *5.5in (14cm) high*

$60-90 **CA**

GLASS

A shoulder decanter, engraved with faux wine label for white wine.

White wine is a rare faux label. Port and madeira are more common.

c1765   11.5in (29cm) high

$1,000-1,200   **JH**

A decanter, with four cut neck rings, flute-cut base and original lozenge stopper.

c1800   11.25in (28.5cm) high

$400-500   **JH**

A set of three blue glass and gilt club-shaped decanters and stoppers, gilt with faux bottle labels for "RUM", "HOLLANDS" and "BRANDY", with ferrous metal and leather mounted tripartite decanter stand.

c1800   9in (24cm) high

$800-1,200   **DN**

A decanter, with three neck rings, sliced cut shoulder and flute-cut base, with mushroom-cut stopper.

c1810   9.5in (24cm) high

$300-400   **JH**

A decanter, with triple neck ring, slice cut shoulders, flute cut base and mushroom stopper.

c1820   9.5in (24cm) high

$400-500   **JH**

A Yeoward sliced cut decanter, with step-cut neck and matching stopper.

c1830   9.5in (24cm) high

$300-400   **JH**

A decanter, with step cut neck and slice cut body.

c1830   9.5in (24cm) high

$300-400   **JH**

A decanter, lens cuts to body, with step-cut neck, hollow blown stopper.

c1835   10in (25.5cm) high

$300-400   **JH**

One of a pair of decanters, diamond and flute cut with blown stopper.

c1830   10in (25.5cm) high

$700-1,000 PAIR   **JH**

A decanter, cut with alternating panels, with diamonds and pillars, hollow blown stopper, one neck ring.

c1840   10.5in (26.5cm) high

$200-300   **JH**

A decanter, with slice and lens cutting.

c1840   14in (35.5cm) high

$100-150   **JH**

A pair of green flashed and clear silver mounted bottle shaped decanters and stoppers, slice cut in staggered bands, the grape embossed collars with conforming stoppers by Henry Manton, Birmingham

1842   14in (35cm) high

$800-1,200   **DN**

A pair of English mid Victorian emerald green decanters with bull's eye stoppers.

11.5in (29cm) high

$1,000-1,500 | **AL**

An unusual Stourbridge decanter in the form of a hunting horn, inscribed with "Foxes Head" and "Tally Ho".

1880 *14.5in (37cm) high*

$1,000-1,500 | **AL**

A late 19thC Stuart decanter, with ribbed body, square section indentations, applied knipped trails.

10.5in (26.5cm) high

$300-400 | **JH**

A Stevens & Williams intaglio cut thistle decanter.

c1890 *9.25in (23.5cm) high*

$1,000-1,500 | **AL**

One of a pair of shaft and globe decanters, engraved with stars, hollow blown stopper.

c1890 *10in (25.5.cm) high*

$300-400 pair | **JH**

A Stevens & Williams 'transparent cameo' decanter.

c1898 *9.5in (24cm) high*

$600-900 | **AL**

An unusual Wrythen decanter, engraved "Brandy" and with blown stopper.

c1900 *12in (30cm) high*

$300-400 | **JH**

A pair of mounted glass lockable decanters, with keys and two silver bottle labels, inscribed "BRANDY" and "WHISKY", with marks for London 1910, maker's mark "B.G. & Sons".

13in (33cm) high

$1,200-1,800 | **L&T**

GLASS

A claret jug, with three neck rings, slice cutting to shoulders and base, with hollow blown stopper.

c1830   10.5in (26.5cm) high

$500-700   JH

A Stourbridge rainbow glass jug.

c1865   8.75in (22cm) high

$600-900   AL

A Richardson's opalescent glass jug.

As can be seen from the above example, Richardson's tended not to put pouring lips on its jugs.

c1865   6.25in (16cm) high

$500-600   JH

A Venetian aventurine colored glass claret jug.

c1870   9.75in (25cm) high

$600-900   AL

A baluster-shaped jug, engraved with roses.

c1845   11.5in (29cm) high

$800-1,000   JH

A claret jug, by Hillebeaur for Whitefriars, with trefoil neck and engraved with an exotic bird.

Hillebeaur was an engraver who worked very close to the Whitefriars showroom. It appears that he and his son did most of the engraving for Whitefriars which had no engravers on its workforce.

c1880   11.5in (29cm) high

$500-600   JH

A claret jug, of classical urn-shape, panels cut diamonds.

c1880   10in (25.5cm) high

$300-400   JH

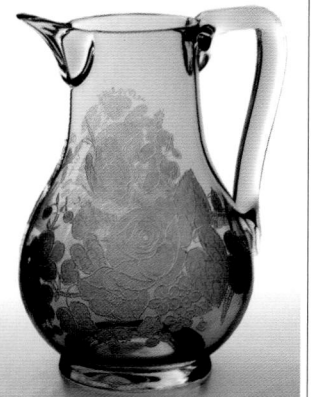

A claret jug, of classical urn-shape, panels cut diamonds.

c1880   10in (25.5cm) high

$300-400   JH

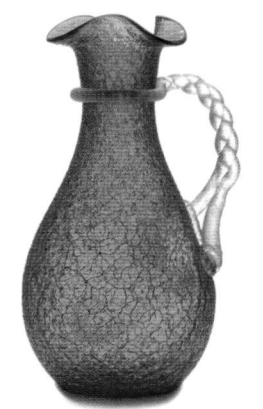

A crackle effect cranberry glass jug with clear glass handles.

c1880   10in (25.5cm) high

$600-800   JH

An Edwardian silver-mounted claret jug, by Joseph Gloster & Sons, Birmingham 1905, with a plain collar, cover and handle over a decoratively cut clear glass body.

7.25in (18.5cm) high

$600-900 CHEF

An engraved club-shaped decanter and faceted stopper, inscribed "JAMES: RAE" and scratched with a date.

1790 *10.25in (26cm) high*

$500-600 DN

A pair of engraved and faceted mallet-shaped decanters with flattened disc stoppers, each decorated with a bird chasing an insect and a flowering plant, between faceted bands.

c1790 *11.75in (30cm) high*

$700-1,000 DN

One of a pair of Regency cut glass conical ship's decanters and stoppers.

$500-600 PAIR SWO

A Regency cut glass claret jug and stopper.

9.75in (25cm) high

$300-400 SWO

A Victorian silver gilt-mounted glass claret jug, engraved with stars, star cut base, the mounts cast with Bacchanalian masks and vines, the hinged cover with lion and shield thumbpiece, by "IF" of London.

c1875 *11.25in (28.5cm) high*

$3,000-4,000 LFA

PAPERWEIGHTS

A Baccarat paperweight, containing chequered spiral and latticino canes, enclosed by basal-cut flutes.

2.25in (6cm) diam

$800-1,000 LFA

A mid-19thC Baccarat paperweight, with a flared bouquet of colored canes encircled by a blue and white band, the base cut with a star, bruised and chipped.

2.75in (7cm) diam

$1,500-2,000 WW

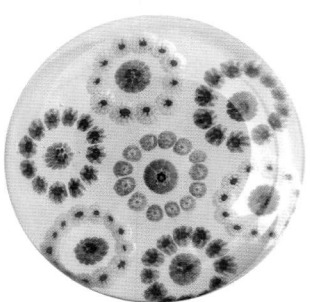

A Baccarat paperweight, with numerous flowerhead roundels.

2.5in (6.5cm) diam

$700-1,000 LFA

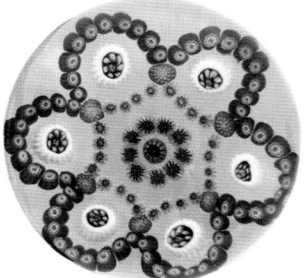

A Baccarat paperweight, with a six-looped garland around millefiori canes.

2.75in (7cm) diam

$700-1,000 LFA

GLASS

A Phoenix Glass Company apricot glass jug, with airtrap decoration.

Phoenix airtrap glass has a slightly coarser finish compared with Mount Washington.

c1885   8.25in (21cm) high

$300-400   **BRK**

A Phoenix Glass Company peachblow glass hobnail pitcher.

c1885   4.5in (11.5cm) high

$300-400   **BRK**

A Stourbridge spirit flagon, acid-etched with a heron in an oasis, shell handle.

c1885   9.5in (24cm) high

$500-600   **JH**

A New England Glass Company 'Wild Rose' peachblow glass jug, with matt finish,

The matt finish, sometimes called 'plush', was achieved using hydrochloric acid vapour.

1885-88   7in (18cm) high

$1,500-2,000   **BRK**

A Mount Washington Burmese glass sugar bowl and creamer, of petticoat shape, with piecrust rim.

c1890   5.5in (14cm) high

$600-900   **BRK**

A tall Stevens & Williams, silver mounted claret jug.

c1895   14in (36cm) high

$5,000-6,000   **AL**

A Stevens & Williams silveria pitcher, signed.

7.5in (17cm) high

$600-900   **AL**

A Stevens & Williams intaglio cut claret jug, silver mount.

1904   11in (28cm) high

$1,000-1,500   **AL**

A 1930s clear Depression glass milk jug.

4in (10cm) high

$10-20   **TAB**

A 1930s Hocking Glass Company clear Depression glass milk jug, with swirled line 'Spiral' pattern.

This pattern came in green and crystal.

1928-30   3.5in (9cm) high

$6-9   **TAB**

A Federal Glass Company of Columbus, Ohio, 'Sharon Cabbage Rose' pitcher.

1933-37   9in (23cm) high

$150-200   **CA**

A Jeanette Glass Company of Jeanette, Pennsylvania, 'Holiday' pink pitcher.

This pattern is also known as 'Buttons and Bows'.

6.75in (18.5cm) high

$60-90   **CA**

A celery vase, with strawberry diamond, lens and flute cutting.

c1825   8.25in (21cm) high

$500-600   **JH**

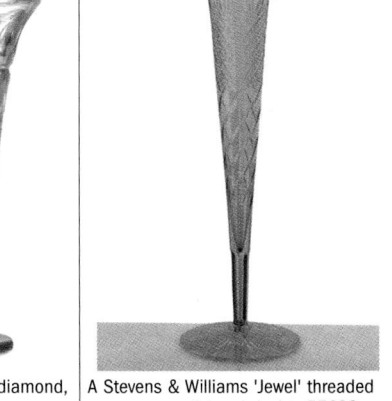

A Stevens & Williams 'Jewel' threaded posy vase, registered design 55693.

c1885   12in (31cm) high

$200-300   **AL**

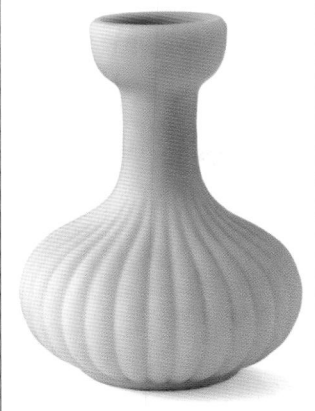
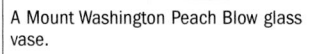

A Mount Washington Peach Blow glass vase.

1886-88.   5in (12.5cm) high

$2,000-3,000   **BRK**

A Stevens & Williams applied glass 'Mistletoe vase'.

c1887

$1,000-1,500   **AL**

A Stevens & Williams 'Jewel' threaded posy vase, registered design 55693.

c1890

$200-300   **AL**

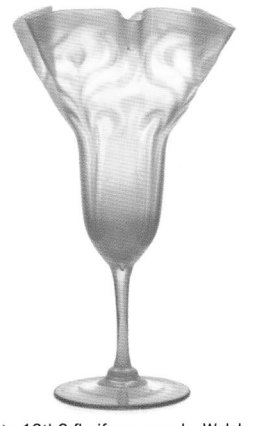

A late 19thC floriform vase by Walsh Walsh.

12.5in (31.5cm) high

$1,000-1,200   **JH**

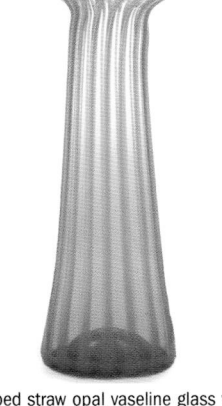

A ribbed straw opal vaseline glass vase.

c1890   10in (25.5cm) high

$280-320   **JH**

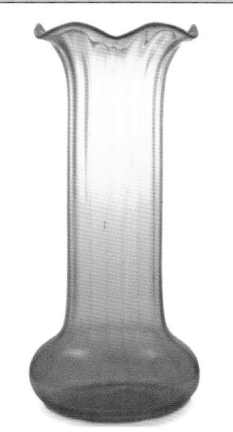

A Whitefriars vaseline glass vase.

c1890   12.5in (31.75cm) high

$400-600   **JH**

A late 19thC James Powell Whitefriars vaseline glass vase.

7.5in (19cm) high

$300-400   **PC**

A Thomas Webb white and cranberry glass vase on three feet.

c1890   7.75in (19.5cm) high

$300-400   **JH**

A glass vase, yellow with white trailed feathering.

c1890   5in (12.5cm) high

$200-300   **JH**

An olive green glass vase.

c1890   4.5in (11.5cm) high

$100-150   **JH**

A Whitefriars Wrythen dimpled posy vase.

c1890 3.5in (9cm) high

$150-200 JH

A pink and opal cased posy vase with green leaf feet.

c1890 3.5in (9cm) long

$80-120 JH

An 'opal over blue' vase with applied leaf decoration.

c1890 4in (10cm) high

$100-150 JH

An American rare Brilliant period center flower holder, possibly by Libbey, cut and polished.

Later on these vases were acid dipped, making the corners less 'sharp'.

$700-1,000 AJK

A Mount Washington Royal Flemish vase, with silver-plated mount, stained glass decoration and gold piping.

Royal Flemish was one of the most ambitious ranges issued by Mount Washington, with a variety of complex shapes.

1890s 7.25in (18.5cm) high

$3,000-4,000 BRK

A Mount Washington Royal Flemish vase, heavily decorated with winged dragon and with mythological beast head, with minute wear to gold trim.

A patent for Royal Flemish glass, a decorated camphor glass with a strikingly dramatic appearance, was issued in 1894 although it had probably already been produced for several years before the patent was received. On such pieces, the surface is typically divided into colored sections by heavy gold lines. On some examples, large open areas are left for elaborate enameling. Many of the same forms and decorations that were used for Crown Milano were used for Royal Flemish. Some pieces are signed with the "R F" monogram with a backward "R".

7.5in (19cm) high

$4,000-6,000 JDJ

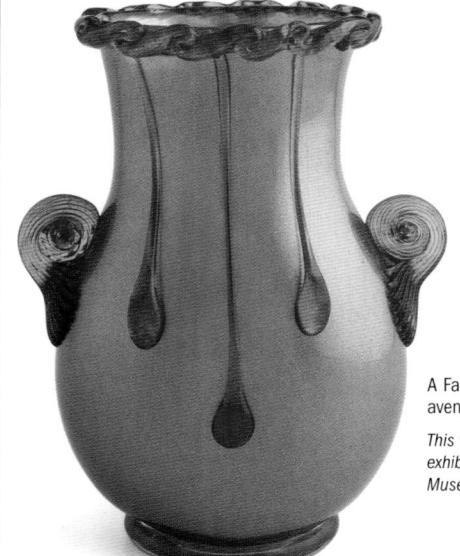

A Farrall Venetian-cut aventurine art glass vase.

This vase has been exhibited in the Smithsonian Museum, Washington.

c1895 8.5in (21.5cm) high

$2,000-3,000 BRK

A Mount Washington Crown Milano glass vase, with roses painted in a solution of gold.

c1895 7in (18cm) diam

$700-1,000 BRK

A Stevens & Williams double case intaglio cut vase, probably by Frederick Carder.

c1900   *12.25in (31cm) high*

$3,000-5,000   **AL**

A Mount Washington Crown Milano rose bowl, shape number 620, with hand painted decoration.

Mount Washington had a large decorating shop and the quality of the painting on its glass is extremely high.

c1895   *2.75in (7cm) high*

$500-600   **BRK**

A green glass vase with a blue trailed snake.

c1900   *4.75in (12cm) high*

$100-150   **PC**

An American Brilliant period flower holder, Hobstar and Cane pattern, by an unknown maker.

12in (30cm) high

$800-1,200   **AJK**

A Val St. Lambert double cased footed vase.

c1915 8.75in (22cm) high

$1,500-2,000   **AL**

A New England Glass Company pressed amberina glass stork vase, designed by Joseph Locke.

Pressed amberina glass is scarce.

c1900   *4.5in (11.5cm) high*

$2,000-3,000   **BRK**

A Val St. Lambert double cased flared vase.

c1915   *11.25in (28.5cm) high*

$400-700   **AL**

A Depression glass Liberty Glass Works lamp in the 'American Pioneer' pattern.

1931-34   *8in (20.5cm) high*

$150-200   **CA**

An Irish glass canoe bowl on molded pedestal base, with scalloped rim.
c1800   10in (25.5cm) high
$1,500-2,000   JH

A fruit bowl, with fan-cut rim above star-cut diamonds.

c1820   10in (25.5cm) wide
$150-200   JH

A cut glass footed bowl.
c1825   5in (12.75cm) high
$500-600   JH

A cut-glass salt.
c1825   3in (7.5cm) diam
$50-70   JH

An oval cut-glass bowl.
c1825   10in (25.5cm) long
$150-200   JH

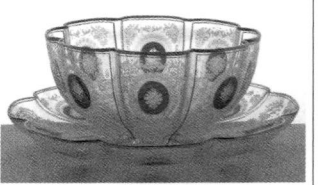

A set of six Lobmeyr bowls and underdishes.
c1875   2.5in (6.5cm) high
$1,000-1,500 set   AL

A blue and opal threaded bowl, with frilled top.
c1880   5cm (12.5cm) diam
$150-200   JH

A Salviati & Co. Venetian revival bowl and underdish.

c1890   3in (8cm) high
$400-600   AL

An opal diamond molded and ruby trailed glass hat.
c1890   2.25in (5.75cm) high
$100-150   JH

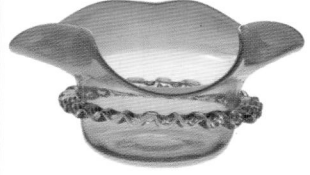

A green and ruby opalescent bowl.
c1890   5.5in (14cm) diam
$150-200   JH

An American Brilliant period two piece egg nog bowl, J. Hoare, in Hobstar pattern.
10in (25cm) high
$800-1,200   AJK

A Stevens & Williams double case bowl.

c1895   *10in (25cm) high*

$1,200-1,500   **AL**

A Powell feather pattern bowl.

c1900   *4in (10cm) diam*

$200-300   **JH**

A Val St. Lambert footed tazza.

c1910   *15.25in (38.5cm) high*

$1,500-2,000   **AL**

One of a set of six scallop-molded finger bowls, with intaglio engraving of swags of bunches of grapes.

c1925   *4.25in (11cm) diam*

$500-600 set   **JH**

A 1930s yellow Depression footed dish.

3in (7.5cm) high

$15-20   **TAB**

A fine 20thC gold-mounted Mouawad quartz and rock crystal garniture, with a purple quartz bowl, swan handles with diamond mounted masks and emerald eyes, gold and seed pearl drops, and two mounted quartz goblets, total diamond wt. 10 ct.

6.5in (16.5cm) high

$6,000-9,000   **FRE**

A Jeanette Jadeite egg-cup

3in (7.5cm) high

$20-30   **PC**

A Bohemian colored vase by Egermann.

c1835   9.5in (24cm) high

$700-1,000   **AL**

A Carlsbad Bohemian two color flared beaker.

c1835   6.25in (16cm) high

$1,000-1,500   **AL**

An early Bohemian flared beaker.

c1840   5.25in (13.5cm) high

$700-1,000   **AL**

A Bohemian uranium glass decanter.

c1840   13in (33cm) high

$500-700   **AL**

A CLOSER LOOK AT A BOHEMIAN GOBLET AND COVER

The snugness of the correct cover is also important, together with the matching design as very often covers are lost, broken and mismatched. Check that covers sit correctly and are in proportion.

Depth of cutting is really only understood by putting one's thumbs into the cuts and across the engraving.

Karl Pfohl (1826-94) is well-known for his lively engravings of galloping horses. The quality and excellence of the piece are more important than the signature.

The 'flashing' is of superior execution and the extra details on the vines is obvious.

The engraving is so fine on the figure you can clearly see his beard, eyes and so on. The horse's reins and tail are clearly done. The reducing lens to rear is well done too with good engraving on the flash resist.

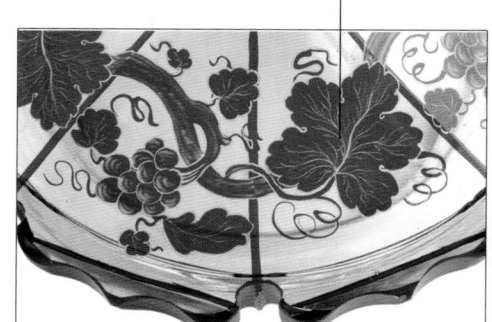

A Bohemian goblet and cover, unmarked but undoubtedly by Karl Pfohl.

18in (45.5cm) high

$45,000-65,000   **AL**

An unusual early Bohemian perfume bottle with chinoiserie decoration and with a reducing lens stopper.

c1845   8.75in (22cm) high

$800-1,200   AL.

A red overlay goblet, by F.P. Zach, Munich, engraved with floral motifs and hunting scene.

c1850   8.75in (22cm) high

$5,000-7,000   FIS

A very rare Masonic double overlay Bohemian beaker, with lodge number.

1859   6.25in (16cm) high

$2,000-3,000   AL

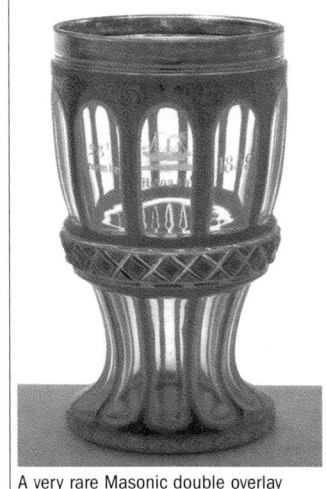

A cobalt blue Bohemian perfume bottle overlaid in white.

c1860   5in (13cm) high

$300-600   AL

A Bohemian ruby flash engraved perfume bottle with rare 'umbrella' stopper.

c1870   8.75in (22cm) high

$1,000-1,500   AL

A very rare Bohemian overlay bottle for the Turkish or Islamic market.

c1870   10.25in (26cm) high

$6,000-9,000   AL

A three color double overlay Bohemian perfume bottle.

c1880   8in (20cm) high

$1,000-1,500   AL

An opalescent engraved and gilded ewer and goblet, by J. & L. Lobmeyr, with a scrolling foliate ground en rocaille and 'jeweled' with opaque white dots, each with monogram mark, foot crack and chip.

c1880   ewer 9.75in (25cm) high

$700-1,000   DN

An exceptionally tall Moser vase with painted birds and applied acorns.

1886   17.5in (44.5cm) high

$3,000-5,000   AL

A 19thC Bohemian cranberry glass beaker, decorated in gilt and silver with a band of scrolled and 'jeweled' flowers and foliage, and scale pattern borders.

4in (10cm) high

$70-100   HAMG

265

SILVER MARKS

- Silver marks were introduced in 14thC England, to indicate that the silver content of a piece of metal was 925 parts in every thousand.
- The name give to this type of silver was 'sterling'. This term may derive from the derogatory name 'Easterling' which English silversmiths gave the standard set by German silversmiths at King John's request.
- English marks are known as hallmarks and typically comprise of four individual marks. These marks represent the silversmith, the date, the assay town where the silver was tested and the 'lion passant' indicating that the metal contains 92.5 per cent silver.
- Not all silver is marked and marks vary from country to country.
- Some Scottish marks include a mark for the assay office master.
- In Pre-Revolution France, marks were used to represent the silversmith, the town, the date and duty. After 1797 the marks were reduced to three: a mark guaranteeing the silver content, a duty mark and the maker's mark.
- The presence of the word "STERLING" in capital letters usually indicates a piece of silver made in the US. Date letters were generally not used and town marks were inconsistent.

The 'Lee' silver tea and coffee service, by William Ball, Baltimore, comprising a hot water pot, coffee pot, tea pot, waste bowl, sugar urn, creamer, teapot stand, and salver, all with with the initials "JLL", each piece marked on base with "W. Ball".

c1795

$80,000-100,000 FRE

A George III tea service, with engraved initials to the cartouches, marks for London, maker's mark "SH, London", and inscriptions to the bases.

1809

$1,200-1,800 L&T

A Coin silver tea service, by Lincoln & Foss, Boston, with oak branch, leaf and acorn repousse decoration, plain lyre handles, comprising hot water pot, teapot, creamer, sugar bowl with cover and waste bowl, 78oz.

c1830

$1,200-1,700 FRE

A five-piece silver tea service, by R. & W. Wilson, Philadelphia, with cabbage finials to lids, grape and leaf-chased mid-band, comprising hot water pot, teapot, covered sugar bowl, teapot, waste bowl marked "R. & W. Wilson Standard" and creamer marked "R. & W. Standard", 147oz.

c1830 *Teapot 12.5in (31.5cm) high*

$3,500-4,500 FRE

An early Victorian Scottish three piece tea service, by J. McKay, comprising teapot, sugar bowl and milk jug, with engraved borders and leaf capped scroll handles, initialled, with marks for Edinburgh, maker's mark, together with Hamilton & Inches King's pattern sugar tongs, Edinburgh.

1839

$1,500-2,500 L&T

A Ball, Black & Co. sterling silver four piece tea service, from New York, with embossed and chased fruiting vine decoration.

1851-1876 *Teapot 10in (25.5cm) high*

$1,500-2,500 FRE

A Victorian sterling silver four piece tea and coffee service, by Samuel Smiley or Samuel Smith of London and retailed by Goldsmiths Alliance Ltd., Cornhill, London, with chased lobed sides.

1869-70 *Coffeepot 10.5in (26.5cm) high*

$2,200-2,800 FRE

A Tiffany & Co. sterling silver four piece tea and coffee service, comprising a kettle on stand, coffee pot, teapot and a sugar bowl.

c1870-75 *kettle 9in (23cm) high*

$6,000-8,000 FRE

An American silver three-piece bachelor's tea set, of circular apple form, on a ring foot, with applied angular scroll milled lip band, ring and scroll handles, by the Gorham Mfg. Co. of Providence, RI, with "EK" monogram.

1877 *largest 3.5in (9cm) high*

$400-500 IHB

A Whiting sterling silver five piece tea and coffee service, with branch form handles, chased and embossed with foliage and fruit, with a Tiffany & Co. sterling silver strainer.

c1880   *Coffee pot 9.5in (24cm) high*

$3,500-4,500   **FRE**

A late 19thC Continental four piece silver tea and coffee service, comprising a coffee pot, teapot, covered sugar bowl and creamer, with crown finials and male term scroll handles, with repousse decoration, 60oz.

Coffee pot 10in (25cm) high

$900-1,200   **FRE**

A Sterling silver six piece tea service, by J.E. Caldwell & Co, comprising a kettle on stand, a teapot, a smaller teapot, a creamer, covered sugar bowl and a waste bowl, together with a silverplated oval tea tray, 129oz.

This form is a copy of a teapot owned and used by George Washington, the original example is in the Philadelphia Museum of Art.

c1890   *Teapot 7.5in (19cm) high*

$1,800-2,200   **FRE**

A late 19thC Chinese silver eight-piece tea and coffee service, comprising a teapot, coffee pot, tea kettle on stand lacking handle, covered sugar bowl, creamer, slop bowl, hot water pitcher, sugar tongs and a tray, each of simulated bamboo form with applied bamboo decoration, signed.

Tray 27.5in (70cm) wide

$6,500-7,500   **FRE**

A late 19thC Continental five piece silver tea and coffee service, with turned ivory acorn finials and fluted sides.

Tea kettle 18in (45.5cm) high

$1,800-2,200   **FRE**

A late 19th to early 20thC South American silver six piece tea and coffee service, chased and embossed with shell, c-scrolls and foliage, minor dents and scratches.

Tray 8.25in (72cm) wide

$4,000-5,000   **FRE**

An early 20thC Canadian Henry Birks & Sons sterling silver six piece tea and coffee service, each with foliate engraved decoration, coffee pot with a replaced finial.

Teapot 4.75in (12cm) high

$1,000-1,500   **FRE**

An early 20thC seven piece Reed and Barton sterling silver tea and coffee service, comprising a teapot, coffee pot, kettle-on-stand, creamer, covered sugar bowl and a tray.

Tray 27in (68.5cm) wide

$5,500-6,500   **FRE**

An early 20thC Tiffany & Co. five piece tea and coffee service, with lobed ovoid sides and scroll handles chased with shells and foliage.

Coffee pot 9.5in (24cm) high

$2,500-3,500   **FRE**

An early 20thC sterling silver eight piece tea and coffee service, comprising tea kettle on stand, teapot, coffee pot, water pitcher, waste bowl, sugar, tea caddy and caddy.

Tea kettle 11.75in (30cm) high

$3,500-4,500   **FRE**

A George V sterling silver tea and coffee service, by Charles Stuart Harris & Sons, London and retailed by James Robinson, 721 Fifth Avenue, New York, chased and embossed, minor dents.

1929   *Tea kettle 11in (28cm) high*

$4,000-5,000   **FRE**

A silver four-piece tea set, of rectilinear hexagonal paneled form having applied gadroon wire rim and wire handles upon a matching plain foot, Birmingham hallmarks, 52.5oz.

1958

$600-1,000   **BIG**

A Victorian tea and coffee service, by Edward Barnard & Sons Ltd, engraved with foliate swags and contained in a fitted wooden case stamped "Widdowson & Veale".

$2,000-2,500   **L&T**

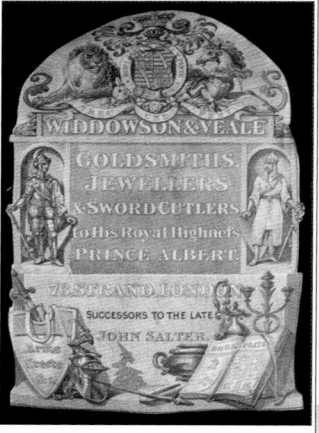

A Sterling silver five piece tea and coffee service, by Black Starr & Frost, comprising a coffee pot, teapot, covered sugar bowl, creamer, waste bowl, with foliate repoussé decoration, with silver plate tray.

Coffee pot 8in (20.5cm) high

$1,500-2,000   **FRE**

A Reed & Barton sterling silver five-piece tea service, in Hampton Court pattern, comprising coffee pot, teapot, covered sugar, creamer, and waste bowl, approx 93oz.

Coffee pot 8.5in (21cm) high

$1,200-1,800   **POOK**

A French Louis XVI style four-piece tea service, by A. Risler et Carre Fils of Paris, comprising a teapot, hot water jug, sucrier and cover and cream jug, chased with floral swags of laurel.

teapot 5.5in (14cm) high

$600-1,000   **L&T**

A Chinese export silver tea service, comprising teapot, tea kettle on stand with burner, sugar bowl with cover and milk jug.

$1,400-2,000   **L&T**

A Sanborns six-piece silver coffee and tea service, comprising coffee pot, sugar, pitcher, water kettle on stand with burner, with lobed side panels, maker's mark.

Sanborns Hermanos is a Mexican department store owned by Grupos Sanborns. It carries its own line of sterling silver flatware and hollow ware.

Coffee pot 10in (25.5cm) high

$900-1,200   **SK**

An Indian silver tea service, cast with foliate scrolls, stiff leaf borders, and dolphin cast finial to the cover, crested and inscribed "AVISE LA FINE".

Motto translates as "CONSIDER THE END" and is associated with the Clan Kennedy.

Teapot 8.75in (22cm) high

$2,500-3,500   **L&T**

A CLOSER LOOK AT A QUEEN ANNE TEAPOT

The age of this piece and the location of manufacture make this piece rare.

The method of manufacturer is unusual as there is a seam to the interior of the pot. The solder to the inside is original.

The crests of Masterman and Sykes have probably been added to this piece to record a marriage.

A rare small Queen Anne Francis Batty of Newcastle pear-shape teapot, with crest of Masterman and Sykes.

1705   8in (20.5cm) wide

$40,000-50,000   **WAL**

A George II Scottish silver bullet teapot, by William Aytoun, assay master Edward Penman, with engraved border and decorative scroll hinge, and marks for Edinburgh.

1729   6.25in (16cm) wide

$6,000-10,000   **L&T**

A scarce George III Scottish tea kettle on stand with burner, by William Gilchrist, assay master Hugh Gordon, with engraved cartouche and marks for Edinburgh.

It is very likely that this kettle had been commissioned by the town council as a Leith Race prize. Gilchrist was Deacon of the Incorporation of Goldsmiths at the time and had a seat on the council.

1753   12.25in (31cm) high

$30,000-40,000   **L&T**

A George III Scottish silver teapot, by William Dempster, with capped spout and engraved border with cartouche, and marks for Edinburgh.

1770   7in (17.5cm) high

$1,200-1,800   **L&T**

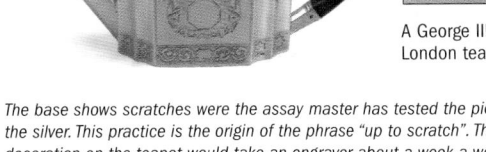

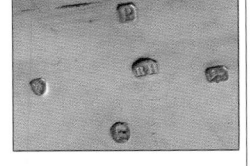

A George III Robert Hennel of London teapot.

The base shows scratches were the assay master has tested the piece for the purity of the silver. This practice is the origin of the phrase "up to scratch". The engraved decoration on the teapot would take an engraver about a week a worth to complete today making it economically unviable.

1790   8in (16cm) high

$2,000-3,000   **WAL**

A Victorian Scottish teapot, by William Marshall, with marks for Edinburgh.

1846-47   7in (18cm) high

$1,000-1,400   **L&T**

A Victorian Irish teapot, by J. Mahoney, with foliate clasped spout, bold leaf clasping and engraved inscription, with a similar cream jug, and marks for Dublin.

1846   *41oz.*

$1,400-2,000   **L&T**

A Victorian Scottish silver tea kettle on stand with burner, by J McKay, decorated with fruit baskets, floral swags, diaper panels and scrolls, with marks for Edinburgh.

1858   *17in (43cm) high*

$3,000-4,000   **L&T**

A Victorian silver bachelor's teapot, by Edward Bernard and John Bernard of London, with bead borders, scroll handle and paneled spout, engraved with two circular vacant cartouches.

1865   *4.75in (12cm) high*

$450-550   **WW**

A four piece American sterling silver tea/coffee service, comprising a coffee pot, teapot and covered sugar bowl.

c1850   *Coffee pot 11.5in (29cm) high*

$2,200-2,800   **FRE**

A late 19thC Reed & Barton six piece sterling silver service, comprising a kettle on a stand, teapot, coffee pot, sugar bowl, slop bowl and creamers, with foliate repousse decoration.

Kettle 14in (35.5cm) high

$4,500-5,500   **FRE**

Two early George III silver tea caddies and covers, by Daniel Smith and Robert Sharp, with gadroon border, chased floral and C-scroll decoration, cartouche later engraved crest, with marks for London.

One caddy is slightly larger, indicating that these are probably the centre piece and one of the smaller side caddies from the traditional set of three.

1762   *5in (13cm) high*

$2,000-3,000   **L&T**

A 19thC Irish tea caddy, possibly by J. Smyth, decorated in the chinoiserie taste, with marks for Dublin, and punched retailer's mark for West & Son, 16oz.

1873   *6.25in (16cm) high*

$3,500-4,000   **L&T**

A George II coffee pot, by Harvey Price, with engraved armorial, with marks for London.

1731   7.5in (19cm) high

$1,500-2,500   **L&T**

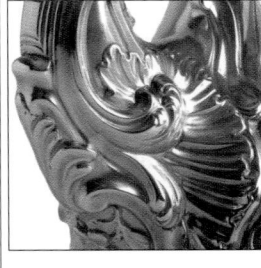

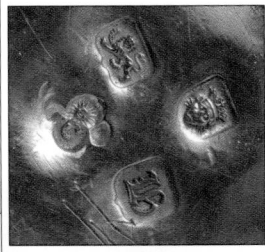

A George II Irish silver coffee pot, probably by Charles Lemaitre, crested, and with marks for Dublin.

c1733   9.5in (24cm) high

$8,000-12,000   **L&T**

A George III Samuel Courtauld London coffee pot, with embossed decoration, ivory handle and marks to base and cover.

Samuel Courtauld is a very collectable silversmith.

1763   11.5in (29cm) high

$6,000-10,000   **WAL**

A George III coffee pot, with chased thistle and floral ground, and leaf clasped spout and handles, with marks for Sheffield, maker's mark indistinct, 31oz.

c1786   10.5in (27cm) high

$1,200-1,800   **L&T**

A silver repousse coffee pot, by Samuel Kirk & Son, the sides chased and embossed with churches and buildings against a foliate ground.

c1846-61   9.25in (23.5cm) high

$2,700-3,200   **FRE**

A Sterling silver Tiffany & Co. coffee pot, with engraved detail, marked "Tiffany & Co 9480M504 Sterling", initialed and dated to the underside "March 22nd, 1891".

9in (22.5cm) high

$600-1,000   **L&T**

A Canadian silver three-piece coffee set, the pot of Georgian baluster form, with baluster creamer and open sugar bowl, by Henry Birks & Sons Ltd of Montreal.

1949   largest 9in (23cm) high

$450-550   **IHB**

A café au lait set, with turned wooden handle, cast fruit and floral finial to the hinged cover, and marks for London, maker's mark "JHR", 16oz.

1913   6.25in (16cm) high

$600-1,000   **L&T**

A café-au-lait set, by Skinner & Co., with marks for London.

1915   6.75in (17cm) high

$450-550   **L&T**

An Edwardian monteith bowl, by Hawksworth Eyre and Co Ltd, the girdled circular bowl with scroll rim, lion mask and ring handles, upon a raised pedestal base.

1901   *8.75in (22.5cm) diam*

$1,200-1,800   **LAW**

A set of four George III twin-handled sauce tureens, by John Schofield, with engraved coat of arms for BARON SHEFFIELD, Peerage of Ireland, with marks for London, and a set of four George III sauce ladles, London.

1782 & 1786   *9.5in (24cm) wide*

$4,000-5,000   **L&T**

A George III Irish silver salt and gilded salt, by Daniel Egan, with reeded borders and one bright engraved and initialed, both with marks for Dublin.

1786   *3in (8cm) high*

$800-1,200   **L&T**

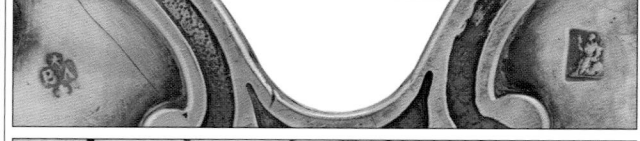

A George III Irish provincial swing-handled basket, by Joseph Gibson, with thread border handle, pedestal foot, and marks for Cork, 7oz.

c1800   *6.25in (16cm) wide*

$2,000-3,000   **L&T**

A William III Britannia Standard monteith bowl, by John Bache, with marks for London 1701-02, with handles issuing from a lion mask, and later cover by John Crouch and Thomas Hannah, with marks for London 1782 and "WE".

1782   *11in (28cm) high*

$33,000-35,000   **L&T**

A George III twin-handled tureen and cover, later embossed with flowers, foliage and C-scrolls, and engraved armorial, marks for London, maker's mark John Edwards III and William Frisbee, 72.5oz.

1791   *11in (28cm) high*

$3,500-4,500   **L&T**

A late 19thC set of four Kirk & Sons Sterling silver compotes, with chased and embossed decoration.

9.5in (24cm) wide

$7,000-9,000   **FRE**

A large Victorian sterling silver punch bowl, by Charles Stuart Harris, London.

1893   *15in (38cm) diam*

$4,000-5,000   **FRE**

A late 19th to early 20thC Russian silver centred bowl, engraved with equestrian and figural shaped reserves, in the Persian taste, against an arabesque and foliate ground, raised on an oval pedestal foot.

19in (48cm) wide

$1,500-2,000   **FRE**

An Edwardian punch bowl, by Henry Wilkinson, embossed with a broad band of flowers and scrolls with shaped blank cartouches, and marks for Sheffield, 44oz.

1902   *11.75in (30cm) diam*

$1,500-2,000   **L&T**

A montieth bowl, by Arthur Martin Parsons and Frank Herbert Parsons, with plated inner liner and marks for London 1934, stamped "TESSIERS LTD, LONDON", 45oz.

9.25in (23.5cm) diam

$2,000-3,000   **L&T**

A silver Edwardian replica of the Warwick Vase, by Elkington & Co, on square pedestal base, with marks for Birmingham.

1906   *10.25in (26cm) high*

$15,000-25,000   **L&T**

273

A 17thC silver single-handled porringer, attributed to John Hull of Boston Massachusetts, with maker's mark twice.

1624-83   *7.25in (18.5cm) wide*

$17,000-20,000   **L&T**

One of a pair of George III sterling silver gilt sweetmeats and underplates, by Paul Storr, London, with trellis pierced sides, silver liners, and leaf cast rims.

1808   *2.5in (6.5cm) high*

$3,000-4,000 pair   **FRE**

A William IV Scottish silver mounted fruitwood luggy, by Peter Arthur, lined and decorated with simple banding on collet foot, with marks for Glasgow.

1833   *4in (10cm) wide*

$500-700   **L&T**

A George II silver covered tureen, Britannia Standard, London, with a berry finial and twin scroll handles, maker's mark B.I., cover slightly warped, some minor dents and bends.

1758   *9.75in (25cm) wide*

$1,700-2,200   **FRE**

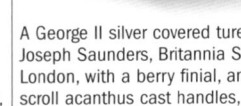

A George II silver covered tureen, by Joseph Saunders, Britannia Standard, London, with a berry finial, and double scroll acanthus cast handles, finial detached.

1735   *5.5in (14in) high*

$1,800-2,200   **FRE**

A colonial curry pan, with removable sliding handles with turned wood grips, three marks for Calcutta, John Mair, thistle, J.M, key, and engraved crest and initials to one side and initials GW to TEE and dated, 20oz.

John Mair was apprenticed to James Gordon of Aberdeen.

1805   *7.5in (19cm) diam*

$3,500-4,000   **L&T**

A Victorian sterling silver gilt covered entree dish, by Paul Storr, London, the base with twin shell form handles, gilt worn with almost total loss to cover.

1838   *12.75in (32.5cm) wide*

$4,200-4,500   **FRE**

An early 20thC sterling silver and silver-gilt plated 'Vitruvian' pattern flower-arranging bowl, retailed by W. W. Wattles & Sons.

15.5in (39.5cm) wide

$1,500-2,000   **FRE**

A pair of continental silver ecuelles and covers, with scroll cast handles, and domed cover with rose cast finial, inscribed "BIDDULPH" in script, 68oz.

6in (15cm) high

$2,000-3,000   **L&T**

An Edwardian large gilded quaich, by David, Herbert and George Edward, with Celtic designs, marks for London and the wooden base stamped "Edward of Glasgow".

1909   *13.75in (35cm) wide*

$2,500-3,500   **L&T**

One of a pair of Irish William III sterling silver salvers, by Joseph Walker, with armorial crests and gadrooned borders, pitting and scratches, Dublin.

1694   10.5in (26.5cm) diam

$6,000-8,000 pair   **FRE**

1734   7.5in (19cm) diam

$1,500-2,500   **L&T**

A George II Scottish silver waiter, by James Taitt, assay master Archibald Ure, of shaped circular form, with pie-crust molded border on three hoof feet, marks for Edinburgh, 9.5oz.

A jeweler and silversmith called 'Tate' accompanied Prince Charles Edward Stuart back to France in 1746 and it is possible that he was the maker of this waiter.

A pair of George II Scottish silver waiters, by Ker & Dempster, assay master Hugh Gordon, with shell and scroll cast edge and molded border, and marks for Edinburgh.

1748 & 1749   8.25in (21cm) diam

$3,000-4,000   **L&T**

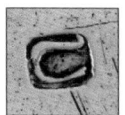 

A George II Edward Lothian of Edinburgh salver, with mark for assay master Hugh Gordon.

c1750   8.25in (21cm) diam

$2,500-3,500   **WAL**

A George III salver, by Richard Rugg of London.

1773   9.75in (25cm) diam

$2,500-3,000   **WAL**

A CLOSER LOOK AT A DUBLIN SALVER

Irish silver is currently very popular, due to its high quality, as a result of Ireland's increased wealth.

Around 40 per cent of Irish silver is undated.

The border of shells in this configuration is particular to Ireland.

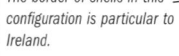

Prominent Irish silversmith Richard Williams was apprenticed to J. Wilme in 1743. Working from 6 Grafton Street in Dublin, he became a master in 1768-9.

A George III salver, by Richard Williams of Dublin.

c1770   14.5in (37cm) diam

$7,000-10,000   **WAL**

A pair of George III ashettes, by Andrew Fogelberg, with gadrooned border and engraved coat of arms, each numbered, with marks for London, 104oz.

1775   *17.25in (44cm) wide*

$3,500-4,500   **L&T**

A pair of George III salvers, with inner molded hare bell swags and an engraved crest to the center, with marks for London, maker's mark "IC", 41oz.

1776   *10in (25cm) diam*

$1,400-2,000   **L&T**

A George III Irish silver waiter, on three fluted feet, with marks for Dublin, maker's mark "RB".

1795   *6.5in (16.5cm) diam*

$800-1,200   **L&T**

A fine set of twelve George III sterling silver gilt dinner plates, by Paul Storr, with gadrooned and shell cast rims, engraved with armorial crests, heavy scratches to underside, London.

1808   *11in (28cm) diam*

$24,000-30,000   **FRE**

A late George III plated salver, by S.C. Young Walker Kitchen & Co., inscribed to the underside "F.W. CROSLAND... HALLS FOUNDRY, BELFAST...", with marks for Sheffield.

1818   *10.25in (26cm) diam*

$600-1,000   **L&T**

One of a set of six silver bread and butter plates, by the Gorham Mfg. Co. of Providence, RI, monogram removed.

1890   *6.25in (16cm) wide*

$500-600 SET   **IHB**

A Victorian sterling silver tea tray, by Richard Martin & Ebenezer Hall, Sheffield, with pierced galleried sides and engraved decoration.

1893   *22.75in (58cm) wide*

$12,000-18,000   **FRE**

A silver compote, of hemispherical form, on a short beaded pedestal, by the Randahl Shop of Chicago, IL.

1940-80   *8.25in (21cm) wide*

$350-450   **IHB**

A William IV silver-gilt two-handled trophy cup and cover, by Barnard Bros of London, with foliate and floral decoration, later base metal bull, inscription and pastoral scene.

1832   17.5in (44.5cm) high

$6,000-7,000   **GORL**

A William IV silver-gilt cup and cover, by Edward, Edward Jnr, John and William Barnard, engraved with a coat of arms inscribed "Rodesse et delectare Simul", with later associated finial depicting Shakespeare, the cover stamped for London, maker's mark "M.R.S.", date rubbed.

1833   19.5in (49.5cm) high

$12,000-18,000   **FRE**

A silver two-handled cup and cover, of early 18thC design, with cut card decoration, London.

1925   11in (28cm) high

$600-1,000   **ROS**

A large 'The King's Cup' trophy cup, by Heming & Co. Ltd., inscribed "Royal Yacht Squadron Regatta, The King's Cup, 1938. Presented by King George VI", marks for London, wooden plinth and case.

1937   19in (48cm) high

$2,500-3,500   **L&T**

A large twin-handled silver trophy cup with cover, by Walker & Hall, with articulated gun finial, inscribed and crested, marks for Sheffield 1939.

c1939   21.25in (54cm) high

$600-1,000   **L&T**

A silver covered cup, by Ilya Shor, New York, the sides decorated with mothers, children and musicians.

c1950   8.5in (21.5cm) high

$20,000-30,000   **FRE**

A George I silver porringer, by William Darker of London, with an engraved coat of arms.

1719   5in (12.5cm) high

$1,500-2,000   **WW**

A George II porringer, possibly by William Fordham or William Fleming, engraved with acorn, stiff leaf and ovolo borders, marks for London.

1730   6.5in (16.5cm) wide

$1,500-2,500   **L&T**

A Victorian silver novelty character container, resembling a gentleman in a powdered wig, probably by Alexander Fisher of London.

1886   2.5in (6.5cm) diam

$600-800   **WW**

METALWARE

A silver tankard, by John Stuart, Providence, Rhode Island, with scrolled thumbpiece, scrolled handle engraved with the initials "W.T.F.", with whistle terminal, marked three times, 29oz.

c1735   8in (20.5cm) high

$12,000-18,000   **FRE**

A pair of early George III tumbler cups, by John Gorham, with engraved crest and gilt interior, and marks for London, 9oz.

1766   3in (7.5cm) diam

$1,500-2,000   **L&T**

An early George III Scottish mounted leather blackjack, by Ker & Dempster, silver lined, with Rococo cartouche inscribed "ESSE QUAM VIDERI" and below "TYNE SILLER, TYNE LITTLE, TYNE FRIENDS TYNE MICKLE, TYNE HEART TYNE A'", with marks for Edinburgh.

1767   7.25in (18.5cm) high

$12,000-18,000   **L&T**

A George II two-handled cup and cover, by Charles Wright of London.

1778   12.35in (31cm) high

$4,000-5,000   **WAL**

A George II twin handled silver cup with cover, maker Francis Spilsbury I, inscribed "This Cup was presented to me on the Anniversary of my Forty Second Birthday by Emma", the opposite side engraved with the coat of arms awarded to Lord Nelson after the Battle of the Nile in 1798, marks for London, 27.5oz.

1739   8.25in (21cm) high

$8,000-12,000   **L&T**

Left: A George III silver tankard, maker probably Thomas Wynne, with scroll handle, marks for London.

1776   6in (15.5cm) high

$1,500-2,500   **L&T**

Right: A George III silver tankard, maker John Langlands, scroll handle, later inscription, marks for Newcastle.

1769   4in (10cm) high

$1,000-1,500   **L&T**

A scarce Scottish provincial egg cup, by Donald Fraser, with central engraved initial R within a garter, with marks for Inverness, marked "DF" and "INS", as well as "DF" to opposite side.

c1830   2.5in (6cm) high

$2,000-3,000   **L&T**

A scarce set of six horn beakers, by William Dunningham and Co, with applied silver shield engraved with a Yacht Club crest, with marks for Edinburgh.

1909   Tallest 5in (12.5cm) high

$1,200-1,800   **L&T**

A Victorian Scottish silver cup and cover, with gilt interior and cast ostrich finial to the domed cover, with marks for Edinburgh, maker's mark "WRC".

1860   *10.25in (26cm) high*

$400-600   **L&T**

A mounted horn beaker, with applied shield with engraved initials, inscribed "JOHN LEIGH" and marked to the rim "I.A, thistle, b, thistle".

5in (12.5cm) high

$1,500-2,000   **L&T**

A pair of Britannia standard reproduction cups and covers, by A. & F. Parsons of Tessiers, with leaf clasped handles, and marks for London, 92oz.

1911   *10.5in (27cm) wide*

$2,000-3,000   **L&T**

A Victorian Scottish lidded jug, by J. & W. Mitchell, with applied decoration and marks for Glasgow.

1852   *11in (18cm) high*

$3,500-4,500   **L&T**

A pair of late George III sauceboats, with marks for London, maker's mark indistinct, later crested and inscribed "TRUE TO THE END, DULCIUS EX ASPERIS".

1814   *4in (10cm) high*

$1,500-2,000   **L&T**

A Victorian wine jug, by Martin and Hall, Sheffield, the elongated neck with cover, scroll handle and ovoid body, with repousse floral and foliate decoration and with embossed angels flanking cartouches.

1895   *12.5in (32cm) high*

$1,500-2,000   **LAW**

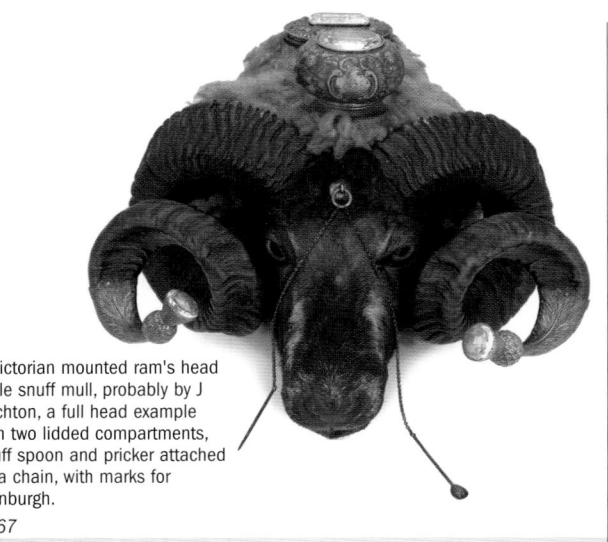

A Victorian mounted ram's head table snuff mull, probably by J Crichton, a full head example with two lidded compartments, snuff spoon and pricker attached by a chain, with marks for Edinburgh.

1867

$6,000-10,000   **L&T**

A Victorian Scottish mounted ram's horn table snuff mull, with cast hinged cover and cairngorm, marks for Edinburgh, and maker's mark "PW".

1870   *7.75in (19.5cm) high*

$3,500-4,500   **L&T**

A Scottish mounted ram's horn snuff mull, apparently unmarked, with thistle decoration and a central plaque to the hinged lid inscribed "Wm Douglas Fordon".

4.25in (11cm) long

$500-700   **L&T**

A Dutch silver tobacco, box of rounded rectangular shape, the cover engraved with a naval trophy, the sides with leafy scrolls and coats of arms, the base with shipping scene.

6.5in (16.75cm) wide

$1,200-1,800   **LAW**

A CLOSER LOOK AT A SCOTTISH SNUFF BOX

This is a rare example of a snuff box by this maker. There are only a few recorded examples.

Robert Dickson silverware pieces feature in the collections of National Museums of Scotland and the Perth Museum and Art Gallery.

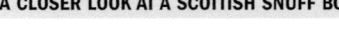

The marks to this piece are interesting as they do not conclusively determine whether they are for Robert Dickson elder or younger. It may have been made in the period where these makers overlap and in fact were most likely using the same punches.

The town punch is of the earlier style used by Dickson elder while the maker's punch is the more distinctive one used by Dickson younger.

A George III Nelson vinaigrette, with portrait of Nelson inscribed 'England Expects Every Man Will Do His Duty', the grille with embossed portrait of H.M.S. Victory and inscription 'Trafalgar Ocr. 21. 1805, by Mathew Linwood, Birmingham.

1806   *1.35in (3cm) wide*

$5,000-7,000   **LAW**

A Scottish provincial snuff box, by Robert Dickson, from Perth, with gilt interior, marked RD, eagle, the hinged lid engraved and inscribed "JOHN PEULLER TO CHARLES BUDD", 4oz.

3.4in (9cm) long

$8,000-12,000   **L&T**

A rare New York silver nutmeg grater, bearing the touch mark of "Sylvester Morris", inscribed "This box given to Miss Elizabeth Putnam by Major General Sir John Vaughan at Newtown Long Island, 1778".

1.5in (4cm) wide

$35,000-40,000   POOK

A rare George III Scottish nutmeg grater, marked with Edinburgh town mark and duty head, no maker's mark apparent, engraved crest of a cockerel and the motto "COURAGE".

c1784-86   1.75in (4.4cm) high

$1,500-2,500   L&T

A George III lidded mustard pot, with scroll pierced sides, and another lidded mustard, both with blue glass liner, marks rubbed, with marks for London 1791, maker's mark "TW".

1791   3.25in (8cm) high

$600-1,000   L&T

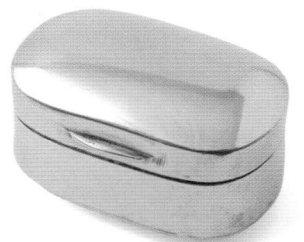

A George III silver nutmeg grater, by Joseph Taylor, of plain oval shape with hinged steel grater, Birmingham.

1809   0.5in (1cm) high

$700-900   CHEF

A 19thC Russian silver box, with rounded corner, with engraved floral decoration, the lid with an antique building, stamped and master's mark "JS".

3in (7.5cm) long

$300-400   KAU

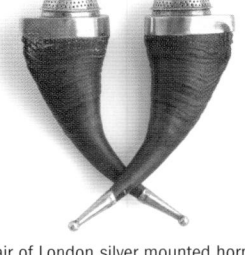

A pair of London silver mounted horn pounce pots, each horn mounted with a silver shoulder and pierced domed oval cap and silver finial to tip.

1885   6in (15cm) long

$550-650   ROS

A Russian silver purse and a cigarette case, the purse engraved with a spider web and spider set with a blue stone cabochon, the cigarette case with applied gold signatures.

c1900

$1,800-2,200   FRE

A LA VIEILLE RUSSIE
Silver gilt trompe l'oeil casket, the cabin trunk with colored cabochons mounted on the side.
Maker: F.W.
St. Petersburg, circa 1900.

A Russian silver gilt trompe l'oeil box, by O.F. Wennerstrom, St. Petersburg, formed as a valise, with applied semi-precious jewelled decoration, with surface scratches.

c1900   4.25in (11cm) wide

$12,000-18,000   FRE

An silver hair receiver, with floral repoussé decoration, the cut glass jar with chanelled sides, the lid marked for A.G. Schultz & Co. of Baltimore, MD.

1910-30   4in (10cm) wide

$250-350   IHB

An H** Mathews oval silver tack box, having a repoussé decorated top with young ladies and musician within a bead border, Birmingham hallmarks.

1924

$200-300   BIG

A small French silver mounted salts bottle, shaped as a horn with plain collar and cap and finial to the clear glass body, fitted with a suspension chain and belt clip, initialled.

3.75in (9.5cm) high

$400-600   CHEF

An early 18thC Continental silver folding spoon, contained in a fitted case, struck with two marks "CPD", "R", with engraved initials and sliding lock.

$800-1,200   **L&T**

An 18thC silver toasting fork, the scrolled trident below a cylindrical knopped and baluster stem with a shaped loop handle, sterling mark only, 5oz.

18.5in (47cm) long

$800-1,200   **CHEF**

Two late 18thC Boston silver spoons, bearing the touch mark of Paul Revere II, 3.9oz.

Paul Revere (1735-1818) was an silversmith, known for his role in the American revolution.

8.75in (22cm) long

$15,000-20,000   **POOK**

A William IV Scottish silver punch ladle, maker William Cunningham, with decorative floral border against a stippled ground with central initialed cartouche, inset with a gilt coin inscribed "Georgius II", wrythen whalebone handle, with marks for Edinburgh.

Popular legend associates coin-inset punch ladles such as this fine example, with the Jacobite cause as each serving presented an opportunity to 'drown' a Hanoverian monarch in the punch.

1830   *13.5in (34cm) long*

$2,500-3,500   **L&T**

A Victorian gilded christening set, by George Adams, stamped "Harry Emanuel Diamond & Pearl Merchant, 18 New Bond St", marks for London.

1863 & 1864

$3,000-4,000   **L&T**

A silver butter knife, with a cast double portrait of Classical warriors, marked sterling only, with "HW" monogram.

1865-80   *6.5in (16.5cm) long*

$80-120   **IHB**

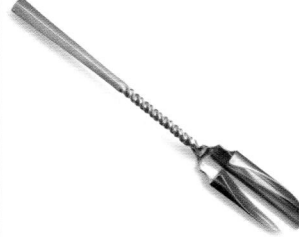

A silver cheese scoop, in the 'Aesthetic Twist #3' pattern, by the Whiting Mfg. Co. of NY,

1880-1900   *9in (23cm) long*

$120-180   **IHB**

A Victorian Scottish bannock fork, the handle of wrythen horn with a plain silver cap, the fork with four tines and ball knop, marks for Edinburgh.

1880   *20.5in (21cm) long*

$600-800   **L&T**

A set of six silver coffee spoons, each having engraved decorated handles, Birmingham hallmarks, cased.

1888

$80-120   **BIG**

A pair of silver sugar tongs, in an early repoussé pattern, with cast and chased claw grips, by S. Kirk & Son of Baltimore, MD.

1890-95   *5in (12.5cm) long*

$70-100   **IHB**

A silver butter pick, in the 'Berain' pattern, with corkscrew tip, by R. Wallace & Sons Mfg. Co. of Wallingford CT.

1907   *5.5in (14cm) long*

$30-40   **IHB**

A set of Norwegian silver gilt and enameled coffee spoons, with six spoons, sugar tongs and a tea strainer, with enamel detail, in a fitted case.

c1930

$800-1,200   **L&T**

A silver cheese fork, in the 'Love Disarmed' pattern, made by Reed & Barton of Taunton, MA.

c1975-2000   *6in (15cm) long*

$80-120   **IHB**

A silver salad fork and spoon, in the 'Versailles' pattern, by the Gorham Mfg. Co. of Providence, RI, with monogram.

9in (23cm) long

$300-400   **IHB**

A Russian Fabergé silver cake server, with shaped blade and plain tapered handle, initialled, and contained in a mahogany case with hinged lid.

12.75in (32.5cm) long

$2,000-3,000   **L&T**

A George III taperstick, by John Carter of London, with Neoclassical column.

1771   7in (18cm) high

$2,000-2,500   **WAL**

A pair of George III silver candlesticks, by John Café of London, of scrolling Rococo style with acanthus leaf detail, with date mark.

1788   9.75in (25cm) high

$3,500-4,500   **GAZE**

An 18th/19thC silver candlestick, decorated with spiral leaf festoons, relief floral decoration, maker's mark.

5.25in (13cm) high

$700-900   **KAU**

A silver chamberstick, by S. Kirk & Son of Baltimore, MD, with a socket riveted through quatrefoil flange and a folk floral design

1880   10.25in (26cm) long

$750-850   **IHB**

An early Victorian candelabra, by John Samuel Hunt, with marks for London.

1848   22.25in (56.5cm) high

$6,000-10,000   **L&T**

A pair of late 19thC Russian silver candlesticks, by A. Riedel, with fruiting vine decoration and foliate capped rusticated feet, with marks for Minsk.

1878   15.25in (39cm) high

$2,000-3,000   **L&T**

A Continental sterling silver large oil menorah, with an eagle finial, flanked by eight graduated outscrolling branches with covered oil font, 38oz.

c1900   18.25in (46.5cm) high

$2,000-3,000   **FRE**

A pair of Edwardian Adam style candlesticks, by Walker & Hall, with marks for Chester.

1906   12in (30cm) high

$2,000-3,000   **L&T**

One of a pair of early 20thC Continental eleven-light sterling silver candelabra, with domed foot and baluster stem.

15.5in (39.5cm) high

$3,500-4,000 PAIR   **FRE**

Three of a set of four Edwardian candlesticks, by Goldsmiths & Silversmiths Co. Ltd, with Corinthian capitals, London marks.

1910   9in (23cm) high

$2,500-3,500 SET   **L&T**

Three of a set of four candlesticks, with marks for London, maker's mark CAA. PRP, and stamped "TESSIERS, LONDON", 63oz.

1985   7in (18cm) high

$2,500-3,500 SET   **L&T**

METALWARE

A large 19thC Neoclassical style sterling silver vase, by Whiting & Co, New York, with swan's mask handles, embossed with a Greek warrior.

24.5in (62cm) high

$8,000-12,000   **FRE**

A George III sterling silver epergne, by Thomas Pitts, London, with foliate chased swag aprons, a pierced shaped oval basket and four conforming dishes, some damage and repairs.

1768   *38in (15in) high*

$30,000-40,000   **FRE**

A pair of late 18thC Russian silver filigree goat's head vases, after a design by Matthew Boulton, the tops reversible to become candleholders, the vase body flanked on either side by goat's heads and decorated with swags.

c1790-1800   *23.5cm (9.25in) high*

$40,000-45,000   **RGA**

A George III cruet, by Peter and Anne Bateman, with engraved silver collars and glass stoppers, with marks for London.

1792   *8.75in (22.5cm) high*

$1,500-2,500   **L&T**

A George III cruet, with a pair of mounted glass bottles and jars, marks for London, and maker's mark Rebecca Eames and Edward Barnard, 28oz.

1818   *11in (28cm) high*

$5,000-6,000   **L&T**

A George IV vase and cover, by John Bridge, one side with a winged angel and two figures, the other with applied armorial and motto "I AM READY", with marks for London.

1827   *15in (38cm) high*

$20,000-30,000   **L&T**

A rare 19thC French silver gilt table salt grinder, engraved with a Ducal coronet and initials, French control marks and no apparent maker's mark.

4.5in (11.5cm) high

$3,000-4,000   **L&T**

A Victorian sterling silver gilt four bottle decanter stand, by Robert Garrard, London, with baluster stem and intertwined scroll handle, and four decanters with engraved decoration, some minor chips to rims of bottles.

1852   *13.5in (34.5cm) high*

$18,000-22,000   **FRE**

A 19th-20thC sterling silver repoussé vase, with a scalloped flaring rim over a graduated relief floral and foliage decorated body on a circular base.

10.25in (26cm) high

$200-300   **FRE**

A pair of late 19th-early 20thC Austrian silver and cut crystal tazzas, retailed by L. Janesich, in flowerhead form, on tree stems and shaped bases bearing a coat of arms, surmounted by deer.

16.5in (42cm) high

$3,500-4,500   **FRE**

A German silver pineapple cup and cover, cast as a huntsman, with lobed and waisted base, the cover surmounted by a vase of flowers finial, 22.5oz.

16.5in (42cm) high

$2,000-3,000   **L&T**

A Continental silver cow creamer, naturalistically cast with foliate decorated hinged cover, and with import marks for London, 3.5oz.

1899   *3.25in (8cm) high*

$1,200-1,500   **L&T**

A 19th/20thC pair of Continental silver table ornaments, modelled as two pheasants, one with wings upraised, with bends to tail feathers and wings.

20in (51cm) long

$3,000-4,000   **FRE**

A large pair of silver game birds, with import marks for London, naturalistically cast.

1926   *Longest 15.25in (39cm) long*

$2,000-3,000   **L&T**

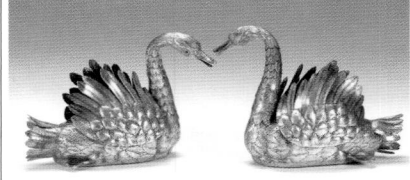

A pair of 20thC Portuguese silver swan centrepieces, by David Ferreira, cast with articulated necks, folding wings and glass eyes.

11.5in (29cm) high

$4,000-5,000   **FRE**

A German sterling silver bonbonnière fashioned as a swan, hinged pressed floral decorated and pierced wings on a lead crystal base, bears UK import marks, London hallmarks.

1958

$300-400   **BIG**

A silver cast model of a labrador, with marks for London, with realistically chased coat.

1970   *3.5in (9cm) high*

$800-1,200   **L&T**

A silver statuette of Francis Humberston MacKenzie, by Elkington & Co, cast with early 19thC full Regimental Highland dress uniform of the Seaforth Highlanders, with marks for Birmingham 1935.

Francis MacKenzie Humberston, or Francis Humberston MacKenzie, Baron Seaforth and MacKenzie (1754-1815), was hereditary clan chief of the MacKenzies. Despite being deaf and for a time dumb, Seaforth enjoyed a distinguished career as a military leader and politician.

1935   *14in (36cm) high*

$4,500-5,500   **L&T**

An ornamental model of a soldier, naturalistically cast and mounted on a green hardstone square base, with marks for London, maker's mark "PCMA".

1987   *7in (18cm) high*

$500-600   **L&T**

An ornamental model of a regimental piper, naturalistically cast and mounted on a green hardstone square base, with marks for London, maker's mark "PCMA".

1987   *6.25in (15.5cm) high*

$600-1,000   **L&T**

METALWARE

A George III silver wine funnel, with reeded borders, monogrammed, makers mark "I.C." and London hallmarks.

1787 *4.75in (12cm) high*

$600-800 **SWO**

A Georgian Scottish silver wine funnel, with rubbed marks for Edinburgh, maker's mark "IH", with reeded borders and stylized floral thumb-piece, 3.5oz.

The stylized floral thumb-piece, seen to the lower strainer part of this wine funnel, resembles the symbolic Jacobite Rose, decoratively employed to represent the House of Stuart. This motif was discreetly used to support the Jacobite cause and was often accompanied by a rose bud representing the Old and Young Pretenders to the throne.

c1819 *5.25in (13.5cm) high*

$1,200-1,800 **L&T**

LEFT A George IV Scottish wine funnel, by J McKay, with well chased fruiting vine decoration, the spout with engraved crest and motto, and marks for Edinburgh, 3oz.

1821 *5.25in (13.5cm) high*

$1,500-2,000 **L&T**

RIGHT A Victorian wine funnel, with marked pull-out strainer, and Gothic style engraving, marks for London, and maker's mark Joseph and John Angel, 4oz.

1848 *6.25in (16cm) high*

$1,600-2,200 **L&T**

A matched pair of Victorian bottle holders, by Charles Stuart Harris, with a crest for PHILLIPS of Shropshire, and marks for London 1896 and 1899, 18oz.

4.25in (11cm) high

$2,000-3,000 **L&T**

A William IV Irish silver crumb brush, with an S-shaped scroll frame with repoussé worked acanthus decoration and a plain handle, Dublin assay.

c1835

$150-300 **BIG**

A late Victorian silver paper knife, with marks for Edinburgh, maker ?H, designed as a miniature broadsword, with quatrefoil and S-pierced and engraved basket hilt, with scarlet cloth liner, 2oz.

The 'S' incorporated into the pierced basket form hilt may be intended to commemorate the Stuart cause, or to refer to Stirling, a center renowned for sword manufacturing.

1895 *10.25in (26cm) long*

$2,000-3,000 **L&T**

A silver blotter, with tooled knop fashioned as a smiling face on plain rectangular base, with London hallmarks.

c1900

$150-250 **BIG**

A silver mounted skean dhu, with marks for Edinburgh, maker's mark "RWF", also stamped "RW Forsyth Ltd, Glasgow & Edinburgh", single fuller blade, the silver mounts cast with Celtic strapwork, with thistle carved cairngorm pommel, contained in a leather scabbard, crested.

1918 *9in (23cm) long*

$3,500-4,500 **L&T**

A Scottish silver dish ring, by Brook & Son, with glass liner and cartouche crested and inscribed "LUX TUA VITA MEA", with marks for Edinburgh.

1922 *7in (17.5cm) diam*

$1,500-2,500 **L&T**

An Edwardian caster, with pierced domed cover, and marks for London, maker's mark rubbed, 13oz.

1904 *8.5in (22cm) high*

$300-400 **L&T**

A pair of captain's calipers/dividers, with engraved floral design, marked to one leg "I.A, thistle, b, thistle".

6.5in (17cm) long

$3,500-4,500 **L&T**

A Scottish Provincial gilt key, by A & J Smith, from Aberdeen, the gilt key with a saltire to the handle, marked "A&JS ABDN" (in one rectangular punch).

4.25in (10.5cm) long

$400-600 **L&T**

SILVER PLATE

- Silver was hugely popular in the 18th century and cheaper alternatives were sought.
- In 1742 Thomas Boulsover discovered the technique of fusing copper and silver using heat. Sheets of fused metal could be shaped to form objects.
- Old Sheffield plate was used from the 1750s to c1840. Pieces were often made in a number of sections and joining seams can sometimes be found running down the centre of objects.
- Plated wear has usually been replated as the original plate would be worn away by handling and polishing.
- Electroplating was introduced by Elkington and Co. in the 1830s and soon replaced Old Sheffield plate. The technique involved depositing a thin layer of pure silver onto a base metal using an electric current.
- Generally electroplated items can appear brighter than Old Sheffield plate as they are covered in a layer of pure silver.

A Victorian silver-plated folding biscuit stand.

8.75in (22cm) high

$100-200   **SWO**

A Victorian Elkington & Co electroplate wine cooler bucket, with twin swing handles, the sides decorated with classical bacchanalian relief, the frieze with a band of fruiting vines, raised on entwined dolphin supports.

c1860   11.25in (28.5cm) high

$2,000-3,000   **FRE**

A CLOSER LOOK AT AN OLD SHEFFIELD PLATE CANDELABRA

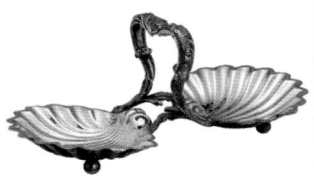

A 19thC silver-plated shell bowl, the two sections united by a rocaille handle.

16in (40cm) long

$120-180   **KAU**

A Victorian electroplate mounted horn centerpiece, designed as a cornucopia, with putto surmount to the cover, and a cast hippocampus.

29in (74cm) high

$2,500-3,500   **L&T**

Old Sheffield plate was introduced c1740 and was made from a fusion of silver and copper.

The candelabra can be identified as Old Sheffield Plate by the lip to the interior of the sconces where the plating joins. After c1840, plating was smoothly built up in sheets.

Decorative balls on Old Sheffield plate pieces were often made in two halves – breathe heavily on the piece to see if a seam can be detected.

18thC Candelabras often have two lights, sometimes with a third 'dummy light' or decorative knop to the centre to balance the appearance. After c1805, three lights are much more common.

A pair of late 18thC George II Old Sheffield plate candelabra.

c1795   15in (38cm) high

$2,000-3,000 PAIR   **WAL**

A pair of Victorian Mappin Bros. plated candelabra, with ram's head decoration.

1870   15.75in (40cm) high

$3,500-4,500 PAIR   **WAL**

An Old Sheffield Plate tray, by Waterhouse Hatfield & Co, with central engraved armorial inscribed "PRO LIBERTATE PATRIAE", on four scroll cast feet.

Motto translates as "FOR THE LIBERTY OF MY COUNTRY".

c1886   29.5in (75cm) wide

$3,000-4,000   **L&T**

An unusual early 20thC silver plated champagne cooler, of campana urn form, with a swivel galleried tray and scroll handles, on a socle base with casters, lacks liner.

21.5in (54.5cm) high

$1,200-1,500   FRE

A late 19thC silver-plated jug, with floral rim and scroll handle.

10in (25cm) high

$120-180   KAU

A late 19thC Victorian silver plated revolving supper set, by Mappin & Webb, London, with a soup tureen, and four outer covered entree dishes and casters.

33.25in (84.5cm) wide

$2,800-3,200   FRE

An Old Sheffield Plate teapot on stand, with bright engraved borders and carved ivory finial, the stand with gadrooned border on four pad feet.

7.5in (19cm) high

$450-350   L&T

A pair of plated silver magnum wine coolers, with lion mask capped ring handles, detachable rims and inner liners, crested, with Hamilton & Inches box.

7.5in (19cm) high

$600-800   L&T

An early 20thC silver plated revolving supper set, with four bakelite turned handles, with covered tureen, four entrée dishes, four blue-glass-lined salts and four Georgian-style casters.

21.5in (54.5cm) high

$1,200-1,800   FRE

A pair of Old Sheffield plate circular wine coasters, of fluted form raised on a barrow of rustic design.

19.25in (49cm) long

$800-1,200   L&T

A set of six Corinthian column Queen's plate candlesticks, by Mappin Brothers, each of circular form on stepped square bases.

4.5in (11cm) high

$800-1,200   L&T

A large silver plated table centerpiece, cast as two stags beneath a fruiting vine, on a petal shaped base with foliate cast border.

18.5in (47cm) high

$1,200-1,800   L&T

A highly unusual 'Roller Skate' plated cruet set designed by William Hutton & Sons, supported on turned wooden wheels and having straps for handle and divisions for the hob nail decorated glass vessels, marked "WH & S".

7in (18cm) high

$800-1,200   JN

A 15thC English Gothic brass candlestick with three knops and circular base.

9.5in (24cm) high

$4,500-5,500   **POOK**

An 18thC iron candle holder, on a lozenge shaped base and four cambered legs.

17.5in (44cm) high

$350-450   **WDL**

A George III pierced brass dog collar, inscribed 'I AND MONT 1793', includes padlock, no key.

4.5in (11.5cm) diam

$6,000-10,000   **L&T**

A pewter plate, of circular form with plain rim, struck with the Laughlin touch "#309", used by Thomas Badger Jr of Boston, MA.

1800-25   *8.5in (21.5cm) diam*

$250-350   **IHB**

A rare set of ten early 19thC bushel measures.

450-550   **MUR**

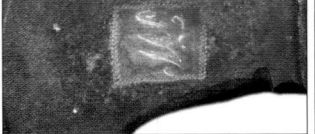

A rare wrought iron pole axe head, dated, with inlaid brass plaque, initialled "JW".

1818   *6.5in (16.5cm) long*

$10,000-15,000   **POOK**

A rare Berks County, Pennsylvania wriggled tin coffee pot, dated, signed "W. Shade", the base inscribed "Catharenah Kline".

1848   *11.25in (28.5cm) high*

$7,500-8,500   **POOK**

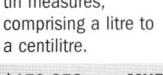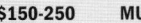

A set of seven 19thC tin measures, comprising a litre to a centilitre.

$150-250   **MUR**

A 19thC cast iron painted trade sign, in the form of a cow and scroll work.

$1,800-2,200   **FRE**

A gold-mounted horn snuff mull, with scroll and animal cast collar, and hinged cover pierced and decorated above a female nude.

4.25in (11cm) long

$2,000-3,000   **L&T**

An English Pewter lidded jug, heart-shaped motifs to body, stamped "0279, Rd421109".

7.25in (18.5cm) high

$80-120   **GAZE**

A pair of painted spelter figures of opposing gentlemen fencers, after L. Raphael, one with rapier, the other pulling on a glove, on square bases and ebonised wooden plinths.

18in (46cm) high

$800-1,200   **L&T**

TALL CASE CLOCKS

A 17thC important ebony-veneered tall case clock, by Johannes Fromanteel, London, the silvered chapter ring signed "Johannes Fromanteel London", the movement with an eight-day internal countwheel striking on a bell, associated case.

71in (182cm) high

$15,000-20,000   **SHA**

A walnut-veneered oak marquetry tall case clock, by Jonathan Lowndes, Pall Mall, London, with the movement by Joseph Knibb.

c1675   *79in (201cm) high*

$70,000-90,000   **RGA**

A William & Mary marquetry tall case clock, by John Berry, London, the brass dial signed "John Berry London", inscribed "Not Chime/Chimes", eight-day grande sonnerie movement, countwheel quarter chiming and rack striking on six bells.

94.5in (240cm) high

$50,000-60,000   **SHA**

A Queen Anne floral marquetry walnut eight-day tall case clock, by Thomas Hickson London, the case has cross grain moldings and marquetry.

c1710   *83in (211.5cm) high*

$50,000-60,000   **RGA**

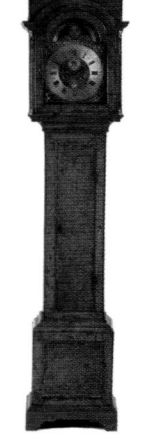

An 18thC Pennsylvania Queen Anne walnut and cherry tall case clock, with eight-day movement, signed, "John Fisher Yorktown".

90in (229cm) high

$5,000-7,000   **POOK**

A late 18thC oak and mahogany crossbanded eight-day tall case clock, by Tobias Fletcher, Barnsley, the twin-train movement with anchor escapement striking on a bell.

87in (221cm) high

$1,500-2,000   **L&T**

A Queen Anne walnut tall case clock, Chester County, Pennsylvania, eight-day brass works with brass face, inscribed "Joshua Humphreys, Charlestown".

c1750   *105in (266.5cm) high*

$35,000-45,000   **POOK**

A fine 18thC burr elm cased eight-day tall case clock, by Thomas Ogden, Halifax, the twin-train movement with anchor escapement, the arched brass dial with painted moon phase.

Thomas Ogden, famed Quaker clockmaker, was known for his unusual cases.

95in (241cm) high

$30,000-35,000   **L&T**

A rare late 18thC walnut tall case clock, Chester County Pennsylvania, attributed to the shop of Isaac Thomas, with a broken arch bonnet over a door enclosing a moon phase movement above a door with carved shell on a base supported by turned feet.

96in (244cm) high

$15,000-20,000   **POOK**

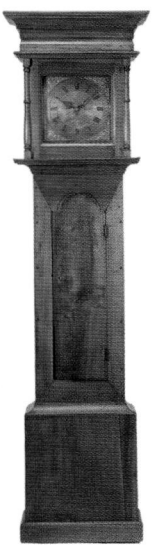

An 18thC walnut tall case clock, by Joseph Wills, Philadelphia, moulded cornice on hood with turned columnettes and glazed door opening to brass dial inscribed "Joseph Wills," tombstone waist door, plinth with molded base.

83in (211cm) high

$7,000-8,000   **FRE**

An 18thC George III walnut tall case clock, with eight-day movement, the brass dial with subsidiary second dial silent and strike, dial signed "Thomas Hill, London".

84in (210cm) high

$2,200-2,800   **FRE**

An 18thC Pennsylvania walnut tall case clock, with broken arch bonnet enclosing an eight-day movement, over case with carved quarter columns on bracket feet.

95in (241cm) high

$12,000-18,000   **POOK**

An 18thC mahogany musical tall case clock, by J. Barns, London, the twin-train movement striking quarters and half on eight bells and hours on one bell.

Many Barns are recorded, stylistically the spandrels are similar to those illustrated in Brian Loome's book indicating 1760-85.

c1770   *96.5in (245cm) high*

$6,000-10,000   **L&T**

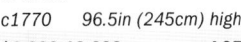

A Philadelphia Queen Anne walnut tall case clock, with sarcophagus shaped top, brass face, signed "George Miller Germantown" with straight case on ogee bracket feet.

c1770   *99in (251cm) high*

$20,000-30,000   **POOK**

A Lancaster County, Pennsylvania Chippendale walnut tall case clock, with brass face works inscribed "Christian Forrer Lampeter".

c1770   *95in (241cm) high*

$30,000-40,000   **POOK**

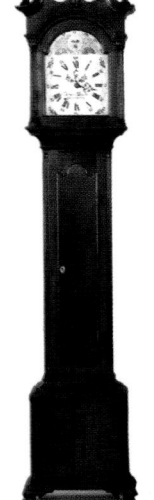

A rare Boston Chippendale mahogany musical tall case clock, dial inscribed "High Water at Boston North America" with three train works with moon phases and seven-tune mechanism.

c1770   *103in (261cm) high*

$25,000-35,000   **POOK**

A Chippendale walnut tall case clock, Pennsylvania, the white painted 30-hour works, inscribed "Johonns Murphy Northampton Co.".

c1775   *96.5in (245cm) high*

$7,000-9,000   **POOK**

A Chippendale walnut tall case clock, Bucks County, Pennsylvania, with white painted face and eight-day works, inscribed "Benjamin Morris, Hilltown", retaining its original dry finish.

c1780   *94in (239cm) high*

$9,000-11,000   **POOK**

A Federal mahogany inlaid tall clock, attributed to Simon Willard, the inlaid base with eagle, shield, and stars, an eight-day brass time-and-strike movement and date and moon's age dials, restoration.

c1800   *90.5in (230cm) high*

$20,000-30,000   **SK**

TALL CASE CLOCKS

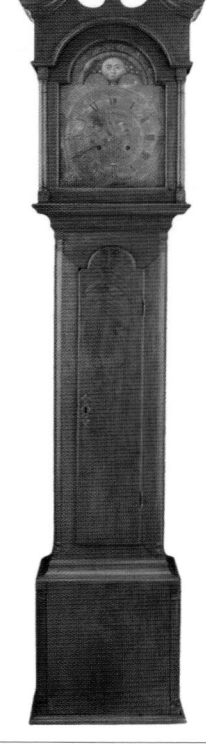

A walnut tall case clock, by Jacob Godshalk, Philadelphia, broken arch cresting with twin roundels, twin engaged columns, brass dial signed by maker, painted moon phase calendar dial, arched cock-beaded pendulum door, feet removed and base molding applied, replaced finials.

89in (226cm) high

$22,000-28,000   **AAC**

A Chippendale walnut tall case clock, Daniel Rose, Reading, PA, brass face has phases of the moon and four season spandrels, signed "Daniel Rose Reading", engraved with two phoenix birds.

c1780   93.5in (237.5cm) high

$22,000-28,000   **FRE**

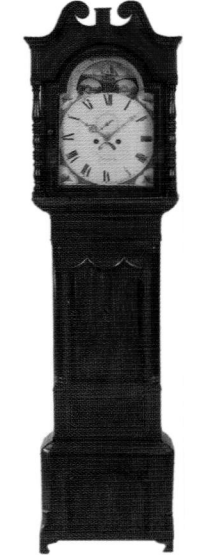

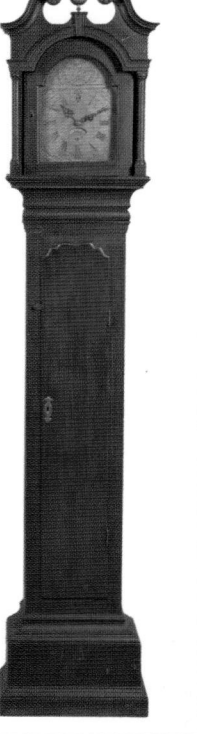

A George III mahogany and oak eight-day tall case clock, possibly by John Beechard, Newcastle, the twin-train movement with anchor escapement.

84.5in (211cm) high

$1,500-2,500   **L&T**

A late 18thC George III mahogany tall case clock, with brass musical eight-day works, signed "Jane Pepper Biggles Wade".

101in (256.5cm) high

$12,000-18,000   **POOK**

A late 18thC inlaid walnut tall case clock, by Samuel Breneiser, Reading, the arched door opens to enameled moon phase face decorated with signs of Zodiac, line inlaid throughout.

94.25in (239.5cm) high

$18,000-22,000   **FRE**

A late 18thC diminutive cherry carved tall case clock, by William Crawford, Oakham, Massachusetts, brass weight-driven movement with drop strike.

According to a letter written in 1934 by the Town Clerk of Oakham, the clockmaker "marched as Sergeant of the Oakham Company, when it responded to the alarm of July 23, 1773, from Rhode Island, and also Sergeant on the alarm of Aug 20 1777, from Bennington. He has also credit for a campaign to Boston, beginning April 1, 1778."

83in (207.5cm) high

$30,000-40,000   **SK**

A George III mahogany eight-day tall case clock, by John Gibson, Edinburgh, the twin train movement with anchor escapement, the brass arched dial with strike/silent dial.

83.5in (209cm) high

$3,000-4,000 **L&T**

A late 18thC walnut tall case clock, Jacob Godshalk, Towamencin Township, Montgomery County, brass face with Roman numeral and Arabic numeral double chapter ring, calendar window, face refinished, later feet.

81.5in (207cm) high

$10,000-15,000 **FRE**

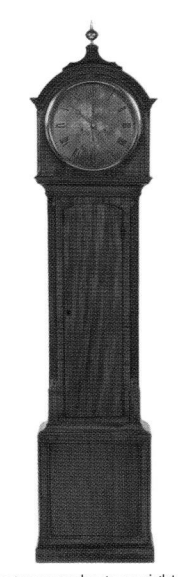

A Regency mahogany eight-day tall case clock, by Green, Edinburgh, the twin train movement with anchor escapement.

79.5in (199cm) high

$4,000-6,000 **L&T**

A late 18thC New Hampshire cherry carved tall case clock, by Stephen Hasham, eight-day brass weight driven movement, with an engraved brass silvered dial showing moon phases, applied chapter ring engraved "S.Hasham", refinished.

94in (239cm) high

$7,000-10,000 **SK**

A late 18thC Pennsylvania walnut tall case clock, with broken arch bonnet enclosing thirty-hour movement, signed "John Heinselman".

89in (226cm) high

$8,000-12,000 **POOK**

A Chippendale applewood tall case clock, Pennsylvania, the broken arch bonnet enclosing an eight-day works with painted dial, inscribed "Thom Lindsey, Frankford".

c1790   97in (246.5cm)

$10,000-15,000 **POOK**

A George III mahogany eight-day tall case clock, by Matthew Lyon, Lanark, the twin-train movement with anchor escapement.

84in (210cm) high

$3,000-4,000 **L&T**

A cherrywood tall case clock, works by Thomas Norton, Philadelphia, painted face with red rose sprays, Roman and Arabic numeral chapter ring, subsidiary Arabic seconds chapter ring, rising sun, some damage.

The case interior inscribed in chalk with dates of cleaning and repair from 1792 to 1860, the largest signed by "John Pittman Oct. 16, 1822".

c1800

$15,000-20,000 **FRE**

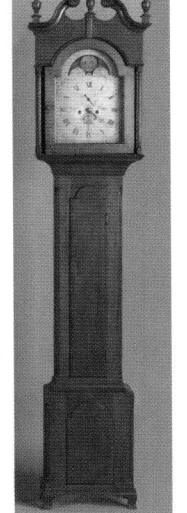

A late 18thC walnut tall case clock, with broken arch bonnet enclosing an eight-day movement with painted dial signed, "Daniel Oyster, Reading".

101in (257cm) high

$10,000-12,000 **POOK**

A George III mahogany eight-day tall case clock, by William Scott, the twin-train movement with anchor escapement, the dial with subsidiary seconds and date aperture.

89.25in (223cm) high

$2,500-3,500 **L&T**

A George III oak eight-day tall case clock, by Walker, Louth, the twin train movement with anchor escapement.

86.5in (216cm) high

$2,500-3,500 **L&T**

TALL CASE CLOCKS

An 18thC George III japanned tall case clock, the later japanned case with a molded cornice on a plinth base, with silvered dial and three subsidiary dials signed "Robert Wyatt, Paradise Row, Chelsea".

85in (216cm) high

$2,800-3,200   **FRE**

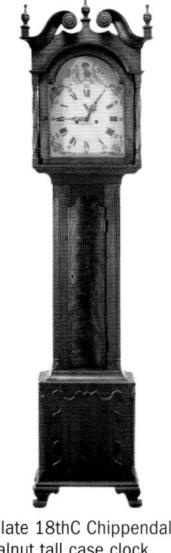

A late 18thC Chippendale walnut tall case clock, Pennsylvania, the case with fluted quarter columns, double arched door with shaped panel, and ogee molded feet.

70.5in (179cm) high

$3,500-4,500   **FRE**

An applewood tall case clock, painted face displaying the phases of the moon, Arabic chapter ring with date crescent above and seconds subsidiary chapter ring.

c1790 101in (256.5cm)

$10,000-15,000   **FRE**

A late 18thC Pennsylvania walnut tall case clock, with broken arch bonnet enclosing an eight-day movement with painted dial.

96in (244cm) high

$7,500-8,500   **POOK**

A mahogany tall case clock, the case attributed to Matthew Egerton Jr., New Jersey, eight-day works with moon phase, case inlaid with urn, conch shell, and eagle.

c1795   96.5in (245cm)

$28,000-32,000   **POOK**

A walnut tall case clock, Pennsylvania, white painted face and eight-day works, inscribed "George Faber, Sumnytown".

c1800 96in (244cm) high

$5,500-6,500   **POOK**

A poplar tall case clock, Pennsylvania, the 30-hour works with painted face, signed "Pr. Miller", over a case with fluted quarter columns supported by ogee bracket feet.

c1800 94in (239cm) high

$4,000-5,000   **POOK**

A Federal mahogany inlaid tall case clock, by Aaron Willard, Boston, the dial lettered "A. Willard".

c1800   92in (233.5cm)

$50,000-60,000   **SK**

A George III mahogany tall case clock, with eight-day musical works, case with arched door, fluted quarter columns with brass plinths and capitals, inlaid base, and straight bracket feet.

c1800   95.75in (243cm)

$8,500-9,500   **POOK**

An early 19thC walnut tall case clock, Pennsylvania, painted face with phases of the moon, with calendar crescent and floral corners, on recessed paneled base of tiger maple with star inlay.

105in (267cm) high

$22,000-28,000   **FRE**

A Federal mahogany tall case clock, with a double scroll cresting with inlaid rosettes, three urn and spire finials, painted face displaying phases of the moon, Arabic chapter ring.

c1800   98in (249cm)

$15,000-20,000   **FRE**

A Berks County Chippendale walnut tall case clock, with eight-day painted dial works, on case with quarter column and applied tulip form panel.

c1800   96in (244cm)

$5,500-6,500   **POOK**

An early 19thC paint decorated tall case clock, J. & H. Twiss, Montreal, Canada, the dial lettered "J. & H. Twiss, Montreal", and wooden weight-driven movement, signed on the door "Alf. Lortie 1922, archt...".

82in (205cm) high

$8,000-12,000 SK

An early 19thC oak 30-hour tall case clock, by W** Tyler, Hinckley, with a cut down box plinth, the four pillar Clerkenwell-type mechanism with anchor escapement and count wheel bell strikes.

80.75in (205cm) high

$1,000-1,500 BIG

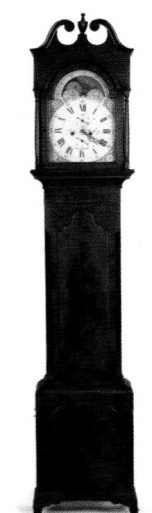

An early 19thC Philadelphia Federal mahogany tall case clock, with eight-day works, signed "David Weatherley Philadelphia".

97.25in (247cm) high

$12,000-18,000 POOK

An early 19thC mahogany eight-day tall case clock, the twin train movement with anchor escapement, indistinctly signed, "Young, Dundee".

84.25in (214cm) high

$4,000-6,000 L&T

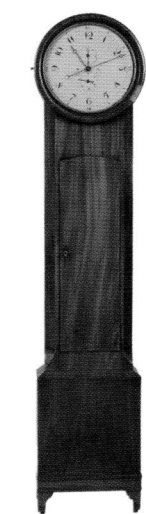

A Regency mahogany eight-day tall case clock, the twin train movement with anchor escapement, the painted dial with subsidiary seconds and date dials.

83.25in (208cm) high

$1,500-2,000 L&T

A New Jersey Federal mahogany inlaid tall case clock, with brass eight-day weight-driven movement, refinished.

c1810   *95in (237.5cm)*

$15,500-16,500 SK

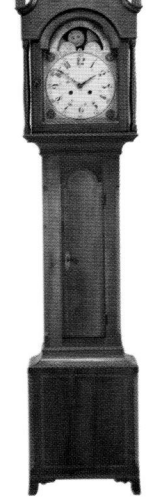

An early 19thC stained mahogany eight-day tall case clock, the twin-train movement with anchor escapement striking on a bell, dial indicating High Water in Leith.

90.5in (230cm) high

$6,000-10,000 L&T

An early 19thC Federal inlaid cherry tall case clock, Pennsylvania, the swan's neck pediment with carved rosettes above arched door, painted moon phase face, turned columnnettes.

96.25in (244.5cm) high

$8,000-12,000 FRE

An early 19thC walnut tall case clock, Pennsylvania, painted face shows moon phases, Arabic numeral chapter ring with subsidiary seconds and date crescent.

97.5in (247.5cm) high

$15,000-20,000 FRE

An early 19thC cherrywood tall case clock, Pennsylvania, the face shows moon phases, Arabic numeral chapter ring with a subsidiary seconds chapter ring, date crescent and mounted with an oval brass monogram plate "BM".

95in (241cm) high

$5,000-6,000 FRE

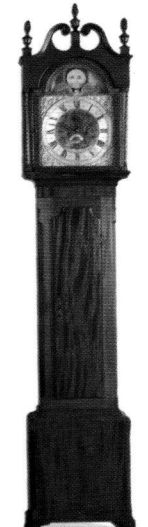

An early 19thC Pennsylvania Federal mahogany tall case clock, with broken arch bonnet enclosing an eight-day movement with brass dial.

95in (241cm) high

$4,500-5,500 POOK

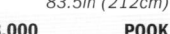

A mahogany band-inlaid tall case clock, by John G. Schmid, Philadelphia, the painted face displaying phases of the moon and fruit corners, Roman numeral chapter ring.

c1820   91in (231cm) high

$3,500-4,500   **FRE**

A George IV mahogany tall case clock, with a silver chapter ring, subsidiary second dials and date aperture, the dial signed "Dan Tribe, Portsmouth".

c1820   82in (208.5cm) high

$3,000-4,000   **FRE**

A Federal mahogany tall case clock, Massachusetts, the broken arch bonnet enclosing an eight-day works with white painted face, inscribed "Ezra Batchelder, Danvers".

c1825   83.5in (212cm)

$7,000-8,000   **POOK**

A fancy painted pine tall case clock, by Silas Houdley, Plymouth, Connecticut, dial with "S. HOADLEY PLYMOUTH", with thirty-hour wooden weight-driven movement.

c1825   90in (225cm) high

$12,000-18,000   **SK**

A paint-decorated tall case clock, by Riley Whiting, Connecticut, the dial with Masonic devices, with wooden weight-driven movement, with some restoration.

c1825   85in (216cm) high

$6,000-8,000   **SK**

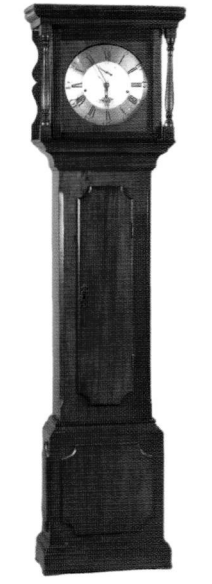

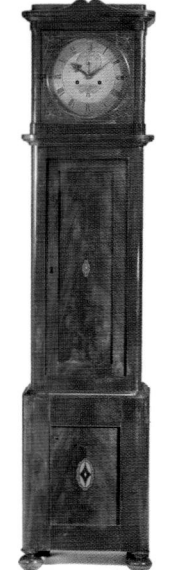

A 19thC Pennsylvania mahogany and pine tall case clock, with thirty-hour movement, painted dial inscribed, "Joseph Blumer".

90in (229cm) high

$2,500-3,500   **POOK**

A 19thC walnut tall case clock, Pennsylvania, enclosing a musical works, brass dial signed "John Gelston Belfast", over a case with canted stiles.

85in (216cm) high

$4,000-5,000   **POOK**

A 19thC cherrywood mahogany finished tall case clock, by Peter Miller, Lynn Township, PA, with moon phases, Arabic numeral chapter ring, subsidiary seconds chapter ring, date movement.

97in (246.5cm) high

$5,000-6,000   **FRE**

A 19thC Continental mahogany and inlaid tall case clock, the associated dial signed "William Smith, London", with subsidiary second dial, date aperture and eight-day movement.

83in (207.5cm) high

$2,000-3,000   **FRE**

A 19thC Pennsylvania Federal walnut tall case clock, with broken arch bonnet with thirty-hour movement signed, "Thomas Plymouth".

99in (251cm) high

$2,500-3,000   **POOK**

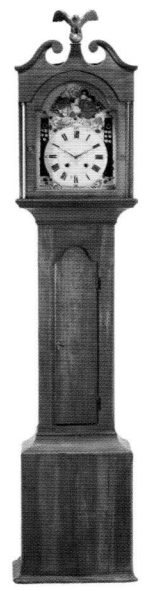
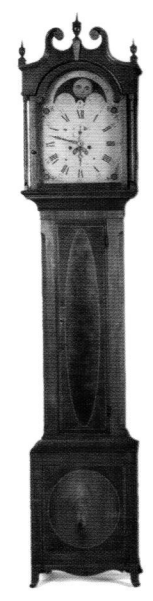

A 19thC cherry tall case clock, the swan's neck pediment centring a plinth with eagle, floral-painted faced, arched waist door, squared plinth, molded base.

$1,200-1,800 FRE

A 19thC Delaware Valley Hepplewhite-style walnut tall case clock, with eight-day movement, broken arch bonnet with star rosettes over a glazed tombstone door.

100in (254cm) high

$8,500-9,500 POOK

A 19thC Maryland Hepplewhite mahogany tall case clock, with flat top bonnet, grapevine inlay enclosing an eight-day movement over an inlaid case.

96in (244cm) high

$7,000-8,000 POOK

A late 19thC Louis XVI-style kingwood tall case clock, the twin train movement with circular white enameled dial with Roman and Arabic chapters, hood with cast and gilt metal figure of Father Time, raised on massive cast paw feet.

89in (226cm) high

$30,000-40,000 L&T

A late 19thC Victorian carved oak tall case clock, the brass dial with silvered chapter ring, subsidiary second dial and an eight-day movement.

102in (255cm) high

$4,500-5,500 FRE

A late 19thC American walnut and marquetry tall case clock, with tiered case decorated with figures and elaborate scrollwork with turned columns.

89in (226cm) high

$1,800-2,200 POOK

A late 19thC Philadelphia mahogany tall case clock, by J.E. Caldwell & Co., with musical brass faced works in elaborately carved case.

99in (251cm) high

$4,500-5,500 POOK

A mahogany tall case clock, by J.E. Caldwell & Co., with a brass face works by Elliot, London and an elaborately carved case.

c1900 97in (246cm)

$10,000-15,000 POOK

A Neoclassical-style mahogany tall case clock, by Elliot of London, with gilt metal blind fret moon face dial, three subsidiary dials and chiming eight-day movement.

c1900 98.5in (250cm)

$7,500-8,500 FRE

A 20thC Pennsylvania folk art tall case clock, with musical mechanism moving a carved carousel in the top section.

89in (226cm) high

$9,000-11,000 POOK

CLOCKS

A Regency rosewood bracket clock, with an acorn finial, white painted convex dial, the sides with twin fruiting basket and loop cast handles, raised on brass ball feet.

c1820   14in (35cm) high

$1,500-2,000   **FRE**

A late Victorian oak-cased eight-day bracket clock, by Mackay and Chisholm, Edinburgh, the twin train fusee movement with anchor escapement striking on a bell and gong.

26.7in (68cm) high

$2,000-3,000   **L&T**

A late 19thC Tiffany & Co. oak case bracket clock, with eight-day chiming movement, two subsidiary dials, slow/fast and silent/chime.

20in (51cm) high

$4,000-5,000   **FRE**

A George III style mahogany and marquetry inlaid bracket clock, with enamel dial, arched case flanked by fluted quarter columns.

c1910   18in (45.5cm) high

$500-600   **FRE**

An unusual George III mahogany bracket regulator, the single train fusee movement with anchor escapement, the hours indicated by sun and moon dial with cottage and ship, the lower half of the dial painted with castle in a landscape.

18.5in (46cm) high

$15,000-20,000   **L&T**

MANTEL CLOCKS

An early 19thC ebony veneered mantel clock, the twin train fusee movement with an engraved steel dial enclosed by foliate scroll spandrels.

13in (33cm) high

$3,500-4,500   **L&T**

A French Empire gilt brass mantel clock, with twin train movement, the case with Classical maiden and a winged boy playing a lyre.

22in (56cm) high

$3,500-4,500   **L&T**

A Neoclassical French cast-brass and mercury-gilded mantel clock, with eight-day striking timepiece with an image of George Washington, on a brass molded base on bun feet, made for the American market, imperfections.

c1810

20in (51cm) high

$75,000-85,000   **SK**

A Neoclassical cast-brass and mercury-gilded mantel clock, made for the American market by Dubuc, Paris, with an eight-day spring-powered clockwork, figure of George Washington on a plinth inscribed "E PLURIBUS UNUM", dial inscribed "Dubuc Rue Michel-le-Comte No. 33A, Paris," swag below reading "WASHINGTON First in WAR, First in PEACE, First in the HEARTS of his COUNTRYMEN," retains gilt, imperfections.

George Washington is dressed in the uniform he wore while commander-in-chief of the military, holding his resignation that he offered to the United States Congress on December 23, 1783. The stance is derived from Trumbull's portrait of Washington at the Battle of Trenton.

c1810   15.5in (39.5cm) high

$35,000-45,000   SK

A French Empire gilt bronze figural clock, depicting the figure of Beauty stung by Cupid, signed "Deniere & Matelin", gilt worn in areas, minor chips.

c1820   22in (56cm) high

$5,000-6,000   FRE

A Charles X gilt bronze mantel clock, engine-turned dial, a flowering basket and butterflies, flanked by an amphora and classical draped maiden with dog.

17in (42.5cm) high

$2,000-3,000   FRE

A rare Norristown, Pennsylvania mahogany pillar and scroll clock, with broken arch bonnet over eight-day works with painted face, signed "J.D. Custer Norristown" supported on carved animal paw feet.

c1835   38in (97cm) high

$50,000-60,000   POOK

A gilt bronze automaton clock, by J.F. Houdin, with a Chinese magician, the dial marked "J F Houdin, Paris", automaton movement engraved "Invente et Execute a la Fabrique D'Horlogerie, J F Houdin Rue Vielle de Temple No. 78 A Paris, 1836".

18in (45cm) high

$25,000-30,000   SWO

A 19thC German gilt bronze figural clock, with enameled dial, flanked by a scholar, signed "4 PH Mourey 71", and "Conrad Felsing Berlin" numbered 2357.

15.25in (38.5cm) high

$1,500-2,500   FRE

A 19thC pollard oak eight-day mantel clock, by Viner, London, the twin train fusee movement with anchor escapement striking on a gong, inscribed to rear "Viner, 235 Regent Street, London", adjustable pendulum.

8.75in (22cm) high

$10,000-15,000   L&T

A 19thC French Empire gilt bronze mantel clock, the engine turned dial with a white enamel chapter ring, case with wheat sheaf and a soldier and weapon trophy, the base inscribed "Honneur et Patrie".

13in (32.5cm) high

$1,800-2,200   FRE

A 19thC French bisque porcelain clock, the enamel dial with Roman numerals, the columnar support flanked by the Three Graces, with relief-decorated panels.

27in (68.5cm) high

$8,000-10,000   FRE

A 19thC French Neoclassical style bronze and Sienna marble clock, with gilt engine turned dial, raised on a stepped Sienna marble base with applied mounts.

24in (61cm) high

$3,500-4,500   FRE

A 19thC gilt brass clock and barometer set, each with silvered circular glazed dial in case fashioned as a ship's wheel on waisted scrolling paneled support and plinth base.

13.5in (34.5cm) high

$4,000-5,000   L&T

A Napoleon III cameo-mounted gilt bronze mantel clock, with engine turned dial signed "Aubert & Co. Regent St. London", and domed case set with profile portraits of classical gods and goddesses.

c1860   18in (45.5cm) high

$2,500-3,000   FRE

A Louis XV-style gilt bronze and marble mantel clock, by Henri Boudebine, with two draped beauties, applied mounts and a central cartouche, on toupie feet, signed "H. Boudebine, Paris".

c1880   *39in (99cm) high*

$22,000-28,000   **FRE**

One of a matched pair of late Victorian walnut Davidson's patent memorandum clocks, by J. Barrie & Sons, Edinburgh, urn lid opens to memorandum mechanism with instructions, one clock with two bone message tablets, the other lacking brass baskets to top.

14.5in (37cm) high

$1,500-2,000 PAIR   **L&T**

A late 19thC French gilt and silvered bronze figural mantel clock, with cornucopias and swags, stamped "Charpentier, Ft de Bronzes 495, A. Paris", no key, areas of loss.

20.5in (52cm) high

$7,500-8,500   **FRE**

A late 19thC Louis XV-style gilt bronze clock, dial signed "Ferdinand Gervais, Paris", surmounted by cupid, with an ornate Rococo scroll base.

15.5in (39cm) high

$1,800-2,200   **FRE**

A late 19thC French gilt bronze and champlevé enamel clock, by Japy Frères, Paris, with white enamel dial, four pilasters on the shaped case with berry finials, on toupie feet.

15in (38cm) high

$2,000-3,000   **FRE**

A late 19thC French marble and gilt bronze clock, in the Turkish taste, with column supports and a crescent moon finial, the works stamped "AD Mougin Deux M'edailles".

22in (56cm) high

$2,000-3,000   **FRE**

A late 19thC Louis XIV-style gilt bronze clock, embossed dial, the case with applied and chased decoration, surmounted by Pallas Athena, the apron decorated with drapery.

25.75in (64cm) high

$2,000-3,000   **FRE**

A late 19thC Louis XV-style gilt bronze and marble mantel clock, the white enamel dial with Roman numerals, flanked by a cherub and globe, supported by a laurel wreath.

13in (32.5cm) high

$500-1,000   **FRE**

A late 19thC French Empire-style gilt bronze mantel clock, the circular foliate dial with white enamel numerals, flanked by a cherub.

18.5in (46cm) high

$3,500-4,500   **FRE**

A late 19thC Louis XV-style gilt bronze and porcelain mounted mantel clock, with inset Sèvres-style painted plaques depicting cherubs and Marie Antoinette, signed illegibly, stamped with initials "J.B.D".

19.25in (49cm) high

$7,500-8,500   **FRE**

A late 19thC French champlevé enamel gilt bronze mantel clock, with enamel dial, Roman numerals, temple-form finial and two draped Classical maidens.

17.5in (44.5cm) high

$2,800-3,500   **FRE**

A late 19thC French champlevé enamel onyx and gilt bronze timepiece, on an onyx wheel, and enameled blind fret molded foliate frieze, impressed "Depose Fizel Aine".

14in (35.5cm) high

$8,000-12,000   **FRE**

A late 19thC Louis XV-style gilt bronze mantel clock, with foliate dial, open Rococo scroll apron, centered by a shell, inscription below the dial.

28.5in (72.5cm) high

$8,500-9,500   **FRE**

A late 19thC Louis XV-style gilt bronze mantel clock, with white enamel dial, rococo scroll case, on a cartouche shaped base.

31in (78.5cm) high

$3,000-5,000   **FRE**

A late 19thC black slate and bronze mounted mantel clock, the movement with anchor escapement striking on a bell, mercury-filled pendulum.

20.5in (52cm) high

$600-1,000   **L&T**

A French champlevé enamel and ormolu mantel clock, the face with key winding mechanism holes, case with scrolls and applied enamel reserves.

c1910   *14in (35cm) high*

$1,500-2,500   **FRE**

CARRIAGE CLOCKS

A rare French two colour bronze automaton, industrial oarsman mantel timepiece, in the form of a ship, the oarsman is the pendulum, the movement impressed "GLT, BTE, SCDC", probably for Guilmet of Paris, the dial inscribed "J W Benson, 25 Old Bond Street, London", on a marble base.

c1900   *16.5in (41cm) high*

$8,000-12,000   **SWO**

An early 19thC brass-cased carriage clock, by Simon Gounouilhou of Geneva, the twin train movement with lever platform escapement striking on a bell.

7in (18cm) high

$2,500-3,500   **L&T**

A 19thC French brass carriage clock, the twin train movement with lever platform escapement and inscribed "Hands/French Make/EM & Co".

6.25in (16cm) high

$1,500-2,000   **L&T**

A 19thC Garnier gilt brass repeating carriage clock, and case, with chaff-cutter escapement, quarter hour striking on two bells, inscription "Paul Garnier" in panel, in a gilt tooled leather case.

Garnier (1801-1869) set up his own business in the Rue Taitbout, Paris, in 1825. He patented his chaff-cutter escapement in 1830 which enabled him to make affordable carriage clocks on a scale unknown before that time. This was the beginning of the Parisian carriage clock industry. He received the order 'Chevalier de la Légion d'honneur' from the French government in 1860.

Case 5.5in (14cm) high

$15,000-20,000   **L&T**

A late 19thC brass cased carriage clock, the twin train movement with lever platform escapement and repeater mechanism, the enamel dial with Roman chapter.

5.5in (14cm) high

$600-1,000   **L&T**

An Edwardian mounted tortoiseshell traveling clock, by Wiliam Comyns, decorated with pique work and harebell border, in a fitted case, with marks for London

1905   *3.25in (8cm) high*

$5,000-6,000   **L&T**

A gilt brass gorge case carriage clock, the enamel dial inscribed "Barraud and Lunds, Vendors, London 7822" with repeater mechanism striking the hours and half hours.

5in (12.5cm) high

$1,500-2,000   **SWO**

A 19thC Louis XV style gilt bronze and lapis lazuli clock garniture, with enamel chapters, inset lapis panels, and five-light candelabra.

Clock 20.25in (51.5cm) high

$10,000-15,000   FRE

A 19thC Louis XV-style gilt bronze mounted marble clock garniture, with urn finial, enamel dial signed "Bouquet, Paris", with a pair of five light candelabra.

Candelabra 22in (56cm) high

$7,000-9,000   FRE

An English Aesthetic slate clock garniture, centred by an amorial crest, with Roman numeral dial signed "D.F. Mangin and Guedin", signed "J. Lefebvre Paris" and numbered 5066.

c1875   *Clock 16.25in (41cm) high*

$3,000-4,000   FRE

A late 19thC Louis XV-style gilt-bronze and marble clock garniture, retailed by Davis Collamore & Co., the clock in the form of three putti supporting a globe, the candelabra as a single putto holding three branches.

Clock 15.5in (39cm) high

$2,500-3,500   FRE

A French champlevé enamel clock garniture, the dial with eight-day movement, surmounted by an urn finial and broken swan neck pediment, the sides decorated with scrolling foliage, the urns of flattened ovoid form with scroll handles.

c1880   *Clock 18.75in (47cm) high*

$4,000-6,000   FRE

A Grecian Revival gilt bronze and slate mantel clock garniture, with gilt dial, Roman numerals, urn finial, base with applied mounts and paw feet, and two ewers on conforming bases.

c1880   *Clock 26.5in (67.5cm) high*

$5,500-6,500   FRE

A late 19thC Louis XV-style cobalt blue porcelain and gilt-bronze mounted clock garniture, enamel dial signed "Leroy, A. Paris", clock surmounted by cherub, the oval base flanked by two children, the candelabra with six candle arms, on socle bases.

Candelabra: 29.5in (75cm) high

$5,500-6,500   FRE

A fine 19thC French chaplevé enamel and gilt bronze clock garniture, retailed Theodore B. Starr, New York, with a cherub, on Rococo scroll feet, with a pair of five-branch figural candelabra.

Clock 19in (48cm) high

$20,000-25,000   **FRE**

A late 19thC Sèvres style porcelain and gilt bronze mounted clock garniture, painted with figures in traditional costume, on scroll feet, and a pair of six-branch candelabra.

Candelabra 24in (61cm) high

$6,000-7,000   **FRE**

A late 19thC French gilt bronze and porcelain mounted assembled clock garniture, the dial signed "Max", painted with a winged cherub, apron inset with a painted porcelain panel, the urns painted with peacocks and foliage, with twin dolphin mask handles.

Clock 13in (33cm) high

$1,000-1,500   **FRE**

A 19thC Louis XV-style white marble and gilt bronze assembled clock garniture, retailed by J E Caldwell, Philadelphia, surmounted by a cupid and maidens, base set with relief panels of putti, the urns with cockerel mask handles, on socle bases.

Clock 14in (35cm) high

$4,000-6,000   **FRE**

A late 19thC French gilt bronze and champlevé enamel assembled clock garniture and a pair of urns with bacchic mask handles raised on toupie feet.

Clock 18in (45.5cm) high

$4,000-6,000   **FRE**

A late 19thC French champlevé enamel and jasperware clock garniture, with urn finial, and a pair of conforming vases raised on socle bases.

Clock 17in (43cm) high

$3,500-4,500   **FRE**

A late 19thC gilt bronze clock garniture, modeled after the Cathedral of Notre Dame, with Gothic style gilt bronze candelabra, the clock works stamped "F. Dumouchel, A Paris, 3 4 6".

Candelabra 22in (56cm) high

$3,500-4,500   **FRE**

A 19thC Louis XVI-style gilt bronze mounted alabaster assembled clock garniture, retailed by Theodore B. Starr, New York.

Clock 20in (51cm) high

$4,000-5,000   **FRE**

A mahogany cased Massachusetts shelf clock, by Aaron Willard, Boston, with an eight-day brass and weight-driven timepiece with passing strike on a bell, marked "A. Willard", dial imperfections.

c1790   *34in (86.5cm) high*
$70,000-90,000   **SK**

A mahogany shelf timepiece, by Samuel Mulliken (1746-1846), Salem Lynn, Massachusetts, painted iron dial, the maker's name "S. Mulliken" in a wreath, and a brass weight-driven movement with a drop-strike mechanism, old surface.

c1802   *40in (100cm) high*
$30,000-40,000   **SK**

A Federal mahogany and veneer pillar and scroll mantel clock, Norris North, Torrington, Connecticut, a wooden thirty-hour weight-driven Torrington-type movement.

c1820   *29.75in (74cm) high*
$5,500-6,500   **SK**

A Federal mahogany and veneer pillar and scroll mantel clock, by Wadsworths & Turners, Litchfield, Connecticut, 30-hour wooden weight-driven movement and the label of the maker, refinished.

c1825   *31in (77.5cm) high*
$2,200-2,800   **SK**

A Federal mahogany pillar and scroll mantel clock by Ephraim Downes, with 30-hour wooden weight-driven movement, restoration.

c1825   *32in (81cm) high*
$1,400-1,800   **SK**

A Classical carved mahogany and veneer mantel clock, possibly by Moses Barrett, Connecticut, with the carved English crest joining square plinths, with 30-hour movement, imperfections.

c1825   *34in (86cm) high*
$3,000-4,000   **SK**

A Federal birch cased shelf clock, attributed to John Taber, Alfred or Saco, Maine, with looking glass, eight-day, weight-powered timepiece with iron plates and brass wheelwork, imperfections.

c1825   *37.5in (95cm) high*
$5,000-6,000   **SK**

A Federal mahogany and veneer pillar and scroll mantel clock, by Eli & Samuel Terry, Plymouth, Connecticut, wooden 30-hour weight-driven movement and the label of the makers.

c1825   *31.25in (78cm) high*
$1,500-2,000   **SK**

A pine and maple cased transitional shelf clock, by William Sherwin, Buckland, Massachusetts, thirty-hour wood, time and strike, weight powered movement and original printed paper label inside.

c1830   *30.5in (77.5cm) high*
$6,500-7,500   **SK**

A mahogany acorn clock, by Forestville, Connecticut, with a white painted face over eglomise panel of landscape with cottage and river.

c1840   24.5in (62cm) high

$18,000-22,000   **POOK**

A rare rosewood shelf clock, by Silas B. Terry, Terry's Ville, Connecticut, the door with a tablet showing "Hancock House Boston", paper dial inscribed by the maker and a brass 30-hour weight-driven movement.

Silas Burnham Terry, a son of Eli Terry, made significant contributions to American clockmaking and the development of the American coiled clock spring.

c1845   22.25in (55.5cm) high

$1,500-2,500   **SK**

A 19thC Federal mahogany miniature shelf clock, inscribed "J.D. Custer" with carved lyre shaped case, on brass ball feet.

                    15in (38cm) high

$3,500-4,500   **POOK**

A Classical rosewood grain-painted and gilt gesso mantel clock, with a tablet of the Merchant's Exchange, Philadelphia, a brass eight-day weight-driven movement, a painted retailer's label "R.W. Patterson & Co., Toronto, Canada West".

R.W. Patterson & Co. retailed clocks in Canada made by Seth Thomas in the 1850s and 1860s.

c1860   32.25in (80.5cm) high

$650-750   **SK**

WALL CLOCKS

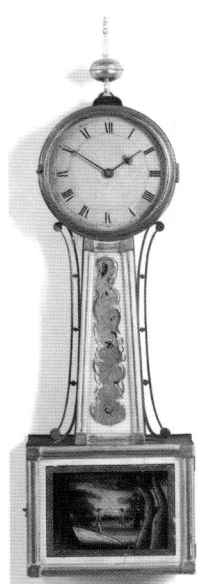

A patent timepiece or 'banjo' clock, attributed to Aaron Willard, Jr., Boston, in a mahogany case with gilded pedestal, brass side ornaments and bezel, eight-day brass weight-powered movement with 'T-bridge' suspension, imperfections.

c1815   42in (106.5cm) high

$10,000-12,000   **SK**

A Federal mahogany and eglomise banjo case wall clock with eight-day brass weight driven movement, possibly Massachusetts, imperfections.

c1820   30in(76cm) high

$2,200-2,800   **SK**

A Federal mahogany gilt-gesso eglomise banjo wall clock, possibly Massachusetts, with eight-day, brass weight-driven movement, imperfections, restoration.

c1820   35in (89cm) high

$1,500-2,500   **SK**

A Federal mahogany eglomise banjo case wall clock, by Elnathan Taber, painted dial inscribed "E Taber" and eight-day brass weight-driven movement, imperfections.

c1820   38in (97cm) high

$5,000-6,000   **SK**

A Boston Federal mahogany banjo clock, with eglomized neck and base above a carved gilt wood drop, signed "Aaron Willard".

c1820   42in (107cm) high

$6,000-7,000   **POOK**

An early 19thC American brass watch safe, with spread winged eagle crest over a swag base.

6in (15cm) high

$500-600   **POOK**

A Federal mahogany mirrored wall clock, possibly by Dewey of New Hampshire, with scrolled crest and base, applied brass rosettes.

c1820   *39in (99cm) high*

$3,000-4,000   **POOK**

A Connecticut mahogany and veneer 'Connecticut Banjo' wall clock, with wooden thirty-hour weight-driven movement, restoration.

c1825   *35in (89cm) high*

$5,000-7,000   **SK**

A 19thC Pennsylvania banjo clock, with inscription "Joseph Fix Maker Reading, PA".

39in (99cm) high

$2,200-2,800   **POOK**

A 19thC Boston Federal mahogany banjo clock, by Aaron Willard Sr., with white painted face over eglomise panel of Neptune on a seahorse.

The Willard brothers invented the banjo clock in 1802. Only about 4,000 were ever made, making them highly collectible today. Working from Grafton and Roxbury, Mass., they also produced tall case, shelf and other wall clocks.

33in (84cm) high

$12,000-18,000   **POOK**

A walnut 'Figure Eight' wall clock, by E. Howard & Co., Boston, painted metal dial inscribed "E. Howard & Co. BOSTON", and brass eight-day weight-driven movement, stamped by the maker.

c1857   *34.25in (85.5cm) high*

$7,500-8,500   **SK**

A Louis XVI-style alabaster and gilt bronze wall clock, dial signed "J.W. Benson, 25 Old Bond St. London", surmounted by cupid and flanked by Classical draped maidens and cornucopia.

c1880   *21.25in (53cm) high*

$4,500-5,500   **FRE**

A Louis XVI-style alabaster and gilt bronze mounted lyre shape clock, dial signed "Festeau Le Jeune, Paris", the white enamel dial flanked by laurel wreaths.

c1880   *38.5in (96cm) high*

$2,000-3,000   **FRE**

A late 19thC Louis XV-style gilt bronze cartel clock, retailed by Tiffany & Co., with an eight-day movement, within a Rococo case and ribbon-tied drapery.

16.5in (42cm) high

$1,800-2,200   **FRE**

A late 19thC walnut regulator clock, by Howard & Co. Boston, Massachusetts.

69in (175cm) high

$40,000-50,000   **POOK**

A Gilbert 31-day oak-cased clock, with reproduction Coca-Cola lower glass panel, wear.

38in (96.50cm) high

$400-500   **JDJ**

A presentation Waltham Riverside open-faced pocket watch, key wound lever movement, the cuvette inscribed: "FROM WILLIAM MORRIS INC, NEW YORK FEB 26th 1910", the reverse inset with 32 single cut diamonds, belcher link chain with reeded spacers each set with a single cut diamond, in a blue velvet fitted case.

A late 18thC silver and gold pocket watch, by John Carrell, Philadelphia, in English silver case.

William Morris was the founder of the William Morris agency, L.A., which is today one of the foremost show business agencies in the US.

1.75in (4.5cm) diam

$1,500-2,500 FRE	**$20,000-30,000** L&T

An Art Deco cocktail watch, with cream dial, and Arabic numerals, set with single cut diamonds, to a ribbon strap, mounts stamped "18ct".

$1,500-2,000 L&T

An Art Deco emerald and diamond cocktail watch, with arabic numerals, calibre cut emeralds and single cut diamonds, with a black moiré ribbon strap.

$2,000-3,000 L&T

A platinum mounted diamond cocktail watch, with silver dial, arabic numerals, blue steel sword hands, and a 9ct white gold snake link bracelet.

$1,000-2,000 L&T

A lady's diamond Jaeger-Le Coultre cocktail watch, with silver dial and dot and baton numerals, steel sword hands, fitted to an integral bracelet box set with round brilliant cut diamonds.

$6,000-10,000 L&T

A lady's diamond Prefis cocktail watch, with gilt baton numerals and hands.

$6,000-8,000 L&T

A lady's 18ct gold Baume & Mercier wristwatch, with satin finished, gold dial with baton numerals, single cut diamond set bezel, tapered interwoven bracelet, with box.

$1,200-1,800 L&T

A lady's gold Cartier wristwatch, with Arabic numerals and steel sword hands, signed, fitted to a patent crocodile skin strap, with box and documents.

$3,000-4,000 L&T

A gentleman's 14ct gold Oyster Perpetual Rolex wristwatch, with enamel dial, gilt numerals and hands, inscribed "SUPERLATIVE CHRONOMETER OFFICIALLY CERTIFIED", with a jubilee bracelet strap, and box.

$2,500-3,500 L&T

A Victorian brass skeleton clock, by E. Mountford, Worcester, open work form, with an inscribed silvered chapter ring, on an ebonized plinth, the twin fusee chain movement striking on a bell.

12.5in (31cm) high

$1,500-2,500   **SWO**

A miniature French silver-gilt and enamel clock, retailed by Dreyfous, 582 Fifth Avenue, New York, the pink guilloche enamel case applied with mounts set with marcasite, in the original tooled red leather case.

c1900   *2.75in (7cm) high*

$4,500-5,500   **FRE**

A Swiss enamel table clock with enamel decoration of maidens and cherubs in ovals on white onyx base.

7in (18cm) high

$4,500-5,500   **JDJ**

A late Victorian easel-back timepiece, by Alfred Clark, with enameled dial, Arabic numerals, and reeded bezel, with marks for London 1901 and stamped "CLARK, 20 OLD BOND STREET".

4.25in (11cm) diam

$1,200-1,800   **L&T**

BAROMETERS

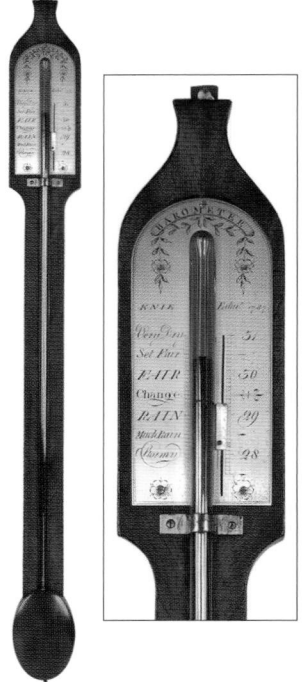

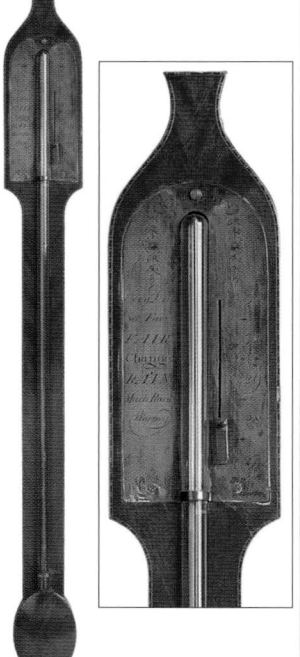

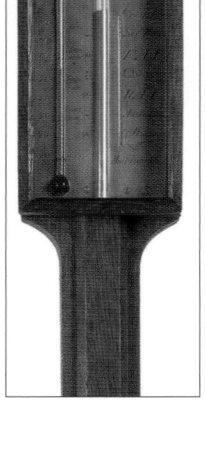

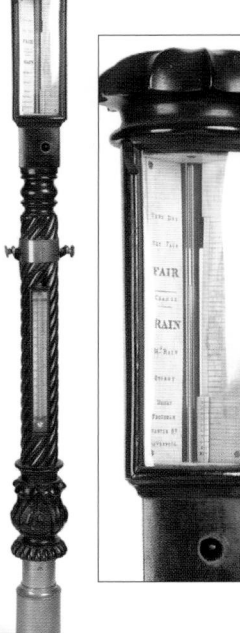

A George III mahogany and chequer strung stick barometer, by Balthazar Knie of Edinburgh, with silvered brass register plate and vernier engraved with a banner inscribed "Barometer", maker's signature and date "1787".

Few dated Knie barometers are believed to exist.

1787   *41.5in (105cm) high*

$4,000-6,000   **L&T**

A George III period mahogany and chequer strung stick barometer, by Balthazar Knie, with brass register plate and engraved vernier, engraved maker's name.

40in (102cm) high

$2,500-3,500   **L&T**

A late George III oak stick barometer, with brass register plate, vernier and thermometer scale bounded by a foliate spray and maker's signature.

37in (94cm) high

$600-800   **L&T**

An early 19thC mahogany cased marine barometer, by Charles Frodsham, Castle Street, Liverpool, with engraved ivory scales, spirally reeded body with brass gimbal mounts set with thermometer.

37.5in (95cm) high

$6,000-10,000   **L&T**

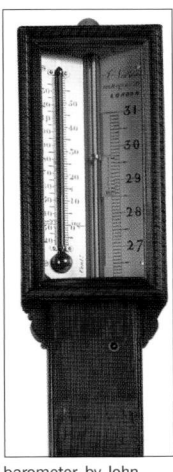

A 19thC oak stick barometer, by John Frederick Newman (fl. 1816-60), signed "Jn Newman, 122 Regent Street, London".

Newman, one of the leading barometer makers of the 19thC, worked from 122 Regent Street between 1827-60. He made the Royal Society's standard barometer in 1822. Newman barometers were used by the Ross Antarctic Expedition and his meteorological station barometers were installed throughout the British Empire.

35.75in (91cm) high

$1,000-1,500   **L&T**

A 19thC mahogany banjo barometer, by Lione and Somalvico, 125 Holbn. Hill, London, the swan neck pediment above a dry/damp dial, central clock, engraved barometer dial and thermometer, all within a shaped case.

49.5in (126cm) high

$3,000-4,000   **L&T**

An early Victorian mahogany double banjo barometer, by Taglia**, 11 Brook Street, Hoban, hydrometer, mercurial thermometer, a level, mirror and mercurial column action faced by a silvered calibrated dial with cast bezel.

38.5in (98cm) high

$600-1,000   **BIG**

SCIENTIFIC INSTRUMENTS

A Russian mahogany and brass bound two-day marine chronometer, with subsidiary seconds and up-and-down dials, within a brass case with gimbal mounts, three tier mahogany case with brass binding.

Dial 4.25in (11cm) diam

$2,000-3,000   **L&T**

A Russian mahogany two-day marine chronometer, the dial with seconds and up-and-down dials, within a brass case with gimbal mounts, a three tier mahogany case with brass mounts, in second mahogany case.

Dial 4.5in (11.5cm) wide

$1,500-2,500   **L&T**

A mahogany and brass bound two-day marine chronometer, by T.S. & J.D. Negus, New York, dial no. 2192, with seconds and up-and-down dials, brass case with gimbal mounts, within three-tier mahogany case with brass binding.

7.5in (19cm) wide

$2,500-3,500   **L&T**

A 18thC ebony octant, with brass mounts and bone scale, inscribed on the cross bar '47'.

13.75in (35cm) high

$1,000-1,500   **L&T**

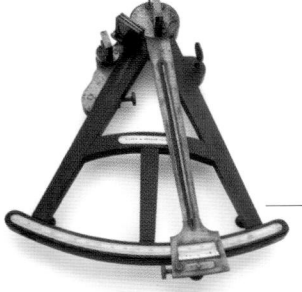

An 18thC ebony octant, by Norrie & Wilson, London, with brass mounts and bone scale, signed on the cross bar 'Norrie & Wilson, London', within fitted mahogany box.

$1,000-1,500   **L&T**

A late 18thC ebony and brass mounted octant, with ivory scale, indistinctly inscribed on the cross bar, '....for Capt. James Grandison, 1789'.

15.75in (40cm) high

$800-1,200   **L&T**

SCIENTIFIC INSTUMENTS

A French 18thC Butterfield-type white metal sundial compass, the bird gnomon engraved with latitude seal 40/60 degrees, reverse engraved with 20 European cities, base engraved with a river landscape, in a shagreen case.

2.25in (6cm) wide

$2,000-3,000   **SWO**

A 19thC gold pocket shipmaster's compass, by Gilbert & Co, London, with white enameled and gilt dial inscribed 'Gilbert & Co, London'.

2in (5cm) diam

$1,000-1,500   **L&T**

A rare brass 'Culpeper-Type' microscope, in the original wooden box with some accessories.

c1800   *12.75in (32cm) high*

$2,000-3,000   **WDL**

A brass ship's binnacle.

A binnacle is a case or box kept on the ship's deck to store navigational instruments such as compasses and sand timers.

55in (140cm) high

$800-1,200   **L&T**

A late 18thC brass pantograph, by Philp, Brighton, the brass with calibrated arms, signed 'Philp, Brighton', in fitted wooden case.

A pantograph is a device made up of angled metal arms, used to copy diagrams and maps.

$350-450   **L&T**

A rare early 'Oberhäuser' drum microscope, by Georges Oberhäuser, Paris, with an old-shaped condenser with lever mechanism.

This extremely rare piece is the tallest drum microscope ever built and is the prototype according to Oberhäuser's patent.

c1840   *12in (30cm) high*

$1,500-2,500   **ATK**

TOOLS

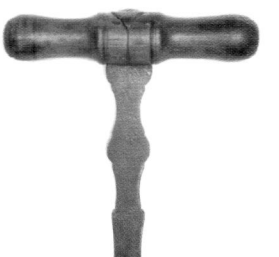

An 18thC vegetable or herb chopper, with wooden handle, in good condition.

$200-300   **MUR**

A very rare 18thC turnscrew or tournevis, with typically shaped decoration, good condition.

5in (12.5cm) long

$120-180   **MUR**

A late 18thC-early 19thC herb or vegetable chopper, with turned black wood handle, good condition.

11in (28cm) high

$600-1,000   **MUR**

A pair of late 17thC/early 18thC iron dividers with ball hinge, good condition.

6in (15cm) long

$100-150   **MUR**

An early surgeon's saw, with horn and ivory handle, the top carved with an eagle's head.

$1,500-2,000   **MUR**

An 18thC hammer, with decorated stock and turned ebony handle.

9.25in (23.5cm) long

$1,200-1,800　　　　　　**MUR**

An 18thC keyhole saw.

$600-900　　　　　　**MUR**

A 17thC hammer, the head decorated with stylized fish and unscrewing to reveal a long spike, marked "1667" and "A.D."

19cm (7.5in) long

$1,200-1,800　　　　　　**MUR**

An 18thC iron axe.

15in (38cm) long

$500-600　　　　**MUR**

A late 19thC decorated iron Guild axe, probably Austrian.

These ceremonial axes where used by the Woodworking Guilds.

9.5in (24cm) long

$500-600　　　　**MUR**

A 17thC iron brace, in the form of two mythical serpents.

$1,200-1,800　　　　**MUR**

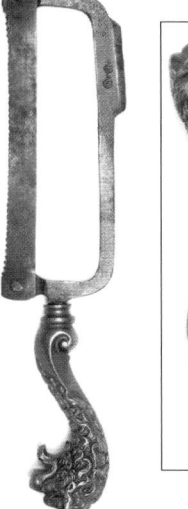

An 18thC-style saw, with bronze handle in the form of a lion and possibly a later addition.

12in (30.5cm) long

$500-600　　　　**MUR**

A rare 18thC plane table rule.

21in (53.5cm) long

$700-1,000　　　　　　**MUR**

An unusual 19thC mahogany boxed walnut and mahogany chisel and mallet.

Box 12in (30.5cm) wide

$400-500　　　**MB**

THE JEWELRY MARKET

The appeal of antique jewelry lies in more than its intrinsic worth. The best pieces immediately identify with the period from which they came and allow us to share the joy the first owner must have felt when wearing them.

Jewelry has traditionally been given as a token of love and emblem of the way in which we would like our relationships to be – the color of the stones is permanent and the metal incorruptible – an ideal relationship would mirror this and be the same at the end as it was in the beginning.

While the cut and quality of any stones and the workmanship of the jeweler are important considerations when assessing value and desirability, so is the style of the piece. Thanks to its high standards of craftsmanship and Modern yet elegant look, Art Deco jewelry from the 1920s and 1930s continues to be highly sought after. Diamond double clips – pins which could be worn

as a single piece or separated to make a pair of pins – made by companies including Van Cleef & Arpels and Cartier are particularly popular at the moment. Examples where the crisp, geometric design is enhanced by rock crystal, onyx or jade command a premium.

Elsewhere, collectors continue to look for "signed" pieces from the 19th and 20th centuries by makers such as Castellani, Giuliano, Lalique, Cartier, Boucheron, Van Cleef & Arpels and Fabergé or jewels that can be identified as being made by a particular maker or sold by a well-known retailer.

In contrast, the market for 18th and early 19th century English diamond work, which tends to lack the bright sparkle of later diamond, is becalmed and pieces continue to represent excellent value for money.

CLASSIC

A scarce Bronze Age gold finger ring, of heavy construction, nearly pure gold, with many digs and scrapes from ploughing.

c1200BC   *6.25in (2.5cm) diam*

$1,500-2,000   **BLO**

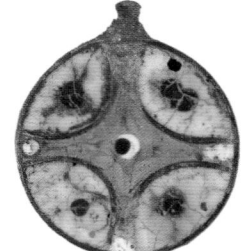

A rare Roman enameled disc pendant, with cruciform arcs design and suspension loop at top, the enamel mostly complete, some adherents to rear.

13.75in (35cm) diam

$500-700   **BLO**

A gold finger ring, the interior engraved "God Gave Me Life To Love" in running script.

c1700

$1,500-2,000   **BLO**

A pair of Queen Anne mother-of-pearl earrings, in gold-plated settings.

c1700   *1.5in (3.75cm) long*

$4,500-5,000   **CSAY**

A pair of Georgian silver and clear paste pendant bow earrings.

c1780   *2.25in (5.75cm) long*

$1,500-2,000   **CSAY**

A pair of Georgian flower and pendant berry motif earrings, comprising foil-backed, silver set clear pastes.

c1780   *1.5in (3.5cm) long*

$2,000-3,000   **CSAY**

A Georgian butterfly brooch, with silver-set pale blue pave enamel bordered with clear pastes.

c1760   *2.5in (6.5cm) wide*

$4,000-5,000   **CSAY**

A Georgian demi-parure, comprising a necklace and bracelet with clear pastes of graduated size in silver settings.

c1790   *Necklace 17in (43cm) long*

$6,000-7,000   **CSAY**

A Georgian gold ring, decorated with clear pastes and faux pearls set against blue enamel.

c1780   *0.75in (2.25cm) diam*

$2,000-3,000   **CSAY**

A Georgian pink tourmaline and diamond cluster ring, with a gold shank engraved with foliage and shells, finger size G.

c1800

$700-1,000   **HAMG**

A Berlin ironwork ring, cast with a burning heart crossed with a cross and an anchor, flanked by foliate forms.

c1820   *0.5in (1.5cm) wide*

$2,000-3,000   **CSAY**

AGATE JEWELRY

- The dramatic landscape of Scotland and Queen Victoria's enchantment with the Highlands fired the Victorian imagination and led to a vogue for all things Scottish.
- Agate jewelry, sometimes known as pebble jewelry, is typically made with agate, granite and other Scottish stones set in engraved silver.
- Agate, a banded and variegated form of chalcedony, has been used in jewelry since Roman times. The rich colors of the different forms of agate mirrored the hues of Scottish landscape and the earthy tones of tartan.
- Inspiration initially came from traditional Celtic jewelry such as the dirk or dagger pin or the hinged circular pin known as the penannular. Motifs included thistles and knots, while the Irish harp was also popular. These were later joined by typical Victorian elements such as the buckle, butterfly and bow.
- Early examples are more sought after, particularly late 18th century pieces. Later examples – often produced in England or Germany to meet demand – are often of lower quality.

A Scottish agate ware pin, with contrasting segments of agate, a citrine and an amethyst paste, and scrolling acanthus decoration to the silver mount, signed by Ellen Dunnet.

c1870	2.5in (6.75cm) long
$1,200-1,800	**YNH**

A Scottish agate ware pin, with segments of contrasting-colored agates, three citrines and an amethyst-colored paste.

1870-80	3in (7.5cm) long
$1,200-1,800	**YNH**

A Scottish agate ware roundel pin, with eight triangular inserts of Aberdeen granite, set within a foliate motif silver frame.

1880-90	6cm (2.25in) diam
$1,000-1,500	**LYNH**

A Scottish agate ware garter pin, with contrasting-colored, silver-set agate segments encircling a prong-set citrine.

1880-90	3in (7.5cm) long
$1,000-1,500	**LYNH**

A Scottish agate ware buckle pin, with contrasting segments of agate in gold-plated settings.

1880-90	2.5in (6.5cm) wide
$1,000-1,500	**LYNH**

A Scottish agate ware knot pin, with interlaced bands of variegated red, orange, pink, gray and black agate set in a silver mount.

1880-90	2.5in (6.5cm) wide
$1,000-1,500	**LYNH**

A Scottish agate ware leaf motif pin, in silver-set segments of polychrome agate, including richly contrasted red and black.

c1880	2.25in (6cm) long
$800-1,200	**LYNH**

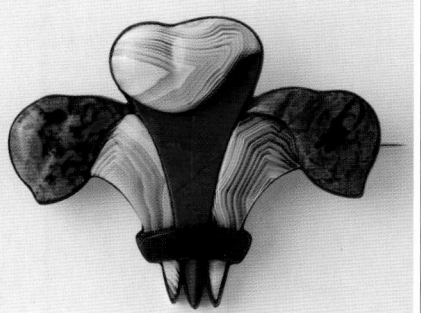

A Scottish agate ware fleur-de-lys pin, in silver-set red and Montrose blue agate.

1880-90	2.25in (6cm) wide
$1,500-2,000	**LYNH**

A Scottish agate ware love knot pin, with interlaced bands of silver-mounted Montrose blue agate, silver chased with scrolling foliate motifs.

1880-90	2.5in (6.25cm) long
$700-1,500	**LYNH**

A Scottish agate ware rosette pin, with carved and polished agate petals set on slate and secured with foliate silver prongs.

1880-90	2in (5cm) diam
$600-800	**LYNH**

A Scottish agate ware stylized sun pin, with radiating silver-set calibre-cut agates of contrasting color, and a variegated yellow and red agate cabochon center.

1890-1900	2.5in (6.25cm) wide
$1,000-1,500	**LYNH**

Two early brass plaid pins, one with Celtic cast border, inscribed "MC 1737", the other crudely engraved with Celtic knotwork borders and inscribed to the reverse.

largest 4.25in (11cm) diam

$1,200-1,800   **L&T**

Plaid pins were traditionally used for fastening fabric at the shoulder. Introduced c200AD, the oldest design was the penannular, an open ring pin with a large pin. Over time, the pins became more decorative and incorporated Celtic designs.

c1890   *2.75in (7cm) diam*

$2,000-3,000   **L&T**

A Scottish provincial mounted pin, by Ferguson & MacBean, with central cairngorm, and marks for Inverness, stamped "F&M, dromedary and INVS".

A Scottish silver mounted plaid pin, with central circular cut cairngorm within a pierced knotwork gallery, and marks for Edinburgh, maker HT.

1910   *3.75in (9.5cm) diam*

$700-1,000   **L&T**

A Scottish silver mounted plaid pin, with a circular cut cairngorm, and a crest inscribed "DALRIADA", with marks for Edinburgh, maker TE.

"DALRIADA" is an ancient Celtic name for Scotland.

1934   *3.75in (9.5cm) diam*

$1,000-1,500   **L&T**

A regimental plaid pin, with four raised Celtic knots, the cypher of the Duke of Argyll, two corresponding crests and a ribbon banner inscribed.

The Duke of Argyll is the chief of the Scottish clan of Campbell. The Earls, Marquesses, and Dukes of Argyll were among the most powerful noble families in Scotland and played a major role in Scottish history throughout the 16th, 17th, and 18th centuries.

3in (7.5cm) diam

$600-900   **L&T**

A Scottish clan pin, with central cast crest for Mackenzie, inscribed "DIA'S MO DHUTAICH-FIDE-PARTA-FIDE".

The Latin motto "FIDE-PARTA-FIDE" translates as "By Faith Obtained, By Faith Increased". Meanwhile the Gaelic inscription "DIA'S MO DHUTAICH" may be interpreted as "God's Own Country".

3.5in (9cm) diam

$1,000-1,500   **L&T**

A Scottish clan pin with applied cast crest for MacLeod, inscribed "HOLD FAST", a matching belt buckle, and a pair of matching shoe buckles.

Buckles 2.75in (7cm) wide

$700-1,000   **L&T**

A Scottish clan pin, with central cast crest for Chisolm, inscribed, also applied with three florets, with a similar cast clan pin and a matching cap badge.

largest 3.25in (8.5cm) long

$500-700   **L&T**

A Scottish plaid pin, with a cast figure of St Andrew, within a thistle and foliate cast surround, within an outer wriggle-work engraved border.

3.75in (9.5cm) diam

$300-400   **L&T**

A Scottish plaid pin, with C-scroll cast edge and foliate cast border, pierced to the center and applied with a cast lion rampant.

3.5in (9cm) diam

$400-600   **L&T**

A Scottish pin, claw set with six purple stones and larger pale purple stone, within a pierced gallery.

4.5in (11.5cm) diam

$1,000-1,500   **L&T**

A cut steel pin, with floral, fruit and foliate motifs.

c1840   1.75in (4.5cm) wide

$300-400   **MARA**

A Victorian silver mounted pin, with pierced thistle and foliate cast border around the central collet set oval cut cairngorm, with marks for London 1849.

3.75in (9.5cm) wide

$1,000-1,500   **L&T**

A Victorian gilt metal 'regard' pin, set with Emerald, Garnet, Amethyst, Ruby and Diamond colored pastes.

c1860   1.75in (4.5cm) wide

$500-600   **CSAY**

A Victorian butterfly pin, with pinchbeck wings and antennae, and a French Jet body and head.

c1860   3in (7.5cm) wide

$800-1,200   **CSAY**

A Victorian sentimental heart-shaped pin, with a black tortoiseshell center set in and framed by gilt metal, and inlaid with a shell floral motif.

c1880   1.5in (3.75cm) long

$600-900   **LYNH**

A basket-shaped pin, carved by J. Johnson from Irish bog wood, with a shield-shaped silver and brass pin by Wm Acheson of Dublin.

c1880   2.75in (7cm) wide

$1,500-3,000   **LYNH**

A late Victorian sentimental pin, fashioned from mother-of-pearl in the form of a hand holding a flower, with three attendant doves.

c1890   2.5in (5cm) wide

$200-400   **LYNH**

A carved mother-of-pearl bird pin.

c1900   4.25in (11cm) wide

$130-270   **LYNH**

A mother-of-pearl floral motif hairpin.

c1900   2.25in (6cm) wide

$200-500   **LYNH**

A gold Egyptian Revival pin, with an entwined-serpents frame and an enamel portrait of an Egyptian woman.

c1900   2.5in (6cm) long

$500-700   **CRIS**

An early Victorian hairpin, with twin gold pins and a floral motif made from Vauxhall glass.

c1850   3in (7.5cm) long

$150-200   **LYNH**

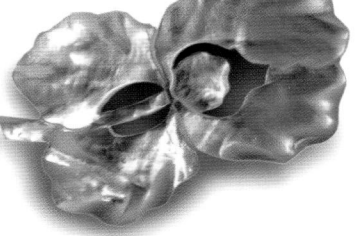

An early Victorian gold hairpin, with a floral motif, and petals made from Vauxhall glass.

c1850   *3in (7.5cm) long*

$100-150   **LYNH**

An early Victorian woven horsehair watch-chain, with 15ct gold links and clasp.

c1840   *16in (40.5cm) long*

$200-300   **MARA**

A Victorian carved jet bead necklace.

c1860   *17.25in (44cm) long*

$200-400   **MARA**

A triple strand baby shell necklace.

c1900   *67.75in (172cm) long*

$200-400   **LYNH**

A 'Mariners' Art' lacquered nut necklace, carved with floral and foliate motifs.

c1840   *17in (44cm) long*

$3,000-4,000   **CSAY**

Detail of a gold twin-pendant necklace, with irridescent blue beetles.

c1900   *1.5in (4cm) long*

$1,500-2,000   **LYNH**

A diamond pendeloque-shaped pendant, with marquise-cut central stone, surrounded by 11 brilliants, on a modern box chain.

A pendeloque is flat on both sides with bevelled edges.

$4,000-5,000   **BIG**

A Victorian pinchbeck bracelet, chased with floral motifs and with a foliate form set under a large citrine cabochon.

c1860   *1.5in (4cm) wide*

$200-400   **MARA**

An oriental silver bangle, with gilt overlay and an applied medallion with a gilt bird and flowers set against black enamel.

c1880   *2.5in (6.5cm) diam*

$1,000-2,000   **LYNH**

A pair of Victorian serpent bangles, in pinchbeck set with French pastes and faux pearls.

c1880

$400-500   **RITZ**

A set of seven enameled gold dress buttons, with old European cut diamonds and enameled surrounds, in a fitted case stamped "Joseph Heming & Co., 28 Conduit Street, London".

$1,000-1,500   **L&T**

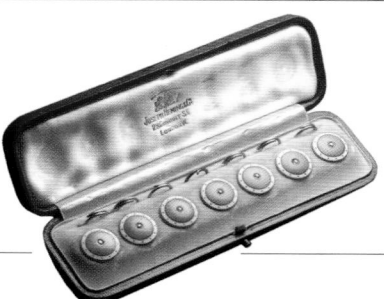

An Edwardian necklace, with silver-linked and prong-set chalcedony-colored faceted pastes.

c1910   *7.75in (20cm) diam*

$600-900   **MARA**

An Edwardian necklace with turquoise and red textured glass beads.

c1910   *26in (66cm) long*

$600-900   **LYNH**

An Edwardian necklace, with silver-set wreaths of small diamante alternated with large, rectangular cut, sapphire blue pastes.

c1910   *7in (18cm) diam*

$500-600   **MARA**

An English Edwardian silver and clear paste necklace with a basket-of-flowers motif, unsigned.

c1914   *15.75in (40cm) long*

$360-430   **RG**

An Arts and Crafts tortoiseshell ladies' haircomb, by Murle Bennett, with a gold band of set amethysts and mother-of-pearl and central blister pearl.

c1900   *11.5cm (4.2in) wide*

$1,200-1,800   **VDB**

An Arts and Crafts pin, in silver and gold-tone metal with ruby red and amber pastes, unsigned.

c1910   *3.5in (9cm) long*

$500-700   **RG**

ART NOUVEAU

An Art Nouveau necklace, with a gold chain and a silver pendant set with turquoise blooms, plique-à-jour, and a pearl drop.

1890-95   *Pendant 2.25in (6cm) long*

$800-1,200   **LYNH**

An Art Nouveau silver and plique-à-jour pendant necklace.

c1900   *Pendant 1.75in (4cm) long*

$1,500-2,000   **RBRG**

A floral motif pendant necklace with silver-set plique-à-jour, clear crystal rhinestones and faceted pink glass stones.

c1900   *Pendant 2.25in (6cm) long*

$1,500-2,000   **RBRG**

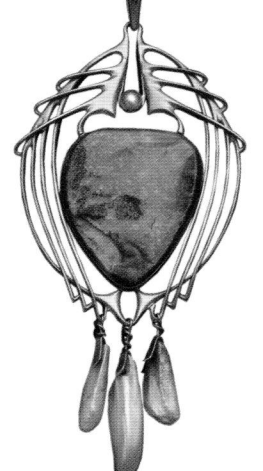

An Art Nouveau gold pendant, by Archibald Knox (1862-1933), for Liberty & Co., model 500/12, collet set with a large boulder opal panel, surmounted by a blister pearl and suspending drop pearls.

c1900-04   *4in (10cm) long*

$12,000-14,000   **L&T**

A George Hunt dress clip, in silver set with blue enamel and a moonstone.

c1915   *1.5in (4cm) long*

$600-800   **RG**

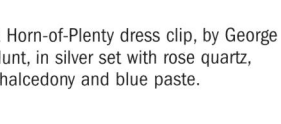

A Horn-of-Plenty dress clip, by George Hunt, in silver set with rose quartz, chalcedony and blue paste.

c1915   *2in (4.5cm) long*

$1,200-1,500   **RG**

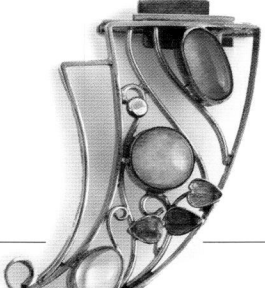

317

JEWELRY

ART DECO JEWELRY

- Art Deco jewelry, fashionable during the 1920s, 1930s and later, is characterized by bold, geometric features. Pieces tended to be elaborately decorated before the mid-1920s, when styles became more abstract.

- Zig-zags, arrow shapes and starbursts were characteristic of innovative Art Deco design that reflected the speed and movement of modern machines, as well as long, loose necklaces and earrings that could move.

- Materials used included semi-precious stones such as aquamarine, topaz and lapis lazuli, metal, jade, plastic and enamels. More expensive pieces were made with diamonds, platinum and pearls. When the supply of gems from India froze during World War II, faux diamonds, rubies and other precious stones were developed.

- Clips and pins were a popular form of Art Deco jewelry. Typically worn on evening dresses and overcoats, they were available in many different designs and materials.

- Important makers included Cartier and Boucheron in Paris, the center of design, as well as Theodor Fahrner in Germany who imitated French designs. Sybil Dunlop, H.G. Murphy and Harold Stabler in Britain took inspiration from Arts and Crafts designs.

- Pieces were rarely marked or signed, although Cartier and Boucheron occasionally stamped their jewelry making these pieces highly sought after.

A very rare French Egyptian-style Art Deco necklace, red glass and chrome beads with chrome button fastening.

1920-30 *12in (30cm) long*

$1,200-1,800 **CRIS**

A French celluloid Auguste Bonaz Art Deco necklace.

c1925 *10in (25.5cm) drop*

$1,000-1,500 **JES**

A French glass tassel choker, with green crystals and stones and brass findings, each with a tassel.

c1930-40 *14in (35.5cm) long*

$2,000-3,000 **DD**

An American Art Deco Miriam Haskell gilded leaf necklace and clip-style earring set, with seed pearls and rhinestones, hand crafted in a Frank Hess design, signed.

1940-50

$2,000-3,000 **DD**

Necklace 15in (38cm) long

DD

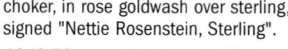

A Trifari Art Deco retro lariat necklace, with rose goldwash in a mesh style flat chain necklace, signed.

1935-40 *14in (35.5cm) long*

$500-700 **DD**

An Art Deco American Marcel Boucher choker, with sapphire and clear rhinestones set in rhodium.

1940-50 *14in (35.5cm) long*

$700-1,000 **DD**

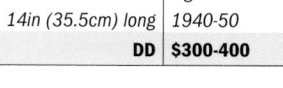

A Nettie Rosenstein Art Deco retro choker, in rose goldwash over sterling, signed "Nettie Rosenstein, Sterling".

1940-50 *Chain 15in (38cm) long*

$300-400 **DD**

A Murano glass necklace, with alternating clear and opaque red glass beads.

1920-30   *30in (76cm) long*

$300-400   **RBRG**

An Italian necklace, with micro-mosaic floral motifs of graduated size and contrasting color.

1920-30   *16.5in (42cm) long*

$400-500   **ECLEC**

An Italian necklace with micro-mosaic floral motifs of graduated size.

1920-30   *16.5in (42cm) diam*

$400-500   **ECLEC**

An Art Deco necklace, in gold-tone metal set with square-cut pink glass stones of graduated size.

1930-40   *17.25in (44cm) long*

$150-200   **ECLEC**

An Art Deco necklace, with gilt metal links and settings, and hollow-center shield motifs of faceted glass in mottled shades of red.

1920-25   *15.25in (39cm) long*

$100-150   **ECLEC**

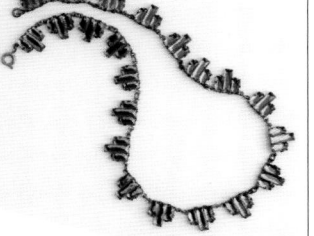

An Art Deco necklace, with silver links and stepped geometric shapes in green mirror glass.

1930-35   *15in (38cm) long*

$200-250   **ECLEC**

A vintage American Art Deco Miriam Haskell poured glass necklace and earrings, with gilded settings.

1940-50   *Necklace 16in (40.5cm) long*

$500-700   **DD**

A Pennino Art Deco set, comprising choker necklace, earrings and bracelet, all clear baguette and round rhinestones set in rhodium, signed.

1940-50   *Necklace 12in (30.5cm) long*

$500-700   **DD**

An American 'Fruit Salad' pendant necklace, with carved emerald, sapphire and ruby-colored rhinestones in silver settings.

c1920   *Pendant 1.25in (3cm) long*

$600-900   **CSAY**

A Marcasite necklace, with pendant bell motifs.

1920-25   *15in (38cm) long*

$400-500   **RBRG**

An Egyptian-Revival pendant necklace, carved from brown Bakelite with red Bakelite beads and a black silk tassel.

1920-30   *Pendant 6.75in (17cm) long*

$400-500   **RBRG**

An American Art Deco lavalliere necklace, with genuine faceted carnelian and marcasite stones, set in sterling.

1930-40   *Chain 16.5in (42cm) long*

$500-700   **DD**

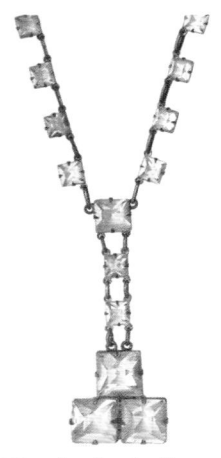

An Art Deco American lavalliere necklace, with French paste, set in sterling.

1930-40   Chain 16in (40.5cm) long

$200-300   **DD**

An Art Deco necklace, with twin tassel pendants, in silver and marbled green plastic, unsigned.

c1930   Necklace 16.5in (42cm) long

$180-220   **ECLEC**

A Krementz Art Deco necklace, with genuine faceted carnelian, onyx and pale citrine stones set in sterling, signed "KREMENTZ STERLING".

1930-40   16.5in (42cm) long

$500-700   **DD**

An Art Deco necklace, with a silver chain and pendant, the latter set with a faceted green glass stone.

1930-40 Necklace 17.25in (44cm) long

$150-200   **ECLEC**

An American Art Deco lavalliere necklace, with genuine faceted sodalite and marcasite stones, set in sterling.

1930-40   Chain 16.5in (18cm) long

$500-700   **DD**

A Trifari Art Deco retro style snake chain necklace, gold-plated with sapphire and clear rhinestone accents.

1940-50   14in (35.5cm) long

$300-400   **DD**

A marcasite pendant necklace, with three small and one large pink pastes.

Pendant 3.25in (8.5cm) long

$550-650   **RBRG**

A Theodor Fahrner pendant pin, in silver and marcasite with a pierced ivory insert and a central blue glass cabochon.

The Fahrner company mass produced affordable sterling and marcasite jewelry between 1855-1979. Theodor Fahrner founded the company in Pforzheim, Germany, where he and his jewelry designers both led and took inspiration from the Art Nouveau, Arts and Crafts, Art Deco, Art Moderne and Contemporary movements.

1920-30   2.5in (6.5cm) long

$1,800-2,200   **RBRG**

A Theodor Fahrner pendant pin, in silver and marcasite with black enamel and pearl highlights.

1920-30   3in (7.75cm) long

$1,800-2,200   **RBRG**

An Art Deco American compact with finger ring, signed,"Richard Hudnut Marvelous".

1930-40   4.5in (11.5cm) long

£120-180   **DD**

An early Art Deco bracelet, in gilt metal set with round-cut clear and amber-colored diamante.

c1920   7in (18cm) long

$400-700   **LYNH**

An early Art Deco bracelet, in gilt metal set with ovoid and rectangular cut clear and emerald-colored diamante.

c1920   7in (17cm) long

$400-700   **LYNH**

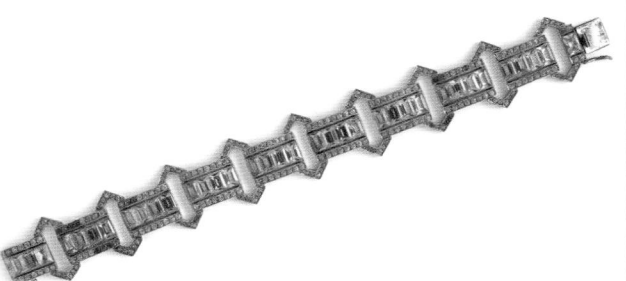

A French Art Deco bracelet, the silver gallery setting with clear crystals.

1920-30   7.5in (19cm) long

$600-900   **CRIS**

A French Egyptian-Revival bracelet, with silver-set and linked polychrome-enameled scarabs alternated with roundels of painted Egyptian scenes.

1920-30   6.5in (16.5cm) long

$300-400   **MARA**

A DRGM (Deutsches Reichs Gebrauchsmuster) bracelet, with 'woven' alloy links, tiny clear crystal rhinestones and a highly polished rhodium-plated clasp.

DRGM translates roughly as German Reich Registered Design and was used to mark many different items designed and registered between 1890 and 1945

c1930

$300-500   **LB**

A rare Fahrner bracelet, with marcasite pineapples and aquamarine baguettes.

This is a very fine Fahrner example using semi-precious aquamarine stones. The baguette cut is typical of cocktail jewelry from this period designed to sparkle and shine for maximum impact.

1930-40   7in (18cm) long

$3,000-4,000   **CRIS**

An Italian chrome bangle, with small polychrome micro-mosaic floral motifs.

1930-40   9in (23cm) long

$50-60   **ECLEC**

An Italian chrome bangle set with alternating pink and green micro-mosaic floral motifs.

1930-40   9in (23cm) long

$50-60   **ECLEC**

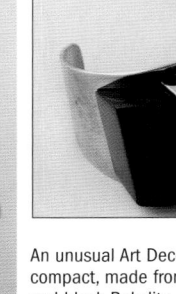

An unusual Art Deco French bracelet-compact, made from gold-plated metal and black Bakelite, with its original box, and marked "Zou Zou".

The design was commissioned by the famous actress Josephine Baker.

Compact 1.75in (4.5cm) wide

1930-35

$1,500-2,000   **LB**

A French Art Deco pin, cast in silver, set with rock crystal of various cuts, including baguette, and a large jade green crystal stone.

This piece was originally commissioned by Queen Mary as a gift to Lady Carmoy, and it retains its original box.

1920-30

$800-1,200   **RITZ**

A marcasite-encased gondola, with gondolier watch-pin.

1920-30   2.75in (6.75cm) long

$700-1,000   **RBRG**

An Italian micro-mosaic pin, of ovoid shape with a center polychrome bouquet within a contrasting floral field and border.

1920-30   2in (5cm) wide

$100-150   **ECLEC**

An Art Deco bracelet in chromed steel and red Bakelite, unsigned.

1925-35

$200-250   **RITZ**

An Art Deco pin of rectangular form carved with floral motifs, in tortoiseshell-like Bakelite and gold-tone metal, unsigned.

Bakelite was patented by Dr.Leo Baekeland in 1907 as an electrical insulator. After the Great Depression in America, bakelite was used for making inexpensive decorative items and jewelry that could be easily mass produced and meet popular demand.

1930-40   2.75in (7cm) wide

$90-110   **JJ**

An Art Deco Jabot pin, the top with two rose diamond sailing ships on a lapis lazuli sea and diamond set arrowhead, set in white precious metal.

2in (5cm) high

$400-600   **WW**

A Reja Art Deco gazelle pin, sterling with rhinestones, signed.

1930-40   3.75in (9.5cm) long

$200-300   **DD**

An Evans American Art Deco leaping gazelle compact, silver with copper accents.

1930-40   3in (7.5cm) diam

$500-700   **DD**

A Reja Art Deco retro set of arrow pins, sterling with a goldwash, ruby and clear rhinestones, signed.

1930-40   2.5in (6.5cm) long

$300-400   **DD**

A French Art Deco paste pin, in a three tier design with clear rhinestones, signed "Sterling".

c1930   2in (5cm) diam

$400-600   **DD**

A Nordic Art Deco atomic pin and earrings set, sterling silver with a goldwash, and ruby and clear rhinestones, signed.

1930-40   pin 3.5in (9cm) long

$300-400   **DD**

A pair of pendant earrings, with micro-mosaic floral motifs in looped, gold-tone wire settings.

1930-40   *1.75in (4.5cm) long*

$70-100   **ECLEC**

An Art Deco rouge compact, with black enamel figural decoration, signed "Richard Hudnut Marvelous".

     1.5in (4cm) diam

$40-60   **DD**

An Art Deco compact, marked "Foreign".

1930-40   *4in (10cm) diam*

$300-400   **JES**

An Art Deco compact, marked "Foreign".

1930-40   *4in (10cm) diam*

$300-400   **JES**

A black Art Deco cigarette case, with lacquer and egg shell on gilded metal.

1925   *4in (10cm) wide*

$1,000-1,500   **JES**

A CLOSER LOOK AT A BOUCHERON COMPACT

Boucheron pieces are highly collectable. Established in 1858 in Paris, the company is known for its fine precious jewelry. The Tsarina of Russia and Queen Isabella of Spain were among its early clients.

During the post-WWI period it became increasingly acceptable for women to be seen in public engaging in intimate activities such as applying make-up. Along with smoking, such daring acts became fashionable and a whole new area of ladies accessories was born.

The compact is complete with matching lipstick holder, making this a rare find. The presence of the original carrying pouches increases the desirability further.

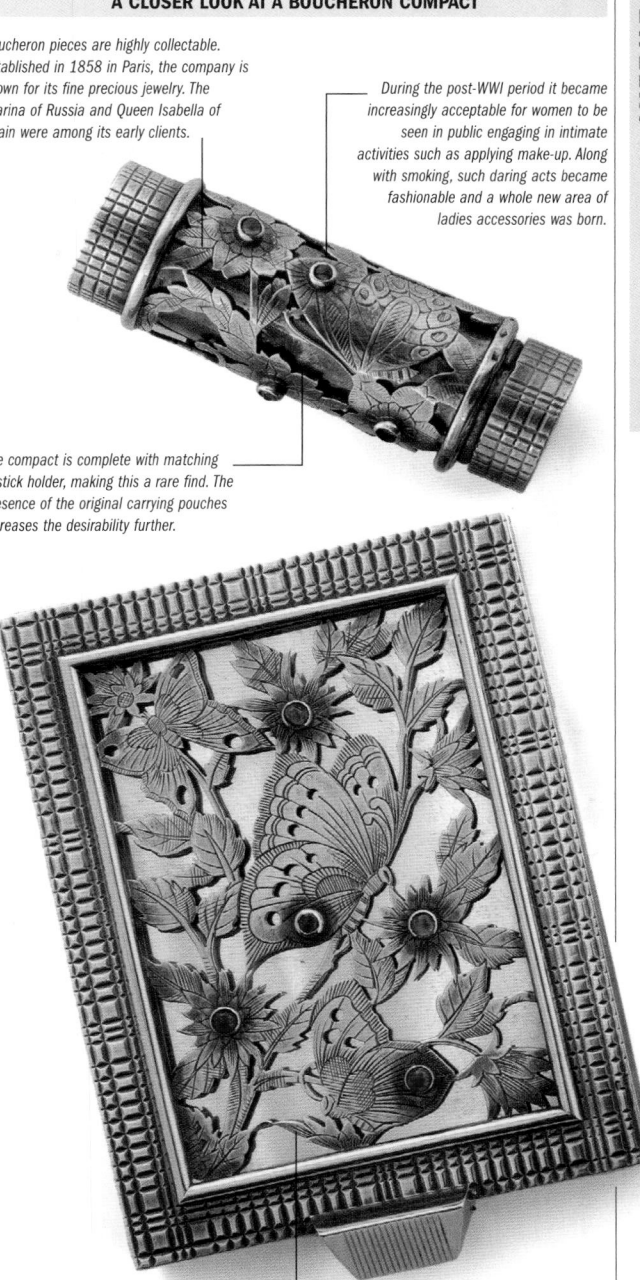

The quality of the decoration, highlighted with cabochon rubies, and the nature of design make this a classic piece.

A ruby set compact and lipstick suite by Boucheron, with cabochon ruby accents, interior swivel mirror and powder compartments, and corresponding lipstick holder, both with French pioncon assay marks, numbered Bt No 875012 and 81.399 for mixed metals, with original black suede carrying pouches and signed "Boucheron Paris".

1940-50

$1,500-2,000   **HAMG**

A Georg Jensen silver tripartite pendant, fixed and hollow, with London import marks.

10.25in (26cm) high

$1,000-1,500 SF

A Georg Jensen stylized silver lily necklace.

Georg Jensen (1866-1935) became know for his simple, unadorned style. The company continues to operate today.

7.25in (18.5cm) diam

$1,500-2,000 SF

A silver abstract 'star-form' bracelet, by Henning Koppel for Georg Jensen.

1960-70 *7.75in (19.5cm) long*

$1,200-1,800 SF

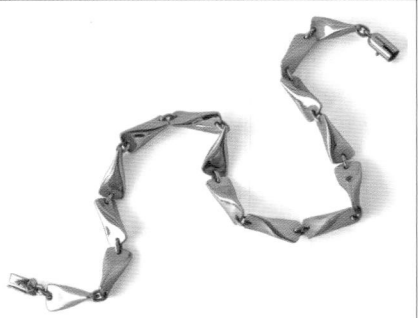

A Georg Jensen silver necklace, constructed of twisted and pinched hollow silver bars.

16in (40.5cm) long

$2,800-3,200 SF

A silver bracelet by Georg Jensen, designed as five industrial scalloped circular links, hallmarked London import 1958, maker's mark G.J.Ld, signed "Georg Jensen sterling Denmark" and numbered "101".

1950-60

$700-1,000 HAMG

A pair of Harry Bertoia hammered and patinated brass earrings, designed as concentric open hoops, without findings, unmarked.

2.75in (7cm) long

$1,200-1,800 SDR

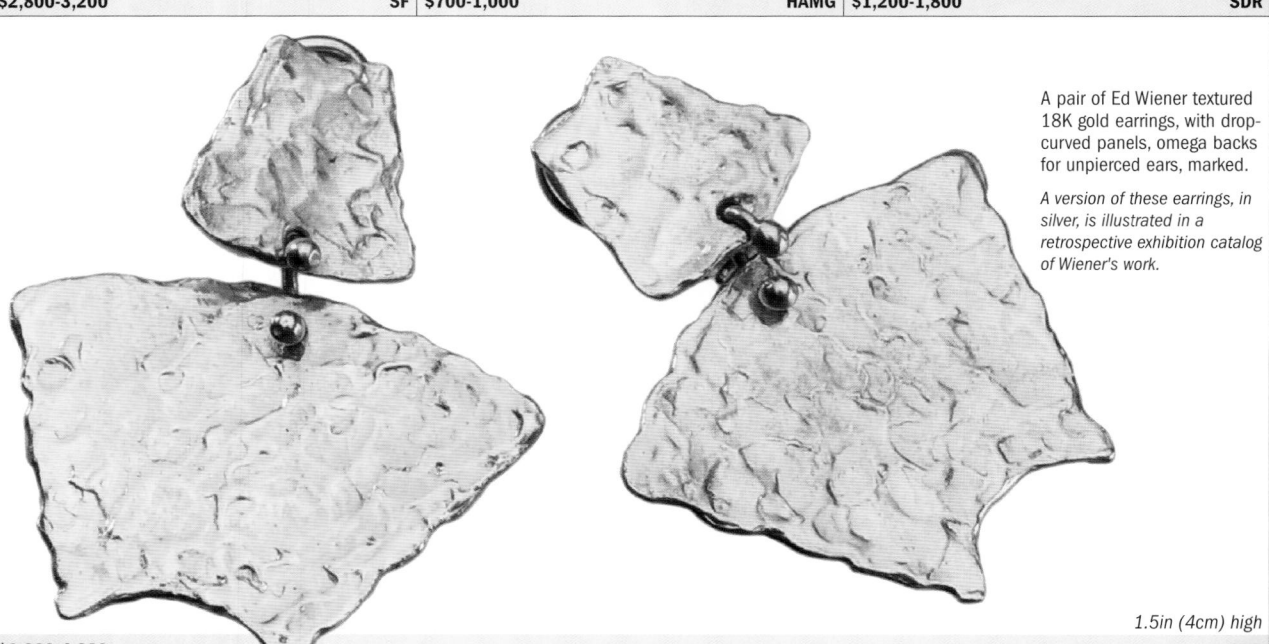

A pair of Ed Wiener textured 18K gold earrings, with drop-curved panels, omega backs for unpierced ears, marked.

A version of these earrings, in silver, is illustrated in a retrospective exhibition catalog of Wiener's work.

1.5in (4cm) high

$2,000-4,000 SDR

A Miriam Haskell bracelet, in gilt metal set with clear and aqua blue rhinestones and three large, milky blue glass stones.

1950-60   *7in (18cm) diam*

$1,000-1,200   **SUM**

A Miriam Haskell necklace, with flower pendant of simulated pearl disks, diamanté and gilded brass flowers, hand wired onto a gilded brass filigree backing.

13.75in (35cm) long

A Miriam Haskell clamper bracelet, the gilded brass with leaves and filigree flowers set with simulated pearls and seed pearls.

1950-60   *2.5in (6cm) diam*

1950-60

$500-700

$200-300   **CRIS**

A Miriam Haskell simulated pearl clamper bracelet, decorated with peridot glass flowers and crystal highlights.

A pair of Miriam Haskell flower earrings, yellow metal set with rose montées.

A pair of Miriam Haskell earrings set with green glass pumpkin cut beads, amber beads and simulated pearls.

1950-60   *2.75in (7cm) diam*

$300-400   **CRIS**

1950-60 1.5in (4cm) diam

$150-200   **CRIS**

1950-60   *1.25in (3cm) long*

$100-150   **CRIS**

A Miriam Haskell necklace, with a pendant of simulated black pearl disks, rose montées and gilded brass leaves, hand wired onto a gilded brass filigree backing.

1950-60   *14in (37cm) long*

$500-700   **CRIS**

ELSA SCHIAPARELLI

- Elsa Schiaparelli (1890-1973) was famous for producing flamboyant jewelry. Born in Rome, she moved to New York to become a script-writer but soon began creating couture and jewelry. In 1928, she opened Schiaparelli Pour le Sport in Paris.
- Possibly her most successful range, her 1936 'Shocking Pink' collection introduced her signature color into jewelry, clothes and cosmetics as well as stirring both outrage and applause from critics.
- She was responsible for setting up one of the first 'ready to wear' retail outlets in New York in 1949.
- Collaborations with Surrealist artists and close friends Salvador Dali, Jean Cocteau and Christian Berard provided inspiration for many of her quirky and highly stylized designs. They also designed some pieces for her.
- After selling her Paris business in 1954, she designed costume jewelry in New York for DeRosa. She used large colorful stones in distinctive bold floral and faunal designs. These continued to be produced until the 1970s.
- Her exotic and often bizarre designs are highly sought after. Pieces from the 1930s are hard to find. Early pieces are rarely signed, but later American and French pieces may carry her signature. Watch out for forgeries and be wary of 1980s reproductions, which are not as desirable.

An Elsa Schiaparelli bracelet, pin and earrings, all in textured gilt metal with lava rock stones and faux pearls.

1950-60   Bracelet 7in (18cm) long

$1,600-1,800   **SUM**

A Schiaparelli feather pin and earrings, yellow metal set with simulated pearls and diamanté accents.

This set is classic Schiaparelli from the 1950s.

1950-60   Pin 3in (8cm) long

$200-300   **CRIS**

An Elsa Schiaparelli pin, in textured gilt metal with lava rock stones and faux pearls.

1950-60   3.25in (8cm) long

$900-1,100   **SUM**

A pair of Schiaparelli brown and green moonstone leaf earrings.

1950-60   1.75in (4.5cm) long

$120-180   **CRIS**

A pair of Schiaparelli acorn and leaf earrings, the yellow metal set with aurora borealis stones.

1950-60   1.5in (4cm) long

$100-150   **CRIS**

A pair of Schiaparelli earrings, with carved rose stones, red aurora borealis navette stones and clear aurora borealis stones.

1950-60   1.5in (4cm) long

$150-200   **CRIS**

A Stanley Hagler two-strand ivorine necklace and matching earrings, with ivorine and citrine glass flower centerpiece.

1960-70   *Necklace 17.75in (45cm) long*

$400-600   **CRIS**

A Stanley Hagler necklace and matching earrings, with emerald green beads and jade crystal rhinestone highlights hand-wired onto a gilt brass filigree backing, signed "Stanley Hagler N.Y.C.".

1960-70   *Necklace 20.5in (52cm) long*

$700-1,000   **CRIS**

A Stanley Hagler faux turquoise and coral three-strand necklace with matching pendant earrings.

1960-70   *Necklace 20.5in (52cm) long*

$400-600   **CRIS**

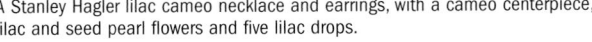

A Stanley Hagler lilac cameo necklace and earrings, with a cameo centerpiece, lilac and seed pearl flowers and five lilac drops.

1960-70   *Necklace 18in (46cm) long*

$500-700   **CRIS**

A Stanley Hagler ivorine and faux coral necklace with matching earrings, with faux coral and ivorine beads handwired onto a gilded brass filigree backing.

1960-70   *Necklace 19in (48cm) long*

$600-700   **CRIS**

A Stanley Hagler peach and champagne carved glass flower necklace and earrings.

1960-70 Necklace 50cm (18.5in) long

$500-600   **CRIS**

A Stanley Hagler necklace with matching earrings, decorated with a foliate clasp which also functions as a centerpiece.

1960-70 Necklace 17.25in (44cm) long

$600-700   **CRIS**

A Stanley Hagler cornelian necklace and earrings, the necklace decorated with a floral centerpiece.

1980-90 Necklace 19in (48cm) long

$500-600   **CRIS**

STANLEY HAGLER

- Stanley Hagler (1923-96), the 'Picasso of jewelry', briefly worked for Miriam Haskell, before setting up on his own in the late 1950s.
- Until Mark Mercy joined him in 1979, he worked alone, experimenting with form and material and paying attention to how each piece would hang and most flatter the wearer.
- Pieces were retailed through up-market shops such as Saks Fifth Avenue in New York and sold to well-known figures such as Wallace Simpson, Duchess of Windsor.
- Hagler specialized in faux pearls, which were made from glass beads dipped in pearl resin up to 15 times to create sheen.
- Flowers formed the inspiration for many of Hagler's designs, but oriental decoration and creatures are recurring motifs.
- Some of his jewelry was multi-purpose and could be modified to a different style. His pieces won him 11 Swarovski awards for 'Great Designs in Jewelry'.
- Pieces from the 1950s are marked "Stanley Hagler" across an oval. He added the initials N.Y.C. in 1983. Examples marked "Stanley Hagler NYC", without periods between the initials, were made by Ian St. Gielar for the company after Hagler's death in 1996.

A Stanley Hagler bracelet, with gold flowers, frosted peridot glass flowers and emerald crystal rhinestone highlights, and signed "Stanley Hagler N.Y.C.".

1960-70   4.25in (11cm) long

$200-300   CRIS

A Stanley Hagler turquoise glass beaded bracelet, the clasp decorated with three jeweled flowers, functioning as a centerpiece.

1960-70   3in (8cm) diam

$200-300   CRIS

A Stanley Hagler coral clamper bracelet, decorated with coral beads and six coral beaded flowers.

1960-70   2.75in (7cm) diam

$200-300   CRIS

A Stanley Hagler pink flower pin.

1960-70   2.5in (6.5cm) long

$100-150   CRIS

A Stanley Hagler baby blue and lilac glass flower and crystal basket pin, the flowers and leaves handwired onto a gilt brass basket.

1960-70   2.75in (7cm) long

$200-300   CRIS

A Stanley Hagler gilt brass flower basket pin, decorated with hand-beaded and glass flowers, signed "Stanley Hagler N.Y.C.".

1960-70   2.75in (7cm) high

$100-150   CRIS

A rare Stanley Hagler large palm tree pin, with beads hand wired onto a gilt brass backing and embellished with glass bananas, parrots and butterflies.

1960-70   2.75in (7cm) long

$200-300   CRIS

A Stanley Hagler jet camellia pin with crystal highlights.

1960-70   3.5in (9cm) diam

$200-300   CRIS

A pair of Stanley Hagler coral and gilded brass three-flower drop earrings.

1960-70   5in (13cm) long

$120-180   CRIS

A pair of Stanley Hagler gilded brass filigree and diamanté drop earrings.

1960-70   3.5in (9cm) long

$100-150   CRIS

A pair of Stanley Hagler flower earrings, with amethyst, peridot and moonstone glass flowers, crystal rhinestone highlights and amethyst drops, signed "Stanley Hagler N.Y.C.".

1960-70   2.25in (6cm) long

$100-150   CRIS

TRIFARI

- One of the largest most admired makers of costume jewelry, Trifari was founded in 1910 in New York by Gustavo Trifari. Leo Krussman joined the firm in 1917 followed by Carl Fishel in 1923 and they became known as Trifari, Krussman and Fishel (T. K. F.)
- The profile of the company was raised by celebrity endorsements and prolific advertising campaigns, which highlighted glamor and good taste. Trifari created exclusive designs for many high profile figures such as First Lady Mamie Eisenhower.
- Alfred Philippe, who joined the company in 1930 and stayed until 1968, is perhaps the pre-eminent Trifari designer. His most commercially successful pieces were his 'Crown' pins and Lucite 'Jelly Bellies'.
- Top-end Trifari pieces are remarkable for their quality. Elaborate techniques were employed such as invisible setting - more frequently associated with precious jewelry.
- Materials included molded and pressed glass, pastes imitating moonstone and chalcedony, and faux pearls and rubies. The company even developed its own non-tarnishing silver substitute, which it named Trifarium.
- Ownership of the company passed to the sons of the original trio in 1964 and then became part of the Monet Group in the 1980s. Liz Claiborne took control of Trifari in 2000.

A Trifari fur clip, rose gold plated and set with faux amethyst stones.

1950-60   *3.5in (9cm) long*

$500-700   **CRIS**

A Trifari brushed gold and diamanté flower pin.

1950-60   *2.5in (6cm) long*

$100-150   **CRIS**

A Trifari poured glass camellia pin with gold highlights.

This pin was inspired by Chanel's camellia pins.

1950-60   *3in (7.5cm) diam*

$100-150   **CRIS**

A Trifari fan pin set with pale blue and moonstone fruit salad pins, designed by Alfred Philippe.

1950-60   *3in (7.5cm) wide*

$700-1,000   **CRIS**

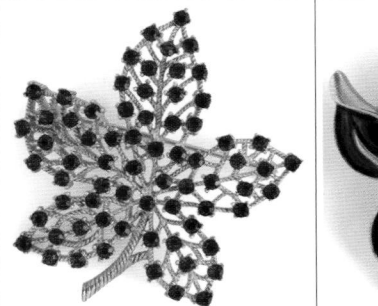

A Trifari open backed maple leaf pin set with faux rubies.

1950-60   *2.5in (6.5cm) long*

$50-80   **CRIS**

A Trifari miniature flower pin, yellow metal set with pale blue and green enamel and red diamanté.

1950-60   *1in (2.5cm) long*

$40-60   **CRIS**

A Trifari feather pin, the white metal set with diamanté.

1930-40   *3.5in (9cm) long*

$200-300   **CRIS**

A Trifari sparrow jelly belly pin, gold wash on white metal with red cabochon eye and clear diamanté accents.

1950-60   *2in (5cm) long*

$300-400   **CRIS**

A Trifari diamanté and citrine sea motif pin, designed by Alfred Philippe.

1940-50   *2.25in (5.5cm) diam*

$200-300   **CRIS**

A Trifari Clipmate, white metal set with clear diamanté stones.

The Clipmate was Trifari's answer to the Coro Duette.

1930-40   *2.75in (7cm) long*

$200-300   **CRIS**

A Trifari rose gold stick pin with square amber glass drop.

1940-50   *3.5in (9cm) long*

$100-150   **CRIS**

A Trifari circle pin with invisibly set faux emeralds and a diamanté border.

1950-60   *2in (5cm) diam*

$150-200   **CRIS**

A pair of Trifari carnation earrings, with red, green and clear diamanté in invisible setting.

1950s   *1.25in (3cm) long*

$200-300   **CRIS**

A pair of Trifari dress clips with matching earrings, the gold plated metal set with aquamarine paste and diamanté.

1940-50   *Clips 2.5in (6cm) long*

$500-700   **CRIS**

A Trifari red and green enamel rose pin and earrings, set with diamanté highlights.

1950-60   *Pin 3.5in (8.5cm) long*

$100-150   **CRIS**

A Trifari pin and earrings, yellow metal with white enamel and turquoise and sapphire cabochons.

1950-60   *Pin 1.5in (4cm) wide*

$100-150   **CRIS**

A pair of Trifari shell-shaped fur clips with matching earrings, the white metal set with simulated pearls, clear paste baguettes and diamanté.

1930-40   *Clips 1.5in (4cm) long*

$400-600   **CRIS**

A Trifari acorn necklace and earrings, with brushed gold metal set with gilded pearls.

1950-60   *Necklace 12in (31cm) long*

$200-300   **CRIS**

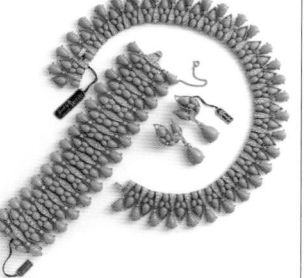

A Trifari turquoise cabochon and clear diamanté parure necklace, bracelet and earrings.

This set was part of a series.

1950-60   *Bracelet 8.25in (21cm) long*

$3,000-4,000   **CRIS**

A Trifari brushed gold geometric bracelet.

1950-60   *7in (17.5cm) long*

$100-150   **CRIS**

An Austrian fruit pin and earrings, with black cherries and green leaves.

1950-60   *Pin 2.25in (5.5cm) long*

$100-150   **CRIS**

An Austrian fruit pin, with red raspberries and green leaves.

1950-60   *2.5in (6cm) long*

$70-100   **CRIS**

An Austrian fruit pin, with red raspberries, green leaves and a red diamanté highlight.

1950-60   *2.5in (6cm) long*

$70-100   **CRIS**

A Boucher piggy bank pin, white metal with gold wash set with multicolored diamanté accents.

1950-60   *1.25in (3.5cm) wide*

$50-70   **CRIS**

A Coppola e Toppo five-strand necklace, with black and clear glass beads and a brass clasp.

Coppola e Toppo, important jewelry designers from the 1940s-80s, started work in Milan and made jewelry for leading fashion designers Schiaparelli, Pucci, Dior and Valentino amongst others. This multiple-strand necklace is a typical design of Coppola e Toppo, and the style that ultimately made brought them their success.

1960-70   *19.5in (50cm) long*

$1,000-1,500   **FM**

A Coppola e Toppo red glass bead parure, consisting of a necklace, bracelet and earrings with characteristic beaded clasps.

1950-60   *Earrings 1.25in (3cm) diam*

$4,000-6,000   **CRIS**

A pair of Coro his and hers penguin pins, enameled pot metal with pink cabochons and diamanté accents.

1950-60   *1.5in (4cm) long*

$200-300   **CRIS**

A floral Coro Duette, gold wash on white metal set with green crystal baguettes and clear crystal rhinestones.

1940-50   *2.5in (6.5cm) long*

$300-400   **CRIS**

A Christian Dior necklace, designed by Mitchell Maer, with floral motifs in rhodium-plated metal with pave-set and pendant clear rhinestone.

1950-60   *Flowers 2.25in (6cm) diam*

$1,500-2,000   **SUM**

A Christian Dior plant-form rhinestone pin, with floral trembler, designed by Mitchell Maer.

1952-56 *3.25in (8.5cm) long*
$500-600 **FM**

A Christian Dior en-tremblant floral pin, designed by Mitchell Maer, in rhodium-plated metal with pavé-set clear rhinestones.

1950-60
$700-1,000 **SUM**

A pair of Eugene earrings, set with turquoise beads and diamanté.

1950-60 *1.5in (3.5cm) long*
$100-150 **CRIS**

An Eisenberg Originals bow pin, the base metal set with clear paste stones.

The chunky metal setting and bow design are typical of 1940s Eisenberg.

1940-50 *3in (7.5cm) wide*
$500-700 **CRIS**

A pair of Maison Gripoix earrings, with blue glass centers encircled by clear crystal rhinestones.

1950-60 *1.25in (3cm) diam*
$400-600 **SUM**

A Dragon pin and earrings set by Har, cast in gold-tone metal with green enameling and ruby, turquoise and aurora borealis rhinestones.

1950-60 *Pin 7cm (2.75in) wide*
$1,200-1,400 **SUM**

A CLOSER LOOK AT A HAR COBRA PARURE

It is harder to find a complete parure than an individual piece as sets were sometimes broken up over the years.

Little is known about the history of Har jewelry, and this has increased its appeal to collectors.

A full parure in such a bold design creates a strong look when worn. The gold enameled green tone metal as well as the dramatic and theatrical nature of this set makes it desirable to vintage fashion enthusiasts.

The cobra motif is typical of Har's fantastical designs, which also included genies, Oriental figures and dragons.

A rare complete cobra parure by Har, comprising a necklace, pin, bracelet and earrings with glass stones, with navette-cut aurora borealis rhinestones.

1950-60 *Necklace 15in (38cm) circ*
$4,000-5,000 **SUM**

A Har dragon necklace and earrings, the enameled yellow metal set with aurora borealis stones.

c1955 *Earrings 1.5in (4cm) long*
$1,500-2,000 **CRIS**

A necklace and earrings set, with floral motifs, by Hobé, in vermeil with high-quality yellow, green, red and clear glass pastes.

1950-60 *Earrings 1.5in (4cm) long*
$1,000-1,500 **SUM**

A pair of Jomaz earrings, white metal set with baguette and round paste stones and simulated pearls.

1940-50 *1.25in (3.5cm) long*
$70-100 **CRIS**

A very rare Joseff silver and red Bakelite leaf pin.

1940-50 *4.75in (12cm) long*
$200-300 **CRIS**

A pair of Kenneth Jay Lane Indian-inspired earrings, with ruby and amethyst glass stones surrounded by clear diamanté.

1960-70   *3.75in (9.5cm) long*

$400-600   **CRIS**

A Kenneth Jay Lane turquoise blue glass and clear rhinestone bib necklace.

This is typical of Lane's extravagant 1960s designs.

1960-70   *Bib 7in (18cm) long*

$2,000-3,000   **CRIS**

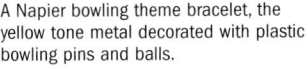

A Napier bowling theme bracelet, the yellow tone metal decorated with plastic bowling pins and balls.

1950-60   *6.5in (17cm) long*

$120-180   **CRIS**

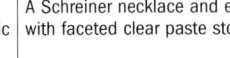

A Schreiner necklace and earrings set, with faceted clear paste stones.

1950-60   *Necklace 14in (34cm) long*

$1,000-1,500   **CRIS**

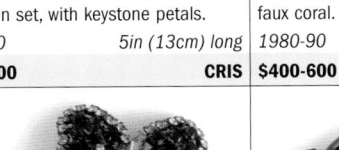

A Vendome feather pin, white metal set with simulated pearls and diamanté.

1950-60   *4.75in (12 cm) long*

$100-150   **CRIS**

A Vendome pink pompom flower pin and earrings, with plastic petals, aurora borealis highlights and yellow metal stem and leaves.

1950-60   *Pin 4.5in (11.5cm) long*

$120-180   **CRIS**

A Vendome yellow pompom flower pin and earrings, the plastic petals with aurora borealis highlights and yellow metal stem with leaves.

1950-60   *Pin 4.5in (11.5cm) long*

$120-180   **CRIS**

A Vendome bracelet, the yellow metal set with faux citrine and topaz cabochons.

1950-60   *2.5in (6.5cm) diam*

$150-200   **CRIS**

A Larry Vrba cerise and clear diamanté flower pin set, with keystone petals.

1980-90   *5in (13cm) long*

$400-600   **CRIS**

A Larry Vrba shell pin, decorated with a diamanté and faux turquoise flower and faux coral.

1980-90   *4.5in (11.5cm) long*

$400-600   **CRIS**

A Larry Vrba amethyst flower pin.

1980-90   *4.75in (12cm) long*

$400-600   **CRIS**

A pair of Weiss earrings, the central pink rough-cut stone surrounded by lilac green and pink baguettes.

1.25in (3cm) long

$70-100   **PC**

A Larry Vrba flower pin, decorated with shells and beads.

1980-90   *5in (13cm) long*

$400-600   **CRIS**

An African carved ivory necklace, with eleven stylized heads, the larger with dark patina and ivory, probably an early tourist piece.

2.25in (6cm) long

$200-300   **SK**

A Murano glass necklace, with polychromatic opaque and vibrantly colored fruit and leaf form glass beads.

1950-60   *16.25in (41cm) long*

$250-300   **LB**

A heron jelly belly pin, with gold wash on silver, red cabochon eye and clear diamanté accents, unsigned.

1940-50   *3.5in (9cm) long*

$600-900   **CRIS**

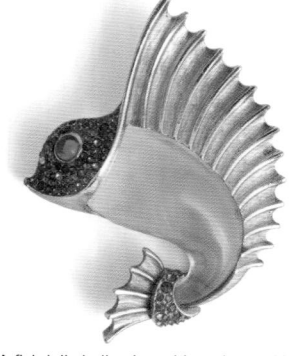

A fish jelly belly pin, gold wash on white metal with green cabochon eye and clear diamanté accents, unsigned.

1950-60   *3in (7cm) long*

$300-400   **CRIS**

A suite of designer jewelry with mussel shell links, comprising necklace, pin/pendant and ear clips, set with cabochon coral stones, and stamped "18kt".

1950-60

$2,000-3,000   **MAX**

A celebrating teddy bear pin, gold plated metal with enamel and diamanté highlights, unsigned.

1.75in (4.5cm) long

$80-120   **CRIS**

A pair of diamond set ear clips, designed as bouquet scrolls, each set with a spray of eight brilliant cut diamonds, to a wire work scroll mount.

1950-60

$700-1,000   **HAMG**

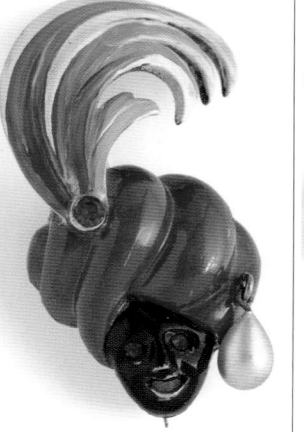

An enameled silver blackamoor pin, set with green and red diamanté and a simulated pearl.

1940-50   *2in (5.5cm) long*

$200-300   **CRIS**

An enamel flower pin, unsigned.

1940-50   *4.5in (11cm) long*

$200-300   **CRIS**

A pair of Dutch man and woman fur clips, unsigned.

1.5in (4cm) long

$120-180   **CRIS**

A Neolitikum redware jug, painted in black and red, with two small handles and ornamental decoration.

2500 BC · 8in (20cm) high
$300-400 · KAU

An Egyptian stone Horos, on a rectangular socle depicting a sitting bird-faced God with entangled arms.

715-332BC · 5in (12.5cm) high
$500-600 · KAU

An Egyptian Ptah, of a standing bald men with skirt, hieroglyphics to the base.

715-332BC · 6.5in (16cm) high
$700-1,000 · KAU

An Egyptian Ptah, of a mummy, glazed in turquoise, holding a scepter.

715-332BC · 7.5in (19cm) high
$500-700 · KAU

A Byzantium green glass light vase, with a conical upper section.

cAD400 · 3.5in (9cm) high
$300-400 · KAU

A Ptolemelian Osiris, glazed in turquoise, sitting on a rectangular base, wearing typical Egyptian clothes, hands on the knees, the skirt with hieroglyphics.

550-250BC · 6in (15cm) high
$500-700 · KAU

A wooden painted Anubis, the God depicted as a laying dog, worm-eaten.

750-632BC · 8.25in (20.5cm) high
$3,000-4,000 · KAU

A small Roman Phönikia amphora, in black glass with colored overlays.

2nd-1stCBC 4.25in (11cm) high
$1,500-2,000 · KAU

A Roman club-shaped vase, in green glass with blue iridescent overlay.

4.5in (11cm) high
$300-400 · KAU

A Roman green glass vase, iridescent overlay.

5.5in (13.5cm) high
$500-600 · KAU

A Roman Puglia brick red ware urn, painted in black and glazed, the egg-shaped body flanked by scroll handles and painted with figures, slightly damaged.

20.5in (51cm) high
$2,000-3,000 · KAU

An Afghanistan jug, with dark patination and a fluted handle.

cAD500 · 5.5in (14cm) high
$200-300 · KAU

A 19thC ivory bust handle lignum vitae cane, the head of Abraham Lincoln carved in the full round on silver collar engraved "C.M.P.", on tapered shaft with silvered metal ferrule.

39in (99cm) high

$3,000-4,000   **FRE**

An ivory topped hardwood cane, the handle in the form of a bust of the first Duke of Wellington, the ring turned shaft with gilt metal ferrule.

35in (89cm) long

$700-1,000   **L&T**

An ivory topped hardwood cane, the handle in the form of a pierrot's head wearing a ruff and a bonnet, the shaft with gilt metal ferrule with steel tip, with silver band with rubbed marks for Birmingham.

1901   35.75in (91cm) long

$300-400   **L&T**

An ivory topped black palm cane, the handle in the form of a hand coming over the eye of an early 19thC gentleman, pulling his nose back, the shaft with silver band and gilt metal ferrule.

36.25in (92cm) long

$400-500   **L&T**

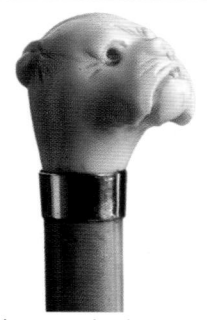

An ivory topped malacca cane, the handle in the form of a pug's head, the shaft with gold band and horn ferrule.

35.75in (91cm) long

$300-400   **L&T**

An ivory topped malacca cane, the handle in the form of a wolfhound's head, with an engraved silver band bearing an inscription from the orchestra at the Theatre Royal, Glasgow to their musical director, 1904-5, with marks for London.

1904   36.25in (92cm) long

$300-400   **L&T**

An ivory topped malacca cane, the handle in the form of an eagle's head, with silver band chased with blank shield, the shaft with gilt metal ferrule with steel tip.

36.25in (92cm) long

$300-400   **L&T**

An ivory topped mahogany cane, the handle in the form of an albatross' head with glass eyes, the shaft with gilt metal ferrule with steel tip.

34.25in (87cm) long

$300-400   **L&T**

An ivory and hardwood cane, the handle in the form of a polka dot leg, the shaft spirally turned with lozenges and gilt metal ferrule with steel tip.

34.25in (87cm) long

$300-400   **L&T**

An ivory topped bone cane, the handle in the form of a fist clutching a serpent, the whalebone shaft with nine ebony bands and ivory tip.

34.25in (87cm) long

$500-600   **L&T**

A George III narwhal and bone walking stick, having a plaited finial to a spiral and ribbed shaft.

35.5in (90cm) long

$3,000-4,000   **WW**

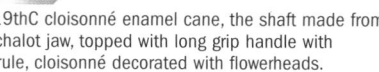

A 19thC cloisonné enamel cane, the shaft made from cachalot jaw, topped with long grip handle with ferrule, cloisonné decorated with flowerheads.

$2,000-3,000   **SEG**

A pair of 18thC Battersea enamel candlesticks, painted and gilded with floral sprays on a white ground with blue cartouches.

9.75in (25cm) high

$1,500-2,000   **L&T**

An 18thC Staffordshire enamel taperstick, of silver shape, landscape printed in puce and bianco sopra bianco scroll work.

6.75in (17cm) high

$1,000-1,500   **LAW**

A late 19thC French 'jeweled' enamel and gilt bronze mounted bijouterie box, gilt and decorated with roses, against a blue ground, with a fitted interior.

10in (25.5cm) wide

$1,200-1,800   **FRE**

A 19thC silver cigarette case with enameled scene to top, and a mark on interior "Alpacca".

3.5in (9cm) wide

$1,500-2,000   **JDJ**

A CLOSER LOOK AT ENAMEL TEA CADDIES

The decoration has been painted in tones of one color – a technique borrowed from ceramic decoration and known as "en camieu".

The rural scenes featuring ancient ruins, rural views and a man fishing by a lake were common in the early 19thC and can be seen on the ceramics of the time.

All three boxes are in good condition, any damage would reduce the value by a third or more.

The gilt metal mounts would have been time-consuming and relatively costly to make, adding to the value and desirability.

A 19thC Staffordshire patch box, painted with two children, and a blue base.

$500-700   **LAW**

A set of three Staffordshire white enamel tea caddies with gilt metal mounts, one with hinged cover, two with push-on covers.

Before 1784, when the enormous taxes on tea were reduced, caddies would have been a luxury item owned by the rich. After this date tea drinking became widely popular and there was a profound increase in the production of tea services and caddies.

3.5in (9cm) high

$7,000-10,000   **LAW**

A late 20thC Russian enamel egg, applied with bees and red cabochons, against pink enamel petals and green leaves, on a silver gilt stand, pseudo marks.

Egg 2.75in (7cm) high

$600-900   **FRE**

An early 20thC framed Limoges enamel plaque by Camille Faure, depicting a figure on a woodland path, signed "Faure, Limoges France".

9.5in (24cm) wide

$800-1,000   **FRE**

FABERGÉ

FABERGÉ

- Carl Peter Fabergé (1846-1920) was the son of a St Petersburg goldsmith of Huguenot descent. After serving an apprenticeship in Frankfurt, Germany, he returned to Russia and took over the family business in 1870.
- He won the Gold Medal at the Pan-Russian Exhibition of 1882 and swiftly gained a reputation for his jewellery and objects d'art, combining the highest artistic flair with attention to detail.
- He came to the notice of the Imperial Court and was commissioned to make the first Easter Egg by Tsar Alexander III in 1884. Over the next 30 years, he won the patronage of several royal houses and established shops in several Russian cities as well as in London.
- In 1917, the Revolution ended the Romanov dynasty and Fabergé's decline paralleled that of his patron, the Tsar. He fled Russia in 1918 and died in Lausanne, Switzerland.
- Fabergé's incomparable skill as a master craftsman was matched by the progressive methods he adopted to run his business. He had a team of workmasters, each with his or her own individual speciality and responsibility.
- Although best known for the 57 Imperial eggs, they created hardstone carvings, flower studies, silver and jewellery as well as functional boxes, bellpushes and frames.

A carved obsidian elephant by Fabergé, with a slightly caricatured manner, and rose cut diamond eyes, chip to one tusk.

c1910   *1.75in (4.5cm) long*

$10,000-15,000   **HAMG**

A carved nephrite elephant by Fabergé, in the caricature manner, with rose cut diamond eyes.

c1910   *1.5in (4cm) long*

$7,000-10,000   **HAMG**

A white chalcedony elephant by Fabergé, with yellow diamond eyes, and chips to both ears and tusks.

c1910   *2in (5cm) long*

$7,000-10,000   **HAMG**

A carved bloodstone elephant by Fabergé, carved in the caricature manner, with cabochon ruby eyes chips to both ears and tail chipped.

c1910   *2in (5.5cm) long*

$7,000-10,000   **HAMG**

A carved bowenite elephant by Fabergé, with cabochon ruby eyes, one eye missing.

c1910   *3in (8cm) long*

$7,000-10,000   **HAMG**

A French 19thC carved ivory plaque, relief carved with Pan as an ass followed by a bacchanalian crowd of maidens, signed "J Pallas".

8.25in (21cm) wide

$5,000-6,000   **L&T**

A French 19thC carved ivory plaque, relief carved with a scene of Pan and a semi-naked dancing nymph and cherubs in a landscape.

9in (23cm) wide

$4,000-4,500   **L&T**

An 18thC French ivory snuff rasp, well-carved with a lady, with shell terminal and iron rasp, cracked and part of shell terminal missing.

8in (20.5cm) long

$3,000-4,000   **BAR**

A 18thC French ivory snuff rasp, well-carved with an elderly couple holding hands walking under a tree, terminating in a shell, lacking iron rasp.

7.5in (19cm) long

$4,000-6,000   **BAR**

A late 18th/19thC carved and painted ivory mechanical Prisoner of War whimsy, the figures dance and spin when crank is turned, within glass dome.

9.25in (23.5cm) high

$7,000-10,000   **FRE**

A French 19thC carved ivory chalice, with the twelve apostles on a bracket inscribed with his name, the underside inscribed with a coat of arms.

6in (15.5cm) high

$4,000-6,000   **L&T**

A 19thC American watercolor on ivory miniature of a young woman.

2in (5cm) high

$2,500-3,500   **POOK**

A Raphael Peale (1774-1825) miniature portrait of a gentleman, in watercolor on ivory, with gilt case set with hair and pearls, unsigned, with initials "M D" at back.

2.75in (7cm) high

$6,000-9,000   **FRE**

An early 19thC watercolor on ivory miniature of Peter Muhlenberg, in a gold locket inscribed, "Peter Muhlenberg March 20th 1787".

2in (5cm) high

$5,000-6,000   **POOK**

An American School 18thC miniature portrait of a gentleman, in oil on ivory and gilt locket case, the reverse bright-cut, unsigned.

2in (5cm) high

$15,000-20,000   **FRE**

An American School 18thC miniature portrait of a lady, in oil on ivory with gilt locket enclosure, unsigned.

1.5in (4cm) high

$2,000-3,000   **FRE**

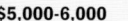

A wooden scale model of a US steam river launch, on molded wooden plinth in glazed brass bound case.

c1880   15.75in (40cm) long

$1,000-1,500   **L&T**

A 20thC model of 'The Marie Sophie of Falmouth', a wooden rig two masted sailing cutter, with a glazed case.

48.5in (121.5cm) long

$600-900   **SWO**

A wooden model of a motor launch, on molded wooden plinth in glazed brass bound case.

c1925   Model 34.5in (88cm) long

$1,200-1,800   **L&T**

A CLOSER LOOK AT A PRISONER OF WAR SHIP

During the Napoleonic Wars, prisoners passed time by producing an array of beautifully crafted decorative items with readily available materials such as wood and bone. Some became highly regarded for their work and were commissioned to make individual pieces with specially supplied materials.

Despite being vulnerable to damage, the ship has survived in very good condition.

The rigging on this model is hugely complex and well realized. Producing this ornate piece would have been a time-consuming task.

The 'rate' of a ship was decided by how many guns it had. First rate ships would have been the biggest ships of the fleet and often the 'flagships'. Rated ships had three square rigged masts.

A fine early 19thC French Prisoner-of-War bone and wood ship's model, of a 120-Gun First Rate Ship-of-the-Line, with three bound masts with yards and booms, the carved figurehead of a Roman warrior.

23.5in (59.5cm) wide

$20,000-30,000   **L&T**

A pair of miniature brass cannons, on stepped wheeled carriages, the barrels with cast coronet and initials "GR".

6.25in (16cm) long

$700-1,000   **L&T**

A glass model of a carronade, with ribbed decoration, on later beech stand with white metal wheels and mounts.

5.75in (14.5cm) long

$400-600   **L&T**

A copper, brass and steel model of a mash tun, on a wooden stand, with label "Bell Brothers, Manchester Ltd.".

21.5in (55cm) high

$2,000-3,000   **L&T**

A copper and brass mounted model of a whisky still, raised on a rectangular oak plinth.

20.5in (52cm) high

$1,000-1,500   **L&T**

A 19thC copper model of a whisky still, of riveted construction with protruding spout.

30.75in (78cm) high

$1,000-1,500   **L&T**

A John Willis Good (1845-1879) finely painted plaster model of the huntsman hallooing, under glass dome.

12in (30cm) high

$6,000-9,000   **CHEF**

A Hoffman perfume bottle, in clear and frosted vaseline crystal, with raised "HOFFMAN" mark.

c1925   6.5in (16cm) high

$1,500-2,000   RDL

An Ingrid perfume bottle, in opaque blue crystal with clear stopper in metalwork with Bakelite rose jewels.

c1925   8.5in (21cm) high

$1,000-1,500   RDL

An 'Ingrid' perfume bottle, in clear crystal with an opaque red stopper.

c1935   4.5in (11.5cm) high

$500-700   RDL

A Czechoslovakian perfume bottle, in amber with a clear and frosted stopper, with enameled and jeweled metalwork, molded "CZECHO-SLOVAKIA" mark.

c1920s   6in (15.5cm) high

$700-1,000   RDL

A Czechoslovakian perfume bottle, in clear crystal with applied birds, stenciled "CZECHOSLOVAKIA" mark.

c1925   6.75in (17cm) high

$800-1,200   RDL

A set of two Czechoslovakian perfume bottles for Ahmed Soliman, in clear crystal with gilt labels, and stoppers, in decorated faux ivory cases and fitted box.

c1935   4.5in (11.5cm) high

$4,000-4,500   RDL

A 'Mon Ame' perfume bottle for Ybry, in purple crystal with stopper, metal cover, label and tasseled box.

c1925   2cm (5cm) high

$700-1,000   RDL

A 'Bouquet' perfume presentation for OTA, of black glass bottles and pearl finished bottles, fitting stopper to base, in display box with label.

c1930   10in (25cm) long

$8,000-12,000   RDL

A Schiaparelli 'Spin & Win' special presentation of 'Shocking' perfume, the four miniature glass bottles revolving when the box lid pops up.

c1940   1.5in (4cm) high

$2,000-3,000   RDL

A pair of Schiaparelli display lamps, with painted vellum shades, the candle-shaped bottle, in clear glass with gold detail, for 'Sleeping' perfume forms the base, used at Place Vendome salon.

c1940   9.25in (23.5cm) high

$800-1,200   RDL

A 'Parfums par Noel' presentation set of 'Cyclamen', 'Night & Day', and 'Blue Grass' for Elizabeth Arden, features blown glass bottles hung in net stockings, stains to box.

c1940   3.5in (9cm) high

$2,000-3,000   RDL

A 'Ballerina' perfume bottle for Marie Earl, in clear glass with gilded detail, sealed and on elaborate ballet shoe display.

c1945   3.5in (9cm) high

$3,000-4,000   RDL

OBJETS DE VERTU

A scrimshaw tusk, engraved by Lt. Theodoric Lee (1826-67), inscribed "Taken at Little Berbey in a skirmish with the natives Dec. 13, 1843, Macedonian", and decorated with a figure of Diana and Captain Kidd, the end inscribed "T. Lee Coast of Africa".

Theodoric Lee, a lieutenant physician in the United States Navy served on the U.S.S. Macedonian, under the command of Commodore Matthew C. Perry and was involved in an attack on the village of Little Berebee on the Ivory Coast to avenge the massacre of U.S. Merchant seamen there two years earlier. The king of Little Berebee was captured and the village set on fire.

c1843

$7,000-10,000 **FRE**

This powder horn was decorated using a method called 'scrimshaw'. Craftsmen would engrave the surface with a knife or pins then rub soot into the surface to make the pattern stand out.

The early age of this piece and the initials inscribed on it add to its rarity, as does the fact that it was designed for use when most were decorative.

The political message inscribed on the bannerette relates to a period of embargo and war in America and is an unusual feature.

Images of the American flag and an eagle also make this horn highly sought after.

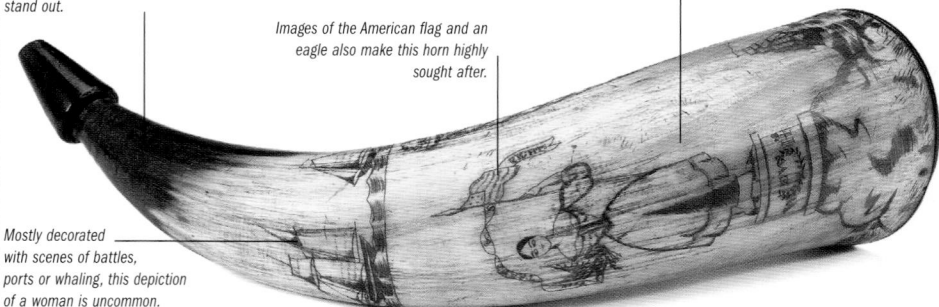

Mostly decorated with scenes of battles, ports or whaling, this depiction of a woman is uncommon.

An American scrimshaw decorated powder horn, inscribed "Free Trade and States R[ight]s.", with the initials "W.H and E.W." and the wooded end of the horn impressed "Heller".

c1830   17in (43cm) long

$25,000-35,000   **FRE**

A 19thC Scrimshaw whale tooth with figure of Lady Liberty with eagle and flag.

7in (18cm) high

$9,000-11,000 **POOK**

A mid-19thC American scrimshaw whale's tooth with etched ship on one side and a family scene on the other.

6in (15cm) high

$800-1,000 **POOK**

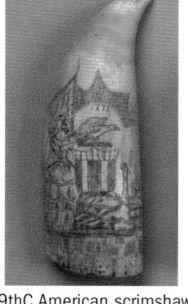

A mid-19thC American scrimshaw whale's tooth with Lady Liberty, dated 1776, reverse with three masted ship.

7in (18cm) high

$2,000-3,000 **POOK**

A mid-19thC American scrimshaw whale's tooth with scene of couple on one side, young girl on reverse.

6in (15cm) high

$1,500-2,000 **POOK**

SHELL

A mid-19thC shell sailors valentine, with an octagonal glazed and hinged frame, one side decorated within a heart, the other a star.

19.75in (50cm) wide

$6,000-9,000 **DN**

An early 19thC sailor's shell valentine hinged octagonal mahogany box, the shells organized in concentric patterns to glazed interiors of lid and base.

9.5in (24.5cm) wide

$3,000-4,000 **L&T**

A pair of shell sailor's valentines, one centered by a heart, the other by a star, formerly hinged together.

Octagonal boxes in the shape of old compass cases served as frames for symmetrical creations using small shells of different colors and shapes.

13.75in (35cm) wide

$12,000-18,000 **L&T**

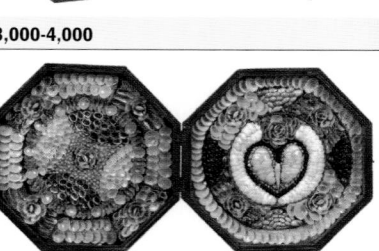

A 19thC sailor's shellwork valentine with flowers and heart decoration.

10in (25.5cm) wide

$7,000-9,000 **POOK**

SNUFF BOXES

- Snuff (finely ground scented tobacco) was not used by the British nobility until the early 18th century when large quantities were seized from captured Spanish ships. Its use soon created a host of conventions and peculiar habits, including specially made boxes.
- Early boxes were made in precious metals, but as snuff became more affordable the practice became more widespread and boxes made from wood and papier mâché became available.
- Enamel boxes were decorated with pictures painted in enamels or gouache on inset panels. Tortoiseshell could be veneered on to a wooden box gessoed white, or colored to give a green or red tinge. Silver was combined with shell or quartz. All the porcelain manufacturers made objets de vertu.
- From 1750, papier mâché became increasingly fashionable as Europe's answer to genuine Oriental lacquer. Papier mâché boxes were painted with chinoiseries, landscapes, portraits, or classical motifs, and sometimes incorporated Wedgwood cameos.
- Many novelty boxes in shapes such as shoes were carved from wood. Boxes of local hard woods with ivory inlays were imported from Vizagapatnam in India.

An 18thC agate snuff box and cover of cartouche shape, with brown stone and gold borders, and fish skin case.

2.5in (6.5cm) wide

$2,000-3,000 **LAW**

An early 18thC red painted tin box and cover, possibly Scandinavian, the cover painted with a portrait of a gentleman.

3.25in (8cm) diam

$300-400 **DN**

A late 18thC French composition snuff box with molded beads, the cover set with a sepia miniature portrait of a female, and a gold border.

3in (7.5cm) diam

$3,000-4,000 **LAW**

A Scottish provincial snuff box, by Robert Keay I, with marks for Perth, stamped "RK" within an oval punch, an eagle displayed and "RK" again, with hinged cover and gilt interior.

c1791 *2.75in (7cm) long*

$1,000-1,500 **L&T**

An 18thC agate and gold snuff box of rectangular shape, with pinkish brown stone and waved gold borders.

2.25in (5cm) wide

$3,000-3,500 **LAW**

An early 19thC Mauchline Ware snuff box, the lid carved with a bust of Napoleon within an ebony molding.

2.5in (6.5cm) wide

$300-400 **DNT**

An early 19thC painted German papier-mâché snuff box, with gilt interior.

4.25in (10.5cm) diam

$500-700 **CHEF**

A mid-19thC German papier-mâché snuff box, the hinged lid printed and overpainted with people listening to traveling musicians on an impromptu stage.

3.5in (9cm) wide

$200-300 **CHEF**

A large 19thC papier-mâché table snuff box.

4.5in (11.5cm) wide

$200-300 **MB**

A Victorian silver mounted ram's head table snuffmull, Edinburgh, maker JM possibly Johnathon Millidge.

c1853 *17in (43.5cm) wide*

$7,000-10,000 **L&T**

A Victorian Scottish mounted ram's head table snuff mull, also suspending six assorted tools from belcher link chains, with marks for Edinburgh, maker's mark "JM".

1894 *16.25in (40.5cm) wide*

$5,000-7,000 **L&T**

An engraved powder horn, decorated with the Coat of Arms of Jamaica and a seated Britannia, dated and signed "James & Lara 1834".

11.5in (29cm) long

$1,000-1,500   **POOK**

A late 18thC horn pipe tamper carved with a caricature head, silver ends engraved with crest and initials.

3.5in (9cm) high

$500-700   **LAW**

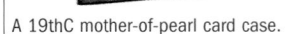

A 19thC mother-of-pearl card case.

4in (10cm) wide

$120-180   **MB**

A 19thC Victorian turtle shell bijouterie box, with removable cover and button handle, opening to reveal a plush fitted interior.

8.5in (21.5cm) long

$1,000-1,500   **FRE**

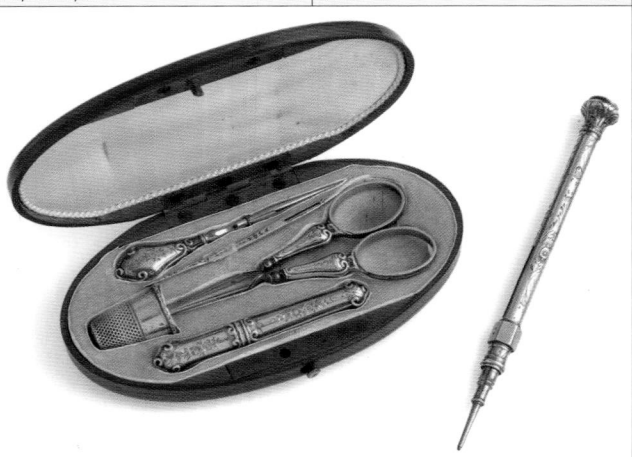

A 19thC French tulipwood etui with gold mounted fittings and gold plated pencil.

4.5in (11.5cm) wide

$500-700   **LAW**

A pair of Georgian/William IV silver framed sunglasses, with part hallmarked silver frame and four hinged half-elliptical green glass sections, with a Regency shagreen and silver-mounted pocket case, various sections bear lion passant and leopard's head marks.

1821-36

$500-700   **BIG**

A 19thC Thomason corkscrew, with bone handle and natural bristle brush, with central cast crest.

9.75in (25cm) long extended

$700-1,000   **L&T**

A 19thC Thomason corkscrew, with bone handle and natural bristle brush, with central cast crest.

9.75in (25cm) long extended

$700-1,000   **L&T**

A pair of early 19thC papier-mâché coasters, each painted with flowers and gilt leaves on a cream ground.

4.75in (12cm) diam

$1,000-1,500   **DN**

A 19thC blue john column, with a brass capital and a square white and black marble base.

16in (41cm) high

$3,000-4,000   **DN**

A Russian silver Samorodok cigarette case, by Karl Gustav Lundell, of bark textured design, with cabochon sapphire thumbpiece, St. Petersburg.

1908-17

$3,000-4,000   **HAMG**

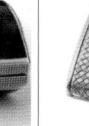

A tortoiseshell-mounted cylindrical cigarette case, with engine turned yellow metal mounts, stamped "585", probably Austrian.

c1940   *3.5in (9cm) wide*

$700-1,000   **DN**

An 18ct woven gold cigarette case, of oval form with plain thumbpiece.

3.5in (9cm) wide

$800-1,200   **WW**

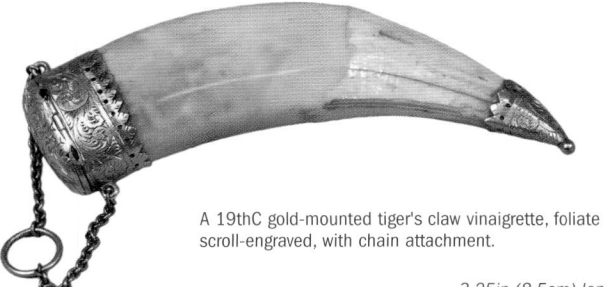

A 19thC gold-mounted tiger's claw vinaigrette, foliate scroll-engraved, with chain attachment.

3.25in (8.5cm) long

$600-900   **SWO**

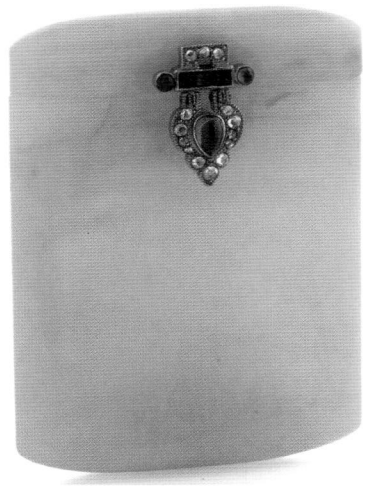

A Belle Epoque jadeite box, by Cartier, Paris, in the Russian style, with rose-cut diamond and caliber-cut sapphire hinges, the thumb piece with a cabochon sapphire lock, signed, French control marks, maker's mark "PD".

c1910

$5,000-6,000   **HAMG**

A 1940s ruby set minaudiere, by Boucheron Paris, with cabochon ruby highlights, with two interior powder compacts, signed Boucheron Paris and numbered "Bt No 875012" and "83.087", with French assay marks for mixed metals, with original suede carrying pouchette.

$2,000-3,000   **HAMG**

An 18ct yellow and white gold lattice work traveling purse clock by Tiffany, the clock with circular gold dial, signed "Tiffany & Co.".

1.25in (3cm) wide

$1,000-1,500   **WW**

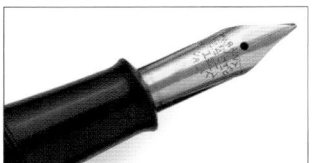

A Victorian gentleman's gilt and engine turned dressing table set, with shaving brush, glass bottle and two glass boxes, crested, inscribed "P & F Schafer, 27 Picadilly", with marks for London, maker's mark "JB".

1875

$300-400   **L&T**

A set of five late 19thC to early 20thC painted horn beakers, each of cylindrical form painted with hunting scenes.

largest 5.25in (13.5cm) high

$2,000-3,000   **ROW**

A Namiki no.6 leverfill fountain pen, with gilt floral sprig decoration on black lacquered ground, character signature.

5in (13cm) long

$1,000-1,500   **GORL**

345

OBJETS DE VERTU

A George III Kit Kat Club cup, the rounded simulated shagreen bowl with a roundel inscribed "Kit Kat Club, 1703" and inscribed beneath "Ranelagh Club", with plated foot and rim.

The Kit-Kat Club was a London political and literary club active from c1700-1720. The membership of some fifty included leading Whig politicians and writers.

5.5in (13.5cm) high

$600-900   **LFA**

An 18thC coral seal, carved with two putti, on a foliate and turned base.

2.5in (6cm) high

$1,500-2,000   **SWO**

An early 19thC Italian micro mosaic panel, depicting figures relaxing in an Arcadian landscape, within gilt brass frame with chased moldings.

3in (7.5cm) wide

$15,000-20,000   **L&T**

A Victorian painted spelter watch holder in the form of a parrot.

6in (15cm) high

$400-500   **SWO**

A Victorian rosewood and porcelain plaque mounted metronome, with Wedgwood style blue jasper ovals in giltmetal frames, on brass ball feet.

12.5in (32cm) high

$1,000-1,500   **L&T**

A Victorian shellwork floral bouquet, shaped and painted as various flower blooms, under a domed glass cover on ebonized circular plinth with flattened bun feet.

15.75in (40cm) high

$400-600   **L&T**

A late 18thC English watercolor on silk picture, with rolled paper and crushed mother-of-pearl, depicting 'The Fortune Teller' after Angelica Kauffmann.

20in (51cm) wide

$5,000-6,000   **POOK**

A late 19thC large swordfish blade, painted in colored enamels with figures in a landscape.

$300-400   **LFA**

A stuffed and mounted black-and-white colobus monkey, standing with arms outstretched, on an African hardwood plinth, bears plaque of "Rowland Ward Ltd, Piccadilly, London".

Rowland Ward (1848-1912) was one of the best known taxidermy businesses in the world.

30in (76cm) high

$600-900   **L&T**

A mounted taxidermy Indian tiger's head, with open mouth in a growl, on oak shield with label on back "Preserved by John MacPherson, taxidermist and furrier, Inglis Street Inverness".

18in (45.5cm) high

$1,200-1,800   **L&T**

PERSIAN CARPET REGIONS

- Bijar rugs are also known as the 'Iron Rugs of Persia', due to their heavy and durable nature. Most were woven by Kurds in the Gerus area. Rugs by the Afshar weavers of the Tekab and Tekkenteppe areas are often among the most sought after.
- Hamadan rugs were made in the city of the same name, south of Bijar. They typically have one heavy cotton shot of weft (single wefted) and are made with thick high quality coarsely woven wool.
- Heriz carpets were produced in the villages of the slopes of Mount Sabalan by Caucasus Shiva Moslems driven south by the Russian military advances.
- Kashan rugs were produced in what was once a major center of the garment trade. Some of the best Kashans are from Ardistan and particularly excellent examples are produced in Yezd and Kashmar.
- Kirman has long been a center for rug production, due to its location and its resistance to invasion. Red and blue shades are typically lighter than in the rugs of other regions and medallion designs are often found.
- Malayer or Malayir-Rugs coming from the large rug producing region south of Hamadan. Examples are single wefted and range from coarse to fine, generally using very good wool.

A late 19thC Bakshaish carpet from North Persia.

250x135in (635x343cm)

$20,000-40,000　　　　　　　**FRE**

A late 19thC Bijar carpet from North Persia.

315x168in (800x426.75cm)

$12,000-18,000　　　　　　　**FRE**

A late 19thC Bijar carpet, from North Persia.

163x125in (414x317.5cm)

$10,000-15,000　　　　　　　**FRE**

An early 20thC Hamadan carpet, from West Persia.

237x137in (602x348cm)

$8,000-12,000　　　　　　　**FRE**

A late 19thC Bijar carpet, from North Persia.

315in (800cm) long

$9,000-12,000　　　**FRE**

A late 19thC Bijar carpet, from North Persia.

161x90in (409x228.5cm)

$2,500-3,000　　　**FRE**

A room-sized Heriz rug, with a central ivory medallion on a red field with blue corners and navy border.

c1900　　　　　　　　　　　　*176in (440cm) long*

$30,000-40,000　　　　　　　　　　　　　　　　**POOK**

An early 20thC Hamadan carpet, from West Persia.

170x122in (432x310cm)

$12,000-18,000　　　**FRE**

One of a pair of Hamadan/Bibikibad rugs, from West Persia.

1925-50　　*58x40in (147.5x101.5cm)*

$1,200-1,800 PAIR　　　**FRE**

A Heriz carpet, from Northwest Persia.

c1900   146x123in (371x312.5cm)

$10,000-15,000   FRE

A late 19thC Heriz carpet, from Northwest Persia.

162x120in (411.5x305cm)

$8,000-12,000   FRE

A Heriz carpet from Northwest Persia.

c1930   156x122in (396.25x310cm)

$8,000-12,000   FRE

A Persian Heriz room-size rug, with eight-point star medallion in shades of cinnabar and brown on an ivory ground within multiple borders.

c1970-80   94x127in (239x322.5cm)

$1,500-2,000   DRA

A Persian Heriz rug, with multiple star medallions and spandrels in shades of red, brown and ivory on a crimson ground.

96x125in (244x317.5cm)

$1,000-1,500   DRA

A 'Mohtashem' Kashan carpet from Central Persia.

c1900   262x159in (665.5x404cm)

$70,000-100,000   FRE

A 20thC Heriz carpet with central medallion on an ivory field with red corners.

124x159in (315x404cm)

$15,000-20,000   POOK

A late 19thC 'Mohtashem' Kashan rug, from Central Persia.

78x50in (198x127cm)

$4,000-5,000   FRE

A late 19thC 'Mohtashem' Kashan prayer rug, from Central Persia, repairs.

79x52in (200.5x132cm)

$6,000-9,000   FRE

An early 20thC Indo-Kashan carpet, machine finished ends with added plain flatweave strip with fringes.

40x105in (102x267cm)

$4,000-6,000   FRE

An early 20thC Manchester Kashan carpet, from Central Persia, inscribed.

206x141in (523x358cm)

$5,000-8,000   FRE

An early 20thC Manchester Kashan carpet, from Central Persia.

225x124in (571.5x315cm)

$8,000-10,000   FRE

A late 20thC Iranian Kashan carpet, in cotton warp and weft with woollen pile, asymmetrical knots, with central medallion with palmette pendants on red floral ground, dark blue spandrels and main border on dark blue ground, with cotton fringe.

81.5x53.5in (204x134cm)

$500-600   **KAU**

A Persian Kashan rug, with scalloped diamond center medallion in shades of blue and ivory on a crimson ground within multiple blue borders.

c1960   *98x146in (249x371cm)*

$2,500-3,500   **DRA**

A Kashan pictorial rug, with a crimson pictorial cartouche and scrolling vine border between bands.

52in (132cm) wide

$1,000-2,000   **L&T**

A Kashan silk rug, the ivory field with central cusped red and light blue medallion suspending pendants.

52in (132cm) wide

$3,000-4,000   **L&T**

A mid-20thC Kazvin carpet, from West Persia.

240x150in (601x381cm)

$3,000-4,000   **FRE**

A Laver Kerman carpet, from Southeast Persia.

c1920   *142x104in (360.5x264cm)*

$3,000-4,000   **FRE**

A Kerman carpet, from Southeast Persia.

c1940   *240x154in (609.5x391cm)*

$5,000-6,000   **FRE**

A mid-20thC Kerman carpet, from Southeast Persia.

142x105in (360.5x26.5cm)

$4,000-5,000   **FRE**

A 20thC room-size Kirman rug with central medallion on an ivory field with multiple borders.

190x144 (483x366cm)

$4,000-6,000   **POOK**

A room-sized Kirman, with overall floral design on an ivory field with multiple borders.

c1915   *138x102in (350.5x259)*

$2,000-3,000   **POOK**

A Persian Kurdish rug, with lozenge medallions and cruciform panels in crimson and ivory on a black-brown ground within multiple borders.

51x110in (129.5x279.5cm)

$650-850   **DRA**

A late 19thC Mahal carpet, from Central Persia.

161x120in (409x305cm)

$4,000-6,000   **FRE**

An early 20thC Malayer corridor carpet, from West Persia, inscribed and dated 1323 (c1905).

199x69in (505.5x175.25cm)

$3,000-4,000   **FRE**

A room-sized Malayer carpet, with overall floral pattern on a blue field with ivory corners and large red border.

c1920   *120x87in (305x221cm)*

$3,000-4,000   **POOK**

A Mashad carpet, from Northeast Persia, inscribed, "Work of Shushtarian".

c1925-50   *221x142in (561x360.5cm)*

$4,000-5,000   **FRE**

A late 19thC Qashqa'i rug, from Southwest Persia.

94x70in (239x178cm)

$3,000-4,000   **FRE**

A Sarouk Fereghan rug, from West Persia.

c1900   *76x48in (193x122cm)*

$4,000-5,000   **FRE**

An early 20thC Malayer Sarouk rug, from West Persia.

78x51in (198x129.5cm)

$2,000-3,000   **FRE**

An early 20thC Malayer Sarouk rug, from West Persia.

78x51in (198x129.5cm)

$2,000-3,000   **FRE**

A Sarouk carpet, from West Persia.

c1920   *164x124in (416.5x315cm)*

$2,000-3,000   **FRE**

A Sarouk carpet, from West Persia, inscribed.

c1920   *165x129in (419x327.5cm)*

$6,000-8,000   **FRE**

A Sarouk carpet, from West Persia.

1920   *180x122in (457x310cm)*

$5,000-6,000   **FRE**

A late 19thC Senneh carpet, with yellow, gold and blue cross-stitching, other end missing some rows of knots, some visible habrash, losses, wear.

300x142in (762x360.5cm)

$10,000-15,000   **FRE**

A late 19thC Senneh rug, from Northwest Persia.

95in (237.5cm) long

$8,000-12,000   **FRE**

An early 20thC partial silk Senneh rug, from West Persia, generally full pile with silk highlights.

83x56in (211x142cm)

$3,000-4,000   **FRE**

A Persian Shiraz rug with tiled center panel of hooked diamonds in shades of blue and red on a crimson ground.

58x8in (147.5x20.5cm)

$300-400   **DRA**

An early 20thC Sultanabad carpet, from west Persia, full pile each end nearly intact, with one end missing some rows of knots in one section, minor losses, wear.

approx. 170x125in (432x317.5cm)

$3,000-4,000   **FRE**

A Tabriz pictorial rug, from Northwest Persia, tan and camel background, generally full pile, small hole.

c1930   *100x66in (254x167.5cm)*

$3,000-4,000   **FRE**

A large Zeigler carpet, the royal blue field with cloud band lattice enclosing plants and medallions, within broad polychrome flowerhead border.

307x212.5in (780x540cm)

$60,000-90,000   **L&T**

A Northwest Persian runner, the blue central ground in rust and cream flanked by stylized animals and figures, within a triple border.

37.75x118in (96x300cm)

$1,200-1,800   **SWO**

A Persian carpet, of claret background with overall floral design, deep leaf and flower border.

$5,000-6,000   **SWO**

A Persian runner with geometric ivory and olive green diamond pattern with geometric border.

234in (585cm) long

$1,000-1,500   **DRA**

A late 19thC Chondoresk rug, Southwest Caucasus.

82x56in (208.25x142.25cm)

$3,000-4,000   FRE

A late 19thC Karabagh runner, from South Caucasus.

224x47in (569x119cm)

$3,000-4,000   FRE

A late 19thC Karachopt Kazak rug, from Southwest Caucasus.

72x48in (183x122cm)

$3,000-4,000   FRE

A 20thC Eagle Kazak throw rug with two medallions on a red field with multiple borders.

90x60in (229x152cm)

$7,000-9,000   POOK

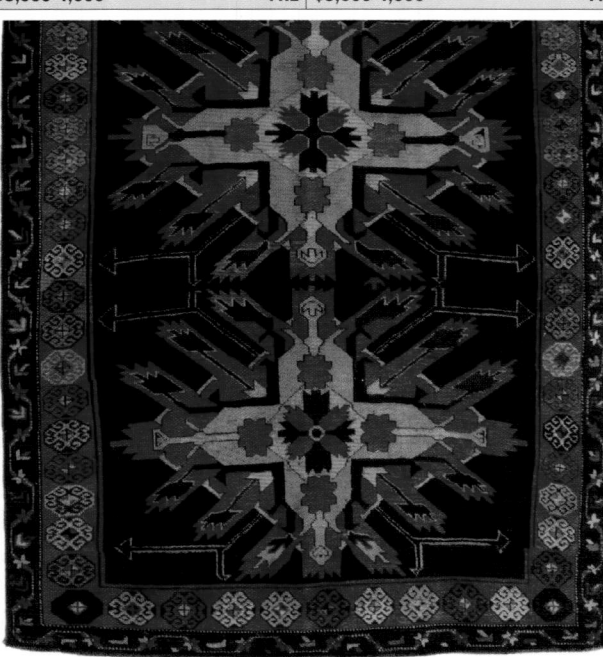

An Eagle Kazak throw rug, with three medallions on a blue field with multiple borders.

106x55in (269x197.5cm)

$3,000-4,000   POOK

A 20thC Kazak throw rug with navy field and multiple borders.

99x50in (251x127cm)

$1,500-2,000   POOK

A Kazak throw rug, with central medallion on red field with sawtooth border.

94x59in (239x150cm)

$7,000-10,000   POOK

A late 19thC Shirvan rug, from East Caucasus.

96x52in (244x132cm)

$5,000-6,000   FRE

A late 19thC Shirvan Leshgi rug, from East Caucasus.

68x47in (173x119.5cm)

$3,400-4,500   FRE

A Shirvan prayer rug, the camel field with a lattice of leaf and geometric motifs, ivory mihrab arch.

72in (180cm) long

$2,000-3,000   L&T

A late 19thC early Shirvan prayer rug, with Akstafa-type design on a navy field with multiple borders.

62x40in (157x101cm)

$7,000-9,000   POOK

A South Caucasian kelleh, within ivory serrated rosette border between polychrome bands.

116.75in (292cm) long

$2,000-3,000   L&T

An Agra rug, with central medallion on a green field with ivory corners and multiple borders.

c1915   113x93in (287x236cm)

$5,000-7,000   **POOK**

An Amritsar carpet, from North India.

c1900   241x132in (612x335.25cm)

$10,000-15,000   **FRE**

An early 20thC Lahore carpet, from North India.

142x111in (696x282cm)

$5,000-6,000   **FRE**

An Indian Serapi Rug with unusual radiating polygon medallion in ivory and crimson on a midnight blue ground within multiple borders.

72x106in (183x269.5cm)

$800-1,200   **DRA**

An Amritsar carpet, from North India.

c1900   125x114in (317.5x289.5cm)

$12,000-18,000   **FRE**

TURKOMAN RUGS

A Turkish wool kelim.

c1965   145.5in (364cm) long

$600-800   **KAU**

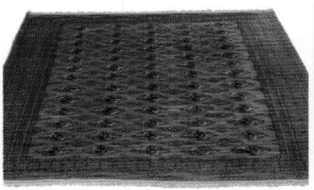

A Tekke, Turkmenistan, woollen rug, asymmetrical knots, Tekke gul with secondary Kurbaghe gul as a filler on red ground, red main border, with Elem above and below, woollen fringe.

c1960   115.2x85.6in (288x214cm)

$600-800   **KAU**

A Turkoman Rug, with center panel of polygons and stars in blue and brown on an au brush cinnabar ground.

c1920   81x87in (205.5x221cm)

$1,500-2,000   **DRA**

A late 19th/early 20thC Turkoman tent band, possibly Yomud.

433x18in (1,100x46cm)

$3,000-4,000   **FRE**

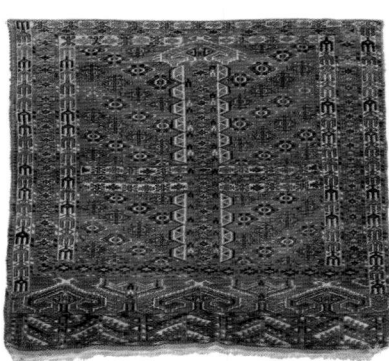

A late 19thC Yomud Turkoman Ensi, from West Turkestan.

61x55in (155x140cm)

$3,000-4,000   **FRE**

A Xinjiang carpet, from East Turkestan, ends generally intact with some minor losses, sides intact, generally full pile, some minor habrash.

c1930   51x88in (129.5x223.5cm)

$400-500   **FRE**

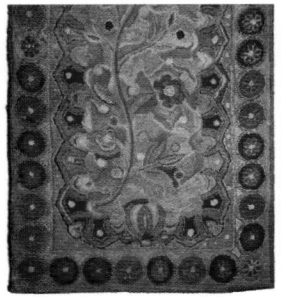

A rare late 19thC very large American hooked runner, with all-over floral pattern.

354in (885cm) long

$8,000-12,000 **POOK**

A Sejshour throw rug, with floral pattern and mustard and navy border.

84in (210cm) long

$3,000-4,000 **POOK**

A 19thC room-sized Mahal rug, with garden design on a blue field with red border.

141in (352.5cm) long

$7,000-8,000 **POOK**

A room-sized Tabriz, with overall floral pattern on a tan field with multiple border.

c1900 *132in (330cm) long*

$40,000-60,000 **POOK**

An early 20thC Spanish Savonnerie carpet.

210x132in (533x335cm)

$5,000-6,000 **FRE**

A Continental Savonnerie carpet.

In 1608 Henry IV initiated the French production of "Turkish style" carpets. Production was soon moved to the Savonnerie factory in Chaillot just west of Paris.

c1925 *128x79in (325x200cm)*

$5,000-6,000 **FRE**

An late 19thC Oushak carpet, from West Anatolia.

136x113in (345x287cm)

$4,000-5,000 **FRE**

An early 20thC Oushak carpet, West Anatolia.

134x99in (340.5x251.5cm)

$6,000-8,000 **FRE**

A room-size floral hand-hooked rug, from Rhode Island, hooked with wool strips on a burlap foundation.

c1955 *108x144in (274x366cm)*

$1,000-1,500 **SK**

A late 19thC framed wool 'penny rug', wool petals in colored tweeds, twills and plaids, arranged in three tiers enclosing woven felt checker-patterned center, some losses.

45.5in (115.5cm) long

$500-600 **FRE**

A CLOSER LOOK AT A ZEIGLER CARPET

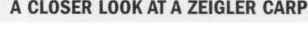

The Manchester-based Zeigler company was established on 1883 to manufacture Persian carpets in Arak, Iran. It employed designers from companies such as Liberty to modify ancient eastern designs.

Zeigler rugs are highly sought after and valuable. One was sold by Lyon & Turnbull in Edinburgh in 2004 for a record breaking $220,000.

This carpet is from Lennoxlove House in East Lothian, property of the present Duke of Hamilton. The origins of the house go back to the 1300s and it is of huge importance in Scottish history due to its architecture, its owners associations with the Royal Stuarts and its furnishings and family portraits. Prior to this it was originally at Hamilton Palace, Hamilton.

Zeigler designs were typically bold and often used a slightly more subdued range of colors than more traditional carpets.

A large Zeigler carpet, the ivory field with allover pattern of scrolling floral vine and palmettes, within rust red abstract vine border between ivory and olive bands.

c1890 *236.25x157.5in (600cm400cm)*

$60,000-80,000 **L&T**

GRENFELL RUGS

- British doctor Wilfred Grenfell went out to Newfoundland to set up a medical mission. The women there made hooked rugs from narrow strips of wool or cotton hooked closely together through linen or burlap backing.
- Grenfell hit upon the idea of supplementing impoverished women's incomes by paying them to make hooked rugs which he would sell to fund his mission work. He gave rug makers kits created by his wife that included everything they needed from materials to burlap backing printed with a pattern.
- Early Grenfell rugs were made of wool and cotton, later examples from donated silk stockings.
- Designs such as fishing scenes and dog teams reflect Newfoundland's craggy environment.
- Select shops in North America, such as Eaton's department store in Toronto, sold Grenfell rugs from 1910 to the late 1940s.

An early 20thC Grenfell hooked picture mat with dog sled scene, Grenfell Labrador Industries, with bleached and dyed rayon and silk strips, a woven maker's label to the reverse, and on a wooden stretcher.

39.5in (100cm) wide

$3,500-4,500   **SK**

An early 20thC Grenfell hooked picture mat with flying ducks, attributed to Grenfell Labrador Industries, Newfoundland and Labrador, composed of rayon and silk strips, with vestiges of a woven maker's label affixed to the reverse.

39.75in (101cm) wide

$6,000-8,000   **SK**

An early to mid-20thC Canadian cotton hooked picture mat with penguins, with rectangular rug composed of cotton strips hooked onto a burlap backing, mounted on a wooden stretcher.

46in (117cm) wide

$4,000-6,000   **SK**

A 19thC American wool hooked rug with leaves and flowers, with an undulating leafy vine accented with red and white flowers, mounted on a wooden stretcher, with minor loss.

51.5in (131cm) wide

$600-800   **SK**

An early 20thC reclining spaniel hooked rug, composed of wool, cotton, and rayon jersey strips hooked onto a burlap backing, and mounted on a wooden stretcher.

34.75in (88cm) wide

$300-500   **SK**

An early 20thC American appliqued cotton and burlap folk art textile panel with cats, with sawtooth edging in assorted cotton fabrics, mounted on a wooden stretcher, with repairs and losses.

55in (139.5cm) wide

$1,000-1,500   **SK**

A pieced cotton quilt with the 'Baskets and Bird' pattern, decorated with pieced red and white baskets containing blossoms and buds alternating with squares of red cutwork double heart blocks, on a white backing.

c1865   *86in (218.5cm) wide*

$1,500-2,000   **SK**

LEFT: A late 19thC appliquéd lily pattern cotton quilt from North Carolina, comprising white blocks with red and green printed cotton lilies, quilted with floral, diagonal, and outline stitches, with white cotton backing.

87in (221cm) high

$1,000-1,500   **SK**

RIGHT: A late 19thC appliquéd 'President's Wreath' cotton quilt, comprised of blocks appliquéd with wreaths of red flowers, enclosed in an undulating budding vine border, quilted with feather, diamond, and outline stitches, with white cotton backing.

86in (218.5cm) high

$3,000-4,000   **SK**

A late 19thC appliquéd and embroidered album quilt, comprised of squares appliquéd with a variety of birds, deer, floral rings and crosses within a berry and leaf border worked with printed and solid cotton patches and yarns, heightened with diamond and conforming quilting.

74in (188cm) high

$3,000-4,000   **FRE**

A late 19thC patchwork quilt, from Lancaster County, Pennsylvania, comprised of printed cotton fabrics in shades of brown, red, green, orange and blue arranged in a sunburst pattern, heightened with diagonal quilting.

92in (233.5cm) high

$500-600   **FRE**

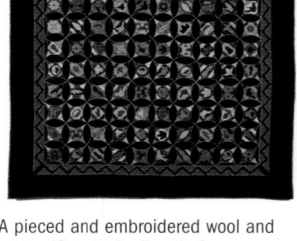

A pieced and embroidered wool and cotton 'Orange Peel' quilt, from Pennsylvania, the diamonds centered with folk motifs including hearts, flowers, birds, houses, baskets, hands and leaves, with red wool binding and black wool backing.

c1880   *78in (198cm) high*

$8,000-12,000   **SK**

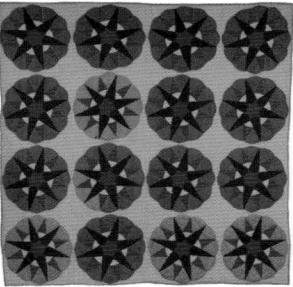

A pieced and appliquéd cotton Pennsylvania German 'Mariner's Compass' quilt, comprising printed calico fabric blocks in shades of red, dark green, blue and yellow, the compasses appliquéd to scallop edged circles in blue calico.

c1885   *73in (185.5cm) wide*

$800-1,200   **SK**

An early 20thC woven cotton runner, from Lancaster County, Pennsylvania, woven with a plaid pattern in shades of blue, black, yellow, green, orange and white.

137.5in (349.5cm) long

$400-500   **FRE**

An appliqué quilt, decorated with red and green calico flowers on an orange ground.

c1900   *95in (237.5cm) long*

$700-1,000   **POOK**

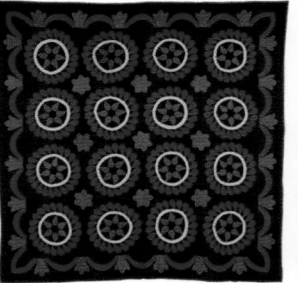

A appliquéd cotton 'Mennonite Wreath' quilt, from Lancaster County, Pennsylvania, comprising appliquéd rosettes in solid colors of red, yellow, and green on an indigo blue ground, with green and red swag border.

c1900   *84.5in (214.5cm) high*

$5,000-6,000   **SK**

An early 20thC pieced quilt, decorated with a sun and grid pattern.

70in (175cm) long

$400-500   **POOK**

QUILTS

- A renewed fascination with craft traditions and folk history has made early American quilts an increasingly popular collecting area.
- Quilting skills arrived in America with the early European settlers. Women organized sewing circles to build friendships and to produce warm and beautiful quilts.
- Early quilts, dating from c1770-1850, are usually the most sought after.
- Baltimore 'album' quilts - made up of separately designed blocks – are generally highly prized and can be worth far more. A fine quality Baltimore album quilt sold for just under $200,000 in the late 1980s and this record set a precedent.
- There are thousands of recognized quilt patterns to choose from such as 'Tumbling Blocks' or 'Bear Paw'. Simple late 19th to early 20thC quilts, with designs such as 'Star' or 'Irish Chain', can be found for as little as $100. More complex patterns, such as the Crazy quilt, popular from the 1870s to c1910, can fetch more.
- Increasingly popular are quilts by African American makers, especially signed examples.
- Attractiveness and quality of the workmanship are keys to value, as is overall condition. Designs with historical significance and strong provenance are very desirable.

A 19thC album-style appliqué quilt, Pennsylvania or Maryland, with 16 blocks with different floral designs within a bow and swag border.

$6,000-8,000   **POOK**

A 19thC Pennsylvania pieced 'Star of Bethlehem' quilt, with panels of tulips and feathers worked in various calico.

95in (241.5cm) wide

$3,000-4,000   **POOK**

A 19thC Pennsylvania vibrant 'Star of Bethlehem' pattern pieced quilt.

$2,000-3,000   **POOK**

A mid-19thC Virginia Indian Plumes quilt, with six-pointed stars within sawtooth surrounds and plume border.

101in (256.5cm) wide

$3,000-5,000   **POOK**

An early 20thC vibrant Mennonite postage stamp quilt.

106in (269cm) wide

$3,000-4,000   **POOK**

COVERLETS

An Indiana jacquard coverlet, inscribed "1848" in navy and white.

91in (231cm) wide

$1,000-1,300   **POOK**

A 19thC New York jacquard coverlet, inscribed "1841 United We Stand Divided We Fall Washington J. Cunningham Weaver. N. Hartford, Oneida. Co. N. York".

84in (213cm) wide

$3,000-4,000   **POOK**

A 19thC jacquard coverlet, inscribed "1869" and "Woven. At. Palmyra. N.Y. by Ira Hadsell" in red and white.

82in (208cm) wide

$1,000-1,500   **POOK**

A 19thC Ohio jacquard coverlet, inscribed "Danniel Bury. New Portage Ohio. 1843" in red, navy, mustard and white.

84in (213cm) wide

$400-800   **POOK**

An Ohio jacquard coverlet, with corner block inscribed "Christian Fasig, Richland, County Ohio 1847", in navy and white.

84in (213cm) long

$800-1,200   **POOK**

A Pennsylvania jacquard coverlet, inscribed "John Smith 1836 L. Walder" with rooster and swag decoration.

102in (259cm) wide

$1,200-1,800   **POOK**

A mid-19thC jacquard coverlet from Pennsylvania or Ohio in red and white.

96in (244cm) wide

$1,200-1,500   **POOK**

A mid-19thC jacquard coverlet inscribed, "Hemfield Railroad" in salmon, navy and white, probably Pennsylvania.

84in (213cm) long

$4,000-6,000   **POOK**

A red and white jacquard coverlet, dated "1852" with animals, buildings and floral decoration, and the initials "HP", dated.

1852   *95in (241.5cm) wide*

$500-600   **POOK**

A Pennsylvania jacquard coverlet, inscribed "Manufactured By Henry. Oberly Womelsdorf. Penn C. Rick".

91in (231cm) wide

$700-1,200   **POOK**

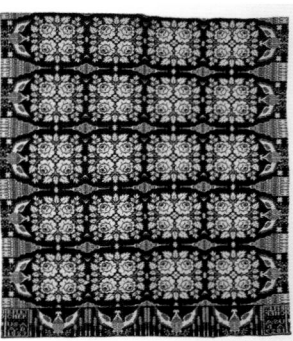

A 19thC jacquard coverlet, inscribed "B.Gletcher U.S.A. A.D. 1829" in navy and white.

89in (226cm) long

$1,200-1,800   **POOK**

A jacquard coverlet, inscribed "John Smith 1836 H. Walder" in red, navy, green and white.

102in (259cm) long

$1,500-2,000   **POOK**

A 19thC jacquard coverlet, inscribed with the names "Washington, Adams, Jefferson, Madison, Monroe, Adams, Jackson, Van Buren, Harrison and Tyler".

91in (231cm) wide

$6,000-8,000   **POOK**

A mid-19thC jacquard coverlet, in red, navy and white.

81in (206cm) long

$1,200-1,500   **POOK**

A mid-19thC jacquard coverlet, inscribed "I.G." in red, navy and white.

89in (226cm) long

$500-1,000   **POOK**

A late 17thC Antwerp 'The Building of Babylon' tapestry, from the Wauters workshop, after the cartoons by Abraham van Diepenbeeck, woven in wools and silks, from the set depicting the Life of Semiramis, with Queen Semiramis being shown the plans of the city.

156in (396cm) wide

$15,000-20,000   L&T

A 17thC verdure tapestry panel, woven in wools with two classical figures resting under trees by a riverbank, in later frame.

75in (190cm) high

$4,000-6,000   L&T

A late 17thC Antwerp tapestry from the Wauters workshop, after the cartoons by Abraham van Diepenbeeck, depicting the Life of Semiramis, showing the child Semiramis being returned to her mother.

In 1906, a dispute over the ownership of these tapestries resulted in two from the set being allocated to the Crown. Those two panels still hang in the Queen's apartment in Holyrood.

121in (308cm) wide

$12,000-18,000   L&T

A late 17thC Antwerp mythological tapestry, from the Wauters workshop, woven in silks and wools, depicting the Life of Semiramis, showing a goddess leaping into the sea.

93.75in (238cm) wide

$10,000-15,000   L&T

A 16thC Flemish tapestry, depicting a scene from Vertumnus and Pomona from Book XIV of Ovid's Metamorphoses.

Vertumnus, the Roman god of autumn, sought to win favor with the wood nymph Pamona by changing his appearance. His disguises included a fisherman, a reaper, a gardener, and, as depicted here, a soldier.

104in (264cm) wide

$15,000-20,000   FRE

A 17thC Continental fragment of a "Diana the Huntress" tapestry.

83in (211cm) wide

$4,000-5,000   FRE

A 19thC Continental needlepoint and petitpoint panel, depicting "Amarillis Crowning Mirtillo with a Floral Wreath".

82in (208cm) wide

$2,000-3,000   FRE

A 19thC Continental tapestry, depicting "Extensive Landscape with Exotic Fowl".

105in (266cm) wide

$3,000-4,000   FRE

A late 17thC English stumpwork marriage scene, with central figures surrounded by various motifs.

20.75in (52cm) wide

$5,000-6,000 POOK

An English silk-on-linen needlework, dated and initialed "MK" with urn full of flowers and gold thread border.

1728 *11.5in (29cm) high*

$5,000-6,000 POOK

A silk needlework picture from Boston, MA, inscribed in beads, "MD 1740" worked in a variety of stitches in colors of red, blue, green, brown, yellow and white in the English needlework tradition.

15in (38cm) wide

$30,000-40,000 POOK

A mid-18thC needlework picture in wool with scene of shepherd, a seated man and the village in the background.

17in (43cm) wide

$15,000-40,000 POOK

An English pictorial needlework with figure in a pastoral landscape, dated, initialed "MP".

1758 *11in (27.5cm) high*

$800-1,200 POOK

A late 18thC wool canvas-work picture, from Salem, Massachusetts, with tent-stitched wool yarns on a linen ground, depicting a hunting scene.

14in (35cm) wide

$60,000-80,000 SK

A CLOSER LOOK AT A CANVASWORK PICTURE

Boston is well known for the quality of its needlework pictures, which were made by young ladies from wealthy families from the mid-18thC onwards. A group of approximately 17 are often known collectively as 'Fishing Lady' embroideries as they share the main motif of a lady fishing at a pond.

It is likely that they were made under the instruction of an experienced teacher who may possibly have run a school, although any records of who the teacher was have since been lost. Patterns, instructions and materials would have been available at speciality shops in Boston.

Other popular motifs, some of which can be seen here, include a promenading couple, racing dogs, exotic birds and leaping deer.

The fishing motif may seem unusual today, but was considered a wholly suitable contemplative pastime for women at the time.

A mid-19thC Boston 'Fishing Lady' school canvaswork picture, wool and silk threads on linen canvas with mica fragments, depicting a pastoral scene with a tall shepherdess with a tiny black shoe peeking out from her hem, in original molded wood frame.

$150,000-200,000 SK

A late 18thC English silk needlework picture, depicting Wilton House in Salisbury.

25.5in (65cm) wide

$6,000-8,000   **POOK**

An early 19thC silk needlework "Samuel's First Prophecy" Biblical picture, embroidered with silk and chenille threads and watercolor on a silk ground, by "Lucy Newberry", original frame.

20in (51cm) high

$3,000-4,000   **SK**

An early 19thC English pictorial needlework with silk and paint on silk depicting two women with a cat by a cottage.

8in (20cm) wide

$1,000-1,300   **POOK**

A silk-on-linen needlework, wrought by Ann Toby, with central verse above a house, dated.

1805   *21in (53.5cm) high*

$6,000-8,000   **POOK**

A silk-on-linen needlework, wrought by Hannah Perce, Delaware Valley, with central basket of flowers with two facing doves within a floral vine, dated.

1809   *8in (20cm) wide*

$4,000-5,000   **POOK**

A Pennsylvania silk, chenille and paint on silk needlework mourning picture inscribed, "In the Memory of My Beloved Mother Ann Currie 1816" with figure, landscape and swags.

17in (43cm) wide

$1,000-1,500   **POOK**

A Philadelphia silk on linen needlework, wrought by Ann Hofman, daughter of Jacob and Susan, with central basket of flowers and script, dated.

1826   *20in (50cm) wide*

$12,000-18,000   **POOK**

A wool needlework, wrought by Adele Lamy Montgomery County, Pennsylvania, with central figure of a blacksmith, dated.

1869   *30in (76cm) high*

$5,000-6,000   **POOK**

A Pennsylvania silk on linen needlework inscribed, "Elizabeth H. Beale work 1832, Parents William + Elizabeth Beale, Mary Morris Ruthrford teacher" with a variety of stitches in shades of green, gold, yellow, blue, white and tan with a central verse surrounded by flowers, birds, vines, trees, and landscape.

25in (64cm) wide

$25,000-30,000   **POOK**

A 19thC English woolwork portrait of a three-masted British ship at sea, framed, some losses.

26in (66cm) wide

$1,500-2,000   **FRE**

A Schwenkfelder woolwork townscape, by Catharine Kriebel (1839-76) of Montgomery County, dated.

This woolwork picture belongs to a small group of related needlework pictures worked in the 1850s in Montgomery county by members of the Schwenkfelder community. It is thought that these pieces were worked in a sewing circle and not a school.

1856   *34.5in (87.5cm) high*

$30,000-40,000   **FRE**

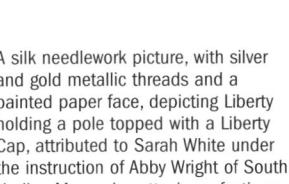

A silk needlework picture, with silver and gold metallic threads and a painted paper face, depicting Liberty holding a pole topped with a Liberty Cap, attributed to Sarah White under the instruction of Abby Wright of South Hadley, Massachusetts, imperfections.

c1805   *16in (41cm) high*

$15,000-25,000   **SK**

An early English band sampler with alphabet, above a folky crewelwork Adam and Eve, dated "March 1744", and verse.

1744   20in (50cm) wide

$65,000-80,000   POOK

A George III English sampler of England and Wales, by Arabella Stone, dated 1800.

20in (51cm) high

1800

$500-600   SWO

An English silk on linen needlework sampler, worked by Elizabeth Goodman with verse over pastoral scene with two figures in landscape surrounded by animals.

1803   16in (40.5cm) long

$3,000-4,000   POOK

An English silk on linen sampler, by Martha Waters, with central verse above a potted flower, dated.

1821   14.25in (36cm) wide

$500-800   POOK

An 18thC Boston silk on linen sampler, with verse flanked by floral vine over a scene of a shepherdess and flock.

13.5in (34cm) high

$15,000-20,000   POOK

A Connecticut silk on linen sampler with inscriptions under bands of alphabets, a large basket of flowers, butterfly, bird within a border of vine and star.

18in (46cm) wide

$9,000-12,000   POOK

A Massachusetts needlework sampler, by "Lydia Gordon born December 11 1786", wrought with silver threads on a linen ground, framed.

1797   22.75in (57cm) high

$10,000-15,000   SK

An 18thC Massachusetts silk on linen sampler, with bands of alphabets and motifs within a foliate border.

19in (48cm) high

$10,000-15,000   POOK

An early 19thC New England silk-on-linen needlework, wrought by Abigail Tufts, with central house surrounded by birds and flowers.

16in (40.5cm) high

$7,000-8,000   POOK

A New Jersey needlework sampler, by Martha Davis, with silk threads and metallic sequins on a linen ground with a verse entitled "Extract".

1813   *26in (65cm) high*

$10,000-15,000   **SK**

A New Jersey silk-on-linen needlework, wrought by "Mary Ann Hollinshead, under the tuition of Eleanor T. Stephens", at the Cream Ridge Seminary.

1827   *17in (43cm) high*

$8,000-12,000   **POOK**

A New York silk on linen needlework sampler, with inscription under scene of Adam and Eve, within a border of strawberries.

16in (41cm) wide

$15,000-20,000   **POOK**

An 18thC Pennsylvania needlework sampler of silk on linen, inscribed, "Henrietta Maria Howell" with verses over family record.

17in (43cm) wide

$4,000-8,000   **POOK**

A Pennsylvania silk-on-linen needlework sampler, wrought by Hannah Maule at the "West-Town Boarding School", Chester County, dated.

1804   *13in (33cm) high*

$4,000-5,000   **POOK**

A Pennsylvania sampler, embroidered silk on linen with four rows of alphabets, with inscription "Jannet Lidsy Aged 10 Years 1807 Collinsburg/Jun 2-Day BG BW".

1807   *13in (33cm) wide*

$8,000-12,000   **SK**

A needlework sampler, possibly Pennsylvania, by "Arianna H. Coles work done in the ninth year of her age", with a pious verse and "An Emblem of industry".

c1820   *18in (45cm) high*

$6,000-8,000   **SK**

A Philadelphia silk on linen needlework sampler inscribed, "Leah Ann Alsop her Work 1823" with a variety of stitches in blue, green, brown, yellow and gold.

20in (51cm) wide

$10,000-12,000   **POOK**

A Pennsylvania silk on linen needlework sampler, wrought by Elizabeth Scofield in Reading, with verse over a double row of flowers, dated.

1826   *19.75in (49cm) high*

$20,000-30,000   **POOK**

A Pennsylvania silk on linen needlework sampler, inscribed, "Jane Fulton aged nine yrs. Done at Mrs. Callan's School. Pittsburgh. April the seventh 1826".

17in (43cm) wide

$7,000-9,000   **POOK**

A Pennsylvania silk on linen needlework sampler, inscribed "Sarah Banes work wrought AD 1830 in the ninth year of her age".

25in (64cm) high

$10,000-20,000   **POOK**

A Pennsylvanian silk-on-linen sampler, wrought by Hannah Wentz, in Chester County, with elaborate still life of flowers, dated.

1834   *25.5in (65cm) wide*

$6,000-8,000   **POOK**

SAMPLERS

- Since the 16th century young women were expected to develop skills in sewing and to show their accomplishment in needlecraft. Samplers were generally produced as stitching practise.
- Usually featuring alphabets, numbers and verses or simple scenes, samplers were often signed and dated, especially from the early 17th century. Early examples are hard to come by and can attract huge sums of money.
- By the 18th century, many samplers featured pious moral or religious verses and even scenes from the Bible. During the 19th century, cross-stitching became dominant and the pictorial element of the sampler began to flourish.
- As formal education for women became more common, the practice of stitching samplers became gradually less widespread.
- Other types of sampler include darning samplers, in which the sampler fabric was cut with holes and 'repaired' with demonstrations of various different weaves, and map samplers, most frequently depicting the home nation of the stitcher.
- Generally, buyers look for intricate and skilfully made samplers with interesting decoration. Condition is crucial, and sun-bleaching or water-staining can reduce value by 50 per cent or more.

A Chester County, Pennsylvania silk on linen needlework family record, inscribed "Elizabeth Yearsleys work in the 17th year of her age 1827, Mary Taylor Teacher", with potted bouquet, verse and family names, over a large elaborate urn flanked by willow trees and perched birds.

30in (76cm) wide

$25,000-30,000   POOK

A silk on linen needlework sampler, inscribed, "Ruth Leach 1732" with bands of tulips over verse.

12in (30cm) long

$10,000-15,000   POOK

A Pennsylvania silk on linen needlework sampler, with central apple tree, two houses over verse enclosed by strawberry vine border.

16in (41cm) wide

$6,000-10,000   POOK

A silk on linen needlework sampler, inscribed "Sarah Jewett born November 6 1745 this sampler I wrought in the year 1761".

23in (58cm) long

$20,000-25,000   POOK

A silk on linen needlework sampler, inscribed, "Deborah Day her sampler made in the year 1777" with bands of alphabets above verse.

17in (43cm) long

$10,000-15,000   POOK

A silk on linen needlework sampler, inscribed, "Ann Jones Her Work Made in the Year 1788" with bands of alphabet.

22in (56cm) wide

$10,000-15,000   POOK

A silk on linen needlework sampler, inscribed, "Charlotte Hough Daughter of Samuel and Susannah Hough Aged 10 years 1799 Sarah Shoemaker" with alphabet, animals, numbers, trees, birds, verse and floral border.

Sarah Shoemaker would have been the child's school mistress.

17in (43cm) wide

$30,000-40,000   POOK

An early 19thC needlework sampler, in a naive style and bearing initials "JP:MS" and inscription "Jessy Paterson Aged 8 years M Grahams School Melrose", in a molded frame.

12.5in (31cm) sq

$3,000-4,000   L&T

A silk on linen needlework sampler, inscribed, "Eufemea Moor August 28th 1816" with house, trees and border in variety of stitches.

20in (51cm) long

$12,000-18,000   POOK

A 19thC silk on linen needlework sampler with inscription in oval with verse surrounded by vines, flowers, birds and butterflies in a scalloped border.

21in (53cm) high

$10,000-13,000   POOK

A large Cantonese asymmetrical fan, painted with figures, the faces of painted ivory and their clothes of silk, the reverse embroidered, with lacquer sticks.

c1870

$200-300   **ROS**

A French painted silk modern fan, by Frédérick, with ivory sticks and guards.

2003   *9in (24cm) high*

$1,200-1,800   **RSS**

A Victorian chinoiserie decorated fan, with Japanned spines.

$120-160   **SWO**

A contemporary silk French erotic fan, by Frédérick, with ivory sticks and guards.

12in (32cm) high

$1,000-1,500   **RSS**

A contemporary French Cleopatra fan, by Sylvain le Guen.

2004   *12.5in (33.5cm) high*

$1,500-2,000   **RSS**

A mother-of-pearl brisé fan, with a detailed carved and etched Oriental scene overall, on both the front and reverse of the fan.

$600-800   **ROS**

TEXTILES

A Victorian woolwork picture, the black ground worked with a house, urns of flowers and sailing ships.

$600-800 SWO

A Victorian woolwork picture of a coastal cutter in full sail, with two smaller boats and a lighthouse, in a maple frame.

18.5in (46cm) wide

$1,000-1,500 SWO

A Victorian woolwork picture of a man-o-war in full sail, in a maple frame.

26in (65cm) wide

$1,200-1,800 SWO

A marine woolwork picture, depicting a twin masted ship, to a shell decorated border, in a bird's eye maple frame.

21in (53cm) wide

$1,500-2,500 WW

COSTUME

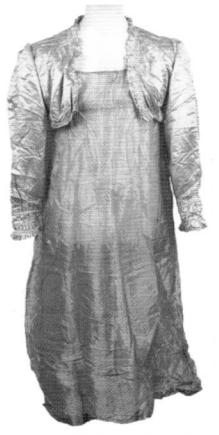

A lady's gown of bright yellow silk shot with gold, with high waisted bodice, draw-string neckline, soft pleated skirt, and a matched bolero jacket.

c1810

$600-1,000 L&T

A lady's gown of eau-de-nil and cream striped silk, with a herringbone pattern, applied pleated eau-de-nil chiffon, silk integral belt to a soft pleated full skirt.

c1820

$800-1,200 L&T

A lady's gown of rose pink silk, with columbine motifs amidst wavescroll vertical stripes, with self-fabric collar, leg of mutton sleeves, and soft pleated skirt.

c1830

$800-1,200 L&T

A lady's high waisted pelisse of silk twill, woven in gold, cream and black with repeat flowerhead motifs against a golden lattice and eau-de-nil colored ground, stand collar and puffed full-length sleeves.

c1820

$1,200-1,800 L&T

A lady's one-piece gown of ribbed pink silk, the boned bodice with pleated neckline, inset 'leg of mutton' full-length deep pink wool sleeves, to a soft pleated full-length skirt.

c1830

$600-700 L&T

VINTAGE FASHION

- Clothing once thought of as second-hand is now often termed vintage and has become very desirable, a trend endorsed by celebrities such as Kate Moss and Sarah Jessica Parker.
- Vintage clothes appeal to established collectors as well as those wanting to create a unique and fashionable look. Buying vintage couture items is also a more affordable way of getting hold of classic designer pieces.
- Important fashion houses such as Chanel, Christian Dior and Yves Saint Laurent generally attract high prices as a result of their status and the quality of their work. Be aware that companies often released different ranges aimed at different levels of the market and this can determine value.
- Iconic designs that sum up the style of an era are particularly popular. Look out for 1950s 'New Look' designs, 1960s 'Mod' style and 1970s psychedelia. 1980s fashion has also become very popular. Classic pieces typical of a label, such as Chanel's famous suits, are very desirable.
- Designer items from recent seasons can maintain their value and may prove to be good investments. Condition is essential and tears or staining should be avoided.

A Chanel rainbow mohair bouclé open front jacket, with variegated yarn applied to a fine black netting and lined with tulle, and semi-precious stone buttons at cuffs.

2003   size 36

$1,500-2,000   FRE

A Chanel pink and pastel houndstooth tweed coat, with piped princess seams and contrasting plaid trim, and belt.

2004   size 36

$1,500-2,500   FRE

A Chanel tweed and printed silk sleeveless dress and blouse, with pleated bodice, fitted mid-section and skirt in a large-scale tweed.

2004   size 36

$800-1,200   FRE

A Dolce & Gabbana silk satin floral print cocktail dress, with 'hydrangea' print, kelly green velvet trim and large rhinestone spray pin.

size 40

$800-1,200   FRE

A Dolce & Gabbana silk-blend stretch satin cocktail dress, with a retro floral watercolor print, taupe velvet trim and jeweled pin detail, original hang tags.

size 40

$600-1,000   FRE

A Gellert-Kaden & Rosenblum full-length mink coat, the nehru collar with hidden hook closures and with long mink tie belt.

1960s   size 2

$4,000-5,000   FRE

A Geoffrey Beene couture silk chiffon print halter dress, with a violet silk applied bow detail, and skirt in sheer layers of fabric.

1970-80   size 2

$120-180   FRE

A Hermès signature striped Rocabar blanket poncho, made from a single piece of felted wool, trimmed in leather and with two buttons.

1990-2000   one size

$800-1,200   FRE

A French Mainbocher black wool and mohair sequined dress coat, labeled "MAINBOCHER / 12 AVENUE GEORGE V".

1930   Size 0/2

$2,000-3,000   FRE

A 1970s Pauline Trigère black wool crepe dress, with a dramatic capelet trimmed with triangular rhinestones.

size 6

$200-300   **FRE**

An Yves Saint Laurent Rive Gauche wool felt skirt suit, with faux horn buttons, Nehru collar and three-button cuffs.

1970-80   *size 40/38*

$100-200   **FRE**

An Yves Saint Laurent Rive Gauche ruffled leather jacket, in supple chocolate brown leather with off-center ruffled button-down closure.

size 36

$500-700   **FRE**

SHOES

A pair of Azzedine Alaïa reptile skin skimmer flats, with slightly upturned pointy toe, in natural snakeskin with a gray bow detail, with box and sleeper bag.

Size 38.5

$80-120   **FRE**

A pair of Balenciaga black multi-buckle high heeled sandals, with five silver buckled adjustable straps, cushioned footbed.

2003   *size 39*

$300-400   **FRE**

A pair of Chanel green quilted ballet flats, in olive green leather with large naturalistic faux python "CC" appliqué on front, clear hard plastic soles.

2005   *size 36*

$80-120   **FRE**

A pair of Chanel peach satin high-heeled mules, with large antiqued jeweled starburst brooch detail on vamp.

size 36.5

$60-100   **FRE**

A pair of Chanel white leather quilted ballet flats, in bright white leather with diamond quilting, with large "CC" appliqué logo in faux python.

2005   *size 36*

$200-300   **FRE**

A pair of Chanel pink suede camelia high-heeled mules, with pink suede straps and flower, gold "Chanel" button, brown ribbon detail, and stacked heel.

size 36

$100-150   **FRE**

A pair of contemporary Gucci peep toe stiletto pumps, in emerald green satin with jeweled signature 'horse bit' detail on front.

Heel 3.5in (9cm) size 6

$80-120   **FRE**

A pair of Manolo Blahnik kitten-heel mules, in white calfskin embroidered with flat silver metal threads and with large rhinestone buckle on vamp.

size 37

$80-120 FRE

A pair of Manolo Blahnik black stiletto pumps, with hour-glass heel and strap detail on vamp.

size 39.5

$100-150 FRE

A pair of Manolo Blahnik tan stiletto pumps, pale calfskin with pointed toe and T-straps.

size 39.5

$100-150 FRE

A pair of Prada formal kitten-heel jeweled mules, in black satin with elaborate violet and crystal rhinestone beading.

size 36

$80-120 FRE

A pair of Prada green satin and violet suede high heel sandals, with gold suede and leather trim, small silver buckle at sides.

size 36

$80-120 FRE

A pair of 1950s N. Porter lady's brown calfskin cowboy boots, with red and white inset design and underslung heel.

$200-300 FRE

A pair of Prada high-heel rose satin and beaded sandals, with ankle straps, grosgrain trim and a small bow detail.

size 36

$120-180 FRE

A pair of 1950s N. Porter lady's cowboy boots, with dramatically underslung heel and multicolor flame stitching.

$200-300 FRE

A pair of Yves Saint Laurent leather sandals, with stacked tapered heel and platform with a cross-strap at vamp and elastic at the ankle.

size 38.5

$150-250 FRE

A pair of Yves Saint Laurent cobalt velvet shoes with leather lacing, and stacked heel platform sole.

size 38.5

$200-250 FRE

TEXTILES

MESHBAGS

- Metal mesh bags were first made from precious metals in the 1820s, and by the end of the century mesh coin and finger purses, inspired by the trend for Medieval fashion, were in vogue. However, they were handmade and therefore expensive.
- In 1908 A.C. Pratt of Newark, New Jersey, patented a mesh machine which meant affordable, mass produced bags could be made and, by 1912, mesh bags were all the rage.
- The major manufacturers included Whiting and Davis (probably the biggest and most famous mesh bag maker and still making mesh bags today), and the Mandalian Manufacturing Co. of North Attleboro, Massachussets (which closed in the 1940s).
- In the 1920s designs started to be screen-printed onto the mesh and so, as a result, bags could be made in a rainbow of colors and designs, including enamel and pearlized finishes.
- Whiting & Davis produced high quality mesh bags since the company's inception in 1876 in Plainville, Massachusetts, to the 1940s and beyond.
- Early bags tended to be fairly plain in decoration, although some top-of-the range examples featured ornate jeweled handles or even tiny clocks.
- As the 1920s progressed, colors got brighter and patterns became bolder and more geometric. Cheaper ranges sometimes featured printed designs rather than the more typical decoration made up of differently colored metals. Some of the most glamorous bags produced by the company were designed in the 1930s by well-known couturiers such as Elsa Schiaparelli and Paul Poiret.
- Mesh bags fell out of favor during the mid-20thC and Whiting & Davis began to concentrate on producing other mesh products such as jewelry. However, mesh bags became popular again during the disco craze of the 1970s.

A Whiting and Davis Art Deco enameled metal mesh purse, geometric borders with a central rose bouquet design in red, green, pink and yellow.

1920s

$200-300   **FRE**

A Whiting and Davis Art Deco enameled metal mesh purse, geometric borders with central rose design.

1920s

$200-300   **FRE**

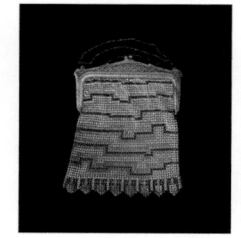

An Art Deco enameled metal mesh purse, stepped-stripe design in coral, black, turquoise and silver.

1920s

$150-200   **FRE**

Left: A Chanel navy quilted chain handle purse, in original white box.

1970s   *10in (25cm) long*

Centre: A Chanel dark brown leather quilted-stripe purse, boxed, as new.

1990s   *8in (20.25cm) long*

A Chanel black patent leather purse, front flap with 'CC' logo detail.

1990s   *7.5in (19cm) long*

LEFT: $800-1,200 CENTER: $1,000-1,500 RIGHT: $400-600   **FRE**

An Art Deco enameled metal mesh purse, green and white geometric tree design.

1920s

$200-300   **FRE**

A Chanel quilted leather bag, with chain handle and 'CC' closure.

This classic design is known as the 2.55 because it was released in February 1955. It is still in production today.

1990   *9in (23cm) wide*

$1,000-1,500   **FRE**

A Hermes navy leather Constance purse, supple and fine leather with bright brass signature 'H' clasp, completely lined in kid, in excellent condition with felt bag and box.

9in (23cm) long

$2,000-3,000   **FRE**

An unusual Hermes canvas and leather bucket purse, natural canvas and navy blue leather with a circular brass 'bracelet' closure which threads through two large openings at the top, attached narrow leather shoulder strap and silk jacquard lining.

1990s

$600-900   **FRE**

Left: A Hermes alligator skin envelope style bag, with gold chain link strap.

Centre: A Hermes navy reptile bag, with chain-detail clasp.

Right: A 1990s Hermes black alligator envelope bag, with gold-plated hardware.

The color of a handbag can have a great effect on value: black is the most desirable color, followed by brown, and collectors will pay a premium for them.

1990s   *9in (23cm) long*

LEFT: $2,000-3,000 CENTER: $1,500-2,000 RIGHT: $2,000-3,000   **FRE**

A Louis Vuitton black Le Fabuleux handbag, in thick luggage-gauge textured leather, with brass details and hardware, lined in signature "micro monogram" acetate.

14in (35.5cm) wide

$2,000-3,000   **FRE**

A 1940-50s Milch brown leather accordion handbag.

12in (30.5cm) wide

$200-300   **MGL**

A Hermès Haut à Courroie Birkin bag, in signature orange luggage-grade calfskin, brass hardware, lock and key, with original receipt, dustbag and box.

The Haute à Courroie is identical in style to the Birkin bag but is of slightly different dimensions.

12.25in (31cm) wide

$5,000-6,000   **FRE**

A 1950s Patricia of Miami lucite handbag, with a racecar-style body with ball feet in avocado green with gold and green confetti dots, hand carved lid decoration.

9.5in (24cm) wide

$400-500   **DJI**

An 18ct woven gold evening purse, with graduated circular cut diamonds set to the rim, mounted with a mirror to the interior.

6in (15.5cm) wide

$4,000-5,000   **WW**

A 1940s evening bag.

9in (23cm) wide

$200-300   **AHL**

A brass-studded and iron-bound leather-covered wooden campaign chest, bearing brass plaque inscribed "Capt Hamilton, Ayrshire Militia", lined with crude green baize and overpainted religious pamphlets, fitted with an array of items partly wrapped in brown paper and newspaper dated 1804.

The chest includes three glass decanters with calf covered bungs, two large platters and six Britannia metal plates, lift out tray with Britannia metal tea pot, four lacquered tin beakers, four tea spoons, a quantity of English blue and white wares including seven various tea bowls (two broken), and seven various saucers (one broken), fitted below with mess tins, kettle, pair of brass candlesticks, flint and strike tin, cruet set, food containers, griddle and more.

24in (61cm) wide

$10,000-15,000   **L&T**

An Asprey of London leather-cased picnic set, with various items including four earthenware plates, cutlery and a wicker covered glass bottle, stamped maker's mark.

22in (56cm) wide

$3,000-4,000   **L&T**

A large early 20thC Louis Vuitton steamer trunk, fully outfitted with carved wooden hangers and shoe box, covered in signature LV canvas with the initials "G.D.W.".

43in (110cm) wide

$6,000-10,000   **FRE**

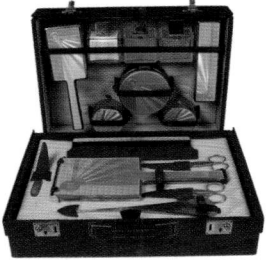

A ladies traveling case, containing silver and enameled dressing table items, makers mark for Albert Carter, Birmingham 1935.

$600-800   **SWO**

DOLLS

THE DOLLS AND TOYS MARKET

This area is composed of separate markets, attracting collectors for different reasons and experiencing varying levels of success. To begin with the positive: demand for teddy bears, trains, die-cast vehicles, the best and rarest dolls and tinplate toys remains strong. The market is less buoyant for automata of all types and dolls and tinplate toys of average or below average quality and rarity.

Looking at the upbeat sections of the market in more detail, teddy bears are the star performers of the toy market. Their appeal is international, to every age group and attracting the specialist collector as well as the first time buyer. There is plentiful information available on the subject which encourages the novice to gain confidence quickly. The winsome expressions on the bears' faces attract some buyers, although experienced collectors will concentrate on early bears in excellent condition. In Europe, bears by German manufacturer Steiff still command the highest prices, although those made by English companies such as Farnell and Chad Valley are rising rapidly in popularity, as are bears made after World War II.

The name Dinky Toy first appeared 1934, Corgi Toys in 1956 and the popularity of the 1/43rd scale die-cast autos and accessories remains strong. However, it must be stressed that condition is of the greatest importance in the die-cast market. Any mass-production toy has to be in as near mint condition as possible and with its original box to command an extraordinary price. There is also an enthusiasm for special editions and rare colorways, with a world record price of $25,300 paid for a pre-war commercial van.

Plastic toys and dolls, including Star Wars figures, Action Man, Barbie, Sacha and Sindy are growing, particularly amongst the nostalgic 30- and 40-somethings. Highest prices are paid for those in original boxes with related accessories and clothes.

Growth in pre-1940s dolls and tinplate toys is hampered by the scarcity of active new collectors with a real passion for the subject and sufficient funds to invest. Prices for many toys and dolls from this period have never been cheaper, in real terms, and this would be an excellent area to start collecting.

Hilary Kay

Jumeau legs were chunky and solid. The stable structure was designed to allow the doll to stand-up.

A large early Jumeau doll, size 15, with fixed wrists and blue mark to body.

c1860-70   32in (81cm) high

$10,000-12,000   **HB**

Jumeau dolls are often marked 'Tête Jumeau' in red to the back of head.

DÉPOSE
TÊTE JUMEAU
Bte S.G.D.G.
15

The pate is made of cork in many pre-1890 Jumeau dolls.

A Tête Jumeau SGDG doll, fully marked head and body with straight wrists, brown paperweight eyes, re-costumed and re-wigged.

c1890-1900   15in (38cm) high

$4,000-5,000   **BER**

A Jumeau doll, with open mouth and molded teeth, unmarked head but label to the body.

Heads are sometimes marked in red or incised with initials.

c1890-1900   22.75in (58cm) high

$3,000-4,000   **HB**

JUMEAU

- Jumeau's bestselling fashion dolls were known throughout the world for their beautifully modeled faces and fashionable Parisian clothing.
- The company was established in the 1840s by Pierre Francois Jumeau and became the first French toymaker to make use of bisque, twice-fired unglazed porcelain.
- The first Bébés - modeled as young girls - began to appear on the market in the 1870s. These were extremely popular and won the company many prestigious awards.
- Jumeau's first Bébé was the Bébé Incassable ('Unbreakable Baby'), then came the Portrait and EJ models, which were followed by the celebrated Jumeau Triste, with its exquisite bisque head commissioned from the sculptor Albert Carriere-Belleuse.
- The quality of materials and craftsmanship and the high cost of production meant the company began to lose out to German manufacturers from the 1890s. In 1899 Jumeau became a member of the Société Française de Fabrication de Bébés & Jouets (SFBJ) until it closed in 1958.
- Not all Jumeau dolls are marked, but look for blue stamps or paper labels on the torso.
- Jumeau dolls are often incised 'E.J' or 'Déposé Jumeau' on the back of the head, or stamped there with 'TÊTE JUMEAU' in red.

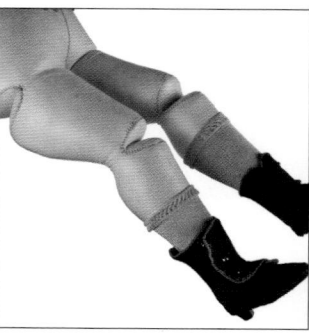

A Jumeau Fashion Lady doll, with kid leather body, paperweight eyes and closed mouth.

The body, with its nipped waist and full thighs and bottom, is modeled on the ideal female form of the period. The kid leather body is held together by internal metal spikes.

c1870-90   13in (33cm) high

$3,000-4,000   **HB**

A Jumeau fashion doll, with original clothes, blue earrings, cut-back head and kid leather body, and red mark to neck.

1880s   *12.5in (32cm) high*

$3,000-3,500   **HB**

A CLOSER LOOK AT A BRU DOLL

The crack to the forehead reduces the value by up to 50 per cent, although this doll remains desirable due to the provenance and the unobtrusive nature of the damage, which is outside the 'mask' or central facial area. A Bru in perfect condition tends to sell for around $30,000.

Produced to the very highest standards using expensive materials and exquisite craftsmanship, Bru dolls were made in France from 1866-1899. Sold in far smaller numbers than Jumeau dolls, the high quality of Bru dolls made them the preserve of the very rich. Even for wealthy youngsters, a Bru doll would have been among the most prized objects in a well-equipped nursery.

This is the best-known type of Bru doll the "Bru Jne". It was made in the 1880s. Heads and lower arms were made from bisque, as were the deep shoulder and breast plates, with small molded breasts. In 1889, a new version known as Bru Jne "R" was launched, but values for these dolls are typically far lower.

The doll is complete with original traditional Romanian dress, needlework and documentation and letters relating to the provenance. It once belonged to the Queen of Romania.

A Bru Jeune doll, with bisque head, shoulder plate and forearms, early molded open mouth showing tongue, paperweight eyes, wearing an original crown in gold metal and lapis lazuli, crack to forehead.

1880s   *21in (53cm) high*

$10,000-15,000   **HB**

An Emile Jumeau doll, brown paperweight eyes, straight wrist body with original finish, incised "Depose E–6J", body stamped in blue "Jumeau Medaille D'or Paris", antique shoes stamped "Bébé Jumeau 6 Paris".

1880-90   *15in (38cm) high*

$5,000-6,000   **BER**

A Jules Steiner Bébé, on original straight wrist fully jointed body, lever eye mechanism, antique mohair wig, incised "SieC", repair, some pronounced coloring.

1880s   *16in (40.5cm) high*

$4,000-5,000   **BER**

A French SFBJ doll, with early five-piece body, dressed as a late Victorian maid.

The price reflects the quality of the doll. The body is simple, made in five sections without articulation and the whole is fairly crude.

c1890   *10.25in (26cm) high*

$300-500   **HB**

A Jules Steiner A-7 Bébé, with original fully jointed body with straight wrists, re-costumed and re-wigged, slight color loss to nose tip.

1880s   *14in (35.5cm) high*

$4,000-5,000   **BER**

SIMON & HALBIG

- The Simon & Halbig porcelain factory began producing dolls in 1869 in Thuringia, Germany, an area previously renowned for its porcelain industry.
- The company began to make dolls in the early 1870s and its output was prolific. It turned out a large number of china and bisque dolls under the Simon & Halbig name, but also supplied heads to the very successful French Jumeau factory and also to the German firm of Kämmer & Reinhardt.
- Simon & Halbig dolls are usually marked. The ampersand was added to the mark in 1905 and it is generally accepted that marks without the ampersand are before that date.
- The quality of Simon & Halbig dolls' heads led to the company supplying heads to many other manufacturers, including Kämmer & Reinhardt, Heinrich Handwerck, Franz Schmidt & Co and Catterfelder Puppenfabrick.
- Rare types or sizes are valuable and include the number 150 and number 153 Character Children, as well as dolls number 1388 and number 1448. Examples of these have all sold in recent years for over $20,000.

A German Simon & Halbig fashion doll, dressed in original clothes complete with bustle, for the French market, with early closed mouth.

c1890	13.5in (34cm) high
$2,500-3,000	**HB**

A Kämmer & Reinhardt Simon-Halbig '121' doll, with blue glass eyes, open mouth and antique wig.

c1900	27in (69cm) high
$1,000-1,500	**BER**

A Kämmer & Reinhardt Simon-Halbig '68' doll with blue glass sleep eyes, on original jointed body with original finish.

c1900	26in (66cm) high
$500-700	**BER**

A Simon & Halbig '151' character girl doll, with an expressively molded face, antique mohair wig, tea dress with pinafore, body with light repainting.

c1910	14in (35.5cm) high
$5,000-7,000	**BER**

A Simon & Halbig '1152' Flapper character doll, with blue glass sleep eyes, original mohair wig, five piece body, re-costumed.

1920s	12in (30.5cm) high
$600-900	**BER**

A Kämmer & Reinhardt Simon & Halbig '126' doll, with 'flirty' glass eyes.

c1920	17in (43cm) high
$700-1,000	**HB**

GERMAN DOLLS

- German doll manufacturers had over taken the French firms by the end of the 19th century and reigned supreme in the doll market from the early 1900s to the 1930s.
- The more sturdy and affordable German dolls were robust enough for children to play with and were popular with middle class children all over Europe and the US.
- Some of the most valuable dolls include character 'Bébés', Googly eye dolls, and fashion dolls.
- Much of the value of these dolls is based on their appealing expressions, the condition, their rarity and their original clothes.
- Early 20th century German dolls vary from their 19th century French counterparts, such as Jumeau and Bru, in a number of ways.
- Heads have a smaller opening positioned at the top and the pate is usually cardboard. "Germany" marks can generally be found to the back of the head
- Faces were often more realistic and child-like, while eyes were often flatter with open/sleep eye lids and lighter eyebrows.
- Ears are not usually pierced and legs are more slender.
- Dolls are typically less finely made using cheaper materials, designed more as a playthings. Clothing was also cheaper and less fashionable.

An Armand Marseille character doll 500, with bisque head, painted eyes, closed mouth and dimples, and a lower quality five-piece straight-limbed body.

c1915   10.5in (27cm) high

$700-1,000   **HB**

An Armand Marseille '390' doll, with brown glass fixed eyes on fully jointed body, redressed, wear.

23.5in (59.75cm) high

$200-300   **BER**

An Armand Marseille Dream Baby, with open/shut glass eyes and light blue dress, dating from c1924.

This well-molded baby doll was hugely popular in the UK and was produced in huge numbers. A number of sizes were produced. This example is fairly small, but not the smallest. A variation was also made with a soft body.

9.5in (24cm) high

$400-500   **HB**

A large Bähr & Pröschild bisque shoulder head doll, with sleeping eyes, earrings, and replaced real hair wig, wearing one brown leather shoe, marked "410".

c1900   24in (60cm) high

$800-1,200   **WDL**

A large German Bruno Schmidt "Wendy" bisque character doll, with deeply molded mouth, glass sleep eyes and molded eyebrows, jointed composition body, antique mohair wig and clothing, marked "2033", and in a heart "B S W 537", small restoration to one finger on each hand.

Bruno Schmidt produced dolls from c1898.

23in (58.5cm) high

$40,000-50,000   **JDJ**

A German Heinrich Handwerck doll, impressed mark to back of head.

c1915-20   24.5in (62cm) high

$500-600   **HB**

A Hertel, Schwab & Co. googly-eyed doll 165-5, with eyes looking to the side and melon mouth, in original shirt, marked to back of neck.

15in (38cm) high

$6,000-7,000   **HB**

A Hertel, Schwab & Co. googly-eyed doll 173-6, in later clothes.

Googlies were inspired by the drawings of Campbells' kids by American illustrator Grace Drayton. They were an immediate success, particularly in the US, due to their cute bisque faces, large side-ways glancing eyes, tiny snub noses and closed smiling watermelon mouths. Bodies tend to be jointed composition. They were produced from c1912-c1938 by many German makers, including J.D. Kestner, Armand Marseille, H. Steiner and Goebel.

15in (38cm) high

$5,000-7,000   **HB**

A Phailibois 'Fisherman' molded and painted papier mâché automaton, with a monkey dressed in late 18thC attire, fishing by glass pond with fish moving beneath surface, working order, glass dome missing.

c1880   22in (56cm) high

$6,000-7,000   **BER**

A Phailibois papier mâché tightrope walker automaton, with composition heads, as the two musicians strum instruments the tightrope walker performs, original glass dome.

c1880   24in (61cm) high

$15,000-20,000   **BER**

A Leopold Lambert Nargileh smoker, as music plays the figure raises and lowers head and arm.

c1885   21in (53cm) high

$6,000-7,000   **BER**

A Leopold Lambert smoking gentleman automaton, with original clothing and unmarked Jumeau head and bisque hands, musical.

c1895   24in (61cm) high

$7,000-8,000   **BER**

A photographer automaton, probably Roullet and Decamps, with open mouth Jumeau head, moves head and lifts glass glide from camera.

c1900   17in (43cm) high

$7,000-8,000   **BER**

A pig in washtub automaton, probably Roullet & Decamps, a large pig scrubs a piglet, with squeal sound.

c1920   14in (36cm) high

$30,000-40,000   **BER**

A No.3 Tête Jumeau automaton, with flange neck, she turns her head and lifts her powder puff, with music, re-costumed.

1890s   18in (46cm) high

$3,000-4,000   **BER**

An early 19thC French clockwork carousel, with figures and horses, label to base, tattered silk canopy.

12in (30cm) high

$3,000-4,000   **BER**

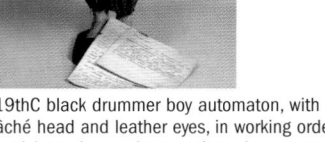

An early 19thC black drummer boy automaton, with papier mâché head and leather eyes, in working order with drum sticks acting as the speed regulator.

30in (76cm) high

$20,000-30,000   **BER**

A Chad Valley teddy bear, the gold plush bear with wide pricked ears, amber colored eyes and vertical stitched snout, jointed limbs and leatherette pads.

1930s   *14.5in (37cm) high*

$600-900   **F**

A Chad Valley golden mohair teddy bear, in original condition with cork-filled limbs and celluloid-covered button.

1930s   *13in (33cm) high*

$1,000-1,500   **LHT**

A Chiltern golden mohair 'Hugmee' teddy bear, with original foot pads, stitched nose, glass eyes and original tag.

1930s-40s   *13in (33cm) high*

$800-1,000   **LHT**

A Chiltern blonde mohair 'Master Teddy' with original clothing, stitched nose and red felt tongue, 'googly' eyes, in good condition.

The 'Master Teddy' was Chiltern's first bear. It went into production in 1915.

c1915   *12.5in (32cm) high*

$1,500-2,500   **LHT**

A Farnell mohair 'Alpha' bear with original paw pads, black boot button eyes and stitched nose, slightly worn.

c1930   *9in (23cm) high*

$1,200-1,800   **LHT**

A Merrythought Cheeky bear, the ears fitted with bells, amber colored eyes and vertical stitched pointed Draylon snout, stitched white felt pads, maker's label.

The Cheeky was first made in 1957 and is still produced today.

1960s   *11in (28cm) high*

$800-1,200   **F**

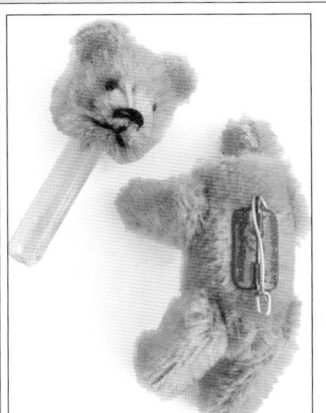

A Schuco peach-colored mohair perfume bottle bear, with brooch back, the head pulls off to reveal a perfume bottle.

1930s   *3.5in (9cm) high*

$800-1,200   **LHT**

A scarce and early gold mohair American teddy bear, with black boot button eyes, card inserts in the feet, original felt pads, stitched nose and claws.

c1905-1910   *24.5in (62cm) high*

$4,000-5,000   **SOTT**

A Steiff cinnamon mohair teddy bear, with blank metal button in ear, worn condition.

c1905   16in (40.5cm) high
$5,000-6,000   **TCT**

A rare Steiff white mohair teddy bear, with original felt pads, boot button eyes and light brown stitched nose, blank metal button in ear, in excellent condition.

c1905   12.5in (32cm) high
$4,000-6,000   **HGS**

A Steiff teddy bear, with pad feet, some exposed straw, stitched nose and claws, boot button eyes.

c1907   13in (33cm) high
$2,000-3,000   **HGS**

A Steiff small brown mohair teddy bear, lacks button in ear.

c1907   10in (25.5cm) high
$800-1,200   **TCT**

A Steiff center seam bear.

c1907   20in (51cm) high
$12,000-18,000   **TCT**

An extremely clean Steiff blonde mohair teddy bear, with original pads, black boot button eyes and stitched nose, in extremely clean condition.

c1908   13in (33cm) high
$1,500-2,500   **HGS**

A Steiff blonde mohair teddy bear, lacks button in ear.

c1907-10   9.75in (25cm) high
$2,000-3,000   **HGS**

A Steiff blonde mohair teddy bear, of typical early form, felt pads, stitched nose and black boot button eyes.

c1910   17in (43cm) high
$4,000-6,000   **LHT**

A Steiff blonde mohair teddy bear, with early face, original pads, stitched nose and black boot button eyes.

1920s   17in (43cm) high
$3,000-4,000   **LHT**

A Steiff white mohair miniature 'Teddy Baby', with velour face and feet.

1950s   3.5in (9cm) high
$700-1,000   **TCT**

A Steiff blonde mohair teddy bear, with original pads, stitched nose and black boot button eyes.

1950s   20in (51cm) high
$600-900   **LHT**

A Steiff white bear, with glass eyes, underscored Steiff button in ear with remnants of orange tag, some fur loss throughout.

1930s	7.5in (19cm) high
$2,000-3,000	**JDJ**

A Steiff teddy bear, with brown glass eyes, jointed body, ear button and yellow "MADE IN Germany" tag.

1950s	13in (33cm) high
$800-1,200	**JDJ**

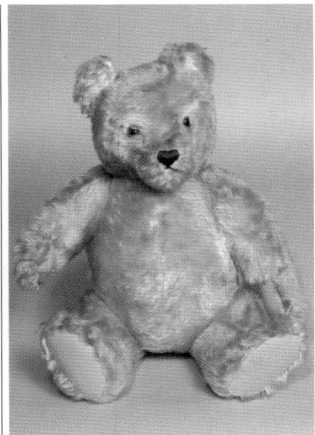

A Steiff bear, with glass eyes, lacking buttons or tags.

1950s-60s	17in (43cm) high
$300-400	**BER**

A yellow mohair Steiff bear, with glass-eyes, partial cloth tag on right arm reading "Made in US Zone, Germany", lacking button and chest tag.

1940s-50s	26in (66cm) high
$3,000-4,000	**JDJ**

A Steiff metal rod monkey, with brown mohair and felt paws and feet, large black button eyes, jointed limbs and neck, some repairs.

c1904	32in (81cm) high
$3,000-4,000	**BER**

A white mohair teddy bear of unknown manufacture, with fully jointed body with glass eyes, original paw pads.

c1920	11in (28cm) high
$500-600	**BER**

A German mohair plush cat with glass eyes, felt sewn on trousers, embroidered shirt.

c1960	32in (81cm) high
$120-180	**BER**

A French papier-mâché bulldog with glass eyes, moving head, chain-operated growl, four wooden wheels.

	19in (48cm) long
$1,000-1,500	**BER**

A stuffed toy bear on wheels with four iron wheels, iron rod base, glass eyes, burlap covering.

c1920	19in (48cm) long
$400-500	**BER**

A small ride-on brown bear with working voice, wood wool stuffed with short mohair fur, glass eyes and pale nose, mounted onto metal frame with wheels, repaired.

	17.25in (43cm) high
$400-600	**WDL**

BING/GUNTHERMANN

BING

- Gebrüder Bing, a German company founded in 1865, began making toys in the early 1880s. They specialized in high quality, hand-painted and mechanical toy boats, cars and trains, and were considered one of the best toy manufacturers in the world.
- Bing perfected the widespread 'Nuremburg style' method of production, which involved lithographically printing sheets of metal, then forming them into toys using tabs and slots.
- Most models were made with highly accurate details like glass windows and wheels that could be steered. These features can add value if still in good condition and working order.
- In 1900, in a lucrative business agreement to expand into the British market, Bing worked with British firm Bassett-Lowke's marketing skills and Henry Greenly's designs. The partnership continued for the next fifteen years.
- Original packaging, features and paintwork are important to collectors. Missing parts or restoration may reduce the value considerably.
- The quality and detail of Bing's toys dropped considerably during the interwar years. By 1933, the Jewish Bing family had moved from Germany to Britain and started the toy company Trix, with Bassett-Lowe.
- Bing models can be identified by marks including the letters "GBN" within a lozenge shape.

A Bing clockwork double Phaeton, hand painted with blue body, red embossed seats, headlamps and glass windshield, spoke wheels, rubber tires, replacements.

c1905-10   15in (38cm) long
$5,000-6,000   BER

A Bing clockwork lithographed tinplate sedan, in blue with light blue striping, electric headlights, seated driver, hood ornament missing.

c1920s   15.25in (38.5cm) long
$3,000-4,000   BER

A Bing clockwork hand painted double Phaeton, in orange with yellow embossed seats, green floor, brown fenders, white rubber tires, spoke wheels, large central headlamp, two nickel headlamps, break to rear spokes.

The detailing is exceptional.

c1905-10
$15,000-25,000   BER

A Bing lithographed tinplate double garage, with pink sedan and blue open roadster, both clockwork, wear.

c1910   8in (20.5cm) long
$600-900   BER

A lithographed clockwork tinplate girl riding a sled, attributed to Bing of Germany, spoke wheels, old solder repair to clockwork.

1920s-30s   6in (15cm) long
$1,000-1,500   BER

A Gunthermann lithographed tinplate clockwork fire truck, with boiler, two firemen, suspended bell, repainted spokes and lamps.

1920s   9.5in (24cm) long
$1,200-1,800   BER

A rare hand painted clockwork Gunthermann fire truck, with brass boiler and railing, composition figures, headlamps and bell, rubber tires and spoke wheels, flaking and retouching.

1920s   12.5in (32cm) long
$4,000-5,000   BER

A rare Gunthermann clockwork hook and ladder fire wagon, hand painted in red with black striping and yellow bench seats, seated fireman, headlamps, spoke wheels, rubber tires, pulling the hose reel.

1920s   12in (30.5cm) long
$5,000-6,000   BER

A scarce Gunthermann clockwork lithographed tinplate fire truck, with hand painted extension ladder on green trestle base, seated firemen, bell, side lamps, rubber tires, spoke wheels.

1920s   12in (30.5cm) total
$3,000-4,000   BER

A Gunthermann clockwork hand painted and lithographed tinplate figure, with vis-à-vis auto, in blue with brown seating, rubber tires, spoke wheels.

c1905   10in (25.5cm) long
$5,000-6,000   BER

A Gunthermann clockwork lithographed tinplate double-decker bus, with enclosed upper deck, seated driver and rear stairwell, Ford Automobiles and Cailler's chocolates advertising.

1930s   9.5in (24cm) long
$1,000-1,500   BER

LEHMANN

- German toymaker Lehmann, founded by Ernst Lehmann in 1881, was known for its high quality hand painted and lithographed tinplate 'novelty' toys, often sold through street vendors.
- The company produced a wide variety of humorous figures, sometimes based on friends and family.
- Germany's colonial interests meant the influence of East African customs, people and animals can be seen in some toys.
- Autos were also popular, but were typically only loosely based on actual examples.
- The high level of detail and the quirky designs meant Lehmann's toys were often copied by other makers across Europe. Most of these copies were of poorer quality and are considered inferior by collectors.
- Ernst Lehmann continued his involvement with design and production until 1931. The company is still in operation today.
- Any Lehmann toys which were only produced for a short period of time can be rare and valuable. Many were prone to rust, so examples should be checked thoroughly, as this can reduce value.

A Lehmann clockwork lithographed tinplate motor coach, with seated driver.

This is one of the earliest of the automotive toys produced by Lehmann.

c1895-1900   5in (12.5cm) long

$500-600   BER

A Lehmann clockwork lithographed tinplate 'Echo Cycle', two wheeled bicycle and rider wearing knee high socks and cap.

c1915   8.5in (21.5cm) long

$1,500-2,500   BER

A Lehmann clockwork lithographed tinplate 'Naughty Boy' toy, hand painted decoration, depicting boy taking steering wheel from adult driver, paint loss.

c1920   5in (12.5cm) long

$500-600   BER

A Lehmann clockwork 'New Century Cycle', with original box, depicting gentleman riding in open cart with attendant holding a parasol.

c1910   5in (12.5cm) high.

$1,500-2,000   BER

A Lehmann lithographed tinplate 'Wild West Bucking Bronco', hand painted, brown horse version, cowboy is bucked off horse when clockwork is activated.

1930s   6in (15cm) long

$1,200-1,800   BER

A rare Lehmann clockwork 'Boxer Rebellion' toy, inspired by the Chinese rebellion of the 1900s, material replaced.

c1900   5in (13cm) high

$20,000-25,000   BER

A Lehmann lithographed and hand painted tinplate "Man Da Rin", with clockwork mechanism.

c1910   7in (18cm) long

$3,000-4,000   BER

A Lehmann clockwork hand painted tinplate Dancing Sailor, wearing blue sailor's uniform and hat with "Dreadnaught" band, in original box.

c1920   7.5in (19cm) high

$1,000-1,500   BER

A rare Lehmann clockwork 'Snik Snak', lithographed tinplate toy, depicting a man walking two dogs pulling in opposite directions.

c1928   8in (20cm) high

$7,000-8,000   BER

A rare Lehmann 'Miss Blondin' lithographed tinplate tightrope walker with box.

c1890   11in (28cm) high

$6,000-7,000   BER

A rare Lehmann 'Tit Bits' money box, pat. 1888, the lithographed tinplate vending bank contains graphics of English and East Indies map.

This was one of the first products from the Lehmann factory.

c1889   6in (15cm) high

$6,000-7,000   BER

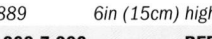

TOYS

A German clockwork tinplate polar sleigh drawn by huskies, depicting the Amundsen South Pole Expedition, one arm replaced.

c1906   10in (25cm) l
$3,000-4,000   BER

A Lehmann "Baker and Sweep" lithographed and painted tinplate toy, of a baker in a cart being hit with a sweeper's broom.

c1915 6in (15cm) long
$10,000-12,000   BER

A German clockwork lithographed tinplate toy of a boy on a three-wheeled scooter.

7.5in (19cm) long
$500-700   BER

A Lehmann lithographed tinplate hot air balloon, with figure standing in gondola.

6in (15cm) high
$7,000-8,000   BER

A Distler clockwork Mickey Mouse organ grinder, in lithographed tinplate, large Mickey pushing cart, and Minnie dancing.

6in (15cm) high
$12,000-18,000 BER

A German clockwork hand-painted tinplate Buster Brown and Tige rocking see-saw.

8.5in (21.5cm) long
$800-1,200   BER

A German clockwork hand painted tinplate clown, playing a double bass, mechanism moves arm holding bow.

8in (20.5cm) high
$800-1,200   BER

A German 'Rollin Rufus' toy, boxed example, depicting full figure atop split barrel, walks when clockwork is activated.

7.5in (19cm) long
$500-700   BER

A German hand painted tinplate springing rabbit, the clockwork mechanism activates hopping motion with pellets once dropping from interior spring tube, paint loss and damage.

6in (15cm) high
$120-180   BER

A rare German lithographed tinplate figural horn, depicting a clown, fading to one side.

$120-180   BER

A clockwork Citroën convertible B2 Torpedo, with nickel plated radiator, full running boards, simulated open soft top, celluloid windscreen.

c1925   *14.25in (36cm) long*
$2,000-3,000   **BER**

A clockwork JEP Renault K2 Torpedo, in black with red lining, seats and running boards, detailed gear mechanism, celluloid windscreen.

c1928   *13in (33cm) long*
$2,000-3,000   **BER**

A JEP clockwork Hispano Suiza, in yellow with red running boards, embossed seating with dual windscreens, nickel headlights, radiator, windscreen frames and side horn, rubber tires, disc wheels, elaborate differential, restored.

Small and respected company Les Jouets Francais joined forces with toymaker Sif in 1909 and began to produce high quality toys under the names JP, J et P and JEP.

c1935   *18.5in (47cm) long*
$6,000-7,000   **BER**

A JEP clockwork luxury 40CV coupe, in blue and yellow, split roof design with open chauffeur's compartment and enclosed passenger seating, engine, electric headlights, restored.

1930s   *17.5in (44.5cm) long*
$4,000-5,000   **BER**

A rare and early Le Jouet Francais tinplate clockwork autocab, painted in red with gold trim and white roof, glass inserts, side lamps and full running boards, repainted.

c1900   *15in (38cm) long*
$15,000-25,000   **BER**

A Fernand Martin 1889 "Exposition Universelle" toy, depicting an Oriental figure pulling a woman in a spoked wheel rickshaw, with flywheel mechanism.

8in (20.5cm) long
$1,500-2,000   **BER**

An early and rare set of Pinard automobiles and garage, three open coupés with gold trim, spoked wheels, rubber tires and clockwork mechanism, tires marked Michelin, garage with three berths and chained front ramps.

22in (56cm) wide
$15,000-25,000   **BER**

A C. Rossignol clockwork luxury sedan, in lithographed tinplate, in green with red running boards, seated driver, electric lights.

1920s   *14in (35.5cm) long*
$1,500-2,500   **BER**

A French clockwork tinplate two-seated open tourer, with upholstered seating, brown body and blue floor, red spoked wheels, rubber tires, replacements and retouching.

14in (35.5cm) long
$3,000-4,000   **BER**

A French clockwork 'Ville de Paris' motorcycle and sidecar, with silver engine detail and leaf pattern stenciling, wire handlebars, disc wheels, rubber tires, side horn.

11in (28cm) long
$3,000-4,000   **BER**

A French clockwork lithographed tinplate three-prop aircraft, with graphic images of seated crew, three propellers.

20in (51cm) wide
$1,000-1,500   **BER**

383

TOYS

A Victor Bonnet and Co. clockwork painted tinplate delivery wagon, with canvas covering stenciled "Gros. Camionnage", seated driver, stains.

1930s   10in (25.5cm) long
$1,000-1,500   BER

A C. Rossignol clockwork lithographed tinplate sedan, in blue with black roof and running boards, embossed driver's back rest, opening doors, seated driver, overprinted.

1920s   13.5in (34.5cm) long
$1,500-2,000   BER

A boxed hand painted tinplate Champion target shooter, a lever to the back controls positioning of rifle, box lid acts as target, paint flaking.

9in (23cm) high
$1,200-1,800   BER

A Lionel Walt Disney Mickey Mouse circus train set with box, three lithographed tinplate cars, and clockwork driven locomotive.

c1934   box 17in (43cm) wide
$3,000-4,000   BER

A rare Nifty Mack clockwork lithographed tinplate, with seated driver, brass finish boiler, hand rails and rear platform, one wheel replaced.

11in (28cm) long
$400-600   BER

A clockwork gas tanker, by Matarazzo of Argentina, of lithographed tinplate, with enclosed cab, gas tank body, fill caps on top, and seated driver, some wear to roof.

11in (28cm) long
$600-900   BER

A Schuco clockwork hand painted tinplate 'Boxer Jack' toy, the felt covered figure swings wildly when activated, cloth sash reads "Boxer Jack".

6in (15cm) high
$500-600   BER

A Japanese clockwork pre-war Nomura Toys lithographed tinplate military auto, rear door opens.

9.25in (23.5cm) long
$600-900   BER

A scarce clockwork touring car, by H. Yamada of Japan, in lithographed tinplate, probably copied from similar 1912 German model, with two open seats, driver and lead mounted head lamps.

11in (28cm) long
$2,000-3,000   BER

A rare Japanese lithographed tinplate clown, holding bats, with cloth outfit.

This model is based on Lehmann's 'Ajax' clown.

6.5in (16.5cm) high
$1,000-1,500   BER

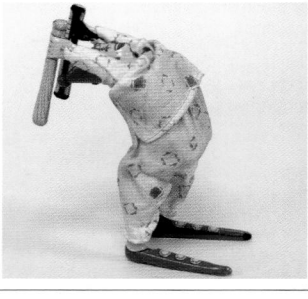

A Spanish lithographed tinplate toy, with two bear cubs riding with a larger bear driving a motorcycle.

9in (23cm) long
$3,000-4,000   BER

A Bing hand painted tinplate clockwork battleship, with gun turrets, cannons, four lifeboats, two stacks and two fire towers with observation platforms.

19.5in (49.5cm) long

$3,000-5,000   **BER**

A Fleischmann hand painted tinplate clockwork warship, in white with wide blue stripe, brown deck, two masts, two stacks, guns on turrets, restored.

c1935   *17in (43cm) long*

$1,500-2,000   **BER**

A Bing 'Kasuga' clockwork hand painted tinplate patrol cruiser, with large gun with covered turret, observation deck and two stacks, repainted.

$1,500-2,500   **BER**

A Märklin hand painted 'Lorelei' paddle wheeler, with covered side wheels, bench seating, railed observation deck, single stack and mast, professionally restored.

13.5in (34.5cm) long

$6,000-9,000   **BER**

A Bing clockwork 'Leviathan' ocean liner, with red and black hull, three stacks, three masts and twelve lifeboats, corrosion and restoration.

29in (73.5cm) long

$6,000-9,000   **BER**

A large Märklin tinplate hand painted clockwork 'Bremen' ocean liner, with three stacks, two masts, lifeboats, steering bridge and detailed appointments on upper deck, professionally restored.

28.5in (72.5cm) long

$20,000-30,000   **BER**

An Orkin pressed steel clockwork 'Pennsylvania' warship, with two fire control towers and guns on wooden turrets, central stack, ventilators, restoration and wear.

29.5in (75cm) long

$3,000-4,000   **BER**

A hand painted Ernest Plank steamboat, with steam powered turbine.

11in (28cm) long

$1,500-2,000   **BER**

A hand painted Ernest Plank 'Jupiter' river boat, steam powered, with box.

18in (46cm) long

$12,000-18,000   **BER**

A Radiguet clockwork patrol boat, with two stacks, cannon with armour shielding and two masts, repainting.

22in (56cm) long

$1,500-2,500   **BER**

A Radiguet steam powered warship, with figurehead, zinc hull, wooden deck, bronze pistons and tubing, re-soldering and repair.

22in (56cm) long

$3,000-4,000   **BER**

An American Weeden tinplate freighter, with light green paint, self standing.

18in (46cm) long

$6,000-7,000   **BER**

A Dinky No. 44b trade box containing six AA motorcycle patrols, excellent condition.

$700-800   VEC

A South African issue French Dinky No. 552 Chevrolet Corvair, pale blue, cream interior, concave chromed hubs, white tires, excellent condition, boxed.

$1,500-2,500   VEC

A scarce prewar Dinky 30 series Rolls Royce car, (30b), with open chassis finished in dark blue with black chassis, white tires, signs of chassis expansion leading to some bowing, minor chips.

1935-1940

$300-400   W&W

A Dinky Thunderbirds FAB1, model 100, finished in luminous pink and complete with Lady Penelope and Parker figures and front rocket, in original box, losses.

$700-1,000   W&W

A Dinky 22 Series Hornby tractor, yellow, blue, red wheels, no hook, good condition.

$1,000-1,200   VEC

A scarce Dinky No. 280 South African issue delivery van, khaki green including ridged hubs, complete with original treaded tires, good condition.

$800-1,000   VEC

A Dinky Toys Pre-war number 28 Series Van marked "Pickfords", deep blue, blue smooth hubs, missing windshield pillar to right-hand side and slight crack to side of van, decals good.

$300-400   VEC

A Dinky Foden flat bed truck, number 905, with chains, with box.

7.25in (18.5cm) long

$300-400   CB

A Dinky Foden 8-wheeled Wagon, number 501, first type cab, brown cab and back, black chassis, silver side flash, brown ridged wheels, herringbone tires, no hook, with box, both in good condition.

$300-400   VEC

A Dinky Pullmore car transporter (982), example with mid blue cab and light blue trailer, complete with loading ramp, both boxed, minor wear.

$300-400   W&W

A Dinky No.935 Leyland Octopus Flat Truck with chains, in a rare colorway, dark blue cab and chassis, primrose yellow cab band and fender, silver grille, pale gray riveted back, gray plastic hubs, yellow box with detailed picture panel. This version is worth twice the value of the green one.

1964-66

$10,000-12,000   VEC

A Dinky lorry mounted cement mixer (960) in orange, with a cement drum painted in mid blue and yellow, boxed.

5in (12.75cm) long

$200-300   W&W

A Corgi No. GS40 "The Avengers" 2-piece gift set comprising, "John Steed's" Bentley, red, black, wire wheels and "Emma Peel's" Lotus, white, black, figure, and three umbrellas, good condition, plus near mint inner pictorial stand and outer blue and yellow picture box.

A Corgi No. 336 "James Bond" Toyota 2000GT taken from the film "You Only Live Twice", white, red aerial, two figures, secret instruction pack containing missiles on sprue, leaflet, missing lapel badge, otherwise near mint condition.

$700-1,000 VEC $600-800 VEC

A Corgi No. GS21 "Chipperfields Circus" gift set comprising of Scammell crane with Menagerie Trailer red, blue, cast wheels, three trailers and Elephant Cage, excellent condition.

A Corgi No. 307 Jaguar E-type, graphite gray, red hood, spun hubs, mint condition with box.

$2,500-3,000 VEC $300-400 VEC

A Corgi No. GS23 "Chipperfields Circus" gift set comprising a Land Rover, six-wheel crane, Bedford Giraffe Transporter, Elephant Cage on trailer and two Animal Cages, excellent condition.

A Corgi No. 333 Mini Cooper "International Rally", red, white roof, spun hubs, racing No. 21, mint, very minor marks, in excellent blue and yellow card box with flash.
c1966

$900-1,100 VEC $300-500 VEC

A Marklin 0-gauge clockwork 4-4-2 Great Northern Railway Atlantic locomotive and tender, in green painted finish with white and black lining.

16in (41cm) long

$2,000-3,000 F

A Marklin 1-gauge 2-B steam "Queen of Scots", locomotive 1443 and a 3-A LNER tender, electric, painted in green, some wear.

$1,000-1,200 LAN

A Marklin 0-gauge 2-B-1 tender locomotive, TCE 66/12920, electrified, partly restored.

1950s

$3,000-4,000 LAN

A Marklin American 0-gauge B-1 steam locomotive AD 1020 with tender, handpainted in black, movement in working order, partly old paint, wear.

12.5in (31cm) long

$6,000-8,000 LAN

A Marklin 1-gauge Emperor's coach 1841, handpainted in green, with crown, 4-A cast iron wheels, four opening doors, with interior decoration, some wear.

c1909 *10.75in (27cm) long*

$3,000-4,000 LAN

A rare Marklin 1-gauge carriage 1912, handpainted in green, 2-A sheet metal wheels.

6.75in (17cm) long

$1,500-2,000 LAN

A Marklin 1-gauge platform carriage 1766, carrying two cars, tinplate wheels, hand-painted.

$2,000-4,000 LAN

A Marklin 1-gauge handcar 1100, hand-painted, with three original figures, the movement in working order, flags replaced, one hat restored.

$15,000-20,000 LAN

A Marklin direction indicator with eight direction signs, handpainted, wear.

8.75in (22cm) high

$400-500 LAN

A Marklin torpedo boat 'Granatiere', sheet metal handpainted, no engine, superstructure not complete, partly overpainted.

22.5in (56cm) long

$2,000-3,000 LAN

A Marklin sheet metal green steam boat, without burner, old finish, wear.

15.25in (38cm) wide

$700-1,000 LAN

A Marklin tinplate 0-gauge track zeppelin SZ 12970, handpainted, electric version, in working order.

c1932-34

$1,000-1,200 LAN

A Hornby O Gauge 0-4-0 No.1 Special Tank loco "Southern" green No.516, clockwork.

$1,200-1,800   **VEC**

A Hornby O Gauge 0-4-0 No.1 Special Tank loco "Southern" black No.A129, clockwork, version issued for 1929 and 30 only.

c1930

$6,000-7,000   **VEC**

A Hornby O Gauge 0-4-0 No.1 special loco and tender, Southern black B343, clockwork, some general retouching to loco overall, front coupling replaced, includes four-wheeled tender with Southern B343 to tender sides.

$1,500-2,000   **VEC**

An E420 locomotive, export 'Eton' locomotive with FCO LNER-pattern tender, with front bulb and no 'Hornby' transfer, varnish discolored and weathered overall.

c1939

$3,000-4,000   **L&T**

A Hornby O Gauge 4-4-0 No.2 loco and tender "L1" No.1759, 20v electric, cab side number has been overpainted, together with 6-wheel tender with Southern "1759" to tender sides, retouching.

$2,500-3,000   **VEC**

A Hornby O Gauge, French manufacture/market, locomotive No0 and tender, "EST" brown, lined splasher, "2910", French type mechanism, small links, old retouching to chimney.

c1931

$1,000-1,500   **L&T**

A Hornby O gauge electric 4-4-2 E320 'Royal Scot' and six-wheel tender, finished in maroon with black smoke box and smoke deflectors, RN6100 to cab sides, LMS to tender in shadow lettering, both in original boxes, with packing and wrapping card, lamps and envelope and track gauge spanner, plus original paperwork.

1937

$1,500-2,000   **W&W**

A Hornby O Gauge No.2 'Special Pullman Set', consisting of 4-4-0 loco and tender LMS maroon "Compound" No.1185, clockwork, early version with "Hornby Made in England limited Liverpool" transfer also includes six-wheeled tender with LMS lettering in plain gold to sides, set also includes Pullman Coach "Iolanthe" and Break Pullman "Arcadia", finished in cream and brown, contained in the correct No.2 Special Pullman box, guarantee and instruction label date coded "11/29".

$4,000-6,000   **VEC**

A Hornby O Gauge E320 'Riviera Blue Train Set' consisting of 4-4-2 No.3 loco and tender "Nord" No.3.1290, 20v electric, includes 2 wagons-lits coaches, dining and sleeping cars, corrugated cover, 12 pieces of curved electric 3-rail track, three boxes of connecting plates and one corridor connector, correct box.

$3,000-4,000   **VEC**

A Hornby Series E3200 Electric Passenger set, 20 volt electric 4-4-2 Royal Scot engine No. 6100 with smoke detectors and tender in maroon LMS livery, together with three LMS coaches and track, front bogie wheels to engine detached with one wheel missing and one fatigued.

$1,200-1,800   **BONC**

A boxed Hornby Dublo EDP2 Passenger Train Set, 4-6-2 black Canadian Pacific loco and 6-wheel tender No.1215, 2 LMS maroon coaches 1st/3rd and break/3rd, oval of track, black controller, spanner and oil bottle, with instructions dated "7/52", also included two layout booklets and other Hornby literature.

1950s

$2,000-3,000   **VEC**

A Karl Bub lithographed tinplate train set, with loco and tender together with coach and track, includes partial distressed box, paper label intact.

13.5in (34.5cm) overall

$600-900   **BER**

An early American Fallows painted tinplate train set, with "ACTIVE" stenciled on boiler.

29in (74cm) long

$4,000-5,000   **BER**

An American hand painted tinplate locomotive, attributed to Fallows, with stenciled "AMERICA" on bell.

12in (30cm) long

$2,500-3,000   **BER**

An American cast iron Hubley elevated railway, with arched tramway, steam locomotive, trestle support, and central clockwork wheel.

c1890   *30in (76cm) diam*

$12,000-18,000   **BER**

An American cast iron Ives No. 40 locomotive, restored.

$1,500-2,000   **BER**

An American Ives "O" gauge passenger electric locomotive with two parlour cars, some restoration.

$1,200-1,800   **BER**

A Western German JH lithographed tinplate miniature train set, with clockwork locomotive and passenger car, complete with original track, boxed.

each car 3.25in (8.5cm) long

$400-600   **BER**

A boxed Meier train set, comprising a tinplate locomotive, tender, coal car, baggage, and two coaches, solder repair.

18in (45.5cm) long overall

$800-1,200   **BER**

A Japanese Nomura Toys lithographed tinplate electric cable car, locomotive and tender, battery operated, boiler lifts for battery placement, includes distressed rubber guide, boxed.

9.75in (25cm) long

$300-400   **BER**

A Voltamp train set with locomotive, three long coaches, repainted.

17in (43cm) long

$3,000-4,000   **BER**

An American hand painted tinplate locomotive, stenciled "SMOKER", with clockwork movement.

12in (30cm) long

$1,200-1,800   **BER**

An American cast iron Ives clockwork locomotive, patented 1884, with key and box.

1880s   *10in (25cm) long*

$5,000-6,000   **BER**

CHESS

- The exact origins of chess are not clear, but a popular view is that it developed from an Indian game called Chaturanga, played from around AD600. By the end of the 11thC chess had become popular amongst the aristocracy in Europe and chess was used for teaching war strategy.
- The earliest European chess pieces ever found were discovered on the Isle of Lewis in 1831. It is believed they were made in Norway around 1150-1200.
- From the end of the 15thC a large variety of sets have been produced, ranging from the very simple to the hugely ornate. Over the years precious materials such as ivory and ebony became popular – even silver and gold were used.
- Jaques Staunton Chess Pieces were launched by John Jaques II, Nathanial Cooke of the Illustrated London News, and Howard Staunton, a chess champion, in 1847. Their distinct shapes made them a great success and have since been used as standard pieces.
- Complete sets command a premium - missing pieces will severely affect the price. However, some very rare sets such as those from before the 18thC, may still reach high prices even if incomplete.

A 13thC ivory chess rook, Islamic or European, cut in crenellation towards bottom and center.

1.75in (4.5cm) high

$10,000-15,000   **BLO**

A late 18thC 'Dieppe style' carved bone figural chess set, Nuremberg, one side with green stained highlights, the other side with pink, in a later mahogany fitted box with two lined presentation trays.

Carved sets such as these, in bone and ivory, are typical of the work found in Northern France and the German state of Nuremberg at the end of the 18thC.

c1780-1800   *king 3in (8cm) high*

$8,000-12,000   **BLO**

A late 18thC to early 19thC Indian 'Central Provinces' ivory figural set, the kings as elephants with princes riding in howdahs, umbrellas carved at a later date, with a copy of Alex Hammond's The Book of Chessmen, Arthur Barker Ltd, 1950, First Edition, signed by the author.

c1780-1820   *king 3in (8cm) high*

$10,000-15,000   **BLO**

An early 19thC Chinese export ivory king chess piece, Cantonese, the figure depicting an Emperor or Chinese Worthy.

c1800-25   *3.5in (9cm) high*

$600-900   **BLO**

An early 19thC English ivory chess set, in the early Calvert style, stained red and left natural, kings and queens with pierced finials.

c1820-30   *king 3.75in (9.5cm) high*

$3,000-4,000   **BLO**

A French 'Europeans vs Moors' bone 'bust' chess set, Dieppe, one side stained brown and representing the Moors, the other natural and representing the Europeans, white queen base replaced in ivory.

This set is an example of the work produced by Dieppe craftsmen at the beginning of the 19thC. In French sets such as these, bishops are typically represented as fools, in an attempt to poke fun at The Church as an institution. The uniforms depicted are typical of the period.

c1810   *king 3.5in (9cm) high*

$8,000-12,000   **BLO**

An early 19thC English Regency silver and silver-gilt 'Bust Set', each piece with a cast three-edged pedestal, the royal pieces, bishops and pawns of bust type, the kings and queens as crowned monarchs, the bishops as jesters, the knights as lions' heads, the rooks as elephants' heads, one silver jester and one silver-gilt rook and pawn with hallmark for London, maker's mark rubbed, bases of varied design.

c1815   *king 3.5in (9cm) high*

$8,000-10,000   **BLO**

A 'Burmese pattern' ivory chess set, Cantonese, stained red and left natural, with carved cartouche decoration, kings and queens with pierced heads and foliate spray finials.

c1830   *king 4.25in (11cm) high*

$3,000-4,000   **BLO**

An Indian 'Crown' ivory chess set, from Vizagapatam, elaborately carved and pierced.

c1830   *king 3.5in (9cm) high*

$10,000-15,000   **BLO**

A 19thC French 'Lyon' wooden and bone mounted chess set, one side dark brown, the other lighter brown, in a wooden box with a sliding lid.

King 3.75in (9.5cm) high

$2,500-3,500 BLO

An English ivory 'Lund-inspired' chess set, one side stained red, the other side left natural, kings with multi-knopped central sections and surmounted with Maltese crosses, queens with feather finials, rooks as raised turrets with ball finials.

c1860 *King 4.25in (11cm) high*

$1,000-1,500 BLO

A 19thC 'Gustavus Adolphus' cast iron figural chess set, by Zimmerman, Hanau, one side gilded, the other side with a black patination, depicting Gustavus Adolphus against Ferdinand of Austria, with foundry stamp to the base.

King 3in (8cm) high

$5,000-6,000 BLO

An early Jaques Staunton 'Yellow Label' weighted boxwood and ebony chess set, in a mahogany box, stamped and labeled "Jaques London", with registration and production numbers.

c1855 *King 4.25in (11cm) high*

$4,000-6,000 BLO

A 19thC Jaques Staunton ivory chess set, stained red and left natural, the white king signed "Jaques London" on the underside of the base.

King 3in (7.5cm) high

$2,500-3,500 BLO

A 19thC Jaques Staunton 'small club' size boxwood and ebony weighted set, stamped "Jaques London", in a mahogany box with a label signed "Jaques & Son, London".

King 4in (10cm) high

$3,000-4,000 BLO

A 19thC Jaques Staunton boxwood and ebony weighted chess set, signed "Jaques London", in a mahogany box with a label signed "J. Jaques & Son, Ltd., London, England".

King 3.5in (9cm) high

$1,400-1,800 BLO

A Jaques Staunton boxwood and ebony weighted chess set, stamped "Jaques London", in a mahogany box with label signed "J. Jaques & Son., Ltd, London, England", some chipping and cracking.

king 4.25in (11cm) high

$2,500-3,500 BLO

A late 19thC Indian silver figural chess set, Jaipur, one side with raised knives, the other side with spears, the kings as princes riding elephants, queens as elephants, bishops as camels, knights as horsemen, rooks as elephants, pawns as footsoldiers.

King 3in (8.5cm) high

$4,000-5,000 BLO

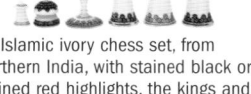

An Islamic ivory chess set, from Northern India, with stained black or stained red highlights, the kings and queens as domed minarets with spires, the pawns of pepperpot shape.

c1920 *King 5.5cm high*

$1,200-1,800 BLO

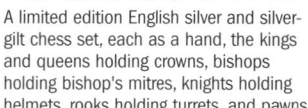

A limited edition English silver and silver-gilt chess set, each as a hand, the kings and queens holding crowns, bishops holding bishop's mitres, knights holding helmets, rooks holding turrets, and pawns holding swords aloft, maker's mark "C J L", hallmarks for London.

1974 *King 3in (8cm) high*

$2,000-3,000 BLO

Dulac, Edmund (1882-1953), 'The Chess Players', watercolour on paper, signed and dated, in a decorative 'chess-patterned' painted frame.

1905 *11.5in (29cm) wide*

$10,000-15,000 BLO

A 19thC English barley corn pattern stained ivory chess set.

King 4.5in (11cm) high

$800-1,200   **SWO**

A 19thC Canton stained and carved ivory chess set, with damage.

c1890

$400-600   **SWO**

A Staunton's-style chess set, in mahogany box.

$250-350   **BIG**

A 20thC pewter and black finished chess set, each piece on a baluster stem and circular base, a mahogany and ply box, and another chess board.

$200-300   **BIG**

A 20thC Dutch painted and glazed ceramic chess board, with relief floral decoration, signed "Delfts".

largest 4.25in (10.5cm) high

$200-300   **KAU**

An early 19thC 'The World With Its Inhabitants' game, by Carl Bauer, comprising a small terrestrial globe with original box, the lid with colored plate, and a 28 page hand-colored engraving concertina depicting figures in national dress, globe retaining some colored decoration and with maker's monogram.

c1825   *2in (5cm) diam*

$2,000-3,000   **GORL**

A Victorian jigsaw map of the world, by Gall and Inglis, Edinburgh, the box with printed sliding cover, marked, dissected maps.

$200-300   **ROS**

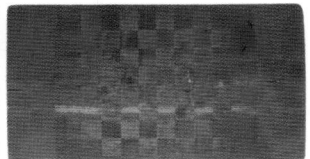

A Canadian game board, with original paint and finish.

c1900   *26in (66cm) high*

$600-800   **ING**

A Victorian child's 'The Little Conjurer' magicians' set, the faux tortoiseshell card box with printed cover, enclosing turned wood implements.

6.75in (17cm) wide

$400-500   **ROS**

An Indian ivory and sandalwood-inlaid chess board, overlaid in mosaic, together with 30 stained ivory backgammon counters.

19.75in (49.5cm) wide

$500-600   **SWO**

GAMES

Six early Islamic gaming die, including a faceted cube in jet, two oval-shaped die, and three further die of cuboid form.

first 1.5in (4cm) high

$1,500-2,500   **BLO**

A 19thC Indian set of bone parcheesi pawns, with leaf-motif stencil decoration, together with three ivory scoring counters.

Parcheesi, the Royal Game of India, can be traced back to 500 B.C. Legend has it that the game was played on palace grounds using slave girls as the pawns.

first 1.5in (4cm) high

$800-1,200   **BLO**

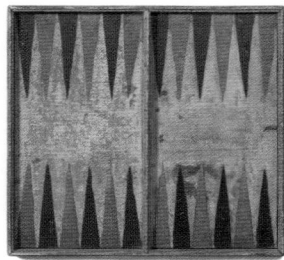

A mahogany cased letters game.

c1840   *10in (25.5cm) wide*

$200-400   **MB**

A 19thC rectangular painted double-sided pine game board, with backgammon to one side and checker board in black and natural paint to reverse.

20in (51cm) long

$1,800-2,200   **SK**

A 19thC painted wooden checker game board, with central field of green and salmon-painted checks, 13 white and dotted squares to each corner.

18in (46cm) wide

$3,500-4,500   **SK**

A 19thC painted pine parcheesi game board, with wide panel and playing field.

24in (61cm) long

$6,500-7,500   **SK**

A 19thC square faux tiger maple painted double-sided wooden game board, with alternating black and faux tiger maple squares, the reverse a parcheesi game, imperfections.

20in (51cm) wide

$1,200-1,800   **SK**

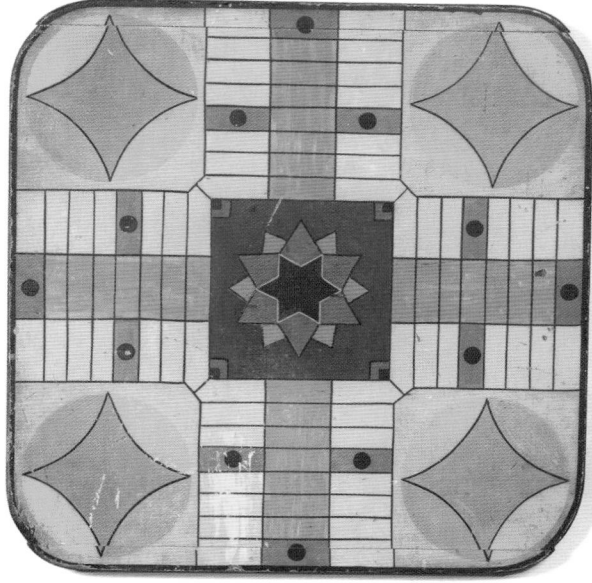

A 19thC square polychrome painted wooden parcheesi game board, with rounded corners, the playing field outlined in black.

19in (48cm) wide

$7,000-8,000   **SK**

A sedeli work ivory-mounted sandalwood board and box, probably either Calcutta or Bombay, for chess and backgammon, secured with two hinges.

c1860   *17.75in (45cm) wide*

$1,000-1,500   **BLO**

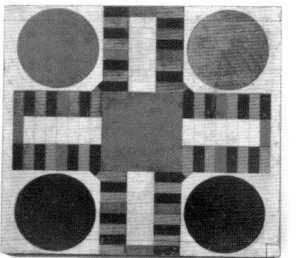

A late 19thC polychrome square painted double-sided wooden game board, one side with a parcheesi game, the reverse painted as checker board in green and black on grey ground.

20in (51cm) wide

$6,000-7,000   **SK**

An English calamander and kingwood-banded games compendium.

c1880   *13in (33cm) wide*

$3,000-4,000   **BLO**

A late 19th to 20thC lithographed paper on wood 'John Bull and Uncle Sam' game, the figures with articulated arm with wire canes, flank channels to marbles, some wear and discolouration to figures.

21in (53.5cm) wide

$750-850   **FRE**

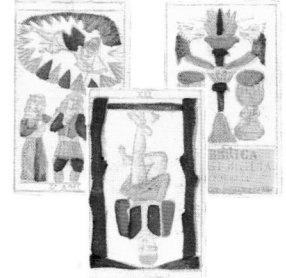

A Dutch 'South Sea Bubble' complete pack of 54 playing cards, Pasquins Windkaart, a satirical depiction of the various financial scams of the period, copper engraving, later mounted on paper.

c1720   *3.25in (8.5cm) high*

$3,500-4,500   **BLO**

A complete pack of 78 Vercelli tarot playing cards, by Luigi Biglia, woodcut with stencil-coloring.

1836   *4.5in (11cm) high*

$1,200-1,800   **BLO**

An incomplete pack of 54 (complete set has 78) Austrian 'Costume' tarot playing cards, by Glanz, Vienna.

c1880   *4in (10cm) high*

$800-1,200   **BLO**

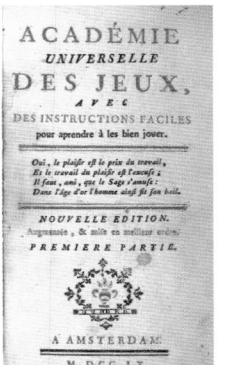

A complete pack of 78 tarot playing cards, by B. Dondorf, Frankfurt, depicting European monarchs and royal residences, in original box with Richard Steinberg's retailer's label, "Berlin W8 Taubenstrasse 14".

c1890   *4.25in (10.5cm) high*

$1,000-1,200   **BLO**

A collection of 13 playing cards and gambling related prints, including 'De Speelkaartemaker','The Wager', and 'Dr Syntax at a Card Party' The Sketch, March 4th, 1908.

$200-300   **BLO**

"Academie Universelle des Jeux", Amsterdam, printed in red and black, with wood-cut illustrations, contemporary calf, spine in compartments, and gilt decorations, minor water-staining, rubbed.

1760

$600-800   **BLO**

An unusual 'Het Vader-Landsch Werp Spel' dice game key, published by J. Verlam, Amsterdam, showing the coats-of-arms of Holland, Gelderland, Zeeland, Vriesland, Gronigen, Utrecht, Overyssel, various worthies and classes, framed and glazed.

1786   *20.75in (53cm) high*

$1,000-1,500   **BLO**

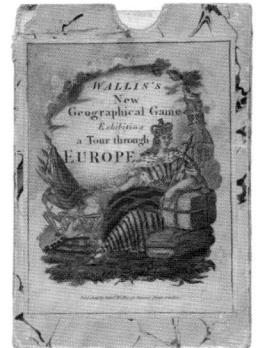

A 'Wallis's Tour of Europe - A New Geographical Pastime' linen-backed game, published by John Wallis, 13. Warwick Square, London, dated March 13th, 1811.

20.5in (52cm) high

$400-600   **BLO**

After Baxter, William Giles (1856-88), 'A Quiet Game of Nap-Spoofed By Jove!', chromolithographic print for Pears and another similar.

$200-300   **BLO**

Rouge et Noir (Pseud.), "The Gambling World", published by Hutchinson & Co, London, with 11 illustrations, original full red cloth, cover with marginal dampstain, title page browned, dated.

1898

$200-300   **BLO**

Henry René D' Allemagne, "Sports et Jeux D'Adresse", Librairie Hachette, Paris, rebound in plain boards with the original pictorial covers preserved as wrappers.

c1904

$1,500-2,000   **BLO**

TOYS

A group of German composition military officer figures, includes Hitler in several poses with podium flag bearer and other officer figures.

3in (7.5cm) high

$400-600   **BER**

A German group of composition soldier figures, includes soldiers in action and other poses, some repainting and breaks.

Largest 4in (10cm) high

$150-200   **BER**

A rare French airplane skittles set, with paper wings and wooden open cockpit fuselage, containing hand painted figures of pilots and French navigators, all original.

9in (23cm) high

$10,000-12,000   **BER**

A clown skittles set, with eight circus performers and animals.

17in (43cm) long

$5,500-6,500   **BER**

A scarce Britains plastic 'Wild West' series 7464 Federal Army gun team and limber, with field canon, ramrods and shells, three soldiers and four horses, boxed, wear.

c1970   *14.75in (37.5cm) long*

$250-350   **W&W**

A late 19th to early 20thC carved and painted shadowbox diorama, with side-wheel steamer and figures, inscribed "Norfolk, Jamestown, Williamsb'g, Hopewell and P.S. Eclipse on the James River 1889".

39.5in (100.5cm) wide

$6,000-7,000   **FRE**

A cast iron money bank, by Shepard Hardware Co., of Jonah and the Whale, with biblical sacrifice activated by push-button, now mounted upon wood coin-box, wear to paintwork.

10.25in (26cm) wide

$1,000-1,500   **GORL**

An unusual early 20thC American painted cast iron 'Shake Hands with Uncle Sam' strength tester, the coin operated arcade machine with dial painted red, white and blue, mounted on an iron stand.

30in (76cm) high

$15,000-20,000   **FRE**

An early and rare 'The Magic Wheel' optical toy, with lithographed rings for viewing, boxed.

$700-1,000   **BER**

A Mahogany and brass biunial magic lantern, by Adams of London, converted for use by Magic Lantern Society Meetings, original insert, two lime and gas illuminates included.

27in (69cm) wide

$6,000-7,000   **BER**

An Edwardian rocking horse 'Patrick', the wooden body on a stained pine safety stand with turned columns and four-bolt swinger brackets, glass eyes, with horsehair mane and tail, metal stirrups, some original leather tack but replacement leather saddle on a red felt saddlecloth, one replacement stirrup, one ear detached at old glued repair.

stand 60.25in (133cm) long

$6,000-8,000   **DN**

An Ayres pony skin rocking horse, the large piebald horse with pricked ears and flared nostrils, baring painted teeth, clear glass eyes, real horse hair mane and tail, with original leather bridle, saddle and red cloth, metal stirrup, and on a wooden safety rocker, minor bald patches.

c1900   *53in (135cm) high*

$1,500-2,500   **BONC**

A rare Edwardian nursery rocking horse, by G. and J. Lines, with saddle, tack, pommels for side saddle riding, etc. and wicker seats to either end, on pedestal supports with cruciform base.

78.75in (200cm) long

$12,000-15,000   **L&T**

An early 19thC painted carousel cow, probably French, possibly The House of Bayol, carved and painted wood, with leather strap and bells, glass eyes, on iron stand, chips, repairs and separations.

40in (102cm) long

$6,500-7,500   **BRU**

LEFT: A late 19thC leather covered rocking horse.

75in (190cm) long

$800-1,200   **POOK**

RIGHT: A late 19thC horsehair rocking horse, with painted base.

50in (127cm) long

$1,000-1,400   **POOK**

A carved and painted 'early prancer' carousel horse, by Gustav Dentzel, Philadelphia, with glass insert eyes and old painted surface.

59in (150cm) long

$16,000-20,000   **POOK**

A 16th/17thC small terracotta Akan figure, from Ghana.

7in (18cm) high

$1,000-1,300   JDB

An *akua-ba* fertility doll, from Ashanti, Ghana, wearing a multi-colored beaded necklace, and having flat round face on body with tiny arms sticking out at sides, and breasts indicated, the doll is carried to aid in pregnancy and childbirth.

12in (32cm) high

$120-180   R

A *kuduo* bronze vessel with figural scene, from Asante, Ghana, used to keep valuables and for religious offerings, with figures on the cover, the body is covered in bands of geometric and floral designs, on raised grill-like foot.

9in (23cm) high

$500-800   R

An early 19thC Asante *acron-kromfi* chair, from Ghana.

Chairs are based on 17thC European models and unlike stools do not have any spiritual function. They are used as prestige objects by important chiefs during festivities or significant gatherings.

42.5in (108cm) high

$15,000-20,000   AC

An *akua-ba* doll, from Ashanti, Ghana, deep black patina with trade dead earrings and necklace.

15.75in (40cm) high

$300-400   LAM

A late 19thC-early 20thC Ashanti wood figure, from Ghana.

8in (20cm) high

$1,600-2,400   BLA

A 20thC Baule mask from the Ivory Coast, in wood with fabric.

12in (30.5cm) long

$3,500-4,500   EL

A Dan Bete warrior's mask, from Ivory Coast.

11in (28cm) high

$8,000-12,000   JDB

An early 20thC wooden Dan mask, from the Ivory Coast.

7.75in (20cm) high

$1,000-1,300   BLA

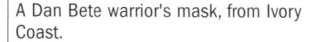

A Dan wooden mask, from the Ivory Coast.

9.75in (24.5cm) high

$9,000-13,000 PC

A late 19thC-early 20thC Dan masculine figure.

17.75in (45cm) high

$2,000-2,400 BLA

A Lega tribe ivory figure, from the Congo region.

7.75in (19.5cm) high

$4,000-4,500 JDB

A 19thC Senufo staff, from the Ivory Coast.

50in (129cm) long

$9,000-13,000 PC

An early 20thC Bambana door lock door, from Mali.

22in (56cm) high

$2,500-3,000 AC

A 16thC Djenne-style (Pre-Dogon) bronze bracelet, from Mali.

3in (7cm) wide

$9,000-13,000 PC

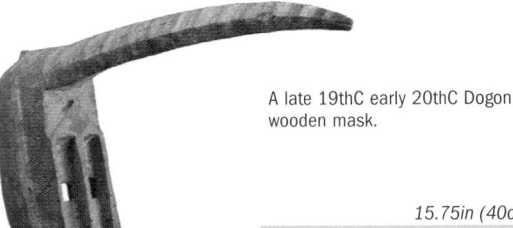

A late 19thC early 20thC Dogon wooden mask.

15.75in (40cm) high

$5,000-6,000 BLA

A Dogon carved wood antelope stylized forehead mask, the long curved horns with zig-zag devices, the human-like face with long nose, small mouth, and glass non-pierced eyes, insect damage.

29 in (73.5cm) high

$1,200-1,800 SK

399

A Dogon 'Master of Ogol' figure, from Mali.

c1930   23.5in (60cm) high

$4,500-5,500   KC

An early 19thC Dogon figure.

13in (33cm) high

$8,000-10,000   AC

A 19thC or later Dogon or Proto Dogon carved Yasa figure, representing a nommo with bowl on head.

9.5in (24cm) high

$1,200-1,600   BLA

A 19thC copper and brass bracelet, Mali, West Africa.

4.25in (11cm) long

$2,000-3,000   PC

A late 19thC Afo figure, from Nigeria.

10.25in (26cm) high

$15,000-20,000   PC

A late 19thC Basenge fly whisk, from Nigeria.

22in (56cm) high

$10,000-14,000   PC

A late 19thC Ekoi crest mask, from Nigeria, made from leopard skin and claws over a human skull.

10.25in (26cm) high

$35,000-40,000   PC

An early 20thC Mama wood mask, from Nigeria.

21.75in (55cm) high

$3,000-3,500   AC

An early 20thC Yoruba wood crest mask, from Nigeria.

12.75in (32.5cm) high

$2,000-3,000   AC

An early 20thC Yoruba figure, from Nigeria.

18.5in (47cm) high

$10,000-14,000   AC

An early 20thC Yoruba fetish figure, from Nigeria.

18.5in (47cm) high

$15,000-20,000   AC

An early 20thC West African carved wood headdress, the hollow conical form with a myriad of unusual animal forms, the two-horned form at the front with 'Picasso'-like twisted face, traces of pigment.

16in (40cm) high

$3,500-4,000   SK

A mid-late 19thC Bangwa prestige stool from Cameroon.

13in (33cm) high

$800-1,200   BLA

A 19thC Cameroon prestige stool, probably Bamileke.

13in (33cm) high

$3,500-4,000   KC

A 19th century wooden Bamun bush cow mask, from Cameroon.

9in (23cm) wide

$4,500-5,500   EL

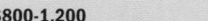

A Mambila mask, from Cameroon.

c1900   *15.75in (40cm) long*

$15,000-20,000   KC

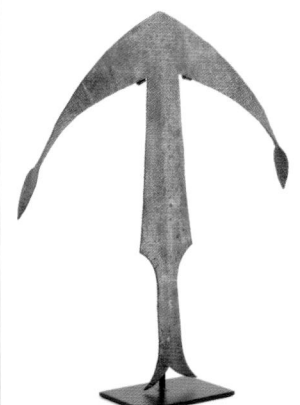

A late 19th or early 20thC Mandjang iron currency, from Cameroon, in the shape of an anchor.

These currencies were exchanged for rubber or ivory until the beginning of the 20thC when they were abolished by colonial settlers.

c1920   *20in (51cm) high*

$800-1,000   EL

An early 20thC carved wooden bellows, by the Mbembe people of Cameroon.

31in (79cm) high

$5,500-6,500   BLA

A Cameroon Grassland mask.

c1870   *16in (41cm) high*

$4,000-5,000   JBB

An early 19thC Suku tribe mask, from the Congo region.

17.75in (45cm) high

$6,000-8,000   AC

An early 20thC Lega tribe stone figure, from the Congo region.

11.5in (29cm) high

$10,000-14,000   AC

An 18thC Mangbetu tapa hammer, with ivory head, for beating textiles, from the Congo region.

11.5in (29cm) high

$9,000-11,000   PC

A Salampasu wood and copper mask, from the Congo region.

22.5in (57cm) high

$3,000-4,000   **PC**

A Yaka whistle, from the Congo region.

16.75in (42.5cm) long

$2,000-2,500   **PM**

An early 20thC Lower Congo figure.

6in (15cm) high

$4,000-5,000   **AC**

A Shona neckrest, from Zimbabwe.

c1880   *6in (15.5cm) high*

$2,000-2,400   **JBB**

A pair of 19thC Shona goblets, from Zimbabwe.

Tallest 11in (28cm) high

$500-600   **KC**

A Shona neckrest, from Zimbabwe.

c1880   *5in (13cm) high*

$3,000-4,000   **KC**

A Songye magical figure, from Zimbabwe.

c1920   *7in (18cm) high*

$1,200-1,600   **JBB**

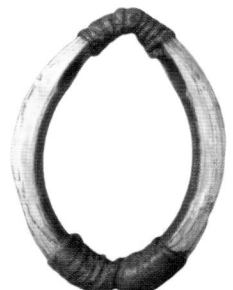

An early 20thC Maasai wild boar tusk bracelet, Kenya.

6in (15cm) high

$160-240   **OHA**

A 20thC circular Maasai beaded necklace, worn by married women, Southern Kenya.

13in (33cm) diam

$80-120   **PHK**

A Tsonga headrest, Mozambique.

6in (15cm) wide

$2,000-2,500   **PHK**

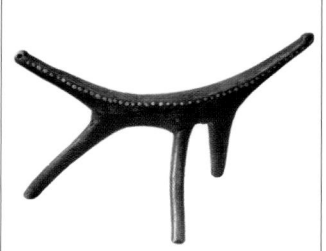

An early 20thC Dinka headrest, Sudan.

6.25in (16cm) high

$600-1,000   **OHA**

A late 19thC dervish jibbeh robe, of appliquéd cotton, Sudan.

In 1881, Muhammad Ahmad proclaimed himself Mahdi (promised prophet of Islam) and declared a jihad against the Egyptian rulers of Sudan. The Mahdi's original supporters were known as dervishes: religious mendicants who were dressed in the roughly patched jibbehs as a statement of the life of austerity and piety to which they were devoted. Later, to differentiate the leaders of the various sections of the Mahdist movement, the patched and appliquéd sections became more design conscious, but the main colors remained beige, brown and blue. These more formal jibbehs were derived from the patched cloths worn by the rank and file. Through humility the leaders demonstrated their nobility.

$6,000-8,000   **EFI**

A 20thC Zande terracotta vessel, Sudan, potted by 'Mbitim'.

10.25in (26cm) high

$1,600-2,400   **PHK**

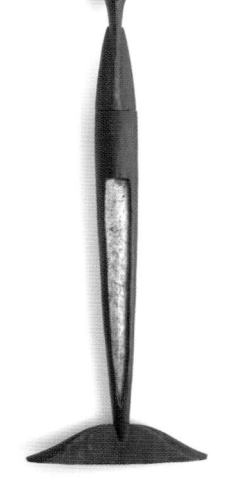

A 20thC Ovambo knife with fish tail base, Namibia, Southern Africa.

16in (41cm) high

$1,200-1,600   **PHK**

A rare Bari headrest, Tanzania.

9.5in (24cm) wide

$1,200-1,600   **PHK**

A mid-20thC Hehe stool, Tanzania.

19.75in (50cm) high

$500-700   **OHA**

Two early 20thC Nyamwezi dolls, Tanzania.

The Nyamwezi make ancestor figures, staffs and high-backed stools carved in relief with male or female attributes.

4in (10cm) high

$200-300   **OHA**

An early 20thC Shambala terracotta sculpture, Tanzania.

6in (15cm) high

$1,000-1,500   **PHK**

GREAT LAKES BEADED DECORATION

- The Great Lakes region covers the area from the eastern coast, west to the Mississippi River, from the northern rim of the Great Lakes to south of the Ohio River valley.
- Tribes include the Huron, Micmac, Ojibwa, Potawatomi and Seneca.
- Due to their geographical location, these indigenous people were some of the first encountered by Europeans. As a result their way of life was changed irrevocably.
- Possessions had traditionally been adorned with porcupine-quill or moose-hair embroidery and pigments, but the introduction of beads was greeted eagerly and beadwork became common.
- By the mid-19th century new tribal art beadwork styles had been developed. People of the eastern regions worked European-inspired lace-like designs, while Plains people typically produced starker geometric pieces.
- Woodlands people largely favored floral motives. The Ojibwa, in particular, decorated their possessions with beaded sprays and scrolling vines.
- Rectangular beaded 'bandolier' bags were popular, especially with the Ojibwa, Potawatomi and Winnebago people, and became an integral part of a man's wardrobe.

A late 19thC Great Lakes loom beaded bandolier bag, Menominee, backed with commercial cloth, the strap with multicolored abstract floral devices, the design and blue background differs on each sides, the pouch with similar floral devices on a white ground, beaded tabs with wool tassels hanging from the bottom.

40in (100cm) long

$2,800-3,200   **SK**

A Great Lakes beaded cloth bandolier bag, Ojibwa, backed in commercial cloth, with multicolored floral devices on a white ground, bugle bead and yarn danglers.

c1900   *47in (117.5cm) long*

$2,000-2,500   **SK**

A late 19thC Great Lakes loom beaded bandolier bag, Ojibwa, backed with commercial cloth, multicolored geometric devices on a clear ground, the tabs with bugle beads and red wool tassels, the red panel above the pocket partially beaded with abstract floral devices.

A Great Lakes beaded cloth man's outfit, Ojibwa, bibbed shirt, half leggings, and breech cloth, all partially beaded with multicolored floral devices using glass and metallic seed beads.

c1900   *33in (82.5cm) long*

$3,500-4,000   **SK**

A mid-19thC Great Lakes carved stone pipe bowl, Ojibwa, the square shank with six small holes, and tapering to the prow in the form of a horse head attached to a human head-form bowl, both with white seed bead eyes, one missing, probably carved on Manitoulin Island.

6in (15cm) long

$20,000-25,000   **SK**

A 19thC Great Lakes massive oval burl bowl, with cutout handles.

22in (55cm) diam

$7,000-10,000   **POOK**

35in (87.5cm) long

$3,000-4,000   **SK**

A late 19thC Northeast birch bark lidded storage box, Eastern Algonquin, rectangular tapered form decorated with avian and foliate devices, minor damage.

13.5in (33.5cm) long

$400-500   SK

A late 19thC Northeast birch bark lidded storage box, Eastern Algonquin, the round lidded form decorated with curvilinear foliate devices, crack across lid.

13.5in (33.5cm) diam

$800-1,000   SK

A pair of early to mid-19thC beaded and quilled hide moccasins, Iroquois, soft sole forms with polychrome geometric quillwork on the vamps and geometrical beadwork with cloth edging on the cuffs, some quill loss.

8.5in (21.5cm) long

$13,000-16,000   SK

A late 19thC Northeast beaded cloth Glengarry cap, Iroquois, with foliate devices done in various size multicolored beads.

9in (23cm) wide

$450-550   SK

A late 19thC Northeast beaded cloth Glengarry cap, Iroquois, multicolored geometric and floral devices on back cloth, metal sequins, red cloth edge binding, includes custom stand, minor bead loss.

9.5in (24cm) wide

$700-1,000   SK

An early 20thC Northeast pictorial birch bark and wood log caddy, Penobscot, the rectangular bark side panels decorated with foliate and animal images, handle broken in one place, damage.

22in (56cm) wide

$9,000-12,000   SK

A 19thC Northeast painted wood splint basket, the round lidded form with stamped and painted decoration.

12.5in (32cm) diam

$600-900   SK

An 19thC Northeast painted wood splint basket, the drum-form with different color splints and black stamped details.

13.5in (34.5cm) diam

$400-600   SK

TRIBAL ART

An early 20thC Northwest beaded hide chief's coat, Athabascan, smoked moose hide with fringe trim and horn buttons, partially beaded with glass and metallic seed beads in a meandering floral pattern,

36in (91.5cm) long

$700-1,000   **SK**

A Northwest polychrome twined and lidded rattle-top basket, Attu, with snowflake devices, the large knob with pinwheel design, one split at the lid's edge.

c1900   *7in (18cm) high*

$5,000-6,000   **SK**

A Northwest polychrome twinned lidded basket, Attu, decorated with colored yarn hourglass devices, wool loss.

c1900   *8in (20.5cm) high*

$1,500-2,000   **SK**

An early 19thC Northwest beaded cloth 'Octopus' bag, Cree, with eight tabs off the bottom, silk appliquéd curvilinear and geometric devices, strands of early trade beads, hide strap with tubular bone beads probably a later addition.

19in (47.5cm) long

$8,000-10,000   **SK**

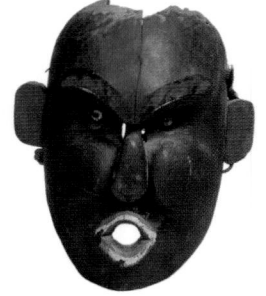

Two mid-19thC Northwest Coast ivory carvings, possibly Haida, one of a European male in a suit and tie, the other a Native female with exposed breasts and wearing a lip labret, both with incised details.

3.75in (9.5cm) high

$1,200-1,600   **SK**

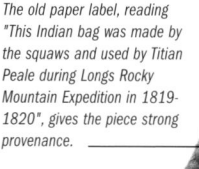

A mid-19thC Northwest Coast carved argillite plate, Haida, the outside with incised curvilinear pattern, the inside with an American eagle clutching an olive branch and arrows, framed with various letters of the alphabet, chips.

9.5in (24cm) diam

$5,000-6,000   **SK**

A CLOSER LOOK AT A CREE BAG

The old paper label, reading "This Indian bag was made by the squaws and used by Titian Peale during Longs Rocky Mountain Expedition in 1819-1820", gives the piece strong provenance.

The association with Titian Peale, an artist, naturalist and member of the well-known Peale family of painters, increases the appeal.

The use of quills in the wrapping of the hide loops is a traditional decorative technique. The beadwork originated with Native American peoples contact with Europeans.

The bag has featured in an exhibition at Monmouth County Library, demonstrating its significance.

A late 19thC Northwest Coast painted cedar wood Tsonoqua mask, Kwakiutl, with projecting mouth, sunken round eyes, and pronounced cheeks and brow line, attached ears and hair moustache, sight holes near nose bridge, red and white painted details on a black ground, possibly spilt and carved in two pieces.

12in (30cm) high

$10,000-15,000   **SK**

An early 20thC Northwest Coast painted wood mask, Kwakiutl, the hollow cedar form pierced at the mouth and eyes, deep stylized carving with human and avian features, commercial pigments.

10.5in (26.5cm) high

$20,000-25,000   **SK**

An early 19thC Northwest quilled cloth pouch, Cree, the U-shaped blue trade cloth form with silk appliqué details, with polychrome geometric, quillwork, with quill-wrapped hide loops and white seed bead spacers below the panels, braided cloth carrying strap, lined with cloth ticking, old paper label, the reverse reads "Holmesburg Feb 4, 1876".

10.75in (27cm) long

$100,000-120,000   **SK**

A late 19thC Northwest Coast polychrome carved mask, Kwakiutl, the hollow cedar form with open mouth, the articulated lower lip secured by a strip of cloth painted to match the wood, with pierced eyes and nostrils, stylized painting, and incised lines overall, remnant nails, probably secured head cloth at one time.

11.5in (29cm) high

$30,000-35,000   **SK**

A late 19thC Northwest Coast polychrome carved wood mask, Kwakiutl, the large cedar form with perforated round nostrils, articulated fins at the top representing a killer whale, articulated lower jaw and side fins representing ravens, stylized painting using black, white, green, and red pigments, remnant string and toggles for articulation, remnant head cloth.

Provenance: Collected by Garnet West in 1941, from R. Scott at Alert Bay, "Probably the Killer Whale mask, good example I believe."

26in (65cm) high

$95,000-115,000   **SK**

A late 19thC Northwest Coast polychrome carved wood mask, Nootka, large cedar form with articulated lower jaw, eyes, and lattice crown, with bold features and painted overall using commercial paints, black, gray-blue, red, yellow, and green stylizations on a cream-colored ground, much of the inner headband with cloth and cedar bark strips remains.

20.5in (51cm) high

$20,000-25,000   **SK**

A 19thC Northwest Coast carved wood figure, Tlingit, possibly a shaman figure, standing with bent knees, the arms held to the lower chest, the large head with ovoid mouth and large stylized eyes and brows, painted details including a European waistcoat.

10in (25.5cm) high

$3,000-4,000   **SK**

A mid-19thC Northwest Coast double-bladed fighting dagger, Tlingit, the tapered metal blades with central ridge, copper covered grip with braided fiber wrapping, long hide wrist strap, includes stand.

24in (61cm) long

$10,000-12,000   **SK**

A late 19thC Northwest beaded cloth wall pocket, Tlingit, the three-panel form partially beaded with an eagle, frog, and bear, each enclosed by multicolored abstract floral devices, bead loss, edge damage.

10in (25.5cm) high

$6,000-8,000   **SK**

An early 20thC Northwest Coast painted wood mask, Tsimsian, with pronounced pierced mouth and cheeks, hollow eye orbits, pronounced arched brown, red and white details on a black surface, long hair hangs from the top.

Provenance: Collected by Garnet West from R. Scott, Alert Bay in 1952, 'Singing Woman'.

11.5in (29cm) high

$5,000-7,000   **SK**

A late 19thC Northwest Coast painted wood mask, Tsimsian, the large cedar form with articulated lower jaw and eyes, the face with human and avian characteristics, with red lips, nostrils, and dash marks over a graphite-like black pigment, cedar bark bundles nailed to the outer edge, part of the articulation mechanism remains, remnant hide strap, patina of use.

Provenance: Collected by Garnet West in 1952 from Rev. Shearman Kitkatla Reserve, Prince Rupert Island, British Columbia and is said to have been worn by Warrior Chief Gum-i-gum, meaning 'Brave Man'.

14in (35cm) high

$280,000-320,000   **SK**

An early to mid-20thC Northwest Coast carved and painted wood raven rattle, with classic iconography and painted red and black.

12.5in (32cm) wide

$2,500-3,000   **SK**

An early to mid-20thC Northwest Coast polychrome wood forehead mask, representing a bird with an articulated lower beak, remnant cedar bark head covering.

18in (45.5cm) long

$3,000-4,000   **SR**

THE GREAT PLAINS

- People of the Great Plains survived by rudimentary farming and buffalo hunting. This animal was of utmost importance and was used for food, clothing and shelter.
- Tribes include the Arapaho, Blackfoot, Cheyenne, Comanche, Cree, Crow, Kiowa and Sioux.
- Many Plains artefacts now found on the market date from the late 19th and early 20th centuries.
- Many are decorated in an ornate ostentatious style, although personal items such as ceremonial drums are sometimes adorned with images perceived in visions.
- The horse, initially introduced in the Southwest by the Spanish, was hugely important for hunting, and many lavish items were made in the animal's honor. The Cree produced beaded pad saddles and the Crow embellished riding gear in brilliant colors.
- Smoking was a social pastime and a sacred rite and the Cheyenne and Arapaho in particular produced ornate smoking paraphernalia, such as hand-carved pipes and flint cases known as 'Strike-a-lites'.

An early to mid-19thC Southern Plains pony beaded cloth and hide man's shirt, probably Comanche, green-dyed with yellow stained hide fringe, barred pony bead decoration,

30in (76cm) long

$7,500-10,000   **SK**

An 1870s Plains-style beaded hide double saddlebags, Ute, the heavily fringed elk hide bags with two beaded panels, bold multicolored hourglass device on a white background.

90in (228.5cm) long

$9,000-12,000   **SK**

A late 19thC Western wood, hide and cloth model cradle, probably Ute, with Comanche style boards unusual beaded and stained hide attachments at the tips, damage.

29in (73.5cm) high

$5,000-6,000   **SK**

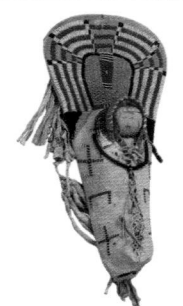

A late 19thC beaded hide and wood model cradle, Ute, the top beaded with a Central Plains barred design, the body with cross and horse track devices, contains a cloth doll.

21in (52.5cm) high

$9,000-11,000   **SK**

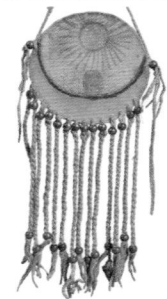

A late 19thC Southern Plains or Ute painted rawhide vision quest amulet, with sun, moon, and human face on one side, an elk on the reverse, fringe with brass beads.

3.75in (9.5cm) diam

$5,000-6,000   **SK**

A late 19thC Plains tomahawk, the buffalo hide drop with multicolored geometric devices, partially replaced, the forged axe head with solid pole.

23.5in (59cm) long

$11,000-13,000   **SK**

A 19thC Plains fringed hide coat, of long form with tapered waist and fringed at all seams, with stand-up collar, cotton cloth trim at opening and wrists, thread-sewn.

44in (110cm) long

$3,000-4,000   **SK**

A mid-19thC Plains/Prairie 'Missouri war axe', the blade with heart cut-out and five-point metal star inlay on one side, the handle possibly Osage orange wood, with brass tacks and incised arrow device, patina of use.

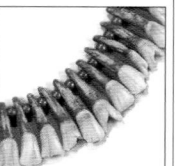

21in (53.5cm) long

$50,000-60,000   **SK**

A mid-to late 19thC Plains animal tooth necklace, strung on cloth, the horse teeth with red paint on the root, hollow brass spacer beads,

21in (53.5cm) long

$1,400-1,600   **SK**

A late 19thC large Plains wood and rawhide drum, the commercial wood body with two drum heads, one painted with the image of a bird, some damage.

24in (61cm) wide

$2,500-3,000   **SK**

A Plains beaded buffalo hide blanket strip, with three large roundels and abstract bears paw devices, thread and sinew sewn, bead loss.

54in (137cm) long

$16,000-20,000   **SK**

A mid- to late 19thC Central Plains wood and rawhide rattle, Arapaho, the head with red and green pigment and brass tack decoration, fur-wrapped handle, and with braided commercial cloth wrist strap.

8.5in (21.5cm) long

$1,000-1,500 SK

A mid-to late 19thC Central Plains beaded and quilled hide pipe bag, Arapaho, the soft hide bag with simple geometric devices, using pink, pumpkin, and black seed beads on a 'pony trader' blue background, multi-colored quill-wrapped rawhide slats and fringe from the bottom, minor restoration, quill loss.

25in (63.5cm) high

$6,000-8,000 SK

A late 19thC Central Plains fully beaded hide vest, Lakota, with geometric and American flag devices, initials "S. S.", red cloth trim, bead loss, old repairs.

20in (51cm) long

$4,500-5,500 SK

A late 19thC Central Plains beaded hide man's vest, Lakota, with calico lining and ribbon trim, with multicolored geometric devices on a white ground, the back with three equestrian warriors wearing leggings and long trailer war bonnets, beaded horses, short fringe.

22in (55cm) high

$15,000-20,000 SK

A late 19thC Central Plains beaded hide man's leggings, Lakota, fringed and with multicolored geometric and cross devices.

37in (94cm) long

$2,000-3,000 SK

A mid-to late 19thC pair of Central Plains beaded buffalo hide moccasins, Lakota, with hard soles, partially beaded with multi-colored geometrical devices, the black and amber 'pony beads', tin cone danglers at the vamps.

10in (25.5cm) wide

$5,000-6,000 SK

A pair of late 19thC Central Plains fully beaded hide moccasins, Lakota, beaded uppers and bottoms with multicolored geometric devices on a white ground, bottle-green 'buffalo tracks', three partially quill-wrapped fringes off the heel.

9.5in (24cm) long

$4,000-5,000 SK

A pair of late 19thC Central Plains beaded hide moccasins, probably Lakota.

According to family history these were given to US Army scout Ned Cook in 1880 for saving an Apache woman from drowning.

9in (22.5cm) long

$24,000-28,000 SK

A pair of Central Plains beaded hide moccasins, Lakota, fully beaded uppers and bottoms with multicolored geometric devices, medium green 'buffalo tracks' and soles.

c1900 *10in (25cm) long*

$3,000-4,000 SK

409

TRIBAL ART

A late 19thC Central Plains beaded hide and cloth saddle blanket, Lakota, the central panel of canvas, the beadwork is on recycled buffalo hide, with multicolored geometric devices on a white background, using glass and metallic seed beads, tab ends with red trade cloth, brass hawk bells, and cowhide fringe.

68in (170cm) long

$2,800-3,200   **SK**

A pair of late 19thC Central Plains beaded buffalo hide possible bags, Lakota, beaded on the font, sides and flap, with multicolored geometric devices on a white ground, red dyed tin cone danglers from the sides and flap, minor bead loss.

21in (53.5cm) long

$11,000-13,000   **SK**

A late 19thC pair of Central Plains beaded hide possible bags, Lakota, beaded on the front and sides with multicolored geometrical devices on a white ground, hide ties.

17in (43cm) long

$3,000-4,000   **SK**

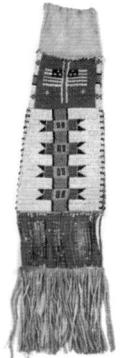

A late 19thC Central Plains beaded and quilled hide pipe bag, Lakota, the oversized beaded panels with multicolored geometric and American flag designs using glass and metallic seed beads, multicolored quilled rawhide slats and fringe from the bottom, quill loss.

31in (78.5cm) high

$4,000-6,000   **SK**

A late 19thC Central Plains pictorial miniature wood and hide tipi or teepee, Lakota, painted with a courting scene, buffalo, remnant quill-wrapped tipi decorations.

***Provenance**: Wistariahurst Museum, collected on a reservation by General Mott Hooton in the 19thC.*

20.5in (51cm) high

$9,000-11,000   **SK**

A late 19thC Central Plains painted muslin dance shield, probably Lakota, stretched over a wood hoop, painted with a hawk framed by crescent moons and dash marks.

17in (43cm) diam

$8,000-10,000   **SK**

A late 19thC carved stone cracker club, Lakota, wood handle wrapped in green-stained rawhide, the oversized head carved as an animal head.

18in (45.5cm) long

$800-1,200   **SK**

A mid-to late 19thC pair of Prairie beaded hide moccasins, Oto, the soft sole forms partially beaded with white outlined multicolored abstract floral devices, edge-beaded tongues.

9.25in (23.5cm) wide

$3,000-5,000   **SK**

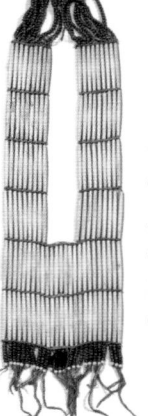

A late 19thC Central Plains woman's bone hairpipe necklace, with rawhide spacers, gold painted wood beads and glass and brass beads.

33in (84cm) long

$2,000-3,000   **SK**

A late 19thC Central Plains beaded hide and tacked cradle board, with buffalo hide and painted parfleche liner, canvas backing, the sack beaded with geometric devices, trade beads and hawk bell drops, the boards with red pigment and brass tack decoration.

44.5in (113cm) high

$90,000-110,000   **SK**

An early to mid-19thC Eastern Plains carved wood ball-headed club, with metal spikes, with ridged butt end, the head blackened and with a hey four-side metal spike, dark patina, crack.

23.5in (59.5cm) long

$7,000-10,000   **SK**

An early to mid-19thC Eastern Plains inlaid stone pipe bowl, the gray brown form with short prow, locomotive-style bowl and central silver band, inlaid with lead in geometrical devices, with two buffalo tracks on the bowl.

5.25in (13.5cm) diam

$1,200-1,500   **SK**

A pair of early 19thC Northern Plains quilled hide moccasins, Cree, the soft sole forms with extremely fine polychrome geometric loom-quilled ankle cuffs, with remnant cloth edging, the vamps with polychrome floral devices.

9.5in (24cm) long

$12,000-18,000   **SK**

A late 19thC Northern Plains beaded hide and cloth martingale, Crow, red cloth inserts and beaded with classic Crow multicolored geometric devices, bead and cloth loss.

31in (78.5cm) long

$7,000-9,000   **SK**

A Northern Plains beaded hide and cloth martingale, Crow, multicolored geometrical devices, partially edged with large milky white beads, large bells and bugle beads from the bottom, cloth loss.

33in (84cm) long

$5,500-6,500   **SK**

An early 20thC Northern Plains beaded hide and cloth mirror bag, Crow, with classic Crow geometrics on one side and multicolored floral devices on the reverse.

18in (45cm) long

$2,000-3,000   **SK**

A late 19thC Northern Plains beaded hide mirror bag, Crow, of diminutive form with classic Crow geometric designs on both sides with strap, fringe from bottom, bead loss, with fringe.

14in (35.5cm) long

$3,000-4,000   **SK**

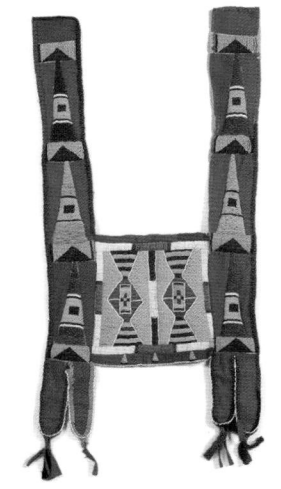

A mid-to late 19thC Northern Plains beaded and tacked hide knife sheath, Crow, buffalo rawhide with hide panel at the top and cut-out belt slot to the side, multicolored geometric devices on a pink ground, using seed, real, and pony beads, 15 remaining brass tacks, traces of red pigment.

$15,000-20,000   **SK**

A late 19thC Northern Plains beaded buffalo hide possible bag, Crow, with thick carrying strap and partially beaded on the front in a traditional Crow design, one bottom tab missing, split in side.

11in (28cm) long

16in (40.5cm) wide

$14,000-18,000   **SK**

A mid-to late 19thC Northern Plains cloth, hide and wood rattle, Crow, the wood handle wrapped with red cloth and hide, the hide head with red and yellow pigments, hide fringe and three hawk bell attachments, patina of use.

10.5in (26.5cm) wide

$1,000-1,500   **SK**

TRIBAL ART

An unusual early 20thC Plateau pictorial beaded cloth, possibly a table cover, beaded on one side with central star and cross, each quadrant with multicolored motifs, partially contoured beadwork with a wide variety of period beads, loop bead edging.

30in (76.5cm) wide

$9,000-12,000   **SK**

A pair of Plateau polychrome parfleche envelopes, with bold geometrical patterns in red, green, blue, and orange, hide ties.

26in (66cm) long

$3,500-4,500   **SK**

An early 20thC Plateau beaded hide man's vest, the front fully beaded with floral devices, the back with floral devices on hide, short fringe at the sides, edged with brass and beaded chain.

22in (56cm) long

$1,000-1,500   **SK**

A pair of Plateau angora saddlebags, the commercial bags covered with orange-dyed woolly panels, beaded cloth saddlebag panel to the top with horse and floral devices, minor bead loss.

40in (102cm) l

$4,500-5,500   **SK**

A late 19thC Plateau beaded wood and hide woman's saddle and stirrups, Flathead, rawhide-covered wood frame with hide covering, and beading, old tag reads, "Indian Woman's saddle made and ridden by Annie Martin Ronan Flathead Res. Mont.", bead loss, damage.

26in (66cm) long

$6,000-8,000   **SK**

SOUTHEAST

A Southeast carved wood mask, Cherokee, by Will West Long, the hollow oval form with grimacing face and small snake on the top of the head, traces of pigment.

Provenance: *Purchased from Will West Long at Ravensford, North Carolina, in 1941.*

10in (25cm) high

$2,500-3,000   **SK**

A Southeast carved wood mask, Cherokee, by Will West Long, the hollow form with pierced mouth and small teeth, large nose, pierced eyes looking to the side, and incised details, animal hair on the top of the head, traces of pigment.

10.5in (26cm) high

$2,000-3,000   **SK**

A 20thC Southeast carved wood mask, Cherokee, by Will West Long, chief collaborator with ethnographer Frank G. Speck, hollowed, tapered form with pierced mouth, nostrils, and eyes, a piece of animal fur attached to top, shiny surface patina.

11.75in (29cm) long

$4,500-5,500   **SK**

A Cherokee carved wood mask, the hollowed form with pierced mouth and two projecting teeth, prominent nose with pierced nostrils, pierced eyes, two short horns, and traces of black and red pigments, signed on the inside "Will West Long."

12in (30cm) high

$2,000-3,000   **SK**

A rare late 19thC Southeast beaded cloth sash, the panel beaded on one side with floral pattern, remnant silk and bead edging, with white pony beaded edging and tassels at the ends.

sash panel 26.5in (66cm) long

$12,000-14,000   **SK**

SOUTHWEST NAVAJO BLANKETS

- The Southwest peoples' adherence to the wisdom and teachings of previous generations helped to foster the creation of an abundance of artistic objects.
- The Navajo of Eastern Arizona and Western New Mexico are famed for their textiles.
- The Navajo people learned from their Pueblo teachers and eventually surpassed them, both in quantity and quality.
- Until around c1880, output consisted almost entirely of blankets. Weaving designs developed from simple striped blankets to complex symmetrical geometrical patterns.
- By the end of the 19th century, weavers were making rugs for non-Native floors.
- Few 19thC blankets produced for local use featured pictorial motifs, but later rugs produced for the commercial market contained human, animal, and other designs.
- Depictions of spirit figures known as 'yeis' were popular as were important elements of the Navajo's world, such as corn, birds and horses.

A late 19thC Southwest late Classic wearing blanket, with natural and commercially dyed homespun wool, in a third-phase chief's pattern with indigo, dark brown, ivory, and aniline-dyed light red stripes overlaid with nine concentric stepped diamonds, edged in red, ivory, and grey tufts.

68in (170cm) long

$22,000-25,000   **SK**

A late 19thC Southwest Germantown weaving, Navajo, vertical black and cream-colored track and arrow pattern down the center, with cross and zig-zag devices down the sides, on a red ground.

86in (215cm) long

$7,000-10,000   **SK**

A late 19thC Southwest Germantown weaving, Navajo, multicolored serrated diamonds on a red ground, fringed at the ends.

50.5in (126cm) long

$6,500-8,500   **SK**

A late 19thC Southwest Germantown weaving, Navajo, tightly woven in a multicolored eye-dazzler pattern, two central red diamonds with crosses, remnant fringed ends.

54in (135cm) long

$4,500-5,000   **SK**

A late 19thC Southwest Germantown weaving, Navajo, two-color striped ends and with an allover multicolored 'eye dazzler' pattern with fringed ends, stains.

77.5in (197cm) long

$14,000-16,000   **SK**

A late 19thC Southwest Germantown weaving, Navajo, an eye dazzler tightly woven of three-ply commercial wool, wool loss to fringe.

76in (193cm) long

$11,000-13,000   **SK**

A late 19thC Southwest Germantown weaving, Navajo, tightly woven saddle blanket with floating serrated diamonds on a red background, fret border and black fringe.

32in (80cm) long

$6,000-8,000   **SK**

A mid-to late 19thC classic Southwest Moki serape, Navajo, indigo blue and natural dark brown striped background overlaid with nine concentric serrated diamond devices, both shades of reds are cochineal dyed, minor damage, stains.

72in (183cm) long

$35,000-40,000   **SK**

A late 19thC Southwest late Classic man's wearing blanket, Navajo, natural and commercially dyed homespun wool, stacked indigo blue and natural ivory-white serrated diamonds on a variegated aniline red background.

70in (175cm) long

$5,000-6,000   **SK**

A late 19thC Southwest late Classic blanket, Navajo, natural and commercially dyed homespun wool, variegated green, deep indigo blue, and ivory-white concentric stepped diamond pattern on an aniline red background.

68in (170cm) long

$12,000-15,000   **SK**

A late 19thC Southwest late Classic serape, Navajo, woven in commercial three-ply aniline red and vegetal green yarn, with hand-spun indigo blue and natural white, with vertical lightning pattern.

69in (172.5cm) long

$7,000-10,000   **SK**

A late 19thC Southwest weaving, Navajo, of softly woven churro wool, with natural brown and white, a pink and faux indigo, done in a third phase chief's blanket revival style.

72in (183cm) long

$5,000-6,000   **SK**

A late 19thC Southwest weaving, Navajo, natural and commercially dyed wool in a fourth phase variation of a woman's shoulder blanket.

51in (129.5cm) long

$10,000-12,000   **SK**

A late 19thC Southwest late Classic wearing blanket, Navajo, tightly woven in a banded pattern, with background in ravelled cochineal-dyed dark red, and aniline-dyed light red, separated by ivory stripes, overlaid with deep indigo blue and ivory zigzag and stepped ivory devices with indigo blue and blue-green stripes.

70.5in (176cm) long

$35,000-40,000   **SK**

A late 19thC Southwest Transitional Period blanket, Navajo, woven in hand-spun merino wool with vertical lightning pattern in aniline red and natural dark brown on a cream-colored ground.

74in (185cm) long

$3,500-4,000   **SK**

A late 19thC Southwest child's blanket, Navajo, woven in a late classic pattern with natural and commercially dyed colors, some dye run, wear.

49.5in (126cm) long

$3,000-4,000   **SK**

A late 19thC Southwest classic woman's wearing blanket, Navajo, with natural and aniline dyed homespun wool, in a second phase woman's pattern with indigo blue and aniline dyed red stripes over natural brown and ivory stripes, wool loss, stains.

52in (132cm) wide

$10,000-12,000   **SK**

An early 20thC Southwest weaving, Navajo, woven in shades of natural brown and white with aniline red accents, large concentric diamond and cross center with three-color fret border, tear, a few repairs.

128in (325cm) long

$3,000-4,000   **SK**

An early 20thC Southwest weaving, Navajo, woven with natural and commercially dyed homespun wool in a first phase revival pattern, stains.

c1900   *46.5in (118cm) long*

$1,800-2,200   **SK**

A late 19thC Southwest painted pottery olla, Acoma, the high shouldered form with a three-band dark brown repeat pattern on a cream-colored slip.

10.5in (26.5cm) diam

$8,000-10,000   SK

A Southwest painted pottery olla, Acoma, with concave base, rounded shoulder and tapered neck, red paint on the bottom and inside of rim, black geometric and hatch devices on a gray-white ground, with clear commercial glaze on the inside.

c1900   11in (28cm) diam

$4,000-5,000   SK

c1900

A Southwest polychrome pottery olla, Acoma, with concave base, high rounded shoulder, and tapered neck, with black, red-brown, and orange geometric, foliate, and stylized parrots on a cream-colored ground.

13.5in (34cm) diam

$30,000-35,000   SK

An early 20thC Southwest painted pottery olla, Acoma, red concave bottom and inner rim, with black on cream geometric and foliate devices, paint loss.

10.5in (26.5cm) diam

$2,000-3,000   SK

An early to mid-20thC Southwestern polychrome pottery olla, Acoma, with high shoulder and four Acoma parrots framed in concentric diamond and floral devices, written on the concave base "Acoma Indian Pottery, Acomita N.M.".

13in (33cm) diam

$1,800-2,200   SK

A 20thC Southwest polychrome pottery olla, Hopi, stylized frog signature on the bottom, the high shouldered form with flared rim and black and red-brown abstract feather devices on a cream-orange ground.

12.5in (31cm) diam

$6,000-8,000   SK

A late 19thC Southwest polychrome pottery olla, Zia, the high shouldered form with a black and red-brown geometric pattern on a cream-colored slip.

12in (30.5cm) diam

$12,000-14,000   SK

An early 20thC Southwest polychrome pottery large olla, Zia, with high shoulder and tapered neck, with black and dark red abstract floral and three large 'Zia' birds.

16.5in (41cm) diam

$11,000-13,000   SK

A late 19thC Southwest pottery polychrome olla, Zuni, the rounded high-shouldered form with concave base and fixture at the top of the underbody, slightly flared rim, cream-colored body with black and red brown geometric and abstract foliate devices and heart-line deer.

14.5in (37cm) diam

$18,000-20,000   SK

A late 19thC Southwest polychrome pottery bowl, Zuni, the high-shouldered form with unusual dark brown underbody and geometric and avian devices, the cream-colored neck with dark brown and red-brown geometric and foliate devices,

9in (23cm) high

$7,000-9,000   SK

415

A late 19thC Southwest polychrome pictorial pottery bowl, Zuni, the deep form with abstract geometric devices on the outer top, the inside with large volutes and two heart-line deer with birds perched on their backs, wear.

14.75in (37.5cm) diam

$4,000-6,000 **SK**

A prehistoric Southwest painted pottery olla, the globular redware form with black and cream-colored abstract pattern, crack to bottom.

14.5in (37cm) diam

$2,000-3,000 **SK**

A late 19thC Southwest polychrome pottery olla, red underbody with black and abstract foliate devices and four large birds on a cream-colored slip, chip at rim.

12in (30.5cm) diam

$15,000-18,000 **SK**

A mid-20thC Southwest large polished blackware pottery vase, Santa Clara, ribbed shoulder, long neck with four 'bear paws' and flared rim, signed "Margaret Tafoya, Santa Clara, New Mexico".

16in (40cm) high

$20,000-25,000 **SK**

A mid-20thC Southwest carved polished blackware pottery bowl, Santa Clara, signed "Margaret" for Margaret Tafoya, oval shaped with deeply carved Avanyu pattern, minor scratches.

8in (20cm) high

$5,500-6,500 **SK**

A Southwest black-on-black pottery vessel, by Maria and Julian Martinez, San Ildefonso Pueblo the tapered neck with Avanyu pattern, minor scratches.

8.5in (21.5cm) diam

$5,000-6,000 **SK**

SOUTHWESTERN BASKETS

A late19thC Southwest polychrome coiled basketry bowl, Apache, with black and dark red maze pattern.

15.75in (40cm) diam

$3,000-4,000 **SK**

A Southwest coiled basketry olla, Apache, the ovoid form with flared rim and decorated with multiple stepped diagonal devices, stitch loss, slight list.

c1900 *22.5in (57cm) high*

$6,000-7,000 **SK**

A Southwest polychrome pictorial basketry olla, Apache, with high shoulder, flared rim, decorated with eight sets of human forms, two rows of animals and verticle stacked diamonds, minor stitch loss.

c1900 *18.5in (47cm) diam*

$40,000-50,000 **SK**

A Southwest coiled basketry olla, Apache, the high-shouldered form with verticle stacked triangles and alternating human figures, stitch loss, rim damage.

c1900 *20in (51cm) high*

$7,000-9,000 **SK**

An early 20thC Southwest pictorial coiled basketry bowl, Apache, the bulbous form with a row of male and female figures, positive and negative dogs, and geometric devices.

7.75in (19cm) diam

$12,000-15,000 **SK**

An early 20thC Southwest coiled basketry lamp, Pima, matching tray and base.

Provenance: *Purchased in 1903 by a doctor from Lowell, Massachusetts.*

shade 10in (25.5cm) diam

$3,500-4,500 **SK**

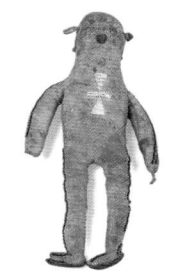

A late 19thC Southwest beaded hide doll, Apache, with hide ears, harness leather, moccasin soles, with blue and black beaded detail, a white cross on the chest, and a large green bead for a nose, minor bead loss.

12.5in (32cm) high

$3,000-4,000   **SK**

A mid-to late 19thC Southwest cloth, hide and wood female doll, Apache, with thread-wrapped head, traces of pigment, commercial leather hair bow, pony beads to the yoke, high-top moccasins, beaded eardrops and necklace.

14in (35.5cm) high

$14,000-18,000   **SK**

A CLOSER LOOK AT A SOUTHWEST KACHINA POLYCHROME DANCE BOARD

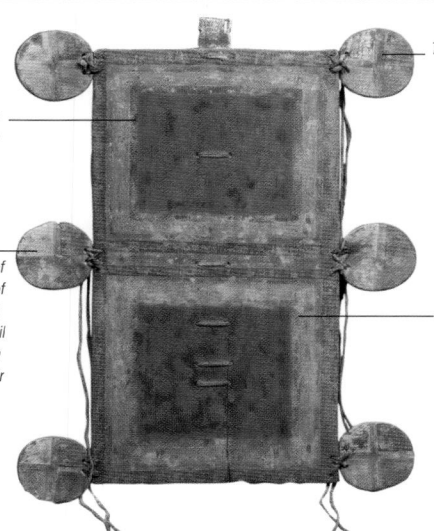

The six discs at the corners and mid-section of the tablet represent the four directions.

Kachina are helper spirits capable of influencing the natural world. The spirits are contacted through dance.

The object, known as a 'moisture tablet', is part of a costume for a number of Hopi kachinam. Important figures such as the red tail hawk and Eagle kachinam wear such devices on their backs.

The green paint is copper carbonate. The Hopi started using copper carbonate during the 1920s. The color would have originally been blue before it oxidized over the decades.

A rare late 19th to early 20thC Southwest kachina polychrome dance board, probably cottonwood, painted on one side with box and border devices, with six circular forms lashed with hide and projecting from the sides, painted with a cross and four-color wedge shapes, cloth waist ties.

19in (48cm) high

$16,000-20,000   **SK**

A Southwest painted dance shield, Hopi, made by S. Benimptewa, art board with wood and paper attachments painted with multicolored symbolic devices.

c1945   *15.5in (39.5cm) diam*

$1,000-2,000   **SK**

A Southwest painted clay doll, Mojave, the body with red striped over yellow pigment, beaded necklace and ear ornaments, limbs reglued.

c1900   *5in (12.5cm) high*

$1,500-2,000   **SK**

An early to mid-20thC Southwest silver and turquoise bow guard, Navajo, stamped silver with rectangular turquoise setting in the center, commercial leather write strap.

Silver 3.25in (8.5cm) wide

$700-1,000   **SK**

An early 20thC Southwest silver, turquoise, and commercial leather bow guards, Navajo, the unusual shape with stamp and repoussé work, and mounted with nine variously shaped turquoise stones, two with serrated bezels, mounted on a commercial leather wrist strap.

silver 5in (12.5cm) wide

$3,000-5,000   **SK**

A 19thC Southwest carved stone fetish figure, probably Zia, with relief-carved legs and arms, the head with broad nose, the eyes inlaid with mica, the chest inlaid with turquoise, and with a string necklace of early green turquoise beads and abalone pendant, smooth patina from handling.

5.5in (14cm) high

$3,000-4,000   **SK**

A 19thC Southwest polychrome carved wood crucifix figure, a graphic depiction of Jesus on the cross, age cracks.

27in (68.5cm) high

$14,000-18,000   **SK**

A Western hide Wild West Show shirt, with multicolored floral embroidery, clamshell buttons and brass studs spelling "IORM TOTE" fringe to seams, tears.

'IORM TOTE' stands for Improved Order of Red Men, a masonic fraternity who's secret password was 'Totem Of The Eagle'.

c1900   *35in (89cm) long*

$1,000-1,200   **SJ**

A large Skookum doll, with blanket, braided leather belt and beaded necklace.

c1925   *33in (84cm) high*

$1,700-2,000   **SK**

Edward Curtis, (American, 1868-1952), 'The Vanishing Race', original photograph, signed, original descriptive Curtis label on the back.

7.5in (19cm) wide

$2,500-3,000	**SK**

Edward Curtis, (American, 1868-1952) 'Canyon de Chelly' signed original orotone photograph, in early frame with descriptive label on the back.

Image 13.5in (34.5cm) wide

$20,000-25,000	**SK**

Will Soule, (American, 1836-1908), large format photograph of a Southern Plains camp, on original card mount, signed "Mow-way or Hand Shakers Camp Fort Sill" lower right.

9.25in (23cm) wide

$2,000-2,500	**SK**

F. Jay Haynes, cabinet card photograph of Chief White Bull, probably Shoshone.

c1883   Card 6.5in (16.5cm) high

$500-600	**SK**

Will Soule, (American, 1836-1908), photograph mounted on card stock, depicting a Southern Arapaho camp scene, the warrior standing at center carrying a tomahawk with a heart cut-out.

9.25in (23cm) high

$2,000-3,000	**SK**

Karl Moon (American, 1878-1948), portrait of an elderly Apache man, stamped "copyright 1908 by Fred Harvey", written on mount "Karl Moon, Nar-i-ke-gi-et-su, Old Apache Scout", small stains.

9.5in (24cm) high

$1,000-1,500	**SK**

Karl Moon (American, 1878-1948), portrait of a Navajo man wearing two necklaces, photo stamped "copyright 1907 by Fred Harvey", mount signed "Karl Moon, Pesothlanny".

Image 9.5in (24cm) high

$1,500-2,000	**SK**

A large matted photograph of a Cheyenne warrior, Hillers, Oklahoma territory, wearing traditional clothing and carrying an elaborate inlaid pipe and pipe bag.

c1875   Image 9in (23cm) high

$1,800-2,200	**SK**

Will Soule (American, 1836-1908), framed cabinet card photograph of Arapaho war chief Powder Face, wearing complete war regalia.

Card 6.25in (16cm) high

$1,000-1,500	**SK**

THE INUIT ART MARKET

Canadian Inuit art has captured the imagination and interest of collectors around the world. Once seen as simply 'arts and crafts', Inuit art now challenges auction records set by international painters, printmakers and sculptors. A growing number of collectors is moved by the artistry of the sculpture and graphics.

The value of Inuit art has increased steadily over the last twenty-five years, with no fluctuation in interest or value, to date. Each new auction sets new price levels and the art finds homes in museums, art galleries and private collections worldwide.

Due to the increasing level of interest in Inuit art and rising prices, it is imperative that collectors conduct adequate research to ensure quality, value and integrity of their acquisition. Value is based on a combination of several factors, the artist, age, subject, material, detail and quality of execution. Emphatically, quality, not size, is the overall determining factor for value.

Works from what is considered the early 'Classic' period (1950-1970) is generally highly valued. Damage to earlier pieces is not a value killer. In fact, missing pieces such as tusks or antlers can be replaced with minimal depreciation. Early stone figures with inset ivory faces also demand a substantial premium. Uniquely, anonymous works from the early (classic) period can be worth as much or more than works by recognized, sought after artists.

Subject matter is also a factor: shamans (transformation or spiritual), bears, caribou, musk ox, hunters, mother and child, and story-telling, are all valued and considered desirable while fish, seals, whales and walrus are less so. A strong, single image is more valued than a 'pegged together' camp or hunting scene made up of several pieces. The dominant graphic artists are mainly from Cape Dorset, Baker Lake and Povungnituk.

- Duncan McLean

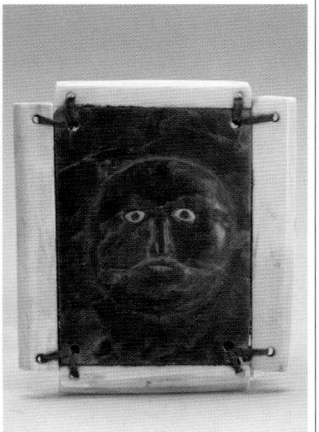

'Framed Face', a soapstone and ivory plaque, by Akeeaktashuk (1898-1954), Inukjuak.

c1950   *4.5in (11.5cm) high*

$20,000-25,000   **WAD**

'Throat Singers' ivory, by Manasie Akpaliapik (1955-), Toronto, signed in syllabics.

4.5in (11cm) high

$4,000-6,000   **WAD**

'Whimsical Figure', soapstone, ivory, antler figure, by Karoo Ashevak, Spence Bay, signed in syllabics.

10in (25.5cm) high

$35,000-45,000   **WAD**

KAROO ASHEVAK

■ From humble beginnings following the traditional Inuit hunting lifestyle, Karoo Ashevak (1940-74) became one of the Arctic's most respected and popular artists.

■ In 1960, he settled in Talurqjuaq, a small community and one of the last to be reached by the outside world.

■ Well-respected in his region and worldwide, he has had huge impact on Kitikmeot artists. His talents were recognized with solo exhibitions in Toronto, Montreal and New York, leading to his most prolific period from 1971 to his death in a house-fire in 1974, generating 250 sculptures.

■ Working mainly in whalebone, with stone, baleen and ivory highlights, his work explores the spirit world, shamanism and mythology.

■ Described as 'Picasso of the North', Ashevak's impeccably finished sculptures are often humorous, grotesque, spiritual and whimsical.

■ His limited output and his skill make his work highly sought-after.

'Shaman', whalebone and sinew figure, by Karoo Ashevak, Spence Bay, signed in syllabics.

c1970   *10in (25.5cm) high*

$25,000-30,000   **WAD**

'Bust', soapstone figure, by Kaka Ashoona (1928-96), Cape Dorset.

c1962   *9in (22.9cm) wide*

$6,000-9,000   **WAD**

'Birth Scene', soapstone figure, by Ennutsiak (1896-1967), Iqualuit, disc number inscribed.

6in (20cm) wide

$13,000-16,000   **WAD**

'Birth Scene', soapstone figure, by Ennutsiak (1896-1967), Iqualuit, disc number inscribed.

6in (20cm) wide

$15,000-20,000   **WAD**

'Figure', in soapstone, by John Kavik (1897-1993), Rankin Inlet, signed in syllabics.

c1960   *5in (13cm) high*

$6,000-9,000   **WAD**

'Sedna', soapstone figure, Kiakshuk (1886-1966), Cape Dorset.

Sedna is the Inuit goddess of the sea, who controls storms, whales and seals. Once she has been pacified by shamans, she releases these animals for the Inuit to eat.

c1962   *10in (25.5cm) wide*

$10,000-15,000   **WAD**

'Mating Polar Bears', a soapstone figure, by Andy Miki (1918-83), Arviat, signed in syllabics.

c1967   *10.5in (27cm) long*

$22,000-28,000   **WAD**

A gray soapstone howling dog, by Andy Miki, Arviat.

10in (25.5cm) high

$18,000-20,000   **WAD**

'Mother and Child', a soapstone figure, by Sheokjuk Oqutaq, (1920-1982), Cape Dorset.

c1960   *5.5in (14cm) high*

$6,000-9,000   **WAD**

'Joyful Bird', a soapstone figure, by Sheokjuk Oqutaq, Cape Dorset.

c1960   *10in (25.5cm) wide*

$15,000-20,000   **WAD**

'Mother and Child', a soapstone figure, by John Pangnark (1920-80), Arviat, signed in syllabics.

c1970   *9.75in (23cm) high*

$22,000-28,000   **WAD**

'Figure', soapstone, by John Pangnark, Arviat.

c1967   *7.5in (18.5cm) high*

$20,000-24,000   **WAD**

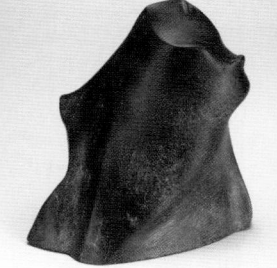

A green soapstone figure of an Inuit mother holding her child, by John Pangnark, Arviat, signed in syllabics.

10in (25cm) high

$7,000-10,000   **WAD**

'Dancing Polar Bear, in soapstone and ivory, Pauta Saila, (1916-), Cape Dorset, signed in syllabics.

19in (48.5cm) high

$28,000-32,000   **WAD**

A brown soapstone dancing polar bear, by Pauta Saila, Cape Dorset, signed in Roman.

This was purchased from the artist in 1975. A short film taken in Cape Dorset in 1975 shows Pauta working on the early stages of carving this piece.

12.5in (31.8cm) high

$12,000-18,000   **WAD**

A dark soapstone musk ox being attacked by Inuit hunters and a dog, by Thomas Sivuraq (1941-), Baker Lake, signed in syllabics.

22in (56cm) high

$10,000-15,000   **WAD**

'Hunter', a soapstone, wood, ivory, sinew figure, by Joe Talirunili, Povungnituk.

16in (40.5cm) high

$20,000-25,000   **WAD**

'Owl', figure in soapstone, by Joe Talirunili, Povungnituk, signed in Roman.

5in (12.7cm) high

$7,000-10,000   **WAD**

JOHN TALIRUNILI

- Joe Talirunili (1893?-1976) was known for both sculpture (mainly in the fifties) and graphics (through the sixties). He was most prolific during the last 15 years of his life.
- He was a famous story-teller in Povungnituk and his work displays a strong narrative theme, relating to his own life on the land: camp-life, hunting and his 'Migration' works; and Inuit legends and stories passed on through oral tradition and visually through his work on paper and in stone.
- His work is famed for its immediacy, enthusiasm and the emotion it elicits, rather than its technical finesse. He would use any material that came to hand. Most pieces have a hallmark 'Joe' carved into them. The owl is an ever-present motif.
- Talirunili was one of the founders of the Povungnituk printshop and contributed over 70 stonecut prints. His prints were carved straight on to stone, without preliminary sketches, and often incorporate syllabics.

'The Migration', a gray soapstone boat with many arctic hares, a dog and an owl, with antler paddles, by Joe Talirunili, Povungnituk.

The Migration series of drawings, sculptures and prints were inspired by an event when he was young, when his family built a umiak, or sealskin boat, to save themselves when stranded on an ice-floe. This piece was commissioned by Steve Chmilnitzky, technical advisor in 1964 to the Povungnituk settlement in Quebec. When it sold in 2006, this was the highest price ever fetched for Inuit art at auction.

12in (30.5cm) long

$220,000-280,000   **WAD**

'Musk Ox', a soapstone and musk ox horn figure, by George Tataniq (1910-1991), Baker Lake, signed in syllabics.

6in (15cm) wide

$7,000-10,000   **WAD**

A dark soapstone figure smoking a pipe, by George Tataniq (1910-1991), Baker Lake, signed in syllabics.

10in (25.5cm) high

$3,000-4,000   **WAD**

'Figure', soapstone, by John Tiktak (1916-81), Rankin Inlet.

c1967   *8in (20.5cm) high*

$15,000-20,000   **WAD**

A gray soapstone bust of an Inuit mother and child, by John Tiktak, Rankin Inlet, signed in syllabics.

7in (18cm) high

$20,000-30,000   **WAD**

A gray soapstone mother and child, by John Tiktak (1916-81), Rankin Inlet, signed in syllabics.

6in (15cm) high

$15,000-20,000   **WAD**

'Family Group near Igloo', soapstone, by Lucy Tasseor Tutsweetok, (b.1934), Arviat.

8in (20.5cm) high

$10,000-15,000   **WAD**

'Family Group', a soapstone figural group, by Lucy Tasseor Tutsweetok, Arviat.

c1975   *24in (64cm) high*

$15,000-20,000   **WAD**

A gray soapstone Inuit community and igloo, by Lucy Tasseor Tutsweetok, Arviat.

13in (33cm) high

$20,000-30,000   **WAD**

'Mother and Child', soapstone, antler, hair, by Judas Ullulaq (1937-1998), Gjoa Haven.

10in (25cm) high

$12,000-18,000   **WAD**

A dark soapstone mother and child, with inset swiveling eyes, teeth and facial tattoos and holding an antler ulu, by Judas Ullulaq, Gjoa Haven.

17in (43cm) high

$15,000-20,000   **WAD**

A green soapstone Inuit woman weaving a mat, by Simeonie Weetaluktuk (b.1921), Inukjuak.

c1955   *7.5in (18.5cm) high*

$6,000-9,000   **WAD**

'Spirit Animal', soapstone, unidentified.

Aspects of the piece show early hints of John Kavik and Andy Miki, both of the Keewatin 'school'. Although the stone's character, the age of the piece and the red inlay detailing indicate an early Port Harrison work.

c1955   *6.5in (16.5cm) long*

$55,000-65,000   **WAD**

A mid-20thC Inuit soapstone carving, depicting a seal eating a large fish, signed.

12in (30.5cm) high

$300-400   **SK**

A green soapstone hunter with inset ivory eyes and inlaid soap decoration, unidentified.

c1955   *16in (40.5cm) high*

$25,000-30,000   **WAD**

A sealskin handbag, by Kenojuak Ashevak, (b.1927), Cape Dorset.

c1958   *10in (25.5cm) wide*

$10,000-15,000   **WAD**

'Birds from the Sea', skin stencil, Kenojuak Ashevak, Cape Dorset, 15/50.

1960   *21.5in (54.5cm) wide*

$10,000-15,000   **WAD**

'Nine Arctic Birds', skin stencil, by Kiakshuk (1886-1966), Cape Dorset.

1960   *22.5in (57cm) wide*

$5,000-6,000   **WAD**

'Eskimo Family Catching Fish', sealskin stencil, by Kiakshuk, Cape Dorset, 9/50.

1961   *37in (94cm) wide*

$6,000-9,000   **WAD**

'Eskimo Summer Tent', skin stencil, by Niviaksiak (1908-59), Cape Dorset.

1959   *13in (33cm) high*

$6,000-9,000   **WAD**

'Untitled', shroud, felt, embroidery floss, thread, by Jessie Oonark (1906-1985), Baker Lake.

c1970   *69in (175cm) high*

$15,000-20,000   **WAD**

'Blue Geese Feeding', sealskin stencil, by Parr (1893-1969), Cape Dorset.

1961   *30in (75.5cm) high*

$6,000-9,000   **WAD**

'Pot Spirits' sealskin stencil, by Sheouak (1923-61), Cape Dorset.

1960   *18in (45.5cm) wide*

$6,000-9,000   **WAD**

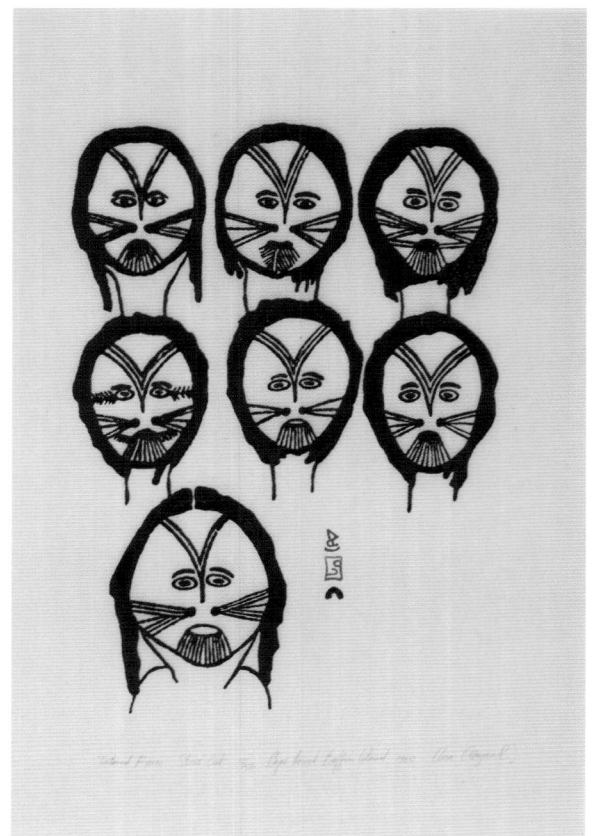

'Tattooed Faces' stonecut, by Jessie Oonark (1906-85), Baker Lake.

1960   *18 x 12in (45.5 x 30.5cm)*

$10,000-15,000   **WAD**

'Running Rabbit', stonecut, by Pudlo Pudlat (1916-92), Cape Dorset, signed in syllabics.

1963   *24in (61cm) high*

$5,000-6,000   **WAD**

'Ready for the Hunt', stonecut, by Joe Talirunili (1893-1976), Povungnituk, signed in syllabics.

1972   *19.5in (49.5cm) wide*

$1,000-1,500   **WAD**

A 20thC framed inuit hide drawing, by George Ahgupukm, depicting various hunting and village scenes, signed lower right corner, minor damage to hide.

image 31in (78.75cm) wide

$10,000-15,000   **SK**

'Untitled' colored pencil drawing, by John Kavik (1897-1993), Rankin Inlet, signed in syllabics.

12in (30.5cm) high

$3,000-4,000   **WAD**

An early 20thC Inuit polychrome carved wood mask, the hollowed oval form pierced at the mouth and eyes, red-brown with black and red details, old tag reads "Indian mask from Ketchikan Alaska".

8.5in (21.5cm) high

$1,500-2,000   **SK**

An early 20thC Inuit carved ivory cribbage board, from Nunivak Island, in the form of a water monster attacking walrus, with relief-carved animal heads along the center, fish on the sides, reverse with engraved kayak and a seal on ice floe, black and red pigment in details.

25in (62.5cm) long

$5,000-9,000   **SK**

A white duffel child's amautik, unidentified, decorated with beadwork in butterfly and striped motifs, trimmed with similar beaded fringes.

42in (106.5cm) high

$5,000-6,000   **WAD**

A Korwar ancestor figure, from the North West Coast of West Papua.

Ancestors are asked via the Korwar for counsel and help in cases of sickness and death and in regard to such undertakings as head-hunting raids and the timing of voyages.

14.5in (36.5cm) high

$900-1,300 **LAM**

A Yangaru figure, wood and natural earth pigments, East Sepik Province, Papua New Guinea.

24.5in (62cm) high

$2,000-2,500 **LAM**

An early Papuan Gulf drum.

35.5in (90cm) high

$500-700 **LAM**

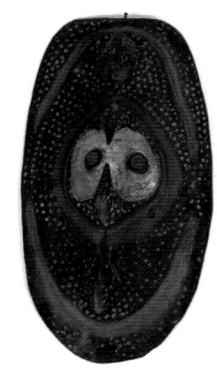

A mask representing the mountain god Garra, from Hunstein, Upper Sepik.

26.75in (68cm) high

$300-400 **LAM**

A large Mina figure, Washkuk area of the East Sepik province, wood decorated with natural earth pigments and classic phallic nose.

75.5in (192cm) high

$400-500 **LAM**

An ancestral figure, from the Washkuk area of the East Sepik province, incised and decorated with trade paints in red, yellow, and blue.

29in (74cm) high

$200-300 **LAM**

A Yam mask, from the Abelam area of the East Sepik province, used in the annual yam fertility festival, woven cane with ochers and trade paint.

24in (61cm) high

$200-300 **LAM**

A Melanesian carved wood Janus-faced club head fragment, Buka Island, with incised detail, blackened areas.

9.25in (23.5in) high

$800-1,000 **SK**

A 19thC Melanesian polychrome carved wood and fiber mask, New Ireland, the hollow, pierced form with highly stylized features, probably had operculum eyes at one time, the elaborate crest of cloth and plant fiber, with highly stylized painting in black, red, and white pigment.

14in (35cm) high

$7,000-10,000 **SK**

A large Melanesian carved wood plate, Vanuatu, the bottom with concentric feet and in the form of a stylized face, cracks.

32in (81cm) high

$1,000-1,500 **SK**

A western Queensland polychrome Aboriginal shield, with striking diamond-based design on the face, the black and white design with traces of yellow.

27in (69cm) high

$800-1,200   **LAM**

An Aboriginal stone axe and an early Australian Aboriginal stone axe, northern Queensland, cane and spinifex handle loosely attached.

longest 17.25in (44cm) long

$300-400   **LAM**

A North Queensland Australian Aboriginal woomera, with patina to the wooden shaft, the top mounted with a notched wooden launch peg attached with a fiber and resin.

35.5in (90cm) long

$500-600   **LAM**

Two Tiwi ceremonial spears, Bathurst Island Northern Australia, handmade with trace of polychrome ocher decoration.

longest 55.5in (141cm) long

$800-1,000   **LAM**

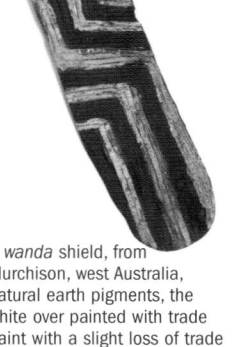

A *wanda* shield, from Murchison, west Australia, natural earth pigments, the white over painted with trade paint with a slight loss of trade paint reveals the ocher still present.

25in (64cm) long

$800-1,200   **LAM**

A Murrawirrie fighting boomerang, Lake Eyre, deep early patination with fluting to both sides.

54in (137cm) long

$3,000-4,000   **LAM**

A 19thC Western Australian hardwood shield.

33.5in (85.5cm) long

$3,000-4,000   **BONA**

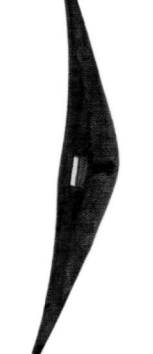

An early South Eastern Australian parrying shield,

34in (86cm) long

$2,000-3,000   **BONA**

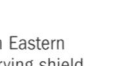

Two stone knives with spinifex resin handles and a large Aboriginal stone axe head.

longest 6.75in (17cm) long

$150-200   **LAM**

An old Ramu river mask, on stand.

21.5in (55cm) high

$2,000-2,500   **LAM**

A pair of late 19thC Louis XV style gilt bronze and rock crystal candelabra, with three branches bearing pear and diamond shaped drops, on openwork triform bases.

27.5in (70cm) high

$5,000-7,000   **FRE**

A rare pair of ormolu mounted glass candlesticks, with facet cut blue glass pedestals probably decorated in the atelier of James Giles.

James Giles (1718-80) was a prominent London ceramic and glass decorator.

c1775-80   12.5in (31cm) high

$20,000-30,000   **WW**

A 19thC pair of Empire gilt and patinated bronze candelabras, with mask motifs, and the stems modeled as two winged draped classical maidens, formerly fitted for electricity.

32.75in (82cm) high

$6,000-9,000   **FRE**

An early 19thC plated candlestick, on a square foot with oval cartouches, fluted stem.

11.5in (29cm) high

$200-300   **KAU**

A pair of patinated and gilt bronze girandoles, with two candle sockets with suspended glass prisms on a bronze base attributed to Fletcher & Day, Birmingham, England.

c1825   18in (46cm) high

$3,000-4,000   **SK**

An exceptionally fine pair of Louis XVI-style ormolu and marble candelabra, by Gervais Maximillian-Eugene-Durand, signed "G. Durand et Fils a Paris".

Gervais Maximillian-Eugene-Durand was born in 1839, the son of Louis Durand who at the time ran an important Parisian workshop. Durand senior worked from a number of locations during the last quarter of the 19thC. His son joined the firm c1890, at which time the name was altered to Durend et Fils. The firm participated in the 1889 Exposition Universelle where they were awarded a silver medal.

c1890   23.75in (59cm) high

$10,000-15,000   **FRE**

A late 19thC pair of Louis XVI-style bisque, porcelain and gilt bronze candelabra, signed "Lagneau", raised on circular bases and toupie feet.

23in (57.5cm) high

$4,000-6,000   **FRE**

A pair of late 19thC Wedgwood Jasperware and lead crystal lusters, with two tiers with faceted pear-shaped pendant drops, and crystal column with brass mountings.

14.75in (37cm) high

$600-800   **BIG**

SAMUEL YELLIN

- Samuel Yellin (1885-1940) was born in Poland and trained as an iron worker and blacksmith. In the early 20th century he left his birth country for the UK before finally settling in the US.
- After further study and teaching in Philadelphia, Yellin opened his own shop in 1909. He moved his business to new, specially designed premises on Philadelphia's Arch Street in 1915 and the company continues to operate from this location today.
- The first quarter of the 20th century saw a rapid increase in new and grand building schemes and Yellin's architectural metalwork work was very much in demand.
- His designs were a feature of many important buildings including the Ford Motor works, the Detroit Institute of Art and Washington National Cathedral. J. P. Morgan, and members of the Guggenheim and Rockefeller families were among his high profile clients.
- He was known for his mastery of metalworking skills but also for his innovative and influential designs.

A pair of late 19thC French Empire style bronze candelabra, with figural stems supporting four scroll branches, and lappet clad reeded ovoid supports.

23.5in (59cm) high

$2,500-3,500   **FRE**

A pair of mid-20thC lead crystal candlestick lusters, each with a shaped sconce, knopped column with pendant faceted drops upon a brass base.

12in (30cm) high

$200-300   **BIG**

A 20thC wrought iron candlestick, by Samuel Yellin, with dish form bobeche, spiral turned standard, stamped "Yellin" on leg.

11in (28cm) high

$10,000-15,000   **FRE**

A 20thC ornamental wrought iron floor lamp, by Samuel Yellin, with adjustable standard, ornate leaf design at the base, and stamped "Samuel Yellin" in leg rim.

82in (208.5cm) high

$15,000-20,000   **FRE**

A pair of Continental wrought iron pricket sticks, with dish tops raised on bobbin turned column stems and open scrollwork triform bases.

65in (162.5cm) high

$2,000-3,000   **FRE**

A pair of polychrome and parcel gilt blackamoor candelabra, modeled holding a cornucopia from which issues eight scrolling branches.

75in (187.5cm) high

$4,000-5,000   **FRE**

A pair of early 20thC carved and polychrome-decorated blackamoor torcheres, modeled as turbanned blackamoors, painted in gilt and enamels and surmounted by 9-branch candelabra.

82.5in (210cm) high

$8,000-12,000   **L&T**

A Guardian Angel miniature lamp, with Nutmeg burner an red glass globe shade, marked "GUARDIAN ANGEL L'ANGE GARDIANI/ C. H. BINKS & CO.", the applied handle covering part of the lettering.

6.5in (16cm) high

$400-500   **WAD**

An Amber Guardian Angel type lamp, with Pet Ratchet burner and red glass globe shade.

6.5in (16.5cm) high

$150-200   **WAD**

A late 19thC pair of Louis XVI-style boulette gilt bronze and alabaster lamps, the oval bases applied with scrolling foliage, with two candle arms, and adjustable tole shades.

27in (67.5cm) high

$1,500-2,000 FRE

A pair of Louis XV style rouge marble and gilt metal mounted urns, with rope twist and husk cast handles and foliate leaf garlands to the front.

20in (51cm) high

$6,000-8,000 L&T

A 20thC wrought iron table lamp, by Samuel Yellin, with twisted standard on a floriform base on three leaf feet.

30in (76cm) high

$4,000-5,000 FRE

A pair of 19thC bronze lamp bases, in a Renaissance manner after Claude Michel Clodion, each formed as an urn supported by a pair of cherubs.

34.5in (80cm) high

$12,000-18,000 L&T

A pair of cast brass Argand lamps, by Thomas Messinger & Sons, Birmingham, England, with manufacturer's plaque, electrified.

c1840 *20in (51cm) high*

$800-1,200 PAIR FRE

A pair of gilt brass electrified argon lamps, Clark & Coit, New York, with cut and etched shades, and lusters, bearing plaque of maker.

c1845 *23in (58.5cm) long*

$2,000-3,000 FRE

A pair of Empire gilt-bronze four branch wall lights, in the form of winged cherub caryatids, with stiff-leaf decorated drip-pans and candle nozzles.

c1820 *20.5in (51cm) high*

$4,000-6,000 FRE

A late 19thC Charles X ormolu and patinated bronze twelve light chandelier, with a frieze cast with patera, flower heads and scrolls, and twelve outscrolling candle arms.

31in (77.5cm) diam

$30,000-50,000 FRE

A pair of brass electroliers, with two graduated tiers of six scrolling branches, supported by a central turned and knopped column.

32in (83cm) diameter

$1,500-2,500 PAIR L&T

An exceptionally large gothic wrought iron lantern and scrolling bracket, by Samuel Yellin, composed of openwork panels, applied leaves, and horned animal heads.

Commissioned by the Central Savings Banks of New York, 1927.

c1927 *63in (160cm) high*

$4,000-6,000 FRE

A large stag's antler chandelier, by Anthony Redmile, London, constructed from intertwined stag's antlers supporting twelve electrified sconces.

52.75in (134cm) diam

$4,000-6,000 L&T

An Edinburgh George III pine and gesso fire surround, with a central tablet of maidens dancing flanked by ribbon tied festoons, and fluted pilasters.

54.75in (139cm) high

$2,000-3,000 **L&T**

An early 19thC Federal pine mantle, with a stepped cornice over a series of reeded pilasters.

69.75in (174cm) wide

$3,000-4,000 **POOK**

An Arthur W. Simpson, Kendal, oak fire surround, with two open plate rack shelves flanked by carved paneled cupboard doors enclosing shelves.

64.25in (163cm) high

$3,000-4,000 **L&T**

An Art Nouveau overpainted cast iron fire surround, cast in the manner of C.F.A. Voysey, with cast marks "Rd. No. 898865" and "No. 152", and a Glasgow style cast iron fender.

55.75in (141.5cm) wide

$1,000-1,500 **L&T**

A steel fireplace set, by Sir Robert Lorimer (1864-1929) and probably executed by Thomas Hadden, comprising an ash shovel and a poker.

stand 18in (46cm) high

$4,000-6,000 **L&T**

A pair of Gustav Stickley andirons, with ring pulls joined by a heavy chain, original patina, replaced back post to one fire dog, and circular Craftsman stamp.

21in (52.5cm) high

$10,000-15,000 **DRA**

A pair of unmarked rectilinear andirons, attributed to Gustav Stickley, some wear and rust to black enamel.

24in (61cm) high

$1,500-2,000 **DRA**

WEATHERVANE

- Instruments used to indicate the direction of the wind have been in use since Roman times. From the Middle Ages, European churches featured 'weather cocks' on their steeples and towers.
- The word 'vane' comes from the old English word 'fane' meaning flag. It is likely that fabric banners were precursors to the weathervanes we know today.
- Weathervanes became increasingly popular in America from the mid-18th century and were particularly widespread in the late 19th century. Animal and patriotic designs were particularly popular and are sought after today.
- Rural workers as well as skilled craftsmen specialized in their production. Well known makers include J.W. Fiske, Harris & Co. and A.L Jewell & Co. Signed examples command a premium.
- The association of weathervanes with folk art and American cultural heritage makes them desirable and valuable. A number of fine examples have sold at auction in recent years for over a million dollars each.

A 19thC large molded copper rooster weather vane, with verdigris surface mounted on copper rod, and black metal stand.

26in (66cm) high

$50,000-80,000   **SK**

A 19thC carved wood and cast iron rooster weathervane, on turned stand, with old breaks.

$3,000-4,000   **FRE**

A cast iron and sheet metal rooster weathervane, mounted on a modern wood stand, with traces of gilt.

$8,000-12,000   **FRE**

A 19thC red painted sheet iron horse weather vane, with reinforced iron straps.

34in (86cm) high

$6,000-8,000   **SK**

A late 19thC small molded and sheet copper eagle weathervane, with iron and sheet copper arrow, and verdigris surface.

arrow 25in (63.5cm) long

$4,000-8,000   **FRE**

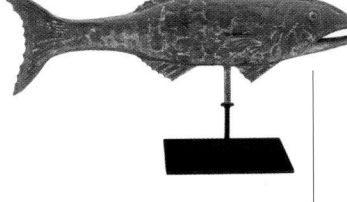

A late 19thC Massachusetts molded and sheet copper fish weathervane, from Waltham, possibly Cushing and White, with traces of gilt.

26in (66cm) long

$15,000-25,000   **FRE**

A molded sheet copper architectural weather vane, by Page Belting Company, Concord, New Hampshire 1893, with copper lettering "P.B. CO.", weathered verdigris finish.

99in (251cm) high

$8,000-12,000   **SK**

A late 19th/early 20thC painted wood, copper and sheet metal whirligig, in the stylized form of a railroad engineer.

46in (117cm) high

$12,000-18,000   **FRE**

A Hackney horse bronze weathervane, Lady Seaton, by Eugene Morahan (American, 1869-1949), signed.

94.75in (240.5cm) high

$35,000-40,000   **SK**

A late 19th/early 20thC molded copper leaping stag weather vane, possibly E.G. Washburne & Co., New York City and Danvers, Massachusetts, including wooden stand, with minor dents.

32in (81.5cm) long

$12,000-18,000   **SK**

Lengths of 19thC cast iron fencing, probably from Philadelphia.

$400-600 FRE

A Samuel Yellin screen from the Equitable Trust Company, New York, with curved dragon heads terminating into spikes, stamped "Samuel Yellin".

This screen represents a partial teller window from the Equitable Trust Company in New York City. It has been modified for architectural use sometime after the bank was dismantled and shows the signs of outdoor usage.

c1926 69in (175.5cm) wide

$6,000-8,000 FRE

A French Art Deco set of wrought-iron gates, with sunburst motifs over diamonds, unmarked, with new black enameled finish.

c1930 97in (246.5cm) high

$8,000-12,000 SDR

Three late 19thC French green painted wirework chairs, including one armchair and two side chairs.

$400-600 FRE

A 19thC painted cast-iron bench, the serpentine scrolled and floral crest above open arch pattern back, and cabriole legs.

62in (157.5cm) long

$1,000-2,000 FRE

A 20thC wrought iron and oak bench, by Samuel Yellin, with straight crest rail flanked with brass mushroom-form stiles, stamped "Samuel Yellin" on crest rail.

54.5in (138.5cm) long

$15,000-20,000 FRE

A pair of possibly 18thC or earlier cast lead urns, each having twin acanthus-scrolled handles, fluted rims, Bacchanalian scenes and egg decorated lower belly.

23.5in (60cm) high

$800-1,000 BIG

One of a pair of cast irons urns of Classical inspiration, the lids with cast leaf decoration topped by a flame finial, the body decorated with a pair of mythical bearded masks united by trailing swags of flowers and a fluted border, the lower section with conforming cast leaf decoration, on a flared socle and squared plinth.

c1780 39in (99cm) high

$30,000-50,000 PAIR RGA

One of a pair of 19thC lead twin-handled garden urns, cast with cartouches held by putti and further decorated with foliate motifs, on a turned base.

17in (43cm) high

$3,000-4,000 PAIR L&T

A late 19thC pair of painted cast iron garden urns on stands, marked "A. Bendroth, NY", with pierced dragon handles, above relief masks.

25in (62.5cm) wide

$8,000-12,000   **POOK**

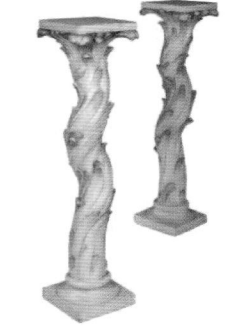

A pair of French Art Deco painted plaster torcheres, Serge Roche (1896-1988), with square top, and painted leafy writhen column.

47.5in (121cm) high

$1,500-2,500   **L&T**

An armillary sphere sundial, Alteration modern, with integral time dial and gnomon in the form of an arrow, on a baluster stone base.

67in (170cm) high

$3,000-4,000   **L&T**

A 19thC Italian statue of Cupid by R. Aurili, the lead figure holding a bow and arrow, on a naturalistic base with flower-filled quiver, with damages.

60.25in (153cm) high

$3,000-4,000   **L&T**

A full bodied painted plaster sculpture of a seated black boy, holding a fishing pole.

c1900   *42in (105cm) high*

$3,000-4,000   **POOK**

A pair of cast bronze lions, in recumbent pose with opposing curled tails, and brown patination.

48in (120cm) long

$3,000-4,000   **L&T**

A late 19thC full bodied copper sculpture of Mercury, retaining old verdigris surface, supported by a large marble plinth.

134in (335cm) high

$40,000-60,000   **POOK**

An 18th/19thC exceptional wrought iron door escutcheon, in the form of a Native American with feathered headdress.

8.25in (21cm) high

$40,000-60,000   **POOK**

An 18th/19thC New England wrought iron thumb latch, the plate in the shape of a man's head.

14in (35.5cm) high

$2,000-3,000   **POOK**

A 19thC painted and decorated Odd Fellows lodge sign, decorated on both sides with a 'hand-in-hand' and inscribed, "Friendly Lodge No. 85 Millerstown".

37in (94cm) high

$5,000-8,000   **FRE**

A late 19thC Continental terracotta bust of a Bedouin, with marks to the base and numbered "1103/21".

24.75in (62cm) high

$700-800   **SWO**

A 20thC white marble figure, depicting a female nude with long curly hair seated on a floral decorated stool and covered with a drape.

48in (120cm) high

$10,000-15,000   **KAU**

A 20thC white marble bust, depicting a laughing woman with a floral dress and frilled hat, on a rectangular socle.

15.25in (38cm) high

$500-600   **KAU**

An Italian white marble figure, modeled as a semi-draped female holding a bouquet of flowers, on a square base.

A 20thC white marble deer, on a naturalistic socle.

38.75in (97cm) high

$800-1,000   **KAU**

A 20thC marble figure of a egret, on a naturalistic base.

27.25in (68cm) high

$300-400   **KAU**

A pair of carved marble lions.

One of a pair of white marble figures, modeled as a rampant lion holding a shield, on a rectangular base, minor damage.

53in (134.5cm) high

$12,000-16,000   **FRE**

16.25in (41cm) high

$1,200-1,800   **SWO**

39in (99cm) high

$10,000-15,000 PAIR   **FRE**

A late 19thC Italian A. Bertozzi marble figure group, with a female nude within a clam shell, signed, Carrara.

22.5in (57cm) high

$6,000-8,000   **FRE**

An 18th/19thC Italian marble bust of a draped classical maiden.

23in (57.5cm) high

$3,000-4,000   **FRE**

A 19thC alabaster architectural model of the Saturn temple in the Roman forum, with three ionic columns, signed.

9.75in (24.5cm) high

$1,500-2,000   **KAU**

Two 19thC marble busts of children, the socles with gilt metal mounts and plinth bases, one gilt metal band later.

15.5in (39cm) high

$1,000-1,500   **L&T**

A 19thC American School marble bust of George Washington, resting on a fluted pedestal with foliate base.

A pair of Napoleon III marble and gilt brass-mounted tazze, each with dished circular tops and stepped plinths with stiff leaf cast moldings.

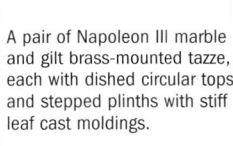

9.25in (23.5cm) high

$3,000-4,000   **L&T**

A late 19thC Italian marble bust of Hermes, together with an alabaster pedestal.

A late 19thC American white marble sculpture of Benjamin Franklin, on a mahogany pedestal.

56in (140cm) high

$15,000-25,000   **POOK**

bust 42in (105cm) high

$2,000-3,000   **FRE**

39.5in (99cm) high

$15,000-25,000   **SK**

A marble bust of James Baird of Elie, by William Birnie Rhind (1853-1933), bears inscription "W.James Baird/ Elie/ executed by/ Birnie Rhind/ 1906".

25in (64cm) high

$6,000-9,000   **L&T**

An Italian 'Socrates' marble bust.

20in (50cm) high

$1,500-3,000   **FRE**

A Florentine Belle Epoque marble figure of a girl by E. Battiglici.

51in (130cm) high

$15,000-20,000   **SHA**

A Phoebe Stabler patinated plaster figure group, depicting a mother with two children, raised on a plinth, signed "Phoebe Stabler".

9.5in (24cm) high

$3,000-4,000   **L&T**

ARCHITECTURAL ANTIQUES

A Canadian painted garden ornament of a bulldog, from Ontario.

c1950   25.25in (64cm) long

$80-120   **RAON**

A novelty bronze bell push, by Bergman, modeled as a head, the nose in the form of a push button which opens the eyes and makes the tongue protrude, stamped marks.

3.5in (9cm) high

$800-1,200   **SWO**

A heavy brass door knocker, by Beardmore of London, cast with a lion's head.

$150-300   **SWO**

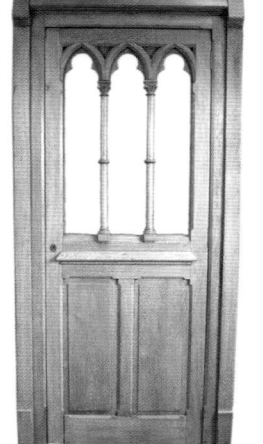

A Victorian oak paneled door and frame, with a twin column pierced opening.

84.5in (211cm) high

$700-800   **SWO**

A pair of arched French windows, with glazing bars and surround.

105in (267cm) high

$3,000-4,000   **SWO**

A late 17thC Italian terracotta relief panel, depicting the Pieta, within a painted and gilt frame.

34.5in (87.5cm) wide

$5,000-6,000   **POOK**

A pair of cast iron stick stands, of elongated form, elaborately cast with three upright supports and shaped rectangular drip trays.

54in (137cm) wide

$5,000-6,000   **L&T**

A 19thC onyx tazza, decorated band of champleve enamel and gilt brass mounts, flanked by cast sphinx handles and raised above a leaf-cast pedestal on square onyx base.

17.25in (44cm) wide

$1,500-3,000   **L&T**

THE BOOK MARKET

Within the book market over the last year prices have remained variable. In the past prices rose steeply for good Natural History and travel books. Several important collections came onto the market, which made excellent prices because of their provenance, but the general market is slower.

The brightest area has to be in Modern First Editions. The point about these is that they have to be in as fine condition as possible, in original cloth and with a dust wrapper. Condition is important for all categories of books.

What has developed over the last few years has been 'The Trophy Book Collector', usually fueled by high City bonuses. In America it saw the rise in popularity of books from the Beat Generation of the Sixties through to Star Wars of the Eighties. In Britain it spanned from J.R.R.Tolkein and C.S. Lewis of the Fifties, and The Beatles through to Harry Potter later on. Such items make 18thC and earlier books look very inexpensive.

A few collectors are looking to the Far East. Many books and manuscripts came from China and the Far East to Europe from travelers and missionaries. While few read Mandarin or Tamil, their books and manuscripts can be very alluring.

The internet has now made it easy for people to see how rare a title is, to view booksellers catalogues, or bid at auction online, which will speed up the business. But the pleasures of holding, assessing and hunting for books in the flesh, cannot be surpassed.

Clive Farahar

THE 'CLASSICS'

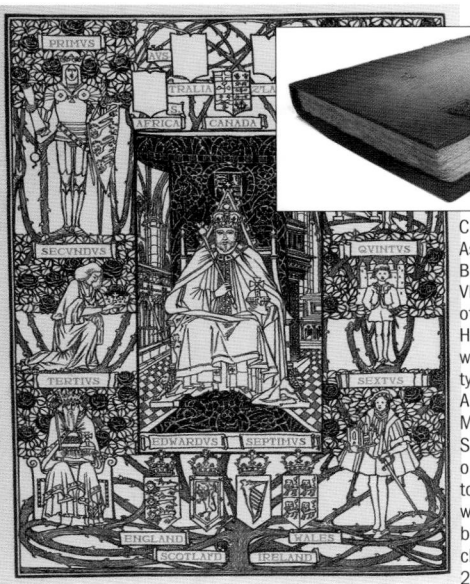

Charles Robert Ashbee "The Prayer Book of King Edward VII", from the Guild of Handicraft, Essex House Press, woodblocks and typeface by C.R. Ashbee, printed by Messrs. Eyre & Spottiswood, London, original oak boards, tooled calf spine, woven leather and beaten pewter clasps, no. 229/400.

1903

$1,500-2,000   L&T

Jane Austen, The Novels, Winchester edition in 12 volumes, half red calf, red cloth boards, spines decorated gilt, Edinburgh, Grant.

1911-12

$7,000-10,000   L&T

Charles Dickens, "Sikes and Nancy, a reading by Charles Dickens with an introduction and a general bibliography of the reading editions by John Harrison Stonehouse", Cosway binding of black crushed morocco, heavily tooled in gilt, with watercolor on ivorine portrait of Dickens by C.B. Currie on the upper cover by Riviere, in its original fleece-lined slipcase, London: Sotheran, no 60 of 250 copies, signed by the publisher.

1921

$7,000-10,000   L&T

Benjamin Franklin, "Pocket Almanac For the Year 1746" by R. Saunders.

$15,000-20,000   POOK

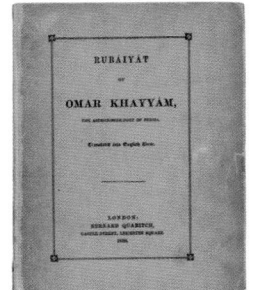

Omar Khayyam, 'Rubaiyat of...', London, Bernard Quaritch, 1 vol., first edition, translator Edward Fitzgerald, original printed tan wrappers, custom cloth fall-down box, with G. Norman imprint on verso of title.

1859

$15,000-20,000   FRE

Rudyard Kipling, "The Jungle Book" and "The Second Jungle Book", first edition, two volumes, full blue morocco gilt by Bayntum Riviere, original cloth bound, marble endpapers, gold over box, some discoloration to backstrips, interior fine.

$3,000-4,000   L&T

William Maitland, "The History of Edinburgh... the Parishes of Canongate, St. Cuthbert and... Leith", Edinburgh: for the author, first edition, folio, folding engraved plan by William Edgar, and 20 engraved plates, modern calf, spine tooled in blind, morocco lettering piece, occasional light marginal dampstaining.

1753

$1,000-1,500   **L&T**

William Cosmo Monkhouse, The Works of Sir Edwin Landseer, R.A. London: Virtue, first edition, 2 volumes, folio, 54 steel engraved plates after Landseer, illustrations, original brown morocco gilt, sides ornately paneled in gilt, spines gilt with dog motifs in compartments.

c1880

$1,500-2,000   **L&T**

William Morris, "The Story of Sigurd the Volsung", 1 vol., 1/160 of 166, Kelmscott Press, London, folio, original vellum, gilt-lettered spine, silk ties, minor wear, with 2 full-page wood-engraved illustrations by Edward Burne Jones.

1898

$6,000-9,000   **FRE**

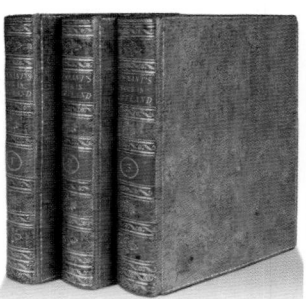

Thomas Pennant, "A Tour in Scotland", MDCCLXIX. London: B. White, fifth edition; "A Tour in Scotland and a Voyage to the Western Hebrides", uniform contemporary tree calf, spines gilt, red morocco lettering pieces, lacking plate 13 in volume 2.

1790

$1,200-1,800   **L&T**

Joseph Ritson, "Memoirs of the Celts or Gauls", London: Payne and Foss, first edition, original cloth spine bound in at end; "Annals of the Caledonians, Picts and Scots"; "and of Strathclyde, Cumberland, Galloway and Murray". Edinburgh: W. and D. Laing, first edition, 2 volumes, together 3 volumes, near uniform brown morocco by Zaehnsdorf with gilt arms on sides, spines gilt, gilt edges.

1827 and 1828

$400-600   **L&T**

John Ross, "A Voyage of Discovery...", London, John Murray, 1 vol, first edition, original gray bands, rebacked with gray cloth, new endpapers, 25 plates, seven maps and charts.

1819

$3,000-3,500   **FRE**

Sir Walter Scott, The Waverley Novels. Edinburgh: A. and C. Black, 48 volumes, engraved titles and frontispieces, illustrations, contemporary half calf, red and green morocco lettering pieces, spines gilt.

1877-78

$3,000-4,000   **L&T**

Sir Walter Scott, "The Border Antiquities of England and Scotland", London: Longman, first edition, 2 volumes, additional engraved titles, 92 engraved plates, contemporary maroon morocco, sides tooled with geometric designs in gilt and blind, spines gilt.

1814

$700-1,000   **L&T**

Thomas H. Shepherd, "Modern Athens", displayed in a Series of Views, or Edinburgh in the Nineteenth Century. London: Jones, additional engraved title and 48 engraved plates, 40 engraved plates, each with two views, lacking the engraved title, 2 works in one volume, contemporary half calf, spine gilt, morocco lettering piece on upper cover.

1829

$500-600   **L&T**

N.P. Willis, "American Scenery", London, Virtue, 1 vol, 2 vols in 1, illustrator W.H. Bartlett, contemporary 3/4 purple morocco or brown pebbled cloth, gilt, gilt-paneled and lettered spine, with engraved map, two hand-colored additional engraved vignette titles, 117 hand-colored steel-engraved plates.

c1840

$3,000-4,000   **FRE**

Louis de Bernieres, "Captain Corelli's Mandolin", first edition, signed by author on title, original white cloth, dustwrapper.

1994

$600-900   **L&T**

Agatha Christie, "Towards Zero", first edition, hardback binding, original cloth covers, published by Collins for The Crime Club.

1944

$500-600   **BIB**

Agatha Christie, "After the Funeral", first edition, hardback binding, with dust wrapper, published by Bodley Head.

1953

$400-500   **BIB**

Agatha Christie, "The Moving Finger", first edition, hardback, with worn dust jacket, published by Dodd, Mead & Co.

1942

$700-1,000   **BIB**

Agatha Christie, "Sparkling Cyanide", hardcover with dustwrapper, first edition, published by Collins for The Crime Club.

This war-time book uses a small typeface, which means less paper was needed.

1945

$400-600   **BIB**

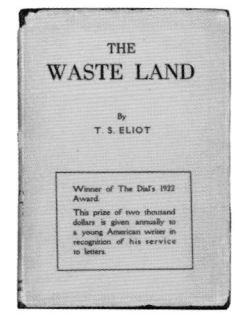

T.S. Eliot, "The Waste Land", New York, Boni & Liveright, 1 vol, first edition in book form, mixed state, no. 64/100, original flexible gilt-lettered black cloth, salmon printed in black, edges untrimmed, mixed state, in flexible cloth with 'mountain' misspelled on p41.

1922

$8,000-10,000   **FRE**

T.S. Eliot, "The Cocktail Party" London: Faber & Faber, first edition, original green cloth, presentation copy, inscribed and signed by T.S. Eliot on front free endpaper recto.

1950

$800-1,200   **FRE**

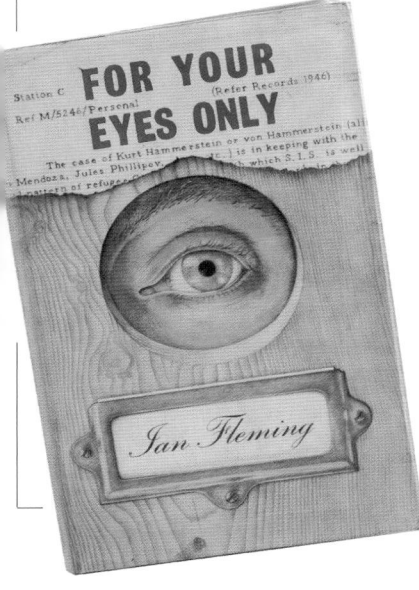

Ian Fleming, "For Your Eyes Only", first edition, published by Jonathan Cape, black cloth boards with gilt title lettering, with dustwrapper.

1960

$1,200-1,800   **BIB**

Ian Fleming, "The Spy Who Loved Me", first edition, publised by Jonathan Cape, hard back, price clipped dust jacket.

1962

$700-1,000   **BIB**

Daphne du Maurier, "The Apple Tree", first edition, hard back with dust jacket, published by Gollancz.

1952

$200-300   **BIB**

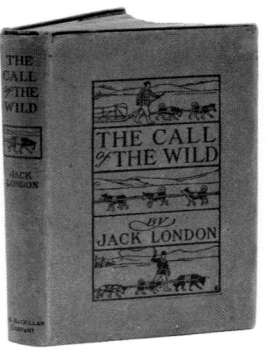

Jack London, "The Call of the Wild", New York, Macmillan, 1 vol, first edition, original gilt-lettered pictorial vertically ribbed green clothfrontis, plus 10 plates, text illustration 2pp adverts, former owner's label on verso of frontis in well-preserved dust jacket.

1903

$5,000-6,000   **FRE**

Ellis Peters, "A Morbid Taste for Bones", facsimile title, "One Corpse Too Many", "Monk's Hood", "Saint Peter's Fair", first editions, original cloth and boards, dust jackets, togther with 17 other titles by the same author.

1977/1979/1981

$2,000-2,500   **BLO**

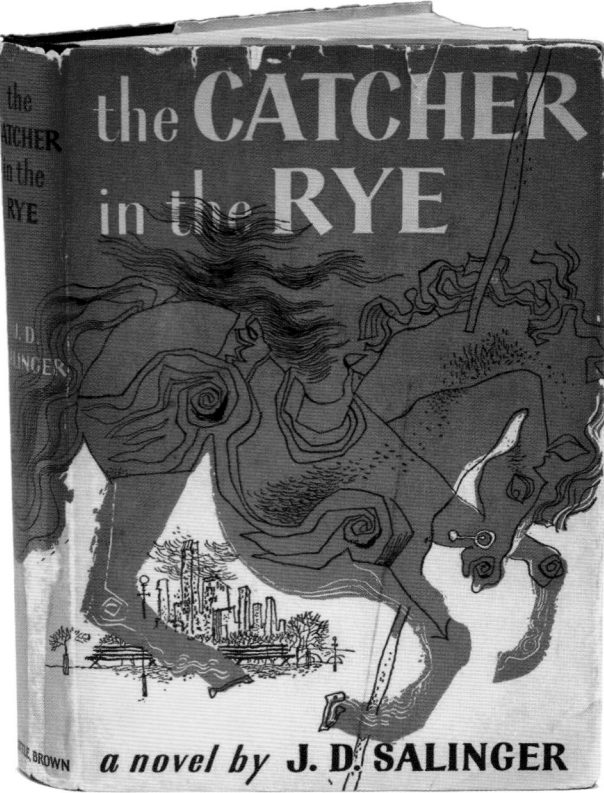

J.D.Salinger, "The Catcher in the Rye", Boston, Little, Brown, 1 vol., first edition, original black cloth, minor wear, first issue with Salinger's photo on back panel.

1951

$3,000-4,000   **FRE**

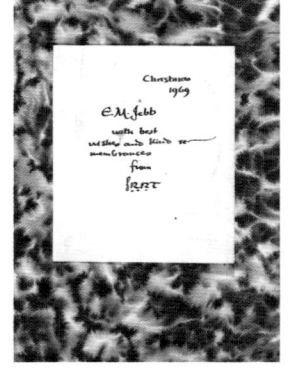

J.R.R. Tolkien, "The Lord of the Rings", 3 volumes in 1 as issued, inscribed by the author on label mounted on front pastedown: "Christmas 1969 E.M. Jebb with best wishes and kind re-memberences from JRRT", original black buckram with gilt, silver and green design on upper cover, slip-case rubbed.

1969

$3,000-4,000   **BLO**

J.R.R. Tolkien, "The Adventures of Tom Bombadil", first edition, illustrations by Paul Baynes, owner's inscription on front free endpaper, light marking to endpapers, original pictorial boards, slightly rubbed at spine ends and corners, dust jacket, torn at corners and spine ends.

1962

$500-600   **BLO**

J.R.R. Tolkien, "The Hobbit or There and Back Again", first edition, frontispiece, one plate and eight illustrations by Tolkien, map endpapers, some very light markings, original decorative cloth, slightly knocked, minor discoloration to spine ends, and top edge, dust jacket badly torn at both ends of spine with loss, large tear from spine into lower wrapper, corners torn and a few other chips from edges.

1937

$10,000-15,000   **BLO**

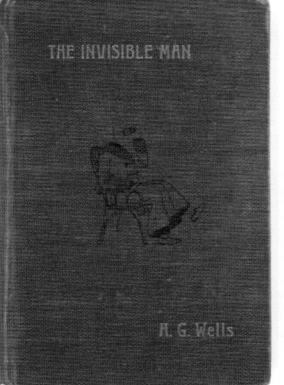

H.G.Wells, "The Invisible Man", London: C. Arthur Pearson Ld., first edition, original red cloth lettered in gilt on spine and on upper cover with design in black, some spotting, some rubbing of extremities, spine soiled.

1897

$600-800   **L&T**

P.G. Wodehouse, "Laughing Gas", London, first edition, original red and black cloth, dustwrapper creased and chipped at edges, interior clean.

1936

$600-900   **L&T**

Richard Adams, "Watership Down", first edition, folding map, original cloth, dust-jacket.

1972

$3,000-4,000   BLO

Hans Christian Andersen, "Fairy Tales", 12 tipped-in color plates, by Kay Nielsen, illustrations, original pictoral moiré cloth, gilt, spine faded and slightly worn at head and foot, corners rubbed.

1911

$800-1,000   BLO

Hans Christian Andersen, "Stories", number 409 of 750 copies, signed by the artist, 28 colored plates by Edmund Dulac including frontispiece, original vellum gilt, slightly stained, hinges neatly strengthened with linen, silk ties, Hodder and Stoughton.

1911

$1,200-1,800   BLO

Samuel Taylor Coleridge, "The Rime of the Ancient Mariner", number 194 of 525 copies signed by the artist, illustrations by Willy Pogàny, modern dark blue morocco with sailing ship of inlaid white and brown morocco blocked in gilt on upper cover, by Asprey, slip-case,

1910

$3,000-4,000   BLO

Edward Gordon Craig, "Book of Penny Toys", number 10 of 550 copies, inscribed by the author "With Greetings from E.C.G. 1900", title with woodcut illustration and partly hand-colored, 20 hand-colored woodcut plates, original buckram-backed hand-colored pictorial boards, uncut, paper label on spine,

1899

$9,000-11,000   BLO

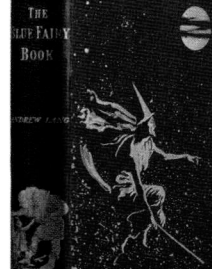

Roald Dahl, "Charlie and the Chocolate Factory", first edition, first issue, illustrations by Joseph Schindelman, original red cloth, dust-jacket, price-clipped, New York.

1964

$3,000-4,000   BLO

C.L. Dodgson, 'Lewis Carroll', "Alice's Adventures in Wonderland", number 85 of 1130 copies, 13 colored plates and other illustrations by Arthur Rackham, original white pictorial buckram gilt, slightly soiled, slip-case strengthened, William Heinemann.

1907

$2,800-3,200   BLO

Nathaniel Hawthorne, "Tanglewood Tales", number 160 of 500 copies signed by the artist, 14 tipped-in color plates by Edmund Dulac, original half vellum, uncut, spine gilt, in morocco-backed cloth crop-back box,

1918

$700-1,000   BLO

Bruno Karberg, "10 Kleine Negerlein", limited to 300 copies, signed by the artist, woodcut title-page, 10 full-page illustrations colored by hand, possibly through stencils, 10 pages of text, and colophon, original cloth-backed boards, label with woodcut title on upper cover, Hamburg, Hans Gotz.

1924

$1,200-1,800   BLO

Andrew Lang, "The Blue Fairy Book", first edition, illustrations by H. J. Ford and G.P. Jacomb Hood, original picorial cloth, gilt, London & New York.

1889

$1,500-2,000   BLO

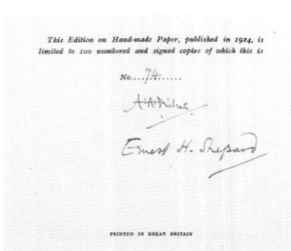

A.A.Milne, "When We Were Very Young", 1st vol., London, Methuen, first edition, large paper copy, illustrated by E.H. Shepard, signed by Milne and Shepard, original burgundy cloth-backed gray bands, paper label, full-page and text illustrations, in custom half blue morocco and cloth slipcase, blue cloth chemise.

1924

$15,000-20,000　　　　　　　**FRE**

A.A. Milne, "When We Were Very Young", second edition, signed on half-title by A.A. Milne, Ernest H. Shepard and Christopher Robin Milne as Billy Moon, illustrations by Ernest H. Shepard, original pictorial cloth, gilt.

December 1924

$8,000-10,000　　　　　　　**BLO**

Beatrix Potter, "The Tale of Johnny Town-Mouse", first edition, first issue with "N" missing from "London" in imprint, color plates by the author, original gray boards, upper cover with pictorial onlay, London & New York.

1918

$1,500-2,000　　　　　　　**BLO**

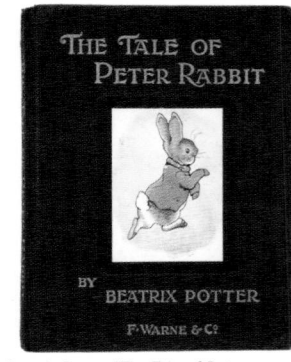

Beatrix Potter, "The Tale of Peter Rabbit", first published edition, fourth printing, with "shed big tears" on p.51, color plates, inscription on half-title dated 1907, original dark gray boards with pictorial inlay, London & New York.

April 1903

$1,200-1,800　　　　　　　**BLO**

Beatrix Potter, "The Tale of Peter Rabbit", first edition, first printing, one of 250 copies, color frontispiece, rest of the plates line drawings, original printed drab boards, ownership inscription of E.D. Blomfield on upper cover, rebacked, privately printed for the author.

December 1901

$20,000-30,000　　　　　　　**BLO**

Arthur Ransome, "Winter Holiday", first edition, frontispiece and illustrations, map endpapers, original cloth, with dust-jacket, price-clipped.

1933

$1,800-2,200　　　　　　　**BLO**

Annie R. Rentoul, "Fairyland of Ida Rentoul Outhwaite", color plates, text-illustrations, original decorative cloth, A.& C. Black.

1931

$1,400-1,600　　　　　　　**BLO**

Dr. Seuss, "How the Grinch Stole Christmas!", first edition, original pictorial paper boards, and dust jacket, Random House, New York.

1957

$3,000-4,000　　　　　　　**BRB**

Louis Wain, "Trip to Catland", 18 full-page color of two-tone illustrations, original cloth-backed pictorial boards, spine defective with hinges pulling,

1915

$500-700　　　　　　　**BLO**

E.B. White, "Charlotte's Web", first edition, original beige cloth and dust jacket, published by Harper & Brothers, New York.

1952

$2,500-3,500　　　　　　　**BRB**

E.B. White, "Stuart Little", first edition, original pictorial beige cloth and dust jacket, published by Harper & Brothers, New York and London.

1945

$1,200-1,800　　　　　　　**BRB**

A William Camden and Robert Morden Britannia folio, portrait frontispiece (loose), eight plates of coins/medals, fifty maps by Robert Morden, all with bright contemporary coloring, later half calf gilt, worn, hinges splitting, map of the West Riding of Yorkshire missing left half.

$4,000-6,000 **L&T**

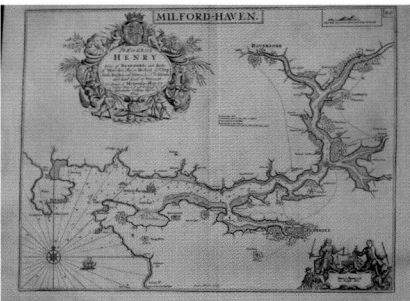

Thirteen Captain Greenville Collins uncolored and hand colored engraved sea charts from Greenville Collins Great Britain's Coasting Pilot, comprising Kingsale Harbour, Approaches to Leith, Dundee, Aberdeen and Montrose, North Sea, Firth of Murray, The Downs, Milford Haven, Yarmouth, Fowey, Scilly Isles and Lands End, Staples, Holy Island and Berwick, Edinburgh, Firth, Rye.

22.75in (57cm) wide

$1,200-1,800 **SWO**

A Hendrick Donker hand colored engraved sea chart, "English Channel".

24.5in (61cm) high

$500-700 **SWO**

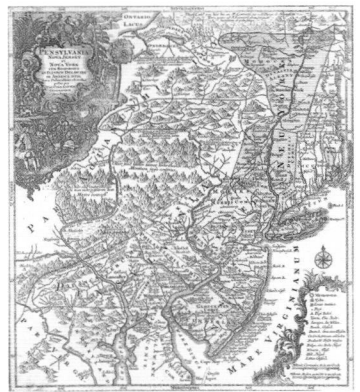

A Sir Robert Dudley engraved sea chart, "Northumbrian Coast".

19in (47.5cm) high

$500-700 **SWO**

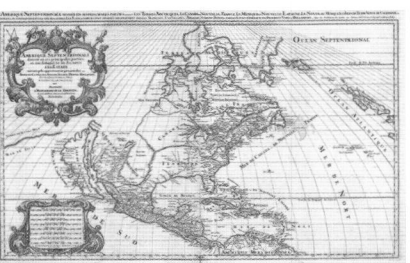

A Charles Hubert Alexis Jaillot engraved map with outline color, "Amerique Septentrionale Divisee en ses Principales Parties", Amsterdam, Pierre Mortier.

1695-1719 *34.75in (88cm) wide*

$1,700-2,000 **FRE**

Two Van Keulen hand colored sea charts, "Southern North Sea" and "Humber and Wash".

24.25in (60.5cm) high

$300-400 **SWO**

A Tobias Conrad Lotter hand-colored engraved map, "Pennsylvania, Nova Jersey et Nova York cum Regionibus ad Fluvium Delaware in America Sitis", Augsburg.

1748-1774 *19.5in (49cm) wide*

$1,200-1,500 **FRE**

A 16thC atlas, by Gerard Mercator, et al., "Tabulae Geographicae, etc", "Duisburg, etc", c1580, 1585, 1589, folio, old wrappers, defective, lacking back wrapper, 75 engraved maps, composite atlas with ten maps by Abraham Ortelius, and 65 maps of France, The Netherlands, Germany, Italy and Greece by Gerard Mercator.

1585, 1589

$2,000-3,000 **FRE**

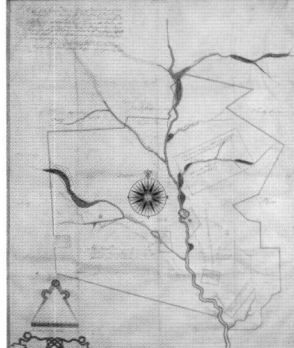

An Ebenezar Miller ink and watercolor hand drawn map, "Map of the Hanour: Thomas Penn & Richard Penn Land at Prince Morris River...", begun in 1748 and completed in 1749, embellished with central yellow, red, and green sun directionals and compass.

25in (62.5cm) high

$2,500-3,000 **POOK**

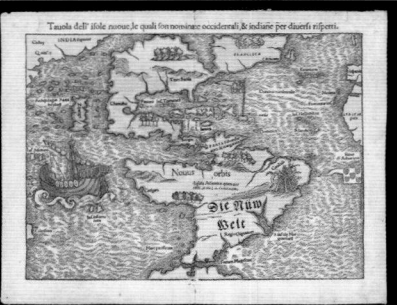

A Sebastian Munster hand-colored woodcut map,
Nova Insulae, "Tavola dell'isole nuove", Basel or
Cologne, Schwartz & Ehrenberg plate 18.

*First published in Munster's edition of Ptolemy's
"Geographia" (Basel, 1540). This is the first map clearly
depicting the New World as a distinct insular landmass.*

1558-75   12.5in (34cm) wide

$5,000-7,000   **FRE**

A John Senex hand-colored engraved map, "North
America Corrected from the Observations
Communicated to The Royal Society at London and
The Royal Academy at Paris", London.

1710   26.25in (66.5cm) wide

$2,500-3,000   **FRE**

A hand colored John Speed map of Europe and the
chief cities.

1626

$1,500-2,000   **L&T**

A Peter Schenk hand-colored engraved celestial map, "Plainsphaerum Coeleste", Amsterdam, depicting the
celestial hemispheres, with smaller hemispheres giving the Tychonica, Ptolemica and Copericana Models,
tides, eclipses & seasons, framed.

c1705   22.25in (56.5cm) wide

$2,500-3,500   **FRE**

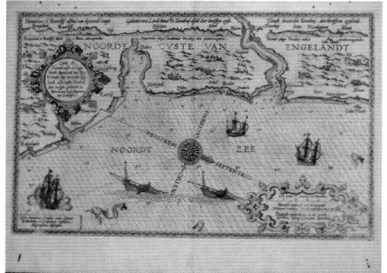

A Lucas Janz Waghenaer engraved chart, "North
East Coast of England", from "Speculum Nauticum".

20.5in (51.5cm) wide

$1,000-1,500   **SWO**

A Frederick de Wit hand-colored
engraved map, "Novissima et
Accuratissima totius Americae
Descripto", Amsterdam, depicting
California as an island, the Great Lakes
as separate bodies of water, ships on the
Atlantic and Pacific, wild animals on the
New Continent, cartouches of Indians &
angels, framed.

1666   22.75in (57.5cm) wide

$2,000-3,000   **FRE**

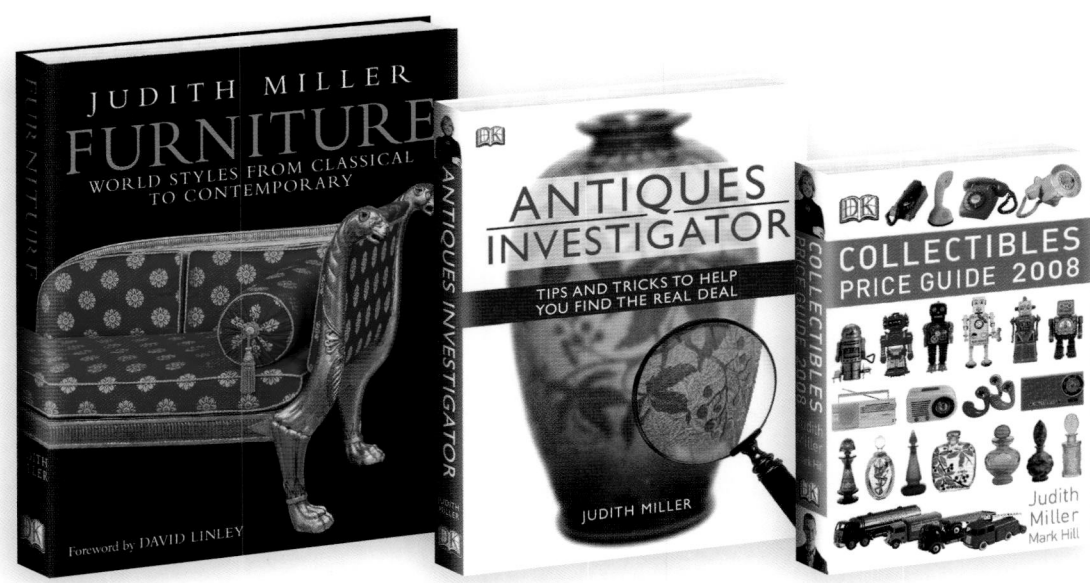

445

A watercolor and ink on paper fraktur, by the Taufzeigen Artist of Montgomery County, Pennsylvania, with a geometric red, blue, and mauve star surmounting a circular cartouche with script flanked by columns with urns and birds, in period frame, dated.

1809   *16.25in (40.5cm) wide*

$2,000-3,000   **POOK**

A hand-drawn watercolor, ink and printed haussegen, by H.W. Villee of Lancaster County, Pennsylvania for Catharina Miller, with central printed script flanked by vibrant hand-drawn tulip trees and spiral columns, flanked by stylized trees arising from pots, dated.

1830   *16in (40cm) high*

$3,000-4,000   **POOK**

A watercolor and ink on paper fraktur, with script surmounted by an eagle with shield and flanked by trailing vines and flowers, dated.

1815   *13in (32.5cm) wide*

$3,000-4,000   **POOK**

An ink and watercolor on paper fraktur, from southeastern Pennsylvania, with central heart surrounded by birds and flowers, dated.

1788   *15in (37.5cm) wide*

$2,000-3,000   **POOK**

A watercolor and ink on paper fraktur, for Maria Kepler, with a banner over lovebirds flanking a crown, above script surrounded by an elaborate border with birds, stars, tulips, and vines with overall pinprick outlined border, in period frame, dated.

1820   *12.5in (31cm) high*

$9,000-11,000   **POOK**

An ink and watercolor bookplate, for Jacob Stauffer of southeastern Pennsylvania, with elaborately stylized letters, dated.

1800   *6.25in (15.5cm) high*

$1,000-1,500   **POOK**

An ink and watercolor bookplate, for David Hartman of southeastern Pennsylvania, with script within a scalloped and floral border, dated.

1816   *6.25in (15.5cm) high*

$1,500-2,000   **POOK**

An ink and watercolor bookplate, for Anna Stauffer of southeastern Pennsylvania, with script within a scalloped and floral border, dated.

1819   *6.25in (15.5cm) high*

$700-1,000   **POOK**

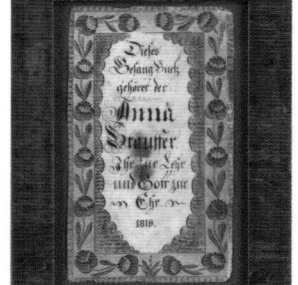

An ink and watercolor on paper vorschrift, from southeastern Pennsylvania, with stylized letters and tulip vine decoration, dated.

1802   *15.75in (39cm) wide*

$2,000-3,000   **POOK**

An ink and watercolor on paper vorschrift, from southeastern Pennsylvania, with script within a tulip border, dated.

1809   *7.75in (19cm) wide*

$700-1,000   **POOK**

An ink and watercolor on paper vorschrift, from southeastern Pennsylvania, with elaborate red and yellow lettering, tulips, and trailing vines, dated.

1829   *12in (30cm) wide*

$700-1,000   **POOK**

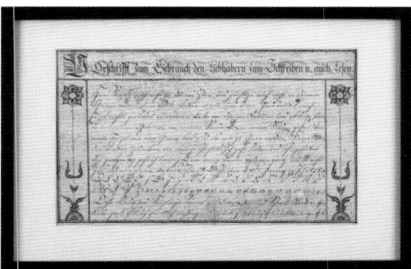

An ink and watercolor vorshrift, by Abraham Dirdorff, with verse flanked by tall flower within red border, dated.

1784   *12.25in (30.5cm) wide*

$1,200-1,800   **POOK**

A Johannes Ernst Spangenberg watercolor fraktur for Andreas Schmidt dated, with central script surrounded by figures, flowers, buildings etc.

Johannes Ernst Spangenberg was active in Northampton County, PA, between 1774-1812.

1774   *16in (41cm) wide*

$2,500-3,000   **POOK**

An 18thC York County, Pennsylvania, watercolor and ink fraktur, by Daniel Peterman, dated and signed, with script, birds and floral vines.

1775   *16in (40.5cm) wide*

$1,500-2,000   **POOK**

A fraktur in ink and watercolor by Daniel Otto, the "Flat Tulip Artist", for Jacob Stover, born 1801, with typical central heart surrounded by tulip vines.

13in (33cm) wide

$2,500-3,000   **POOK**

A watercolor and ink on paper birth record for Anna B. Cochran, born July 6, 1804, depicting the birth inscription flanked by two fanciful birds perched on fruiting branches.

6.25in (15.75cm) wide

$5,000-7,000   **SK**

A fraktur in ink and watercolor on paper by Joseph Lochbaum, the "Nine Hearts Artist", for Samuel Lehman with typical heart format.

Joseph Lochbaum was active in southeastern Pennsylvania between 1800-06.

15.5in (39.4cm) wide

$2,500-3,500   **POOK**

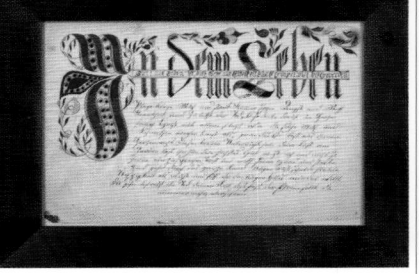

A watercolor on paper fraktur drawing, Middletown, Pennsylvania, inscribed "Ahinoam Smedley 1805" with urn with tulip and floral tree with perched bird.

10in (25.5cm) high

$4,000-5,000   **POOK**

An early 19thC Schwenkfelder ink and watercolor vorschrift, by Maria Heebner (1807-1868), Montgomery County, Pennsylvania.

13in (33cm) wide

$600-900   **POOK**

A Daniel Peterman, York County, Pennsylvania watercolor and ink fratur, with central script surrounded by typical birds, flowers, and two large female figures, signed lower right "Made by Daniel Peterman", dated.

1823   *14in (35.5cm) wide*

$4,000-6,000   **POOK**

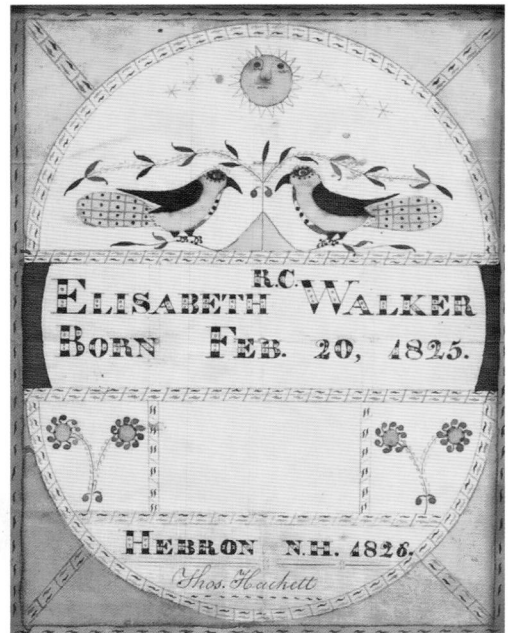

A 19thC American School birth record for Elisabeth Walker, born Feb. 20, 1825, watercolor and ink on paper, depicting the birth inscription flanked by two fanciful birds, the sun, and flower motifs, signed "Hebron N. H. 1826 Thos. Hackett".

7in (17.75cm) wide

$7,000-10,000   **SK**

A house blessing for Peter and Susanna Umbehauer, in watercolor and ink on paper, attributed to Heinrich Engelhard (active 1820-1836).

c1830   *12.75in (33cm) wide*

$2,000-3,000   **FRE**

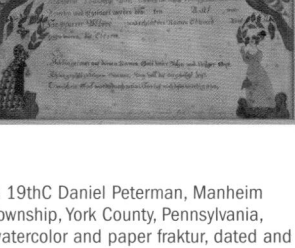

A 19thC Daniel Peterman, Manheim Township, York County, Pennsylvania, watercolor and paper fraktur, dated and signed, with script, tulips, parrots and two female figures.

1834   *15.75in (40cm) wide*

$3,000-4,000   **POOK**

A Jonas Kriebel, Montgomery County, Pennsylvania, vibrant Schwenkfelder ink and watercolor on paper fraktur vorschrift, with bold fanciful lettering, signed lower right "Jonas K. Kriebel", dated.

1842   *17in (43cm) wide*

$1,200-1,800   **POOK**

A "Heart and Hand Artist" family record for the Batchelder family, watercolor and ink on paper, the last entry date by the artist's hand is Feb 27, 1842.

The artist was active in Maine, Vermont, and New Hampshire from 1830-1856.

c1840   *10.75in (27.5cm) wide*

$7,000-10,000   **SK**

A Heinrich Engelhard, southeastern Pennsylvania, active 1829-1836, watercolor and ink on paper haus-segen, done for Jonathan Berbe, with typical vibrant format with elaborate colorful lettering over script and basket.

1831   *9.75in (24.75cm) wide*

$6,000-9,000   **POOK**

A "Heart and Hand Artist" family record, for the Davis family, watercolor and ink on paper commemorating the births, marriages, and deaths of Stephen Davis and Sally J. (Dyer) Davis and their thirteen children, inscribed "Present date Dec. 28, 1856".

14in (35.5cm) wide

$18,000-20,000   **SK**

A southeastern Pennsylvania watercolor fraktur for George Schrader, with bird and flowers over script, retaining a 19thC frame with its original red and yellow stripe decoration, dated.

1846   *frame 7.35in (18.5cm) wide*

$10,000-15,000   **POOK**

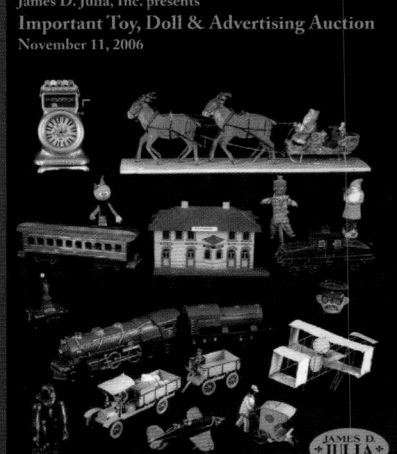

449

GOLF

GOLF

- Many items relating to golf are highly collectible, but early equipment, such as golf clubs and balls, is especially sought-after.
- The earliest record of professionally made golf clubs dates back to 1502, when James IV of Scotland commissioned a bow maker to produce a specially made set of clubs. Although it would be almost impossible to find equipment dating from this period, Scottish-made clubs that predate the introduction of the steel shaft in the 1920s are popular.
- Mid-19th century long nose examples can be worth from around $2,000 to $90,000. Many later clubs, dating from the 1930s onwards, can still be picked up for relatively low sums, but may have the potential to rise in value if rare.
- The earliest golf-balls, known as 'featheries', were introduced in the early 17th century. A featherie by an unidentified maker can be valuable, but an example by a named maker, such as Andrew Dickson or Henry Mills, can easily fetch over $18,000.
- Featheries were replaced in the mid-19th century by gutta percha balls, invented by Rev Adam Paterson of St. Andrews. Genuine gutta percha balls by notable makers, such as Allan Robertson or Archie Simpson, are sought after.
- Early twentieth century golf books or rare later publications are also sought-after, as are ceramics by notable makers.

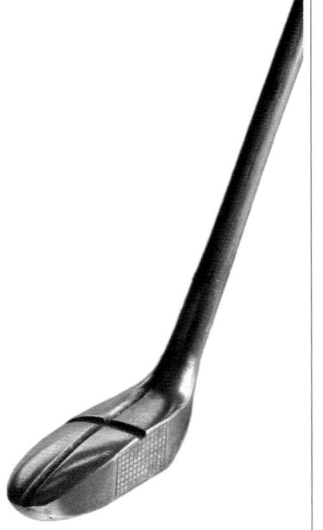

A George Bennie of Bute 'Bennie No. 2' aluminum-headed putter, hickory-shafted, together with an original advertising poster.

$600-700   L&T

A W. Clark wooden head center shaft putter, with brass face plate, and hickory shaft.

$500-600   L&T

A Willie Dunn Jr. Pyralin head putter, with brass face plate.

3.25in (8.5cm) long

$1,200-1,400   MSA

A Elephant Brand 'Phosphor Bronze' patent putter, with smooth alloy head, and hickory shaft.

$400-600   L&T

An R. Forgan longnose playclub, the fruitwood head stamped with maker's name and Prince of Wales feathers, horn insert, lead counterweight, hickory shaft, and wrapped leather grip.

$2,000-3,000   L&T

A hickory shaft, by Hendry & Bishop Ltd, Edinburgh The Giant 'Cardinal' Special niblick.

$700-1,000   L&T

A rare Scottish 'The Perwhit' iron putter, by Hendry & Bishop, with concave head, patent No. 247116.

4.25in (10.5cm) long

$900-1,100   MSA

A Kroydon Clubs, center-shafted pendulum putter, hatched face, hickory shaft.

$500-600   L&T

A long nose spoon, by McEwan of Musselburgh, the shaft stained near the grip "D MCGREGOR".

c1875   head 6.25in (16cm) long

$3,000-3,500   MSA

A McEwan longnose play club, leather insert to face, horn insert to sole and lead counterweight, with hickory shaft, and wrapped leather grip.

$1,200-1,800   L&T

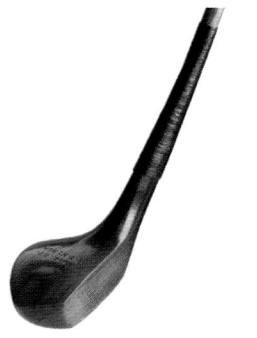

An unusual horn headed spliced driver, hickory-shafted, and stamped "Made by A. T. Mizra".

c1895-1900

$600-700   **L&T**

A T. Morris longnose putter, the scared head with horn insert to the sole, lead counterweight, hickory shaft, and wrapped leather grip.

$2,000-3,000   **L&T**

A Tom Morris of St. Andrews putter, with fruitwood head and silver collar to the shaft, and hickory shaft.

c1865-70

$3,000-4,000   **L&T**

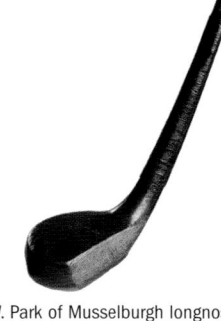

A W. Park of Musselburgh longnose putter, hickory shaft.

c1885

$1,000-1,500   **L&T**

A CLOSER LOOK AT A GOLF CLUB

This club comes with a letter from the vendor describing his acquisition of the club for his collection in 1985.

The provenance is extremely strong. Harry B. Wood received this club directly from Tom Morris, the Scottish champion and club-maker, and eventually gave it to the North Manchester Golf Club. There is a picture of the club in Wood's book Golfing Curios and The Like.

Wood had special cards printed for attachment to the shafts and the Philp putter has a card that details its previous ownership by Old Tom and Young Tom Morris.

It is likely that the club was used by Tom Morris in several Opens. He kept the club for many years suggesting its importance to him.

Hugh Philp (1782-1856) is considered the premier long nose clubmaker. In 1819 he was appointed the clubmaker to the Society of St. Andrews (later named Royal and Ancient).

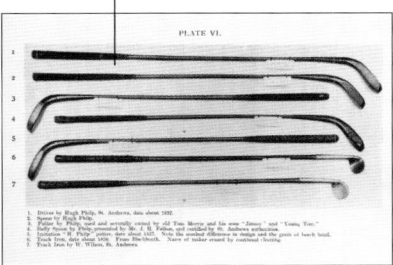

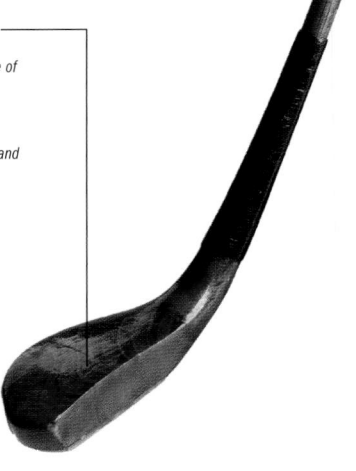

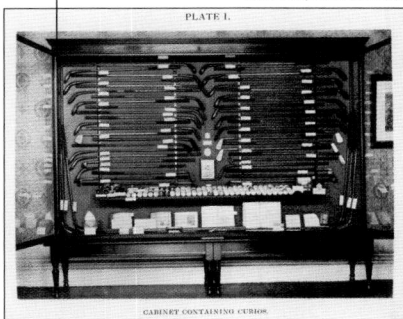

An important, rare and historical H. Philp longnose putter, owned by Tom Morris, from the Harry B. Wood Collection, with paper label and ties.

$120,000-180,000   **L&T**

A Schenectady putter, patent March 24, 1903, the center shafted alloy head stamped "Harry C. Lee & Co., NY.", with hickory shaft.

$400-500   **L&T**

A Spalding Kro-Flite, Robert T. Jones Calamity Jane putter, hickory shaft.

$400-500   **L&T**

A Spalding Kro-Flite, J. Hepburn National Links patent pitcher, with waterfall grooved face, and hickory shaft.

$500-700   **L&T**

A Standard Mills Co. 'McP' model long nose putter, hickory shaft.

$700-1,000   **L&T**

A Wright & Ditson deep groove mashie niblick, hickory shaft, with waterfall face pattern, Bee-line patented 20.4.20.

c1920

$600-900   **L&T**

A Sunday stick, the scared head formed as a wood, with ebony insert, greenheart shaft, silver plaque inscribed "E.R.A. Hunter", hallmarked London.

1898

$200-300   **L&T**

A Sunday stick, the socket head formed as a wood, stamped "A. James, Special", with ivorine insert to face and horn insert to sole, lead counterweight, hickory shaft.

$300-400   **L&T**

An early rut iron, the blacksmith manufactured head with long crimped hosel, replacement hickory shaft and wrapped leather grip, slight loss adjacent to securing hole at top of hosel.

$1,000-1,500   **L&T**

An unnamed feather golf ball, the stitching visible.

$2,000-3,000   **FRE**

An unused smooth gutta ball.

c1860

$400-600   **L&T**

A 'Heavy Colonel' green dot bramble golf ball, with large dimples.

c1910

$700-1,000   **L&T**

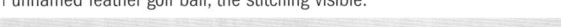

A mesh pattern gutty ball, by A J. & D. Clark, Musselburgh, in unused condition.

A Halley the Ocobo 27 mesh pattern gutty ball.

$1,000-1,200   **FRE**   **$1,000-1,200**   **FRE**

Atherton, Edward, "Songs of the Links", with engraved illustrations, privately printed by the Knot Club, St. John N.B., and signed in pencil by the artist.

c1900

$2,000-3,000　　　　　　　**L&T**

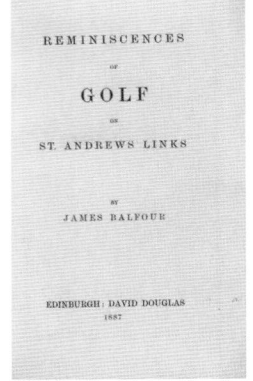

Balfour, James, "Reminiscences of Golf on St. Andrews Links", first edition, rebound in vellum cover, with decorative end papers, Edinburgh, David Douglas.

c1887

$1,500-2,000　　　　　　　**L&T**

"Golfer's Guide for the United Kingdom", edited by W. Dalrymple, first edition, Edinburgh, White & Co., with photographs, diagrams, maps, and advertisements.

1895

$1,000-1,500　　　　　　　**L&T**

Duncan, David S, "The Golfing Annual 1898-1899 Vol XII", and "The Golfing Annual 1900-1901 Vol XIV", London, Horace Cox, with cloth cover, gilt lettering and decoration.

$1,000-1,500　　　　　　　**L&T**

After John Hassall, 'Seven Ages of Golf', published by Bemrose, comprising eight humorous golfing depictions, chromolithographic prints, each inscribed "J. Hassall".

14.75in (37.5cm) high

$1,500-2,000　　　　　　　**L&T**

Hopkinson, Cecil "Collecting Golf Books 1743-1938", first edition in cloth cover, with gilt lettering to spine, London, Constable & Co.

c1938

$1,000-1,500　　　　　　　**L&T**

Hughes, H.E., "Chronicles of Black Heath Golfers", first edition, London, Chapman & Hall, portrait frontispiece of Edmund Hegan Kennard, illustrated, with cloth cover, gilt lettering and stamp to cover, and George Nicol book plate.

1897

$1,500-2,000　　　　　　　**L&T**

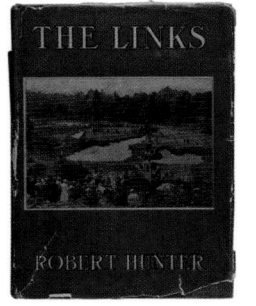

Hunter, Robert, "The Links", first edition, New York, Charles Scribner's Sons, with black and white plates and diagrams, decorative cloth cover and end-papers, and original dust jacket.

c1926

$1,000-1,500　　　　　　　**L&T**

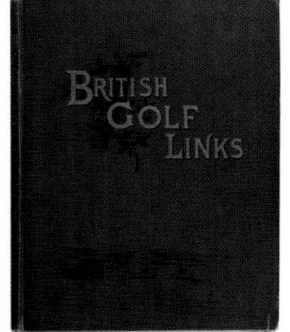

Hutchinson, Horace, "British Golf Links", first edition, London, Virtue & Co., frontispiece, illustrated throughout, gilt decorative cloth boards.

c1897

$1,000-1,500　　　　　　　**L&T**

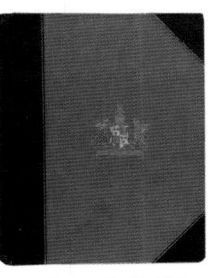

Hutchinson, Horace G., "Golf, The Badminton Library", first edition, London, Longmans, Green, with contributions by Lord Wellwood, Sir Walter G. Simpson, Bart., A.J. Balfour and others, illustrated by Thomas Hodge and Harry Furniss, gilt lettered spine, large paper edition.

c1890

$2,000-3,000　　　　　　　**L&T**

J.A.C.K., "Golf in the Year 2000 or What We Are Coming To", first edition, London, T. Fisher Unwin.

c1892

$2,000-3,000　　　　　　　**L&T**

Kerr, John, "The Golf Book of East Lothian", first edition, Edinburgh, T. & A. Constable, number 127 of 250 copies, illustrated, with gilt decorated cover and spine.

c1896

$3,000-4,000   L&T

MacLennan, R.J., "Golf at Gleneagles", first edition, Glasgow, McCorquodale & Co., with photographs, drawings and advertisements, in original publisher's packaging.

c1921

$1,000-1,500   L&T

McPherson, J. Gordon, "Golf & Golfers, Past & Present", first edition, Edinburgh, William Blackwood & Sons, with portrait frontispiece.

c1891

$1,000-1,500   L&T

Pearson, Issette, Pascoe A. Bennet and others, "Our Lady of the Green, A book of Ladies' Golf", first edition, London, Lawrence & Bullen Ltd.

c1899

$1,000-1,500   L&T

Tulloch, W.W., "The Life of Tom Morris with glimpses of St. Andrews and its golfing celebrities", first edition, London, T. Werner Laurie, illustrated.

c1908

$1,000-1,500   L&T

Wethered, H.N., and Simpson, T., "The Architectural Side of Golf", first trade edition, London, Longmans, Green & Co., with preface by J.C. Squire, illustrations by the author, engraved plate and course plans.

c1929

$2,000-3,000   L&T

Wood, Harry B., "Golfing Curios and 'The Like'", London, Sherratt & Hughes, with appendix comprising a 'Biography of Golf'.

c1910

$2,000-3,000   L&T

The Golfer's Handbook 1904, Edinburgh, The Golf Agency, illustrated with photographs and advertisements, red cloth cover.

c1904

$1,500-2,000   L&T

Unknown, "The Foursome, Rhymes", hand-written, with decorative paper wrappers, undated.

$1,200-1,500   L&T

"History of the Warrender Golf Club", with brown paper wrappers.

$1,500-2,000   L&T

A Doulton Lambeth stoneware jug, decorated in relief with figures of golfers within stylized Art Nouveau floral decoration.

5.75in (14.5cm) high

$1,500-2,000   L&T

An early 20thC Hohr-Grenzhausen pottery stein, decorated with a scene of a golfer, with pewter mount and hinged lid, impressed numerals to the underside.

c1900   8.5in (22cm) high

$1,000-1,500   L&T

A Lenox pottery tankard, decorated in monochrome green, with a scene of golfers, and printed marks to the underside.

5.25in (13.5cm) high

$2,000-3,000   L&T

A Royal Doulton 'Morrisian Ware' baluster vase, decorated with golfing figures on a gilt-decorated crimson and yellow ground.

5.75in (14.5cm) high

$1,500-2,000   L&T

An early 20thC Lenox pottery tankard, decorated in monochrome green, with a scene of golfers, gilt rim, and printed marks to the underside.

Ceramic designer Walter Scott Lenox (1859-1920) established his own business in New Jersey, US, in 1889. The firm is still in operation today.

5.75in (14.5cm) high

$2,000-3,000   L&T

A Royal Bonn transfer-printed pottery tankard, with golfers putting on a seaside course.

6.5in (16.5cm) high

$2,000-3,000   L&T

A Weller 'Dickensware' pottery mug, incised and polychrome-decorated with a golfer, with impressed mark and numbered 592/14 to the underside.

5.5in (14cm) high

$1,500-2,000   L&T

A sterling silver spirit flask, by William B. Kerr & Co., engraved with a scene of three golfers and inscribed "One Up and Two To Go".

8in (20cm) high

$400-600   L&T

A Wood & Wood biscuit barrel, decorated with a scene of golfers with mountains behind, with plated swing handle and circular lid.

6in (15.5cm) high

$1,000-1,500   L&T

An ivory and embossed gilt metal golf club-shaped walking stick or umbrella handle, with barley twist carving, and engraved name "J GARVEN".

9.5in (24cm) high

$1,700-2,000   MSA

A late Victorian silver-plated golf trophy, engraved with inscriptions to the obverse and reverse, on three crossed golf club supports, the base mounted with three mesh pattern balls, the cover surmounted by a figure of a golfer.

15in (38cm) high

$1,500-2,000 **L&T**

A silver-plated golfing trophy, in the form of a diabolical golfer standing beside a bag of clubs, on a molded circular base and ebonized wooden stand with attached plaque, inscribed "Lucifer Golfing Society".

The Lucifer Golfing Society was founded in 1921 by Sir Hedley le Bas and friends.

6.5in (16.5cm) high

$600-900 **L&T**

A silver and gold Master's Tournament Augusta National Low Amateur Cup, with decorated handles, applied gold disks.

This cup was won by Harvie Ward Jr. in 1957 when he was an amateur and fourth in the tournament. It was the first known cup of this type to be offered at public auction.

$25,000-35,000 **L&T**

A Victorian silver-plated deskstand, comprising a shield-shaped base surmounted by a pen-holder formed as crossed long nose clubs supported by a fence, flanked by two mesh-patterned golf ball inkwells with hinged covers, on three ball supports.

9in (23cm) wide

$500-600 **L&T**

A Victorian ram's horn inkwell, with silver-plated mount, surmounted by a figure of a golfer addressing a ball, with lidded circular inkwell formed as a mesh-pattern ball.

8.5in (21.5cm) high

$2,000-3,000 **L&T**

A presentation silver-plated ink stand, surmounted by a cast figure of a golfer, flanked by twin lidded circular section inkwells and pen recess, on four bun feet.

1906 *8.75in (22cm) wide*

$500-600 **L&T**

A silver watch holder, embossed to the back with a golfing scene, surmounted by a folding handle, on four bun feet, hallmarks for Birmingham.

1910 *2.75in (7cm) high*

$1,000-1,500 **L&T**

A silver clock, relief-decorated to the frieze with a golfer in the follow through, fitted with a Swiss watch movement, with hallmarks for Birmingham.

1927 *6.75in (17cm) high*

$400-500 **L&T**

A two-part cast iron dimpled golf ball press, marked "5598" and "SPECIAL 5606".

4in (10cm) wide

$700-1,000 **MSA**

A stuffed and mounted roach, with label inscribed, "Taken by Mr. J. Budd/in the Thames at/ Harvey Island/ 8th Novr. 1877/ Wgt. 1lb. 3ozs."

23.5in (60cm) wide

$1,000-1,500   **L&T**

A stuffed and mounted roach, in a naturalistic river setting, within a bowed glazed case inscribed, "ROACH Caught by JDS. Smith in the River Severn, 1910. Weight 7ln 131/4 ozs".

20cm (51cm) wide

$700-1,000   **L&T**

A stuffed and mounted chub, with label inscribed, "Chub/ caught on Oct. 30th 1910/ in the River Wye, Hereford/ by Mr. B. Hundley/ member of the/ Worcester Angling Society/ Weight 4lbs 2 ozs".

14.5in (37cm) wide

$200-400   **L&T**

A stuffed and mounted perch, with label inscribed "Caught at Chertsey by D.B. Heather, January 27th 1911 Weight 1lb 15ozs".

19in (48cm) wide

$600-700   **L&T**

A stuffed and mounted perch, with label inscribed "Perch, caught by J.T.R. Cary, Chipping Norton, September 1st 1914, weight 14ozs, 2 dams".

19in (48cm) wide

$700-1,000   **L&T**

A stuffed and mounted roach, with label inscribed "Roach caught by S. Martin on the Wye, 4th October 1923", and with preserver's label.

21in (53cm) wide

$1,000-1,500   **L&T**

A stuffed and mounted perch, bears inscription, "Perch 11b 9oz Caught at Tottenham Reservoirs by G. Gillson. 4th March 1925".

19in (48cm) wide

$700-1,000   **L&T**

A stuffed and mounted roach, with label inscribed "Rudd, Slapton Ley, July 9th 1953, Wgt. 1lb 15ozs".

19.25in (49cm) wide

$600-700   **L&T**

A stuffed and mounted pike, with label inscribed "Pike 25 1/2lbs caught by J.A. Harvey on the River Witham, Tattershall at 4.30 p.m. March 13 1957".

49.25in (125cm) wide

$600-900   **L&T**

A stuffed and mounted roach, in a naturalistic river setting, within a rectangular case with bowed glazed front.

23.25in (59cm) wide

$600-700   **L&T**

A stuffed and mounted pike, and a label inscribed "Pike, taken on a Perch dead bait, Loch Lomond, January 16th 1976, 18lbs 1oz".

45.5in (115.5cm) wide

$700-1,000   **L&T**

MEDALS

- Awards for courageous soldiers have been around since the earliest days of organized warfare. In the 3rd century BC, King Alexander awarded a medal to Jonathon the High Priest for his leadership of the Jews. This is the first recorded mention of a medal.
- British medals mostly commemorated a war or event until the mid-19th century, when gallantry was also awarded. The first British medal of this kind, awarding soldiers in all ranks, was the Victoria Cross in 1856.
- Most are marked with the recipient's name and details, making it possible to find out more details about the soldier.
- Medals from World War II do not usually include names because of the large number of people involved, but details can sometimes be found on the allocation sheet if a medal comes with its original documentation.
- Campaign medals were issued with clasps and bars recording particular battles and locations. Medals with multiple bars are rare and consequently tend to be more valuable, as do medals with demonstrable provenance such as photos and letters.
- Faked clasps, tampered details and re-strikes (molds of originals) are common and can be avoided by checking for filing on the rim, unclear lettering and design, and cross-referencing details.

A toned Defeat of the Spanish Armada silver medal, by G. V. Bijlaer, with fleet of ships and armorial shield of Prince Maurice, inscription and date 1588.

2in (5cm) diam

$2,000-3,000　　　　　　　　　　　　　　　　　**BLO**

A toned Charles, Prince of Wales silver medal, by N. Briot, with bust, Prince of Wales plumes, and inscription.

1638　　　　　　　　　　　　　　　*1in (3cm) diam*

$3,000-4,000　　　　　　　　　　　　　　　　　**BLO**

An extremely fine James I silver badge or naval reward, in the manner of Nicholas Hilliard, with badge of the Order of the Garter with legend "+JACOBVS.DG.MAG.BRITA.FR.ET.HI.REX.", and an arc on the sea with legend "STET.SALVS IN VNDIS", probably cast and chased.

The inscription "STET.SALVS IN VNDIS" roughly translates as "may it stand safe amid the waves".

2.25in (6cm) high

$1,500-3,000　　　　　　　　　　　　　　　　　**BLO**

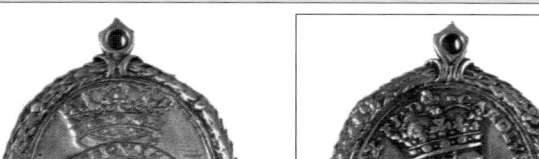

A Charles I gilt cast silver Royalist Badge, after Rawlings, with bust of King and Royal Arms, integral suspension loop, and wear to high points of plating.

2.5in (6cm) high

$1,500-2,000　　　　　　　　　　　　　　　　　**BLO**

A very fine Charles I silver-gilt Royalist cast oval medal, by T. Rawlins, with bust of King, incuse inscription, and Royal Arms.

1.5in (3cm) high

$1,500-2,000　　　　　　　　　　　　　　　　　**BLO**

An Oliver Cromwell, Lord Protector cast silver medal, after T. Simon, with bust of Cromwell, and arms of Cromwell and the Commonwealth.

1653

$300-400   **BLO**

A very fine silver gilt medal commemorating the marriage of Charles II and Catherine of Braganza, struck by G. Bower, dated, with inscription and catalogue number painted on reverse, scratch behind neck of Catherine.

1662

$1,500-2,000   **BLO**

A very fine silver medal commemorating the Dukes of Monmouth and Argyle Beheaded silver, by R. Arondeaux, with slight edge bruising.

1685   *2.25in (6cm) diam*

$600-800   **BLO**

A toned Naval Victory against Holland silver medal, by J. Roettiers, with bust and the King Charles II as a Roman General with inscription "Pro Talibvs Avsis".

1665   *2.25in (5.5cm) diam*

$2,000-3,000   **BLO**

A toned Accession of George I silver medal, by G. Vestner, with a bust and with stars in the midst of constellation of Leo, with inscription.

1714

$800-1,200   **BLO**

A very fine Capture of Portobello bronze medal, with bust of Admiral Vernon Took, and Portobello harbour, No.22, some wear to high detail, an unusual raised rim.

1739   *1.5in (4cm) diam*

$150-300   **BLO**

A toned Majority of George, Prince of Wales silver medal, by T Pingo, with "Georgivs Walliae Princeps", and figure of Tellus, with inscriptions above and below.

1759

$1,000-1,500   **BLO**

A scarce 18thC Russian Order of St. Anne, second class civil neck badge in gold and enamel by Kiebel.

$1,500-2,000   BLO

A rare Vatican Order of St. Gregory the Great, a Military Knight Commander's neck badge in gold and enamel, the back gold with blue enameled center.

c1830

$1,000-1,200   BLO

A scarce Sicilian Royal Order of Francis I, a magnificent Knight Commander's neck badge with crown, in gold and enamel, with chips to white enamel.

c1830

$10,000-12,000   BLO

A Military General Service medal, naming Charles King, Serjt, 7th Hussars.

1793-1840

$1,500-3,000   BLO

A Kaiser-I-Hind silver medal, Victorian issue, 2nd Class, with pin buckle and in Garrard case of issue.

$600-800   BLO

An Indian Attendants gold badge, with portrait of Queen Victoria, surrounded by a sunburst with gold crown suspension.

$6,000-8,000   BLO

A Most Honourable Order of the Bath, Knight Commanders (K.C.B.) gold medal set, civil division, with hallmarked gold neck badge and breast star in Garrard case of issue.

1864

$3,000-4,000   BLO

A scarce Ceylon Diamond Jubilee gold medal, with legend and date "1837-1897", and the inscription "To Commemorate sixty years of Her Majesty's Reign, The Rt. Hon. Sir J. West Ridgeway, K.C.B., K.C.M.G. Governor", in Phillips Brothers and Son, London case of issue, with lid embossed "Commemoration Medal Queen's Diamond Jubilee, 1897, G.I.A. Skeen, Government Printer, Ceylon".

1897

$2,000-3,000   BLO

The awards of Sir William Wyllie G.C.B., Indian Army, The Most Honourable Order of the Bath, Knight Grand Cross (G.C.B.) Military Division, hallmarked 1871, breast star with full sash, Ghuznee 1839, and Scinde Medal for Meeanee 1843 (Major W. Wyllie, 21st Regt. Bomb. N.I.), impressed in small block lettering.

$12,000-18,000   BLO

A Russian Order of St. Vladimir, fourth class gold and enamel civil breast badge, with no makers mark.

$1,500-2,000   BLO

The awards of Surgeon-General Sir Pardey Lukis, K.C.S.I., Indian Medical Service, The Most Exalted Order of the Star of India, Knight Commanders (K.C.S.I.) set, the neck badge with onyx cameo, and a breast star, both with motto set with diamonds, in "Victor Crichton" case of issue with Indian Volunteer Forces Decoration, G.V.R. issue, reverse engraved "The Honourable Surgn Genl Sir C.P.Lukis, K.C.S.I., I.M.S, 1st Bn.C.V.R.".

$12,000-18,000   BLO

An Order of British India, 2nd class neck badge, in gold with dark blue center and surround.

$1,200-1,800   **BLO**

An Order of British India, 1st Class neck badge, in gold with sky blue center and surround.

The Order was established in 1837 by the East India Company.

$1,500-2,000   **BLO**

An Order of British India, 1st Class neck badge, in gold with light blue center and dark blue surround.

$1,500-3,000   **BLO**

A 20thC Patiala Order of Krishna second class set, with sash badge engraved "Spink & Sons Ltd, London, No.8", and a breast star with Spink backplate.

$6,000-9,000   **BLO**

A scarce Bahawalpur Order of Imtiaz-i-Satlej, second class set, with neck badge and a breast star, each with Spink backplate reading "Medallists to H.M. the King".

$2,000-3,000   **BLO**

A Most Eminent Order of the Indian Empire, Knight Commanders (K.C.I.E.) medal set, with a neck badge and a breast star in Garrard case of issue.

$6,000-8,000   **BLO**

A Most Eminent Order of the Indian Empire, Companions (C.I.E.) neck badge, in gold and enamel and in Garrard case of issue.

The Order was founded in 1877 to reward British and native officials who served in India.

$1,200-1,800   **BLO**

A Kaiser-I-Hind gold medal, Edward VII issue, 1st Class, with pin buckle and in Garrard case of issue.

$2,000-3,000   **BLO**

A very fine and scarce German Zeppelin clasp, by C.E. Juncker of Berlin, in bronze with traces of silvering.

1914-18

$300-400 BLO

A German first class Iron Cross, of 'clam' type screw-back with uniform support pin, and makers mark "I59".

1914

$300-400 BLO

A Bahawalpur Silver Jubilee silver medal, unnumbered, with slight edge knocks.

1931

$150-200 BLO

An American Legion of Honor Nile Temple medal in silver, with blade engraved "Nile", reverse engraved on gold-plate "Col. Robt. M. Watkins, Commander 1937 from Legion of Honor Nile Temple A.A.O.N.M.S. Seattle".

$150-200 BLO

A German Luftwaffe air-gunners clasp, by Imme & Sohn, Berlin, in blue case of issue marked "Luftwaffen Fliegersshutzen Abzeitchen".

$500-700 BLO

A group of four 20thC medals to Color Sergeant-Major Wilfred A. Burchall, with Warwick box of issue, certificate and original chindit cloth badge, and also 17 silver Football and Sports medals to W.A. Burchall.

$1,000-1,500 BLO

A Kaiser-I-Hind medal, George VI issue, 2nd Class, with silver bar and pin buckle, in Garrard case of issue, dated.

1947

$1,000-1,500 BLO

A group of four medals to Miss Dorothy Jobson, V.A.D., Royal Red Cross, GVR second class, with 1914-15 star, War (with MID oakleaf) and Victory (D. Jobson, VAD).

$1,000-1,500 BLO

A group of three medals to Nursing Sister M.M. Hutheson (nee Cross), Queens South Africa (Nursing Sister M.Cross), British War (erased) and Victory Medals (T-Nurse Mrs M.M. Hutcheson).

$600-800 BLO

A group of six 19th and 20thC medals to Captain John Goldsmith (Indian Medical Service), with script engraving.

$2,000-3,000 BLO

A WWII Military medal group of seven to Ambulance Driver A. R. Payne, Royal Army Medical Corps, awarded during the North African Campaign, 1942.

The ribbons on British World War II medals carry symbolic meaning. Pale blue is for the Air Crew Europe, black edges for night flying, and yellow stripes for enemy searchlights.

$3,000-4,000 BLO

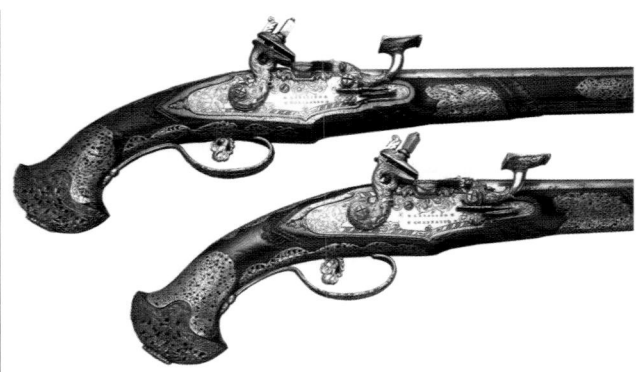

A pair of 17thC Brescian pierced steel mounted snaphaunce holster pistols, the locks engraved with a double eagle and foliate scrolls, neck cocks in the form of grotesque beasts, square head top jaw screws, dark walnut full stocks, signed "LAZARINO COMINAZZO".

The snaphaunce first appeared in the mid-16thC. It had fallen out of fashion in most countries by the end of the 17thC.

23.5in (59.5cm) wide

$40,000-50,000   **L&T**

A Pressburg pistol, probably 18thC, iron and wood, rounded wooden handle with rocaille decoration, floral engraved mountings, signed.

14.5in (36cm) wide

$3,000-4,000   **KAU**

A Philadelphia tiger maple percussion long rifle, with elaborated brass patch box, the lock inscribed "Jas Gotcher Philad.", the barrel inscribed "Samuel Walley".

barrel c1800   *39in (97.5cm) long*

$2,000-3,000   **POOK**

A brass-barreled flintlock blunderbuss with spring bayonet, by Thomas & Storrs of London, the barrel engraved "London", the plate engraved "Thomas & Storrs".

c1810   *29.5in (75cm) long*

$5,000-6,000   **W&W**

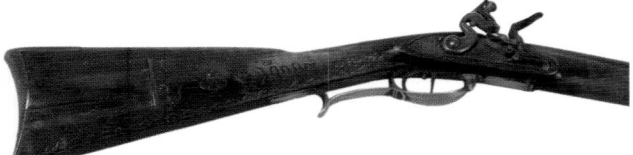

A Lancaster County, Pennsylvania, tiger maple flintlock long rifle, the barrel signed "J. Dickert" and the brass patch box bearing the initials of John Shearer, dated.

1811   *60.5in (150cm) long*

$20,000-30,000   **POOK**

A brass barrelled flintlock blunderbuss with spring bayonet, by Thomas & Storrs of London, with bell mouth barrel, octagonal breech bearing Birmingham proofs and engraved "London".

c1820   *29.5in (75cm) long*

$4,000-6,000   **W&W**

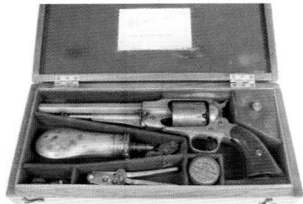

A Remington six shot revolver, new model series, patented Sept 14, 1858, serial no. 115872, in a fitted box with accessories.

$3,000-4,000   **SWO**

A Colt Army model 1860 percussion revolver, with a six shot cylinder and eight inch barrel, with walnut grips and brass trigger guard, struck "Address Col. Saml. Colt, New York, U.S. America" conforming serial numbers throughout No.64140, with leather holster.

$2,000-3,000   **SWO**

A 5 shot .36 RF conversion from Colt Model 1862 Police percussion revolver, spring-loaded ejector on right, pale walnut grips, the frame and butt straps bright nickel plated, re-engraved with a New York address, number "2699" on all parts except loading gate which is numbered "2691".

9.5in (24cm) long

$1,500-2,000   **W&W**

A six shot 5mm pinfire 'Apache' pepperbox revolver, knuckleduster and dagger combination, with a German silver frame stamped "I. Dolne Invur".

7.75in (19.5cm) long unfolded

$3,000-4,000   **W&W**

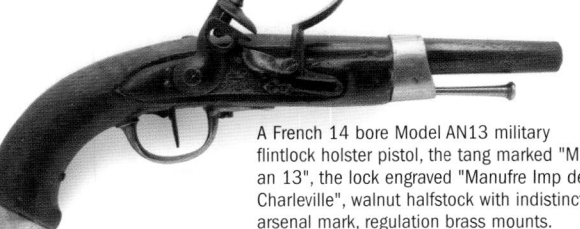

A French 14 bore Model AN13 military flintlock holster pistol, the tang marked "M an 13", the lock engraved "Manufre Imp de Charleville", walnut halfstock with indistinct arsenal mark, regulation brass mounts.

14in (35.5cm) long

$1,200-1,800   **W&W**

MILITARIA

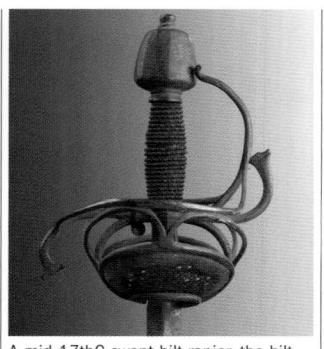

A mid-17thC swept hilt rapier, the hilt with pierced inner shell hand guard resting on side rings, damage and wear.

blade 39in (99cm) long

$5,000-6,000   **L&T**

A 17thC Scottish all steel sword, the basket hilt pierced with hearts and roundels, the chaneled blade with integral clip.

blade 31in (78.5cm) long

$3,000-4,000   **LFA**

An early 18thC Scottish basket hilted broad sword, blade signed "ANDRIA FRERARA", damage.

blade 33in (84cm) long

$4,000-5,000   **L&T**

A George III presentation saber, with Royal Cypher, shagreen grip with wire binding and leaf-cast stirrup hilt, the leather scabbard stamped "Gibson, Thomson & Craig, Edinburgh".

$3,000-4,000   **SWO**

A third quarter 19thC English-made Bowie knife, the clipped blade marked "Wragg and Sons, Sheffield" and "California Hunting Knife", German silver and leather sheath, damage.

8in (20.5cm) long

$4,000-5,000   **SK**

A Middle Eastern dagger with copper gilt grip and circular pommel, decorated with gilt copper and paste jewels.

The dagger was presented to Lt. Commander Joseph Rushton RNVR by T.E. Lawrence (Lawrence of Arabia) in recognition of his naval support for military actions.

17in (43cm) long

$1,000-1,200   **L&T**

A rare late 18thC American silver hilt sword, bearing the touch "DS", possibly David Smith, retaining its original trefoil blade with leather scabbard.

35in (89cm) long

$15,000-25,000   **POOK**

A 19thC silver-mounted Indo-Persian Jambiya, with silver decoration and wiring, silver and leather scabbard, later felt appliqué to rear, some pitting to blade and regluing of scabbard tip.

blade 6.25in (16cm) long

$200-300   **BLO**

A 19thC Indian Pesh Kabz dagger, with decorated brass hilt, red inlaid ivory grips, and woven leather scabbard, the tip of scabbard showing wear.

blade 9.5in (24cm) long

$400-600   **BLO**

An Argentinian gaucho's dagger, in silver scabbard by J.S. Ferra, in .900 silver hilt, with 'LSB' monogram in gold and stamp, some minor blade oxidation.

c1900   *blade 6.25in (16cm) long*

$400-600   **BLO**

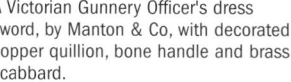

A Victorian Gunnery Officer's dress sword, by Manton & Co, with decorated copper quillion, bone handle and brass scabbard.

$500-600   **BLO**

A mid-19thC American carved powder horn, attributed to Timothy Tausel (1810-1852) with a typical spread winged eagle holding a banner, inscribed "E. Pluribus Unum", the reverse with four leaping deer.

8.75in (22cm) long

$4,000-5,000   **POOK**

An American engraved powder horn, inscribed "Isaiah Thomas" and dated "1775", with elaborate mermaid, ship and pinwheel decoration.

Isaiah Thomas was a patriot during the American Revolution and founder of the American Antiquarian Society.

4in (10cm) long

$30,000-40,000   **POOK**

A Jacob Gay (American, active 1758-1787), engraved powder horn, with inscription "This Horn made at Fort Edward May 15, 1758. Samuel McNeill, I powder with my brother ball: most hero like doth conquer all", over a family crest.

This horn incorporates many of Gay's fanciful techniques including the use of faces, hearts, and decoration within letters.

11in (28cm) long

$45,000-55,000   **POOK**

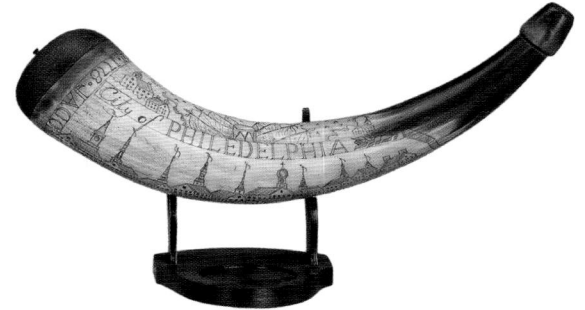

An engraved powder horn, inscribed "Jacobus deHart II Pa. RegT. 1778" and "City of Philadelphia," decorated with a townscape and ships.

1778   *14in (35.5cm) long*

$5,000-6,000   **FRE**

A rare example of original quilted grape shot, comprising nine balls in three tiers around an iron spike and bound in canvas and twine, with red oxide finish.

A grapeshot consists of a cluster of nine iron balls contained with in canvas and was made to be shot from a cannon.

6in (15cm) high

$2,000-3,000   **W&W**

A mid-19thC American painted military snare drum, manufactured by William Hall & Son, decorated with 'Liberty and Prosperity', and inscribed "City Battalion".

16.5in (42cm) wide

$6,000-7,000   **POOK**

A 19thC ceremonial painted wooden drum, with "CADETS 1786" and the motto "MONSTRAT VIAM" (It Points the Way), interior label with "From H. Prentiss 33 Court St. Boston".

The First Corps of cadets has been one of the major organizations of the Massachusetts National Guard for over 250 years.

17.5in (44.5cm) high

$4,000-5,000   **SK**

A early 19thC 3rd Ayrshire Yeomanry Local Militaria tailed jacket, of red and yellow broadcloth, Lieutenant Colonel, with associated gilt metal buttons, and an Ayrshire Yeomanry sabre tash.

$8,000-12,000   **L&T**

An original leather fire bucket from HMS Victory, painted with the ship's name and "GR" with "1803" below, copper bound at rim and copper studs.

10in (25.5cm) high

$2,000-3,000   **W&W**

An officer's gilt and silver-plated helmet plate of The Princess of Wales' Own Regiment, with original fittings and black velvet center backing.

The regiment was created on 16 January 1863 and was named following the wedding of the Prince of Wales (later Edward VII) to Princess Alexandra of Denmark.

$1,000-1,500   **W&W**

DECORATIVE ARTS

THE DECORATIVE ARTS CERAMICS MARKET

It's best to view the Arts and Crafts market as an organic beast, running here, sleeping there, growing in different years at different speeds. The current beast is alive and well, though he's not quite as peppy.

American Art Pottery is doing considerably better than other areas, though prices for some key makers have seen better days. For every George Ohr, the mischievous mad potter of Biloxi, whose work is bought at ever higher prices by arts and crafts collectors, art collectors, folk art collectors, there is a Grueby, strong, stoic, vegetal, and selling for under the money.

British wares that seem to go through the roof are Minton pâte-sur-pâte by Solon, Royal Worcester reticulated ware by George Owen and vases painted with sheep by Harry Davis, highland cattle by John Stinton and swans by Charles Baldwyn. In pottery, fine lustre wares by William de Morgan and others,

and saltglaze by the Martin Brothers, especially the bird-headed jars, are selling well. Majolica has had a rocky ride, although the best vessels of George Jones and Minton are holding up their heads proudly.

Instead of attempting to mimic the intensely integrated interiors of the period, where the right colors and the right textures needed to marry with the right everything else, perhaps it's time to see the Arts and Crafts for what it's always been, the team player of the decorative arts. The simple lines, the balancing of weight and mass, the power of its philosophy manifest in the process of its creation are ultimately, in the end product, all compelling aspects of this infectious material. Arts and Crafts can more than hold its own in a sea of its later 20th century brethren but unlike much of what was to follow, Arts and Crafts are centered in its soul.

David Rago

BOCH FRÈRES

- Boch Frères was founded by Pierre-Joseph Boch in Luxembourg in 1767 and was passed down through subsequent generations.
- It became Villeroy and Boch in 1836 when the faience factory of Villeroy merged with Boch in the face of competition from English porcelain manufacturers.
- In 1841, the Belgium branch of the Boch family set up the Keramis factory at La Louvière and traded as Boch Frères.
- The Boch Frères company became well known for its Art Deco ceramics. Pieces were of high quality and simple in form.
- Charles Catteau (1880-1966) was one of the factory's leading designers. He had worked as a potter at Sèvres and Nymphenburg before joining Boch Frères as Design Director in 1907. He was influenced by Japanese and African design as well as the Avant Garde and Bauhaus movements.
- Catteau joined the 'Circle of Friends of the Fine Arts' in 1908. His Art Deco work won him a grand prix at The International Exhibition of Decorative Arts in 1925.
- The company is still in production today.

A large Boch Freres 'Keramis' ovaiform vase, decorated with a broad frieze of deer against a crackled ground between geometric borders, marked "Keramis" to base.

14in (35.5cm) high

$2,000-2,500   **JN**

A Boch Freres ovoid vase by Charles Catteau, with stylized flowers on black ground, marked "LL/W5 1184/Ch Catteau/ Keramic/ Made in Belgium/ 875".

12in (30.5cm) high

$1,500-2,000   **SDR**

A Boch Freres ceramic lamp base, attributed to Charles Catteau, stamped "Boch Freres/Gres Keramis/914C".

12in (30.5cm) high

$900-1,100   **SDR**

A Boch Freres ovoid floor vase, by Julius Ernest Chaput painted with stylized Art Deco birds and flowers, hand written "Chaput.J" and "38/B.F.K./UNIQUE/472 CB".

This piece commands a high price as it is rare, striking, large, well-painted and in perfect condition.

19.25in (49cm) high

$20,000-25,000   **SDR**

A Boch Freres ovoid vase, enamel decorated with birds, on a crackleware ground, stamped "Keramis Made in Belgium/D1322".

12in (30.5cm) high

$1,200-1,500   **SDR**

A Boch Freres Art Deco pottery vase, molded with leaping gazelle vase, signed to base.

c1925   *10in (25.5cm) high*

$1,200-1,500   **DD**

A second quarter 20thC Boch Freres art pottery vase, with a crackle ground decorated with penguins and lower geometric border design, black ink mark and "D1104".

c1930   *14.5in (37cm) high*

$10,000-14,000   **SK**

A vase, attributed to Boch Freres, of leaping stags in ivory glossy glaze over terra cotta ground, marked "BFK/ DL339/ LN".

8in (20cm) high

$500-600   **SDR**

CARLTON WARE

- The Wiltshaw & Robinson company was established in 1890, and the bright, modern and hugely diverse pieces produced during the 20th century are known as Carlton Ware.
- When Frederick Cuthbert Wiltshaw, the son of the founder, took over the company in 1918, output was revolutionized and in light of successes at Wedgwood, a range of decorative luster ware was introduced.
- Luster pieces featured glossy designs of flowers in more than 12 different colors, creatures and Oriental and Egyptian motifs Patterns included 'Floral Comets', 'Dragon and Cloud' and 'Secretary Bird'.
- After the 1925 Paris Exhibition of Decorative Arts, designs became more geometrical and stylized. Items that display patterns well, such as chargers or large vases, tend to receive more interest.
- Luster ware was relatively time-consuming to produce and during the late 1920s, the 'Handcraft' range, with matt glazes and simpler floral designs was introduced.
- Also popular, though typically less valuable today, was Carlton Ware's range of naturally colored table wares modeled as salad leaves, two-dimensional flowers and fruit.

A Carlton Ware 'Chinese Bird and Cloud' pedestal bowl, pattern number 3275, printed and painted marks.

9.75in (25cm) high

$800-1,000   WW

A Carlton Ware 'Chinese Bird and Cloud' vase and cover, pattern number 3275, printed and painted marks, restored.

14.5in (37cm) high

$800-1,200   WW

A Carlton Ware 'Floral Comets' vase, pattern number 3387, printed and painted marks, faint hairline to top rim.

6in (15cm) high

$600-900   WW

A Carlton Ware 'Forest Tree' vase, pattern number 3253, printed and painted marks, restored top rim.

11.5in (29cm) high

$700-1,000   WW

A Carlton Ware 'Jagged Bouquet' vase, pattern no.3457, printed and painted marks.

6in (15.5cm) high

$800-1,000   WW

A Carlton ware 'Flies' vase painted in colors and gilt on a blue luster ground, printed and painted marks.

11in (28cm) high

$600-800   WW

A Carltonware luster ginger jar and cover, printed and painted in gilt and colored enamels in the 'Paradise Bird & Tree' pattern, with printed and painted marks, no. 3154.

10in (25.5cm) high

$700-1,000   L&T

A Carltonware 'Rouge Royale' vase and cover, decorated with floral motif, original paper label, printed and painted marks.

11in (28cm) high

$600-700   WW

A Carlton Ware 'Towering Castle' wall plaque, pattern no.3458, printed and painted marks.

12.5in (31.5cm) diam

$600-700   WW

A Carlton Ware Handcraft charger, pattern no 3673, painted with daisy flowers in colors on a blue ground, printed and painted marks.

12.75in (32cm) diam.

$900-1,000   WW

A Carlton Ware 'Reproduction of Old Swansea' vase, pattern 624, printed and painted in colors and gilt on a blue Imari ground, designed by Horace Wain, blue crown mark, 'Reproduction Old Swansea' mark.

c1912   *9in (22.5cm) high*

$500-600   WW

CLARICE CLIFF

CLARICE CLIFF

- Clarice Cliff (1899-1972) was born in Tunstall at the heart of the Staffordshire potteries. After learning free-hand painting and enameling at Linguard Webster & Co., she joined A.J.Wilkinson of Burslem in 1916.
- She began experimenting with decorating discarded 'blank' tablewares with bright colors and bold geometric shapes in her Newport studio, acquired in 1920. She launched her instantly successful 'Bizarre' range in 1928.
- Cliff designed over 500 shapes and 2,000 patterns during the Art Deco years with her team of mostly female decorators, known as 'The Bizarre Girls'. She also produced a novelty range of wall masks and figures, which is highly collectable, as is the 'Circus' series designed by Dame Laura Knight.
- Rarity, pattern, shape and condition usually determine the value. Pre-war pieces are usually the most collectable.
- Watch out for fakes, which can often be identified by poor-quality painting and a murky glaze.
- She marked many of her wares with the pattern name alongside a facsimile of her signature until the 1960s. She retired from A.J. Wilkinson in 1963.

A Clarice Cliff Fantasque 'Autumn' bowl, with variously colored trees, printed mark in black.

7.25in (18.5cm) diam

$400-600   **GORL**

A Clarice Cliff 'Applique Orange Avignon' grapefruit bowl, printed and painted marks.

6.25in (16cm) diam

$700-1,000   **WW**

A Clarice Cliff "Bridgwater Orange" sugar sifter, of bonjour shape, with a white ground and stylized scenery, marked on base, hand painted "Bizarre, Made in England".

5in (13cm) high

$800-1,200   **LAW**

A Clarice Cliff Bizarre conical sugar sifter, with the 'Green Capri' pattern, printed mark.

5.5in (14cm) high

$600-900   **WW**

A Clarice Cliff Bizarre 'Red Carpet' cup and saucer, with printed mark, restored.

3in (7.5cm) high

$700-1,000   **WW**

A Clarice Cliff Fantasque Bizarre 'Orange Chintz' 362 vase, with printed mark.

8.25in (21cm) high

$1,000-1,500   **WW**

A Clarice Cliff Fantasque Bizarre 'Orange Chintz' Perth jug, with shape number "24", printed mark, restored spout.

6in (15cm) high

$600-900   **WW**

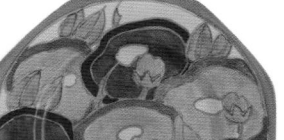

A Clarice Cliff Fantasque Bizarre 'Blue Chintz' octagonal plate, with printed mark, overpainting to blue.

8.75in (22cm) wide

$400-600   **WW**

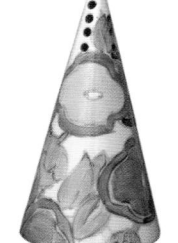

A Clarice Cliff 'Blue Chintz' sugar shaker, with 14 holes, black printed marks.

5.5in (14cm) High.

$1,500-2,000   **BRI**

A Clarice Cliff Bizarre 'Cornwall' conical sugar sifter, with printed mark, restored tip.

5.5in (14cm) high

$1,000-1,500   **WW**

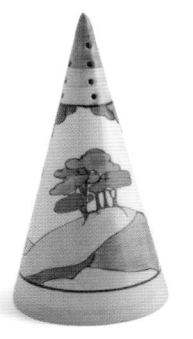

A Clarice Cliff Bizarre 'Coral Firs' conical sugar sifter, with printed mark.

5.5in (14cm) high

$1,200-1,800   **WW**

A Clarice Cliff Bizarre 'Crocus' pattern octagonal milk jug.

6in (15cm) high

$500-600   **JN**

A Clarice Cliff Bizarre 'Crocus' pattern circular jam pot and cover.

3.5in (9cm) high

$200-400   **JN**

A Clarice Cliff Bizarre Stamford 'Crocus' pattern teapot and cover, printed mark.

4.75in (12cm) high

$900-1,100   **WW**

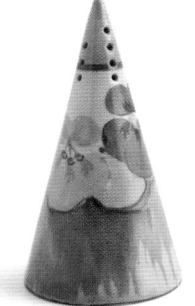

A Clarice Cliff Bizarre 'Delecia Pansies' conical sugar sifter, with printed mark, restored.

5.5in (14cm) high

$500-600   **WW**

A Clarice Cliff Bizarre 'Green Erin' conical coffee cup and saucer.

2.75in (7cm) wide

$500-700   **WW**

A Clarice Cliff 'Floreat' Fantasque Bizarre mei ping vase.

$700-1,000   **WW**

Part of a Clarice Cliff Bizarre Conical 'Gibraltar' painted coffee service for six, comprising coffee pot and cover, milk jug, six cans and six saucers, with printed marks, dated.

1931   *Pot 7in (18cm) high*

$9,000-11,000   **WW**

A Clarice Cliff 'Gloria Autumn' Bizarre daffodil bowl, printed mark.

13.5in (34cm) wide

$500-700   **WW**

A Clarice Cliff Fantasque Bizarre 'House and Bridge' plate, with printed mark, minor restoration to back rim.

9in (23cm) diam

$500-600   **WW**

A Clarice Cliff Bizarre 'Applique Idyll' wall plaque, printed and painted marks.

13.5in (34cm) diam

$3,000-4,000   **WW**

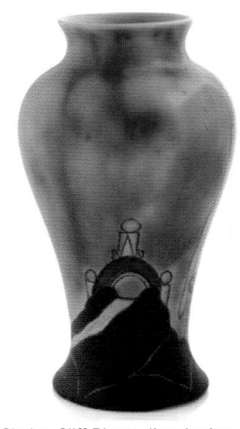

A Clarice Cliff Bizarre 'Inspiration Caprice' meiping vase, with painted marks.

9in (23cm) high

$1,500-2,000 WW

A Clarice Cliff Bizarre 'Inspiration' pattern 269 vase, with printed and painted marks.

7.75in (19.5cm) high

$700-1,000 WW

A Clarice Cliff Fantasque Bizarre 'Melon' meiping vase, with printed mark.

9in (23cm) high

$1,500-2,000 WW

A Clarice Cliff Fantasque Bizarre 'Melon' pattern conical bowl, printed mark, restored rim.

6in (15.5cm) diam

$600-700 WW

A Clarice Cliff Fantasque Bizarre 'Melon' twin-handled lotus vase, printed mark.

11.75in (29.5cm) high

$1,200-1,800 WW

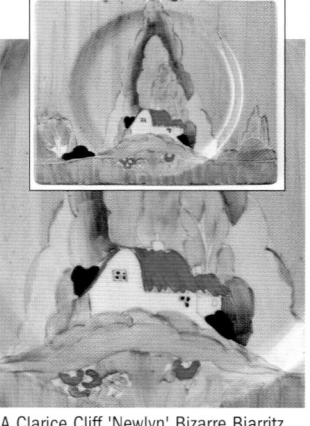

A Clarice Cliff 'Newlyn' Bizarre Biarritz plate, printed mark.

10.25in (26cm) wide

$1,200-1,500 WW

A Clarice Cliff 'Pansies' conical sugar shaker, marked on the base "Pansies, Bizarre by Clarice Cliff, Newport Pottery".

5.25in (13cm) high

$800-1,000 LAW

A Clarice Cliff Fantasque Bizarre 'Red Roofs' conical cup and saucer, with printed marks.

2.25in (6cm) high

$1,000-1,200 WW

A Clarice Cliff Fantasque Bizarre 'Red Roofs' plaque, with printed mark.

11.75in (30cm) diam

$3,000-3,500 WW

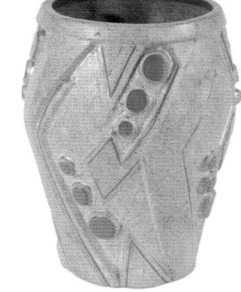

A Clarice Cliff Art Deco 'Scraphito' vase, with a deeply molded abstract pattern, marked "Painted/Bizarre by Clarice Cliff/Newport Pottery/England" and impressed "470".

8.75in (22.25cm) high

$1,800-2,200 SDR

A Clarice Cliff Bizarre 'Summer Cottage' pattern low cylindrical preserve pot, with metal cover, printed factory mark.

3.75in (9.5cm) diam

$300-400   ROS

A Clarice Cliff 'Taormina' pattern circular wall plaque, printed marks.

17.5in (44.5cm) diam

$1,000-1,200   L&T

A Clarice Cliff Bizarre 'Orange Trees and House' bowl, with printed mark.

8.75in (22cm) diam

$400-600   WW

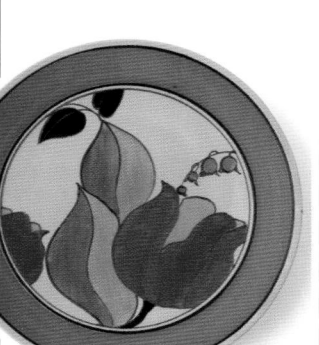

A Clarice Cliff Fantasque 'Red Tulip' Bizarre wall plate, printed mark.

10.5in (26.5cm) diam

$1,000-1,200   WW

A Clarice Cliff large Fantasque Bizarre 'Windbells' meiping vase, with the printed mark.

14.25in (36.5cm) high

$3,000-3,500   WW

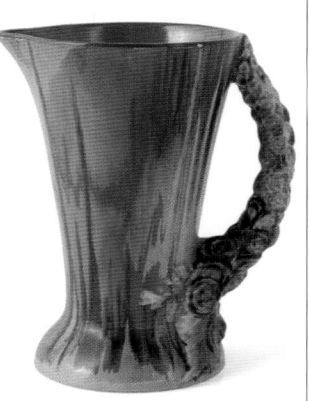

A Clarice Cliff Bizarre jug, with Delecia effect drip glaze and embossed autumnal flowers to the handle, factory marks to underside.

9.25in (23.5cm) high

$150-200   ROS

A Clarice Cliff pottery pitcher, decorated with oranges and lemons, on ribbed body with handle, mark on base.

12in (30.5cm) high

$1,000-1,200   SK

A Clarice Cliff 'Original Bizarre' 268 vase, printed mark.

7.75in (20cm) high

$1,000-1,200   WW

A Clarice Cliff fish vase, model 329, printed mark.

10.5in (27cm) high

$200-300   WW

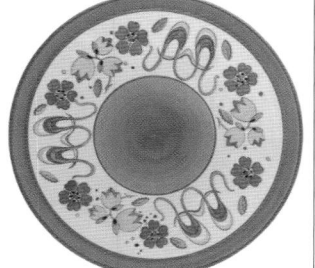

An unusual Clarice Cliff charger, painted with a border of flowers and foliage, printed mark.

18in (45cm) diam

$800-1,000   WW

A Clarice Cliff pottery bowl, with wide rim decorated with geometric shapes, mark on base.

18in (45.75cm) diam

$1,000-1,500   SK

A William De Morgan 'Bedford Park Daisy' tile.

This tile was made for Norman Shaw's Bedford Park housing development.

6in (15cm) wide

$900-1,100   **PC**

A panel of two William De Morgan 'Barnard Bishop & Barnard' tiles surrounded by other de Morgan tiles.

This tile was made for the Bank of England, Norwich. The varying shades of the outer tiles are caused by different firing temperatures.

$5,000-7,000   **PC**

A William De Morgan 'Chicago' tile, painted in the Iznik style with interlocking flowers, and set within converted ebonized stool, impressed Merton Abbey mark.

9.25in (23.5cm) sq

$3,000-4,000   **L&T**

A William De Morgan 'Elsley' pattern two-tile panel, each decorated with thorny branches of flowering roses.

each 6in (15cm) wide

$1,000-1,500   **L&T**

A William De Morgan 'K L Rose' tile, in aubergine.

Tiles such as this would mainly have been used in fireplaces.

6in (15.25cm) wide   c1890

$900-1,100   **PC**

A large William De Morgan circular charger, decorated by Charles Passenger, with a fantastical winged beast on a foliate ground, painted marks "W. De Morgan & Co., Fulham, C.P., 2079".

16in (40.5cm) diam

$40,000-45,000   **L&T**

A William De Morgan 'Persian Frieze' tile.

6in (15cm) wide

$800-1,000   **PC**

A William De Morgan 'Poppy' pattern tile, designed by William Morris, in manganese pink and green, unmarked.

5in (13cm) wide

$900-1,100   **SWO**

A William De Morgan tile.

6in (15cm) wide

$800-1,000   **PC**

A William de Morgan panel of four tiles, for Morris & Co. comprising two pairs of tiles, each painted with flowering foliage in an Iznik design, impressed mark.

each tile 6in (15.25cm) wide

$800-1,200   **L&T**

Two William de Morgan Fulham period tiles, one painted with carnations in blue and green and the other with a flowerhead in purple, impressed mark.

1898   *6in (15.5cm) wide*

$1,200-1,800   **L&T**

A William de Morgan eight inch tile, with a carnation, late Fulham period, impressed mark verso.

c1898   *8in (20.5cm) wide*

$2,800-3,200   **L&T**

A William De Morgan pottery Persian tile, painted with a bird, carnation flowers, impressed Sand's End mark.

6in (15cm) wide

$4,000-4,500   **WW**

A William De Morgan tile, decorated with flowering leafy stems on a turquoise ground, impressed mark.

8in (20.5cm) wide

$4,000-5,000   **L&T**

A William de Morgan six tile panel, painted with a large Persian vase decorated with flowers inside a floral border, one tile cracked.

23.5in (60cm) high

$12,000-14,000   **WW**

A Bodley & Son luster plate, possibly by William De Morgan, painted in ruby luster with two classical dolphins, impressed "Bodley & Son".

c1875   *9in (23cm) diam*

$1,000-1,500   **WW**

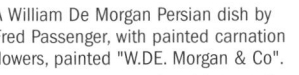

A William De Morgan Persian dish by Fred Passenger, with painted carnation flowers, painted "W.DE. Morgan & Co".

c1890   *8in (20.5cm) diam*

$5,000-6,000   **WW**

A William De Morgan pottery charger with painted winged creatures in ruby luster on a white ground, indistinct impressed mark, imperfections in the glaze.

c1880   *14in (36cm) diam*

$5,000-6,000   **WW**

A William de Morgan circular charger, painted in ruby luster with opposed beasts on a foliate ground, decorated verso with concentric bands.

14in (35.5cm) diam

$2,000-3,000   **L&T**

A William De Morgan 'Persian' vase, by Joe Juster, with painted scrolling foliage, painted "D M Fulham JJ 14", small glaze chip to base rim.

c1890   *9in (22cm) high*

$4,000-6,000   **WW**

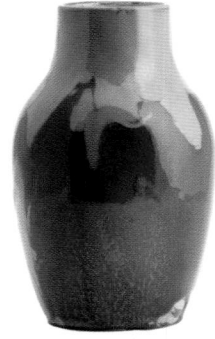

A Dedham experimental vase, by Hugh Robertson covered in a khaki green over blue and green glaze, incised "Dedham Pottery HCR".

The Dedham pottery was established in Dedham MA, US by Hugh Robertson in 1895. It closed in 1943.

8in (20cm) high

$1,500-2,000   DRA

A Dedham experimental baluster vase, by Hugh Robertson covered in thick white and beige glaze over a frothy green ground, incised "Dedham Pottery HCR", in ink "DP 71B".

9in (23cm) high

$3,000-4,000   DRA

A Dedham Pottery experimental vase, by Hugh Robertson with thick emerald green opaque glaze, over a white orange peel ground, loss to part of one drip, probably from manufacture, marked "Dedham Pottery HCR", in ink "DP 23E".

6in (15cm) high

$2,000-3,000   DRA

A Dedham Experimental vase by Hugh Robertson, covered in mottled brown and green volcanic glaze. Incised Dedham Pottery/HCR/ink DP10B.

8in (20cm) high

$2,000-3,000   DRA

A Dedham Experimental vase by Hugh Robertson in thick brown and green glaze, incised "HCR Dedham pottery DP71B".

8.5in (22cm) high

$2,500-3,000   DRA

A Dedham Crackleware plate no. 2 in the Tapestry Lion design, indigo and impressed stamps.

8.25in (21cm) diam

$2,000-3,000   DRA

A Dedham Crackleware crab plate with seaweed design, indigo stamp.

8.5in (22cm) diam

$1,500-2,000   DRA

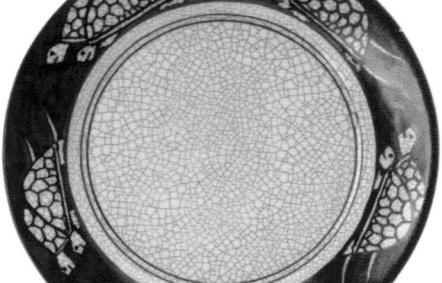

A Dedham Crackleware plate, No.2, the Turtle, chip to footrim, indigo stamp.

8.25in (21cm) diam

$2,500-3,000   DRA

DOULTON

- John Doulton established Doulton & Co. in Lambeth, South London in 1815, initially selling stoneware industrial and commercial products. From the 1830s onwards Doulton produced a range of commemorative wares.
- His son Henry transformed the company by opening an art pottery studio employing students from the Lambeth School of Art in 1871. Doulton's success in the 1880s helped the company grow enormously.
- By 1877, the firm set up a factory in Burslem producing tableware such as the 'Dubarry' dinner service, and in the 1920s and 1930s, a highly successful and very collectable range of Art Deco decorative figures.
- Doulton became Royal Doulton after King Edward awarded the company the first of five royal warrants in 1901.
- Production at Lambeth ended in 1956 but continues today in Burslem. Many of the most popular figures, such as 'The Balloon Seller', which has been in production since 1929, and 'Top o' the Hill', since 1937, are still being made.
- Female figures, particularly those designed by Arthur Leslie Harradine, are usually the most collectable. However, if a piece is not in mint condition, it is very unlikely to command the highest prices.
- Doulton marked pieces with the factory name, date and initials of the artist.

An early Doulton Lambeth stoneware baluster vase, by Hannah Barlow and Frank Butler, with ponies between formal borders, marks for 1875 and artists' monograms, three panels signed "HBB".

12.75in (32.5cm) high

$2,200-2,800   JN

An early Doulton Lambeth stoneware slender ewer, by Hannah Barlow, incised with ponies, pigs and goats in a sparse landscape, with formal beaded borders, factory marks, dated "1876" with artist's monogram numbered "643".

9in (23cm) high

$1,000-1,500   JN

A Doulton Lambeth stoneware jug, by Hannah Barlow, incised with ponies, between formal beaded and foliate borders, plated collar and cover, factory marks, dated 1884, artist's monogram and Lucy Barlow as assistant.

8.25in (21cm) high

$1,000-1,500   JN

A Doulton Lambeth stoneware vase, by Hannah Barlow, decorated with a band of incised donkeys, impressed marks to base.

14.5in (37cm) high

$1,000-1,500   JN

A large Doulton Lambeth stoneware vase, by Hannah Barlow, decorated with a band of deer, impressed marks to base.

16.5in (42cm) high

$1,500-1,700   JN

A Doulton Lambeth stoneware ewer, by Hannah Barlow, incised with hunter and hounds, between formal foliate borders, rosette mark and artist's monogram.

11.5in (29cm) high

$2,000-3,000   JN

An early Doulton Lambeth stoneware jug, by Hannah Barlow, incised with a horse and a frog, with scrolling foliage and stiff leaf borders, factory marks and "HBB" monogram.

7.75in (19.5cm) high

$1,000-1,500   JN

A Doulton Lambeth stoneware two handled loving cup, by Frank Butler, decorated with shaped panels of leaves on an oatmeal ground with a silver rim.

6.5in (16.5cm) high

$600-900   JN

A Doulton Lambeth stoneware jug, by Frank Butler, decorated with blue and brown foliage and beading.

8.75in (22cm) high

$900-1,100   JN

A Doulton Lambeth stoneware jug, with three embossed circular panels, monogram mark for Francis E. Lee and dated, marked and monogram "MA".

1877   *9in (23cm) high*

$500-600   LAW

DECORATIVE ARTS

A Doulton Lambeth stoneware salad bowl, by Edith Lupton, decorated with intricate foliate banding between formal bands of florets, rosette mark dated and artist's initials, replaced silver collar, 1980.

1881   10.5in (26.5cm) diam

$600-900   **JN**

A highly important Doulton Burslem 'Diana' vase, modeled by Charles Noke and painted by George White and Fred Hancock, painted with the adoration of Diana the Huntress, griffin handles, printed marks, restoration, wear.

The vase was first exhibited at the World's Columbian Exhibition in Chicago 1893 and was illustrated in an article in Royal Doulton magazine "Gallery" Volume 19, Number 2 Summer, 1999.

c1895   39in (100cm) high

$10,000-12,000   **FRE**

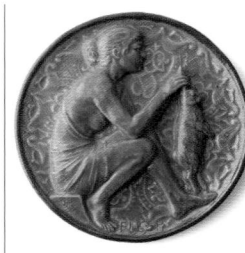

A Doulton stoneware plaque, 'Flesh' by George Tinworth, incised with allegorical maiden holding a hare by its ears, with blue glazing, incised "GT".

9in (24cm) diam

$2,000-3,000   **WW**

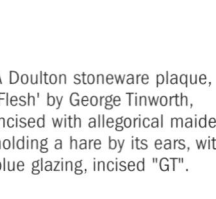

A Doulton Lambeth stoneware 'Mouse on a Bun' figure, by George Tinworth, impressed Lambeth rosette, incised monogram.

3in (7.5cm) high

$2,000-3,000   **WW**

A rare Doulton Lambeth 'Tea Time Scandal' stoneware mouse group, by George Tinworth, with impressed mark, "GT" monogram, small chip.

3.75in (9.5cm) high

$5,000-6,000   **WW**

A rare Doulton Lambeth 'The Combat' stoneware mouse and frog, by George Tinworth, glazed in colors with impressed mark, "GT" monogram.

4in (10cm) high

$4,000-5,000   **WW**

A Doulton Lambeth stoneware Bibelot, modeled as a kookaburra on a boat, impressed marks.

4.25in (11cm) high

$300-400   **WW**

A pair of Doulton, Burslem vases, printed and painted in blue and gilt with tulips, with printed marks.

7.5in (19.5cm) high

$700-1,000   **L&T**

A Doulton Lambeth 'Worlds Colombian Exposition' stoneware commemorative jug, with stars and stripes, a portrait of Washington and Christopher Columbus and an American crest, impressed marks to base.

7.5in (19cm) high

$500-700   **JN**

A Doulton Lambeth stoneware silver mounted jack, impressed marks, rim stamped "London".

1890   8.25in (21cm) high

$200-300   **WW**

A Doulton Lambeth Aesthetic Movement framed tile, the Minton blank painted with a contemplative Classical maiden, bears monogram and painted Doulton mark.

tile 8.5in (22cm) high

$1,000-1,500   **L&T**

A Doulton Lambeth boat shaped stoneware lighter, printed with "Tough & Henderson, 53 Upper Ground St, Blackfriars Bridge, S.E.I, Telephone 611 Hop", impressed marks.

7in (18cm) long

$600-700   **DN**

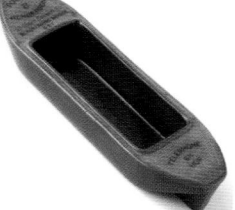

A Doulton Lambeth boat shaped stoneware lighter, printed with "Downey, 4 Pratt At, Lambeth S.E, Telephone 858 P.O. Victoria", impressed mark and "Rd 411218", restored chip.

7in (18cm) long

$500-600   **DN**

A Royal Doulton 'Nelson and his captains' jug, with blue glaze and buff colored panel of Nelson and his Captains, Hardy, Miller, Troubridge and Collingwood.

8.5in (22cm) high

$500-600　　　　**LAW**

A Royal Doulton Lord Nelson earthenware loving cup, decorated with Nelson and comrades with the inscription 'England Expects', the reverse with a naval scene and inscription 'Twas in Trafalgar Bay', marked number "376 of an edition of 600" on its base, with certificate.

10in (26cm) high

$1,000-1,200　　　　**LAW**

A Royal Doulton Seriesware earthenware mug, with monks, painted by Charles Noke.

5.5in (14cm) high

$300-400　　　　**JN**

A Royal Doulton flambé Sung vase, by Charles Noke, shape number 1261, with decoration of prunus blossom, covered in rich flambé glaze, printed mark and Sung mark.

10in (25cm) high

$2,000-3,000　　　　**WW**

A Royal Doulton Sung bone china vase, by Charles Noke, with painted blossom under a streaked flambé glaze, printed mark, Sung and facsimile signature.

13in (33.5cm) high

$2,000-3,000　　　　**WW**

A Royal Doulton stoneware baluster vase, by Eliza Simmons, painted with a geometric design of grapes, vine leaves and trellises, factory marks and artist's monogram, numbered "968", illegible date code.

16.5in (42cm) high

$900-1,100　　　　**JN**

A Royal Doulton stoneware vase, by Emily Stormer, with incised flowers and leaves upon a blue ground, impressed marks to base.

15in (38cm) high

$600-700　　　　**JN**

A Royal Doulton 'The Regency Coach' earthenware jug, showing the London to Brighton coach, no. 353 of 500, inscription, marked, with certificate.

10.75in (27cm) high

$600-700　　　　**LAW**

A Royal Doulton Cambridge rowing tyg, presented to the Scratch Fours, 29th March 1902, with crossed oars and floral patterns, monogram mark for Francis E. Lee and Royal Doulton mark, chip to rim.

6in (15cm) high

$200-300 LAW

A Royal Doulton figure of 'Angela', number HN1204, designed by Leslie Harradine, printed and painted marks, fan extensively restored.

c1940 *7.5in (19cm) high*

$1,000-1,200 DN

A Royal Doulton 'Carmen' figurine, number HN1267.

7in (17.5cm) high

$700-1,000 SWO

A Royal Doulton 'Sweet and Twenty' figure, number HN1298, depicting a seated woman fanning her face.

6in (15cm) high

$400-500 ROS

A Royal Doulton 'Bonnie Lassie' figure, number HN1626, designed by Leslie Harradine and issued between 1934-1953, marked on base, chip.

5.25in (13cm) high

$300-400 LAW

A Royal Doulton figure, 'Spring' HN2085.

7.5in (19cm) high

$220-280 SWO

A Royal Doulton 'The Mask' figure, number HN656, designed by L. Harradine, printed and painted marks, restored.

1924-38 *6.75in (17.25cm) high*

$3,000-3,500 WW

A Fulper baluster vase, covered in a fine frothy Cat's Eye glaze, incised "D536".
Fulper Pottery was produced in Flemington, NJ, US from 1860 to 1955.

13.25in (33cm) high

$500-600　　　　**DRA**

A tall, narrow Fulper vase, covered in a fine frothy Cat's Eye flambé glaze, with vertical mark.

16in (40.5cm) high

$5,000-6,000　　**DRA**

A large Fulper bullet-shaped vase covered in a fine ivory to mauve frothy flambé glaze, small grinding chip to base, with vertical mark.

13in (33cm) high

$3,500-4,500　　**DRA**

A Fulper bullet vase, covered in an ivory to blue flambé glaze, vertical ink race track mark.

10.5in (26.5cm) high

$400-500　　　　**DRA**

A Fulper Temple jar, covered in Mirrored Black glaze, with light abrasion around rim of jar, vertical mark and paper label.

14in (35.5cm) high

$1,500-2,500　　**DRA**

A Fulper early Vasekraft cylindrical vase with four buttresses beneath an embossed tapering top, covered in Cafe-Au-Lait crystalline glaze, with 9in hairline, vertical mark and paper label.

12.25in (31cm) high

$1,500-2,000　　**DRA**

A Fulper Effigy bowl, with three gargoyles covered in matte gray glaze, supporting a bowl in Chinese blue flambé glaze, vertical mark.

7.5in (19cm) high

$700-900　　　　**DRA**

A pair of Fulper tall candlesticks covered in Mirror Black flambé glaze, some scratches to base of one, with vertical marks.

11.5in (29cm) high

$500-600　　　　**DRA**

A pair of Fulper Vasekraft bookends, modeled with Aztec masks and covered in Mission Matte glaze, vertical marks, with Vasekraft paper label.

6in (15cm) wide

$400-600　　**DRA**

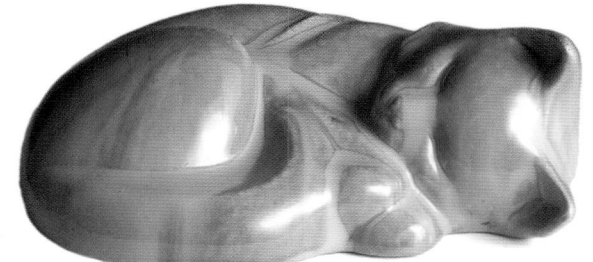

A Fulper sleeping cat figure or doorstop, covered in green flambé glaze, impressed horizontal mark.

8.5in (21cm) wide

$1,100-1,400　　**DRA**

An early Fulper white rabbit figure with pink glass eyes, impressed horizontal mark "#883".

5.5in (14cm) high

$2,000-2,500　　**DRA**

479

GOLDSCHEIDER

- Friedrich Goldscheider founded The Goldscheider Manufactory and Majolica Factory in Vienna, Austria in 1885. It was renowned for making mostly female figures and wallmasks.

- In the interwar years Goldscheider faithfully interpreted the styles and fashions of the Art Deco period, giving the figures long dresses, cropped hair with Marcel waves, cloche hats, and borzoi hounds, in rich, bright colors.

- The pieces were composed of several sections 'luted' together with slip and then fire-glazed, so that seams could be cleaned up. This complicated process gave them detail which set Goldscheider apart from other firms.

- Rarity, size and condition determine price. Beware of damage as terracotta is prone to chipping. Figure groups were particularly difficult and time consuming for the ceramicist, making them rare and very desirable.

- In the late 1930s Goldscheider collaborated with Myott, Son & Co. in Staffordshire. From then on the mark "Goldscheider made in England", or "Myott and Goldscheider" was used.

- Austrian pieces tend to be more sought after, as are pieces bearing the mark of Ludwig Goldscheider, which are rarer. The factory closed in 1954.

A 19thC Goldscheider terracotta figure, modeled as a seated 'Mercury', after the antique, on an oak pedestal, bears "Goldscheider" plaque.

48in (122cm) high

$5,000-7,000   **FRE**

A late 19thC Goldscheider-style pottery figure of a bearded banjo player, with turquoise jacket, on marbled plinth, unmarked.

29.5in (75cm) high

$5,000-7,000   **L&T**

A Goldscheider pottery figure of Rigoletto, model number 170, impressed marks, restored neck.

38.5in (98cm) high

$700-1,000   **WW**

A Goldscheider glazed earthenware butterfly girl figure, decorator's signature, factory mark and country of origin, numbered.

c1935

$3,000-4,000   **SK**

A Goldscheider earthenware figure, by Dakon, with impressed marks, no. 5815.

15in (38.5cm) high

$2,000-3,000   **L&T**

A Goldscheider earthenware figure, by Dakon, modeled as a girl seated on a wall feeding a biscuit to her dogs, with impressed marks, no. 7423.

9.5in (24.5cm) high

$2,500-3,500   **L&T**

A Goldscheider earthenware figure, modeled as a girl seated on her suitcases, with impressed marks, no. 7172.

10in (25.5cm) high

$3,000-4,000   **L&T**

A Goldscheider terracotta bust, with marks and original tags intact.

c1935   *15in (38cm) high*

$3,000-4,000   **DD**

A Goldscheider terracotta bust, with marks and original tags intact.

c1935   *11in (28cm) high*

$3,000-4,000   **DD**

GRUEBY

- The American potter William H. Grueby founded the Grueby Faience Company in 1884, in Boston. Although successful, the company was not profitable and in 1908 it went bankrupt.
- Most Grueby pottery was produced between 1892 and 1907. Grueby continued potting with the Grueby Faience and Tile Company.
- The company specialized in handmade tiles and slip-cast vessels with thick matt glazes, the pieces are organic and highly stylized.
- The most important glaze was the matt green glaze, considered to be the finest in American art pottery.
- Work often featured details such as petals and these works tend to be more valuable than plainer pieces. Polychrome wares are also more sought after, as are single color pots with deep tooling.
- Grueby tiles are were incredibly popular at the beginning of the 20thC. They were found in hotels, restaurants and also on the walls of many stations in the New York Subway.
- Gustav Stickley used only Grueby tiles to complement his furniture. The tiles are of superb quality and highly sought after by collectors.

A Grueby early bulbous vase incised with long leaf-forms, covered in feathered matte green glaze, with vertical stamp "Grueby BOSTON".

7in (18cm) high

$2,500-3,000　　　　**DRA**

A Grueby bulbous vase with impressed oval leaves, covered in frothy matte green glaze, with circular Faience mark.

7.5in (19cm) high

$2,000-2,500　　　　**DRA**

A Grueby ovoid vase, covered in a frothy matte green glaze, with 2in stilt pull chip, Grueby Pottery circular stamp.

7.5in (19cm) high

$800-1,200　　　　**DRA**

A Grueby gourd-shaped Kendrick vase with two rows of tooled and applied leaves under a fine matte green glaze. (Recently discovered in a Montreal home, this vase shows a rare combination of perfect glazing and organic form), a few nicks to leaf edges and one to base, circular pottery stamp 33.

12in (30cm) high

$25,000-30,000　　　　**DRA**

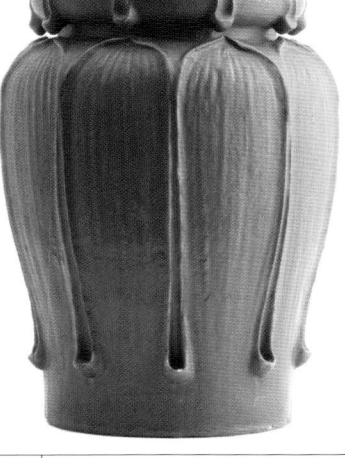

A Grueby vase with tooled and applied full-height leaves covered in a superior matte green glaze, alternating with yellow buds, a few nicks to leaf edges and small grinding chip, "Grueby Faience" circular stamp.

12in (30cm) high

$11,000-13,000　　　　**DRA**

A Grueby squat vase, by Ruth Erickson, with two rows of curled, rounded leaves covered in oatmealed green glaze, restored chip at rim, "Grueby Pottery" circular stamp, artist signed "RE".

6in (15cm) wide

$1,200-1,500　　　　**DRA**

A Grueby bulbous vase, covered in thick, oatmealed, matte indigo glaze, some glaze misses allow buff clay to show through, circular pottery stamp and "211".

6in (15cm) high

$700-1,000　　　　**DRA**

A Grueby Pottery decorated tile, from Boston, Massachusetts in shades of blue, green, ocher and cream glaze.

9in (23cm) diam

$8,000-1,000　　　　**SK**

A Grueby tile, designed by Addison LeBoutillier and decorated in cuenca with a frieze of ivory horses, with professional restoration to lower right side, signed "K.C."

6in (15cm) wide

$3,000-4,000　　　　**DRA**

A Grueby tile, "The Pines," decorated in cuenca, with glazed sides, artist-signed "RD."

6in (15cm) wide

$4,000-5,000　　　　**DRA**

A large Minton majolica game pie dish, cover and liner, typically molded and colored with basket weave and dead game, some damage.

1859   *15.75in (40cm) long*

$1,500-2,000   **SWO**

A Minton majolica teapot and cover, modeled as a lemon issuing flowers and leaves, the cover formed as a mushroom, faintly impressed mark.

c1860   *7in (18cm) long*

$4,000-6,000   **WW**

A Minton majolica game pie dish, the lid molded with a hare, duck and moorhen with sprig handle, the base decorated with oak leaves against a basket weave ground, dated, restored.

1864   *13in (33cm) wide*

$1,200-1,500   **GORL**

A Minton majolica oval game-pie tureen and cover, the ozier-molded base with trailing oak leaves, the cover molded with a coot, rabbit and mallard.

c1865   *12.75in (32cm) wide*

$1,200-1,500   **DN**

A pair of Minton Majolica sweetmeat figures, modeled as a young boy and girl kneeling beside a basket and raised on mottled bases, impressed marks and date codes, damaged

1870   *7.75in (19.5cm) wide*

$600-900   **WW**

A Minton majolica teapot and cover modeled as a Japanese dwarf with Noh mask, impressed marks, shape 1838, year cypher, replacement chip to spout.

1875   *9in (22cm) wide*

$1,000-1,800   **DN**

A Minton majolica teapot and cover, in the Aesthetic style, with molded panels of three friends based on a Chinese Kangxi biscuit porcelain original, large crack to base.

1879   *5in (15cm) high*

$2,500-3,000   **SWO**

A Minton Majolica three division nut dish, with a blue interior, rope twist handles and a blue speckled base, impressed "Mintons", no 783.

10.5in (26.5cm) wide

$1,000-1,200   **JN**

A Minton Majolica oval game pie dish and cover, pattern number "668", with pale blue base and interior, the lid with dead game in relief, with green basketwork sides decorated with oak leaves, impressed "Minton"

13in (33cm) wide

$1,000-1,200   **JN**

A Minton majolica large platter, with brown cattails and white lotus blossoms on large green lily pads, stamped "MINTON 827".

24in (61cm) wide

$6,000-8,000   **DRA**

A George Jones majolica oval dressing table tray, molded with two swallow tail butterflies and flowering lilies, minor rubbing, impressed monogram and registration diamond to base.

c1870   *11in (28cm) wide*
$1,500-2,000   **SWO**

A late 19thC George Jones majolica stilton dish and cover, the cover with butterflies, lilies and bulrushes on a pale blue ground, with molded base.

11in (28cm) diam
$2,000-3,000   **SWO**

A late 19thC George Jones oval twin-handled Majolica tureen, the border formed as rustic branches extending to form handles, the blue ground relief molded with a hare and two leverets amidst ferns on green glazed plinth, relief molded diamond registration mark.

14.5in (37cm) wide
$700-1,000   **L&T**

A Wedgwood majolica wall charger, modeled in low relief with sea nymph, Thetis, mother of Achilles riding a sea serpent, scrolling foliage on rim, herons standing on classical dolphins, impressed Wedgwood mark, small chip to back rim.

15in (38cm) diam
$1,500-2,000   **WW**

A late 19thC Continental majolica four-tier oyster stand, of tapered form with eel-loop handle and revolving base, painted with colored glazes, old metal rod repair through the middle.

12in (22cm) high
$600-700   **DN**

A late 19thC Continental majolica basket.

$70-100   **DN**

An exceptional Marblehead corseted vase, incised by Arthur Baggs, with a geometric pattern of long vertical stems and small squares, with ship mark/"AB/T".

This piece commands a high price because it is rare, the better of only two known, designed and perfectly executed by a master and more Viennese than American in style.

8.5in (21.5cm) high
$75,000-85,000   **DRA**

A Marblehead pottery vase, executed by Arthur Baggs, with a stippled green body, pottery mark, initials for Mr. Baggs and "T" possibly for Hannah Tutt.

Arthur Baggs became director in 1908. Hannah Tutt worked at the pottery around 1912.

c1912   *4in (10cm) high*
$7,000-7,500   **SK**

A Marblehead pottery vase, decorated by Hannah Tutt, in five colors and grapevine pattern, pottery mark, artist's initials on base, tight rim hairline.

c1912   *3.5in (9cm) high*
$3,000-4,000   **SK**

A Marblehead Pottery vase, by Hannah Tutt, rim hairline.

The Marblehead Pottery was established by Herbert J. Hall in Marblehead MA, in 1904. It closed in 1936.

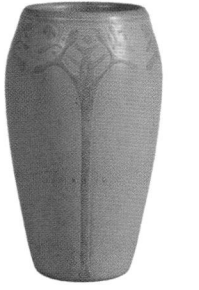

c1912   *7in (18cm) high*
$2,000-2,500   **SK**

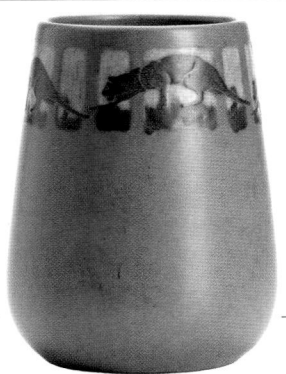

A Marblehead vase, by Hannah Tutt, with black crouching panthers in front of green stylized trees and an amber sky, hairline to rim, possibly from firing, glaze thinness near base, stamped ship mark.

c1912   *7in (18cm) high*
$35,000-40,000   **DRA**

A Marblehead cat-decorated two-color pottery vase, impressed pottery mark.

c1907   7.5in (19cm) diam
$12,000-15,000   SK

A rare Marblehead vase, excised with panels of crouching gray panthers in front of a yellow ground, with green grass and blue trees, 1in tight line to rim, and ship mark.

                    6.5in (16.5cm) high
$25,000-30,000   DRA

A Marblehead four-color decorated pottery vase, with incised decoration, impressed pottery mark and pottery label.

                    7in (17.75cm) high
$5,000-6,000   SK

A Marblehead corseted vase covered in smooth indigo matte glaze, 3in Y-shaped line from rim, mark covered in glaze.

                    8.75in (22cm) high
$400-600   DRA

A Marblehead vase, decorated in wax resist with stylized trees in blue-gray with indigo on smooth speckled ground, small chip, ship mark.

                    8in (20cm) high
$5,000-7,000   DRA

A Marblehead barrel-shaped vase, incised with stylized butterflies and blooms in polychrome on a matte mustard ground, and ship mark.

                    4.5in (11.5cm) high
$5,000-6,000   DRA

A Marblehead four color vase, decorated in caramel color with tree trunks in medium colored caramel, with blue/green leaves, initials of potter and decorator.

c1904   4in (10cm) high
$4,000-6,000   SK

A Marblehead ovoid vase, matt-painted with a grapevine in blue-green, brown, and green, on a mustard ground, with ship mark and paper label.

                    5in (12.5cm) high
$2,000-3,000   DRA

An unusual Marblehead teapot, by Arthur Baggs, with a geometric pattern in black on dark green, ship stamp and "AEB/HT".

                    6in (15cm) high
$9,500-11,500   DRA

A Marblehead small tapered vessel, covered in smooth matte gray-purple glaze, with oval paper label.

                    3.5in (9cm) diam
$300-400   DRA

A rare Marblehead vertical plaque, incised with a landscape of evergreens, mounted in period Arts & Crafts frame, three short firing lines, one continues into deep crazing line, with two ship medallions.

plaque 9.75in (24.75cm) high
$70,000-80,000   DRA

MARTIN BROTHERS

- Best known for their highly original and striking salt-glazed pottery grotesque birds, the Martin Brothers were Robert, modeler; Walter, thrower; Edwin, decorator; and Charles, part-time business administrator.
- After Robert studied at the Lambeth School of Art and trained as a stone carver, he led the family enterprise in their pottery studio in Fulham, London, which opened in 1873. They moved to a larger studio in Southall in 1877.
- Their animals usually have detachable heads and can be used as tobacco jars. Sporting humanistic grins, they were clearly inspired by the Gothic Revival. Martin Brothers also produced a range of vases with Japanese and naturalistic incised decoration.
- The quality of the design and the condition usually determine the value. While Martin Brothers hollow-wares tend to command lower prices, animals groups on wooden stands are rarer and therefore highly sought after.
- Marks include "RW Martin & Brothers", "Martin Brothers", and early pieces are signed "Martin", along with the date, a number and often a location.
- Production slowed around the time of the outbreak of WWI until the factory finally closed in 1915, although a small amount of work was produced until 1923.

A Martin Brothers stoneware miniature bird, modeled with wings outstretched and beak open, in shades of blue and green on a buff ground, incised "Martin Bros 10-1900 London".

1900   *3.75in (9.5cm) high*

$9,000-11,000   **WW**

A Martin Bros. stoneware bird jar with cover with shades of blue, green and ocher, original label to wood base incised "Martin Bros, London & Southall 4-1901" to head and base.

9.5in (24cm) high

$20,000-25,000   **WW**

A Martin Brothers stoneware 'Monk' bird jar and cover, modeled standing with shaven head and solemn expression, in shades of blue, green and brown, incised "RW Martin London & Southall 10-1905" to head, restored.

1905   *9.5in (24cm) high*

$12,000-18,000   **WW**

A Martin Brothers stoneware miniature bird jar and cover, modeled standing upright, the head cast slightly to the right, in shades of ocher and blue, on ebonized wooden base, incised "Martin Bros, London & Southall", hairline to back rim of cover.

4.25in (11cm) high

$5,000-7,000   **WW**

A rare Martin Brothers stoneware monkey vase and cover, by Robert Wallace Martin, modeled on haunches with arms resting in front with forward-looking stare, in shades of brown, blue and ocher, incised "R W Martin & Bros, London & Southall", restored rims.

A monkey is an unusual animal for Robert Martin to model and this figure might relate to his sister's death caused by a monkey bite.

10.75in (27cm) high

$18,000-22,000   **WW**

A Martin Ware three-handled loving cup, incised with three pictorial panels, and inscribed "Morning", "Noon", and "Night", with incised marks "R. W. Martin/ London/ 4-1875".

1875   *6in (15.5cm) high*

$3,000-4,000   **L&T**

An early Martin Brothers stoneware jug, incised and painted with Narcissi, incised "Martin London & Southall".

c1880   *8.75in (22.5cm) high*

$900-1,100   **WW**

An early Martin Brothers stoneware jug, incised with simple leaves, incised "Martin London & Southall".

c1880   *8.75in (22.5cm) high*

$900-1,100   **WW**

A Martin Brothers stoneware jug, incised with sunflowers, in shades of blue, green and brown on an ocher ground incised "4-10-81 Martin London", restored chip to inside of top rim.

1881   *9.75in (25cm) high*

$700-1,000   **WW**

A Martin Brothers stoneware jug, the body incised with a frieze of leaves, the handle modeled as a grotesque head, in shades of brown and green on a buff ground, incised "Martin London & Southall 4-82", restoration to exterior of neck.

1882   *9.5in (24cm) high*

$1,500-2,000   **WW**

A Martin Brothers stoneware flask incised and painted in the Aesthetic style with butterflies flying past iris and bulrushes in shades of ocher and blue on a buff ground with plated metal stopper incised "10-1892, Martin Bros, London & Southall".

1892   *9in (24cm) high*

$4,000-5,000   **WW**

An unusual Martin Brothers stoneware face mug, by Robert Wallace Martin, each side modeled with a smiling face, in shades of brown highlighted in black and white, incised "R W Martin & Bros London & Southall 7.2.1911".

1911   *4.75in (12cm) high*

$5,000-7,000   **WW**

A Martin Brothers stoneware face jug, modeled with grimacing and smiling face, covered in a blue/green glaze, incised "R.W.Martin & Bros, Southall".

5.25in (13.5cm) high

$2,000-3,000   **WW**

An early Martin Brothers stoneware beaker vase by Robert Wallace Martin, manufactured at Pomona House, incised with a band of stiff leaf decoration above lappet bands, in shades of green and blue on an ocher ground incised "F 11 R W Martin Fulham 8-74", minor hairline to top rim.

1874   *4.25in (11cm) high*

$1,000-1,200   **WW**

An early Martin Brothers stoneware vase, by Robert Wallace Martin, cylindrical form, incised with roundels and radiating foliate panels in shades of blue on a gray ground incised "R W Martin, London 2-1877 N17", restored.

This vase shows similarities in style to examples produced by the French potter Jean-Charles Cazin, engravings of which were published in Revue de l'Art Ancien et Moderne. These engravings published in 1901 were drawn by Edgar Kettle who worked at the Martin Brothers pottery and date from before 1875 when Cazin left the nearby Fulham Pottery.

1877   *14.25in (36.5cm) high*

$900-1,100   **WW**

A Martin Brothers stoneware vase, incised with butterflies and wild flowers, below chevron bands, in shades of green, brown and white on a buff ground, incised "1.9.83 R W Martin & Bros, London & Southall", restored neck.

1883   *9.75in (25cm) high*

$1,400-1,600   **WW**

A Martin Brothers stoneware vase, incised with birds and a butterfly flying past blackberry sprays in shades of blue, green and brown on an ocher ground, incised "10-1886 R W Martin & Bros, London & Southall".

1883   *9in (23cm) high*

$1,500-2,000   **WW**

A Martin Brothers stoneware vase, of tall and slender form, incised "R.W. Martin & Bros London & Southall", base of neck restuck.

1888   *15in (38.5cm) high*

$600-800   **SWO**

A Martin Brothers vase, of tall and slender form decorated with herons in a naturalistic landscape, incised base "R W Martin & Bros, London and Southall, dated 2/1888", base of the neck restuck.

1888   *15.25in (38.75cm) high*

$600-700   **SWO**

A Martin Brothers stoneware vase by Robert Wallace Martin, incised with white opium poppies and butterflies, in shades of white, green and brown on a buff ground, incised "7-1889, RW Martin Bros, London & Southall".

1889   *13in (33cm) high*
$3,000-4,000   **WW**

A Martin Brothers stoneware vase incised with grotesque scaly fish and eels in green and brown on a gray/blue ground, with carved foliage frieze on the pierced shoulder, incised "5-1890 Martin Brothers London & Southall".

1890   *6in (16cm) high*
$5,000-6,000   **WW**

A Martin Brothers stoneware vase, by Walter and Edwin Martin, incised with comical birds standing, perched and flying past foliage sprays, finely modeled and painted in shades of white, blue, green and brown on an ocher ground, mounted with lamp fittings, incised "5-1893 Martin Bros, London & Southall", hairline to top rim, drilled base.

1893   *7.75in (20cm) high*
$1,000-1,500   **WW**

A Martin Brothers stoneware gourd vase, by Edwin Martin, incised with veins in shades of blue and green, incised "10-1898 Martin Bros, London & Southall", star crack to base.

1898   *8.75in (22cm) high*
$2,000-3,000   **WW**

A Martin Brothers stoneware miniature vase, incised with jellyfish, in shades of green on a buff ground, incised "11-99 Martin Bros, London".

1899   *3in (7.5cm) high*
$1,000-1,200   **WW**

A Martin Brothers stoneware vase, incised with dragons, in shades of brown on a pale blue ground, incised "12-1899, Martin Bros London & Southall", restored crack to rim.

1899   *9.5in (24cm) high*
$5,000-7,000   **WW**

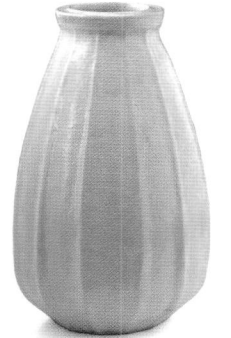

A Martin Brothers stoneware gourd vase, by Robert Wallace Martin, covered in a white glaze, incised "R W Martin & Bros, London & Southall".

10.75in (27cm) high
$800-1,200   **WW**

A Martin Brothers stoneware gourd vase, by Edwin Martin, tall twisted neck, glazed in shades of green and blue, incised "Martin".

5.75in (14.5cm) high
$800-1,200   **WW**

A Martin Brothers stoneware gourd vase, twisted body with incised detailing, in shades of green, blue and brown, incised "Martin, London".

5in (13cm) high
$600-900   **WW**

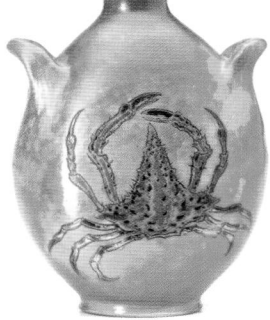

A Martin Brothers urn, incised with crabs, restoration to body line, incised "6-1903/Martin Bros/London + Southall".

1903   *7.5in (19cm) high*
$700-1,000   **DRA**

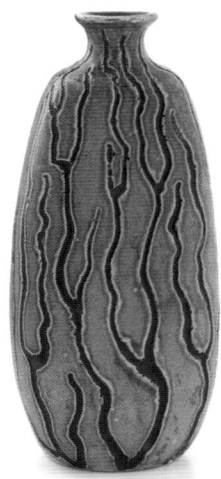

A Martin Brothers stoneware gourd vase, by Edwin and Walter Martin, incised with ribs, in shades of green on an ocher ground, incised "5-1904 Martin Bros London & Southall", "Harriman Judd" label, minor restoration to top rim.

1904   3.75in (9.5cm) high

$500-700   **WW**

A Martin Brothers stoneware gourd vase, by Edwin and Walter Martin, with five loop handles applied to the shoulder, covered in a mottled blue/brown glaze with green detailing, incised "6 - 1905 Martin Bros, London & Southall"

1905   6.25in (16cm) high

$1,800-2,000   **WW**

A Martin Brothers stoneware gourd vase, by Walter and Edwin Martin, painted in shades of blue and green, incised "6-1901 Martin Bros, London & Southall", hairline body crack.

1901   3.25in (8.5cm) high

$500-700   **WW**

A Martin Brothers stoneware miniature vase, incised with fish, crabs and shell fish, in shades of green and brown, incised "12-13 Martin Bros, London & Southall", minor burst air bubbles in glaze firing.

3.25in (8.5cm) high

$1,200-1,500   **WW**

A Martin Brothers stoneware vase and cover, by Walter and Edwin Martin, incised with grotesque and scaly fish amongst jellyfish and sea creatures, the cover modeled with a limpet, in shades of blue and gray, incised "2-1912 Martin Bros London & Southall" to base and inside cover.

1912   5.5in (14cm) high

$2,000-3,000   **WW**

A Martin Brothers stoneware baluster form vase with incised slipper orchids, flies and dragonflies in shades of brown on a buff ground, incised "Martin Bros, London & Southall".

8in (21cm) high

$2,000-3,000   **WW**

MOORCROFT

- Born to a Staffordshire ceramics painter, William Moorcroft (1872-1945) familiarized himself with historic pottery whilst at college. This knowledge is evident in the range of forms of his early work.
- In the 1890s, he joined James Macintyre & Co., in Burslem. His early Arts and Crafts 'Aurelian' vases were printed patterns, whilst 'Florian Ware', was decorated in the emerging Art Nouveau style.
- Moorcroft set up his own company in 1912 with financial assistance from Liberty & Co.
- By this time, Moorcroft's patterns, including 'Pomegranate', 'Wisteria' and 'Hazeldine', were simpler and bolder, usually with dark grounds and a clear glossy glaze that enhanced the rich colors.
- Success led to the firm receiving a Royal Warrant in 1929. Walter Moorcroft took over the works after his father's death in 1945 and it is still in production today.
- Early Moorcroft pottery can be found in museums throughout the world, including the Victoria and Albert Museum, London.

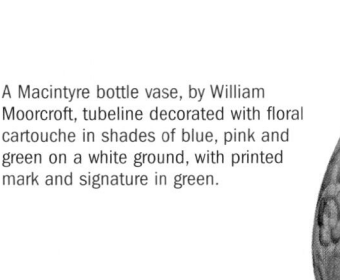

A Macintyre bottle vase, by William Moorcroft, tubeline decorated with floral cartouche in shades of blue, pink and green on a white ground, with printed mark and signature in green.

13.5in (34cm) high

$4,000-5,000 **WW**

A large Moorcroft Florianware vase, of shouldered baluster form, boldly tube-line decorated with panels of irises in shades of blue, printed marks, signed in green, painted mark "M 1059".

16in (40.5cm) high

$3,000-4,000 **L&T**

A Moorcroft Florianware egg cup with raised decoration in shades of blue, signed "W.M." in green and with printed mark to base.

2in (5cm) high

$900-1,100 **JN**

An unusual Moorcroft cylindrical vase, decorated with a landscape in blue and white, on pewter base, "MOORCROFT/Signature/Made in England/281".

1920s *10.5in (26.5cm) high*

$3,500-4,500 **DRA**

A Moorcroft red vase decorated in the "African Lily" pattern, under flambé glaze, on raised circular foot, impressed and signed in blue.

7.5in (19cm) diam

$1,000-1,200 **MAX**

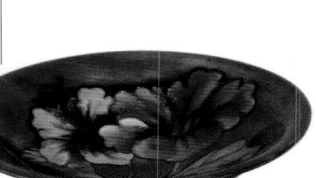

A Walter Moorcroft shallow dish, 'Anemone' pattern, signed and with paper label.

9.5in (24cm) diam

$220-280 **MAX**

A large Moorcroft bulbous vase painted in the 'Anemone' pattern in red on a cobalt ground, ink script signature, stamped "MOORCROFT MADE IN ENGLAND", Queen Mary paper label.

12.5in (32cm) high

$3,000-4,000 **DRA**

A tall early Moorcroft bottle-shaped vase painted in the 'Claremont' pattern with mushrooms in blue-greens and maroon, in script "W. Moorcroft Des.", stamped "RD/NO/420081/MADE FOR SPAULDING & CO".

16.5in (42cm) high

$4,000-5,000 **DRA**

An early Moorcroft biscuit jar, in the 'Eventide' pattern, with original silvered cover and handle, with small glaze flake to rim, on edge of silver, "MOORCROFT/Signature/Made in England", hallmarks on silver.

6.5in (16.5cm) high

$2,000-3,000 **DRA**

MOORCROFT

A Moorcroft 'Finches' pattern baluster vase, designed by Sally Tuffin, decorated in shades of blue, green and red against a blue ground.

c1990   *7.5in (19cm) high*

$300-400   **GORL**

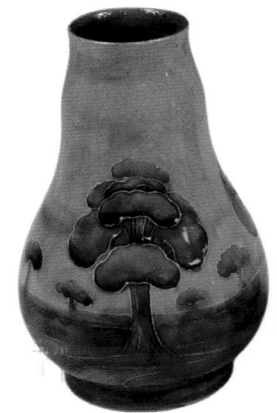
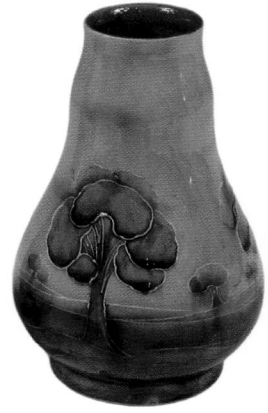

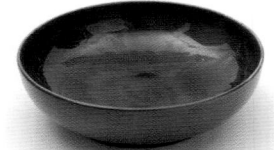

A Moorcroft 'Fish and Seaweed' pattern luster bowl, decorated in a mottled blue red glaze, painted signature and impressed Burslem marks.

8in (20.5cm) diam

$400-500   **GORL**

A pair of Moorcroft 'Hazeldene' pattern vases, printed mark "Made For Liberty & Co", painted signature.

c1910   *6.5in (16cm) high*

$4,000-5,000   **SWO**

A Moorcroft 'Plum' pattern vase, with a slender neck and bulbous body, the body decorated in a blue glaze with fruits and leaves, marked "Moorcroft, Made in England", with the signature and number "M156".

c1920   *9.25in (23cm) high*

$500-700   **LAW**

An early Moorcroft urn in the 'Pomegranate' pattern, stamped "MOORCROFT BURSLEM ENGLAND 5", with signature.

8.5in (21.5cm) high

$1,500-2,000   **DRA**

A pair of Moorcroft 'Pomegranate' pattern baluster slender neck vases, impressed and signed in green.

8.5in (21.5cm) high

$1,200-1,800   **MAX**

A large Moorcroft baluster vase, decorated in the 'Pomegranate' pattern against a blue ground, impressed and signed in blue.

12.5in (32cm) high

$2,000-3,000   **MAX**

A pair of Moorcroft 'Spring Flowers' pattern lamp bases, impressed marks, initialed in blue, bears 'By Appointment' labels.

13in (33cm) high

$2,000-3,000   **L&T**

A Moorcroft vase by Anji Davenport, 'Angel's Trumpet' pattern, produced for Moorcroft Collector's Weekend, limited edition number 134, with factory and artist marks.

1998   *7.5in (19cm) high*

$400-600   **ROS**

NEWCOMB COLLEGE

- Newcomb College, was established in New Orleans in 1895 as a vocational training institution for young women artists. Active until 1940, it provided employment for graduates at a time when there were few work opportunities for women.
- The studio produced some 70,000 pieces designed by approximately ninety women artists. Its founder, designer Ellsworth Woodward (1861-1939), saw the department as a vehicle for training a new generation of women potters.
- The distinguished potter Mary G. Sheerer of Cincinnati was hired to teach pottery-making and decorating. Talented designers and instructors such as Sadie Irvine, Harriet Joor, Anna Frances Simpson, and Henrietta Bailey contributed their talents to the success of the pottery.
- Influenced by the Arts and Crafts movement, their designs exhibited unique imagery of flora and fauna native to the southern United States.
- Newcomb pieces were given soft curvaceous shapes inspired by peasant pottery and Oriental wares. They are best known for their unique soft blue and green glazes.
- The company won international acclaim at the Paris Exposition of 1900. Newcomb College pottery is collectable today, commanding higher prices for earlier pieces.

A Newcomb College early vessel, carved by Marie de Hoa LeBlanc, with five stylized blue and white rabbits, marked "NC/MHL/U/K5X/JM".

Exhibited in "Newcomb Pottery, An Enterprize for Southern Women 1895-1940," the Newcomb College of Tulane University and the Smithsonian Institution Traveling Exhibits Services, 1984-87, cat. no. 48.

1902   9.5in (24cm) wide

$90,000-110,000   **DRA**

An early Newcomb College squat vase, painted by Marie de Hoa LeBlanc, with poinsettia, two hairlines from rim, minor colored-in nick to base, marked "NC/MHSB/JM/0048/W/".

1904   6in (15cm) high

$10,000-12,000   **DRA**

An early Newcomb College large three-handled vase, carved by Marie de Hoa LeBlanc, with yellow crocuses on green stems against an indigo ground, firing bubbles under top of handles, marked "NC/MHLB/W /JM/DE8".

Exhibited in "A Century of Ceramics in the United States 1878-1978," Everson Museum of Art, Syracuse, New York, 1979.

1909   9.5in (24cm) wide

$22,000-28,000   **DRA**

A Newcomb College vase, carved by Sadie Irvine, with tall pines in blues and greens, incised "NC/SI/K/ET9/JM".

1911   12in (30cm) high

$13,000-15,000   **DRA**

A Newcomb College transitional bulbous vase, carved and painted by Sadie Irvine with blue narcissus on a light green ground, "NC/JM/SI/FQ61".

1913   7.25in (18.5cm) high

$2,000-2,500   **DRA**

A large Newcomb College squat vessel carved by Sadie Irvine with a full moon behind live oaks and Spanish moss, "NC/SI/JH/49/TB78".

1931   6.75in (17cm) high

$4,000-5,000   **DRA**

A Newcomb College vase, carved by Sadie Irvine with blue blossoms on a blue ground, "NC/JM/SI/0011/79".

1925   7.5in (19cm) high

$2,000-3,000   **DRA**

An early Newcomb College biscuit jar with cover, carved by Harriet Joor, with blue and yellow water lilies, restored chip and tight hairline to rim of jar, marked "NC/HJ/JM/JJ34/W".

Exhibited in Newcomb Pottery, An Enterprize for Southern Women 1895-1940, the Newcomb College of Tulane University and the Smithsonian Institution Traveling Exhibits Services, 1984-87, cat. no.84.

1903   7in (18cm) high

$10,000-15,000   **DRA**

An early Newcomb College bulbous vase, by Ada Lonnegan, with fleshy gardenias on a cobalt ground, marked "NC/JM/Lonnegan/XX63/Q".

Exhibited in "A Century of Ceramics in the United States 1878-1978," Everson Art Museum, Syracuse, New York, 1979.

1904   7in (16cm) high

$12,000-15,000   **DRA**

DECORATIVE ARTS

A Newcomb College bud vase, by Joseph Mayer, with floral decoration, impressed "NC" and "JM" marks with painted date code "JJ40".

1918   *5.5in (14cm) high*

$4,000-5,000   **FRE**

An early Newcomb College tall candlestick, carved by Leona Nicholson, with three large whimsical frogs pointing to crescent moons, chip to base from firing, marked "LN/H38X".

c1902   *11.5in (29cm) high*

$17,000-20,000   **DRA**

A Newcomb College vase, carved by Mazie Ryan, with clusters of wisteria on a pale blue ground, incised "NC, M.T.RYAN, 1904 MRYAN, JM NNZ Q".

1904   *9in (23cm) high*

$45,000-50,000   **DRA**

A Newcomb College vase carved by A. F. Simpson with tall pines under a moonlit sky, incised "NC/AFS/JM/KC7/ 133 1/2".

1919   *8in (21cm) high*

$10,000-12,000   **DRA**

A Newcomb College bulbous vase, sharply carved by A.F. Simpson, with live oak trees and Spanish moss in a landscape with yellow sky, 1920, "NC/AFS/LE47/275".

1920   *5in (13cm) high*

$3,000-3,500   **DRA**

A Newcomb College squat bowl, carved by A.F.Simpson with blue and yellow daffodils on a blue ground, "NC/JM/AFS/KV45/256".

1920   *6.5in (16.5cm) wide*

$2,000-3,000   **DRA**

A Newcomb College tall cylindrical vase, carved by A.F. Simpson, with tall trees laden with Spanish moss in front of a full moon, 1925, "NC/JM/AFS/ OQ32/229", paper label.

1925   *10.25in (26cm) high*

$5,000-7,000   **DRA**

A Newcomb College vase, decorated by A.F. Simpson with a moonlit bayou scene, 1928, incised "NC/RC51/144/ AFS/JH".

1928   *11in (28cm) high*

$16,000-18,000   **DRA**

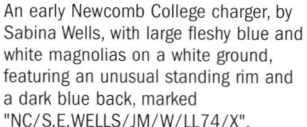

An early Newcomb College charger, by Sabina Wells, with large fleshy blue and white magnolias on a white ground, featuring an unusual standing rim and a dark blue back, marked "NC/S.E.WELLS/JM/W/LL74/X".

Exhibited in "Newcomb Pottery, An Enterprize for Southern Women 1895-1940."

1903   *9in (23cm) diam*

$10,000-12,000   **DRA**

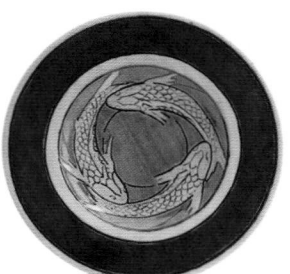

A Newcomb College Pottery bowl, with trumpet form flowers in cream glaze, matte blue body, marked with impressed potter's cipher, decorators initials, numbered.

9in (23cm) diam

$1,500-2,000   **SK**

A tall and early Newcomb College vase, carved by Sadie Irvine, with pine trees on bright blue trunks against a blue-green and ivory ground.

1909   *15.25in (38.5cm) high*

$100,000-120,000   **DRA**

A Newcomb College hand-built tile, modeled with a woman holding a black umbrella in glossy polychrome, mounted in a fine Arts & Crafts frame, restored firing line, light abrasion to surface, unmarked.

tile 4.75in (12cm) high

$700-1,000   **DRA**

A George Ohr pinched, notched, and folded vessel, with scalloped rim covered in an unusual copper gunmetal glaze with bright orange interior, signature.

5in (13cm) high

$7,000-9,000   **DRA**

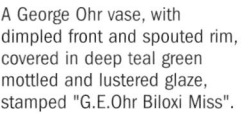

A George Ohr vase, with dimpled front and spouted rim, covered in deep teal green mottled and lustered glaze, stamped "G.E.Ohr Biloxi Miss".

5in (13cm) diam

$6,000-8,000   **DRA**

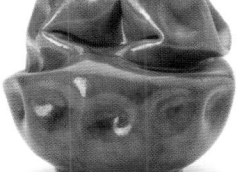

A George Ohr dimpled and folded vessel, covered in a sheer green glaze, the buff clay showing through, stamped "BILOXI MISS. GEO. E. OHR".

3.5in (9cm) high

$10,000-12,000   **DRA**

A George Ohr straight-walled vessel, with folded rim, covered in a blood red, yellow, brown, and lime green dripping and mottled leathery matte glaze, several short firing lines in crooks of folds, clearly from manufacture, with script signature.

George E. Ohr (1857-1918) has been called the first art potter in the US.

5in (13cm) diam

$35,000-40,000   **DRA**

A George Ohr spherical vase, with deep in-body twist to shoulder and rim, covered in gunmetal and deep green speckled glaze, stamped "G.E. Ohr Biloxi Miss".

4in (10cm) high

$6,000-8,000   **DRA**

A George Ohr tall vase, with two ribbon handles, covered in a spectacular red and green mottled glaze, stamped English Text "G.E. OHR, Biloxi, Miss.".

Featured in a period trick photograph of the potter, published in Robert Blasberg's "George E. Ohr and his Biloxi Art Pottery," 1973.

8.5in (21.5cm) high

$90,000-110,000   **DRA**

An exceptional George Ohr bulbous vase, the upper part covered in an unusual raspberry and green matte leathery glaze, the lower in blue-green semi-matte glaze, with script signature.

6.75in (17cm) high

$18,000-20,000   **DRA**

A George Ohr bisque clay pitcher, by with two deep in-body twists and a ribbon handle, script signature.

6in (15cm) high

$7,000-9,000   **DRA**

A rare George Ohr milk can-shaped vase, with single curled handle and accordion snake, covered in green and indigo gunmetal glaze, stamped "G.E.Ohr Biloxi Miss".

6in (15cm) high

$16,000-18,000   **DRA**

A large and unusual George Ohr bulbous vase and cover, covered in vertical strips of raspberry, yellow, black, and amber glaze, the cover a cup-shape with finial, base stamped "G.E.Ohr Biloxi, Miss.", cover stamped "GEO. E. OHR BILOXI, MISS".

7in (18cm) high

$14,000-16,000   **DRA**

A George Ohr open and squashed vessel, with folded and rounded rim, covered in a raspberry, aquamarine, and indigo speckled and mottled glaze, stamped "Biloxi, Miss, Geo. E. Ohr".

5in (13cm) wide

$13,000-16,000   **DRA**

A George Ohr ashtray/ matchholder with floriform top in mottled gunmetal and green glaze on yellow base, the back printed with "A Biloxi Welcome" stamped "G.E. OHR, Biloxi, Miss".

4.75in (12cm) wide

$1,500-2,000   **DRA**

A Pilkington's Lancastrian pottery jug, by Gordon Forsyth, with golden brown luster over orange, flowers, impressed mark, artist cypher date mark.

1910   4in (11cm) diam.
$4,000-5,000   WW

A Pilkington's Lancastrian pottery vase and cover, by Gordon M. Forsyth, shape 2229, with painted columns of lilies and scrolling flowers, inscribed "Ave Maria Gratia Plena" with gold luster on ruby, impressed mark, artist cypher, hairline to cover.

1919   17in (43cm) high
$5,000-7,000   WW

A Pilkington's Lancastrian pottery vase, by Richard Joyce with painted galleon, in gold and ruby luster on a graduated green ground, impressed mark, applied paper label.

1908   7in (19cm) high
$3,000-4,000   WW

A Pilkington's Lancastrian pottery vase, by Richard Joyce, shape 2809, with painted carnations in shades of ruby and copper luster on greenish blue ground, impressed marks, some restoration.

1909   6in (15cm) high
$1,500-2,000   WW

A Pilkington's Lancastrian wall charger, designed by Walter Crane and painted by Richard Joyce with a knight on a rearing horse, the rim with a ferocious dragon in vivid gold and red luster on a cream ground, inscribed "Un Chevalier Sans Peur et Sans Reproche", with impressed factory mark, painted artist and designer cyphers and date mark.

1912   19in (48cm) diam
$35,000-55,000   WW

A Pilkington's Lancastrian pottery solifleur vase, by Richard Joyce, with painted running stags, in gold on a gold luster ground, impressed mark.

1913   9in (24cm) high
$2,000-3,000   WW

A Pilkington Lancastrian Heraldic vase with cover, by Richard Joyce, with painted frieze of three mounted knights, in gold on a blue ground, impressed mark with date, artist cypher and date, restoration to top.

1917   17in (42cm) high
$5,000-6,000   WW

A Pilkington's Lancastrian vase and cover, by Richard Joyce, painted with a frieze of courting hares in a landscape in deep ruby luster on amber ground, impressed marks, painted artist cypher and date code.

1919   5in (13cm) high
$4,000-5,000   WW

A Pilkingtons Lancastrian vase, by Richard Joyce, decorated in a green luster, depicting two knights in armour with a central crest of an English lion, the vase embellished with gilt luster decoration and showing a religious cross to the reverse, monogram for Richard Joyce on the base, damaged and restored.

13in (33cm) high
$600-700   LAW

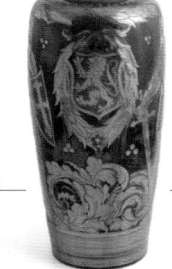

A Pilkington's Lancastrian pottery vase by Richard Joyce, with frieze of mounted Greek warriors in gold and ruby luster on red ground, impressed marks, artist cypher.

11in (28cm) high
$4,000-5,000   WW

A Pilkington's Royal Lancastrian vase, by William Mycock, with painted flowers in shades of gold and purple luster on blue ground.

1924   *9in (23cm) high*

$2,000-3,000   **WW**

A Pilkington's Lancastrian vase, by William Mycock, with lobed form, painted heraldic panel flanked by panels of scrolling flowers and foliage in shades of copper and gold luster on ruby luster ground, impressed mark, painted artist cypher.

1919   *13in (33cm) high*

$3,000-4,000   **WW**

A Pilkington's Lancastrian vase and cover, by William S Mycock, shape 2229, with painted galleons on either side of a heraldic lion shield in copper and ruby luster on a lime green ground, impressed mark, original label, faint hairline to rim of cover.

1911   *17in (43cm) high*

$7,000-10,000   **WW**

A Pilkington's Lancastrian vase, by Walter Crane, painted by William Mycock with heraldic lions above Tudor rose and heart design in shades of red and gold, the interior glazed gold, with impressed mark, painted artist cyphers and date code.

1912   *8.75in (22cm) diam*

$5,000-6,000   **WW**

A Pilkington's Royal Lanastrian vase, by William Mycock, painted with heraldic lions amid Tudor rose and cypresses, in shades of gold and ruby luster on a vivid blue ground, the neck with fleur de lys, impressed mark, painted artist cypher and date.

1917   *8.5in (21.5cm) high*

$3,000-4,000   **WW**

A Pilkington's Royal Lancastrian vase, by William Mycock, painted with chrysanthemums in shades of gold and ruby luster on a blue ground, impressed mark, painted artist cypher and date mark.

1923   *8.75in (22.5cm) high*

$4,000-6,000   **WW**

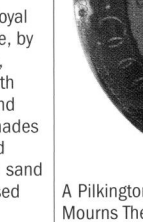

A Pilkington's Royal Lancastrian vase, by William Mycock, shape 3107, with painted birds and sunflowers in shades of ruby and gold luster on a pale sand ground, impressed mark.

11in (28cm) high

$4,000-6,000   **WW**

A Pilkington Lancastrian charger, 'The Conquered Mourns The Conqueror is Undone', by Gladys Rogers, with shield decoration to well, the rim with inscription, impressed and painted marks on reverse, minor faults.

1911   *19in (48.5cm) diam*

$4,000-5,000   **WW**

An early 20thC Royal Lancastrian 'uranium orange' glazed bowl, mounted on a Tudric pewter circular foot.

8.5in (21.5cm) diam

$280-320   **SWO**

ROOKWOOD POTTERY

- Maria Longworth Nichols originally founded the Rookwood Pottery in 1880.
- William Watts Taylor took over its running in 1890 and hired German chemist, Karl Lagenbeck to produce original glazes including their unique matte glaze.
- Laura Fry patented their famous airbrush technique while Kataro Shirayamadani introduced an oriental feel to designs.
- From 1905, Rookwood introduced a more economical production line, where decoration was embossed in the mold and not hand applied.
- The pottery won a number of awards including the Exposition Universelle in Paris in 1889 and the World Columbian Exposition in Chicago in 1893.
- Pieces are marked profusely, including a die-stamped flame designation, a Roman numeral date, shape number, clay composition, and the incised signature of the artist.
- Arthur Townley currently runs Rookwood and produces a limited number of pieces each year from the original molds.

A Rookwood Standard glaze dark baluster vase, painted by Matt Daly, with a day lily on dark brown ground, glazing inconsistency over leaves, uncrazed, "ROOKWOOD 1884/117C/MAD".

1884　　　*7.75in (19cm) high*

$250-450　　　**DRA**

A Rookwood Standard glaze stoppered jug, painted by E.T. Hurley, with branches of leaves and amber berries, flame mark/ETH, several scratches.

c1898　　　*9in (23cm) high*

$700-900　　　**DRA**

A Rookwood standard glaze bulbous vase, painted by Mary Nourse, with brown nasturtiums, abrasion around shoulder, flame mark/M.N.

1902　　　*7in (18cm) high*

$400-500　　　**DRA**

A Rookwood Standard glaze vase, painted by Mary Nourse, with oak leaves and acorns, flame mark.

1903　　　*10in (25cm) high*

$600-900　　　**DRA**

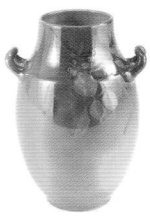

A Rookwood standard glaze two-handled vase, painted by O.G. Reed, with branches of leaves and berries, restoration to one handle, flame mark/OGR.

1893　　　*7.5in (19cm) high*

$400-600　　　**DRA**

A Rookwood standard glaze vase with flat shoulder, painted by O.G. Reed, with amber clover blossoms, a few scratches, flame mark/OGR.

1895　　　*5in (13cm) high.*

$400-500　　　**DRA**

A rare Rookwood carved Standard glaze vase, by John D. Wareham, with red-hot pokers in relief against a dark brown ground, a few short scratches, seconded mark for glaze, misses around bottom, with flame mark and "732B/JDW/X".

1900　　　*10.25in (26cm) high*

$6,000-8,000　　　**DRA**

A Rookwood rare carved Standard glaze narrow vase, incised and painted probably by K. Shirayamadani, with amber fish on bottle green ground, the surface with long drips, minor flake on footring, flame mark/589E/0.

1900　　　*8.25in (21cm) high*

$4,000-5,000　　　**DRA**

A Rookwood Standard glaze vase, decorated by Kataro Shirayamadani, decorated with yellow flowers, pottery mark and date, artist's mark and "X" to base.

c1900　　　*11.5in (29cm) high*

$5,000-6,000　　　**SK**

A monumental Rookwood vase, decorated by Albert R. Valentian, with autumn leaves, pottery and date mark, artist's initials over the letter "D".

1990　　　*21in (53.5cm) high*

$3,500-4,500　　　**SK**

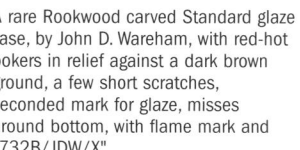

A Rookwood Standard Glaze light ewer, with Gorham silver overlay, painted by Mary Nourse with poppies, the silver with poppies and leaves, flame mark/496C/W/M.N./L/Gorham Mfg. Co/R40.

1892　　　*10.5in (26.5cm) high*

$3,000-4,000　　　**DRA**

ROOKWOOD GLAZES

- The Standard glaze was developed in 1884, discontinued 1909. A translucent high gloss with a yellow tinge, Standard glaze gives the underlying design a darker aspect.
- Also developed in 1884, Iris is a clear lead-based glaze with a high sheen created by the extremely high lead content which by 1912 was recognised as a health hazard. Pieces often incised W for white glaze. At Rookwood the Iris glaze was known as white glaze because it is white in its unfired state.
- Another high gloss glaze, Sea Green confers a blue-green color to the underglaze decoration and was thus suited to seascapes.
- Rookwood devised its own version of Grueby's successful matt glaze, simply called Matte, around 1900.
- Vellum was introduced c1900. Usually clear, sometimes with green and yellow tints, it creates hazing on the underglaze.
- Rookwood's Jewel Porcelain, introduced in 1916, is clear gloss glaze with tiny air bubbles that produce a similar effect to the Vellum glaze but without a waxy appearance.

A Rookwood iris glaze bulbous vase, beautifully decorated by Lenore Asbury, with branches of white hollyhocks, and wonderful subtle gradations of tone, flame mark/X/1278C/LA.

Iris Glaze is one of the finest glaze lines produced at the Cincinnati pottery. The name derived from the iris plant – known for its luminosity and opalescence. The glaze is unsurpassed for the clarity, richness of color and depth that it imparts to the objects it covers. It is highly refractive and made the surface very shiny, although it is prone to crazing.

1910   12in (30.5cm) high

$8,000-10,000   **DRA**

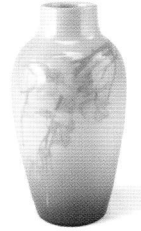

A Rookwood Iris glaze vase, painted by Sarah Coyne, with pale pink roses and celadon leaves, restoration to drill hole on bottom, flame mark/V/940C/Artist cipher.

c1905   10.75in (27.5cm) high

$1,000-1,200   **DRA**

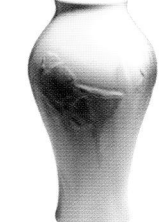

A Rookwood relief Iris glaze baluster vase, carved by Matt Daly, with purple and red irises on a butter yellow glossy ground, restored drilled hole on bottom, flame mark.

1900   11.25in (28cm) high

$1,500-2,000   **DRA**

A Rookwood Iris glaze ovoid vase, painted by Ed Diers, with violets on a purple ground, 1902, minor glaze flake to rim, flame mark/II/732C/ED/W.

1902   6.25in (16cm) high

$1,000-1,500   **DRA**

A Rookwood Iris glaze corseted vase, painted by Ed Diers, with branches of cherry blossoms on a blue-to-pink ground, uncrazed, flame mark, "XI/1659E/W/ED".

1911   7.25in (18cm) high

$1,700-2,000   **DRA**

A Rookwood Iris glaze baluster vase, slip-decorated by Elizabeth Lincoln, with wisteria clusters, flame mark.

1910   8in (20cm) high

$1,400-1,800   **DRA**

A Rookwood Iris glaze ovoid vase, painted by Elizabeth Nourse, with blue violets on a celadon ground, flame mark/IX/939D/E.N./W.

1909   7in (18cm) high

$2,500-3,000   **DRA**

A Rookwood Iris glaze ovoid vase, painted by Fred Rothenbusch with pink trumpet vines on a mauve ground, flame mark/I/917D/FR.

1901   6.5in (16.5cm) high

$1,500-2,000   **DRA**

A rare Rookwood miniature Iris glaze pitcher, painted by Sarah Sax, with branches of yellow flowers on pink ground, flame mark/1670F/ W/Artist cipher.

1900   3in (7.5cm) high

$1,000-1,300   **DRA**

A Rookwood Iris glaze tapering vase, painted by Carl Schmidt, with diaphanous white irises on a black-to-pink shaded ground, uncrazed, neatly drilled bottom, flame mark, "W", artist cipher.

1910   9in (22.5cm) high

$5,000-6,000   **DRA**

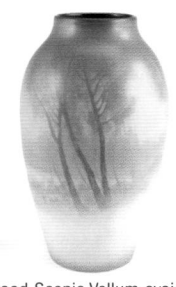

A Rookwood Scenic Vellum ovoid vase, painted by Sally Coyne, with a snowy landscape at dusk, flame mark/XXIII/900C/V/SEC.

1923   8.5in (21.5cm) high

$2,500-3,000   **DRA**

A Rookwood tall Scenic Vellum flaring vase, painted by E.T. Hurley, with a river landscape at dusk with with pink sky, flame mark/XVII/1369D/E/ V/E.T.H.

1917   9.25in (23.5cm) high

$2,500-3,500   **DRA**

A Rookwood pottery Scenic Vellum vase, painted by Sallie E. Coyne, depicting tall pines against a snowy landscape, with impressed marks.

1916   6.25in (16cm) high

$2,500-3,000   **FRE**

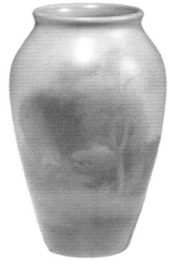

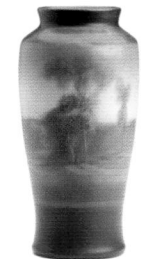

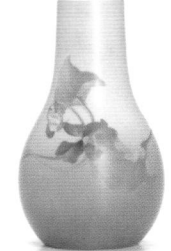

A Rookwood Scenic Vellum ovoid vase, painted by Fred Rothenbusch, with trees in a hilly landscape, uncrazed, flame mark.

1937   7.75in (19cm) high

$3,000-4,000   **DRA**

A Rookwood Scenic Vellum vase, by Fred Rothenbusch, with maker's mark, artist's signature and numbered "952 D V" to base, burst bubble.

1920   9.5in (24cm) high

$3,000-4,000   **SK**

A Rookwood Scenic Vellum vase, painted by Fred Rothenbusch, with a landscape on a cobalt ground, flame mark, "XXXI/1664D/FR".

1931   10.5in (26cm) high

$3,000-4,000   **DRA**

A Rookwood vellum vase, painted by Fred Rothenbusch, with violets on a shaded ground, with flame mark/V/989D/FR.

1905   8.25in (21cm) high

$1,000-1,500   **DRA**

A large Rookwood Scenic Vellum plaque, painted by Ed Diers, with a Venetian scene in mauves and ivory, 'On the Riva', uncrazed, original frame, ED/flame mark.

plaque 14.5in (37cm) wide

$16,000-20,000   **DRA**

A large Rookwood Scenic Vellum plaque, painted by E.T. Hurley, with a mountainous lake landscape in pink hues, mounted in its original ivory-enameled frame, light and sparse crazing, with flame mark and "XLVI/ETH".

1946   14in (37cm) wide

$15,000-18,000   **DRA**

A fine Rookwood Scenic Vellum plaque painted by Sara Sax, 'The Road to the River,' with a snowy mountain road in browns, blues and greens, mounted in original frame, some restored patches to gilding, flame mark/XIX/Sax.

1919   12.5in (32cm) wide

$10,000-14,000   **DRA**

A Rookwood Scenic Vellum plaque, painted by Sara Sax, The Road to the River, with a snowy mountain road in browns, blues and greens, mounted in original frame. Flame mark/XIX/Sax.

1919   12.5in (32cm) wide

$12,000-15,000   **DRA**

A Rookwood Wax Matte tall vase, painted by Elizabeth Barrett, with red dogwood blossoms on a brown butterfat ground, post-factory drill to base, flame mark/artist cipher.

1924   *12in (30.5cm) high*

$500-700   **DRA**

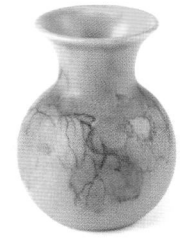

A Rookwood Wax Matte bulbous vase, painted by Katherine Jones, with blue flowers and green leaves on a pink and blue ground, flame mark/KJ.

1927   *6.25in (16cm) high*

$500-700   **DRA**

A large Rookwood Wax Matte vase, painted by Elizabeth Lincoln, with birds and sunflowers, flame mark/XXV/324/LNL.

1925   *17.25in (44cm) high*

$6,000-8,000   **DRA**

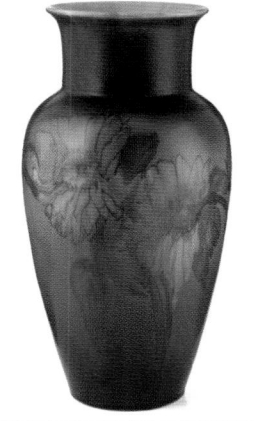

A Rookwood Wax Matte bulbous vase, painted by K. Shirayamadani, with orange and blue crocuses on a shaded ground, flame mark, "XXXV/S", artist cipher.

1935   *6.5in (16cm) high*

$1,500-2,000   **DRA**

A Rookwood Production tall ovoid vase, embossed with jonquils under a bright matte yellow glaze, flame mark.

1922   *9.5in (24cm) high*

$500-600   **DRA**

A Rookwood Z-Line inkwell, with frog lid and organic design to body, covered in matte green glaze, crude restoration to rim chip.

1903   *2.75in (7cm) wide*

$400-500   **DRA**

A pair of Rookwood Production bookends, designed by William McDonald, with tall ships, covered in turquoise crystalline glaze, chip to one, chip and hairline to other, flame mark/WMCD.

1924   *5.5in (14cm) wide*

$250-400   **DRA**

A pair of Rookwood Production owl bookends, designed by William McDonald, and covered in a mat green glaze, flame mark/XXV11/2565/WMC.

1921   *7.25in (18.5cm) high*

$1,000-1,500 pair   **DRA**

A pair of Rookwood Production St. Francis bookends, the saint petting a fox and a bird, flame mark.

1945   *7.5in (19cm) high*

$300-400   **DRA**

A Rookwood Production vase, with tulips covered in a brown glaze.

1914   *10.5in (26.5cm) high*

$300-400   **DRA**

A Rookwood Production vase, covered in a pink glaze, with crazing.

    6in (15cm) high

$70-100   **DRA**

A Rookwood Production vase, embossed with large poppies under a light green matte glaze, flame mark/VII/1005.

1907   *9.75in (25cm) high*

$70-100   **DRA**

A Rookwood Jewel Porcelain lamp base, painted with purple magnolia on an ivory ground and mounted in its original base fixture, mark hidden by base.

13.5in (34.5cm) high

$550-750   DRA

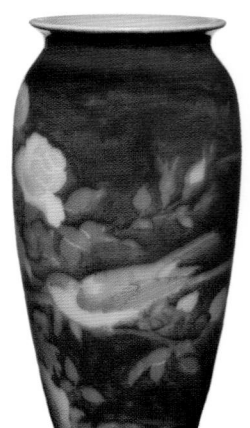

A Rookwood Jewel Porcelain vase, by Jens Jensen, with blue and white dogwood blossoms with brown leaves on ivory ground, flame mark/artist signature.

1944   *9in (23cm) high*

$1,000-1,300   DRA

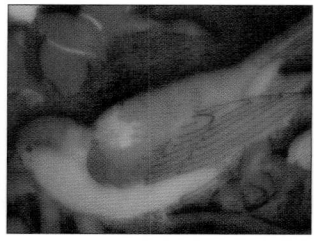

A Rookwood jewel porcelain vase, painted by Arthur Conant, with a bird in a peony garden, a few glaze specks have earned it a seconded mark, flame mark/XX1/2544/artist's cipher/X.

1921   *8in (20.5cm) high*

$2,500-3,500   DRA

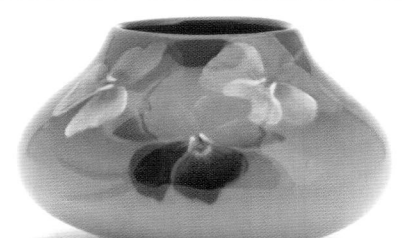

A Rookwood Sea Green squat vessel, painted by Constance F. Baker, with white and gray pansies on a shaded ground, flame mark/IV/536E/C. A. B./X, etched "51".

1904   *5in (12.5cm) wide*

$700-900   DRA

A Rookwood Squeezebag urn, decorated by Wilhelmine Rehm, with stylized foliage in brown on a verdigris ground, with flame mark/XXX/6010E/WR.

1930   *8in (20.5cm) high*

$700-1,000   DRA

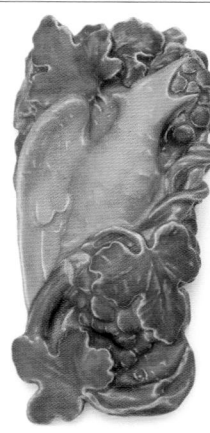

A large Rookwood Faience wall pocket, heavily modeled with a bird perched on a grapevine, with flame mark/XVI/2279.

1916   *14in (35.5cm) h*

$2,000-2,500   DRA

A Rookwood French Red tall baluster vase, painted and carved by Sara Sax, with enamel-type orange, blue and pink flowers on a gun-metal ground, with restoration to section of base, and flame mark/XX1/2551/artist's cipher.

French Red
A rose semi-translucent gloss glaze often used in combination with gloss enamels and/or mat colors on an object with an incised decoration. The rose color is most often seen in combination with a gloss and/or mat black.

1921   *14in (35.5cm) high*

$1,200-1,800   DRA

A Rookwood Faience tile, modeled with a pink magnolia and blue leaf on gray ground, mounted in a fine Arts & Crafts frame, stamped "ROOKWOOD FAIENCE 1714Y/C/730".

6in (15cm) wide

$300-500   DRA

A Rookwood trivet tile, modeled with three white geese in a verdant landscape, flame mark.

1930   *5.75in (14cm) wide*

$300-500   DRA

ROSEVILLE

- Roseville was established in Zanesville, Ohio in 1890. It produced hand painted artistic and functional wares with richly colored glazes that largely offered an inexpensive alternative to Rookwood.
- From 1900 the company produced a range known as 'Rozane Ware', under the art director Frederick Hurten Rhead. The factory soon became more innovative and experimental, bringing out new ranges such as 'Della Robbia' and 'Woodland'.
- Methods moved towards molding as demand for hand-painted wares fell after World War I. Among the most successful and collectable of the Roseville ranges are geometric Art Deco 'Futura' pieces, introduced in 1928, and the 'Fuchsia' range introduced in the 1930s.
- While 'Experimental' pieces are unique and highly desirable, the more common 'Pinecone' line tends to be less sought after. Value can be determined by color range. As taste and fashion varies, demand fluctuates.
- Many Roseville pieces are unmarked, although over half of all 'Rozane' wares made before 1907 were marked. Watch out for forgeries.
- Roseville ceased production in 1954.

A Roseville Art Deco Futura range pink four-sided vase, 399-7" with chevron design in green, unmarked.

$600-700　　　　　　　　**DRA**

A Roseville Art Deco Futura range two-handled vase, in green and orange with a stepped neck, 1in bruise to body, unmarked.

8.5in (21.5cm) high

$200-300　　　　　　　　**DRA**

A Roseville Art Deco Futura range pink and green star-shaped vase, restoration around the base.

9.5in (24cm) high

$150-250　　　　　　　　**DRA**

A Roseville Art Deco Futura range pink and green bulbous vase, with stepped neck, restoration around the base, paper label.

8.5in (21.5cm) high

$200-300　　　　　　　　**DRA**

A Roseville Art Deco Futura range four-sided buttressed vase, covered in a a speckled blue glaze, unmarked.

6in (15.25cm) high

$500-600　　　　　　　　**DRA**

A Roseville Art Deco Futura range faceted "Aztec" bowl, unmarked.

8in (20cm) wide

$400-500　　　　　　　　**DRA**

A Roseville Art Deco Futura range blue flat vase, unmarked, 81-5".

$400-600　　　　　　　　**DRA**

A Roseville Art Deco Futura range faceted bowl, 188-8", in orange and green, chip and fleck to the rim, unmarked.

8in (20cm) wide

$250-300　　　　　　　　**DRA**

A Roseville Art Deco Futura jardinière, with leaves in pink and purple against a gray green ground, unmarked.

10.5in (26.5cm) wide

$300-350　　　　　　　　**DRA**

A Roseville Art Deco Futura range blue four-sided flaring vessel, embossed with branches of green leaves, nick to underside of two buttresses, unmarked.

8.5in (21.5cm) wide

$300-400　　　　　　　　**DRA**

A Roseville Art Deco Futura range "Balloons Bowl", 187-8, touch-ups to a few nicks around the rim, some interior painted over, unmarked.

8.5in (21.5cm) wide

$180-220　　　　　　　　**DRA**

A Roseville Azurean bulbous vase, painted by W. Myers, restoration to underside of base, no visible mark.

8in (20cm) high

$1,500-2,000   **DRA**

A tall pink Roseville Baneda vase, unmarked, with chip to one handle, and bruise to the other.

12.5in (32cm) high

$800-1,000   **DRA**

A blue Roseville Fuchsia jardinière and pedestal set, with raised mark, fleck and a few very minor scratches.

8in (20.5cm) high

$1,500-1,800   **DRA**

A large Roseville Pauleo vase, covered in an exceptional marbleized lustered glaze, unmarked.

13.5in (34.5cm) high

$1,200-1,500   **DRA**

A large and rare Roseville blue Pine Cone urn 912, with impressed mark.

15in (38cm) high

$2,000-3,000   **DRA**

A Roseville Sunflower umbrella stand, crisply decorated with strong color, some faint spiderlines on bottom, unmarked.

20.25in (51.5cm) high

$3,000-5,000   **DRA**

A Roseville Vista umbrella stand, unmarked and with restoration to area at base, long line from rim, and faint line to interior.

20in (51cm) high

$600-900   **DRA**

A Roseville Blue Windsor vase, crisply decorated with ferns on both sides, and unmarked.

7.5in (19cm) high

$700-1,000   **DRA**

A large Roseville brown Wisteria vase, with ribbed base and flaring rim, and foil label.

12.5in (32cm) high

$900-1,200   **DRA**

An early 20thC Roseville Pottery jardinière, with gray body, geometric designs in glossy glaze colors of green, blue, yellow and dark red, "R" mark on base.

12in (30.5cm) diam

$250-350   **SK**

ROYAL WORCESTER

- The Worcester factory, established by Dr John Wall and William Davis in 1751, became the Worcester Royal Porcelain Co. in 1862.
- Products of the late Victorian period tended to be elaborate and richly gilded.
- Reticulated pieces by George Owen imitated pierced ivory.
- Pieces from the 1870s and 1880s expressed the fashion for Japonaiserie.
- Particularly collectable are the figures by James Hadley.
- By 1900, alongside the production of everyday wares, extravagant bone china pieces decorated with skilful depictions of landscapes, animals and flowers were produced.
- Of note are vases painted with sheep by Harry Davis, highland cattle by John Stinton and swans by Charles Baldwyn.
- In the 1930s and '40s a highly successful series of ceramic sculptures were produced.
- Most collectable are the bird figures modeled by Dorothy Doughty and the equestrian portraits modeled by Doris Lindner.
- In 1976 the company merged with Spode.

A Royal Worcester ewer, painted by C. Baldwyn, with swans flying through reeds, on a matt blue ground, green marks, date code, shape no. 2259.

1903   *6in (15cm) high*

$4,500-5,500   **DN**

A Royal Worcester boxed coffee set, decorated with songbirds on a pale yellow ground with gilt rim and handle, comprising six coffee cups and six saucers in a lined black leather box, all signed "E. Barker", puce marks, and painted mark "Z793".

1933

$8,000-9,000   **L&T**

A Royal Worcester ewer, painted by Harry Davis with hill sheep in a Highland landscape, puce printed marks, shape no.1209, date code, restored section to handle.

1903   *17in (42.5cm) high*

$8,000-12,000   **DN**

A Royal Worcester globular pot-pourri vase and cover, painted by Harry Davis with views of Durham Cathedral, puce printed marks, date code, shape number 1515, inscribed "Durham Cathedral".

1912   *8.5in (21cm) high*

$6,000-7,000   **DN**

A Royal Worcester oviform vase and cover, painted by Harry Davis with hill sheep in a Highland landscape, puce printed marks, date code, shape no. 2158, restored cover.

1912   *11in (28cm) high*

$6,000-7,000   **DN**

A Royal Worcester slender oviform vase and cover, painted by Harry Davis with hill sheep in a Highland landscape, puce printed marks, date code, shape no.1957, finial of cover restored.

1920   *14in (35.5cm) high*

$7,000-10,000   **DN**

A Royal Worcester slender ovoid vase, painted by Harry Davis with hill sheep in a Highland landscape, puce printed marks, date code.

1914   *9in (22cm) high*

$6,000-7,000   **DN**

A Royal Worcester oviform vase, painted by Harry Davis, with hill sheep in a Highland landscape, puce printed marks, shape no.287/H, date code.

1922   *8in (20.5cm) high*

$5,000-6,000   **DN**

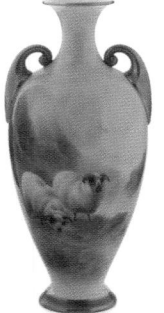

A Royal Worcester spill vase, painted by Harry Davis, with lowland sheep in a meadow landscape, with a pierced gilt japanesque lower section, puce printed mark, shape no.6/161, date code, small chipped and cracked section to foot.

1922   *6.5in (16.5cm) high*

$3,000-4,000   **DN**

A Royal Worcester ovoid vase with flared neck, painted by Harry Davis, with lowland sheep in a meadow landscape with bluebells, puce printed mark, shape no.202/H, date code.

1926   *6.5in (16.5cm) high*

$8,000-9,000   **DN**

CLOSER LOOK AT A ROYAL WORCESTER TEAPOT

Pieces by James Hadley (1837 - 1903) are collectable in their own right. He worked as chief modeler for Royal Worcester between 1870 and 1875 before setting up his own studio to supply his former employer.

'Aesthetes' were the subject of derision during the period and this teapot, depicting an Aesthetic young man and women picks up on this trend. The background and humor make this an appealing piece.

The lily and the sunflower were promoted by Oscar Wilde, a leading Aesthetic figure, as beautiful examples of natural design and they appear here on the teapot as representations of Aesthetic taste.

The modeling reflects the general discomfort with the Aesthetic movement's take on gender roles, while the inscription mocks its more superficial tendencies.

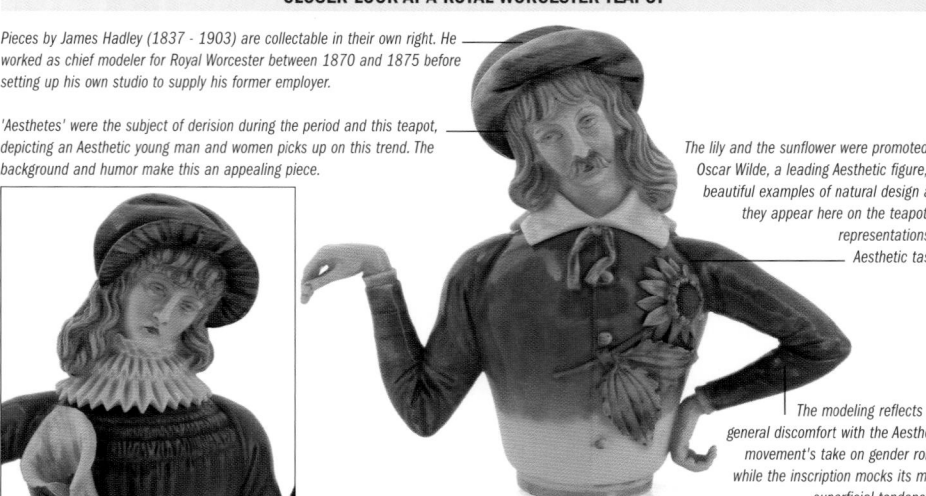

A Royal Worcester Aesthetic Movement teapot and cover, probably designed by R.W. Binns and modeled by James Hadley, one side modeled as a satire of Oscar Wilde, the other a female, their mutual arm and limp wrist forming the spout, the other handle, the base signed "Budge" and inscribed "Fearful consequences through the laws of natural selection and evolution of living up to one's teapot".

c1882   *6in (15cm) high*

$7,000-10,000   **ROS**

A Hadley's Royal Worcester oval basket group, formed on a rustic base as a young boy and girl leaning on tree trunks either side of an oval basket, the upright posts modeled as logs, incised "Hadley's", with printed mark to base and number "1233".

18.5in (47cm) wide

$3,000-4,000   **JN**

A Royal Worcester oviform vase and cover, painted with roses by W Jarman, with gilt slender neck, shape 2194, tip of the finial lacking. date code.

1912   *12.5in (32cm) high*

$400-500   **DN**

A Royal Worcester pot pourri vase and pierced cover, of globular form with pierced neck and painted with roses by H. Martin, green painted marks, shape 6293, date code, some sticky tape marks.

1911   *7.5in (19cm) high*

$900-1,100   **DN**

A Royal Worcester Sabrina ware vase, decorated with flamingos in a landscape, with flared neck painted with birds in flight, signed Walter Powell, shape 2199.

7.5in (19cm) high

$1,500-2,000   **BRI**

A Royal Worcester pot pourri vase and cover, painted with roses, signed "Sedgley".

c1922   *9.25in (23.5cm) high*

$1,200-1,500   **WW**

A Royal Worcester vase and cover, the baluster body with twin lion's head handles, painted with ducks in flight above a lake, signed "Jas Stinton", printed mark and date code.

1908   *16.5in (41.5cm) high*

$9,000-11,000   **L&T**

A Royal Worcester urn-shaped two-handled pedestal vase, painted by H. Stinton with Highland cattle in a landscape, puce printed marks, shape 1969, date code for 1912.

6.75in (17cm) high

$4,000-6,000   **DN**

A Royal Worcester dish, painted with fruit, signed "E Townsend", impressed and printed marks,

4.75in (12cm) wide

$500-600   **SWO**

A large Royal Worcester Moresque vase, of baluster form, the tapering neck with pierced floral decoration, above molded gilt panels of stylized flowers, the body applied with panels of gilt scrolling foliage, with stylized columns forming cartouche panels painted with floral scenes above further scrolling foliage, the circular foot with panels of molded foliage, the handles with molded flowers above curved gilt foliate supports, puce printed mark and date code, registered mark "63498", shape "1200" and further gilt printed mark.

1886   18.25in (45.5cm) high

$4,000-6,000   **L&T**

A large Royal Worcester blush ground pot pourri vase and cover, the pierced neck decorated with griffins, foliage and applied swags, the main body with painted floral sprays heightened with gilding, shape 1428, date code, pinnacle of finial restored.

1892   15.25in (39cm) high

$2,800-3,200   **SWO**

A Royal Worcester Art Nouveau vase, printed and impressed marks, restored.

16in (41cm) high

$200-300   **SWO**

A Royal Worcester boxed coffee set, comprising six coffee cups and six saucers, decorated in bright yellow with gilt stylized shell and swag design and white jeweling with gilt interior, handle and well, puce printed mark, and additional puce printed mark of a Viking long boat, painted mark "C899"; together with six silver and guilloché enameled coffee spoons, in a fitted black leather box marked "Brook & Son, Goldsmiths to the King, 87 George Street, Edinburgh".

The longboat symbol was the mark of the dealers Mather.

1922

$1,000-1,500   **L&T**

A pair of Royal Worcester porcelain figures, modeled by James Hadley, formed as a Japanese gentleman and his companion, each standing beside a table, on shaped bases, printed and impressed marks.

c1873   15.5in (39.5cm) high

$6,000-8,000   **FRE**

A pair of Royal Worcester Limited Edition 'Madeleine' and 'Elizabeth' bone china figures, one with a feather boa, the other with a red parasol and handkerchief.

c1960s   9in (23cm) high

$1,500-2,000   **SHF**

A pair of Royal Worcester Limited Edition 'Caroline' and 'Beatrice' bone china figures, one holding a fan, the other holding a parasol.

c1960s   9in (23cm) high

$2,200-2,800   **SHF**

A Royal Worcester group of three fox cubs, shape number 3131, printed mark in black, modeled by Doris Lindner.

1954   2.25in (5.5cm) high

$300-400   **LFA**

DECORATIVE ARTS

A Ruskin high-fired vase, of slender baluster form, covered in streaked glazes in white, red and purple, with green spotting, impressed marks, dated.

1907   *12in (30.5cm) high*
$2,500-3,000   **L&T**

A Ruskin pottery high-fired stoneware vase, with lavender over silver-gray, liver red speckled with turquoise glaze, impressed "Ruskin Pottery West Smethwick".

1908   *6in (15cm) high*
$3,500-4,000   **WW**

A Ruskin Pottery high-fired stoneware vase, covered in a running sang-de-boeuf over silverglaze, impressed "Ruskin".

1911   *10.25in (26cm) high*
$3,000-4,000   **WW**

A Ruskin Pottery high-fired vase, of shouldered form with everted rim, covered in a lavender and purple glaze, the shoulder with a band of diffusing turquoise, impressed "Ruskin".

1912   *9.25in (23.5cm) high*
$3,000-4,000   **WW**

A Ruskin pottery stoneware 'Kingfisher' luster ginger jar with cover, impressed "Ruskin".

1912   *5in (13cm) high*
$900-1,100   **WW**

A Ruskin pottery high-fired stoneware 'Elephant's Foot' vase, with tall cylindrical shape covered in sang de boeuf, purple and turquoise glaze, impressed "Ruskin England".

1916   *12in (30cm) high*
$4,000-6,000   **WW**

A Ruskin pottery high-fired stoneware 'Elephant's Foot' vase, with cylindrical shape with lavender and purple speckled glaze over sang de boeuf, impressed "Ruskin Pottery".

1917   *8in (21cm) high*
$3,000-4,000   **WW**

A Ruskin pottery high-fired stoneware vase with slender stem, knopped body, glazed in 'air brushed' sang de boeuf over silver gray, impressed "Ruskin England".

1920   *12in (31cm) high*
$4,000-5,000   **WW**

A Ruskin pottery high-fired stoneware vase, in baluster shape, glazed in liver red and purple, white glaze to the neck rim with mint green spots, impressed "Ruskin England".

1922   *9in (22cm) high*
$1,200-1,400   **WW**

A pair of Ruskin earthenware candlesticks, each with an all over yellow luster glaze and low spread bases, impressed mark and dated.

1924   *6in (15cm) high*
$180-220   **BIG**

A Ruskin pottery stoneware single handled vase, glazed with streaked lavender and sang de boeuf over silver with turquoise spots, impressed "Ruskin England".

1933   *8in (22cm) high*
$1,500-2,000   **WW**

A Ruskin pottery stoneware high-fired stoneware vase with mottled lavender and turquoise gaze with mint spots, impressed "Ruskin Pottery West Smethwick".

13in (32cm) high
$6,000-9,000   **WW**

A Saturday Evening Girls Pottery goose decorated four-color bowl, with some imperfections, signed, AH/5-14 SEG.

c1914   12in (30cm) diam
$5,000-6,000   **SK**

A Saturday Evening Girls Pottery five color decorated bowl, decorated with incised landscape of trees, sky and earth, initialed "SG", numbered.

c1916   9in (23cm) diam
$2,500-3,000   **SK**

A Saturday Evening Girls Pottery large centerbowl, decorated in cuerda seca with geese on a yellow ground, 3in (7.5cm) hairline, marked "SEG 217".

                  10.5in (26.5cm) diam
$5,000-6,000   **DRA**

A Saturday Evening Girls Pottery vase, decorated in cuerda seca with trees in a landscape against a yellow ground, signed "S.E.G. 4-19".

8in (20cm) high
$4,000-5,000   **DRA**

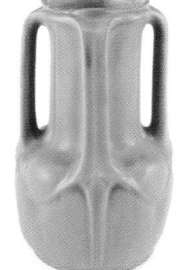

A Saturday Evening Girls Pottery tall bud vase, decorated with a band of yellow daffodils in cuerda seca, in a five-color landscape, marked "SEG/TB 5-13".

1913   8in (20.5cm) high
$4,000-5,000   **DRA**

A Saturday Evening Girls Pottery bud vase with a band of trees, signed "SEG/514".

Saturday Evening Girls Club started meeting in Boston Library in 1899. By 1907 they had opened a pottery. In 1908 it became the Paul Revere Pottery. It closed in 1942.

8in (20.5cm) high
$3,000-4,000   **DRA**

A large Teco vase, with four webbed handles, covered in smooth matte green glaze, restoration to small chip on one handle, short bruise to body, small glaze flake on bottom, stamped "Teco".

14in (35.5cm) high
$7,000-9,000   **DRA**

A Teco small vase, with bulbous base and two angular handles, covered in smooth matte green glaze, restoration to small chip on handle, stamped "Teco".

3.75in (9.5cm) high
$900-1,100   **DRA**

A Teco vessel, with four buttressed handles, covered in an unusual frothy dark brown glaze with some over firing to glaze causing bubbles, restoration to a couple of base chips, stamped "Teco 175".

14in (36cm) high
$3,000-4,000   **DRA**

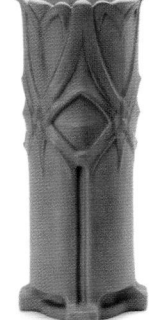

A rare Teco tall vase, embossed with a Prairie School design, covered in matte green glaze with charcoaling details, restoration to several hairlines, stamped "Teco".

17in (43cm) high
$10,000-12,000   **DRA**

A rare Teco tall three-lobed vase, covered in matte green with charcoaling details, short scratch to body, stamped "Teco 163".

18in (45.75cm) high
$10,000-12,000   **DRA**

A Teco tall pitcher, with twisted handle, covered in smooth matte green glaze, no visible mark.

13in (32.5cm) high
$2,000-2,500   **DRA**

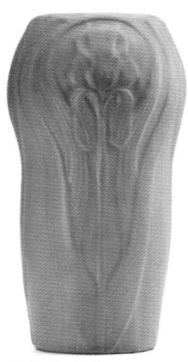

A tall, early Van Briggle bulbous vase, embossed with irises under a dark blue-green and bright green glaze.

1903   *15in (38cm) high*

$30,000-35,000   **DRA**

A tall early Van Briggle vase, embossed with bell-shaped flowers and swirling leaves under a smooth matte green glaze, marked "AA VAN BRIGGLE".

1902   *10.5in (26.5cm) high*

$3,000-4,000   **DRA**

A rare and early Van Briggle three-color bulbous vase, sharply embossed with purple poppies on bright green stems against a mottled light blue-green ground.

1902   *8in (20.5cm) high*

$30,000-35,000   **DRA**

A Van Briggle bulbous vase, embossed with poppy pods under a dark green to medium green matte glaze, "AA 1916".

1916   *7.75in (19.5cm) high*

$1,200-1,500   **DRA**

A Van Briggle vase, embossed with jonquils and covered in a fine and unusual bright green and rose matte glaze, marked "AA VAN BRIGGLE/1905 /40".

1905   *11in (28cm) high*

$2,000-2,500   **DRA**

A Van Briggle vase embossed with peacock feathers and covered in light blue and sheer white glaze, the clay showing through, marked "AA VAN BRIGGLE 1904 III 23".

1904   *11in (28cm) high*

$1,500-2,000   **DRA**

An early Van Briggle squat vessel, modeled with spade-shaped leaves and peacock feathers and covered in dead-matte mustard glaze, "AA/Van Briggle/1904/151".

1904   *5.5in (14cm) wide*

$2,000-2,500   **DRA**

An early Van Briggle vase, embossed with stylized morning glories and covered in raspberry glaze with green accents, "AA VAN BRIGGLE".

Artus Van Briggle (1869-1904) and his wife Anna founded the Van Briggle art pottery in Colorado Springs, Colorado in 1899. Having worked as a decorator at the Rookwood Pottery in Cincinnati, Ohio, Artus brought to the new enterprize a taste for slip-cast ceramic vessels in organic shapes decorated with sumptuous matte glazes. The company's output varied widely, ranging from high-quality innovative studio wares to ordinary commercial merchandise. Vases were typically molded and decorated with embossed patterns featuring stylized Art Nouveau flowers and leaves or Native American designs. Occasionally the factory produced vessels that were embellished with molded animals or human figures – the best known being 'Despondency' and the celebrated 'Lorelai' vases.

The Van Briggle pottery produced its finest work before the death of Artus in 1904, although until Anna sold the factory in 1912 the company continued to create quality art wares decorated with rich matte finishes in a variety of distinctive hues.

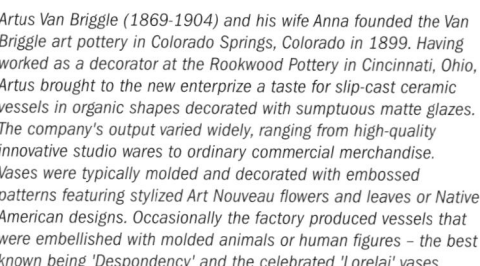

1905   *7in (18cm) high*

$1,500-2,000   **DRA**

CHARLES VYSE

- The pottery run by Charles Vyse (1882-1971) and his wife Nell (1892-1967) is probably best known for its small production of figurines of London characters.
- They also made studio pottery, both revivals of oriental forms and glazes and hand-decorated stoneware in the Art Deco style.
- Charles' family had been involved in the Staffordshire pottery industry for generations. He was apprenticed to Doulton as a modeler and designer, and won a scholarship to the Royal College of Art (1905-1910) where he studied sculpture.
- He was a member of the Royal Society of British Sculptors (1911) and attended the Camberwell School of Arts and Crafts (1912).
- Nell researched the 19thC texts which allowed them to recreate early Chinese glazes.
- In 1940 the studio was damaged in an air raid and at around that time they parted. Charles continued to produce figurative pieces and taught modeling and pottery at Farnham School of Art.

A Charles Vyse painted pottery figure 'The Tulip Woman', painted "CV 1922 Chelsea" to base.

1922   10in (26cm) high
$2,500-3,000   WW

A Charles Vyse figure group, 'The Macaw', depicting a young boy standing beside a seated cat, a parrot perched upon his shoulder, molded flora to cushion base, signed "VYSE CHELSEA", on an octagonal wooden plinth.

c1924   12.5in (32cm) high
$6,000-7,000   GORL

A Charles Vyse figure group, 'La Folie Bergere', depicting a child leap-frogging Pan, whilst Pan cradles a lamb, on a canted rectangular base, incised signature "C. VYSE CHELSEA".

c1927   12in (30.5cm) high
$5,000-6,000   GORL

A Charles Vyse ceramic group, 'The Gypsies', modeled as a woman and her child with a man carrying cabbages, raised on a plinth, with painted marks to base "CV 1924 Chelsea".

10.6in (27cm) high
$10,000-15,000   L&T

A Charles Vyse stoneware vase, of compressed globular shape, painted with white flowers, foliage and two butterflies against a pale celadon ground, signed "C. Vyse".

1928   4.5in (11.5cm) high
$400-600   JN

A Charles Vyse pottery figure, 'Autumn Leaves' painted in colors on wood base, impressed "CVyse 1929 Chelsea".

10in (25cm) high
$2,500-3,000   WW

Two views of a Charles Vyse pottery figure, 'Dancing Gypsies' painted in colors, restored arms.

11in (28cm) high
$4,000-6,000   WW

A rare Charles Vyse painted pottery 'Barnet Fair' figure, on ebonized wood base, impressed "C Vyse Chelsea".

11in (29cm) high
$12,000-14,000   WW

509

A Wedgwood black 'Fairyland' luster bowl, of circular footed form, printed and painted in gilt and colored enamels with the 'Poplar Trees' pattern to the exterior, and 'Woodland Elves V - Woodland Bridge' to the interior with a 'Mermaid' roundel to the center, printed and painted marks, "Z4698".

7.75in (28cm) diam

$12,000-14,000   **L&T**

A pair of Wedgwood black Fairyland luster vases and covers, each of baluster form with domed covers, printed and painted in gilt and colored enamels in the 'Jeweled Tree' pattern with 'Cat and Mouse' and 'Copper tree' panels, printed and painted marks, "Z4968".

7.75in (28cm) high

$6,000-7,000   **L&T**

A large Wedgwood Fairyland luster plaque, designed by Daisy Makeig-Jones, with the 'Imps on a Bridge and Treehouse' pattern number 3082, printed and painted in colors and gilt on a midnight blue ground, in original ebonized wood frame.

14.75in (37.5cm) high

$20,000-25,000   **WW**

An important Wedgwood Fairyland luster vase, designed by Daisy Makeig-Jones, decorated in the 'Bubbles' pattern on a midnight blue ground, printed and painted in colors and gilt, with printed Wedgwood mark and original paper label.

Daisy Makeig Jones took inspiration from the Buddhist tale of Kwannon the Divine Mother, who poured the Water of Creation over the Earth. The water fell in a series of bubbles, each containing a baby child, but many of them were snatched by a dragon before they reached the ground.

21.25in (54cm) high

$40,000-50,000   **WW**

An exceptional Wedgwood Fairyland luster malfrey pot, shape 2312, pattern Z4968 with 'Demon Tree' decoration on body, 'Owls of Wisdom' on cover, 'Pan-Fei' border to rim and base.

14in (36cm) high

$60,000-70,000   **JDJ**

A Wedgwood Fairyland luster vase with 'Tree House' design on main body, signed "Wedgwood Made in England Z4968".

17in (43cm) high

$45,000-50,000   **JDJ**

A Wedgwood Fairyland luster vase with 'Tree Serpent' pattern, shape 3150, pattern Z5360, some minor wear to rim of vase.

12in (30cm) high

$18,000-22,000   **JDJ**

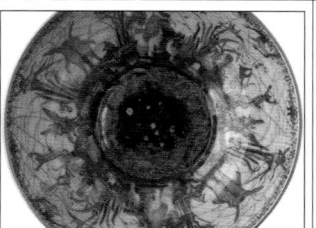

An unframed Wedgwood Fairyland luster plaque with blue and yellow scene with elves on a black sky ground, signed "Wedgwood England".

11in (28cm) high

$120,000-25,000   **JDJ**

An unusual Wedgwood Fairyland luster Imperial bowl, designed by Daisy Makeig-Jones, the exterior with 'Poplar Trees' on a black luster ground, printed factory mark, painted "Z4968".

9in (22cm) diam

$6,000-8,000   **WW**

A Wedgwood Fairyland luster 'Fairy Gondola' lily tray, designed by Daisy Makeig-Jones, the exterior a black luster ground printed with birds, factory mark.

13in (33cm) diam

$4,000-6,000   **WW**

A Wedgwood fairyland luster 'Candlemas' vase, designed by Daisy Makeig-Jones, decorated with panels of candles and ceremonial figures, and printed gilt Portland mark.

c1920   *8.75in (22cm) high*

$8,000-10,000   **FRE**

A large 19thC Wedgwood black basalt 'Brainstone' vase, the oval bowl with swan-neck handles mounted upon winged sphinxes on a rectangular plinth molded with a key fret, impressed "Wedgwood", restored.

This vase shape was in production by 1777 and produced intermittently until 1938.

12.5in (32cm) long

$5,000-6,000   **WW**

A late 19thC Wedgwood Arts and Crafts luster vase, by Alfred Powell, painted in pink luster with three panels of life at Chavenage, Cirencester, with impressed marks, painted monogram.

8in (20.5cm) high

$700-1,000   **L&T**

Left: An Alfred Powell Wedgwood Arts & Crafts earthenware comport and cover, painted in spiral bands, painted monograms and number 427 to base and cover, chip to foot rim.

13.75in (35cm) high

Right: An Alfred Powell Wedgwood Arts & Crafts earthenware comport and cover, painted in spiral bands, painted monograms and number 430 to base and under cover.

13.75in (35cm) high

LEFT: $4,000-4,500 RIGHT: $5,000-5,500   **L&T**

A Wedgwood pottery figure by John Skeaping, modeled as a lying duiker, covered in a cream glaze, impressed "J Skeaping, Wedgwood".

7in (17.5cm) wide

$150-200   **WW**

A Wedgwood 'Age of Jazz' limited edition figure, in original box with certificate, printed marks.

These were made for the Clarice Cliff Collectors' Club.

7.5in (19cm) high

$500-600   **WW**

A Wedgwood 'Age of Jazz' figure, in original box with certificate, printed marks.

7.5in (19cm) high

$500-600   **WW**

A Keith Murray blue shoulder vase, designed for Wedgwood.

1930s   *11in (28cm) high*

$600-800   **FRE**

A pair of brass jardinières, inset with Wedgwood 'Old English Series' tiles, each with a lead lining, enclosing four 'Month' tiles, one September, October, November and December, the other, January, February, March and April, minor surface scratches, the March title is cracked in two.

7.5in (19cm) high

$1,200-1,500   **DN**

WEMYSS

- Wemyss ware was produced by the Fife Pottery in Kirkcaldy, Scotland from the early 1880s. Owner Robert Methven Heron worked with Karel Nekola, the chief decorator, to create a new concept in decoration.
- Nekola was largely responsible for introducing the bold, bright designs that became the blueprint for all future Wemyss ware.
- The popularity of Wemyss in Scotland was shortly followed by that in England when Thomas Goode & Co. of Mayfair, London obtained the sole selling rights.
- Notable commissions include a series of commemorative pieces for Queen Victoria's Diamond Jubilee in 1897 and the coronation of George V in 1911.
- The factory in Scotland closed in 1930 but Wemyss ware continued to be produced by the Bovey Pottery in Devon. Later the rights were sold to Jan Plichta, who, along with Nekola's son Joseph, produced a popular series of small animals. In 1957, Plichta sold the rights to Royal Doulton.
- Pre-1930 wares are impressed "Wemyss" and are usually also stamped "R.Heron & Son" and/or "T. Goode & Son", with a painted 'Wemyss' mark. Pieces after 1930 were not impressed but carry either the Bovey Pottery or Jan Plichta stamp.

A Wemyss spill vase, of cylindrical form with everted rim, painted with pink cabbage roses, impressed mark "Wemyss".

6.5in (16cm) high

$600-700 L&T

A large Wemyss 'Kenmore' vase, of baluster form, with pierced shoulder and molded body, painted with pink cabbage roses, impressed and painted marks "Wemyss".

14.5in (36.5cm) high

$4,000-5,000 L&T

A rare Wemyss flower vase, of ovoid form with domed base, painted with pink cabbage roses on a yellow ground, apparently unmarked.

5.75in (14.5cm) high

$800-1,200 L&T

A large Wemyss 'Lady Eva' vase, of waisted form, painted with pink cabbage roses, impressed and painted marks "Wemyss", with restoration.

11.5in (29cm) high

$800-900 L&T

A Wemyss matched ewer and basin, painted with pink cabbage roses, ewer with impressed and painted marks "Wemyss" and blue printed retailer's mark, the basin with painted mark "Wemyss T. Goode & Co. London", and impressed mark "Wemyss", minor damage.

basin 15.5in (39cm) wide

$2,000-3,000 L&T

A Wemyss footbath, of elongated and molded cylindrical form, with twin handles, decorated with cabbage roses, some restoration.

19.25in (49cm) diam

$2,000-3,000 L&T

An early 20thC Wemyss inkwell, of heart shape with removable covers, painted with rooster, impressed marks, damage to covers and discoloration.

7in (18cm) wide

$500-600 SWO

Left: A rare Fife Pottery twin-handled vase, of flattened and tapering form, molded to the front with a rooster chasing a fly, and painted on the reverse with flowering spotted dead nettle, the sides with applied rosette bosses, painted mark "Fife Pottery", some damage.

Right: A Wemyss twin-handled vase, of flattened and tapering form, molded in relief to the front with a rooster chasing a fly, and painted on the reverse with fruiting apples, the sides with applied rosette bosses, painted mark "Wemyss Ware R.H. & S." and with blue printed retailer's mark, restoration.

both 15.5in (39cm) high

LEFT: $3,000-4,000 RIGHT: $1,500-2,000 L&T

A Wemyss muffin dish and cover, painted in back, red and green enamels with domestic fowl in long grass, impressed mark and retailer's mark for Thomas Goode & Co, cracked.

9in (23cm) diam

$700-1,000 DN

An early 20thC Wemyss pottery bowl, painted with a band of black domestic fowl with red wattles, within red-line borders, script mark, some crazing.

9in (23cm) wide

$900-1,100 DN

A Wemyss tray, of square form, painted with flying bees around a bee skep, printed factory mark, painted serial no. "W43".

7.5in (19cm) wide

$700-1,000   **L&T**

A Wemyss tray, of square form, painted with flying bees around a bee skep, impressed mark "Wemyss", green printed retailer's mark.

7.5in (19cm) wide

$600-700   **L&T**

A Wemyss quaich, of circular form, with twin lug handles, painted with bees around a bee skep, painted marks "Wemyss", restoration.

10.25in (26cm) wide

$1,200-1,500   **L&T**

A Wemyss comb honey dish, cover and tray, each of square form, painted with flying bees around bee skeps in a landscapes, dish with painted marks 'Wemyss', tray with impressed mark "Wemyss", restoration.

tray 7.25in (18.5cm) wide

$600-900   **L&T**

A Wemyss comb honey dish, cover and tray, each of square form, painted with flying bees around bee skeps in a landscapes, tray with impressed mark "Wemyss".

tray 7.25in (18.5cm) wide

$1,600-1,800   **L&T**

A Wemyss comb honey dish, cover and tray, the tray matched, each of square form, painted with flying bees around bee skeps, dish with painted mark "Wemyss Made in England", tray with impressed and painted marks "Wemyss", restoration.

tray 7.5in (19cm) wide

$900-1,100   **L&T**

A Wemyss honey pot and cover, decorated with bees around a beehive, damage and staining, painted mark.

c1910   *4.74in (12cm) high*

$600-700   **SWO**

A Wemyss honey pot and cover, of cylindrical form, painted with bees flying around a bee skep in a landscape, painted mark "Wemyss".

4.75in (12cm) high

$1,500-2,000   **L&T**

A Wemyss miniature honey pot and cover, of cylindrical form, painted with bees around a bee skep, painted marks "Wemyss", cover restored.

2.75in (7cm) high

$800-1,200   **L&T**

A Wemyss honey pot and cover, modeled as a bee skep with 'thatched' cover, painted with flying bees, painted marks "Wemyss, T. Goode & Co., London".

7.25in (18.5cm) high

$4,000-5,000   **L&T**

A Wemyss pottery money box, with a white ground, with black sponged decoration, the feet, ears and face highlighted in pink, painted mark underneath.

5.75in (15cm) long

$1,000-1,500   **PC**

A large Wemyss pig, seated on its haunches, painted with black on white markings with pink details, impressed mark "Wemyss R.H. & S.", with restoration.

17.75in (45cm) long

$8,000-10,000   **L&T**

A small Wemyss pig, seated on its haunches, painted allover with shamrocks, impressed mark "Wemyss", with restoration.

6.25in (16cm) long

$800-1,200   **L&T**

A small Wemyss pig, seated on its haunches, painted allover with shamrock leaves, impressed mark "Wemyss", painted mark "T. Goode & Co. London".

6.25in (16cm) long

$1,500-2,000   **L&T**

A Wemyss pig painted with sprays of thistles, painted mark "Wemyss Made In England".

c1930   *16in (40.5cm) long*

$3,000-4,000   **DRA**

A Wemyss cat, in seated pose, with applied glass eyes, painted with pink cabbage roses, painted marks "Wemyss", with damage.

12.75in (32.5cm) high

$7,000-10,000   **L&T**

A Wemyss cat, in seated pose, with applied glass eyes, painted with pink cabbage roses, painted marks "Wemyss Ware, Made in England".

12.75in (32.5cm) high

$7,000-10,000   **L&T**

A Wemyss pottery cat, seated with painted cabbage rose, glass eyes, painted marks "Wemyss Ware Made in England".

13in (32.5cm) high

$7,000-10,000   **WW**

A Wemyss tabby cat, modeled in a seated upright position with smiling face and with applied green glass eyes, painted mark "Wemyss".

12.75in (32.5cm) high

$35,000-45,000   **L&T**

A Wemyss tabby cat, modeled in a seated upright position with smiling face and applied green glass eyes, impressed mark "Wemyss Ware R.H. & S.", puce printed retailers mark.

13in (33cm) high

$15,000-20,000   **L&T**

A pair of Wemyss cats, modeled in an upright seated position, with smiling face and applied glass eyes, glazed in green, impressed mark "Wemyss".

12.5in (32cm) high

$6,000-7,000 each   **L&T**

A Wemyss 'Apples' pattern twin-handled pail, of tapering cylindrical form, with twin lug handles.

11in (28cm) high

$2,000-3,000   L&T

A Wemyss slop bucket, of tapering cylindrical form, with cane swing handle, painted with cherries, impressed mark "Wemyss R.H. & S.", puce retailers mark, restoration.

11.5in (29cm) high

$1,500-2,000   L&T

A Wemyss preserve jar and cover, of cylindrical form, painted with blackcurrants, the lid with applied fruiting stem in relief, painted mark "Wemyss".

3.25in (8cm) high

$1,500-2,000   L&T

A Wemyss twin-handled serving dish, of oblong outline, painted with oranges, painted mark "Wemyss", minor damages.

13.5in (34cm) wide

$1,200-1,800   L&T

A large and rare Wemyss tyg, painted with swimming Carp, impressed marks.

9.25in (23.5cm) high

$7,000-10,000   L&T

A rare Wemyss bread and butter plate, of circular form, painted with a frieze of cows and a bull in a landscape, impressed mark "Wemyss, R.H. & S." with minor damage.

6in (15cm) wide

$3,000-4,000   L&T

A Wemyss tray, painted with a black pig, within green scalloped border, impressed mark "Wemyss", with a fine hairline.

7.5in (19cm) wide

$3,000-4,000   L&T

A pair of Wemyss 'Fife Pottery' vases, each of tapering lozenge section, painted in yellow, green and blue with foliate panels on a white ground, one vase marked "W.W./ R.H.&S./F.P.", the other marked "Wemyss Ware/ R.H.&S./F.P.", damages.

22in (56cm) high

$2,000-3,000   L&T

A Wemyss 'Lady Eva' vase, painted with flowering chrysanthemums, impressed and painted marks "Wemyss".

8in (20cm) high

$1,500-2,000   L&T

A large Wemyss basin painted with sprigs of white broom, within black line borders, impressed and painted marks "Wemyss", with minor damages.

15.5in (39cm) diam

$1,800-2,200   L&T

A Wemyss soap dish, liner and cover, painted with trailing ivy branches, painted mark "Wemyss", with minor damages.

5.5in (14cm) wide

$1,500-2,000   L&T

A tall Zsolnay bulbous vase, painted with sunflowers in rich lustered glazes, with professional restoration to several hairlines, five castle medallion/7879/ 36/18.

17in (43cm) high

$9,000-11,000   **DRA**

A tall Zsolnay buttressed and bulbous vase, modeled with blue bell flowers on a lustered orange ground, restoration around rim, five churches medallion, 367660.

19in (48cm) high

$4,000-6,000   **DRA**

A large Zsolnay vase modeled by M.L. with a maiden embracing a tree, covered in green and purple lustered glaze, raised five churches medallion/5955/ML.

17.5in (44cm) high

$4,000-5,000   **DRA**

A Zsolnay tall tankard, completely covered with oak branches and large beetles, covered in lustered glazes, five churches medallion, 4115/10/36.

The Zsolnay pottery and porcelain factory opened in Pecs, Hungary in 1853.

16in (41cm) high

$25,000-30,000   **DRA**

A Zsolnay four handled vase, etched and gilded with clusters of red flowers on a cobalt ground, restoration to one handle, five churches medallion, 6184, 23.

9in (23cm) high

$4,000-6,000   **DRA**

A Zsolnay vase, modeled with stylized ferns in a lustered gold glaze on purple ground, four opposing hairlines, five churches medallion, 8331,36.

9in (23cm) high

$3,000-4,000   **DRA**

A Zsolnay center dish modeled with a squirrel, brown, blue and green lustered glazes, touch-up to ear, short scratch, raised five churches medallion, 5776/36/48.

c1900   *13in (33cm) wide*

$2,000-3,000   **DRA**

A Zsolnay vase, molded with three owls, and covered in lustered purple glaze, with three minor flakes, five castle mark/ZSOLNAY PECS 5286.

11.75in (29.75cm) high

$5,500-6,500   **DRA**

A Zsolnay Ketupa Ceylonensis figure of an owl clutching a fish, in green and purple lustered glaze, with restoration to a few chips on base and wing tip, raised five churches medallion/5771 5643/title.

13in (33cm) high

$2,000-3,000   **DRA**

A Zsolnay green copper luster figure of a comical alert fox, and a similar figure of a rabbit eating a lettuce leaf, both with printed marks to base.

Fox 4.5in (11.5cm) high

$200-300 pair   **JN**

An Austrian Art Nouveau Amphora pitcher modeled with a pink, green, and gold Iris blossom on long green leaves, with reglued spout petal, stamped "AMPHORA 55/3683/", artist signed "HE" or "TM".

18.5in (47cm) high

$3,000-4,000   DRA

A tall Amphora lustered vase, embossed with water lilies and lily pads and twisted stems for handles, stamped "crown/3850/AMPHORA/AUSTRIA/45", wear and restoration.

19.25in (49cm) high

$1,000-1,500   DRA

A Henry van de Velde Art Nouveau vase, with twisting body and three handles at rim, covered in green and brown flowing glazes, restoration to two small chips at base, a couple glaze flakes to handles, firing lines near rim, unmarked.

11.25in (28cm) high

$1,000-1,400   DRA

An American Arequipa large squat vessel, covered in lavender semi-matte glaze, incised Arequipa Cal, 859, 19. *Arequipa Pottery was founded by Philip King Brown & Henry Bothin in Farifax, CA, US. It closed in 1918.*

11in (28cm) wide

$900-1,100   DRA

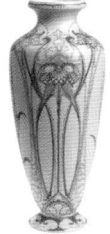

An Arnhem large shouldered vase, with everted rim, painted in colors with panels of flowering irises, with printed mark, painted monogram and no. 178.

20in (51cm) high

$3,000-4,000   L&T

An Ault twin-handled bottle vase, designed by Christopher Dresser, glazed in a streaked green glaze, impressed facsimile signature, no. 247H.

19.25in (49cm) high

$9,000-11,000   L&T

A late 19thC set of twelve Bodley and Son porcelain plates, by J. Birbeck, and retailed by Bailey, Banks & Biddle, Philadelphia, each painted with different game bird, printed mark.

9in (23cm) diam

$2,000-2,500   FRE

A Bough circular charger, decorated by Elizabeth Amour with a panel of sweet peas, with painted marks "EA/ BOUGH/ 52".

14.5in (37cm) diam

$1,000-1,500   L&T

A Bretby 'Jewel' ware jug, impressed, mark, "1612" with Liberty paper label to base.

c1905   *12.5in (32cm) high*

$400-500   GAZE

A Bretby 'Jewel' ware small jug, impressed marks, "1617".

c1905   *8.25in (21cm) high*

$300-400   GAZE

A Bretby 'Jewel' ware jug, with impressed mark, "1588".

c1905   *7.5in (19cm) high*

$300-400   GAZE

A rare Brouwer tall vase, with bands of dark brown glaze dripping over a flame-painted lustered ground, "Ceramic Flame Co." paper label, signature, drilled hole, flakes.

12in (30.5cm) high

$4,000-6,000   DRA

A Brouwer vase, with small nicks around rim, signed flame.

Brouwer Pottery (Middle Lane Pottery) was founded by Theophilus A Brouwer in 1894 in East Hampton, NY, US. It closed in 1946.

6in (15cm) diam

$1,800-2,200   DRA

A late 1880s large and impressive Burmantofts faience vase, painted in the 'Anglo-Persian' style with swimming fish on a foliate ground, impressed factory marks, decorators initials, painted marks "Design 43, 166".

All Burmantofts 'Anglo-Persian' wares bear the initials of the as yet unknown decorator 'L.K.'. These wares made their first documented appearance at the Saltaire Exhibition in 1887 and were inspired by the 'Persian' wares of William de Morgan. Large pieces such as this piece were expensive to produce and are rare examples.

21.25in (54cm) high

$20,000-25,000   L&T

A rare Burmantoft's faience dragon vase, with tall tapering neck, applied with a coiled dragon and with gilt, impressed marks.

13.5in (34.5cm) high

$2,000-3,000   **WW**

CLOSER LOOK AT A COWAN BOWL

Bright geometric pieces with bold Art Deco styling evoking the 'Age of Jazz' and are hugely desirable.

Designs inspired by skyscrapers and other types of radical modern architecture are particularly popular with collectors. The depiction of nightclubs adds to the overall sense of urban energy, excitement and glamour.

This Cowan punch bowl is from a total edition of around 50, and as a result is extremely rare. Three versions were produced: the original large etched parabolic shape, a smaller flared bowl and a similar 'poor man's' version without etching. The original design can be worth around twice as much as he 'poor man's' version.

The bowl was designed by important industrial designer Viktor Schreckengost for Eleanor Roosevelt.

A rare bowl by Viktor Schreckengost for Cowan, "New Year's Eve in New York City" (otherwise known as the 'Jazz Bowl'), carved with Art Deco renderings of New York skyscrapers and nightclubs, in Persian Blue and black glaze, minor rim chip, stamped Cowan, signed "Viktor Schreckengost".

1931   *14in (35.5cm) diam*

$55,000-65,000   **DRA**

A Burmantoft faience vase, incised with irises and painted with colored glazes, impressed marks.

13.75in (35cm) high

$400-600   **DN**

A Bushey Heath pottery vase by Fred Passenger, printed Bushey Heath mark, painted "FP" monogram.

8in (20cm) high

$5,000-6,000   **WW**

A Ceramic Art Company porcelain bulbous vase, painted by W.H. Morley with chrysanthemums, gilded rim, green ink stamp, artist signature.

12in (30.5cm) high

$1,000-1,500   **DRA**

Four China-Painting vertical tiles, finely hand painted in Delft blue with characters from Shakespeare's Midsummer Night's Dream: 'Lion', 'Moonshine', 'Pyramus', and 'Thisbe', on roughly-cut English blanks, unmarked.

China-painting is usually fairly artisanal in quality. These are extremely professional and clever.

6in (15cm) wide

$300-400   **DRA**

A Chelsea Keramic Art Works vase, covered in oxblood glaze with orange peel texture, stamped "CKAW".

9in (23cm) high

$8,000-10,000   **DRA**

A pair of Cowan figurines, by F. Luis Mora, of a Native Indian couple with child, in polychrome majolica glazes, both stamped "Cowan" and artist-signed.

tallest 18in (45.5cm) high

$8,000-10,000   **DRA**

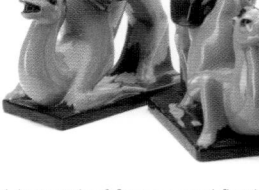

A large pair of Cowan camel figurine bookends by Alexander Blazys, in beige and brown crackled glaze, floral stamp.

1927-31   *9.5in (24cm) high*

$4,000-6,000   **DRA**

A Russell Crook stoneware vase, decorated with a gray moose on a black ground, with minor flakes to rim, unmarked.

8in (20.5cm) high

$7,000-9,000   **DRA**

An Essevi pottery figure, from a model by Sandro Vachetti, raised on an ebonized wooden base, with painted marks.

12in (30.5cm) wide

$6,000-7,000   **L&T**

A Paul Dachsel 'Artichoke' vase, with blue/green mottled glaze with gilt enhancements, and impressed number "103/2".

c1905   *6in (15cm) high*

$2,500-3,000   **FRE**

A Dagobert Peche coffee service, manufactured by Parma, printed and painted in gilt and colored enamels with a grid design, with printed factory marks.

Coffee pot 8.5in (22cm) high

$800-1,200   **L&T**

A Theodore Deck twelve-tile panel painted by Ernest Carriere with ducks above a pond, restoration to glaze on three tiles, signed "TH.DECK." and "ERNEST CARRIERE".

each tile 10in (25.5cm) wide

$6,000-7,000   **DRA**

A De Porceleyne Fles long horizontal tile, decorated in cuenca with a deer hunt in the snow, some grout to back, stamped bottle, "TL, Delft".

17.25in (44cm) long

$800-1,000   **DRA**

A pair of De Porceleyne Fles vertical plaques decorated in cuenca, each with a peacock on a brick wall in front of an ivy-covered window, unmarked.

12.25in (31cm) high

$1,200-1,600   **DRA**

A large Dunmore jardiniere and stand, the lobed ovoid jardiniere raised on a stand molded with three griffin caryatids on a concave triform plinth, the whole covered in streaky green and sang de boeuf glazes, restored base.

45in (114cm) high

$900-1,100   **L&T**

A pair of 19thC Fischer Budapest earthenware vases, each of tapered ovoid form, with lid having gilded lion finial, bold polychrome and floral decoration.

18in (46cm) high

$120-180   **BIG**

A Foley 'Intarsio' circular wall plaque, printed and painted in colors with two Art Nouveau maidens within a band of waterlilies, printed factory marks "3066" and "330300".

15in (38cm) diam

$1,500-2,000   **L&T**

An early Gallé pottery farmyard scene vase, with scene of rooster, hen and chicks in farmyard, signed "M. Latoche" on painted surface, signed on underside "E.G.", impressed "244".

7in (18cm) high

$2,000-3,000   **JDJ**

A Gouda basket-shaped vase, decorated in the Rozenburg style with pastel blossoms, signed and numbered "170".

14in (35.5cm) high

$2,500-3,000   **DRA**

A Greenwood porcelain vase, with gilded decoration, purple stamp "GREENWOOD ART POT'RY Co. N.J.".

12.5in (31cm) high

$3,500-4,000   DRA

A tall Haviland & Co. red clay vase, designed by Eugene Chaplet and decorated by Albert Damousse, covered in yellow, green and gold glazes, a few small chips to handles and rim, stamped "H&Co. R.V.3.1, 47, A.V".

15.5in (39cm) high

$4,000-6,000   DRA

A fifteen-piece pottery tea service by Raoul Lachenal consisting of six cups and saucers, teapot, covered milk jug and sugar bowl, painted Lachenal and monograms in orange.

c1930   *6.5in (16.5 cm) high*

$700-1,000   SK

A Hartford faience architectural tile, embossed in high relief, covered in rich matte glazes with period wooden box frame, some damage, stamped "The Hartford Faience Co. Hartford, Conn 17".

13in (33cm) square

$17,000-20,000   DRA

A Lenci pottery figure, from a model by Helen König Scavini, with painted marks, dated "7-4-32".

9.5in (24cm) high

$6,000-10,000   L&T

A Lenox gourd-shaped pitcher, with gilded branch handle, decorated with two tall birds in the Asian style, purple CAC stamp.

10.25in (26cm) high

$3,000-4,000   DRA

A Lenox urn, painted by William Morley, green Lenox CAC stamp.
Walter Scot Lenox opened the Ceramic Art Company in 1889 in Trenton NJ, US. In 1906 it was renamed Lenox Inc. It is still operating.

13.25in (33.5cm) high

$5,000-6,000   DRA

A Linthorpe Pottery vase, designed by Christopher Dresser, incised with geometric bands under a thick brown and green glaze, impressed marks, facsimile signature.

11.5in (29cm) high

$1,200-1,500   WW

A large pair of Linthorpe vases, designed by Christopher Dresser, of shouldered tapering form with cylindrical necks, each molded in relief with a frieze of waterlilies and flowering plants and covered in treacle, green and turquoise glazes, impressed marks, no. 168 with monogram.

19in (48cm) high

$1,000-1,500   L&T

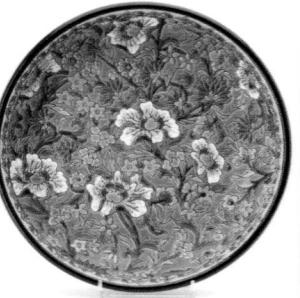

A Longwy Chinese Art Deco enameled footed bowl with blossoms in polychrome, green heraldic stamp with "LONGWY FRANCE/1252/223".

10.5in (26.5cm) diam

$1,500-1,800   DRA

A rare Maling figure, by Norman Carling, painted and incised marks "Maling, England" and "N. Carling/39", minor chips to flowers.

11.25in (28.5cm) high

$4,000-6,000   L&T

A rare Maling figure, by Norman Carling, modeled as a mermaid, rising from the waves, printed mark "Maling/Made in England".

Norman Carling (1902-1971) was a skilled modeler who brought a new three-dimensional aspect to Maling pottery. He joined Maling in 1935 from A.J. Wilkinson, and produced a number of quality Art Deco models. Most of his models were produced as a one-off or in very small quantities but none went into full production. This figure of a mermaid is believed to be one of only two still in existence and is reputed to be a depiction of his wife.

10.5in (27cm) long

$6,000-7,000   **L&T**

A CLOSER LOOK AT A MINTON CHARGER

Henry Stacy Marks was a prominent British painter known for his depictions of historical and Shakespearean scenes. He was also known in artistic circles for his high spirits and sense of humor.

The designs were reproduced on a series of rectangular plaques and on vases by Mintons Art Pottery Studio.

Marks originally created these designs for the painter Miles Birkett Foster for his house at Witley, Surrey. They were also used at Eaton Hall, Cheshire for the Duke of Westminster.

Each plate has been individually painted and depicts a different scene making this an expensive and time-consuming series to produce.

A set of seven Minton chargers depicting Shakespeare's Seven Ages of Man, by Henry Stacey Marks (1829-1898) for Minton's Art Pottery Studio, London, each painted in gilt and colored enamels, and signed "H.S.Marks", impressed and painted factory and painters marks verso.

1873   *19.25in (49cm) diam*

$30,000-40,000 set   **L&T**

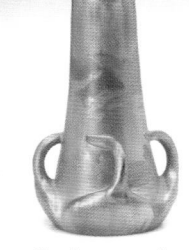

A Jerome Massier vase, painted with flying ducks over four organic handles, covered in a fine matte lustered glaze, small burst bubbles on one handle and to rim, signed "Jerome Massier Vallauris".

18.25in (46cm) high

$5,000-6,000   **DRA**

A Maw & Co. Aesthetic Movement luster plate, by Lewis F. Day, with grotesque beast amongst foliage, and molded and painted marks.

9in (23cm) wide

$1,000-1,500   **L&T**

A Maw two-tile panel attributed to Lewis Day or George Maw, painted with an Elizabethan falconer, framed, tiles embossed "MAW & BENTHALD WORKS/FLOREAT SALOPIA/BROSELEY/SALOP/165C".

c1883   *tiles 16in (40.5cm) high*

$1,500-2,000   **DRA**

A Meissen model of a World War I field gun in the white, first modeled in 1916.

c1925   *14in (35.5cm) long*

$2,000-3,000   **PC**

An Australian Melrose-ware bowl, green glaze, printed maker's marks, original decal label.

c1920

$600-700   **SHA**

A Minton pottery lazy susan, with printed stylized decoration, on a low base, impressed marks, restoration to rim.

1881   *21.5in (55.5cm) diam*

$600-700   **SWO**

A Minton Aesthetic Movement brass and tiled jardiniere, each side with a Mintons hand-painted tile depicting scenes from Classical antiquity, and with molded marks.

10.5in (27cm) high

$5,000-6,000   **L&T**

A Minton 'Suspense' cabinet plate, painted by Henry Mitchell, gilt frame on bleu celeste ground, printed retail stamp for Daniel of London.

9.5in (24cm) diam

$700-1,000   **NEA**

A group of six Minton Aesthetic Movement tiles, printed with birds, molded marks verso "Minton Hollins & Co. Stoke on Trent".

c1875   *6in (15cm) wide*

$600-700 set   **L&T**

A pair of Montigny Sur Loing vases, painted with spring flowers and insects on a buff ground, with painted marks and initialled "G.C.".

8.25in (21cm) high

$700-1,000   **L&T**

A Moravian pair of Persian Antelope tiles.

The Moravian Pottery and Tile Works was founded by Henry Chapman Mercer in 1898 in Doylestown, PA, US. It is still operating.

7in (17.5cm) high

$500-600   **DRA**

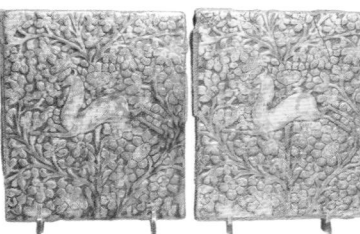

A Morrisware vase, designed by George Cartlidge, tube line decorated with clover flowers in purple on a mottled blue ground, printed marks, facsimile signature, impressed model mark.

7in (18cm) high

$900-1,100   **WW**

A porcelain bowl by Bernard Moore, with carp-like scaly fish on a midnight ground on the interior, the exterior decorated in flambé with waves, incised "BM".

9in (24cm) diam

$3,000-4,000   **WW**

A Moravian mosaic medallion, 'Silva Vocat,' with a red bird on blooming branch, some restoration, stamped pottery mark.

17.5in (44.5cm) diam

$6,000-7,000   **DRA**

A large Mougin gourd-shaped vase covered in a fine amber mottled crystalline glaze, stamped "Mougin Nancy, 7.Z".

11in (27.5cm) high

$2,000-3,000   **DRA**

A Mougin Art Deco vase, carved in high relief with stylized mechanic design in black over a bright green ground, impressed "MOUGIN/ NANCY/ 177-JB1S".

6.25in (15.5cm) high

$500-600   **SDR**

A William Staite Murray stoneware vase, with a crackled celadon glaze, impressed seal mark.
William Staite Murray (1881-1962) was one of the most important British potters of the first half of the 20thC.

4in (11cm) high

$600-900   **WW**

A Muresque fine tile panel, with a wind-blown pine and a mission on the Californian coast, three small chips to edges, stamped "Muresque Tiles INC".

16in (40.5cm) wide

$3,000-4,000   **DNS**

A Nippon vase, decorated in Coralene with pink and russet peonies on a shaded ground, gilt around rim worn off, wear to gilt around base, stamped US Patent 917, Feb 9.1909.

8.25in (21cm) high

$1,000-1,500   **DRA**

A Nonconnah covered bisque-fired vessel cameo decorated with a wreath of ivy, small chip to rim of vase and cover, signed "Nonconnah 22".

4in (10cm) high

$1,000-1,500 DRA

A North Dakota School of Mines circular trivet, decorated in squeezebag by Flora Huckfield, in beiges against a blue ground, blue ink stamp "Huck 4288".

5in (12.5cm) diam

$400-600 DRA

CLOSER LOOK AT AN OVERBECK VASE

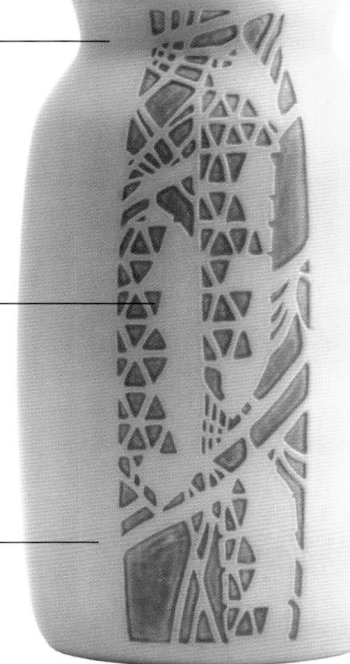

The Overbeck Pottery was established by four of six sisters in Cambridge City IN, US. The sisters were all involved in production between 1911 and 1955. It has long been held in high esteem and won many international design awards. In recent years interest has grown and prices have risen.

This vase was made by two of the most significant members of the Overbeck family – Hannah, known as 'the ultimate designer' and Elizabeth, known as 'the ultimate potter' and named as a fellow of the prestigious American Ceramic Society in 1936.

Overbeck pieces are relatively rare and this is a fine example.

A North Dakota School of Mines vase, excised by Julia Mattson, with cowboys and lassos against a mountain background, in blue-gray and ivory and with indigo stamp and "JM".

4.25in (11cm) high

$4,500-6,000 DRA

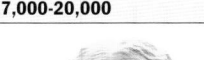

An Ott & Brewer bottle-shaped vase, with a polychromatic bird and gilded accents, early crescent moon red stamp.

10in (25.5cm) high

$7,500-10,000 DRA

A vase by Elizabeth and Hannah Overbeck, finely excised with conventionalized pine cones in matte mustard and forest green glazes, incised "OBK, E, H".

9in (23cm) high

$17,000-20,000 DRA

An Ott & Brewer pitcher, red crown and sword stamp.

Ott and Brewer was founded in 1863 in Trenton, NJ, US.

17.25in (44cm) high

$3,000-4,000 DRA

An Ott & Brewer parian bust of the Virgin Mary, rendered by Isaac Broome, possibly for the Philadelphia Centennial Exposition, 1876, hand-incised "BROOME SCULPTOR 1876".

1876 *15.25in (39cm) high*

$4,000-5,000 DRA

An Ott & Brewer parian bust of Jesus Christ, rendered by Isaac Broome, possibly for the Philadelphia Centennial Exposition, 1876, hand-incised "BROOME SCULP' 1876".

1876 *15.25in (39cm) high*

$4,000-5,000 DRA

An Overbeck pitcher, incised and painted with blue-gray stylized trees or blossoms on a smooth matte brown ground, incised "OBK/F".

9.5in (24cm) wide

$4,000-5,000 DRA

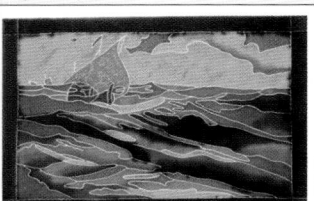

A large Owens tile, decorated in cuenca with a sailboat on the water, some edge chips, unmarked.

17.75in (45cm) wide

$2,500-3,000 DRA

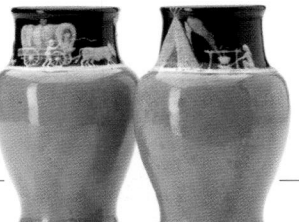

A pair of Pisgah Forest baluster vases, each with a band of cameo decoration, both on black over a turquoise base, potter's wheel mark with "WB Stephen".

1930 *7.5in (19cm) high*

$2,000-3,000 DRA

OTHER FACTORIES

DECORATIVE ARTS

A twin-handled Purmerends vase, with frilled rim, painted in bold colors with fantastical fish swimming through water plants, and painted marks.

11in (28cm) high

$4,000-5,000   **L&T**

A Carter's Poole pottery tile in the style of Edward Bawden, decorated with a modeler at work in the Poole factory.

5in (13cm) square

$600-800   **WW**

An Art Deco Poole pottery vase, in pattern AX painted by Margaret Holder, impressed mark, painted artist cypher, small chip to inside of base rim.

11in (28.50cm) high

$2,000-3,000   **WW**

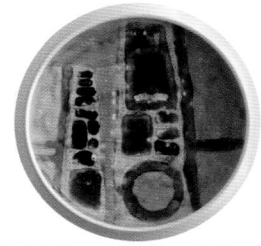

A Poole Pottery studio plaque, by Tony Morris, of circular form with inverted rim, painted with a geometric abstract design in shades of blue, impressed Poole Studio mark and painted "TM" monogram.

10.75in (27.5cm) diam

$3,000-4,000   **WW**

An Art Deco Primavera figure group, modeled as an embracing couple in colorful costume, printed and painted marks.

9.75in (25cm) high

$1,000-1,500   **L&T**

A Royal Dux model of a young lady feeding a doe, upon a green naturalistic base, impressed number and applied mark to base.

15in (38cm) high

$900-1,100   **JN**

A Poole pottery studio charger, by Tony Morris, painted with an abstract design of Corfe Castle, printed studio mark, painted "TM" monogram.

14in (35cm) diam

$2,000-3,000   **WW**

A Quenvitt 'Minstrel' box and cover, the cover molded as a mask, the base with frilled 'ruff', and molded maker's marks.

8.25in (21cm) wide

$400-600   **L&T**

A Rosenthal porcelain figure 'Princess with Frog King', designed by Lore Friedrich Gronau, looking at the crowned frog with a golden ball, green maker's mark and model number "1793".

1948   *8.25in (20.5cm) high*

$400-500   **KAU**

An Ernst Wahliss 'Royal Vienna' Art Nouveau figure, of a maiden in flowing robes, holding flower garlands, applied blue lozenge mark "Royal Vienna/Wahliss", impressed and painted marks "4731 873H".

$1,000-1,200   **L&T**

A Rye Pottery ewer, typically decorated with applied foliage.

7in (18cm) high

$400-500   **GORL**

A Shelley Art Deco tea service, each printed and painted in the 'Green Block' pattern with geometric motifs, with printed and painted marks, no. P 11785.

$1,500-2,000   **L&T**

A Shearwater baluster vase, incised with birds, beetles, and flowers in black and brown on ivory ground, with circular stamp.

c1935   *9in (23cm) high*

$15,000-20,000   **DRA**

A terracotta of Penthesilia, Queen of the Amazons, signed, with Susse Freres founders stamps.

34in (86cm) long

$1,500-2,000   **L&T**

A Rosenthal porcelain figure of a girl with a chick, designed by Lore Friedrich-Gronau, signed, green maker's mark and model number "1640".

1937   *5in (12.5cm) high*

$400-600   **KAU**

A Turn Wien porcelain vase and cover, with reticulated decoration and Japanese style branches in gilt on a sage green ground, printed and impressed marks, small chip to cover.

12.25in (31cm) high

$200-300   **DN**

An Upchurch stoneware ewer with streaked salmon pink glaze incised.

14in (35cm) high

$400-500   **WW**

A Villeroy & Boch Jugendstil vase, with four long buttresses and a band decorated with stylized mushrooms, with V&B glaze stamp.

21.25in (54cm) high

$1,500-2,000   **DRA**

A Charles Volkmar four-footed jardiniere, painted in barbotine with a fox-hunting scene, signed "Chas. Volkmar".

15in (38cm) wide

$1,000-1,500   **DRA**

A C. F. A. Voysey framed Maw & Co. four-tile panel, with tube-lined decoration of a bird in a tree, in a stained beech frame.

c1898   *11.5in (29cm) wide*

$2,000-2,500   **L&T**

A Joseph Wackerle Nymphenberg figure group, modeled as a masked 'Pierrot & Columbine', impressed and incised marks 175, signed and dated.

1905   *12in (31cm) high*

$3,000-4,000   **L&T**

A Phillip Wadsworth stoneware vase, of shouldered form, with cylindrical neck and collar rim, covered in a pale celadon glaze, incised "PSW P/50".

Phillip Wadsworth, the son of a director at Minton's, studied under William Staite Murray at the Royal College of Art between 1931 and 1936.

12.5in (32cm) high

$500-600   **WW**

An Ernst Wahliss 'Serapis Fayence' vase, printed and painted in gilt and colored enamels, with printed and impressed marks, no. 9680.

14in (36cm) high

$2,000-3,000   **L&T**

A W.J. Walley vase, covered in an unusual red and ivory marbleized flambé glaze, small chips to base and rim, stamped WJW.

4.75in (12cm) wide

$2,500-3,000   **DRA**

A Dorothea Warren O'Hara tall china-painted vase in a Persian style, in black on amber. Signed Dorothea Warren O'Hara in cartouche.

14in (35.5cm) high

$1,500-2,000   **DRA**

A Watcombe Pottery teapot with lid, designed by Christopher Dresser, with a painted flying crane, Watcombe mark.

4.5in(11.5cm) high

$600-800   **WW**

An early 20thC Weller Pottery 'Woodcraft' pattern planter, decorated with branches covering a tree trunk with a den of foxes peering out from the side.

8in (20cm) diam

$300-500   **SK**

DECORATIVE ARTS

A rare matt green Weller architectural-form vase, with buttressed handles, unmarked, the body with faint impressed decoration, and very minor grinding chip.

11.5in (29cm) high

$1,000-1,500   DRA

A Wheatley vase with ridged shoulder covered in a good feathered matte green glaze, row of burst bubbles at shoulder and shaved glaze around base, from manufacture, unmarked.

5.5in (14cm) high

$400-500   DRA

A Geoffrey Whiting stoneware cut-sided vase, with olive green and tenmoku glaze, impressed marks.

9in (24cm) high

$400-500   WW

A Wiener Werkstatte tin glazed bowl and cover, attributed to Hilda Jesser, painted with flowers and leaves, impressed and painted marks, 268 and 824.

c1920   *7.5in (19cm) high*

$1,000-1,500   L&T

A Wileman & Co. Foley 'Urbato' bowl, two-handled, the exterior tube-lined with stylized leaves against a peach ground, pattern number 4404.

7.5in (19cm) wide

$550-650   GORL

A pair of Willetts Belleek scalloped urns painted by Walter Marsh with purple grape clusters, restoration to one, artist-signed and green serpent mark.

12.5in (32cm) wide

$1,500-2,000   DRA

A Willetts Belleek tankard with dragon handle painted by George Houghton, 1906, signed on side and bottom, brown crown stamp.

15.25in (38.5cm) high

$2,500-3,000   DRA

A pair of French Japonism chargers, with painted characters from 'The Mikado', and gilt decorated rims, impressed "B & Ch Montereau" mark, one bearing paper retailer's label, "Rue Helevy, 6, a cote du Nouvel Opera, Mon. Toy/Ancienn Ch**/Paris".

c1885   *17.75in (45cm) diam*

$1,500-2,000   FRE

A Vally Wieselthier ceramic sculpture of a head, 'Cella', some breaks and touch ups to hair strands, signed and titled on base.

14.5in (37cm) high

$6,000-7,000   SDR

An Aesthetic Movement teapot and cover, printed blue and white decoration, impressed registered diamond.

6.5in (16.5cm) high

$200-300   WW

An Austrian Art Deco faience sculpture with a mythical female figure sitting astride a unicorn, in polychrome majolica glazes, restoration to several areas, unmarked.

22in (56cm) wide

$800-1,200   SDR

A late 19thC Sèvres style porcelain Art Nouveau vase, with gilt bronze finial, sides painted with a bust-length portrait of a young beauty and a gilt-enriched ground, on a socle base.

26in (66cm) high

$4,000-5,000   FRE

THE DECORATIVE ARTS GLASS AND LAMP MARKETS

The market remains very strong for high quality art glass and lighting. Even with high demand and limited supplies we are seeing some changes happening in this market. While the highest end of the glass and lamp market continues to get stronger and stronger, we have seen over the past year a slight weakening in prices for the mid to lower range items.

Even though two pieces by the same maker, in the same pattern may look identical, there are subtle differences that can make a large difference in price. A collector needs to not only know which patterns are rare and more valuable but also needs to be aware of the subtle differences that affect value. One of the most important factors in valuing fine art glass can be color. Colors will vary in depth of shade and in beauty, which in turn will affect the price of a piece. For instance, a fine Tiffany vase in blue favrile can have different tones of blue and can also vary in the degree of iridescence. The richer the more beautiful the blue and the brighter the iridescence, the more valuable the vase.

When looking at artistic glass that is created by workman's hands, such as French cameo glass, the workmanship comes into play in determining value. You may find two Daum blackbird vases of the same size and shape and yet one will have deeper and more detailed cutting and the contrasting colors of black

and white may be more intense in one vase than the other. This variation in color and in workmanship could lead to the better vase being valued at as much as twice that of the lesser vase.

The past year has seen some very strong and impressive prices realized at auctions of fine art glass and lighting. A rare Quezal Jack in the Pulpit vase with extremely fine decoration and bright iridescence set a new record for the factory selling for $36,800. James D. Julia Auctioneers in Fairfield, ME discovered a rare Pairpoint Puffy Owl lamp. Previously there were only five known examples, and this lamp was the sixth. It sold for a very strong $86,250. High quality Steuben Aurene continues to be extremely strong and last year saw several rare red Aurene vases come to the market with an 8in (20cm) beautifully decorated vase selling for $33,350. In the French cameo glass market Daum, seems to be taking center stage while fine cameo glass by Emile Gallé continues to be very strong at the upper levels .

A final word of caution. With prices continuing to rise, and with the constant improvement in technology and techniques, reproductions of art glass are getting better and better. This makes it more important than ever for the collector to improve their knowledge and expertise.

Dudley Browne

ARGY-ROUSSEAU

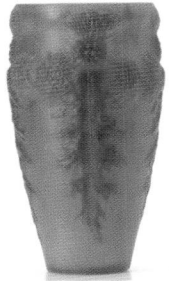

A Gabriel Argy-Rousseau pâte-de-verre vase, patterned with four naturalistic thistles on purplish ground, molded "G. Argy-Rousseau".
c1920   6in (15cm) high
$4,000-5,000   DRA

A Gabriel Argy-Rousseau pâte-de-verre vase, patterned with a band of masks of tragedy and comedy in deep purple, molded signature "G. Argy-Rousseau".
c1920   10in (25.5cm) high
$10,000-15,000   DRA

A Gabriel Argy-Rousseau pâte-de-verre 'Tetes de Lion' vase, the lip molded with six bosses carved with lion heads in shallow relief, molded "G. Argy-Rousseau".
c1925   8.25in (21cm) high
$10,000-15,000   DRA

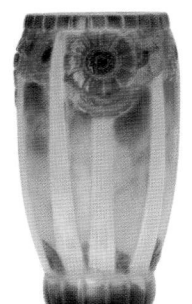

A Gabriel Argy-Rousseau pâte-de-verre vase, with stylized poppies, molded signature G. Argy-Rousseau, molded "France" on base.
c1925-30   6in (15cm) high
$10,000-15,000   DRA

A Gabriel Argy-Rousseau pâte-de-verre vase, with a band of satyr, faun and nymph, in indigo, aqua, and purple, molded signature "G. Argy-Rousseau".
      9in (23cm) high
$8,000-10,000   DRA

A Gabriel Argy-Rousseau pâte-de-verre vase, with colored chrysanthemums on mottled gray ground, molded signature "G. Argy-Rousseau".
      5.75in (14.5cm) high
$8,000-10,000   DRA

A Gabriel Argy-Rousseau pâte-de-verre vase, with fronds on frosted, mottled ground, molded "G. Argy-Rousseau" on body and "France" on base.
      6.5in (16.5cm) high
$6,000-8,000   DRA

A Gabriel Argy-Rousseau pâte-de-verre box and cover, patterned with formalized honesty leaves in autumnal colors on mottled ground, based molded "G. Argy-Rousseau, France".

c1920   3.75in (9.5cm) high

$3,500-4,500   **DRA**

A Gabriel Argy-Rousseau pâte-de-verre footed bowl, bordered with a band of four birds of prey on a ground of stylized flowers, molded signature "G. Argy-Rousseau".

c1925   6.25in (16cm) high

$3,000-4,000   **DRA**

A Gabriel Argy-Rousseau pâte-de-cristal footed bowl, modeled as a stylized poppy head in naturalistic colors on a clear foot, molded signature "G. Argy-Rousseau".

c1925   4in (10cm) diam

$2,000-3,000   **DRA**

A Gabriel Argy-Rousseau pâte-de-verre veilleuse lamp, patterned with three masks in deep purple, with original wrought-iron illuminating base, marked G. Argy-Rousseau.

c1925   5.5in (14cm) high

$10,000-12,000   **DRA**

A Gabriel Argy-Rousseau pâte-de-verre veilleuse lamp, patterned with three masks in bright coral colors, with original wrought-iron illuminating base, marked "G. Argy-Rousseau".

5.5in (14cm) high

$9,000-11,000   **DRA**

A Gabriel Argy-Rousseau pâte-de-verre veilleuse lamp, patterned with three stylized peonies in pinkish red, with original wrought-iron illuminating base, marked "G. Argy-Rousseau".

c1925   6.75in (17cm) high

$10,000-12,000   **DRA**

A Gabriel Argy-Rousseau pâte-de-cristal pendant, with poppy pattern in white and yellow on clear ground, engraved "G.A.R."

2.25in (5.5cm) high

$1,500-2,000   **DRA**

A Gabriel Argy-Rousseau pâte-de-verre lampshade, modeled as a stylized peony in exceptionally deep shades of deep violet, red and brown, lightening towards the center, molded signature "G. Argy-Rousseau".

12.5in (30.5cm) wide

$15,000-20,000   **DRA**

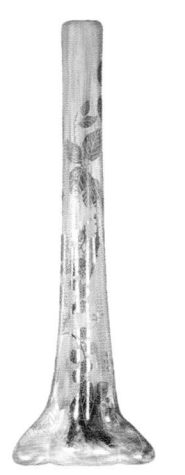

A fine large Daum Nancy trefoil cameo glass vase, decorated with blackberries, signed "Daum Nancy" with cross of Lorraine.

23.5in (59.5cm) high

$6,000-7,000 **GHOU**

A Daum acid-etched and enameled solifleur bud vase, patterned with blackberries in mauve and orange on frosted and shaded lemon-yellow ground, cameo signature "Daum Nancy" with cross of Lorraine.

9.25in (23.5cm) high

$1,500-2,000 **DRA**

A Daum cameo amphora-form vase, decorated with berried branches in violet-blue, green and mottled glass over a shaded and frosted orange ground, engraved signature "Daum Nancy" with cross of Lorraine.

10in (25.5cm) high

$10,000-15,000 **DRA**

A tall Daum etched and enameled cameo glass vase, with red and orange rosehips and green leaves, signed "DAUM NANCY" with cross of Lorraine.

19.75in (50cm) high

$5,000-6,000 **DRA**

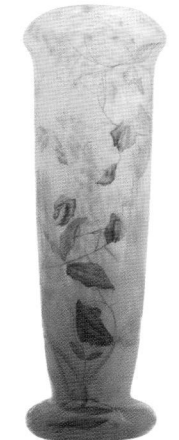

A Daum monumental etched and enameled glass vase, patterned with morning glories in naturalistic colors against a frosted and mottled ground shading to amber, cameo signature "DAUM NANCY" with cross of Lorraine.

c1900 *20in (51cm) high*

$7,000-10,000 **DRA**

A Daum etched and enameled vase, patterned with beech leaves in naturalistic colors against a mottled yellow, green and clear ground, cameo signature "Daum Nancy" with cross of Lorraine.

9.75in (25cm) high

$1,500-2,000 **DRA**

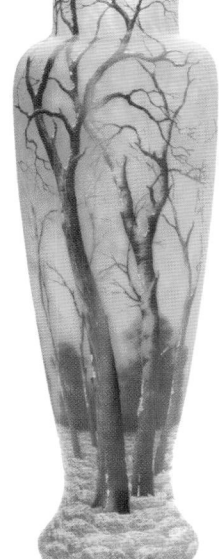

A Daum etched and enameled landscape scenic vase, with winter wooded landscape painted in naturalistic enamels against a shaded lemon-orange interior ground, painted "Daum Nancy Lorraine" on base.

17.25in (44cm) high

$15,000-20,000 **DRA**

A Daum etched and enameled vase, with gilt decoration patterned with violets on a mottled and frosted ground shading to purple at foot, with cameo "Daum Nancy" signature with cross of Lorraine.

9.5in (24cm) high

$10,000-12,000 **DRA**

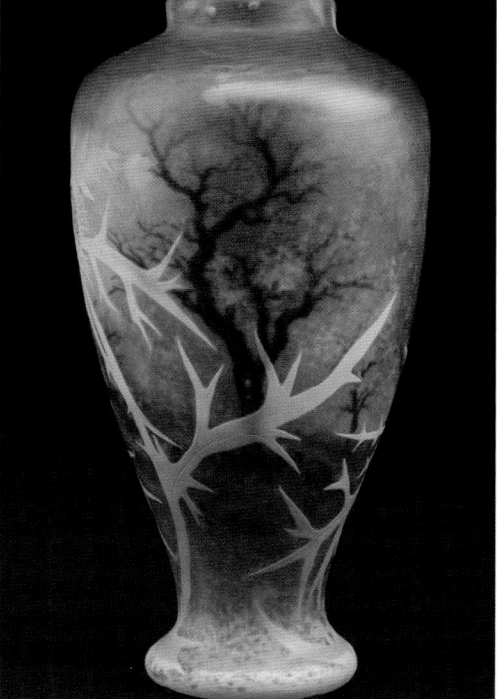

A Daum cameo vase with internal decoration with black trees overlaid with thistle decoration, wheel-carved signature "Daum Nancy"

8in (20cm) high

$50,000-55,000 **JDJ**

529

A Daum cameo vase, with acid cut grape and vine pattern in autumn colours with addition of two wheel carved snails applied to surface of vase, signed with engraved and gilded signature, "Daum Nancy".

13in (33cm) high

$20,000-25,000   **JDJ**

A rare Daum cameo vase with acid etched and enameled blackbird decoration, signed in enamel, "Daum Nancy".

10in (25cm) high

$20,000-25,000   **JDJ**

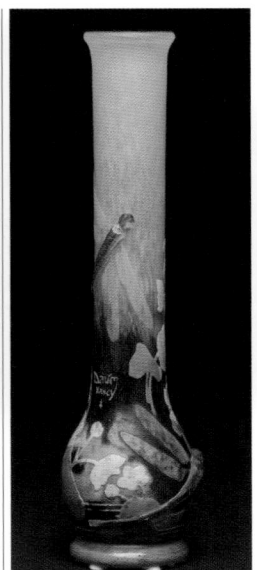

A Daum cameo vase, with applied and wheel-carved dragonflies, signed "Daum Nancy".

12in (39cm) high

$40,000-50,000   **JDJ**

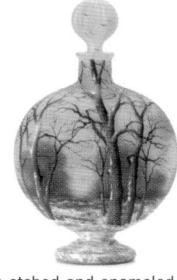

A Daum etched and enameled vase, decorated with tiger lilies in naturalistic colors against a frosted pink, yellow and white ground, cameo signature "Daum Nancy" with cross of Lorraine.

4.75in (12cm) high

$3,000-4,000   **DRA**

A Daum scenic cameo vase, with burnt-orange lakeland scene against a mottled yellow and orange shaded ground, with cameo signature.

4.5in (11.5cm) high

$1,500-3,000   **DRA**

A Daum scenic cameo vase, with wooded lakeland landscape, cameo signature "Daum Nancy" with cross of Lorraine.

5.5in (14cm) high

$2,000-3,000   **DRA**

A padded and wheel-carved Daum cameo glass vase, with mottled inclusions, acid-etched and carved, "Daum, Nancy", small chip to foot rim.

3.75in (9.5cm) high

$5,000-6,000   **L&T**

A Daum etched and enameled scenic perfume bottle and stopper, painted signature "Daum Nancy" and cross of Lorraine with rare Majorelle retail label.

7.75in (19.5cm) high

$12,000-18,000   **DRA**

A Daum wheel-carved cameo glass martele vase, patterned with blossoms in orange and green against a clear martele ground, engraved signature "DAUM NANCY" and cross of Lorraine.

c1895   *7in (18cm) high*

$5,500-6,500   **DRA**

A Daum scenic cameo jardinière, with wooded lakeland scene in shades of green on lemon and orange shaded ground, cameo signature "Daum Nancy" with cross of Lorraine.

10in (25.5cm) diam

$7,000-10,000   **DRA**

An exceptional Daum rain scene lamp with signature in enamel "Daum Nancy".

14in (36cm) high

$30,000-40,000   **JDJ**

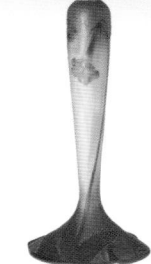

An Art Nouveau Daum slender table lamp, decorated with trumpet lilies in deep red shades on mottled pale yellow ground, shade engraved "Daum Nancy" with cross of Lorraine.

18.75in (47.5cm) high

$18,000-22,000   **DRA**

A Daum etched and enameled three-handled vase, patterned with herons flying among tendrils, above a pond of waterlilies, painted "Daum Nancy" with Cross of Lorraine in gilt.

11in (28cm) high

$30,000-35,000 DRA

An Art Deco Daum acid-etched vase, with a pattern of stylized flora in amber over internally speckled ground, wheel-cut "Daum Nancy France".

10in (25.5cm) high

$1,500-2,000 DRA

An Art Deco Daum acid-etched vase, with shell pattern, wheel-cut "Daum Nancy" with cross of Lorraine.

6in (15cm) high

$1,500-2,000 DRA

An Art Nouveau Daum tall-necked vase, of square, tapering form, internally decorated and enameled with vertical streaks in autumnal tones, engraved "Daum Nancy" with cross of Lorraine.

24in (61cm) high

$3,000-4,000 DRA

An Art Nouveau Daum tall-necked vase, with mottled, matte finish in shades of pink and mauve, half inch conchoidal chip at neck, engraved "Daum Nancy" with cross of Lorraine.

29in (73.5cm) high

$800-1,200 DRA

A Daum footed vase, internally decorated with gilt foil inclusions on shaded green, amber and blue ground, wheel-cut "Daum Nancy" with cross of Lorraine.

13in (33cm) high

$1,500-3,000 DRA

A Daum etched and enameled glass vase, patterned with wisteria in shades of mauve and green, engraved signature "DAUM NANCY" with cross of Lorraine.

c1900 *7in (18cm) high*

$3,500-4,000 DRA

A CLOSER LOOK AT A DAUM LAMP

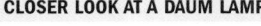

French metalworker Edgar Brandt was a hugely influential and highly respected craftsman. He produced architectural elements for important buildings as well as working with fashionable manufacturers.

The design is unusual and would be an interesting addition to a Daum collection.

The piece is marked both Daum and Brandt. As well as Daum art glass, Brandt metalware is collectable in its own right, making this lamp doubly desirable.

A Daum Nancy internally decorated blown glass vessel, with wrought iron mounts, c1910-1925, signed "Daum Nancy" with cross de Lorraine.

c1915 *6in (15cm) high*

$1,800-3,000 FRE

A Daum pâte-de-verre vide-poche by Amalric Walter, in the form of a frog and lily pad, etched "Daum, France" mark to the underside.

c1930 *6.25in (16cm) wide*

$2,000-2,500 FRE

An extremely rare Daum Nancy perfume burner, with applied and wheel-carved dragonflies, with hallmarked silver lid, lamp signed "Daum Nancy".

6in (15cm) high

$15,000-20,000 JDJ

A Daum/Edgar Brandt wrought-iron and glass table lamp, the bullet-shaped shade internally decorated with gilt foil inclusions on blue and mauve mottled ground and held in an ornamental armature, base stamped "E. Brandt", shade engraved with cross of Lorraine.

c1925 *18in (45.5cm) high*

$30,000-35,000 DRA

A De Vez scenic cameo vase, with moonlit landscape of gondola and village in deep brown and red on a shaded lemon-yellow ground, with cameo signature.

10in (25.5cm) high

$1,500-2,000　　　　**DRA**

A De Vez scenic cameo vase, with mountain goat and conifers in green, blue and white in mountain landscape against a shaded pink sky, with cameo signature.

10.25in (26cm) high

$1,500-2,000　　　　**DRA**

A De Vez scenic cameo vase, decorated with a lakeland landscape with village and fishing boat in mauve and pale green against a shaded lemon-yellow and orange ground, with cameo signature.

17in (43cm) high

$2,000-3,000　　　　**DRA**

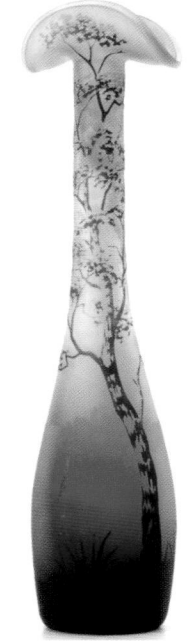

A scenic cameo vase, attributed to De Vez, patterned with a birch tree against a lakeland landscape in shades of brown and green on shaded blue ground, indistinct signature.

10.75in (27.5cm) high

$900-1,100　　　　**DRA**

A De Vez scenic cameo vase, patterned with an eagle alighting a nest in a wooded landscape, in browns on pink frosted ground, with cameo signature.

7.5in (19cm) high

$900-1,100　　　　**DRA**

A De Vez scenic cameo vase, with wooded mountain lakeland scene in green and red on shaded lemon-yellow and white ground, cameo signature.

12.25in (21cm) high

$1,200-1,800　　　　**DRA**

A De Vez scenic cameo vase, with Alpine scene in blue and lemon-yellow cut back to white clouds and snow capped mountains, the shoulder decorated with pinecones shading to pink at the neck, with cameo signature.

10.5in (26.5cm) high

$1,500-2,000　　　　**DRA**

A De Vez scenic cameo vase, with tropical mountainous landscape in shades of blue, green and yellow on shaded, opalescent amber ground. cameo signature "De Vez".

10in (25.5cm) high

$1,000-1,500　　　　**DRA**

EMILE GALLÉ

■ The son of a glass and faience factory owner, Emile Gallé (1846-1904) immersed himself in the arts and in 1874, took over the family business in Nancy, Lorraine.

■ Gallé loved the natural world and wild animals and under his lead, the factory initially produced clear colored glass with enameled floral decoration.

■ These pieces were artistically successful and he was awarded four gold medals at the 1878 Paris International Exhibition.

■ This exhibition opened his eyes to the work of other glassmakers and enabled him to start work on the spectacular cameo vases.

■ The cameo technique involved layering colored glass, and then etching them to reveal the surfaces beneath and create detailed landscape and foliate designs.

■ Gallé's early pieces were entirely handmade and unique but after 1899, production of more commercial 'standard' art glass began. Modern techniques such as acid-etching and wheel-carving were used.

■ The "Gallé" signature appears in many different versions on cameo glass; a star next to the mark indicates pieces produced after Gallé's death in 1904.

■ The factory ceased production in 1936.

An Emile Gallé artistic cameo vase, patterned with lilies in violet and shades of green on an internally streaked green and opalescent ground, cameo signature "Gallé" in Japanese taste.

c1900   13.5in (34.5cm) high

$9,000-11,000   **DRA**

An Emile Gallé scenic cameo vase, with mountain landscape in shades of mauve, green, and blue on frosted and shaded lemon-yellow ground, with cameo signature.

11.75in (30cm) high

$3,500-4,000   **DRA**

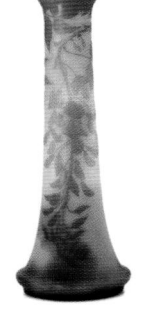

An Emile Gallé monumental cameo glass vase, with wisteria pattern in shades of mauve on mottled ground, with cameo signature.

18.75in (47.5cm) high

$4,000-5,000   **DRA**

An Emile Gallé solifleur cameo bud vase patterned with bellflowers in deep mauve on frosted amber ground, with cameo signature.

5.25in (13.5cm) high

$800-1,200   **DRA**

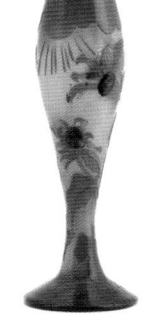

An Emile Gallé applied and internally decorated cameo vase, with gold foil inclusions, engraved signature on base.

1900   13in (33cm) high

$6,000-8,000   **DRA**

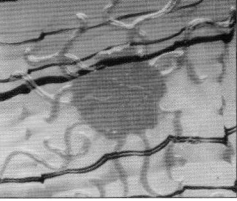

An Emile Gallé artistic marine cameo and internally decorated vase, patterned with undersea plants and creatures in amber on internally decorated mauve, amber and frosted ground, cameo signature formed as jellyfish tentacles.

8.5in (21.5cm) high

$18,000-24,000   **DRA**

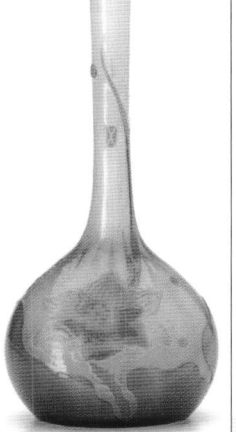

An Emile Gallé 'Verre Parlant' cameo vase, decorated with roses in deep red on shaded pale ground, the tall neck with "bonheur" vertically depicted in cameo, vertical cameo signature.

8in (20cm) high

$4,000-5,000   **DRA**

An Emile Gallé cameo solifleur bud vase, decorated with clematis in mauve on shaded lemon yellow ground, with cameo signature.

10.5in (26.5cm) high

$3,000-4,000   **DRA**

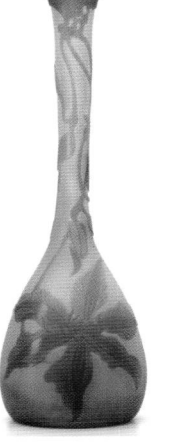

An Emile Gallé cameo vase, decorated with violets in green and brown on shaded lemon-yellow ground, the base fire polished, with cameo signature.

4.25in (11cm) high

$1,200-1,800   **DRA**

An Emile Gallé cameo vase, decorated with honeysuckle in mauve against a shaded lemon-yellow ground, cameo signature.

9.5in (24cm) high

$2,000-3,000   **DRA**

An Emile Gallé solifleur cameo bud vase, decorated with red orchids over frosted lemon-yellow ground, with cameo signature.

8.25in (21cm) high

$3,000-4,000   **DRA**

An Emile Gallé scenic cameo vase, in dark browns over shaded green ground, with cameo signature.

6.5in (16.5cm) high

$1,000-1,500   **DRA**

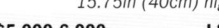

A tall Gallé cameo glass vase, the pale gray body overlaid and acid etched with pine trees in a mountain landscape, cameo signature mark.

15.75in (40cm) high

$5,000-6,000   **L&T**

An Emile Gallé scenic cameo vase, decorated with a condor in deep brown against a mountainous landscape, with cameo signature.

11in (28cm) high

$6,000-8,000   **DRA**

An Emile Gallé cameo vase, decorated with hydrangea in shades of red on frosted yellow ground, with cameo signature.

18in (45.5cm) high

$10,000-15,000   **DRA**

An Emile Gallé cameo vase, decorated with clematis in deep and light purple on shaded and fire polished ground, cameo signature.

6.5in (16.5cm) high

$4,000-6,000   **DRA**

An Emile Gallé scenic cameo vase, with a continuous mountainous landscape in shades of mauve, green, blue and yellow against a shaded orange ground, the base fire polished, cameo signature "Gallé".

14in (35.5cm) high

$9,000-11,000   **DRA**

An Emile Gallé cameo footed vase, decorated with camellias in mauve on shaded lemon-yellow ground, the base fire polished, with cameo signature.

6.5in (16.5cm) high

$900-1,200   **DRA**

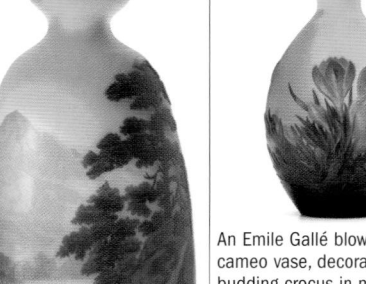

An Emile Gallé cameo vase, decorated with bell-flowers in shades of mauve and green on shaded lemon-yellow ground, with cameo signature.

15in (38cm) high

$5,000-6,000   **DRA**

An Emile Gallé blown-out cameo vase, decorated with budding crocus in mauve and green against a shaded orange ground, with cameo signature.

8in (20cm) high

$4,500-5,000   **DRA**

An Emile Gallé cameo glass pillow vase, with scooped rim decorated with oak leaves and acorns in brown and green on shaded red ground, with cameo signature.

9in (23cm) high

$3,000-4,000   **DRA**

An Emile Gallé scenic cameo vase, with wooded lake scene in deep mauve against a shaded blue background, engraved signature.

4.5in (11.5cm) high

$2,000-3,000   **DRA**

An Emile Gallé cameo glass vase, of shouldered tapering form, the gray and lemon glass body overlaid in blue and amethyst glass and acid-etched with trees in a mountain landscape, cameo mark "Gallé".

13.75in (35cm) high

$6,000-7,000   **L&T**

An Emile Gallé blown-out cameo vase, decorated with clematis on shaded lemon-yellow ground, old surface crack to interior of base, possibly in manufacturing, with cameo signature.

9.5in (24cm) high

$4,000-5,000   **DRA**

An Emile Gallé cameo vase decorated with pansies in purple and green on shaded lemon-yellow ground, with cameo signature.

5in (12.5cm) high

$1,500-2,000   **DRA**

An Emile Gallé cameo glass vase, with acid etched decoration of trees in a mountain landscape, and cameo mark "Gallé".

6in (15.5cm) high

$4,000-5,000   **L&T**

An Emile Gallé cameo glass vase patterned with dahlia blossoms in shades of blue and violet, partly fire-polished against a frosted lemon yellow ground, cameo signature.

c1900   *10in (25cm) high*

$5,000-7,000   **DRA**

An Emile Gallé cameo blown-out vase, in water lily soufflé with brown, green and lavender-white on sky blue ground, signed in cameo.

10in (25cm) high

$20,000-25,000   **JDJ**

An Emile Gallé 'Verre Parlant' floriform cameo vase, decorated with orchids in blood red, engraved "O Beaute", and the base engraved "Cristallerie de Gallé Nancy".

The neck is engraved with the opening lines from Baudelaire's 'Les Fleurs de Mal'.

7.5in (19cm) high

$20,000-30,000   **DRA**

An Emile Gallé cameo footed plate, patterned with morning glories in violet on frosted pale ground, the border crimped, small flake to rim, cameo signature formed as a tendril.

10.25in (26cm) diam

$2,000-3,000   **DRA**

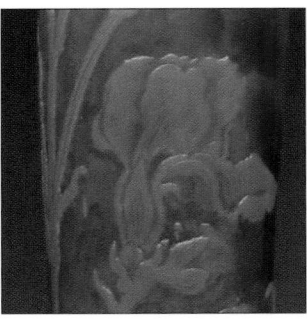

An early wheel-carved Gallé vase, with bright green textured ground with wheel-carved irises, leaves and stems, signed "Cristallerie E. Galle Nancy Modeo et Décor Depose".

15in (38cm) high

$12,000-14,000 **JDJ**

An Emile Gallé floriform vase, internally decorated and modeled as an arum lily with a pattern of tendrils in deep brown on speckled amber and clear ground, base etched "Gallé" on polished pontil.

10.75in (27.5cm) high

$5,000-7,000 **DRA**

An Emile Gallé enameled glass hexagonal vase, decorated with thistles and wild flowers in applied polychrome enamel, gilt and engraving on smoky ground, base with ornamental gilt "E. Gallé" signature.

8.5in (21.5cm) high

$3,000-4,000 **DRA**

An Emile Gallé enameled glass trefoil bowl, decorated with trailing anemone in naturalistic polychrome enamels and gilt on pale green frosted ground, base engraved "Gallé Nancy" within a leaf device.

6.75in (17cm) diam

$3,000-3,500 **DRA**

An Emile Gallé enameled glass perfume bottle with stopper, enameled "E. Gallé" and with retailer's paper label for "Au Vase Etrusque Paris".

c1910 *4in (10cm) high*

$1,800-2,200 **DRA**

A Gallé marquetry glass 'Crocus' vase, with overlay decoration, etched Gallé mark.

c1900 *13.5in (34.5cm) high*

$25,000-30,000 **FRE**

A Lalique opalescent 'Bacchantes' glass vase, the sides molded in high relief with dancing nudes, etched "Lalique, France".

1927   9.5in (24cm) high

$8,000-10,000   **FRE**

A Lalique 'Biches' vase, frosted and stained, signed.

6.75in (17cm) high

$1,200-1,800   **GHOU**

A Lalique 'Malesherbes' vase, in opalescent glass with green patina, stencilled "R. LALIQUE" mark, engraved "France No. 1014".

c1927   9in (22.5cm) high

$3,000-4,000   **RDL**

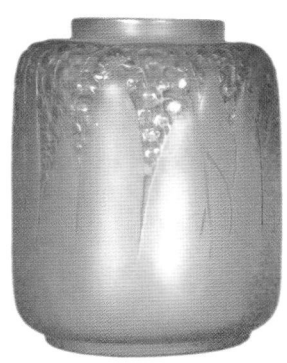

A Lalique 'Muguets' vase, frosted and gray stained, signed.

6.25in (16cm) high

$1,500-2,000   **GHOU**

A Lalique 'Fougères' frosted blue glass vase, of ovoid form, molded with bands of foliage, etched mark "R. Lalique".

6in (15cm) high

$7,000-8,000   **L&T**

A Lalique monumental clear and frosted crystal glass vase and cover, of shouldered tapering form, molded in relief with fern fronds and to the shoulders with four masks, the slightly domed lid similarly decorated, etched marks "Lalique, France".

After 1945   18.5in (47cm) high

$6,000-7,000   **L&T**

A Lalique oval vanity mirror, tulip pattern, signed "Lalique France".

10in (25.5cm) high

$300-400   **FRE**

A Lalique 'Flausa' molded glass perfume bottle for Roger & Gallet, the bottle molded "Flausa" and "Roger & Gallet", the stopper molded "Lalique", with silk cord seal and parfum, in the original box.

c1912   Bottle 4.5in (11.5cm) high

$4,500-6,000   **FRE**

A Lalique opalescent glass bowl, the broad flaring rim molded with lily of the valley, blue staining, stenciled mark "R. Lalique, France".

12.5in (31.5cm) diam

$1,500-2,000   **L&T**

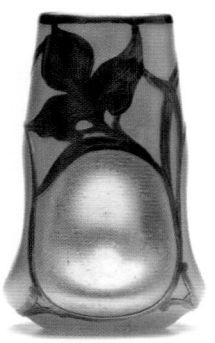

A Loetz silver overlay vase, in gold iridescence patterned with silver orchids, polished pontil, silver with maker's symbol for Alvin and stamped "Patented 925/1000".

6.25in (16cm) high

$1,400-1,600   **DRA**

A Loetz Art Nouveau glass vase, with silver overlay, decorated with iridescent trailing tendrils.

c1900   *4in (10cm) high*

$3,000-3,500   **DRA**

An Art Nouveau Loetz vase, with silver floral pattern overlay and rim, with trefoil lip, polished pontil, loss to one silver leaf tip.

5in (12.5cm) high

$1,000-1,500   **DRA**

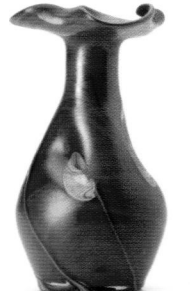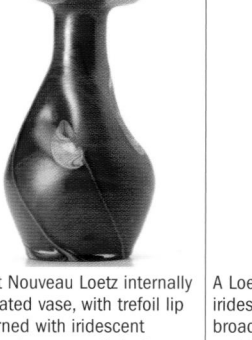

A Loetz gilt metal mounted iridescent glass vase, designed circa 1903 for E. Bakalowits, the gourd-shaped body with peacock iridescence held by cast leafy mounts.

c1903   *13in (33cm) high*

$5,000-6,000   **L&T**

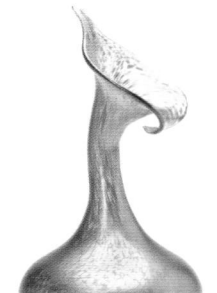

A Loetz-style handled glass vase, the body of concave shape, decorated in a purple iridescent color, unmarked.

8.5in (22cm) high

$250-300   **PC**

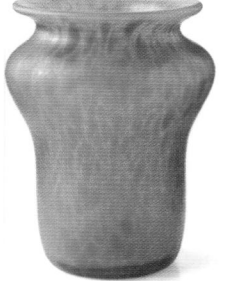

A small Loetz-style iridescent glass vase, with thistle shaped neck, exhibiting a peacock blue and mauve sheen.

5in (13cm) high

$200-300   **JN**

A Loetz iridescent vase, patterned with gold stylized leaves on wavy ground, polished pontil engraved "Loetz Austria".

6.75in (17cm) high

$4,000-5,000   **DRA**

An Art Nouveau Loetz internally decorated vase, with trefoil lip patterned with iridescent swirling lappets, polished pontil.

6.75in (17cm) high

$3,000-4,000   **DRA**

A Loetz 'Jack-in-the-Pulpit' iridescent green glass vase, the broad rim above tapering neck and bulbous body.

9in (23cm) high

$1,000-1,500   **L&T**

A Loetz monumental lily vase, of naturalistic floriform with iridescent oil spot decoration, unmarked.

18in (46cm) high

$3,000-4,000   **DRA**

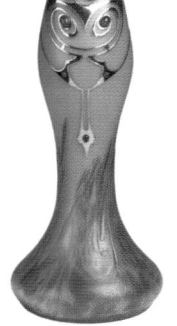

A Loetz iridescent glass vase, with amber iridescence to the body, overlaid in silver to the bulbous neck and inset with green cabochon stones.

12.5in (31.5cm) high

$3,000-4,000   **L&T**

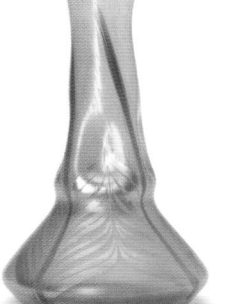

A Loetz iridescent vase, of pinched form with pulled-feather decorations, polished pontil engraved "Loetz Austria".

9.75in (25cm) high

$3,500-4,000   **DRA**

A small Loetz-style iridescent glass vase, of tapering shape with everted rim, exhibiting a green-golden lustrous sheen.

6in (15cm) high

$240-280   **JN**

A Loetz iridescent vase, with waved ground in shades of blue with blue interior, polished pontil engraved "Loetz Austria".

8.75in (22cm) high

$2,000-3,000   **DRA**

MONART

- The Moncrieff glassworks in Perth, Scotland initially produced functional clear glass items. The Monart range of art glass was introduced in 1924.
- The range was created by glassblower Salvador Ysart, who had worked at Schneider. He was encouraged by Isabel Moncrieff, the wife of the factory owner.
- Ysart and his sons designed over 300 Monart shapes, inspired predominantly by Chinese ceramics, between 1924 and 1933.
- Pieces were decorated with crushed enamel flecks of varying sizes, prior to being free-blown.
- Decoration was often concentrated towards the top of an object. Sometimes a 'Paisley Shawl' finish was added by pulling the design on the surface of the molten glass.
- On occasions, specks of silver or copper were introduced and other techniques were developed, such as cloisonné, which involved plunging the hot glass into cold water to produce a decorative cracked surface.
- Production of Monart ceased in 1939 and was resumed on a smaller scale after the war under Paul Ysart, the eldest son of Salvador, who set up Vasart glass with two of his brothers.
- Collectors identify Monart by its distinctive body and ground pontil mark. Paper labels are desirable.

A Monart glass vase, of tapering ovoid form, the green body with green stripes, graduating to amethyst stripes at the neck with red and aventurine inclusions, A shape.

8in (20.5cm) high

$1,000-1,500   **L&T**

A Monart glass vase, of striped peppermint color with mica inclusions, MF shapes.

8.75in (22.5cm) high

$1,000-1,200   **L&T**

A Monart glass vase, with cylindrical neck above ovoid body, with mottled blue and green inclusions, and darker blue stripes, bears traces of paper label, B shape.

10in (25.5cm) high

$1,500-3,000   **L&T**

A large Monart glass vase, of tapering cylindrical form the body with mottled blue and green inclusions and blue swirls, QA shape.

10.5in (27cm) high

$1,500-2,000   **L&T**

A Monart glass vase, of tapering cylindrical form, the mottled red body graduating to green towards the rim, with amethyst and aventurine inclusions, OE shape.

9in (23cm) high

$800-1,200   **L&T**

A Monart glass jar and cover, the mottled green body and cover each with amethyst and aventurine inclusions to rim, bears traces of paper label, Z shape.

8.5in (22cm) high

$1,000-1,500   **L&T**

A Monart glass vase, of globular footed form, the mottled blue body with darker blue and aventurine.

6.5in (17cm) high

$1,500-2,000   **L&T**

A Monart 'stoneware' glass vase, with cylindrical neck above squat ovoid body, with pulled decoration in pink amethyst and green, bears torn paper label, GA shape.

7.5in (19cm) high

$3,000-4,000   **L&T**

A Monart glass vase, of tapering ovoid form, the lemon body with orange, yellow, green and aventurine inclusions and brown stripes, KC shape.

8.75in (22cm) high

$1,500-2,000   **L&T**

A Monart glass vase, mottled yellow with green, orange, light and dark blue, amethyst, pink and bubble inclusions, bears paper label "VII+.295E", ZD shape.

7in (17.5cm)

$1,000-1,500   **L&T**

A Monart glass vase, of ovoid form, with mottled orange inclusions graduating to brown at the rim, and large bubble pattern, bears torn paper label, QB shape.

6.75in (17cm) high

$800-1,200   **L&T**

A Monart glass vase, with mottled red to mottled green neck, original paper label "IV FB 52", FB shape.

14in (35.5cm) high

$1,500-2,000   **WW**

A Monart glass vase, with flared rim, above tapering ovoid body, with mottled and striped blue inclusions, UB shape.

8in (20cm) high

$700-1,000 **L&T**

A pair of footed Monart glass vases, with everted rims, mottled body, and central swirling band with blue and aventurine inclusions, TC V shape.

11.5in (29.5cm) high

$1,200-1,800 **L&T**

An early Monart 'Stoneware' bowl, with pale gray body overlaid with mottled bands of brown and royal blue, shape XV.

9.5in (24cm) diam

$2,000-3,000 **L&T**

A large Monart glass bowl, with flaring rim, the mottled red body with green amethyst, lemon and aventurine inclusions, bears paper label.

12.25in (31.5cm) diam

$1,000-1,500 **L&T**

A large Monart glass bowl, of flared footed form, the clear glass with white webbed pattern and aventurine inclusions to the rim, bears paper label "IV.AI.386".

12in (30cm) diam

$600-800 **L&T**

SCHNEIDER

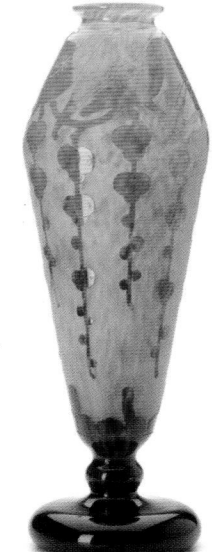

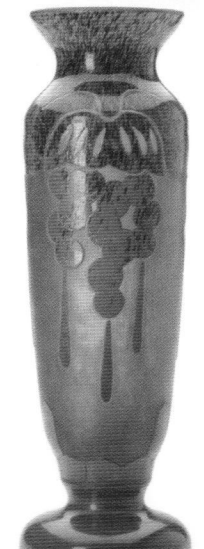

A Charles Schneider etched and enameled vase, decorated with Morning Glories shading from red to mauve on mottled ground, engraved "Le Verre Français".

15.5in (39.5cm) high

$2,000-3,000 **DRA**

A Charles Schneider etched and enameled vase, decorated with stylized bellflowers shading from red to mauve on mottled ground, engraved "Le Verre Français".

15in (38cm) high

$2,500-3,000 **DRA**

A Charles Schneider etched and enameled vase, decorated with stylized bellflowers in red shading to mauve on mottled ground, engraved "Le Verre Français".

16.5in (42cm) high

$2,000-3,000 **DRA**

A Charles Schneider etched and enameled beetle vase, in aubergine over clear yellow-orange ground, engraved "Le Verre Français", base with inlaid glass cane.

11.75in (30cm) high

$4,000-5,000 **DRA**

A Charles Schneider etched and enameled vase, decorated with stylized fruiting branches in cinnabar on frosted amber ground, cameo signature "Charder".

16.5in (42cm) high

$2,500-3,000 **DRA**

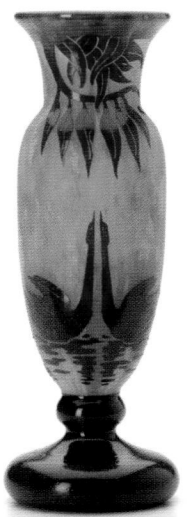

A Charles Schneider etched and enameled vase, decorated with stylized swans under leafage in purple on mottled and frosted orange and yellow ground, cameo signature "Charder".

10.5in (26.5cm) high

$3,500-4,500   **DRA**

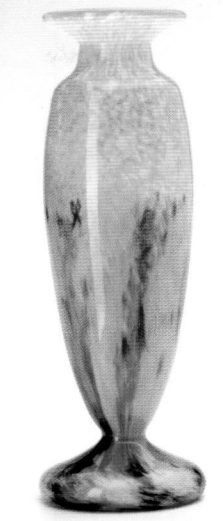

A Charles Schneider baluster vase, in mottled shades of pink, blue, and purple, stenciled "Schneider" on foot, base stenciled "France Avignon".

14in (35.5cm) high

$1,500-2,000   **DRA**

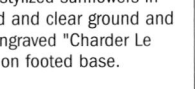

A Charles Schneider acid-etched vase, decorated with stylized sunflowers in green on frosted and clear ground and shaded base, engraved "Charder Le Verre Français" on footed base.

14.5in (37cm) high

$3,000-3,500   **DRA**

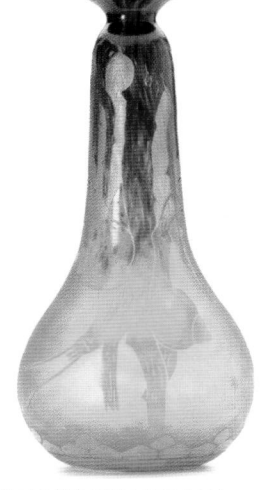

A Charles Schneider etched and enameled vase, decorated with snails on trailing branches in brown shading to orange on mottled lemon-yellow ground, base with inlaid glass cane, engraved "Le Verre Français".

15in (38cm) high

$5,000-6,000   **DRA**

A Charles Schneider etched and enameled vase, with stylized Art Deco pattern in rare blue color, inlaid glass cane signature, engraved "Le Verre Français".

3.5in (9cm) high

$1,500-2,000   **DRA**

A Charles Schneider etched and enameled vase, decorated with stylized nightshade in turtle shell on mottled and matte orange and yellow ground, engraved "Le Verre Français".

15in (38cm) high

$2,500-3,500   **DRA**

A Charles Schneider overlaid and etched glass vase, decorated with stylized wisteria in purple over blue frosted and shaded ground, cameo mark "Charder", etched "Le Verre Français".

6in (15cm) high

$1,500-2,000   **DRA**

A Schneider-style cameo glass vase, of squat shape tapering to a rectangular neck, the amber tinted body overlaid with blue glass acid-etched with stylised flowers, signed with colored glass "cane".

4in (10cm) wide

$300-400   **JN**

A Charles Schneider etched and enameled vase, patterned with stylized pansies in blue and orange on yellow ground, engraved "Le Verre Français".

14.75in (37.5cm) high

$3,500-4,000   **DRA**

A Charles Schneider footed vase, the bowl in deeply mottled orange and yellow tones on applied mottled purplish stem and foot, engraved "Schneider France".

11.75in (30cm) high

$1,000-1,500   **DRA**

A Steuben gold Aurene floriform vase, engraved "Aurene 346".

12in (30.5cm) high

$1,500-2,000 DRA

A Steuben gold Aurene floriform vase, engraved "Aurene 346".

10in (25.5cm) high

$1,200-1,800 DRA

A Steuben gold Aurene floriform vase, engraved "Aurene 2699".

12in (30.5cm) high

$1,500-2,000 DRA

A Steuben gold Aurene 'three-log' vase, engraved "Steuben Aurene 2749".

6in (15cm) high

$1,000-1,500 DRA

A Steuben vase, in conical shape with heart and vine decoration with iridescent blue glaze, signed "Steuben Aurene 1278"

10in (25cm) high

$5,000-6,000 JDJ

A Steuben vase, with decoration of applied leaf and vine, signed "Steuben Aurene 6299", minor scratches.

6in (15cm) high

$8,000-9,000 JDJ

A pair of Steuben blue Aurene table candlesticks, with spiral twisted stems, each engraved "Aurene 989".

6in (15cm) high

$2,000-3,000 DRA

A Steuben Rosaline glass vase, patterned with blossoming peony in acid-etching.

6.5in (16.5cm) high

$1,500-2,000 DRA

A Steuben Tyrian vase, with gold heart and vine decoration on a greenish/blue to purple/gray, signed "Tyrian".

7in (18cm) high

$18,000-22,000 JDJ

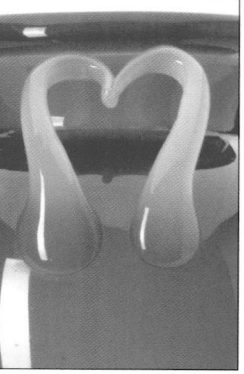

A Steuben acid-cutback vase, with black stylized foliate design cut to green, unmarked.

10in (25.5cm) high

$7,000-9,000 DRA

A Steuben large jade-green vase, with applied alabaster glass handles of unusual form.

$3,000-4,000 DRA

12in (30.5cm) high

$3,000-4,000 DRA

A Steuben blue bubbly vase, with quilted pattern, stenciled mark.

8in (20cm) high

$2,000-3,000 DRA

LOUIS COMFORT TIFFANY

■ Louis Comfort Tiffany (1848-1933), son of jewelry maker Charles Louis Tiffany, studied painting and glass-blowing before establishing a successful interior design company.

■ Inspired by the work of the glass designer Emile Gallé, he also began to experiment with glass.

■ In 1881 he patented his 'Favrile' iridescent glass, which utilized sprayed metallic lusters.

■ In 1885 Tiffany established a new company, which was later named Tiffany Studios, to focus on the development of innovative freeblown glass vases - produced commercially from 1894.

■ Simpler vase shapes were decorated with a huge variety of complex techniques such as the peacock pattern, feathering, painting and threading. Pieces were sometimes marvered – a technique that involved pressing hot glass into the surface of a vase to created floral shapes.

■ Other innovations included the iridescent 'Lava' range and the pitted 'Cypriote' range, as well as the hugely valuable leaded lamp shades.

■ Tiffany Studios finally closed in 1932. Tiffany & Co. are still in business.

A Tiffany Furnaces gilt bronze and enamel trumpet vase, the flaring base decorated in peacock blue enamel shading to gold and white, stamped "LOUIS C. TIFFANY FURNACES INC. FAVRILE 165".

13.5in (34.5cm) high

$600-900   **DRA**

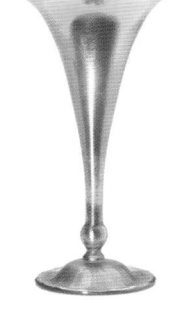

A Tiffany Studios gold Favrile glass trumpet vase, with domed ribbed base and folded foot, base engraved "L.C. TIFFANY Favrile" with partially obscured design number, "9???D".

14in (35.5cm) high

$2,000-3,000   **DRA**

A Tiffany Favrile bronze mounted trumpet form vase, incised butterfly decoration inside rim, signed "Favrile", base stamped "Louis C. Tiffany Furnaces Inc. Favrile 158".

17.5in (44.5cm) high

$900-1,200   **FRE**

A Tiffany gilt bronze and Favrile glass feather design floriform vase, base stamped "Tiffany Studios New York 1043", glass signed "LCT".

14in (35.5cm) high

$1,000-1,500   **FRE**

A Tiffany Studios gold Favrile glass vase, with pulled feather design on pinecone base, glass engraved "L.C.T".

c1910

$3,000-4,000   **DRA**

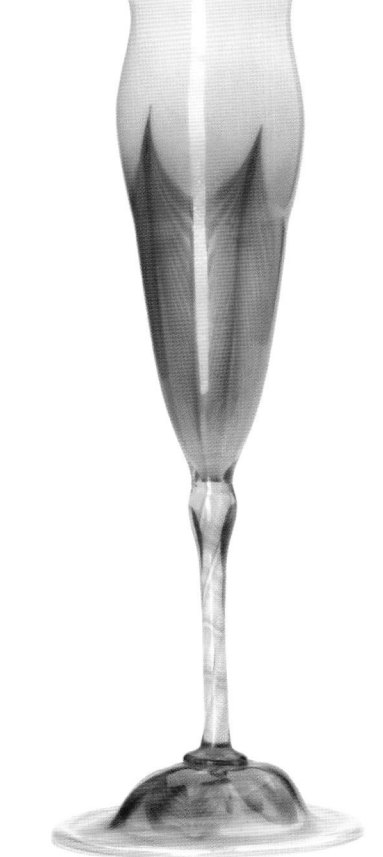

A Tiffany Studios Favrile glass floriform vase, with green and gold pulled feather decoration on foot shading to pink and opalescent at the rim, engraved "Tiffany Favrile 2549D".

12.25in (31cm) high

$6,000-8,000   **DRA**

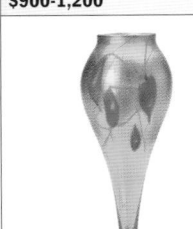

A Tiffany Studios gold Favrile glass floriform vase, internally decorated with green and white trailing vines, engraved "LC Tiffany-Favrile 8835H".

6in (15cm) high

$3,000-4,000   **DRA**

A Tiffany Studios gold Favrile ribbed floriform pedestal vase, marked "1526 6835L/L.C. Tiffany/Favrile".

12.5in (31.5cm) high

$1,500-2,000   **DRA**

A Tiffany Studios Favrile glass floriform vase, closed floriform in pulled feather design in opalescent and green, engraved "L.C.T. W4050".

12.75in (32.5cm) high

$6,000-8,000   **DRA**

DECORATIVE ARTS

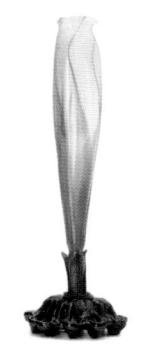

A Tiffany floriform vase, on molded glass and metal foot (probably associated), unsigned.

c1900   15.5in (38.5cm) h
$3,000-4,000   DRA

A Tiffany Favrile glass 'Floriform' vase, with feather decoration, raised on a slender striated shaft and domed foot, signed "LCT" and numbered 4880B.

c1905   11.25in (28.5cm) high
$5,000-7,000   FRE

A Tiffany Favrile glass 'Floriform' vase, with feather decoration and a striated slender shaft, signed "LCT" and numbered "4879B".

c1905   11.5in (29cm) high
$5,000-7,000   FRE

A Tiffany Studios gold Favrile glass Jack-in-the-Pulpit vase, engraved "L.C.T Y5465" and with paper label.

17.5in (44.5cm) high
$18,000-22,000   DRA

A Tiffany Studios gold Favrile glass vase, decorated with green leaves in bronze holder with swirls, original dark patina. "L.C.T./Tiffany Studios/New York/711".

14in (35.5cm) high
$3,000-4,000   DRA

A Tiffany Studios gold Favrile glass vase, with hexagonal rim on polychrome enameled foot, base impressed "Louis C. Tiffany Furnaces Inc. 151" beneath monogram.

13.5in (34.5cm) high
$3,000-4,000   DRA

A pair of Tiffany Studios green Favrile glass floriform vase, gold with green leaf decoration, each engraved "L.C.TIFFANY Favrile 1501", engraved control number "8499", "8500".

The consecutive control numbers on these vases indicate they were made, and have always been, together as a pair.

8in (20cm) high
$4,000-6,000   DRA

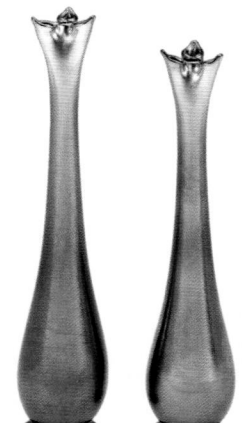

A rare Tiffany blue favrile glass exposition vase, signed "L.C. Tiffany, Favrile, Alaska-Yukon Pacific Ex, 2145 E", with a similar larger example signed "L.C. Tiffany, Favrile 2538 E".

Made for the 1909 Alaska-Yukon Pacific Exposition in Seattle.

c1909   larger 17in (43cm) high
$15,000-20,000   FRE

A CLOSER LOOK AT A TIFFANY VASE

Introduced by Louis Comfort Tiffany in 1884, Favrile glass is created by dissolving salts of metallic oxides in molten glass and then spraying the surface with chloride to create a lustrous iridescent finish.

Inspired by the woodland flower, 'Jack-in-the-Pulpit' vases originated in England and were produced by a number a glassmakers. Tiffany examples are particularly valuable.

Tiffany glass was free-blown and this fine shape was very difficult to produce.

Tiffany produced a variety of floriform vases that reflected Art Nouveau interest in the aesthetics of the natural world.

A Tiffany Studios gold Favrile glass Jack-In-Pulpit vase, c1900 - 1910, engraved "L.C.T - FAVRILE 1636H".

c1900   20in (51cm) high
$20,000-25,000   DRA

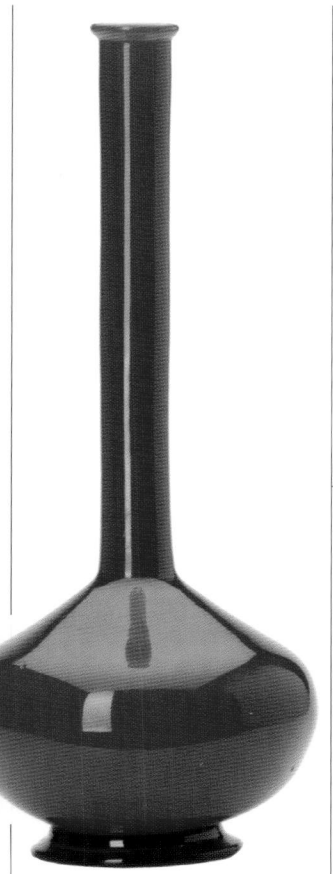

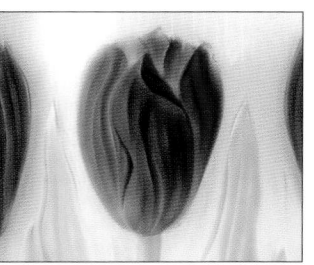

A Tiffany Studios carved overlay and internally decorated glass vase, patterned with purple headed tulips with green leafage below a neck of scrolled lappets, engraved "L.C. Tiffany Favrile, # 4182A".

11.75in (30cm) high

$30,000-35,000 **DRA**

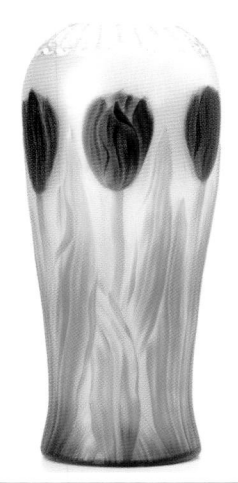

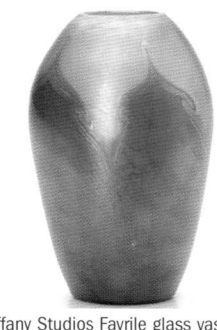

A Tiffany Studios Favrile glass vase, internally decorated with stylized Moorish leafage in green and iridescence on gold ground, engraved "L.C.T. 6436".

6.5in (16.5cm) high

$2,500-3,000 **DRA**

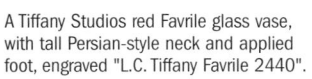

A Tiffany Studios red Favrile glass vase, with tall Persian-style neck and applied foot, engraved "L.C. Tiffany Favrile 2440".

12in (30cm) high

$10,000-15,000 **DRA**

An L. C. Tiffany Favrile glass cabinet vase, with blue pulled-feather decoration on deep bottle-green ground, etched "L.C.T./?Y3826".

2.25in (5cm) high

$2,500-3,000 **DRA**

An early 20thC Tiffany Favrile glass paperweight vase, with gold iridescent pulled-feather decoration to the rim, internally decorated in orange and green, marked "LC Tiffany Favrile V210".

6.75in (17cm) high

$25,000-30,000 **FRE**

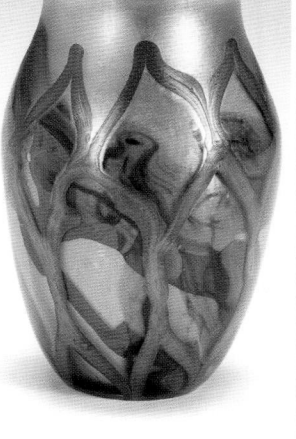

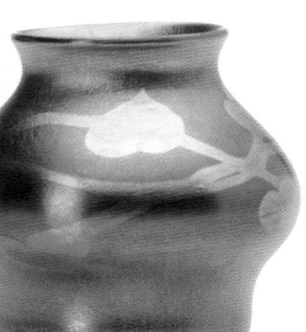

A Tiffany Studios blue Favrile glass vase, patterned with a band of silvery trailing vines on blue ground, engraved "L.C.T. 644B" and with paper label.

3.25in (8.5cm) high

$2,000-3,000 **DRA**

A Tiffany Corona Favrile glass vase, blue to gold iridescence, signed "Corona".

In 1892, Louis Comfort Tiffany began producing Favrile glass (trademarked 1894) at his factory in Corona, Queens, New York, marking the initial pieces Corona. However after about four weeks of production, the furnace was lost in a fire. After this point, Tiffany changed the markings to Favrile glass, making the surviving Corona-marked pieces rare.

1892   3.75in (9.5cm) high

$3,000-4,000 **FRE**

A Tiffany Favrile-style iridescent glass vase, of double-ogee form with flared neck, rim exhibiting a golden sheen with vivid tones of peacock blue on the interior.

1909   3.5in (9cm) high

$300-400 **JN**

A Tiffany Studios gold Favrile bowl, engraved "L.C. Tiffany Favrile 8964 K", together with an iridescent lapis compote engraved "L.C. Tiffany Inc. Favrile".

Bowl 11in (28cm) diam

$2,000-3,000 **DRA**

DECORATIVE ARTS

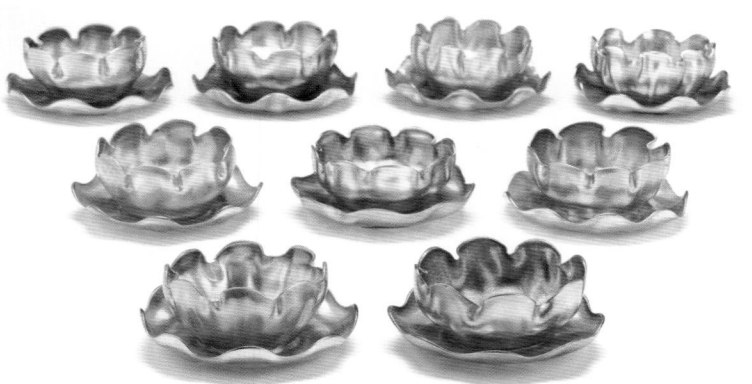

An early 20thC set of nine Tiffany Favrile glass finger bowls and saucers, etched "L.C.T.", the lobed gold iridescent bowls and saucers with undulating rims.

Bowls 4.5in (11.5cm) diam

$3,000-4,000   FRE

An L.C. TIFFANY Gold Favrile scalloped bowl, its interior acid-etched with a branch of leaves, etched "L.C.Tiffany-Favrile/7035".

2.5in (6cm) high

$2,000-3,000   DRA

A Tiffany Studios Favrile glass footed center bowl, in white pastel shading to green at the rim and with feather quilted interior, applied clear foot, engraved "L.C. Tiffany 8861".

12in (30.5cm) diam

$1,000-1,500   DRA

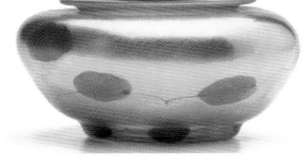

A Tiffany Studios gold Favrile glass fruit bowl, vertically ribbed with scalloped rim, engraved "L.C.T."

11in (28cm) diam

$1,000-1,500   DRA

A Tiffany Studios gold Favrile glass vase, patterned with trailing vines in iridescent green, engraved "L.C. Tiffany Favrile 373K".

7.5in (19m) high

$2,000-3,000   DRA

Six Tiffany gold Favrile glass goblets, etched "L.C.T. Favrile".

6in (15cm) high

$2,000-3,000   DRA

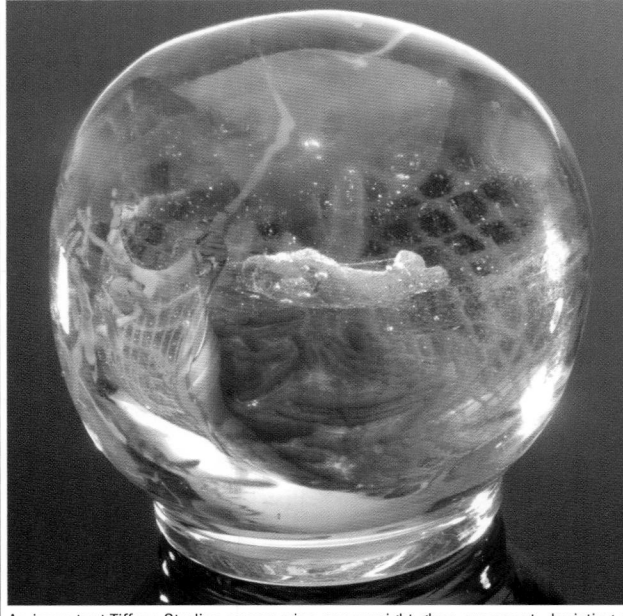

An important Tiffany Studios aquamarine paperweight glass ornament, depicting a single fish swimming against a background of aquatic foliage in an aquamarine sea, engraved "L.C.Tiffany Inc. Favrile 6508N".

6.25in (16cm) high

$20,000-25,000   DRA

Two Tiffany Studios gold Favrile glass table candlesticks, with ribbed, baluster stems, each engraved "L.C.T Favrile 1825".

11.75in (30cm) high

$4,500-5,500   DRA

A Tiffany Favrile glass experimental rondel.

9.25in (23.5cm) diam

$1,200-1,400   FRE

A Tiffany two-handled ovoid vase, of lustred gold and purple glass, marked "L.C Tiffany/Favrile/9388J".

8.5in (21.5cm) high

$2,000-3,000   DRA

A Tiffany Studios red glass vase, internally decorated with opalescence streaking, engraved "LCT 7078A".

5.75in (14.5cm) high

$2,500-3,000   DRA

An Amalric Walter pâte-de-verre covered box, with chestnut knop.

Amalric Walter (1870-1959) worked at Daum and later ran his own studio. His name is often spelled Almaric. Amalric is used by the Musée des Arts Decoratifs in Paris.

6.25in (16cm) high

$9,000-10,000   **DRA**

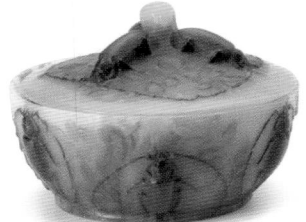

An Amalric Walter pâte-de-verre covered box, designed by Henri Berge, with beetle decoration, cover and box with molded "A Walter Nancy" and box with "Berge Sc".

c1920   7in (18cm) wide

$7,000-10,000   **DRA**

An Amalric Walter pâte-de-verre covered box, designed by Henri Berge, with snail knop, over with molded "AWN" and artists monogram, base molded "A Walter Nancy AH".

4.5in (11.5cm) diam

$5,000-6,000   **DRA**

An Amalric Walter pâte-de-verre covered box, designed by Henri Berge, with snail knop, cover with molded "AWN" and artist's monogram, base molded "A. Walter Nancy AH".

4.5in (11.5cm) diam

$4,000-6,000   **DRA**

An Amalric Walter pâte-de-verre covered box, designed by Henri Berge, decorated with a frieze of oak leaves and acorns, the cover knop in the form of a snail, engraved signatures "A. Walter Nancy" and "Berge Sc".

4.5in (11.5cm) diam

$5,000-6,000   **DRA**

An Amalric Walter pâte-de-verre covered cigarette box, with two compartments, cover molded "AWN" and artist's monogram, box with molded "A Walter Nancy" signature.

9in (23cm) wide

$9,000-10,000   **DRA**

An Amalric Walter pâte-de-verre vide poche, designer by Henri Berge, the wall and two handles with stylized lotus in green and blue on lemon-yellow ground, engraved "A. Walter Nancy" and "H. Berge".

10.5in (26.5cm) long

$1,200-1,800   **DRA**

An Amalric Walter pâte-de-verre lobed dish, designed by Henri Berge, molded "A Walter Nancy" and "Berge Sc".

7.75in (19.5cm) high

$1,200-1,800   **DRA**

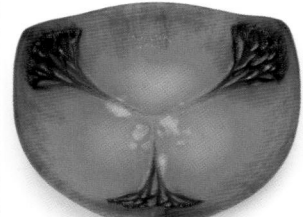

An Amalric Walter pâte-de-verre dish, patterned with stylized flora, engraved "A. Walter Nancy".

c1925   7in (18cm) diam

$2,000-3,000   **DRA**

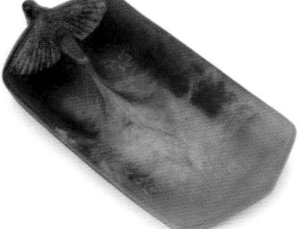

An Amalric Walter pâte-de-verre dish, designed by Henri Berge, decorated with a moth, molded "A. Walter Nancy" and "Berge Sc".

c1920   4.5in (11.5cm) high

$2,000-3,000   **DRA**

An Amalric Walter pâte-de-verre paperweight, designed by Henri Berge, decorated with beetles, molded "A. Walter Nancy" and "Berge Sc".

c1920   2.75in (7cm) high

$3,000-4,000   **DRA**

An Amalric Walter pâte-de-verre chameleon paperweight, molded signature "A. Walter Nancy" and artist's monogram.

c1920   3.25in (8.5cm) diam

$5,000-6,000   **DRA**

A Webb Gem cameo vase, enameled and gilded by Jules Barbe, neck decorated with carved gold gilt panels with enameled flowers, the body with gold gilt medallions separated by flowing bands, signed "Thomas Webb & Sons Gem Cameo".

The cutting on this vase was probably the work of George or Thomas Woodall.

8in (20cm) high

$10,000-12,000   **JDJ**

An English glass epergne, with three crystal and amber leaves on clear stems, central yellow trumpet with cranberry rigaree and rim, on a bevelled six lobed mirror, unsigned.

15in (38cm) high

$5,000-6,000   **JDJ**

A Thomas Webb & Sons cameo glass vase, with trailing white vines and a butterfly on a citron and blush ground, glassworks mark to side.

c1900   7in (17.75cm) high

$1,200-1,800   **SK**

A Thomas Webb & Sons cameo glass vase, with trailing white vines and a butterfly on a blue ground, maker's mark in semicircle with cameo to base.

c1900   7.5in (19cm) high

$1,200-1,800   **SK**

A Thomas Webb & Sons cameo glass vase, patterned with morning glory in white and red on lemon yellow ground.

5in (13cm) high

$2,000-3,000   **DRA**

A Thomas Webb rainbow-cased glass vase, with a pattern of fruiting apple branches on opaque chalk-white ground.

c1890   14in (35.5cm) high

$10,000-12,000   **DRA**

OTHER FACTORIES

A D'Argental scenic cameo vase, with wooded lakeland scene in shades of brown and orange on frosted, lemon-yellow ground, the base fire-polished, with cameo signature.

10in (25.5cm) high

$1,200-1,800   **DRA**

A D'Argental scenic cameo vase, with a mountainous lakeland landscape, cut to opalescence, each panel with cameo signature "D'Argental".

12in (30.5cm) high

$3,000-4,000   **DRA**

A François Decorchemont pâte-de-cristal bowl, cut with a pattern of facets and 'thumbprints' molded on lemon-yellow ground, small bruise to outer rim, roundel signature.

6in (15cm) diam

$1,000-1,500   **DRA**

An Andre Delatte cameo vase, decorated with blackberries in polished reds on shaded and mottled lemon-yellow and white ground, cameo signature "A. Delatte Nancy".

5.75in (14.5cm) high

$1,000-1,200   **DRA**

An early pâte-de-verre figural panel, attributed to George Despret, decorated with the figure of a bull in mauve bordered by green foliage on mottled blue and white ground, some surface cracks.

10in (25.5cm) long

$700-1,000   **DRA**

A James Couper Clutha vase designed by Christopher Dresser, with frilled rim, and decorated with aventurine and bubble inclusions.

15.75in (40cm) high

$3,000-4,000   **L&T**

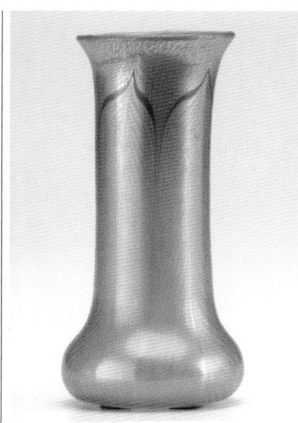

A Kew-Blas gourd-shaped vase, with gold cartouche pattern against a green, ivory and gold swirled and marbleized ground, unmarked.

10in (25.5cm) high

$1,500-2,000   **DRA**

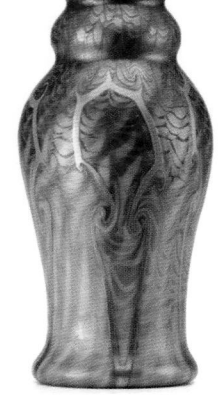

A Kew-Blas gold iridescent glass vase, with pulled feather decoration in green, engraved "Kew-Blas".

7.75in (19.5cm) high

$800-1,000   **DRA**

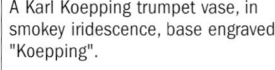

A Karl Koepping trumpet vase, in smokey iridescence, base engraved "Koepping".

4.75in (12cm) high

$700-1,000   **DRA**

A Legras scenic cameo vase, with wooded lakeland scene with sailboats in green and white over a shaded lemon-orange ground, with cameo signature.

7.5in (19cm) high

$1,600-2,000   **DRA**

An Ernest-Baptiste Leveille cameo glass marine vase, patterned with aquatic life in shades of deep brown and red over internally decorated orange, yellow and sea-green ground, base engraved "E. Leveille 1890 No. 353".

1890

7in (18cm) high

$35,000-40,000   **DRA**

A CLOSER LOOK AT A LIBERTY & CO. CYMRIC DECANTER

Liberty's Cymric and Tudric ranges were introduced to showcase ornate metalware design. Cymric pieces were made from silver and were at a higher end the market than the more affordable pewter Tudric range.

As well as its rarity, the association of the three important names of Liberty, Knox and James Powell & Sons, makes this an appealing piece.

Archibald Knox was Liberty's most famous designer. He was inspired by Celtic art.

James Powell & Sons Whitefriars glassworks reflected the fashions of the day, working with leading designers such as William Morris and the Guild of Handicraft.

A rare Cymric silver-mounted decanter, designed by Archibald Knox (1864-1933) for Liberty & Co., the ovoid green glass body probably James Powell & Sons, with tall cylindrical neck and applied ribbed band, the silver collar, decorated with Celtic strapwork, having a shaped spout and curved handle, the stopper with tapering handle similarly decorated, hallmarked Birmingham, maker's stamp "L&C", "Cymric".

1903

10in (25.5cm) high

$15,000-20,000   **L&T**

A Legras etched and enameled vase, decorated with autumn leafage in purple on shaded orange ground, cameo signature "Legras".

11.5in (29cm) high

$1,200-1,800   **DRA**

A Mont Joye monumental etched and enameled vase, with horse chestnut design in naturalistic colors in silver and gilt on frosted mauve ground, gilt stamp on base.

27in (68.5cm) high

$4,000-6,000   **DRA**

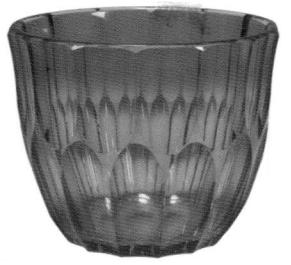

A Moser-style Art Deco glass topaz bowl with two rows of faceted panels, maker's mark to base.

8in (20cm) high

$400-600 **SK**

A Muller Frères carved cameo glass vase patterned with blossoming carnations in deep red and yellow on polished and mottled red ground, engraved signature.

c1900 *17in (43cm) high*

$3,000-4,000 **DRA**

An Orrefors graal vase, by Knut Bergkvist, decorated with stylized flora, base engraved "Graal Orrefors 19 KB J-W".

4.5in (11.5cm) diam

$2,000-3,000 **DRA**

A floriform vase, possibly Quezal, decorated with vertical leafage in green and gold.

10.5in (26.5cm) high

$1,000-1,200 **DRA**

A Quezal gold iridescent glass vase, with pulled feather decoration in gold and green on ivory ground, with gold interior, engraved "Quezal A776".

9.25in (23.5cm) high

$2,000-3,000 **DRA**

A Eugene Rousseau enameled and applied glass vase, in Japanese taste, base engraved "E. Rousseau Paris".

9.5in (24cm) high

$1,500-2,000 **DRA**

A Stevens & Williams Dolce Relievo Aesthetic vase, patterned with peacocks between three applied horn handles in mauve on ivory ground.

3.5in (9cm) high

$3,000-4,000 **DRA**

A group of five Art Nouveau glasses, in the manner of Theresienthal, painted in gilt and colored enamels, with painted marks "W.W./ D/ 416".

9.25in (23.5cm) high

$4,000-5,000 **L&T**

A Whitefriars glass bowl, designed by William Wilson, pattern no. 8988, cut with comets, unsigned.

1934 *11in (28cm) diam*

$1,500-2,000 **WW**

A pair of tall leaded-glass windows, by Arthur Huen, with an arrow motif in green, yellow, and gold-leaf on clear glass ground, mounted in original zinc frames.

Glass manufactured by the Chicago firm Gianni and Hilgard, who also produced work for Frank Lloyd Wright.

46in (117cm) high

$6,000-9,000 **DRA**

An Arts & Crafts stained, painted and leaded glass panel, depicting two deer.

9.75in (25cm) wide

$1,000-1,500 **L&T**

Four stained, painted and leaded glass panels, attributed to John Moyr Smith, depicting a Grecian god and goddess, amusing animal and insect studies, within geometric borders.

approx 32.5in (82.5cm) high

$8,000-12,000 **L&T**

TIFFANY LAMPS

- Currently the most desirable of Tiffany & Co.'s extensive output, lamps were the most commercially successful area of production at the time.
- Louis Comfort Tiffany (1848-1933) was fascinated by stained glass windows and realized that the effect could be recreated using artificial light. Lampshades would be a perfect medium for his work.
- The first leaded shades included 'Nautilus', 'Dragonfly' and 'Wisteria'. By 1906, over 125 different types were on sale.
- Generally hemispherical in shape, shades were made from tiny fragments of glass held together by lead to form a foliate scene or an abstract design.
- Earlier pieces tended to be simple with geometric designs using only one or two colors.
- After extensive experimentation, Tiffany had over 5,000 colors at his disposal, which reproduced the subtle tones and textures found in nature.
- In time, decoration gradually became more complex and colorful, featuring flowers, fruit and insects in highly ornate arrangements.
- Natural designs and forms that featured irregular shaped borders required the highest level of skill to produce and are consequentially extremely highly valued today. Prices reach over a million pounds for the most rare and exquisite examples.
- Tiffany Studios finally closed in 1932.

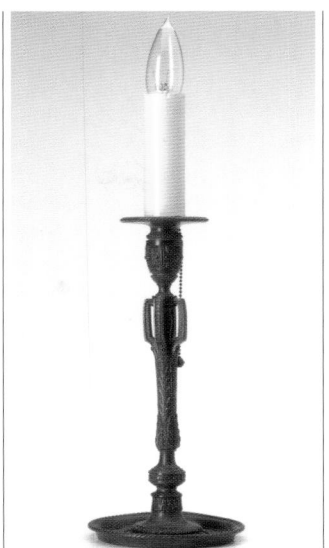

A Tiffany Studios 'Acanthus' pattern candlestick lamp, no. 621, with verdigris patina, stamped "Tiffany Studios New York" on base.

14.5in (37cm) high

$1,500-2,000   **DRA**

A Tiffany Studios bronze candlestick, original light brown patina, worn in places, impressed "Tiffany Studios New York 1210".

10in (25.5cm) high

$1,000-1,500   **DRA**

A Tiffany Studios bronze tripod candlestick, the bobeche set with a band of glass cabochons, impressed marks.

12.25in (31cm) high

$3,000-4,000   **DRA**

A Tiffany bronze twin branch candelabrum, stamped "Tiffany Studios New York 4292".

12.5in (32cm) high

$2,500-3,000   **FRE**

A Tiffany Studios four-light glass and bronze candelabrum, the bobeche blown with opaque green glass, the base set with coordinating green cabochons, de-patinated, base impressed "S1040".

13in (33cm) high

$3,500-4,000   **DRA**

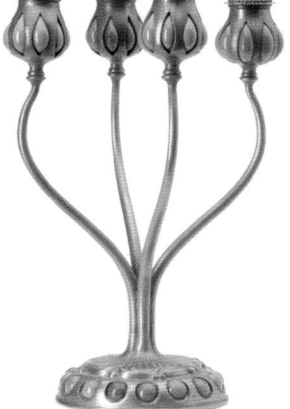

A pair of Tiffany candlestick lamps with blown glass heads with pulled feather shades, shades signed, bases signed "Tiffany Studios".

18in (46cm) high

$25,000-30,000   **JDJ**

A Tiffany Studios bronze six-light candelabrum, with original snuffer in fitted cavity, original condition, gilt patina worn in places, impressed mark "Tiffany Studios New York 1290".

22in (56cm) wide

$5,000-6,000   **DRA**

A Tiffany Studios favrile glass and bronze candelabra, the double-gourd form shades of opalescent glass with clambroth decoration, the base stamped.

17.75in (45cm) high

$8,000-10,000   **FRE**

A Tiffany Studios three-light lily lamp, with gold Favrile glass shades on a gilt-parcel base, flake to one fitter, stamped "Tiffany Studios New York/306", shades etched "L.C.T."

16.5in (42cm) wide

$7,000-10,000   **DRA**

A Tiffany Studios seven-light lily lamp with gold Favrile shades on a bronze base with "TIFFANY STUDIOS NEW YORK/29788', impressed fleur-de-lys, shades marked "LCT".

20in (51cm) high

$25,000-30,000 DRA

A Tiffany 12-light lily lamp with gold dome finish, original sockets, signed "Tiffany Studios New York 332" on base, shades signed.

20in (51cm) high

$30,000-35,000 JDJ

A Tiffany bronze lily lamp, triple branch with gold favrile shades, signed "LCT", base stamped "Tiffany Studios New York 320", one shade cracked at base, repaired with glue and tape.

8.5in (21.5cm) high

$3,000-4,000 FRE

A Tiffany Studios bronze and turtle-back swivel lamp, ornamented with bead and wire work, signed on base and numbered "D801".

14in (35.5cm) high

$15,000-17,000 SK

A Tiffany Studios double-turtleback desk lamp, the shade set with two green turtleback tiles both with original opalescent liners and the base set with a band of glass cabochons, base impressed "Tiffany Studios New York D801", one tile cracked through the center.

14.25in (36cm) high

$10,000-15,000 DRA

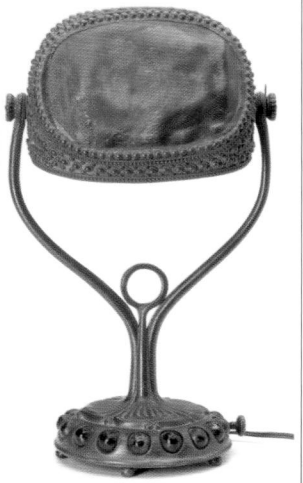

A Tiffany gilt bronze desk lamp and shade, base stamped "Tiffany Studios 688".

14in (37cm) high

$2,000-2,500 FRE

A Tiffany Studios desk lamp, with green Favrile glass shade, signed lower center "Favrile", over a bronze counter balance.

c1900 *16in (40.5cm) high*

$10,000-12,000 POOK

A Tiffany Studios table lamp, bronze and glass, the linenfold glass and bronze shade over three light candlestick lamp with pulled feather cylindrical socket covers.

20in (51cm) high

$17,000-20,000 SK

A Tiffany Studios Moorish bronze lamp, with iridescent green glass prisms divided by ball chains, base stamped "Tiffany Studios, New York 50182".

22in (56cm) high

$35,000-38,000 FRE

A Tiffany Studios New York bronze and glass double student lamp, decorated with wirework frame, adjustable reservoir, glass shades, one numbered 22503.

c1902 *29in (73.5cm) high*

$12,000-18,000 SK

A Tiffany Studios, New York bronze d'ore and Favrile glass table lamp, with lemon iridescent shade and molded base inset with mother of pearl roundels, maker's marks.

15.5in (39.5cm) high

$6,000-8,000 L&T

An early 20thC Tiffany Studios Favrile glass and bronze lamp, with a damascene shade on a "baby-bullet" urn form bronze base, shade signed "L.C.T.", the base stamped "Tiffany Studios, New York 23568".

18in (46cm) high

$12,000-18,000   **FRE**

A Tiffany Studios table lamp, bronze and iridescent glass, heat cap with wirework fitted with three screws to hold large gold damascene shade, signed "Tiffany Studios New York".

26in (66cm) high

$28,000-32,000   **SK**

A Tiffany Studios table lamp, with a bell-shaped Favrile glass shade spirally decorated on green ground with white interior, bronze base with brown patina, shade engraved "L.C.T.", base impressed "Tiffany Studios New York 606".

15.25in (38.5cm) high

$6,000-7,000   **DRA**

A L. C. Tiffany gold Favrile candlestick lamp, with a twisted base and ruffled shade, the shade and base etched "L.C.T.".

13in (33cm) high

$2,000-2,500   **DRA**

A Tiffany gold Favrile glass candlestick lamp, signed "L.C.T." on fitter, removable candlestick.

15in (38cm) high

$1,500-2,000   **SK**

A Tiffany gold Favrile glass candlestick lamp, signed "L.C.T." on fitter, removable candlestick.

17.25in (44cm) high

$1,200-1,800   **SK**

A Tiffany Studios table lamp, with geometric shade of rectangular green glass on fluted floral three-socket base with bronze patina, a few short breaks to glass, both shade and base stamped "Tiffany Studios New York", the shade marked "1496", and the base marked "368".

25.5in (65cm) high

$28,000-32,000   **DRA**

A Tiffany Studios table lamp, with a glass geometric shade on a three-socket bronze urn base, four short breaks to glass, marked "TIFFANY STUDIOS NEW YORK 444/TIFFANY STUDIOS NEW YORK 1013".

22in (56cm) high

$25,000-30,000   **DRA**

A Tiffany Studios acorn table lamp, with a band of green leaves on shaded yellow ground, stick base with gilt finish, shade with tag impressed "Tiffany Studios New York 1435", base impressed "Tiffany Studios New York 588".

15.75in (40cm) diam

$15,000-17,000   **DRA**

A Tiffany Studios table lamp, with acorn green and white slag glass on bronze base with three-light swirling cluster, seven short breaks to glass, stamped "TIFFANY STUDIOS NEW YORK".

22in (56cm) high

$10,000-15,000   **DRA**

A Tiffany Studios Art Nouveau table lamp, pomegranate mosaic glass and d'ore bronze base, the domed shade in green glass with pomegranate border stamped "TIFFANY STUDIOS NEW YORK 1457".

21in (53.5cm) high

$25,000-30,000   **SK**

A Tiffany Studios glass and bronze turtleback tile lamp, on conforming base, shade with iridescent green 'turtleback' tiles on mottled dichroic green geometric ground, impressed "TIFFANY STUDIOS NY 5086".

c1910   23in (58cm) high

$45,000-50,000   **DRA**

A Tiffany Studios table lamp, with geometric shade bordered with Greek Key band in amber and green over a bronze urn base, original patina, stamped "TIFFANY STUDIOS NEW YORK 1444-7".

22in (56cm) high

$22,000-28,000   **DRA**

An outstanding Tiffany peacock lamp, with peacock feather design on shade on an original peacock feather bronze base, unsigned.

25in (64cm) high

$120,000-160,000   **JDJ**

A Tiffany Studios poinsettia table lamp, with domed shade of red flowers in a wide band on a base with water lily and twisted stem, the shade marked "Tiffany Studios New York 1558", the base marked "Tiffany Studios New York 443".

26in (66cm) high

$100,000-120,000   **POOK**

An early 20thC Tiffany Studios peony leaded glass and bronze table lamp, with peonies against a striated ground, stamped "Tiffany Studios, New York 1505-5", the verdigris-brown patinated stick base, stamped "Tiffany Studios, New York 531".

32.25in (82cm) high

$150,000-170,000   **SK**

A Tiffany Studios table lamp, with golden pansies on a lapis ground, over a faceted bronze base with three feet, breaks to glass, sockets possibly replaced, base and shade stamped "Tiffany Studios New York".

21.5in (54.5cm) high

$90,000-100,000   **DRA**

A Tiffany Studios table lamp with Apple Blossom shade on hammered bronze base, original patina, a few breaks to shade, base and shade stamped "TIFFANY STUDIOS".

23in (58cm) high

$25,000-35,000   **DRA**

An early 20thC Tiffany Studios bronze 'Tyler' lamp, with leaded glass shade, on an urn-shaped base, shade marked "Tiffany Studios, New York".

22in (56cm) high

$15,000-20,000   **FRE**

A Tiffany Studios floor lamp, bronze shaft with paneled linenfold amber glass shade, both stamped "TIFFANY STUDIOS NEW YORK".

64.5in (163cm) high

$16,000-20,000   **DRA**

A Tiffany Studios floor lamp with a bronze adjustable harp top and acorn shade in green slag glass, both stamped "TIFFANY STUDIOS NEW YORK".

57.5in (146cm) high

$18,000-22,000   **DRA**

A Tiffany Studios floor lamp, in bronze and glass, the harped shade with green glass revealed through a fretwork frieze, impressed "Tiffany Studios New York 502".

55in (139.5cm) high

$7,000-10,000   **DRA**

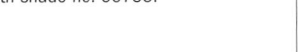

A Handel glass and metal desk lamp, with shade no. 66755.

c1919   13.5in (34.25cm) wide

$1,500-2,000   **SK**

An adjustable Handel desk lamp, with faceted slag glass shade, on a single socket bronzed base, with original on/off key, and shade stamped "Handel".

Shade 5in (12.75cm) high

$2,500-3,000   **DRA**

A Handel reverse-painted table lamp, maker's mark and pat. "979664" on three-socket standard with gray-green patina.

24in (61cm) high

$7,000-10,000   **SK**

An early 20thC Handel reverse-painted table lamp, decorated with a tropical island scene, shade and base marked.

23in (58.5cm) high

$9,000-11,000   **SK**

An early 20thC Handel gridded metal overlay and caramel slag glass table lamp, the apron backed by maroon slag glass, three socket standard, and base marked "Handel"

20.5in (52cm) high

$4,000-5,000   **SK**

A rare Handel reverse-painted table lamp, with all over reverse painting of flowering hydrangea in large pink and white clusters on light green ground, bronze pear-shaped base with acid finished patina.

22in (56cm) high

$15,000-20,000   **JDJ**

A Handel metal overlay table lamp, with textured conical shade, hammered copper overlay, strap work in stylized tulip design, signed "Handel", on domed base with bronzed metal finish, impressed "Handel" on base of shade.

25in (63.5cm) high

$3,000-5,000   **SK**

A Handel table lamp, with acid-etched glass shade having reverse-painted tropical island scene, with a bronzed base, original patina and acorn pulls, shade marked "HANDEL", lamps patent No. 63911A

24in (61cm) high

$8,000-10,000   **DRA**

A Handel table lamp, its etched glass shade enamel-painted with a Venetian harbour scene by John Bailey, over a bulbous three-socket bronzed base, some scratches and wear to patina on base, one minor flea bite to bottom rim of shade, shade marked "Handel 6757" and "John Bailey", base stamped "Handel".

23in (58.5cm) high

$20,000-30,000   **DRA**

A Handel table lamp, etched glass shade reverse-painted with scene of cranes flying through tall bamboo, with bronzed base.

23.5in (59.5cm) high

$18,000-22,000   **DRA**

A Handel table lamp, with acid-etched shade reverse-painted with a tropical scene with parrots, with a bronzed base.

23in (59cm) high

$12,000-18,000   **DRA**

A rare Handel table lamp, the shade painted with a Thomas Hart Benton-type landscape, and the bronzed base embossed with a woven rattan pattern, shade painted "Handel 5889/JB".

26in (66cm) high

$10,000-15,000   **DRA**

A CLOSER LOOK AT A HANDEL LAMP

While leading contemporaries concentrated on floral designs, Handel also became known for landscape and non-floral pieces. The peacock epitomizes the style and color palette of the period.

Reverse-painting took a great deal of skill. As well as possessing a mastery of watercolor techniques, the artist would need to understand how the image would be affected by light and glass.

Bases were made by Handel after 1902 and were designed to compliment the shape of the shade.

The number refers to the painted design. Original watercolors were approved and numbered before being copied onto a blank shade. Copies varied depending on the skill of the artist making each piece unique.

A Handel table lamp, with large faceted slag-glass shade, with brown and green catkins over a bronzed base.

28in (71cm) high

$50,000-60,000   **DRA**

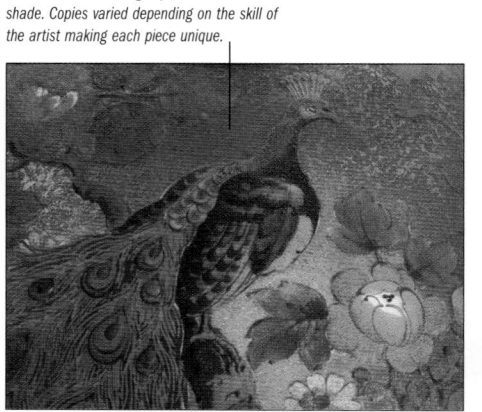

A Handel table lamp, its glass shade obverse-painted and etched with peacocks on prunus branches, over a three-socket classical bronzed base, very minor manufacturing imperfection to the inside of shade, gilding in excellent condition, shade etched "7126", base has cloth label.

24in (61cm) high

$25,000-30,000   **DRA**

A Handel table lamp, its etched glass shade reverse-painted with a Dutch landscape, shade stamped "Handel Lamps" with patent, signed "Handel #7067", its base stamped "Handel".

23in (59cm) high

$3,500-4,000   **DRA**

A Handel table lamp, with reverse-painted glass shade, over a bronzed lobed three-socket base, shade stamped "Handel lamps", painted "Handel 6625", the base with cloth tag.

24in (61cm) high

$8,000-10,000   **DRA**

A tall Handel table lamp, with Gothic green amber and ruby slag glass shade, bronzed five-socket base, breaks to a few panes, base marked "Handel".

31in (78.75cm) high

$4,000-5,000   **DRA**

A Handel table lamp, its large faceted slag-glass shade with brown and green catkins over a bronzed base, base is stamped "Handel".

28in (71cm) high

$5,000-6,000   **DRA**

A Handel table lamp, reverse-painted with landscape scene of a pond and stream with a waterfall surrounded by trees and rocks, signed, over double sockets with ball pulls, decorated shaft and base, marked "Handel".

22in (55.75cm) high

$2,000-3,000   SK

An early 20thC Handel table lamp, reverse-painted with a riverside landscape, with a shaded green and amber interior, metal rim stamped "Handel".

22in (55.75cm) high

$4,000-5,000   SK

A Handel table lamp, reverse-painted with a winter landscape at sunset on domed shade over double sockets with bell form pulls with conforming decoration on glass base, within gilt metal framework, circular base, signed "Handel".

22in (55.75cm) high

$1,500-2,500   SK

A Handel boudoir lamp, the domed shade with floral decoration, signed "Handel 5449 EL.", over single socket on cylindrical standard flaring to circle foot with raised decoration, cloth label on base.

13in (33cm) high

$1,500-2,500   SK

A Handel table lamp, reverse-painted domed shade with landscape scene, signed, paper label inside.

16in (40.5cm) high

$3,000-4,000   SK

A leaded glass chandelier with six geometric panels of leaded glass in mottled colors of green, red and blue, a heavy cast flower and leaf motif design framing the leaded glass, original heavy bronze chain.

29in (74cm) diam

$7,000-10,000   JDJ

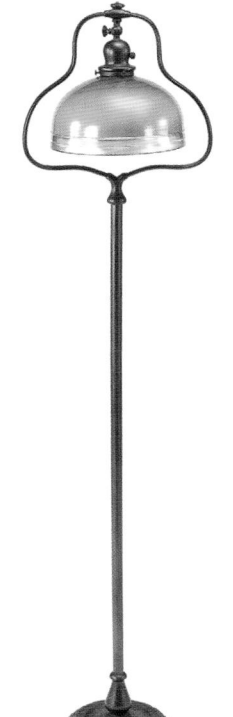

A Steuben brown Aurene glass domed shade with applied internally decorated intarsia rim and Calcite interior on a Handel bronzed metal harp floor lamp base with embossed foot, felt removed from base, unmarked.

58in (147.5cm) high

$3,500-4,000   DRA

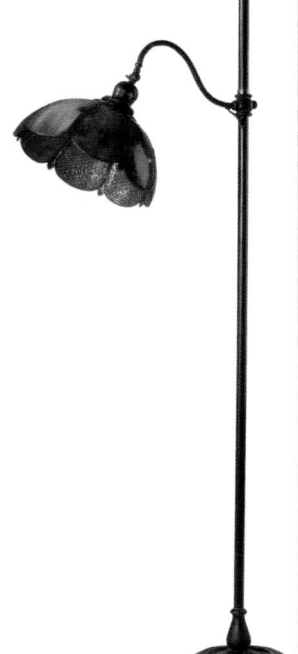

A Handel adjustable floor lamp, with period hemispherical leaded glass shade in blue, green and purple slag glass, with original patina, unmarked.

62.5in (158.75cm) high

$2,500-3,000   DRA

A rare Handel ceiling fixture, with lustred glass shade, painted with parrots, hanging from a single-socket bronzed mount, marked "6997 Handel PR".

22in (66cm) high

$5,000-6,000   DRA

557

A Roycroft hammered copper single-socket table lamp, with a Steuben gold Aurene flaring ribbed shade, with original patina to base, new patina to cap, a few small chips to shade fitter, base stamped orb and cross mark, shade unmarked.

18.5in (47cm) high

$3,000-4,000   **DRA**

A Roycroft hammered copper and glass table lamp, designed by Dard Hunter, the shade made of bright green and purple leaded glass, orb and cross mark on base.

18.5in (47cm) high

$30,000-35,000   **DRA**

A pair of Roycroft hammered copper table lamps with square bases topped by newer laced-up conical shades, medium patina, early orb and cross marks.

Provenance: The Roycroft Inn.

19.5in (49.5cm) high

$4,000-5,000   **DRA**

A Roycroft brass-washed hammered copper table lamp, with helmet shade, pierced and with mica lining, the shade and square base with wood grain patina, with some pitting and light wear to brass wash, original mica, with orb and cross mark.

14in (35.5cm) high

$2,500-3,500   **DRA**

A Roycroft/Steuben hammered copper and glass table lamp, its hemispherical shade of lustered amber glass with a contrasting band, over a three-socket base with three hammered bands, fine original patina, some chipping to glass fitting under metal cap, orb and cross mark on base.

16in (40.5cm) high

$6,000-8,000   **DRA**

A pair of Roycroft Secessionist copper and silver candlesticks, designed by Dard Hunter, with small squares on circular bases, dent to one cup, fine original finish, orb and cross marks.

8.25in (21cm) high

$20,000-25,000   **DRA**

A Roycroft Secessionist wall sconce, designed by Dard Hunter, with a copper and silver frame and a cylindrical green and purple leaded glass shade, short break to one green piece.

14.5in (37cm) high

$35,000-45,000   **DRA**

A Bigelow, Kennard and H.G. Cleaveland table lamp, shade stamped "BIGELOW, KENNARD & CO. BOSTON, BIGELOW STUDIOS", base stamped "HG CLEAVELAND BOSTON".

19.5in (49.5cm) high

$10,000-15,000   **DRA**

A Bradley and Hubbard slag glass and metal overlay table lamp, with caramel glass panels, manufacturer's marks.

c1908   *19.25in (49cm) high*

$400-500   **SK**

An early 20thC Bradley and Hubbard metal overlay and slag glass table lamp, manufacturer's mark, base numbered "261", some wear.

14.5in (37cm) high

$500-600   **SK**

A Bradley and Hubbard iron and slag glass table lamp, its faceted shade pierced in a feather pattern and lined with panels of glass, covered in forest green enamel, embossed "B&H 216".

24in (61cm) high

$800-1,200   **DRA**

A hammered copper, glass and mother-of-pearl table lamp, in the style of Elizabeth Burton, with faceted lit base and conical shade, single-socket, with fine original patina, missing two screws, dent to top of shade, unmarked.

22.5in (57cm) high

$4,000-5,000   **DRA**

An early 20thC EM & Co. metal overlay and bent caramel slag glass table lamp, two socket standard and ribbed base with manufacturer's mark on base.

21.75in (55.25cm) high

$500-700   **SK**

A rare and early Fulper Vasekraft table lamp, with two-socket column base, under a flat shade with red and yellow leaded slag glass inserts, covered in a fine matte brown flambe glaze dripping over a frothy matte mustard ground, some short, dark crazing lines around rim of shade, from firing, vertical Fulper stamp, circular Vasekraft stamp, and "Tests Pending the United States and Canada...France and Germany".

18.5in (46cm) high

$20,000-30,000   **DRA**

A rare Fulper mushroom-shaped lamp, covered in a Leopard-Skin crystalline glaze, the shade inset with leaded glass, some damage, vertical mark.

17in (43cm) high

$35,000-50,000   **DRA**

A Fulper mushroom-shaped table lamp, covered in Flemington Green flambé glaze, its shade inset with green, pink and caramel leaded slag glass, shade restored, vertical mark and "21".

17in (43cm) high

$10,000-15,000   **DRA**

A Fulper chandelier inset with leaded glass pieces in green and white against a Leopard Skin crystalline glaze, some damage, vertical mark.

16in (40cm) wide

$15,000-20,000   **DRA**

A rare Fulper lantern made to imitate copper, with faux rivets and straps surrounding leaded glass panes, with a café-au-lait glaze, restored, unmarked.

Only three of these are known.

lantern 13.25in (33.5cm) high

$6,000-7,000   **DRA**

An early 20thC Gorham Company swivel bronze and metal desk lamp, with gold iridescent glass jewels, base impressed "Gorham Co. N.Y."

$1,500-2,500   **SK**

An early 20thC Jefferson table lamp, reverse-painted shade decorated with a land and waterscape scene in earth tones with yellow sky, signed on rim.

23.25in (59cm) high

$2,000-2,500   **SK**

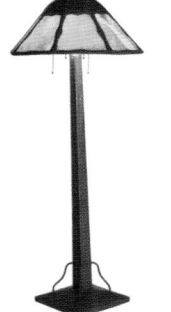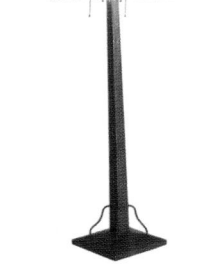

A hammered copper floor lamp, attributed to Limbert, the shade lined with green and brown slag glass over an eight-socket, four-sided base, original dark patina, unmarked.

68in (170cm) high

$15,000-20,000   **DRA**

A Limbert hammered copper table lamp, pierced with peacocks and roses, lined in caramel slag glass, three-socket base lights up, two replaced glass panes, unmarked.

25in (64cm) high

$15,000-20,000   **DRA**

A Morgan large etched glass hanging fixture, reverse-painted with blue birds of paradise, two panels cracked.

62in (157.5cm) wide

$3,000-3,500   **DRA**

A Muller Frères glass and painted metal chandelier, shades signed, aperture chipped.

c1935   *33in (84cm) high*

$1,500-2,000   **SK**

A CLOSER LOOK AT A GRUEBY/BIGELOW KENNARD TABLE LAMP

Recently discovered in a Massachusetts estate, this lamp was assembled by Grueby and Bigelow Kennard when made. Original conversions are extremely rare.

Many manufacturers of relatively affordable leaded lamps in the Tiffany style did not mark their pieces. Boston jeweler Bigelow Kennard, established in c1830, were an exception.

Modeler Ruth Erickson has been associated with some of the finest and most valuable pieces of Grueby.

The matt green glaze, a hallmark of Grueby, was considered to be the finest of all early 20th century American art potters.

A Grueby/Bigelow Kennard table lamp with a Grueby Kendrick vase with seven handles covered in matte green glaze, signed by Ruth Erickson, and topped by a Bigelow Kennard green leaded glass shade in geometric pattern, over an electrified oil font, paper label to base, "C. P.? 4-7-6", and circular pottery mark, shade stamped "BIGELOW, KENNARD & CO. BOSTON".

28in (71cm) high

$55,000-65,000   **DRA**

An NW Art Shade Company table lamp, with gilt metal overlay and slag glass

32in (81cm) high

$4,000-5,000   **SK**

An Old Mission Kopper Kraft hammered copper and mica table lamp, four-panel flaring shade atop a four-arm single-socket bulbous base, original patina and mica with stamped mission mark.

24in (61cm) high

$8,000-10,000   **DRA**

A Revere copper and slag glass lamp, its faceted shade with glass panes on a flaring four-sided base with three sockets, stamped "REVERE STUDIOS NEW YORK".

24in (61cm) high

$2,000-3,000   **DRA**

An early 20thC Salem Bros. metal and slag glass overlay table lamp, with caramel glass panels, manufacturer's mark to base and numbered "13".

13in (33cm) high

$500-700   **SK**

A Gustav Stickley floor lamp, with a silk lined wicker shade, hammered copper arm with a single pivoting socket, original finish and patina, "Als-ik-kan" die stamp.

58in (147cm) high

$12,000-14,000   **DRA**

A Gustav Stickley table lamp with a hammered copper three-socket base and a silk-lined wicker shade, original patina, some tears to original silk, re-patinated or new shade cap. "Als-ik-kan" stamp.

21.5in (54.5cm) high

$7,000-10,000   **DRA**

A Suess table lamp, its leaded glass shade in slag glass, over a matching three-socket bronze base, breaks to a few glass pieces, original patina, unmarked.

24in (61cm) high

$4,000-5,000   **DRA**

A hammered copper and mica table lamp, by Dirk Van Erp, with panel shade over three socket bulbous, riveted base, open box mark.

18in (46cm) high

$10,000-12,000   **DRA**

A Dirk Van Erp hammered copper and mica table lamp, with three-socket tapering base, new patina and mica, shallow dent, stamped Windmill mark.

20in (50.75in) high

$6,000-8,000   **DRA**

An extremely rare hammered copper and mica table lamp, by Dirk Van Erp, with unusual shade lined in parchment over mica, on a four-arm base with electrified oil font, excellent original condition, remnants of original hand-painted flowers on parchment, windmill stamp "Dirk Van Erp" with remnant of "D'Arcy Gaw".

Dirk Van Erp (1860-1953) was a Dutch immigrant to the US who settled in California in 1886. He was an active Arts and Crafts metalworker from 1908, and his son William Van Erp continued his work in his studio until 1944. He specialized in meticulously hand-hammered copper with exposed riveting and strapwork decoration.

23in (58cm) high

$110,000-130,000   **DRA**

An early 20thC table lamp, with reverse-painted shade with green foliate decoration, shade and base signed.

22in (56cm) high

$4,000-5,000   **POOK**

An Arts & Crafts period lantern, with leaded glass panels of stylized Glasgow roses in polychrome slag glass, without chain, one corner needs soldering

10in (25.5cm) high

$2,000-3,000   **DRA**

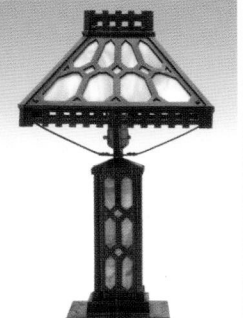

A Gothic table lamp of black enameled cast iron lined in green slag glass, unmarked.

20in (51cm) high

$500-700   **DRA**

A New York hammered brass and caramel slag glass lantern.

c1912   *23in (58.5cm) high*

$800-1,000   **SK**

An Arts & Crafts brass electrolier, in the style of W.A.S. Benson.

33.5in (85cm) high

$800-1,200   **L&T**

An Arts & Crafts silvered hanging candelabra, supported by four chains suspended from a domed rose.

15in (38cm) diam

$800-1,200   **L&T**

An early 20thC American Arts and Crafts brass and slag glass hanging lamp, with caramel and lavender glass.

16in (40.5cm) wide

$1,200-1,800   **SK**

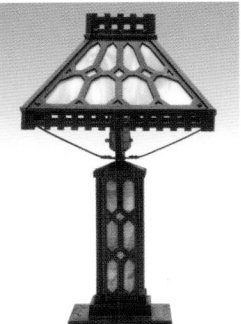

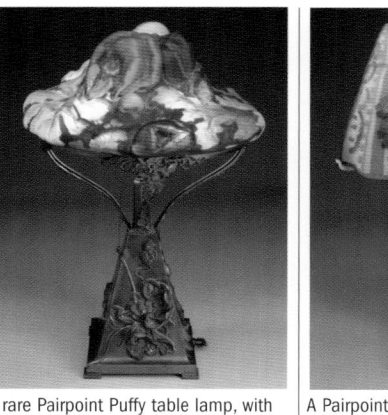

A rare Pairpoint Puffy table lamp, with white, orange and purple flowers on the shade, matching poppy decorated base signed, "Pairpoint Mfg. Co. 3049" together with "P" in a diamond.

22in (56cm) high

$20,000-25,000   **JDJ**

A Pairpoint Puffy table lamp, with shade of garlands of flowers on a quilted ground, square base with raised floral decoration, shade signed "The Pairpoint Corp", base signed, "Pairpoint MF'G Co. "B3020" with "P" in diamond.

22in (56cm) high

$12,000-14,000   **JDJ**

A Pairpoint Puffy lamp, reverse-painted with violet roses and yellow and blue butterflies, gold tone accent on the outside of shade, over single bulb with pull chain, signed "Pairpoint Corp".

15in (38cm) high

$1,800-2,200   **SK**

A Pairpoint Puffy table lamp, reverse-painted with orange, yellow, and blue chrysanthemums and a hummingbird, base raised on three feet.

13.5in (34cm) diam

$3,000-4,000   **SK**

A Pairpoint Puffy lamp, reverse-painted glass and metal, decorated with pink and blue flowers on a yellow background with trees in the ground, illegible signature.

14.5in (37cm) high

$1,200-1,800   **SK**

A Pairpoint Papillion lamp, with red and pink roses, multi-colored butterflies on dark green ground, signed in gold.

22in (56cm) high

$10,000-12,000   **JDJ**

An early 20thC Pairpoint lamp, with reverse-painted shade with landscape decoration, shade and base signed.

$2,500-3,000   **POOK**

An early 20thC Pairpoint table lamp, with seascape decorated shade on a dolphin base, shade and base signed.

22in (56cm) high

$6,000-7,000   **POOK**

A Pairpoint table lamp, reverse-painted with farmland scene of haystacks and horses, marked "Pairpoint Co".

21.5in (54.5cm) high

$2,000-2,500   **SK**

A Pairpoint table lamp, reverse-painted shade glass and metal, decorated with a formal garden scene, unsigned.

22in (56cm) high

$2,000-2,500   **SK**

$6,000-8,000   **JDJ**

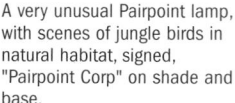

A very unusual Pairpoint lamp, with scenes of jungle birds in natural habitat, signed, "Pairpoint Corp" on shade and base.

21in (53cm) high

A Quezal glass and slag glass chandelier, with six pulled feather shades, Signed "Quezal", two shades with nicks.

8.5in (21.5cm) high

$4,000-5,000   **SK**

A Quezal chandelier, silver plated square undulating ceiling mount, suspended with five links, the center one adjustable, with five glass shades, signed.

39in (99cm) high

$4,000-6,000   **FRE**

A Quezal glass and silvered metal hanging lamp, shades with gold iridescent interior, white exterior, signed Quezal, may have had center shade.

with shade 44in (111.76cm) high

$1,500-2,500   **SK**

A Quezal brass table lamp, topped by Quezal floriform shades, a few chips to fitters, two shades cracked and reglued, shades etched "Quezal", base unmarked.

26.5in (67.5cm) high

$6,000-7,000   **DRA**

A Quezal bronze wall sconce, with two pulled-feather iridescent signed shades.

11.5in (29cm) high

$2,500-3,000   **SK**

ART NOUVEAU LAMPS

An Apollo Studios Art Nouveau hammered copper lamp, lined with opaque glass, stamped "Apollo Studios, New York Real Copper 264", minor knicks to base and shade.

22in (56cm) high

$1,500-2,500   **FRE**

An Art Nouveau André Delatte cameo glass and wrought-iron three-light chandelier, the glass bowl and three shades with bold grape-vine pattern in shades of brown on frosted orange ground, in conforming wrought-iron frame applied with grape vines, suspended by original chains and foliate ceiling cap, bowl and each shade with cameo signature "A. Delatte Nancy".

25in (63.5cm) diam

$3,500-4,000   **DRA**

A Muller Frères cameo scenic table lamp, the bullet shaped-shade and slender form base decorated with desert oasis scene in shades of deep brown on frosted and shaded orange ground, shade and base with cameo signature "Muller Fres. Luneville".

25.5in (65cm) high

$6,000-8,000   **DRA**

A Bigelow & Kennard floor lamp with shade of conical shape of small brickwork design, squares in three rows separated by pine cone design at shoulder, three metal pulls for three sockets on Renaissance-style floor base on three legs on paw feet, unsigned.

65in (165cm) high

$6,000-8,000   **SK**

A pair of Paul Nicolas scenic cameo vases, mounted as table lamps with period gilt-metal fittings, each decorated with a pair of pheasants in wooded landscape in shades of red on frosted lemon-yellow ground, cameo signature "P. Nicolas".

8in (20cm) high

$2,000-2,500 DRA

An early 20thC mosaic glass hanging lamp, with dome shade decorated with grape vines decorated in colors of green, red, purple, yellow and purple attributed to Seuss Ornamental Glass Works.

24in (61cm) diam

$4,500-5,000 SK

An early 20thC American art glass domed hemispherical shade, with geometrical slag glass and metal cap, chain and ceiling mount.

22.5in (57cm) diam

$1,400-1,600 SK

An Art Glass mosaic ceiling lamp shade, domed shape with colored glass segments, unsigned.

20in (51cm) diam

$500-600 SK

An early 20thC American large dome Art Glass shade, with scalloped top rim in red, yellow and green glass, unsigned.

22in (56cm) diam

$1,200-1,800 SK

An early 20thC large Art Glass mosaic shade, with scalloped decorated with cherries, apples, pears and grapes, unsigned.

25in (63.5cm) diam

$500-600 SK

A 20thC American reverse-painted glass and metal table lamp, depicting a woodland scene at sunset, on two socket standard, base with painted scenes and gilt-metal, some wear.

23.5in (59.5cm) diam

$3,000-3,500 SK

An American Art Nouveau leaded glass and metal table lamp, the paneled shade set with opalescent jewels on a bronzed figural and whiplash base with three sockets, unmarked.

c1905   *24in (61cm) diam*

$2,000-2,500 DRA

A late 19thC French Art Nouveau bronze table lamp, full bodied figure of a woman with hands upholding a single socket, flanked by two sockets, pink floral beaded shades.

shades 4.25in (10.75cm) high

$1,000-1,200 SK

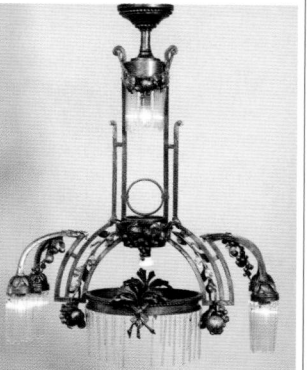

A French Art Nouveau hanging lamp, silvered iron and glass, relief decorated with fruit and leaves.

c1905   *34in (86cm) wide*

$1,000-1,500 SK

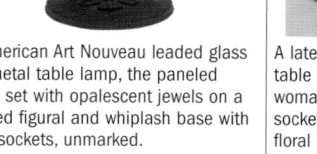

An Art Nouveau copper alloy ceiling light, in the manner of W.A.S. Benson, with vaseline glass shade.

19in (48cm) high

$2,000-2,500 L&T

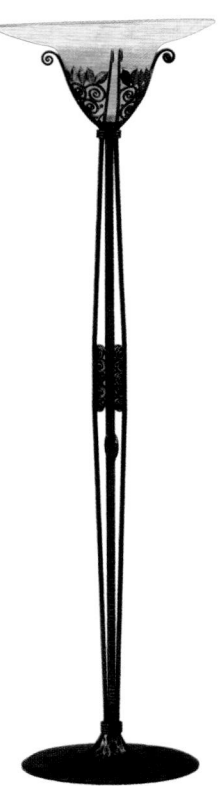

An early 20thC French aluminium plant-form lamp, by Charles & Fils, fitted with a single socket and raised on a square block plinth, marked.

21in (53cm) high

$3,000-4,000   **SK**

Two French Art Deco pendant chandeliers, by Degue, on reticulated metal frames with frosted glass shades in floral motif, both complete with ceiling caps.

33in (83.75cm) high

$2,500-3,000   **SDR**

A 1940s Christian Dell/Geb. Kaiser & Co. 'Scissor' wall lamp, of black enameled metal, with wall bracket, marked "Kaiser-Idell Original".

$800-1,200   **SDR**

An Edgar Brandt (1880-1960), wrought iron floor lamp, with Daum, Nancy glass shade, signed, scratches/scuffs to the shade caused by the leaf decoration on the frieze, losses to the patination and some surface corrosion, copper highlights to the base.

c1925   *68in (172.75cm) high*

$15,000-20,000   **FRE**

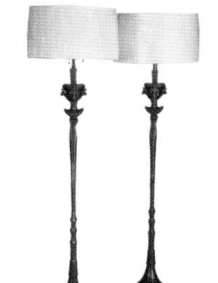

A pair of floor lamps, attributed to T.H. Robsjohn-Gibbings, each with two sockets, white drum shades, and ram's head shaft with hoof feet, covered in bronzed finish, unmarked.

65.5in (166cm) high

$2,500-3,000   **SDR**

A rare 'Circus' lamp base, designed by Dame Laura Knight and produced by Clarice Cliff for the 1934 Art and Industry exhibition, modeled as a totem pole of clowns and acrobats, printed "Bizarre" mark, first edition, hairline crack.

19in (48.5cm) high

$10,000-12,000   **WW**

A Monart glass lamp and shade, with mottled mushroom shade and swirling inclusions to the rim, on a corresponding baluster base.

22in (56cm) high

$7,000-10,000   **L&T**

A Monart 'Paisley Shawl' glass table lamp, by Salvador Ysart, with mushroom shade, and blue and red 'enameled' decoration, on a corresponding baluster base.

24.5in (62cm) high

$10,000-15,000   **L&T**

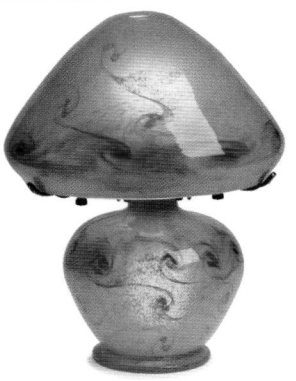

A Monart glass lamp and shade, with mottled mushroom shade decorated to the rim with swirling inclusions, on a corresponding base with applied foot.

12in (31cm) high

$2,000-2,500   **L&T**

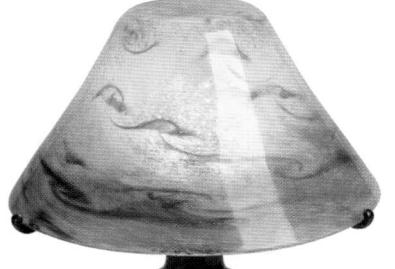

A Monart glass lamp and shade, with mottled inclusions to the body and rim, surmounted by a corresponding shade of tapering cylindrical form.

15.25in (39cm) high

$5,000-6,000   **L&T**

565

A Roland Paris Art Deco bronze and marble lamp stand, on stepped marble base decorated with carved ivory and enameled metal figures, etched "Roland Paris".

27in (69cm) wide

$15,000-20,000   **SDR**

A WMF silver-plated Art Deco table lamp stand. no 11987.

12in (30.5cm) high

$300-400   **GAZE**

An Art Deco chrome desk lamp, with arched single-socket fixture and two semicircular opaque glass panels, mounted on marbelized caramel-colored bakelite shaft and chrome base with spherical ball decoration, some looseness, and minor pitting to chrome, unmarked.

11in (27.5cm) wide

$300-400   **SDR**

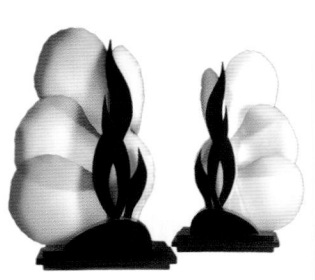

An Art Deco pair of organic table lamps, with petal shades in peach, amber and white, on ebonized wood bases, unmarked.

$400-600   **SDR**

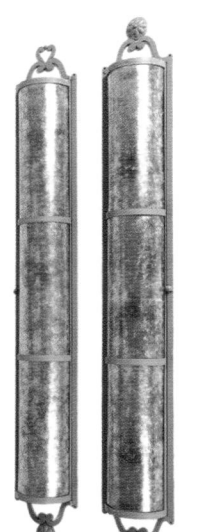

A pair of French Art Deco fine and unusual vertical wall sconces with green enameled metal frames, and mica shades, unmarked.

$800-1,200   **SDR**

A pair of Art Deco gilt bronze skyscraper design torcheres, raised on four stepped feet.

c1930   *69in (175.5cm) high*

$3,000-3,500   **SK**

An Art Deco bronze torchere, with flaring alabaster shade, and scroll-foot base, unmarked.

71in (177.5cm) high

$3,000-4,000   **SDR**

An Art Deco glass and wrought iron floor lamp, with orange and blue mold-blown shade within a wrought iron framework.

c1930   *68in (173cm) high*

$3,000-4,000   **SK**

A French Art Deco molded glass and silvered bronze ceiling lamp, with ten fan shape colorless glass panels, in a metal framework creating a circular form suspended on a decorated shaft.

c1930   *34in (86.5cm) diam*

$3,000-4,000   **SK**

A French Art Deco hand-forged iron chandelier, with reticulated frame and original frosted glass starburst shades, a few chips to shade collars, unmarked.

32.5in (82.5cm) long

$600-1,200   **SDR**

A Liberty Tudric pewter clock designed by David Veazey, model number 0150, cast in low relief with honesty seedheads, stamped marks.

14in (35cm) high

$4,000-5,000   **WW**

A Liberty Tudric hammered pewter mantle clock with enameled face in blue and green, Roman numerals, small dent to back foot, stamped "MADE IN ENGLAND "TUDRIC" 01319".

14in (36cm) wide

$2,000-3,000   **DRA**

A Liberty & Co. silver mantel clock, by Archibald Knox, with single train movement, enameled dial, and stylized Arabic numerals, and hallmarked "Birmingham".

1903   *4in (10cm) high*

$8,000-12,000   **L&T**

A Tiffany Studios desk clock, with key in 'Greek Key' pattern, marked "Tiffany & Co. New York" on clock face and stamped on back "Tiffany Studios New York 1121".

6in (15cm) high

$5,000-6,000   **DRA**

An Albin Müller patinated cast iron and enamel table clock, manufactured by Fürstlich Stolbergsches Hüttenwerk, the twin-train movement with anchor escarpment, enameled.

c1904   *55.5cm high*

$15,000-20,000   **L&T**

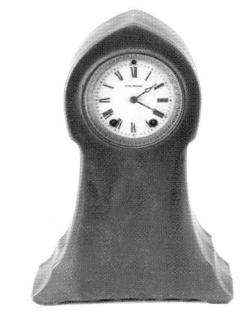

A mantel clock, possibly Hampshire, with Seth Thomas movement, hairlines to face, missing glass, chips and hairline to base and back, unmarked.

15in (38cm) high

$300-400   **DRA**

An Australian Arts and Crafts, with silky oak long case clock, the broken pedestal top with arched glazed door enclosing a domed brass dial, above a long door decorated with carved flannel flowers and ribbon motif, above a boxed base decorated with a boomerang, some losses and splits, movement unknown.

103in (262cm) high

$5,000-7,000   **BONA**

A French gilt bronze and champleve enamel 'Japonism' clock, formed as a gong, with polychrome decorated dial and pilasters, and shaped base surmounted by fu-lions.

c1875   *15.5in (39.5cm) high*

$4,500-5,000   **FRE**

An Austrian Art Nouveau terracotta clock, the brass dial surmounted by two draped lovers, flanked by a baby climbing stairs whilst an elderly man with long beard looks on, impressed seal.

c1900   *31in (77.5cm) high*

$1,500-2,000   **FRE**

A French bronze Art Nouveau figural clock, signed "Sam Grün" and with "Jollet & Co." foundry seal, on a gilt-bronze-mounted green marble base.

16.5in (42cm) wide

$6,000-8,000   **FRE**

An Art Nouveau patinated spelter mantel clock, by A. De Ranieri, with enamel dial painted with flowers, flowing organic molded case surmounted a young girl, signed on the base.

22.75in (58cm) high

$1,500-2,000   **L&T**

A J. & J. G. Low rare mantel clock with tiles on each side and top, embossed with bees and foliage under olive green glossy glaze, with New Haven Clock Co. works with ivory enameled face, complete with weight and key, tiles stamped "J.&J.G.LOW PATENT..."; Clock face stamped "Made by the New Haven Clock Co. New Haven Conn. USA".

14.25in (36cm) high

$6,000-8,000   **DRA**

A General Electric Art Deco alarm clock, 'Circe', model 7H92, with stylized floral medallion to reverse-painted arched glass face, on stepped chrome base, die-stamped marks, small chip to edge of one numeral.

8in (20cm) wide

$600-900   **SDR**

An Art Deco bronze Zodiac eight-day mantel clock, circular form, rectangular plinth.

11.5in (29cm) high

$1,300-1,500   **FRE**

An Art Deco clock, Telechron '700 Electroalarm' 'Vinylite' electric mantel clock, by Warren Telechron Co of Ashland, Massachusets, skyscraper shape in 'walnut', the glass dial with mirrored border, linear brass ornament and red accents, maker's mark on reverse with numbers 233645A, some damage.

This clock is thought to have been designed by Paul Frankl but there is no proof of his involvement in the factory's records. This was the first Telechron alarm clock made.

c1932   *8in (20cm) high*

$700-1,000   **SK**

CHRISTOPHER DRESSER

- Dr Christopher Dresser (1834-1904) has been called the first independent industrial designer and has emerged as one of Glasgow's most influential sons.
- Dresser turned his hand to everything from ceramics and glass to botany and retail. His metalware designs are arguably his greatest legacy.
- His clean designs foreshadowed the modern movement by a quarter of a century, but were rejected by some in his day as too eccentric for Victorian tastes.
- Dresser differed from William Morris and other Arts and Crafts designers in his belief that new technologies and industrialization should be harnessed for their power to democratize design.
- Working with firms such as Hukin & Heath, Elkington & Co. and James Dixon, Dresser produced a great variety of teapots, toast racks, kettles, candleholders and tureens.
- There was a discernable difference in Dresser's work after he traveled to Japan in 1876. Ancient Andean and Egyptian forms, Classical antiquity and feudal Europe were also influential.

A Christopher Dresser copper and brass tea kettle and cover, manufactured by Benham & Froud Ltd.

This tea kettle was probably produced by Benham and Froud for the Art Furnishers Alliance for which Dresser was the 'Art Manager'.

c1880   8.25in (21cm) high

$12,000-18,000   L&T

A Christopher Dresser three-piece silver plate tea service, manufactured by Elkington & Co., comprising a teapot with hinged cover and with rosewood handle and knob, a milk jug, with rosewood handle and a sugar bowl, each piece inscribed with a crest, stamped marks "Elkington & Co. 16675".

1885   teapot 5.5in (14cm) high

$7,000-8,000   L&T

A three-piece silver plate tea service by Christopher Dresser, manufactured by James Dixon & Sons, comprising a lidded teapot with ebony handle, a milk jug, and a sugar bowl, each stamped with facsimile signature "Chr. Dresser", and marked "J.D. & S. 2278".

1880   teapot 5.25in (13.5cm) high

$30,000-35,000   L&T

A Dresser silver teapot, manufactured by Heath and Middleton, silver with wicker covered twin handles, the body inscribed with initials "FMS", hallmarked for London, also with retailers mark "W Thornhill & Co, New Bond Street W".

1881   3.75in (9.5cm) high

$2,000-3,000   L&T

A Hukin & Heath electroplated silver tureen and cover designed by Christopher Dresser with ebonized wood rod handles and finial with stamped marks.

9in (23cm) high

$15,000-20,000   WW

A Christopher Dresser silver plate claret jug, manufactured by James Dixon and Sons, stamped marks "J.D. & S. 2522".

9.75in (24.5cm) high

$3,000-4,000   L&T

A Christopher Dresser silver plate ribbed milk jug, shape 16678, manufactured by Elkington & Co., stamped marks "Elkington & Co.", registration mark.

1885   3in (7.5cm) high

$2,000-2,500   L&T

A Christopher Dresser silver plate and glass claret jug, manufactured by Hukin and Heath, stamped marks "H & H 2120".

The shape of this claret jug derives from ancient Greco-Roman Askos: leather bags or wine skins. The shape has been widely adapted and was particularly popular in the 1830s to 50s – silver manufacturers such as Paul Storr and William Elliott in London were making silver-mounted examples at this time.

1880   7in (18cm) high

$15,000-20,000   L&T

A Christopher Dresser silver plate hot water jug, probably manufactured by Richard Perry, Son & Co., ebonized handle, stamped marks "G1 2c".

1876-80   8in (20cm) high

$3,000-4,000   L&T

DECORATIVE ARTS

A Christopher Dresser silver and glass lidded decanter, manufactured by Heath and Middleton, bears crest, hallmarks for London, bears maker's marks and retailer's mark "G.W.S.S.&Co. 166 Regent St W".

1882   *9in (23cm) high*
$4,000-6,000   **L&T**

A Christopher Dresser silver and glass cased decanter and four glasses, manufactured by Heath and Middleton, comprising a lidded decanter with ebony handle, and four glasses, each bears stamped makers' marks, and hallmarks for London 1882-3.

1882-3   decanter 9.75in (25cm) h
$10,000-15,000   **L&T**

A Christopher Dresser (1834-1904) tall glass and silver mounted decanter, by Heath and Middleton, with ebonized handle, hallmarked Birmingham.

1880   14.5in (37cm) high
$12,000-14,000   **L&T**

A silver plate tantalus, by Christopher Dresser, manufactured by Hukin and Heath, with glass and ebonized wood, stamped marks "Designed by Dr C Dresser" and "H & H 2046", registration mark.

1879   11.5in (29cm) high
$7,000-10,000   **L&T**

A Christopher Dresser silver plate and glass lidded decanter & stopper, manufactured by Hukin and Heath, stamped marks "Designed by Dr C Dresser", and "H & H 2045", registration mark.

1879   9.5in (24.5cm) high
$32,000-36,000   **L&T**

A Hukin & Heath electroplated decanter stand, by Christopher Dresser, stamped "Designed by Dr C Dresser", stamped marks "H & H 1936", registration mark, also with retailers mark "Collins, Silversmith, Brighton".

1878   12.25in (31cm) high
$1,500-2,500   **L&T**

A Hukin & Heath glass and electroplate decanter, by Christopher Dresser, with stamped marks.

8.5in (22cm) high
$1,500-2,500   **L&T**

A Christopher Dresser silver plate and glass circular cruet set manufactured by Elkington & Co., with ebony handle, stamped marks "Elkington & Co. 17282", with registration mark.

1885   6in (15cm) high
$15,000-20,000   **L&T**

A Christopher Dresser silver plate cruet set, manufactured by Elkington & Co, stamped marks "Elkington & Co. 17286".

4.75in (12.5cm) high
$400-500   **L&T**

A Christopher Dresser silver plate and glass condiment set, manufactured by Hukin and Heath, stamped marks "H & H 2239", registration mark.

1879   5in (13cm) high
$800-1,200   **L&T**

A Christopher Dresser silver plate creamer and sugar on stand, manufactured by Hukin and Heath, stand with stamped marks "H & H 3911", creamer and sugar with registration marks.

1884   6.5in (16.5cm) high
$1,500-2,000   **L&T**

A Christopher Dresser silver plate and glass cruet set, manufactured by Hukin and Heath, inscribed with crest, stamped marks "Designed by Dr C Dresser", and "H & H 1918", registration mark.

1878   8.25in (21cm) high
$4,000-5,000   **L&T**

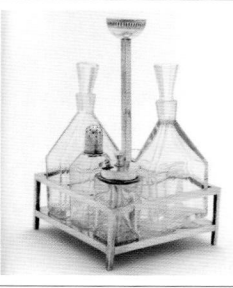

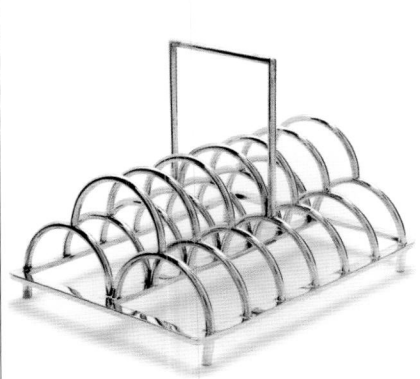

A Christopher Dresser silver plated toast rack, designed 1879, manufactured by James Dixon & Sons, indistinct stamped marks, numbered "66".

5.5in (14cm) high

$12,000-18,000   **L&T**

A Christopher Dresser silver plated toast rack, designed for James Dixon and Son, Sheffield, with conjoined lancet arches, stamped marks "J.D. & S. 72'".

c1885   *4.5in (11.5cm) wide*

$3,000-3,500   **L&T**

A Christopher Dresser silver plated toast rack, manufactured by Hukin and Heath, stamped marks "Designed by Dr C Dresser", and "H & H 1987", registration mark.

1881   *5.25in (13.5cm) high*

$8,000-10,000   **L&T**

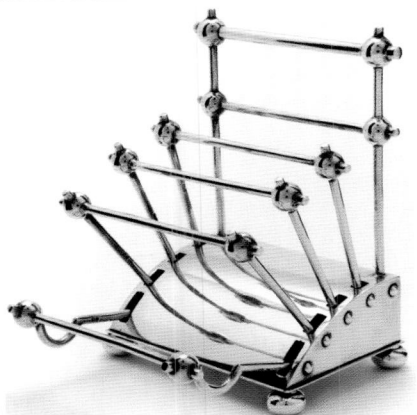

An articulated silver letter rack by Christopher Dresser, manufactured by Hukin and Heath, incorporating a pen rest, stamped marks "H & H 14775" with hallmarks for Birmingham.

1909   *5in (13cm) high*

$4,000-5,000   **L&T**

An articulated silver plated letter rack by Christopher Dresser, manufactured by Hukin and Heath, stamped marks "H & H 2555".

4.75in (12.5cm) high

$3,000-4,000   **L&T**

A Christopher Dresser electroplated toast rack with adjustable arms, marked "H&H" with hallmarks, numbered "2555" with inscription "E.J.T to B. C. Oct. 23/84".

6in (15cm) wide

$3,000-4,000   **SDR**

A four piece electroplated tea and coffee service, by Christopher Dresser, designed for James Dixon and Sons, and comprising a lidded coffee pot, a lidded teapot, a milk jug and a sugar bowl, each of tapering form cast with a decorative foliate band, bears stamped facsimile signature and factory marks, no. 2293.

coffee pot 8in (20cm) high

$8,000-12,000   **L&T**

A Christopher Dresser silver-plated tureen and cover, designed for Elkington & Co, with ebonized handles, stamped "Elkington & Co. 12780" and "22366" for 1885.

1885   *13.5in (34cm) diam*

$9,000-10,000   **L&T**

Six glasses and stand by Christopher Dresser, manufactured by Hukin and Heath, silver plate and glass, the handle inscribed with initial "D", stamped marks "Designed by Dr C Dresser", and "H & H 2268", registration mark.

1878   *6in (15.5cm) high*
$2,500-3,000   **L&T**

A Christopher Dresser silver plate tureen, cover and ladle manufactured by Hukin and Heath, with ebony handles and knob, stamped marks "Designed by Dr C Dresser" and "H & H 2168", indistinct registration marks.

1880   *7.75in (19.5cm) wide*
$18,000-22,000   **L&T**

A Christopher Dresser silver plate spoon warmer, manufactured by Hukin and Heath, with ebony handle, stamped marks "H & H 2693".

c1880   *5in (13cm) high*
$3,000-3,500   **L&T**

A Christopher Dresser silver plated spoon warmer, manufactured by Hukin and Heath, with ebony handle, stamped marks "H & H 2857".

c1880   *5.75in (14.5cm) high*
$3,000-3,500   **L&T**

A rare staved oak circular bowl, by Christopher Dresser for Hukin and Heath, with electroplated mounts and with applied opposed cartouches and twin handles, raised on tapering feet, later frosted glass liner, stamped marks "H&H 2466".

A design for an uncovered bowl in oak was registered by Hukin and Heath in 1880. This rare example would originally have had a porcelain liner, now replaced with frosted glass.

c1880   *13in (33cm) diam*
$8,000-12,000   **L&T**

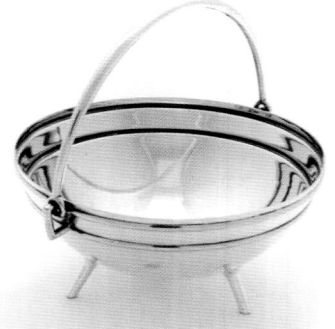

A Christopher Dresser silver plate sugar basket, manufactured by Hukin and Heath, with swing handle, stamped marks "Designed by Dr C Dresser", and "H & H 2072".

5.5in (14cm) diam
$8,000-10,000   **L&T**

A silver plated double serving dish, by Christopher Dresser for Hukin and Heath, with loop handle and prong legs, stamped marks "H&H 2523".

10.5in (26.5cm) wide
$1,000-1,500   **L&T**

A Tudric pewter lidded jug, designed by Archibald Knox for Liberty & Co., the tapering body cast with stylized foliage, the hinged lid with shaped thumbpiece, the applied handle rush-covered, stamped factory marks, no. 0301.

8in (20.5cm) high

$500-600   **L&T**

A Liberty Tudric jug, in the manner of Archibald Knox, with a beaten finish and a decorative Art Nouveau handle, marked underneath, made by Liberty & Co., 066.

5in (13cm) high

$300-350   **LAW**

A Liberty Tudric pewter and enamel fruit bowl, with green glass liner, designed by Archibald Knox, cast in low relief with Art Nouveau foliage enameled in shades of blue and green, stamped marks.

9in (24cm) diam

$2,500-3,000   **WW**

A Liberty & Co. silver twin-handled bowl, by Archibald Knox, decorated with Celtic knotted line and inlaid with shaped panels of turquoise enamel, hallmarked Birmingham.

1902   *6.75in (17cm) wide*

$8,000-10,000   **L&T**

A pair of Liberty & Co. Tudric pewter candlesticks formed as candle sconces, each supported on four shaped and tapering legs to a shaped hollow base, stamped to base "Liberty & Co, English Pewter, Tudric" and number "0222".

4in (10cm) high

$1,500-2,000   **JN**

A Liberty & Co. pewter desk stand, by Archibald Knox, with ivorine calendar cards, foliate frame and stylized plant forms, fitted with two inkwells and a pen holder.

10.25in (26cm) wide

$1,000-1,500   **L&T**

A Liberty & Co. pewter part tea service and tray, by Archibald Knox, all with stylized Celtic foliage and seed heads, stamped marks, no. 0231.

tray 19.25in (49cm) wide

$1,200-1,800   **L&T**

A Liberty & Co. Art Nouveau two-handled pewter vase, designed by Archibald Knox, No.029, base with small hole.

10in (25.5cm) high

$150-200   **GAZE**

A Liberty & Co. hammered silver six division toast rack with circular handle and demi-lune divisions, impressed decoration, marks to base number "50252" and maker's mark "L & Co. Birmingham".

1933   *4.75in (12cm) wide*

$600-800   **JN**

A Roycroft hammered copper baluster vase with flaring rim, of heavy gauge, some pitting and wear to original patina, orb and cross mark.

8.25in (20.5cm) high

$400-600 **DRA**

A rare Roycroft hammered copper cylindrical vase, incised with full-length leaves alternating with buds beneath a verdigris-patinated hammered top, orb and cross mark.

8.25in (20.5cm) high

$2,500-3,000 **DRA**

A Roycroft hammered copper tall American Beauty vase, original dark patina, stamped "THE G.P.I. AMERICAN BEAUTY VASE MADE EXCLUSIVELY FOR GROVE PARK INN BY THE ROYCROFTERS", orb and cross mark.

22in (56cm) high

$5,000-6,000 **DRA**

A Roycroft copper bottle-shaped Ali Baba vase with long neck covered in a verdigris patina, some scratches, pitting, and dents, orb and cross mark.

15in (38cm) high

$2,000-3,000 **DRA**

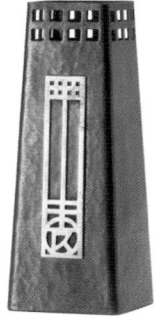

A rare Roycroft hammered copper and silver four-sided vase, designed by Dard Hunter, with overlay and a silver panel featuring "R", and orb and cross mark.

6.75in (17cm) high

$10,000-12,000 **DRA**

A Roycroft hammered copper four-sided tapering vase, pierced with two rows of small squares, minor cleaning to patina, and orb and cross mark.

7in (18cm) high

$7,000-10,000 **DRA**

A pair of Roycroft hammered copper candlesticks with three curved legs, original patina, orb and cross marks.

9in (23cm) high

$7,000-10,000 **DRA**

A Roycroft American half dollar piece.

Provenance: Purported to be Elbert Hubbard's first earnings from writing, saved by his wife as a pocket piece until found by his offspring, kept in a hand carved wooden box. From the Estate of Miriam Hubbard Roelofs, Elbert Hubbard's daughter.

1872

$1,100-1,300 **DRA**

A Roycroft hammered silver plated dog bowl with straight sides, monogrammed "ADA", orb and cross mark.

6.25in (15.5cm) wide

$1,200-1,800 **DRA**

A Roycroft hammered copper five-piece smoking set in the Trillium pattern with an ashtray/matchbox stand, match holder, and cigarette holder, on a circular tray, medium patina, orb and cross marks.

tray 9.75in (25cm) diam

$1,200-1,800 **DRA**

An L.C. Tiffany copper-clad earthenware vase, with rolled-in rim embossed with a band of densely packed dogwood blossoms under a dark brown patina, "LCT BP170".

7in (17.5cm) wide

$5,000-6,000   **DRA**

An L.C. Tiffany copper-clad earthenware vase, embossed with Virginia creeper leaves under a dark brown patina, "LCT P125, L.C. Tiffany Favrile Pottery".

6.5in (16cm) wide

$3,500-4,000   **DRA**

A large L.C. Tiffany copper-clad vase, with squat shoulder embossed with a band of Virginia creeper, original dark patina, interior firing lines, "LCT/L.C. Tiffany – Favrile Bronze Pottery/B.P. 235".

The interior firing lines are not uncommon with this type of technique.

12in (30cm) wide

$7,000-10,000   **DRA**

A Tiffany grapevine pattern inkwell with green patinated pierced bronze panels, green and white glass sides, one side cracked, with original clear glass well, stamped "Tiffany Studios, New York 884".

4in (10cm) wide

$700-800   **SWO**

A Tiffany Studios gilt-parcel inkwell in the grape pattern with mother-of-pearl dots, complete with glass liner, normal wear to gilt, stamped "TIFFANY STUDIOS NEW YORK 1157".

3.75in (9.5cm) wide

$900-1,100   **DRA**

A pair Tiffany Studios gilt bronze candlesticks, with a textured finish, stamped "TIFFANY STUDIOS, NEW YORK, 1213", bobeches lacking.

c1910   *18.5in (47cm) high*

$1,500-2,000   **FRE**

A pair of Tiffany Studios bronze tripod candlesticks, gadrooned cups, bases embossed with medallions reading "FIRST PANEL SHERIFF'S JURY 1905-1906", stamped "TIFFANY STUDIOS NEW YORK".

8in (20.5cm) high

$1,500-1,700   **DRA**

A Tiffany Studios bronze candelabra with tall swirled stem and oval base, stamped "TIFFANY STUDIOS NEW YORK/1230", and circular stamp.

9in (23cm) high

$3,000-3,500   **DRA**

A Tiffany brass and enameled three piece inkstand, bottle form lift lid ink well, on circular footed twin handled base, with putti decoration, together with pair of matching candlesticks, stamped "Tiffany & Co."

sticks 7.75in (19.5cm) high

$600-1,200   **FRE**

A rare and unusual Tiffany bronze inkstand, naturalistic blue point crab with articulated top shell, holding oyster shell inkwell in claws, signed on base "Tiffany Studios New York 23547", small rear chip to oyster shell.

8.5in (21.5cm) wide

$10,000-12,000　　　**FRE**

A Tiffany Studios bronze paperweight of a crouching lioness in acid-etched finish, stamped "TIFFANY STUDIOS NEW YORK 932".

5in (12.5cm) long

$1,300-1,500　　　**DRA**

A Tiffany Studios bronze letter holder in the Zodiac pattern, original verdigris patina, touch-ups to back, "TIFFANY STUDIOS NEW YORK 1009".

9.5in (24cm) wide

$500-600　　　**DRA**

A Tiffany bronze and gem Byzantine five piece desk set, consisting of pair of end panels for desk pad, lift lid notepad, pen tray and blotter, stamped "Tiffany Studios New York", original finish, all marked.

$4,000-6,000　　　**FRE**

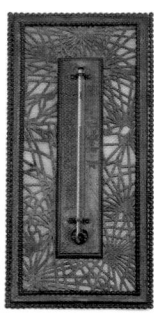

A Tiffany Studios bronze Pine Needles thermometer, c1900, stamped "Tiffany Studios New York 1013".

1900　　　*8.75in (22.25cm) high*

$1,200-1,800　　　**FRE**

Tiffany Studios large bronze desk frame in the Zodiac pattern covered in a fine original verdigris patina, stamped "TIFFANY STUDIOS NEW YORK 920".

14in (35.5cm) high

$5,000-6,000　　　**DRA**

A Tiffany Furnaces Brass desk frame with gold Favrile glass, stamped "LOUIS C. TIFFANY FURNACES INC/56", circular stamp.

10.5in (26.5cm) high

$3,000-4,000　　　**DRA**

ARTS & CRAFTS SILVER

■ Victorian mass-production had reduced the value of metalware, but Arts & Crafts craftsmen sought to elevate it once again to a fine art.

■ Arts & Crafts was one of the most influential design movements of the late 19th and early 20th centuries. Exponents rejected industrial production in favor of traditional craftsmanship.

■ Arts & Crafts metalwork saw design as subordinate to function. As a result forms were clean and simple, laying the foundations for modern design.

■ Shapes recalled design eras predating industrialization, such as the medieval or Tudor past.

■ Important makers include Charles Robert Ashbee founder of the Guild of Handicrafts. The community of artist craftsmen, in operation from 1887-1908 produced high quality, handmade silverware, metalware and furniture.

■ Metalworkers Omar Ramsden and Alwyn Carr were responsible for some of the most beautifully crafted pieces of the period. Influenced by historical styles, their work involved hand-hammered decoration and inset enamel or precious stones.

■ Liberty & Co. and Tiffany both introduced high quality yet commercially successful Arts & Crafts style pieces.

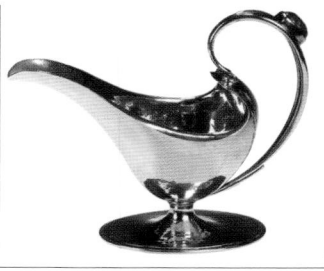

A Ramsden and Carr silver cream jug, mounted to the handle with a turquoise enamel cabochon, hallmarked London, inscribed to the base "Ramsden & Carr Made Me".

1904　　　*5.5in (14cm) long*
$4,000-6,000　　　**L&T**

An Arts & Crafts silver caddy spoon, by Omar Ramsden & Alwyn Carr, with planished finish, and central red enameled panel, with marks for London, 1oz.

1906　　　*3.25in (8cm) long*
$3,000-4,000　　　**L&T**

A silver box and cover by Alwyn Carr with lobed decoration, the cover with scroll and ball finial and set with five green stones.

1921　　　*4.25in (11cm) wide*
$6,000-8,000　　　**LAW**

An Arts & Crafts silver quaich, by Omar Ramsden, with planished finish, and waisted handles, with marks for London, and inscribed "OMAR RAMSDEN ME FECIT", 4oz.

1923　　　*6in (15cm) wide*
$2,000-3,000　　　**L&T**

An Edwardian silver porringer, designed by Charles Robert Ashbee, Guild of Handicraft Limited, with looped handle inset with a green chrysoprase stone, London hallmarks.

1902　　　*7.75in (19.5cm) wide*
$6,000-8,000　　　**SWO**

An Ian A.R. Davidson silver powder bowl and cover, with lobed finial set with moonstone and red cabochons, and marks for Edinburgh, sponsor's mark "BH" (Bernard Harrington).

1952　　　*6.75in (17cm) high*
$3,000-4,000　　　**L&T**

A pair of Arts and Crafts silver candlesticks, by James Dixon & Sons, with dished drip tray above square tapering column, hallmarked Sheffield.

1928　　　*8.5in (22cm) high*
$1,500-2,500　　　**L&T**

An Arts and Crafts silver pedestal bowl, by Goldsmith's and Silversmith's Co. Ltd, of London, with a spot-hammered bowl.

1918
$500-600   **B**

A pair of silver candlesticks, Goudji, Paris, with blue agate collar, square bases, inlaid blue agate panels around a stag motif, and a hand beaten finish.

9.75in (19.5cm) high
$5,000-6,000   **L&T**

An Arts and Crafts silver comport, by A. E. Jones, of elliptical form, with twin looped handles and pierced leaf medallions, the whole raised on a spreading square foot with faux rivet decoration, hallmarked "Chester", indistinct maker's marks.

1915   *9.25in (23.5cm) wide*
$1,000-1,200   **L&T**

A Kalo hammered sterling silver faceted pitcher, monogrammed "M", stamped mark/4 pints.

8.25in (21cm) high
$4,000-5,000   **DRA**

A sterling silver chalice chased with a latin motto, Shepheard & Co., hallmarked S & Co., English.

5in (13cm) diam
$2,000-3,000   **DRA**

An Arts & Crafts silver spill vase, hallmarks for Birmingham, with registered design mark 467044, marked "WHH", some damage.

9in (23cm) high
$100-120   **GAZE**

An unusual Arts and Crafts box and cover fashioned from a brazil nut case applied with silver-metal mounts set with foil-backed green enameled plaques.

5.5in (14cm) high
$400-600   **JN**

A small Arts and Crafts silver two-handled bowl, of compressed form, applied with a pair of pierced stampwork handles, maker's mark worn, London.

1905   *3.5in (9cm) wide*
$120-180   **B**

A Guild of Handicrafts electroplated muffin dish and cover, by C. R. Ashbee (1863-1942), of circular dished form with applied beaded rim and hot water compartment below, the domed lid with basket finial set with amethyst-colored cabochon, apparently unmarked.

8.75in (22.5cm) diam
$2,000-3,000   **L&T**

Three electroplated jam spoons, Charles Rennie Mackintosh (1868-1928), manufactured by E. Bingham & Company for Miss Cranston's Tearooms, Glasgow, comprising two small and one larger, each with trefoil terminals, stamped marks.

c1905   *largest 6in (15cm) long*
$1,500-2,000   **L&T**

A Charles Rennie Mackintosh set of four electroplated teaspoons, manufactured by E. Bingham & Company for Miss Cranston's tearooms, Glasgow, stamped marks.

c1905   *5in (13cm) long*
$1,100-1,300   **L&T**

An 18-piece suite of electroplate cutlery, designed by Charles Rennie Mackintosh for Miss Cranston's tearooms and comprising seven forks, six bearing stamped marks "Miss Cranston's"; six dessert spoons, six bearing stamped marks "Miss Cranston's"; and five fish knives, unmarked, each with trefoil terminals.

c1905
$6,000-8,000   **L&T**

A Charles Rennie Mackintosh set of six forks, designed for Miss Cranston's Tearooms, Glasgow, with ebonized handles and electroplated prongs, stamped "Miss Cranston's".

c1898   8in (20.5cm) long

$1,500-2,500   **L&T**

A pair of Dirk van Erp silver-plated hammered copper quadruple low candlesticks on oval bases, stamped "Dirk Van Erp" with windmill.

12in (30cm) wide

$1,500-2,500   **DRA**

A Dirk van Erp silver-plated hammered floriform center bowl, stamped windmill, handwrought Dirk Van Erp, San Francisco.

14.5in (37cm) diam

$1,200-1,800   **DRA**

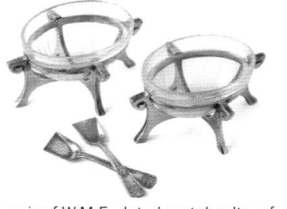

A pair of W.M.F. plated metal salts, of oval shape with oval cut glasses dishes supported in oval frames with stylized handles and supported on curved legs, complete with matching spoons with engraved decoration, bears stamped maker's marks.

3.5in (9cm) wide

$600-800   **JN**

A pair of Kalo silver-gilt candlesticks, monogrammed "M", with stamped marks.

12in (30.5cm) high

$5,000-6,000   **DRA**

An Arts and Crafts copper wall mirror, by Frank Bazely, cast and chased in relief, with domed cartouches, surmounted with the figure of an owl.

11.5in (29.5cm) wide

$3,000-4,000   **L&T**

A pair of W.A.S. Benson & Co. copper and brass chamber sticks, each with turned nozzles and curved handles with leaf terminals, above stamped flowerhead drip trays, stamped marks.

7in (17.5cm) diam

$1,000-1,500   **L&T**

A pair of W.A.S. Benson copper and brass chambersticks, each with a loop handle and a petal shaped base, both stamped "Benson and W.A.S. Benson".

7in (17.5cm) diam

$800-1,200   **SWO**

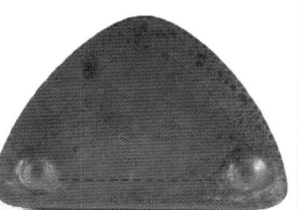

A pair of Albert Berry hammered copper triangular bookends, stamped "BERRY'S CRAFT SHOP, THEIR MARK", wear to patina.

5.5in (14cm) wide

$300-400   **DRA**

A hammered copper and fossilized walrus tusk lamp base, by Albert Berry, with three sockets, fine original patina, and stamped hammer mark, "Berry Craft Shop Seattle".

base 25in (63.5cm) high

$9,000-10,000   **DRA**

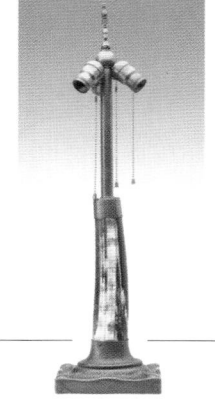

A Rebecca Cauman hammered copper candy dish with a flaring top and foot joined by a glass ball, original patina, scratches, stamped "Cauman".

6.75in (17cm) wide

$1,000-1,500   **DRA**

A Dirk van Erp hammered copper closed-in vessel, some cleaning to patina, a few shallow dents, windmill mark, remnants of D'Arcy Gaw.

5.75in (14cm) wide

$1,500-1,700   **DRA**

A pair of Dirk van Erp hammered copper bookends, each with a pierced lunette featuring a scrub oak tree, fine original patina, open box mark.

5.5in (14cm) wide

$1,800-2,200   **DRA**

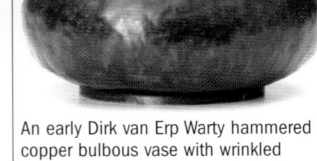

An early Dirk van Erp Warty hammered copper bulbous vase with wrinkled neck, with scattered deep red blush, with closed box mark.

8.5in (21.5cm) high

$10,000-12,000   **DRA**

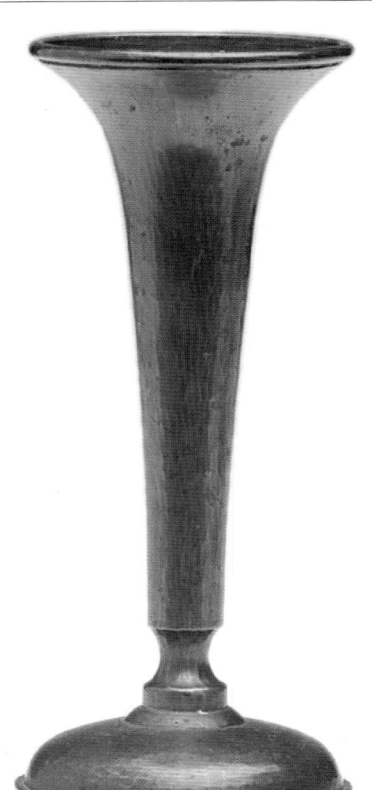

A Dirk van Erp hammered copper flaring bud vase, fine original dark patina, scratch to side, open box mark.

7.5in (19cm) high

$1,000-1,200   **DRA**

An Arts and Crafts embossed copper box, by S. Parker, the hinged lid embossed with grapes and vines, flanking two blue ceramic plaques, possibly Ruskin, the front and sides with embossed foliate motifs, engraved to base "S. Parker, Benthal Rd School, Clapton, E11".

15.25in (38.5cm) wide

$1,200-1,400   **JN**

An Arts and Crafts John Pearson copper charger, the rim decorated with a raised border of shells and seaweed, the central panel depicting a shoal of fish around a galleon, the surface of the dish overlaid with a black lacquered finish, signed on the back "J. Pearson 1890", 335.

15in (38cm) diam

$3,000-4,000   **LAW**

An Arts and Crafts John Pearson copper dish, the rim decorated with a raised border of acorns and leaves, the central panel depicting birds and foliage, the surface of the dish overlaid with a black lacquered finish, signed on the back "J. Pearson 1890, 329".

12in (32cm) diam

$1,000-1,500   **LAW**

A large Newlyn-style patinated copper charger, in the manner of John Pearson, of circular form, the central panel repoussé decorated with a galleon in full sail, enclosed by a rim of swimming fish.

24in (61cm) diam

$800-1,200   **L&T**

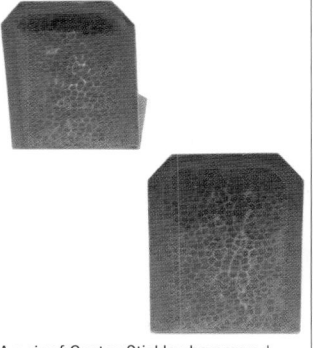

A pair of Gustav Stickley hammered copper rectangular bookends, with clipped corners, original patina, "Als Ik Kan" stamp.

5.5in (14cm) high

$1,300-1,500   **DRA**

An unusual Gustav Stickley hammered copper inkwell with riveted base and old applied owl figurine, possibly not original to piece, original dark patina to most, "Als Ik Kan" stamp, area cleaned on base, no liner.

5.5in (14cm) diam

$500-600   **DRA**

The Arts Crafts Shop five-piece enameled copper desk set, letter holder, inkwell, pen tray, card tray, and four blotter corners, original patina, several chips to enamel, most stamped "The Art Crafts Shop Buffalo NY".

$1,000-1,200   **DRA**

An Arts and Crafts copper-framed wall mirror, with a hammer-beaten surround, relief decorated with stylized floral designs with blue enamel flowerheads.

20.75in (53cm) high

$500-600   **SWO**

An Arts and Crafts hammered copper riveted mirror frame, with original bevelled glass, original dark patina, unmarked.

37.75in (94cm) high

$3,000-4,000   **DRA**

A Scottish Arts and Crafts copper wall mirror, repoussé decorated with floral roundels reserved on punched line border above a moth motif.

34.5in (88cm) wide

$1,200-1,800   **L&T**

A Hammered copper Fine Arts & Crafts sign of repoussé copper, for the Pond Applied Art Studio, fine original patina.

Theodore Pond owned the Pond Applied Art Studio in Baltimore, MD, from 1911-1914

16.5in (42cm) high

$7,000-8,000   **DRA**

An Arts and Crafts brass and copper casket, with enameled cartouche.

8.5in (22cm) wide

$500-600   **GAZE**

An Arts and Crafts copper coal scuttle, the cylindrical body with riveted brass straps on three heavy-cast legs.

22.5in (57cm) long

$800-1,000   **L&T**

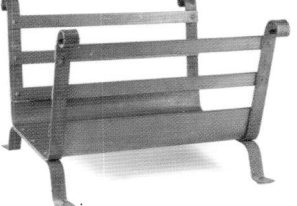

An Arts and Crafts wrought-iron and copper riveted log holder, wear to finish, unmarked.

20in (51cm) wide

$800-1,200   **DRA**

A Scottish Arts and Crafts brass-framed mirror, in the manner of P.W. Davidson, repoussé decorated with flying swallows amongst stylized trees, dated.

1926   *20.5in (52cm) wide*

$1,500-2,500   **L&T**

A Scottish Arts and Crafts brass charger, attributed to Margaret Gilmour, repoussé decorated with a central boss enclosed by a band of Celtic knotwork.

19.5in (49.5cm) diam

$800-1,200   **L&T**

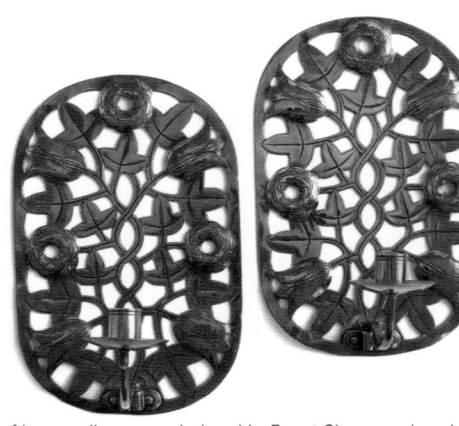

A pair of brass wall sconces, designed by Ernest Gimson and made by Alfred Bucknell, each backplate pierced and embossed with tulips and roses, with a detachable candle arm.

11in (28cm) high

$22,000-28,000　　　　　　　　　　　　　　　　　　**LFA**

A pair of brass candlesticks, possibly Ernest Gimson, with faceted base and stem, probably manufactured by Alfred Bucknell, unmarked.

10in (25cm) high

$2,500-3,000　　　　　　　　　　**DRA**

A Jarvie brass candelabra with two rivetted coils supporting long and tapering candle holders, missing bobeches, some cleaning to patina, stamped "Jarvie".

10in (25.5cm) high

$5,000-6,000　　　　　　　　**DRA**

A Jarvie card tray embossed with holly leaves and berries, unpatinated, signed "The Jarvie Shop".

6in (15cm) diam

$1,500-2,500　**DRA**

An Archibald Kendrick & Sons Aesthetic brass door knocker, the design attributed to Christopher Dresser, of angular outline in two parts, cast and pierced with stylized foliate decorations , cast marks "406 A.K & Sons".

8.25in (21cm) high

$600-800　**L&T**

A pair of Scottish Arts & Crafts brass plated vases, by Sir Robert Lorimer, embossed with foliate panels, inscribed under base "Gifted to/The South Church/ Creiff/ by Elizabeth R. Birch/ Oct. 1929/Designed by Sir Robert Lorimer".

The South Church, Creiff alterations were one of Lorimer's final commissions.

9.5in (24.5cm) high

$800-1,200　**L&T**

A large Iona Alexander Ritchie circular brass charger, repoussé decorated with Celtic knotwork, two hanging mounts to rear, unmarked.

This is an unusually large size for a charger.

26in (68.5cm) diam

$4,000-5,000　**L&T**

An Iona brass inkwell, by Alexander Ritchie, with hinged lid enclosing a glass liner, and opposed panels of sailing galleons and Celtic knotwork.

5.5in (14cm) high

$1,200-1,800　**L&T**

A large brass Glasgow style planter, repoussé decorated with flowering thistles.

11.5in (29cm) high

$800-1,200　**L&T**

A Scottish School Arts & Crafts brass planter, of rectangular form with separate liner, the sides repoussé-decorated with stylised rose motifs, the angles with rivetted brackets, ring handles to the ends, ball feet.

20in (51cm) wide

$800-1,000　**L&T**

A pair of Scottish School brass vases, of square section tapered form, with liners, in the style of Alexander Ritchie, Iona, each of footed tapering form decorated with repoussé panels of Celtic designs.

12.25in (31cm) high

$800-1,000　**L&T**

A Scottish Arts & Crafts brass wall mirror, with beaten brass frame, pierced and repoussé decorated with two panels of stylized flowering roses.

41.25in (105cm) wide

$4,000-6,000　**L&T**

A wood and brass three-footed Arts & Crafts cylindrical vessel, possibly Newcomb College, the brass inlay of foliate branches, cleaned patina, unmarked.

4in (10cm) wide

$700-1,000　**DRA**

A tall Heintz sterling-on-bronze vase, overlaid with poppies on verdigris ground, restoration to finish on rim, discoloration and dent to base, stamps "HAMS".

12.5in (31cm) high

$400-800   **DRA**

A pair of tall Heintz sterling-on-bronze candlesticks, overlaid with a Greek key pattern, touch-ups to patina near silver, stamped "HAMS" patent.

11.5in (29cm) high

$600-800   **DRA**

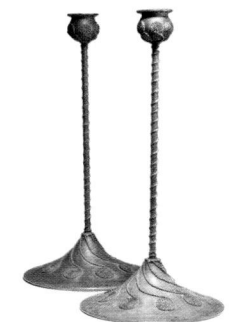

An Arts & Crafts pair of bronze tall candlesticks, with coiled rope pattern on verdigris ground, unmarked.

15.5in (39cm) high

$200-400   **DRA**

An Arts & Crafts cast metal hinged inkwell embossed with a stylized pattern and covered in a bronze patina, unmarked.

6.5in (16.5cm) wide

$300-400   **DRA**

A Scottish Arts & Crafts cast and wrought iron fire grate, in the manner of Sir Robert Lorimer, with slatted grate, scrolling supports, and perching birds.

39.5in (100cm) wide

$2,000-3,000   **L&T**

A set of three Cotswold School Arts & Crafts steel fireirons, with boldly turned knop terminals.

approx 33in (84cm) long

$2,000-3,000   **L&T**

A Scottish Arts & Crafts wrought iron three hinged panels, scrolling foliage and bird roundel, and backed by a glazed panel.

30.25in (77cm) high

$3,000-4,000   **L&T**

A pair of Louis Sullivan cast-iron balusters from the Guaranty Building in Buffalo, NY, 1894-1896, original finish.

30in (76cm) high

$6,000-8,000   **DRA**

The log fork from a composite set of four Scottish Arts & Crafts steel fireirons, attributed to Sir Robert Lorimer, with scrolling foliate terminals.

log fork 27.5in (70cm) long

$3,000-4,000   **L&T**

A William Connell pewter hinged box with heart-shaped and circular cabochons, stamped "PEWTER 02163".

8in (20cm) diam

$700-1,000   **DRA**

A Cellini Craft hammered aluminum large tray, inset with a Hispano-Mooresque California tile, surrounded by four almond-shaped dimples, stamped "ARGENTAL/HANDWROUGHT/MW/CELLINI-CRAFT".

17in (42.5cm) diam

$200-400   **DRA**

DECORATIVE ARTS

A Georg Jensen sterling silver bowl, with everted rim and hammered finish raised on stylized leaf and berry, on a spreading circular base, with stamped marks.

5in (13cm) high

$1,500-2,500   **L&T**

A pair of silver fish servers, by Evald Nielsen.

11in (28cm) long

$800-1,200   **PC**

A Reed & Barton Art Nouveau sterling silver punch bowl, applied with flowerheads.

The fine Art Nouveau modeling suggests an attempt by Reed & Barton to rival Gorham's Martele.

c1900

$12,000-14,000

20.5in (52cm) wide

FRE

An Art Nouveau WMF double-handled silver-plated tazza, lacks liner, stamped "I/O OX" and "NS".

9.5in (24cm) wide

$90-110   **GAZE**

A WMF Art Nouveau electroplated chamber stick, of triangular form, applied with a looped handle, the nozzle and each corner decorated with an entrelac design, stamped marks.

6.5in (16.5cm) wide

$300-400   **B**

A pair of WMF Art Nouveau electroplated jardinieres, with blue glass liners and twin handles, the frame cast with opposed Art Nouveau maidens, and stamped marks.

12.25in (31cm) wide

$1,200-1,800   **L&T**

A WMF silver plated vase, number 304, with a pair of stylized handles and relief panels from classical mythology and a green glass liner.

13in (33cm) high

$700-1,000   **SWO**

A WMF Art Nouveau baluster vase, of naturalistic organic form beneath a shaped rim and set with a figure, on foliate spreading base.

9in (23cm) high

$150-250   **NEA**

An Art Nouveau silver-plated vase.

6.5in (16.5cm) high

$120-180   **GAZE**

A pair of gilt bronze Art Nouveau vases, by Louis & Francois Moreau, 'Spring & Summer' signed "L&F Moreau", on round onyx bases.

23in (58.5cm) high

$15,000-25,000   **FRE**

A French Art Nouveau gilded metal mirror.

c1905

$1,200-1,800   **TDG**

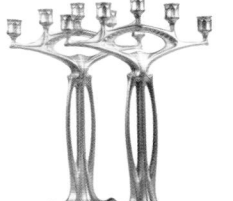

A pair of Art Nouveau five-candle candelabra in gilt-parcel finish, probably German or Austrian, stamped "89".

19in (48cm) high

$3,000-4,000   **DRA**

A Secessionist oval copper tray, fitted with brass gallery and twin oval handles, the whole with pierced chequer decoration.

23.75in (60.5cm) long

$400-600   **L&T**

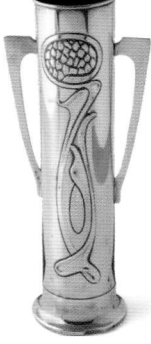

An Art Nouveau repoussé vase, with foliate decoration.

$120-140   **GAZE**

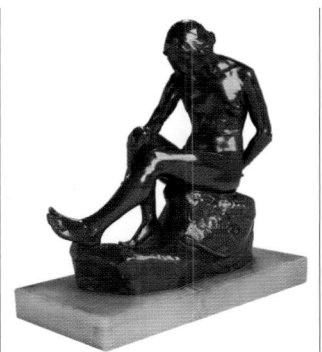

A bronze figure of the seated 'Eve' by David Alexander Francis ARSA, with an apple and a serpent on a rock, on an onyx plinth.

12.5in (32cm) high

$1,200-1,800   **L&T**

A Charles Marion Russell (American 1864-1926) bronze, 'Indian with Rattle Snake', brown patina, signed "C.M.Russell" and with artist symbol, dated, B. Zoppo foundry, NY.

1914   *4in (10cm) high*

$3,000-4,000   **FRE**

After Michelangelo (Italian, 1474-1564), 'Lorenzo de Medici, Il Pensieroso', medium brown patina, the base incised "Reduction Sauvage".

19in (48.5cm) high

$1,000-1,500   **FRE**

An equestrian statue after Andrea Verocchio (Italian, 1435-1488), from the Colleoni Monument, dark brown patina and gilt bronze, on a marble plinth with cast bronze relief.

20.25in (51.5cm) high

$2,000-3,000   **FRE**

A bronze Figure of a discus thrower.

$120-180   **BRI**

A bronzed metal figure of a child entitled 'Bonne Fete', on wood base, and signed "A.J. Scott".

16in (40.5cm) high

$120-180   **MAX**

A 19thC bronze figure of a woman, with two cherubs riding a dolphin.

15.75in (40cm) high

$700-1,000   **SWO**

A late 19thC Continental equestrian bronze, depicting a Roman figure on horseback, patinated and gilded.

12.5in (31cm) high

$800-1,200   **FRE**

A French 'Mercury' bronze bust, with a dark brown patina, raised on a socle base.

9in (23cm) high

$800-1,200   **FRE**

After Pierre Puget, (French, 1620-1694), a 'Milo of Crotona' bronze, greenish brown patina, signed "Puget".

8.25in (20.5cm) high

$400-600   **FRE**

A 19thC French School bronze 'Figure of Pan', raised on a turned rouge marble plinth.

11.75in (30cm) high

$1,500-2,000   **L&T**

A 19thC French Diana Moreau bronze sculpture, signed in the bronze "Moreau, Sculpt."

18in (46cm) high

$2,000-3,000   **L&T**

A pair of 19thC French School bronze Assyrian figures.

$2,000-3,000   **L&T**

Two late 19thC Grand Tour bronzes, after the Antique 'Cymbal Player' and 'Dionysus'.

tallest 15in (38cm) high

$2,000-3,000   **L&T**

A Sir John Steell RSA (1804-1891) bronze, of 'Alexander taming Bucephalus', signed in the bronze "Jn. Steell sculpt. Edinr.1833".

This is a reduction of the bronze which stands in the courtyard of The City Chambers, High Street, Edinburgh.

19.5in (49.5cm) high

$7,000-10,000   **L&T**

A pair of late 19th/early 20thC French bronze figures of 'Mercury' and 'Fortuna', after Giambologna, decorated with a bronze relief of putti.

Mercury 34in (86cm) high

$4,000-5,000   **L&T**

Two French bronze figures of Mercury and Fortuna, after Giambologna, on marble and cherub cast bases.

c1900   *Mercury 32in (81cm) high*

$3,000-4,000   **L&T**

A pair of late 19thC patinated bronze figures, cast as a male and a female Bacchic follower, on inlaid square marble plinths.

tallest 14.5in (37cm) high

$3,000-4,000   **L&T**

A CLOSER LOOK AT AN EQUESTRIAN BRONZE

The bronze is a reduction of a large original shown at the 1851 Great Exhibition and this well-known connection increases its desirability.

Thomas Thornycroft was a highly respected Victorian sculptor and this was one of his most prominent works.

The original sculpture was subsequently commissioned for distribution by The Art Union of London. Thornycroft produced all fifty casts.

The depiction of Queen Victoria, in a less solemn pose than is more commonly found, means this bronze has appeal for collectors of royal commemoratives, as well as those interested in bronzes.

A Thomas Thornycroft (1814-1885) equestrian bronze statue of Queen Victoria, signed in the bronze "T. Thornycroft. fecit, London 1853" and marked "Art Union of London 1851".

21.5in (55cm) high

$10,000-15,000   **L&T**

An Abastenia St. Leger Eberle Indian and Buffalo bronze tobacco jar, inscribed "St. Eberle SC", the underside inscribed "Copyrighted 1905 by Gorham Co." and stamped "Q438 Gorham Co. Founders."

7in (18cm) high

$7,000-10,000   **FRE**

A Gaston Veuvendt Leroux Aida (1854-1942) bronze figure, seated on Pharoah's head and holding gold-tone cymbals, multi-patinated, artist's signature and foundry medallion "Bronze Guarnate au Titre".

29in (72.5cm) high

$12,000-18,000   **FRE**

A bronze mother and child group, after Eugene-Antoine Aizelin (1821-1902), with a dark brown patina, signed "Aizelin".

12in (30cm) high

$1,200-1,800   **FRE**

An Alfred Barye 'Racehorse With Jockey' bronze ,with brown patina, inscribed "Alfred Barye fils, Sculpteur 1868".

17in (42.5cm) wide

$6,000-7,000   **FRE**

A CLOSER LOOK AT AN AUGUSTUS SAINT-GAUDENS BRONZE

Irish-born Augustus Saint-Gaudens (1848-1907) is rated among the greatest monument sculptures of the late 19thC, making this an important piece.

This cast is version two. Saint-Gaudens was unhappy with his first attempt and tried again. However, he eventually decided to base the statue's head on his earlier model.

The piece is of museum quality. The Metropolitan Museum of Art in New York has a 'Head of Victory' in its collection.

This bronze began as a study for the Sherman Monument, dedicated to the Civil War general William Tecumseh Sherman (1820-1891). The monument depicts the General on horseback and stands outside New York's Central Park in the Grand Army Plaza.

An Aim-Jules Dalou (1838-1902) 'Tete de Paysan, Etude' bronze, with a brown patina, inscribed "DALOU" and with "CIRE PERDUE/A.A. HEBRARD" foundry stamp.

c1895   *12.75in (32cm) h*

$3,000-4,000   **FRE**

An early 19thC Empire gilt bronze Venus plaque, probably for Jacob Freres, Paris, mounted on a silk panel and framed.

17.5in (44.5cm) high

$1,500-2,500   **L&T**

A large Marius Jean-Antonin Mercie (1845-1916) 'Gloris Victis' bronze group, signed "A Mercie", foundry marks for Ferdinand Barbedienne, wood pedestal.

42.5in (106cm) high

$6,000-7,000   **FRE**

An Augustus Saint-Gaudens 'Head of Victory, Nikh-Eiphnh, Second Version' bronze sculpture, with a brown/green patina, signed and dated "A. SAINT GAVDENS M.C.M." and inscribed "COPYRIGHT MCMVII BY AUGUSTUS SAINT GAUDENS".

8.25in (21cm) high

$150,000-200,000   **SK**

A Charles-René Saint-Marceaux (1845-1915) 'Seated Classical Draped Man' bronze, with dark brown patina, signed "St Marceaux", Valsuani foundry seal, on a green marble base.

6in (15cm) high

$1,000-1,500   **FRE**

A Charles-René Saint-Marceaux (1845-1915) 'Recumbent Classical Male' bronze, with a dark brown patina, signed "STM", Valsuani foundry seal, on a green marble base.

5.5in (14cm) high

$1,500-2,000   **FRE**

An Alexandre Pierre Shoenewerk (1820-1885) bronze group, modeled as two dancing cherubs, with a brown patina, signed "Shoenewerk, Scpte and L. Maichaud, Edte."

11in (27.5cm) high

$1,500-2,000   **FRE**

A Joseph Uphues black marble and bronze male nude sculpture, with dark patination, signed and marked "Aktiengesellschaft Gladenbeck Berlin", arrow missing.

27in (67.5cm) high

$1,500-2,500   **KAU**

An Austrian Franz Bergman cold-painted bronze figure of an Arab tribesman, with a flint lock rifle resting on his shoulder, Bergmann stamped mark.

4in (10cm) high

$600-800   **DNT**

A pair of French Debut 19thC patinated bronze figures, depicting a North African man and woman, each signed "Debut", one with stamp "Bronze Garanti au Titre, Paris", both with plaques inscribed "Prix de Rome".

taller 15.5in (39cm) high

$1,500-2,500   **L&T**

A Gilbert Dutch bust of a girl, in bronze on an onyx base, inscribed and dated.

1919   *13.75in (35cm) high*

$800-1,200   **SWO**

An A. Gory 'Laughing Girl' patinated bronze head and shoulders bust, on a green marble base, signed in the bronze.

15in (38cm) high

$3,000-4,000   **L&T**

A partially silvered bronze figure group, cast from a model by Kelety, signed in the bronze.

9.25in (23.5cm) high

$2,000-4,000   **WW**

An A. Petro bronze bust of a girl, signed in the bronze, inscribed "Usine de Bronzes, R Debraz, Bruxelles".

23in (58cm) high

$1,200-1,800   **L&T**

A pair of late 19thC bronze figures of putti, emblematic of summer on square marble bases.

8.25in (21cm) high

$1,500-2,000   **SWO**

A Russian 'Standing Cossack with Rifle' bronze, signed in Cyrillic, brown patina, on a naturalistic base.

18.5in (46cm) high

$12,000-18,000   **FRE**

An Antoine Louis Barye bronze model of a tiger, modeled prowling on all fours, the rectangular base stamped "Barye".

15in (38cm) wide

$6,000-8,000 GORL

A 19thC Bergman cold-painted bronze grouse, cast mark to underside.

22.5cm (8.75in) high

$1,500-2,500 SWO

Two Franz Bergman cold painted bronze birds, a 'Woodcock' & 'Robin', each with maker's mark to the undersides.

2.5in (6cm) high

$500-600 ROS

An Isidore Bonheur figure of a 'Standing Bull', on an oval base.

6.5in (16cm) wide

$3,000-4,000 SWO

A late 19thC pair of Louis XVI-style gilt-bronze chenets, cast by Bouhon Frères, Paris, modeled as recumbent roaring lions, on shaped plinth bases, stamped "Bouhon Fres".

12.75in (32cm) wide

$6,000-8,000 FRE

A Donald Greig bronze group, depicting a troop of five elephants.

8.75in (22cm) wide

$1,500-2,000 LFA

A bronze model of two pointers on a naturalistic oval mound base, after P J Mêne, cast signature mark.

17.75in (45cm) wide

$2,000-3,000 LFA

An E. Steenacker patinated bronze figure of a hound, toying with a snail, on a naturalistic oval base with branches, leaves and ivy, signed in the bronze.

20in (51cm) wide

$4,000-6,000 L&T

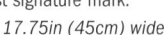
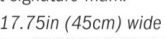

A bronze animalier group, after Pierre Jules Mêne (1810-1879), with two Pointers on an oblong naturalistic base, signed "P.J. Mêne".

18in (46cm) wide

$4,000-6,000 WW

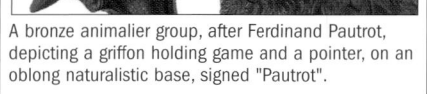

A bronze animalier group, after Ferdinand Pautrot, depicting a griffon holding game and a pointer, on an oblong naturalistic base, signed "Pautrot".

17in (43cm) wide

$4,000-6,000 WW

An Australian cold painted bronze group of six cats.

c1900   *6.5cm (2.5in) high*

$1,500-2,000 SWO

A 19thC Italian bronze and red griotte marble tazza, the round bowl being held by three figures of Neptune on a round base with paw feet.

6in (15cm) diam

$500-700   **DN**

A late 19thC French gilt bronze Neoclassical style urn, decorated in high relief with fruiting vines, masks and lion pelt, on a marble base.

13in (32.5cm) wide

$1,000-1,500   **FRE**

A pair of Neoclassical style bronze urns, with relief foliate swag decoration and lion's mask and loop handles, surmounted by winged cherubs.

31.5in (80cm) high

$4,000-6,000   **FRE**

A Francois Pompon bronze model of a bear cub, with deep brown patination, and signature to base "pompon".

c1920-30   *4.75in (12cm) high*

$700-1,000   **ROS**

A Victorian bronze inkwell in the form of a bear, with hinged head opening to reveal a well.

8.5in (21cm) high

$400-600   **SWO**

A French 'Pointer' bronze, after Jules Moignez (1853-1894), with a dark brown patina, raised on a green marble base, signed "J. Moignez".

11in (27.5cm) wide

$600-700   **FRE**

A cold painted bronze figure of a seated terrier.

2.5in (6cm) high

$200-300   **LAW**

A bronze inkwell, after Francesco Fanelli, in the form of a triton holding a hinged shell whilst rising a dolphin, tip of the tail missing.

4.5in (11.5cm) high

$1,200-1,800   **WW**

A late 19thC Louis XV-style bronze inkwell, decorated in relief with Bacchic masks, on three bull's mask hoof feet, and a marble base.

7.5in (19cm) high

$400-600   **FRE**

A cold painted bronze figure of a bull.

4in (10cm) high

$200-300   **LAW**

A Louis Ernest Barrias (French 1841-1905) young girl of bou-saada, in gilt bronze, signed "E. Barrias", with Susse Freres Editeurs, Paris, foundry seal and mark.

13in (33cm) high

$17,000-20,000 FRE

An early 20thC Luis Domenech y Vincente Art Nouveau bronze figural lamp, with green and gilt bronze patina, signed "L. Domenech" with foundry seal, numbered 9736.

12.5in (32cm) high

$2,000-3,000 FRE

An Art Nouveau 'L'Ame des Fleurs patinated spelter figure, signed "A. Foretay".

29.25in (74cm) high

$1,400-1,700 L&T

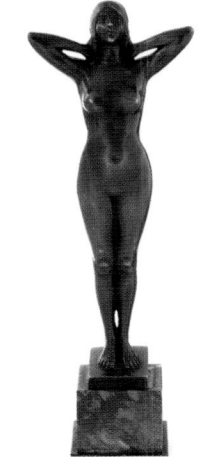

A bronze Hofer standing female nude with arms upon her neck on a marble plinth, signed.

15in (38cm) high

$1,200-1,400 JN

A French gilt bronze table lamp in the form of the American dancer Loie Fuller with backswept hair, lightly veiled nude body, signed Raoul Larche.

c1900

17in (43cm) high

$8,000-10,000 SK

An Emmanuel Villanis bronze, 'L'eclipse', with dark brown patina, signed "E. Villanis", with "Societé des Bronze de Paris" foundry seal, stamped "E 1037".

42.5in (108cm) high

$8,000-12,000 FRE

An Emmanuel Villanis (French 1858-1914) bronze, 'Shackled', with dark brown and green patina, modeled as a slave girl with a removable cloth across her lap, signed "E. Villanis".

16in (40.5cm) high

$6,000-8,000 FRE

An Ernest Wante (Belgian, 1872-1960) bronze, Andromeda & Rebecca, with gold and dark brown patinas, on shaped wood bases, each signed "E. Wante".

tallest 12.25in (31cm) high

$4,000-5,000 FRE

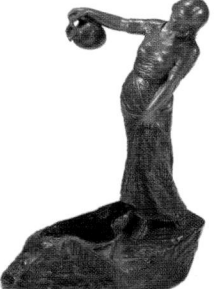

A late 19th/early 20thC Art Nouveau bronze figural jardiniere, with red brown patina, modeled as a female farm labourer standing on a rock.

28in (71cm) high

$3,000-4,000 FRE

A female warrior with sword and shield bronze figure, by Marcel Bouraine, on a stepped circular marble base, signed in the bronze.

18.5in (47cm) high

$2,500-3,000   **L&T**

A bronze sculpture of a stalking lion, by Brault, signed in the bronze, bears foundry stamp, raised on slate plinth.

34.75in (88cm) wide

$2,000-3,000   **L&T**

An early 20thC Spanish Jose Cardona Bronze, 'Boy With Cigar', green/brown patina, signed "J Cardona", foundry seal "BRONZE/ GARANTI/ AU/ TITRE/ L.V/ DEPOSE".

14in (35.5cm) high

$800-1,200   **FRE**

A Claire-Jeanne-Roberte Colinet (French 1910-1940) bronze, 'Danseuse de Thebes', with gold brown patina, signed "Colinet", on a rectangular marble base.

21in (53.5cm) wide

$5,000-6,000   **FRE**

A Pierre Feliz Fix-Masseau (French 1869-1937) bronze, 'Le Secret', with dark green/brown patina, signed "Fix Masseau" and foundry seal, "SIOT / DECAUVILLE / PARIS / FONDUER", numbered 1594.

24.5in (62cm) high

$8,000-12,000   **FRE**

A patinated bronze Dancer, by Maurice Guirard-Riviere, signed in the bronze.

19.5in (50cm) high

$1,500-2,000   **L&T**

An Art Deco bronze, seated figure of a woman with a bowl and monkey, stamped "HAGENAU 1934"

9in (23cm) high

$600-800   **FRE**

A Hagenauer olivewood and bronze figure of Jesus Christ, with stamped marks.

9.5in (24cm) high

$1,000-1,500   **L&T**

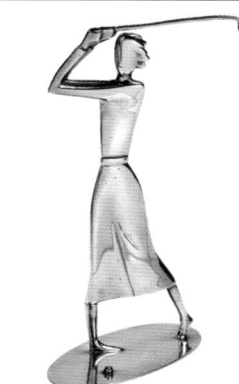

A Hagenauer nickel figure, depicting a lady golfer, with stamped marks.

8.5in (22cm) high

$1,500-2,000   **L&T**

A Max LeVerrier Art Deco (French 1891-1973) 'Janle' chromed metal sculpture on black marble base, signed and titled.

12.5in (31.75cm) high

$1,500-2,000   **SDR**

A Josef Lorenzl patinated bronze dancer, on a marble plinth.

18.5in (47cm) high

$1,500-2,500   **L&T**

An Art Deco Lorenzl figure of a nude dancing girl, black patinated bronze, signed upon a cylindrical marble base.

19.5in (49.5cm) high

$4,000-5,000   **JN**

A Josef Lorenzl patinated bronze dancer, on a faceted onyx base.

18.5in (47cm) high

$5,000-6,000   **L&T**

A Bertram MacKennal (1863 - 1931) bronze figure of Salome, with green marble base inscribed on base "B. Mackennal" and "London".

14in (35.5cm) high including base

$8,000-10,000   **SHA**

A verdigris bronze figure, cast from a model by Morante, on a marble base, signed in the bronze.

15.25in (38.5cm) high

$1,300-1,500   **WW**

A Charles Raphael Peyre (1872-1949), Assyrian Maiden, bronze, partly gilded with verdigris patination, the semi-clothed figure with long skirt and peacock headdress, holding a snake and leaning on a pedestal, raised on associated stepped black marble plinth.

40in (102cm) high

$4,000-6,000   **L&T**

A German V. Seifert bronze model of a standing female nude holding and drinking from a vessel upon a square marble plinth, signed with Gladenbeck foundry marks.

14.75in (37.5cm) high

$2,500-3,000   **JN**

A Szirmai gilt bronze figure of a young woman on a circular marble base, signed and with founders' marks for F. Costenoble, Paris.

16.25in (41.5cm) high

$2,500-3,000   **JN**

A silvered bronze figure of a dancer, cast from a model by R. Varnier, on a stepped marble base, signed in the marble.

13.75in (35cm) high

$1,200-1,800   **WW**

A Lilli Wislicenus (German 1872-1939) bronze slave girl, with light brown patina, signed "L. Wislicenus", and inscribed "Finzelberg" with stamped "12" to base.

26.5in (67.5cm) high

$3,000-4,000   **FRE**

A Phillipe Wolfers (Belgian 1858-1929) bronze, 'Princess of the Nile', dark green patina, inscribed and numbered "1/6 Ph. Wolfers, sere perdue" raised on marble base.

19.5in (49.5cm) long

$10,000-15,000   **FRE**

An early 20thC European School bronze figure of a man.

19.25in (49cm) high

$2,000-3,000   **L&T**

An early 20thC European School bronze figure of a running boy, on a veined marble plinth.

6.25in (16cm) high

$3,000-4,000   **L&T**

An early 20thC European School bronze figure of a dancing couple.

14.75in (37.5cm) high

$1,500-2,500   **L&T**

An Art Deco gilt metal figure, on alabaster base unsigned.

7.5in (19.5cm) high

$400-500   **WW**

An Art Deco gilt metal figure, modeled balancing on one foot, on alabaster base, unsigned.

10in (25cm) high

$400-500   **WW**

A patinated bronze figure of a girl, on a stepped marble base, unsigned.

11.5in (29cm) high

$1,100-1,300   **WW**

A Demêtre H. Chiparus figure of a schoolgirl, gilt bronze and ivory figure of a schoolgirl holding her portfolio case, raised on an onyx base, inscribed "D Chiparus 1430".

6.75in (17cm) high

$1,100-1,300   **FRE**

A CLOSER LOOK AT A CHIPARUS BRONZE FIGURE

Romanian born Demetre H. Chiparus (1886-1947) worked in Paris was one of the best-known sculptures of the Art Deco period.

This design of a woman with two borzoi hounds was hugely popular and as a result was copied by other makers. Such examples are less valuable than the hard to find original.

He was skilled at chryselephantine, the art of combining bronze and ivory to create stylized sculptures.

Period Chiparus pieces have well defined detailing and are of elegant proportions. Themes are drawn from the more glamorous side of Parisian life during the era.

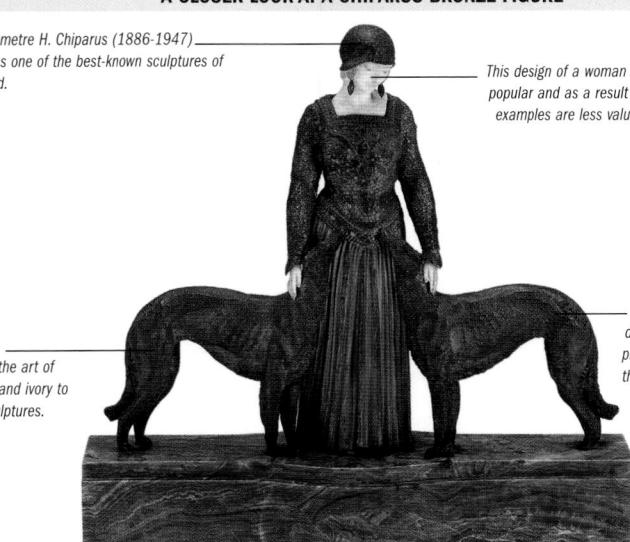

A Demêtre H. Chiparus 'Friends Forever' carved ivory, gilt and cold painted bronze figure, with onyx base signed "Chiparus".
1886-1947   *11in (28cm) high*

$20,000-30,000   **FRE**

An Egyptian Dancer by George Gori, a cold painted bronze and hand carved ivory figure of an exotic dancer in full costume standing on an onyx base, signed by the artist.

c1925   *13.5in (34cm) high*

$16,000-18,000   **RGA**

A Hans Harders patinated bronze and ivory figural lamp, cast as a figure of a Japanese girl, cast mark "Harders".

24in (67cm) high

$7,000-10,000   **L&T**

A Lucienne Antoinette Heuvelmans Madonna and Child in bronze and ivory, with stepped black slate base, signed in the bronze.

13in (33cm) high

$2,000-3,000   **L&T**

A Jaeger bronze and ivory figure of 'Athena' on marble base, modeled as the warrior maiden, wearing a plumed helmet, 'medusa' breastplate and holding a long spear, signed on back also with founder's mark for Rosenthal und Maeder.

$3,000-4,000   **JN**

Pierre Le Faguays 'Dandy' c1932, patinated silver and guilt bronze figure holds scissors in his right hand, ivory head and hands resting on shaped red and brown marble base, incised "P. Le Faguays" to top left corner of base.

1932   *12in (31cm) high*

$10,000-12,000   **SHA**

A gilt, bronze and ivory Omerth figure, modeled as a young woman wearing a ribboned bonnet, pleated dress and apron, she holds a bouquet of flowers in her arms, Mexican onyx base, signed on back of dress.

13in (33cm) high

$2,500-3,000   **JN**

A bronze and ivory 'Girl Fishing' figure, Ferdinand Preiss (1882-1943), raised on a faceted slate plinth.

6.75in (17cm) high

$2,500-3,000   **L&T**

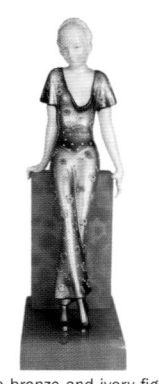

An Art Deco bronze and ivory figure, in the style of Ferdinand Preiss, a lady reclining against a wall, painted bronze ivory and onyx, some damage.

8.5in (21.5cm) high

$1,800-2,200 **SWO**

A Ferdinand Preiss bronze and ivory figure of a boy, 'Oriental Waiter', with stained face and wearing a turban, jacket and trousers and holding a tray with a vessel and two beakers, on green onyx base, engraved "F. Preiss".

7in (18cm) high

$3,000-4,000 **GORL**

A Ferdinand Preiss Sonny Boy and Hoop Girl pair of patinated bronze and ivory figures, each raised on a green onyx base, signed on the base "F. Preiss".

8.25in (21cm) high

$12,000-18,000 **L&T**

A Schrimpf bronze figure of a dancing girl, bronze with metal sépatina, carved ivory on a marble base in a bronze frame, on a wooden base, signed.

c1935   *13.5in (34cm) high*

$2,000-3,000 **DOR**

An Art Deco patinated bronze and ivory figure, of a lady, raised on a green onyx plinth.

8in (20.5cm) high

$2,000-2,500 **L&T**

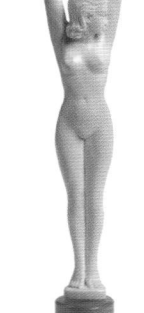

An early 20thC French school ivory nude figure, on a turned green onyx base.

$1,200-1,800 **L&T**

An Art Deco bronze figure of a nude, modeled as a standing figure balancing an ivory ball on her hand, on an onyx base, signed "Lorenzl".

c1930   *12.75in (32.5cm) high*

$3,000-4,000 **FRE**

A continental Art Deco gilt bronze and bisque porcelain figure of a clown, raised on a gray marble base, signed "Zabo".

c1930   *13in (33cm) high*

$1,500-2,000 **FRE**

A Continental gilt bronze and porcelain figure of a girl herding geese, on a naturalistic oval base, mounted as a lamp, signed indistinctly.

7in (18cm) high

$300-500 **FRE**

An Ian A.R. Davidson six-piece silver tea and coffee service, with marks for Edinburgh, sponsor's mark "BH" (Bernard Harrington), and carved rosewood handles and finials.

1952 coffee pot 12.5in (32cm) high
$8,000-12,000   L&T

A B.H. Edlunds three piece tea set, Swedish, oval form, ebonized "C" form handle, 28oz.

1946   6.25in (16cm) high
$5,000-6,000   FRE

An Hirata & Co. sterling silver tea/coffee and dessert service, early 20th century, after a design by Georg Jensen, comprising a coffee pot, tea pot, creamer, covered sugar bowl, two tazzas, a covered dish opening to reveal a compartmented interior, and a pair of oval trays, 147oz.

teapot 8.5in (21.5cm) high
$5,000-6,000   FRE

A Georg Jensen three-piece silver and ivory coffee set, comprising a coffee pot, sugar bowl and milk jug.

pot 8in (20.5cm) high
$3,000-4,000   PC

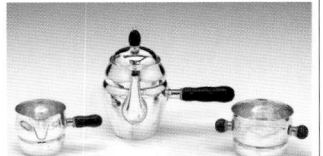

A Georg Jensen sterling silver coffee pot, model number 30A, with ivory handle and bud finial, together with a Georg Jensen sterling silver sugar bowl and creamer model number 80A.

c1930
$2,500-3,000   FRE

A Georg Jensen sterling silver three piece tea service, comprising a teapot, sugar bowl and a creamer, with turned wood handles, finial slightly loose, some minor dents.

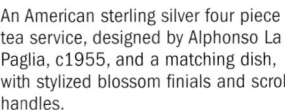

c1930   teapot 6in (15cm) high
$1,500-2,000   FRE

A cased Georg Jensen five piece sterling silver coffee service by Johan Rohde, with ivory handles.

1925-30   tray 24.5in (62cm) wide
$25,000-30,000   FRE

A Puiforcat four-piece silver plated coffee and tea set, together with matching twin handled tray, half-reeded canisters with applied silver bead hardwood covers and "C" form handles, consisting of coffee pot, teapot, covered sugar and milk jug, 1930's, each stamped "Puiforcat" and "EP" with flanked penknife mark.

coffee pot 5.5in (14cm) high
$8,000-12,000   FRE

An American sterling silver four piece tea service, designed by Alphonso La Paglia, c1955, and a matching dish, with stylized blossom finials and scroll handles.

tray 16in (40.5cm) wide
$4,000-6,000   FRE

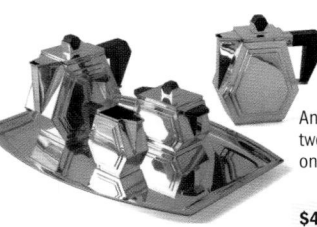

An Art Deco silver teaset, comprising two pots, a sugar bowl and a milk jug on a tray.

tray 16.5in (42cm) long
$4,000-6,000   PC

An Art Deco silver vase designed by Charles Boyton, knopped base and ropework decoration, maker's mark "T D & S" for Birmingham and designer's facsimile signature.

1940   *9in (23cm) high*

$900-1,100   **JN**

An Evald Nielsen silver and ivory candlestick.

6.25in (16cm) high

$600-800   **PC**

A 20thC set of twelve Japanese Hirata & Co sterling silver beakers, of cylindrical form with flared rims, with a bellflower openwork foot, stamped "Sterling, Hirata & Co, 950", 81oz.

6.75in (17cm) high

$2,000-3,000   **FRE**

A mid-20thC Napier silver plated Art Deco cocktail shaker, in the form of a penguin.

12.5in (32cm) high

$2,000-2,500   **FRE**

A Danish form sterling silver circular footed bowl, with pierced floral decorated base, stamped "STERLING 162", 32oz.

5.25in (13.5cm) high

$700-1,000   **FRE**

An Art Deco twin-handled silver bowl, of square tapering form with stepped base and green-stained ivory fin handles, hallmarked "Sheffield", maker's and retailer's mark for Wilson & Sharples, Edinburgh.

1933   *9.75in (25cm) wide*

$4,000-5,000   **L&T**

An American Art Deco vanity case, sterling engine turned dimensional case, multiple compartments inside for cosmetics, a tortoise shell comb and a mirror, hallmarked.

c1935   *4.5in (11.5cm) wide*

$1,500-2,000   **DD**

A 1930s H. Harders Art Deco plaque, silver-plated on molded sheet copper with large central figure surrounded by an array of industrial motifs, in ebonized oak frame, stamped "H. Harders FC."

Harders was a sculptor whose majority of works were produced in the 1920s/30s. His primary medium was bronze but he also designed many pieces in porcelain for the Germany manufactory, Fraureuth.

12.25in (31cm) high

$2,000-3,000   **SDR**

An Edgar Brandt pair of wrought-iron gates with floral and vine design, signed "Edgar Brandt".

52in (132cm) high

$8,000-12,000   **SDR**

599

THE AESTHETIC MOVEMENT

- The Aesthetic Movement flourished in Britain and America in the 1870s and 1880s.
- Its essence was a rejection of the fashionable influences in art at the time – both the morality and realism proposed by Ruskin and others, and the French Revival style – in favor of the intrinsic beauty of art being its only necessary justification.
- Key supporters were artists James McNeill Whistler and Frederic Leighton, writer Oscar Wilde and architect E.W. Godwin.
- Inspiration came from 'exotic' sources such as Japonisme, Egyptian and Moorish, and the Gothic Revival. Japan especially influenced design when its ports opened for trade with Europe in 1859 and the fashion for Japonisme took off.
- Forms were Asian influenced: simple lines, symmetrical, rectilinear, ebonized wood, spindle legs, based on E.W. Godwin's work, and featured gilded highlights, spindles and painted or marquetry panels.
- Key motifs were bamboo, flowers, birds, insects, peacock feathers and sunflowers, which became more extensive and elaborate as the movement progressed.

An Aesthetic movement carved walnut sideboard, attributed to Frank Furness (1839-1912) and Daniel Pabst (active 1854-96), Philadelphia, the super structure with mirrored panels and raised mirrored-door cupboard; the lower section with carved chamfered-edge panels, two drawers and two cupboard doors, plinth base.

$7,000-8,000   **FRE**

An Aesthetic Movement ebonized sideboard, by John Moyr Smith (1839-1912) for Cox and Sons, with gilded incised decoration, painted with a Jester and a Nobleman, flanked by two glazed doors enclosing shelves, paneled sides painted with lattice motifs.

71.5in (182cm) wide

$3,500-4,500   **L&T**

An Aesthetic movement oak and ebonized pot cupboard, with spindle ledge back, molded top and single door with carved and incised panel, on turned and incised supports.

16.25in (41cm) wide

$300-400   **L&T**

An Aesthetic movement carved oak settee, attributed to Allen and Brother, Philadelphia (1870-1875), the crestrail with an owl over a coffered and upholstered back, incised stiles with urn form finials, arms carved with flowerheads at handholds, ring-turned spindles, the carved and fluted legs, carved seat rail, fan and line carved brackets, turned feet, old oilcloth upholstery with label.

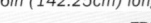

56in (142.25cm) long

$8,000-12,000   **FRE**

Two of a set of four Gothic Revival oak dining chairs, with stuffover seats in cut velvet enclosed by paneled frame with applied rosettes and front rails.

c1860

$2,000-3,000   **L&T**

An Aesthetic Movement ebonized armchair, the design in the manner of E.W. Godwin, the latticed square back above curved open arms and stuffover seat, on turned and reeded legs.

$1,200-1,800   **L&T**

An Aesthetic Movement rosewood center table, the design attributed to E.W. Godwin for William Watt.

35.75in (91cm) diam

$4,000-6,000   **L&T**

A Gothic Revival oak coal box, in the manner of Bruce Talbert.

20.75in (53cm) wide

$600-1,000   **L&T**

A Gustav Stickley spindled Morris chair, with corbels under flat arms, its drop-in spring seat and loose back cushion covered in medium brown leather, original finish.

38in (96.5cm) high

$9,000-11,000   DRA

A Gustav Stickley open-arm Morris chair, (no. 346) with original vinyl upholstery to seat, different back pillow, worn original finish, missing washers, red decal.

40in (101.5cm) high

$1,500-2,000   DRA

A Gustav Stickley drop arm settle and armchair with rush seats, some imperfections to seats, original finish, red decal on both pieces.

c1902

$8,000-1,200   SK

A Gustav Stickley massive even arm settle, with paneled back and sides and loose cushions upholstered in dark brown leather, original finish.

84.75in (215cm) wide

$15,000-20,000   DRA

A Gustav Stickley Morris chair, (no. 2342), with flat arms, five slats to the floor, and loose seat and back cushions covered in original, green, laced leather, original finish, cane deck, and cushions. "'02-'04" decal under arm, wear to finish on arms, pegs/washers original, small chips to edges.

40in (101cm) high

$30,000-40,000   DRA

A New York Gustav Stickley oak hall bench, with paneled backrest with shaped arms, lift seat with storage compartment, Gustav Stickley decal.

c1904   *47in (119cm) wide*

$9,000-11,000   SK

A Gustav Stickley occasional table, with circular top and stacked arched cross-stretchers topped by finial, refinished top, original finish to base, large red decal.

30.25in (77cm) diam

$2,500-3,500   DRA

A Gustav Stickley lamp table, with circular top, its legs joined by arched cross-stretchers, original finish, split to stretcher, staining to top, branded mark.

20in (51cm) diam

$1,200-1,800   DRA

An early Gustav Stickley tea table, with shaped legs joining a floriform top and lower shelf, original finish, color added, unmarked.

23.25in (59cm) high

$9,000-11,000   DRA

A Gustav Stickley pedestal dining table (no. 656), with circular top and split pedestal with four shoe feet, four 11" leaves, refinished, new hardware, unmarked.

54in (137cm) diam

$7,000-8,000   DRA

A Gustav Stickley director's table, with a large overhanging top, a broad, canted apron, and massive shoe feet, original finish with overcoat, several chips, large red decal under top, one chip from leg edge, two from top of base under top, minor seam separations to shoe feet, top has been reglued.

96in (244cm) wide

$17,000-24,000   DRA

DECORATIVE ARTS

A Gustav Stickley drop-front desk, (no. 518) with iron strap hinges and escutcheon, chamfered sides and front panel, red decal on back, remnants of paper label, wear, stains.

51.5in (129cm) high

$10,000-15,000   DRA

A Gustav Stickley chalet desk, with drop front, gallery interior, the top and lower shelf mortised through the sides with keyed through-tenons, original finish, split, warping, unmarked.

46in (115cm) high

$2,200-2,800   DRA

A Gustav Stickley sideboard, with plate rack, red decal in top drawer, original dark finish with overcoat to top.

48in (120cm) wide

$4,000-5,000   DRA

A Gustav Stickley sideboard, (no. 814) with hammered copper V-pulls and strap-hinges, original finish, decal inside drawer, paper label, damage, wear.

62in (155cm) wide

$7,000-8,000   DRA

A rare and early Gustav Stickley server, with plate rack, large red decal, refinished, bow to plate rail.

59.5 (149cm) wide

$12,000-18,000   DRA

An early Gustav Stickley server, with two small drawers over a single long drawer, chamfered sides, and wooden pyramidal knob-pulls, dark brown original finish, large red decal.

c1900   *59in (147.5cm) wide*

$55,000-65,000   DRA

A Gustav Stickley three-drawer server, (no. 818) with backsplash and oval iron pulls, red decal, refinished, repaired, reglued.

48in (122cm) wide

$1,800-2,200   DRA

A Gustav Stickley server, with three small drawers over a linen drawer, original finish, large red decal, minor seam separations.

75in (119cm) wide

$18,000-22,000   DRA

A Gustav Stickley magazine stand, (no. 547) with square beveled top over three shelves and paneled sides, red decal, some wear and damage.

15.25in (38.5cm) wide

$4,500-5,500   DRA

A Gustav Stickley magazine stand, (no. 72) with overhanging top, three shelves, arched sides, paper label and branded mark, light overcoat, minor scuffs.

22in (56cm) wide

$3,500-4,500   DRA

A Gustav Stickley magazine stand, with D-shaped cut-out handles with arched toe board, original finish, wear and staining, seam separation, unmarked.

40in (100cm) high

$1,800-2,200   DRA

A Gustav Stickley magazine stand, (no. 548), with paneled sides and four shelves, refinished, seam separation to lower shelf, unmarked.

44in (110cm) high

$2,200-2,800   DRA

GUSTAV STICKLEY

- Gustav Stickley (1858-1942) followed the principles of the Arts & Crafts Movement closely, establishing a workshop in 1898 which looked to Morris' designs.
- Trained as a stonemason before apprenticing himself to his uncle's chair factory, he was fascinated by the construction of furniture. This is reflected in the details he emphasized, such as the dovetailing or exposed dowel-ends.
- In 1898, he traveled to England, where he met key players in the Arts & Crafts movement, and became enthralled by the ideas of John Ruskin and William Morris.
- In 1901, he dedicated the first issue of his monthly design magazine, 'The Craftsman', to William Morris.
- 'The Craftsman' was originally designed as a marketing tool for Gustav's furniture but expanded to cover philosophy and architecture, featuring work by Harvey Ellis, whose more delicate approach tempered Gustav's austerity of style.
- His statement that furniture must 'fill its mission of usefulness' was reflected in its simple, rectilinear designs.
- He selected natural materials, such as oak, leather and rush and drew attention to the woodgrain through his hallmark fumed-ammonia finish.

A rare and early Gustav Stickley sideboard, with three drawers over three cabinet doors with butterfly joints and four-sided iron and copper pulls, thick top and bottom joined through sides with keyed through-tenons, refinished, pulls and backplates replaced, unmarked.

75.75in (179.5cm) wide

$15,000-20,000 **DRA**

A Gustav Stickley eight-leg sideboard, with four central drawers, two paneled cupboard doors with hammered copper hinges, original finish, and seam separations to top.

69.5in (176.5cm) wide

$20,000-25,000 **DRA**

A Gustav Stickley bride's chest, with paneled sides, each inset framed by interior corbels, a paneled top, cedar lining, and iron hasps and hardware, refinished.

41in (104cm) wide

$15,000-20,000 **DRA**

A Gustav Stickley gout stool, with four short flaring feet, covered in original hard leather with pyramidal tacks, dryness and a few spots to leather, dry original finish, reglued split to one leg, red decal and a paper label.

12in (30cm) wide

$2,800-3,200 **DRA**

A Gustav Stickley spindled footstool, with mortised stretchers, missing upholstery, partially removed varnish overcoat, unmarked.

20in (51cm) wide

$1,200-1,800 **DRA**

A Gustav Stickley child's wardrobe, with two paneled doors, interior drawers and shelves, and hammered copper V-pulls, original finish, touch up to finish on front, good condition, red decal inside top drawer, paper label on back.

60in (152cm) wide

$25,000-30,000 **DRA**

A Gustav Stickley triple-door, mitred-mullion bookcase, with 12 panes per door, three fixed interior shelves per section, copper ring-pulls, original finish with light overcoat, red decal on back.

73in (185cm) wide

$15,000-20,000 **DRA**

A Stickley Brothers magazine stand, with three shelves, remnant of paper label, original finish, edge wear, loose.

38.5in (96cm) high

$1,200-1,800 **DRA**

A Stickley Brothers mahogany magazine stand, with slats all around, paper label, original finish, some scuffs.

43in (107.5cm) high

$1,000-1,500 **DRA**

A Stickley Brothers magazine stand, with slatted sides and back around five shelves, branded mark, original finish.

47in (117.5cm) high

$1,000-1,500 **DRA**

A Stickley Brothers plant stand, with curved aprons over double stretchers, partial paper label, refinished.

22in (55cm) high

$1,800-2,200 **DRA**

A Stickley Brothers plant stand, with broad cloud-lift apron and canted legs, metal Quaint tag, original finish, some losses and seam separation.

33.75in (84cm) high

$1,500-2,000 **DRA**

A Stickley Brothers nightstand, with closed cabinet on bottom, original finish and condition, stenciled number, bail missing.

18in (45.5cm) wide

$2,000-3,000 **DRA**

A Stickley drink stand, with copper top, arched aprons and tapering legs, refinished, repair, staining, unmarked.

27.5in (69cm) high

$600-700 **DRA**

A Stickley Brothers sewing stand, with drop sides, metal Quaint tag, refinished.

29.25in (73cm) high

$1,500-2,000 **DRA**

A Stickley Brothers coat rack/umbrella stand, with Macmurdo feet and spindled sides under curved stretchers, original finish, losses, wear and damage, unsigned.

88in (223.5cm) high

$1,500-2,000 **DRA**

A Stickley Brothers sideboard, with plate rack, original finish, branded mark, some staining and wear to top.

54in (135cm) wide

$4,000-5,000 **DRA**

A Stickley Brothers sideboard, no. 8840, with plate rack, branded Stickley Brothers Grand Rapids, metal tag, stenciled number, overcoated original finish, small burn to top.

50in (127cm) wide

$2,500-3,500 DRA

A Stickley Brothers server, with plate rack, original finish, ghost of metal tag, missing two copper floral tacks, loose back.

501in (127cm) wide

$2,500-3,500 DRA

A Stickley Brothers writing desk, with gallery top, single drawer and slatted sides, stenciled "918B", refinished.

35.25in (89.5cm) wide

$2,000-3,000 DRA

A Stickley Brothers postcard desk, with shaped backsplash and letter holes, brass hardware, refinished, unmarked.

36in (90cm) high

$1,000-1,500 DRA

A drop-front desk with three drawers, attributed to the Stickley Brothers, with a walnut interior, refinished, roughness around keyhole on lid, unmarked.

47.5in (120.5cm) wide

$1,200-1,900 DRA

An early 20thC Stickley Brothers inlaid oak chest, with tapered posts, silver metal inlay and two posts for a mirror, replaced pulls.

44in (112cm) wide

$2,500-3,500 SK

A Stickley Brothers double bed, with paneled head and footboard, original finish, Quaint tag.

80in (203cm) wide

$4,500-5,500 DRA

A Stickley Brothers log holder, with vertical slats and cut-out pulls, metal tag, new finish, chips, loss to part of one copper strap.

20in (50cm) wide

$1,200-1,800 DRA

A Stickley Brothers slatted waste basket, with cut-out handles, original finish, stamped mark and Quaint tag, some wear and edge chips.

18in (45.5cm) high

$1,200-1,800 DRA

A Stickley Brothers tea cart, with slatted sides, large wheels and removable glass-bottom tray, branded mark, dry original finish, split and a few stains.

33in (84cm) wide

$700-800 DRA

A Stickley Brothers hammered copper coal bin, with two riveted handles and straps, medium patina, repair, unmarked.

15.75in (39cm) wide

$2,800-3,200 DRA

An L. & J.G. Stickley open-arm Morris chair, with corbels under flat arms, "The Work of..." decal under arm, recovered in russet leather, original finish with overcoat, some alligatoring.

39in (97.5cm) high

$2,800-3,200   **DRA**

An L. & J.G. Stickley Prairie armchair, (no. 408) ghost of a label, refinished.

32in (81.5cm) high

$4,000-5,000   **DRA**

An oversized L. & J.G. Stickley armchair, (no. 452) with three vertical slats and long corbels under flat arms, "The Work of..." decal, original finish, wear.

40in (101.5cm) high

$1,500-2,000   **DRA**

An L. & J.G. Stickley Morris rocker, with drop-in spring seat and loose back cushion, handcraft decal on back stretcher, wear.

37in (92.5cm) high

$1,500-2,000   **DRA**

An L. & J.G. Stickley Prairie rocker, (no. 409) with slatted sides and back, seat recovered in celadon green leather, branded "The Work of...", chip, refinished.

32in (81.5cm) high

$4,000-5,000   **DRA**

An L. & J.G. Stickley stationary back Morris rocker, (no. 475) the drop-in spring seat and back pillow covered in red vinyl, "The Work of..." decal, wear to arms.

37in (94cm) high

$3,500-4,500   **DRA**

An L. & J.G. Stickley settle and armchair, settle refinished and with L. & J.G. decal, armchair with overcoated original finish and branded "The Work of...".

Settle 52.75in (134cm) wide

$2,000-3,000   **DRA**

An L & J.G. Stickley rocker, with drop-in spring cushion covered in maroon vinyl, original finish with overcoat, metal "Work of..." tag, split to one arm at back.

35in (87.5cm) high

$700-800   **DRA**

An L. & J.G. Stickley drop arm settle and armchair, with drop-in spring cushions, original finish, Handcraft decals, replaced upholstery, wear.

Settle 64in (160cm) wide

$2,800-3,200   **DRA**

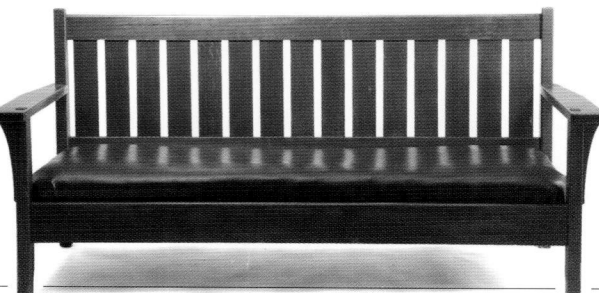

A drop arm settle with slatted back, attributed to L. & J.G. Stickley, original finish, chip, unmarked.

75in (187.5cm) wide

$1,800-2,200   **DRA**

An extremely rare L. & J. Stickley mousehole trestle table, with two up-ended stretchers, branded mark, refinished, separations, reshaped stretcher edges.

84in (210cm) wide

$7,000-8,000   DRA

An L. and J.G. Stickley hexagonal games table, (no. 563) with 'wagon-wheel' base with large, decorative keyed through-tenons, branded signature, heavy overcoat on worn original finish, top refinished, loose.

48in (122cm) diam

$3,500-4,500   DRA

An L. & J.G. Stickley lamp table, the lower shelf supported by cross stretchers, original finish on base, stenciled "4341.540" under top, restoration.

29.25in (73cm) high

$2,200-2,800   DRA

An early L. & J.G. Stickley large tabouret, (no. 559) the legs mortised through the octagonal top, Handcraft decal, original finish.

18in (45.5cm) wide

$2,000-3,000   DRA

An L. & J.G. Stickley octagonal tabouret, the legs mortised through the top, "Work of..." decal, worn original finish to top, repair to one stretcher.

20in (50cm) high

$1,000-1,500   DRA

An L. & J.G. Stickley octagonal tabouret, with the legs mortised through the top, original finish, color loss to top, paint spots on legs, unmarked.

20in (50cm) high

$1,500-2,000   DRA

An L. & J.G. Stickley clipped-corner tabouret, with square apron and arched stretchers, Handcraft decal, original finish with light overcoat.

18in (45.5cm) high

$1,500-2,000   DRA

An L. & J.G. Stickley clip-corner tabouret, with arched stretchers, "The Work of..." decal, original finish with color added to top.

16in (40.5cm) wide

$1,200-1,800   DRA

A large L. & J.G. Stickley mahogany stand, (no. 542) with exposed through-tenons, overcoated original finish, top refinished, light scuffs, unmarked.

30in (73.5cm) diam

$1,000-1,500   DRA

An L. & J.G. Stickley plant stand with clipped corners, original finish, "The Work of..." decal, stains to top.

29in (72.5cm) high

$1,500-2,000   DRA

An L. & J.G. Stickley copper-top drink stand, (no. 22) with four flaring legs joined by arched cross-stretchers, remnant of decal on leg, original finish, minor checking to legs.

28.5in (72.5cm) high

$5,000-6,000   **DRA**

An L. & J.G. Stickley magazine stand with slatted sides, arched toe-boards and four shelves, "The Work of..." decal, refinished, split seam.

42in (106.5cm) wide

$1,800-2,200   **DRA**

An L. & J.G. Stickley magazine stand, branded "The Work of...", uneven original finish, some stains to surfaces.

39.5in (97.5cm) high

$1,500-2,000   **DRA**

An L. & J.G. Stickley magazine stand, with two shelves, tapering legs and a single slat on each side, original finish, Handcraft decal, seam separations and stains.

36in (90cm) high

$1,500-2,000   **DRA**

A rare Onondaga Shops server, with paneled sides and five drawers, restoration to original finish, small hole to one drawer, replaced runners on two, unmarked.

47.5in (119cm) wide

$8,000-12,000   **DRA**

An Onondaga Shops server, with three drawers, hammered copper ring pulls and a backsplash, refinished, some edge chips, unmarked.

44in (110cm) wide

$1,500-2,000   **DRA**

An early Onondaga Shops double-door bookcase, (no. 519) keyed through-tenons and copper pulls, remnant of label, refinished, seam separations, added bead, cleaned patina to pulls.

52in (132cm) wide

$8,000-12,000   **DRA**

An Onondaga Shops cellaret, with butterfly joinery and hammered copper pull, interior shelf and bottle holder, decal inside drawer, refinished, filled hole, chip.

32.5in (81cm) high

$3,000-4,000   **DRA**

An L. and J. G. Stickley oak bookcase, (no.641) the single door with 16 panes of glass and original hammered hardware.

Leopold and Julius George (L. & J.G.), two of Gustav Stickley's five brothers, are considered to be his most talented successors.

56.75in (144cm) high

$2,500-3,500   **SWO**

A L. & J.G. Stickley single-door bookcase, with 16 panes and hammered copper pull with original key, branded "The Work of...", two drilled holes.

55.5in (139cm) high

$5,000-6,000   **DRA**

An L. & J.G. Stickley double-door china cabinet, (no. 729) with hammered copper hardware, original finish, Handcraft decal on back, seam separations to top, losses.

70in (175cm) high

$12,000-18,000   **DRA**

An L. & J.G. Stickley sideboard, (no.709), with corbelled plate rack, six small drawers and two cabinet doors over a linen drawer, original finish, Handcraft decal, chip to veneer on left door panel.

54in (137cm) wide

$4,000-5,000   **DRA**

L & J.G. STICKLEY & THE STICKLEY BROTHERS

- Leopold (1869-1957) and John George (1871-1921) Stickley were the next oldest brothers after Gustav, and astute businessmen. In contrast to Gustav's techniques Leopold and John George favoured highly efficient, mechanical production methods, but their style did reflect the influence of their older brother in their simple, Arts & Crafts inspired designs.
- Leopold had worked with Gustav before but set out alone in 1904 under the name Onondaga Shops. Meanwhile John George had been working for brother Albert in Michigan.
- In 1904 the two brothers united to establish "L & J.G. Stickley" in Fayetteville, New York, (renamed 'Handcraft' in 1906 and later called 'The Work of L. & J.G. Stickley' from 1912).

- The "Stickley Brothers Company" name was adopted by John George and Albert (1862-1928) in Grand Rapids, Michigan in 1891, referring to the name Albert and Charles had used previously while they worked with Gustav in New York.
- John George left to work with Leopold, but Albert continued the business under the family name. He often worked in a different vein to his brothers, sometimes using more decorative elements to his work.
- John George's furniture is marked with the "Quaint" logo.
- Albert had a strong affinity with the designs of English and Scottish cabinetmakers and had a showroom in London until 1902.

An L. & J. G. Stickley Prairie settle, with paneled sides, with broad and flat top overhanging the back and arms and supported by long corbels, and a drop-in spring cushion covered in dark brown leather.

$18,000-22,000   **DRA**

An L. & J.G. Stickley rare triple-door bookcase, (no. 647) with gallery top, 12 panes per door, keyed through-tenon construction, chamfered back, original copper hardware, refinished, minor checks to edges, good condition, Handcraft decal.

72.5in (184cm) wide

$12,000-18,000   **DRA**

An L. & J.G. Stickley bow-arm Morris chair, with drop-in spring seat, upholstered in faded tan leather, original finish has normal wear to arms, Handcraft label.

34in (86cm) wide

$12,000-18,000   **DRA**

A Limbert even-arm settle, with broad slats all around, recovered in light brown leather, original finish, branded inside back stretcher, wear.

73.75in (184cm) wide

$4,000-5,000   **DRA**

A Limbert daybed, with shaped sides and drop-in spring bench cushion, paper label, refinished, replaced leather.

78.5in (189cm) wide

$2,500-3,500   **DRA**

A Limbert library table, with turtle top, single blind drawer, thin original finish, top refinished, branded mark, seam separation, scratches.

47.75in (121.5cm) wide

$2,800-3,200   **DRA**

A Limbert library table, with blind drawer containing lift-top desk, inkwell and pen holders, original finish with wax, branded inside drawer left, stain, burn, wear.

36in (90cm) wide

$1,000-1,500   **DRA**

An oval Limbert library table, (no. 158), with plank legs and cut-out stretchers supporting an oval-shaped lower shelf, original finish, branded under shelf.

48in (120cm) wide

$15,000-20,000   **DRA**

A Limbert single oval lamp table, with corbels supporting the top, canted, cut-out sides, cleaned original finish, branded under shelf.

45in (112.5cm) wide

$4,500-5,500   **DRA**

A Limbert pedestal dining table, (no. 466) complete with two leaves, original finish, branded mark, chips, wear.

45in (112.5cm) wide

$1,500-2,000   **DRA**

Part of a complete Limbert original dining room set, consisting of a china cabinet, sideboard with mirrored back splash, dining table and a set of seven dining chairs, branded marks.

Cabinet 58.5in (146cm) high

$10,000-15,000 SET   **DRA**

A Limbert oak writing desk, with arched backsplash and single drawer with wooden pulls, refinished, branded inside drawer, minor rings to one cubby.

36in (90cm) wide

$2,500-3,000   **DRA**

A Limbert three-door bookcase, (no. 373) original finish, branded mark and "373", one cracked pane, missing hardware.

65in (165cm) wide

$3,000-4,000   **DRA**

An early Limbert double-door bookcase, with leaded glass doors, original finish, paper label and stenciled "No. 321", damage, wear.

43.5in (110cm) wide

$5,000-6,000   **DRA**

A Limbert two-door bookcase, with bookshelf top and square cut-out sides, overcoated original finish, paper label on back, chips, scratches and damage.

63.75in (159cm) high

$7,000-8,000   **DRA**

ROYCROFT

- The Roycroft community of craftsmen (known as the Roycrofters) was founded in East Aurora, New York, by Elbert Green Hubbard.
- Inspired by the ideas of William Morris, Hubbard developed a unique interpretation of the Arts & Crafts Movement.
- Roycroft initially produced leatherwork, lighting and wrought metalware as well as simple Mission furniture.
- From 1896, the woodworkers produced souvenirs for visitors to the workshop.
- Roycroft furniture is considered some of the finest of the time.
- Forms were rectilinear and constructed from oak with traditional pins, pegs and mortise-and-tenon joints.
- Patinas are typically warm brown.
- Pieces were often marked with an orb and cross symbol or "Roycroft".
- When Hubbard died in the Lusitania tragedy in 1915, his son Elbert Jnr took over the firm and established Roycroft departments in stores throughout the US.
- The company closed in 1938.

A rare Roycroft hand-tooled and embossed leather covered chair, with vertical seat-rail slats and tapered legs, carved orb and cross mark, original finish.

Provenance: *From the estate of Elbert Hubbard, and the salon of the Roycroft Inn. This is one of two chairs pictured in period photos of the room.*

37.5in (94cm) high

$30,000-40,000   **DRA**

A rare oversized Roycroft armchair, with tacked on replaced green leather seat, carved "Roycroft" on front stretcher, refinished.

38in (96.5cm) high

$1,500-2,000   **DRA**

A Roycroft meditation chair, covered in original tacked-on leather, original finish, carved orb and cross mark on front, wear, straps broken.

34.25in (87cm) high

$2,000-3,000   **DRA**

A Roycroft child's chair, with seat, original finish, carved orb and cross mark, replaced vinyl seat.

25in (62.5cm) high

$1,000-1,500   **DRA**

A Roycroft dining chair, with single broad vertical slat, carved orb and cross mark, refinished, new upholstery.

41in (104cm) high

$1,000-1,500   **DRA**

A Roycroft mahogany drop-front writing desk, with Macmurdo feet, hammered copper and original key, with side chair with new tacked-on leather, both have original finish and orb and cross marks.

Desk 44in (110cm) high

$5,000-6,000   **DRA**

A rare Roycroft 'Ali Baba' bench, with half-timber on flaring legs, original finish, carved orb and cross mark, water line, splits, chips.

44.25in (112cm) wide

$7,500-9,000   **DRA**

A Roycroft 'Ali Baba' bench, with lower stretcher mortised through the sides and half-log seat, original finish, carved orb and cross mark.

42in (105cm) wide

$8,000-10,000   **DRA**

A Roycroft cestnut library table, with Macmurdo feet, overcoated original finish, carved orb and cross mark, minor roughness to edges.

30in (76cm) wide

$1,800-2,200   **DRA**

DECORATIVE ARTS

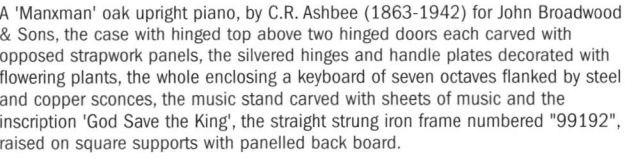

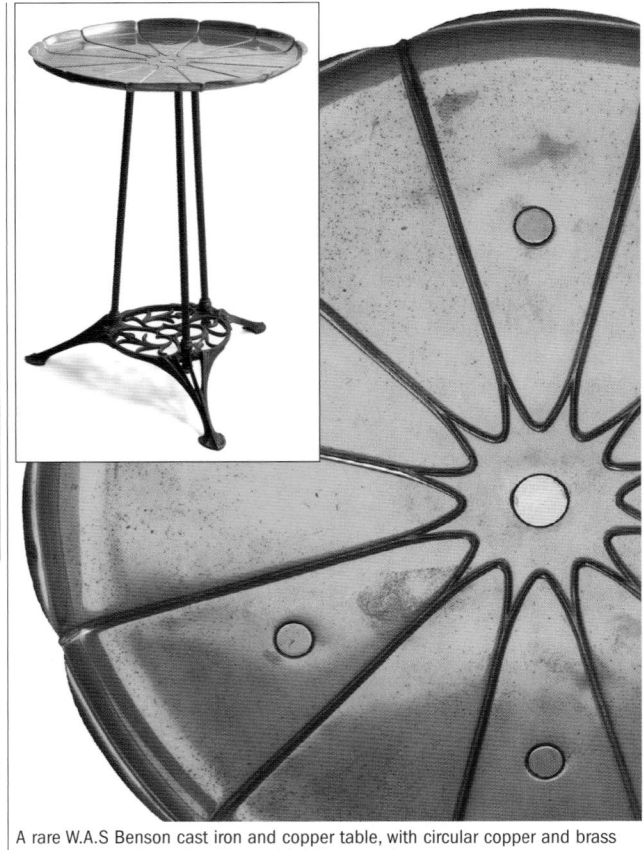

A 'Manxman' oak upright piano, by C.R. Ashbee (1863-1942) for John Broadwood & Sons, the case with hinged top above two hinged doors each carved with opposed strapwork panels, the silvered hinges and handle plates decorated with flowering plants, the whole enclosing a keyboard of seven octaves flanked by steel and copper sconces, the music stand carved with sheets of music and the inscription 'God Save the King', the straight strung iron frame numbered "99192", raised on square supports with panelled back board.

54.25in (138cm) wide

$6,000-10,000　　　　　　　　　　　　　　　　**L&T**

A rare W.A.S Benson cast iron and copper table, with circular copper and brass tray top on cast iron tripod base with foliate panels.

27in (68cm) high

$20,000-30,000　　　　　　　　　　　　　　　　**WW**

An Arts & Crafts oak settle, designed by George Montague Ellwood for J.S. Henry, the shaped back and sides with open shelf above an upholstered panel.

c1900　　　　*63.5in (161cm) high*

$4,000-5,000　　　　　　　　**L&T**

A Gillows four-fold oak draught screen, designed by Bruce J. Talbert, each reversible fold with upholstered panel within a molded frame with pierced gallery and turned finials.

75.25in (191cm) high

$2,500-3,500　　　　　　　　**L&T**

An Arts & Crafts Larkin leaded glass oak bookcase, New York, with turquoise glass and top over two clear glass doors, paper label.

57.5in (146cm) wide

$600-800　　　　　　　　**SK**

A Liberty & Co. Arts & Crafts oak lady's and gentleman's armchairs, the gentleman's chair with upholstered panel, the ladies chair with lower back.

$2,000-3,000　　　　　　　　**L&T**

An Arts & Crafts oak refectory table, designed in the manner of Thomas Jekyll, the rectangular top with molded edge.

72in (183cm) long

$2,000-3,000　　　　　　　　**L&T**

A copper-framed wall mirror, designed by Archibald Knox (1864-1933) for Liberty & Co. Ltd., London.

35in (89cm) wide

$4,000-6,000　　　　　　　　**L&T**

A Lifetime drink stand, with circular top and apron on four flaring legs joined by arched cross-stretchers, excellent original finish to base, top refinished, some nicks to top, ghost of a label.

18in (45.5cm) diam

$1,800-2,200 **DRA**

A Morris & Co. mahogany and inlaid sideboard, manufactured by Arthur W. Simpson of Kendal, the rectangular reverse breakfront top with satinwood crossbanding.

85.5in (217cm) wide

$10,000-15,000 **L&T**

An Arts & Crafts lamp table, with circular top and shelf, some wear to original finish, four holes under bottom shelf, possibly moved.

24in (61cm) diam

$1,200-1,800 **DRA**

A Morris & Co mahogany-framed sofa, upholstered in 'Squirrel' pattern wool, on spirally fluted turned legs with brass caps and pot castors.

72.75in (185cm) wide

$2,500-3,000 **L&T**

An E.G. Punet Arts & Crafts oak and ebony-inlaid chair, made by William Birch, High Wycombe, England, with rush panels and seat and an inlaid plant motif.

$3,500-4,500 **L&T**

A Rose Valley carved oak side chair, with pierced Gothic carving to splat, carved rose and 'V' upon a ribbon with date, shaped saddle seat and pierced-carved trestle base with stretcher.

Rose Valley, a utopian Arts and Crafts community, was founded in 1901 near Moylan, PA, by William Lightfoot Price, a Philadelphia architect. They were inspired by the advocates of the British Arts and Crafts movement, John Ruskin and William Morris. Rose Valley furniture is considered rare. At most, a few hundred pieces were made by a small team of craftsmen before the furniture shop closed in 1906.

1902 *36in (91.5cm) high*

$15,000-20,000 **FRE**

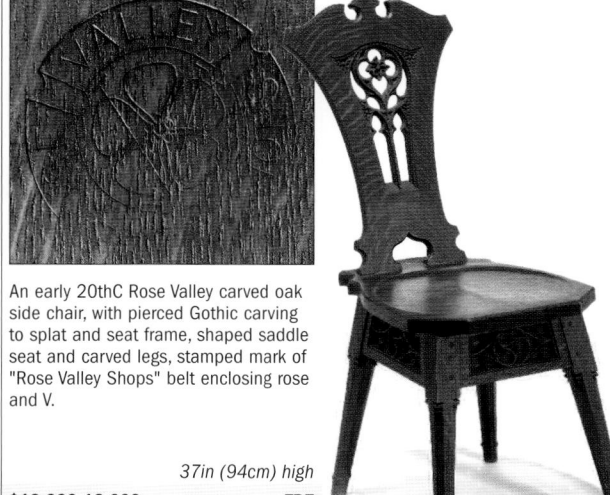

An early 20thC Rose Valley carved oak side chair, with pierced Gothic carving to splat and seat frame, shaped saddle seat and carved legs, stamped mark of "Rose Valley Shops" belt enclosing rose and V.

37in (94cm) high

$12,000-18,000 **FRE**

A rare early pair of Tiffany Studios Gothic style chairs, with turned posts, carved stretchers, original dark finish, solid quarter-sawn oak, pinned construction, reupholstered with historically correct tacked-on burgundy leather, branded "REPRODUCTION BY TIFFANY STUDIOS".

$4,500-5,500 **DRA**

A Glasgow School oak open armchair, in the style of George Walton, the slender back with heart-shaped toprail, inlaid with a heart shape and embellished with punched markings, the outswept arms of 'cacateuse' form above a circular moulded seat on square legs linked by stretchers.

$800-1,200   **L&T**

A Scottish Arts & Crafts brass wall mirror, in the manner of Marion Henderson Wilson, with repoussé waterlillies and beveled plate.

13in (33cm) wide

$1,500-2,000   **L&T**

A CLOSER LOOK AT AN ARTS & CRAFTS CABINET

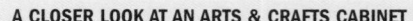

The cabinet was made by George Walton for The Phillippines, Brasted Chart, near Westerham, Kent.

Walton decorated the drawing room at The Phillippines from 1902 and the scheme marked a change of direction for his work to a more formal, classical style.

The use of architectural detailing on the cornice of this cabinet is reflected in the wall paneling, as are the gilded embellishments which also adorn the cornice shelf around the room.

An Arts and Crafts walnut display cabinet, by George Walton (1867-1943), with gilt embellishments, the later projecting cornice with gently curved outline decorated to the underside with Classical Greek architectural mutules, over a single glazed door with chamfered astragals and carved and gilded foliate motifs, flanked by further corresponding glazed panels and enclosing freestanding concave shelves supported by pegged uprights, the base with a central drawer with inset copper-backed handle, flanked by drawers with inset horn handles, the whole raised on square tapering legs.

77.25in (196.5cm) high

$15,000-20,000   **L&T**

A Wylie and Lochhead mahogany display cabinet, flanked by twin panels each marquetry inlaid with stylized plant forms.

59.75in (152cm) high

$1,000-1,500   **L&T**

A Wylie and Lochhead mahogany framed sofa, by E. A. Taylor (1874-1951), the rectangular back and arms with loose cushions above an upholstered seat with arched rails raised on square legs linked by stretchers.

$3,000-4,000   **L&T**

A Wylie and Lochhead mahogany and inlaid armchair, designed by George Logan.

$600-1,000   **L&T**

A Scottish Arts & Crafts oak open bookcase, the ledge back above rectangular molded top and an arrangement of four open shelves flanked by the cupboard doors with stained and leaded glass panels, over a further arrangement of six open shelves raised on a plinth.

$3,000-4,000   **L&T**

A pair of stained oak Glasgow School armchairs, with shaped back pierced with six square apertures, and curved open arms with paneled side.

c1900

$6,000-10,000   **L&T**

A Scottish Arts and Crafts oak tub armchair, the curved top rail above slats extending to a lower stretcher and enclosing an upholstered seat with loose cushion, checker inlaid decoration.

$700-900   **L&T**

A Scottish Arts and Crafts tin wall mirror, repoussé decorated with Celtic knotwork and set with turquoise Ruskin roundels.

16in (41cm) wide

$600-1,000   **L&T**

An Arts & Crafts oak-framed open armchair, the narrow rectangular back with upholstered panel above curved arms and upholstered panel seat, the whole raised on three plank supports.

$800-1,200   **L&T**

An English Arts & Crafts Hall stand, with open wood work and central mirror.

c1912   *60in (152.5cm) wide*

$1,000-1,500   **SK**

An Arts and Crafts oak sideboard, with overhanging cornice and raised on bracket feet, with decorative iron handles and hinges.

63in (160cm) wide

$2,000-3,000   **L&T**

An overpainted bedroom suite, in the style of Charles Rennie Mackintosh, comprising a wardrobe, with a chest of drawers, a dressing table and a pair of double bed ends.

65in (165cm) wide

$600-800 SET   **L&T**

An early 20thC English Arts & Crafts oak mirrored chest of drawers, wear and refinished.

54in (137cm) wide

$800-1,200   **SK**

A Liberty & Co. Arts and Crafts oak linen press, raised on stile feet.

84.25in (214cm) high

$4,000-5,000   **L&T**

A Shop of the Crafters armchair, inlaid in metal and fruitwood, original finish, paper label, check to one arm post, missing cushions.

37in (92.5cm) high

$3,000-4,000   **DRA**

A J.M. Young Morris chair, with slats to floor under flat arm, leather upholstery, refinished, damaged back bar.

The J.M. Young Furniture Company was founded by a Scotsman in Camden, New York in 1872. In 1902 his two sons joined him. In 1904 they produced a range of Arts & Crafts furniture following the style of the Stickleys. They continued to produce an Arts & Crafts range throughout the 1930s and '40s. The business closed in 1979.

37in (94cm) high

$3,500-4,500   **DRA**

A rare J.M. Young wing-back rocker, with drop-in spring seat and tacked-on back covered in original brown naugahyde, original finish, splits to seat, roughness, unmarked.

34.75in (88.5cm) high

$800-1,200   **DRA**

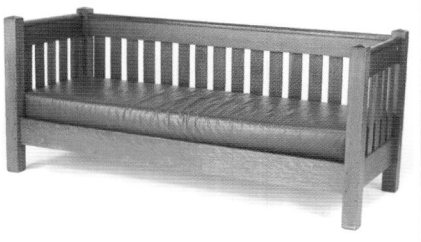

A J.M. Young even-arm settle, with vertical back slats, overcoated original finish, paper label.

78in (198cm) wide

$2,500-3,500   **DRA**

A J.M. Young oversized settle, recovered in chocolate brown leather, refinished, damage and wear, unmarked.

83in (207.5cm) wide

$2,000-3,000   **DRA**

An Arts and Crafts cube settle, with narrow slats all around and drop-in spring seat, new fabric upholstery, rot, chip, unmarked.

46.5in (118cm) wide

$1,000-1,500   **DRA**

An Arts & Crafts cube settle, with drop-in spring seat, recovered with tan leather, original finish, seam separation, tears and stains to upholstery, unmarked.

78in (198cm) wide

$1,800-2,200   **DRA**

An Arts & Crafts Morris chair, with three slats under flat arms, recovered in green vinyl, wear, damage, unmarked.

38in (95cm) high

$1,200-1,800   **DRA**

A large Arts & Crafts dining table, the lower shelf mortised with keyed through-tenons, refinished, minor separation, unmarked.

96in (240cm) long

$4,000-5,000   **DRA**

An Elenore Plaisted Abbott (American, 1875-1935), Rose Valley, oil on canvas, four part folding screen, each panel with wooded landscape with nudes.

c1903   79in (197.5cm) wide

$20,000-30,000   **POOK**

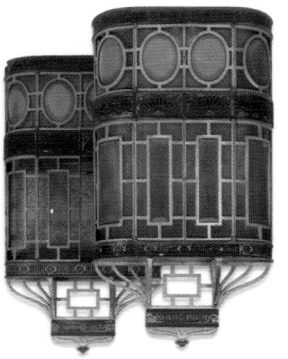

A pair of cast iron overmantel Coalbrookdale cabinets, with pierced gallery, glazed panels, twin doors and a cast frieze, enclosing a backplate cast with stylized foliage.

Formerly the sides of an overmantel mirror and cabinet.

1882   44in (112cm) high

$3,000-4,000   **L&T**

An Art Nouveau mahogany music cabinet, designed by George Montague Ellwood for J.S. Henry.

c1900   54in (137cm) high

$2,000-3,000   **L&T**

An Émile Gallé chestnut marquetry folding tea table, the top inlaid with a panel of tulips and flora in colored woods, engraved signature "Émile Gallé Nancy" with monogram "EG" and cross of Lorraine.

26.5in (67.5cm) high

$3,500-4,500   **DRA**

A Josef Hoffmann for J&J Kohn four-piece Secessionist bentwood furniture suite, a settle and two armchairs with full-height spindles and fabric upholstery, and a glass-topped side table with matching fabric insert and planished metal base, unmarked.

Settle 49.5in (126cm) wide

$4,500-5,500   **SDR**

A CLOSER LOOK AT A GALLÉ CASKET

In 1885, Gallé added a cabinet-making and marquetry workshop to his glassworks, taking his love of nature, sinuous forms and sophisticated materials into wood.

Subtly shaded exotic woods are used to make veneers for the marquetry. Here, they are used to depict tulips swaying in a breeze.

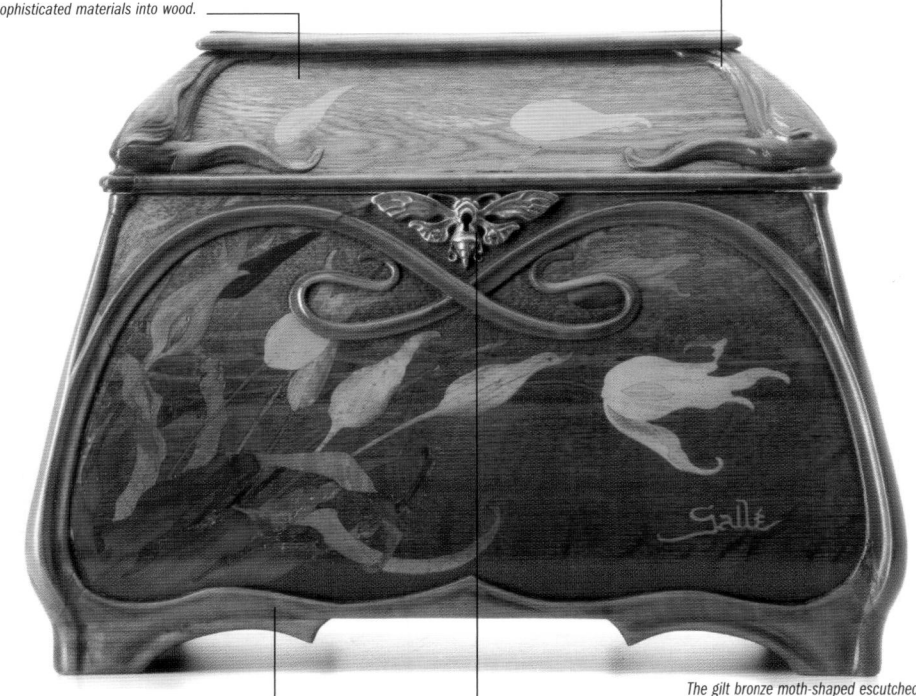

The relief carving is sinuous and organic in form, a typical feature of Gallé's work.

The gilt bronze moth-shaped escutcheon is typical of the naturalistic motifs used by Art Nouveau cabinetmakers.

An Emile Gallé marquetry and gilt bronze casket, the sides and lid decorated with tulips, the hinged lid carved with tulips and tendrils framing the panels at the corners, gilt bronze moth escutcheon, inlaid "Gallé".

c1900

$15,000-20,000   **DRA**

A Scottish Art Nouveau draught screen, by William McWhannel Petrie, depicting a study of music in four gilt panels, in oil on canvas, with copper edging, signed "Wm. M Petrie".

68.5x20.5in (174x52cm)

$8,000-12,000   **L&T**

A pair of 'English New Art' mahogany chairs, inscribed "Design for a chair to be executed in mahogany, P.J.M. inv. at. delt. Nov. 1908".

1908

$600-800   **L&T**

A Shapland and Petter Art Nouveau mahogany and inlaid bureau, lock stamped "S. & P. B.".

52.25in (133cm) high

$1,500-2,000   **L&T**

An Art Nouveau Harold Stabler tin wall mirror, with repoussé-worked columns and stylized, signed and dated with hammered mark "Harold Stabler 1902".

13.5in (34cm) wide

$4,000-6,000   **L&T**

A Scottish Art Nouveau bureau bookcase, attributed to E.A. Taylor for Wylie & Lochhead, Glasgow.

79.5in (202cm) high

$5,500-6,500   **L&T**

An Art Nouveau stained beech open armchair, the back with upholstered panel and waved rails above shaped open arms and upholstered panel seat raised on turned and blocked legs linked by stretcher.

$800-1,200   **L&T**

An Art Nouveau mahogany and pewter inlaid wing armchair.

$1,200-1,800   **L&T**

A 20thC European Art Nouveau carved wood chair, relief-carved in the form of lily pads, unsigned.

41in (104cm) high

$4,000-5,000   **SK**

A Secessionist Inlaid mahogany barrel-back armchair with a shaped seat, worn original finish, cracks crest rail, unmarked.

30in (76cm) high

$1,000-1,500   **DRA**

A late 19thC to early 20thC English Art Nouveau wardrobe, with glass door and figural wood panels,

52in (132cm) wide

$600-800   **SK**

A Continental Art Nouveau walnut bedroom suite comprising: a wardrobe, a dressing table, and a double bed end.

Wardrobe 74in (188cm) wide

$400-600   **L&T**

An Art Nouveau mahogany and inlaid bedroom suite, comprising a wardrobe with central mirrored panel and twin marquetry inlaid paneled doors, with a dressing table.

69.75in (177cm) wide

$1,200-1,800   **L&T**

An Art Nouveau mahogany and inlaid display cabinet.

48in (123cm) wide

$2,000-3,000   **L&T**

An Art Nouveau mahogany display cabinet, two paneled doors inlaid with specimen woods and mother-of-pearl depicting flowering plant forms.

75.25in (191cm) high

$3,000-4,000   **L&T**

An Art Deco Belmet Products Inc., New York, chrome and Bakelite-veneered smoke stand, Belmet tag.

23.25in (59cm) wide

$450-550 SDR

A Paul Frankl Art Deco table, with raised sides, open storage compartment, and flared pedestal base, entirely covered in original faux tortoiseshell finish, unmarked.

36in (91.5cm) wide

$2,500-3,500 SDR

A Heals Art Deco dining room suite, ebonized with coromandel wood veneers, comprising a dining table, a set of four chairs, and a sideboard, stamped serial numbers.

52.25in (133cm) wide

$2,500-3,500 SET L&T

A Laszlo Hoenig Art Deco satin birch chest, the rectangular top with gilt inset panel and glazed preserve, above two short over three long drawers, each with reeded turned handles and brass backplates, raised on molded outswept legs.

Laszlo Hoenig was a designer and decorator, based in South Audley Street, London, England.

53.25in (135cm) wide

$1,000-1,500 L&T

A Wolfgang Hoffmann for Howell three-piece sectional sofa, with tubular chrome frame and loose cushions upholstered in cowhide and black leather, unmarked.

c1936 *79.5in (199cm) wide*

$3,500-4,500 SDR

A European Art Deco console table, with layered rectangular top on double-banded semi-circular base, unmarked.

58.5in (148.5cm) wide

$2,500-3,500 SDR

A pair of Art Deco console tables, in chrome and exotic wood veneer, on platform base with triple-banded supports, unmarked.

48in (122cm) wide

$2,000-3,000 SDR

A CLOSER LOOK AT A MARIE ZIMMERMANN WOODEN BOX

This piece was designed by Marie Zimmermann (1878-1972), an acclaimed craftsman who brought the Arts & Crafts principles to her Deco influenced work.

Zimmermann often combined metals for texture and cabochon stones such as jade and amethyst to create a sophisticated design on a simple form.

The Egyptian-influenced geometric design in rich colours reflect the exoticism of the Deco period.

Her busy central New York workshop allowed her to remain in touch with and adapt to the range of artistic styles that influenced America in the 1930s.

A Marie Zimmermann carved wooden box, studded with cabochon jewels of amethyst and semi-precious quartz, lined in silk, with some paint loss.

c1935 *12.5in (31cm) wide*

$120,000-150,000 DRA

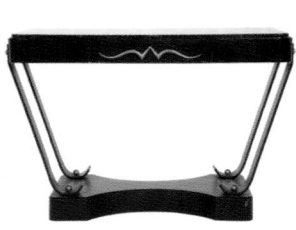

A small Art Deco occasional table, with black granite top on metal base with matte black finish, and gold-accented details, unmarked.

32.5in (82.5cm) wide

$850-950   **SDR**

An Art Deco extension dining table, with broad oak top and one integrated leaf, on curved plank-leg base with stretcher, unmarked.

closed 50in (127cm) wide

$450-550   **SDR**

Two chairs from an Art Deco walnut dining room suite, comprising a dining table, and a set of six chairs.

Table 35.75in (91cm) wide

$2,500-3,500 SET   **L&T**

One of a pair of Art Deco burl wood Classical-inspired backless chairs, in the style of Jules Leleu, with black velvet upholstery, unmarked.

27.75in (70.5cm) high

$2,500-3,500 PAIR   **SDR**

An Italian Art Deco pair of armchairs with deeply-channeled beige fabric upholstery, on olive wood frames, with brass sabots, unmarked.

32.5in (82.5cm) high

$3,500-4,500   **SDR**

An Art Deco crescent-shaped sofa and matching armchair with channeled light gray velvet upholstery, and swirling ribbed trim with ebonized finish, unmarked.

81in (205.75cm) wide

$2,500-3,500   **SDR**

A pair of Art Deco burl wood and mahogany console tables, with single cabinet door concealing a mirrored interior and glass shelf, unmarked.

39.5in (100cm) wide

$1,200-1,800   **SDR**

An unusual Art Deco black lacquered vanity, with a circular beveled mirror with embossed leather panel to back, and three drawers with chrome hardware, unmarked.

47.5in (120.5cm) wide

$1,800-2,200   **SDR**

A French Art Deco demi-lune oak commode, with pink and brown marble top, parchment covered exterior, three drawers with silvered metal drop pulls, on ebonized ovoid feet, unmarked.

33in (84cm) high

$7,500-8,500   **SDR**

An Art Deco fluted corner cabinet, of stepped form with single door concealing a stationery shelf, unmarked.

47.5in (120.5cm) high

SDR

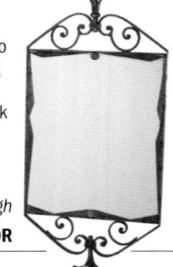

A French Art Deco iron wall-hanging mirror, with scrolled openwork frame, stamped "France".

60in (152cm) high

$850-950   **SDR**

An Art Deco oval wall-hanging mirror, in wrought-iron frame with beveled glass and stylized floral panels, unmarked.

17.25in (43.75cm) wide

$1,000-1,500   **SDR**

$900-1,100

WILLIAM MORRIS

- William Morris (1834-1896) is credited as one of the founding fathers of the Arts and Crafts movement. Deeply opposed to mechanical production methods and lamenting the decline of ancient skills, he campaigned for the revival of traditional techniques to create beautiful, handcrafted objects.

- His London-based design firm Morris, Marshall, Faulkner & Company promoted an integrated style of interior that was largely inspired by medieval sources, and which looked to local and natural materials and handicraft traditions to produce highly original ceramics, textiles, wallpaper, carpets and furniture.

- He began making hand-knotted rugs in c1878. Having learnt the skill himself, he then taught others and in 1880 organized an exhibition of finished carpets and rugs based on his collection of historical Eastern rugs.

- In 1881 carpet-weaving was moved to Merton Abbey in South London. The carpets produced at Merton in the 1880s and 90s are the largest objects the firm produced and were extremely expensive to produce. Along with their tapestry production they represent the most luxurious of Morris and Co.'s output.

- The hand-knotted rugs were referred to as Hammersmith rugs to distinguish them from the machine woven carpets which the firm also produced at the time.

- Only a few designs for Hammersmith carpets are known because there are no day books available to indicate which designs were made up and in what quantities. As a result they are difficult to date. Of the few examples that are known they tend to be named after the houses for which they were made, for example 'Clouds', the 'Hurstbourne', or the 'Bullerswood' carpets. Alternatively they were named after the patron who commissioned them, as in the 'McCulloch', however the designs for these carpets may have had their origins in earlier works.

A fine William Morris Hammersmith hand-knotted carpet, cotton warps, jute binding wefts with woollen knots, the indigo ground with an allover design of flowering branches on a fine tendril field, within red ground border of meandering parrot tulips and multiple guard bands, the outer border with marbleized green and blue pile, the ends with 'Soumak' fringing.

The ground and border of the carpet show strong stylistic characteristics of both Morris' 'Holland Park' (1883) and the 'Clouds' (1887) carpets. Holland Park carpet is said to be Morris's most original carpet design and shows traces of all his greatest influences: medievalism, floral realism and eastern precision. From 1883 to around 1889 Morris had adopted a more classical and symmetrical format for his carpet designs. They displayed, as in this instance, a quartered design (where each quarter of the design is the same but reversed as a mirror) often with a central medallion.

c1889-94   193x138in (491x351cm)

$150,000-200,000   **L&T**

A Morris & Co. wool hanging, woven in 'Bluebell' pattern, blue cotton lining.

'Bluebell' was designed by J.H. Dearle

c1905-10   56.25in (143cm) long

$4,000-5,000   **L&T**

A Morris & Co. wool hanging, by William Morris, in the 'Tulip and Rose' pattern.

1875   82.75x32.5in (210x82.5cm)

$3,000-4,000   **L&T**

A William Morris bolt of 'Cray' pattern printed cotton, printed marks to selvedge and to one end "Regd. Morris and Company".

1884   585in (1,500cm) long

$5,000-6,000   **L&T**

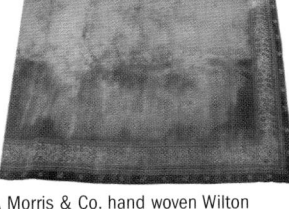

A Morris & Co. hand woven Wilton carpet, the green field within a leafy border.

214.5in (545cm) long

$5,000-6,000   **L&T**

A large Morris-style carpet, decorated with stylized natural motifs.

214in (545cm) long

$1,000-1,200   **SWO**

A William Morris-style runner with stylized poppy and scroll motif in ivory, coral and brown on an ocher ground.

32x165in (81.5x419cm)

$500-600   **DRA**

A silver gilt framed embroidery by Sir Edward Maufe (1883-1974) and Vernon Hill 'Morse', worked in colored silks and gold threads and depicting the Lamb of God, enclosed within triptych frame engraved with a lattice design, hallmarked London, with maker's mark 'CSAC'.

1953   *5x7in (13x18cm)*

$1,500-2,500   **L&T**

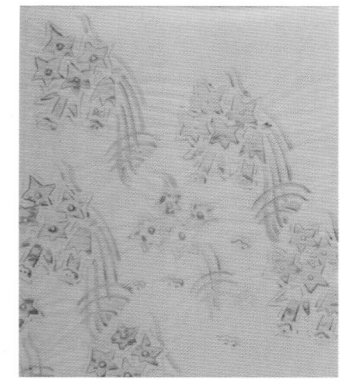

Jessie M. King (1875-1949), design for a batik, watercolour, unsigned.

10.25in (26cm) high

$700-800   **L&T**

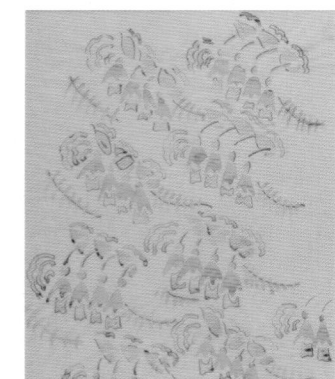

Jessie M. King, design for a batik, watercolor, unsigned.

10.25in (26cm) high

$700-800   **L&T**

An Ann Macbeth silk and linen portiere, with stylized flowers embroidered and appliqued, some fading to centre, a couple of stains, restoration to a few small tears.

Ann Macbeth was a designer and teacher, and member of the Glasgow School. This portiere's design was published in the 1906 Studio Yearbook.

.

c1900   *102in (259cm) high*

$10,000-15,000   **DRA**

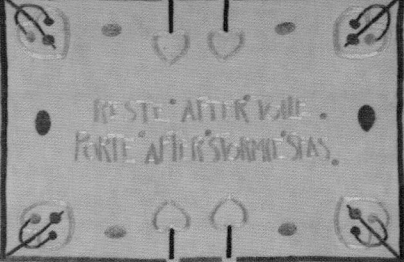

A Gustav Stickley, rare embroidered linen by Newcomb College decorator Harriet Joor, with gold and green dragonflies on a natural linen ground, some discoloration to one end, unmarked.

60in (152.5cm) long

$13,000-15,000   **DRA**

A wallpaper or textile design by C.F.A. Voysey (Charles Francis Annesley Voysey (1857-1941), an artist's woodblock proof, designed for Scott Morton & Co. for the Essex range, framed and glazed, pencil marks "Essex A.17".

c1900   *29.25in (74.5cm) high*

$7,000-10,000   **L&T**

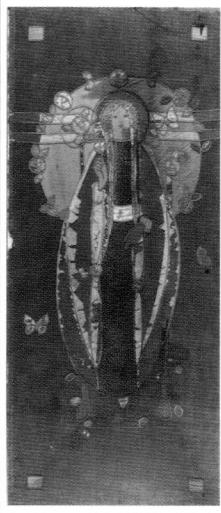

A Scottish School embroidered panel, worked in colored silks with a maiden in a rose bower reserved on a linen ground, framed and glazed.

c1900 57in (145cm) h

$800-1,200   **L&T**

A Scottish School Arts and Crafts framed embroidered panel, worked in colored silks on a linen ground.

16cm (41cm) wide

$700-1,000   **L&T**

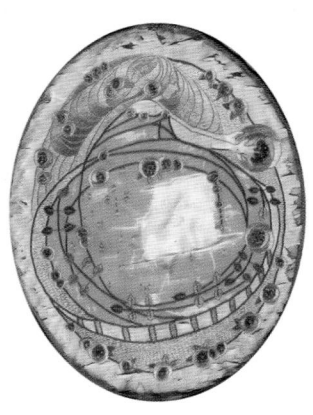

A Scottish School Art Nouveau silkwork panel, worked in the manner of Margaret or Frances Macdonald, with a maiden, holding a stylized rose within a flowerhead and foliate border, oval frame.

14.25in (36cm) high

$1,500-1,700 L&T

A rare Jugendstil textile embroidered by Margarethe von Brauchitsch, with stylized blossoms in black and ivory on a natural linen ground, some staining and minor thread wear, embroidered "MvB".

Von Brauchitsch studied with Koloman Moser in Vienna, and was a founding member of the Vereinigte Werkstatten (Munich Secession movement).

1902

60in (152.5cm) long

$2,500-3,000 DRA

A Duncan Grant wool carpet, probably woven by Wilton Royal, with baskets of flowers.

c1935

143.25in (364cm) long

$15,000-20,000 L&T

A Belgian curtain panel in the style of Henri van de Velde, with stylized gray satin flowers appliqued on maroon wool, some discoloration, few stains, wear to satin.

121in (307.5cm) long

$500-700 DRA

'Cupid and my campaspe played...', by Annie French (1872-1965) in pen, ink and watercolor, bears initials "A.F.".

9.5x8.5in (24.5x22cm)

$4,000-6,000 L&T

'Spring', by Jessie I. Dunlop, oil on canvas.

36.25in (92cm) high

$3,000-4,000 L&T

'La Journée', a group of four watercolor studies, by Ethel Larcombe, each bears artist's monogram.

approx 10.25in (26cm) high

$4,000-6,000 L&T

An Arts & Crafts plaster panel, in the manner of Phoebe Stabler, modeled in relief as a triptych with molded Celtic knotwork frame, enclosing three panels.

27x62.25in (69x158cm)

$4,000-6,000 L&T

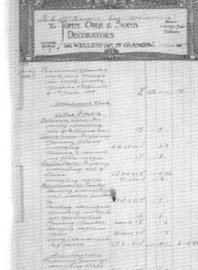

A Charles Rennie Mackintosh Art Nouveau printed invoice, for John Orr & Sons, Decorators, 101 Wellington Street, Glasgow, bears printed initials "C.R.M.", with another sheet of headed notepaper from the same firm, printed in the Aesthetic style, dated.

1897

7.75in (19.5cm) long

$1,000-1,500 L&T

MODERN FURNITURE

THE MODERN MARKET

In the last ten years the fashion for cleaner lines and uncluttered, if not minimal, living has revolutionized the way many of us decorate our homes. Affordable copies of iconic designs by Charles and Ray Eames and Arne Jacobsen have started to appear in furniture stores and so the move away from "old" and "antique" began.

Marcel Breuer's Wassily chair, Mies van Der Rohe's Barcelona chair and the iconic 670 lounge chair of Charles and Ray Eames are becoming as ubiquitous in a way their creators could only have dreamed. As a result contemporary remakes of what tend to be scarce mid-20th century originals, now have a firm and profitable place on the secondary market.

Meanwhile, the more fluid and craftsman-like forms of Finn Juhl and the masterly combinations of Piero Fornasetti, which seamlessly mesh classical and surreal designs with 20th century items, continue to win new admirers. The same can be said of Pennsylvania's own New Hope School, and its star pupil Paul Evans. Manufacturers such as Knoll, Herman Miller, and Dunbar also have their followers.

Modern ceramics continue to be a major growth area, from the great classic studio potters Hans Coper and Lucie Rie to Peter Voulkos and Beatrice Wood.

The second half of the 20thC has seen the great renaissance of glass from Murano. While the Dale Chihuly phenomenon goes from strength to strength, other names to conjure are Dante Marioni and Marvin Lipofsky.

John Sollo

WENDELL CASTLE

A Wendell Castle walnut Crescent rocking chair with ecru fabric, signed "WC76".

1976	*39.5in (100.5cm) high*
$20,000-23,000	**SDR**

An important and monumental Wendell Castle 'Desk Clock' desk, with fiddle back mahogany and curly maple veneer, inlaid with mother-of-pearl and abalone, drop-front component enclosing drawers and shelves, with gold-plated brass-faced clock with chiming pendulum movement, branded "Wendell Castle 1985".

1985	*94in (239cm) high*
$70,000-100,000	**SDR**

A Wendell Castle wall sculpture/table, "Autumn Drive," of mahogany, Madrone burl veneer, and oil pastel on illustration board, composition signed "Castle 91".

1991	*82.5in (209.5cm) high*
$6,000-9,000	**SDR**

A Wendell Castle four drawer chest, carved and painted in polychrome with bulbous spayed feet, signed "Castle 93".

1993	*60in (152cm) wide*
$15,000-20,000	**SDR**

A Wendell Castle wall-hanging bookshelf and counter, with six blind drawers.

124in (315cm) wide	
$20,000-25,000	**SDR**

A Wendell Castle conference table, oak veneer top on patinated metal legs, with seating capacity for twenty people.

185in (470cm) wide	
$20,000-25,000	**SDR**

CHARLES & RAY EAMES

- Charles and Ray Eames defined the American post-war modern movement. Their work with venerable institutions such as the Smithsonian placed them at the heart of the rapid development of American design.
- Charles established his own architectural office in 1930, and soon began to diversify into other areas of design. He is most famous today for the iconic chairs he designed with his wife Ray, an avant-garde artist.
- Their goal was to create furniture that could be mass-produced, was affordable, and performed well. They began to experiment with plywood and one of their first products was the molded plywood chair, which was developed with Eero Saarinen.
- After WWII, the pair began to use the revolutionary material fiberglass, which could be molded into any shape. Combined with plastic, it allowed the construction of a seat from a single piece of material.
- Charles and Ray continued to design pieces throughout the 1950s and 1960s, most of them made and distributed via Herman Miller. Some of these, such as the '670' lounge chair and '671' ottoman, are instantly recognisable.
- Reproductions of Eames designs are still made today.

A Charles & Ray Eames rosewood framed armchair and ottoman, model nos. 670 and 671, upholstered in black leather.

$1,500-2,000　　　　**L&T**

An Eames 670 and 671 lounge chair and ottoman, for Herman Miller, rosewood and red leather.

$4,500-6,500　　　　**FRE**

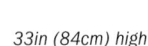

Two early 21stC Charles & Ray Eames for Herman Miller lounge chairs, with black leather upholstered seats on molded plywood walnut finish shells, manufacturer's label.

33in (84cm) high

$2,000-3,000　　　　**SK**

Four Charles & Ray Eames for Herman Miller dowel-leg side chairs, with original bikini-pad fabric upholstery, Herman Miller factory tags.

32.25in (82cm) high

$3,000-4,000　　　　**SDR**

A pair of Charles & Ray Eames for Zenith gray fiber glass shell armchairs with rope-edge back, on black metal bases, checkerboard label.

31in (78.5cm) high

$800-1,200　　　　**SDR**

A Charles & Ray Eames for Herman Miller fiberglass shell armrocker, with stitched white seat cover on cat's cradle base with birch runners, Herman Miller factory label.

27.5in (70cm) high

$600-900　　　　**SDR**

A mid-20thC Charles & Ray Eames for Herman Miller Tandem seating unit, two off-white composite seats and a laminate table, on aluminum legs, designed for airport seating, manufacturer's label.

71.5in (181.5cm) wide

$400-600　　　　**SK**

A Charles & Ray Eames for Herman Miller molded plywood child's stool, unmarked.

Compared to many of Eames' designs this is comparatively scarce.

10.25in (26cm) wide

$1,500-2,000　　　　**SDR**

A Charles & Ray Eames for Evans early CTM table, with molded plywood top on polished chrome legs, early Evans decal.

34in (86.5cm) diam

$600-900　　　　**SDR**

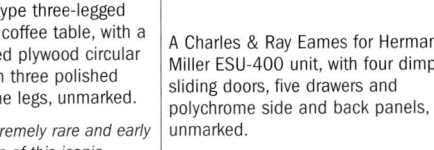

A Charles & Ray Eames for Herman Miller prototype three-legged 'CTM' coffee table, with a molded plywood circular top on three polished chrome legs, unmarked.

An extremely rare and early version of this iconic Eames design.

34.25in (87cm) diam

$12,000-15,000　　　　**SDR**

A Charles & Ray Eames for Herman Miller ESU-400 unit, with four dimpled sliding doors, five drawers and polychrome side and back panels, unmarked.

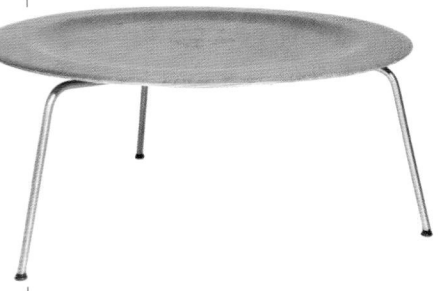

48.25in (122.5cm) wide

$10,000-14,000　　　　**SDR**

MODERN DESIGN

A Wharton Esherick walnut coffee table, with free-form top on splayed legs, and two pencil drawings on paper depicting plans for the table.

1970   *61in (155cm) length*

$30,000-40,000   **SDR**

A stool, by Wharton Esherick, with three flared dowel legs mortized through the seat, and graduated stretchers, carved "WE 1966".

1966   *16.5in (42cm) wide*

$4,000-6,000   **SDR**

A stack-laminated tabletop mirror, by Wharton Esherick, with sculptural frame and recessed glass, incised "WC74".

1974   *11.25in (28.5cm) wide*

$3,000-4,000   **SDR**

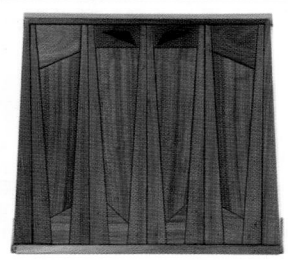

A Wharton Esherick padouk Victrola cabinet, with pull-out counter slabs and folding doors, carved with abstract primitive forms, with original Capehart Victrola user's manual and additional carved items from the original installation, carved "WHARTON ESHERICK MCMXXX+J.S".

1930   *52in (132cm) wide*

$100,000-150,000   **SDR**

A Wharton Esherick sculpted maple wall mounted corner shelf, signed "1963 W.E".

This biomorphic, organic form is typical of Esherick's designs.

1963   *120in (305cm) long*

$35,000-45,000   **SDR**

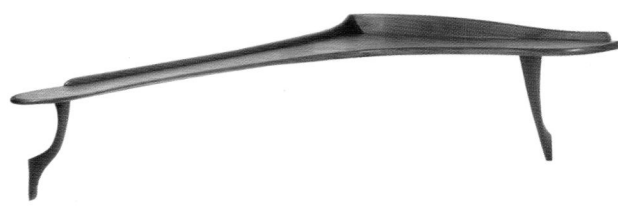

PAUL EVANS

- Paul Evans (1931-87) trained as a silversmith before establishing his own studio and beginning to accept commissions for pieces of monumental furniture.
- During the 1960s, he headed Directional Furniture, a North Carolina company known for its progressive designs. By the late 1970s he was working from his own studio.
- Evans' work is hugely sculptural in appearance and his large scale pieces, such as his room dividers, act as works of art as well as furniture.
- His early experience in metalwork gave him an understanding of these materials and they featured frequently in his pieces. His stalagmite-form tables, with bronze supports and plate-glass tops, are typical of his work.
- Echoes of Paul Frankl's 1920s Skyscraper line can be seen in Evans' Cityscape range.
- Success enabled Evans to open a showroom in New York in 1979 and bring his work to a wider audience.
- His work is hugely popular today and prices have risen dramatically in recent years.

A Paul Evans sculpted steel dining table, with a rectangular plate glass top resting on two crescent-shaped supports decorated with pinwheels, stars, and geometric motifs covered in red, gold, and black patinas, welded mark, "PE 68".

1968   *72in (183cm) wide*

$3,000-5,000   **SDR**

A Paul Evans skyline coffee table, with plate glass top, the base covered with treated paints and gold finish.

60in (152cm) wide

$15,000-18,000   **SDR**

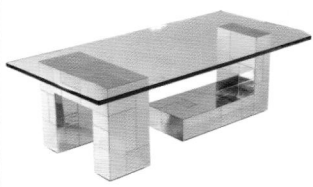

A Paul Evans 'Cityscape' coffee table with rectangular glass top on two geometrically-shaped supports, covered in polished brass and chrome patchwork, one support signed "An Original Paul Evans".

50in (127cm) wide

$2,000-3,000   **SDR**

A Paul Evans sculpted bronze dining table, with round-edged plate glass top resting on a serpentine stalagmite base, signed "PE 6?".

87.75in (223cm) wide

$9,000-11,000   **SDR**

A Paul Evans skyline dining table, with plate glass top, signed "Paul Evans 76".

1976   *96in (244cm) wide*

$30,000-35,000   **SDR**

A Paul Evans sculpted bronze coffee table, with circular glass top resting on stalagmite base, unmarked.

41.5in (105.5cm) diam

$2,000-3,000   **SDR**

A Paul Evans sculpted bronze dining table, with rectangular plate glass top resting on a six-legged base, marked "PE 68".

1968   48in (122cm) wide

$3,000-4,000   SDR

A Paul Evans copper, bronze and pewter patchwork parson's table with slate top.

52in (132cm) wide

$3,000-5,000   SDR

A Paul Evans sculpted steel coffee table, with oval slate top.

66in (167.5cm) wide

$18,000-20,000   SDR

An unusual parson's-style coffee table, by Paul Evans, covered in metallic plate patchwork, hand-hammered and machine abraded, visibly nailed to frame, inset with slate top.

68in (172.5cm) long

$2,000-3,000   FRE

A Paul Evans wall-hanging shelf, with rectangular plate glass top resting on two sculpted bronze supports, marked "PE 71".

1971   glass 60in (152.5cm) wide

$1,000-1,500   SDR

A Paul Evans painted and perforated steel front cabinet, with four bi-fold doors, slate top, plinth base, signed "Paul Evans 63 D".

The first of only three made, this piece was an original floor sample in Evans' studio in New Hope, PA for nearly a decade.

1963   72in (183cm) wide

$55,000-65,000   SDR

A rare six-door cabinet on raised plinth, by Paul Evans, the entire surface worked in parquetry olive burl veneer, three compartments each with adjustable shelf.

c1970   90in (228.5cm) wide

$15,000-20,000   FRE

A rare Paul Evans two door cabinet, with copper, pewter and bronze patchwork, slate top.

42in (107cm) wide

$20,000-30,000   SDR

A Paul Evans sculpted bronze wall-hanging cabinet, with inset slate panel to top, and two bi-fold doors concealing shelves and green-painted interior, signed "PE 68".

1968   52in (132cm) wide

$5,000-7,000   SDR

A Paul Evans unusual sculpted bronze wall-hanging cabinet, with two slate panels to top and bi-fold doors, inset with silvered metal geometric forms, marked "PE 70".

1970   84in (213cm) wide

$4,000-6,000   SDR

A Paul Evans custom-designed wall-hanging cabinet in sculpted bronze and rosewood, with three interior shelves, signed "PE 70/DR".

A rare and exceptional piece.

1970   139in (353cm) wide

$50,000-55,000   SDR

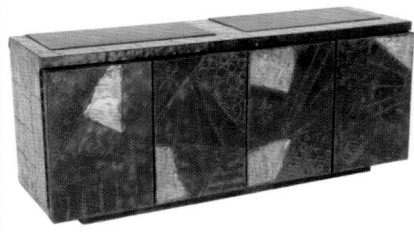

A Paul Evans four door painted patchwork steel credenza, with two piece slate top.

72in (183cm) wide

$20,000-30,000　　　　　　　SDR

A Paul Evans sculpture-front wall-mounted four-door buffet with slate top, and interior drawer and shelves, signed "Paul Evans 76".

1976　　　　　　　　　*72in (183cm) wide*

$90,000-100,000　　　　　　SDR

A Paul Evans sculpted steel wall-hanging cabinet, with slate top, riveted metal patchwork covering to top and sides, and two sculpted doors, welded mark, "Paul Evans '70".

1970　　　　　*36in (91.5cm) high*

$3,000-5,000　　　　　　　SDR

A Paul Evans faceted burl walnut wall cabinet, with black mirrored glass over original brown fiberglass.

82in (208cm) wide

$50,000-60,000　　　　　SDR

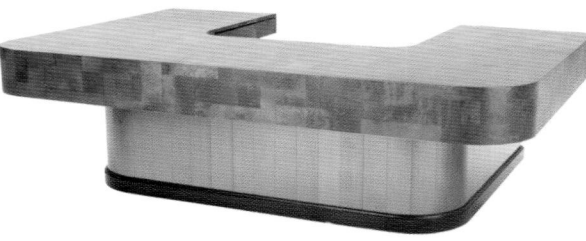

A Paul Evans u-shaped three drawer chrome and burl patchwork desk, signed "Paul Evans".

96in (244cm) wide

$20,000-30,000　　　　　　SDR

A pair of Paul Evans sculpted steel cube chairs, with gold velvet upholstery on swivel bases.

30in (76cm) wide

$27,000-32,000　　　SDR

A Paul Evans double stalagmite sculptural room divider, of oxidized steel blades decorated with welded geometric and swirling patterns.

c1965　　*136in (345cm) high*

$15,000-20,000　　　SDR

A Paul Evans sculpted bronze fireplace surround with chrome patchwork frame and folding glass doors, signed "PE 75".

1975　　*82in (208cm) wide*

$20,000-30,000　　　SDR

A Paul Evans sculpted bronze disc bar with two semi-circular doors concealing an interior cabinet, single drawer and storage cubicles, unmarked.

72in (183cm) wide

$6,000-9,000　　　SDR

A Jean-Michel Frank for Comte Ltd. three drawer desk, in light wood with brass escutcheons with sabot feet, unmarked.

43.5in (110.5cm) high

$4,500-6,500 SDR

A large limed oak console table, by Jean-Michel Frank for Chanaux & Co., stamped "J.M. Frank/Chanaux & Co." along footboard.

c1930 *78.25in (199cm) wide*

$40,000-70,000 SDR

A pair of parchment-covered pedestals, by Jean-Michel Frank for Comte Ltd., with scalloped aprons, made in South America, unmarked.

c1940s *15.75in (40cm) wide*

$5,000-6,000 SDR

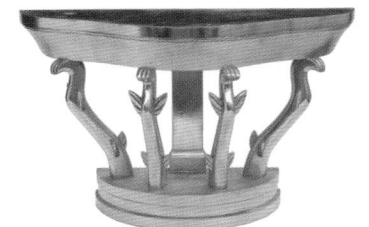

A demi-lune console table, by the Rockerfeller Foundation after a design by Jean-Michel Frank and Diego Giacometti, in gold leaf finish with a scalloped top and four branched supports on a stepped base, unmarked.

c1960 *51.75in (131.5cm) wide*

$4,000-6,000 SDR

A games table, attributed to Jean-Michel Frank, with inset oak top on black iron base with sharply tapered legs, unmarked.

This table was in the Hotel Provincial Mar Del Plata in Argentina.

35.75in (91cm) wide

$3,000-4,000 SDR

A 'Wiggle' chair, by Frank Gehry, from the 'Easy Edges' series, of laminated cardboard construction, unmarked.

22in (56cm) high

$2,500-3,500 SDR

A pair of Frank Gehry 'Power Play' armchairs with bent and woven maple laminate, design series 1989-92, Knoll, USA.

32in (81.5cm) wide

$2,500-3,500 SK

A cork and corrugated cardboard wine rack, by Frank Gehry, with nine bottle capacity, unmarked.

14.25in (36cm) wide

$1,200-2,000 SDR

A Frank Gehry 'Easy Edges' coffee table of laminated cardboard construction, Easy Edges paper tag.

38in (96.5cm) wide

$2,500-3,000 SDR

A Finn Juhl for Niels Vodder #53 settee and matching armchair, upholstered in light blue fabric, both have branded manufacturer's mark.

Settee 50.5in (128cm) wide

$5,000-7,000   **SDR**

A Finn Juhl for Niels Vodder NV-53 settee, on sculpted walnut frame upholstered in red fabric.

51in (130cm) wide

$3,000-5,000   **SDR**

A Finn Juhl teak armchair, upholstered in teal wool.

32in (81cm) high

$3,000-5,000   **SDR**

A Finn Juhl set of six rosewood armchairs, covered in black leather.

25in (63.5cm) wide

$20,000-30,000   **FRE**

A Finn Juhl for Baker Unit 22 walnut and sycamore cabinet, the rectangular top fitted with twin-paneled doors enclosing two drawers and two open shelves.

1952   *30in (76cm) high*

$1,000-1,500   **FRE**

A Finn Juhl for Baker Unit 24 walnut and sycamore chest, straight front fitted with four drawers, bar pulls, cylindrical tapering legs.

1952 30in (76cm) high

$1,200-2,000   **FRE**

A Finn Juhl rosewood extension dining table, oval top, cylindrical tapering legs, with two additional table boards.

118in (300cm) long extended

$9,000-12,000   **FRE**

A Finn Juhl teak side table, for France & Son, Denmark, rectangular tray top, tapering molded legs, apron stretcher, circular metal tag.

15in (38cm) high

$500-700   **FRE**

A Vladimir Kagan for Dreyfuss walnut contour armchair, upholstered in blue leather with Kagan-Dreyfuss paper label.

35in (89cm) wide

$5,000-7,000　　　　　　　**SDR**

A Vladimir Kagan armchair with original upholstery, on walnut base, with Kagan-Grosfield tag.

29.75in (75.5cm) wide

$12,000-18,000　　　　　　**SDR**

A Vladimir Kagan Model 100B high-back barrel chair and ottoman, with terracotta-colored ultrasuede upholstery on sharply-tapered legs, unmarked.

Chair 35in (89cm) high

$4,500-6,500　　　　　　　**SDR**

A Vladimir Kagan sculptured walnut rocker with ottoman, in original Knoll tweed fabric upholstery.

The original fabric found on this rocker increases the value.

42in (107cm) wide

$10,000-15,000　　　　　　**SDR**

A Vladimir Kagan 'Erica' chaise, no. 6910-L, with single contoured arm, fully-upholstered in rust-colored brushed fabric on cruciform lucite base, unmarked.

52in (132cm) wide

$6,000-9,000　　　　　　　**SDR**

A Vladimir Kagan set of six 'Matrix' chairs, with bentwood frames, covered in tufted purple mohair, with "Vladimir Kagan Design Inc." tags.

36in (91.5cm) high

$3,000-4,000　　　　　　　**SDR**

A Vladimir Kagan for Dreyfuss set of twelve walnut Sling dining chairs, two no. VK102 armchairs and ten no. VK101 side chairs, with original rust-colored velvet upholstery, Kagan-Dreyfuss tags.

Armchairs 24.5in (62cm) wide

$28,000-32,000 SET　　　　**SDR**

A late 1960s Vladimir Kagan ottoman, with original fabric upholstery in dark brown with cream squares, on lucite plank supports with polished chrome connectors, accompanied by photocopy of a letter from Kagan authenticating this piece, unmarked.

25.5in (64.5cm) wide

$1,500-2,000　　　　　　　**SDR**

A Vladimir Kagan sofa, from the Grosfeld House Collection upholstered in oatmeal-colored fabric on walnut whalebone legs.

96in (244cm) wide

$10,000-15,000　　　　　　**SDR**

A Vladimir Kagan sofa, with original upholstery on walnut base.

98in (249cm) wide

$15,000-20,000　　　　　　**SDR**

A Vladimir Kagan 150BC 'Cloud' sofa, fully-upholstered in royal blue wool on ebonized wood supports, unmarked.

136in (145.5cm) wide

$8,000-10,000　　**SDR**

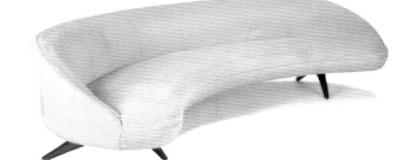

A Vladimir Kagan sofa, with original upholstery on walnut base, Kagan-Dreyfuss tag.

101.5in (258cm) wide

$15,000-20,000　　**SDR**

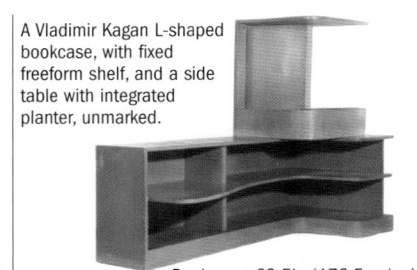

A Vladimir Kagan L-shaped bookcase, with fixed freeform shelf, and a side table with integrated planter, unmarked.

Bookcase: 69.5in (176.5cm) wide

$2,000-2,500　　**SDR**

A Vladimir Kagan three-piece custom-built wall unit in burlwood veneer, the top with glass front doors, mirrored interior and three glass shelves, resting on a dark brown lacquered slab with two blind drawers, over a two-door cabinet, unmarked.

88in (223.5cm) high

$3,000-4,000　　**SDR**

A Vladimir Kagan serving cart, its hinged top inset with tan laminate, over removable glass tray on sculptural walnut frame with brass-capped feet, and casters, unmarked.

36in (91.5cm) wide

$800-1,200　　**SDR**

A Vladimir Kagan occasional table, with oval plate glass top resting on a sculpted walnut base, unmarked.

52in (132cm) wide

$1,500-2,000　　**SDR**

A Poul Kjærholm three legged stool, in brown leather on brushed aluminum frame, marked on frame.

22in (56cm) diam

$7,000-10,000　　**SDR**

A 'PK27' easy chair, by Poul Kjærholm and E. Kold Christensen, with laminated ash frame, rubber support blocks and reddish-brown leather seat pad, unmarked.

28in (71cm) wide

$4,000-6,000　　**SDR**

A pair of Poul Kjærholm PK22 chairs, with black vinyl on chrome bases.

30in (76cm) wide

$2,500-3,500　　**SDR**

A set of three 'PK71' nesting tables, by Poul Kjærholm, with square steel frames and black acrylic tops.

largest 11in (28cm) wide

$3,000-4,000　　**SDR**

A 'PK61' coffee table, by Poul Kjærholm and E. Kold Christensen, with square plate glass top inset and chrome-plated steel base, signed with stamped manufacturer's mark and "Denmark".

31.75in (80.5cm) wide

$3,500-4,500　　**SDR**

A Philip & Kelvin Laverne bronze coffee table, with verdigris patina, depicting an Asian scene with pagoda, signed "Philip Kelvin Laverne."

54in (137cm) long

$6,000-8,000   SDR

A rare Philip & Kelvin Laverne "Tao" bronze dining table etched with an Asian village scene sparsely colored with red, yellow, blue and green paint, signed "Philip and Kelvin Laverne."

84in (213cm) long

$10,000-15,000   SDR

A Philip & Kelvin Laverne pedestal table, decorated with an Asian courtyard scene in bronze and pewter with enameled details, top artist signed.

47in (119.5cm) diam

$7,000-10,000   SDR

A Philip & Kelvin Laverne oval coffee table, its top decorated with Asian figures against a brass, pewter, and enameled patina, top signed "Philip Kelvin Laverne."

66in (167.5cm) long

$5,000-6,000   SDR

A Paul McCobb Planner Group dining table, cylindrical canted legs, with two additional table boards.

29in (73.5cm) high

$500-700   FRE

A Paul McCobb Planner Group desk, fitted with three small, one long drawer and file drawer.

20.25in (51.5cm) high

$400-600   FRE

A 1950s Paul McCobb maple sideboard, with two sliding doors concealing four drawers and single shelf, on flared leg base, unmarked.

60in (152.5cm) wide

$800-1,200   SDR

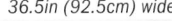

A Paul McCobb for Winchendon four-drawer jewelry chest, with segmented drawer fronts and small brass knob pulls, unmarked.

c1950   *36.5in (92.5cm) wide*

$700-1,000   SDR

A Paul McCobb side table, the circular top with small brass inlay to center, on pedestal base with three canted legs, unmarked.

22in (56cm) diam

$700-1,000   SDR

A rare Paul McCobb for Arbuck wrought-iron dining table, with cat's cradle stretcher beneath a plate glass top, unmarked.

59.5in (151cm) wide

$3,000-4,000   SDR

A Paul McCobb two-piece open shelving unit, of brass rods with white enameled wooden shelves, unmarked.

76in (193cm) high

$1,000-1,500   SDR

A Paul McCobb three-seat armless sofa, with woven fabric upholstery in black, brown, beige and white, on tapering wood legs, unmarked.

80in (203cm) long

$700-1,000   SDR

A James Mont nightstand, with black matte finish, and three drawers with combed fronts and circular gilt wood pulls, unmarked.

25.25in (64cm) high

$1,500-2,000   SDR

A James Mont pair of pickled oak bookmatched end tables, with carved medallions and gold finish, each marked "James Mont Design".

20.5in (52cm) wide

$10,000-15,000   SDR

A James Mont three-door cabinet, with red enameled finish and large brass drop-pulls, three interior drawers and single shelf.

60in (152.5cm) wide

$10,000-15,000   SDR

A James Mont ebonized dresser, with two drawers and doors, carved and painted bamboo details in silver leaf, with painted ring pulls.

96in (244cm) wide

$7,000-10,000   SDR

A James Mont sideboard, with two doors and carved pulls.

72in (162cm) wide

$3,000-4,000   SDR

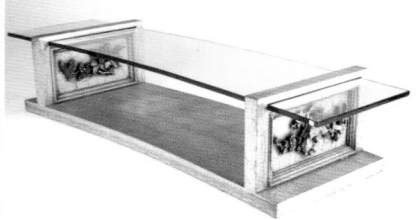

A James Mont silver-painted coffee table with curved glass insert top.

78in (198cm) wide

$6,000-9,000   SDR

A George Nakashima conoid chair, with hickory spindles and walnut saddle seat, marked with owner's name under seat.

c1969   *35.5in (90cm) high*

$8,000-12,000   SK

A George Nakashima walnut chair, with curved crest rail over hickory spindles joined to walnut saddle seat on cantilevered legs, accompanied by original receipt.

c1982

$12,000-15,000   SK

A 20thC George Nakashima massive walnut conoid lounge chair, with a wide low seat and a tall, slightly curved spindle back.

34in (86.5cm) wide

$12,000-15,000   FRE

A George Nakashima walnut lounge chair, with single free-edge writing arm, spindled back, and saddle seat, on tapering dowel legs, unmarked.

32.5in (82.5cm) high

$7,000-15,000   SDR

A pair of 20thC George Nakashima walnut 'Mira' stools, spindle-back with shaped tri-corner seat, cylindrical tapering legs conjoined by t-form stretcher with footrest.

33.75in (85.5cm) high

$4,000-6,000   FRE

Part of a George Nakashima set of six grass-seated chairs, with curved rail.

c1957   *27in (68.5cm) high*

$10,000-15,000 SET   SK

A George Nakashima walnut conoid bench, free edge seat with butterfly joint and applied with shaped spindles for the backrest.

c1975   *84in (213cm) wide*

$45,000-55,000   **FRE**

A George Nakashima walnut table, with free edge jutting over median shelf with wide board sides, accompanied by copy of original sketch by George Nakashima.

1976   *21in (54.25cm) wide*

$20,000-30,000   **SK**

A CLOSER LOOK AT A GEORGE NAKASHIMA TABLE

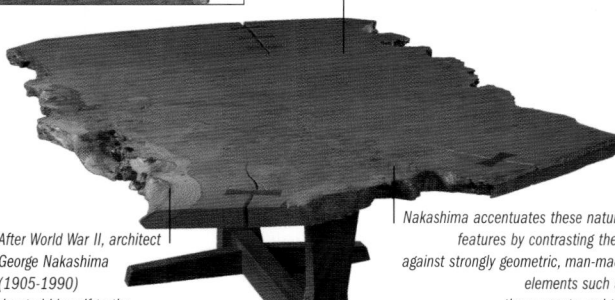

The dramatic natural, unfinished edge is typical of his work, as is the rich color and focus on the burls.

Nakashima chose his wood carefully, ensuring each piece would exemplify the natural beauty of wood – this is a particularly large and successful example.

After World War II, architect George Nakashima (1905-1990) devoted himself to the creation of unique wooden furniture from his studio in New Hope, Pennsylvania.

Nakashima accentuates these natural features by contrasting them against strongly geometric, man-made elements such as the supports and the inlaid butterfly joints.

A large George Nakashima walnut table, with free edge burl walnut top on two canted supports joined by cross stretchers balanced by two perpendicular supports.

87in (221cm) wide

$200,000-300,000   **SK**

A George Nakashima coffee table, the thick Tiger's eye maple burl top on a walnut 'Minguren I' base.

1988   *59in (150cm) long*

$30,000-35,000   **FRE**

A George Nakashima walnut conoid dining table, with four butterfly joints, signed "George Nakashima, New Hope Feb. 1971".

72.5in (184cm) wide

$30,000-40,000   **SK**

A George Nakashima walnut free-edge dining table, of two panels with three butterfly joints in the center on tapering rounded legs, with original work order and bill of sale, signed.

1955   *71.5in (181.5cm) long*

$4,500-6,500   **FRE**

A George Nakashima free-edge burl walnut conoid coffee table.

75.5in (192cm) wide

$32,000-36,000   **SDR**

A late 1960s George Nakashima walnut highboy, with pinned and dovetailed case construction, and single blind drawer over six larger ones with recessed pulls, unmarked.

52.75in (134cm) high

$25,000-30,000   **SDR**

A George Nakashima walnut chest of drawers, dovetail top board over straight front, fitted with five graduated drawers, recessed bar pulls.

39in (98.5cm) high

$12,000-15,000   **FRE**

A George Nakashima walnut sideboard, with dovetailed corners, two sliding doors with burled panels and three oak sliding drawers, signed in black script "George Nakashima February 1980".

60in (152cm) wide

$12,000-18,000   SK

A George Nakashima cherry eight-drawer dresser, with pinned and dovetailed case construction, marked with original owner's name on back.

60in (152.5cm) wide

$15,000-20,000   SDR

A George Nakashima walnut plain front sideboard, with sliding doors enclosing six drawers and two shelves with dovetail edges, with original work order and bill of sale dated and signed.

1955   *72in (183cm) long*

$10,000-15,000   FRE

A George Nakashima small walnut credenza, rectangular free-edge top over twin slatted grass cloth sliding doors, cylindrical tapering legs enclosing dividers with dovetail joints at the sides.

56in (142cm) wide

$12,000-15,000   FRE

A George Nakashima cherry eight-drawer dresser, with pinned and dovetailed case construction, marked with original owner's name on back.

60in (152.5cm) wide

$18,000-20,000   SDR

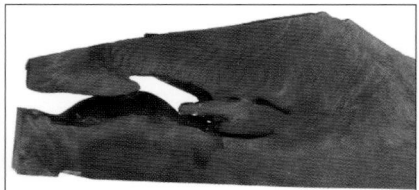

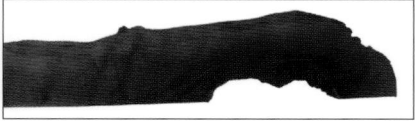

A George Nakashima walnut double pedestal desk, with single-board, free-edge top, single rosewood butterfly key, and six drawers, the top marked with original owner's name.

65in (165cm) wide

$30,000-35,000   SDR

A late 1960s George Nakashima walnut free-standing rectangular mirror, with overhanging and beveled top rail, exposed tenons along top and sides, unmarked.

From the original owner, accompanied by signed and dated pencil sketch.

36in (91.5cm) high

$10,000-15,000   SDR

A rare and unusual George Nakashima walnut music stand, with a free-form top on an adjustable rectangular shaft and geometric base, signed "George Nakashima, Jan 1976".

1976   *58in (147.5cm) high*

$45,000-55,000   FRE

A George Nakashima walnut free-form wall-hanging shelf, marked with original owner's name along back edge.

119.75in (304cm) long

$20,000-25,000   SDR

A George Nelson for Herman Miller ebonized cabinet, with single door, two interior shelves, and three drawers, all with chrome knob pulls, on plank-leg base, Herman Miller foil label.

29.75in (75.5cm) wide

$900-1,200   **SDR**

A George Nelson for Herman Miller thin edge rosewood veneer credenza with three doors, four drawers, and chrome pulls.

80in (203cm) wide

$4,000-6,000   **SDR**

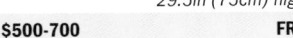

A George Nelson for Herman Miller white and yellow laminated chest, of three drawers.

29.5in (75cm) high

$500-700   **FRE**

A George Nelson for Herman Miller white yellow and orange laminated cabinet, fitted with single drawer and twin sliding doors.

29.5in (75cm) high

$500-700   **FRE**

A George Nelson coconut chair with ottoman, upholstered in red wool.

33in (84cm) wide

$5,000-7,000   **SDR**

A George Nelson for Herman Miller Primavera chest of drawers, no. 4620, with mahogany finish and metal tag.

1962   *39.5in (100.5cm) wide*

$900-1,200   **SK**

A George Nelson for Herman Miller Primavera bedroom suite, comprising two chests with metal tags, two headboards and a night stand, wear, one pull broken.

c1962   *Chest 39.5in (100.5cm) wide*

$2,000-3,000   **SK**

A George Nelson for Herman Miller swag-leg desk, with white laminate top, painted cubby dividers, wood veneer frame and chrome legs, Herman Miller label.

39in (99cm) wide

$6,000-9,000   **SDR**

Two George Nelson for Herman Miller planter end tables, with two lamps, composite top and drawer, label on drawer interior.

45.5in (115.5cm) wide

$1,200-1,500   **SK**

A George Nelson for Herman Miller 'Sling' sofa, with dark brown leather upholstery on tubular polished chrome frame, embossed mark.

85.75in (218cm) wide

$2,000-3,000   **SDR**

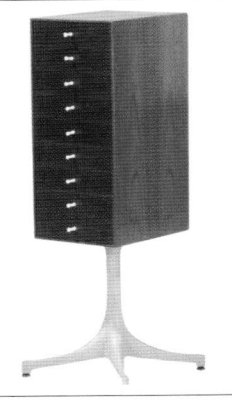

A George Nelson for Herman Miller rosewood jewelry chest on enameled metal pedestal, with white ceramic pulls.

38in (97cm) high

$12,000-15,000   **SDR**

MODERN DESIGN

A Tommi Parzinger for Parzinger Originals extension dining table, with parquetry inlay to mahogany top, and brass details to feet, includes two 18in leaves in storage rack, marked "Parzinger Originals".

closed 72in (183cm) long

$10,000-15,000   SDR

A Tommi Parzinger for Charak dining table, with inset parquetry top in an ebonized frame, includes two 18in leaves, stored underneath.

closed 66in (167.5cm) wide

$2,000-4,000   SDR

A Tommi Parzinger for Charak coffee table, inset with four beige marble slabs, paper label "This piece was handmade in the workshops of Charak, Bolton, Mass", with model number and date.

38in (96.5cm) diam

$2,000-3,000   SDR

A Handsome sofa, attributed to Ico Parisi, reupholstered in tufted black vinyl, black metal legs and brass feet, unmarked.

c1955   *65.5in (166cm) wide*

$1,200-1,800   SDR

A Tommi Parzinger four poster mahogany king size bed with original receipt.

85in (216cm) wide

$20,000-30,000   SDR

A Charlotte Perriand console table, with a rectangular blonde-wood top on double-pedestal base of black enameled iron, unmarked.

c1958   *59in (150cm) wide*

$2,000-3,000   SDR

A Charlotte Perriand rectangular pine table, with black enameled metal base.

61.5in (156cm) wide

$2,000-3,000   SDR

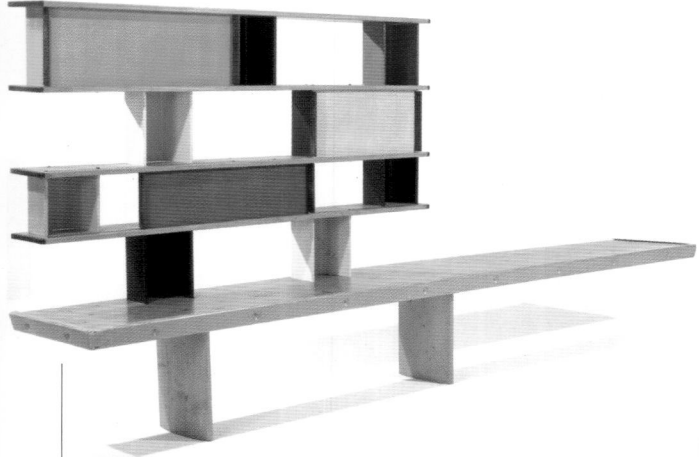

A Charlotte Perriand and Jean Prouve bibliotheque, with enameled aluminum and pine shelving unit on pine long bench.

1953   *138in (351cm) wide*

$90,000-120,000   SDR

A Charlotte Perriand pine lighted wardrobe, with single sliding door enclosing interior shelves with drawers.

68in (173cm) high

$5,000-7,000   SDR

An American Gaetano Pesce black and white 'Nobody's Chair', comprised of panels of colored polyurethane based elastic resin clipped together, painted on the inside "05/09/02".

2002   *35in (88cm) high*

$700-1,000   **GM**

An Italian Zero Disegno limited edition 'Nobody's Chair' for Etro, comprised of panels of colored polyurethane based elastic resin inlaid with Etro design silk fragments, and with random coloring clipped together, numbered on the inside "08/99", designed by Gaetano Pesce.

2004   *35in (88cm) high*

$1,500-2,000   **GM**

An Italian limited edition Bernini 'Broadway 6' chair, with thermochromatic plastic seat mounted on a tubular metal frame with nine sprung feet, numbered 0080 from an edition of 1,000, designed by Gaetano Pesce.

This chair was available in blue, red or black, with the color changing slightly with the heat of the sitter. The sprung feet give a pleasant 'cushioned' and rocking feeling.

2001   *29.5in (75cm) high*

$1,000-1,500   **GM**

A pair of Gaetano Pesce armchairs, upholstered in red and green plush cotton.

34in (86cm) high

$3,000-4,000   **SDR**

A Gaetano Pesce poured resin Waffle table, from the office of the Chiat-Day advertising agency.

44.5in (113cm) wide

$10,000-15,000   **SDR**

A Gaetano Pesce for Nobody's 'Nobody's Low Round Side Table', comprised of panels of red and clear colored polyurethane based elastic resin clipped together, painted "23.7.02", designed by Gaetano Pesce.

2002   *19.5in (49cm) high*

$500-700   **GM**

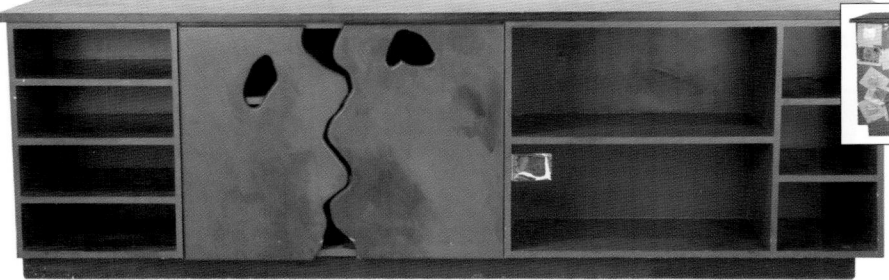

A Gaetano Pesce painted sideboard, with two carved doors, shelving space, back affixed with paper flyers.

96in (244cm) wide

$5,000-7,000   **SDR**

A Harvey Probber eight-drawer jewelry chest, with knob pulls and ebonized oak case, unmarked.

36.5in (92cm) high

$3,000-4,000 SDR

A Harvey Probber cabinet, with two doors, on ebonized frame with brass-capped feet, with Probber metal tag.

54.5in (138cm) wide

$1,000-1,500 SDR

A Harvey Probber special order wall unit, interior fitted for bar, with tambour doors originally designed for a television and caned panel sliding doors fitted for shelves, with copy of original buyer's receipt.

This unit in situ was originally tension mounted, floating on a wall opposite a sofa. This piece would be expensive to reproduce by today's standards.

1967 *133in (338cm) wide*

$3,000-4,000 SK

A Harvey Probber pair of ten-sided end tables, each with single drawer over cabinet door concealing two shelves, with Probber metal tag.

24in (61cm) wide

$5,000-7,000 SDR

Two Harvey Probber bent mirror aluminum and upholstered armchairs, paper label, with copy of original buyer's receipt.

c1969 *27.5in (70cm) wide*

$5,000-7,000 SK

A Harvey Probber single-drawer desk, with bleached African rosewood top on mahogany legs.

Provenance: Commissioned for President Lyndon B. Johnson in 1968 and accompanied by a notarized letter of provenance from a former Probber designer.

98.5in (250cm) wide

$10,000-15,000 SDR

A Gilbert Rohde for Herman Miller double-pedestal Paldao desk, with exotic wood veneer, over a pull-out shelf and six drawers, the case with tacked-on green leatherette details, stenciled number.

56.5in (143cm) wide

$3,500-4,500 SDR

A Gilbert Rohde for Herman Miller vanity, in contrasting woods, with plate glass top raised over a bank of three drawers with horizontal pulls, stenciled "3626" on back.

52.5in (133cm) wide

$1,600-2,000 SDR

A Gilbert Rhode 'All in One chest', with breakfront top unit on lower base unit fitted with pigeonholes flanked by open compartments over drawers, two side doors, American Ash Group "no 4021, 4020".

52in (132cm) wide

$2,000-3,000 SK

A Gilbert Rohde for Herman Miller tiger maple veneer tier table, from Palladio group serial no. 41-83 with square top on bottom tier with diagonal divide on tapered legs.

43in (109cm) wide

$1,000-1,500 SK

A Karl Springer three-drawer desk, the top covered in dyed and lacquered parchment veneer, with V-shaped back, on ebonized wood supports, signed on drawer.

29.25 (74.5cm) wide

$5,000-7,000   SDR

A Karl Springer occasional table, covered in a lacquered batik finish.

26in (66cm) wide

$3,000-4,000   SDR

A Karl Springer massive coffee table, covered in tortoiseshell, horn and bone inlay.

70.5in (179cm) wide

$3,000-4,000   SDR

A Karl Springer three-legged coffee table, covered in snakeskin.

Formerly in the Imelda Marcos collection.

40in (101.5cm) diam

$20,000-25,000   SDR

A Karl Springer coffee table, with lacquered and dyed parchment finish, on plinth base, unmarked.

48in (122cm) wide

$2,000-3,000   SDR

A Karl Springer set of four steel barstools, with leather upholstered seats.

29in (73.5cm) high

$7,000-10,000   SDR

A Hans Wegner 'Papa Bear' chair, with tufted orange wool upholstery, exposed teak armrests, and flaring dowel legs, unmarked.

38.75in (98.5cm) wide

$1,500-2,000   SDR

A pair of Hans Wegner for Johannes Hansen 'The Chair' sculpted dining chairs, unmarked.

29.75in (75.5cm) high

$6,000-8,000   SDR

A Hans Wegner for Getama teak daybed, with new ivory fabric upholstery, on tapered legs, Getama mark.

77in (195.5cm) wide

$2,000-3,000   SDR

A Hans Wegner three-piece child's set, 'Peter's Table and Chairs', the table with keyed-through tenons, the chairs with oval cut-out to sides, black FDB stamp mark.

Wegner designed these pieces to mark the birth of Borge Mogensen's son, Peter. The chairs come apart and can be easily re-assembled by a child, without the use of tools. The FDB stamp mark on each piece indicates an early manufacturing co-op that Wegner was associated with before becoming commercially successful.

c1959   Chairs 19in (48cm) high

$2,000-3,000   SDR

A Hans Wegner for Andreas Tuck teak drop-leaf table, with on X-leg base, branded mark.

closed 50.5in (128cm) wide

$4,000-6,000   SDR

A rare Edward Wormley for Dunbar Oregan pine server, with two drawers over sliding doors concealing shelves, on tapering legs, Dunbar metal tag.

70.75in (180cm) wide

$4,000-6,000　　　　　　　**SDR**

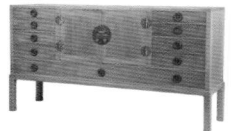

An Edward Wormley for Dunbar sideboard, with eight drawers flanking a two-door cabinet with interior glass tray and shelf, over a linen drawer, all with brass hardware, unmarked.

70in (178cm) wide

$5,000-7,000　　　　　　　**SDR**

An Edward Wormley for Dunbar walnut and mahogany sideboard, with wooden drop pulls and brass backplates and two interior shelves, brass Dunbar tag.

65in (165cm) wide

$10,000-15,000　　　　　　　**SDR**

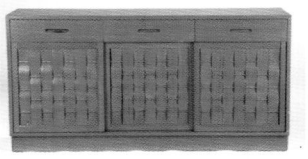

An Edward Wormley for Dunbar walnut and brass sideboard, no. 4469, the interior with six drawers and two shelves, detached Dunbar factory tag.

61.5in (156cm) wide

$3,500-4,500　　**SDR**

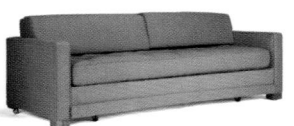

An Edward Wormley custom-designed sofa/trundle bed, with brown mini-check fabric upholstery, wooden block legs to front and brass casters to back, unmarked.

1957　　　*90in (228.5cm) wide*

$3,500-4,500　　**SDR**

An Edward Wormley for Dunbar pair of Janus lounge chairs, upholstered in pink and gold fabric, Dunbar metal tags.

27in (68.5cm) high

$5,000-6,000　　**SDR**

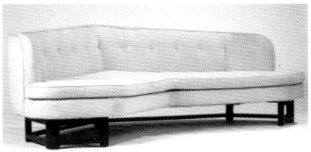

An Edward Wormley for Dunbar corner sofa, upholstered in its original ivory fabric, on wood base, fabric label.

101in (256.5cm) long

$4,500-5,500　　**SDR**

An Edward Wormley for Dunbar pair of brass and rosewood occasional tables, with original smoked glass tops, brass "D" tags.

27.5in (70cm) diam

$7,000-10,000　　**SDR**

An Edward Wormley for Dunbar walnut Longjohn bench, with center drawer, green Dunbar tag.

72in (183cm) long

$2,000-3,000　　**SDR**

An Edward Wormley for Dunbar birch and walnut magazine tree table, with middle supported five graduated shelves, metal label for Dunbar Berne Indiana.

24in (61cm) high

$3,500-4,500　　**SK**

An Edward Wormley three-tier trolley, on casters.

29.5in (75cm) high

$400-600　　**FRE**

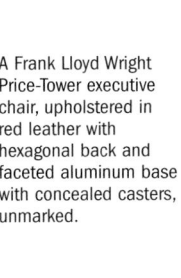

A Frank Lloyd Wright Price-Tower executive chair, upholstered in red leather with hexagonal back and faceted aluminum base with concealed casters, unmarked.

A pair of Frank Lloyd Wright dining chairs, with canted crestrails, plank sides, and drop-in seat, and set of three drawings, drawings marked "Frank Lloyd Wright/Architect/1950".

32.5in (82.5cm) high

$5,000-7,000   **SDR**

A Frank Lloyd Wright metal occasional table, unmarked.

This is smaller than most Biltmore tables and most likely is a prototype.

26in (66cm) wide

$3,000-4,000   **SDR**

A Dunbar lounge chair, with emerald green upholstery on dark-stained wood base, unmarked.

36.5in (92.5cm) high

$600-900   **SDR**

36in (91cm) high

$15,000-20,000   **SDR**

A pair of Dunbar leather chairs, on ebonized wood frames with brass "D" tags.

35in (89cm) high

$4,000-6,000   **SDR**

A Dunbar three-seat sofa, with oak trim to sides, fully upholstered in tan velvet, marked Dunbar on decking, with factory tag.

86in (218.5cm) wide

$1,500-2,000   **SDR**

A Dunbar table, with inset parquetry top, and single drawer, on ebonized frame, Dunbar metal tag.

54in (137cm) wide

$700-1,000   **SDR**

A Dunbar conference table, in walnut with ebonized trim, Dunbar D tag.

May be configured into multiple tables or as one larger unit.

157in (354cm) length

$8,000-10,000   **SDR**

A Dunbar circular coffee table, with inset glass top, and lower shelf, in dark brown finish, brass "D" tag.

40in (101.5cm) diam

$700-1,000   **SDR**

A Dunbar sideboard with three drawers, one cabinet door and one tambour door, brass pulls and brass base.

73in (185cm) wide

$8,000-10,000   **SDR**

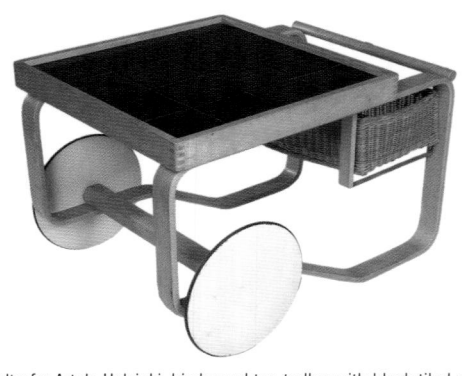

An Alvar Aalto for Artek, Helsinki, birchwood tea trolley, with black tiled panel top, above a wicker basket with continuous bentwood support, the painted wheels with rubber rims.

Aalto produced two designs for similar trolleys. The first, without the wicker basket, was designed in 1936 and first exhibited at the Milan Triennial of that year. The second, as above, was first exhibited the next year at the Paris World Fair.

c1937   35.75in (91cm) long

$2,000-3,000   **L&T**

An Alvar Aalto lounge chair, with closed loop birch frame with blue fabric upholstery, unmarked.

c1950   28in (71cm) high

$2,500-3,500   **SK**

A pair of early Alvar Aalto birch three drawer chests.

36in (91cm) wide

$8,000-10,000   **SDR**

An Eero Aarnio/Asko 'Ball' chair, with red fiberglass shell and lavender fabric-upholstered interior, on swivel base of red enameled metal, unmarked.

48in (122cm) high

$1,500-2,000   **SDR**

A small Jacques Adnet revolving two-tier gueridon, with black leather-covered surfaces on an enameled steel frame with brass accents and ball feet, unmarked.

12.25in (31cm) wide

$5,000-7,000   **SDR**

A Jacques Adnet valet, covered in leather.

43in (109cm) high

$5,000-6,000   **SDR**

A pair of Ron Arad for One Off Pair of 'Rover' chairs, with black leather upholstery on tubular steel frame with dark gray enameling, marked "One Off".

This notable design is typical of the 1980s fad for commenting on consumerism by recycling and using objets trouvés. Here, an old car seat is combined with what looks like scaffolding poles.

35in (89cm) high

$15,000-20,000   **SDR**

An Andre Arbus sycamore veneer console table with semi-circular top with lower shelf, ormolu mounts.

33in (84cm) high

$5,000-7,000   **SDR**

An Archizoom Associati/Poltronova Modular Safari sofa, with white fiberglass frame, upholstered in red and purple fabric, unmarked.

102in (259cm) wide

$7,000-10,000   **SDR**

A pair of wrought-iron demi-lune console tables, designed by Oscar Bach, with black marble tops and reticulated aprons with Renaissance mask motifs, unmarked.

25.5in (65cm) wide

$3,000-4,000   **SDR**

A pair of Baker ebonized lounge chairs, with windowpane backs and woven oatmeal-colored upholstery, "Baker" metal tags.

28.5in (72cm) high

$2,000-3,000 SDR

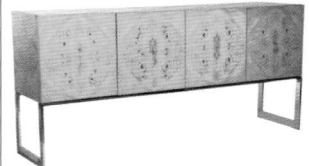

A Milo Baughman four-door buffet, in burlwood veneer, the interior with single shelf and two tray-style drawers, on an angular polished steel base, inspection tag on base.

1972 *72in (183cm) wide*

$3,000-4,000 SDR

A Milo Baughman for Thayer Coggin wood console table, inlaid with two polished brass bands, Thayer Coggin tag.

60in (152.5cm) wide

$800-1,200 SDR

A Gary Knox Bennet large steel console table, with mottled brown patina on metal leg, marked "In Oakland/GKB/Anno/'92".

39.35in (99.5cm) high

$4,000-5,000 SDR

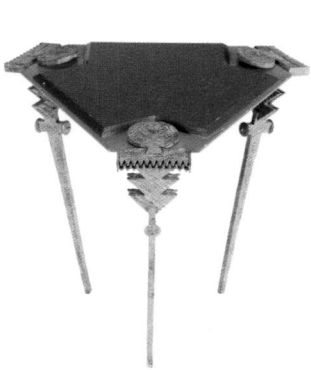

A Gary Knox Bennet 'Table #8', in patinated bronze with arrow-shaped top, on three tapered legs, unmarked.

19in (48cm) high

$2,500-3,000 SDR

A Post Design 'Sgaboo' multicolored solid foam rubber and plastic stool, designed by Markus Benesch.

2005 *17.5in (44cm) high*

$500-700 GM

A Samson Berman special-order single-pedestal desk, in walnut with champagne formica top and mother of pearl handles, accompanied by a shelf and a desk chair upholstered in white naugahyde, with original invoice, unmarked.

1962 *desk 65in (165cm) wide*

$1,000-1,500 SDR

A pair of Samson Berman special-order walnut chests, each with a champagne formica top, with mother-of-pearl inlay to handles, on brass base, with original invoice, unmarked.

1962 *60in (152.5cm) wide*

$1,500-1,800 SDR

A late 20thC Bernini rosewood desk, with fitted compartment and drawers, labeled.

51in (129.5cm) wide

$4,500-6,500 SK

A rare Harry Bertoia child's chair.

21.75in (55cm) high

$450-650 MG

An Osvaldo Borsani for Techno L77 single adjustable bed, on iron frame with red fabric upholstery, Techno labels.

76in (193cm) long

$6,000-9,000 SDR

A Osvaldo Borsani mahogany cabinet, with ribbed doors with brass pulls hiding two interior shelves, standing on brass capped legs.

55in (140cm) wide

$7,000-9,000 SDR

A two seat teak and ash settee, with gray upholstered padded back and seat on teak frame with curved arms, stretchers, tapered legs, branded mark for Bovirke Cabinetmakers.

1953   *51in (129.5cm) wide*

$1,000-1,500   **SK**

A 1960s Marcel Breuer for Gavina reclining chair, with bright red upholstery to undulated seat on laminated and bentwood blonde-wood frame, unmarked.

49in (124.5cm) wide

$1,500-2,000   **SDR**

A pair of Andy Buck 'Lounge Lizards' chairs, with sleigh-shaped frames in ebonized mahogany and burgundy wool upholstery, unmarked.

1999   *38in (96.5cm) high*

$5,000-6,000   **SDR**

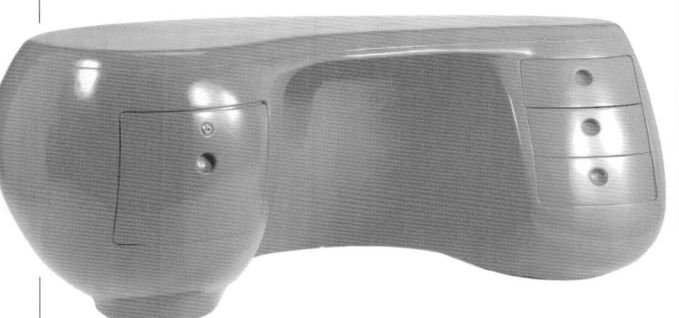

A Maurice Calka for Leleu-Deshay rare 'Boomerang' desk, of biomorphic form in orange fiberglass, its four drawers with circular recessed pulls, unmarked.

70in (178cm) wide

$10,000-15,000   **SDR**

Two of a set of four side dining chairs, by Franco Campo and Carlo Graffi, with shaped high backs, flaring wooden legs with black sabers and red leather upholstery, unmarked.

19.25in (49cm) wide

$15,000-20,000 SET   **SDR**

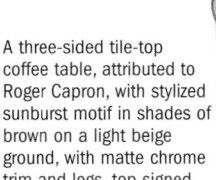

A three-sided tile-top coffee table, attributed to Roger Capron, with stylized sunburst motif in shades of brown on a light beige ground, with matte chrome trim and legs, top signed illegibly.

35in (89cm) wide

$2,500-3,000   **SDR**

A Roger Capron coffee table, its top with geometrically shaped tiles covered in ocher, green, brown, black, and ivory crackled glazes, on black iron base, artist-signed.

47.75in (121cm) wide

$4,000-5,000   **SDR**

Eight late 20thC Cassina red leather armchairs, Italy, with cushion seat and ball feet, manufacturer's label.

33in (84cm) high

$2,000-2,500   **SK**

A Sandro Chia cast bronze 'Sedia' chair with verdigris patination, in an edition of 25 pieces.

1989   *37.75in (92cm) high*

$6,000-8,000   **GM**

A Michael Coffey 'Serpent' biomorphic coffee table, of Bubinga wood with plate glass insert along the top, on cantilevered base with Lucite plank support, incised "M. Coffey".

1989   *57in (145cm) wide*

$20,000-30,000   **SDR**

A CLOSER LOOK AT A SANDRO CHIA TABLE

Italian artist, Sandro Chia was a part of the Neo-Expressionist 'Transvanguardia' art movement. The swirling, nature-inspired form of the base has echoes of his oil paintings.

The unusual cast bronze base is shaped to form the letters in his surname.

Chia's pieces have been exhibited in a number of major museums, such as the Museum of Modern Art in Paris. This status increases the desirability of his furniture.

This table is from a limited edition of just 25 pieces increasing the rarity and desirability.

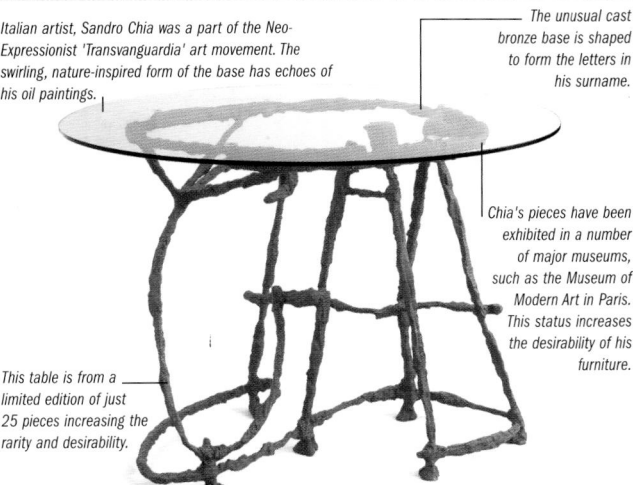

A limited edition Italian cast bronze 'Tavolo' table, with with verdigris patination, glass top, designed by Sandro Chia.

1989   *31.5in (80cm) high*

$12,000-18,000   **GM**

A Jonathan Cohen Studio Furniture chest on stand, with concave doors, signed "Jonathan Jacob Cohen. Stephen Barney".

42in (106.5cm) wide

$4,000-6,000   **SK**

A Joe Colombo for Stendig "Elda" chair, in bright yellow fiberglass with red military wool upholstery, Stendig label.

37.25in (94.5cm) high

$2,000-4,000   **SDR**

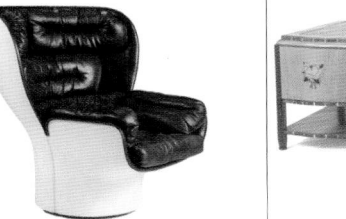

A Joe Colombo 'Elda' chair with black leather upholstery on white fiberglass swivel frame, upholstery in as-found condition, unmarked.

38in (97cm) high

$1,000-1,500   **SDR**

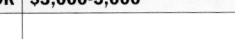

A Rene Crevel for Krieger mahogany and fruitwood partners' desk, the top lined in brown leather, four cabinet doors inlaid with roses, over two shelves, on reeded quarter-column legs.

c1925   *69.5in (176.5cm) wide*

$3,000-5,000   **SDR**

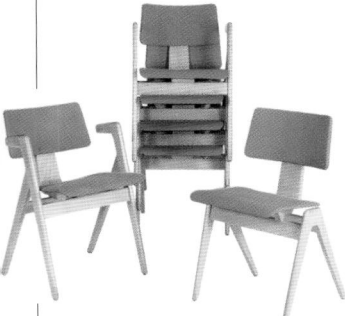

A Robin Day set of six blonde wood chairs, with emerald green vinyl upholstery, unmarked.

29.75in (75.5cm) high

$700-1,000   **SDR**

An Italian Memphis, Milan 'Kristall' table, patterned laminated wood and plastic covered steel, designed by Michele de Lucchi.

A highly popular Postmodern design, this plays on a number of themes key to the movement. These include the use of different materials, surface decoration, bright colors and an unusual form – which in this case almost looks like a four-legged animal.

1981   *19.75in (50cm) high*

$1,000-1,500   **GM**

A Donald Deskey dining table, with black formica top on chrome base, formica label.

60in (152cm) wide

$9,000-12,000   **SDR**

MODERN DESIGN

A Donald Deskey painted mahogany four-drawer dresser, in green and ivory with chrome detailing.

72in (183cm) high

$1,000-1,500   **SDR**

A Danish teak and fabric chair with ottoman, by Povi Dinesen, with tall back with shaped wood arm rests raised on tapered cylindrical legs, matching ottoman with cut-out carrying handles, cabinet maker's mark to base.

c1960   *41in (104cm) high*

$2,000-3,000   **SK**

A Canadian A. J. Donahue coconut-style lounge chair, with original beige pile upholstery on dark brown bent plywood frame, with flared metal legs, unmarked.

29.25in (74.5cm) high

$2,000-3,000   **SDR**

A French Charles Douduy dining table, with broad rectangular top, and leaf extensions at either end, unmarked.

closed 67.5in (171cm) wide

$700-1,000   **SDR**

A Dorothy Draper for Heritage three-drawer dresser, in black and gold finish with circular brass pulls, and matching wall-hanging mirror, dresser marked "Heritage".

31.5in (80cm) wide

$2,000-3,000   **SDR**

A John Dunnigan cherry and mahogany billiards table, with slate top, black leather pockets and green rayon tassels, includes seven pool cues and a bridge, signed "John Dunnigan #9215".

1993   *100.5in (255cm) long*

$12,000-18,000   **SDR**

A German Fabricus & Kastholm for Alfred Kill set of six dining armchairs, with brown hard leather upholstery on three-legged swivel metal base with ball casters, unmarked.

1965   *36.5in (92.5cm) high*

$15,000-20,000   **SDR**

A pair of rare Fabricus & Kastholm ottomans, with channeled mahogany leather upholstery on polished chrome frame, unmarked.

28.5in (72.5cm) high

$4,000-6,000   **SDR**

One of a pair of Grant Featherston B210 armchairs, manufactured by Emerson Brothers, Australia, with timber frame and brown mottled upholstery.

c1956

$3,000-4,000 PAIR

A Grant Featherston R160 Contour armchair, designed c1953, manufactured by Emerson Brothers, Australia; timber frame, gray mottled upholstery, restored.

$1,500-2,000

One of three Grant Featherston A310H dining chairs, designed c1953 manufactured by Emerson Brothers, Australia; timber frames with pink upholstery.

$2,000-3,000 SET   **SHA**

A Thomas Hucker console table, of Pau Ferro and wenge woods, anodized aluminum and steel, the slatted top wrapped with waxed linen lashing, with opening invitation for Hucker's one-man show at the Peter Joseph Galley, depicting the console, unmarked.

$5,000-9,000   **SDR**

A Marshall Fields three-seat 1800 sofa, with walnut frame, gold brocade upholstery, and ball casters.
1964   *102in (259cm) long*

$12,000-18,000   **SDR**

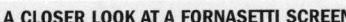
A CLOSER LOOK AT A FORNASETTI SCREEN

Piero Fornasetti's love of surface ornamentation caused shockwaves in a design context that promoted rational and unadorned forms.

Disregarded by his contemporaries, his work was popular with the buying public in the 1950s, and began to undergo a renaissance in the 1980s. Today his pieces are sought after and valuable.

Motifs were usually taken from the Classical Roman and Greek world.

Patterns were applied by lithographed transfers, often in black or gold on a white background.

A Piero Fornasetti three-panel room screen, the front decorated with an ancient Roman cityscape in black and cream, the back covered in red lacquered finish, on casters, unmarked.

each panel 53.25in (135cm) wide   **SDR**

$4,500-6,500   **SDR**

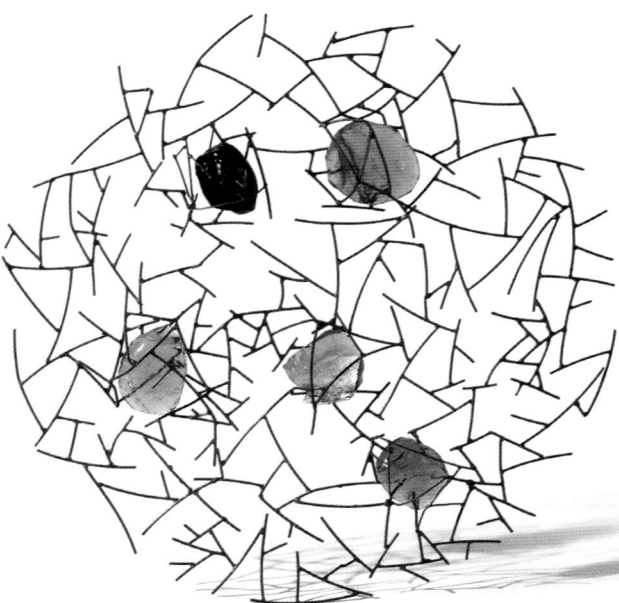

A large circular steel wire screen, embedded with pieces of molten glass, by Claire Falkenstein, unmarked.

35.5in (90cm) diam

$30,000-40,000   **SDR**

A Piero Fornasetti small side table, decorated with classically rendered portraits of a man and woman in profile, in black and white on mottled green ground over corsetted brass tripod base, marked with label, "Fornasetti/Made in Italy".

22in (56cm) diam

$1,500-2,000   **SDR**

A Piero Fornasetti three-panel folding screen, one side decorated with musical instruments, the other with postcards and floral bouquets in polychrome.

each panel 19.5in (49.5cm) wide

$4,500-5,500   **SDR**

A Piero Fornasetti four-panel screen, decorated with hot air balloons, on casters, marked "Fornasetti Milano, Made in Italy".

each panel 19.5in (49.5cm) wide

$10,000-15,000   **SDR**

MODERN DESIGN

A large coffee table, attributed to Tsuguharu Foujita, of burl walnut, satinwood and sycamore, the center inlaid with assorted motifs in rare woods and ivory, on ivory sabot feet.

20.25in (51cm) wide

$4,000-6,000 SDR

A Paul Frankl long coffee table, with overhanging rectangular top of brown laminated cork, raised on angular base with dark brown finish, unmarked.

22in (56cm) wide

$1,500-2,500 SDR

A Paul Frankl Skyscraper armchair, with silver-leaf frame with scalloped base, upholstered in navy blue and silver fabric.

28in (71cm) wide

$2,500-3,500 SDR

A pair of Paul Frankl-style lounge chairs and an ottoman, in chartreuse velvet upholstery.

Chairs 31.5in (80cm) wide

$6,000-9,000 SDR

A Pedro Friedeberg Butterfly chair, with human head and feet, the seat painted with Op Art designs on red painted base, signed "PEDRO FRIEDEBERG".

20in (51cm) wide

$12,000-18,000 SDR

A Jeffrey Greene solid walnut rocking chair, with corseted spindles all around a sculptural single-plank seat, signed "Jeffrey Greene/1992/I".

1992 *48in (122cm) high*

$2,000-3,000 SDR

A Jeffrey Greene large wall-hanging storage cabinet, of rosewood and walnut with interior shelves.

1981 *90in (229cm) high*

$1,500-2,000 SDR

A pair of Eileen Gray Bibendum chairs, with chrome frames upholstered in gray leather.

36in (91cm) wide

$3,000-4,000 PAIR SDR

An early 1970s Martin Grierson lounge chair, with tufted black leather upholstery, and black hard plastic grips to laminated rosewood frame, on aluminum swivel base, unmarked.

32.5in (82.5cm) high

$1,000-1,500 SDR

A Greta Magnusson Grossman walnut and black laminate cabinet, with ebonized wood pulls, on four drawers flanking a cabinet with five interior tray drawers, on black metal legs with ball feet, unmarked.

33.5in (85cm) wide

$4,000-6,000 SDR

A Grosfeld House black lacquer carved mirror and console table.

Mirror 52in (132cm) high

$5,000-7,000 SDR

A Piet Hein for Fritz Hansen occasional table, with a circular top, stamped mark and foil label.

39.5in (100.5cm) high

$1,000-1,500 SDR

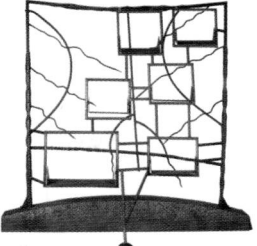

A Warren Holzman for Artists@Work (Philadelphia) sculptural welded iron wall unit, with six shelves, resting on curved base.

c1999   95.5in (241.5cm) wide

$4,000-5,000 SDR

A Michael Hurwitz painted bentwood ash rocking chaise longue.

86in (218cm) wide

$10,000-15,000 SDR

A Hvidt-Nielsen set of six teak tables, with leaf-shaped tops on tubular brass legs, one has France & Son logo with John Stuart tag.

26in (66cm) wide

$2,000-3,000 SDR

An Arne Jacobsen for Fritz Hansen Swan chair, with green fabric upholstery on seat and back on aluminum pedestal swivel base, early label on base.

1958   33in (84cm) high

$1,500-2,000 SK

An Arne Jacobsen for Fritz Hansen Swan chair, on steel swivel base with pink wool upholstery, stamped "FH", made in Denmark.

30in (76cm) wide

$1,000-1,500 SDR

An E. Jacquemin coffee table, with chrome and plate glass top and rosewood veneer base.

26.5in (67cm) diam

$4,000-5,000 SDR

One of a pair of wood armchairs, attributed to Pierre Jeanneret, the back and seat upholstered in cream colored fabric.

30in (76cm) wide

$3,000-4,000 PAIR SDR

A pair of Paul Kiss wrought-iron pedestals, with gold marble tops, stamped "P. Kiss/Paris".

38in (96.5cm) high

$35,000-45,000 SDR

A pair of Paul Kiss wrought-iron side tables, with pink marble tops, stamped "P. Kiss".

20in (51cm) diam

$20,000-24,000 SDR

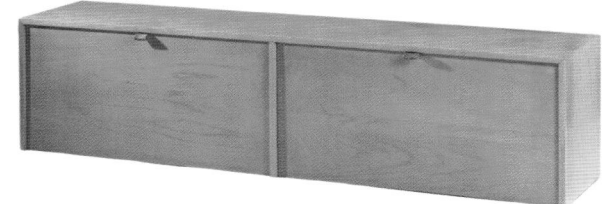

A Florence Knoll hanging cabinet, fitted with twin fall front doors with leather pulls, enclosing four sections.

72in (183cm) long

$2,000-3,000 FRE

KNOLL

- Hans Knoll founded Knoll Furniture in New York in 1938. Born in Stuttgart, Germany, he was a great admirer of the Bauhaus movement and of Modern designers such as Marcel Breuer and Ludwig Mies van der Rohe.
- Florence Schust, a talented young designer, joined the firm during WWII. She played a leading role in the company's development and in 1946, married Hans Knoll.
- The pair encouraged and worked with emerging Modernist designers and believed in crediting each by name. Eero Saarinen, Jens Risen and Harry Bertoia created key works for Knoll, and the company also acquired the rights to pieces by Breuer and van der Rohe.
- The post-war boom in architecture fueled demand for well-made modern furniture and the company thrived. Knoll also enjoyed success with its business furniture and played a significant role in revolutionising the appearance of post-war offices.
- Manufacturing was based in Pennsylvania, an area chosen for its tradition of high quality craftsmanship. In the 1950s, the company acquired property in East Greenville and continues to operate from these premises today.

A Florence Knoll for Knoll credenza, with grass doors, leather pulls and tapering legs.

72in (183cm) long

$12,000-15,000   SDR

An Alan S. Kushner custom-designed entertainment unit, executed for a designer show house, with large two door cabinet flanked by shelves, with lighting to base, unmarked.

84in (213cm) wide

$1,500-2,000   SDR

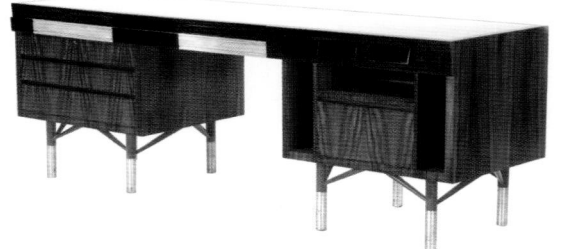

A Paul Laszlo rosewood veneer desk, with 11 drawers, white leather top on steel capped feet, Paul Laszlo metal tag.

80in (203cm) wide

$10,000-15,000   SDR

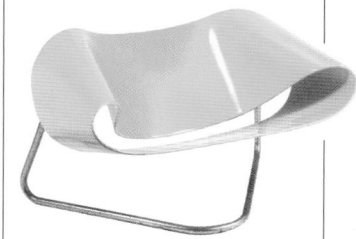

A rare Cesare Leonardi for France Stagi 'Ribbon' chair, model no. CL9, with yellow molded fiberglass seat on cantilevered base of tubular chromed steel, Fiarm label.

39.75in (101cm) wide

$1,500-2,000   SDR

One of a pair of Christian Liagre for Holly Hunt lounge chairs, in ebonized mahogany with black hard leather sling seats.

22.5in (57cm) wide

$10,000-15,000 PAIR   SDR

A Sam Maloof adjustable music stand, with cantilevered music tray on swiveling shaft.

44in (111.5cm) high

$28,000-32,000   SDR

An Italian Driade 'SOF SOF" chair, designed by Enzo Mari, with metal wire frame supporting a leather upholstered cushion.

1971   *31in (79cm) high*

$1,000-1,500   GM

An Italian Castelli 'Box' chair, designed by Enzo Mari, with injection molded polypropylene seat and back on a collapsible tubular metal frame.

1976   *32in (81cm) high*

$300-400   GM

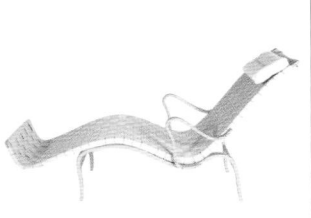

An early Bruno Mathsson for Karl Mathsson chaise longue, with oatmeal-colored webbing, and attached headrest, on laminated bentwood frame, Bruno Mathsson/Karl Mathsson labels.

53.5in (134cm) wide

$1,000-1,500   SDR

A Bruno Mathsson for Karl Mathsson 'Pernilla' lounge chair, with oatmeal-colored cotton webbing on laminated bentwood frame, Bruno Mathsson/Karl Mathsson branded marks.

43.5in (110.5cm) high

$900-1,200   SDR

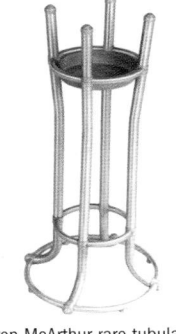

A Warren McArthur rare tubular aluminum plant stand, with integrated metal shelf, outline of McArthur decal.

30.25in (75.5cm) high

$3,500-4,500   SDR

One of a pair of Richard Meier for Knoll black lacquered barrel-back armchairs.

28in (71cm) high

$6,000-8,000 PAIR   SDR

A Borge Mogensen for Frederica Stolefabrik settee, with tan leather upholstery on wood legs, manufacturer's label, upholstery with discoloration and tears.

61.75in (157cm) wide

$2,500-3,500   SDR

A 1950s Borge Mogensen for Frederica Stolefabrik rare solid oak coffee table, stenciled number.

35.5in (90cm) wide

$1,200-1,800   SDR

A Henry Morandière walnut dining table, the top with extensions, branded maker's mark.

c1962   *84in (213cm) wide*

$2,000-3,000   SK

An Oliver Mourgue 'Djinn' two seat sofa, with colorful floral and palm motive upholstery, unmarked.

46in (117cm) wide

$2,000-3,000   SDR

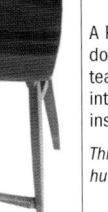

Two Jere Osgood walnut stools, unmarked.

c1970   *25in (62.5cm) high*

$2,000-3,000   SDR

A Pace rounded-edge three-door credenza, in Japanese teamo wood, with three interior shelves, Pace label inside one door.

This credenza can be wall-hung or placed on a base

72in (183cm) wide

$2,500-3,000   SDR

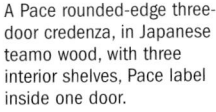

A pair of Verner Panton 1-2-3 lounge chairs, upholstered in blue boucle fabric.

33in (84cm) wide

$2,000-4,000   SDR

A Pierre Paulin for Artifort ribbon chair, covered in original Jack Lenor Larson stretch jersey fabric on a black lacquered wood base, Artifort label.

38.5in (98cm) high

$2,500-3,500   SDR

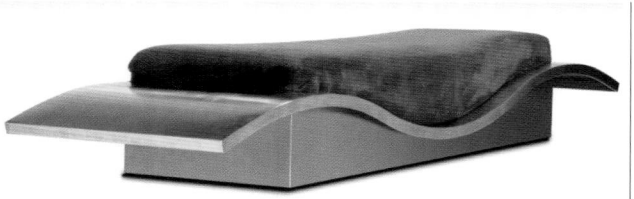

A Maria Pergay Flying Carpet daybed, in stainless steel with fabric cushion.

118in (300cm) long

$90,000-100,000　　　　**SDR**

GIO PONTI

- After graduating in 1921, Italian architect Gio Ponti (1891-1979) joined the porcelain manufacturers Richard Ginori where he developed an interest in clean modern forms adorned with elegant Neo-classical-style decoration.
- By the mid-1930s he was working on large-scale architecture commissions and later became responsible for the iconic 1956 Pirelli tower in Milan and the 1958 Alitalia offices in New York.
- Ponti's unifying approach to design also lead him to develop furniture. His believed that furniture and architecture and should be integrated and this concept reached it logical conclusion in his 'organized walls', which consisted of in-built shelving, lighting and furniture.
- His eclectic and decorative approach to design was at odds with the belief among contemporaries that modern forms should be rational and unadorned. In 1940, artist Piero Fornasetti (1913-88) began to produce patterns for his furniture.
- Perhaps his most famous work was the 1957 Superleggera (Super Light) chair, produced for Cassina, a company with whom he collaborated for several years.
- As well as furniture, Ponti exceled in other areas of commercial design, producing stage sets, glass designs and car bodies.

A Gio Ponti walnut two-drawer desk, designed for the University of Padua, with brass pulls.

55in (139.5cm) wide

$7,000-10,000　　　　**SDR**

A Jean Prouve wood and metal wardrobe, with two sliding doors ending in long vertical pulls concealing a clothes rack and two wood shelves, gold enameled metal panels and feet.

63.25in (160.5cm) high

$20,000-30,000　　　　**SDR**

A John Michael Pierson Portfolio-Review table, composed of geometric forms, a large golf tee at one end, unmarked.

Pierson is currently head of furniture design at the University of North Carolina.

1984　　　　*74in (188cm) wide*

$800-1,200　　　　**SDR**

A Warren Platner for Lehigh-Leopold two-drawer desk with leather top and chrome base.

81.5in (213cm) wide

$15,000-20,000　　　　**SDR**

A 'Supperleggera' chair, with original wicker seat, designed by Gio Ponti in 1955 and manufactured by Cassina from 1957.

32.75in (83cm) high

$700-1,000　　　　**GM**

An unusual Phillip Lloyd Powell coffee table, with two free-form planks fastened with butterfly keys and joined by ornate brass hinges, on three chip-carved plank legs with exposed tenons, unmarked.

55in (140cm) wide

$1,300-1,800　　　　**SDR**

A set of Phillip Lloyd Powell double paneled folding doors, with carved curvilinear design.

72in (183cm) high

$35,000-55,000　　　　**SDR**

A Jean Prouve wall-hanging cabinet, with single sliding door and enameled metal compartments in light yellow and royal blue, with two interior shelves, unmarked.

116.5in (256cm) long

$17,000-20,000　　　　**SDR**

A Jean Prouvé oak bench, on enameled metal frame.

56in (142cm) wide

$18,000-20,000   **SDR**

A pair of Jacques Quinet gueridon tables, with broad apron, metal sabot feet.

23.5in (60cm) high

$10,000-15,000   **SDR**

A Isokon Penguin Donkey Mark II bookcase, designed by Ernest Race, with opposed white-painted shelves on square supports.

c1963   *21in (53cm) wide*

$400-600   **L&T**

A Dieter Rams for Braun model 'MM4' hi-fi stereo unit, with teak console, including a record player, four speakers and radios, in working condition with original owner's manual.

44.5in (112.5cm) wide

$1,000-1,500   **SDR**

A Jens Risom dining table, with circular top and T-shaped legs, Jens Risom label.

28.75in (73cm) diam

$500-700   **SDR**

A T.H. Robsjohn-Gibbings for Widdicomb set of four walnut lounge chairs, with fabric upholstery.

26in (66cm) wide

$10,000-15,000   **SDR**

A John Risley wire chair and ottoman, with stylized female figure chair, with circular ottoman.

c1955

$2,000-3,000   **SK**

A Serge Roche baroque style sideboard, of oxidized mirrored panels fastened with star-shaped pegs.

100in (254cm) wide

$25,000-35,000   **SDR**

A Serge Roche Baroque style two-door cabinet, of oxidized mirrored panels with red leather.

71in (180cm) high

$35,000-45,000   **SDR**

An Eero Saarinen for Knoll 'Womb' chair and matching ottoman, with original upholstery, on black metal bases, upholstery tag to ottoman.

Chair 36in (91.5cm) high

$2,000-3,000   **SDR**

An Eliel Saarinen cabinet, with parquetry drop-front door on both sides, concealing a mirror interior with two shelves, over lower shelf on caster, unmarked.

42in (106.5cm) wide

$1,500-2,000   **SDR**

A Saporiti chaise longue, with polished chrome frame and plum-colored ultrasuede cushions, Saporiti Italia label.

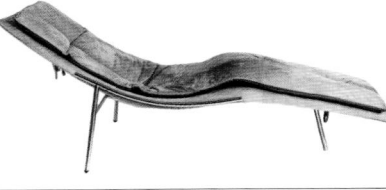

72in (183cm) wide

$1,500-2,000   **SDR**

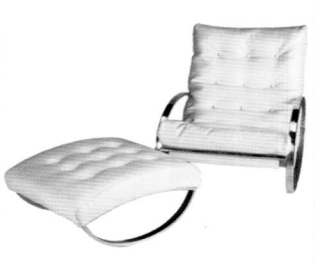

A modern rocking lounge chair and ottoman, upholstered in tufted butter yellow vinyl, on flat polished chrome frames, W. & J. Sloane paper tags.

1974   *Chair 37in (94cm) high*

$800-1,200   **SDR**

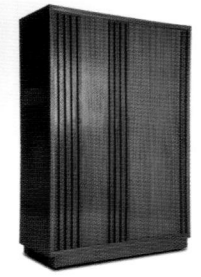

An André Sornay mahogany wardrobe, with two sliding doors concealing one fixed shelf and four adjustable ones, the case with fine microdot brass inlay, branded mark and numbered 1354.

44in (112cm) wide

$7,000-10,000   **SDR**

A Wendy Stayman wall-mounting tie cabinet, of mixed woods, both doors ending in full-height pulls, its interior with brass hangers and three drawers, unmarked.

46.25in (117.5cm) high

$3,000-4,000   **SDR**

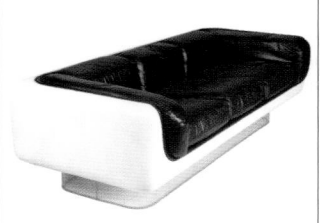

A Steelcase sofa, with black upholstery on molded white fiberglass frame, and Lucite base, steelcase label.

81in (205.5cm) wide

$2,500-3,000   **SDR**

A Studio Modern custom-designed credenza, the top and six bi-fold doors decorated with a running geometric pattern in ivory, black, and browns, concealing tray drawers and a small cabinet, on plinth base, illegible inscription with date, on side.

1977   *96in (244cm) wide*

$3,000-4,000   **SDR**

A Studio sculpted wood dining table and set of eight side chairs.

Table 81.5in (207cm) long

$9,000-12,000   **SDR**

A 1960s Asko 'Mademoiselle' vblack lacqueredchair, designed by Ilmari Tapiovaara.

1958   *35in (89cm) high*

$1,000-1,500   **GM**

A 1960s Asko 'Crinoletto' white lacquered wooden chair, designed by Ilmari Tapiovaara.

1962   *28.75in (73cm) high*

$2,000-3,000   **GM**

A Michael Taylor for Baker set of three small side tables, in ebonized wood with brass accents, and travertine tops, unmarked.

20in (51cm) wide

$1,500-2,000   **SDR**

A pair of Vladimir Kagan Trisymmetric lounge chairs, on bronze bases upholstered in tan leather.

34in (86cm) high

$10,000-15,000   **SDR**

A Smokey Tunis side chair, with mottled plexiglass panel back, and patchwork leather upholstery to seat, on a dark gray enameled wood frame, unmarked.

44in (112cm) high

$800-1,200   **SDR**

An Aldo Tura two-door bar cabinet, with dyed-green parchment covering, its case with polished brass studs, strap hardware, drop pulls, its illuminated and mirrored interior with glass shelves, on trestle base, Tura paper label.

51in (129.5cm) high

$2,000-3,000   **SDR**

A Smokey Tunis enameled wood shutter, with textured brownish-gray finish, and two hinged panels with geometric cut-outs.

51.5in (131cm) wide

$1,200-2,000   **SDR**

A Mies Van Der Rohe for Knoll 'Barcelona' daybed, with tan leather upholstery to bolster and to tufted cushion, on wood frame with polished metal legs, cushion has Art Metal/Knoll Associates tag.

73in (185.5cm) long

$4,000-6,000 **SDR**

A CLOSER LOOK AT A PAIR OF KNOLL CHAIRS

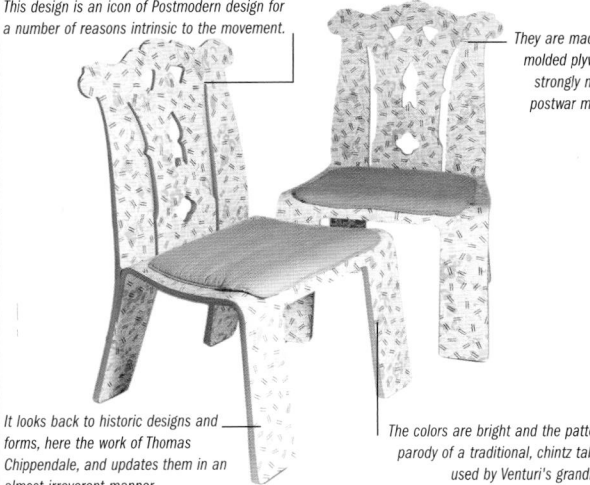

This design is an icon of Postmodern design for a number of reasons intrinsic to the movement.

They are made from molded plywood, a strongly modern, postwar material.

It looks back to historic designs and forms, here the work of Thomas Chippendale, and updates them in an almost irreverent manner.

The colors are bright and the pattern is a parody of a traditional, chintz tablecloth used by Venturi's grandmother.

A pair of Mies Van Der Rohe for Knoll 'Barcelona' chairs, with tufted black leather cushions, and black hard leather strap supports, on polished steel X-frames, Knoll Associates label.

30in (76cm) high

$2,000-3,000 **SDR**

A Mies Van Der Rohe for Knoll Barcelona chair, chromed steel frame, with tan tufted leather upholstered cushions.

$800-1,200 **FRE**

A Robert Venturi for Knoll pair of 'Chippendale' chairs, in the 'Grandmother's Tablecloth' pattern, with attached seat pillows covered in original Knoll fabric, showroom models, unmarked.

37.5in (95cm) high

$10,000-13,000 **SDR**

A Maurice Villency set of six tall-back dining chairs, with chocolate brown suede upholstery on polished chrome frames, unmarked.

44.5in (114cm) high

$2,000-3,000 **SDR**

A Heywood Wakefield six-drawer double-pedestal desk, with whalebone pulls, and an armchair with fabric-covered seat pad, unmarked.

Desk 47in (119.5cm) wide

$2,000-3,000 **SDR**

A K.E.M. Weber for Lloyd Mfg. Co. lounge chair, on chrome-plated steel frame with wood armrests in black, manufacturer's label.

34.5in (87.5cm) wide

$1,200-1,800 **SK**

A Robert Whitley tall stool, with maple burl seat on tapering dowel legs with stretchers, marked "Original Design 1951/Robert Whitley/Designed June 1990".

1990 *26in (66cm) high*

$1,200-1,500 **SDR**

An A.L. Wilson textured steel figural side chair, depicting an artist in profile with painter's palette seat, signed "A.L. Wilson".

1979 *79.5in (86cm) high*

$2,000-4,000 **SDR**

A Russell Woodard five-piece patio set, consisting of four armchairs with ivy motif along crestrail, and a pedestal table, all with green enameled finish, unmarked.

T<None>able 47.5in (120cm) diam

$700-1,000 **SDR**

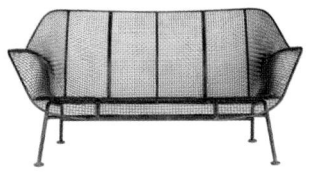

A Russell Woodard mesh settee, with black enamel finish on tubular iron frame, unmarked.

53.5in (135.5cm) wide

$3,000-4,000 **SDR**

A pair of Russel Wright for Conant Ball "American Modern" tall chests, each with five drawers and long horizontal pulls, American Modern/Conant Ball decal.

46.75in (118.5cm) high

$1,000-1,500 **SDR**

A Russel Wright for Statton Furniture Co. 'Easier Living' lounge chair, on ball casters with blond-wood frame and adjustable back, upholstered in black and cream striped fabric, unmarked.

30.25in (77cm) high

$700-1,000 SDR

A Russel Wright for Conant Ball Morris chair, with fabric-covered seat support, Conant Ball decal.

c1936 *35in (89cm) high*

$1,000-1,500 SDR

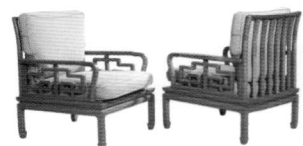

A pair of mid-20thC American Asian-inspired lounge chairs, later cushions, unsigned.

Many designers took inspiration from Asia including James Mont and T.H. Robsjohn-Gibbings.

33in (84cm) high

$2,000-3,000 SK

A pair of Danish rosewood lounge chairs, each with three pairs of slats to rounded back, and fabric-upholstered cushions, unmarked.

26.5in (67.5cm) high

$700-1,000 SDR

A mid-20thC pair of wirework armchairs with wire frames, burl wood armrests, attached fabric seat and back rest, on spring wire base with four prong feet, unmarked.

32in (81.5cm) high

$400-500 SK

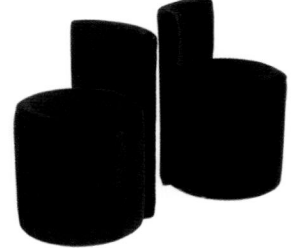

A Modern pair of slipper chairs, upholstered in black velvet, unmarked.

26.75in (68cm) high

$600-900 SDR

A 1970s white fiberglass egg chair and ottoman, the chair with reading light and two speakers to interior, covered in dark brown shag upholstery, unmarked.

Chair 52in (132cm) high

$2,000-3,000 SDR

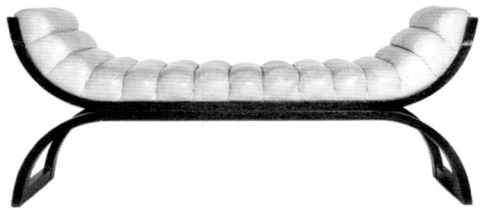

An Italian daybed, with channeled ivory leather upholstery on limed oak frame with ebonized finish, unmarked.

65in (165cm) wide

$3,000-4,000 SDR

An Edward Zucca maple and poplar Roman chest, with three divided compartments with hinged lids, the exterior painted in green and the interior painted blue, signed "Edward Zucca 2000 A.D./Made in Woodstock, Connecticut USA S.P.Q.R."

2000 *58in (147cm) wide*

$6,000-9,000 SDR

An Italian Illuminated cabinet-on-stand, with beveled and floral-decorated glass panes, two cabinets with mirrored and fitted interior, and three drawers on scallop-edged base, unmarked.

51.5in (131cm) wide

$2,000-2,500 SDR

A Norwegian 'Desk in a Box', with rosewood veneer case, and two doors concealing interior shelves, cubicles, and a desk light, replaced.

closed 45.25in (115cm) wide

$2,000-2,500 SDR

A Swedish teak desk, of sugar bin shape, recessed brass pulls, unmarked.

45.5in (115.5cm) wide

$700-1,000 SDR

A console table, with slab top and legs laminated in parchment, unmarked.

59in (147.5cm) wide

$12,000-15,000 SDR

A Modern coffee table, with a metal ribbon base with serrated edges, coated in a terracotta patina, supporting a circular glass top.

47in (119cm) diam

$1,200-1,500 SDR

POSTMODERNISM

- From the 1970s onwards, Postmodernism was an eclectic genre which rejected the 'form follows function' tenet of Modernism. Instead, designers challenged preconceived ideas of what was 'good' design.
- Designers borrowed styles from the past and motifs from several different eras might be combined on one piece. The aim was to present archaic forms in an unexpected, irreverent way.
- Costly materials such as marble and semiprecious metals were combined with cheap ones such as plastics or synthetic textiles. Cheaper materials were also given an expensive finish. Wood was often painted to look like marble.
- Surface decoration and visual impact was often seen as being as important as form. Plastic laminates which imitated anything from animal skin to wood were popular coverings.
- Some designers rejected precision manufacturing and modern materials and returned to traditional crafts such as handblown glass or the potter's wheel.
- Minimalism, geometry, architecture and popular culture all had an influence on Postmodern design.

An Italian Alchimia 'Kandissa' lacquered wood framed mirror, designed by Alessandro Mendini.

Due to a lack of money Alchimia was unable to pay its manufacturers for orders, meaning that only a very few examples (probably less than 10) of this mirror exist. The wildly clashing colours and asymmetric forms are an important aspect of Postmodernism.

1978   39.5in (100cm) high

$6,000-8,000   **GM**

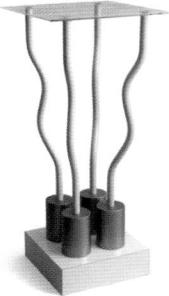

An Alchimia Belux 'Le Strutture Tremano' table, the glass top supported by colored plastic finished shaped tubular supports, on a white laminated wooden box stand, designed by Ettore Sottsass in 1979.

No longer in production.

c1985   19.75in (50cm) wide

$2,000-3,000   **GM**

A unique Alchimia 'Maschere 2' wall lamp, with hand painted papier-mâché mask and neon tube lighting, and transformer, mounted on a gold painted wooden board, designed by Lapo Binazzi.

1981   15in (38cm) high

$3,000-4,000   **GM**

An Italian Alchimia 'Cariatidi' aluminium decorative furniture finial sculpture, designed by Andrea Branzi.

These were placed on furniture when displayed in shops.

1979   12in (30.5cm) high

$2,500-5,500   **GM**

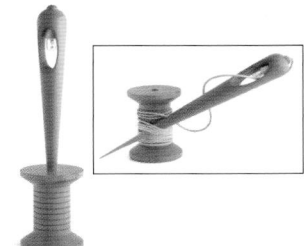

A unique Alchimia 'Needle and Spool' table lamp, comprised of a turned wood cotton reel and needle, the eye of the needle holding the bulb and the electric cable acting as the thread, designed by Lapo Binazzi.

This is typical of the humor of much Postmodern design, where another household form is appropriated in an unexpected manner.

1982   Needle 21.25in (54cm) long

$3,500-4,000   **GM**

An Alchimia 'Lassu' bronze sculpture of a chair on a pyramid, designed by Alessandro Mendini.

Larger, useable wooden examples of this design also exist, but only in an extremely limited number.

1983   11.5in (29cm) high

$4,000-6,000   **GM**

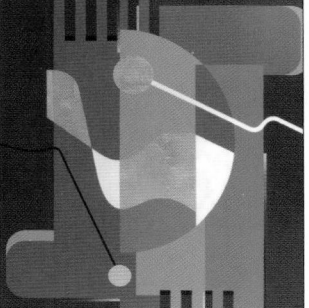

An Italian Alchimia 'Atropo' table, with gold colored metal legs and handpainted table top with gold foil highlights, signed 'Alessandro Mendini', designed by Alessandro Mendini.

1984   28in (71cm) high

$6,000-7,000   **GM**

An Italian Museo Alchimia 'Decoration Olo' wood and metal blue arch sculpture, with removable flags and stylized heads, designed by Alessandro Mendini.

1988   12in (30.5cm) high

$1,000-1,500   **GM**

SOTTSASS

- Best known for founding the Memphis design group of the 1980s, Italian designer Ettore Sottsass (1917-) is considered one of the most influential designers to work in every decade from the 1950s to the turn of the century.
- Whilst training as an architect, Sottsass began to move away from functional Modernist designs and develop a freer, more sensual and colorful style.
- In 1957, Sottsass began work at office equipment firm Olivetti and soon became primary designer. He also experimented with glass and ceramics.
- During the 1970s Sottsass briefly became part of Allesandro Mendini's Studio Alchimia, which eroded the prevailing idea that design was essentially a practical pursuit.
- Sottsass formed the successful Memphis group in 1980. Although there was no specific agenda, the group sought to move away from slick, plain design and embrace color and playfulness.
- Sottsass' designs are typically colorful and exuberant. Influences included Art Deco, Pop Art and tribal designs. Pieces sometimes parodied tradition forms. 1980s objects were often made of plastic laminates and had bold surface patterning.

A limited production 1960s Italian Bitossi 'Totem' handpainted ceramic sculpture, designed by Ettore Sottsass, comprized of eleven components bolted together through the middle with an iron rod and signed "E.SOTTSASS BITOSSI".

21in (53.5cm) high

| $1,000-1,500 | GM |

A 1960s Italian Il Sestante yellow ceramic ashtray, with painted marks to base, designed by Ettore Sottsass.

Unlike many of Sottsass' other ceramic designs, especially those by Bitossi, this design was only produced in the 1960s, so is scarcer.

5.25in (13.5cm) wide

| $3,500-4,500 | GM |

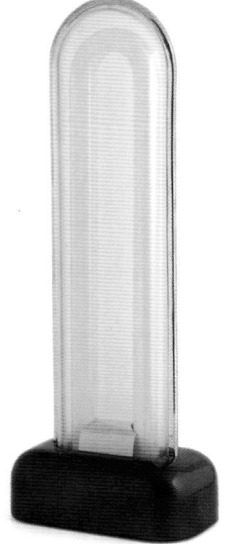

An Italian Poltronova 'Asteroide' table lamp, designed by Ettore Sottsass, with metallic blue finished base, fluorescent tube bulb and perspex cover with chrome plated trim.

1968   *28.5in (72cm) high*

| $7,000-10,000 | GM |

A 1960s Italian Fontana Arte 'Vase 410H', the bow tie shaped glass vase, comprized of glass panels glued together, designed by Etorre Sottsass.

1979/80   *18in (45.5cm) high*

| $3,000-4,000 | GM |

An Italian Vistosi limited edition 'Veniera' glass jar, with black lid, numbered 249 from an edition of 250, designed by Ettore Sottsass.

1972   *10.25in (26cm) high*

| $3,000-4,000 | GM |

An Italian Vistosi limited edition red and black glass 'Aulica' footed bowl, numbered 235 from an edition of 250, designed by Ettore Sottsass.

1972   *8in (20cm) high*

| $3,000-4,000 | GM |

A limited edition Italian Vistosi 'Bailissa' glass vase, with bulbous hollow black base, numbered 164 from an edition of 250, designed by Ettore Sottsass.

1972   *9.25in (23.5cm) high*

| $3,500-4,500 | GM |

An Ettore Sottsass for Vistosi fruit bowl, of transparent green and opaque white glass, etched "E. Sottsass/Vistosi/77" and numbered "69/250".

1977   *12.5in (31.5cm) wide*

| $800-1,200 | SDR |

An Italian Stilnovo 'Don' lacquered metal table lamp, with removable hat shaped shade clipped to the bulb, designed by Ettore Sottsass.

1977   *16.5in (42cm) high*

| $700-1,000 | GM |

An Italian Stilnovo 'Sinus' red and white plastic table or desk lamp, designed by Ettore Sottsass.

1970   *12.75in (32.4cm) high*

$1,000-1,500   **GM**

A very rare American Swid Powell silver plated baby's cup, made in Argentina, designed by Ettore Sottsass.

1985   *2.25in (5.5cm) high*

$1,200-1,800   **GM**

A pair of American Swid Powell silver plated 'Silvershade' candlesticks, designed by Ettore Sottsass.

Only a few of these candlesticks were made. Other, similar designs include 'Moonlight' and 'Starlight'.

1986   *13.5in (34.5cm) high*

$2,000-3,000   **GM**

A Collection Bharata 'Ringhiera Rossa' display piece or vase, with a ribbed marble column on a carved wooden base, with a pink marble disc and brass tubular frame to top, designed by Ettore Sottsass.

1988   *21in (53.5cm) high*

$4,500-5,500   **GM**

An Italian Compagnia Vetreria Muranese limited edition 'Le Connessoni Con Il Resto' glass vase, with everted conical rim from the Rovine (Ruins) collection, numbered 3 from an edition of 9, distributed by Design Gallery Milan, designed by Ettore Sottsass.

1992   *18.5in (47cm) high*

$10,000-15,000   **GM**

A limited edition Italian Compagnia Vetreria Muranese 'Sempre Piu Nel Mezzo' glass vase, from the Rovine (Ruins) collection, numbered 4 from an edition of 9, distributed by Design Gallery Milan, designed by Ettore Sottsass, with engraved marks to clear foot.

1992   *21.75in (55cm) high*

$10,000-15,000   **GM**

A limited edition silver plated salt shaker, numbered 18 from an edition of 99, with stamped facsimile signature to base, designed by Ettore Sottsass.

1994   *2.5in (6cm) high*

$700-1,000   **GM**

An Italian Venini limited edition 'Nebulosa Millenium III' glass display piece/vase, designed by Ettore Sottsass, comprized of four pieces of glass and numbered 58 from an edition of 99 and engraved 'venini Millenium III 58/99 E.Sottsass'.

Produced to celebrate the millennium.

1999   *21.5in (54.5cm) high*

$4,500-5,500   **GM**

An Italian Venini limited edition glass and Potoro marble 'Marito e Moglie' vase sculpture, the glass fitting into the marble on posts, engraved "E. Sottsass venini 2003 20/99", numbered 20 out of an edition of 99, designed by Ettore Sottsass.

2003   *24in (61cm) high*

$5,000-7,000   **GM**

An Italian Memphis 'Bay' protoype table lamp, with lacquered metal base, shaped glass column and perspex discs, designed by Ettore Sottsass.

1983   *19.25in (49cm) high*

$3,000-4,000   **GM**

A Giotto desk mirror, with wooden base and faux columns, pink lacquered wood 'pediment' and GIOTTO plaque to side, designed by Ettore Sottsass.

26in (66cm) high

$3,000-4,000   **GM**

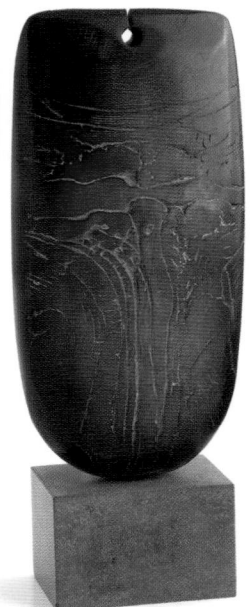

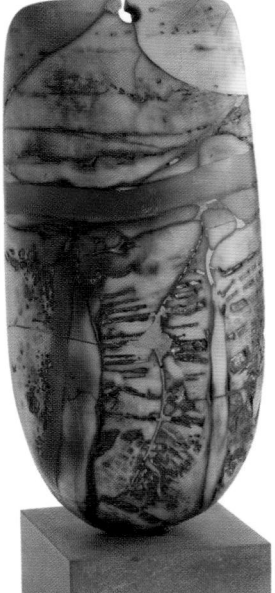

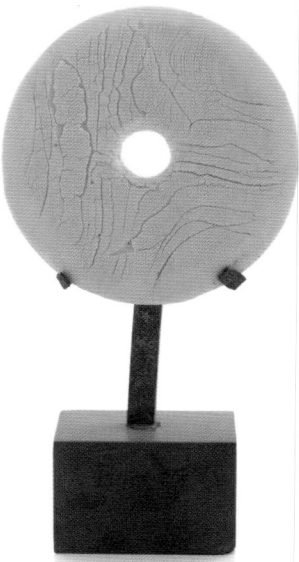

A Peter Hayes stoneware bust, of abstract form, covered with a matt black glaze, on marble base, signed and dated.

2000 12.5in (32cm) high

$400-600 **WW**

A Peter Hayes burnished keyhole raku vase, on a granite base, signed and dated.

2004 10.25in (26cm) high

$600-700 **WW**

A Peter Hayes raku bow-form keyhole sculpture, internally decorated with a blue resin band, on a slate base, signed and dated.

2005 13in (33cm) high

$700-1,000 **WW**

A small Peter Hayes porcelain disk form, on a granite base, unsigned.

9.5in (24cm) high

$300-400 **WW**

A ceramic figure by Pamela Kelly, 'One Great Ape', with raku glaze.

2004 23in (58.5cm) wide

$7,000-9,000 **DRG**

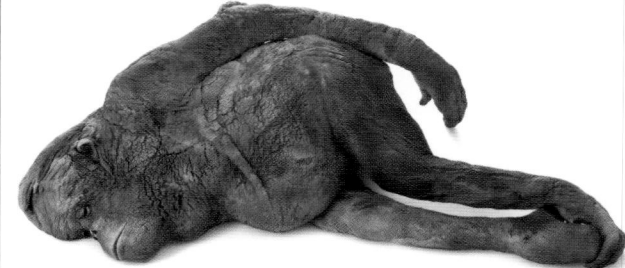

A ceramic figure by Pamela Kelly, 'Resting', with raku glaze.

2004 34in (86.5cm) long

$7,000-10,000 **DRG**

A ceramic sculpture by Pamela Kelly, 'Us', with raku glaze.

2004 6.5in (16.5cm) high

$2,000-2,500 **DRG**

A ceramic figure by Pamela Kelly, 'White Bull', with raku glaze.

2005 10in (25.5cm) high

$3,000-4,000 **DRG**

A Pablo Picasso for Madoura bowl, painted with fish, with raised 31.3.55, small flakes, stamped "MADOURA/EMPREINTE ORIGINALE DE PICASSO".

7in (17.5cm) diam

$1,000-1,500 SDR

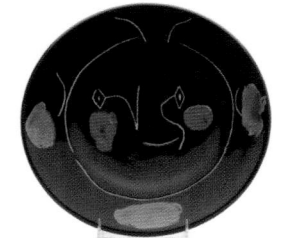

A Pablo Picasso for Madoura, incised and painted portrait plate, signed "EDITION PICASSO" and stamped "MADOURA/PLEIN FEU/EDITION/PICASSO".

9.5in (24cm) diam

$3,000-4,000 SDR

Two Pablo Picasso for Madoura small bowls, painted with birds and covered in ivory and celadon glaze, signed "EDITION PICASSO" and stamped "MADOURA/PLEIN FEU/EDITION PICASSO".

6in (15cm) diam

$3,000-4,000 SDR

A Pablo Picasso for Madoura bowl with green and black glossy glaze around a matte center, a few glaze flakes to rim, in ink "EDITION PICASSO", stamped "MADOURA PLEIN FEU".

5.25in (13.5cm) diam

$2,000-3,000 SDR

A Pablo Picasso for Madoura pitcher, decorated in wax resist with black and white masks, signed "EDITION PICASSO", stamped "Madoura".

5.5in (14cm) high

$3,000-4,000 SDR

A Pablo Picasso for Madoura fish-shaped water pitcher, marked "EDITION PICASSO/MADOURA" and stamped "MADOURA/PLEIN FEU".

9in (23cm) wide

$5,000-6,000 SDR

A faïence charger, by Henry Varnum Poor, incised with a fruit basket still life in polychrome, signed "HVP 57".

1957   *12.5in (32cm) diam*

$1,000-1,500 SDR

A faïence charger, by Henry Varnum Poor, incised with a medallion of a Pilgrim in glossy crackled polychrome, signed "HVP 57", some glaze chips.

1957   *12.75in (32.5cm) diam*

$1,000-1,500 SDR

A faïence charger, by Henry Varnum Poor, incised with a coffee pot and fruit bowl still life in crackled polychrome, some damage, signed "HVP 57".

1957   *12.5in (32cm) diam*

$1,000-1,500 SDR

A corsetted footed vase, by Henry Varnum Poor, of buff clay, with two ear-shaped handles, incised with a face and painted in white, green, brown and black majolica glaze, incised "HVP/58".

1958   *13in (33cm) high*

$5,000-7,000 SDR

LUCIE RIE

LUCIE RIE

- Lucie Rie (1902-1995) was born in Vienna and studied at Kunstgewerbeschule, the art school associated with the Weiner Werkstätte. She set up her first studio in 1925 and exhibited in her first international exhibition in Paris.
- In 1938 she settled in London and began to make ceramic buttons for Bimini Glass and Jewelry Workshop.
- After the war, Rie returned to experimenting with art pottery, drawing influence from Scandinavian Modernism, Asian ceramics and the British ceramic tradition.
- Shapes were modern and architectural and the influence of English Abstraction can be seen in her white glazes. Pieces were typically functional wares, including stem bowls and bottles.
- In 1948, Rie acquired a kiln and her work began to develop into the style most associated with her today. The kiln allowed further experimentation and glazes varied, ranging from pitted volcanic glazes to intricate sgraffito filigree.
- In the late 1940s, Rie hired art potter Hans Coper and he became her partner in the studio.
- She stopped making pottery in 1990 and was made a dame in 1991.

A Lucie Rie footed conical stoneware bowl, glazed golden metallic around the rim and running on to the off-white pitted body, signed with "LR" seal.

10.5in (26.5cm) diam

$3,000-4,000   **JN**

A Lucie Rie porcelain bowl, of flaring conical form covered with a pale blue glaze, impressed seal mark.

8.5in (21.5cm) diam

$4,500-6,500   **WW**

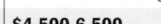

A Lucie Rie flaring porcelain bowl, radiating with sgraffito lines on bronze glaze interior and matte white exterior, marked "LR".

9in (23cm) diam

$7,000-9,000   **SDR**

A Lucie Rie stoneware vase, of flaring form with waisted collar, incised with vertical and horizontal sgraffito lines visible through a manganese glaze, impressed "LR" seal mark.

c1960

$1,500-2,000   **WW**

An early Lucie Rie Austrian earthenware bowl, with gently rounded sides, the red body covered with an almost lemon colored glaze with random streaks of amber and brown, signed "L.R.G." for Lucy Rie Gompertz and "Wien", some chipping to rim.

11in (28cm) diam

$2,000-3,000   **JN**

A slender Lucie Rie stoneware vase, of shouldered form with narrow neck and flared rim with dark brown edge, otherwise pale bluey-oatmeal tones, signed with "LR" seal.

10in (25.5cm) high

$3,500-4,500   **JN**

A Lucie Rie porcelain vase, of shouldered form with narrow cylindrical neck and flaring rim, covered in a bronze glaze with sgraffito bands to shoulder and top rim, impressed seal mark.

8.75in (22.5cm) high

$12,000-18,000   **WW**

A Lucie Rie porcelain bottle vase with collar rim, the body and neck with sgraffito lines, covered in a golden glaze to shoulder and rim over bronze impressed "LR" seal.

c1978   *9.5in (24cm) high*

$6,000-9,000   **WW**

A Lucie Rie stoneware bottle vase, of swollen form with cylindrical neck and broad flaring rim, covered in a pitted white glaze with bronze bands, inlaid with green stripes to shoulder and inside top rim, impressed seal mark.

9.75in (24.5cm) high

$12,000-18,000   **WW**

A Lucie Rie porcelain vase with flaring rim, under bronze glaze with blue and incised pinstripe rim and shoulder, marked with artist's LR cipher.

7.5in (19cm) high

$18,000-20,000   **SDR**

A framed photograph of Lucie Rie in black and white by Terry Day.

20in (50.5cm) wide

$500-700   **WW**

A ceramic and mixed media sculpture by Bill Stewart, 'J. Fred Muggs, Frieda the Cat & The Fabulous Porkers'.

2004   *83in (211cm) high*

$12,000-18,000   **DRG**

A ceramic 'Sky Dancer', by Bill Stewart.

2004   *13.5in (34.5cm) long*

$700-1,000   **DRG**

A ceramic 'Sky Dancer', by Bill Stewart.

2004   *9in (23cm) long*

$700-1,000   **DRG**

A ceramic and mixed media sculpture by Bill Stewart, 'Checking For Bugs Before take Off'.

2004   *37in (94cm) long*

$10,000-15,000   **DRG**

A Toshiko Takaezu ceramic vessel, with modeled buttresses under a flattened top, in brown glazes, signed "TT".

16.5in (42cm) diam

$10,000-12,000   **SDR**

A Toshiko Takaezu stoneware sculptural garden stool, covered in amber and mahogany matte glaze, complete with internal rattle, hairlines, incised initial.

13in (33cm) high

$2,500-3,500   **SDR**

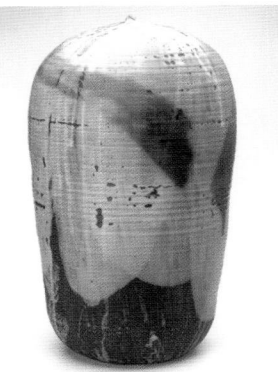

A Toshiko Takaezu large stoneware moon pot, covered in lavender, celadon and brown dead-matte glaze, with internal rattle, marked "TT".

23.5in (60cm) high

$7,000-10,000   **SDR**

A Toshiko Takaezu moon pot covered in speckled and mottled brown glazes, with internal rattle.

7in (18cm) high

$4,000-6,000   **SDR**

A ceramic sculpture by Dalit Tayar, 'Structure (Man)'.
2003   20.75in (52.5cm) high
$7,000-10,000   DRG

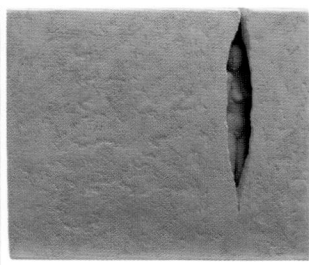

A ceramic sculpture by Dalit Tayar, 'Structure (Woman)'.
2003   18.5in (47cm) high
$7,000-10,000   DRG

A ceramic sculpture by Dalit Tayar, 'Structure (Angel Emerging)'.
2003   18.5in (47cm) high
$7,000-10,000   DRG

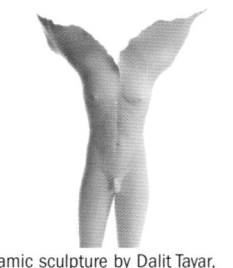

A ceramic sculpture by Dalit Tayar, 'Large Angel'.
2003   14in (35.5cm) high
$3,000-4,000   DRG

A ceramic sculpture by Dalit Tayar, 'Small Angel', with polychrome decoration.
2003   6.5in (16.5cm) high
$3,000-4,000   DRG

A ceramic sculpture by James Tyler, 'Guillermo'.
2005   35in (89cm) high
$10,000-15,000   DRG

A ceramic sculpture by James Tyler, 'Female Torso'.
2003   18in (45.5cm) high
$3,000-4,000   DRG

A ceramic sculpture by James Tyler, 'Brick Torso'.
2003   48in (122cm) high
$7,000-10,000   DRG

A ceramic sculpture by James Tyler, 'Small Brick Head'.
2003   8in (20.5cm) high
$1,000-1,500   DRG

An earthenware teapot by Noi Volkov, 'Bosch', with polychrome oxide glazes depicting faces after Heironymous Bosch.

2005 *12in (30.5cm) long*

$4,000-6,000 **DRG**

An earthenware teapot by Noi Volkov, 'Dali Landscape Teapot', with polychrome oxide glazes and painting after Dali.

2005 *14in (35.5cm) high*

$3,000-4,000 **DRG**

An earthenware sculpture by Noi Volkov, 'Marilyn', with polychrome oxide glazes.

2005 *12in (30.5cm) high*

$5,000-7,000 **DRG**

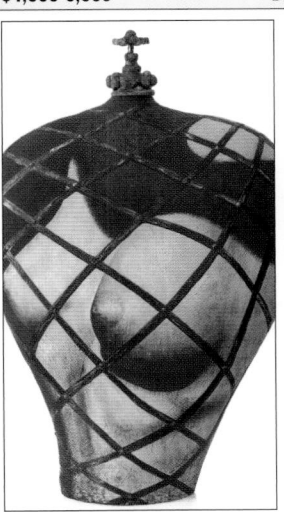

An earthenware baluster-form sculpture by Noi Volkov, 'Pearl Earring', with polychrome oxide glazes and painting after Vermeer.

2003 *26in (66cm) high*

$10,000-15,000 **DRG**

An earthenware sculpture by Noi Volkov, 'Pants of Van Gogh', decorated with polychrome oxide glazes and painting after Van Gogh, also incorporating mixed media including a pair of jeans.

2004 *57in (145cm) high*

$10,000-15,000 **DRG**

An earthenware water pot by Noi Volkov, 'Van Gogh/Venus', with polychrome oxide glazes and painting after Botticelli and Van Gogh.

2004 *17in (43cm) high*

$7,000-10,000 **DRG**

An earthenware teapot by Noi Volkov, 'Van Gogh Grecian Teapot', with polychrome oxide glazes and painting after Van Gogh.

2004 *19in (48.5cm) high*

$4,000-6,000 **DRG**

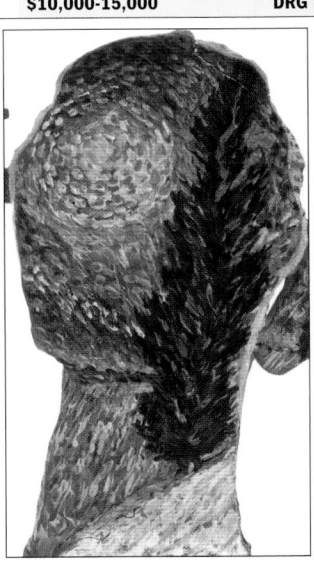

A Peter Voulkos large stoneware charger, incised with a woman's face under a cobalt, gray and brown glaze, signed "Voulkos".

18in (46cm) diam

$10,000-15,000   SDR

A Peter Voulkos flaring stoneware bowl, painted with abstracted fish in brown on a pale green matte ground, signed "Voulkos".

12in (30cm) diam

$2,000-3,000   SDR

A Peter Voulkos stoneware bottle, with bulbous middle, both sides painted with abstract floral pattern in light blue, black and brown on a speckled matte white ground, crack around neck.

13.75in (35cm) high

$1,000-1,500   SDR

A Peter Voulkos handbuilt vessel of Oriental form, covered in areas of thick matte glazes, in white, royal blue, blue-green and brown, a few glaze chips, possibly from firing, signed "Voulkos".

Abstract impressionist Jackson Pollock famously redefined art as a process rather than a product. Peter Voulkos (1924-2002) was the first of a generation of potters to apply this idea to clay-making him an important and influential ceramic artist.

1961   *12.5in (32cm) high*

$20,000-25,000   SDR

A Peter Voulkos tall ridged stoneware bottle, covered in gunmetal glaze.

18.75in (48cm) high

$6,000-9,000   SDR

BEATRICE WOOD

- Beatrice Wood (1893-1998), the daughter of San Francisco socialites, studied at the Académie Julian in Paris before settling in New York.
- Here she fell in with a group of creative individuals including actors and Dadaists. Her relationship with Marcel Duchamp and Henri-Pierre Roché is supposed to have inspired the novel *Jules et Jim*.
- Wood did not become interested in ceramics until she was in her 40s, by which time she had become an adherent to the Theosophical Society and moved to California.
- Pieces are primarily sculptural in form. Many feature small apertures and are not intended for practical use.
- Wood developed a range of volcanic glazes in a range of bright colors and earth tones and characterized by pitted surfaces.
- Other pieces featured applied decoration inspired by India.

A Beatrice Wood charger, painted with a woman holding blooming branches, 1950, signed "Beato".

13in (33cm) diam

$3,000-4,000   SDR

A Beatrice Wood charger, painted with cross-legged figure, "Meditation", signed "Beato".

15in (38cm) diam

$4,000-5,000   SDR

A Beatrice Wood charger, painted with Madonna and Child, signed "Beato".

13.25in (35cm) diam

$4,000-5,000   SDR

A Beatrice Wood chalice, modeled with four couples and covered in celadon volcanic glaze, signed "Beato".

6.5in (16.5cm) high

$3,000-4,000   SDR

MODERN DESIGN

A Beatrice Wood chalice, in chartreuse dead-matte glaze, signed "Beato".

6.75in (17cm) diam

$4,000-5,000   SDR

A Beatrice Wood two handled chalice, in lustred gold glaze, signed "Beato".

8in (20cm) high

$8,000-10,000   SDR

A Beatrice Wood tapering vase, covered in oxblood and celadon crystalline glaze, signed "Beato/N", restored to rim.

10in (25.5cm) high

$800-1,200   SDR

A Beatrice Wood Ring flask, with two loop handles, under mottled green glaze, signed "Beato".

19.25in (26cm) high

$3,000-4,000   SDR

A Beatrice Wood pair of centerpiece hollow arc-shaped candleholders, covered in mottled lustred glaze, signed "Beato".

each 10in (25.5cm) wide

$3,000-4,000   SDR

A Beatrice Wood ceramic sculpture, 'Coffee Break', with figures around a bench in lustred green glazes on a lustred mauve ground, firing line to seam, a few hairlines to extremities, titled and signed "Beato".

15.5in (39.5cm) high

$10,000-15,000   SDR

A Beatrice Wood ceramic bust, 'Surplus', signed "Beato".

14in (36cm) high

$3,000-4,000   SDR

A porcelain group by Chris Anteman, 'Red Meat', decorated with enamel, decals and lustre glaze.

2003   *18in (45cm) high*

$2,000-3,000   DRG

A porcelain group by Chris Anteman, 'Poppy Fields', decorated with enamels, decals and lustre glaze.

2003   *18in (45cm) high*

$3,000-6,000   DRG

A large ceramic vessel by Rudy Autio, 'Razz-ma-Tazz'.

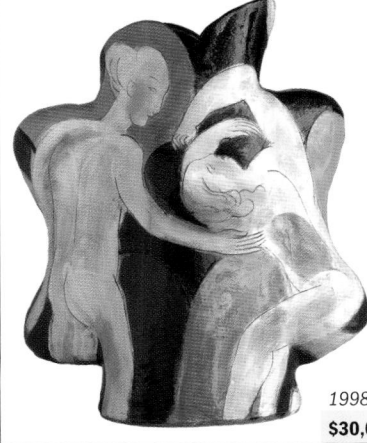

1998   *31.5in (80cm) high*

$30,000-40,000   DRG

A pit-fired earthenware sculpture by Bennet Bean, 'Two Dahlias', with gilded and painted decoration.

2004   *18.5in (47cm) wide*

$4,500-5,500   DRG

A pit-fired earthenware sculpture by Bennet Bean, 'Black & White Tulips', with painted decoration.

2004   *27in (68.5cm) wide*

$10,000-15,000   DRG

A pit-fired earthenware sculpture by Bennet Bean, 'Dancing Tulips', with gilded and painted decoration.

2004   *28.5in (72.5cm) wide*

$10,000-15,000   **DRG**

A Harding Black gourd-shaped vase, embossed with floral medallions and covered in a Chinese blue flambé glaze over dark brown ground, small nick to medallion, signed "Harding Black, 1957".

1957   *9.25in (23.5cm) high*

$600-900   **SDR**

A large Feelie, by Rose Cabat, covered in mauve vellum crystalline flambé glaze, on a turquoise ground, signed "Cabat".

9.5in (24cm) high

$3,000-4,000   **SDR**

A Paul Chaleff stoneware flaring low bowl, with four large circles in sand or brick red on a rich dead-matte green ground, signed "Paul Chaleff 1979".

15.25in (39cm) wide

$600-900   **SDR**

A Jean Cocteau red clay charger, painted with a flute-playing Pan, signed "Jean Cocteau" on front, marked "Edition originale de Jean Cocteau/Atelier Madeline-Jolly" verso.

12in (30cm) diam

$2,000-4,000   **SDR**

A Chinese-style 'Patom' garden stool, by Claude Conover, embossed in two different patterns and rubbed with an ivory matt glaze.

17in (43cm) high

$4,000-6,000   **SDR**

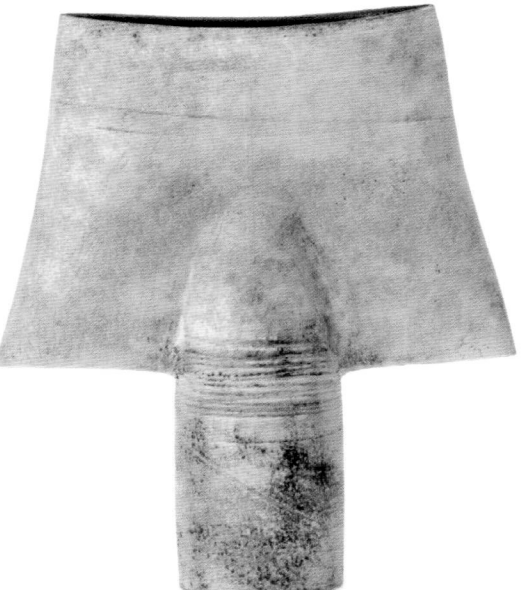

A Hans Coper spade-form stoneware vessel, rubbed with oxides, signed "HC".

8.75in (22cm) high

$20,000-25,000   **SDR**

A melon-shaped 'Tzum' Asian garden stool, by Claude Conover, with vertical and random etching, covered in light and dark brown glaze, signed and titled.

16in (40.5cm) high

$6,000-8,000   **SDR**

A Claude Conover stoneware vessel, signed "Claude Conover Ixcit".

20in (51cm) high

$6,000-9,000   **SDR**

A Wilhelm Hunt Diederich large faïence bowl, painted with a brown rooster on gray and yellow ground, signed on front.

15in (38cm) diam

$10,000-15,000   **SDR**

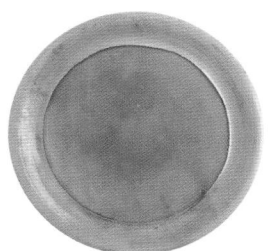

A large John Dunn raku bowl, of shallow form, the interior glazed a pale celadon lustre, impressed seal mark, minor glaze loss.

22.5in (57cm) diam

$450-550   **WW**

A John Dunn raku cylinder vase, unsigned.

17.25in (44cm) high

$600-900   **WW**

A Gambone geometric dish, in red and yellow glazes, signed with donkey and "Gambone Italy".

dish 10.25in (26cm) high

$2,000-3,000   **SDR**

A Gambone bottle-shaped vase, in crackled glaze decorated with red and brown square pattern, signed "Gambone Italy".

13.5in (34cm) high

$1,500-2,000   **SDR**

A David Gilhooly large sculptural covered vessel, modeled with frogs as Mt. Rushmore icons, a few minor nicks to pine trees, some minor chips to inner rim, incised "D667".

This is the first of Gilhooly's frog pots, exemplifying the artist's fascination with frogs anthropomorphizing, a theme he was to explore for a large part of his early career.

13in (33cm) high

$4,000-5,000   **SDR**

A David Gilhooly large sculptural piece, with pigeons perched on an imposing frog-like face, minor restoration and touch-ups to several birds, firing cracks to base.

22.5in (57cm) high

$7,000-10,000   **SDR**

A ceramic bust of a young woman, by Grailhe, covered in matt black glaze, signed "Grailhe".

16in (40.5cm) high

$1,000-1,500   **SDR**

An Erick Gronborg whimsical ceramic teapot, with applied clay strips glazed green, a fire engine-red handle and spout, and a nude finial, marked with "Erick Gronborg" in cartouche.

15.5in (39.5cm) wide

$500-700   **SDR**

A Shoji Hamada low stoneware bowl, painted in quadrants, remnant of paper label.

12in (30cm) diam

$5,500-7,000   **SDR**

Two Josh Herman ceramic vessels covered in volcanic glazes, vase marked with artist's "JH" cipher.

larger 9in (23cm) high

$600-900   **SDR**

A George Jouve bulbous ceramic vase, with applied plaque incised with bird, moon and starts on a gunmetal ground, signed "JOUVE".

14in (36cm) high

$20,000-30,000   **SDR**

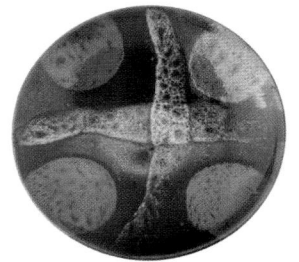

A Bernard Leach framed drawing of an owl, for a design for a tile, "BL" monogram, from the Janet Leach collection, back stamped.

1935

$600-900   **GAZE**

MODERN DESIGN

A Bernard Leach framed drawing of his dog Peter, from Janet Leach collection, back stamped.

c1940s

$700-1,000   **GAZE**

A CLOSER LOOK AT A NATZLER VASE

The highly influential Natzlers were a husband and wife team – Otto was responsible for developing and applying the glazes, Gertrud for the design and potting of the forms.

The form is well-proportioned and the crystalline glaze is desirable, with its strong and varying colors.

This piece reached a world record price for Natzler pottery, and is noted as one of the most accomplished pieces they produced.

This is a very large example, which is scarce as it would have required great skill to throw and form on a potter's wheel.

A Natzler exceptional tall bulbous vase with blue crystalline glaze, signed "Natzler", label K301.

19in (48cm) high

$250,000-300,000   **SDR**

An untitled suite of six ceramic vessels, by Andrew Lord, each of white clay covered in gunmetal black glaze with gold drips, some damage and restoration to three vessels, unmarked.

largest 29in (73.5cm) high

$35,000-55,000   **SDR**

A Bruce Elwin McGrew untitled ceramic of four separate components.

27in (67.5cm) high

$400-600   **SDR**

A tall bottle-shaped vase, by Harrison McIntosh, of red clay painted with vertical butter yellow lines on a matt blue-green ground, stamped "HM".

14.25in (36cm) high

$4,000-6,000   **SDR**

A Natzler flaring vase, covered in fine, active white with light blue volcanic glaze, signed.

This 'volcanic' style glaze is typical of the influential Natzlers' ceramics.

8in (20cm) high

$5,000-7,000   **SDR**

A Natzler flaring vessel, covered in mottled yellow glaze, marked "Natzler" and "N909".

3.5in (8cm) high

$4,000-6,000   **SDR**

An American Postmodern Swid Powell 'Little Dripper' transfer-printed tea or coffee pot, with milk jug, sugar bowl with spoon and coffee filter holder, designed by Michael Graves.

The color symbolism in terms of pattern is interesting: the red represents the heat under the teapot and the blue waves the water in the teapot. The forms also recall the work of Christopher Dresser.

1987   *Teapot 9.25in (23.5cm) wide*

$1,200-1,800   **GM**

A spherical stoneware vase, by Antonio Prieto, incised and painted with concentric circles in light and dark brown, signed "Prieto/sp/mia".

10in (25.5cm) high

$4,500-5,000   **SDR**

A chimney-shaped stoneware vessel, by Daniel Rhodes, with ridges and dimples, sagger-fired, signed "Rhodes".

c1978   *10.5in (26.5cm) high*

$700-1,000   **SDR**

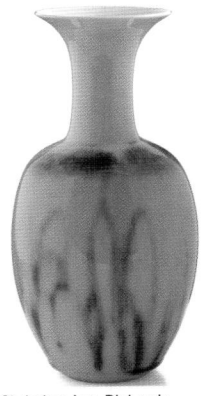

A Christine Ann Richards porcelain vase, the white body splashed with sang-de-boeuf, impressed seal mark.

12.5in (31.5cm) high

$600-900   **WW**

A Phil Rogers stoneware vase, of cut sided form with horizontal hatching, covered in a speckled glaze, with impressed seal mark.

8in (20.5cm) high

$200-300   **WW**

A Scheier stoneware jar and cover, embossed and incised with female fertility figures under a bronze volcanic glaze, signed "Scheier 83".

1983   *16in (41cm) high*

$7,500-9,500   **SDR**

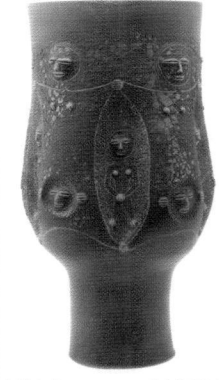

A Scheier monumental footed vase, incised with faces and figures outlined in blue on dark gray matte ground with bronzed mottling, incised "Scheier 66".

1966   *22in (56cm) high*

$7,500-9,000   **SDR**

A hand-built raku vessel, by Paul Soldner, with stamped, cut and modeled decoration, impressed mark, chip to rim.

12in (30.5cm) high

$1,000-1,500   **SDR**

A wood-fired stoneware charger, by Paul Soldner, painted with a mother and child in blue-green, gray and burgundy matt glazes, signed "Soldner".

16.5in (42cm) diam

$2,000-3,000   **SDR**

A Rudolph Staffel porcelain flaring vase, incised with vertical and horizontal lines on a light blue to indigo body, signed "Rudolph Staffel".

8.75in (22cm) high

$5,000-6,000   **SDR**

A tall tapered vase, by Stonelain, painted with stylized skyscrapers on a mottled amber ground, stamped "Stonelain" with bottle motif.

16.5in (42cm) high

$4,000-7,000   **SDR**

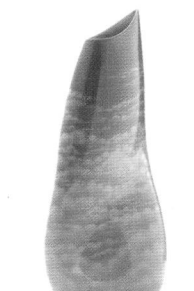

A tall folded and bent china vase, by Giuseppe Vallini, painted with white clouds on a shaded blue to pink ground, marked "Vivi Torino/Made in Italy".

18.5in (47cm) high

$1,200-1,800   **SDR**

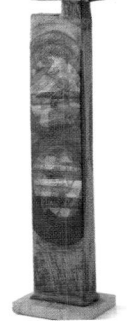

A tall four-sided ceramic vessel, by William Wyman, painted with medallions, one etched "Stay here, don't go now, stay here! Do not go away from me again", on an etched ground, signed "Wyman 64".

27in (68.5cm) high

$2,000-2,600   **SDR**

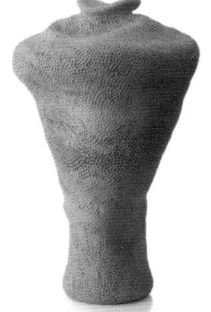

A white clay vase by Michal Zehavi, 'Untitled Jar #1004-6'.

2004   *26in (66cm) high*

$4,000-6,000   **DRG**

A white clay vase by Michal Zehavi, 'Untitled Jar #1004-4'.

2004   *21in (53.5cm) high*

$4,000-6,000   **DRG**

An Italian faïence wall-hanging mask of tribal figure, cut-out and covered in turquoise semi-matte glaze, marked "Italy" with cipher.

17.25in (43cm) high

$300-400   **SDR**

A Fulvio Bianconi for Venini 'Commedia Dell'Arte' figure in white lattimo glass with red, blue, and green applied decoration, unmarked.

12.5in (31.75cm) high

$700-1,000   SDR

MURANO

■ The island of Murano, in the Venetian lagoon, has been famed for glass production since the 13thC. The 20thC saw a renaissance in Murano glass, with many innovative techniques being introduced.

■ From the 1940s, Italy came into its own as a center of design. Fine artists were commissioned by Murano to produce pieces in organic 'new look' shapes.

■ Colors were vibrant and decoration was abstract. Glassworkers also reworked traditional Venetian techniques, such as mosaics, murrine, tesserae and sommerso cased and colored glass.

■ Key factories included Arte Vetraria Muranese (AVEM), Barovier & Toso, Seguso Vetri d'Arte, Venini and Vetreria Vistosi. Many of these are still in production today.

■ A number of important Modern designers produced glass designs for Murano companies including Gio Ponti, Fulvio Bianconi and Carlo Scarpa. Hand-blown pieces by important factories tend to be the most sought after.

■ Pieces range from decorative items such as vases to figures and ornaments for the tourist trade.

A Gio Ponti for Venini floor lamp base, of stacked red and cobalt glass elements.

glass 58in (147cm) high

$11,000-15,000   SDR

A Davide Salvadore organically shaped matte black glass vase, with a marbleized kidney-shaped base, acid etched "Davide Salvadore/Murano/2000".

16.5in (42cm) high

$2,000-3,000   SDR

A Carlo Scarpa spherical vase, in opaque black glass with applied red rim, on flared foot, unmarked.

5.5in (14cm) high

$2,000-3,000   SDR

A rare Archimede Seguso sfumato basket shaped glass vessel, in ruby red with gold leaf inclusions.

10in (25cm) high

$2,000-4,000   SDR

An Archimede Seguso large three-lobed Polveri glass vase, in aubergine, orange, and clear, with gold inclusions, remnants of foil labels to body and to base.

13.75in (33cm) high

$3,000-4,000   SDR

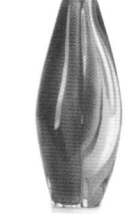

A Livio Seguso Sommerso glass sculpture, with iridescent infant, signed "Livio Seguso", gallery tag.

14in (36cm) high

$6,000-8,000   SDR

An A.V.E.M. Bizzantino glass floor vase, with multi-colored murrines and canes against a ruby ground, with gold and silver foil inclusions, marked with remnant of "Made in Italy" foil label, also paper label with "1338" in pencil.

This is sometimes known as the 'Tutti Frutti' vase.

20.5in (52cm) high

$3,000-4,000   SDR

A large Venini fazzoletto smoked glass vase, with white zanfirico rods, stamped "Venini/Murano/Italia".

11.5in (29cm) high

$2,000-3,000   SDR

Two Venini blown glass Clessidre, one in shades of blue, the other in yellow and gray.

larger 7.5in (19cm) high

$1,500-2,000   SDR

A Venini rooster figure, in opaque polychrome glass, base stamped "Venini/Murano/Italia".

6.75in (17cm) high

$2,000-3,000   SDR

A Dale Chihuly five-piece Seaform, set in cranberry glass with brown concentric rings, and blue-green lip wrap, largest element signed "Chihuly 1986".

1986   *15.75in (40cm) wide*

$16,000-20,000   **SDR**

A Venetian Dale Chihuly blown and hot worked glass, accented with gold leaf, etched "Chihuly 90".

1990   *23in (58cm) high*

$10,000-15,000   **SDR**

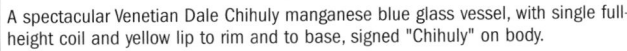

A spectacular Venetian Dale Chihuly manganese blue glass vessel, with single full-height coil and yellow lip to rim and to base, signed "Chihuly" on body.

1991   *31.75in (80.5cm) high*

$25,000-35,000   **SDR**

A Dale Chihuly large soft cylinder, with random striations in yellow, red and green on a mottled white, lavender and clear ground, with yellow wrap, unsigned.

23in (58.5cm) high

$15,000-20,000   **SDR**

MODERN DESIGN

A glass sculpture by Laura Donefer, 'Little Red Witch Pot', incorporating beads and other mixed media.

2004   6in (13.5cm) high

$2,000-3,000   **DRG**

A glass sculpture by Laura Donefer, 'Icestorm Amulet Basket', incorporating beads and other mixed media.

2004   12.5in (32cm) high

$4,000-5,000   **DRG**

A Michael Glancy blown and carved glass vessel, with "Golden Orb" elector-formed with gold leaf interior and exterior, etched "Michael M. Glancy 1986", stylized "MG" cipher on bottom.

1986   5in (13cm) diam

$8,000-10,000   **SDR**

A clear glass sculpture, by Sidney Hutter, '90 Degrees of 4 Colorwheel: Jerry Vision Vase #195', with orange, yellow and blue dyed glue.

2003   16.5in (42cm) high

$18,000-20,000   **DRG**

A clear glass sculpture, by Sidney Hutter, 'Two Views of 4 Color Wheel: Jerry Vision Vase # 176', clear glass plates with red, yellow and blue dyed glue.

2004   18.5in (47cm) high

$18,000-20,000   **DRG**

A Jon Kuhn optical and lead glass crystal sculpture, "Cube", 1998, signed Jon Kuhn 1998.

11in (28cm) high

$12,000-15,000   **SDR**

A Vicke Lindstrand for Kosta large 'Trees in Fog' glass vase, with white shaded rim and deep amethyst tree silhouettes cased in clear, stamped "Lindstrand/ Kosta" in square, also etched LW2205", small, shallow chip to base.

12.5in (31.5cm) high

$2,000-2,500   **SDR**

A glass sculpture by Marvin Lipofsky, 'California Loop Series #3', with flocking and electroformed copper.

1969   17in (43cm) long

$15,000-18,000   **DRG**

A glass sculpture by Marvin Lipofsky, 'California Loop Series (Purple)', with flocking and electroformed copper.

1969   *28in (71cm) long*

$24,000-28,000   **DRG**

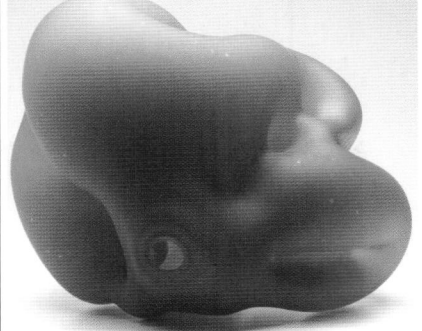

A Marvin Lipofsky Pitchuck Series 1984-85 No.17 (Pacific Sunset), with cut, sandblasted and polished mold blown glass, 1984-85, fully signed.

16in (41cm) wide

$7,000-10,000   **SDR**

A cast glass sculpture, by John Littleton and Kate Vogel, 'Lotus Hands'.

2004   *15in (38cm) high*

$10,000-18,000   **DRG**

A cast and hot-formed glass sculpture, by John Littleton and Kate Vogel, 'Of The Forest', with gold leaf.

2002   *14.5in (37cm) high*

$10,000-13,000   **DRG**

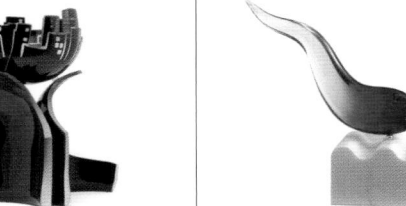

A Concetta Mason carved and laminated glass two piece sculpture, 'Urban Twilight,' signed, titled and dated, with artist's cipher.

1991   *15in (38cm) high*

$4,000-6,000   **SDR**

An Italian Museum Market limited edition 'Phlox' sculpture, comprised of a blue and clear glass fish mounted on a white marble base carved to mimic a stylized sea, designed by Alessandro Mendini.

1993   *20in (51cm) high*

$2,500-3,000   **GM**

A Tom Patti sculpture of stacked, fused, blown and polished glass, etched "Patti 78".

1978   *6in (15cm) wide*

$11,000-15,000   **SDR**

A blown glass sculpture, by Danny Perkins, 'Malibu', with painted decoration.

2005   *47in (119.5cm) high*

$10,000-13,000   **DRG**

A blown glass sculpture, by Danny Perkins, 'Stone', with painted decoration.

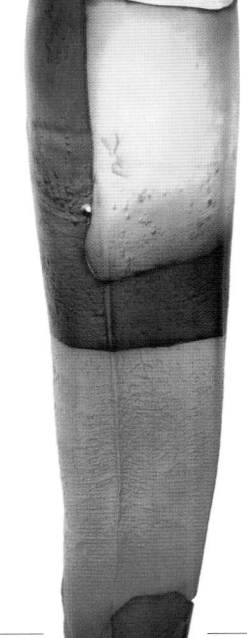

2005   *40in (101.5cm) high*

$10,000-13,000   **DRG**

A large blown and sculpted glass vessel, by Jennifer Pohlmann & Sabrina Knowles, 'Migration-Ceremonial Bird Pot Series', decorated with beads.

2004   *38in (96.5cm) high*

$10,000-13,000   **DRG**

A blown and hot-sculpted glass sculpture, by Ross Richmond, 'Stargazer'.

2004   *11.75in (42.5cm) high*

$4,000-5,000   **DRG**

A solid blown and hot-sculpted glass bust, by Ross Richmond, 'Bust #71'.

2005   *14in (35.5cm) high*

$4,000-5,000   **DRG**

A Dutch Schulze Dreamscape glass vessel, from Oregon, in shaded transparent blue and turquoise glass, internally decorated with opaque twisted glass cane and murrini, signed by artist, dated "96" and numbered "3-90" on the base.

1996   *18in (45.5cm) high*

$1,500-2,000   **SK**

A spherical vessel of cut, sandblasted and polished dark green glass, by Frantisek Vizner, unmarked.

c1975   *5.75in (14.5cm) diam*

$4,000-6,000   **SDR**

A Tapio Wirkkala for IItalia swirled glass vase in clear with internal bubbles, etched "Tapio Wirkkala/Iitalia/VI-48?", few minor nicks and scratches.

6in (15cm) high

$400-800   **SDR**

A gray-blue bowl of cut, sandblasted and polished glass, by Frantisek Vízner, unsigned.

1987   *11in (28cm) diam*

$12,000-18,000   **SDR**

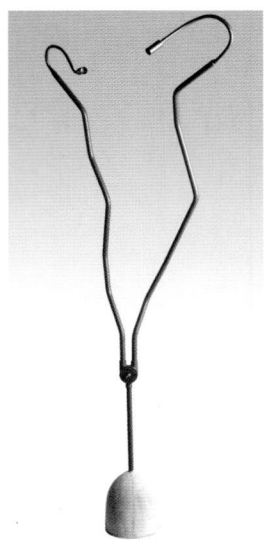

A Ron Arad for One-Off tree light, with concrete base and enameled metal adjustable stems, stem marked "BARTON/MADE IN ENGLAND/MALL 8".

1984   *75in (190.5cm) high*

$10,000-15,000   **SDR**

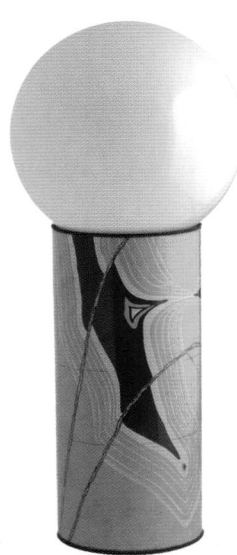

A 1960s Archizoom for Poltronova 'Tizio-Caio-Sempronio' printed tin and opaque white glass table lamp, printed "ARCHIZOOM DESIGN CENTRE".

c1967   *21.75in (55cm) high*

$1,000-1,500   **GM**

An Arredoluce six-light floor lamp, with enameled metal shades on white enameled metal base.

72in (183cm) high

$3,000-4,000   **SDR**

An Oscar Bach table lamp base, with two sockets and red enameled decoration on stem, marked "Oscar Bach" in script, remnant of label, needs re-wiring.

34.75in (88.5cm) high

$4,000-6,000   **SDR**

A pair of Oscar B. Bach Gothic form bronze candlestick table lamps, signed "Oscar B. Bach".

33in (84cm) high

$2,500-3,000   **FRE**

A pair of Barbini table lamps, with clear and opaque glass ovoid globes resting on white enameled metal bases, Barbini labels.

17in (43cm) high

$7,000-10,000   **SDR**

A wrought-iron torchere, in the style of Edgar Brandt, with a leaf and coiled vine motif to shaft and tripod base, unmarked.

75in (190.5cm) high

$1,200-2,000   **SDR**

An Italian Wireless 'WL01c' wire and papier-mâché shade table lamp, designed by Andrea Branzi and distributed by Design Gallery Milan.

1992   *16.25in (41cm) high*

$1,200-1,800   **GM**

A Christian Dell cream-colored chrome and tole desk lamp.

13in (33cm) high

$700-1,000   **FRE**

A Walter Dorwin Teague for Polaroid Corporation executive desk lamp no. 114, in brown bakelite with aluminum shaft, paper label on base, missing diffuser.

12.5in (32cm) high

$1,000-1,500   **SDR**

A Fantoni tall four-sided lamp base, impressed with geometric decoration and covered in chartreuse, amber and rust dead-matte glazes, mounted on wood base obscuring the signature.

18in (45.5cm) high

$700-1,000   **SDR**

A Fontana Arte polished brass floor lamp, with ivory enameled metal shade, and adjustable-height shaft, on boomerang-shaped plate glass base, unmarked.

63in (160cm) high

$3,500-4,500   **SDR**

A Fontana Arte table lamp, with five adjustable brass arms with enameled metal shades on a clear glass base.

25in (63.5cm) wide

$6,000-9,000   SDR

A Pierre Guariche floor lamp, with yellow enameled metal shade cantilevered over tripod base.

60in (152cm) high

$3,000-4,000   SDR

An Heifetz pair of chromed metal table lamp bases, with fin-shaped elements to shaft, on white marble bases, some chips to marble, unmarked.

34.75in (88cm) high

$800-1,200   SDR

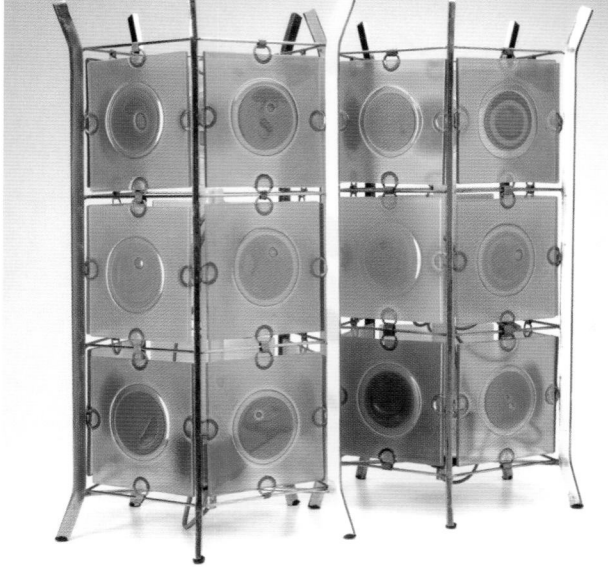

A pair of Higgins Rondo table lamps, each with 15 multi-colored glass panels fastened on a metal pentagonal base.

22.75in (58.5cm) high

$10,000-15,000   SDR

A Laurel lamp, white frosted shade, chromium base.

12in (30.5cm) high

$100-200   FRE

A Lightolier swing-arm floor lamp, with three enameled metal shades on brass shaft and marble base.

60.5in (154cm) high

$2,000-3,000   SDR

A pair of Dino Martens for Aureliano Toso mezza filigrana table lamp bases, with swirling canes, on acrylic bases.

36.25in (92cm) high

$4,500-5,500   SDR

A pair of James Mont carved wood table lamps, covered in gold leaf with gold leaf shades.

36in (91cm) high

$2,000-3,000   SDR

A pair of James Mont gessoed and gilded wood gargoyle table lamps.

22in (56cm) high

$10,000-15,000   SDR

A 20thC floor lamp, by George Nakashima, the tall drum form shade on an upright base of burl and rosewood, some creases and tear to one panel.

62in (157.5cm) high

$16,000-20,000   FRE

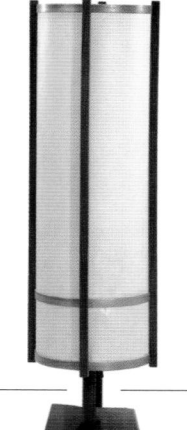

A 20thC table lamp, by George Nakashima, drum-form shade over twin cylindrical standards, burl free-form base.

27.5in (70cm) high

$7,000-9,000   **FRE**

A George Nakashima rosewood floor lamp, with free-form base.

58.5in (148.5cm) high

$32,000-35,000   **SDR**

A late 20thC Nessen lamp.

48in (122cm) high

$200-300   **SK**

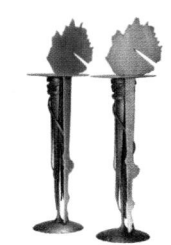

An Albert Paley pair of 'Sunrise' tall candlesticks, of forged milled steel.

Designed for the American Ballet Theater.

1993   *21.5in (54.5cm) high*

$4,000-6,000   **SDR**

An Albert Paley table lamp of forged steel, stamped "ALBERT PALEY 1992".

1992   *41in (104cm) high*

$20,000-25,000   **SDR**

A Tommi Parzinger for Dorlyn Silversmiths five-arm polished brass wall sconce, with etched sunburst motif to backplate, stamped mark.

21.5in (54.5cm) high

$600-900   **SDR**

A Tommi Parzinger gilt metal four-light floor lamp.

74.5in (189cm) high

$6,000-9,000   **SDR**

An American limited production Gaetano Pesce 'Osso' table lamp, with a shaped and textured faceted cast metal bronze base and a multicolored polyurethane plastic shade, produced in a series of 10 different examples, each with random coloring.

1989   *37.5in (95cm) high*

$14,000-26,000   **GM**

An Italian Arteluce 'Nr 607' halogen table lamp, the metal frame with with lightly textured gray finish, designed by Gino Sarfatti in 1971.

This was the first lamp to use halogen bulbs.

12.25in (31cm) high

$1,500-2,000   **GM**

A unique Italian green finished metal framed vanity mirror and halogen lamp, with cherub finial, designed by Nanda Vigo.

1986

$5,000-7,000   **GM**

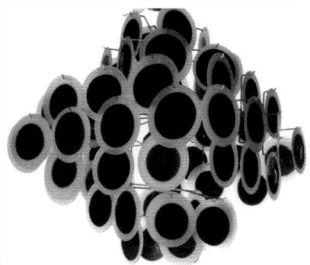

A Vistosi large chandelier, with circular blown glass discs in deep purple and white, suspended from a multi-pronged stainless steel frame, unmarked.

34in (86cm) wide

$2,000-3,000   **SDR**

A Canadian Birks Sterling ring box, with applied double "B" motif to lid.

c1970   *1.5in (4cm) high*

$300-400   **TCF**

A Nord Bowlen for Lunt 74-piece sterling silver and nylon flatware service, in the Contrast pattern, all marked "LUNT/STERLING".

c1954

$7,000-10,000   **SDR**

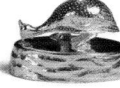

A pair of American Swid Powell silver plated stepped small candlesticks, designed by Robert and Twix Haussmann.

     2.75in (7cm) high

$1,000-1,500   **GM**

A pair of American Swid Powell metal verdigris style finish candlesticks, designed by Steven Holl, the underside of the bases with stamped facsimile signature.

1986   *20in (51cm) high*

$2,000-3,000   **GM**

A Los Castillos unusual and whimsical hammered silver-plated water pitcher, with a figural handle of a monkey with hardstone cabochon eyes, shallow dent to body, minor plate wear to figure, stamped "Plateado/Emilia Castillo/Mexico M.R./TD-85".

     10.5in (26.5cm) high

$2,000-4,000   **SDR**

A set of 12 Patrick Mavros silver animal place card holders, including meerkats, a frog, a zebra, a hippo, an ostrich, each mounted on an oval base, boxed.

Zimbabwean silversmith Patrick Mavros, has been creating sculptures of wildlife in silver for the last 25 years. Manufactured using the ancient technique of lost-wax casting these naturalistic pieces are highly detailed and often humorous.

$1,800-2,200   **L&T**

An Italian limited edition Cleto Munari .925 silver jug, with gilt wash to interior and stamped marks to base, numbered 87 from an edition of 300, designed by Angelo Mangiarotti.

1981   *8.75in (22cm) high*

$400-600   **GM**

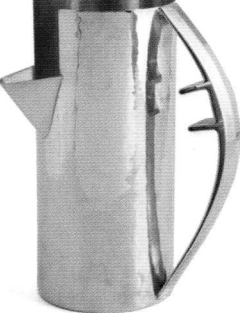

A Italian limited edition Cleto Munari .925 silver jug, with hammered effect, gilt wash to interior and stamped marks to base, numbered 22 from an edition of 300, designed by Carlo Scarpa.

1984   *8.75in (22cm) high*

$2,000-3,000   **GM**

An Italian Cleto Munari .925 silver double cone goblet, with gilt wash to interior, designed by Angelo Mangiarotti.

1981   *8in (20cm) high*

$400-600   **GM**

A French Cristofle .925 silver 'Bascule' tea/coffee pot and milk jug, with stamped marks to base, designed by Lino Sabatini.

1960   teapot 4.75in (12cm) high

$1,000-1,500   **GM**

An Italian Cleto Munari .925 silver tulip shaped goblet, with gilt wash to interior, designed by Angelo Mangiarotti.

A set of six silver goblets, with textured lower sections, hollow base, bowl interiors with gold wash, London hallmarks and maker's mark "YPB".

1981   8in (20cm) high | *1974*   6.25in (16cm) high

$3,000-4,000   **GM** | **$1,000-1,500**   **GAZE**

An Egmont Arens for The Hobart MFG. Co. aluminum and steel Streamliner meat slicer, Model-410, with rubber foot pads, metal tag and paper label.

A wonderful example of Machine Age design.

20.5in (51cm) wide

$1,200-1,500   **SDR**

A cast bronze textured Priapo sculpture of a stylized man with a large penis, designed by Andrea Branzi in 1986, from a series of six.

12.5in (31.5cm) high

$5,000-7,000   **GM**

A pair of 1970s Italian chrome metal curving candlesticks, designed by Luigi Colani.

13in (33cm) high

$700-1,000   **GM**

An Italian 'Mouse' cast bronze sculpture of a stylized standing man with large ears, designed by Andrea Branzi, from a series of four.

1986   23.25in (59cm) high

$5,000-7,000   **GM**

A Eugen Gaus (American 1905-1988) bronze sculpture of a man, untitled, on wood base, signed and dated.

1946   26.75in (68cm) high

$15,000-20,000   **SDR**

A pair of Hagenauer polished bronze double candelabra with elaborate bird and grapevine central motif.

14in (36cm) high

$11,000-15,000   **SDR**

A 'Heavenly Chorus' charger enameled metal, manufactured by Bernard Hesling, Australia, signed and dated.

1972   25.5in (65cm) diam

$600-900   SHA

A Josef Hoffmann for Wiener Werkstatte brass-washed copper teapot, with tin lining, rosewood handle and acorn finial, marked with "JH" cipher and "WIENER/WERK/STATTE".

10in (25.5cm) wide

$7,000-10,000   SDR

A Boris Lovet-Lorski bronze, untitled, signed "Lovet Lorski".

19in (47.5cm) high

$2,500-4,000   SDR

A David Mellor 'Pride' electroplated tea service, for Walker and Hall, comprising a teapot and cover, a hot water jug and cover, a milk jug and a sugar bowl, each with stamped marks "53722".

1959

$800-1,200   L&T

A Philip & Kelvin Laverne cast metal small table/stool, "The Kiss," after Constantine Brancusi, in verdigris patina, on casters.

21in (53cm) high

$12,000-18,000   SDR

A 'Maestrale' chrome-plated metal conical table fan, the slot with attached pink silk cloth that flaps when the fan is turned on, designed by Denis Santachiara.

Two large door handles of forged steel, designed by Albert Paley.

72in (183cm) long

$14,000-18,000   SDR

1988   27.25in (69cm) high

$1,500-2,000   GM

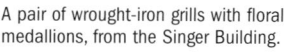

A set of twelve Gio Ponti stainless steel knives, stamped "Ponti Fraser's Italy".

7.25in (18cm) long

$600-800   SDR

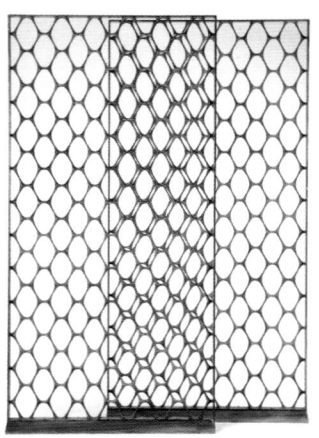

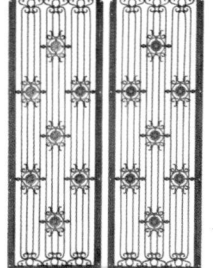

A pair of wrought-iron grills with floral medallions, from the Singer Building.

1906-08   54in (137cm) high

$4,000-5,000   SDR

A pair of room dividers of sculpted bronze in a steel frame, on wood bases.

81in (205.5cm) high

$16,000-20,000   SDR

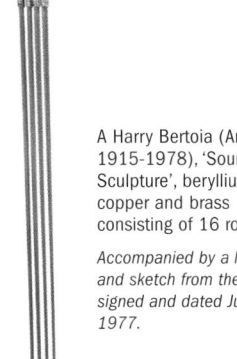

A Harry Bertoia (American 1915-1978), 'Sound Sculpture', beryllium copper and brass consisting of 16 rods.

Accompanied by a letter and sketch from the artist signed and dated July 1, 1977.

103in (261.5cm) high

$65,000-85,000 FRE

A Harry Bertoia 'Sound Sculpture', beryllium copper and brass consisting of 13 rods.

Accompanied by a photocopy of a sketch signed by the artist.

78in (198cm) high

$40,000-55,000 FRE

A Harry Bertoia 'Sound Pod', welded sheet steel, accompanied by mallet.

96in (244cm) high

$40,000-55,000 FRE

A Harry Bertoia 'Sonambient', with X-base in beryllium copper.

34in (86cm) wide

$70,000-90,000 SDR

A Harry Bertoia 'Sonambient Sound Sculpture', 25 brass and aluminum rods.

Originally created for the McMaster Memorial Gardens.

c1970   53.5in (136cm) high

$45,000-50,000 SDR

A Harry Bertoia 'Willow' sculpture, stainless steel rods on stainless steel base.

96in (244cm) high

$115,000-125,000 SDR

A Harry Bertoia untitled bronze, with verdigris patina.

20in (51cm) high

$30,000-35,000 SDR

A Joe Brown (1909-1985) bronze sculpture "Running Back", American, on marble plinth, green-brown patina.

9.5in (24cm) high

$1,000-1,500 FRE

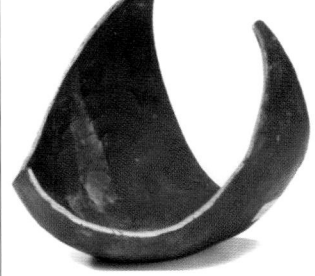

A Paul Evans lead table sculpture, with gold trim, unmarked.

c1970s   5.75in (14.5cm) high

$1,000-1,500 SDR

A rare Paul Evans Argente welded aluminum sculpture, on black enameled pedestal base.

This rare piece was part of Evans' 1968 'Sculptures in the Fields' series. He created only three Argente masterpieces and photographed them in a Bucks County field. The Field series is considered to be among the rarest and most important of all of Evans' work. Accompanied by copy of original photo.

78in (198cm) high

$35,000-45,000 SDR

A Frank Gehry prototype bird sculpture, with shaped laminate chips forming feathers, mounted in deep square box frame, unsigned.

c1980   26in (66cm) wide

$7,000-10,000   **SK**

A Klaus Ihlenfeld (German/American, 20thC) untitled bronze with verdigris patina, signed.

7in (17.75cm) diam

$6,000-9,000   **SDR**

A set of 12 'Thanks Tablets', enamel on cast hydro cal visible markers, 2000, each signed by Allan McCollum, dated and numbered.

each 4in (10cm) diam

$5,000-7,000   **SDR**

A Belgian Herman Muys lightbox sculpture, comprised of etched and applied glass pieces depicting an array of electronic themes and motifs, in ebonized wood frame.

Commissioned for the European headquarters of IT&T Corporation.

1996   45.5in (115.5cm) high

$6,000-8,000   **SDR**

A magnesite sculptural relief, by Isamu Noguchi, possibly a maquette for a playground design, incised "IN" to rear.

16.5in (42cm) wide

$180,000-270,000   **SDR**

A metal sculpture by Lindsay Rais, 'Small Spiralling Basket', incorporating pistachio nut shells, anti-tarnish silver wire, stainless steel mesh, coated copper, and beads.

2003   8in (20.5cm) high

$800-1,100   **DRG**

A Morris Singer abstract 'Candida' bronze head, signed "2/5" and foundry stamp.

9.5in (24cm) high

$350-450   **JN**

An Edward Zucca sculpture 'Caveman TV', poplar, hemlock, oak, ash, maple, bark, cowhide, paper, rush, horn, bones, chamois and Connecticut fieldstone, signed, titled, dated and inscribed.

1993   74in (188cm) high

$7,000-10,000   **SDR**

A marquee sign, 'The Sound of Music', the white enameled letters traced with lightbulbs within, mounted to a steel frame.

This was the short marquee used during The Sound of Music's run at the Mark Hellinger Theater on Broadway from November 1962. The Sound of Music originally opened on Broadway at the Lunt-Fontanne Theater in 1959.

1962-63   *letters 14.5in (37cm) high*

$3,000-4,000   **FRE**

A marquee sign, 'the musical', the enameled letters traced with rows of lightbulbs within, mounted to a steel frame.

This sign is purported to have been part of the marquee for La Cage Aux Folles during its run at the Palace Theater on Broadway.

1983-87   *18.25in (46.5cm) high*

$4,500-6,000   **FRE**

A 'Once Upon a Time' neon theater sign, in unmounted neon tubing, thought to have been created for a 1960s television show.

13.5in (34cm) high

$3,000-4,000   **FRE**

A neon profile of Bob Hope, in unmounted neon tubing, thought to have been originally created for a Hollywood restaurant decorated with caricatures of the stars.

c1945   *24in (61cm) high*

$1,500-2,000   **FRE**

An 'S' from the 42nd street subway station sign, New York City, in enameled metal with over one-hundred pink light bulbs which undulate across the surface with a mechanical flasher.

c1985   *61in (155cm) high*

$8,000-10,000   **FRE**

A model 'i' from the 'Biography' sign on 1775 Broadway, 1998-2005, in enameled metal with red neon tubing, the 'dot' a separate piece.

1998-2005   *69.75in (177cm) high*

$7,000-10,000   **FRE**

A mid-20thC neon sailboat, unmounted neon tubing, the red boat with white sails and a green flag on a wavy blue sea under an orange/yellow sun, within a blue border.

21.75in (55.25cm) wide

$1,000-1,500   **FRE**

A model for the Coca-Cola Spectacular at 2 Times Square, carved, painted and molded wood and plastic, with related materials including rolled blueprints, a framed elevation print and reproduction photographs of the Spectacular in place.

The Coca-Cola Times Square Spectacular remained in place from 1992 to 2003, when it was replaced by another Coca-Cola sign featuring digital imagery.

1990   *55in (140cm) high*

$25,000-30,000   **FRE**

A Planters Peanuts Times Square 1952 Spectacular large-scale replica, in enameled metal and paint with neon, depicting Mr. Peanut and a can of Planters Cocktail Peanuts.

Planters Peanuts has a long history of signs in Times Square going as far back as the thirties with an early Spectacular which spilled peanuts onto Broadway. The Planters sign was installed around 1952. This replica was made by Artkraft Strauss in 1997 and was painted by French artist, Sam Quinones.

1997   *90in (229cm) high*

$4,000-6,000   **FRE**

MODERN DESIGN

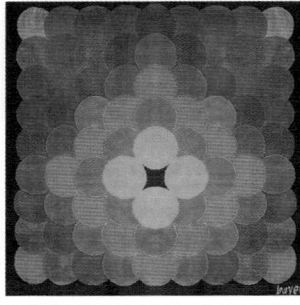

A Herbert Bayer 'Ordered Amassment III' pile woven wool tapestry, with "Bayer" woven into the tapestry lower right recto.

77.5in (194cm) high

$4,000-6,000 SDR

An Edward Fields wool area rug, in the wave pattern, signed "Edward Fields".

102in (259cm) wide

$1,000-1,500 SDR

A Lucienne Day panel of 'Calyx' pattern fabric, in brown, designed for the festival of Britain and subsequently produced by Heals & Sons Ltd.

1951 *48in (123cm) wide*

$800-1,200 L&T

An Edward Fields Agros wool rug in the floral pattern, "Edward Fields" label.

1971 *61.5in (156cm) wide*

$800-1,000 SDR

EDWARD FIELDS

- Edward Fields Inc. (New York) has been producing custom rugs since 1935.
- The more transitory lifestyle led by Americans from the 1950s meant that homeowners were reluctant to invest in fixed furnishings that could not be taken to a new property. Edward Fields pioneered the 'area rug' which was intended to cover an entire living room floor without being a permanent fixture.
- In partnership with Raymond Loewy, Fields introduced a range of five rugs with futuristic designs, including 'Infinite Star', 'Heavenly', 'Legend' and 'Stella'.
- Edward Fields' rugs became known for their high quality and strong designs. He received prestigious commissions including the White House and Air Force One.
- In recent years, the five original designs have been re-released creating a renewed interest in vintage examples.
- The rugs became a huge success and went on sale at Lord's & Taylor's on Fifth Avenue, New York. Other designers such as Pierre Cardin followed suit, aiming to bring street fashion into the home. The company is still in business today.

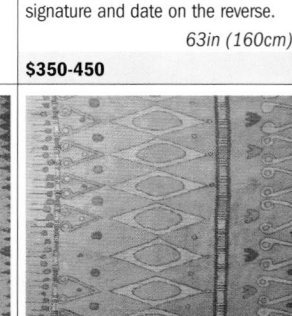

A mid-20thC geometric textile wall hanging, by Aurelia Munoz, composed of multiple pieced geometric shapes and fabrics of various textures, artist's stitched signature and date on the reverse.

63in (160cm) high

$350-450 SK

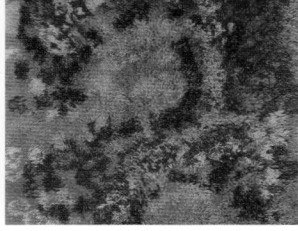

A Danish Rya rug, with abstract design in red, brown and orange.

137in (342.5cm) long

$300-400 SDR

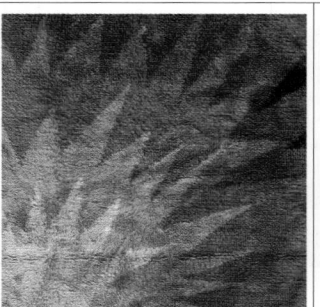

A Rya-style area rug, with starburst pattern in brown, orange and yellow, unmarked.

97in (242.5cm) long

$400-600 SDR

A Danish modern shag area rug, with sunburst pattern and flame border in salmon, red and brick on an ivory ground.

108in (270cm) long

$250-350 SDR

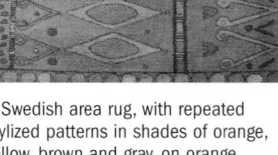

A Swedish area rug, with repeated stylized patterns in shades of orange, yellow, brown and gray, on orange ground, unmarked.

118in (299.5cm) wide

$900-1,200 SDR

A shag rug, with overall abstract pattern, in red, orange and brown.

79in (197.5cm) long

$400-600 SDR

688

A Pedro Friedeberg three legged figural mahogany clock painted in red and gold, with battery movement enclosed in hinged and pegged back leg panel, signed "Pedro Friedeberg" inside back panel.

23in (58cm) high

$3,000-4,000   **SDR**

A postmodern table clock, by Gary Knox Bennett, with black and white case and whimsically designed shadowbox face with enameled hands in yellow, orange, blue and white, signed "In Oakland/GKB/ANNO 94".

18.25in (46.5cm) high

$3,000-4,000   **SDR**

A 'Yellow Clock', by Gary Knox Bennett, of painted wood with recessed dial and ivory hands, signed "In Oakland/GKB/Anno 92".

14in (35.5cm) high

$2,000-4,000   **SDR**

A Paul Evans for Phillip Lloyd Powell walnut charger, with radiating pewter inlay, marked "Designers Inc. * Paul Evans".

17.5in (44.5cm) diam

$1,200-1,500   **SDR**

A walnut and metal clock, by Gary Knox Bennett, with 'winged' case, purple lustred concave face with flaming heart hands and Cupid, unmarked.

1979   *24.5in (62cm) high*

$1,000-1,500   **SDR**

A Herman Miller desk clock, in angular wood frame with circular face, face marked "Herman Miller".

9.75in (25cm) wide

$4,000-5,000   **SDR**

A Trucks 'HF5563' limited edition pink lacquered wood jewelry box, with three carved acrylic removable finials, numbered 2 from an edition of 12, designed by Johanna Grawunder.

1986   *13.5in (34.5cm) wide*

$3,000-4,000   **GM**

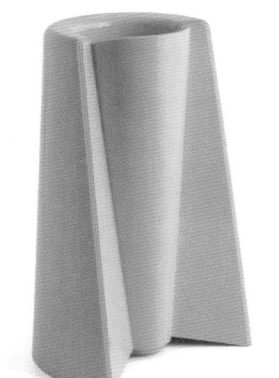

A 1970s Italian Danese 'Pogo Pogo' injection molded ABS plastic vase, designed by Enzo Mari.

1969   *12in (30cm) high*

$500-700   **GM**

A 1970s Italian Danese gray plastic vase, designed by Enzo Mari.

1969   *16.5in (42cm) high*

$600-900   **GM**

An Italian Danese injection molded gray striated plastic watering can, designed by Enzo Mari.

This is the prototype, produced under Mari's guidance.

1997   *19.25in (49cm) long*

$700-1,000   **GM**

A figured tulipwood spherical vessel, by Ed Moulthrop, with closed-in rim, signed "Ed Moulthrop/Figured Tulipwood/808921-U".

c1980   *9.5in (24cm) diam*

$4,000-6,000   **SDR**

689

"La Dame Aux Camelias", by Alphonse Mucha, printed by F. Champenois, Paris, depicting the actress Sarah Bernhardt clothed in magnificent costume against a background of silver stars, framed, creases.

1896   *80in (203cm) high*

$15,000-20,000   **SWA**

"Job", designed by Alphonse Mucha, and printed by F. Champenois, Paris, with the bust of a woman with extravagant hair.

1896   *24in (61cm) high*

$28,000-32,000   **SWA**

"La Samaritaine", by Alphonse Mucha, printed by F. Champenois, Paris, depicting the near-life size actress with a halo behind her head and flowing hair and gown, framed.

1897   *68.25in (173.5cm) high*

$20,000-25,000   **SWA**

"Vin Des Incas", designed by Alphonse Mucha, on paper.

Vin des Incas was one of the many varieties of fortified wine that were popular at the turn of the century. Distilled from various herbs, these tonics were sold as medication targeting various illnesses, and in this case specifically aimed at convalescents.

1897   *5.5in (13.5cm) high*

$6,000-8,000   **SWA**

CLOSER LOOK AT A MUCHA POSTER

This poster, designed by the hugely popular Czech artist Alphonse Mucha (1860-1939), is advertising luxury champagne. He was also well known for his stage performance posters and magazine covers.

Here the artist employs the elongated format which he liked so much. The stars, another of his signature design motifs that worked so well when first used in his famous poster advertising the play 'La Dame Aux Camelias' for Sarah Bernhardt, here serve as the sparkling bubbles of the champagne.

With his immediately recognizable style, Mucha was soon trusted to advertise for many prestigious brands, such as Moet & Chandon, Vin Des Incas, Job and here Ruinart.

The extravagant flowing hair that was Mucha's hallmark is no longer based on reality here, and becomes an entirely decorative element. It is said to also subtly convey the effervescent quality of the champagne.

"Champagne Ruinart", by Alphonse Mucha, printed by F. Champenois, Paris, tape repair, creases.

1896   *69.25in (176cm) high*

$10,000-15,000   **SWA**

'Rose', designed by Alphonse Mucha, and printed by F. Champenois, Paris, expertly replaced margins.

1898   *40.5in (102.5cm) high*

$6,000-8,000   **SWA**

"Les Arts", designed by Alphonse Mucha (1860-1939), a group of four decorative panels.

1898

22in (56cm) high

$55,000-65,000

SWA

"Job", designed by Alphonse Mucha, and printed by F. Champenois, Paris, depicting a girl sitting in a circle with brown hair and a pink dress.

This poster is considered to be Mucha's best advertising piece.

1898

61in (155cm) high

$12,000-15,000

SWA

"Dawn & Dusk", designed by Alphonse Mucha, and printed by F. Champenois, Paris, a set of two posters depicting two maidens at opposite ends of the day couched beneath the boughs of a tree, framed.

Only 1000 copies of these posters were printed.

1899

18.5in (46.5cm) high

$15,000-20,000

SWA

"Cocorico", designed by Alphonse Mucha, trial proof printed on silver foil paper and hand signed in ink, creases.

Cocorico was a fashionable magazine that included essays, poetry and art. Between 1898 and 1902 sixty-three issues of the magazine were published, each with a cover designed by a well-known poster artist. Of all the great artists involved, Mucha was the major contributor. His design for the frontispiece was used continuously from 1899.

1899

12.25in (31cm) high

$7,000-10,000

SWA

"Exposition De St. Louis", designed by Alphonse Mucha, and printed by F. Champenois, Paris, depicting a maiden within a halo hand-in-hand with a Native American, framed, restored and repaired.

1903

39.5in (100.5cm) high

$8,000-10,000

SWA

"Divan Japonais", designed by Henri De Toulouse-Lautrec.

1893   *32in (81cm) high*

$30,000-35,000   **SWA**

"Le Deuxieme Volume De Bruant", designed by Henri De Toulouse-Lautrec, and printed by Chaix, Paris, repaired tears.

Lautrec designed more posters for Bruant than for anyone else. This poster, which exists in several variants, shows the performer, dressed in his trademark black velvet suit, hat and boots, turning his back on viewers.

1893   *31.5in (80cm) high*

$5,000-7,000   **SWA**

"L'Argent", designed by Henri De Toulouse Lautrec, and printed by Eugene Verneau, Paris, depicting Monsieur and Madame Reynard walking away from a table.

Both the Théâtre de l'Oeuvre and the Théâtre Libre commissioned Toulouse-Lautrec to design illustrated programs. "L'Argent" is said to be among the best he designed.

1895   *12.5in (32cm) high*

$15,000-20,000   **SWA**

'Oscar Wilde Et Romain Coolus', designed by Henri De Toulouse Lautrec, advertising Coolus's "Raphaël", and Wilde's "Salomé" and depicts Wilde against an outline of the British Houses of Parliament.

Wilde's play had been banned in Britain, and the aesthete himself was in jail at the time of this production. The play had its world premiere February 10, 1896, at the Théâtre de l'Oeuvre.

1896   *12.75in (32.5cm) high*

$10,000-15,000   **SWA**

"Troupe De Mlle Eglantine", designed by Henri De Toulouse Lautrec, depicting four dancers, water damage, faded, folds.

This poster was for the troupe's appearance at the Palace Theatre in London, where it performed the Quadrille Naturaliste, a popular dance from the French music halls. Lautrec bathes the dancers in the yellow glow of the stage lights. Their darkly clad legs emerging from the large white space of their petticoats was both alluring and risqué.

1896   *24in (61cm) high*

$28,000-32,000   **SWA**

"May Milton", designed by Henri De Toulouse Lautrec, pinholes.

May Milton was an English dancer. This is one of the best examples of Lautrec's use of blank paper to help to create an image.

31in (78.5cm) high

$20,000-25,000   **SWA**

A "Lippincott's November" 1890 lithograph signed, Will Cargueville, framed.

22in (56cm) long

$400-600   **SK**

"Folies Bergere/Les Girard", designed by Jules Cheret, and printed by Cheret, Paris.

This is one of Cheret's rarest posters. Cheret designed two versions of this poster for the Girards. This version, the first and most rare, was printed when the troupe appeared at the Folies Bergère.

1877   *22in (56cm) high*

$8,000-10,000   **SWA**

"Champagne Hau", designed by Walter Crane, a Dionysian goddess draped in harvest orange is walking through a similarly-colored autumnal vineyard and extracting champagne straight from the ripe, red grapes, orange lettering, restored, matted and framed.

1894   *22.5in (57cm) high*

$2,000-3,000   **SWA**

"Librairie Romantique", designed by Eugene Grasset, and printed by J. Bognard, Paris, with a young woman in old-fashioned vestment from the 1830s sitting on a pile of old books, with the Notre Dame in the background, framed, repaired tears.

1887   *50.5in (128.5cm) high*

$3,000-4,000   **SWA**

'Grafton Gallery', designed by Eugene Grasset, and printed by Verdoux, Ducourtioux & Huillard, with a symbolist young woman enveloped in her flowing scarf, picking flowers, water damage, discoloration, tears.

This image was used to advertise a decorative arts exhibition at the Grafton Gallery in London.

1893   *28.25in (72cm) high*

$1,000-1,500   **SWA**

"Hermann Scherrer", designed by Ludwig Hohlwein, printed by G. Schuh, Munich, repaired tears, folds.

This image was so striking that it became an emblem of the company, which used it on catalogue covers and on their clothing labels.

1907   49in (124.5cm) high

$10,000-15,000   **SWA**

"Automobile Club De France/6EME Exposition", designed by Privat Livemont, and printed by J. Barreau, Paris, with a woman driving past the Grand Palais.

The French Automobile Club was founded in 1895 and organized its first exhibition in 1898. In 1902, Privat Livemont was commissioned to design the poster advertising the fifth Auto Show, and then later to design two more, this poster being one of them.

1903   14.5in (37cm) high

$6,000-9,000   **SWA**

"La Lanterne", designed by Eugene Oge, and printed by Charles Verneau, Paris, with the image of a priest-like vampire grasping the church of Sacre Coeur, repaired tears, folds.

La Lanterne was an anti-clerical magazine that began publication on April 22, 1877.

1902   55.25in (140.5cm) high

$3,000-4,000   **SWA**

A "Harper's Snow Shoes 1896" signed, Edward Penfield lithograph, framed.

16in (40.5cm) long

$400-600   **SK**

"Zegepraal", designed by Sluyters, and printed by Scheltens & Giltay, Amsterdam, framed, tape stains, repaired tears.

1904   45.25in (115cm) high

$7,000-10,000   **SWA**

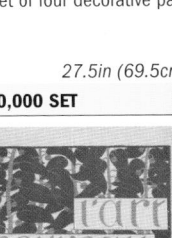

"Fleurs", designed by Elizabeth Sonrel, one of a set of four decorative panels, on paper.

27.5in (69.5cm) high

$7,000-10,000 SET   **SWA**

"Théâtre De Loie Fuller", designed and printed by Manuel Orazi, with a dancer swirling beneath a falling bouquet of roses transforming into snowflakes, framed.

This poster is for Loie Fuller's special theatre at the 1900 Paris World's Fair.

1900   77.5in (197cm) high

$45,000-55,000   **SWA**

"Exposition A La Bodiniére", designed by Theophile-Alexandre Steinlen, and printed by Charles Verneau, Paris, depicting two of his cats, creases, folds.

La Bodiniere was the exhibition hall of the Théâtre d'application, which offered a variety of attractions from art exhibits by Paris's avant garde artists to shadow plays. Steinlen chose a horizontal format for this exhibition poster, exceedingly rare for the genre.

1894   29.75in (75.5cm) wide

$7,000-10,000   **SWA**

"Delftsche Slaolie", designed by Jan Toorop (1858-1928).

This poster for salad oil by the Dutch artist Jan Toorop is probably the best-known example of Art Nouveau produced in the country.

1895   34in (86.5cm) high

$10,000-12,000   **SWA**

"L'Art Nouveau Exposition Permanente", designed by Felix Vallotton, printed by Lemaergier, Paris, with a very simple and sensitive stylized vegetal motif, repaired tears.

This is an extremely rare document, of both historical importance and artistic merit.

c1896   23.5in (59.5cm) high

$16,000-20,000   **SWA**

"Vers New York/Hamburg-Amerika Linie", designed by Albert Fuss, repaired tears and creases.

c1930   *39.5in (100.5cm) high*

$700-1,000   SWA

"Los Angeles/United Airlines", designed by Stan Galli, repaired tears and overpainting.

c1960   *40in (101.5cm) high*

$800-1,000   SWA

"Air Algérie", by Guy Georget, and printed by Aljanvic, Paris, with a passenger plane flying in the sky above red and white stripes, framed.

39.25in (99.5cm) high

$900-1,100   SWA

"Air Afrique", designed by F. Joseph. and printed by Reboul et Fils, Paris, advertising Air Afrique's North Africa route, with the silhouette of a Bloch 220.

1938   *36.5in (93cm) high*

$1,500-2,000   SWA

"New York/Fly TWA", designed by David Klein, with a geometric, abstract, kaleidoscopic view of Times Square.

This is the rare, earlier variation of the poster which features a detailed image of a TWA Constellation. Later versions depict the silhouette of a jet plane.

25.25in (64cm) high

$2,000-3,000   SWA

"Le Maroc Par Marseille", designed by Jacques Majorelle, and printed by Lucien Serre, Paris.

1926   *41.75in (106cm) high*

$4,000-6,000   SWA

"United States Lines", designed by Edmond Maurus, and printed by Publix, Paris, restoration along folds.

c1935   *39.25in (99.5cm) high*

$6,000-9,000   SWA

"American Airlines/Washington", designed by Edward McKnight Kauffer, repaired tears losses.

In 1948, Kauffer designed a poster for American Airlines which presented a view of the Capitol with red, white and blue typography. This more sophisticated design suggests it was an earlier design.

c1947   *39.75in (96cm) high*

$1,500-2,000   SWA

"The New 20th Century Limited", designed by Leslie Ragan, and printed by Latham Litho., Long Island, with a powerful Art Deco image of one of this century's most famous American trains.

In the 1930s, when the Art Deco movement began to reflect the sleek, aerodynamic lines new technology, the new 20th Century Limited, designed by Henry Dreyfus, was the pride of the New York Central Line, running from New York to Chicago. This image has been featured by the United States Postal Service on a series of stamps commemorating the 1930s, and is among the top American Art Deco posters ever designed.

1938   *40.75in (103.5cm) high*

$25,000-30,000   SWA

"Air France/Israel", designed by Renluc, and printed by Hubert Baille & Cie, depicting highlights of Israeli life, such as industry, architecture, history, recreation and agriculture, on a map of the Mediterranean coast.

1951   *39.5in (100.5cm) high*

$1,500-2,000   SWA

"Amerique Du Sud/Air France", designed by Bernard Villemot, printed by Courbet, Paris, with local gathering by a large Spanish-style church, on paper.

1958   *39.25in (99.5cm) high*

$800-1,000   SWA

"Britain/Qantas", by an anonymous designer, with a brown, white and gray bull dog sitting against a blue background.

39.25in (99.5cm) high

$500-700   SWA

"Mont Tremblant", designed by Herbert Bayer, with a tinted photomontage of a skier looking up towards a Canadian leaf and a skier, restored and repaired.

1939   *40.5in (102.5cm) high*

$5,000-6,000   **SWA**

"Winter In Sweden/Swedish Air Lines", designed by Rene Crispen, and printed by J. Olsens Litho., Stockholm, a color photograph of a blond holding her skis over her shoulders in front of a plane, restored and repaired.

1948   *39in (98.5cm) high*

$700-900   **SWA**

"Winter Holiday/Snow Valley", designed by Fritz Dillman, with skiers in red, white, blue and yellow circling a snowman.

     18in (45.5cm) high

$1,000-1,500   **SWA**

"Dartmouth Winter Carnival", designed by T. M. Joanethis, with a skier in a red hat and gloves virtually exploding out of the poster.

1938   *33.5in (85cm) high*

$6,000-7,000   **SWA**

"Davos Parsenn", designed by Herbert Leupin, and printed by Wolfsberg-Druck, Zurich, with skiers skiing along the sides of a star.

     40in (101.5cm) high

$1,000-1,500   **SWA**

"Come To Snow Valley", designed by Sascha Maurer, and printed by Argus Graphic Arts, New York, with a waving snowman wearing a blue scarf, red mittens and a hat.

     22.5in (57cm) high

$1,000-1,500   **SWA**

"Mob", designed by Martin Peikert, and printed by Klausfelder Vevey, with a woman sitting atop a speeding train, repaired tears and creases.

     40in (102cm) high

$2,500-3,000   **SWA**

"Sun Valley Idaho", designed by Dwight Shepler and Arnold, with a skier pausing to listen to a man playing an accordion, restored and repaired.

     38in (96cm) high

$2,500-3,000   **SWA**

"Chamonix/Mont Blanc", designed by Francisco Tamagno, and printed by Emile Pecaud & Cie., Paris, depicting a couple executing a perfectly synchronized ski jump, repaired tears, folds.

Tamagno created this at a time when skiing was so new that it was virtually unknown, and skiing advertising even more so.

1910   *42.5in (107.5cm) high*

$13,000-15,000   **SWA**

"Les Vosges", designed by Louis Tauzin and printed by F. Champenois, Paris, depicting families and couples sledding, skating and skiing.

The poster exists with several text variations, including one from as late as 1913 promoting the 7th International Skiing Competition.

     41.5in (105.5cm) high

$6,000-9,000   **SWA**

"Mt. Buffalo National Park, Victoria", designed by Percy Trompf, printed by Robert Harding Litho., Melbourne, expert overpainting, repairs and folds.

Australia's Mt. Buffalo National Park was established in 1898, in Victoria, northeast of Melbourne. The Mt. Buffalo Chalet was built in 1910 and from then on the area became a destination for skiers.

c1930   *40in (101.5cm) high*

$6,000-9,000   **SWA**

"Yosemite Winter Sports", by an anonymous designer, with a skier before of one of Yosemite's mountains, restored losses, repaired tears.

At Badger Pass, in 1928, the first American ski school was established, and Yosemite still offers visitors downhill runs and cross-country skiing trails.

     22in (56cm) high

$1,000-1,500   **SWA**

"Soave-Bertani", designed by Araca, printed by Grafiche Baroni, Milan, with a stylized Art Deco graphic of a man pouring the last drops of wine from a bottle, horizontal fold.

1931   *55.5in (141cm) high*

$5,000-7,000   **SWA**

"Back Him Up Buy War Bonds", by Frank Brangwyn, printed by Avenue Press, London, with a vivid battle front scene of a British Tommy bayoneting a German soldier, repaired tears and creases.

1940   *60in (152.5cm) wide*

$800-1,000   **SWA**

"Maison Prunier", designed by A.M. (Adolphe Mouron) Cassandre, framed.

By 1934, Cassandre had abandoned his geometrical style of design and switched to a warm, sensuous line. His poster for Maison Prunier clearly represents this change in style. Already well-established in Paris, this poster was designed to announce the opening of Prunier's London branch. The rendering of the table, fish, shell and lobster are marvellously drawn with warm tones. But Cassandre's magic also relies on the subtle way the table is positioned beneath a halo of typography with the restaurant's name located right beneath the corner of the table, as if being highlighted by an arrow.

59.5in (151cm) high

$25,000-30,000   **SWA**

"If You Want To Fight! Join The Marines", by Howard Chandler Christy, creases, repaired tears.

An early sexy, taunting, challenging and daring recruitment poster designed two years before the United States entered the war.

1915   *40in (101.5cm) high*

$2,000-3,000   **SWA**

"Lippincott's For August", designed by Joseph J. Gould, with a woman reading a copy of Lippincott's under a porch, tears and creases.

1897   *18.5in (47cm) high*

$800-1,200   **SWA**

"Lionel Hampton", designed by D'Apres Serge Jacques, and printed by Aussel, Paris, with a photographic rendering of Hampton playing his drums, repaired tears and creases.

46.75in (118.5cm) high

$2,000-3,000   **SWA**

"Fly With The Marines", designed by H. H. L., and printed by the Alpha Litho., Co., Camden, New Jersey, with an eagle feasting on a Japanese fighter plane.

1942   *39.5in (100.5cm) high*

$600-900   **SWA**

"On The Job For Victory", designed by Jonas Lie, and printed by W. F. Powers Co., New York, with hulls amidst the cranes and scaffolding of a busy shipyard, minor tears and creases.

c1918   *54.75in (139cm) wide*

$2,000-3,000   **SWA**

"Ballets Russes" after Pablo Picasso, printed by Watelet-Arbelot, Paris, on paper, the image affixed to poster, losses, tears and creases.

Serge Diaghilev founded the Ballets Russes in 1909 and premiered with a revolutionary show and first season at the Théâtre Chatelet that transfixed Paris and transformed the artistic landscape. For years they performed at the Théâtre des Champs Elysees, on the cutting edge of all the artistic disciplines featuring (among many other talents) music by Stravinsky, sets and costumes designed by the best Cubist artists and some the great ballet dancers of all time. In 1917, at the suggestion of Jean Cocteau, Diaghilev commissioned Picasso to design the sets and costumes for Parade. The image on this poster is a lithograph after a costume drawing of Picasso's which the Ballet Russes used on their posters. Both in Paris and Monte Carlo (where they also performed) they had typographic posters printed listing the program of their season, around a blank space into which they would glue this image.

1939   *39.5in (100.5cm) high*

$3,000-4,000   **SWA**

"Save Wheat", designed by Edward Penfield, with French women pulling a plow through rocky ground, repaired tears and creases, folds.

Penfield's image is based on a photograph which appeared on another U.S. Food Administration poster.

1918   *35in (89cm) high*

$1,000-1,500   **SWA**

"Starve The Squander Bug", by Theodor Seuss Geisel, and printed by the Government Printing Office, in typical Seussian style, with a "Squander Bug" eating money, creases and fold.

Long before he began his illustrious career as a children's book illustrator, Dr. Seuss did political cartoons for newspapers in New York City.

c1943   13.5in (34.5cm) high
$600-900   SWA

"Teamwork Builds Ships", designed by William Dodge Stevens, and printed by Forbes, Boston, with men labouring on the hull of a ship, tears, creases.

c1918   50in (127cm) wide
$2,500-3,000   SWA

"Official United States War Films", designed by Stoner, and printed for Alpha Litho., Co., New York, with soldiers carrying their bayonets as they charge into battle, folds and repairs.

41in (104cm) high
$3,000-5,000   SWA

"Negrita. Le Rhum.", designed by Bernard Villemot and printed by Bedos, Paris, with a woman leaning against a palm tree, silhouetted against a sunset, creases and minor tears.

1974   89in (226cm) wide
$4,000-6,000   SWA

"Contrex", designed by Bernard Villemot, and printed by Martin, Paris, with a woman against a geometric background, on paper.

c1975   68.5in (174cm) high
$600-900   SWA

"Book Week", designed by Jessie Wilcox Smith, with young children browsing through the books that line the library's shelves, repaired tears, pinholes.

In America, Book Week was introduced in 1919 to focus attention on the need for quality children's books and the importance of childhood literacy.

1921   21.25in (54.4cm) high
$600-900   SWA

"I-Me-My-Mine", by an anonymous designer, printed by Mather & Co., Chicago, with a musician playing a saxophone.

1925   47.5in (120.5cm) high
$2,000-3,000   SWA

"Steer Straight For Success", by an anonymous designer, printed by Mather & Co., Chicago, with a ship leaving behind a trail of black steam as it makes its way through the water, creases.

1925   48in (122cm) high
$1,200-1,500   SWA

"Ringling Bros. and Barnum & Bailey/ Pallenburg's Wonder Bears", by an anonymous designer, and printed by The Erie Litho Co., Erie, PA., with brown bears roller skating, riding bikes, playing music, dancing and walking on stilts, tears and creases.

c1920   41in (104cm) wide
$2,000-3,000   SWA

"Kaffee Hag", by an anonymous designer, printed by Fretz, A. G., Zurich, with a red heart and a white outline of a coffee cup, repaired tear, folds.

50in (127cm) high
$400-600   SWA

FIGURATIVE

THE PAINTINGS MARKET

It was another annus mirabilis for the art market with many auction houses posting their best results yet. Underpinning this stellar performance were the extraordinary prices achieved in the Modern and Contemporary categories. A Christie's Modern and Impressionist auction in New York last November fetched $492 million – a record total for a single auction. Such sales clearly bolstered New York's enduring reputation as the art world's capital city. It should be noted, however, that London equaled the Big Apple in totals for Contemporary art.

Another significant factor in the overall market has been the influx of new buyers with a seemingly unquenchable thirst for 'the new' in art. This last year has seen the inexorable rise of the markets for Indian and Chinese contemporary art. Chinese painters such as Zhang Xiaogang, Fang Lijun and Liu Xiaodong and the Indian artists Frances Newton Souza and Tyeb Maht, now regularly fetch six and seven figure sums at auction.

Looking to the future, it would seem to be a safe prediction that Russian Contemporary Art will be next to see a dramatic surge.

Here in the USA it was a solid year for American paintings of all periods. At Freeman's in Philadelphia, where I work, it was our strongest year yet with Pennsylvania Impressionist art contributing considerably to the totals. Other regional houses performed well again largely due to strong local support for the indigenous art that they handle be it from California Impressionism to Western Art. Floridian subjects have also proved increasingly popular of late.

Two other strong collecting areas have again been Illustration art – a Norman Rockwell painting sold for over $15 million – and also for works by African American artists.

Alasdair Nichol

FIGURATIVE PAINTINGS

Thomas Hargreaves (British 1775-1846), Half length portrait of Sir William Hortham, watercolor on ivory.

A native of Liverpool, Hargreaves was assistant and pupil of Sir Thomas Lawrence from 1793. He exhibited at the Liverpool Academy, The Society of British Artists and at the Royal Academy.

4x3in (10x7.5cm)

$12,000-18,000   **L&T**

Constantino Brumidi (Italian 1805-1880), portrait of Rob and Tom Lindsay, unsigned, oil on canvas, framed.

An Italian-American painter, Brumidi painted in the Vatican before emigrating to the US in 1852. Other works include the Apotheosis of Washington in the canopy of the Rotunda.

c1860   62x78in (157.5x198cm)

$12,000-18,000   **FRE**

Jacob Eichholtz (American 1776-1842), an oil on canvas portrait, probably Edward Everett (former president of Harvard).

30in (76cm) high

$4,000-5,000   **POOK**

Otto Eerelman (Dutch, 1839-1926), an oil on canvas of a father and bride riding a carriage, signed lower left "O. Eerelman".

24in (61cm) wide

$6,000-9,000   **POOK**

Richard Cosway R.A., (British, 1742-1821), 'Mrs Tickell', oil on copper, oval, inscribed "Cosway" verso, within a red leather folder.

7x6in (17.5x15cm)

$20,000-25,000   **FRE**

A Neoclassical maiden, oil on canvas, bears signature and date "Joseph Coomans 1870" but by a follower of Pierre Olivier Joseph Coomans (Belgian, 1816-1889).

27x19.25in (68.5x49cm)

$15,000-20,000   **FRE**

Sir John Hoppner, attributed (British, 1758-1810), an oil on canvas portrait of Mrs. Goldsmith and daughter, remnants of 19thC label reads "her daughter Hester".

30in (76cm) high

$8,000-12,000   **POOK**

Attributed to Jacob Maentel, (American, 1763-1863), watercolor portrait, inscribed lower left on tombstone "Georg Oberdorf geboren 1781 den 1 Septemb. ab gemalt 1819".

9.25x7.5in (23.5x19cm)

$4,000-5,000   **POOK**

Sarah Miriam Peale (American, 1800-1885), an oil on canvas portrait of William Jessop (b. 1800).

30in (76cm) long

$10,000-15,000   **POOK**

Ammi Phillips (American, 1788-1865), oil on canvas portrait of Garret DuBois.

30.5x24in (77.5x61cm)

$5,000-6,000   **POOK**

Eunice Griswold Pinney (American, 1770-1849), watercolor of two women and a child in a landscape, retaining an early faux tiger decorated frame.

8.25x9.5in (21x24cm)

$6,000-7,000   **POOK**

The circle of Allan Ramsay (Scottish, 1713-1784), a half length portrait of a lady, oil on canvas.

30x24.75in (76x63cm)

$4,000-6,000   **FRE**

Jacob Maentel (American, 1763-1863), an unusual oversized Pennsylvania watercolor and ink on paper portrait of hatter John Mays of Schaefferstown, Lebanon County.

16in (40.5cm) long

POOK

A 17thC portrait of a gentleman and his wife, Anglo-Dutch School, oil on canvas.

43.5x53.5in (110.5x135.5cm)

$30,000-35,000   **FRE**

An American school 19thC portrait of two children, oil on canvas, in a contemporary grain painted wood frame, unsigned, relined, repairs, retouch.

c1830   *36x31in (91.5x79cm)*

$10,000-15,000   **SK**

$500,000-600,000

Jules Breton (French, 1837-1906), an oil on canvas portrait of four peasant girls, signed lower left.

20in (51cm) wide

$7,000-10,000   **POOK**

John George Brown (American, 1831-1913), "Bird Nesting", oil on canvas, signed and dated.

This painting may be based on a sketch entitled "After Gull's Eggs" executed in 1877, at Grand Manan Island.

1878   *30in (76cm) wide*

$400,000-500,000   **FRE**

David Burliuk (Russian, 1882-1967), "Peasant Woman with Horse", oil on canvas, signed "BURLIUK." lower right.

14x10in (35.5 x25.5cm)

$15,000-25,000   **SK**

Dean Cornwell (American, 1892-1960), an oil on canvas illustration of a saloon with young girl displaying her portfolio, signed lower left "Dean Cornwell 1916".

30in (76cm) wide

$22,000-28,000   **POOK**

Arthur Drummond (British, 1871-1951), "The Flower Seller", oil on canvas, signed and dated "A Drummond 89" bottom right.

27.5x22in (70x56cm)

$12,000-18,000   **FRE**

Rudolf Ernst (Austrian, 1854-1932), "Avaricious Eyes", oil on panel, signed.

32x25in (81.5x64cm)

$140,000-160,000   **FRE**

William Gilbert Gaul (American, 1855-1919), "Rainy Day In The Garret", oil on canvas, signed inscribed and dated "Gilberty Gaul NY – 78".

27x34in (68.5x86.5cm)

$90,000-100,000   **FRE**

Edward Atkinson Hornel (Scottish, 1864-1933), "Maytime In The Orchard", oil on canvas, signed and dated.

1916   *25x30in (63x75cm)*

$35,000-45,000   **L&T**

Edgar Hunt (British, 1876-1953), "Ponies, Goat And Chickens In A Farmyard", oil on board, signed and dated.

1940   *11.75x13in (30x34cm)*

$25,000-30,000   **L&T**

Robert Gemmell Hutchison R.B.A., R.O.I., R.S.A., R.S.W. (British, 1860-1936), "Tug O' War", oil on board, signed.

7x10in (17.5x25.5cm)

$22,000-28,000   **L&T**

Henri Martin (French, 1860-1943), "Jeunes Filles Au Jardin", oil on panel, signed.

16x12.5in (41x32cm)

$30,000-40,000   **L&T**

Josephine Paddock (American, 1885-1964), "Taking Tea", oil on canvas, signed and dated 1935 verso.

40x40in (101.5x101.5cm)

$15,000-25,000   **FRE**

William McCance (Scottish, 1894-1970), "The Thriller", oil on board, signed and dated.

McCance's paintings of the twenties occupy a unique place in Scottish art. With the exception of William Johnstone, no other Scottish painter responded with such imagination and vigour to the Cubist and Surrealist movements, which had emerged in France in the preceding years.

1928   *14x10in (35.5x25.5cm)*

$25,000-30,000   **L&T**

Norman Rockwell (American, 1894-1978) "The Silhouette", oil on canvas, signed.

44in (112cm) wide

$300,000-400,000   **FRE**

Jack Vettriano (Scottish, b. 1954) "Study for the Sun Seekers", signed, oil on canvas.

1996   *12 x 9.75in (30 x 25cm)*

$30,000-40,000   **L&T**

Edward Arthur Walton R.S.A., P.R.S.W., H.R.W.S. (Scottish, 1860-1922), "Portrait of Miss Emmy Mylne", oil on canvas, signed.

40.5x30.25in (103x77cm)

L&T

William Aiken Walker (American, 1838-1921), oil on board double portrait of two cotton pickers, signed lower left "W.A. Walker".

9x12in (23x30.5cm)

$35,000-45,000   **POOK**

Theodore Wores (American, 1859-1939), "The Candy Seller", oil on canvas, signed and with artist's device, inscribed "Th. Wores / Tokio 1885", some damage.

20.75x27in (52x68.5cm)

$25,000-30,000   **FRE**

$12,000-18,000

PAINTINGS

William James Blacklock (British, 1815-1858), "By The Lakeside", oil on canvas, signed and dated.

1855   *16x24in (41x63cm)*

$30,000-40,000   **L&T**

John Brett A.R.A. (British, 1831-1902), "The Lizard", oil on canvas, inscribed and dated "Lizard July 19, '76".

                                    10x19in (25.5x48.5cm)

$25,000-30,000   **L&T**

Federico Del Campo (Peruvian, 1837-1927), "Napoli", oil on panel, signed.

                          8x5in (20x12.5cm)

$15,000-20,000   **FRE**

Ernest Chateignon (French), "A Rest From Their Labors", oil on canvas, signed.

c1865   *18.25x24in (46.5x61cm)*

$15,000-20,000   **FRE**

Hermann Davids Salomon Corrodi (Italian, 1844-1905), "Busy Street Scene, Rome", oil on canvas, signed and inscribed.

              60x38.5in (152.5x77.5cm)

$80,000-110,000   **FRE**

Charles Theodore Frere (French, 1814-1888), "A North African Market", oil on canvas, signed.

              16x24.5in (40.5x62cm)

$50,000-55,000   **FRE**

Nicolas De Gyselaer (Dutch, 1590-1654), "Feast In The House Of The Rich Man", oil on panel, signed and dated "ND (conjoined) Giselaer 1672".

              18.75x27in (47.6x68.5cm)

$6,000-9,000   **FRE**

Attributed to Jonathan Orne Johnson 'J.O.J' Frost (American, 1852-1928), 'Street Scene, Marblehead, Massachusetts', oil on paperboard, unsigned, in a contemporary frame.

Joseph H. Hidley (American, 1830-1872), oil on panel, view of a Rensselaer County, New York farmstead.

c1860   *12.5x17in (32x43cm)*

$130,000-140,000   **SK**

J.O.J. Frost was an untrained artist and native of the seaside town of Marblehead, Massachusetts. He ran a seafood restaurant for most of his life, but after his wife's death in 1919, he began to sculpt and paint scenes of Marblehead life to educate the citizens of Marblehead in their town's history.

32in (80cm) wide

$70,000-80,000   **SK**

William Bradley Lamond R.B.A. (British, 1857-1924), "A Flock Of Sheep In The Shade", oil on canvas, signed.

13.75x17.75in (35x45cm)

$6,000-9,000 | L&T

Edmund Darch Lewis (American, 1837-1910), oil on canvas river scene, titled "Summer with Cattle", signed lower right "Edmund D. Lewis 1886".

49.75in (126.5cm) high

$6,000-9,000 | POOK

Jacob More F.S.A. (British, 1740-1793), "Landscape With A Storm", oil on canvas.

16x12.5in (40.5x32cm)

$20,000-25,000 | L&T

Alexander Nasmyth (British, 1758-1840), "A Wooded River Landscape With Figures By A Waterfall", oil on canvas, signed.

18.5x25in (47x64cm)

$20,000-25,000 | L&T

Alfred De Bréanski Senior (British, 1852-1928), "Near Keswick, Cumberland", oil on canvas, signed.

24x36in (62x92cm)

$45,000-50,000 | L&T

J. Stroman (American, mid-19thC) vibrant oil on canvas Pennsylvanian farm scene, inscribed verso "Landscape near York by J. Stroman 1867".

$60,000-70,000 | POOK

Alfred Sisley (French, 1839-1899), "La Passarelle – Matinée De Septembre", oil on canvas, signed and dated.

This painting shows the footbridge of the river Orvanne, in Moret, a region in the Ile de France. Sisley moved there in 1880 and stayed there for rest of his life. The painting engages with all the elements Sisley was fascinated with. The large expanse of luminous sky is very characteristic of this period and Sisley explains its significance in a letter to Adolphe Tavernier: "The sky is not simply a background: its planes give depth and the clouds give movement to a picture. What is more beautiful than the summer clouds floating across the blue sky. What movement and grace. Don't you agree? They are live waves at sea, one is uplifted and carried away."

1890

21x25in (53.5x63.5cm)

$1,000,000+ | L&T

Walter Emerson Baum (American, 1884-1956) Philadelphia Academy of Fine Arts (PAFA), "Zion Hill", oil on canvas, signed.

32x40in (81.5x101.5cm)

$30,000-35,000   **FRE**

Maurice Braun (American, 1877-1941), "View to the Distant Hills", oil on canvas, signed "Maurice Braun-" lower right, framed.

15.75x20in (40x51cm)

$20,000-25,000   **SK**

Johann Berethelsen (American, 1883-1972), oil on panel New York City winter street scene with Old Trinity Church in the distance and the American flag in the foreground, signed lower right.

15.5x11.5in (39.5x29cm)

$25,000-30,000   **POOK**

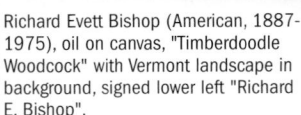

Richard Evett Bishop (American, 1887-1975), oil on canvas, "Timberdoodle Woodcock" with Vermont landscape in background, signed lower left "Richard E. Bishop".

27in (69cm) wide

$35,000-40,000   **POOK**

Bernadus Johannes Blommers (Dutch, 1845-1914) "The Toy Boat", watercolor, signed.

11x17.5in (28x45cm)

$20,000-30,000   **FRE**

Hugh Henry Breckenridge (American, 1870-1937), "A Moonlit Path", oil on canvas.

24x20in (61x51cm)

$15,000-25,000　　　　　**FRE**

Laurence A. Campbell (American, b. 1940), An oil on canvas of Fifth Avenue, New York City, signed lower right.

48in (122cm) high

$100,000-120,000　　　　　**POOK**

Fern Isabel Coppedge (American, 1888-1951), "The Delaware Valley", oil on canvas, signed and inscribed.

Fern Isabel Coppedge was a Philadelphia Impressionist.

38in (96.5cm) wide

$300,000-400,000　　　　　**FRE**

John Steuart Curry (American, 1897-1946), oil on canvas of a cornfield, signed lower left "John Steuart Curry".

18x24in (45.75x61cm)

$50,000-60,000　　　　　**POOK**

Carlo Fornara (Italian, 1871-1968), Quiete Lunare, signed "C Fornara" bottom right, indistinctly inscribed verso, signed and inscribed on two partial labels verso, oil on canvas.

27.25x19.75in (69x50cm)

$65,000-75,000　　　　　**FRE**

Franz Johnston (Canadian, 1888-1949), "Banff, Al'Ta", oil on canvas board, signed and inscribed verso, unframed.

9.5x13in (24x33cm)

$15,000-25,000　　　　　**L&T**

James Kay R.S.A., R.S.W. (Scottish, 1858-1924), "Exeter Cathedral", oil on canvas, signed.

24.5x29in (62x74cm)

$12,000-18,000　　　　　**L&T**

Stepan Kolessnikoff (Russian, 1879-1955), "The Old Tree", oil on panel, signed, indistinctly inscribed and artist's stamp verso.

25x20.25in (63.5x51.5cm)

$20,000-30,000　　　　　**FRE**

William Langson Lathrop (American, 1859-1938), "Plowing Time", oil on canvas, signed and inscribed.

19x25in (48.5x63.5cm)

$40,000-50,000   FRE

Harry Leith-Ross (American, 1886-1973), oil on canvas landscape titled verso "March Afternoon", signed lower left "Leith-Ross".

24x30in (61x76cm)

$55,000-65,000   POOK

Giovanni Martino (American, 1908-1998), oil on canvas landscape titled verso "Winter", signed lower right "Giovanni Martino", retaining a National Academy of Design label verso.

30x36in (76x91.5cm)

$12,000-18,000   POOK

Roy C. Nuse (American, 1885-1975) PAFA, "Cabin Run, Tohickon", oil on canvas, signed and dated '21.

30x25in (76x63.5cm)

$50,000-55,000   FRE

Mary Elizabeth Price (American, 1877-1965) PAFA, "From On High – Washington's Rock", oil on canvas, signed, inscribed and dated 1935 verso.

22x30in (56x76.5cm)

$40,000-50,000   FRE

Ferdinand Loyen Du Puigaudeau (French, 1864-1930), "Sunset On The Breton Coast", oil on canvas, signed.

15x18.25in (38x46.5cm)

$15,000-25,000   FRE

Edward Willis Redfield (American, 1869-1965) PAFA, "A Misty Morning", oil on canvas, signed, inscribed and dated, in a Harer frame.

1940   *25x30in (63.5x76cm)*

$250,000-300,000   FRE

William Trost Richards (American, 1833-1905) "Waves Breaking On A Deserted Shore At Sunset", oil on canvas, laid down on board, signed and dated.

Richards was a member of the Philadelphia Academy of Fine Arts (PAFA).

1883 21x36in(53x91cm)
$110,000-140,000 FRE

Robert Shaw (American, 1859-1912), oil on canvas landscape with young boys swimming in the nude, signed lower right "R. Shaw 1883".

30x40in (76x101.5cm)
$30,000-40,000 POOK

Eric Sloane (American, 1905-1985), oil on masonite winter landscape with hunter, titled lower left "February", signed lower right "Sloane".

17.5x24in (44.5x61cm)
$20,000-30,000 POOK

Eric Sloane (American, 1905-1985), oil on masonite landscape with hunters walking along a coast, titled "Quiet Morning", signed lower right "Sloane"

24in (61cm) wide
$15,000-20,000 POOK

Bela De Tirefort (American, 1894-1993), oil on canvas New York City snow scene, signed lower right "De Tirefort '36".

20in (51cm) high
$12,000-18,000 POOK

Ben Turner (American, 1912-1966), An oil on board landscape, signed lower left "Ben Turner".

47in (119cm) high
$15,000-25,000 POOK

Maurice Utrillo (French 1883-1955), inscribed, signed and dated "Bessines (Haute-Vienne), Moulin de Lavaugrasse Maurice, Utrillo, V, Juin 1923", gouache on paper, laid down on card, unframed.

10.25x13.75in (25.5x35cm)
$25,000-35,000 FRE

Guy Carlton Wiggins (American, 1883-1962), "Columbus Monument", oil on board, New York street scene titled verso, signed lower left and dated 1918.

7.75x9.75in (19.5x24.75cm)
$60,000-80,000 POOK

PAINTINGS

Antonio Nicolo Gasparo Jacobsen (Danish/American, 1850-1921), a portrait of an American Ship, signed, oil on canvas, in a molded giltwood frame.

21.75x36in (55x91.5cm)

$40,000-50,000　　　　**SK**

Hermanus Koekkoek (Dutch, 1836-1909) An oil on canvas harbor scene with ships in choppy waters, signed lower left.

23in (58cm) wide

$60,000-70,000　　　　**POOK**

William Pierce Stubbs (American, 1842-1909), an oil on canvas ship portrait of the schooner, Harry A. Barry, signed lower left "Stubbs".

26in (66cm) wide

$12,000-18,000　　　　**POOK**

Attributed to William Pierce Stubbs (American, 1842-1909), a portrait of the American racing sloop Vigilent (sic), oil on canvas, unsigned, vessel identified on the bow.

22x36in (56x91.5cm)

$15,000-20,000　　　　**SK**

An early 19thC China trade oil on canvas ship portrait, with central three-masted British ship flanked by two Chinese boats, inscribed verso "Capt. P. Brown RN's East Indiaman Ship Charlotte".

26.5in (67.25cm) wide

$6,000-9,000　　　　**POOK**

William Gay Yorke (British, 1817-1892) oil on canvas, signed, with a three-masted vessel in water with figures on deck being pursued and fired upon by other vessels, in a gilt-gesso frame.

28in (71cm) high

$10,000-15,000　　　　**SK**

A 19thC Massachusetts folk art oil on board of a whaling scene, dated.

1845　　　　*10x10in (25x25cm)*

$8,000-12,000　　　　**POOK**

A 19thC American School portrait of a four masted ship, oil on canvas, unsigned, framed.

16x30in (40.5x76cm)

$6,000-9,000　　　　**FRE**

George Binet (French, 1865-1949), "On The Promenade, Le Havre", oil on canvas, signed.

18x25in (46x63cm)

$15,000-25,000   L&T

Francis Campbell Boileau Cadell, (British, 1883-1937) "Sound of Mull from Iona", signed, oil on board.

14.5x17.5 in (37x44cm)

$130,000-140,000   L&T

Jean Dufy (French, 1888-1964), "Honfleur", signed "Jean Dufy" bottom right, inscribed "Honfleur II" in pencil on stretcher verso, oil on canvas.

13x18.25in (33x46.5cm)

$40,000-50,000   FRE

William Mervyn Glass R.S.A., P.S.S.A. (British, 1885-1965), "White Sands, Iona", oil on board, signed with initials.

14x17.5in (36x44cm)

$5,000-7,000   L&T

Sir Herbert James Gunn R.A., P.R.P, R.S.W. (British, 1893-1964) "St. Ives", oil on canvas, signed.

14x18in (35.5x46cm)

$45,000-55,000   L&T

William Lee-Hankey R.W.S. (British, 1869-1952), "Le Cheval Blanc, Honfleur", oil on canvas, signed.

12x14in (30x34.5cm)

$6,000-9,000   L&T

John MacLauchlan Milne R.S.A. (Scottish, 1886-1957) Cuillins From Morar.

50x60cm (19.75x23.75in)

$50,000-60,000   L&T

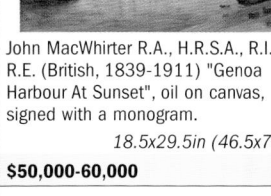

John MacWhirter R.A., H.R.S.A., R.I., R.E. (British, 1839-1911) "Genoa Harbour At Sunset", oil on canvas, signed with a monogram.

18.5x29.5in (46.5x75cm)

$50,000-60,000   L&T

Walter Elmer Schofield (American, 1867-1944), "Breakers on the Shore", oil on canvas, signed and dated .

1903   21x27in (53.5x68.5cm)

$12,000-18,000   FRE

Laurence Stephen Lowry (British, 1887-1976), "Glasgow Docks, 1947", oil on canvas, signed and dated.

"Some people like to go to the theater, some like to watch television, I just like watching ships" – L.S. Lowry in the Daily Telegraph, November 1963. Lowry's reputation rests on the incredible popularity of his work, depicting the Lancashire working classes at work and at leisure with humor and freshness. This work is a rare and important depiction of Glasgow docks, dating from 1947. Born in Salford in 1887, Lowry rarely left Great Britain, despite exhibiting in Europe, and France in particular. He used particular markers and motifs throughout his work. One such motif is the dark mast, rising above the bustle of the scene below, as seen in "The Junction" from 1956. With its multitude of verticals densely populating the space, "Glasgow Docks" may indeed be also read as a scene presided over by Lowry himself. Another, darker iconography frequently present in his work is that of the vessel, be it a cart, a taxi or a ship, which with his dark sense of humor and fatalistic attitude to life, Lowry saw as a metaphor for death. He is recorded as remarking about a ship entering a harbor in Sutherland, "Oh it was beautiful, like a coffin floating towards you."

20x24in (51x61cm)

$1,000,000+

L&T

Patrick William Adam R.S.A. (British, 1854-1929), "The White Flower Stand", oil on canvas, signed.

33x13.5in (84x47cm)

$6,000-7,000   L&T

Mary Armour R.S.A., R.S.W. (British, 1902-2000) "Still Life With Garlic", oil on canvas, signed and dated.

1982   *22x26in (56x66cm)*

$25,000-30,000   L&T

Mary Armour R.S.A., R.S.W. (British, 1902-2000), "Still Life With Striped Cloth", oil on board, signed.

19.5x23in (50x58.5cm)

$15,000-20,000   L&T

Rutherford Boyd (American, 1884-1951), watercolor still life of irises, signed lower right "R. Boyd '26".

27in (69cm) wide

$15,000-20,000   POOK

Patrick Henry Bruce (American/French, 1881-1937), oil on canvas still life, "Green Jug of Roses", signed lower right "Bruce".

22in (56cm) wide

$50,000-60,000   POOK

Patrick Henry Bruce (American/French, 1881-1937), oil on canvas still life of anemones, signed lower right "Bruce".

24in (61cm) wide

$30,000-35,000   POOK

Samuel Coleman, (American, 1832-1920), "Hollyhocks", oil on canvas, framed, signed and inscribed "Sam' Coleman. ...ington On Hudson" lower left.

30.5in (76cm) high

$8,000-12,000   SK

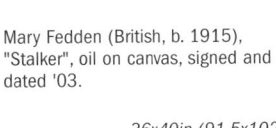

Joan Eardley R.S.A. (British, 1921-1963), "A Still Life Of Mixed Flowers", oil on canvas, signed verso.

12x11in (30.5x28cm)

$60,000-70,000   L&T

Mary Fedden (British, b. 1915), "Stalker", oil on canvas, signed and dated '03.

36x40in (91.5x102cm)

$60,000-70,000   L&T

George Loftus Noyes (Canadian/American, 1864-1954), "Still Life with Fish and Radishes", oil on canvas, signed "G. Noyes" lower right, repaired puncture, retouch, craquelure, framed.

20x30in (51x76cm)

$12,000-18,000   SK

711

Samuel John Peploe R.S.A. (Scottish, 1871-1935) "A Still Life of Apples and Pink Roses", signed oil on canvas.

This is a richly composed still life of Peploe's most typical subject matter, roses. The genre captivated the artist throughout his career, allowing him to experiment with composition, tone, hue and color. He regarded painting as an intellectual exercise and, as a purist, sought to paint 'the perfect still life'.

22x18in (56x46cm)

$450,000-500,000 **L&T**

Levi Wells Prentice (American, 1851-1935), oil on canvas still life of apples and basket, signed lower right "L. W. Prentice".

10in (25cm) wide

$8,000-12,000 **POOK**

Anne Redpath (Scottish, 1895-19650) O.B.E., R.S.A., A.R.A., L.L.D., "Summer flowers in a jug", signed, oil on board.

16x20.5in (41x52cm)

$100,000-120,000 **L&T**

A Joseph Stella (Italian/American, 1877-1946), untitled floral still life oil on canvas, signed.

13in (33cm) high

$25,000-35,000 **SDR**

Anne Redpath O.B.E., R.S.A., A.R.A., L.L.D., A.R.W.S., R.O.I., R.B.A. (Scottish, 1895-1965), "Still Life Of Roses In A Teapot", watercolor, signed.

13x13in (33x33cm)

$25,000-30,000 **L&T**

Adam Bruce Thomson R.S.A., R.S.W. (British, 1885-1976), oil on canvas, signed.

20x16in (51.5x41cm)

$6,000-9,000 **L&T**

Ben Austrian (American, 1870-1921), oil on canvas of a hen sitting in basket with sixteen chicks, signed lower right "Ben Austrian 1911".

26in (66cm) wide

$35,000-40,000   **POOK**

Ben Austrian (American, 1870-1921), oil on canvas of a hen and seventeen chicks, signed lower right "Ben Austrian 1908".

26in (66cm) wide

$50,000-70,000   **POOK**

William Merritt Chase (American, 1849-1916), "The Copper Kettle", oil on canvas. 9in (23cm) wide

$20,000-30,000   **FRE**

Carl Reichert (Austrian, 1836-1918), an oil on panel interior scene of two dachshunds, signed lower left "C. Reichert".

13in (33cm) wide

$15,000-20,000   **POOK**

Simon Saint-Jean, (French, 1808-1860) "French Partridge At Evening", oil on canvas, signed and dated 1839.

29.75x37.5in 73x95cm)

$40,000-50,000 L&T

A portrait of a black cat on a tasseled pillow, oil on academy board, in a molded and gilded frame, signed "A.S.".

9.75x8in (25x20.5cm)

$6,000-9,000   **SK**

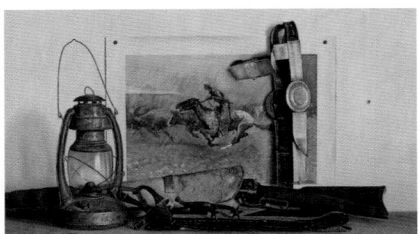

William Acheff (b.1947), "Yesterday", oil on canvas.

26x46in (66x117cm)

$70,000-80,000   **ALT**

William Acheff (b. 1947), "Late Summer", oil on canvas.

12x28in (30.5x71cm)

$30,000-40,000   **ALT**

Harry Adamson "Evening Flotilla-Canvasbacks", oil on canvas, signed.

36in (90cm) wide

$20,000-30,000   **RENO**

Harry Adamson "Aleutian Throne Room – Emperor Geese", oil on canvas, signed and dated.

1984   36in (90cm) wide

$20,000-25,000   RENO

Harry Adamson "A Flurry of Blacks", oil on canvas, signed.

1976   36in (90cm) wide

$25,000-30,000   RENO

ADAMSON

- Born in Seattle in 1916, Harry Adamson has studied wildlife for over 50 years. The majority of his work features wildfowl.
- Adamson studied under Paul J. Fair, a nationally recognized sculptor and wildlife photographer. A period of book illustration at the Museum of Vertebrate Zoology in Berkeley, California, also contributed to his early training.
- After serving for more than four years in World War II, the artist began painting fulltime. He is still painting today.
- Throughout his career, Adamson has observed, studied and painted the massive annual waterfowl migration. Although best known for his landscapes with flocks of mallards and pintails, he has also painted sheep, condors, falcons and tropical birds.
- Adamson's work has frequently been displayed nationally and internationally in the prestigious 'Birds in Art' exhibitions, and at the Smithsonian Art Museum, the Carnegie Museum of Natural History, Pittsburgh, and the British Museum, among others. He was named the first California Waterfowl Association Artist of the Year and 1979 Ducks Unlimited Artist of the Year.

Carl Brenders "Late Snow – Great Blue Heron", gouache, signed, was released as a limited edition print by Mill Pond Press in November 1986.

36in (90cm) high

$25,000-30,000   RENO

Ken Carlson "Rams in Late Light", oil on board, signed.

Of this painting Ken Carlson writes, "One of the rewards of researching for Dall Sheep paintings is the opportunity to travel to spectacular high country. Early fall provides color that at its peak and late light enhances the dynamic contrast of the white sheep."

36in (90cm) wide

$40,000-50,000   RENO

Philip R. Goodwin (1881-1935), "Lucky Catch", oil on canvas, signed.

c1910   36in (90cm) high

$70,000-100,000   RENO

Herman W. Hansen (German/American, 1854-1924), "Bad News at a Pony Express Station", oil on canvas, signed "H-W-Hansen-", titled in an inscription on the reverse, framed.

32x39.25in (81x99.5cm)

$15,000-25,000 SK

Carl Rungius (1869-1959), "In the Yukon Territory 1919", oil on canvas.

18x24in (46x61cm)

$70,000-80,000 ALT

Charles M. Russell "Trails Plowed Under", pen and ink, signed.

12in (30cm) wide

$50,000-55,000 RENO

Charles M. Russell (1864-1926), "Meeting of Sacajawea and Her Relatives of the Shoshone Tribe", pen and ink, signed, on the reverse is an unfinished sketch.

22.25in (55.5cm) wide

$120,000-180,000 RENO

CHARLES M. RUSSELL

- Charles M. Russell (1864-1926) was raised in Missouri and left for the Montana Territory aged 16. He spent a decade working as a ranch hand and cowboy.
- At 19, Russell completed his earliest watercolors which derived from sketching what he had seen.
- As a self-taught artist, his sketches were crude but showed an observant eye, a feel for anatomy and a flair for depicting action.
- His paintings, watercolors and sketches capture the spirit of the vanished era of American history, documenting the old west and Native Americans. Russell's work reflected the public's demand for authenticity, but also revealed the soul of a romantic.

Charles M. Russell (1864-1926), "First American News Writer", pen and ink, signed and dated.

1910 *19in (47.5cm) high*

$60,000-80,000 RENO

Charles M. Russell (1864-1926), "Thurston Held Mona Somewhat Tighter Than He Need To Have Done", watercolor and gouache, signed.

15.5in (39cm) high

$60,000-80,000 RENO

PAINTINGS

Birger Sandzen (1871-1954) "Southwestern Landscape", oil on canvas, signed.

23.5in (59cm) wide

$35,000-50,000   **RENO**

Joseph H. Sharp "Pueblo Indian", oil on board, signed.

According to John C. Pickett, the location of this painting is behind Sharp's Taos studio on Kit Carson Road. On the reverse is a grocery list written by Sharp on a cardboard insert.

14in (35cm) wide

$50,000-55,000   **RENO**

Olaf C. Seltzer (1877-1957) "Deer in a Mountain Landscape", oil on canvas, signed.

24in (60cm) wide

$40,000-50,000   **RENO**

Theodore Van Soelen (1890-1964), "Cienega In Spring", oil and egg tempera on canvas.

35.5x45.5in (90x115.5cm)

$40,000-50,000   **ALT**

Olaf Wieghorst (1899-1988), "The Challenge", oil on canvas.

25x30in (63.5 x76cm)

$30,000-35,000   **ALT**

Olaf Wieghorst (1899-1988), "Navajo Girl on Burro", oil on canvas.

16x20in (40.5x51cm)

$25,000-35,000   **ALT**

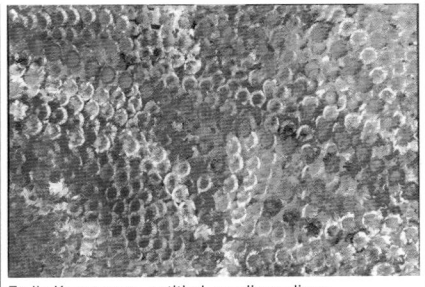

Emily Kngwarreye, untitled, acrylic on linen.
27x22.75in (69x58cm)

$4,000-6,000　　　　　　　　**BONA**

Lorna Brown Napanangka, Women and Bush Foods.
2003

$3,000-4,000　　　　　　　　**BONA**

Nurapayia Nampitjinpa, Yumarra Rockhole Site.
1999

$3,000-4,000　　　　　　　　**BONA**

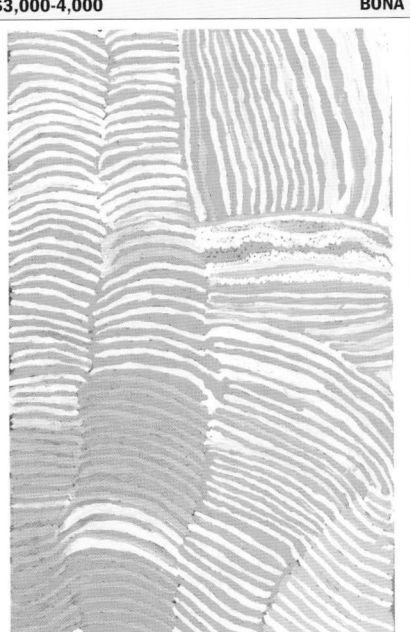

Makinti Napanangka, Untitled, acrylic on linen
47.25x23.75in (121.5x61cm)

$4,000-6,000　　　　　　　　**BONA**

Evelyn Pultara, untitled, acrylic on linen.

$5,000-6,000　　　　　　　　**BONA**

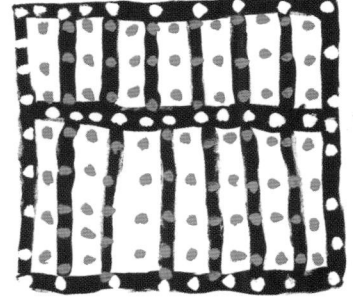

Prince of Wales, Body Marks, acrylic on linen.

$4,000-6,000　　　　　　　　**BONA**

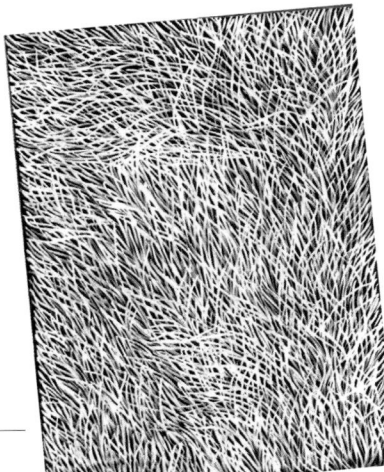

Barbara Weir, Grass Seed, acrylic on canvas.

$3,000-4,000　　　　　　　　**BONA**

John Banting (1902-1970), "String Music", oil on canvas.

24x36in (61x91cm)

$10,000-15,000   **L&T**

Romare Bearden, "Alone (Seul)", acrylic and collage mounted on masonite, signed in pencil, upper right recto.

9in (23cm) wide

$15,000-25,000   **SWA**

John Bellany, (b. 1942), "Self Portrait With Owl Mask", oil on canvas.

74x62in (188x158cm)

$20,000-30,000   **L&T**

John Bellany R.A (b.1942), "Self Portrait With Cat", oil on canvas, signed, unframed.

67x59in (170x150cm)

$25,000-35,000   **L&T**

John G. Boyd R.P., R.G.I (1940-2001), "The Farmer's Wife", oil on canvas, signed.

48x40in (122x102cm)

$8,000-12,000   **L&T**

Raoul Dufy (French 1877-1953), 'Landscape at Langres', oil on canvas, signed bottom right, "Raoul Dufy".

This painting probably dates from the mid-1930s when the artist consistently worked near Langres. From 1935, he experimented with thinner layers of paint which allowed light to travel through it, a technique comparable to watercolor work.

28.75x24in (73.5x61cm)

$200,000-250,000   **FRE**

Elizabeth Blackadder O.B.E., R.A., R.S.A., R.W.S, R.G.I., D.Litt. (b. 1931), "Girvan", watercolor, signed and dated '69.

26.5x39.5in (67x100cm)

$6,000-9,000   **L&T**

Henri Gaudier-Brzeska (French, 1891-1915), "L'Homme Pisse", pen and ink, signed, inscribed and dated 1913.

Horace Brodzky has confirmed this drawing to be a self-portrait.

$15,000-20,000   L&T

Patrick Heron (British, 1920-1999) "Orange Horizon", signed on the stretcher, oil on canvas,

'Color is the only direction in which painting can travel.' This statement, made in 1962, defines Patrick Heron's development as an artist. He was one of the first British artists to embrace abstraction or rather 'non-figuration' as he emphasized.

17.75x14in (45x35cm)

$70,000-100,000   L&T

Frances Hodgkins (New Zealand, 1869-1947) "Crossroads, Barcelona", oil on panel, signed.

20x26.5in (51x67cm)

$10,000-15,000   L&T

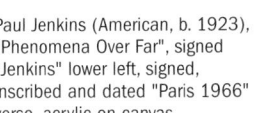

Paul Jenkins (American, b. 1923), "Phenomena Over Far", signed "Jenkins" lower left, signed, inscribed and dated "Paris 1966" verso, acrylic on canvas.

38.25x63.75in (97x162cm)

$10,000-15,000   FRE

William Johnstone O.B.E. (1897-1981), "Garden Of The Hesperides (Nocturne)", oil on canvas, signed and dated 1929 verso.

25x29in (63x75cm)

$35,000-50,000   L&T

A portrait of Andy Warhol IV, by Peter Max (b.1937), signed upper right, framed.

28x22in (71x56cm)

$4,000-5,000   ISA

Sir William McTaggart P.R.S.A., R.A., Hon. R.S.W. (1903-1981),"Gnarled Trees", oil on canvas, signed.

28x36in (71x91cm)

$30,000-40,000   L&T

Alberto Morrocco R.S.A., R.S.W., R.P., R.G.I., L.L.D (1917-1999), "Vera In Turkish Costume", oil on canvas, signed.

43x53in (109x135cm)

$30,000-40,000   L&T

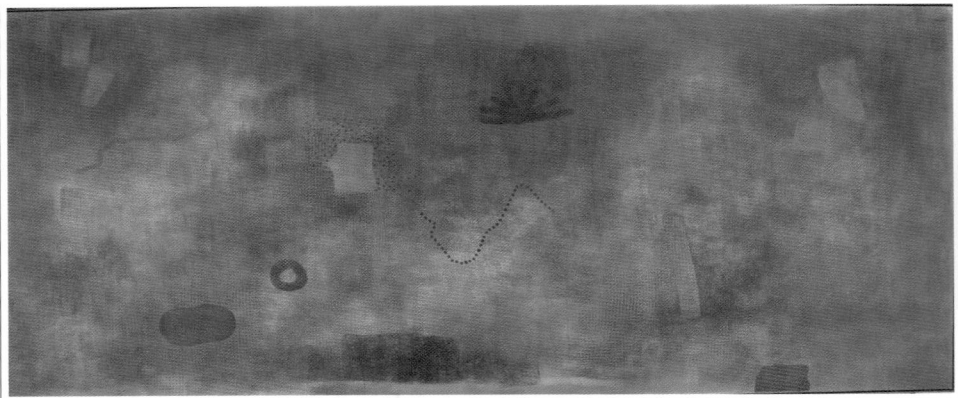

A Robert Natkin framed acrylic on canvas, untitled from the Intimate Lighting Series

1977   *144in (366cm) wide*

$15,000-20,000   **SDR**

Mary Newcomb (b. 1922), "Horse And Trap, Run And Rest", oil on board, signed and dated '79.

28x31in (70x78cm)

$20,000-30,000   **L&T**

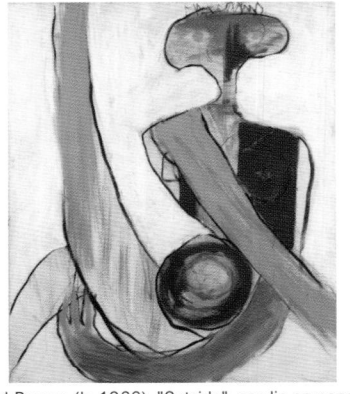

David Rayson (b. 1966), "Outside", acrylic on panel.

David Rayson has forged an international reputation as one of the UK's leading painters, he is also Senior Painting Tutor at the Royal College of Art.

2001   *39.5x45.5in (100x115cm)*

$35,000-50,000   **L&T**

Jenny Saville (b. 1970), "Self Portrait", pencil on paper.

1992   *28x20in (71x51cm)*

$60,000-80,000   **L&T**

William Scott R.A. (1913-1989), "Seated Figure With Cat II", charcoal.

9x8in (23x17cm)

$10,000-15,000   **L&T**

John Wells (1907-2000), untitled, oil on board, dated 1970 on backboard.

1.75x12in (4.5x30.5cm)

$6,000-9,000   **L&T**

William Scott R.A. (1913-1989), untitled, gouache.

Scottish born of Northern Irish descent, Scott studied with Henry Moore's contemporary and friend Kathleen Bridle. From a young age he was exposed to the works of Cezanne, Derain, Picasso and Modigliani long before studying at the Royal Academy schools in London. His work rapidly progressed towards abstraction.

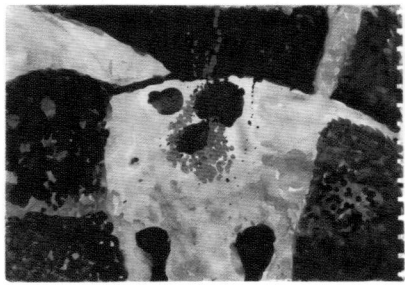

9.75x13.75in (25x35cm)

$10,000-15,000   **L&T**

Adrian Wiszniewski (b. 1958), "Silent Mutations", oil on canvas, signed, unframed.

96x96in (244x244cm)

$30,000-40,000   **L&T**

A mid-19thC lithograph, identified in the matrix as "The American National Game of Base Ball. Grand Match for the Championship at the Elysian Fields, Hoboken, NJ", with hand-coloring on paper, in a molded giltwood frame, some damage.

c1866   24x33in (61x84cm)

$90,000-100,000   **SK**

A hand-colored lithograph, "A View from the American Side", by Sarony & Major, Litho, NY, together with a William Henry Bartlett (American) hand-colored engraving, "View from Hyde Park".

c1850   lithograph 11.5x15in (29x38cm)

$600-800   **POOK**

A framed hand-colored lithograph on paper identified by inscription in matrix "The Road, Winter, 1853", published by Nathaniel Currier.

26in (66cm) wide

$3,000-4,000   **SK**

A framed hand-colored lithograph on paper identified in inscription in matrix, "THE LIFE OF A FIREMAN, The race. -'jump her boys, jump her!'" 1854, published by Nathaniel Currier.

30in (76cm) wide

$5,000-6,000   **SK**

A framed hand-colored lithograph on paper identified, "Wild Duck Shooting. A good day's sport", 1854, published Nathaniel Currier.

30in (76cm) wide

$6,000-8,000   **SK**

A framed hand-colored lithograph on paper identified in inscription in matrix, "The Last War Whoop, 1856", published by Nathaniel Currier.

31in (79cm) wide

$8,000-12,000   **SK**

After John James Audubon, Bien edition chromolithograph titled "Great White Heron", the background of early Key West.

1860   24.5x36.5in (62x92.5cm)

$8,000-10,000   **POOK**

Augustus Kollner (American, 1813-1900), a colored lithograph of Albany, New York by Deroy.

7.25x11in (18.5x28cm)

$500-600   **POOK**

A framed chromolithograph on paper identified in inscription in matrix, "The Yacht Squadron at Newport, 1872", publishers Currier & Ives (1857-1907).

32in (81cm) wide

$10,000-15,000   **SK**

PAINTINGS

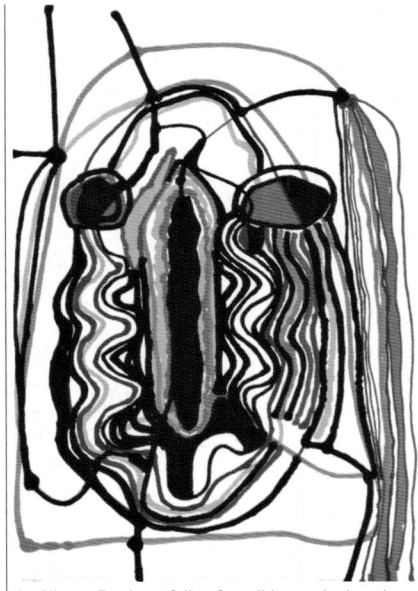

Alexander Calder (American, 1898-1976), Spirals Composition, pencil signed and inscribed "E.A." Color lithograph.

26x38in (66x96.5cm)

$2,000-2,500   FRE

George Russell Drysdale (1912-1981), 'Two Children', lithograph on paper, ed. 66/75, inscribed l.l.c. "Two Children 66/75" and l.r.c. "Russell Drysdale".

21.25x30in (54x76cm)

$2,000-3,000   SHA

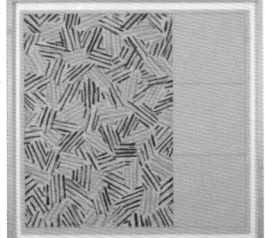

An eleven-color lithograph, by Jasper Johns (American, b. 1930), published in 1976 by Gemini G.E.L, signed in pencil and stamped lower right numbered 6/60.

30in (76cm) wide

$8,000-12,000   POOK

An Alberto Burri portfolio of ten lithographs in colors, signed and numbered, from private collection.

11in (28cm) high

$12,000-14,000   SDR

A set of four acrylic and silkscreen prints titled "Four Maos" by Richard Pettibone, 1975, signed and dated.

each 4in (10cm) sq

$20,000-25,000   SDR

A framed acrylic and silkscreen on canvas titled "Roy Lichtenstein Tex, 1962", 1969, by Richard Pettibone, signed, dated.

15in (38cm) wide

$90,000-110,000   SDR

Andy Warhol (American, 1928-1987), Marilyn Monroe (Marilyn), 1967, pencil signed on verso, "Factory Additions, New York", publisher, Aetna Silkscreen Products, Inc., New York, printer, color silkscreen.

6in (15.25cm) sq

$8,000-10,000   FRE

A lithograph by Robert Rauschenberg (American, b. 1925) titled "Week in Review", signed in pencil lower right and numbered "53/250".

30in (76cm) high

$900-1,100   POOK

A mid-19thC American whole plate daguerreotype of a gentleman wearing a top hat, the image portraying a half-length seated bearded gentleman wearing a double-breasted coat with a velvet collar, mounted in a rectangular scroll and floral embossed gilt brass frame.

8.5in (21cm) high

$1,500-2,500 SK

A daguerreotype of Colonel Stephen Crosby (1788-1857), Utica, New York,

c1850 *one-fourth plate*

$400-500 FRE

A tintype of a mason, one-fourth plate, hand-tinted and silvered.

c1860

$400-500 FRE

A tintype of North Carolina confederates with musical instruments and dog, one-sixth plate.

c1860

$900-1,100 FRE

One of two Ambrotypes of William Sherrill, North Carolina senator, c1870, one- fourth plate and one-sixth plate, one in a mother-of-pearl and hand-painted papier- maché case.

$700-1,000 set FRE

An ambrotype of a New England meeting house, one-fourth plate.

c1860-1880

$150-250 FRE

An albumen print photograph, signed "Geronimo", by Wyman, H.W., St. Louis: Murillo, 1904. , with slightly faded signed attestation of E(dward) B(allard) Lodge on verso, "The autograph was done for me by Geronimo at St. Louis Exposition of 1904.".

5.5x4in (14x10cm)

$7,000-10,000 FRE

Lindbergh, Charles (1902-1974), American pilot, photograph of Charles Lindbergh standing before the Spirit of St. Louis, inscribed To Waterman Granton Pen (?) and signed by Lindbergh lower right.

The aviator Charles Lindbergh piloted the first solo non-stop flight across the Atlantic in 1927.

$1,200-1,800 L&T

723

KEY TO ILLUSTRATIONS

EVERY ANTIQUE ILLUSTRATED in *DK Antiques Price Guide 2008* by Judith Miller has a letter code which identifies the dealer or auction house that sold it. The list below is a key to these codes. In the list, auction houses are shown by the letter Ⓐ and dealers by the letter Ⓓ. Some items may have come from a private collection, in which case the code in the list is accompanied by the letter Ⓟ. Inclusion in this book in no way constitutes or implies a contract or a binding offer on the part of any of our contributors to supply or sell the goods illustrated, or similar items, at the prices stated.

AA Ⓓ
Albert Amor
37 Bury Street, St James's,
London SW1Y 6AU
Tel: 020 7930 2444
www.albertamor.co.uk

AHL Ⓓ
Andrea Hall Levy
PO Box 1243, Riverdale, NY 10471
Tel: 001 646 441 1726
barangrill@aol.com

AJK Ⓓ
Antiques by Joyce Knutsen
Tel: 001 315 637 8238 (Summer)
Tel: 001 352 567 1699 (Winter)
knutsenglass@aol.com

AL Ⓓ
Andrew Lineham Fine Glass
Mob: 07767 702 722
www.antiquecolouredglass.com

ALT Ⓐ
Altermann Galleries
Santa Fe Galleries, 225 Canyon Road,
Santa Fe, New Mexico 87501
Tel: 001 505 983 1590
www.altermann.com

B Ⓐ
**Dreweatt Neate, Tunbridge Wells
(formerly Bracketts)**
The Auction Hall, The Pantiles,
Tunbridge Wells, Kent TN2 5QL
Tel: 01892 544500
www.dnfa.com/tunbridgewells

BAR Ⓐ
**Dreweatt Neate, Bristol (formerly
Bristol Auction Rooms)**
St John's Place, Apsley Road, Clifton,
Bristol BS8 2ST
Tel: 0117 973 7201
www.dnfa.com

BD Ⓓ
Barry Davies Oriental Art Ltd
PO Box 34867, London W8 6WH

BEA Ⓐ
Beaussant Lefèvre
32 rue Drouot, 75009 Paris,
France
Tel: 00 33 1 47 70 40 00
www.beaussant-lefevre.auction.fr

BER Ⓐ
Bertoia Auctions
2141 Demarco Drive, Vineland NJ
08360 USA
Tel: 001 856 692 1881
www.bertoiaauctions.com

BIB Ⓓ
Biblion
1/7 Davies Mews, London W1K 5AB
Tel: 020 7629 1374
www.biblion.com

BIG Ⓐ
Bigwood
The Old School, Tiddington,
Stratford-upon-Avon Warwickshire
CV37 7AW
Tel: 01789 269415
www.bigwoodauctioneers.co.uk

BLA Ⓐ
Blanchet et Associés
3 rue Geoffroy Marie, 75009 Paris,
France
Tel: 00 33 1 53 34 14 44
blanchet.auction@wanadoo.fr

BLO Ⓐ
Bloomsbury Auctions
Bloomsbury House, 24 Maddox
Street, London W1 S1PP
Tel: 020 7495 9494
www.bloomsburyauctions.com

BMN Ⓐ
Auktionshaus Bergmann
Möhrendorfestraße 4, 91056
Erlangen, Germany
Tel: 0049 9 131 450 666
www.auction-bergmann.de

BONA Ⓐ
Bonhams & Goodman
7 Anderson Street, Double Bay
NSW 2028, Australia
Tel: 0061 02 9327 9913
www.bonhamsandgoodman.com.au

BRB Ⓓ
Bauman Rare Books
535 Madison Avenue, New York, NY
10022, USA
Tel: 001 212 751 0011
www.baumanrarebooks.com

BRI Ⓐ
Brightwells Fine Art
Fine Art Saleroom, Easters Court,
Leominster, Herefordshire HR6
0DE
Tel: 01568 611122
www.brightwells.co.uk

BRK Ⓓ
Brookside Antiques
44 North Water Street, New Bedford,
MA 02740 USA
Tel: 001 508 993 4944
www.brooksideartglass.com

BRU Ⓐ
Brunk Auctions
Post Office Box 2135, Asheville, NC
28802, USA
Tel: 001 828 254 6846
www.brunkauctions.com

CA Ⓐ
Chiswick Auctions
1-5 Colville Road, London W3 8BL
Tel: 020 8992 4442
www.chiswickauctions.co.uk

CATO Ⓓ
Lennox Cato
1 The Square, Church Street,
Edenbridge,
Kent TN8 5BD
Tel: 01732 865 988
www.lennoxcato.com

CHEF Ⓐ
Cheffins
Clifton House, 1&2 Clifton Road,
Cambridge, Cambridgeshire CB1
7EA
Tel: 01223 213343
www.cheffins.co.uk

CLV Ⓐ
Clevedon Salerooms
The Auction Centre, Kenn Road, Kenn,
Clevedon, Bristol, BS21 6TT
Tel: 01934 830 111
www.clevedon-salerooms.com

CRIS Ⓓ
Cristobal
26 Church Street, Marylebone, London
NW8 8EP
Tel: 020 7724 7230
www.cristobal.co.uk

CSA Ⓓ
Christopher Sykes Antiques
The Old Parsonage, Woburn, Milton
Keynes MK17 9QJ
Tel: 01525 290 259/ 290 467
www.sykes-corkscrews.co.uk

CSAY Ⓓ
Charlotte Sayers FGA
313-315 Grays Antique Market, 58
Davies Street ,
Tel: 020 7499 5478

DA Ⓓ
Davies Antiques
c/o Cadogan Tate, Unit 6, 6-12 Ponton
Road, London SW8 5BA
Tel: 020 8947 1902
www.antique-meissen.com

DB Ⓓ
David Bowden
Stand 07 Grays Antique Markets,
58 DaviesStreet, London W1K 5LP
Tel: 020 7495 1773

DD Ⓓ
Decodame.com
853 Vanderbilt Beach Road,
PMB 8,
Naples, FL 34108, USA
Tel: 001 239 514 6797
www.decodame.com

DJI Ⓓ
Deco Jewels Inc
131 Thompson Street, NY, USA
Tel: 001 212 253 1222
decojewels@earthlink.net

DN Ⓐ
Dreweatt Neate
Donnington Priory Salerooms,
Donnington, Newbury, Berkshire
RG14 2JE
Tel: 01635 553553
www.dnfa.com/donnington

DNT Ⓓ
**Dreweatt Neate Tunbridge Wells
(formerly Bracketts)**
Auction Hall, The Pantiles,
Tunbridge Wells, Kent TN2 5QL
Tel: 01892 544500
www.dnfa.com/tunbridgewells

DOR Ⓐ
Dorotheum
Palais Dorotheum, A-1010 Vienna,
Dorotheergasse 17, Austria
Tel: 0043 1 515 600
www.dorotheum.com

DRA Ⓐ
David Rago Auctions
333 North Main Street,
Lambertville, NJ 08530, USA
Tel: 001 609 397 9374
www.ragoarts.com

DRG Ⓓ
R. Duane Reed Gallery
7th Floor, 529 West 20th Street, New
York, NY 10011 USA
Tel: 001 212 462 2600
www.rduanereedgallerynyc.com

ECLEC Ⓓ
Eclectica
2 Charlton Place, Islington, London N1
8AJ
Tel: 020 7226 5625
www.eclectica.biz

EFI Ⓐ
Esther Fitzgerald Rare Textiles
28 Church Row, London NW3 6UP
Tel: 020 7431 3076
www.estherfitzgerald.co.uk

F Ⓐ
Fellows & Sons
Augusta House, 19 Augusta Street,
Hockley, Birmingham, B18 6JA
Tel: 0121 212 2131
www.fellows.co.uk

FIS Ⓐ
Auktionhaus Dr Fischer
Trappensee-Schößchen, D-74074
Heilbronn, Germany
Tel: 0049 71 31 15 55 70
www.auctions-fischer.de

FM Ⓓ
Francesca Martire
F131-137, Alfies Antique Market,
13 Church Street, London NW8 8DT
Tel: 020 7724 4802

FRE Ⓐ
Freeman's
1808 Chestnut Street,
Philadelphia, PA 19103, USA
Tel: 001 215 563 9275
www.freemansauction.com

GAZE Ⓐ
Thos. Wm. Gaze & Son
Diss Auction Rooms, Roydon Road,
Diss, Norfolk, IP22 4LN
Tel: 01379 650306
www.twgaze.com

GHOU Ⓐ
Gardiner Houlgate
Bath Auction Rooms, 9 Leafield Way,
Corsham, Nr Bath, SN13 9SW
Tel: 01225 812 912
auctions@gardiner-houlgate.co.uk

GK Ⓐ
Gallerie Koller
Hardturmstrasse 102, Postfach, 8031
Zürich, Switzerland
www.galeriekoller.ch

GM Ⓓ
Galerie Maurer
Kurfurstenstrasse 17, D-80799
Munchen, Germany
Tel: +49 89 271 13 45
www.galerie-objekte-maurer.de

GORL Ⓐ
Gorringes
15 North Street,
Lewes, East Sussex BN7 2PD
Tel: 01273 472503
www.gorringes.co.uk

H&L Ⓐ
Hampton and Littlewood
The Auction Rooms, Alphin Brook
Road, Alphington,
Exeter, Devon EX2 8TH
Tel: 01392 413100
www.hamptonandlittlewood.co.uk

HAMG Ⓐ
**Dreweatt Neate Godalming
(Formerly Hamptons)**
Baverstock House, 93 High Street,
Godalming, Surrey GU7 1AL
Tel: 01483 423567
www.dnfa.com/godalming

HB Ⓓ
Victoriana Dolls
101 Portobello Rd, London, W11 2BQ
Tel: 01737 249 525
heather.bond@totalserve.co.uk

HGS Ⓓ
Harpers General Store
301 Maple Avenue, Mt. Gretna, PA
17064
Tel: 001 717 865 3456
www.harpergeneralstore.com

IHB Ⓓ
Imperial Half Bushel
831 N Howard Street,
Baltimore, MD 21201, USA
Tel: 001 410 462 1192
www.imperialhalfbushel.com

ING Ⓓ
Ingram Antiques
669 Mt. Pleasant Road,
Toronto, Canada M4S 2N2
Tel: 001 416 484 4601

ISA Ⓐ
Ivey Selkirk Auctioneers
7447 Forsyth Boulevard, Saint
Louis, MI 63105, USA
Tel: 001 314 726 5515
www.iveyselkirk.com

JDB Ⓓ
Jo De Buck
43 Rue Des Minimes, B-1000
Brussels, Belgium
Tel: 0032 2 512 5516
jdb-tribalart@belgacom.net

JDJ Ⓐ
James D Julia Inc
PO Box 830, Fairfield, ME 04937,
USA
Tel: 001 207 453 7125
www.juliaauctions.com

JH Ⓐ
Jeanette Hayhurst Fine Glass
32A Kensington Church St.,
London W8 4HA
Tel: 020 7938 1539

JHD Ⓓ
John Howard @ Heritage
Heritage, 6 Market Place, Woodstock,
Oxon, OX20 1TA
Tel: 0870 444 0678
www.antiquepottery.co.uk

JN Ⓐ
John Nicholsons
The Auction Rooms, 'Longfield',
Midhurst Road, Fernhurst,
Haslemere, Surrey GU27 3HA
Tel: 01428 653727
www.johnnicholsons.com

KAU Ⓐ
Auktionhaus Kaup
Schloss Sulzburg, Hauptstrasse
62, 79295 Sulzburg, Germany
Tel: 0049 7634 5038 0
www.kaupp.de

KC Ⓓ
Kevin Conru
8a Rue Bodenbroek, B 1000
Brussels, Belgium
Tel: 0032 2 512 7635

L&T Ⓐ
Lyon and Turnbull Ltd.
33 Broughton Place,
Edinburgh, Midlothian EH1 3RR
Tel: 0131 557 8844
www.lyonandturnbull.com

LAM Ⓓ
Lawson Menzies
212 Cumberland Street, Sydney, NSW
2000, Australia
Tel: 02 8274 1851
www.lawsonmenzies.com.au

LAW Ⓐ
Lawrences' Auctioneers
The Linen Yard, South Street,
Crewkerne, Somerset TA18 8AB
Tel: 01460 73041
www.lawrences.co.uk

LB Ⓓ
Linda Bee
Stand L18-21, Grays Antique Market,
1-7 Davies Mews, London, W1K 2LP
Tel: 020 7629 5921
lindabee@grays.clara.net

LFA Ⓐ
Law Fine Art Ltd.
Ash Cottage, Ashmore Green,
Newbury, Berkshire, RG18 9ER
Tel: 01635 860033
www.lawfineart.co.uk

LH Ⓓ
Lucy's Hat
1118 Pine Street, Philadelphia, PA,
USA   shak06@aol.com

LHS Ⓐ
L.H. Selman Ltd.
123 Locust Street, Santa Cruz, CA
95060 USA
www.selman.com/pwauction/

LHT Ⓓ
Leanda Harwood Teddy Bears
www.leandaharwood.co.uk

LYNH Ⓓ
Lynn & Brian Holmes
Tel: 020 7368 6412

MARA Ⓓ
Marie Antiques
G107&136-137 Alfies Antique Market,
13 Church Street, , London NW8 8DT
Tel: 020 7706 3727
www.marieantiques.co.uk

MAX Ⓐ
Maxwells
133A Woodford Road, Woodford,
Cheshire SK7 1QD
Tel: 0161 439 5182

MGL Ⓓ
Mix Gallery
17 South Main Street,
Lambertville, NJ 08530, USA
Tel: 001 609 773 0777
www.mix-gallery.com

MG Ⓓ
Mod-Girl
c/o South Street Antiques Centre, 615
South 6th Street, Philadelphia, PA
19147-2128 USA
Tel: 001 215 592 0256
modgirljill@comcast.net

MSA Ⓓ
Manfred Schotten Antiques
109 Burford High Street, Burford,
Oxfordshire OX18 4RH
Tel: 01993 822 302
www.schotten.com

NA Ⓐ
Northeast Auctions
93 Pleasant Street, Portsmouth, NH
03801 USA
Tel: 001 603 433 8400
www.northeastauctions.com

NAG Ⓐ
Nagel
Neckarstrasse 189-191,
70190 Stuttgart, Germany
Tel: 0049 711 649 690
www.auction.de

NEA Ⓐ
Dreweatte Neate (Formerly Neales)
The Nottingham Salerooms, 192
Mansfield Road, Nottingham, NG1
3HU
Tel: 0115 962 4141
www.dnfa.com/neales

OHA Ⓓ
Owen Hargreaves & Jasmine Dahl
Stall 16 Portobello Antiques Market
Tel: 0207 253 2669
www.owenhargreaves.com

P Ⓓ
Posteritati
239 Centre Street, New York, NY
10013, USA
Tel: 001 212 2226 2207
www.posteritati.com

PAR Ⓓ
Partridge Fine Arts Plc
144-146 New Bond Street, London
W1S 2PF
Tel: 020 7629 0834
www.partridgeplc.com

PC ⒫Ⓒ
Private Collection

725

PHK Ⓟ©
Philip Keith Private Collection
www.philipkeith.co.uk

POOK Ⓐ
Pook & Pook
463 East Lancaster Avenue,
Downington, PA 19335, USA
Tel: 001 610 269 4040/0695
www.pookandpook.com

R&GM Ⓓ
R & G McPherson Antiques
40 Kensington Church Street,
London W8 4BX
Tel: 020 7937 0812
www.orientalceramics.com

RAON Ⓟ©
R.A. O'Neil Private Collection

RB Ⓓ
Roger Bradbury
11 Church Street, Coltishall, Norwich,
Norfolk, NR12 7DJ
Tel: 01603 737 444

RBRG Ⓓ
RBR Group at Grays
158/168, Grays Antique Market, 58
Davies Street, London, W1K 5LP
Tel: 020 7629 4769
rbr@grays.clara.net

RDER Ⓓ
Rogers de Rin
76 Royal Hospital Road, Paradise
Walk, Chelsea, London SW3 4HN
Tel: 020 7352 9007
www.rogersderin.co.uk

RDL Ⓐ
**David Rago/Nicholas Dawes Lalique
Auctions**
333 North Main Street, Lambertville, NJ
08530, USA
Tel: 001 609 397 9374
www.ragoarts.com

RENO Ⓐ
The Coeur d'Alene Art Auction
PO Box 310, Hayden, ID 83835, USA
Tel: 001 208 772 9009
www.cdaartauction.com

RGA Ⓓ
Richard Gardner Antiques
Swan House, Market Square, Petworth,
West Sussex GU28 0AH
Tel: 01798 343 411
www.richardgardenerantiques.co.uk

ROS Ⓐ
Rosebery's
74-76 Knight's Hill, West Norwood,
London SE27 0JD
Tel: 020 8761 2522
www.roseberys.co.uk

ROW Ⓐ
Rowley Fine Arts
8 Downham Road, Ely, Cambridge,
Cambridgeshire CB6 1AH
Tel: 01353 653020
www.rowleyfineart.com

RP Ⓓ
Rosie Palmer
26-28 High Street, Otford, Kent TN15
9DF
Tel: 01959 522 025
www.otfordantiques.co.uk

RSS Ⓐ
Rossini SA
7, rue Drouot, 75009 Paris, France
Tel: 00 33 (0)1 53 34 55 00
www.rossini.fr

SDR Ⓐ
Sollo:Rago Modern Auctions
333 North Main Street, Lambertville, NJ
08530 USA
Tel: 001 609 397 9374
www.ragoarts.com

SF Ⓓ
The Silver Fund
1 Duke of York Street, London SW1Y
6JP
Tel: 0207 839 7664
www.thesilverfund.com

SHA Ⓐ
Schapiro Auctioneers
162 Queen Street, Woollahra, NSW
2025, Australia
Tel: +612 9326 1588
www.shapiro.com.au

SHF Ⓓ
Steppes Hill Farm Antiques
Steppes Hill Farm, Stockbury,
Sittingbourne, Kent, ME9 7RB
Tel: 01795 842 205

SJH Ⓐ
S. J. Hales
S.J.Hales, Tracey House Salerooms,
Newton Road, Bovey Tracey, Newton
Abbot, Devon, TQ13 9AZ
Tel: 01626 836684
www.sjhales.com

SK Ⓐ
Skinner Inc.
The Heritage on the Garden,
63 Park Plaza Boston MA 02116,
USA
Tel: 001 617 350 5400
www.skinnerinc.com

SOTT Ⓓ
Sign of the Tymes
12 Morris Farm Road, Lafayette, NJ
07848 USA
Tel: 001 973 383 6028
www.millantiques.com

STE Ⓓ
Cloud Glass
info@cloudglass.com
www.cloudglass.com

SUM Ⓓ
Sue Mautner Costume Jewellery
Mob: 07743 546 744

SWA Ⓐ
Swann Galleries Image Library
104 East 25th Street, New York, New
York 10010
Tel: 001 212 254 4710
www.swanngalleries.com

SWO Ⓐ
Sworders
14 Cambridge Road, Stansted
Mountfitchet, Essex CM24 8BZ
Tel: 01279 817 778
www.sworder.co.uk

TAB Ⓓ
Take-A-Boo Emporium
1927 Avenue Road, Toronto, Ontario,
M5M 4A2
Tel: 001 416 785 4555
www.takeaboo.com

TAM Ⓓ
Antiques & Militaria
Toronto Antiques Centre, 276 King
Street West, Toronto, Ontario, M5V 1J2
Canada
Tel: 001 416 345 9941
www.antiquesandmilitaria.com

TCF Ⓓ
Cynthia Findlay
Toronto Antiques Centre,
276 King Street West, Toronto,
Ontario M5V 1J2, Canada
Tel: 001 416 260 9057
www.cynthiafindlay.com

TCT Ⓓ
The Calico Teddy
www.calicoteddy.com

TDG Ⓓ
The Design Gallery
5 The Green, Westerham, Kent, TN16
1AS
Tel: 01959 561 234
www.designgallery.co.uk

VA Ⓐ
Johannes Vogt Auktionen
Antonienstraße 3, 80802 Munich,
Germany
Tel: 0049 89 33079139
www.vogt-auctions.de

VDB Ⓓ
Van Den Bosch
Shop 1, Georgian Village, Camden
Passage, Islington N1 8DU
www.vandenbosch.co.uk

VEC Ⓐ
Vectis Auctions
Fleck Way, Thornaby, Stockton on
Tees,
County Durham TS17 9JZ
Tel: 01642 750 616
www.vectis.co.uk

W&W Ⓐ
Wallis and Wallis
West Street Auction Galleries,
Lewes, East Sussex BN7 2NJ
Tel: 01273 480 208
www.wallisandwallis.co.uk

WAD Ⓐ
**Waddington's Auctioneers &
Appraisers**
111 Bathurst St., Toronto,
Ontario M5V 2R1, Canada
Tel: 001 416 504 9100
www.waddingtons.ca

WAL Ⓓ
William Walter Antiques Ltd
Vault 3, London Silver Vaults, Chancery
House, Chancery Lane, London, WC2A
1QS
Tel:020 7242 3248
www.williamwalter.co.uk

WW Ⓐ
Woolley and Wallis
51-61 Castle Street, Salisbury,
Wiltshire SP13SU
Tel: 01722 424 500
www.woolleyandwallis.co.uk

NOTE

For valuations, it is advisable to contact the dealer or auction house in advance to confirm that they will perform this service and whether any charge is involved. Telephone valuations are not possible, so it will be necessary to send details, including a photograph, of the object to the dealer or auction house, along with a stamped addressed envelope for response. While most dealers will be happy to help you, do remember that they are busy people. Please mention *DK Antiques Price Guide 2008* by Judith Miller when making an enquiry.

COLLECTING ON THE INTERNET

The internet has revolutionized the trading of both antiques and collectibles, especially for smaller pieces, such as ceramics and metalware, which are are easily defined, described and photographed. Shipping is also comparatively easy for smaller items. The Internet has provided a cost-effective way of buying and selling, away from the overheads of shops and auction rooms. Around the world, antiques are offered for sale and traded daily, with sites varying from global online marketplaces, such as eBay, to specialist dealers' websites.

When searching online, remember that some people may not know how to accurately describe their item or may use special terminology. General category searches, even though more time consuming, and even deliberately misspelling a name, can yield results. Also, if something looks too good to be true, it probably is. Using this book to get to know your market visually, so that you can tell the difference between a real bargain and something that sounds like one, is a good start.

As you will understand from buying this book, colour photography is vital – look for online listings that include as many images as possible and check them carefully. Be aware that colours can appear differently, even between computer screens.

Always ask the vendor questions about the object, particularly regarding condition. If there is no image, or you want to see another aspect of the object – ask. Most sellers (private or trade) will want to realize the best price for their items so will be more than happy to help – if approached politely and sensibly.

Sellers should describe their item accurately. Include as much detail as possible including maker, size, colour, any other marks, condition, and damage. Always include as many digital photographs as possible. These should be shot in focus and in clear, preferably natural, light. Try to find out likely shipping and packaging costs in advance and aim to include them on your listing, along with methods of payment you will accept. Have the item at hand and be ready to answer questions promptly from potential buyers.

As well as the 'e-hammer' price, you will probably have to pay additional transactional fees such as packing, shipping, and possibly regional or national taxes. It is always best to ask for an estimate for these additional costs before leaving a bid. This will also help you tailor your bid as you will have an idea of the maximum price the item will cost if you are successful.

As well as the well-known online auction sites, such as eBay, there is a host of other online resources for buying and selling, for example fair and auction date listings.

INTERNET RESOURCES

Live Auctioneers
www.liveauctioneers.com
info@liveauctioneers.com
A free service which allows users to search catalogs from selected auction houses in the US and Europe. Through its connection with eBay, users can bid live via the Internet into salerooms as auctions happen. Registered users can also search through an illustrated archive of past catalogs and receive a free newsletter by email.

invaluable.com
www.invaluable.com
sales@invaluable.com
A subscription service which allows users to search selected European auction house catalogs. Also offers an extensive archive for appraisal uses.

The Antiques Trade Gazette
www.atg-online.com
The online version of the UK trade newspaper, comprising British auction and fair listings, news, and events.

Maine Antiques Digest
www.maineantiquesdigest.com
The online version of America's trade newspaper including news, articles, fair and auction listings, and more.

La Gazette du Drouot
www.drouot.com
The online home of the magazine listing all auctions to be held in France at the Hotel de Drouot in Paris and beyond. An online subscription enables you to download the magazine online.

AuctionBytes
www.auctionbytes.com
Auction resource with community forum, news, events, tips, and a weekly newsletter.

Internet Auction List
www.internetauctionlist.com
Auction news, online and offline auction search engines and live chat forums.

Go Antiques/Antiqnet
www.goantiques.com
www.antiqnet.com
An online global aggregator for art, antiques and collectables dealers who showcase their stock online, allowing users to browse and buy.

eBay
www.ebay.co.uk
Undoubtedly the largest of the online auction sites, allowing users to buy and sell in an online marketplace with over 52 million registered users. Collectors should also view eBay Live Auctions (www.ebayliveauctions.com) where traditional auctions are combined with online bidding allowing

users to interact with the saleroom.

Tias
www.tias.com
An online global aggregator for art, antiques and collectibles dealers who showcase their stock online, allowing users to browse and buy.

Collectors Online
www.collectorsonline.com
An online global aggregator for art, antiques and collectibles dealers who showcase their stock online, allowing users to browse and buy.

Antiques and The Arts
www.antiquesandthearts.com
Website of Antiques and the Arts weekly newspaper. Calendar of events, auctions, shows, and book reviews.

PayPal
www.paypal.com
An online transaction site, allowing payment to be made and accepted in a secure environment.

BidPay
www.bidpay.com
An online transaction site, allowing payment for goods by Western Union money order, sterling cheque or payment to a US bank account.

KEY TO ADVERTISERS

CLIENT	PAGE NO	CLIENT	PAGE NO
Lyon & Turnbull	16	Dorling Kindersley	445
Skinner Inc	72	James D Julia	449
Freeman's	118	Rago Arts & Auction Center	599
Jeanette Hayhurst Fine Glass	246		

DIRECTORY OF AUCTIONEERS

THIS IS A LIST OF AUCTIONEERS that conduct regular sales. Auction houses that would like to be included in the next edition should contact us by 1 February 2008.

Alabama

Flomaton Antique Auction
PO Box 1017, 320
Palafox Street,
Flomaton 36441
Tel: 251 296 3059
Fax: 251 296 1974
info@flomatonantiqueauction.com
www.flomatonantiqueauction.com

Jim Norman Auctions
201 East Main St,
Hartselle, 35640
Tel: 205 773 6878

Vintage Auctions
Star Rte Box 650,
Blountsville, 35031
Tel: 205 429 2457
Fax: 205 429 2457

Arizona

Dan May & Associates
4110 North Scottsdale Road,
Scottsdale, 85251
Tel: 480 941 4200

Old World Mail Auctions
PO Box 2224
Sedona, 86339
Tel: 928 282 3944
marti@oldworldauctions.com
www.oldworldauctions.com

Star Auction Inc
P. O. Box 1232, Dolan Springs,
86441-1232
Tel: 602 767 4774
Fax: 602 767 3900

Arkansas

Hanna-Whysel Auctioneers
3403 Bella Vista Way,
Bella Vista, 72714
Tel: 501 855 9600

Ponders Auctions
1203 South College,
Stuttgart, 72160
Tel: 501 673 6551

California

Bonhams & Butterfields
7601 Sunset Blvd,
Los Angeles, 90046-2714
Tel: 323 850 7500
Fax: 323 850 5843
info@butterfields.com
www.butterfields.com

Bonhams & Butterfields
220 San Bruno Ave,
San Francisco, 94103
Tel: 415 861 7500
Fax: 415 861 8951
info@butterfields.com
www.butterfields.com

I.M. Chait Gallery
9330 Civic Center Drive,
Beverly Hills, 90210
Tel: 310 285 0182
Fax: 310 285 9740
www.chait.com

Cuschieri's Auctioneers & Appraisers
863 Main Street,
Redwood City, 94063
Tel: 650 556 1793
info@cuschieris.com
www.cuschieris.com

eBay, Inc
2005 Hamilton Ave, Ste 350,
San Jose, 95125
staff@ebay.com
www.ebay.com

San Rafael Auction Gallery
634 Fifth Avenue, San Rafael,
San Rafael, 94901
Tel: 415 457 4488
Fax: 415 457 4899
sanrafaelauction@aol.com
www.sanrafael-auction.com

L. H. Selman Ltd
123 Locust St,
Santa Cruz, 95060
Tel: 800 538 0766
lselman@got.net
www.paperweight.com

Slawinski Auction Co
PO Box 67059
Scotts Valley, 95067
antiques@slawinski.com
www.slawinski.com

North Carolina

Robert S. Brunk Auction Services, Inc
P. O. Box 2135, Asheville 28802
Tel: 828 254 6846
auction@brunkauctions.com
www.brunkauctions.com

Historical Collectible Auctions
24 NW Court Square,
Suite 201, Graham 27253
Tel: 336 570 2803
auctions@hcaauctions.com
www.hcaauctions.com

South Carolina

Charlton Hall Galleries, Inc
912 Gervais St,
Columbia 29201
Tel: 803 799 5678
info@charltonhallauctions.com
www.charltonhallauctions.com

Colorado

Pacific Auction
1270 Boston Ave.,
Longmont, 80501
Tel: 303 772 9401
ojpratt@pacificauction.com
www.pacificauction.com

Pettigrew Auction Company
1645 South Tejon Street,
Colorado Springs, 80906
Tel: 719 633 7963

Priddy's Auction Galleries
5411 Leetsdale Drive,
Denver, 80222
Tel: 800 380 4411

Stanley & Co
Auction Room,
395 Corona Street, Denver
Tel: 303 355 0506

Connecticut

Norman C. Heckler & Company
79 Bradford Corner Rd,
Woodstock Valley, 06282-2002
Tel: 860 974 1634
info@hecklerauction.com
info@hecklerauctin.com

Lloyd Ralston Toys
350 Long Beach Blvd,
Stratford, 06615
Tel: 203 386 9399
lrgallery@sbcglobal.net
www.lloydralstontoys.com

Winter Associates, Inc
Auctioneers & Appraisers,
21 Cooke St,
P. O. Box 823,
Plainville, 06062
Tel: 860 793 0288

North Dakota

Curt D. Johnson Auction Company
4216 Gateway Drive,
Grand Forks, 58203
Tel: 701 746 1378
merfeld@rrv.net
www.curtdjohnson.com

South Dakota

Fischer Auction Company
238 Haywire Ave,
P. O. Box 667,
Long Lake, 57457-0667
Tel: 800 888 1766/
605 577 6600
figleo@hotmail.com
www.fischerauction.com

Delaware

Remember When Auctions, Inc
42 Sea Gull Rd,
Swann Estates,
Selbyville, 19975
Tel: 302-436-4979
sales@history-attic.com
www.history-attic.com

Florida

Auctions Neapolitan
1100 1st Ave South.,
Naples 34102
Tel: 239 262 7333
info@autionsneapolitan.com
www.auctionsneapolitan.com

Burchard Galleries/Auctioneers
2528 30th Ave North,
St Petersburg, 33713
Tel: 727 821 1167
mail@burchardgalleries
www.burchardgalleries.com

Arthur James Galleries
615 East Atlantic Avenue,
Delray Beach
Tel: 561 278 2373
arjames@bellsouth.net
www.arthurjames.com

Kincaid Auction Company
3809 East Hwy 42,
Lakeland 33801
Tel: 800 970 1977
kincaid@kincaid.com
www.kincaid.com

Albert Post Galleries
809 Lucerne Ave,
Lake Worth, 33460
Tel: 561 582 4477
a.postgallery@juno.com
www.albertpostgallery.com

Georgia

Arwood Auctions
26 Ayers Ave, Marietta, 30060
Tel: 770 423 0110

Great Gatsby's
5070 Peachtree Industrial Blvd,
Atlanta, GA 30341
Tel: 770 457 1903
internet@greatgatsbys.com
www.greatgatsbys.com

My Hart Auctions Inc
PO Box 2511,
Cumming, GA 30028
Tel: 770 888 9006
myhart@antiquefurniture.us

Red Baron's Auction Gallery
6450 Roswell Rd,
Atlanta, 30328
Tel: 404 252 3770
rbarons@onramp.net

Southland Auction Inc
3350 Riverwood Parkway,
Atlanta, GA 30339
Tel: 770 818 2418

Idaho

The Coeur d'Alene Art Auction
PO Box 310, Hayden, 83835
Tel: 208 772 9009
cdaartauction@cdaartaution.com
www.cdaartauction.com

Indiana

Kruse International
PO Box 190,
Auburn, 46706
Tel: 219 925 5600/
800 968 4444

Lawson Auction Service
923 Fourth St,
Columbus, 47265
Tel: 812 372 2571
dlawson@lawsonauction.com
www.lawsonauction.com

Curran Miller Auction & Realty, Inc
4424 Vogel Rd, Ste. 400,
Evansville, 47715
Tel: 800 264 0601
email@curranmiller.com
www.curranmiller.com

Schrader Auction
209 West Van Buren St,
Columbia City, 46725
Tel: 219 244 7606

Slater's Americana
5335 North Tacoma Ave, Suite 24,
Indianapolis, 46220
Tel: 317 257 0863

Stout Auctions
529 State Road East,
Williamsport, 47993
Tel: 765 764 6901
info@stoutauctions.com
www.stoutauctions.com

Strawser Auctions
Michael G. Strawser,
200 North Main, P. O. Box 332,
Wolcotville, IN 46795
Tel: 260 854 2859
info@strawserauctions.com
www.strawserauctions.com

Illinois

Butterfield & Dunning
755 Church Rd,
Elgin, 60123
Tel: 847 741 3483
info@butterfields.com
www.butterfields.com

Hack's Auction Center
Box 296, Pecatonica, 61063
Tel: 815 239 1436

Hanzel Galleries
1120 South Michigan Ave,
Chicago, 60605-2301
Tel: 312 922 6247

Joy Luke Auction Gallery

300 East Grove St,
Bloomington, 61701-5232
Tel: 309 828 5533
robert@joyluke.com
www.joyluke.com

Susanin's Auction
228 Merchandise Mart,
Chicago, 60654
Tel: 888 787 2646/
312 832 9800
info@susanins.com
www.susanins.com

Iowa

Jackson's Auctioneers & Appraisers
2229 Lincoln St,
P. O. Box 50613,
Cedar Falls, 50613
Tel: 319 277 2256
jacksons@jacksonsauction.com
www.jacksonsauction.com

Tubaugh Auctions
1702 8th Ave,
Belle Plaine, 52208
Tel: 319 444 2413
www.tubaughauctions.com

Kansas

AAA Historical Auction Service
P. O. Box 12214,
Kansas City, 66112
www.manions.com,

CC Auction Gallery
416 Court, Clay Center, 67432
Tel: 785 632 6062

Spielman Auction
2259 Homestead Rd, Lebo, 66856
Tel: 316 256 6558

Kentucky

Hays & Associates, Inc
120 South Spring St,
Louisville, 40206-1953
Tel: 502 584 4297

Steffen's Historical Militaria
P. O. Box 280,
Newport, 41072
Tel: 859 431 4499
www.steffensmilitaria.com

Louisiana

Estate Auction Gallery
3374 Government St,
Baton Rouge, 70806
Tel: 504 383 7706

Neal Auction Company
4038 Magazine Street
New Orleans,
Louisiana 70115
Tel: 504 899 5329
Toll Free: 800 467 5329
Fax: 504 897 3808

New Orleans Auction Galleries
801 Magazine St,
New Orleans, 70130
Tel: 504 566 1849
info@neworleansauction.com
www.neworleansauction.com

Maine

Cyr Auctions
P.O. Box 1238, Gray,
Maine 04039
Tel: 207 657 5253
Fax: 207 657 5253
info@cyrauctions.com
www.cyrauction.com

James D Julia Auctioneers Inc
Rte 201, Skowhegan Rd,
P. O. Box 830, Fairfield,
ME 04937
Tel: 207 453 7125
jjulia@juliaauctions.com
www.juliaauctions.com

Thomaston Place Auction Galleries
P. O. Box 300,
Business Rt 1,
Thomaston, ME 04861
Tel: 207 354 8141
auction@kajav.com
www.thomastonauction.com

Maryland

Hantman's Auctioneers & Appraisers
P. O. Box 59366,
Potomac, 20859-9366
Tel: 301 770 3720
hantman@hantmans.com
www.hantmans.com

Isennock Auctions & Appraisals, Inc
4106B Norrisville Rd,
White Hall, 21161-9306,
Tel: 410 557 8052
isennock@starix.net
www.isennockauction.com

Richard Opfer Auctioneering, Inc
1919 Greenspring Dr,
Lutherville,
Timonium, 21093-4113
Tel: 410 252 5035
info@opferauction.com
www.opferauction.com

DIRECTORY OF AUCTIONEERS

Sloans & Kenyon
4605 Bradley Boulevard
Bethesda, MD 20815
Tel: 301 634-2330
Fax: 301 656-7074
www.sloansandkenyon.com

Massachusetts

Douglas Auctioneers
Rte 5, South Deerfield, 01373
Tel: 413 665 2877
www.douglasauctioneers.com
info@douglasauctioneers.com

Eldred's
P. O. Box 796,
East Dennis, 02641-0796
Tel: 508 385 3116
info@eldreds.com
www.eldreds.com

Grogan & Company Auctioneers
22 Harris St,
Dedham, 02026
Tel: 781 461 9500
grogans@groganco.com
www.groganco.com

Shute Auction Gallery
850 West Chestnut St,
Brockton, 02401
Tel: 508 588 0022/
508 588 7833

Skinner Inc.
63 Park Plaza, Boston,
MA 02116
Tel: 617 350 5400
info@skinnerinc.com
www.skinnerinc.com

Skinner, Inc
357 Main St,
Bolton, MA 01740
Tel: 978 779 6241
info@skinnerinc.com
www.skinnerinc.com

Willis Henry Auctions, Inc
22 Main St,
Marshfield, 02050
Tel: 781 834 7774
wha@willishenry.com
www.willishenry.com

Michigan

DuMouchelle Art Galleries Co
409 East Jefferson Ave,
Detroit, 48226
Tel: 313 963 6255
info@dumouchelles.com
www.dumouchelles.com

Ivey-Selkirk Auctioneers
7447 Forsyth Boulevard
Saint Louis,
Missouri 63105
Tel: 314 726 5515
Toll: 800 728 8002
Fax: 314 726 9908
iveyselkirk@iveyselkirk.com
www.iveyselkirk.com

Minnesota

Buffalo Bay Auction Co
5244 Quam Circle,
Rogers, 55374
Tel: 612 428 8480
buffalobay@aol.com

Tracy Luther Auctions
2548 East 7th Ave,
St. Paul, 55109
Tel: 612 770 6175

Rose Auction Galleries
3180 Country Drive,
Little Canada, 55117
Tel: 612 484 1415
auctions@rosegalleries.com
www.rosegalleries.com

Missouri

Ivey Selkirk Auctioneers
7447 Forsyth Blvd,
Saint Louis, 63105
Tel: 314 726 5515
www.iveyselkirk.com

Simmons & Company Auctioneers
40706 East 144th St,
Richmond, 64085
Tel: 816 776 2936/800 646 2936
www.simmonsauction.com

Montana

Allard Auctions
PO Box 1030,
St. Ignatius, MT 59865
Tel: 460 745 0500
www.allardauctions.com

Stan Howe & Associates
4433 Red Fox
Dr, Helena, MT 59601
Tel: 406 443 5658/
800 443 5658

New Hampshire

Northeast Auctions
694 Lafayette Rd,
P. O. Box 363,
Hampton, 03483
Tel: 603 926 9800

New Jersey

Bertoia Auctions
2141 Dearco Dr,
Vineland, NJ 08360
Tel: 856 692 1881
toys@bertoiaauctions.com
www.bertoiaauctions.com

Craftsman Auctions
333 North Main Street,
Lambertville, NJ 08530
Tel: 609 397 9374
info@ragoarts.com
www.ragoarts.com

David Rago Auctions
333 North Main Street,
Lambertville, NJ 08530
Tel: 609 397 9374
info@ragoarts.com
www.ragoarts.com

Dawson & Nye
128 American Road,
Morris Plains, NJ 07950
Tel: 973 984 8900
info@dawsonandnye.com
www.dawsonandnye.com
info@dawsons.org www.dawsons.org

Greg Manning Auctions, Inc
775 Passaic Ave,
West Caldwell, NJ 07006
Tel: 973 882 0004/
800 221 0243
info@gregmanning.com
www.gregmanning.com

Rago/Dawes Lalique Auctions
333 North Main Street,
Lambertville, NJ 08530
Tel: 609 397 9374
info@ragoarts.com
www.ragoarts.com

Sollo:Rago Modern Auctions
333 North Main Street,
Lambertville, NJ 08530
Tel: 609 397 9374
info@ragoarts.com
www.ragoarts.com

New Mexico

Altermann Galleries
Santa Fe Galleries,
203 Canyon Road,
Santa Fe, 87501
info@altermann.com
www.altermann.com

New York

Christie's
502 Park Ave,
New York, NY 10022
Tel: 212 546 1000
info@christies.com
www.christies.com

Christie's East
219 East 67th St,
New York, NY 10021
Tel: 212 606 0400
info@christies.com
www.christies.com

Samuel Cottone Auctions
15 Genesee St,
Mount Morris, 14510
Tel: 716 658 3180

William Doyle Galleries
175 East 87th St,
New York, 10128-2205
Tel: 212 427 2730
info@doylegalleries.com
www.doylegalleries.com

Framefinders
454 East 84th Street,
New York 10028
Tel: 212 396 3896
framefinders@aol.com
www.framefinders.com

Guernsey's Auction
108 East 73rd St,
New York, 10021
Tel: 212 794 2280
auctions@guernseys.com
www.guernseys.com

William J. Jenack Auctioneers
62 Kings Highway Bypass, Chester,
NY 10918
845 469-9095
845 469-8445
info@jenack.com
www.jenack.com

Mapes Auction Gallery
1729 Vestal Parkway,
West Vestal, 13850-1156
Tel: 607 754 9193
info@mapesauction.com
www.mapesauction.com

North River Auction Gallery
1293 Route 212
Saugerties, NY 12477
Tel: 845 247 9130
Fax: 845 247 9134

Phillip's, De Pury & Luxemburg
450 West 15 Street,
New York, NY 10011
Tel: 212 940 1200
info@phillipsdepury.com
www.phillipsdepury.com

Sotheby's
1334 York Ave,
New York, NY 10021
Tel: 212 606 7000
info@sothebys.com
www.sothebys.com

Stair Galleries
549 Warren St
Hudson NY 12534
Tel: 518 751 1000
Fax: 518 751 1010
www.stairgalleries.com

Sterling Auction House
40 Railroad Ave
Montgomery, NY 12549
845-283-326
www.sterlingauctionhouse.com

Swann Galleries, Inc
104 East 25th St,
New York, NY 10010-2977
Tel: 212 254 4710
swann@swanngalleries.com
www.swanngalleries.com

Ohio

Belhorn Auction Services
PO Box 20211,
Columbus, OH 43220
Tel: 614 921 9441
www.belhorn.com

Cowan's Historic Americana Auctions
673 Wilmer Avenue,
Cincinnati, 45226
Tel: 513 871 1670
info@historicamericana.com
www.historicamericana.com

DeFina Auctions
1591 State Route
45, Austinburg, 44010
Tel: 440 275 6674
info@definaauctions.com
www.definaauctions.com

Garth's Auction, Inc
2690 Stratford Rd,
P. O. Box 369,
Delaware, 43015
Tel: 740 362 4771
info@garths.com
www.garths.com

Oregon

O'Gallery
228 Northeast Seventh
Avenue Portland,
Oregon 97232
Tel: 503 238 0202
Fax: 503 236 8211
www.ogallerie.com

Pennsylvania

Noel Barrett
P.O. Box 300,
Carversville, 18913
Tel: 215 297 5109
toys@noelbarrett.com
www.noelbarrett.com

Dargate Auction Galleries
5607 Baum Blvd,
Pittsburgh, 15206
Tel: 412 362 3558
dargate@dargate.com
www.dargate.com

Freeman's
1808 Chestnut St,
Philadelphia, 19103
Tel: 610 563 9275/
610 563 9453
info@freemansauction.com
www.freemansauction.com

Hunt Auctions
75E. Uwchlan Ave.
Suite 130, Exton, 19341
Tel: 610 524 0822
Fax: 610 524 0826
info@huntauctions
www.huntauctions.com

Pook & Pook, Inc
P. O. Box 268,
Downington, 19335-0268
Tel: 610 269 0695/
610 269 4040
info@pookandpook.com
www.pookandpook.com

Sanford Alderfer Auction Company
501 Fairgrounds Rd,
P. O. Box 640,
Hatfield, 19440-0640
Tel: 215 393 3000
info@alderfercompany.com
www.alderfercompany.com

Skinner's Auction Company
170 North Hampton Street,
Easton, 18042
Tel: 610 330 6933

Rhode Island

Gustave White Auctioneers
37 Bellevue, Newport, 02840-3207
Tel: 401 841 5780

Tennessee

Kimball M Sterling Inc
125 West Market St,
Johnson City, 37601,
Tel: 423 928 1471
kimsold@tricon.net
www.sterlingsold.com

Texas

Austin Auctions
8414 Anderson Mill Road,
Austin, 78729-5479
Tel: 512 258 5479
austinauction@cs.com
www.austinauction.com

Dallas Auction Gallery
1518 Slocum Street
Dallas, TX 75207
Tel: 214 653 3900
Fax: 214 653 3912
info@dallasauctiongallery.com
www.dallasauctiongallery.com

Utah

America West Archives
P. O. Box 100,
Cedar City, 84721
Tel: 435 586 9497
info@americawestarchives.com
www.americawestarchives.com

Vermont

Eaton Auction Service
RR 1, Box 333,
Fairlee, 05045
Tel: 802 333 9717
eas@sover.com
www.eatonauctionservice.com

Virginia

The Auction Gallery
225 Gun Club Road,
Richmond, 23221
Tel: 804 358 0500
www.estate-services.com

Ken Farmer Auctions & Estates
105 Harrison Street,
Radford, 24141
Tel: 540 639 0939
info@kfauctions.com
www.kenfarmer.com

Phoebus Auction Gallery
14-16 East Mellen St,
Hampton, 23663
Tel: 757 722 9210
bwelch@phoebusauction.com
www.phoebusauction.com

Washington DC

Seattle Auction House
5931 4th Avenue South, Seattle
Washington 98108
Tel: 206 764 4444
Fax: 206 764 0556
www.seattleauctionhouse.com

Weschler's
909 East St NW,
Washington, 20004-2006
Tel: 202 628 1281/
800 331 1430
www.weschlers.com

Wisconsin

Milwaukee Auction Galleries
1919 North Summit Ave,
Milwaukee, 53202
Tel: 414 271 1105

Schrager Auction Galleries, Ltd
P. O. Box 10390,
2915 North Sherman Blvd,
Milwaukee, 53210
Tel: 414 873 3738
www.schragerauctions.com

DIRECTORY OF CANADIAN AUCTIONEERS

Alberta

Arthur Clausen & Sons, Auctioneers
11802 - 145 Street,
Edmonton, Alberta,
Canada, T5L 2H3
Tel: 780 451 4549
arthur.clausen@telus.net
www.clausenauction.com

Hall's Auction Services Ltd
5240 1A Street S.E.,
Calgary, Alberta,
Canada, T2H 1J1
Tel: 403 640 1244
info@hallsauction.com
www.hodginshalls.com

Hodgins Art Auctions Ltd
5240 1A Street S.E.,
Calgary, Alberta,
Canada, T2H 1J1
Tel: 403 640 1244
info@hallsauction.com
www.hodginshalls.com

Lando Art Auctions
11130-105 Avenue N.W.,
Edmonton, Alberta,
Canada, T5H 0L5
Tel: 780 990 1161
mail@landoartauctions.com
www.landoartauctions.com

British Columbia

All Nations Stamp & Coin
Hudson's Bay Company
4th Floor, 674 Granville Street,
PO Box 54023, Vancouver,
British Columbia,
Canada, V6C 3P4
Tel: 604 689 2230
collect@direct.ca
www.allnationsstampandcoin.com

Maynards Fine Art Auction House
415 West 2nd Avenue,
Vancouver, British Columbia,
Canada, V5Y 1E3
Tel: 604 876 6787
www.maynards.com

Robert Derot Associates
P.O. Box 52205, Vancouver,
British Columbia,
Canada, V7J 3V5
Tel: 604 649 6302
robert@robertderot.com
www.robertderot.com

Waddington's West
3286 Bellevue Road, Victoria,
British Columbia,
Canada, V8X 1C1
Tel: 1 250 384 3737
www.waddingtonsauctions.com

Ontario

Empire Auctions
165 Tycos Drive,
Toronto, Ontario,
Canada, M6B 1W6
Tel: 416 784 4261
www.empireauctions.com

Grand Valley Auctions
154 King Street East,
Cambridge, Ontario,
Canada
Tel: 519 653 6811
www.grandvalleyauctions.ca

A Touch of Class
92 College Crescent,
Barrie, Ontario,
Canada, L4M 5C8
Tel: 1 888 891 6591
info@atouchofclassauctions.com
www.atouchofclassauctions.com

Estate and Antiques Sales
2030 Eglinton Avenue West,
Toronto, Ontario,
Canada, M6E 3S4
Tel: 416 780 9101
www.estateandantiquesales.com

Gordon's Auction Center
1473 Princess Street,
Kingston Ontario,
Canada, K7M 3E9
Tel: 613 542 0963
mail@gordonsauction.com
www.gordonsauction.com

Ritchies
288 King Street East,
Toronto, Ontario,
Canada, M5A 1K4
Tel: 416 364 1864
www.ritchies.com

Waddington's
111 Bathurst Street,
Toronto, Ontario,
Canada, M5V 2R1
Tel: 416 504 9100
www.waddingtonsauctions.com

Walkers
81 Auriga Drive, Suite 18
Ottawa, Ontario,
Canada, K2E 7Y5
Tel: 613 224 5814
www.walkersauctions.com

Quebec

Empire Auctions
5500, rue Paré,
Montréal, Québec,
Canada, H4P 2M1
Tel: 514 737 6586

Iegor - Hôtel des Encans
872, rue Du Couvent,
Angle Saint-Antoine Ouest,
Montréal, Quebec,
Canada, H4C 2R6
Tel: 514 842 7447
information@iegor.net
www.iegor.net

Montreal Auction House
5778 St. Lawrent Blvd.,
Montreal, Quebec,
Canada, H2T 1S8
Tel: 514 278 0827
maison.des.encans@videotron.ca
www.pages.videotron.com

Pinneys Auctions
2435 Duncan Road (T.M.R.), Montreal, Quebec,
Cananda, H4P 2A2
Tel: 514 345 0571
pinneys@ca.inter.net
www.pinneys.ca

Ritchies
1980, rue Sherbrooke O.
Suite 100 (Ground Floor),
Quebec, Canada, H3H 1E8
Tel: 514 934 1864
www.ritchies.com

The Canadian Antique Dealers Association
PO Box 131
Bloor Street West, Toronto,
Ontario, Canada, M5S 3L7
Tel: 416 483 1481
cada@bellnet.ca
www.cadinfo.com

Canadiana

Antiquites Gerard Funkenberg & Jean Drapeau
900 Massawippi,
North Hatley, Quebec,
Canada J0B 2C0
Tel: 819 842 2725

The Blue Pump
178 Davenport Road,
Toronto, Ontario,
Canada, M5R 172
Tel: 416 944 1673
john@thebluepump.com
www.thebluepump.com

Ingram Antiques & Collectibles
669 Mt. Pleasant Road, Toronto,
Ontario, Canada, M4S 2N2
Tel: 416 484 4601

Old Canada Country Antiques
#407-17765 65a Avenue
Surrey, British Columbia,
Canada V3S 5N4
Tel: 604 575 2577
Fax: 604 575 2573
& 2227 Granville St,
Vancouver, Canada V6H 3G1
Tel: 604 731 2576
www.oldcanadacountry.com

Ceramics

Cynthia Findlay
Toronto Antiques Centre,
276 King Street West, Toronto,
Ontario, Canada, M5V 1J2
Tel: 416 260 9057
call@cynthiafindlay.com
www.cynthiafindlay.com

Pam Ferrazzutti Antiques
Toronto Antiques Centre,
276 King Street West, Toronto,
Ontario, Canada, M5V 1J2
Tel: 416 260 0325
pam@pamferrazzuttiantiques.com
www.pamferrazzuttiantiques.com

Staffordshire House
1 Chestnut Park Road, Toronto,
Ontario, Canada, M4W 1W4
Tel: 416 929 3258
jjd@aol.com
www.staffordshirehouse.com

Fine Art

Barbara M. Mitchell
Tel: 416 699 5582
fineartsbarbara@hotmail.com

Furniture

Croix-Crest Antiques
49 Mary St., St. Andrews,
New Brunswick, Canada E5B 1S5
Tel: 506 529 4693
Fax: 506 529 8734

Faith Grant The Connoisseur's Shop Ltd.
1156 Fort Street, Victoria,
British Columbia, Canada V8V 3K8
Tel: 250-383-0121
Fax: 250-383-0121
nfo@faithgrantantiques.com
www.faithgrantantiques.com

Howard & Co.
158 Davenport Rd., Toronto, Ontario,
Canada, M5R 1J2
Tel: 416 922 7966
bhoward@on.aibn.com

Jonny's Antiques
21 Avenue Road,
Four Season's Hotel,
Toronto, Ontario,
Canada, M5R 2G1
Tel: 416 928 0205
jonnysantiques@rogers.com

Lorenz Antiques Ltd.
701 Mount Pleasant Road,
Toronto, Ontario,
Canada, M4S 2N4
Tel: 416 487 2066
info@lorenzantiques.com
www.lorenzantiques.com

Maus Park Antiques
176 Cumberland Street,
Toronto, Ontario,
Canada, M5R 1A8
Tel: 416 944 9781
mauspark@bellnet.ca
www.mausparkantiques

Milord Antiques
1870 Notre-Dame St W.,
Montreal, Quebec,
Canada H3L 1M6
Tel: 514 933 2433
Fax: 514 933 2539
www.milordantiques.com
showroom@milordantiques.com

The Paisley Shop
77 Yorkville Avenue, Toronto,
Ontario, Canada M5R 1C1
Tel: 416-923-5830
Fax: 416-923-2694
www.paisleyshop.com

Richard Rumi & Co. Antiques
55 Woodlawn Avenue,
Mississauga, Ontario,
Canada L5G 3K7
Tel: 905-274-3616
Fax: 905-274-3617
www.rumiantiques.com

Shand Galleries
Toronto Antiques Centre,
276 King Street West, Toronto,
Ontario, Canada M5V 1J2
Tel: 416.260.9056
Fax: 001 416.260.9056

R.H.V. Tee & Son (England) Ltd.
7963 Granville Street,
Vancouver, British Columbia,
Canada V6P 4Z3
Tel: 604 263 2791
Fax: 604 263 2339
info@teeantiques.com
www.teeantiques.com

General

Floyd & Rita's Antiques and Collectables
Toronto Antiques Centre,
276 King Street West, Toronto,
Ontario, Canada M5V 1J2
Tel: 416 260 9066
antiques@floydrita.com
www.floydrita.com

Toronto Antiques Centre
276 King Street West, Toronto,
Ontario, Canada, M5V 1J2
Tel: 416 345 9941
www.torontoantiquectr.com

Jewelry

Fraleigh Jewellers – Gemmologists
1977 Yonge Street, Toronto,
Ontario, Canada, M4S 1Z6
Tel: 416 483 1481
rfraleigh@sympatico.ca

Oriental

Pao and Molkte Ltd.
Four Seasons Hotel, 21 Avenue Road, Toronto,
Ontario, Canada, M5R 2G1
Tel: 416 925 6197
paomoltke@mail.com

Topper Gallery
1111 Finch Avenue West, Toronto, Ontario,
Canada, M3J 2E5
Tel: 416 663 7554

Silver

Richard Flensted-Holder
86 Gloucester Street,
Toronto, Ontario, Canada, M4Y 2S2
Tel: 416 961 3414
(by appointment only)

Louis Wine Ltd.
140 Yorkville Avenue, Toronto, Ontario, Canada,
M5R 1C2
Tel: 416 929 9333
louiswine@rogers.com
www.louiswine.com

DIRECTORY OF SPECIALISTS

SPECIALISTS WHO WOULD LIKE TO BE INCLUDED in the next edition, or have a change of address or telephone number, should contact us by 1 February 2008.

Readers should contact dealers by telephone before visiting them to avoid a wasted journey.

American Paintings

James R Bakker Antiques Inc
248 Bradford Street, Provincetown, MA 02657
Tel: 508 487 9081

Jeffrey W. Cooley
The Cooley Gallery Inc,
25 Lyme Street, Old Lyme, CT 06371
Tel: 860 434 8807
info@cooleygallery. com
www.cooleygallery. com

Americana and Folk Art

Augustus Decorative Arts Ltd
Philadelphia
Tel: 215 587 0000
elle@portraitminatures.com

Axtell Antiques
1 River Street,
Deposit, NY 13754
Tel:607 467-2353
Fax: 607 467-4316
www.axtellantiques.com

Thomas and Julia Barringer
26 South Main Street, Stockton, NJ 08559
Tel: 609 397 4474
Fax: 609 397 4474 tandjb@voicenet.com

Bucks County Antique Center Route 202,
Lahaska, PA 18931
Tel: 215 794 9180

J M Flanigan American Antiques 1607 Park
Avenue, Baltimore, MD 21217
Tel: 410 225 3463
jmf745i@aol.com

Frank Gaglio, Inc
56 Market St., Suite B, Rhinebeck NY 12572
Tel: 845 876 0616

Sidney Gecker
226 West 21st Street,
New York, NY 10011
Tel: 212 929 8769

Pat and Rich Garthoeffner Antiques
122 East Main Street, Lititz, PA 17543
Tel: 717 627 7998
Fax: 717 627 3259
patgarth@voicenet.com

Allan Katz Americana
25 Old Still Road, Woodbridge, CT 06525
Tel: 203 393 9356
folkkatz@optonline.net

Nathan Liverant and Son
168 South Main Street, P.O. Box 103, Colchester,
CT 06415
Tel: 860 537 2409
www.liverantantiques.com
mail@liverantantiques.com

Judith and James Milne Inc
506 East 74th Street, New York, NY 10021
Tel: 212 472 0107
www.milneantiques.com
milneinc@aol.com

Olde Hope Antiques Inc
P.O. Box 718, New Hope, PA 18938
Tel: 215 297 0200
Fax: 215 297 0300
info@oldehopeantiques.com
www.oldehopeantiques.com

Pantry & Hearth,
994 Main Street South, Woodbury, CT 06798
Tel: 203 263 8555
gail.lettick@prodigy.net

Sharon Platt
1347 Rustic View, Manchester, MO 63011
Tel: 636 227 5304
sharonplatt@postnet.com

Raccoon Creek Antiques
Box 276, 208 Spangsville Road, Oley, PA 19547
www.raccoonantiques.com

J. B. Richardson
6 Partrick Lane, Westport, CT 06880
Tel: 203 226 0358

Marion Robertshaw Antiques
P.O. Box 435, Route 202, Lahaska, PA 18931
Tel: 215 295 0648

Cheryl and Paul Scott
P.O. Box 835, 232 Bear Hill Road, Hillsborough,
NH 03244
Tel: 603 464 3617
rivrebend@mcttelecom.com

The Splendid Peasant
Route 23 and Sheffield Road, P. O. Box 536,
South Egremont, MA 01258
Tel: 413 528 5755
folkart@splendidpeasant.com www.splendid-peasant.com

The Stradlings
1225 Park Avenue, New York, NY 10028
Tel: 212 534 8135

Patricia Stauble Antiques
180 Main Street, PO Box 265, Wiscasset, ME
04578
Tel: 207 882 6341
pstauble@midcoast.com

Throckmorton Fine Art
145 East 57th Street, 3rd Floor, NewYork, NY
10022
Tel: 001 212 223 1059
Fax: 001 212 223 1937
www.throckmorton-nyc.com

Jeffrey Tillou Antiques
33 West Street & 7 East Street, P.O. Box 1609,
Litchfield, CT 06759
Tel: 860 567 9693
webmaster@tillouantiques.com

Paul and Karen Wendhiser
P.O. Box 155, Ellington, CT 06029

Antiquities

Frank & Barbara Pollack
1214 Green Bay Road, Highland Park, IL 60035
Tel: 847 433 2213
FPollack@compuserve.com

Architectural Antiques

Garden Antiques
Katonah, NY 10536
Tel: 212 744 6281
gardenantiques@pipeline.com
www.bigardenantiques.com

Cecilia B Williams
12 West Main Street, New Market, MD 21774
Tel: 301 865 0777

Books

Bauman Rare Books
535 Madison Avenue,
New York, NY 10022
Tel: 212 751 0011
www.baumanrarebooks.com

Carpets and Rugs

John J Collins
Jr Gallery, P.O. Box 958, 11 Market Square,
Newburyport, MA 01950
Tel: 978 462 7276
www.bijar.com
bijar@telcity.com

Karen and Ralph Disaia
Oriental Rugs Ltd, 23 Lyme Street, Old Lyme,
CT 06371
Tel: 860 434 1167
www.orientalrugsltd.com
info@orientalrugsltd.com

D B Stock Antique Carpets
464 Washington Street, Wellesley, MA 02482
Tel: 781 237 5859
www.dbstock.com
douglas@dbstock.com

Ceramics

Charles & Barbara Adams
289 Old Main St, South Yarmouth, MA 02664
Tel: 508 760 3290
adams_2430@msn.com

Jill Fenichell
by appointment only
Tel: 212 980 9346
jfenichell@yahoo.com

Mark & Marjorie Allen
6 Highland Drive, Amherst, NH 03031
Tel: 603 672 8989
mandmallen@antiquedelft.com
www.antiquedelft.com

Mellin's Antiques
P.O. Box 1115, Redding, CT 06875
Tel: 203 938 9538
rich@mellin.us

Philip Suval, Inc
1501 Caroline Street, Fredericksburg, VA 22401
Tel: 540 373 9851
jphilipsuval@aol.com

Costume Jewelry

Aurora Bijoux
Tel: 215 872 7808
www.aurorabijoux.com

Deco Jewels Inc
131 Thompson Street, NY
Tel: 212 253 1222
decojewels@earthlink.net

Junkyard Jeweler
www.tias.com/stores/thejunkyardjeweler

Million Dollar Babies
Tel: 518 885 7397

Terry Rodgers & Melody
1050 2nd Avenue,
New York, NY 10022
Tel: 212 758 3164
melodyjewelnyc@aol.com

Roxanne Stuart
PA
Tel: 215 750 8868
gemfairy@aol.com

Bonny Yankauer
bonnyy@aol.com

Clocks

Kirtland H Crump
387 Boston Post Road,
Madison, CT 06443
Tel: 203 245 7573
kirtland@sbaglobal.net
www.crumpclocks.com

Decorative Arts

Sumpter Priddy Inc
323 South Washington Street, Alexandria, VA 22314
Tel: 703 299 0800
info@sumpterpriddy.com

Leah Gordon Antiques
Gallery 18, Manhattan Art and Antiques Center, 1050 Second Avenue, New York, NY 10022
Tel: 212 872 1422

Lillian Nassau
220 East 57th Street New York, NY 10022
Tel: 212 759 6062
lilnassau@aol.com
www.lilliannassau.com

Susie Burmann
23 Burpee Lane, New London, NH 03257
Tel: 603 526 5934 rsburmann@tds.net

H L Chalfant Antiques
1352 Paoli Pike, West Chester, PA 19380
Tel: 610 696 1862
chalfant@gateway.net

Brian Cullity
18 Pleasant Street, P.O. Box 595, Sagamore, MA 02561
Tel: 508 888 8409
info@briancullity.com
www.briancullity.com

Gordon and Marjorie Davenport Inc
4250 Manitou Way, Madison, WI 53711
Tel: 608 271 2348 GMDaven@aol.com

Ron and Penny Dionne
55 Fisher Hill Road, Willington, CT 06279
Tel: 860 487 0741

Peter H Eaton Antiques
24 Parker Street, Newbury, MA 01951
Tel: 978 465 2754 peter@petereaton.com
www.petereaton.com

Gallery 532
142 Duane Street, New York, NY 10013
Tel: 212 964 1282
www.gallery532.com

Stephen H Garner Antiques
P.O. Box 136, Yarmouth Port, MA 02675
Tel: 508 362 8424

Samuel Herrup Antiques
35 Sheffield Plain Road (Route 7), Sheffield, MA 01257
Tel: 413 229 0424
ssher@ben.net

High Style Deco
224 West 18th Street,
New York, NY 10011
Tel: 001 212 647 0035
Fax: 001 212 647 0031
www.highstyledeco.com

R Jorgensen Antiques
502 Post Road (US Route 1), Wells, ME 04090
Tel: 207 646 9444
info@rjorgensen.com
www.rjorgensen.com

Leigh Keno American Antiques 127 East 69th Street, New York, NY 10021
Tel: 212 734 2381
leigh@leighkeno.com
www.leighkeno.com

Bettina Krainin
289 Main Street, Woodbury, CT 06798
Tel: 203 263 7669

William E Lohrman
248 Route 208, New Paltz, NY 12561
Tel: 845 255 6762

Lorraine's
23 Battery Park Avenue
Asheville, NC 28801
Tel: 828 251 1771
Fax: 828 254 9490
lorrainesantiques@cs.com

Gary and Martha Ludlow Inc
5284 Golfway Lane, Lyndhurst, OH 44124,
Tel: 440 449 3475
ludlowantiques@aol.com

Macklowe Gallery
667 Madison Ave., New York, NY 10021
Tel: 212 644 6400
www.macklowegallery.com

Milly McGehee
P.O. Box 666, Riderwood,
MD 21139
Tel: 410 653 3977
millymcgehee@comcast.net

Jackson Mitchell Inc
5718 Kennett Pike, Wilmington, DE 19807
Tel: 302 656 0110
JacMitch@aol.com

Perrault-Rago Gallery
333 North Main Street, Lambertville, NJ 08530
Tel: 609 397 9374
info@ragoarts.com
www.ragoarts.com

James L Price Antiques
831 Alexander Spring Rd, Carlisle, PA 17013
Tel: 717 243 0501
jlpantiques@earthlink.net

RJG Antiques
P.O. Box 60, Rye, NH 03870
Tel: 603 433 1770
antiques@rjgantiques.com
www.rjgantiques.com

John Keith Russell Antiques Inc
110 Spring Street, P.O. Box 414,
South Salem, NY 10590
Tel: 914 763 8144
info@jkrantiques.com
www.jkrantiques.com

735

DIRECTORY OF SPECIALISTS

Israel Sack
730 Fifth Avenue, Suite 605, New York, NY 109
Tel: 212 399 6562

Lincoln and Jean Sander
235 Redding Road, Redding, CT 06896
Tel: 203 938 2981
sanderlr@aol.com

Kathy Schoemer American Antiques
P.O. Box 429, 12 McMorrow Lane, North Salem,
NY 10560
Tel: 603 835 2105

Thomas Schwenke Inc
50 Main Street North, Woodbury, CT 06798
Tel: 203 266 0303
schwenke@schwenke.com
www.schwenke.com

Jack and Ray Van Gelder
Conway House, 468 Ashfield Road, Conway,
MA 01341
Tel: 413 369 4660

Van Tassel/Baumann American Antiques
690 Sugartown Road,
Malvern, PA 19355
Tel: 610 647 3339

Furniture

American Antiques
161 Main Street, P.O. Box 368, Thomaston,
ME 04861
Tel: 207 354 6033
acm@midcoast.com

American Spirit Antiques
P.O. Box 11152, Shawnee Mission, KS 66207
Tel: 913 345 9494
Tedatiii@aol.com

Barbara Ardizone Antiques
P.O. Box 433, 62 Main Street, Salisbury,
CT 06068
Tel: 860 435 3057

Artemis Gallery
Wallace Road, North Salem, NY 10560
Tel: 914 669 5971
artemis@optonline.net www.artemisantiques.com

Carswell Rush Berlin, Inc
P.O. Box 0210, Planetarium Station, New York,
NY 0024 0210
Tel: 212 721 0330
carswellberlin@msn.com
www.americanantiques.net

Joanne and Jack Boardman
522 Joanne Lane, DeKalb, IL 06115
Tel: 815 756 359
boardmanantiques@aol.com

Boym Partners Inc
131 Varick Street, 915, New York, NY 10013
Tel: 212 807 8210
www.boym.com

Joan R. Brownstein
24 Parker Street,
Newbury, MA 01951
Tel: 978 465-1089
Fax: 978 465-2155
www.joanrbrownstein.com

Evergreen Antiques
1249 Third Avenue,
New York, NY 10021
Tel: 212 744 5664
www.evergreenantiques.com

Eileen Lane Antiques
150 Thompson Street,
New York, NY 10012
Tel: 212 475 2988
www.eileenlaneantiques.com

Lost City Arts
18 Cooper Square,
New York, NY 10003
Tel: 212 375 0500
www.lostcityarts.com

Lili Marleen
www.lilimarleen.net

Alan Moss
436 Lafayette Street,
New York, NY 10003
Tel: 212 473 1310
Fax: 212 387 9493

General

Bucks County Antiques Center
Route 202, 8 Skyline Drive, Lahaska PA 18914
USA
Tel: 001 215 794 9180

Camelot Antiques
7871 Ocean Gateway
Easton, Maryland 21601
Tel: 410 820 4396
camelot@goeastern.net
www.about-antiques.com

**Manhatten Arts
and Antiques Center**
1050 Second Avenue, bet.
55th-56th Street,
New York, NY 10022
Tel: 212 355 4400 ·
Fax: 212 355 4403
info@the-maac.com
www.the-maac.com

Showcase Antiques Center
At entrance to Old Sturbridge Village, Route 20,
Sturbridge, MA 01566
Tel: 508 347-7190
Fax: 508 347-5420
www.showcaseantiques.com

South Street Antique Markets
600 Bainbridge St
Philadelphia, PA 1914

Glass

Brookside Art Glass
44 North Water Street, New Bedford, MA 02740
Tel: 508 993 4944
www.brooksideartglass.com

Holsten Galleries
Elm Street, Stockbridge, MA 01262
Tel: 413 298 3044
www.holstengalleries.com

Antiques by Joyce Knutsen
Tel: 315 637 8238 (Summer)
Tel: 352 567 1699 (Winter)

L.H. Selman Ltd
123 Locust Street,
Santa Cruz, CA 95060
Tel: 800 538 0766
www.selman.com/pwauction/

Paul Reichwein
2321 Hershey Avenune, East Petersburg,
PA 17520
Tel: 717 569 7637

Jewelry

Ark Antiques
P.O. Box 3133,
New Haven, CT 06515
Tel: 203 498 8572
www.ark-antiques.com

Arthur Guy Kaplan
P.O. Box 1942, Baltimore, MD 21203
Tel: 410 752 2090

Marine Antiques

Hyland Granby Antiques
P.O. Box 457, Hyannis Port,
MA 02647
Tel: 508 771 3070
alan@hylandgranby.com
www.hylandgranby.com

Metalware

Wayne and Phyllis Hilt
176 Injun Hollow Road,
Haddam Neck,
CT 06424
Tel: 860 267 2146
philt@snet.net
www.hiltpewter.com

Modern

Mix Gallery
17 South Main Street,
Lambertville, NJ 08530
Tel: 609 773 0777
www.mixgallery.com

736

Moderne Gallery
111 North 3rd Street,
Philadelphia, PA 19106
Tel: 215 923 8536
www.modernegallery.com

Modernism Gallery
800 Douglas Road, Suite 101,
Coral Gables, FL 33134, USA
Tel: 305 442 8743/
001 305 632 4725
www.modernism.com

Oriental
Marc Matz Antiques
By appointment
368 Broadway,
Cambridge, MA 02139
Tel: 617 460 6200
www.marcmatz.com

Scientific Instruments
Edison Gallery
Susanin's 900 S. Clinton St., Chicago, Il 60607
Tel: 617 359 4678
www.edisongallery.com

Silver
Chicago Silver
www.chicagosilver.com

Jonathan Trace
P.O. Box 418, 31 Church Hill Road, Rifton,
NY 12471
Tel: 914 658 7336

Imperial Half Bushel
831 N Howard Street,
Baltimore, MD 21201
Tel: 410 462 1192
ihb@imperialhalfbushel.com
www.imperialhalfbushel.com

Textiles
Stephanie's Antiques
28 West 25th Street,
New York NY 10010
Tel: 212 633 6563

Colette Donovan
98 River Road, Merrimacport, MA 01860
Tel: 978 346 0614
colettedonovan@adelphia.net

M Finkel & Daughter
936 Pine Street, Philadelphia, PA 19107
Tel: 215 627 7797
mailbox@finkelantiques.com
www.samplings.com

Cora Ginsburg
19 East 74th Street New York, NY 10021
Tel: 212 744 1352
coraginsburg@rcn.com
www.coraginsburg.com

Nancy Goldsmith
New York, NY
Tel: 212 696 0831

Andrea Hall Levy
PO Box 1243,
Riverdale, NY 10471
Tel: 646 441 1726
barangrill@aol.com

Stephen & Carol Huber
40 Ferry Road, Old Saybrook, CT 06475
Tel: 860 388 6809
hubers@antiquesamplers.com
www.antiquesamplers.com

Fayne Landes Antiques
593 Hansell Road, Wynnewood, PA 19096
Tel: 610 658 0566

Charlotte Marler
Booth 14,
1528 West 25th Street,
New York, NY 10010
Tel: 212 367 8808
char_marler@hotmail.com

Tribal Art
Arte Primitivo
Howard S. Rose Gallery, 3 East 65th Street -
Suite 2,
New York, NY 10021
Tel.: 212.570.6999
www.arteprimitivo.com

Marcy Burns American Indian Arts
525 East 72nd Street, New York,
NY 10021
Tel: 212 439 9257
marcy@marcyburns.com
www.marcyburns.com

Domas & Gray Gallery
Tel: 228 467 5294
www.domasandgraygallery.com

Elliot & Grace Snyder
P.O. Box 598, South Egremont, MA 01258
Tel: 413 528 3581

Jamieson Tribal Art
Golden Chariot Productions,
468 Wellington West Street, Suite 201, Toronto,
Ontario, Canada M5V 1E3
Tel: 001 416 569 1396
www.jamiesontribalart.com

Morning Star Gallery
513 Canyon Road, Santa Fe,
NM 87501, USA
Tel: 001 505 982 8187
www.morningstargallery.com

Myers & Duncan
12 East 86th Street, Suite 239,
New York, NY 10028
Tel: 212 472 0115
jmyersprimitives@aol.com

Trotta-Bono American Indian Art
PO Box 34,
Shrub Oak, NY 10588
Tel: 914 528 6604
tb788183@aol.com

GLOSSARY

A

albarello jar An Italian tin-glazed earthenware pharmacy jar.

albumen print Photographic paper that is treated with egg white (albumen) to enable it to hold light sensitive chemicals.

ashet A large plate or dish.

astragal Architectural molding with a semi-circular section.

aventurine A translucent glass given a sparkling appearance by the incorporation of flecks of oxidized metal. Can also be used as a glaze on ceramics.

B

Bakelite An early synthetic plastic which was patented in 1907.

balance An escape mechanism that is used in clocks without pendulums.

baluster A curved form with a bulbous base and slender neck.

Baroque An ornate and extravagant decorative style which was popular in the 17th and 18thC.

bergère The French term for an upholstered armchair.

bezel The groove or rim on the inside of the cover or lid on vessels such as teapots.

bianco-sopra-bianco A technique involving painting opaque white glaze on to a greyish ground.

boulle A type of marquetry that includes tortoiseshell and metal.

brassing Wear to plating that reveals the underlying base metal.

break-front A term for furniture with a projecting center section.

broderie anglaise White thread embroidered onto white cloth, used after the 1820s.

C

cabochon A protruding, polished, but not faceted, stone.

cabriole leg A leg with two gentle curves that create an S-shape.

cameo Hardstone, coral or shell that has been carved to show a design in a contrasting color.

cameo glass Decorative glass made from two or more layers of differently colored glass, which are then carved or etched to reveal the color beneath.

caryatid An architectural column in the form of a woman.

cased glass Glass encased with a further layer of glass.

celadon A distinctive gray/green or blue/green glaze.

center seconds hand A seconds hand that is pivoted at the center of the dial.

chamfered A surface that has been cut with a slanted edge.

champlevé A type of decoration where enamel is applied to stamped hollows in metal.

chapter ring The ring of hour and minute numbers on a clock dial.

character doll A doll with a face that resembles a real child.

charger A large plate or platter, used for display or serving.

chasing The technique of decorating the surface of silver by punching it with small tools.

chinoiserie Oriental-style lacquered or painted decoration featuring figures and landscapes.

chronometer A timekeeper used for calculating longitude at sea.

clock garniture A matching clock and candelabra set.

cloisonné A decorative technique whereby metal cells are filled with colored enamels.

commode A decorated low chest of drawers with a curved form.

composition A mixture including wood pulp, plaster and glue and used as a cheap alternative to bisque in the production of dolls.

core forming An early form of glass-making where molten glass is wound around a mud core.

crackle A deliberate crazed glaze effect used on porcelain.

credenza The Italian term for a side cabinet with display shelves at both ends.

crewelwork A wool embroidery technique used on linen.

cricket cage A small box designed to amplify the chirping of a cricket contained therein.

D

daguerreotype An early type of photograph, from c1839 until the 1850s.

davenport A small writing desk. In America, a large parlor sofa.

dentils Small teeth-like blocks that form a border under a cornice.

Deutsche Blumen Floral decoration found on 18thC faience and porcelain.

diecast Objects made by pouring molten metal into a closed metal die or mold.

ding A very small dent in metal.

dovetailing A method of joining two pieces of wood together by interlocking mortises and tenons.

dump A doorstop made from left-over glass, often with decoration.

E

earthenware A type of porous pottery that requires a glaze to make it waterproof.

ebonized Wood that has been dyed black to resemble ebony.

egg and dart A classical molding that incorporates egg and 'v' shapes used to enrich Neoclassical wares.

enamel Colored glass paste that is applied to surfaces to create a decorative effect.

escapement The mechanical part of the clock or watch that regulates the transfer of energy from the weights or spring to the movement of the clock or watch.

escutcheon A protective plate, as for a keyhole

F

faïence Earthenware treated with an impervious tin glaze.

fairing A small porcelain figure made in Eastern Germany and given away as prizes or sold inexpensively at fairs.

Fazackerley A style of floral painting found on English delft.

Fazackerley colors The bright enamel colors used to decorate pieces of English delft. The name probably derives from a pair of Liverpool delft mugs, dedicated to Thomas and Catherine Fazackerley, which were destroyed in WWII.

festoon A decorative motif in the form of a garland or chain of fruit, flowers and ribbons suspended on a loop.

figuring A natural pattern created by the grain in the wood.

finial A decorative knob on a terminal or cover of a vessel.

flatware Any type of cutlery.

free blown Glass blown and manipulated into shape without the use of a mold.

fretwork Geometric pierced decoration.

frieze A piece of wood supporting a table top or cornice.

frit Powdered glass added to white clay to produce a soft-paste porcelain. Also describes impurities found in old glass.

fusee A grooved device found in clocks that offsets the force of the spring as it runs down.

G

gadroon A decorative border of flutes or reeds.

gesso A paste mixture applied to timber then carved and gilded.

gnomon The part of a sundial which casts the shadow.

Greek key A Classical motif of interlocking lines.

grosse point A stitch that crosses two warp and two weft threads.

guilloché An engraved pattern of interlaced motifs, sometimes with translucent enamels.

H

hard-paste porcelain Porcelain made from kaolin, petuntse and quartz.

harlequin set A set of ceramics or furniture, in which the pieces are similar rather than identical.

hiramakie A Japanese decorative technique whereby a powdered charcoal design is coated with a layer of transparent lacquer.

honey gilding A decorative technique using gold leaf mixed with honey for a reddish tinge.

hotei The Japanese god of contentment and happiness.

I J K

intaglio Cut or engraved decoration on glass.

japanning The process of coating objects with layers of colored varnish in imitation of lacquer.

knop The knob on lids and covers and also the bulge on the stem of a candlestick or glass.

kovsh A Russian shallow drinking vessel with a handle.

kraak ware Late Ming Chinese blue and white porcelain exported by Dutch traders in ships known as 'carracks.'

L

lacquer An oriental varnish made from tree gum with a gloss finish.

lead glass or crystal A particularly clear type of glass with a high lead oxide content.

lead glaze A clear glaze with a lead based component.

longcase clock A weight-driven, free-standing clock.

luster An iridescent finish found on pottery and produced using metallic oxides.

M

manganese A mineral used to produce a purple glaze.

maiolica Italian tin-glazed earthenware produced from the 14thC.

marqueterie sur verre A method of decorating glass in which a hot glass shape is pressed onto the surface of a shape.

marquetry A decorative veneer made up from colored woods.

married A term uses to describe a piece that is composed of parts that were not originally together.

Meiji A period in Japanese history dating from c1868-1912.

Mon A Japanese family crest. A common example is the 16 petal chrysanthemum flower.

movement The entire time-keeping mechanism of a clock or watch.

N O

netsuke A small toggle used to secure pouches and boxes hung on cords through the belt of a kimono.

ogee An S-shaped shallow curve.

okimono A Japanese ornamental carving.

opalescent An opal-like, milky glass with subtle gradations of color.

opaline glass A translucent white glass made with the addition of oxides and bone ash.

ormolu Bronze gilding used in 18thC and early 19thC France as decorative mounts.

overglaze Enamel or transfer-printed decoration on porcelain that is applied after firing.

ovolo A quarter-circle shaped molding.

P

parian A semi-matte type of porcelain, made with feldspar, that does not require a glaze.

parquetry A variant of marquetry where veneers are applied in symmetrical designs.

parure A jewelry set usually comprising a matching necklace, pair of earrings, bracelet and a brooch.

paste The mixture of ingredients that make up porcelain. Also a compound of glass used to make imitation gemstones.

patina A surface sheen on objects that is produced over time through polishing and handling.

pavé setting A method of mounting jewels so that each stone is set close to the next.

pearlware English earthenware with a blue tinted glaze, developed by Wedgwood.

penwork Indian ink decoration applied with a pen.

petit point Finely worked embroidery with stitches that cross one warp or weft thread.

pinion A small toothed gear within a clock movement.

piqué A decorative technique where small strips or studs of gold are inlaid onto ivory or tortoiseshell on a pattern and secured in place by heating.

plique-à-jour Technique where enamel is set into an openwork metal frame to create an effect similar to stained glass.

porcelain A mixture of china clay and china stone that becomes hard, translucent and white when fired. Hard-paste porcelain is fired at a higher temperature than soft paste.

pounce pot A small pot for gum dust used to prevent ink from spreading.

press-molded Ceramics formed by pressing clay into a mold. Pressed glass is made by pouring molten glass into a mold and pressing it with a plunger.

Q R S

repoussé A French term for the raised, 'embossed', decoration on metals such as silver.

sabot The metal 'shoe' on the end of a cabriole leg.

saber leg A leg shaped like the curved blade of a saber.

salt glaze A thin glaze used on stonewares and made with the addition of salt during firing.

sautoir A long chain with gems or pearls set at intervals along the length.

scagliola Imitation marble made with plaster.

seat rail The horizontal bar that joins the chair legs directly below a chair seat.

serpentine A curved form with a projecting middle used in case furniture.

sgraffito A pattern of scratched decoration that reveals a contrasting color beneath.

skiver The sheepskin leather inset found in the top of writing tables and desks.

slip A mixture of clay and water used to decorate pottery and to produce slip-cast wares.

slip-casting Method of manufacturing thin-bodied vessels by pouring slip into a mold.

socle A plain block that forms the base of a sculpture, vase, or column.

soda glass Formed by the addition of soda to the batch to produce a light glass with a yellow or brown tint.

soft-paste porcelain Porcelain made from kaolin, powdered glass, soapstone and clay.

splat The central upright in a chair back.

squab A stuffed cushion.

sprigged ware Pottery decorated with ornaments applied with slip.

staining (glass) A method of coloring glass with metal oxides which are painted on and then fired.

sterling silver A standard of silver where the silver content is 92.5 per cent pure silver.

stretchers The bar between two legs on tables and chairs used to stabilize the structure.

stoneware A type of ceramic similar to earthenware and porcelain and made of high-fired clay mixed with stone, such as feldspar, which makes it non-porous.

stuff-over seat A chair with an upholstered seat rail.

stumpwork Raised embroidered needlework.

subsidiary dial A secondary dial set in the main dial that indicates seconds or the date.

swags Decorative ornaments similar to a festoon made up of fruit, flowers, husks, or nuts, or a loop of cloth.

swan-neck cresting or pediment Formed when two S-shaped curves almost meet.

T

tallcase clock A weight-driven, free-standing clock.

tantulus A lockable frame holding cut-glass spirit decanters.

tazza A shallow bowl or cup on a pedestal foot.

terracotta A red earthenware that is lightly fired and usually unglazed.

thrown ware Hollow vessels made by hand on a wheel.

tin-glaze An opaque, white glaze used on earthenware such as delftware, faïence, and maiolica and produced using tin oxide.

tinplate Toys made from thin steel covered with a coating of tin to guard against rust, which could then be painted or decorated with lithography.

toile Cotton fabric printed with a monochrome design.

torchère A portable stand with a table top to support a candle or lamp.

train A set of interconnected wheels and pinions that transfers energy from the spring or wheel to the escape mechanism.

transfer printing A method of decorating ceramic objects. An image is transferred to paper from an inked engraving and then to the vessel.

transitional The Chinese period around the transition from the Ming to the Qing dynasty.

trefoil A motif incorporating three lobes or leaves.

U V W Y

underglaze Decoration painted on to a biscuit body before glazing.

veneering A technique used in furniture making which involves using fine woods to cover or decorate the surface of less expensive woods.

vermeil Gold-plated silver.

wax doll Dolls with heads and occasionally bodies made from either molded or carved wax.

wheel engraving A method of engraving into the surface of glass by holding a rotating wheel of stone or metal against it.

white metal Precious metal that is possibly silver, but not officially marked as such.

yellow metal Precious metal that is possibly gold, but not officially marked as such.

INDEX